the
AMERICANA
ANNUAL

1991

GROLIER

AN ENCYCLOPEDIA OF THE EVENTS OF 1990
YEARBOOK OF THE ENCYCLOPEDIA AMERICANA

This annual has been prepared as a yearbook for general encyclopedias. It is also published as *Encyclopedia Year Book*.

Grolier Enterprises, Inc. offers a varied selection of both adult and children's book racks. For details on ordering, please write:

Grolier Enterprises, Inc.
Sherman Turnpike
Danbury, CT 06816
Attn: Premium Department

The Year in Review

© Laski/Sipa

A promise of peace that was unheard of in recent memory and that came with the thaw of the Cold War in late 1989 and early 1990 was replaced suddenly with the threat of international conflict on Aug. 2, 1990. On that day, Saddam Hussein's troops swept over a near-defenseless Kuwait within a matter of hours, but the Iraqi leader could not have anticipated the international reaction to the invasion.

In passing 12 resolutions against Iraq, the United Nations took its strongest stand since the Korean conflict, nearly 40 years earlier. With UN backing, an international force, led by the United States, was preparing for war to free Kuwait. Meanwhile, the era of East-West cooperation continued as the United States and the Soviet Union voted together at the UN and worked toward progress in disarmament. Meanwhile the most tangible example of reconciliation in 1990 was the joining together of East and West Germany as a unified nation for the first time since World War II.

There, however, was disturbing news from the East as well. Dissidents in Romania, for example, accused government officials of being Communists in disguise, and other Eastern Europe democracies experienced growing pains. Action toward independence and greater freedom within the Soviet re-

The Alphabetical Section

Entries on the continents, major nations of the world, U.S. states, Canadian provinces, and chief cities will be found under their own alphabetical headings.

Contents

Feature Articles of the Year

publics and massive food shortages threatened to tear the Soviet Union apart. Soviet problems were so serious that President Mikhail Gorbachev's foreign minister and longtime ally, Eduard Shevardnadze, resigned and warned of a coming dictatorship. For many Soviets it was ironic that President Gorbachev was named the 1990 recipient of the Nobel Peace Prize. He remained popular outside his homeland, however.

There was also the paradox of continuing conflicts and the promise of peace elsewhere in 1990. The civil war in Lebanon showed signs of ending as Syrian troops forced the Christian renegade leader Gen. Michel Aoun to abandon his rebellion against the government. Israel was rocked by controversy over the deaths of Palestinian demonstrators. In South Africa the celebration over the release from jail of antiapartheid leader Nelson Mandela and the liberalization of government policies was tempered by ethnic violence. Liberia endured a bloody civil war.

As ousted Panamanian dictator Manuel Antonio Noriega awaited trial in Miami, his country faced the task of rebuilding; in Nicaragua, Violeta Barrios de Chamorro upset Sandinista Daniel Ortega in presidential elections but had problems governing. An era ended in Great Britain with Margaret Thatcher resigning as prime minister after a leadership struggle in her Conservative Party. In Poland, Lech Walesa, the shipyard electrician who rose to prominence as the head of Solidarity, was elected president. Playwright Václav Havel turned statesman and was leading Czechoslovakia.

Americans were concerned not only about the crisis in the Persian Gulf but also about an economy that was sputtering into a recession. President Bush lost some political support when he went back on his "read-my-lips" promise not to raise taxes. However, his choice for the Supreme Court, David Souter, easily won Senate approval.

Citizens everywhere stopped to observe the 20th anniversary of Earth Day. A flaw in the lens of the Hubble Space Telescope obscured astronomers' view of the heavens. An international conference on AIDS was held in San Francisco. The era of the "junk" bond ended, but a crisis in the savings and loan industry continued.

In sports, the underdog Cincinnati Reds swept the Oakland Athletics to win the 1990 World Series. Boxer Buster Douglas came from nowhere to knock out seemingly invincible heavyweight champion Mike Tyson, but later was knocked out himself. West Germany took soccer's World Cup. People turned to romantic films, such as *Ghost* and *Pretty Woman*. The younger audience thrilled to the exploits of the "Teenage Mutant Ninja Turtles." "The Simpsons," a bug-eyed animated family, became a hit both on television and in merchandising, and Bugs Bunny turned 50. Ken Burns' rich documentary on the Civil War was public television's highest-rated show.

The world lost composer-conductor Leonard Bernstein, Muppets creator Jim Henson, fashion designer Halston, and singer-dancer Sammy Davis, Jr. It also lost a short-lived peace dividend.

THE EDITORS

Leaders from all the nations of Europe (excluding Albania), Canada, and the United States gathered in Paris, Nov. 19–21, 1990, for a summit of the Conference on Security and Cooperation in Europe (photo). The signing of a treaty aimed at reducing conventional weapons in Europe was a highlight of the meeting.

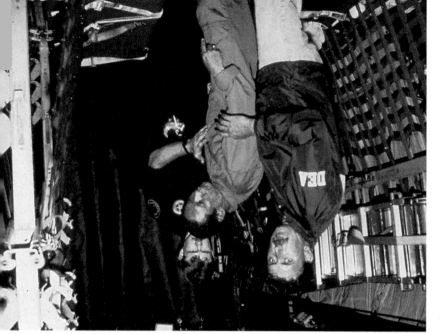

AP/Wide World

January

1 Two Roman Catholic nuns are killed and a bishop and another nun are wounded in northeastern Nicaragua.

3 Ten days after taking refuge in the Vatican embassy in Panama, Panamanian strongman Gen. Antonio Noriega surrenders to U.S. authorities. He then is flown to Florida to face drug charges.

10 China's Premier Li Peng announces the lifting of martial law in Beijing.

11 As Soviet President Mikhail Gorbachev begins a visit to Lithuania, some 250,000 people stage an independence demonstration in the republic.

12 Romania becomes the first Soviet-bloc nation to outlaw the Communist Party.

15 The Soviet government sends troops to the republic of Azerbaijan as Muslim Azerbaijanis and Christian Armenians engage in a virtual civil war.

The Campeau Corporation files for bankruptcy protection for its Federated Department Stores Inc. and Allied Stores Corp.

20 The U.S. space shuttle *Columbia*, with a five-member crew, lands at Edwards Air Force Base in California after a ten-day mission during which it retrieved a scientific satellite from failing orbit and deployed a communications satellite.

23 The second session of the U.S. Congress convenes.

The Central Committee of the ruling Albanian Workers' (Communist) Party endorses a program of modest reforms during a two-day meeting.

28 The San Francisco 49ers overwhelm the Denver Broncos, 55–10, in professional football's Super Bowl XXIV.

29 U.S. President George Bush sends to Congress a $1.23 trillion budget for fiscal 1991.

31 During his first State of the Union address, President Bush proposes that the United States and the Soviet Union reduce their respective conventional forces in central and eastern Europe to 195,000 troops.

February

1 El Salvador's President Alfredo Cristiani confers with President Bush in Washington.

Pope John Paul II concludes an eight-day visit to Africa.

4 In Costa Rica, Rafael Angel Calderón Fournier of the opposition Social Christian Unity Party is elected president.

Nelson Mandela, the 71-year-old South African black nationalist leader who had spent more than 27 years in prison, is greeted warmly by supporters following his release on February 11.

7 At the conclusion of a three-day plenum in Moscow, the Central Committee of the Soviet Communist Party votes to disavow the party's constitutionally guaranteed monopoly on political power.

An oil tanker spills nearly 400,000 gallons (1.5 million l) of crude oil a few miles off Huntington Beach, CA.

11 In South Africa black nationalist leader Nelson Mandela is freed following more than 27 years in prison. On February 2, South Africa's President F.W. de Klerk announced that his government was lifting the 30-year ban against the African Nationalist Congress (ANC), the principal black group fighting to end white minority rule and apartheid.

James (Buster) Douglas knocks out boxing's undefeated heavyweight champion Mike Tyson in the tenth round of a fight in Tokyo.

13 The foreign ministers of the 16 nations of the North Atlantic Treaty Organization and seven nations of the Warsaw Pact conclude an unprecedented conference in Ottawa, Ont.

The securities firm of Drexel Burnham Lambert Group Inc. files for bankruptcy protection.

West Germany's Chancellor Helmut Kohl and East Germany's Premier Hans Modrow agree to open talks on a unified currency for the two nations.

15 Communist Party and government leaders in the Soviet republic of Tadzhikistan resign in the wake of ethnic violence.

Meeting in Cartagena, Colombia, the presidents of Bolivia, Colombia, Peru, and the United States pledge to cooperate in the fight against illegal drug trafficking.

Great Britain and Argentina agree to restore full diplomatic relations, severed during the 1982 war over the Falkland Islands.

March

U.S. President George Bush and Japan's Prime Minister Toshiki Kaifu discussed economic issues, including the U.S. trade deficit with Japan, in Palm Springs, CA, March 2–3.

AP/Wide World

1 Luis Alberto Lacalle is inaugurated as president of Uruguay.

At least 32 persons are killed as Indian security forces fire on pro-independence marchers in Srinagar, capital of Jamma and Kashmir. Some 70 persons had been killed in similar disturbances in late January.

The U.S. Nuclear Regulatory Commission approves a full-power license for the Seabrook (NH) nuclear-power plant.

4 The U.S. space shuttle *Atlantis*, with a five-member crew, completes a secret military mission. The shuttle had been launched on February 28 after several postponements.

Local and legislative elections are held in the Soviet republics of Russia, Byelorussia, and the Ukraine.

7 Following several weeks of turmoil in South Africa's black tribal homelands, bloody protests break out in Bophuthatswana. South African troops had been sent to Ciskei after a March 4 military coup.

18 Japan's ruling Liberal Democratic Party retains control of the lower house of the Diet (parliament) in general elections.

19 Striking miners at Pittston Co. mines vote to ratify a new contract and end a ten-month strike.

20 Great Britain announces that it will lift a ban against new investment in South Africa on February 23.

21 Czechoslovakia's President Vaclav Havel addresses a joint session of the U.S. Congress.

25 In national elections in Nicaragua, Violeta Barrios de Chamorro of the National Opposition Union defeats incumbent Sandinista President Daniel Ortega Saavedra.

West German Chancellor Helmut Kohl ends two days of talks with President Bush at Camp David, MD.

26 The USSR begins to withdraw its troops from Czechoslovakia under an agreement signed in Moscow.

Elections in Nicaragua: Violeta Barrios de Chamorro of the National Opposition Union and her running mate, Virgilio Godoy Reyes of the Independent Liberty Party, acknowledge victory over incumbent President Daniel Ortega Saavedra in national balloting February 25. Mrs. Chamorro asked all Nicaraguans "to work for the reconciliation" of their country.

© Alex Quesada/Matrix

April

1 Zimbabwe's ruling African National Union-Patriotic Front (ZANU-PF) is declared the winner of March 28–29 elections.

2 The University of Nevada at Las Vegas (UNLV) defeats Duke University, 103–73, to win the National Collegiate Athletic Association's Division I basketball title.

11 Following victories by non-Communists in legislative elections in Lithuania on February 24 and March 4, the Soviet republic's parliament formally declares a restoration of Lithuania's independence from the USSR.

Patricio Aylwin takes office as president of Chile.

13 In Haiti, Supreme Court Justice Ertha Pascal-Trouillot is sworn in as interim president. Lt. Gen. Prosper Avril had resigned the presidency on March 10 in the face of increasing antigovernment unrest.

President Bush removes economic sanctions against Nicaragua.

14 The Central Committee of Mongolia's Communist Party votes to end its monopoly on power and replaces its entire leadership.

15 A four-day meeting of the Soviet Congress of People's Deputies ends. During the session, the Soviet parliament repealed the Communist Party's monopoly on political power, revamped the office of president, and elected Mikhail Gorbachev to a five-year term as the new-style executive president.

Fernando Collor de Mello is sworn in as president of Brazil.

In Iraq, Farzad Bazoft, an Iranian-born British journalist, is hanged after being convicted of espionage.

In Israel the government of Prime Minister Yitzhak Shamir falls in a vote of no-confidence.

18 Two persons disguised as policemen break into the Isabella Stewart Gardner Museum in Boston and steal 12 pieces of art, including paintings by Vermeer, Rembrandt, Degas, and Manet, valued at some $200 million.

19 Following four months of negotiations, representatives of major-league baseball owners and players reach agreement on a new four-year collective-bargaining agreement.

21 Namibia, formerly South-West Africa, officially becomes an independent nation, ending 75 years of South African rule.

Taiwan's National Assembly reelects President Lee Teng-hui to a six-year term.

22 In a state court in Anchorage, AK, Joseph J. Hazelwood, captain of the oil tanker *Exxon Valdez* that ran aground off the coast of Alaska in March 1989, is acquitted of a felony charge of criminal mischief and of two misdemeanor charges of operating a vessel while intoxicated and reckless endangerment. He, however, is convicted of negligent discharge of oil, a misdemeanor.

23 The Nicaraguan contras agree to dismantle their camps in Honduras prior to the inauguration of President-elect Chamorro.

24 Australia's ruling Labor Party of Prime Minister Robert J. Hawke is returned to power in national elections.

25 Eighty-seven persons are killed in a fire in an illegal social club in the Bronx, NY. A 36-year-old Cuban immigrant later is arrested and charged with arson and murder.

31 Riots break out in London, England, in protest against a new system of local taxation that is to become effective April 1.

Jessica Tandy was awarded an Oscar as best actress on March 26 for her role in "Driving Miss Daisy."

© Barr/Gamma-Liaison

In federal court in Washington, DC, April 7, John M. Poindexter, former national security adviser to President Reagan, is convicted of five felony charges for his role in the Iran-contra affair.

8   Following nearly two months of prodemocracy demonstrations in Nepal, King Birendra drops the nation's ban on political parties.

England's Nick Faldo wins the Masters golf tournament.

9   Four British soldiers are killed in a bomb attack in Northern Ireland.

10   A Frenchwoman, her Belgian companion, and their daughter are released in Beirut, Lebanon, after being held hostage for more than two years. Palestinian officials claim that their release is part of a French-Libyan deal.

President Bush and Canada's Prime Minister Brian Mulroney meet in Toronto.

11   Constantine Mitsotakis is sworn in as premier of Greece after his New Democratic Party won half of the nation's parliamentary seats in April 8 elections.

12   In East Germany, Lothar de Maizière, the leader of the conservative Christian Democratic Union, is installed as premier of a "grand coalition" government. Free national elections were held on March 18.

13   President Bush and British Prime Minister Margaret Thatcher confer in Bermuda.

15   Swedish-born movie actress Greta Garbo dies in New York City.

19   President Bush and France's President François Mitterrand exchange ideas in Key Largo, FL.

22   People throughout the world mark the 20th anniversary of the original Earth Day.

Pope John Paul II concludes a two-day visit to Czechoslovakia. The restoration of diplomatic ties between the Vatican and Czechoslovakia was announced on April 19.

23   Li Peng becomes the first premier of China to visit the USSR since Zhou Enlai in 1964.

24   U.S. junk-bond dealer Michael Milken pleads guilty to six felony counts of securities fraud.

Campaign posters help publicize March-April parliamentary elections in Hungary. A new government was formed in May.

25   Violeta Barrios de Chamorro is sworn in as president of Nicaragua, ending some 11 years of rule by the Sandinista National Liberation Front.

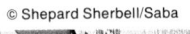

Former U.S. hostage Robert Polhill, left, welcomes Frank Reed home to the United States following his release from captivity in Beirut on April 30. Polhill himself had been set free in Lebanon eight days earlier.

© Brad Markel/Gamma-Liaison

The U.S. space shuttle *Discovery*, which was launched on April 24 with a crew of five, deploys the Hubble Space Telescope in an orbit 381 mi (613 km) above Earth.

28 *A Chorus Line*, the longest-running show in Broadway's history, closes after a run of nearly 15 years.

30 The Chinese government announces the lifting of martial law in Lhasa, the capital of Tibet.

Representatives of the United States and Panama sign three agreements on fighting drug trafficking.

May

2 South Africa's President F. W. de Klerk and Nelson Mandela, the leader of the African National Congress (ANC), hold the first formal talks between the government and the ANC.

3 In Hungary, Jozsef Antall, the head of the center-right Democratic Forum, which won a parliamentary majority of seats in March-April elections, is asked to form a government.

4 Latvia's Supreme Soviet (parliament) votes in favor of a declaration of independence from the USSR.

16 Entertainer Sammy Davis, Jr., and puppeteer Jim Henson die in Los Angeles and New York City, respectively.

22 Pro-Western North Yemen and pro-Soviet South Yemen merge into the Republic of Yemen.

24 During a banquet in Tokyo for visiting South Korean President Roh Tae Woo, Japan's Emperor Akihito expresses his "deepest regret" for Japan's occupation of Korea (1910–45).

The Edmonton Oilers capture hockey's Stanley Cup.

© Halawani/Sipa

The slaying of seven Palestinians inside Israel by an Israeli Jew described as "mentally deranged" on May 20 led to widespread rioting in the Israeli-occupied Gaza Strip and West Bank.

27 In Colombia, César Gaviria Trujillo, the candidate of the ruling Liberal Party and a supporter of the government's campaign against the drug cartels, is elected president.

In the first free, multiparty elections in Myanmar (Burma) in 30 years, the opposition National League of Democracy wins a majority in the National Assembly.

29 Boris Yeltsin is elected president of the Russian Federation.

31 The United States vetoes a UN Security Council resolution that would have sent an observer mission to the Israeli-occupied West Bank and Gaza Strip.

© Laski/Sipa

Supporters of Boris Yeltsin, who was chosen chairman of the Russian Federation on May 29, gather in Moscow's Red Square, above, to await election results. At the time, Soviet President Mikhail Gorbachev, whose policies had been criticized by Yeltsin, was preparing for a summit meeting with President Bush. In the East Room of the White House, June 1, the two presidents signed a series of bilateral agreements, protocols, and understandings.

June

3 Soviet President Gorbachev concludes a four-day visit to Washington during which he and President Bush signed accords on strategic arms, chemical weapons, trade, and other issues.

4 Soviet President Gorbachev and South Korea's President Roh Tae Woo confer in San Francisco.

9 Forty-eight political prisoners are freed in South Africa. On June 7, President de Klerk had lifted the four-year-old state of emergency in three of the nation's four provinces.

10 Alberto Fujimori, 51-year-old agricultural engineer, is elected president of Peru, defeating novelist Mario Vargas Llosa in runoff elections.

Flaming oil is spilled into the Gulf of Mexico after a series of explosions occurs aboard a Norwegian supertanker.

11 Ending a three-month government crisis in Israel, the Knesset (parliament) approves a new right-wing coalition cabinet led by Yitzhak Shamir as prime minister.

John Poindexter, former U.S. national security adviser who in April was convicted of five felony counts in connection with the Iran-contra affair, is sentenced to six months in prison.

12 In local elections in Algeria, the Islamic Salvation Front wins a majority of provincial and municipal races.

© P.F. Gero/Sygma

© Farnood/Sipa

13 In Czechoslovakia, the Civic Forum and Public Against Violence alliance is declared the winner of June 8–9 parliamentary and regional elections.

14 The Detroit Pistons capture their second consecutive National Basketball Association championship, defeating the Portland Trail Blazers, four games to one.

Flash floods devastate parts of Ohio, West Virginia, and Pennsylvania.

17 Bulgaria's ruling Socialist Party gains a parliamentary majority following runoff elections.

18 In Jacksonville, FL, James E. Pough, a 42-year-old construction worker, goes on a shooting rampage with a semiautomatic rifle, killing eight persons and seriously injuring five before taking his own life.

20 The United States declares that it is suspending its diplomatic contact with the Palestine Liberation Organization (PLO) in light of the PLO's failure to condemn an abortive seaborne assault against Israel.

Ion Iliescu, the leader of Romania's National Salvation Front which won national elections on May 20, is sworn in as president. Romania had been hit by severe violence, June 13-15, as progovernment coal miners clashed with antigovernment students. Several hundred persons were injured.

Nelson Mandela, South African black nationalist leader, arrives in New York, beginning an 11-day, eight-city U.S. tour.

21 A proposed U.S. constitutional amendment permitting the prosecution of those who destroy the U.S. flag is defeated in the House of Representatives. On June 11 the U.S. Supreme Court declared unconstitutional a 1989 federal law banning the desecration of the flag.

More than 40,000 persons are killed as northern Iran is struck by a devastating earthquake.

23 Canada's Prime Minister Brian Mulroney acknowledges that his plan to grant special constitutional status to Quebec (the Meech Lake accord) has failed and warns that the nation needs time to "mend divisions and heal wounds."

Jean Chrétien of Quebec is elected leader of Canada's opposition Liberal Party.

25 Fang Lizhi, China's most prominent dissident, and his wife, Li Shuxian, are permitted to leave China.

26 Breaking a campaign pledge, President Bush acknowledges that any agreement with Congress to reduce the budget deficit would require "tax-revenue increases."

An Iranian woman tries to console herself as she sits amid the ruins of a devastating earthquake in Iran. Some 40,000 persons were killed in the June 21 catastrophe.

Following the June 22 collapse of Canada's Meech Lake accord, a series of constitutional measures to grant Quebec special status, some 200,000 Quebeckers celebrated St. Jean-Baptiste Day, the province's traditional holiday, by marching in a Montreal parade in support of a "free Quebec."

© Canadawide/Sygma

29 The republic of Lithuania agrees to suspend its declaration of independence for 100 days in exchange for talks with Moscow and the lifting of economic sanctions.

Ninety-three nations agree that by the year 2000 they will halt the production of chemicals that destroy the atmosphere's protective ozone layer.

The National Aeronautics and Space Administration (NASA) announces that it is grounding indefinitely all space-shuttle flights until an elusive fuel leak has been fixed. The agency had reported a major flaw in the light-gathering mirrors of the Hubble Space Telescope on June 27.

30 Santa Barbara and Los Angeles County, CA, are declared federal disaster areas as fires kill at least two persons and destroy more than 500 homes.

© J. Langevin/Sygma

Albania's Communist government gave in to international pressures on July 8 and allowed several thousand of its citizens to emigrate. The Albanians, many of them young, had taken refuge in various embassies in the capital city of Tiranë following a series of prodemocracy demonstrations in late June-early July.

July

1 A state treaty establishing a unified economic and monetary system for East Germany and West Germany becomes effective.

Marking Canada Day at Parliament Hill in Ottawa, Ont., Queen Elizabeth II calls for Canadian unity.

2 In a U.S. federal court in New York City, Imelda Marcos, wife of former Philippine President Ferdinand Marcos, is acquitted of charges of racketeering, fraud, and obstruction of justice. Her codefendant, Saudi Arabian financier Adnan Khashoggi, is acquitted of obstruction of justice and mail fraud.

Some 1,500 Muslim pilgrims are killed in a stampede in a pedestrian tunnel leading to the holy city of Mecca, Saudi Arabia.

6 During a two-day meeting in London, the leaders of the North Atlantic Treaty Organization (NATO) agree to a series of major changes in military policy, including the scaling back of front-line defenses.

8 West Germany wins the World Cup soccer tournament.

Representatives of the United States and Greece sign an agreement calling for continued U.S. military presence in Greece.

Sweden's Stefan Edberg wins the men's singles tennis title at Wimbledon. On July 7, Martina Navratilova had taken the women's singles championship for a record ninth time.

11 The leaders of the seven major industrial democracies conclude their 16th annual summit in Houston, TX. Accords were signed on trade, agriculture, Soviet aid, and the environment.

The government of Kenya announces that 20 persons have been killed and more than 1,000 arrested in street protests and rioting stemming from President Daniel arap Moi's crackdown against political opponents favoring a multiparty system.

13 The 28th Congress of the Communist Party of the Soviet Union ends. Highlights of the meeting included the reelection of President Gorbachev as Communist Party general secretary, the resignation of Boris Yeltsin from the party, and the election of Ukraine President Vladimir A. Ivashko, a Gorbachev ally, to the new post of Communist Party deputy general secretary.

17 In Moscow, West German Chancellor Helmut Kohl and Soviet President Gorbachev reach a consensus regarding the unification of Germany. Under the agreement, Germany would be a member of NATO and the German-Polish border would be guaranteed.

20 A three-judge panel of the U.S. Court of Appeals in Washington overturns one and suspends the other two felony convictions of Oliver North in the Iran-contra affair.

23 President Bush names David H. Souter of New Hampshire an associate justice of the U.S. Supreme Court. The 50-year-old U.S. Court of Appeals judge would succeed William J. Brennan, Jr., who resigned on July 20.

25 The U.S. House of Representatives votes to sustain President Bush's veto of a bill permitting time off from work to care for newborn or adopted children or to care for seriously ill family members.

26 President Bush signs into law a bill prohibiting discrimination against the disabled.

The U.S. House of Representatives votes, 408–18, to reprimand Rep. Barney Frank (D-MA) for improper use of his office to aid a male prostitute. On July 25 the U.S. Senate had voted, 96–0, to denounce Sen. David Durenberger (R-MN) for improper financial dealings.

27 In the Caribbean nation of Trinidad and Tobago, a group of black Muslims surrenders to authorities after staging an unsuccessful coup attempt. Prime Minister Arthur N.R. Robinson and other cabinet members were taken hostage during the revolt.

30 Ian Gow, a Conservative member of Britain's Parliament, is killed by a car bomb in Hankham, East Sussex. The Provisional Irish Republican Army takes responsibility for the attack.

August

1 Bulgaria's Grand National Assembly (parliament) selects Zhelyu Zhelev, 55-year-old head of the Union of Democratic Forces, as the nation's president. Petar Mladenov had resigned the office on July 6 amid antigovernment protests.

2 Iraqi troops and tanks seize control of oil-rich Kuwait. Hours later the UN Security Council condemns the action.

3 Hungary's parliament elects Arpad Goncz, a writer and former dissident who has served as the nation's acting president since May, president.

Only tanks and a few parked cars were visible in the streets of Kuwait after Iraqi troops invaded the oil-rich sheikdom on August 2. Later in the month, Iraqi President Saddam Hussein was shown on national television meeting with a group of Western hostages who were being detained in the troubled area.

Iraqi TV Taped Broadcast

6 Pakistan's President Ghulam Ishaq Khan dismisses the government of Prime Minister Benazir Bhutto, accusing her of "corruption and nepotism." A state of emergency is declared, and elections are scheduled for October 24.

8 Iraq's President Saddam Hussein annexes Kuwait as tensions mount in the Persian Gulf. On August 6 the UN Security Council had voted to impose a trade embargo against Iraq, and on August 6–7 President Bush had ordered a major U.S. military buildup in Saudi Arabia to prevent Iraqi aggression.

Soviet cosmonauts Anatoly Solovyov and Aleksandr Balandin return to Earth after a six-month mission aboard the Soviet space station *Mir*.

10 Washington, DC, Mayor Marion Barry is convicted on one misdemeanor drug charge and acquitted on a second. A mistrial is declared on 12 other misdemeanor and felony charges.

16 Dominican Republic's President Joaquín Balaguer is sworn in for a second consecutive term. On June 11 he was declared the victor of a highly contested presidential election on May 16.

23 The parliament of the Soviet republic of Armenia votes to declare independence from the USSR.

24 Brian Keenan, a teacher from Belfast, Northern Ireland, who had been held hostage in Lebanon for more than four years, is released in Beirut. Two Swiss hostages, kidnapped Oct. 6, 1989, had been freed earlier in the month.

The South African government imposes a limited state of emergency in 19 magisterial districts as violence escalates in the black townships around Johannesburg, an outgrowth of the three-year-old interblack conflict in eastern Natal province.

September

© Greg Locke/First Light Toronto

Robert Keith (Bob) Rae, a 42-year-old lawyer with a graduate degree in politics from Oxford, led his New Democratic Party (NDP) to an upset victory in Ontario's provincial elections on September 6.

4 In New Zealand, Geoffrey Palmer resigns as prime minister and leader of the ruling Labour Party. He is succeeded by Mike Moore.

6 In provincial elections in Ontario, the New Democratic Party, led by Bob Rae, ousts the Liberal government of Premier David Peterson.

The premiers of North Korea and South Korea conclude two days of talks in Seoul.

9 Following seven hours of talks in Helsinki, Finland, President Bush and President Gorbachev issue a statement calling upon the "government of Iraq to withdraw unconditionally from Kuwait, to allow the restoration of Kuwait's legitimate government, and free all hostages now held in Iraq and Kuwait."

Tennis star Pete Sampras wins the men's singles title at the U.S. Open. Argentina's Gabriela Sabatini had taken the women's singles crown on September 8.

10 Liberia's President Samuel K. Doe is killed by one of the two rebel factions that had been fighting for months to overthrow him. A multinational force seeking a cease-fire in the civil war had landed in Monrovia, Liberia, August 24. U.S. marines had airlifted more than 1,000 from the country, August 16 and 19.

After two days of talks in Jakarta, Indonesia, Cambodia's four warring factions accept a UN plan to end their civil war.

11 President Bush addresses a joint session of Congress on the Iraq crisis.

12 Representatives of East Germany, West Germany, France, Great Britain, the USSR, and the United States sign the Treaty on the Final Settlement with Respect to Germany.

16 In a videotaped broadcast on Iraqi television, President Bush warns the Iraqi people that Saddam Hussein has taken them "to the brink of war" by invading Kuwait.

17 U.S. Air Force Chief of Staff Gen. Michael J. Dugan is fired for discussing confidential Persian Gulf strategy with the press.

18 The 45th session of the United Nations General Assembly convenes; Malta's Guido de Marco is chosen as president.

Atlanta is chosen as the site for the 1996 Olympics; Athens reacts with bitter disappointment at being bypassed.

19 In Poland, Gen. Wojciech Jaruzelski asks parliament to set a date for ending his term of office as president.

24 South Africa's President F. W. de Klerk meets with President Bush at the White House.

27 Using a little-known constitutional provision, Canada's Prime Minister Brian Mulroney adds eight temporary members to the federal Senate. The move is an attempt to gain more votes for the proposed goods and services tax.

Vietnam's Foreign Minister Nguyen Co Thach and U.S. Secretary of State Baker discuss the Cambodian civil war in the highest-level meeting between the two countries since the Vietnam War.

30 The Soviet Union and South Korea formally establish diplomatic relations to the consternation of North Korea, the Soviet Union's longtime Communist ally.

The first World Summit for Children is held at the United Nations, attracting 71 world leaders to discuss youth-related issues.

October

1 The Supreme Soviet passes a new law guaranteeing freedom of religion in the USSR.

2 At least 132 persons die in the crash of a Chinese passenger plane after hijackers attempt to divert the aircraft from Guangzhou (Canton) to either Taiwan or Hong Kong.

3 East and West Germany are rejoined, forming a unified Germany for the first time since World War II. West German Chancellor Helmut Kohl becomes chancellor of all Germany.

5 In Cincinnati, OH, a jury acquits the Contemporary Arts Center of obscenity charges stemming from the museum's exhibitions of photographs by Robert Mapplethorpe.

Great Britain agrees to join the European Community's Exchange Rate Mechanism (ERM), a move initially opposed by Prime Minister Margaret Thatcher, who feared a loss of control over monetary policy.

6 In Louisiana, state Rep. David Duke (R), a former Ku Klux Klan grand wizard, polls a surprising 40% of the vote in his losing bid to unseat U.S. Sen. J. Bennett Johnson (D).

7 The Socialist Party of Chancellor Franz Vranitzky is returned to power in Austria's general elections.

The 11th Asian Games conclude in Beijing.

8 David Souter, 51, is sworn in as the 105th U.S. Supreme Court justice.

10 The U.S. space shuttle *Discovery* completes a four-day mission.

11 General Motors unveils the Saturn compact car, made by the Saturn Corp., its first new division since it acquired Chevrolet in 1918.

12 With U.S. backing, the UN Security Council adopts a resolution criticizing Israel for the killing of at least 18 Palestinians during an October 8 riot in Jerusalem.

The Eastman Kodak Company is ordered to pay Polaroid Corp. $909.5 million for infringement on instant photography patents.

13 In Lebanon, Christian renegade leader Gen. Michel Aoun abandons his rebellion against the government in the face of a Syrian-led military offensive.

15 The Norwegian Nobel Committee awards the Peace Prize to Soviet President Mikhail Gorbachev.

18 Receiving Hungary's Premier Jozsef Antall at the White House, President Bush announces that the United States will extend $47.5 million in agricultural credits and loan guarantees to Hungary for the purchase of grain.

20 The underdog Cincinnati Reds complete a four-game sweep of the Oakland Athletics to win the 1990 World Series.

21 In Malaysia, Prime Minister Mahathir bin Mohamad wins a third term of office.

24 The U.S. Senate fails by one vote (66–34) to override the presidential veto of the Civil Rights Bill of 1990. President Bush had vetoed the measure because it would ''introduce the destructive force of quotas.''

Nawaz Sharif (below front) and Ghulam Mustafa Jatoi of Pakistan's Islami Jamhoori Ittehad (IJI) campaign prior to October 24 national elections. The IJI captured 105 of 207 contested seats, and Sharif, 42, took office as prime minister on November 6. Jatoi had served as interim prime minister following the removal of Benazir Bhutto from the post in August.

27 In New Zealand, Jim Bolger's opposition National Party sweeps to victory in parliamentary elections.

28 The 101st session of the U.S. Congress adjourns. A deficit-reduction package had passed the previous day after five months of debate; it calls for budget cuts of $496.2 billion over five years.

31 In Australia, Prime Minister Bob Hawke and the leaders of the country's eight states and territories agree to a government restructuring.

November

3 In Norway, Labor Party leader Gro Harlem Brundtland succeeds Jan Syse as premier. Syse's center-right coalition had collapsed on October 29.

5 Rabbi Meir Kahane, the founder of the Jewish Defense League in the United States and leader of the anti-Arab Kach party in Israel, is assassinated in New York City.

6 Elections are held throughout the United States. Despite a perceived anti-incumbent sentiment, only one U.S. senator (Republican Rudy Boschwitz of Minnesota) and 15 House members are defeated; six of 23 incumbent governors fail to win another term.

8 As tensions in the Persian Gulf continue, President Bush decides to double the number of U.S. troops deployed in the area to 400,000 soldiers by early 1991.

9 Soviet President Gorbachev becomes the first foreign leader to pay an official state visit to a reunified Germany.

Mary Robinson, 46, is the first woman to be elected president of Ireland.

10 In India, Chandra Shekhar is sworn in as prime minister with the support of Rajiv Gandhi's Congress(I) Party. Vishwanath Pratap Singh had resigned as prime minister on November 7 after losing a no-confidence vote.

13 Wendell Ford (D-KY) is named majority whip of the U.S. Senate, replacing an ailing Alan Cranston (D-CA).

15 The U.S. Senate Ethics Committee opens hearings to determine whether the "Keating five"—Senators Alan Cranston (D-CA), Dennis DeConcini (D-AZ), John Glenn (D-OH), John McCain (R-AZ), and Donald W. Riegle, Jr. (D-MI)—exerted undue influence in interceding with federal regulators in behalf of savings and loan executive Charles H. Keating.

19 In Paris leaders of the Conference on Security and Cooperation in Europe sign an agreement to reduce conventional weapons.

20 In El Salvador the Farabundo Martí National Liberation Front (FLMN) launches an offensive in seven of the country's 14 provinces.

The U.S. space shuttle *Atlantis* completes a secret, six-day military mission.

On November 12, Emperor Akihito was enthroned officially as the 125th monarch to sit on the Chrysanthemum Throne of Japan. The ancient ceremonies were performed with some modifications, most of which were to emphasize that the emperor is not the object of worship.

21 Junk-bond dealer Michael R. Milken is sentenced to ten years in prison for securities fraud.

President Bush spends Thanksgiving Day with U.S. troops stationed in the Persian Gulf.

27 In Mexico, President Carlos Salinas de Gortari and President Bush conclude two days of talks focused on trade and the Persian Gulf.

28 In Great Britain, John Majors, 47, the chancellor of the exchequer, is chosen prime minister after being elected leader of the Conservative Party on November 27. He succeeds Margaret Thatcher, who announced her resignation on November 22 after failing to win reelection as party leader on the first ballot.

In Singapore, Goh Chok Tong becomes prime minister, succeeding Lee Kuan Yew, who resigned after holding the post for 31 years.

The presidents of Argentina and Brazil sign an agreement renouncing the use and deployment of nuclear weapons.

29 The United Nations Security Council approves a resolution authorizing the use of force against Iraq if it failed to withdraw its forces from Kuwait by Jan. 15, 1991.

30 Chinese Foreign Minister Qian Qichen meets with President Bush in Washington, the highest-level talks between the two countries since the crackdown against the prodemocracy movement in China in 1989.

President Bush names outgoing Florida Gov. Bob Martinez to succeed William Bennett as director of the Office of National Drug Control Policy.

In an effort to bring peace to the Persian Gulf, President Bush announces that he would send Secretary of State James Baker to Iraq and would receive Iraq's foreign minister at the White House.

December

Gary Kasparov successfully defends his world chess title against Anatoly Karpov.

AP/Wide World

1 The United States wins tennis' Davis Cup for the first time since 1982.

2 Chancellor Helmut Kohl's Christian Democratic Union is victorious in Germany's first elections as a reunified nation.

3 An antigovernment uprising in Argentina is put down by forces loyal to President Carlos Saúl Menem.

Continental Airlines Holdings Inc. files for bankruptcy protection.

4 In Chad, Gen. Idris Deby declares himself president; the rebel general's troops had forced Hissein Habré, president since 1982, to flee the country on December 1.

5 In Panama, Col. Eduardo Herrera Hassan, former leader of the national police, surrenders to U.S. Army troops after a coup attempt. Hassan had escaped from jail and barricaded himself in the national police headquarters.

6 In Bangladesh, Shahabuddin Ahmed takes power as interim president. Hussain Mohammad Ershad had resigned on December 4 in the face of growing protest to his rule.

Iraq's President Saddam Hussein announces that all foreigners detained in Iraq and Kuwait will be freed.

7 Bulgaria's Grand National Assembly elects Dimitar Popov as premier.

The General Agreement on Tariffs and Trade Uruguay Round of multinational trade talks are suspended without agreement.

8 President Bush concludes a six-day, five-nation tour of Latin America.

9 In Poland, Lech Walesa, the shipyard electrician who rose to prominence as the leader of Solidarity, is elected president, defeating Polish-Canadian businessman Stanislaw Tyminski in a run-off election.

10 The space shuttle *Columbia* lands at Edwards Air Force Base, CA, after a nine-day astronomy mission.

12 President Bush approves up to $1 billion in federal loan guarantees for the Soviet Union and also promises shipments of food and medicine to help the Soviets combat a severe economic crisis and food shortage.

14 A judge in Missouri gives permission to the parents of Nancy Beth Cruzan to remove her feeding tubes. Cruzan, 33, who has been in a vegetative state since an automobile accident in 1983, has become a focal point of the right-to-die movement.

16 Jean-Bertrand Aristide, 37, an expelled Roman Catholic Salesian priest, is elected president in Haiti's first free election.

Thailand's Premier Chatichai Choonhavan reshuffles his cabinet amid pressure from the military.

17 President Bush nominates former Tennessee Gov. Lamar Alexander to succeed Lauro F. Cavazos as secretary of education. On December 14 he had named outgoing Rep. Lynn Martin to succeed Elizabeth Dole as secretary of labor.

18 The U.S. Federal Reserve Board votes to cut its discount rate from 7% to 6.5%.

20 Soviet Foreign Minister Eduard Shevardnadze resigns, warning that conditions in the Soviet Union could create a dictator.

27 Gennadi I. Yanayev is confirmed as vice-president of the USSR, a new position.

29 Poland's new President Lech Walesa names Jan Krzysztof Bielecki as premier.

Japan's Prime Minister Toshiki Kaifu reshuffles his cabinet.

31 Gary Kasparov of the USSR retains the world chess championship, defeating fellow countryman Anatoly Karpov. In the 24-game contest, Kasparov took four games, Karpov won three, and 17 were drawn.

Lech Walesa and his wife Danuth vote in Poland's runoff presidential elections on December 9. The leader of Solidarity and Nobel Peace Prize winner was elected easily and was sworn in as president on December 22.

© Sygma

The Iraq-Kuwait crisis of 1990 was like no other. It was the first, but not the last, crisis of the post-World War II era in which the fear or reality of Soviet or other Communist aggression played no part. The traditional motives of national ambition and greed, not the ideological rivalry of superpowers, were the mainspring. The crisis arose from the aggressive ambitions of a despotic ruler (Saddam Hussein) of a not particularly important but well-armed and strategically located state in the Middle East (Iraq). In this situation, the United States and the Soviet Union acted in concert, not in opposition to each other. Curiously, only in one other Middle East crisis, the strange and isolated episode of the Suez crisis of 1956, had this happened.

Background. The Iraqi conquest of Kuwait in early August perhaps should not have caused as much surprise as it did. When Kuwait became independent of Britain in 1961, Iraq—then ruled by Abdul Karim Kassem—immediately threatened to take it over. The Kuwaiti emir called back in British troops for protection, and those were replaced a short time after by a

IRAQ CRISIS

By Arthur Campbell Turner

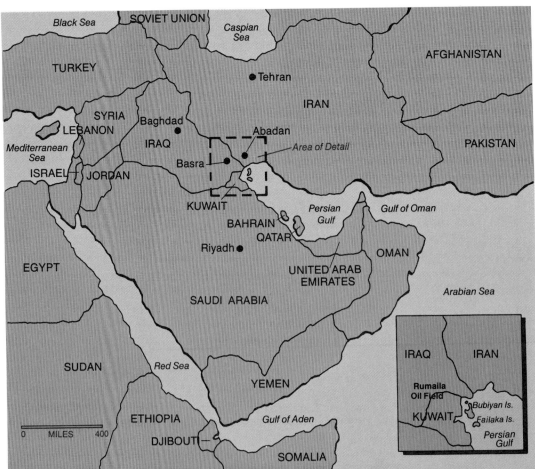

joint Arab force. The threat receded, but it was renewed in 1973 and in the 1980s. For Iraq always has regarded its rich neighbor, Kuwait, as its own.

The Iraqi claim, however often reiterated, has little substance. Many people have a confused idea that Kuwait is a British invention, created as quasicolonial territory and "carved out" of Iraq at the end of World War I. It also often is thought that it is somehow unfair that part of the great Rumaila oil field (a small part) is in Kuwait. In fact, Kuwait as a political entity has existed, and under the same dynasty—the Al-Sabah family—since the 1750s. It is Iraq that is the political upstart, a state created by the British at the end of World War I and patched together by combining the three administrative districts *(vilayets)*—Mosul, Baghdad, and Basra—of the former Ottoman Empire, which disappeared in 1918. It is true that Kuwait was part of the Ottoman Empire, but it was on the very fringes of that empire, and Turkish authority was always nominal, never real. It was the fear of the then ruler of Kuwait that his independence might be curbed by Ottoman, or German, or Wahhabi power that induced him to ask for British protection in the 1890s. As for the Rumaila field, oil production there began only in the 1970s.

Shadows Before. Also, portents of immediate dangers to come in the actions of Saddam Hussein of Iraq were not lacking in the first seven months of 1990. The cessation of warfare between Iran and Iraq in 1988 had left Saddam Hussein possessing the temptation of an army, experienced and estimated to be 1 million strong, and on the Persian Gulf to the south of Iraq a number of very rich and vulnerable neighbors. He also had, as a result of the war (a war which Iraq had started), a foreign debt to non-Arab states of some $40 billion, and was under some pressure at least to service interest payments. His utter contempt for foreign opinion was shown in the execution on March 15, for alleged spying, of the London *Observer* journalist Farzad Bazoft; while his readiness to violate whatever fragile stability the Middle East had, and his perfervid anti-Israeli attitudes, were exhibited in his making ominous arrangements for military cooperation with Jordan. His speeches to the Arab Cooperation Council in Amman (February 24) and to the emergency Arab summit in his own capital at the end of May were threatening in tone. The blatant purpose of these activities was to proclaim, indeed flaunt, anti-Western and anti-Israeli attitudes, and to advance his ambition to establish hegemony in the region. Among the Arab masses, these gambits met with some success; less so with most Arab rulers.

Oil Grievances. The Organization of the Petroleum Exporting Countries (OPEC) had made little headway in 1990 in curbing overproduction of oil. An emergency OPEC session in Geneva in early May produced an agreement on curbing production which, by July, clearly was not being observed. The Iraqi deputy prime minister was openly critical of overproduction by the United Arab Emirates (UAE) and Saudi Arabia at

Editor's Note: As this publication was going on press, Iraq ignored the United Nations deadline for evacuating from Kuwait and hostilities broke out in the Persian Gulf.

In August, Iraq under the leadership of Saddam Hussein, page 24, invaded and conquered its oil-rich neighbor, Kuwait, leading to the first international crisis following the end of the Cold War. Hussein's action was condemned immediately by the United Nations, and a massive multinational force, led by the U.S. military, below, was dispatched to the Persian Gulf.

AP/Wide World

About the Author. A long-time observer of the Middle East scene, Arthur Campbell Turner is a professor of political science at the University of California, Riverside. A graduate of the University of Glasgow, Oxford, and the University of California, Berkeley, he also has taught at such institutions as Berkeley, the University of Toronto, Claremont Graduate School, and UCLA. Professor Turner is author of *The Unique Partnership: Britain and the United States* (1971) and coauthor of *Tension Areas in World Affairs* (1964) and *Power and Ideology in the Middle East* (1988). He is a former member and chairman of the Editorial Committee of the University of California Press.

With oil refineries and storage facilities such as the one below, Kuwait is a leading world oil producer. In fact, Kuwait and Iraq together account for 40% of world oil production. Although crude-oil prices rose and the U.S. consumer saw a big price increase at the gas pump following the August invasion, the crisis had little effect on the oil supply overall.

the end of June and during a tour of the UAE. At Jiddah, Saudi Arabia, July 10–11, Kuwait and the UAE agreed to limit production until the desired "reference price" ($18 a barrel) was attained.

However, no more than a week later, Iraq launched a bitter denunciation of Kuwait accusing it of undermining Iraq during the eight years of war with Iran; of advancing into Iraqi territory; of stealing oil rightfully Iraq's from the Rumaila field; and reproaching Kuwait for not canceling Iraqi debts incurred during the war. In plain fact, Kuwait during the war, at considerable risk to itself, had been of enormous assistance to Iraq not only by lending interest-free some $20 billion not in the least likely ever to be repaid, but by serving as the main port of entry for imports to Iraq at a time when the Iraqi Gulf ports were unusable. Kuwait responded on July 19, in a circular note to Arab League states, that the Iraqi charges had no factual basis.

Saddam Hussein's language became ever more belligerent as July progressed, and he is believed to have made lavish promises to various parties, including Egypt, Jordan, Yemen, Tunisia, and the Palestine Liberation Organization (PLO) of a share in the loot if they would go along with an annexation of Kuwait by Iraq. Egypt's President Hosni Mubarak, at any rate, turned him down flat, and in the last days of July received (along with Jordan, Saudi Arabia, and Kuwait itself) emphatic assurances that Iraq would not attack Kuwait. One bizarre result of this lying ploy was that the 20,000-man Kuwaiti armed forces, on alert status since mid-July, were taken off it again—even though there were thousands of Iraqi troops deployed on the border, and on August 1, Iraq had walked out of negotiations with Kuwait.

International Reaction to the Conquest of Kuwait. The conquest of Kuwait by Iraq, which began when Iraqi tanks rolled across the border early on the morning of August 2, was a

© Gilles Bassignac/Gamma-Liaison

© Harriet Logan/Sipa

matter of only hours. Nevertheless it was a mistake (just as Iraq's attack on Iran ten years before had been). Saddam Hussein did not foresee, and few would have foretold, the astounding vigor and near unanimity of the world community's reaction against him. If he was surprised there was, perhaps, some excuse. Only the previous day, U.S. Assistant Secretary of State John Kelly, appearing before a congressional subcommittee, had refused to respond to questions about U.S. attitudes in the event of an Iraqi invasion of Kuwait; while in the same period, April Glaspie, the U.S. ambassador in Baghdad, had assured Hussein that his quarrels with Kuwait were a purely local affair in which the United States had no interest.

Course of the Crisis. On August 3, when the conquest of Kuwait was virtually complete, an estimated 100,000 Iraqi troops and 300 tanks had massed on the Kuwait-Saudi border. President Bush warned that the integrity of Saudi Arabia was a vital U.S. concern; in Moscow the U.S. and Soviet foreign secretaries jointly condemned the invasion and called for an immediate withdrawal from Kuwait. A crucially important decision was taken on August 6 when King Fahd of Saudi Arabia agreed to permit deployment of U.S. troops to deter an attack. The next day saw the beginning of "Operation Desert Shield," when an initial contingent of U.S. troops and planes was ordered to Saudi Arabia. From this modest start there ensued rapidly the most massive deployment of U.S. troops on foreign soil since the Vietnam war (*see* accompanying article). At the end of August, U.S. intelligence had estimated the number of Iraqi troops in Kuwait at 265,000, and by September 18 the number was thought to have grown to 360,000. On November 8 the president announced plans to double the U.S. forces in the Gulf; on November 19, Iraq riposted that it would pour 250,000 more troops into Kuwait. Thus the stakes progressively increased, and with them the presumed risk of war.

Paratroopers from France and R.A.F. Coltishall "Jaguars" from Britain, above, were part of the international force that was assembled in the Gulf. Below, Iranian women seem to forget that their nation only recently had fought a devastating war against Iraq and express their displeasure with the U.S. policy.

© Eslami Rad/Gamma-Liaison

Secretary-General Javier Pérez de Cuéllar (left) presided as the United Nations passed 12 Security Council resolutions involving Iraq's invasion of Kuwait. The resolutions included calling for the establishment of a sea and air blockade against Iraq and authorizing the use of force against Iraq if it did not withdraw from Kuwait by Jan. 15, 1991. Represented by Foreign Minister Eduard Shevardnadze (center), the USSR joined with the United States in voting against Iraq.

UN Actions. Among the most surprising, and welcome, aspects of the crisis was the series of concerted actions by the UN Security Council, which brought into being a worldwide embargo on trade with Iraq, and legitimated and encouraged the creation of a multinational force in Saudi Arabia. This, of course, was possible only because of the acquiescence of the Soviet Union and China—permanent Council members with veto power under the UN Charter.

During August five resolutions were passed by the Security Council whose combined effect was: to condemn the Iraqi invasion of Kuwait and demand immediate and unconditional withdrawal (August 2); to impose mandatory economic sanctions on Iraq, banning import or export of all products, with some exceptions for medical supplies and foodstuffs (August 6); to declare the Iraqi annexation of Kuwait (by this time organized as a new 19th province) null and void (August 9); to call for the release of all foreign nationals held against their will in Iraq and Kuwait (August 18); and to authorize a sea and air blockade of Iraq and the inspection of ships at sea (August 25, Cuba and Yemen abstaining). While the August 25 resolution did not authorize in so many words the use of force, it did sanction ''measures commensurate to the specific circumstances''—a phrase regarded by the United States and Britain as in fact authorizing force.

The multinational force gathered in Saudi Arabia and the Persian Gulf continued to lack a unified command structure. This was an unfortunate difference from the Korean case and might prove highly dangerous in the event of actual fighting. At any rate, in the course of four months the totals grew to formidable numbers, with contributions from some 26 states

(Continued on page 32.)

The U.S. Viewpoint

With the end of the Cold War Americans heaved a collective sigh of relief and looked to 1990 as a year of peace and international stability. But these high hopes did not survive the summer when the fading menace of Soviet aggression was replaced abruptly by the threat posed by Iraqi ruler Saddam Hussein. By invading neighboring Kuwait on August 2 and laying an iron grip on that tiny oil-rich country, Hussein jolted the United States out of its euphoria and pushed it to the brink of war.

Tension over the Middle East dominated the final five months of the year, and during this period attitudes on the U.S. front shifted. At first Americans were caught up in the drama of the military buildup for Operation Desert Shield, and overwhelmingly supportive of President Bush's demand that Hussein retreat from Kuwait. But as the months dragged on, though backing for the president's main objective remained steadfast, more questions were

Photos, AP/Wide World

raised about his strategy and tactics. And by year's end the nation was embroiled in a full-scale debate over whether Bush was moving too fast down the road to war.

Ironically, though Bush himself from the start condemned the Iraqi invasion as "naked aggression," he initially said that American intervention was not under consideration. But a few hours later he said: "We're not ruling any options out." Over the next few days the president hardened his stand. On August 3, concerned about the possibility of an Iraqi invasion of Saudi Arabia, the president declared that "the integrity" of that country was one of the United States' "vital interests." Just as significant, Bush announced that the conquest of Kuwait was "unacceptable."

On August 6, after extensive phone conversations with Saudi King Fahd, Bush announced the dispatch of U.S. ground, air, and naval forces to Fahd's country to defend it against aggression. Although at first Defense Department officials talked of a force of about 50,000 troops, that number in reality would more than triple in the next three months.

Attempting to establish a rationale for his policy, Bush in televised remarks on August 8 likened the Iraqi attack to Nazi Germany's aggression which touched off World War II. "Appeasement does not work," Bush said and laid down four principles as guides to U.S. policy—Iraqi withdrawal from Kuwait, restora-

Through the UN-imposed economic sanctions and its biggest military buildup since the Vietnam War, the United States hoped to persuade Iraq to evacuate Kuwait. Secretary of Defense Dick Cheney (extreme left) and Joint Chiefs of Staff Chairman Colin Powell directed the U.S. deployment.

tion of the preinvasion Kuwait government, defense of the security of the Persian Gulf, and protection of the lives of American citizens abroad—hundreds of whom were being held hostage in Iraq and Kuwait. Bush emphasized that the mission of U.S. armed forces involved in Operation Desert Shield was "wholly defensive," adding: "Hopefully they [the troops] will not be needed long." The seriousness of the U.S. commitment was underlined August 22 when the president announced a call-up of military reserves, most of whom would be shipped to the Persian Gulf.

Early Support. The president's actions initially received overwhelming backing, as opinion surveys reflected. A *Los Angeles Times* poll published August 31 showed that 73% of those interviewed approved of the way "Bush is handling the Iraqi situation." Inevitably though, given the complexity of the undertaking, questions arose about how the United States would achieve its objectives and no easy answers were forthcoming.

Actually, the United States appeared to be counting heavily on the UN-approved trade embargo against Iraq to force Hussein to withdraw. But no one could predict how long it would take for the weight of these sanctions to be felt. Meanwhile, the United States was feeling economic pain itself as the crisis led to a sharp rise in oil prices which brought complaints from consumers and undermined an already shaky economy.

Underlying the questions about the U.S. role in the Gulf was uncertainty about the reasons for the commitment. Though Bush had emphasized the need to resist aggression, and likened Hussein to Hitler, critics contended that the comparison with the Nazi leader was overdrawn. Another cause for skepticism about the soundness of Bush's policy was the tolerance of Hussein's regime by the administration prior to the Kuwait invasion. This attitude had reflected Iraq's hostility toward Iran, the United States' Middle East adversary throughout the 1980s, and Iraq's importance as an export market for U.S. grain.

Along with citing the principle of resisting aggression, Bush defended Operation Desert Shield on more practical grounds. On August 15 he declared: "Our jobs, our way of life, our own freedom and the freedom of friendly countries around the world" would be endangered if Iraq seized control of "the world's great oil reserves." But this emphasis on oil seemed crass to some critics who contended that Americans should not be asked to risk their lives to keep the cost of fuel down.

Nevertheless, the president stood his ground. In a televised address on the Gulf crisis on September 11, Bush told a joint session of Congress, "vital issues of principle are at stake" in the Middle East. He backed up that assertion with the implied warning that military action might become necessary if the trade embargo did not force Iraq out of Kuwait.

A small but vigorous protest movement against the buildup and the threat of war began to develop. The movement had roots among both conservatives and liberals. In addition resistance to the idea of a Middle East war was bolstered by the participation of the families of troops who had been shipped to the Gulf region. By October 20 the protest movement was strong enough to stage demonstrations in more than a dozen cities. But the movement's influence was limited. On Capitol Hill, Congress rejected suggestions from administration critics that it invoke the 1973 War Powers Resolution, which could have placed a time limit on the commitment of U.S. forces in the Middle East in the absence of a declaration of war. Instead, the House of Representatives and the Senate overwhelmingly adopted resolutions giving support for actions so far taken by the president in the Middle East, without authorizing future use of military force.

Policy Shift. For nearly two months the Middle East situation appeared stalemated as the president was preoccupied with domestic concerns, notably the debate over the budget deficit and the congressional elections. But no sooner was the campaign over than Bush acted to increase dramatically the pressure on Hussein, in the process also intensifying criticism at home. On November 8, Bush announced that the United States would deploy more than 150,000 additional troops to the Persian Gulf, nearly doubling the size of the force committed to Desert Shield. The reinforcements were needed, the president said, to establish "an adequate offensive option" to force Iraq out of Kuwait. This was the first explicit public declaration that the U.S. forces might play an offensive role by launching an attack to drive Iraqi forces out of Kuwait. Moreover, the United States followed up the announcement

For the U.S. soldiers stationed in the Saudi Arabian desert, letters from home helped morale. Americans were encouraged to write to members of Operation Desert Shield.
© Delahaye/Sipa

Amid reports that Iraq was stockpiling biological and chemical weapons, U.S. forces dressed in protective suits and masks were undergoing biowarfare drills. Meanwhile there was some U.S. sentiment favoring simply bringing the troops home.

AP/Wide World

© Jim Levitt/Impact Visuals

of the reinforcements by prodding the UN Security Council into adopting on November 29 a resolution authorizing the United States and its allies to "use all necessary means" to uphold previous resolutions demanding the Iraq withdrawal from Kuwait.

The policy shift caused concern in Congress and led to calls for a special session, both from the president's critics and supporters. But the idea was dropped after House leaders told the president on November 29 that they could not assure him of strong backing from both parties for a resolution which would endorse the use of force. But this decision did not keep the president's newly aroused critics on Capitol Hill from speaking out in hearings conducted by the Senate Foreign Relations and Armed Services Committees on the Persian Gulf. Perhaps the most prominent of the critics, because of his widely acknowledged expertise on national-security matters, was Democratic Sen. Sam Nunn of Georgia, chairman of the Armed Services Committee. "Time is working on our side," Nunn said when his committee's hearings opened November 27, in arguing that the United States would be served better by waiting for the sanctions to take effect. Similar views were heard from James R. Schlesinger, defense secretary in the Nixon and Ford administrations, and from two former chairmen of the Joint Chiefs of Staff, Adm. William J. Crowe and Gen. David Jones.

The well-publicized warnings against hasty military action on the Hill apparently had their impact on the president. On November 30 in a dramatic gesture intended to demonstrate he wanted to "go the extra mile for peace," Bush announced that he would send Secretary of State James A. Baker III to Baghdad to look

Saddam Hussein "in the eye" and persuade him to pull out of Kuwait before the January 15 deadline. But even as he made a move toward peace, the president stressed that he was determined to go to war if necessary. Moreover, if it came down to the use of force, Bush promised, in an allusion to the irresolute way the Vietnam War was conducted, he would not settle for halfway measures. " . . . If there must be war," he said, "we will not permit our troops to have their hands tied behind their backs."

Bush's effort at diplomacy was matched by a gesture fully as dramatic from Saddam Hussein. On December 6 he announced that he had decided to free all the foreigners held hostage in Iraq and Kuwait since the August 2 invasion, in hopes of encouraging diplomatic efforts to avert hostilities. But while Bush welcomed the action, he stressed that it in no way would alter his determination to make Iraq leave Kuwait.

As the year ended, Americans seemed split over what course to follow in the Middle East. A *New York Times* poll taken December 9-11 showed that if Iraq failed to withdraw from Kuwait by the January 15 deadline, 48% of those interviewed thought the United States should continue to wait for the impact of the economic sanctions to be felt while 45% favored an immediate military attack. Said Frank Newport, editor of the *Gallup Report*: "Bush will face a divided public if in fact we go to war. There is by no means a consensus."

ROBERT SHOGAN

Editor's Note: Robert Shogan has been national political correspondent in the Washington bureau of the *Los Angeles Times* since 1973. Mr. Shogan's books include *None of the Above: Why Presidents Fail & What Can Be Done About It*, a study of the American presidency.

© J. Pavlovsky/Sygma

© Andy Hernandez/Sipa

By late 1990, Iraq had a military force of some 430,000 in and around Kuwait. Additional recruits, including women, were being trained for the People's Army in Baghdad.

at a great variety of levels, ranging from the 30,000 troops promised by Britain and Egypt and the 21,000 Syrians, to a few hundred and a few ships from such states as Belgium, Senegal, Spain, and Argentina. Some countries—for example, South Korea and Japan—pledged financial aid, not troops. Saudi Arabia itself had almost 70,000 troops and the UAE, 40,000. Syria and Turkey also added significantly to the pressure on Iraq by stationing massive forces on their borders with it.

Arab Divisions and Sanctions. The crisis deeply divided the Arab world as no other series of events had done. The first attempt to formulate a response, at an Arab League ministers' meeting in Cairo on August 3, resulted in a condemnation of Iraq's actions endorsed by 14 of the league's members. The other seven members either opposed the motion, abstained, or did not participate. A more formal meeting on August 10 in Cairo, at which Egypt's President Mubarak strongly condemned Iraq, approved military aid to Saudi Arabia and was carried by 12 votes of the 21 members.

The effect of economic sanctions remained uncertain. Since Iraq and Kuwait have no exports worth mentioning, except oil, and at the same time must import food and many other products, sanctions would appear to have a good chance of effectiveness in the long run provided there are no leaks in the embargo. It was not at all clear by year's end, however, that they were having a major effect. What was reasonably certain was that the absorption of Kuwait had not yielded the expected profit. Kuwaiti oil could not be marketed, and Kuwait's enormous wealth in other forms was beyond Iraq's reach. For some years, Kuwait's income from its investments (only 2% of which is invested in the Arab world, and which is administered from London) has exceeded its oil revenues. Kuwaiti funds, at first frozen (like Iraq's) by the United States and other Western states, soon were released, unlike Iraq's, so the emir's government, in exile in Taif in Saudi Arabia, had ample funds for its support and for aiding the anti-Iraqi effort.

Even though the two states, Iraq and Kuwait, between them produce more than 40% of current world oil production, the effect of the embargo on the outside world was surprisingly slight. An immediate rise in the price of crude to more than $40 a barrel over a few weeks was followed by a substantial decline, as Saudi Arabia, the UAE, and other producers more than filled the gap; by early December oil supply had ceased to be a problem.

Hostages and Embassies. The aspect of the crisis which had the most psychological impact on the West was Iraq's detention of more than 10,000 foreigners resident in Iraq and Kuwait against their will. Some 3,500 were Americans. Attention first was directed to their plight on August 7; the U.S. government at first avoided using the term "hostages," until President Bush declared on August 20 that the 3,000 remaining "are, in fact, hostages." Most were rounded up in hotels; some were located as "human shields" as possible target areas; some remained hidden.

President Kurt Waldheim of Austria visited Iraq in late August and secured the release of some 80 Austrian hostages. There then ensued over months a curious pilgrimage to Baghdad of relatives of hostages, out-of-office politicians both European and American, sport and entertainment celebrities, generic "peace activists," and (it seemed) publicity seekers. All this must have been gratifying to Saddam Hussein, and enabled him to earn cheaply a reputation for goodwill by releasing, in response to these appeals, a driblet of persons in this or that group, none of whom should have been detained in the first place.

© Barry Iverson, "Time" Magazine

Egypt's President Hosni Mubarak (extreme left), a severe critic of Iraq's action against Kuwait and a supporter of the multinational force, and Syria's President Hafiz al-Assad, also an opponent of Iraq as well as a rival of Hussein for leadership of the Arab world, hold a summit. Above, volunteers enlist in the Saudi National Guard. Since Saudi Arabia was a prime target for further Iraqi aggression, it undertook military preparations of its own.

© Thomas Hartwell, "Time" Magazine

A related question was the long effort to keep open Western embassies in Kuwait and so demonstrate nonrecognition of the conquest. Iraq on August 10 reportedly ordered all embassies to close by the end of the week; on August 22 the United States and other countries stated their intention to defy this order. Under extreme difficulties for the diplomatic staffs, this was done. However, when on October 20, Canada abandoned its embassy in Kuwait, only U.S., French, and British missions remained. By early December there were only the United States and Britain.

Climactic Events of December. The events from August through December had a clearly defined shape. The great rush of events in August created a situation—a confrontation rather than a crisis—which was maintained without essential change until the very end of November and early December. Then, in a concentrated period, the situation was redefined and sharpened. Though President Bush all along had said that continued Iraqi occupation of Kuwait was unacceptable, it had not been clear whether the military deployment was intended merely to protect Saudi Arabia, pending the hoped-for result of the imposition of sanctions.

On November 29 six weeks of intensive diplomatic lobbying by the United States bore fruit when the UN Security Council passed Resolution 678 (the 12th on this crisis) which authorized member states "to use all necessary means" to make Iraq withdraw from Kuwait if it had not done so by January 15. The vote was 12 to two, with Cuba and Yemen against and China abstaining. A Rubicon had been crossed. The immediately following events encouraged hopes of a peaceful resolution. President Bush at his press conference of November 30 offered to send Secretary of State Baker to Baghdad and to invite Iraqi Foreign Minister Tariq Aziz to

© P. Howell/Gamma-Liaison

More than 10,000 foreigners, including some 3,000 Americans, were caught unwillingly in Iraq and Kuwait following the August 2 invasion. Many were rounded up in hotels, while others were "human shields" in target areas. Some were released through the intermediacy of family members, politicians, and others. On December 6, President Hussein announced that all remaining Westerners would be freed soon. Those Americans desiring to leave, including the group at right, were released in time for the holidays with their families.

Washington. He was emphatic, however, that nothing less was acceptable than complete Iraqi withdrawal from Kuwait. The same day, Iraq delivered fruit and food to the besieged U.S. embassy in Kuwait. The offer of talks in Baghdad and Washington was accepted by Iraq on December 1, but with an insistence on a wider agenda that would include discussion of "Palestine and other occupied lands"—an attempted linkage that the United States had rejected consistently.

One week after the passing of Resolution 678 came Iraq's announcement that it would free all remaining hostages by Christmas; the U.S. response was to state its readiness to close its Kuwait embassy if the hostages indeed were released. Both things happened.

Reflections. As 1990 drew to a close the U.S. government was facing extraordinarily difficult decisions. Peace with Saddam Hussein appeared to call for some compromise. The outlines of a possible compromise had been bruited throughout the fall: Iraqi withdrawal from Kuwait, but with some concessions in regard to the Rumaila oil field, and possible cession to Iraq of Warbah and Bubiyan islands at the mouth of the Shatt al-Arab. Such a settlement was possible or even, in the long run, likely; but it would amount to giving some reward for aggression; while, even without concession, any outcome that left in existence Iraq's military might, plus a probable acquisition of nuclear weapons in the not-distant future, evoked nightmarish scenarios of future actions. Everything hung on Saddam Hussein's willingness to comply with the unprecedented UN ultimatum. The future course of events in the Middle East, and the world, turned on whether he would decide to play the peace card.

See also articles on the individual countries in the Alphabetical Section; BIOGRAPHY—*Hussein, Saddam;* UNITED NATIONS.

The troops of Operation Desert Shield not only had to adjust to unfamiliar surroundings, including living in camouflage tents, above, but also had to endure the wait to see how the Iraq crisis would develop—if there would be a resolution or if war would break out.

A view of
Europe as the
Cold War Ends

By F. Roy Willis

Celebrations of "unity day," such as the one above, were held throughout Germany in early October as the Federal Republic and the Democratic Republic were rejoined into one nation. The reunification was perhaps 1990's clearest sign of the dawn of a new Europe.

For Europeans 1989 had been an *annus mirabilis*—an unbelievable year. Both in words and actions, the leaders of the Western and Eastern blocs had shown that the Cold War was virtually at an end. One after another, the authoritarian Communist regimes of Eastern Europe had collapsed or been overthrown, and a great surge of democratic reform had spread to most if not all of those countries. Western Europe's prosperity continued unabated, offering a material example that the East European countries hoped quickly to emulate, while remodeling their political systems upon those of the West. The 12-member European Community (EC) had continued to forge ahead with its plans for full economic union by 1992, as well as for greatly increased political integration. After so many heady events, it hardly was surprising that many in Europe wondered if 1990 might not be a time of letdown and disappointment and perhaps even of disillusionment.

Strengthened East-West Relations. All Europeans were aware that maintenance of Soviet-U.S. reconciliation was central to the continuance of the process of democratization in Europe, as was the success of Soviet President Mikhail Gorbachev's reform program within the Soviet Union. As former dissident and new Czech President Václav Havel told the U.S. Congress in February, "You can help us most of all if you help the Soviet Union on its irreversible but immensely complicated road to democracy."

Gorbachev's strengthening personal relationship with U.S. President George Bush and harmonization of Soviet and U.S. foreign policy brought to Europe not only a relief from the tensions of the Cold War but direct practical benefits. In December 1989, at their first summit meeting off Malta, the two leaders had agreed to accelerate negotiation of treaties on nuclear and conventional arms and had welcomed the political changes in Eastern Europe. In June, during Gorbachev's six-day whirl across the United States, he and Bush signed a framework agreement on reducing strategic nuclear weapons that would cut U.S.-USSR long-range nuclear missiles by about 30% and an agreement to eliminate most of their chemical weapons, while Bush offered a trade treaty intended to aid the faltering Soviet economy by reducing tariffs on Soviet exports.

At Stanford University, Gorbachev summarized the extraordinary new era that East-West relations were entering: "The Cold War is now behind us. Let us not wrangle over who won it . . . It is in the common interest of our two countries and nations not to fight this trend toward new cooperation, but rather to promote it." Only two months later, with the Iraqi invasion and annexation of Kuwait, the Soviet Union and the United States for the first time since 1945 stood firmly united in a major world crisis, in their condemnation of Iraq, as Bush and Gorbachev emphasized in their third, brief summit meeting in Helsinki, Finland, in September.

Toward a New Military Balance. In this favorable atmosphere, arms-reduction talks between the 16-member North Atlantic Treaty Organization (NATO) and the seven-member Warsaw Pact made steady progress. Meeting in Ottawa, Canada, in February, the foreign ministers of NATO and the Warsaw Pact quickly agreed to an "open skies" proposal that would permit unarmed planes, after notification, to monitor military activity on the other's territory. The Conventional Forces in Europe (CFE) negotiations between the alliances, which had been making only slow progress since they opened in Vienna in March 1989, however, seemed to be overtaken by events in Eastern Europe. President Gorbachev gave in one by one to the demands of the new East European governments that Soviet troops be withdrawn from their territory. In July the Soviet Union unexpectedly agreed to a united Germany being a member of NATO and announced that it would have no troops in Eastern Europe after its withdrawal from East Germany in 1994. The Vienna negotiators, therefore, concentrated on levels of weapons systems that each alliance could maintain in the whole area from the Atlantic to the Ural mountains. By October they had agreed to limit each alliance to 20,000 tanks, 30,000 armored combat vehicles, and 2,000 helicopters. This CFE treaty was signed at the November meeting of the 34-nation Conference on Security and Cooper-

About the Author. F. Roy Willis has been a professor of history at the University of California, Davis, since 1964. He recently returned from two years of service at the University of Montpellier, France. A European specialist, Professor Willis is the author of such books as *The French in Germany* (1962), *Europe in the Global Age* (1968), *Italy Chooses Europe* (1971), and *The French Paradox* (1982). Born in Lancashire, England, and a graduate of Cambridge University and Stanford University, he was a fellow of the Rockefeller Foundation in Paris and of the Guggenheim Foundation in Rome.

Improved relations between the United States and the Soviet Union as well as a strong working relationship between their two presidents, Mikhail Gorbachev and George Bush, were credited with bringing the Cold War to an end and leading to significant agreements on nuclear and conventional armaments.

© Joyce C. Naltchayan/The White House

U.S. Vice-President Dan Quayle and House Speaker Thomas Foley (top right) applaud as Czechoslovakia's President Václav Havel addresses a joint session of Congress on Feb. 21, 1990. The former playwright declared that "for another 100 years, American soldiers should not be separated from their mothers because Europe is incapable of being a guarantor of world peace. Sooner or later, Europe must recover and come into its own."

ation in Europe (CSCE), whose role as a guarantor of European military security was winning enthusiastic Russian and German approval but little support from France, Britain, and the United States.

Meanwhile, the mutual relationship and character of the two alliances changed rapidly. Although the Warsaw Pact leaders had declared in December 1989 that Europe should retain its existing frontiers and military alliances, at their summit meeting in Moscow the following June, at which four of the seven government heads were non-Communists, they decided to transform the pact into a political rather than a military alliance and declared that confrontation with NATO was "no longer in line with the spirit of the time." The Hungarian Prime Minister Jozsef Antall even called for the abolition of the pact by 1991.

With the waning of the Communist threat in Europe, which it had been created to repel, NATO searched for a new role. At a NATO summit meeting in London in July, the NATO leaders declared that the two alliances were no longer adversaries, and, as a corollary, gave up their strategy of "forward defense," by which NATO troops had been massed along the border with the Warsaw Pact countries, and stated that use of nuclear weapons would be a "last resort." Although favoring the strengthening of CSCE, the leaders shied away from using it to replace NATO.

Paradoxically, the Western powers were concerned that this new harmonious relationship in Europe was threatened not by the strength of their former adversaries but by their economic weakness, especially in the Soviet Union, and sought means to aid their recovery. The collapsing economy of East Germany was to become, after unification, largely the responsibility of West Germany, which expected to spend between $30 billion and $60 billion annually on its development,

With the Warsaw Pact proclaiming that the West is no longer an "ideological enemy" and with Soviet troops being withdrawn from Eastern Europe, Czech tanks, right, were being turned into scrap as part of the movement toward arms reduction.

© Chamussy/Sipa

and to a lesser extent of the European Community, which would spend $650 million annually. In Paris in May the European Bank for Reconstruction and Development, known as BERD, formally was created with the participation of 40 countries. The bank was to use its capital stock of some $12 billion to make loans to Eastern Europe and the USSR for rebuilding their economies, especially in the private sector. West Germany took the lead in promising to aid the Soviet Union with $3 billion in loans, and Italy and France also offered aid. President Bush, who had been reluctant to offer more than technical assistance until the USSR cut its military spending further, finally followed their lead in December by offering $1 billion in loans for food purchases. The same month the European Community leaders at their summit in Rome authorized an additional $1 billion in medical supplies and food.

Leaders of the North Atlantic Treaty Organization (NATO) met in London, July 5–6, for what would be a historic summit. The leaders agreed to a series of dramatic changes in military strategy, including a scaling back of the frontline defenses.

Shadows Over the New Eastern Europe. In most of Eastern Europe the wave of political reform continued to swell. On March 18 the East German voters gave the former Communists only 16% of the vote and put in power a coalition headed by Christian Democrat Lothar de Maizière, pledged to unite the two Germanys. In two-stage elections on March 25 and April 18, Hungary elected an anticommunist coalition dominated by the center-right Democratic Forum, under Jozsef Antall. The new parliament in Czechoslovakia, elected on June 8 and 9, chose Marian Calfa of the Civic Forum/Public Against Violence alliance as premier and confirmed Václav Havel as president. In Poland, President Wojciech Jaruzelski, the Communist general who had imposed martial law in 1981, asked parliament to cut his term in office to permit democratic presidential elections to take place. In the first round on November 25, Premier Tadeusz Mazowiecki ran a poor third because of dissatisfaction with his economic policies and dropped out. On December 9, Solidarity leader Lech Walesa was elected in a landslide. Even in Albania the repressive Communist regime of Ramiz Alia promised greater religious freedom and foreign travel, as well as increased consumer goods, and, after student riots in December, authorized the formation of a non-Communist opposition party.

The glaring exceptions to the rejection of the Communists in popular elections were Bulgaria and Romania. The Bulgarian Socialist Party, the renamed and reformed Communist Party, received 47% of the vote in elections in June after the 16-party Union of Democratic Forces, the principal anticommunist grouping, failed to win support outside the cities. But tension remained high, and anticommunist crowds burned and ransacked the Socialist Party headquarters in Sofia. Rancor was even stronger in Romania, where in elections on May 20 the National Salvation Front composed mainly of former Communists won 66% of the vote and its leader, Ion Iliescu, became president with an 85% majority. Accusing the Front

Free, multiparty elections became common in East Europe in 1990. Residents of Prague, below left, check some campaign posters prior to June 8–9 parliamentary and regional elections. The Civic Forum-Public Against Violence alliance finished first in the balloting. In Bulgaria, Petar Mladenov, the former Communist Party general secretary who in April was named to the new post of executive president in anticipation of June elections, takes a campaign stroll. The Socialist Party won a solid parliamentary majority in a runoff election. Meanwhile in Romania, after the National Salvation Front, composed mainly of former Communists, captured a majority of the May 20 vote, supporters of the opposition staged a sit-in, protesting that the election was rigged. As the protest continued and turned violent, some 10,000 progovernment coal miners, bottom, routed the demonstrators.

© Shepard Sherbell/Saba

© Miladivonic/Sipa

AP/Wide World

Europe also is undergoing major economic change. For example, East Europe's first stock exchange, left, opened in Budapest, Hungary, June 21, 1990.

of intimidation and election rigging, supporters of the opposition organized a two-month-long sit-in which was broken up by unarmed police. But after the antigovernment crowds turned violent, Iliescu called into Bucharest club-wielding miners who indiscriminately beat up any suspected opponents of the regime. In the Balkans, old ways seemed hard to change.

The new governments of Eastern Europe were faced by even greater problems of economic breakdown than expected, and the proposed remedies, though painful, were far from guaranteed of success. COMECON, the East European economic community, was falling apart, as its members sought to shift their trade to the West. From 1991 on, all transactions were to be in hard currency, replacing the frequent use of barter among the partners. Even Soviet oil, selling at vastly higher prices after the Gulf crisis, had to be paid for in hard currency which Russia intended to use to purchase Western goods rather than the outmoded East European products. East Germany planned to phase out its contracts with its former COMECON partners.

Where harsh economic plans had been implemented to hasten the transition to a market-style economy, the immediate results seemed to be inflation and unemployment. Hungary, the East European country that had taken the lead in privatization of industry and services, creation of a stock exchange, and freeing of most prices, was burdened with a $20 billion foreign debt and a growing budget deficit. Poland's sudden abolition of price controls and subsidies, as a form of shock therapy for installation of a capitalist economy, had reduced inflation from 78% per month in January to only 4% in May while filling the shops with goods. However, industrial output had fallen, almost 500,000 were unemployed, and inefficient state companies were on the point of collapse. The harshness of Poland's example discouraged President Gorbachev from engaging in a similar reform program; and while their political leaders disputed how to create a market economy the Soviet citizens saw the disintegrating system unable even to maintain the low level of consumption to which they were accustomed. In April *The Economist* of London voiced a widely held fear: "There is a strong chance that the revolution which began in 1989 will not just be painful—that much is certain—but that it will go both economically and politically wrong.''

Germany Unified. By contrast with the uncertainty of Eastern Europe, the West Europeans felt certain of embarking on a decade of rapid economic progress, stimulated by German unification and the creation of EC's single market in 1992. German unification was remarkably smooth. The Christian Democratic-led government of East Germany quickly accepted West German terms for economic and monetary union, which was implemented on July 1, making the West German mark the common currency. On August 31 representatives of the two German states signed a complex treaty detailing how their widely differing systems were to be harmonized at unification. In Moscow on September 12, Britain, France, West and East Germany, the United States, and the Soviet Union signed the Treaty on the Final Settlement With Respect to Germany, giving up the occupation rights assumed in 1945, and in effect formally ending World War II. On October 3 jubilant crowds assembled before the floodlit Reichstag building to witness the unfurling of the red, black, and gold federal flag of the united country which, with 78 million inhabitants and a gross national product of $1.8 trillion, seemed likely to dominate the continent. On December 2, Chancellor Helmut Kohl's coalition of Christian Democrats and Free Democrats won an overwhelming victory in the first election in a unified Germany.

But there were shadows over the unification. Estimates of the cost to West Germans of bringing their new compatriots to an equal standard of living roused resentment at the prospect of higher taxes. Unemployment was soaring in the East, reaching some 350,000 in August, and was expected to top 1 million by 1991, at a time when prices and rents also were jumping. Overall, German economists predicted, the united nation would achieve a growth rate of only 1.5% in 1991 compared with West Germany's 4% in 1990.

Toward 1992. Disputes among EC members over such matters as monetary unification seemed minor in relation to the clear determination to complete the achievement of a single Community-wide market by 1992, as they had agreed by passage in 1986 of the Single European Act. This act, the first major revision of the 1957 Treaty of Rome, had ended a decade of stagnation in the Community by streamlining voting procedures in the Council of Ministers, increasing the powers of the European Parliament, and laying down a detailed list of changes that by 1992 would abolish barriers within the Community not only to agricultural and industrial trade but to Community-wide banking, insurance, and services. By 1990 three fifths of these changes had been made. At the European Council meetings of heads of state or government in June and December 1989, it had been agreed that an Economic and Monetary Union (EMU) should be created. Meeting in Dublin in June 1990, the leaders of the EC nations went further and

"What a long way the world has come."

**Mikhail Gorbachev
Paris, Nov. 19, 1990**

"It is the first time in history that we witness a change in depth of the European landscape that is not the outcome of a war or a bloody revolution."

**François Mitterrand
Paris, Nov. 19, 1990**

For the first time in some 40 years, Easter Sunday services are held in St. Alexander Nevsky Cathedral in Sofia, Bulgaria. A new era of increased religious freedom in the USSR and the former Communist nations of East Europe was another indication of a new era on the European continent.

decided that in December they would open intergovernmental conferences not only on the EMU but also on greater political union.

The drive of EC to increased union had repercussions for all Europe. The number of countries pressing for or considering membership increased greatly. After East Germany's acceptance into EC without a treaty of accession, as part of unified Germany, Austria increased its pressure for acceptance, as did Turkey. In July, Malta and Cyprus applied to join. Norway, Sweden, and Finland were considering applications, while the East European countries, led by Czechoslovakia and Hungary, made clear their goal of joining eventually. Although the Community intended to block further expansion at least until 1992, it however did begin negotiations with the six-member European Free Trade Association (Switzerland, Austria, Norway, Sweden, Iceland, and Finland) for creation of a European Economic Space (EES) in which their economic laws would be harmonized.

The magnet to the would-be members was of course the prosperity of EC's members. The average growth rate in 1990 was expected to be 3%–3.5%, with Spain and Germany each reaching or exceeding 4%. Inflation was tumbling, except in Britain. Government deficits were dropping in most countries. Unemployment, though high, was stable at about 9%. Newer EC members, such as Portugal and Spain, were enjoying booms as their economies adjusted to the stimulus of the wider market. But Iraq's invasion of Kuwait brought home to Europeans the vulnerability of a prosperity dependent upon abundant oil supplies from the unstable Middle East and reminded them that the ending of the Cold War in Europe was far from freeing them from the danger of war altogether. Nevertheless, the common condemnation of Iraq by both Western and Eastern Europe provided encouraging proof that the extraordinary political changes of 1989–90 henceforth would permit all Europeans to act together for the first time since 1945 in the cause of world peace and justice.

See also articles on the individual countries within the Alphabetical Section.

© Hans J. Buckard/Bilderberg/Saba

The Union Republics of the USSR

By Robert Sharlet

With a housing development and a monument of Lenin as backdrops, a wedding party takes time out for photographs in Bratsk, Siberia. Demands for sovereignty and greater freedom focused international attention on the union republics of the Soviet Union during 1990.

Future historians of Russia and the Soviet Union well may mark the year 1990 as the beginning of the disintegration of the state forged by Lenin—the Union of Soviet Socialist Republics or the USSR. By the end of the year, all 15 of its constituent union republics had declared their sovereignty, calling into question the de jure status of the USSR if not its very de facto existence as a unified nation-state. At the Fourth Congress of People's Deputies in December, USSR President M. S. Gorbachev struggled valiantly to regain control of the separatist tendencies which his reform program *perestroika*, or "restructuring," launched in the mid-1980s, had released unintentionally. As the world watched, Gorbachev seemed destined to lose the contest with the powerful centrifugal forces tearing the mighty Soviet Union apart as the decade of the 1990s opened.

History of the Soviet State. The USSR was formed in 1922. Following the Bolshevik Revolution of 1917 and the ensuing Civil War, the former csarist Russian empire fell into disarray as a number of the captive peoples under Russian domination sought their independence. This resulted in the emergence of the independent states of Finland, Lithuania, Latvia, and Estonia, and the reconstitution of Poland as a nation-state from the wreckage of the Russian, Prussian, and Austrian empires. Other nationalities of the former czarist empire, such as the Ukrainians and Georgians, enjoyed newfound autonomy for a brief time, before the Bolsheviks began to reassert Russian primacy and refashion a new imperial order under Soviet rule.

Under the guiding influence of the Communist Party, the Union of Soviet Socialist Republics was created in 1922. The four parties to the first Treaty of Union were the Russian, Ukrainian, Byelorussian, and Transcaucasian republics which now were styled "union republics." In 1925 the Uzbek and Turkmen union republics were carved out of Russian central Asia, and joined the USSR. By 1936 there were 11 union republics, three more created out of former Russian Turkestan (the Kazakh, Kirghiz, and Tadzhik union republics), and the Armenian, Azerbaijan, and Georgian union republics which emerged from the subdivision of the Transcaucasian union republic into its three predominant ethnic components. Five more union republics were added to the USSR in 1940 by dint of threat and force against neighboring countries. Romania and Finland were pressured and forced to yield parts of their territories which respectively became the Moldavian and Karelian-Finnish union republics, while the erstwhile czarist Baltic provinces were annexed directly by military occupation and incorporated into the USSR as the Lithuanian, Latvian, and Estonian union republics. On the eve of the Nazi invasion of the USSR in 1941, the union comprised 16 union republics encompassing a bicontinental landmass one sixth the size of the moon and reaching from the border of Europe to the Pacific, and extending from the Arctic Circle to the Middle East.

In the period after Joseph Stalin's death in 1953, the USSR contained 15 union republics (the Karelian-Finnish republic having been reduced in status in 1956), 20 autonomous republics (most within the giant Russian union republic), eight autonomous regions, and ten autonomous districts. This vast, populous, internal empire, long ruled mainly by Russian Communist Party leaders from Moscow, comprises more than 100 nationalities which speak approximately 130 different languages, only 70 of which include literary languages.

In theory, the USSR appears to be a federal state, but in practice, it has operated as a centrally controlled unitary state. The basic concept of the various union and autonomous administrative entities was to afford space for the titular nationality of the area to exercise a degree of cultural autonomy. In the course of industrializing the country, however, the Communist Party colonized many of the union republics bordering on the Russian republic (RSFSR) with Russian workers and administrators. As a result, some 20 million to 25 million Russians live outside the RSFSR and constitute a sizable part of the populations of two of the three tiny Baltic republics and several of the sparsely settled Central Asian republics as well as the approximately 11 million Russians living in the Ukraine. This Russian demographic presence as well as the party's ten-

(Continued on page 48.)

About the Author. Robert Sharlet, professor of political science at Union College in Schenectady, NY, specializes in Soviet and East European affairs. The author of three books and numerous articles and essays, he was graduated from Brandeis and Indiana universities and was an exchange fellow at Moscow University Law School. The recipient of various grants from the Ford Foundation and other institutions, Dr. Sharlet has testified before the U.S. Congress, appeared as a guest expert on various television programs, and is consulted regularly by leading newspapers and magazines. He spent part of 1990 taking a firsthand look at the situation in the USSR.

0	500
	MILES

Arctic Ocean

FINLAND
POLAND
Estonia
Latvia
Lithuania
Byelorussia
Moldavia
Ukraine
Black Sea
TURKEY
Georgia
Armenia
Caspian Sea
IRAQ
Azerbaijan
Turkmen
IRAN
Kazakhstan
Uzbekistan
Kirghizia
Tadzhikistan

Russian Soviet Federated Socialist Republic

Sea of Okhotsk

CHINA
MONGOLIA

The Union Republics

Armenian Union Republic. The Armenian people have lived in the region between the Black Sea and the Caspian Sea since ancient times. The Kingdom of Armenia, which lasted from around 190 B.C. to around 1070 A.D., included not only the present Armenian Republic, but also a large slice of what is now eastern Turkey. The country later was divided between Persia and the Ottoman Empire. Persian Armenia, annexed by Russia in 1828, became an independent republic after the breakup of the Russian Empire in 1918. It was incorporated into the USSR in 1922, and became the Armenian Soviet Socialist Republic in 1936. Since 1988 it has been involved in an armed conflict with neighboring Azerbaijan.

The Armenians were the first nation to adopt Christianity (300 A.D.) officially. Their church, the Armenian or Gregorian Church, is an independent body. Armenia is mountainous, but vineyards, fruit, and tobacco are cultivated in the valleys. It has a chemical industry, and its mineral products include copper and gold. **Area:** 11,500 sq mi (29 800 km²); **Population:** 3,305,000 (1990 est.); **Capital:** Yerevan.

Azerbaijan Union Republic. Situated on the western shore of the Caspian Sea, this republic is the northern part of the larger region of Azerbaijan, the rest of which is in Iran. It was annexed by Russia in 1813, and became a union republic of the USSR in 1936. It includes the Nakhichevan Autonomous Republic (which is separated from it by Armenia) and the territory of Nagorno-

Karabakh, which triggered the recent conflict between Armenia and Azerbaijan. Azerbaijan's most important products are petroleum and natural gas. Its people are mostly Muslim, speak a Turkic language, and have strong sentimental ties to their fellow Azeris in Iran. **Area:** 33,400 sq mi (86 500 km²); **Population:** 7,145,600 (1990 est.); **Capital:** Baku.

Byelorussian Union Republic. Byelorussia, or White Russia, was part of Poland until the late 1700s, when it was annexed by Russia. The republic, established in 1919, was enlarged by territory taken from Poland in 1939. Its people are related closely to the Great Russians in language and culture. Its chief industrial products include cement, steel, and TV sets. Byelorussia has a seat in the United Nations. **Area:** 80,151 sq mi (207 590 km²); **Population:** 10,200,000 (1990 est.); **Capital:** Minsk.

Estonian Union Republic. The northernmost of the three Baltic states, Estonia was ruled by the German Teutonic Knights, Poland, and Sweden before being conquered by Russia in 1721. Like its Baltic neighbors, the country was independent from 1918 until 1940, when it was annexed by the USSR. In 1990 it declared that it intended to reclaim its independence. The Estonians, who comprise about 60% of the population, are mostly Lutheran and are related closely to the people of nearby Finland. Ethnic Russians make up 34% of the population and generally are opposed to the inde-

pendence movement. Electric motors and paper products are manufactured, and oil shale is mined in the northeast for use as fuel. **Area:** 17,400 sq mi (45 065 km²); **Population:** 1,600,000 (1990 est.); **Capital:** Tallinn.

Georgian Union Republic. Georgia, on the eastern shore of the Black Sea, was annexed by Russia in 1801 and became a union republic of the USSR in 1936. The Georgians, a proud mountain people who constitute 69% of the population, elected a non-Communist government in 1990, and declared their intention of seeking independence. They have been Christians since the 4th century A.D., and have their own Orthodox Church. The Georgian language belongs to the Caucasian group, which is native to the region. Notable Georgians have included Joseph Stalin and Eduard Shevardnadze, Mikhail Gorbachev's foreign minister from 1985 to 1990. Other peoples in the republic include the Abkhaz, who are also Caucasians, the Turkic Adzhars, and the Ossetians, who speak an Iranian language. Wine, tea, and fruit are important Georgian agricultural products, and manganese is a major mineral resource. **Area:** 27,000 sq mi (70 000 km²); **Population:** 5,449,000 (1989); **Capital:** Tbilisi.

Kazakh Union Republic. Kazakhstan covers a large area of Central Asia. Traditionally the domain of the Kazakhs, nomadic horsemen who were subdued by the Russians in the 18th and 19th centuries, it became a union republic of the USSR in 1936. Today the Kazakhs, a Turkic-Mongol people, comprise 36% of the population. The first region to experience ethnic violence in the wake of the Gorbachev reforms, Kazakhstan is one of the main grain-producing areas of the USSR; coal mining and electric power are major industries. **Area:** 1,049,155 sq mi (2 717 300 km²); **Population:** 16,600,000 (1990 est.); **Capital:** Alma-Ata.

Kirghiz Union Republic. Kirghizia, a mountainous country on the Chinese border, was formerly part of the Khanate of Kokand, annexed by Russia in 1876. The Kirghiz people, who are Muslim and speak a Turkic language, form 52% of the population. Mineral resources include coal, petroleum, natural gas, and uranium. Kirghizia's Ashtar movement has led the fight for greater local autonomy. **Area:** 76,640 sq mi (198 500 km²); **Population:** 4,372,000 (1990 est.); **Capital:** Frunze.

Latvian Union Republic. Latvia, one of the Baltic republics, was part of medieval Livonia, ruled by the Teutonic Knights; later divided between Sweden and Poland, it was absorbed into the Russian Empire in the 1700s. It was independent from 1918 to 1940, when it was annexed by the USSR. In 1990 the Latvian government declared its intention to reclaim its independence. The Latvians, or Letts, who constitute 52% of the population, are mostly Lutheran, and speak a Baltic language related to Lithuanian. Latvia's products include transportation and electrical equipment, and chemicals. **Area:** 24,600 sq mi (63 700 km²); **Population:** 2,700,000 (1990 est.); **Capital:** Riga.

Lithuanian Union Republic. Lithuania is the southernmost of the three Baltic republics. A small country today, in medieval times it ranked as a grand duchy and was one of the great powers of Eastern Europe. In 1386 it was united with Poland; the resulting kingdom of Poland-Lithuania included most of what is now Byelorussia and the Ukraine. Annexed by Russia in 1795, Lithuania regained its independence in 1918, but was subjected to Soviet rule along with Estonia and Latvia in 1940. Gorbachev's *glasnost* policy encouraged a revival of Lithuanian nationalism, represented by the Sajudis Party. The republic was the first to declare itself independent in 1990, an action that the USSR took steps to prevent. The Lithuanian people are traditionally Roman Catholic and speak a Baltic language related to Latvian; they comprise 80% of the population. Electric power and the manufacture of textiles and fertilizers are major industries. **Area:** 25,174 sq mi (65 200 km²); **Population:** 3,700,000 (1990 est.); **Capital:** Vilnius.

Moldavian Union Republic. Formerly known as Bessarabia, the Moldavian Republic is the eastern part of the historic region of Moldavia, the rest of which lies in neighboring Romania. Annexed by Russia in 1812, it belonged to Romania from 1918 to 1940, when it was incorporated into the USSR. The Moldavians, a Romanian-speaking people who form about 64% of the population, generally support the Moldavian Popular Front, which formed a government in 1990 and tried to make Romanian the republic's official language. This was resisted by the Gagauzi, a Turkish-speaking minority, and by the ethnic Russians who live along the Dniester River. **Area:** 13,000 sq mi (33 700 km²); **Population:** 4,341,000 (1989); **Capital:** Kishinev.

Russian Union Republic. The Russian Soviet Federated Socialist Republic (RSFSR) is by far the largest and most powerful of the union republics of the USSR. Extending from the Baltic Sea across the Russian heartland and the vast reaches of Siberia to the Pacific Ocean, it occupies three quarters of the total area of the Soviet Union, and contains 51% of its population. The majority (83%) of the republic's inhabitants are ethnic Russians, but it also includes more than 38 other national groups, many of them living in the 16 autonomous republics, five autonomous regions, and ten national areas under the jurisdiction of the RSFSR. The Russian Republic is responsible for about 70% of the agricultural and industrial output of the USSR. It produces about 90% of the nation's petroleum, 81% of the timber, and 75% of the natural gas.

In 1990, led by its president, Boris Yeltsin, the RSFSR emerged as a new and independent force in Soviet affairs, and Yeltsin challenged Mikhail Gorbachev's primacy in the Soviet power structure. In June the RSFSR declared that its laws took precedence over those of the central government; in August it concluded a treaty on trade and economic cooperation with Lithuania, the first such agreement between two Soviet republics; in September the Russian parliament approved a radical 500-day plan shifting its economy to a free-market system; as 1991 began, Yeltsin was engaged in hard bargaining with Gorbachev over the amount of the RSFSR's contribution to the Soviet budget. **Area:** 6,592,812 sq mi (17 075 303 km²); **Population:** 147,386,000 (1989); **Capital:** Moscow.

Tadzhik Union Republic. Tadzhikistan, one of the Central Asian republics, borders on Afghanistan and China. Formerly part of the Emirate of Bukhara, it was organized as an autonomous republic in 1924 and became a union republic in 1929. The Muslim Tadzhiks, who comprise 59% of the population (23% are Uzbeks) speak an Iranian language and have close ties to their fellow Tadzhiks in Afghanistan. Tadzhikistan is a major cotton-growing region. **Area:** 55,251 sq mi (143 095 km²); **Population:** 5,112,000 (1989); **Capital:** Dushanbe.

Turkmen Union Republic. Established in 1924, the Turkmen Republic is north of Iran on the eastern side of the Caspian Sea. Its main physical feature is the Kara Kum desert. The Turkmen people, who make up 68% of the population, are Muslim and speak a Turkic language. The republic is a major producer of petroleum, natural gas, and cotton. **Area:** 188,455 sq mi (488 096 km²); **Population:** 3,621,700 (1990 est.); **Capital:** Ashkhabad.

Ukrainian Union Republic. Like the Byelorussians, the Ukrainians, who comprise 75% of the Ukraine's population, are Slavs and close ethnic relatives of the Great Russians. The Ukraine belonged to Poland from the 1300s to the 1600s, and some areas (Galicia and Carpatho-Ukraine) did not join the USSR until 1945. Galicia is the stronghold of the Ukrainian Catholic Church, a minority religious group outlawed by Moscow in 1946. The status of this church remains a source of conflict between the Galicians and the Soviet government. The majority of Ukrainians belong to the Orthodox faith.

In the fall of 1990 the Ukraine experienced a rash of strikes and protest demonstrations that forced its hitherto conservative Communist government to take a more independent stance toward the central government. Considerable resentment still exists over the government's handling of the Ukraine's Chernobyl nuclear accident in 1986.

The Ukraine is the second-largest Soviet republic in population. It is rich in coal and iron deposits and produces more than 40% of the nation's steel. In agriculture, it accounts for as much as 25% of the grain supply and 60% of the sugar. **Area:** 233,089 sq mi (603 677 km²); **Population:** 51,704,000 (1989); **Capital:** Kiev.

Uzbek Union Republic. Uzbekistan is the most populous of the Central Asian republics. Its cities, including Samarkand and Tashkent, were major centers of Islamic civilization in the Middle Ages. More recently it was ruled by the Muslim states of Bukhara and Khiva, which came under Russian control in the 1800s. The Uzbeks, who make up 69% of the population, are a Turkic people. Uzbekistan is an important cotton-growing region. **Area:** 172,740 sq mi (447 400 km²); **Population:** 19,906,000 (1989); **Capital:** Tashkent.

dency to seed the administrations of the outlying union republics with Soviet Russian party and governmental officials effectively ensured Russian control of the USSR since its inception in the early 1920s.

Thus, Soviet nationality policy has been skewed consistently toward ethnic Russian domination from Lenin to Gorbachev. Stalin paid lip service to Soviet federalism by having a purely symbolic right of secession clause written into the Constitution of 1936. In 1945 at the founding conference of the United Nations in San Francisco, he sought to obtain separate seats for each of the union republics. Rebuffed by the West, he settled for three delegations—the USSR, the Soviet Ukraine, and Soviet Byelorussia. In the post-Stalin period, Nikita Khrushchev was confronted by the first shoots of ethnic nationalism in the western Ukraine, which had been taken from Poland after World War II. The western Ukrainian ethnic dissidents, who sought more real cultural autonomy within the USSR, were repressed judicially, but the movement for more ethnic rights took root in the Ukraine and in several other republics as well. Leonid Brezhnev, who took office as party leader in 1964, soon faced diverse forms of ethnic dissent in Lithuania and Georgia as well as the Ukraine, and among the Crimean Tartars, a smaller nationality. The Brezhnev administration continued the policy of repression, but the problem continued to grow through the 1970s and into the early 1980s, with even a Great Russian nationalist movement arising from the shadows of history.

© Kimmo Raisanen/Lehtikuva Oy/Saba

Members of the nationalist Latvian National Front stage a rally prior to March-April 1990 elections for the Supreme Soviet in Latvia. Following the balloting, Latvia's newly elected Supreme Soviet, with a majority of delegates loyal to the Popular Front, proclaimed its independence on May 4 but took a more cautious line than its Baltic neighbors.

Perestroika and the Union Republics. Coming to power in 1985 as Communist Party chief, Gorbachev soon launched his ambitious program, called *perestroika*, for reforming the Soviet system. The three principal domestic policies of Gorbachev's reform program were *glasnost*, or more openness and access to public information; democratization, or greater civic involvement in the political process; and economic restructuring of the overly centralized, heavily bureaucratized planned state economy.

Glasnost and, in particular, democratization very quickly began to have a significant impact on the ethnic dimension of Soviet society. Prior to Gorbachev, unauthorized public demonstrations were nearly nonexistent in the USSR; the rare outburst by intellectual dissidents or, occasionally, disgruntled workers invariably were suppressed by unbridled displays of the state's immense police power. Thus the first major outburst of the Gorbachev era caught both him and the leadership by surprise. In violation of long-standing, unwritten political custom, Moscow appointed an ethnic Russian to the post of first secretary (not the usual second secretaryship) of a union republic Communist Party, in effect as boss of Kazakhstan. In

ЗА РЕАЛЬНЫИ ТРУД, РЕАЛЬНУЮ ЗАРПЛАТУ.

© Laski/Sipa

December of 1986 thousands of Kazakhs responded by going into the streets to protest. Although the demonstrators were quelled, a precedent had been established in the heretofore quiescent Soviet society.

Many Soviet citizens began to take Gorbachev's encouraging calls for democratization, especially as a lever against reform-resistant economic bureaucrats, in directions he did not anticipate. In the summer of 1987 a group of Crimean Tartars from the south startled the Kremlin and the world by boldly demonstrating in Red Square, airing their ethnic grievances a stone's throw from Lenin's Mausoleum. In the glare of *glasnost* and the new openness in the Soviet media, Gorbachev and the party leadership had no choice but to negotiate peacefully with the protesters, setting another important precedent for political behavior in the USSR. By early 1988 hundreds of thousands of Armenians were taking to the streets and squares of the union republic capital of Erevan with impunity, to protest against neighboring Azerbaijan over a territorial issue.

The examples of the Kazakhs, Crimean Tartars, and Armenians in turn had emboldened other ethnic groups, which long had nursed grievances in relative silence against the central government, the Russians, the Communist power, or all three. So-called popular fronts were organized by the majority nationality in several union republics. At first these fronts tiptoed rather tentatively into the public arena, unsure of the limits of the regime's tolerance. Initially, in a number of places, mass ethnic activism was directed against environmentally offending projects, such as nuclear reactors in the wake of the 1986 Chernobyl disaster, imposed on the republics by

On March 11, 1990, Lithuania became the first of the union republics to declare its independence and elected Vytautas Landsbergis, below, a 57-year-old music professor and political activist, as president. For the first time members of independent and unofficial organizations were allowed to participate in Moscow's May Day celebrations in 1990, above. Some of the protesters expressed support for Lithuania's independence.

© Chip Hires/Gamma-Liaison

the center. Gradually, as fear of retribution ebbed, the popular fronts took on cultural issues, such as the language rights of the majority, and then progressively more explicit political matters with the tone of ethnic activism becoming steadily stronger, more daring, and even strident. If anything, the rather precipitous collapse of the Communist regimes of East Europe in the last months of 1989 accelerated the political education of Soviet activists, as ethnically driven disputes between various non-Russian groups such as Armenians and Azeris, between Russians and non-Russians such as the Moldavians, and between the center and a union republic as exemplified by Georgia's bitter dispute with Moscow over the Soviet army's violent dispersal of a peaceful demonstration in the spring of 1989—moved ethnic disputes to center stage in Soviet politics at the beginning of the 1990s.

The Union in Disarray. Nineteen-ninety was a tumultuous year in the history of the union republics. Early January saw renewed brutal attacks by Azeris against Armenians, necessitating Soviet military intervention in Baku, capital of Azerbaijan and home to a variety of nationalities like many large multiethnic Soviet cities. In March, Lithuania became the first union republic to declare its independence from the USSR. Simultaneously, Gorbachev rushed through the legislative process the first Soviet law on secession, insisting that a union republic only could secede from the union in accordance with its provisions, which among other things entail a five-year waiting period. Lithuania defied the law and Gorbachev replied with an economic embargo of the republic. By summer,

The year opened with the Soviet government dispatching troops to the southern republic of Azerbaijan to stop ethnic violence between Muslim Azerbaijanis and Christian Armenians. Sporadic violence between the two ethnic groups had been occurring since 1988. Claims to Nagorno-Karabakh, a predominantly Armenian autonomous region within Azerbaijan, was the contentious point.

© Novosti/Lehtikuva Oy/Saba

Thousands of Soviet Georgians packed the streets of the republic's capital, Tbilisi, April 8–9, 1990, to commemorate the first anniversary of the killing of 19 pro-independence demonstrators in Tbilisi by Soviet troops. An evening memorial rally, left, was part of the demonstration.

stalemate had occurred and a process of negotiations was opened between Moscow and its rebellious republic.

Indeed, Gorbachev had prevented immediate secession, but his was a Pyrrhic victory as the contagion of separatism rapidly spread across the Soviet Russians' enormous internal empire. Throughout the summer of 1990, one by one other union republics took the less dramatic step of issuing proclamations of sovereignty as expressed in the declarative precedence of republic legislation over federal law. The Estonians and Latvians declared themselves sovereign; the Russian republic now led by the erstwhile party boss, Boris Yeltsin, followed suit along with the Moldavians, Ukrainians, Uzbeks, Georgians, and others. Last to join the rush to presumptive independence was the Kirghiz union republic in December.

The chain reaction of sovereignization, however, did not stop in the union republic capitals. Soviet public authority began to unravel visibly as lesser units of the USSR took their cues from their union republics, and autonomous republics, regions, districts, and, in some areas, even cities clamored to add their voices to the rising chorus of sovereign claims. This included most of the autonomous entities of the RSFSR, the Osset and Abkhaz minorities in the Georgian union republic, and the Gagauz people as well as several predominantly Russian-populated cities, respectively, in Moldavia. As the union republics frayed the fabric of the USSR, the ethnic minorities of the federated republics in turn pressed similar demands on their titular nationalities. While Yeltsin of the RSFSR, for the time being at least, fielded the diverse claims of sovereignty with diplomatic aplomb, the Georgians and Moldavians reacted to internal ethnic challenge more aggressively. The Georgian republic abrogated the sovereignty declarations of the Ossets and Abkhazians and even rescinded their status as autonomous republics, while the Moldavians threatened the Gagauz with mob violence and engaged in armed conflict with their Slavic neighbors who provocatively had proclaimed the so-called Trans-Dnieper republic in the midst of the Moldavian union republic. By the end of 1990 the Union of Soviet Socialist Republics was in serious disarray.

The Future of the USSR? To rephrase the question above, does the USSR have a future? President Gorbachev still thinks so, but this may be wishful thinking, as can be seen in the demurral of a thoughtful Soviet lawyer at a conference in New York in the fall of 1990, who simply but unequivocally stated, ''The Soviet Union no longer exists.'' By this he meant that the historic conception had been shattered by uncontrollable forces, and the shards of union now lay about in myriad patterns. While the lawyer's pronouncement might have been premature, the evidence suggests that the relevant question is no longer, ''Will the Soviet Union break up?,'' but, ''How and when will the implosion occur?''

The planned division of economic labor in the state economy is breaking down as factories fail to fulfill contractual obligations and union republics begin to refuse to ship goods beyond their borders. Republican custom posts and border guards even have begun to appear in a few places to enforce local economic nationalism. Significant shortfalls in the semiannual spring and fall conscriptions for the Soviet armed forces surfaced in 1990 as draft avoidance in the non-Slavic republics became rampant, and a number of union republics asserted the right to retain ethnic servicemen of their nationality on republic territory. Several republics have begun to conduct their own foreign economic relations, while others have bypassed Moscow and established by agreement and treaty new relationships among themselves. At least one union republic, namely the Ukraine, experimented during the year with the idea of a separate currency. Possibly the most dramatic evidence of the incipient disintegration of the USSR is the extraordinary, multisided legal conflicts which emerged in 1990 between the Soviet state and its union republics. Federal and republic law routinely clash on a wide range of issues,

Workers assemble electrical household meters in a factory in Vilnius, Lithuania. The republic is a major producer of electrical power and exports electricity to its neighbors. After Lithuania's declaration of independence in March, Tass, the Soviet news agency, issued a statement pointing out that ''all installations and projects in Lithuania'' are the ''property of the USSR.''

© Filip Horvat/Saba

© Edward Igor/Sipa

with a consequent kind of legislative gridlock in which many contradictory new laws are passed, but few are implemented. This phenomenon described as the "war of laws" already has eroded public authority seriously at all levels of government in the USSR, leading Gorbachev in December to dub the republican challenge to federal writ a "quiet counterrevolution."

As the year drew to a close, President Gorbachev strove to keep the country intact by offering the union republics a new deal, the draft version of a new Treaty of Union which was published for discussion in late November. While the draft was designed to transform constitutionally the USSR (to be renamed the Union of Sovereign Soviet Republics) from a unitary state masquerading as a federation into an actual federal system, it might have been too late in the race to rein in a number of runaway republics. The spectrum of their dissent spanned a preference for no relationship with the USSR to a weak confederation at most. As a way of going over the heads of the rejectionist republics, Gorbachev at the opening of the Fourth Congress of People's Deputies on December 17 called for an all-union referendum on the proposed Treaty of Union. Even if he might prevail at the ballot box, however, it was doubtful that a number of maverick republics would abide by the outcome, leaving Gorbachev one final option, the resort to force. Whatever the future may hold for the foundering Soviet state in the decade of the 1990s, one thing is certain—the opening line of the national anthem with its stirring reference to the "unbreakable Union of freeborn Republics" surely will need to be revised.

About two thirds of the 3.6 million people of the Turkmen Union Republic live in rural areas. Islam is the republic's chief religion and its citizens speak a Turkic language. With borders on Iran and Afghanistan, the republic declared its sovereignty on Aug. 23, 1990.

Earth Day Turns 20

© LeRoy Henderson/Black Star

A greater awareness of environmental concerns developed between the first Earth Day, April 22, 1970, (photo above) and Earth Day 1990 (right).

Part celebration, part sickbed vigil, Earth Day 1990, April 22, captured the attention and imagination of uncounted millions in 140 countries. The organizers, led by those who ran the first Earth Day 20 years earlier, said that this time it was the largest grass-roots demonstration in history.

On Earth Day itself, a balmy Sunday in most of the United States, there were rallies and concerts, tree plantings, litter cleanups, cere-

---

"I am only one, but I can do something."

GAYLORD NELSON
Cofounder
Earth Day 1970

monies to honor Brazilian rain forests and to protest against pollution in Eastern Europe and against development in a hundred environmentally sensitive sites. In the days leading up to the event, there were countless announcements by industrial companies of steps they had taken, or would take soon, to ease the burden on Mother Nature. Big corporations still stressed commercial angles, but they had an "earthier-than-thou" touch, each arguing its environmental virtue, and with rival engineers debating, for example, whether styrofoam was really any worse for the environment than cardboard.

In the United States, in zoos and parks and on street corners, employees of the Environmental Protection Agency (EPA) handed out leaflets on environmental problems and progress. In Washington legislators groped toward a new Clean Air Act. And on computer bulletin boards, programmers posted new environmentally conscious software, like a program that takes the words that normally would fill three or four pages of printer paper and squeezes them onto one. The sentiment was unambiguous: The human race must leave a gentler footprint on the planet. But the trail leading to Earth Day 1990 was not so promising.

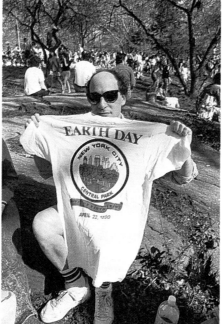

© Halebian/Gamma-Liaison

© Brad Markel/Gamma-Liaison

© Jennie Jones Photography Inc.

The Cuyahoga River in Cleveland, OH, was so polluted in the summer of 1969 that it caught on fire, trapping a tug in the process. It since has been cleaned up to the extent that Clevelanders today welcome a visit to the riverfront, above.

© "The Plain Dealer," Cleveland

THE ENVIRONMENT
A World of Challenges

Editor's Note: In recognition of Earth Day 1990, Matthew L. Wald, a reporter specializing in coverage of the environment and the energy field in the business and financial news department of *The New York Times*, wrote "Guarding Environment: A World of Challenges." The article appeared in the April 22, 1990, issue of the *Times*, © 1990 by The New York Times Company. Excerpts from the report appear on the following pages and are reprinted with permission.

Twenty years after the first Earth Day, the Cuyahoga River no longer caught fire on its way through Cleveland, and bald eagles, once threatened by DDT, had increased nearly seven-fold in the continental United States, enough for government biologists to consider promoting the population to "threatened" from "endangered."

From Streams to Stratosphere. There were scores of other examples of modest environmental progress. But the targets had shifted. Once concern was centered on narrow problems: the stream in the valley, the dump nearby, tiny snail darters or giant pandas. By 1990, the issues were systemic: industrial gases acting like glass in a greenhouse to trap heat around the Earth, the destruction of the protective ozone layer. Scientists had discarded the image of Mother Nature with a black eye for one of Mother Nature stumbling toward a cliff.

"The ozone hole is the smoking gun," said Michael Oppenheimer, a senior scientist at the Environmental Defense Fund, who called the thinning of the protective ozone layer "real proof that humans threaten life on Earth." The near-global agreement in Montreal in January 1989 to cut production of chlorofluorocarbons, which destroy ozone, was cited by many experts as a watershed event, a sign that would be seen in the future as the point at which the human species realized there is more to life than being at the top of the food chain. Around the United States, however, progress on the environment was mixed with frustration. Examples abound:

• Utilities in the United States were burning more than twice as much coal for electricity as they did in 1970, yet emitted 15% less sulfur dioxide, the coal by-product that causes acid rain. Still, 4,000 lakes in the United States and 164,000 in Canada were acidified or threatened, by environmentalists' count.

• The tail pipes of new cars were emitting 96% less carbon monoxide and hydrocarbons and 76% less nitrogen oxides than older models. But there were so many more vehicles and so much congestion that half of Americans lived in counties that violated federal clean air standards in 1988.

• Fish had returned to the Cuyahoga River and to Lake Erie, into which it empties, and other Great Lakes. But the flesh of many Great Lakes fish carried toxic chemicals that made them dangerous to eat, and cast doubt on the wisdom of restocking the lakes.

"This is not the way to reconcile people with nature, and the public knows that," William K. Reilly, head of the Environmental Protection Agency, said of the poisonous fish. Reilly, who carries a business card of brown recycled paper, is himself a symbol of the ascent of environmentalism, if not the environment, an insider at the White House who is a former president of the World Wildlife Fund-United States.

The U.S. Environmental
Protection Agency

During a Jan. 24, 1990, news conference, President Bush endorsed a proposal elevating the Environmental Protection Agency (EPA) to cabinet status. The president said that he was convinced that the challenges facing the environment "are so important that they must be addressed from the highest level of our government." Bush also pointed out that "many countries have environmental ministers" and that cabinet status for EPA "would help influence the world's environmental policies." Various members of Congress agreed with the president, and legislation elevating the EPA to the Department of the Environment was introduced in both houses of Congress. The House of Representatives passed a bill in March, but that bill died in a Senate committee. A separate Senate bill also died without a Senate vote. In early January 1991 a new House bill on the subject was introduced.

In supporting the measure, William Howard, the executive vice-president of the National Wildlife Federation, noted that EPA "has a larger budget than either the State Department or the Department of Commerce and employs more people than the Education Department or HUD [the Department of Housing and Urban Development]."

The EPA was established as an independent agency in 1970 "to permit coordinated and effective government action on behalf of the environment."

Human Ecology

Feb. 7, 1969, Senator Muskie, center, Sen. Alan Cranston, and Adm. Chester Bender inspect damage from an off-shore oil-drilling leak.

by Edmund S. Muskie

Editor's Note: At the dawn of the environmental movement, in 1969, Edmund S. Muskie, then a U.S. senator from the state of Maine and one of the first promoters of the environmental cause, wrote an article titled Human Ecology for the *Encyclopedia Year Book*. Excerpts from the summary appear on this page. It is interesting to note that many of the senator's warnings remain as pertinent in the 1990s as they were on the first Earth Day.

In 1969 an era came to an end. It was an era of exploration, outreach, and headlong advance. Interrupted by two world wars, slowed by a constant tug between peace and war, and fueled by the eager consumption of technology and material accomplishment, man had forced his way out of the environment and landed on the moon. No matter how far afield our explorations take us, however, we must always return to Earth.

In some future time, we may find another environment in which we can live without artificial assistance. But for the foreseeable future we have but one natural environment. If we do not begin to repair the damage we have caused as we have flexed our technological muscle, we will soon be economic orphans—faced with an environment that cannot support simple human existence, much less the exploration of our outer space.

So as we embark on a new era, it would be the greatest of human failures if we neglected to make some elementary decisions as to what our focus for this era must be. Our responsibility on Earth—for our own survival—is to maintain that which is not defiled, enhance that which is degraded, and restore that which has been destroyed. While we may dream of frontiers of space, we must act on the frontier of recovery. If we set goals for the future, this must be one of them. If we are to embark on a romantic adventure this must be it. There is no time to lose.

The environmental crisis is unlike any other we have ever faced. There is no one moment at which the critical point is reached. In fact, there is no such thing as a critical point. Mankind may simply reach the day when there is not enough air, water, and land to support life on this Earth. We may reach a day when the task of restoration is too great. And we may reach a day when the task of replacement is impossible. We are in the midst of the environmental crisis, not approaching it. Whatever our past performance, we can change course. We can make a commitment to a livable environment—if it is important enough to us.

In contrast to classic environmental problems like the dwindling population of eagles, newly recognized global problems may require solutions before the symptoms are understood plainly. Kenneth H. Keller, a chemical engineer who is a former president of the University of Minnesota, wrote: "Our ability to affect our ecological niche is accompanied by an inability to assess the effects of doing so. In contrast to similar problems in the past, we are faced with the situation that the negative effects may be irreversible if we do not act to correct them, but that forces us to act before we can be sure that we understand them."

That understanding may be needed most in the developing countries, where population and economic activity were growing far faster than in industrial nations. If huge populations were to attain Western standards of consumption without some corresponding leap in efficiency, nature would reel, experts predicted. "We need to alter the presumption that increased consumption and economic growth are essential to prosperity," said Peter Dykstra, a spokesman for the Washington office of Greenpeace.

Changing Views—Many Shades, All of Them Green. If the physical picture was mixed in 1990, the political message was not, especially after the *Exxon Valdez* impaled herself on Bligh Reef in March 1989 and the Chernobyl reactor spewed radiation across the Ukraine and much of Europe three years earlier. Concern for nature had claimed hearts and minds around the world. As Yogi Berra might have said, suddenly the environment was all around us. For example, a New York Times/ CBS News Poll asked a random sample of Americans if they

Toxic waste and damage caused by spills from big oil tankers are two major environmental concerns. After the "Exxon Valdez" ran aground in the Gulf of Alaska in March 1989 and an explosion occurred on the Norwegian supertanker "Mega Borg," below, off the coast of Texas in June 1990, the U.S. Congress passed comprehensive oil-spill liability, cleanup, and prevention legislation. Although a survey released by the Environmental Protection Agency (EPA) in 1990 showed a decline in the amount of toxic substances released by industry from 1987 to 1988, experts pointed out that the exact amount of toxic pollution remained unknown. Many companies are not required to release their emissions standards.

© "Houston Post"/Sygma

© Dennis Capolongo/Black Star

agreed that "protecting the environment is so important that requirements and standards cannot be too high, and continuing environmental improvements must be made regardless of cost." When the question first was asked, in September 1981, 45% said yes. In April 1990, 74% did.

Some suspected that the 1990 fever of interest was an unsustainable fad. But to be an environmentalist was to be in the mainstream, as demonstrated by Edgar S. Woolard, Jr., the chairman of E.I. du Pont de Nemours & Company, which once advertised "Better Living Through Chemistry." "Industrial companies will ignore the environment only at their peril," he said. "Corporations that think they can drag their heels indefinitely on genuine environmental problems should be advised: Society won't tolerate it, and Du Pont and other companies with real sensitivity and environmental commitment will be there to supply your customers after you're gone."

The idea that the public would reward companies that struck a protective pose toward nature seemed demonstrated by the experience of Conoco, a Du Pont subsidiary that is the world's 20th-largest oil company, which announced that it was changing the recipe of its gasoline to reduce air pollution. From coast to coast, Conoco said, it received telephone calls asking where its gasoline could be bought.

The reasons for the shift toward environmentalism were not clear even to the victors. Some traced it to a merger of two popular concerns: preservation of the wilderness and fear of cancer. A recurrent theme of environmental decay was the presence of new chemicals, often man-made, that are suspected or confirmed carcinogens. The global nature of problems like diminishing stratospheric ozone, deforestation, and hunger had its own effect on attitudes, blurring the boundaries between nations, some experts said. The environmentalists' response to the Chernobyl disaster—that a nuclear accident anywhere is an accident everywhere—had parallels that applied to pollution. Political change also brought nations together; countries in the European Community moved as a single unit to impose tail-pipe emission standards.

Heightened consciousness added up to an important change for the environment, experts said, perhaps more than any invention, regulation, or other development of the last two decades. What remained to be seen was how long the attitude, which also seemed dominant on previous Earth Days, would endure. But in the spring of 1990, longtime environmental advocates were basking. James Gustave Speth, president of the World Resources Institute in Washington, said the biggest development since the first Earth Day was "the steady and sometimes spectacular growth of worldwide public concern about environmental degradation, and of citizen action and organization to meet these challenges." John C. Sawhill, president of the Nature Conservancy, called it "the gradual 'mainstreaming' of environmental activism."

Michael Deland, chairman of President Bush's Council on Environmental Quality, said an "environmental ethic" had

Beach pollution is another troubling problem. Various U.S. beaches have been forced to close at the height of recent summer seasons after debris, including medical waste, has washed up on shore. Federal legislation ending the dumping of sewage into the ocean after 1991 was enacted in 1988.

© Najlah Feanny/Black Star

(Continued on page 64.)

As Eastern Europe took to democracy, it came out that the area is beset with environmental problems. The Romanian town of Copsa Mica, above, the home of two chemical plants, is covered by a haze of noxious fumes.

Air Pollution

Between the Earth Day celebrations in 1970 and 1990, few arenas achieved greater progress in environmental protection than air quality, according to the 20th annual report of the President's Council on Environmental Quality (CEQ), issued on June 5, 1990. "Despite continued air-pollution problems in many places, primarily cities," it reported, "the country's efforts to protect air quality have been substantial. Not only have total annual emissions of the most common air pollutants declined or remained fairly constant over the past two decades, but they have done so in spite of strong economic and population growth."

Notwithstanding, new research indicated that air pollutants—both natural and human-made—continue to pose the most potent risks to the planet's health.

Trends. Concentrations of sulfur dioxide, smog ozone, and nitrogen oxides—three pollutants long used as a general index of air quality—were at an all-time high in the United States around 1970. By 1988 (the most recent year for which data were available), levels of sulfur dioxide had fallen by 40%, nitrogen-oxide levels had dropped about 25%, and smog-ozone concentrations had been reduced about 18%. In an April 5, 1990, address on urban air-quality trends, U.S. Environmental Protection Agency Administrator William K. Reilly also noted that just since 1980, lead levels have plummeted by almost 90%, ambient carbon-

monoxide levels have fallen 28% and concentrations of particulates (dirt, dust, and soot) have dropped 20%. Overall, however, these changes have not been sufficient to return urban air quality in the United States to acceptable levels, he said. He noted, for example, that "112 million people are living in areas still exceeding the smog standards, while almost 30 million are living in areas exceeding the carbon-monoxide standard, and over 25 million are in areas violating the particulate standard."

Data his agency released to Congress three months earlier on pollutants emitted into the air by U.S. companies in 1987 also indicated that billions of pounds of toxic chemicals are emitted each year. According to Rep. Henry A. Waxman (D-CA), chairman of the House Subcommittee on Health and the Environment, these data are "very troubling. It shows that a great number of [industrial] plants potentially pose extremely high cancer risks to the public." In a letter to Waxman, Administrator Reilly said "we take very seriously the potential problems these emissions could present and thus have . . . entered into discussions with industry to get emissions reductions before a new clean air act requires them."

Clean Air Act. The June CEQ report credited much of the two-decade-long progress in air-pollution control to U.S. enactment of a Clean Air Act in 1970. This sweeping new legislation regulated the sulfur dioxide, nitrogen oxides,

© Cameramann International Ltd.

© Stuart Cohen/Comstock

Although the quality of the air in the United States has improved substantially since the first Earth Day, serious problems remain. Smog, not only in California, right, but elsewhere as well, is a major concern. In fact, about 45% of Americans live in areas exceeding smog standards. As part of the campaign to combat smog and clean the air, several states, including California and New York in 1990, have adopted stricter pollution standards for the growing number of autos.

carbon monoxide, particulates, hydrocarbons, and lead emitted by automobiles, electric power plants, and industrial boilers. By 1980, however, it became clear to many people that the act needed substantial strengthening and an expansion of responsibilities.

Though many lawmakers tried to revise the act throughout the 1980s, they met insurmountable opposition from President Ronald Reagan. Five months into his term, President George Bush reversed that stance by proposing tough changes to the act; 17 months later, after intense political compromise on controversial provisions in the 868-page bill, a revised Clean Air Act was signed into law.

It called for annual reductions in emissions of chemicals that contribute to the formation of smog ozone—hydrocarbons and nitrogen oxides; mandatory marketing of "reformulated" gasoline (containing lower levels of ozone-forming constituents) in the smoggiest cities; guaranteed annual reductions of 10 million tons of sulfur dioxide and 2 million tons of nitrogen-oxides emissions—the two leading contributors to acid rain; and new industrial controls on the air releases of at least 189 potentially cancer-causing chemicals.

Acid Rain. On Sept. 30, 1990, the National Acid Precipitation Assessment Program (NAPAP) ended its ten-year, $535 million mission to investigate the production and effects of sulfur- and nitrogen-based air pollutants. Its final report, issued on September 5, concluded that roughly 75% of acidified surface waters in the eastern United States owe their biological fate to fossil-fuel pollutants. But it found that "with the possible and notable exception of high-elevation red spruce in the northern Appalachians," few North American forests suffer much from these emissions. The health of crops and people also appeared relatively unaffected by most acidic pollutants, NAPAP concluded. But haze remained acid rain's most visible symptom.

The human eye should be able to distinguish features up to 143 mi (230 km) away. But in 1990, haze limited visibility in the United States to about 93 mi (150 km) in rural regions west of the Mississippi and to just 15.5 mi (25 km) in areas east of the Mississippi. About 85% of eastern haze and 50% of western haze stems from air pollution. NAPAP analyses concluded that sulfates—the leading constituent of acid rain—were responsible for 60% of haze affecting eastern regions and for 30% of the haze obscuring western vistas.

NAPAP's final report also estimated some of acid rain's many costs: between $1 million and $13 million per year in losses to recreational fishing in the Adirondacks, $1 billion to $3 billion annually in reduced crop yields from the ozone that acidic emissions foster, and visibility losses in the eastern United States valued at between $3 billion and $13 billion a year.

NAPAP's "death" was short-lived—a mere six weeks. One provision in the revised Clean Air Act not only revived the program but also expanded its responsibilities to assess the effectiveness of the new law's acid-rain controls through long-term monitoring of key pollutants and sensitive ecosystems.

Global Warming. Current emissions of "greenhouse" gases—such as carbon dioxide and methane—could raise average global temperatures roughly 1°C by 2025 and 3°C by 2100, according to a blue-ribbon committee of roughly 250 scientific experts convened by the United Nations Intergovernmental Panel on Climate Change (IPCC). This would constitute a rate of warming faster than at any time during the past 10,000 years, they noted. Stabilizing the now rising atmospheric levels of these pollutants will require dramatic changes, said NASA's Robert T. Watson, a member of IPCC's science committee. For example, Watson pointed out that it might take cutting carbon dioxide and chlorofluorocarbon (CFC) emissions by 60% to 85% and methane releases by 15% to 20%.

Adding urgency to the global-warming threat was the mid-August report of an unexpected increase in the rate of carbon dioxide's buildup in the atmosphere. Researchers at the National Oceanic and Atmospheric Administration in Boulder, CO, reported that the annual increase in atmospheric concentrations of this gas—the leading contributor to the anticipated global warming—has risen 22% to 43% faster over the past four years than the rate that had been typical for the previous 15 years.

Responding to concerns about such data, Australia, Canada, Japan, New Zealand, and 18 other nations, including all 12 members of the European Community, independently announced that they soon would adopt formal carbon-dioxide-emissions limits. The announcement made during the ten-day World Climate Conference in Geneva, Switzerland, which ended in early November, was intended to help pressure representatives of the other 113 participating nations to adopt formally a treaty setting specific carbon-dioxide limits. However, when the United States and the USSR—the two leading greenhouse-gas emitters—refused to commit to any such limits, the attendees agreed merely to urge the initiation of greenhouse-gas-limiting strategies and to set goals for capping the carbon-dioxide emissions.

Stratospheric Ozone Protection. In the September 5 issue of *Nature*, Michael Proffitt of the University of Colorado and his colleagues reported new data indicating that chlorine-based air pollutants—such as CFCs—are destroying up to 35% of the ozone in high-latitude Arctic air each winter. That is three times the amount previously indicated. Since at least 1985, the same chlorine-based pollutants have caused a seasonal hole to form in stratospheric ozone over the Antarctic. However, Proffitt's team said, owing to different atmospheric conditions over the Arctic, an ozone "hole" does not form there.

On June 29, 59 nations agreed to halt the production of chemicals that destroy Earth's protective layer of stratospheric ozone. Production of CFCs and halons are to end by the year 2000. This augments a 1987 international treaty known as the Montreal Protocol, which would have required only a halving of CFC production by 2000 and an eventual freeze on halon use. The accord also expanded the list of chlorine-based chemicals that will be phased out to include methyl chloroform, carbon tetrachloride, and hydrochlorofluorocarbons.

As part of the revised Clean Air Act, the United States agreed to even tougher controls. Such controls will speed the phaseout of methyl-chloroform production, phase out hydrochlorofluorocarbons (substitutes for many CFCs), and require the recycling and safe disposal of CFCs from air conditioners and other appliances that are repaired or disbanded.

JANET RALOFF

About the Author. Janet Raloff is environment/policy editor of *Science News*, published by Science Service, Inc., in Washington, DC. As such, Ms. Raloff has been following and writing about developments related to air pollution and other environmental issues since the late 1970s.

Acid rain, above, and the loss of the world's tropical rain forests are two other current environmental issues. A ten-year, $500 million U.S. study concluded in 1990 that acid rain does cause damage, but the amount of damage is less than once feared. Some experts, including scientists in Canada, which has been affected by the problem, questioned the findings. "World Resources 1990–91," a report prepared by the World Resources Institute in collaboration with the United Nations, stated that some 40 million to 50 million acres (16.2 million to 20.2 million ha) of tropical rain forests, which are important for controlling global climate, are cleared annually for agriculture and other development. The Institute estimated that 1.9 billion acres (769.2 million ha) of such forest remained.

emerged nationally and internationally since the first Earth Day. Where this ethic was leading was less clear. Individual choices of Americans often pointed away from environmentally sound practice. For example, the average gas mileage of new cars declined 4% from the model year 1988 to 1990 after rising about 50% in the previous decade. Americans still preferred heavier cars with bigger engines and better acceleration, the automakers said. And the number of miles Americans drove rose about 2% a year.

Despite individual choices, sometimes regulation forces steps that bring measurable progress. For example, tests showed that concentrations of the pesticide DDT in human tissue fell from an average of 8 parts per million in 1970 to 2 in 1983 as a result of a federal ban. (Concentrations fell in bald eagles, too, leading to their partial recovery.) Lead concentrations in blood fell 40% from 1975 to 1981, and the number of people with more than 1 part per million of cancer-causing polychlorinated biphenyls declined from about 70% of the population in 1972 to about 10% in 1983. In the absence of a comprehensive yardstick of environmental progress, perhaps the closest thing is a broad measure of human health: life expectancy. In 1990 it was 75 years, up from 70.9 years in 1970, according to the Census Bureau.

Staying Inventive—Living Cleaner, Living Smarter. All these signs of environmental progress and even degradation are actually a result of overall human progress, said Julian Simon, a professor at the University of Maryland business school who espouses the unconventional view that a bigger population is a plus because it means more human creativity and more progress. "The list of things we can worry about is

© Jack Fields/Photo Researchers

The mining and smelting of nickel dominate the economy of New Caledonia, left, a French territory in the southwest Pacific. Since the waste from such strip (surface) mining can devastate surrounding land, efforts to regulate it have been an objective of environmentalists.

reasonably short,'' he said. ''We can worry about getting fed, the safety of our children, having a car, things like that. Now we don't worry about our children dying of smallpox; as we successively solve one problem after another, we work our way down the list, and we've worked our way down to the environment.''

Simon's thesis that progress brings environmentalism seemed to be headed for a test in Eastern Europe, where the collapse of communism exposed environmental exploitation and an aspiration not only for political freedom, but also for clean air and healthy forests, and an end to what Dykstra of Greenpeace called ''environmental repression.'' Even less sanguine experts agreed that the cure lay in part in new invention. With encouragement from the government, scientists and engineers were laying the foundations for an economy that would not consume scarce resources or continuously pollute.

The most promising invention of the last 20 years, said Oppenheimer of the Environmental Defense Fund, is the photovoltaic cell, which turns sunlight into electricity. The price of such cells was still too high to compete with electricity produced from oil but was falling rapidly; the Electric Power Research Institute, a utility research consortium, said some utilities might find solar cells cheaper than oil for some power needs by the middle of the 1990s.

That was in the future. Smaller technological advances in the 1980s helped Americans use energy more efficiently. And some experts said this could point the way for other countries. Progress in efficiency was important because the United States, with about 2% of the world's population, was using 24% of its energy, about twice as much as Western Europe and Japan per unit of output. China, with about 20% of the

Nearly 100,000 dolphins, one of nature's more intelligent creatures, have been killed annually when they are caught inadvertently in tuna nets. In April 1990 the three largest sellers of tuna in the United States declared that they no longer would market tuna caught by methods harmful to the popular mammal.

© Cannon/Greenpeace

world's population, was using 9% of its energy. This was a result not of virtue but of poverty. If China were to achieve the same rate of energy consumption as the United States, that nearly would double world consumption. The fuel would be coal, vastly increasing output of carbon dioxide and sulfur dioxide.

The developing world was least likely to operate efficiently; it was polluting more and enjoying it less. A study by the Department of Energy found that in the United States, about 8% of electricity was lost in transmission before it reached the consumer. For Pakistan, the figure was 28%. It took China 37% more energy to make a ton of paper than it took the United States, the study reported. Some experts said that moving to very efficient practices would help the environment and also the poor. This stood in contrast to the idea common in past decades that saving the environment conflicts with economic development. Deland of the White House said, "A sound and safe environment and a flourishing economy are two sides of the same coin."

Enduring Growth—More Mouths, Less Land. Many experts said technological invention and economic progress would reach their limits in the face of rising population, which was now 5.3 billion and probably would be 1 billion higher by the turn of the century. That population appeared to be putting more and more pressure on the planet. In Genesis, God gave Adam and Eve "every herb bearing seed, which is upon the face of all the earth, and every tree," and Dr. Peter M. Vitousek, a Stanford biologist, said humans had taken a huge chunk of the gift. Of the total amount of energy captured by green plants worldwide, he calculated, nearly 40% was controlled or consumed by humans. The figure included trees cut for lumber or paper, and grain harvested as animal feed. God's other creatures got the leftovers. A growing population could be fed with new plants that put more of their product into food and less into roots and leaves, he said. But right now, he went on, farmers were pumping well water for irrigation faster than it could be replenished, poisoning water with fertilizer, and carrying out other steps that could not be sustained for long. "Our present mix of technology and population is too high," he said.

© Jack Wilburn/Animals Animals

Environmental and economic issues can and have come into conflict. For example, in the Pacific Northwest of the United States, the survival of the northern spotted owl, whose population has dwindled to an estimated 2,000 nesting pairs, was threatened by the timber industry. Accordingly, in mid-1990 the U.S. Fish and Wildlife Service declared the spotted owl a "threatened" species and, thereby, subject to federal protection. Efforts also were made to placate the lumbermen, who feared the loss of jobs.

Some damaging practices already were taking their toll. Researchers at the Worldwatch Institute said population was rising faster than grain production. Erosion, over-irrigation, and other practices were ruining farmland. The loss of protective ozone allowed the entry of radiation that stunted plants as well as hurting animals. According to Worldwatch, grain output per person rose 26% in the 1970s, but fell 2% in the 1980s and would fall 7% more in the 1990s. The most productive land was in the middle and northern latitudes, where scientists said the greenhouse effect would be strongest.

The solution may lie in strategies to have to set fewer plates. "The best technologies in the world," said Michael Fischer, executive director of the Sierra Club, "will not save us if there are too many mouths to feed."

© Dan Helms/Compix

The Garbage Crisis

As the cartoon character Shoe stands in his kitchen, putting his groceries away, he mutters to himself: "It's one of those great mysteries of life in America—in just one day, how do two bags of ordinary groceries . . . turn into three bags of garbage?."

The Problem. The question posed by the popular cartoon character is one for all Americans to consider, as individually they throw out an average of 3.5 lbs (1.58 kg) of trash daily. This represents a collective total of something equivalent to 160 million tons annually and is only a start. Annual estimates soar as high as 11 billion tons, when such disposables as drilling muds, mining wastes, and sludge are included.

The quantities are growing. The U.S. Environmental Protection Agency (EPA) predicts that the 160 million tons will swell to 190 million by the end of the 1990s; presumably other estimates increase at comparable rates. EPA Administrator William Reilly considers solid waste "the environmental issue of the coming decade." But as quantities grow, the nation is swiftly running out of places to dispose of its garbage and other wastes. In 1990 about 80% was compacted and buried in landfills, but according to EPA projections, more than one third of the 6,000 operating landfills will be full by 1993.

With communities resisting the siting of new dumps—the ubiquitous "not-in-my-back-yard" (NIMBY) syndrome—trash is being hauled further and at greater costs to a final resting place. Garbage from New Jersey is buried in Ohio and, as Staten Island's Fresh Kills landfill, which takes in 24,000 tons daily, dots the skyline with its 250-ft-(76-m-) high garbage hills, increasing quantities of New York's trash are hauled away for disposal elsewhere. William Aguirre, the landfill's supervisor, has noted that Fresh Kills has it all—"your plastics, your Styrofoams, even stoves and refrigerators. It was a valley when it started [in 1948]. Now it's a mountain."

Today's mounting garbage problem was forecast two decades ago by farsighted environmentalists who worried about the impact of a "disposable society," but the public paid scant attention to a situation that was not as frightening or as immediate as the toxic-waste scares at such sites as Love Canal, NY. To most Americans, garbage was someone else's problem, something that disappeared forever once put at the curb or behind the back fence or in the dumpster.

Solutions. Now, as disposal costs increase and dump space disappears, communities are looking for new solutions. Most experts see a multiple approach to the garbage crisis: reducing the amount of waste, recycling and reusing as much as possible, burning what cannot be reused, then burying whatever is left. That approach has prompted considerable interest in just what Americans throw away. Many products that were durable two decades ago, such

67

as diapers, razors, and pens, now are disposable, and the quantities of other throwaways, including junk mail, glossy catalogs, foam cups, and food containers, keep growing. Dumps are not full of just foam cups, plastic bottles, and disposable diapers. One EPA study shows nearly 40% of what Americans throw out is made of wood, paper, or paper products. Glass, metals, and food products each account for another 10% of what goes in the trash, yard wastes for 20%, and plastics for only slightly more than 7%.

Another analysis comes from garbage archaeologist William Rathje of the University of Arizona, who has excavated dumps to find out what happens to garbage after it is buried. Rathje discovered much of what Americans throw out is extremely durable. Forms of paper —not just newspapers but solid items such as telephone books—take up about 55% of the

space and still are readable decades later, and about half of the food debris, for example, corncobs, peach pits, and hot-dog buns, still is recognizable. Also, he has found that, by volume, plastics account for about 14% of what is in a dump—a percentage that has remained constant over the years—that food packaging takes up a scant .24% of the space, and disposable diapers only 1.8%. According to Professor Rathje, "practically nothing decomposes in a landfill."

Many believe the most effective first step in solving the garbage crisis is simply to reduce the amount that is thrown away. Toward this goal, manufacturers are finding ways to minimize the use of packaging materials, use less plastic and glass in containers, and design more durable goods. Products in refillable containers are appearing on shelves, and shoppers are starting to bring their own tote bags to carry home the groceries.

Incineration, in new "waste-energy" facilities with environmentally protective scrubbers and filters, is considered another piece of an integrated trash solution and a sure way to reduce volume. Modern facilities reduce volume by about 90%, producing some energy in the process and leaving behind ash that must be buried. Environmentalists worry about potential air-pollution problems and the fact that the ash may be toxic.

Recycling. The garbage crisis has created renewed enthusiasm for recycling throughout the United States. In the early 1970s, many environmentally conscious citizens carefully sorted their bottles by color, peeled labels from their tin and aluminum cans, bundled their newspapers, and hauled the various items to a recycling center. But the effort waned as markets failed to develop, and recycling all but disappeared. Now, as waste experts and communi-

© J. Chenet/Woodfin Camp & Associates

© David Sears/Gamma-Liaison

The polystyrene-foam containers that help keep fast-food products warm pose a special waste problem. Many communities have restricted such environmentally damaging containers, and efforts to recycle them are under way. Recycling centers, such as the one at right, *pound the polystyrene into plastic pellets that can be turned into various products, including cassette boxes and yo-yos.*

Garbage trucks wait to enter an incinerator and power plant near Peekskill, NY. Built during the early 1980s, the plant burns the waste to produce electricity. Such "waste-energy" facilities are seen as an answer to the trash problem, but construction costs are high and environmentalists worry about related air-pollution problems.

© Zeva Oelbaum

ties alike see recycling as a major part of the solution to their garbage problems, the practice has returned. Once again, citizens are bundling papers and sorting glass, metal, and—this time —plastic containers. But that is only a start. According to one EPA official, "most people think they put out the glass, aluminum, and paper and they have recycled. In fact, all they've done is separate."

This time there is a significant difference that may make recycling succeed. In growing numbers, manufacturers are searching for new markets and new uses for recycled materials. More newspapers are starting to use recycled newsprint, and companies like Procter and Gamble are making new product containers from old plastic drink bottles. Used plastics also are being turned into insulation, building materials, and a host of other useful substances. For example, Heinz has announced a plan to turn spent ketchup bottles into carpeting.

As the 1990s begin, about 10% of what Americans throw out is recycled. About half the aluminum cans that are used annually, some 42.5 billion, are recycled. Since turning raw bauxite into aluminum costs about ten times what it does to reprocess old cans, there is ample economic incentive. Some 10% of glass is reused and about 30% of paper is recycled as packaging, cereal boxes, toilet tissue, and, as mills develop the capacity to use it, newsprint.

But the effort is only beginning. The EPA has set a 25% recycling target by 1992. Many environmentalists think that is not enough and have raised their sights to at least 50%. They point to the fact that the Japanese already reuse half of what they throw away and that such European nations as Sweden and West Ger-

many have perfected the art of turning waste into energy at the same time they reuse valued materials. At least one U.S. environmental group, the Environmental Defense Fund (EDF), has made a major commitment to recycling. "We throw away as waste what others see as resources," says EDF head Frederic Krupp. "People want to be involved in things that make this life better. If we can make it convenient, I think we can get the whole country recycling."

Ultimately, economics will dictate solutions to the waste problem. Because landfills are subsidized by local governments and costs are included in a general-services bill, most Americans have no idea what it costs to throw away their garbage. But they are starting to find out. Communities that have experimented by charging a flat fee per trash can or by increasing the cost as more is thrown out found a quick reduction in the amount of waste as citizens tried to cut down their bills. To encourage recycling, various cities including New York have begun fining citizens and landlords who do not comply.

Consumer awareness is only a start. Easing the garbage crisis will require a coordinate effort beginning with manufacturers and including all segments of society. At the point that raw materials become more expensive than the reprocessing of used materials, conserving resources will be essential, markets for recycled goods will flourish, and the strains on the rapidly filling landfills will ease.

MARY HAGER

About the Author. Mary Hager is a correspondent in the Washington Bureau of *Newsweek*. A specialist in the science and health field, Ms. Hager contributed to the magazine's Nov. 27, 1989, cover story on the waste crisis.

West Indian (Florida) Manatee
© W. Gregory Brown/Animals Animals

California Condor
© M. Austerman/Animals Animals

endangered species:
An Update

Black Rhinoceros
© Michael Blate/Tom Stack & Assoc.

American Alligator
© Zig Leszcynski/Animals Animals

Bald Eagle
© Leonard Lee Rue III/The Image Bank

Since the U.S. Endangered Species Act was enacted in 1973, there have been additions, deletions, and corrections to the list of wildlife endangered or threatened by extinction. For example, the Florida manatee now is endangered in part because of the increasing number of pleasure boats, while the American alligator, once near extinction because of its valuable hide, has made a major recovery. Although the California condor, the whooping crane, and the black-footed ferret remain endangered, specific programs have brightened their future. Bald eagles have increased to the extent that officials were considering changing their status from endangered to threatened. The Bactrian camel and the black rhinoceros were classified as endangered in 1976 and 1980, respectively. The grizzly bear is threatened in the 48 conterminous states. A treaty banning trade in the threatened African elephant and its ivory was ratified by 76 nations in 1989.

Bactrian Camel © George Holton/Photo Researchers

Brown (Grizzly) Bear © C.J. Ott/Photo Researchers

Whooping Crane © C.C. Lockwood/Animals Animals

Black-footed Ferret © Jane T. Camenzind

African Elephant © E.E. Kingsley/Photo Researchers

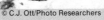

The Big Business of Dieting

By Jenny Tesar

© Lester Sloan/Woodfin Camp & Associates

Baseball manager Tommy La-Sorda and television star Oprah Winfrey (page 73) helped publicize the business of dieting by losing a great deal of their own weight through liquid diets.

About the Author. Jenny Tesar, a free-lance writer living in Connecticut's Fairfield County, specializes in the fields of science, medicine, and technology. She is the author of the forthcoming *Global Warming* and five other books on environmental issues as well as a book for young adults on forensic science. A computer enthusiast, Ms. Tesar has written a variety of educational programs.

"I lost over 100 lbs without dieting."
"Lose 7 lbs in one week."
"Burn fat overnight."
"We succeed where diets fail you."
"Ultimate Solution Diet!"

Buoyed by such cheerful promises and desirous of quick, easy weight loss, American adults—25% of whom are classified officially as obese and untold millions of whom think they are—have turned dieting into a major industry. They spend a hefty $33 billion per year on diet books, audio- and video-tapes, appetite suppressants, low-calorie prepared foods, diet sodas, commercial weight-loss programs, and other products. According to MarketData Enterprises, a marketing-research company in Lynbrook, NY, the figure is expected to exceed $50 billion by 1995.

That is a hefty sum for something that does not necessarily work. Despite the impressive claims of guaranteed success made by many diet programs and products, an estimated 90% of the people who lose 25 lbs (11 kg) in a diet program regain that weight within two years. In addition to being ineffective, diet plans may be dangerous. For instance, some women who have used commercial diet plans have suffered from gallstones and have had to have their gallbladders removed. Rapid weight loss also has been linked to heart malfunctions, neurological problems, arthritic conditions, swelling of the limbs, dizziness, and depression.

These health-safety problems plus misleading promotional practices, untrained providers, and charges of hard-sell tactics have been the focus of recent U.S. congressional investigations into the diet industry. In 1990 the House of Representatives' Subcommittee on Regulation, Business Opportunities, and Energy held hearings on what chairman Ron Wyden (D-OR) called a "largely unregulated health business." Of particular concern to the subcommittee were commercial weight-loss clinics and physician-supervised weight-loss programs.

Weight-Loss Programs. The best weight-loss program has two aspects: the intake of fewer calories and more exercise. The simplest, least expensive, and most successful way to lose weight is on one's own, by cutting back on high-calorie foods and by establishing an ongoing regimen of walking, swimming, or some other type of calorie-burning exercise. Many people, however, find they lack initiative and feel they need outside help if they are to lose weight. This has given rise to a broad range of diet programs.

Each year seems to mean a new craze. There was the Grapefruit Diet, the Scarsdale Diet, the Atkins Diet, and more recently, the liquid diet. The day that Oprah Winfrey told viewers of her television show that she had lost 67 lbs (30 kg) on a liquid-formula diet called Optifast, the manufacturer of the diet, Sandoz Nutrition Corporation, reported receiving hundreds of thousands of telephone calls requesting information on the product. Physicians and hospitals also were inundated: "We had 500 calls the day Oprah talked about her diet," said Leslie Katz, director of the preventive-medicine center at Graduate Hospital in Philadelphia.

Medically Supervised Liquid Diets. Very-low-calorie liquid diets designed to replace normal food entirely for weeks at a time have been around for many years. In the 1970s, more than 50 deaths resulted from liquid diets, which contained poor-quality protein and lacked essential minerals and carbohydrates. Today's formulas are much more balanced, containing all basic food groups. They are available through hospitals and doctors' offices. Each program has three phases. During the initial "fasting" period, patients consume only the liquid diet, which consists of a powdered food mixed with water. This is drunk five times a day, giving a patient a daily food intake of 400 to 800 calories. This first phase lasts three or more months, and the dieter usually loses three to ten lbs (1.4–4.5 kg) weekly. In the program's second "refeeding" phase, the liquid gradually is replaced with low-calorie meals. The third "maintenance" phase is designed to help patients continue sensible eating habits taught during the program. Weekly physical examinations are an essential part of each program, to ensure that medical problems caused by rapid weight loss are caught and dealt with. Typical side effects, including mild anemia, hair loss, dizziness, constipation, swollen joints, and fatigue, are temporary.

© Donna Zweig/Gamma-Liaison

Theoretically, these liquid-diet programs are only for people who are at least 20% above their ideal weight; some medical experts believe they should be available only to those who are 50% or more overweight. Patients should be free from medical conditions such as diabetes, cancer, heart and liver

WEIGHT AND HEIGHT

In March 1983 the Metropolitan Life Insurance Company released its latest tables, indicating the "ideal weight" an adult person, aged 25–59, should maintain to live a long life. The tables were based on mortality research of millions of policyholders.

Men				Women			
Height[1]	Weight[2]			Height[1]	Weight[2]		
	Small Frame	Medium Frame	Large Frame		Small Frame	Medium Frame	Large Frame
5'2"	128–134	131–141	138–150	4'10"	102–111	109–121	118–131
5'3"	130–136	133–143	140–153	4'11"	103–113	111–123	120–134
5'4"	132–138	136–145	142–156	5'0"	104–115	113–126	122–137
5'5"	134–140	137–148	144–160	5'1"	106–118	115–129	125–140
5'6"	136–142	139–151	146–164	5'2"	108–121	118–132	128–143
5'7"	138–145	142–154	149–168	5'3"	111–124	121–135	131–147
5'8"	140–148	145–157	152–172	5'4"	114–127	124–138	134–151
5'9"	142–151	148–160	155–176	5'5"	117–130	127–141	137–155
5'10"	144–154	151–163	158–180	5'6"	120–133	130–144	140–159
5'11"	146–157	154–166	161–184	5'7"	123–136	133–147	143–163
6'0"	149–160	157–170	164–188	5'8"	126–139	136–150	146–167
6'1"	152–164	160–174	168–192	5'9"	129–142	139–153	149–170
6'2"	155–168	164–178	172–197	5'10"	132–145	142–156	152–173
6'3"	158–172	167–182	176–202	5'11"	135–148	145–159	155–176
6'4"	162–176	171–187	181–207	6'0"	138–151	148–162	158–179

[1]In shoes with 1-inch heels. [2]Wearing indoor clothing (5 lbs for men; 3 lbs for women). Courtesy, Metropolitan Life Insurance Company.

Regimented exercise is one of the most important ingredients of any weight-loss effort. Accordingly, health clubs have sprung up across the United States and become a big business of their own.

© Arthur Shay

The Nathan Pritikin diet plan emphasizes aerobic exercise and foods low in fat and high in complex carbohydrates and fiber. Classes in "life-style" education and stress management are offered at his Longevity Centers.

© Lief Skoogfors

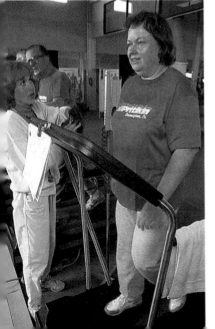

diseases, and psychiatric problems. The three major liquid-diet programs are Optifast, Health Management Resources (HMR), and Medifast. Costs are high, generally ranging up to $3,000 over a six-month period.

Mass-Market Powders. Some liquid-diet foods are available in supermarkets and drugstores without a prescription. The best-known of these are Slim-Fast and Ultra Slim-Fast, which comprise about 80% of the market. These milkshake-like drinks are designed to replace one or two meals a day, *not* to be a person's only source of calories. Cost is less than $1 per serving.

Special Foods. Some programs are based on the use of special prepackaged foods and food supplements. Among these are Nutri/System, Diet Center, and Jenny Craig International Weight Loss Centres. The foods and food supplements these companies sell account for more than half of their revenues. Programs typically cost $600 to $1,200. For example, the 16-week Jenny Craig program costs $185 plus approximately $10 per day for the prepackaged foods. The programs include counseling and follow-up maintenance help. "People think of diets as something you go on and off," said Craig. "Ours is a lifestyle." In contrast, Weight Watchers relies on ordinary store-bought foods, which dieters must weigh according to Weight Watchers guidelines. The program is relatively inexpensive and flexible, leaving the initiative up to participants.

Self-help Programs. Several nonprofit organizations operate informal, low-cost programs in which dieters meet weekly to offer one another encouragement and emotional support. The best known are Overeaters Anonymous and TOPS (Take Off Pounds Sensibly). Others are sponsored by community health centers and various groups.

An Underregulated Business?. "While potions and weight-losing nostrums have been around for generations, our research indicates that a new mix of questionable products, untrained providers, and deceptive advertising is exposing our citizens to unexpected health risks," said Representative Wyden as he opened his subcommittee's hearings on the nation's diet industry. The House subcommittee pointed out that while some clinics and products offer safe and effective weight loss when properly used and administered, "it's impossible for consumers to know which are good ones and which are bad."

The subcommittee's efforts included an overall assessment of the industry, including a survey of the training of people who offer professional services and a look at the research supporting claims for various products and services: "Consumers are buying health based on the smooth patter of salesmen with meaningless credentials who use unscientific success rates to separate health conscious consumers from their money. These professional counselors, nutritionists, and behaviorists are frequently poorly trained laymen who dispense information with no proof or scientific basis." Indeed, witnesses alleged that patients in some diet programs have received advice by untrained personnel that led to life-threatening emergencies.

Another major area of interest to the subcommittee was federal enforcement efforts to control false and deceptive advertising and to ensure that products being marketed are safe. "In this Madison-Avenue-gone-mad environment, the qualified and the unqualified compete side-by-side. Bogus gimmicks share shelf space with bona fide products," said the subcommittee. According to the subcommittee, such government agencies as the Food and Drug Administration (FDA) and the Federal Trade Commission (FTC) have taken action

Clients at Health Management Resources (HMR), must count and compare calories. Like Optifast and Medifast, the program lasts several weeks and includes three phases—"fasting," "refeeding," and "maintenance."

only against the most blatant frauds, such as the Fat Magnet diet pills that purportedly acted like tiny magnets to attract and eliminate fat cells.

Among current practices and deceptions singled out by the subcommittee were half-hour "infomercials." These television programs have the appearance of talk shows or news programs but in reality are paid advertisements. "Doctors" wearing white coats and stethoscopes tout "original clinical studies," "scientific breakthroughs," and "doctor-recommended programs" with dramatic testimonials from grateful patients.

Concerns also were raised that people's understanding of the dynamics of weight loss are colored by three major misconceptions:

Misconception Number 1—people believe that if a diet food, drug, or gadget is dangerous, the government will prevent its use. Not necessarily true, said the subcommittee: "Many bogus products simply slip through the cracks. Such is the case with the grapefruit pills which are said to 'give faster weight loss.' It looks like a drug; it's marketed like a drug, but the FDA considers it a food product—and one that's correctly labeled, at that."

Misconception Number 2—people think that their failure to take off weight is due to their own lack of willpower—not the fault of the products they have tried. They also believe that dieting is safe. "Diets by their nature are artificial—and temporary," said the subcommittee. "Consumers assume that after starving themselves and losing 20 or 30 lbs [9–13.6 kg], they can return to eating 'normally.' But research now suggests that starving inevitably leads to stuffing. The weight is gained back faster and it's lost more slowly the next time around."

Misconception Number 3—the experts know what they are doing. The subcommittee pointed out that despite their medical degrees, many physicians lack an understanding of the complicated physiological and psychological factors involved in obesity. Meanwhile, liquid-diet manufacturers lure them with promises to improve their "competitive edge" for little capital investment. "A sample come-on suggests that a physician can net over $22,000 yearly treating only 20 patients, and over $70,000 if treating 100. Hyping the ease of start-up and offering an all-inclusive marketing and training package, companies can easily find willing physicians to sign on," said the subcommittee.

"I JUST LOVE FAD DIETS. I'M ON FOUR OF THEM RIGHT NOW."
© Sidney Harris

Caveat Emptor. About 34 million Americans are severely overweight, according to the National Center for Health Statistics. Many have lost weight, only to regain it when they went back to bad eating habits and a sedentary life-style. And so they return to the weight-loss regimen they used before, or try a different system in hopes that it will be the last diet they ever will need. When evaluating a weight-loss product or service, medical experts advise the consumer to employ the prin-

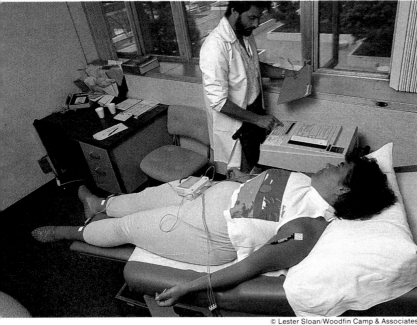

A dieter undergoes an electro-cardiograph. People seeking to lose weight are encouraged to do so under careful medical supervision.

ciple of caveat emptor—let the buyer beware. Here are some questions that should be asked:

• What is the daily calorie intake of the plan or program? If it is under 1,000 calories, people who are only mildly overweight are likely to lose muscle tissue instead of fat tissue.

• What is the nutritional content of the products involved? Do they provide sufficient vitamins and minerals? Is fat content minimal?

• How much weight can one be expected to lose each week? Rapid weight loss can cause health problems.

• What medical risks are associated with the program or product?

• What are the training and qualifications of the program's counselors? Is the program supervised by a physician? How often should one be examined by a physician?

Anyone who plans to undertake major weight loss should begin by having a complete physical examination—one that includes an electrocardiogram to ensure the heart muscle is normal and a blood count to check that there are no mineral deficiencies. The diet should be conducted under a doctor's supervision, with regularly scheduled appointments to monitor blood pressure, urine content, electrolyte levels, and other processes.

In the world of diets and dieting, the potential for abuse—both by customers and to customers—is high. As long as people believe one never can be too thin or too rich, problems are likely to exist. In the words of Representative Wyden, "the science of diet and weight control is largely unexplored territory. We need to know much more in order to evaluate and improve weight-control programs, and to protect consumers' health and safety."

A CHORUS LINE
Broadway's Longest Run

By John Milward

A Chorus Line was, in the words of one of the musical's songs, a singular sensation. It stands as the longest-running show in the history of Broadway. But the theatrical institution that gave new meaning to the term "legs" is no more. On April 28, 1990, after 6,137 performances, the curtain finally came down on the show. Above the marquee of the Shubert Theater, where A Chorus Line had been in residence since 1975, an electric sign comforted theatergoers with a line from "What I Did For Love," another of the show's popular songs: "Kiss today goodbye and point me toward tomorrow."

A Chorus Line broke the rules of the traditional musical, where dialogue and song blend to tell a single story. A Chorus Line did not even have a plot. Instead it captured the drama of an audition where 17 dancers—or "gypsies" in theatrical slang—competed for eight spots in a fictitious musical. In the process, and between bursts of choreographic razzmatazz, the dancers reflected on their lives and revealed their hopes and fears. On closing night, the audience, which included many of the players who had originated the various roles, was primed particularly to share those emotions.

Toward the end of the play, when the fictitious director was about to make his final choices for the cast, he told the

About the Author. John Milward is a free-lance writer and critic. His work appears regularly in a variety of publications, including *The Philadelphia Inquirer*, *New York Newsday*, and *The Chicago Tribune*. Mr. Milward's book, *The Beach Boys Silver Anniversary*, was published by Doubleday in 1985.

17, "Before I start eliminating, I want to say you're all ter-rific." The Shubert audience broke into a long and rapturous ovation. After the final number, Joseph Papp, director of the New York Shakespeare Festival which produced the play and profited by its immense success, reiterated that notion when he spoke to all present and past members of the production. According to Papp, "the characters in *A Chorus Line* are for the most part based on the lives and experiences of Broadway dancers. This show is dedicated to anyone who has ever danced in a chorus or marched in step anywhere."

Michael Bennett, the show's director, co-choreographer, and driving force, was not around to take his bow. Stricken with AIDS, he had died of lymphoma at the age of 44 on July 2, 1987. Bennett was not the only person connected with *A Chorus Line* who died of AIDS, a disease that has cut a brutal path across the theatrical community. Yet it was Bennett's absence in particular that added poignancy to the closing of *A Chorus Line*, a play about the troubles and triumphs of danc-ers that reflected a more innocent time when the only life-or-death matter facing a performer was whether or not he or she would get the part.

Significantly, the show was not about stars but about sup-port players, the extras who are hired to make the top-billed talent look good. Furthermore, the show did not tell a single story as much as introduce the viewer to a whole milieu. It also opened at a time when, due to a declining number of Broadway shows, professional dancers were becoming some-thing of an endangered species.

"A Chorus Line," Broadway's singular sensation that opened in 1975, closed on April 28, 1990, after a record 6,137 perfor-mances. Director Joseph Papp, members of the original cast, and a packed house attended the finale.

Photos Wide World

© Martha Swope

Its Success and Influence. *A Chorus Line* was both an artistic and financial success. The musical first was presented on April 16, 1975, at the 299-seat Newman Theater, part of Papp's Public Theater complex in New York City. It moved to the Shubert on July 25, 1975, and had its official opening on October 19 of the same year. A critical smash, the show collected nine Tony Awards and the Pulitzer Prize. More than 6.5 million people saw the play at the Shubert Theater; millions more, in 22 countries, saw road-show productions.

Numbers like those added up to a financial windfall. By the time the show closed in New York, its total gross was approximately $280 million, with nearly $150 million coming from the Broadway production. More than $38 million went into the coffers of Papp's nonprofit New York Shakespeare Festival, the city's premier Off-Broadway showcase. Besides helping to finance a host of new plays and a complete cycle of Shakespeare productions, revenue from *A Chorus Line* also was used to establish an endowment designed to sustain free productions of Shakespeare in New York's Central Park.

A Chorus Line reminded many that a high kick, a good song, and an effervescent smile can make for grand theater. It also influenced the way in which Broadway plays are developed, a process that has become dramatically more expensive since the blockbuster was launched for $1,147,000. The show was developed in a workshop, a process of collaborative germination long used in avant-garde theater but rarely in productions that are aimed for Broadway. The workshop process also added to the emotional appeal of *A Chorus Line*, for its book and songs were greatly influenced by the real-life tales of theatrical gypsies.

© Jon Blau/Camera Press London
from Globe Photos

"Grease," the hit rock 'n' roll musical that evoked memories of the 1950s, ran in New York from 1972 until 1980. Jacqui Ann Carr and Richard Gere, above, were featured in the show's London version. Broadway's first long-running musical, "Oklahoma," has been performed innumerable times, by high-school, local, and professional acting companies.

© Photofest

© Martha Swope

© Photofest

The Long Run. When *A Chorus Line* was performed on Sept. 29, 1983, for the 3,389th time, it succeeded *Grease*, the popular rock 'n' roll musical of the 1970s that evoked nostalgic memories of the 1950s, as the longest-running show in Broadway history. Earlier, *Grease* itself had overcome such musical phenomenons as *Fiddler on the Roof* (3,242 performances), *Hello Dolly* (2,844), and *My Fair Lady* (2,717), as well as such dramatic successes as *Life with Father* (3,224) and *Tobacco Road* (3,182), to gain the top spot. Since 1983, *Oh Calcutta* (5,959) and *42d Street* (3,486) have achieved milestones of their own by surpassing *Grease* on the long-run chart.

The performance record established by *A Chorus Line* would not be surpassed immediately. The combination of the tremendous expense of staging a major Broadway production, especially musicals, which generally tend to run longer than dramas, and the high cost of the Broadway-theater ticket work against the long run. For example, *Jerome Robbins' Broadway*, the hit of 1989 and the winner of six Tony Awards, closed in September 1990 following a run of less than two years. The show, Broadway's most expensive endeavor ever, recovered only slightly more than 50% of its original investment. A large cast was particularly expensive for the Robbins production. The only show running in 1990 with a viable shot to catch *A Chorus Line* was *Cats*. However, the Andrew Lloyd Webber hit would have to play until 1996 to approach the magic number of 6,138.

After *A Chorus Line* closed, memorabilia from the show, including a strip of the stage, was auctioned off. For the many dozens of dancers who hoofed across the Shubert floorboards singing "I really need this job," being in *A Chorus Line* was indeed the opportunity of a lifetime. And for Broadway, it remains a singular sensation that will not be topped easily.

Other Long Runs. Wanda Richert, above left, portrayed an overnight theatrical success in "42nd Street"; Tevye the dairyman (Zero Mostel) dreamed of being a rich man in "Fiddler on the Roof"; and Carol Channing was the first Dolly Levi in "Hello Dolly."

© Photofest

HIGH-TOPS AND TWO-WHEELERS

RACING INTO THE NINETIES

About the Author. Jeffrey H. Hacker has been associated with this annual as an editor/contributor for more than ten years. Mr. Hacker is the author of four books for young adults and has done extensive promotional writing for various consumer products. When time permits, he enjoys taking a bike ride while wearing his favorite "sneaks."

By Jeffrey H. Hacker

Remember that ratty old pair of sneakers you wore every day to play baseball, fish in the pond, deliver newspapers, go to the movies, or just hack around the neighborhood? They did not seem special then, those U.S. Keds or P.F. Flyers or Converse All-Stars. High-tops or low-cuts, black or blue or white, they were really all the same: rubber on the bottom, canvas on top (with a round rubber patch on the ankle), and a powerful odor from the inside. They were your "sneaks," and you lived in them.

And remember your first "two-wheeler"—that old bicycle you took to school, the Little League field, the candy store, or nowhere in particular as long as there was a steep hill to race down? Maybe it was a Raleigh or a Huffy or a Columbia Western Flyer with a chrome fin and colored streamers flying from the handlebars. Sure it weighed more than a tank. Sure it had fat balloon tires. Sure you had to stand up and back-pedal to apply the brake. But it worked just fine, and what a battering it took!

Sentimentalism? Sure. Rose-colored memories? Maybe so. But if you have shopped for sneakers or a bicycle lately you probably have noticed that U.S. Keds and three-speed "racers" have gone the way of Victrolas and Volkswagen Beetles. Welcome to the age of $170 bioengineered athletic shoe/status symbols and $4,000 computer-designed composite-fiber aerospace bicycles. High-tech, high-priced, largely

Far East-made, and as specialized as the medical profession, sneaks and bikes have come of age with the baby-boom generation. For signs of the consumer times, you need not look any farther.

Pumped Up. The arch principle in sneaker commerce today is specialization. The all-purpose gym shoe is all but extinct now, its place in the evolutionary chain assumed by a myriad mutant species in every imaginable color: shoes for tennis, basketball, running (short-, middle-, and long-distance), walking, hiking, cycling, aerobics, boardsailing, name it. Nike, which by mid-1990 was Number 1 in the sneaker industry, offers 300 models (for 24 sports) in 900 styles. Reebok, its chief rival, sells 175 models in 450 colors and patterns. And then, of course, come all the also-rans: Adidas, Asics, Avia. . . . The closest thing to your reliable all-purpose P.F. Flyers is the cross-training shoe, same as Bo Jackson wears.

© Nike

The pitch, of course, is performance enhancement and preservation of physical integrity (running faster and avoiding injury). The jargon is straight out of NASA, with running shoes leading the way: Asics feature a "vertical extension midsole collar and extended stabilizing pillar"; Saucony's Courageous line boasts a "tri-density compression plug mid-sole, with increasing EVA foam densities across the rear-foot and mid-foot region."

As the 1990s began, mountain biking (page 82) was the latest sports craze; sneakers were available in hundreds of models, colors, and styles, and at correspondingly high prices; and big-name athletes, including teenage tennis star Michael Chang (below), were promoting their favorite brand of high-tops.

Flexibility, stability, and cushioning are the three words athletic-shoe engineers have tacked to their bulletin boards. You can see these qualities on the undersole; you can see them in the material (even leather has been left in the dust); and you can feel them in the fit. Whatever your requirements, whether you are flat-footed or high-arched, you will find what you need—heel supports, arch supports, torque enhancers, molded collars, thermoplastic ankle straps—and a whole lot more.

© William Stevens/Gamma-Liaison

Reebok in 1989–90 introduced four new "technologies," three of which—The Energy Return System (ERS), Hexalite, and Energaire—got lost in the fuss over the fourth: The Pump, the amazing inflatable sneaker. Air is pumped into the lining by squeezing a basketball-shaped button on the tongue of each shoe; a valve on the heel releases pressure as desired. Nike's counterpart, Air Pressure, contains an air bladder in the ankle-collar that can be inflated (with a hand-held pump) for a snug fit.

The cutting edge of high technology costs money, of course. A pair of Pumps sells for $170, with Air Pressures not far behind; Nike's hugely popular Air Jordans fetch a modest $125. You still can do better than triple figures, certainly, but $12.95 high-tops went out with the Mercury space program.

But here is the kicker: According to a recent industry survey, 80% of athletic shoes sold in the United States are not even used for athletics! All that engineering, all that torque-talk, all that *money*, and the shoes still are being worn to go to

© Cameramann International Ltd.

Comfortable sneakers for walking are a definite part of the wardrobe of the working woman of the 1990s.

the movies and hack around the neighborhood. So it is style and status that sell after all, Detroit's secret recipe seeping into sportswear. Talk about pumped! The U.S. sneaker industry generated nearly $5 billion in sales during 1989, twice the volume of 1985.

The elevation of sneakers to high-priced status symbols and the exorbitant sums being spent on flashy, celebrity-studded advertising have garnered the industry some stiff criticism. A flurry of reports about teenagers murdered for their shoes, the popularity of luxury sneaks among inner-city gangs and cash-rich drug dealers, and the awarding of six-figure contracts to college basketball coaches for outfitting their teams in a particular shoe all have muddied the stark-white image of some manufacturers. The explanations, of course, go much deeper than Air Jordans or Reebok Pumps. To blame sneaker companies for urban crime and the professionalization of college sports is like blaming aspirin makers for the high cost of health care.

When you get right down to it, it is not the shoes that have changed so much. It is the times.

Who's Pedaling What. If high-tech sneakers were born of the 1970s running boom, the children of the 1990s are state-of-the-art, computer-designed, light-as-a-feather specialty bicycles. The bike is back, as any glance at the side of the road will confirm. At least 90 million Americans took a spin in 1990, up from 72 million in 1983. More than 3 million use their bikes for commuting to work and other basic transportation. Long-distance cycling is the hottest fitness/recreation activity since video aerobics. About 70% of new riders are women and, for the first time in memory, adult riders outnumber kids; 35- to 40-year-olds represent the fastest-growing cycling segment.

Cycle Composites, Inc.

In the age of vintage bikes, the Schwinn Company offers the Kestrel. It is made of carbon fiber, a light, strong, nonmetallic composite.

What can explain these things? Maybe (despite tri-density compression plug midsoles) all that bouncing and pounding took their toll on aging baby-boomer knees. Maybe an environmentally sound alternative to cars—and the chance to beat gridlock—started the wheels turning. Or maybe three-time Tour de France champion Greg LeMond made it fashionable to wear Lycra shorts and a half-melon helmet.

Whatever the consciousness-raising, bike mania has been fueled by basic advances in engineering and design. From spokes to seat, the new cycles are geared for easy riding. It starts with the frame, now available in strong, lightweight aluminum, titanium, carbon fiber, and other miracle materials. The popular Kestrel 4000 features a molded, one-piece, carbon-fiber frame. Price (frame only): up to $1,700.

The safety helmet now is available in an array of types. Legislation mandating helmets for children riding in bike carriers was enacted in New York and California and considered in other states.

© Tavernier/Sipa Sport

Specialized Bicycle Components

In wheels, the mid-1980s innovation of solid Kevlar disks has given way to a three-spoke design made of carbon fiber, epoxy resin, Kevlar, and aluminum. Price: $750 each.

State-of-the-art shifting systems are more like the automatic transmission in a car than anything you ever have imagined on a bike. Sure you still can buy a ten-speed, but some new bikes have as many as 21 gears. Other options include a push-button gear shift and an electronic micro-motor sprocket changer. Price: $300 or more.

Hydraulic brakes (up to $200), a computerized cyclometer ($40-$350), and, inevitably, an inflatable seat can round out the package. Total price: standard models, $150-$2,500; for something really souped up, an easy $4,000.

Hand in hand with the advances in component engineering have come increasing competition and specialization among bike makers. The new demand has spawned a cottage industry of small, specialty companies. Beyond your basic tour bikes and racing bikes, you now can buy "mountain" (or all-terrain) bikes, hybrid bikes (a cross between a racing bike and mountain bike), city messenger bikes, bikes for women, even fold-up bikes. Recognizing that basic models in basic colors just do not cut it anymore, a market-savvy entrepreneur in Santa Monica, CA, does a big business in customized bike painting and restoration.

The current rage, following (or leading) the rush to long-distance recreational cycling, is the inappropriately named mountain bike. Sturdy-framed, soft-saddled, and fast, these models are designed for all terrains, on or off the road. For balance and durability, they even have fat tires. Strip away the high tech, drop a zero from the price tag, hang on some streamers, and you almost are back to that Columbia Western Flyer of a long, long time ago.

So pump up those sneaks, tune up those bikes, and listen very carefully. What you hear—the *ppssssssstt* of your Nikes or Reeboks and the gentle whir of three-spoked wheels—are the sounds of technical innovation, marketing hype, and a generation growing up, mostly.

Aerospace technology and computer-aided design have revolutionized bicycle manufacturing. Three-spoke wheels (above), hydraulic brakes, and automatic gearshifts are some of the latest features.

The bicycle has become a convenient means of getting to and from work in today's traffic-infested city.

© Piero Guerrini/Gamma-Liaison

People, Places, and Things

Weddings Around the World. Two prominent Democratic political clans were united on June 9, 1990, as Kerry Kennedy, right, daughter of the late Sen. Robert F. Kennedy, married Andrew Cuomo, son of New York Gov. Mario Cuomo. The bride has been directing an international human-rights organization and the groom has been a political aide to his father. On February 9, Susan Eisenhower, the granddaughter of the late president, married Roald Z. Sagdeyev, a prominent Soviet physicist, in Moscow. The couple had met at a conference on U.S.-Soviet affairs.

AP/Wide World

© P.F. Gero/Sygm

Japan's Prince Aya, Emperor Akihito's second son, was married to Kiko Kawashima, a commoner, in a sacred Shinto shrine deep in the woods on the grounds of the Imperial Palace on June 29. The newly named Prince Akishino, who had completed two years of graduate work at Oxford, planned to continue his study of catfish. Princess Kiko would go on with her study of psychology - sociology.

© Sygm

© Luigi Baldelli/Contrasto/SABA

Sports Celebrations. *At Rome's Baths of Caracalla on the eve of the World Cup soccer finals in July, the world's three leading tenors (left to right)—Placido Domingo, José Carreras, and Luciano Pavarotti—joined together for a benefit concert. Conducted by Zubin Mehta, the concert featured operatic and popular tunes and later was released on a compact disc. There was joy in Atlanta as the International Olympic Committee chose the Georgia capital over five other cities as the site of the 1996 Summer Olympics. The city planned to spend some $1.2 billion in private funds on the games.*

© Ann States/SABA

THE ATLANTA DREAM TEAM
Atlanta 1996
Atlanta 1996

© F. Hibon/Sygma

Big Macs, Blades, and Bart. *After McDonald's debuted in Pushkin Square in January 1990, Muscovites waited for up to 90 minutes to enter the 700-seat establishment. After "Big Mak" prices doubled in October, however, the lines shortened. Meanwhile in the United States, blading became the latest sports craze and the television hit "The Simpsons" led to the latest merchandising fad. Introduced by a small company based near Minneapolis, the new skates have a single row of polyurethane rollers. By midyear some 70 spinoff "Bart" products were on the market.*

© Phil Huber/Black Star

© Nathan Bilow/Allsport

© R. Maiman/Sygma

© Jack Lynn

Yesterday, Today, and Tomorrow. *Leaders from more than 70 nations assembled at the United Nations in late September for the World Summit for Children. Canada's Prime Minister Brian Mulroney (above, left) was cochairman. In early July the Richard King Mellon Foundation of Pittsburgh gave some 100,000 acres (40 485 ha) of wildlife refuge and historic land, including an area along the Alligator River in North Carolina, above, to the United States. Presidents Reagan, Bush, and Ford were on hand for the July dedication of the Richard Nixon Library and Birthplace in Yorba Linda, CA.*

AP/Wide World

© Ted Hardin

© Rick Falco/Sipa Press

To honor the immigrant heritage of the United States, Ellis Island in upper New York Bay was re-opened in September 1990. The island had been the gateway to America for millions of immigrants. The focal point of an eight-year, $156 million restoration project, funded by corporate and private donations, is the new Ellis Island Immigration Museum. Located in the island's main building, *left*, which was built in 1900 in French Renaissance style, it offers the visitor a chance to follow the path of the original immigrants. At the museum's dedication on September 9, Vice-President Dan Quayle called the center ''nothing less than the triumph of the American spirit.''

The Alphabetical Section

ABORTION

Both supporters and opponents of legalized abortion in the United States looked in 1990 to the November midterm elections as an opportunity to garner support for their cause. As U.S. armed forces headed for the Persian Gulf and the U.S. economy took a downward turn, however, abortion suddenly waned as a significant factor in the election's outcome.

The Elections. Nonetheless, abortion remained a contentious issue in many campaigns, but the results of the November 6 contests gave no clear victory to either side. In states where candidates for governor were on opposite sides of the abortion debate, for example, voters sent pro-choice candidates to the statehouses in Florida, Georgia, Rhode Island, Minnesota, New Mexico, and Texas, but they elected antiabortion governors in Iowa, Kansas, Michigan, Ohio, and Pennsylvania.

Likewise, voters failed to issue a clear mandate to lawmakers in Washington concerning the increasingly restrictive federal abortion policy. As a result of legislative actions in 1990, federal funds remained unavailable for abortions except in cases where continued pregnancy threatened the woman's life, international family-planning agencies that promote abortion were denied U.S. assistance, and the District of Columbia was barred from using local tax revenues to pay for abortions. Although antiabortion forces lost eight votes in the House and two votes in the Senate, pro-choice legislators remained too few to override President George Bush's strongly antiabortion stance.

The only unequivocal expression of voter support for the right to abortion came in three ballot initiatives. Voters in Oregon rejected two measures—to restrict legal abortions and to notify in advance the parents of minors seeking abortions. Voters in Nevada codified that state's statute allowing abortion through the 24th week of pregnancy.

State Legislatures. The voters' ambiguous message on abortion came as a disappointment to pro-choice advocates, who had attracted a groundswell of public support in the wake of the Supreme Court's 1989 decision in *Webster v. Reproductive Health Services*. That decision granted the states greater power to write their own laws on abortion and was seen as a step toward overturning the court's 1973 *Roe v. Wade* ruling that legalized abortion. Jolted into action by the *Webster* decision, pro-choice advocates succeeded in 1990 in blocking most state legislatures' attempts to restrict access to the procedure.

Of the 41 states that tried to enact new restrictions on abortion after the *Webster* decision, only three—Pennsylvania, South Carolina and West Virginia—succeeded. Pennsylvania's new law required married women to notify their husbands before having abortions; imposed a 24-hour waiting period; and banned most abortions in public hospitals, all abortions after the 24th week of pregnancy, and all abortions undertaken as a means of selecting the gender of children. In August a federal district judge struck down several provisions of the law, but the ruling was being appealed. South Carolina's law required parents to be notified before a minor could obtain an abortion. West Virginia placed new restrictions on public funding for abortion. In July the Louisiana legislature passed a bill outlawing abortion except when necessary to save the woman's life or in cases of incest or "violent" rape that had been reported to authorities within seven days. The law was so restrictive that Gov. Buddy Roemer, an abortion opponent, vetoed it. A restrictive law in Guam also was struck down by the courts.

Supreme Court. The future of abortion policy was clouded further by the appointment of David Souter to the U.S. Supreme Court. Bush's first nominee to the court received Senate confirmation on October 2 after steadfastly evading lawmakers' attempts at uncovering his position on abortion. His stance should become clearer when the Supreme Court issues its decision on the one case concerning abortion that it accepted for the 1990–91 term. That case, *Rust v. Sullivan*, involves a regulation that the Reagan administration issued in 1988, barring doctors at about 4,000 federally funded family-planning clinics from discussing abortion with their patients, even upon request. Whatever the outcome in *Rust v. Sullivan*, the court was not expected to address the key issue in the debate—the constitutional right to abortion enshrined in *Roe v. Wade*—until 1991–92 at the earliest.

RU-486. In the final analysis, technological advancement ultimately may settle the abortion issue. RU-486, the French "abortion pill," proved to be a safe alternative to the clinical procedure when taken early in pregnancy and under medical supervision. The Food and Drug Administration (FDA) banned RU-486 imports for "personal use," meaning abortion, but researchers found further evidence in 1990 that the drug may prove invaluable in the treatment of certain cancers, an adrenal-gland disorder called Cushing's syndrome, and other illnesses caused by hormonal disorders. In November lawmakers heard testimony from experts challenging the FDA ban, which they said discouraged the drug's manufacturer, Roussel-Uclaf, from providing adequate shipments of RU-486 for legal research purposes in the United States. Advocates on both sides of the debate agreed, however, that if RU-486 were made more available, even for research purposes, it soon would be used for its original purpose.

MARY H. COOPER
"Editorial Research Reports"

ACCIDENTS AND DISASTERS

AVIATION

Jan. 15—A small passenger plane crashes in the mountains south of San José, Costa Rica; all 21 aboard are feared dead.

Jan. 19—Seven are killed when a twin-engine corporate jet crashes while trying to land during a storm at the Little Rock, AR, airport.

Jan. 23—A military transport plane crashes into a hillside near Caracas, Venezuela, killing all 24 aboard.

Jan. 25—A Colombian jetliner runs out of fuel and crashes in Cove Neck, NY, while waiting to land at Kennedy International Airport; 73 are killed and many more injured.

Feb. 14—Ninety-three are killed when an Indian Airlines jet crashes when trying to land at Bangalore, India.

May 5—A Miami-bound U.S. civilian cargo plane crashes into a residential neighborhood in Guatemala, killing three crew members and at least 14 on the ground.

May 10—A small plane carrying passengers to see Pope John Paul II crashes while trying to land in southeastern Mexico, killing at least 27.

May 11—Seven persons are killed when fire sweeps through a Philippine airliner preparing for takeoff at Manila.

Sept. 11—A Peruvian jet en route from Malta to Miami, FL, is lost off the coast of Newfoundland, leaving 18 persons dead.

Oct. 2—At least 132 are killed when a hijacked Chinese passenger jet crashes into two other jets while attempting to land at an airport in Guangzhou, southern China.

Nov. 14—An Italian airliner crashes while preparing to land at Zurich, Switzerland, killing all 40 aboard.

Nov. 21—At least 37 persons are killed when a turboprop plane crashes in heavy rain while trying to land on Koh Samui island, Thailand.

Dec. 3—A jet waiting for takeoff from Detroit (MI) Metropolitan Airport becomes lost in the fog and is clipped by another jet whose takeoff path it had wandered into, leaving eight passengers dead.

FIRES AND EXPLOSIONS

Jan. 14—An electrical fire breaks out in a discotheque in Zaragoza, Spain, killing 43 persons.

March 7—A gas explosion and resulting fire in a restaurant in Frankfurt, West Germany, kills at least 11.

March 18—Thirteen are left dead when a gas explosion destroys a four-story building and starts a large fire in Teheran, Iran.

March 25—In the worst fire in New York City in 79 years, 87 persons at an illegal social club in the Bronx are killed in a fire started by an arsonist.

April 6—A fast-moving fire sweeps through a hotel in Miami Beach, FL, killing nine persons.

June 8—Two crewmen are killed when an explosion and fire occur on the Norwegian supertanker *Mega Borg* in the Gulf of Mexico.

June 20—An explosion rocks the U.S. aircraft carrier *Midway*, causing a fire and leaving three crewmen dead.

July 6—Seventeen persons are killed and five injured in an explosion at an Arco Chemical Co. plant in Channelview, TX.

Aug. 26—A gas explosion tears through a coal mine in central Yugoslavia, killing 178 miners.

Oct. 19—At least 21 are left dead when a methane gas blast tears through a coal mine in Karvina, Czechoslovakia, and causes a fire in the mine.

LAND AND SEA TRANSPORTATION

Jan. 4—At least 210 persons are killed when an overcrowded passenger train collides with a freight train in Sukkur, Pakistan, in Pakistan's worst rail disaster in history.

Jan. 5—A crowded bus plows into a tractor-trailer northwest of Kampala, Uganda, killing more than 30.

Jan. 14—A ferry carrying about 150 passengers sinks in the Dhaleswari River near Mushiganj, Bangladesh, leaving at least 100 dead.

Jan. 16—Eighteen Argentine tourists are killed when their bus overturns near Porto Alegre, Brazil.

Jan. 24—A van carrying farm workers plunges into a canal in heavy fog in Clewiston, FL, leaving ten Mexican migrants dead.

Jan. 30—A Greek-registered cargo ship disappears during a storm in the English Channel; all 19 crew members are feared dead.

Feb. 16—A passenger bus collides head-on with a gas tanker near Chetumal, Mexico, killing 12 Guatemalan refugees.

March 7—Three are killed and 150 are injured when a subway train derails and crashes in Philadelphia.

March 22—A fishing trawler capsizes and sinks in the Bering Sea off the Alaskan coast, killing nine fishermen.

April 6—A ferry overturns and sinks while traveling in high winds on the Gyaing River in Myanmar, leaving more than 200 dead.

April 7—At least 166 persons are killed when fire breaks out aboard a Danish-owned passenger ferry in the North Sea.

April 14—A delivery truck carrying hitchhikers loses its brakes and overturns near Pantar in the southern Philippines, killing at least eight persons.

April 16—At least 80 are killed when a leaking gas cylinder explodes in a commuter train near Kumrahar, India, and sets off a fire.

May 19—A freight train plows into the back of a stationary passenger train near the Black Sea in Soviet Georgia, killing at least 11 persons.

July 26—A fuel truck runs into a hotel in Shtaura, eastern Lebanon, bursting into flames and leaving 12 dead.

Sept. 1—A bus slides off a bridge into a river outside Seoul, South Korea, leaving 20 dead.

Sept. 25—Eleven persons are killed when a bus plunges over a cliff in Queensland, Australia.

Dec. 22—A ferry returning U.S. Navy sailors from shore leave in Israel to the aircraft carrier *Saratoga* capsizes in the eastern Mediterranean, killing 21.

STORMS, FLOODS, AND EARTHQUAKES

Feb. 28—At least 168 persons in Western Europe are left dead after a series of severe storms swept the area over the previous month.

April 26—A strong earthquake in central China kills 126 persons.

May 12—More than 200 are killed and millions are left homeless when India's worst storm in a decade sweeps through the southeastern portion of the country.

May 30—At least nine persons are killed when a strong earthquake centered north of Bucharest, Romania, rocks Eastern Europe.

May 30—An intense earthquake shakes northern Peru, leaving 135 persons dead and injuring hundreds.

June 3—Tornadoes and violent storms leave at 13 persons dead in the U.S. Midwest.

June 14—Twenty-six persons are left dead when flash floods inundate the eastern Ohio village of Shadyside after severe thunderstorms.

June 21—A major earthquake registering 7.7 on the Richter scale, followed by several major aftershocks, strikes northwestern Iran, leaving at least 40,000 dead and more than 400,000 homeless.

June 25 (reported)—A typhoon strikes the Philippines and Taiwan, leaving at least 47 dead, and goes on to sweep China's eastern coast, killing ten persons there.

July 13—An avalanche caused by an earthquake strikes Lenin Peak in the Pamir Mountains in Soviet Central Asia, killing 40 mountain climbers.

July 16—More than 1,600 are killed when a strong earthquake rocks Luzon, the main island of the Philippines.

Aug. 25—Severe flooding due to monsoons kills at least 50 people in western India.

Aug. 28—A severe tornado sweeps through northern Illinois, killing at least 28 persons.

Sept. 11—Record rains cause landslides and widespread flooding in South Korea, leaving at least 45 persons dead and 31 missing.

MISCELLANEOUS

Feb. 27—At least 21 persons die when a mudslide sweeps through the Peruvian jungle village of San Miguel de Rio Mayo.

March 12—A blast furnace at a steel mill in Gansu province, China, collapses, killing 19 persons.

July 2—Some 1,500 Muslim pilgrims suffocate or are trampled to death in a stampede in a pedestrian tunnel leading to the sacred city of Mecca, Saudi Arabia.

ADVERTISING

An uneasy U.S. economy hit the U.S. advertising and media industries hard in 1990. Advertisers tightened their budgets and reduced ad spending, sparking recessionary conditions and layoffs at some ad agencies. Mergers and acquisitions among major, multinational agencies, a mainstay of the booming 1980s, also dwindled.

Controversies. Tobacco and liquor marketers came under fire in 1990 for the placement of billboard ads in low-income areas of major cities. Special-interest groups defaced several billboards, accusing marketers of targeting minorities excessively in ads for cigarettes and alcohol-related products.

The protests led to new recommendations from the Outdoor Advertising Association of America that billboard ads for cigarettes and alcohol not be placed within 500 ft (152 m) of schools, churches, and hospitals. At the same time, several tobacco companies agreed to replace cigarette billboards in minority areas with ads for other products. The moves were expected to cut the amount of outdoor advertising spending by tobacco companies, which accounted for $187.8 million in 1989. Beer, wine, and liquor marketers spent $57.4 million on outdoor ads in the same period. A U.S. House of Representatives subcommittee spurned proposed legislation calling for restrictions on tobacco advertising.

Both houses of Congress passed legislation limiting advertising on children's television programming. The bill, which President Bush allowed to become law without his signature, limits commercials on children's television programs to ten and one half minutes per hour on weekends and to 12 minutes per hour on weekdays.

Another controversy erupted in the television industry over the issue of ratings guarantees, which ABC, NBC, and CBS traditionally offer advertisers who purchase airtime. Ratings guarantees are a promise to marketers that programs they advertise on will receive a certain level of ratings points, which are tabulated by Nielsen Media Research. If the program falls short, the networks provide "make goods," or free airtime on other shows. But in 1990 the three networks claimed the methodology used by Nielsen to determine ratings was inaccurate and that ratings for many shows were too low. The networks then adopted a complicated formula that effectively decreased the amount of "make goods" available for advertisers. The advertising community protested, and the three networks began negotiations with Nielsen on how to improve the research company's methods.

Media Recession. An oversaturated magazine industry felt the crunch in 1990 when advertisers cut their budgets, and smaller titles were forced to close. At the same time, the tight economy and the fear of war in the Middle East led tense advertisers to cut ad spending across the board. The cuts led to layoffs at several agencies.

Lord, Geller, Federico, Einstein, an agency that was rocked in 1988 when its top executives walked out to form their own shop, was merged into Brouillard Communications. Both Brouillard and LGFE are owned by London-based WPP Group, and the new agency was renamed Brouillard LGFE. Saatchi & Saatchi, once the most expansion-minded agency in the world, began the year burdened with heavy debt from years of acquisitions and named Robert Louis-Dreyfus as new chief executive to bring the company back to financial health.

Ad Volume. The McCann-Erickson ad agency had predicted that U.S. ad spending would increase 6% to $132 billion in 1990. But in May the agency revised its forecast to between 5% and 6% to $130 billion. At the same time, the Publishers Information Bureau reported that magazine ad pages were down 3.3% for the first half of 1990 compared with the same period in 1989. In April the Newspaper Advertising Bureau halved its advertising-revenue-increase projection for 1990 to between 3% and 4%. The three major TV networks, CBS, NBC, and ABC, along with Fox Broadcasting, reported a record $4.3 billion in the 1990–91 network TV upfront market.

Creative. The most celebrated TV ad in recent years was ousted from creative competition at the International Advertising Film Festival in Cannes, France. Festival judges labeled the spot, which had been created by Chiat/Day/Mojo in 1989 for Eveready Battery Co.'s Energizer battery, a copycat. The ad featured a pink mechanical bunny wearing sunglasses who walks his way through the battery ad and disappears, only to return later in what appear to be ads for separate products. The judges ruled that the commercial was similar in concept to another campaign that ran previously in the United Kingdom for Carling Black Label Beer.

American Express Co. scored a creative coup when it snared actor Paul Newman to appear in his first television commercial.

Acquisitions. Interpublic Group of Companies, which owns ad agencies McCann-Erickson and Lintas:USA, became the first agency to establish a third agency network by acquiring London-based Lowe Group. D'Arcy Masius Benton & Bowles bought Yellowhammer, a large London agency made vulnerable by Britain's slow economy. Also, a handful of U.S. agencies opened offices in several Eastern European nations, while many others, including Bozell and BBDO, formed joint operations with companies in the Soviet Union to provide clients with access to what they hope will become an open marketplace.

JOHN WOLFE, *"Advertising Age"*

AP/Wide World

From Pakistan, resistance leader Gulbuddin Hekmatyar (right) gave his support to an unsuccessful March coup attempt, led by Shahnawaz Tanai, against the Afghan regime.

AFGHANISTAN

In 1990 the tragedy of the forgotten civil war in Afghanistan continued. The world's largest refugee population—3.3 million Afghans in Pakistan and more than 1 million in Iran—remained trapped abroad, while the fighting at home, though somewhat less intense than in 1989, continued to take its steady toll. Ranged against the Soviet-installed Republic of Afghanistan (RA) under President Najib (also known as Najibullah) was a motley assortment of resistance forces, often hostile to each other, that patiently pursued their common goal of destroying this last vestige of the Soviet occupation. By virtue of adroit political maneuvering and a massive Soviet arms supply, Najib still clung to power at year's end, but his position remained tenuous.

Internal Political Developments. The most dramatic political development during the year was a failed coup attempt in March by Gen. Shahnawaz Tanai, the RA defense minister and unofficial head of the Khalqi (Masses) faction of the People's Democratic Party of Afghanistan (PDPA). Khalq was the bitter enemy of the dominant Parcham (Banner) faction, whose head was President Najib. Tanai had made at least two other attempts, in August and December 1989, and he moved this time just as some 127 persons implicated in the December plot, including 11 generals and many ranking PDPA members, were facing trial. Aircraft

from Bagram air base dropped bombs near Najib's office, narrowly missing the president, but key military officers remained loyal, and the coup miscarried. Tanai and his cohorts fled to Pakistan, where they were received by Gulbuddin Hekmatyar, one of the leaders of the *mujahidin* resistance forces. Although Hekmatyar's Hezb-e-Islami (Islamic Party) were Muslim fundamentalists and the Tanai-led Khalqis were militant and atheistic Communists, it later was revealed that Tanai and Hekmatyar had been collaborating for a long time.

About one third of the top leadership of the RA and PDPA were implicated in the plot. Najib ceremoniously purged them from their party and state posts, but by then most had escaped to Pakistan, where they joined forces with Hekmatyar.

Although the coup attempt had damaged his regime badly, Najib took advantage of the defection of the hard-line Marxist Khalqis to make changes that he previously had been unable to carry through because of their opposition. These included changing the name of the PDPA to the Watan (Homeland) Party so as to improve its image, and shifting the mandate for complete political control to a so-called Peace Front. Eight other political parties that were willing to be part of the Peace Front were to have some say in decision-making, though not in the key areas of defense, security, police, or foreign affairs.

On the surface, Najib seemed committed to opening the door to political pluralism. His declared program included the holding of internationally supervised free elections, with a commitment to abide by their results. He tried unsuccessfully to talk the former king, Zahir Shah, into returning from exile in Italy to join in a new government. In April he chose a supposedly nonparty prime minister, Fazl Haq Khaliqyar, who formed a 36-person cabinet that included only 13 identified PDPA members, though these were all in key posts. Most of the others were people who had not been prominent previously, though all but six were known to have collaborated with the regime, including two women who had been party activists. Finally, during Najib's trips abroad in the summer of 1990, he left in charge such ostensibly non-PDPA figures as Khaliqyar and Vice-President Abdul Rahim Hatef.

There was, however, skepticism both inside and outside Afghanistan that the real nature of party rule had changed, despite Najib's repeated denials that the PDPA, let alone the Watan Party or the newly formed Peace Front, had ever been Communist or even Marxist. The Peace Front, for example, was to be headed by Farid Ahmad Mazdak, former chief of the party's youth group and the youngest, most energetically capable member of the PDPA's ruling Politburo. Of the eight other collaborating Peace Front parties, at least two also

---

AFGHANISTAN • Information Highlights

Official Name: Republic of Afghanistan.
Location: Central Asia.
Area: 250,000 sq mi (647 500 km²).
Population: (mid-1990 est.): 15,900,000.
Chief Cities (March 1982): Kabul, the capital, 1,127,417; Kandahar, 198,161; Herat, 155,858.
Government: Najibullah, general secretary, People's Democratic Party (appointed May 1986) and president; Fazil Haq Khaliqyar, prime minister (named April 1990). *Legislature*—bicameral National Assembly.
Monetary Unit: Afghani (50.6 afghanis equal U.S.$1, August 1990).
Gross Domestic Product (1989 est. U.S.$): $3,000,-000,000.
Foreign Trade (1989 U.S.$): *Imports*, $798,000,000; *exports*, $238,000,000.

---

changed their names, leading to suspicions that they were merely rump parties following the old PDPA's lead. Najib himself rejected demands that he step down from power before the elections were held.

Moreover, none of Najib's maneuvers impressed the resistance, which, though split on many other issues, was united in its uncompromising opposition to any government headed by the PDPA or other pro-Soviet group, by whatever name.

Just as the failed March coup attempt had removed the difficult and uncompromising figure of Tanai from the RA, so it estranged the similarly hard-line Hekmatyar from the Afghan Interim Government (AIG), the resistance's loose, Pakistan-based confederation. The remaining AIG members would not forgive Hekmatyar his collaboration with Tanai, a dedicated Communist.

Military Developments. There were few important victories or defeats on either side during the year. Both government and resistance forces rained inaccurate rockets on each other but failed to inflict strategic damage. Tanai, who had been born near Khowst, joined the Hekmatyar attack on this outpost, but it successfully withstood a summer-long siege.

In early October the resistance's Jamiat Islami (Islamic Society) scored its most important victory of the year when it seized Tarin Kot, capital of the centrally located Uruzgan province. Uruzgan thus became the fifth province (after Kunar, Takhar, Paktika, and Bamian) to fall under full resistance control. A week later, however, Hekmatyar failed in an attack on Kabul made without the support of the other resistance factions.

The Economy. According to government figures of unknown reliability, Afghanistan's gross national product (GNP) for the first nine months of 1989 was 1,971 billion afghanis (approximately $3.75 billion at the market rate of 525 afghanis per dollar, or $15.8 billion at the official rate of 125 afghanis per dollar). In February the inflation rate was listed as 10%.

From March through September 1989, Afghanistan imported $373 million and exported $104.9 million worth of goods. The main exports were rugs, karakul pelts, fruits, medicinal herbs, and cumin. Some 95% of agriculture, the main source of these exports, was in private hands at the start of the year. The export of natural gas to the USSR, suspended for several years because of resistance activity, was slated to resume in April, but by year's end there was no confirmation that it had.

Imports were fuel, electricity (from Soviet Central Asia), transportation equipment, chemicals, medicine, and construction materials. Most of these items, especially fuel, remained in short supply throughout the year. Foreign aid, most importantly grain, came from many foreign donors, especially from the USSR. In an unusual reverse flow, Kabul provided Moscow with 1.5 tons of cigarettes to alleviate a Soviet shortage. Soviet border troops, who are under the secret police (KGB), handled the shipment.

According to official statistics in April, some 53% of Afghan dwellings had been destroyed by the war and another 18% damaged. Basic foodstuffs were rationed and acute food shortages were reported from various parts of the country, especially in the north, where a plague of locusts worsened an already bad situation.

The economic development budget for 1990 was set at 16.1 billion afghanis ($128 million at the official rate), of which about 59% would be generated internally and the remaining 41% would come from outside sources.

Outside Powers' Involvement. Soviet and U.S. arms deliveries to their respective clients continued. For the USSR, total economic aid (of which arms accounted for more than 90%) remained at roughly the same level in 1990 as in 1989, or about $5 billion per year. The United States, whose arms aid to the resistance had peaked at about $650 million per year in 1987–88, had dropped its military support to about $300 million annually in 1989–90, and expected to cut that figure to about $200 million in 1990–91. Other governments playing a role in arms deliveries were Saudi Arabia, which financed much of the arms flow to the resistance, and Pakistan, which controlled distribution of the weapons and funneled most of them to its favorite, Hekmatyar. Iran was active in supporting resistance groups loyal to the Shia branch of Islam.

During 1990 the United States and USSR groped cautiously toward a formula for peace. They agreed in principle on free, internationally supervised elections, but the interim roles of the present RA government, the PDPA, and particularly of Najib, remained in dispute. Washington and the resistance viewed all of these as Soviet puppets and insisted that Najib abandon his hold on the army, the intelligence service, and security forces before any elections could be held. Moscow, however, only would concur in having Najib share power with other factions' leaders during this time.

On several occasions during the year, notably before the June summit meeting between U.S. and Soviet leaders and at an August conference between the two powers in the Soviet city of Irkutsk, it was reported that the two sides were very close to a compromise agreement, but a final understanding never was reached. Part of the difficulty in reaching an accord may have stemmed from the internal Soviet political situation, where the still-powerful KGB may have insisted on protecting their longtime protégé Najib at all costs.

Another key Soviet consideration was the fate of some 300 Soviet soldiers missing in action (MIA) during the ten years of occupation. Many of these were thought to be still alive and prisoners of the resistance. Soviet attempts to talk with the resistance directly foundered when its leaders demanded as a precondition that all Soviet aid to Najib cease.

Pakistan, whose burden of supporting the Afghan refugees was alleviated only partly by $52 million from the United Nations, still was hoping for military victory via Hekmatyar.

Prospects for peace in 1991 were dimmed by Pakistani support for Hekmatyar, Soviet support for Najib, and the Afghan resistance's refusal to condone a role in postwar Afghanistan for either.

ANTHONY ARNOLD
Hoover Institution, Stanford

AFRICA

The year 1990 was marked by extraordinary political changes in sub-Saharan Africa. However, by the end of the year it remained unclear how permanent those changes were or where they would lead. Historians may look back on 1990 as marking the beginnings of the spread of democracy in much of the region, or they may conclude that the year was one of false hopes and promises.

South Africa and Namibia. The most momentous changes appeared to be occurring in South Africa. The government decided in February to release Nelson Mandela (*see* BIOGRAPHY), the most prominent black South African opponent of apartheid, who had been jailed for more than a quarter of a century. In addition, the long-outlawed African National Congress (ANC), which had spearheaded much of the resistance to white rule in South Africa, of which Mandela was the best-known leader, was legalized and the state of emergency that had been in place for several years was lifted. The government of F. W. de Klerk (*see* BIOGRAPHY) began talks with Mandela and his ANC colleagues on organizing more formal negotia-

J. Isaac/UN Photo

Namibia's flag was raised at the United Nations headquarters for the first time on April 23, 1990, as the new African nation became the 160th member of the world body.

tions on a future constitution for South Africa. A new constitution would permit the participation of all races in government, reforming a system where whites, representing about 15% of the population, monopolize political power.

As promising as the changes in South Africa appeared, there also were problems. Violence escalated among black groups in Natal province, as the Zulu-supported Inkatha movement struggled for predominance with the ANC and the United Democratic Front. The violence also was interpreted as a struggle by Mangosuthu Buthelezi, leader of Inkatha, to win acceptance by Mandela and the South African government as a national political leader and participant in negotiations over South Africa's future constitution.

Right-wing whites also began protesting the dialogue between the government and the ANC, and there were suspicions that some of the ongoing violence in South Africa was a result of their opposition to change. Revelations of past human-rights abuses and assassinations by secret army death squads shocked white South Africans, adding one more element to the growing sense of uncertainty about the morality of past government policies and the future direction of the country.

While political change appeared to be accelerating in South Africa, a major political advance was consolidated in neighboring Namibia. This arid land long had been a United

Nations trusteeship of South Africa. Despite pressures and protests by the international community, the government in Pretoria had refused to relinquish its control of the territory. But in 1989 the South Africans had agreed to withdraw from Namibia as part of a regional agreement which included the withdrawal of Cuban troops from Angola. After constitutional negotiations among various Namibian political groups, and a UN-sponsored election, Namibia was declared independent on March 21, 1990. It attained independence as a multiparty, liberal democracy with a bill of rights and an independent judiciary. Sam Nujoma, the former leader of the insurgency group, South West Africa People's Organization (SWAPO), was elected the first president. He named a cabinet of mixed racial, ethnic, and political complexion and announced policies encouraging private investment to help the country develop. Namibia's auspicious beginning as an independent country was another hopeful sign that multiparty, multiracial democracy might work in Africa.

Other Democratic Developments. Democracy appeared to be breaking out in other parts of the continent as well. The Nigerian military government continued its commitment to free elections in 1992 and to handing over power to a civilian government. However, the military leadership did not like the six political parties which an election commission recommended be permitted to participate in that election. As a result, Nigerian President Ibrahim Babangida simply decreed the establishment of two political parties—one slightly left of center and one slightly right of center. It was an innovative way of establishing political parties from above; but it was unclear how well it would work.

Sustained and deepening economic problems provoked a series of major riots in a number of autocratic, one-party states and fed demands for political liberalization. Various presidents had their armies or police put down demonstrations in 1990 but many leaders also promised a degree of political liberalization. Positive developments involved the creation of national commissions to consider their countries' political futures, referenda on changes in the political system, permission for opposition political parties to be formed, or elections. Countries following these patterns included the Ivory Coast, Gabon, Zambia, Tanzania, Cape Verde, São Tomé and Principe, Guinea-Bissau, Guinea, Benin, Zaire, the Congo (Brazzaville), and Angola. Governments in Kenya, Togo, Ghana, Cameroon, Sierra Leone, Malawi, and elsewhere resisted pressures for democratization, although political changes were occurring so rapidly in the region that there was no telling how long these and other governments could hold off liberalization.

What was not clear in all of these changes, and promises of change, was their meaning and likely direction. They occurred under external as well as internal pressures. Western governments, including the United States, warned Africans that they would have to improve the quality of their governance and move toward more open political systems if they were to continue receiving foreign aid on which most of their governments depend heavily. Pressure for change also derived in part from frustrations with the slow progress toward economic recovery and lagging investment which was, in turn,

A bloody civil war raged in Liberia during 1990. Prince Johnson (center), who had broken with rebel leader Charles Taylor in midsummer, led the faction that ambushed and killed President Samuel K. Doe in September.

AP/Wide World

In Rwanda members of the minority Tutsi tribe, who tried in the fall of 1990 to topple the national government controlled by the majority Hutu tribe, are interrogated in a jail in Kigali, the nation's capital.

© P. Versele/Gamma-Liaison

likely a result of poor governance. Both domestic and foreign investors were reluctant to risk their resources in countries lacking transparent policy-making and public accountability for politicians. Too often the rule of law was the exception and corruption by public officials was legion.

Another major source of pressures for political liberalization in Africa was the extraordinary move toward political liberalization in Eastern Europe. Both Africans and their foreign supporters had begun to ask: If multiparty and democratic systems were possible in Eastern Europe, why not in Africa?. But politicians in Africa, as elsewhere, are rarely eager to give up power and the personal wealth that often accompanies it. What the world saw in Africa in 1990 may not be the beginnings of real democracy but only a mirage, as politicians attempted to retain their foreign support and calm down their own discontented populations. Only time would tell whether African leaders would turn away from political liberalization as soon as they felt it was safe to do so, or whether they could maintain control of the process of opening up their political systems and avoid losing their jobs or lives.

Conflicts. If some hope was to be found in the beginnings of democracy in much of Africa, only despair appeared to emerge from most of Africa's conflicts. The wars in the Horn of Africa ground on. Eritreans, demanding independence from Ethiopia, captured Massawa, a major port city, underlining the inability of the Ethiopian army to subdue them. Nevertheless, Ethiopia's President Mengistu Haile-Mariam refused to negotiate with the Eritrean rebels and a political stalemate continued. Fears grew of renewed famine in the country.

The civil war between the Arab, Muslim north and the south of Sudan (primarily African with a mix of Christian and traditional religions) also continued with no promise of resolution. The north refused to budge on the implementation of Muslim Sharia law throughout the entire country, and the non-Muslim southerners refused to accept that Sharia law. Reports of human-rights abuses by the government in Khartoum increased, while fears of a major human catastrophe, involving starvation for millions of Sudanese, particularly in the south, rose with the failure of the rains to appear. Nevertheless political conditions continued to deteriorate and foreign-relief organizations withdrew their personnel and closed down their programs.

The civil war in Somalia continued with reports of government massacres of dissidents, particularly in the north where political opposition to President Mohammed Siad Barre was the strongest. But human-rights abuses and an apparent massacre also occurred in the capital, Mogadishu, during the summer as opposition to Barre and his reported corruption continued to grow.

The major conflict in West Africa, a bloody civil war in Liberia which began in December 1989, continued during much of 1990. The largest rebel group was headed by Charles Taylor, a former government official who had been accused of embezzling $1 million from Liberia, and who had escaped from jail in the United States while awaiting extradition. Taylor reportedly was supported by Libya and Burkina Faso. It also was likely that Ivory Coast at least turned a blind eye to the shipment of arms to Taylor across its borders.

Taylor's ragtag but successful army was accused of brutality, particularly against the Krahns—ethnic supporters of President Samuel K. Doe. The government was accused, in turn, of massacres and brutality directed

Port Gentil, the economic and oil center of Gabon, was the scene of antigovernment unrest in May following the mysterious death of an opposition leader. A state of siege was declared and French troops were called in to evacuate French citizens.

© Chamussy/Sipa

against the ethnic groups supporting Taylor, primarily the Gios and Manos. By midsummer a new rebel army led by Prince Johnson had broken off from Taylor's group. The competing rebels fought their way into the capital of Monrovia but could not dislodge Doe and the remnants of his army, who barricaded themselves in the presidential palace.

In an attempt to end the civil war, West African leaders belonging to the Economic Community of West African States (ECOWAS) created a cease-fire monitoring force. It was made up of 3,000 troops from several neighboring West African countries, including Nigeria, Ghana, Guinea, Sierra Leone, and Gambia. Its avowed goal was to set up an interim government to manage Liberia until new elections could be held. Johnson supported the intervention but Taylor opposed it, attacking the West African force after it entered Liberia. In September, Doe was ambushed on a visit to ECOWAS headquarters. The Liberian president, who himself had come to power in a bloody coup in 1980, was tortured and murdered by Prince Johnson's forces. But the remnants of his army remained barricaded in the presidential palace. In the meantime, Francophone African countries began openly to criticize the ECOWAS mission, fearing it would become a tool of Nigerian policies. Although a cease-fire was accepted in late November, no interim government was in place, and the future was uncertain.

As September ended the central African nation of Rwanda was invaded by a rebel army of refugee tribesmen. The rebels from the minority Tutsi tribe were suppressed in about two weeks by government troops aided by forces from Zaire, Belgium, and France. The Hutu tribe made up 88% of the country's population and controlled the government.

Two conflicts in Africa showed some promise of resolution. The principal protagonists in the Angolan conflict, the MPLA government in Luanda and the UNITA rebels based in the south, began negotiations in Portugal on a political settlement. In Mozambique the government held preliminary negotiations with representatives of Renamo, an insurgent group challenging that government for political power. By late 1990 neither conflict had come to an end but the possibility of political settlement looked encouraging for the first time in many years.

Overview. If change was in the air, so was a measure of continuity. Attempted coups in Nigeria, Zambia, Madagascar, and Sudan occurred but failed. Structural adjustment programs, implemented throughout much of the region, continued with World Bank, International Monetary Fund, and foreign government support. The results remained meager but African and foreign officials remained hopeful. Meanwhile the conflict in the Persian Gulf and the rapid run-up in petroleum prices brought welcome financial relief for the oil-exporting countries of Nigeria, Cameroon, Congo (Brazzaville), Gabon, and Angola. The rest of Africa, which must import petroleum, saw its import bill spiral up yet again and faced still worsening economic problems.

In 1990 there was a sprinkling of good and bad news for the masses of Africa. The good news was that the soccer team of Cameroon unexpectedly fought its way into the quarterfinals of soccer's World Cup. The Cameroonians did not get to the final but they put Africa on the world soccer map. The bad news was that AIDS continued to spread, with a surprisingly large number of HIV carriers found in Ivory Coast for the first time. The full scope and ultimate human and developmental costs of this terrible disease in Africa still were unknown but each successive study brought ever larger estimates.

CAROL LANCASTER, *Georgetown University*

© David R. Frazier, Photography

U.S. wheat is loaded for export from Galveston, TX, during 1990, a record year globally for wheat production and one in which U.S. agriculture benefited from rising exports of farm products.

AGRICULTURE

The year 1990 was favorable for world agricultural production. Preliminary data indicate the global wheat yield set a new record, and yields of corn, rice, soybeans, and other protein crops were good. Favorable yields were much needed, since world grain stocks had been in a steep downtrend, dropping slightly below accepted minimum standards for food security. Larger crops should increase the world's reserve grain supplies modestly to help offset future adverse weather.

U.S. red-meat production declined slightly during the year, as farmers reduced output in response to 1988 and 1989 financial losses. Production of chicken, turkeys, and catfish continued the strong upward trend of recent years, providing U.S. consumers with ample supplies. Summer fruit and vegetable crops were good, but down from previous records. U.S. citrusfruit production, however, dropped substantially because of a winter cold snap. Internationally, world production of meat animals increased slightly, along with a continued longterm upward trend in poultry production.

U.S. agriculture benefited from rising exports of farm products in 1990, including feed grains, soybeans, red meat, and poultry. The U.S.-Canadian Free Trade Agreement, in its second year of operation, gave Canadian farmers improved access to U.S. markets for durum wheat and oats, while increasing competition from U.S. products in its fruit and vegetable markets. The United States and Mexico agreed to begin talks on a similar agreement in 1991.

Farming and the Environment. Environmental concerns were important in global agriculture in 1990. The industry was facing the challenge of supplying food and fiber to an ever-expanding world population through increased efficiency, while at the same time minimizing adverse impacts on the environment. In two California counties, manure from livestock operations was reported to be polluting water supplies. Similar problems have developed in northern Europe.

In the U.S. Midwest, corn growers expanded their use of a newly developed test to measure soil-nitrogen content, thus helping to avoid excessive use of nitrogen fertilizer that can pollute groundwater. In South America, where clearing of tropical rain forests has been a major concern, research focused on systems of sustainable agriculture to maintain long-term productivity in tropical grasslands. This research may reduce the pressure to convert rain forests to agricultural uses. In the United States environmental concerns were incorporated in new farm legislation.

Biotechnology. Progress continued in biotechnology, an emerging field of study that can increase agricultural productivity through improvements in plant and animal breeding, genetic transfers, and new biochemical processes. (*See also* BIOTECHNOLOGY.) In 1990 a new variety of orange that briefly can resist temperatures as low as 20°F (6°C) without damage became available in Florida.

Biotechnology also has led to an infant industry producing biodegradable garbage bags made partly from cornstarch. Research continues on other potential uses of starch-based plastics, including biodegradable disposable diapers and food containers. Two recent biotech products—BST (bovine somatotropin) and PST (porcine somatotropin), both naturally occurring hormones—moved closer to commercial application in 1990. They were held back due to consumer or producer concerns and the need for further testing. Use of BST can increase milk production per cow by 10% to 20%. University research indicates PST can lower the feed required to produce pork by 12% to 20%, thus reducing production costs. PST also produces leaner pork to meet the needs of today's health-conscious consumers.

In industrial markets, printers' ink is a new and rapidly growing market for soybean oil because of quality characteristics and environmental benefits. Industrial demand for corn may receive a boost in the next few years from 1990 clean-air legislation. Tighter air-quality standards will affect the type of gasoline that can be sold in up to 40 cities of the United States. The new regulations create potentially increased demand for ETBE, a corn-based motor-fuel additive that reduces certain automotive exhaust emissions.

Decline in Processors. Farmers depend heavily on agribusiness firms to supply needed inputs and to buy and process their products. The number of input and processing firms declined sharply in the 1980s in the United States, although the downward trend had slowed by late 1990. Increased concentration of ownership in meat-packing caused farm groups to be concerned about possible adverse effects on competition in livestock-buying. In some areas, only one buyer exists for certain types of livestock. Concentration of ownership has occurred as older, less efficient packing plants were closed down and replaced by fewer and larger new plants.

International Developments

Eastern Europe and the USSR took major steps in 1990 to decentralize their economies and revitalize agriculture by providing economic incentives. Several other countries reduced tariff or quota barriers on imports of farm products, and negotiators from nearly 100 countries worked jointly to reduce trade-distorting agricultural subsidies.

The Soviet Union. Weather was favorable for good crops in the USSR. Preliminary reports indicated the country's grain production was the largest in several years. However, rain during harvest and a shortage of machinery, drying equipment, transportation, and storage facilities were believed to have increased spoilage losses. Also, Soviet farms were reluctant to sell grain, preferring to store it as protection against economic and political uncertainty. These developments and confusion resulting from decentralized decision-making led to widespread food shortages, particularly of meat. Despite limited foreign exchange and lack of credit, the Soviet Union would be an importer of grain, protein meal, flour, and possibly meat and vegetable oil in 1991.

The Supreme Soviet gave President Mikhail Gorbachev sweeping powers to convert the USSR's economy to a market-directed system. In late 1990 it remained uncertain whether farmers would be allowed to own land, but future decisions about what farm products to produce were expected to be guided by market prices and profitability. The shift to a market economy eventually may boost lagging agricultural productivity. However, to achieve full potential, time will be required to generate needed investments in roads, railroads, grain storage and drying facilities, a retail farm-supply sector, a farm-credit system, and futures markets for price discovery and risk management. Management skills will have to be developed and local resistance to change overcome. During the transition period, Soviet imports of basic agricultural products likely will remain large and highly variable from year to year. Availability of food will continue to be important in maintaining political stability.

Eastern Europe. After more than four decades of attempting to keep its agricultural system innovative and progressive within a government-directed economy, Eastern Europe abruptly shifted to a market-based system. Its farmers and agribusinesses were struggling to learn Western-style management techniques for capitalizing on market opportunities and dealing with market risks. The shift to democracy and a market-directed economy brought temporarily increased grain, meat, and protein-meal imports, credit, and technical assistance from Western neighbors. Changes got under way that might position Eastern Europe to increase farm productivity substantially in the next few years, perhaps regaining its pre-World War II status as Europe's breadbasket.

With German reunification, competitive pressures from more efficient West German farms made temporary protection of East German agriculture necessary. Over time, however, unifying the nation's farm policies will become a more important goal as the new Germany becomes more of an agricultural exporter.

The European Community. The European Community (EC) maintains price supports encouraging self-sufficiency in agriculture to prevent food shortages such as in the immediate post-World War II years. Performance of the EC's farm sector in 1990 confirmed that its emergence as a leading agricultural exporter is not temporary. The Community is now one of the world's largest exporters of wheat and protein meal, and the largest exporter of pork and beef.

In 1990 the EC worked out several details of its planned economic unification, which will begin in 1992. Initially, the EC will unify health and sanitary regulations across borders. Unification also will require equal tax treatment and government financial assistance to farmers from one member nation to another. Unification should increase the efficiency of EC agriculture, making it a stronger competitor in world markets. At the same time, U.S. firms wishing to export to the EC will find the task easier with a single set of EC health and sanitary regulations.

Latin America. Agriculture in Brazil and Argentina was restrained by sluggish economies as both governments tightened fiscal reins to control inflationary pressures and meet repayment requirements on foreign debt. Tight economic controls led to inadequate credit for farm inputs along with low farm-product prices, exchange-rate problems, and export taxes on some Argentine farm products. Even so, Argentine farmers harvested a record soybean crop and better yields of corn and sunflowers than in 1989 because of generally favorable weather. Brazil's crops were large but below previous records, due in part to slightly reduced soybean production after years of expansion.

Mexico and Venezuela, major oil exporters, benefited from rising petroleum prices stemming from the Middle East crisis. Increased per capita incomes late in the year led to growing demand for meat products in these two countries. Agriculture elsewhere in the region remained stable, limited by inadequate credit, high interest rates, and high inflation.

Asia. Crops were good in Asia, including the most densely populated countries, India and China. India again accumulated a moderate food-grain surplus, partially rebuilding stocks depleted after a severe drought in 1987. Strong Western demand for textiles, automobiles, electronics, and other items maintained economic growth along the Pacific Rim, in turn expanding Far East demand for U.S. agricultural products such as red meat, poultry, feed grains, protein meal, and vegetable oil.

In response to growing demand and U.S. political pressure, Japan, South Korea, and Taiwan reduced import restrictions on several farm products, including meat. However, Japan and Korea refused to remove restrictions on rice imports. These two countries view domestic rice production as a form of insurance against possible disruptions in imported food supplies due to war, labor strikes, political embargoes, or other unforeseen events.

Growth in China's agricultural production slowed in 1990 from the rapid pace of the previous ten years, as changing government policies reduced incentives to expand grain output and slowed consumer-demand growth. Its government also took action to slow the conversion of scarce cropland to industrial and residential development. Several million acres (hectares) were shifted from agriculture to these uses in the 1980s.

Vietnam has overtaken the United States to become the world's second-largest rice exporter, with its farmers producing more in response to profit incentives. Indonesia also expected to expand its rice exports in the next few years in response to larger production. Increased meat production in Thailand substantially reduced its availability of corn for export to neighboring countries. Thailand usually is the world's third- or fourth-largest corn exporter.

Africa. Africa continued to struggle with the world's most serious food problems. Except for South Africa, a few of its southern neighbors, and the northern tier of countries, agricultural production has lagged behind population growth for more than a decade. In late 1990 a food crisis again was emerging in interior Ethiopia, although production had improved some in neighboring countries to the south and west.

Africa's agricultural problems reflect variable rainfall, lack of fertilizer, inadequate research on crops adapted to the area, rapid population growth, gradual expansion of the Sahara desert, and policies that keep farm prices low. A promising new approach to reduce these problems is intercropping, which involves alternating strips of trees and shrubs with strips of crops. Nitrogen-producing trees and crops are used to add soil fertility. Trees and shrubs control soil erosion. They also provide material for mulching, which conserves soil moisture and adds nutrients to the soil. Moreover, the trees provide fuel wood for cooking and heating, reducing the need to burn soil-nourishing crop residue and animal dung.

See also FOOD.

ROBERT N. WISNER, *Iowa State University*

ALABAMA

The elections and racial conflict in Selma made headlines in Alabama during 1990.

The Elections. Incumbent Gov. Guy Hunt, elected in 1986 as the state's first Republican governor in 112 years when the Democratic primary failed to produced a clear winner, was reelected easily in November with 52% of the vote. His opponent, Paul Hubbert, leader of the state teachers' union, received 48% of the vote after surviving a primary runoff election in June to become the Democratic nominee. During the campaign Governor Hunt had stressed his success in bringing industry to the state. Democrats won all other major offices. U.S. Sen. Howell Heflin easily won reelection, and in House races Democrats maintained their five-to-two advantage. The party also maintained its solid grip on the state legislature.

The Legislature. During the legislative session, Governor Hunt made numerous proposals, but few of them became law. The main

In March 1990 some 5,000 persons gathered in Selma to mark the 25th anniversary of the 1965 U.S. civil-rights march from Selma, AL, to the state capital at Montgomery that was led by the Rev. Martin Luther King, Jr., in a drive to register black voters.

© Linda Schaefer/Sygma

work of the assembly was the passage of a record $2.5 billion education budget and an $800 million plus general-fund appropriation bill. Hunt signed the budget enactments on May 3, but declined a public ceremony because of the amount of "pork" they contained.

The legislature also set up a committee, chaired by former state Supreme Court Chief Justice C. C. Torbert, to examine the state's tax structure. In public hearings during the summer, reform groups supported a comprehensive tax overhaul, while representatives of large farms and timber companies argued against increases in property taxes.

In May a lawsuit against state officials was filed by representatives of revenue-deficient school systems seeking a more need-based distribution formula.

Racial Controversies. In January, Federal Bureau of Investigation (FBI) agents began an investigation of junk dealer Robert Wayne O'Ferrell in connection with the mail-bomb death on Dec. 16, 1989, of federal Judge Robert Vance at his Mountain Brook home. However, suspicion of O'Ferrell ended when Walter Leroy Moody of Rex, GA, was arrested on November 7 for the murders of Vance and Savannah Alderman Robert Robinson.

The 25th anniversary of the attack on civil-rights protesters by state troopers in Selma was commemorated on March 7. Earlier the city again was engulfed in turmoil after the white-controlled school board, in a clear racial split, ended the contract of Norward Roussell, its first black school superintendent, in December 1989. He was reinstated temporarily in February, but the severity of protests by black school patrons forced the cessation of classes for several days. Roussell resigned in May, and an agreement was reached in August, providing for equal representation of blacks and whites on the school board.

National attention also was focused on Alabama prior to the August Professional Golfers' Association (PGA) tournament at the exclusive Shoal Creek club near Birmingham. Shortly before the tourney, it was revealed that the club had no black members and little interest in integration. However, when civil-rights organizations threatened to picket the tournament and national television advertisers began pulling their commercials, the first black member was recruited. The controversy's national implications were demonstrated when the PGA decided that future tournament-location clubs actively must solicit minority members.

Military Crisis. In late August following Iraq's invasion of Kuwait, seven Alabama military reserve units were sent to the Persian Gulf as members of Operation Desert Shield. Ala-

---

ALABAMA • Information Highlights

Area: 51,705 sq mi (133 915 km²).
Population (1990 census prelim.): 3,984,000.
Chief Cities (July 1, 1988 est.): Montgomery, the capital, 193,510; Birmingham, 277,280; Mobile, 203,820; Huntsville, 159,450.
Government (1990): *Chief officers*—governor, Guy Hunt (R); lt. gov. Jim Folsom, Jr. (D). *Legislature*—Senate, 35 members; House of Representatives, 105 members.
State Finances (fiscal year 1989): *Revenue,* $8,278,000,000; *expenditure,* $7,401,000,000.
Personal Income (1989): $56,112,000,000; per capita, $13,625.
Labor Force (June 1990): *Civilian labor force,* 1,899,200; *unemployed,* 139,500 (7.3% of total force).
Education: *Enrollment* (fall 1988)—public elementary schools, 521,650; public secondary, 203,101; colleges and universities, 103,936. *Public school expenditures* (1989–90), $2,200,000,000.

bama reportedly had more mobilized National Guard units than any other state.

Floods. In February and March disastrous floods drenched south Alabama. Hardest hit was Elba where 14 died, primarily as a result of a river-levee break on March 17. Property damage reached about $100 million.

WILLIAM H. STEWART
The University of Alabama

ALASKA

The year 1990 was a tumultuous one for Alaska in important political, social, and economic areas. The year also saw one of the worst forest-fire seasons in the history of the state.

Government and Politics. In politics, the major issue was the gubernatorial victory of Walter J. Hickel as the standard-bearer of the Alaska Independence Party (AIP). A former Republican governor elected in 1966, Hickel resigned after two years to become secretary of the interior (1969–70) in the Richard Nixon administration. Neither Hickel nor his running mate, Jack Coghill, ran in the primary election as AIP members, although Coghill did win the Republican primary nomination for lieutenant governor. Democratic Gov. Steve Cowper did not seek reelection.

In other contests, Alaska's voters mirrored national trends. Ted Stevens (R), the senior U.S. senator from Alaska, was reelected by a wide margin, while Don Young (R), in an extremely close race with a relatively unknown Democratic challenger, was reelected narrowly to the lone seat in the House of Representatives. Meanwhile, the state legislature continued its tradition of coalition organizing. Alaska's new 20-member Senate, evenly divided between Democrats and Republicans, would feature a majority organization of all

ALASKA · Information Highlights
Area: 591,004 sq mi (1 530 700 km²).
Population (1990 census prelim.): 546,000.
Chief Cities (1980 census): Juneau, the capital, 19,528; Anchorage (July 1, 1988 est.), 218,500; Fairbanks, 22,645; Sitka, 7,803.
Government (1990): *Chief Officers*—governor, Steve Cowper (D); lt. gov., Stephen McAlpine (D). *Legislature*—Senate, 20 members; House of Representatives, 40 members.
State Finances (fiscal year 1989): *Revenue,* $5,112,000,000; *expenditure,* $4,448,000,000.
Personal Income (1989): $11,407,000,000; per capita, $21,656.
Labor Force (June 1990): *Civilian labor force,* 262,600; *unemployed,* 17,200 (6.5% of total force).
Education: *Enrollment* (fall 1988)—public elementary schools, 78,518; public secondary, 27,963; colleges and universities, 28,361. *Public school expenditures* (1989–90), $808,060,000.

members led by Republicans, with no minority organization, while the state's 40-member House of Representatives featured a majority coalition led by 24 Democrats and at least three Republicans.

During the year a team of five federal agencies took over management of hunting on all federal land in Alaska (60% of the state) as a result of the Alaska Supreme Court ruling in *McDowell et al v. State of Alaska* that the state's subsistence hunting and fishing laws were unconstitutional. The Arctic Regional Fish and Game Council, representing several northern Alaska Iñupiat villages, filed suit in a U.S. district court claiming the new regulations were inconsistent with Iñupiat customs and traditions, and asking that villages be given more control over hunting and fishing on public lands. In the meantime, the Alaska Boards of Fish and Game declared that several state-controlled hunting and fishing areas were open to all residents as subsistence users. In a related issue, Governor Cowper issued an executive order that in some cases recognized Alaska Na-

Capt. Joseph J. Hazelwood (right), former master of the "Exxon Valdez" oil tanker involved in the March 1989 oil spill in Alaska's Prince William Sound, appeared in the Anchorage, AK, Superior Court in March where he was convicted of negligence and sentenced to 1,000 hours of community service—helping in cleanup operations—and fined $50,000.

tive villages as tribal governments, representing a change from previous state policy on tribal-government status that occurred after a series of defeats for the state in the U.S. court system.

Governor Cowper, because of state revenue projections, deleted several million dollars from the fiscal year 1991 budget, cutting certain social-service programs at the local level. After vociferous criticism by many groups, most of these funds were restored. However, without the record-level surge in crude oil prices due to the Persian Gulf crisis that began in August, it was doubtful that sufficient revenues would have been available. It was likely that incoming Governor Hickel also would face a need for budget cuts in 1991. In September the Atlantic Richfield Company (ARCO) announced that it was paying $287 million to the state in settlement of a 13-year dispute over North Slope oil royalties.

Economy. While revenues from oil production on the North Slope appeared to be declining, other areas of the economy seemed more upbeat. A major international economic conference was held in Anchorage in September, attracting representatives from northern-region nations and the Pacific Rim countries to promote trade and commerce. Alaska Airlines announced that it had acquired a route between Alaska and the Soviet Union, with service beginning in 1991, that further encouraged trade and passenger traffic between the two points. In addition, for the first time since the beginning of the Cold War, Alaska Natives were able openly to visit friends and relatives on the east coast of Siberia and have those visits returned.

Oil and the Environment. Some acrimony remained in the relations between the state, Alyeska Pipeline Company, Exxon, and the U.S. Coast Guard at the end of the second year of cleanup following the 1989 *Exxon Valdez* oil spill. The state continued cleanup operations after the Exxon efforts were completed, promoting its own standards regarding the success of all cleanup work.

Finally, a major area of controversy was the push to open the Arctic National Wildlife Refuge to oil development. Concerns ranged from those focusing on the amount of revenues available to the state to those of conservationists about maintaining the integrity of the refuge. A similar controversy concerned offshore drilling. While a moratorium existed on drilling in Bristol Bay because of potential damage to commercial fishing from an oil spill, similar environmental concerns by Iñupiat Eskimos about an oil spill in the Arctic waters of the Beaufort Sea and its effects on the migratory Bowhead whale population were not met with equal sympathy.

CARL E. SHEPRO
University of Alaska

ALBANIA

During 1990, Albania became the last Marxist nation to be influenced by the historic political and economic changes that swept Eastern Europe.

Domestic Affairs. On January 1, Ramiz Alia, head of state and first secretary of the Albanian Workers' (Communist) Party, predicted that the popular uprisings that had ended Communist rule in most of Eastern Europe in late 1989 and "bourgeois reformism" would not affect Albania. Nevertheless, rumors of widespread demonstrations and riots, the declaration of a state of emergency, and brutal crackdowns by security forces flowed from the tightly isolated country. *Zeri i Popullit*, the party newspaper, accused Albanian exiles of fomenting unrest and trying to restore royal rule under Leka, son of the last monarch. In March, apparently in an attempt to contain popular discontent (primarily among the young) through a controlled revolution from the top, Alia and the party's Central Committee announced a limited, gradual "democratization" of the country's draconian institutions and laws, one that would continue to preserve the prevailing "socialism" but "with more realism." Albanians were to be granted basic rights of free speech, assembly, religious practice (although Albania would continue to be atheist officially), and travel. Citizens who were at least 16 years of age would be eligible for passports.

Though political pluralism was rejected, contested elections by secret ballot were to be held for governmental and party positions, and terms of office were to be set for party and governmental officials and parliamentary deputies. Reforms of the legal system were to include a new minister of justice (Enver Halili), the appointment of defense lawyers for persons accused of crimes, and a sharp reduction in the number of capital crimes from 24 to 11, with defection no longer labeled a capital crime and no capital punishment at all for women. A limited free-market mechanism was to be introduced and would include decentralized economic decision-making in industry, agricul-

---

ALBANIA • Information Highlights

Official Name: People's Socialist Republic of Albania.
Location: Southern Europe, Balkan peninsula.
Area: 11,100 sq mi (28 750 km²).
Population (mid-1990 est.): 3,300,000.
Chief City (mid-1987): Tiranë, the capital, 225,700.
Government: *Head of state,* Ramiz Alia, chairman of the Presidium (took office November 1982) and first secretary of the Albanian Workers' Party (April 1985). *Head of government,* Adil Carçani, chairman, Council of Ministers—premier (took office January 1982). *Legislature* (unicameral)—People's Assembly, 250 members.
Gross National Product (1989 est. U.S.$): $3,800,-000,000.

Although Albanian pedestrians present a business-as-usual picture of life in a Socialist state, in fact, the waves of democratic change, which first came with the fall of East Germany's Berlin Wall in late 1989, began to be felt across Albania, a last outpost of European Marxism.

© Michel Setboun/J.B. Pictures

ture, and commerce; the legalization of small-scale private enterprises and agricultural plots and controlled international joint ventures; and permitted variations in the prices of consumer goods and personal incomes. In May the Albanian People's Assembly (parliament) unanimously approved legislation to convert these promises into law.

Mass demonstrations of thousands of people continued, however. Some were organized in support of the government's reform program. Others expressed, with increasing violence, growing dissatisfaction with the cautious and limited nature of the changes, and the slow pace of putting them into practice, especially the issuing of passports. An avalanche of discontent developed between June 28 and July 6, when between 4,500 and 6,000 Albanians stormed about a dozen foreign embassies in Tiranë, demanding asylum and the right to emigrate. At first the authorities denounced them and the police fired upon them, but after a deluge of diplomatic protests from abroad, the Albanian regime agreed to let them leave.

In an apparent attempt to defuse popular anger and to avoid the sort of bloody mob violence that had taken place in Romania in late 1989, the Communist Party and government met hastily and announced the removal of prominent conservatives from the Politburo and various ministries (including Interior Minister Simon Stefani and Defense Minister Prokop Murra), a 20% wage hike for the lowest-paid workers, and the legal privatization of small trade and service industries. Beginning in July about 25,000 Albanians were permitted to travel abroad. Despite these reforms, the populace, plagued by Europe's lowest standard of living, serious shortages of food and energy, and a 30% rate of inflation, remained suspicious and restive. The Albanian writer Ismail Kadare, perhaps the most popular figure in Albania, sought asylum in France in October and denounced the Albanian regime. On December 12 the formation of Albania's first opposition party, called the Democratic Party, was announced in Tiranë. Leaders swiftly applied for legal status through the Ministry of Justice, and the government indicated that it would authorize the creation of independent parties. The Communist Party indicated, however, that perhaps parliament and not the party was the proper authority for changing the law from one-party rule.

Foreign Affairs. Albania continued to signal its readiness to end its self-imposed isolation and to open itself to the outside world. In March direct telephone links with Great Britain, France, and Canada were set up. In April, Prime Minister Adil Carçani announced that Albania was willing to resume its long-interrupted diplomatic relations with the United States, the Soviet Union, and Great Britain. Prominent Albanian-Americans and ''friendly'' members of the U.S. Congress were invited to visit Albania. The Soviet Union and Albania formally agreed to normalize their relations on August 1. In May, Javiér Perez de Cuéllar became the first United Nations secretary-general to visit Albania. In July, Albania was granted ''observer status'' by the Conference on Security and Cooperation in Europe. Tiranë hosted the foreign ministers of the five other Balkan states in an October meeting.

JOSEPH FREDERICK ZACEK
State University of New York at Albany

ALBERTA

The staging of the national Liberal Party leadership convention and the appointment of Canada's first elected senator were among the highlights of 1990 in Alberta.

Politics. In June an estimated 10,000 delegates, observers, and news media personnel descended on Calgary to see Jean Chrétien elected leader of the federal Liberal Party after beating Paul Martin and Sheila Copps.

Politically more dynamic, though, was the sudden growth of the Reform Party. Founded by Preston Manning, son of longtime Social Credit Premier E. C. Manning, the party's platform was to cut government spending and taxation and stress a right-wing policy in other areas. Public-opinion polls throughout 1990 showed it with some 40% support, higher than any other political party in Alberta. Although the party planned to seek only federal seats, pressure was growing for it to challenge Premier Don Getty's ailing Progressive Conservative government, which with a C$9 billion accumulated deficit and high taxation policies trailed the Reform Party, Liberals, and socialist New Democrats in popularity.

A stunning achievement was the appointment by Prime Minister Brian Mulroney of war hero and businessman Stanley Waters to the Canadian Senate. Waters thus became the first elected senator in Canadian history, since the Senate is an appointed body. Getty had held a precedent-setting Senate election race in 1989 to pressure Mulroney into turning the Senate into an elected body amid growing calls for changing the Upper House in Ottawa. Waters, a Reform Party candidate, won. Mulroney at first refused to accept Waters' victory, but public pressure made him change his mind.

Economy and Business. The Middle East crisis gave a boost to the province's oil industry, the major economic foundation of Alberta. After oil prices collapsed in 1986 to $11 per barrel from $27, provincial revenues and real-estate values fell drastically, and unemployment rose. By late 1990, oil prices had surged from less than $20 a barrel—deemed a barely sustainable level for Alberta's economy—to $38. Provincial Treasurer Dick Johnston predicted a windfall from royalties of perhaps C$500 million if oil prices stayed high.

The largest share offering in Canadian history hit a snag in 1990 when Technology Minister Fred Stewart revealed that a company taking part in the province's ambitious plan to privatize Alberta Government Telephones had overestimated its earnings by 50%. Novatel, Ltd., in fact, had yet to make a profit and had lost C$25 million in the past two years. Stewart said it would cost taxpayers C$21 million to make the share offering viable, and some assessments predicted the eventual cost to taxpayers might be as much as C$171 million.

Scandal. Alberta's biggest financial scandal, the collapse in 1987 of the C$1.2 billion Principal Group of Companies, continued to haunt investors, the provincial government, and the corporation's former management. Some 67,000 investors lost money in the financial services and trust company operation, and the provincial government generally was blamed for not keeping the corporation under strict supervision. After a major judicial inquiry, the company's founder and three associates were charged with misleading advertising and faced the possibility of five years' imprisonment.

Queen's Visit. The biggest social event of the year took place with the visit to Calgary and Red Deer of Queen Elizabeth II. Unlike her later visit to Hull, Que., there were no incidents or political protests during her Alberta tour.

PAUL JACKSON, *"The Calgary Sun"*

ALGERIA

After 27 years of single-party politics, Algeria experienced a torrent of political activity in 1990. In June the voters rejected the long-ruling National Liberation Front (FLN) in local elections that gave control over municipal and provincial affairs to the Islamic Salvation Front (FIS) in most of the country's districts and all the major cities. President Chadli Benjedid announced late in July that he would dissolve the National Assembly and hold new legislative elections in the first quarter of 1991.

Multiparty Politics. Throughout the spring the media bombarded Algerians with interviews with the leaders of the new parties that sprouted across the political landscape following the constitutional revision of 1989. Marches, demonstrations, and rallies became everyday occurrences as the new parties mobilized their supporters. By the end of the year, some 30 parties had registered officially under

Algerian Muslims gather for prayer. In June the Islamic Salvation Front, which had campaigned in favor of transforming the nation into an Islamic state and implementing the Muslim legal code, swept to victory in local elections.

© Albert Facelly/Sipa

the new laws. Most of the new parties were too small to have much impact, and some of the more significant ones, such as Hocine Ait Ahmed's Socialist Forces Front (FFS), made the tactical error of boycotting the June local elections.

The Islamist Front led by Abassi Madani was ready in June to challenge the FLN, and swept to a stunning victory. Capitalizing on widespread popular dissatisfaction with those in power and drawing on its organizational base in the mosques, the FIS captured 54% of the vote. With 28%, the FLN managed to hold onto about one third of the towns and provincial assemblies. Said Saadi's Rally for Culture and Democracy ran well in such Berber strongholds as Kabylie.

After President Benjedid gave in to pressure from the FIS to call national legislative elections, the reeling FLN split into factions for and against the government of Prime Minister Mouloud Hamrouche. The president of the National Assembly, Rabah Bitat, resigned in protest over Hamrouche's economic-liberalization policies, while former Prime Minister Kasdi Merbah withdrew from the FLN to form yet another party. In September, Ahmed Ben Bella, the country's first president, returned from ten years of exile, hoping to harness some of the Islamist sentiment and some of the dissent of the fragmenting FLN behind his Movement for Democracy in Algeria. However, relatively small crowds turned out to greet the former leader. Meanwhile the FIS threw itself into the task of providing municipal services and instituting Islamic practices in the towns that it now governed. Women's groups were among those to express concern about acts of intolerance carried out by Muslim activists.

As political parties proliferated, Benjedid sought to establish himself as a presidential arbiter above the fray. One such strategy was to transfer his function as minister of defense to Gen. Khaled Nezzar, former chief of staff of the armed forces. The appointment was welcomed by the FIS. Similarly, the abolition of the military secret police shortly after the resignation of its director, known as an opponent of the Islamists, appeared designed to placate the strongest of the new parties.

Foreign Policy. Like most Arab countries, Algeria was affected by the crisis surrounding Iraq's invasion of Kuwait. The Algerian government criticized both the Iraqi action and the deployment of foreign, mainly U.S., forces in

---

ALGERIA • Information Highlights

Official Name: Democratic and Popular Republic of Algeria.
Location: North Africa.
Area: 919,591 sq mi (2 381 740 km²).
Population (mid-1990 est.): 25,600,000.
Chief Cities (Jan. 1, 1983): Algiers, the capital, 1,721,607; Oran, 663,504; Constantine, 448,578.
Government: *Head of state,* Chadli Benjedid, president (took office Feb. 1979). *Head of government,* Mouloud Hamrouche, prime minister (appointed Sept. 16, 1989).
Monetary Unit: Dinar (8.847 dinars equal U.S.$1, July 1990).
Gross Domestic Product (1988 est. U.S.$): $54,100,000,000.
Foreign Trade (1987 U.S.$): *Imports,* $7,029,-000,000; *exports,* $8,186,000,000.

Saudi Arabia. It abstained on the Arab League resolution to send forces to the Persian Gulf, but individual political leaders, such as Madani and Ben Bella, called for Algeria to defend Iraq in case of attack. President Benjedid met with King Hassan of Morocco and King Hussein of Jordan in September in an effort to find a diplomatic solution—to no avail.

The Arab Maghreb Union (AMU), an association of Algeria, Libya, Mauritania, Morocco, and Tunisia formed in 1989, met in Tunis in January and in Algiers in July. The AMU accomplished little in 1990, in part because the Western Saharan issue continued to divide Algeria and Morocco. The organization failed to agree upon a site for permanent headquarters, but the member states did declare that they would form a regional customs union by 1995.

Economics. Algeria profited from the increase in oil prices, using the revenues to pay off various debts incurred by its strapped economy, while keeping a tight lid on imports. Led by Minister of the Economy Ghazi Hidouci, the government stuck resolutely to its program of introducing market reforms. With a record output of 17.2 billion m³ (22.5 billion cubic yards) in 1989, Algeria moved into second place among world exporters of liquefied natural gas. It explored plans for additional pipelines to Italy and Spain, and welcomed foreign investment on a much larger scale than in the past, but shortages of food and housing and high unemployment continued.

ROBERT MORTIMER, *Haverford College*

ANGOLA

Angola's 15-year civil war between the ruling Movement for the Popular Liberation of Angola (MPLA) and the rebel National Union for the Liberation of Angola (UNITA) continued throughout 1990.

Conflict. Peace efforts by Zaire and seven other African nations in January were rejected by MPLA President José Eduardo dos Santos because the proposed cease-fire was linked to the demands by UNITA leader Jonas Savimbi for a multiparty political system. In April 1990 a new round of official talks took place between the movements at Evora, Portugal, through the

efforts of the Portuguese government. Unofficial meetings continued throughout the year, even as UNITA increased its attacks on MPLA-controlled cities and railroads and, in turn, as the MPLA launched a 20,000-troop offensive against the UNITA stronghold of Mavinga. By mid-June, however, the MPLA was forced to retreat in the face of high casualties and an infusion of U.S. military equipment which seemed to tip the balance in favor of UNITA. In part, their retreat led to concessions by the MPLA in the Portuguese-orchestrated negotiations.

The MPLA eventually accepted that UNITA candidates could run as independents but would not budge on its insistence that Jonas Savimbi would have to go into voluntary exile and that UNITA forces would have to be integrated into an MPLA-controlled national army. UNITA's demands included a cease-fire followed by the drafting of a new constitution and multiparty elections.

The improved international climate between the United States and the Soviet Union also seemed to have a positive effect in bringing the conflict closer to a solution. Although the superpowers agreed in October to broker future negotiations, the Soviets announced continued support for the MPLA. In 1990 such support amounted to $800 million in direct aid and the stationing of more than 1,000 Soviet military advisers in Angola. Meanwhile the United States announced $60 million in additional military support for UNITA until a peace settlement was signed.

Economy. In May the government agreed to permit the reintroduction of small-scale private businesses and to reduce its role in the economy. This led to speculation that such changes eventually could open the way for increased aid and investment from the United States and other Western nations. While there only has been marginal development of Angola's rich mineral resources because of the war, oil in the Cabinda area brought in more than $2 billion in revenues. There also were reports of important new offshore deposits.

On the other hand, after a number of years of drought, the central and southern regions faced a renewed threat of famine exacerbated by refugees from the war and other economic dislocations. In October the United Nations pledged $70 million in food aid, which would feed nearly 2 million people. Southeastern Angola, controlled by UNITA, was hit hardest and relief efforts were complicated by the MPLA's previous refusal to allow UN relief organizations to transport medical supplies and food to the affected areas. The first successful aid delivery across battle lines was a modest one organized by the International Red Cross in October.

PATRICK O'MEARA and N. BRIAN WINCHESTER
Indiana University

ANGOLA • Information Highlights

Official Name: People's Republic of Angola.
Location: Western Africa.
Area: 481,351 sq mi (1 246 700 km²).
Population: (mid-1989 est.): 8,500,000.
Chief City (1982 est.): Luanda, the capital, 1,200,000.
Government: *Head of state and government,* José Eduardo dos Santos, president (took office 1979). *Legislature*—People's Assembly.
Gross Domestic Product (1987 est. U.S. $): $4,700,-000,000.

ANTHROPOLOGY

In 1990 anthropologists questioned widespread notions about modern human anatomy; a fossil skull sparked debate over early human ancestors; and a controversial theory attempted to explain why humans have big brains.

Modern Human Origins. Two investigators challenged the generally accepted view that a group of approximately 100,000-year-old fossils found in caves at the mouth of South Africa's Klasies River belonged to anatomically modern humans. Many anthropologists contend the remains, including several jawbones and a number of teeth, critically support the view that modern humans originated in Africa as early as 200,000 years ago and then spread throughout Europe and Asia. But Rachel Caspari and Milford Wolpoff of the University of Michigan reported that the Klasies individuals most likely belonged to an early form of *Homo sapiens* that later evolved into anatomically modern humans.

The South African fossils' anatomy differs in important respects from that of humans who inhabited the same area several thousand years ago, according to Caspari and Wolpoff's controversial analysis. Their conclusion supports the theory that modern *Homo sapiens* evolved simultaneously in several parts of the world.

The size and thickness of the Klasies specimens vary considerably from one individual to another, and similar anatomical variations occur between groups of modern people living in different regions, the researchers said. Thus the definition of "anatomically modern humans" remains unclear, they argued.

Ancient Skull. The discoverers of a 9- to 10-million-year-old skull in Greece said it may have been a direct ancestor of hominids, the evolutionary family that includes modern humans. The skull possibly represents the earliest hominid species yet found, contended a scientific team led by Louis de Bonis of the University of Poitiers in France.

In some ways, the new skull—assigned to the species *Ouranopithecus macedoniensis*—resembles the remains of several ancient apes considered ancestral to modern orangutans, the researchers acknowledged. But the size and shape of its teeth more closely favor *Australopithecus afarensis*, a 3.5-million-year-old hominid species that includes the famous partial skeleton of "Lucy," according to de Bonis and his associates.

Ouranopithecus may have split off from gorillas and chimpanzees around 12 million years ago and become a direct forerunner of hominids, the scientists maintained. Most anthropologists currently hold that hominids diverged from African great apes between 5 million and 10 million years ago. But several scientists familiar with the Greek find disputed its proposed hominid ties. In their view, the skull closely parallels several species of orangutan that lived throughout central Europe and Asia from about 15 million to 7 million years ago.

Brain Cooling. A network of veins draining the brains of one line of early hominids allowed for large jumps in brain size among human ancestors over the last 2 million years, asserted Dean Falk of the State University of New York at Albany. Bony channels on the inside of fossil braincases indicate the venous system began to form in "Lucy" and other members of the species *Australopithecus afarensis* found at an Ethiopian site, Falk asserted. The dense web of veins expanded along with brain size in the descendants of Lucy and her kin, who eventually evolved into modern humans, in Falk's view.

Falk noted that recent experiments on living humans suggested blood in cerebral veins cools down near the surface of the scalp and then reverses direction back into the heat-sensitive brain during strenuous exercise or prolonged sun exposure. This venous "radiator" allowed for brain expansion among human ancestors, who survived on hot African savannas, Falk maintained. Other early hominids who became extinct lived in wooded areas and lacked the brain-cooling veins, she added. Other researchers rejected the importance of an extensive venous network for brain enlargement. Venous blood in a sinus near the nasal cavities effectively cools blood entering the brain, they pointed out.

BRUCE BOWER
"Science News"

ARCHAEOLOGY

The discoveries of a 3,500-year-old calf figurine, an engraved limestone pebble 15–20 centuries old, and the earliest known Maya city were among the highlights of 1990 in archaeology.

Eastern Hemisphere

Calf Figurine. Archaeologists digging at the site of the ancient Canaanite city of Ashkelon in Israel uncovered a 3,500-year-old calf figurine, the oldest such object known.

The silver, bronze, and copper figurine—intact except for one missing horn—provides evidence that a commonly used religious symbol was in place by about 1550 B.C. Old Testament accounts mention the worship of golden calves, similar in form but considerably larger than the Ashkelon find, from the 13th to the 8th centuries B.C. A pottery shrine the size of a football encased the calf, which is about 4.5 inches (11.4 cm) long, 4.25 inches (10.8 cm) tall, and weighs nearly 1 lb (.45 kg). Both artifacts were found in the rubble of a temple.

© Shlomo Arad/Sipa

A 3,500-year-old silver, bronze, and gold calf figurine, the possible prototype of the biblical "golden calf," was discovered in the Canaanite city of Ashkelon in mid-1990.

Iraqi Temple. Evidence unearthed at a huge Iraqi temple indicated that it was dedicated to the Babylonian goddess of healing and may have served as an early treatment facility for physical ailments. The temple lies within an ancient religious center known as Nippur. Archaeologists examined a layer of the temple dating to between 1600 B.C. and 1200 B.C.

Several artifacts in the temple were dedicated to Gula, the Babylonian goddess of healing. A lapis lazuli disk contained an inscription to Gula, and six dog figurines resembled objects associated with worship of the same goddess at other Babylonian sites. Investigators also found several human figurines, each making a gesture referring to a physical ailment, such as an upset stomach.

Early Riders. Humans domesticated and rode horses about 6,000 years ago, much earlier than many researchers had assumed, according to an archaeological study of horse teeth from a site in the Soviet Ukraine. Two cheek teeth from the lower jaw of a horse buried at the site show microscopic features that develop when a bit—the part of a bridle placed in a horse's mouth—rubs against the teeth as the horse is ridden. The same dental features, including tiny enamel fractures within polished patches, appear in living horses that are ridden, but not among wild horses.

Scientists who studied the prehistoric horse teeth said horseback riding was the first major innovation in human land transport, preceding the invention of the wheel by approximately 500 years.

Fertility Pit. Archaeologists digging at Mosphilia, a settlement on the Mediterranean island of Cyprus dating to between 4000 B.C. and 2500 B.C., discovered an oblong, flat-bottomed pit containing more than 50 objects apparently used in a prehistoric fertility ritual. Stone and pottery figurines in the pit portray women, many of whom possess swollen bellies and sit on birthing stools used during childbirth. The heads of several figurines were cleanly, and probably deliberately, broken off. Investigators found the figurines in and around a large bowl resembling a circular building at Mosphilia that may have been a birthing house. Pits and cracks on the bowl indicated it had been burned intentionally before its burial.

A 4,000-year-old Babylonian temple, discovered by University of Chicago archaeologists in Mesopotamia's ancient religious center of Nippur, may shed new light on the early practice of medicine.

AP/Wide World

Minoan Culture. New evidence suggested that the advanced Minoan civilization of ancient Crete was not destroyed by a devastating volcanic eruption, as many archaeologists had assumed previously. Excavations on Crete, an island near Greece, indicate the Minoans immediately rebuilt their dwellings on top of large quantities of volcanic ash soon after a major eruption on the nearby island of Santorini around 1600 B.C. A large, three-room house at the Minoan site lies on top of a layer of volcanic ash covering 23 sq ft (2.14 m²).

The Minoan culture rose to prominence 4,000 years ago and developed a sophisticated economy and trading system. Mycenaeans from mainland Greece may have conquered the Minoans around 1450 B.C.

Symbolic Pebble. An engraved limestone pebble found at an Israeli archaeological site dating to between 19,000 and 14,500 years ago possesses a sophisticated design intended to transmit some type of message, according to a new analysis by an Israeli archaeologist. Unlike Europe, where cave paintings, engraved bones, and other artwork abound from the same time period, such finds rarely occur in the Middle East.

The 4-inch- (10-cm-) long and 2.5-inch- (6.35-cm-) wide pebble contains incised lines on both its sides that form ladders with rungs and a crosshatch design. The meaning of the engraved patterns remains unclear, although similar designs have been found carved into limestone slabs in a 12,000-year-old Israeli cave.

Western Hemisphere

Supernova Bowl. A study of a 900-year-old bowl made by the Mimbres Indians of southwestern New Mexico indicated that a painting on its surface depicts a massive star explosion, or supernova, that created the Crab nebula. Astronomers in China and Japan documented the appearance of the same supernova on July 5, 1054 A.D.

The Mimbres bowl, discovered in the mid-1930s, features a 23-pointed circular object that apparently symbolizes the supernova and the 23 days it was bright enough to be seen during daylight hours. A black rabbit curled into a crescent shape lies above the supernova image. Stylized rabbit representations commonly symbolize the moon in many Southwest Indian cultures. The bowl's curved rabbit and supernova image are positioned in the same orientation as that reported in Asian documents for the lunar crescent and supernova.

Florida Fisheries. A network of circular canals and earthen mounds in southern Florida may represent North America's earliest known fisheries, reported an archaeologist who has excavated most of the nearly 40 "earthworks." Some of the sites date to as early as 450 B.C., while others originated in the 16th century A.D.

The carefully engineered earthworks indicate that prehistoric hunter-gatherers living more than 30 mi (48 km) inland developed socially stratified societies based on fish harvesting. The sites feature circular ditches, some up to 1,450 ft (442 m) in diameter and 6 ft (1.8 m) deep, located in savannas and floodplains adjacent to lakes, creeks, and rivers. Drainage canals extend out from gaps in the man-made circles and connect to the nearby water sources. Indians easily could have blocked the channels to trap fish that swam into the ditches.

Anasazi Pits. Investigations of pit dwellings constructed by the mobile Anasazi Indians, who lived in what is now the southwestern United States from 450 A.D. to 1300 A.D., indicated that members of the tribe often moved because their sunken quarters deteriorated and became infested with insects, or as a ritual response to a pit dweller's death.

Some archaeologists had suggested the Anasazi abandoned and sometimes burned pit structures because of disease, natural disasters, or warfare. But burned pit structures at a sample of 35 Anasazi sites were not located in villages that had experienced intense warfare or disasters. However, the dwellings had grass and earth roofs that well may have been infested by insects. Also, some modern southwestern Indians burn houses after the death of an occupant.

Maya City. Archaeologists announced the discovery of the earliest known Maya city. Excavations at Nakbe, in northern Guatemala, yielded nearly 100 stone temples and buildings, carved monuments depicting kings, and thousands of stone tools and pottery fragments.

Nakbe was a flourishing city by about 600 B.C., said its discoverers. Researchers previously thought the Maya did not build urban centers before 200 B.C. Evidence of an earlier village lies beneath the urban ruins at Nakbe and may provide clues to the cultural forces that transformed a rural outpost into a major metropolis.

Maya Codex. A rare bark-paper book—known as a codex—turned up at a Maya site in El Salvador. In 600 A.D., a volcanic eruption buried the site in ash and preserved many of its structures and material goods. Only a few other Maya bark-paper books have been found, and the paint on most of them had decomposed into tiny fragments. However, volcanic ash preserved some of the painted decoration on the newly discovered codex, which now is under study.

Excavators of a communal building at the Maya site found the codex in a niche underneath a large bench. The niche also contained a clam shell and three bowls. One bowl still bore the finger impressions of someone who apparently had scooped out some food with three fingers.

BRUCE BOWER, *"Science News"*

Photos, © Timothy Hursley

Fay Jones was awarded the American Institute of Architects' 1990 Gold Medal. His Thorn-crown Chapel in Eureka Springs, AR, right, was honored in 1981 by the AIA and illustrates his admiration of the Gothic style.

ARCHITECTURE

A purely American architectural style has become more difficult to define. This was more apparent in 1990 than ever before. Leaders in the field grew increasingly apart in their ideas of what should be built. Much of this was credited to the increasing ease of crossing international borders.

The Overseas Market. Indeed, U.S. architectural firms looked as never before for work overseas—in part because of a soft economy at home and an increasing recognition of the growing unity of the global economy. Firms doing substantial portions of their work abroad included EDAW (planning for Euro Disneyland in France), CRSS, Swanke Hayden Connell, SOM, DMJM, Pei Cobb Freed, Perkins & Will, RTKL, Heery International, 3D/I, Kohn Pedersen Fox, and HOK. Nothing like the scale of the new work abroad had been seen since architect Daniel Burnham made "no little plans" for the total redevelopment of Manila, the Philippines, early in the century.

The biggest market for U.S. services was Europe (which generated some $1.3 billion in commissions), but the Asian nations of the Pacific Rim were catching up ($1.1 billion). Even Eastern Europe, just a few years before out of bounds for U.S. firms, offered new opportunities for such firms as Emery Roth (which opened an office in Budapest, Hungary), Gunnar Birkets, and William McDonough. The lat-

ter is a small firm that won the commission to design the Warsaw (Poland) Trade Center in the form of a rocket incorporating stones from the ruins of the Warsaw ghetto in its base. Indeed the U.S. Department of Commerce looked increasingly to service firms and architects, in particular, to help make up for the United States' massive deficits in the balance of trade in goods.

Why were U.S. architectural firms becoming so popular abroad? Not necessarily because of their ability to design efficient buildings as might be suspected, according to many of the firms, but because of their ability to design buildings that fit preconceived ideas of American appearance. This would account especially for the Japanese demand for well-known, avant-garde designers such as SITE, Inc., Michael Graves, and Peter Eisenman. Arquitectonica, best known for producing buildings with a colorful tropical flair in Miami, was designing a headquarters for the Bank of Luxembourg on that city's main avenue. Robert Stern was designing a palatial hotel for Euro Disneyland meant to recall the Edith Wharton era.

Observer Nicholas Polites called the trend a reversal of the turn of the century when American moguls plundered European palaces for antique paneling and other trappings with foreign associations. Still, observed Easley Hamner of The Stubbins Associates, the majority of commissions abroad, especially in the Pacific Rim, had to be "traditional modern" to be liked by the clients. Certainly a massive "festival marketplace" in Osaka by the Cambridge Seven followed this formula.

U.S. Buildings. The growing international unity had repercussions on U.S. design as well. Italian architect Aldo Rossi won the year's Pritzker Prize for his influence on architecture in "following the lessons of classical architecture without copying them." A 25-story headquarters outside of Denver for developers, the John Madden Company, was designed by U.S. architects, the Urban Design Group, to resemble an Italian Renaissance campanile. There were practical advantages. The enclosed space, raised on tall open arches, was at the top (where the bells would be in the prototype), providing panoramic views and visibility for the building as well. The urge for architecture with romantic associations of any kind became ever more ingrained in the American psyche.

For the Crown American Corporation in Johnstown, PA, Michael Graves designed a headquarters redolent with images of ancient Egypt and Greece mixed with modern industrial Italy. For Home Savings in downtown Los Angeles, architects Albert C. Martin and Associates provided offices resembling a high-rise, turn-of-the-century Plaza Hotel in New York. For a resort in Lake Buena Vista, FL, Wimberly Allison Tong & Goo designed a hotel resembling the late 19th-century Grand Hotel on Mackinac Island. For the NBC Tower in Chicago, SOM designed a building reminiscent of Rockefeller Center in New York. Most favored were styles with indigenous precedent as part of a growing interest in creating a sense of singular locale.

The winner of the American Institute of Architects' annual gold medal was Arkansas architect Fay Jones, whose individualistic "organic" buildings had been called Ozark style. Orlando announced plans for a new city hall in quiet neoclassic style traditionally associated with government buildings by architects Heller Leake, complete with a huge copper dome. A similar building by The Grad-Partnership was announced for Newark to house federal offices. A new community in Florida with strict design requirements for West Indies architecture, Caribe, was opened only miles away from Seaside, a pioneering planned community with similar design controls. But as seasoned journalist Donald Canty put it, the biggest breakthrough may not have been in styles at all, but in a growing recognition that aggressive designs meant to assert individuality were no longer desirable, that buildings should be "building blocks of neighborhoods, not isolated objects."

Architects Frank Gehry and Stanley Tigerman teamed up on a 400,000-sq-ft (37 160-m²) factory in California for furniture manufacturer Herman Miller, proving that even the strongest of egos could find it possible to get along. The muscular result was a building of diverse forms that together formed a complex with the stamp of Italian modernism in the 1930s.

Remodeling. Partially a result of the new longing for romantic associations and partially a result of the slow pace of the U.S. economy, renovation and restoration took up ever more of architects' work. Among notable remodelings and renovations of early 19th-century buildings in Florida alone were the Alfred I. du Pont house in Jacksonville (into a yacht club by Pappas Associates), Freedom Tower in Miami (into offices and a banquet facility by R.J. Heisenbottle), and Venetian Pool in Coral Gables by Carlton Decker. New Orleans saw the restoration of the Howard Memorial Library by Errol Barron and Michael Toups and Richmond witnessed the restoration and conversion of federal-style row houses into an inn by Glave Newman Anderson, Architects.

A massive lighted sign that had dominated the main waiting room of New York's Grand Central Station came down as part of a restoration by Harry Weese & Associates and Beyer Blinder Belle. The latter architects together with Notter Finegold + Alexander were responsible for perhaps the largest restoration project in history, Ellis Island, the facility in New York harbor through which flowed millions of immigrants after the first buildings were built in 1892 and in which a museum was opened in 1990. (*See* page 90.)

Professional Trends. Another effect of the slowing economy was that many firms were trying to diversify the type of buildings they designed. For instance, Kohn Pedersen Fox had made a meteoric rise to prominence by designing office buildings in postmodern style, using boldly adapted historic precedent in details and proportions. Now the company was trying to shake that image while it shifted into building types for which there was stronger current demand, including health-care facilities, prisons, and factories.

An effect of increased competition was that architects were beginning to think of themselves as being in a service industry (as opposed to being purely professionals). Such marketing techniques as advertising, once strictly taboo, were becoming normal. Architects wrestled with the increasing complexity of the building process caused by larger projects, stricter government and community controls, technological advances in construction techniques and in the functions for which buildings would be used, and the ever-swelling body of information required to put buildings together. While architects agonized over low fees and pay levels, the federal government hit the American Institute of Architects with an injunction for restricting free trade by frowning on its members bidding the cost of their work, which, of course, would drive fees even lower.

CHARLES K. HOYT, *"Architectural Record"*

ARGENTINA

In 1990 the government of Argentine President Carlos Saúl Menem survived a military revolt and continued the difficult process of trying to straighten out the country's chaotic economy.

Government and Politics. Antonio Ermán González became the third economy minister to serve in the Menem cabinet on Dec. 15, 1989. González, who moved from the social-welfare portfolio, also had served under Menem in the La Rioja provincial government. In January, Menem named his second defense minister, Humberto Romero, who replaced Italo Luder. Menem himself assumed leadership of the official Peronista party in August, replacing Buenos Aires provincial Gov. Antonio Cafiero.

At the opening session of congress, Menem attacked the bloated state bureaucratic apparatus for its inefficiency and corruption. Irregularities at the Central Bank were addressed with the removal of 15 top officers and a restructuring of the institution. Outright fraud and other corrupt practices resulting in an estimated 13%-14% loss of earnings were uncovered at the publicly owned Greater Buenos Aires Power Company. The government also began publishing the names of tax dodgers in the press.

A May Day protest against Menem's policies drew some 60,000–70,000 people to the presidential palace. It was organized by the Trotskyist Movement toward Socialism (MAS). Dissident unionists under the leadership of Saúl Ubaldini had rallied a like number of protesters four weeks earlier.

As factionalism in congress made obtaining its approval of proposed legislation increasingly difficult, Menem relied more and more on government by decree. Among the more controversial edicts was that issued in February authorizing men in uniform to intervene in civilian affairs whenever social unrest mounted.

Mutiny. On December 3, just two days before a scheduled visit from U.S. President George Bush, the Carapintadas, or "painted faces," an ultranationalist military faction, staged the latest of several coup attempts for which they have been responsible since the restoration of civilian rule late in 1983, and the first since Menem took office. One of its leaders, Col. Mohammed Alí Seineldin, had been placed under house arrest by the government in October. The revolt was put down by loyal troops with air support after several hours of fighting in which 21 men were killed. President Bush, who arrived on December 5, praised Menem for his firmness in containing the dissidents. Bush's visit was the first by a U.S. president to Argentina in 30 years.

Economy. Antonio Ermán González took on a desperate economic situation. Inflation rose to 80% in his first full month in office. Unemployment and underemployment reached 18%, and Argentina had not been able to make payments on its foreign debt since 1988. In order to implement President Menem's economic reform—consisting of an open economy, privatization, and increased trade—Ermán González abolished price and foreign-exchange controls,

In early December 1990 forces loyal to Carlos Saúl Menem suppressed an antigovernment revolt in Buenos Aires. The Argentine president called for an end to "these ridiculous antics that have hurt the country so much."

© C. Carrion/Sygma

ended state subsidies to private companies, and lowered import barriers, while reducing taxes on exports. By July he had cut inflation to less than 11%. For the purpose of stabilizing the exchange rate, he blocked all seven-day deposits. Investors could recover only 1 million australes ($800). Deposits above that amount were converted into government dollar bonds. To help raise tax revenue from 18% to 23% of gross domestic product (GDP), an ad valorem tax of 13% was introduced in February. Electricity and telephone rates, which accounted for 30% of federal revenues, were raised periodically. A favorable trade balance for 1990 of $7 billion was projected on November 4, largely resulting from greater grain exports.

The centerpiece of Menem's economic-reform program was privatization of the state-owned sector, starting with the national telecommunications company and the government airlines, Aerolíneas Argentinas. The Argentine telephone company ENTEL was split into two companies and sale of a 60% share of each was completed on November 8. The southern operation went to Telefónica, the Spanish telephone company, and Citicorp (U.S.); the northern operations were purchased by Italian and French phone companies and by J.P. Morgan. Sale of a majority share of the national airline was pending at the end of the year to a group headed by Iberia Airlines of Spain. Other state activities offered for sale included energy, railroads, and eight industrial concerns operated by the armed forces.

Implementation of the Menem economic program was opposed bitterly by organized labor, including many Peronista unions. Even though the minimum wage was increased to the equivalent of $124 per month on September 25, it was calculated at the time that, to cover basic necessities, a family would need $400 monthly. Strikes were frequent among workers in the companies being privatized, as well as among bus drivers and hospital employees. In mid-October the president issued a decree restricting the right to strike among workers in the public sector.

Foreign Debt. In desperate need of fresh capital, but blocked from drawing on earlier loans because of its failure to satisfy accompanying conditions, Argentina negotiated with lenders from the public sector. On May 24 negotiators were able to get a $239 million installment on a $1.4 billion standby agreement signed in November 1989 with the International Monetary Fund. Disbursements had been frozen in February because of Argentine noncompliance with loan stipulations. Under the May accord, Argentina agreed to control inflation, a budget deficit, and balance of payments, while increasing tax revenues.

Although no new funding was extended by the commercial banks that had lent Argentina more than $30 billion, and on which $6.1 billion

---

ARGENTINA • Information Highlights

Official Name: Argentine Republic.
Location: Southern South America.
Area: 1,068,297 sq mi (2 766 890 km²).
Population (mid-1990 est.): 32,300,000.
Chief Cities (1980 census): Buenos Aires, the capital, 2,922,829; Cordoba, 970,570; Rosario, 794,127.
Government: *Head of state and government,* Carlos Saúl Menem, president (took office July 8, 1989). *Legislature*—Senate and Chamber of Deputies.
Monetary Unit: Austral (4,880 australs equal U.S.$1, financial rate, Dec. 20, 1990).
Gross National Product (1989 est. U.S.$): $72,000,-000,000.
Economic Indexes (1989): *Consumer Prices* (1983 = 100), all items, 3,294,600; food, 3,186,500. *Industrial Production* (1980 = 100), 79.
Foreign Trade (1988 U.S.$): *Imports,* $5,322,000,000; *exports,* $9,137,000,000.

---

in interest was past due, a token payment of $40 million was made during talks that opened in New York on June 7 as a tangible sign that Argentina wanted to regain access to world financial markets. The talks were aimed at negotiating a debt-forgiveness package. Debt-rescheduling talks on $2.8 billion of a $5.5 billion portion of Argentina's commercial debt extended by 16 Western creditor nations belonging to the Paris Club, had been concluded on Dec. 22, 1989, in Paris. Repayment was stretched over ten years, with a six-year grace period.

Foreign Relations. In response to the Iraqi invasion of Kuwait, Argentina dispatched two warships and 450 men to the Persian Gulf on September 25. The contingent was requested by a member of Kuwait's government-in-exile and its participation was to be funded by Kuwait. Approval of the decision to send the naval force was not submitted to congress for its approval. Public opinion heavily opposed Argentina's participation in the Gulf crisis, and congressional support was unsure. The Menem administration's action was supported by the United States and members of the European Community.

Relations with Great Britain were normalized, beginning in December 1989, when consular ties were resumed. Reestablishment of direct flights between Buenos Aires and London came in January, after an eight-year lapse that followed the Malvinas (Falklands) war with Great Britain. Argentine merchant ships were allowed in waters surrounding the British-held Malvinas Islands. Full diplomatic relations were restored in February, at which time an exclusive military zone around the islands effectively was removed. Argentina was unsuccessful in gaining removal of some 2,000 British troops from the area, but Argentine families were allowed to visit grave sites on the islands where Argentine dead were buried following the armed conflict in 1982.

LARRY L. PIPPIN
University of the Pacific

ARIZONA

The lingering influence of a former impeached governor, an indecisive gubernatorial election, and yet another defeat of a proposed Martin Luther King, Jr., holiday were the leading news stories in Arizona in 1990.

Politics. Evan Mecham, who was elected governor with 40% of the vote in a three-way race in 1986 and was impeached and removed from office in 1988 following charges of financial improprieties, continued to influence Arizona politics in 1990. In 1990, Mecham ran for governor again, but was defeated by a two-to-one margin by Phoenix developer J. Fife Symington III in a five-way Republican primary. Symington faced Democrat Terry Goddard, former mayor of Phoenix, in November's general election. Symington received 4,200 more votes than Goddard, but a former Mecham aide running as an antiabortion write-in candidate gained more than 10,000 votes, enough to deny the Republican a majority.

In 1988, Arizona's constitution was amended to require a simple majority for election and a runoff between the top two votegetters. Unfortunately, the legislature had failed to pass laws necessary to implement a runoff election. So Gov. Rose Mofford was forced to call a special legislative session in November and a runoff election was scheduled for February 1991.

The November election resulted in significant changes in the legislature. The 30-member Senate went from a 17–13 Republican majority to a Democratic majority by the same margin. The 60-member House gained 11 new members with a 33–27 Republican majority.

Both of Arizona's U.S. senators, Dennis DeConcini (D) and John McCain (R), were among five senators—the Keating five—under Senate scrutiny for their involvement with Charles Keating, a key figure in the savings and loan scandal. (*See* UNITED STATES—*Domestic Affairs*.)

King Holiday. The issue of a state holiday honoring Martin Luther King, Jr., continued to cause controversy. Governor Mecham had achieved notoriety in 1987 when he canceled a King holiday that former Gov. Bruce Babbitt had proclaimed by executive order. A special legislative session in November 1989 passed a bill that dropped Columbus Day as a state holiday in favor of King Day. This upset people of Italian heritage who joined anti-King Mecham supporters to circulate referendum petitions against the measure. They were successful in holding the holiday in abeyance until the election of 1990. Voters then were given the ballot options of the Columbus Day swap or a proposal for a new King Day holiday. Both proposals were defeated.

The economic fallout of the defeat of the King holiday was immediate as National Foot-

---

ARIZONA · Information Highlights

Area: 114,000 sq mi (295 260 km²).
Population (1990 census prelim.): 3,619,000.
Chief Cities (July 1, 1988 est.): Phoenix, the capital, 923,750; Tucson, 385,720; Mesa, 280,360; Tempe, 140,440; Glendale, 140,170.
Government (1990): *Chief Officers*—governor, Rose Mofford (D); secretary of state, Jim Shumway (D). *Legislature*—Senate, 30 members; House of Representatives, 60 members.
State Finances (fiscal year 1989): *Revenue,* $7,578,000,000; *expenditure,* $7,157,000,000.
Personal Income (1989): $56,196,000,000; per capita, $15,802.
Labor Force (June 1990): *Civilian labor force,* 1,752,300; *unemployed,* 101,700 (5.8% of total force).
Education: *Enrollment* (fall 1988)—public elementary schools, 417,579; public secondary, 157,311; colleges and universities, 257,786. *Public school expenditures* (1989–90), $2,185,384,000.

---

ball League Commissioner Paul Tagliabue recommended that the 1993 Super Bowl game be moved from Phoenix. Hope also dwindled for a major-league baseball franchise in Arizona, and several college teams refused to play in postseason bowl games in the state

Economy. The economy reeled from commercial overdevelopment with vacancy rates exceeding 25%. In midsummer business-bankruptcy rates in Tucson were the highest in the nation. Yet, unemployment was less than the national average as other segments of the economy remained strong.

The Navajos. Political instability continued its reign on the Navajo reservation. On October 17 suspended tribal chairman Peter MacDonald was convicted of 41 counts of bribery in tribal district court. This compelled the tribal council to declare him ineligible for reelection. In the presidential election, which had been postponed until November 20, Peterson Zah, the tribal chairman from 1983 to 1987, emerged the victor. Meanwhile, MacDonald faced a second trial on conspiracy charges.

PETER GOUDINOFF, *University of Arizona*

ARKANSAS

Politics dominated 1990 news in Arkansas.

Elections. Incumbent Gov. Bill Clinton (D) was reelected, defeating former utilities company executive Sheffield Nelson (R). A former Democrat, Nelson had defeated another former Democrat, U.S. Rep. Tommy F. Robinson, in the May 29 GOP primary. If Clinton completes his historic fifth gubernatorial term, he will have served longer than any other chief executive in the state's history. In the race for lieutenant governor, Jim Guy Tucker (D) defeated Kenneth Muskie Harris, a black who had been chosen over Ku Klux Klan supporter Ralph F. Forbes in the much-publicized GOP runoff primary.

U.S. Sen. David Pryor was unopposed in his bid for a third term. Ray Thornton resigned as president of the University of Arkansas to become a victorious Democratic candidate for the U.S. House of Representatives in the 2d District. Arkansas' other member of the U.S. House—Bill Alexander (D), J.P. Hammerschmidt (R), and B.F. Anthony, Jr., (D) were returned to office. Court-ordered redistricting, the result of a lawsuit filed by individuals seeking greater minority representation in the state legislature, led to some incumbent state legislators being assigned to predominately new districts. Twenty percent of the state senators and 15% of the state representatives were replaced by the voters. The percentage of black legislators in the new General Assembly doubled. The makeup of the new General Assembly was affected by a number of senior members, including the leader of the senate, who either were defeated or chose not to seek reelection.

A proposed constitutional amendment, filed by an initiated petition, to establish a state-licensed lottery was voided by the state Supreme Court due to vagueness in the title. Voters defeated both a proposed amendment to the state constitution raising interest rates on commercial loans and a proposal raising the salaries of the state's seven elected statewide officers. A 1956 amendment legalizing racial segregation was repealed. Initiated acts to establish a standard of ethics for political candidates and to create a method for financing construction costs for colleges and universities also passed.

Controversy was a major part of 1990's political scene. State Attorney General Steve Clark, after first announcing as a gubernatorial candidate, was forced out of the campaign by disclosures that he improperly used a state expense account. He later resigned as attorney general after being convicted of a felony.

Weather. Weather played its usual role in the state's economy. Massive flooding in the Mississippi delta damaged more than 2 million

AP/Wide World

Arkansas was struck by unusually heavy flooding during 1990. The Arkansas River overflowed its banks north of Pine Bluff, above, and elsewhere in the state in the spring.

acres (809 717 ha) of farmland and caused an estimated \$235 million in crop and livestock losses. The Arkansas River crested at 4 ft (1.2 m) above flood stage at Little Rock, the highest it had been in more than 60 years, and did more than \$10 million in damage to roads and bridges.

Other News. The military crisis in the Persian Gulf hurt Arkansas' farm economy as economic sanctions prevented Iraq, the state's chief customer for its rice, from purchasing the grain and drove up the cost of fuel oil by more than \$.50 per gallon.

The 8th Circuit Court of Appeals accepted the school-desegregation plans submitted by the three Pulaski County school districts, thus ending eight years of litigation.

Environmental concerns—ranging from clear-cutting the Ouachita National Forest, to incinerating dioxins, and proposed commercial mining at the state's Crater of Diamonds State Park—also attracted national attention.

C. FRED WILLIAMS
University of Arkansas at Little Rock

ARKANSAS • Information Highlights

Area: 53,187 sq mi (137 754 km²).
Population (1990 census prelim.): 2,337,000.
Chief Cities (1980 census): Little Rock, the capital (July 1, 1988 est.), 180,090; Fort Smith, 71,626; North Little Rock, 64,288; Pine Bluff, 56,636.
Government (1990): *Chief Officers*—governor, Bill Clinton (D); lt. gov., Winston Bryant (D). *General Assembly*—Senate, 35 members; House of Representatives, 100 members.
State Finances (fiscal year 1989): *Revenue,* \$4,300,000,000; *expenditure,* \$3,840,000,000.
Personal Income (1989): \$31,035,000,000; per capita, \$12,901.
Labor Force (June 1990): *Civilian labor force,* 1,125,200; *unemployed,* 81,700 (7.3% of total force).
Education: *Enrollment* (fall 1988)—public elementary schools, 309,268; public secondary, 127,119; colleges and universities, 84,550. *Public school expenditures* (1989–90), \$1,087,987,000.

ARMS CONTROL AND DISARMAMENT

The reduced Cold War tensions between the United States and the Soviet Union set the stage in 1990 for the most impressive disarmament ever attempted by modern nations. The scheduled reductions covered conventional forces on both sides and the tremendously more destructive strategic nuclear weapons kept by the two military superpowers.

Conventional Disarmament. What began in 1973 as the Mutual and Balanced Force Reduction talks became reality 17 years later when U.S. Secretary of State James Baker and Soviet Foreign Minister Eduard Shevardnadze agreed in October to reduce U.S. and Soviet forces stationed in Europe, and those of each nation's allies, down to the same level. The requirement for equality between the force levels had been a long-standing demand by Washington. The basic ceilings agreed to were 20,000 tanks for the United States and the North Atlantic Treaty Organization (NATO) with the same for the Soviet Union and the Warsaw Pact nations; 20,000 artillery pieces for each side; and 30,000 armored vehicles each. The logic behind those particular numbers was that each side should retain sufficient forces to defend itself from attack, but neither side should have enough to support offensive operations.

The Soviets and Warsaw Pact nations always have deployed far more military equipment and troops in Eastern Europe than have the United States and its NATO partners. Thus, to reach equal levels of forces would require the Soviets and their allies to withdraw much more equipment than the United States and West Europeans. Until the events of 1989 which ended the Cold War this had been a nonnegotiable point from Moscow's perspective. However, the USSR altered its opposition in 1990 and the one-sided reductions agreed to included more than 20,000 more tanks removed for the Soviets than for the United States, and nearly 30,000 more artillery pieces.

By late 1990 the world picture had changed considerably. The downfall of the Communist regimes in Eastern Europe made the Warsaw Pact increasingly irrelevant. For this reason, and because the United States redeployed heavy armored divisions to the Persian Gulf in response to Iraq's invasion of Kuwait, it appeared the numbers of forces remaining in Europe would be lower than the agreed ceilings.

Tactical Nuclear Weapons. Remaining to be negotiated were the battlefield nuclear weapons which both sides have deployed over the years in their respective areas of control in Europe. These are small atomic weapons with short ranges. Already agreed to, and in the process of being destroyed, were the intermediate-range nuclear forces such as the U.S. Pershing II ballistic missiles and cruise missiles, and

USSR's SS-20s. These weapons were covered in the Intermediate Nuclear Forces (INF) Treaty signed in the final months of the Reagan administration. By late 1990 the phased destruction of the INF weapons was progressing smoothly with inspectors of each nation in the other country to verify compliance to the treaty.

Strategic Nuclear Weapons. The most fearsome weapons ever developed are the long-range bombers which carry thermonuclear bombs and nuclear-tipped cruise missiles, the Intercontinental Range Ballistic Missiles (ICBMs) with multiple thermonuclear warheads, and the Submarine Launched Ballistic Missiles (SLBMs) with multiple thermonuclear warheads, which are carried aboard nuclear-powered submarines. While the upper numbers of these types of weapons have been placed under ceilings by previous agreements, such as the Strategic Arms Limitation Talks I and II, there had not been any disarmament of them. That changed in 1990 with a U.S.-USSR agreement in principle to the terms of the Strategic Arms Reduction Talks (START), which began during the Reagan administration.

The basic figure in the proposed START treaty is 1,600. This is the total number of strategic nuclear delivery vehicles (SNDVs), i.e., long-range bombers, ICBMs, and SLBMs, which may be deployed by the United States and the Soviet Union. The 1,600 number approximates a 30% reduction in the strategic nuclear forces possessed by the two superpowers.

The success of all U.S.-USSR arms-control and disarmament agreements depends upon the reliability of the means to verify compliance to the agreements. Thus, as both nations moved toward acceptance of the START accords, considerable preparatory work was required to develop mutually satisfactory inspection and verification procedures. Several such procedures were tested in 1990 and pronounced acceptable to both sides. One involved the development of inspection techniques designed to demonstrate features that distinguish heavy bombers equipped to carry nuclear-armed air-launched cruise missiles (ALCMs) from bombers that only can carry bombs. Another important verification procedure was developed to prove how many reentry vehicles, or warheads, are being carried by a particular ballistic missile, either an ICBM or an SLBM. By late 1990 both the U.S. and Soviet negotiators were positive that the START treaty would be signed in 1991. The picture was complicated, however, by domestic turmoil in the USSR.

In another development, a group of technologically advanced, industrialized nations formed the Missile Technology Control Regime, the purpose of which was to prevent the sale of technology to nations suspected of wanting to develop their own ballistic missiles.

ROBERT M. LAWRENCE
Colorado State University

A guard stands watch at the scene of the world's largest known art theft. Works valued at at least $200 million, including paintings by Vermeer, Rembrandt, Degas, and Manet, were stolen March 18, 1990, from the Isabella Stewart Gardner Museum in Boston, when two robbers dressed as policemen overpowered security guards.

© R. Maiman/Sygma

ART

The year 1990 witnessed the continued growth of the museum-going audience and the expansion of existing museums and construction of new ones to meet the public's increasing interest in art. However, many museums were finding themselves in a financial squeeze and were selling or even trading works in their collections to buy new works of greater importance to their acquisition policies. Auction prices for art continued to set records, although at a slower pace than in 1989 (*see* page 124).

Exhibitions. The highlight of the 1990 museum exhibition schedule was the highly praised traveling exhibition of Monet's series paintings (*see* page 123). Except for the Monet show, the only other major exhibitions of Impressionist art were found in collector shows. One splendid such show included works from Leningrad's Hermitage and Moscow's Pushkin museums. Entitled "From Poussin to Matisse: The Russian Taste for French Painting," the exhibit opened at New York's Metropolitan Museum of Art in May with 50 paintings. Its outstanding paintings were ten Matisses from 1908 to 1913—among the artist's finest works. The show traveled to the Art Institute of Chicago in September.

The work of Matisse was seen again in a stunning show entitled "Matisse in Morocco," which opened at the National Gallery of Art in Washington, DC, in March and moved to the Museum of Modern Art (MoMA) in New York in June. Though small—comprising only about 20 of Matisse's 1912–13 paintings, plus a number of drawings—the show was a gem.

Matisse also was included in "The Fauve Landscape," subtitled "Matisse, Derain, Braque and Their Circle, 1904–1908," an examination of the Fauve period, which premiered at the Los Angeles County Museum.

The New York School of painting received its due with a retrospective of the German-born American Hans Hofmann, whose works appeared at the Whitney Museum of American Art in the summer. Hofmann long was considered more important as a teacher of art than as one of the leading Abstract Expressionists.

The influence of commercial culture on high modernism was examined in an interesting show entitled "High and Low: Modern Art and Popular Culture," which opened at New York's MoMA in the fall. The exhibition was divided into four sections: graffiti, caricature, comics, and advertising. The show would travel to the Art Institute of Chicago and The Los Angeles Museum of Contemporary Art (MoCA) in 1991.

A contemporary show with a compelling idea was San Francisco's Museum of Modern Art's "Elegiac Paintings: Art at the End of the 20th Century." The 40 paintings exhibited contained a dual theme, being literal elegies and also engaging the idea of the death of painting. Kiefer, Levine, Schnabel, Rothko, and Warhol were among the artists featured.

An exhibition with a historical perspective was "Facing History: The Black Image in American Art, 1710–1940," which opened at Washington's Corcoran Gallery of Art in January and moved to the Brooklyn Museum in April with more than 100 paintings, drawings, and sculptures. It included works by Eakins, Homer, Sargent, and Marsh and examined the effect of culture and history in the artistic representation of blacks in the United States.

The first major show of George Caleb Bingham in more than 20 years opened at the St. Louis Art Museum, with 29 genre paintings depicting idealism and westward expansionism of the Jacksonian era, plus 20 portraits, 44 drawings, and four prints. The show went on to the National Gallery (minus the portraits and drawings) in the summer.

Also at the National Gallery, and appearing there only, were featured works of two great Old Master painters. "Titian: Prince of Painters" opened in late October with 50 of his more famous works. The show was organized in combination with the city of Venice to celebrate the quincentenary of Titian's birth. A show of 90 paintings by the Flemish Baroque painter Anthony Van Dyck opened at the National Gallery in November, commemorating the 350th anniversary of his death in 1641.

Significant shows of non-European art included works from Mexico, Japan, Indonesia, and the Islamic world. In October a panoramic survey of Mexican art ranging from the pre-Columbian period to the 20th century opened at the Metropolitan. Entitled "Splendors of Thirty Centuries," the show included 400 works and would travel to the San Antonio Museum of Art, and the Los Angeles County Museum in 1991. Also opening in October was an exquisite exhibition entitled "Courtly Splendors: Twelve Centuries of Rare Treasures," which revealed the refined life of the aristocracy throughout Japanese history. The show, organized exclusively for the Boston Museum of Fine Arts by the Japanese Agency of Cultural Affairs, celebrated the enthronement of Emperor Akihito. A nationwide U.S. celebration of Indonesian culture opened at the National Gallery in November with 125 works in a show entitled "Sculpture of Indonesia." The show moved to Houston's Museum of Fine Arts in December and would travel to other museums in 1991. The year closed with an exhibition, "Islamic Art and Patronage," opening in December at the Walters Art Gallery in Baltimore and featuring 107 works from Kuwait. It would travel in 1991 to other museums.

Museums. One word that cropped up often in museum news in 1990 was controversy. The Guggenheim Museum in New York, for example, came in for its share of controversy when it sold three paintings by Kandinsky, Chagall, and Modigliani at Sotheby's in May to help pay for Minimalist art from the collection of Count Giuseppe Panza di Biumo. The deal also included the land and buildings of the Panza family estate near Milan, Italy. The Panza collection would not be seen until the museum's reopening in 1991. The Guggenheim closed April 29 until the fall of 1991 to begin a $40 million renovation and expansion which was to include a ten-story tower and new galleries.

Another matter of some controversy was the request in March 1990 of the Board of Trustees of the Whitney Museum of American Art for the resignation of Thomas Armstrong III, the museum's director for the previous 15 years. Jennifer Russell, associate director, was appointed acting director. Also in March, the Kimbell Museum in Fort Worth, TX, after a great public protest, announced its "indefinite postponement" of a planned expansion designed by Romaldo Giurgola.

Theft followed closely on the heels of controversy in 1990 museum news. On an early Sunday morning, March 18, two men posing as police officers broke into the Isabella Gardner Museum in Boston and carried off a dozen artworks valued at $200 million. Included in the heist were Vermeer's *The Concert*, valued at $100 million, Rembrandt's *A Lady and a Gentleman in Black* and *The Storm on the Sea of Galilee*, and Manet's *Chez Tortoni*. It was the largest art theft in U.S. history and the largest in the world since the 1911 robbery of the *Mona Lisa*. A $1 million reward was offered for information leading to recovery of the pieces. They were not insured against theft.

Gifts to museums in 1990 included a $6 million donation to the Kansas City Art Institute by R. Crosby Kemper, Jr., to establish the Kemper Museum of Contemporary Art and Design. The site for the Kemper Museum was donated by the Hall Family Foundation. The building was scheduled for completion in 1992. Another museum gift was the Tobishima Corporation's unrestricted gift of $5 million to the Guggenheim.

One of the only museum projects actually to be completed in 1990 was the expansion and renovation of the Indianapolis Museum of Art. The project was designed by architect Edward Larrabee Barnes at a cost of $32.5 million. The four-story Mary Fendrick Hulman Pavilion increased the museum's exhibition space by more than 80%.

In April the Art Museum at Princeton opened its newly designed galleries for its collection of Far Eastern art. Also in April, construction began on the $31 million expansion of the Brooklyn Museum. Eventually, the size of the museum would be doubled at a projected cost of $250 million.

New appointments and changes in personnel in 1990 included the appointment of W. Richard West, Jr., as director of the new National Museum of the American Indian; of Richard Muhlberger as director of the Knoxville Museum of Art; and of Dr. Lee Hall as director of the National Museum of Women in the Arts in Washington, DC. Also, Andrew Pekarck resigned as director of Asia Society Galleries in New York to found a new museum of Asian art in New York, and William S. Woodside announced his retirement as president of the Whitney Museum.

Notable acquisitions included the Art Institute of Chicago's purchase of Constantin Brancusi's 1919 bronze sculpture, *Golden Bird*, from the Arts Club of Chicago for $12 million. Also in 1990, The Museum of Modern Art in Fort Worth acquired 19 works by Milton Avery, including two paintings.

MARGARET BROWN HALSEY
New York City Technical College

Monet in the '90s

A landmark exhibition of series paintings by the French Impressionist Claude Monet (1840-1926) was mounted in 1990. Entitled *Monet In the '90s: The Series Paintings*, the international exhibit was the most comprehensive show ever of Monet's series, perhaps the least known of his works. Almost 100 pieces, dated from 1889 to 1900, and representing all 16 of the series, were assembled. Each series consists of several paintings of the same scene, made at different times of the day or year. The show opened in February at the Museum of Fine Arts, Boston, traveled to The Art Institute of Chicago in May, then went to the Royal Academy in London in September, closing in December.

Among the works displayed, which ranged in subject from grainstacks in the French countryside to scenes in Japan and England, were a view of the sunlight effect on the Creuse Valley (*below*), and the façade of the Rouen Cathedral (*right*). The paintings, one critic stated, " . . . produce an overwhelming sense of harmony and peace."

Photos courtesy of the Museum of Fine Arts, Boston

The Art Market

Auction prices for works of art ran the gamut during 1990, with Impressionist and Postimpressionist works bringing the highest bids. In the spring the market seemed strong, as a Van Gogh and a Renoir broke all previous price records at their respective sales at the Christie and Sotheby auction houses. By year's end, however, prices had fallen. In November sales at both auction houses had failed to reach their presale estimates, and works by many major artists passed unsold or fell well below their presale estimate. Although some claimed the art market remained very much alive, prices at auctions in November were about 25% to 30% less than six months earlier.

The highest-priced paintings—Van Gogh's "Portrait du Dr. Gachet" (which sold for $82.5 million at Christie's May 15 New York auction-house sale) and Renoir's "Au Moulin de la Galette" (which sold for $78.1 million at Sotheby's May 17 auction)—soared beyond the record $53.9 million paid for Van Gogh's "Irises" in 1987 (sold again in 1990 to the Getty Museum for an undisclosed price) or the $51.3 million for Picasso's "Pierrette's Wedding" of 1989,

thus breaking all past records. Both paintings were purchased by Hideto Kobayashi for Japanese collector and paper manufacturer Ryoei Saito. At Christie's November sale a Van Gogh drawing broke a record when William Acquavella, a New York art dealer, paid $8.4 million for "Garden of Flowers." At the same auction, however, bids for Van Gogh's "Vase with Cornflowers and Poppies" from 1890 rose only to $9 million—below the house estimate of $12 million to $16 million. Indeed, the fate of that Van Gogh was more in keeping with the art market's general economic trend, which fell in 1990 except for isolated cases.

The top prices for other Impressionist and Postimpressionist works were paid for Van Gogh's "Self Portrait" of 1888 and Manet's "The Bench" of 1881, which fetched, respectively, $26.4 million and $16.5 million at Christie's May 15 sale. From the collection of Henry Ford II came Renoir's "Cup of Chocolate" from 1878, which sold for $18.2 million in November.

Modern art continued to bring the highest prices after Impressionist and Postimpressionist paintings. Picasso's "Les Tuileries" brought

Van Gogh's "Portrait du Dr. Gachet," painted just six weeks before the artist's suicide in July 1890, brought a record auction price of $82.5 million at Christie's in May.

Renoir's "Au Moulin de la Galette," an Impressionist painting of an open-air, dance-hall scene, brought $78.1 million at Sotheby's in May, the second-highest price ever paid at auction.

$24.06 million at Christie's June 25 sale. Wassily Kandinsky's 1914 "Fugue" brought $20.9 million and Chagall's 1923 "Birthday" brought $14.9 million at Sotheby's the month before; both works were sold by the Guggenheim Museum. Other modern artists whose works sold for more than $10 million were Toulouse-Lautrec, Matisse, Modigliani, and Vlaminck. The highest price for a modern sculpture was brought by Brancusi's cast of "The Blond Negress," which sold for $8.8 million, a record, at Sotheby's May sale.

Prices for Old Master paintings fell below the prices for both Impressionist and Modern paintings. The top price for an Old Master painting went to Rembrandt's "Saint Peter in Prison," which sold for $9.5 million (well below its presale estimate) in New York in May.

The contemporary art market, though leveling off, set new auction records for 20 contemporary artists, including Richard Diebenkorn, Jean Dubuffet, Roy Lichtenstein, Adolph Reinhardt, and Cy Twombly. The top price for a painting went to Willem de Kooning's landscape "July," purchased in May for $8.8 million, below the $20.68 million for his 1955 "Interchange," sold in late 1989.

The U.S. art market experienced a slowdown. The year's top lot was Thomas Eakins' "John Biglen in a Single Scull" for $3.52 million, a record for a 19th-century watercolor.

Nineteenth-century European painting prices also retreated, but at Sotheby's February sale, Léon Gérôme's "Bathsheba Observed by King David" brought a record $2.2 million. The strongest groups were the British Pre-Raphaelites and Victorian painters. Lord Leighton's "Dante in Exile" brought $1.9 million at Sotheby's London in June. Sotheby's New York June 19 sale of antiquities from the collection of former Texas billionaires Nelson and

William Hunt saw a fragmentary red figure calyx krater (circa 510 B.C), signed by the painter Euphronios, go for $1.76 million—an auction record for a Greek vase.

The market for Chinese works of art was stronger than ever for the best works but otherwise weak. The highest-priced work was a large famille rose and doucai moonflask vase, which in June brought $825,000.

A world record for a Japanese screen was established in Christie's March sale with "Scenes In and Out of the Capital (Kyoto)," one of a pair of six paneled screens from the first half of the 17th century.

Top prices in the Latin American market went to Fernando Botero's "Man with a Cane," which brought a record $3.82 million at Sotheby's; Frida Kahlo's "Diego and I," which sold for $1.43 million; and Roberto Matta's "The Disasters of Mysticism," which sold for $1.155 million, followed by paintings which brought prices between $500,000 and $900,000 by Rufino Tamayo, Diego Rivera, and Wilfredo Lam. The upsurge of interest in Latin American art was due partly to the rapidly increasing population of Latin Americans in the United States. Nationalism in art sales was a current trend.

African art established a new record with "The Bangwa Queen," which sold for $3.4 million at Sotheby's April 11–12 auction. The celebrated figure of a dancing woman is considered the finest expression of movement in African art. Sotheby's April sale of the Franklin Collection of African Art brought $7 million and set an all-time record at auction for tribal art.

Finally, in the midst of falling art prices in November, film star Greta Garbo's collection of art works and furniture were sold above Sotheby's presale estimates.

MARGARET BROWN HALSEY

The Question of Obscenity

© Mark Lyons/NYT Pictures

Dennis Barrie, director of the Contemporary Arts Center in Cincinnati, was acquitted in an October 1990 obscenity trial relating to the museum's Robert Mapplethorpe exhibit.

Campaigns against obscenity in the United States commonly target materials sold under the counter or in sleazy stores, but during 1989 and 1990 the assault on obscenity broadened to include serious films, photographs, and popular music. Museum directors, artists, record-store owners, and pop singers all were targets of obscenity prosecutions. Intensifying the debate was the question of whether federal money should be spent on art, especially controversial art.

Mapplethorpe. At the center of both the obscenity argument and the battle over government financing was a retrospective exhibition of photographs by Robert Mapplethorpe, who died in 1989 of complications from AIDS. The exhibition, "Robert Mapplethorpe: The Perfect Moment," consisted mostly of photographs of celebrities, flowers, and traditional nudes, but a few depicted homosexuality, sadism, masochism, and child nudity. The photographs were exhibited in three cities with little opposition. In Washington, however, one gallery canceled the show rather than run the risk of losing its federal funding, and in Cincinnati, the show provoked an obscenity trial.

After the Mapplethorpe show opened at Cincinnati's Contemporary Arts Center in April 1990, local authorities charged the art gallery and its director, Dennis Barrie, with exhibiting obscene materials. At issue were seven photographs depicting homosexual or sadomasochistic acts or showing children with their genitals exposed. Germane to the case were the standards that the U.S. Supreme Court had established as criteria for judging a work to be obscene—those being that it must appeal to the prurient interest; depict sexual activities in a patently offensive manner; and lack serious literary, artistic, political, or scientific value. The prurient appeal and patent offensiveness are judged by local community standards, but the literary, artistic, political, or scientific value must be judged by a national standard.

Barrie's lawyers based their defense on the artistic-value issue and brought in various art experts to testify to the merit of Mapplethorpe's photographs. In October jurors acquitted Barrie and the art gallery.

Federal Support. The Cincinnati verdict relieved museums and their directors of one threat, but another repercussion from the Mapplethorpe exhibition was congressional action to restrict federal funding for the arts. Opposition to arts spending already was simmering in June 1989, and the use of federal funds distributed by the National Endowment for the Arts (NEA) to underwrite the Mapplethorpe exhibition brought the issue to a boil.

Opponents of the endowment say that financing the arts is not a job for the federal government and that the arts best can prosper through funding from private donors and buyers, but that if the government does underwrite the arts, it should make sure the money is spent in ways taxpayers would approve. Those who favor federal support argue that private donors do not support art that is controversial or innovative, and that individuals who buy art often prefer to invest in safe, established artists. Supporters also say that arts projects are able to attract private money only after receiving government grants.

In 1989 the opponents of federal funding were persuasive enough to get a law passed that prohibited the use of federal money for artworks deemed obscene under the Supreme Court's three-part test. In 1990, however, Congress compromised on the issue, replacing the language prohibiting grants for obscene works with a new provision stating that artists who use NEA money to produce works that later are judged obscene by the courts then must return the money and would be ineligible for federal grants for three years. The measure also required that the grant-review panels include nonartists, and it provided for a three-year extension of the NEA.

Pop Music. While some communities worried about obscenity in art museums and galleries, officials elsewhere scoured record stores for the albums of the rap music group 2 Live Crew. In Broward County, FL, Sheriff Nick Navarro decided that the 2 Live Crew album *As Nasty as They Wanna Be* was too nasty for local residents. Armed with a federal judge's determination that the album was obscene, Navarro and his deputies arrested a record-store owner who sold the album and three members of 2 Live Crew after they sang at an adults-only concert.

Prosecutors said *As Nasty as They Wanna Be* was nothing but a catalogue of profanities that encouraged the abuse of women. Defenders of 2 Live Crew say the group's songs are examples of comedic exaggeration typical of African-American street culture. Others wondered why officials labored to suppress rap music while ignoring sexist and sexual performances by white entertainers. At the October trials, the record-store owner was convicted on obscenity charges, while the members of 2 Live Crew were acquitted.

The 2 Live Crew incident proved to some people that sex, drugs, and violence were themes that permeated popular music. Organizations concerned about this trend have demanded warning labels on records.

The Parents Music Resource Center, a leader of this movement, wants voluntary, not mandatory, record labeling. Nevertheless, bills that would require record labels were introduced in several states in 1990. The proposals varied but usually required labels on any records advocating suicide, violence, or sex and provided fines and jail terms for retailers who sold objectionable records without labels. The record industry responded by instituting voluntary labeling, agreeing to place on the cov-

ers of potentially offensive albums a warning label, "Parental Advisory—Explicit Lyrics." Because of a 1985 agreement with the Parents Music Resource Center, some record makers already had labels, but they were not uniform. The new labels all will be the same.

Motion Pictures. Meanwhile, the motion-picture industry's rating system was under attack from filmmakers and critics. The issue was the X rating given to certain 1990 films. The rating system, devised in 1968 by the Motion Picture Association of America (MPAA), is voluntary, but all major producers submit their films for review. The ratings (G, PG, PG-13, R, and X) are supposed to tell parents whether the movies are suitable for children.

An X rating means that persons under 17 are not admitted. The MPAA, which oversees the rating system, copyrighted all of the letters except the X. Unfortunately, the X rating soon became the almost exclusive property of the pornographers. Many movie theaters refused to show X-rated movies, and often newspapers would not accept advertisements. Because these policies made it difficult for X-rated movies to make money, major studios began requiring directors to deliver R or PG movies.

The system usually worked well, but several 1990 films were exceptions. The films most often mentioned were *The Cook, the Thief, His Wife and Her Lover*; *Henry: Portrait of a Serial Killer*; and *Tie Me Up, Tie Me Down!*. On one point film critics usually agreed: The movies were serious attempts at art, not pornography. When the films received the X rating, the producers and directors usually chose to release the films unrated rather than make cuts to win an R, but the lack of a rating diminished the films' ability to reach an audience. Critics of the system suggested a new copyrighted rating for movies that are too strong for an R rating but not pornographic.

The MPAA's president, Jack Valenti, objected, saying that the only purpose of the rating system was to help parents decide what movies their children should see, not to judge a film's artistic value. Nevertheless, in October the MPAA announced the creation of a new category, NC-17, to replace the X rating. NC-17, which means that no children under 17 may be admitted, will be copyrighted so that pornographers cannot use it.

Whether the recording industry's voluntary labeling or the new film-rating system could gain support while protecting artistic freedom remained to be seen, but the attempt to define and separate art from obscenity no doubt will continue for some time.

JOHN R. BENDER
University of Nebraska—Lincoln

ASIA

The Asia-Pacific rim—Japan, South Korea, and Taiwan in the north, the member states of the Association of Southeast Asian Nations or ASEAN (Malaysia, Indonesia, Singapore, Thailand, the Philippines, and Brunei), and Australia and New Zealand in the south—constitutes one of the world's fastest-growing economic regions. With almost two thirds of the globe's population, Asia is a $3 trillion market. Education provides its competitive edge. Led by Japan with 94% of its young people obtaining a secondary education and South Korea with more people with doctorates per capita than any country in the world, Asia's general commitment is to an open world economy.

APEC. Concerned about the prospect of regional economic blocs in both Europe and North America, the capitalist Pacific rim states, minus Taiwan but together with the United States and Canada, created a new consultative mechanism of their own, the Asia-Pacific Economic Cooperation Council (APEC), in 1989. Its first two annual meetings were held in Canberra, Australia, in 1989 and in Singapore in 1990. Sensitive to the concerns of ASEAN that the new organization not dilute the Southeast Asian group's bargaining power, APEC is not foreseen as an incipient common market for the Pacific but rather as an opportunity for its members to convene regularly to support trade liberalization and encourage regional economic-policy coordination.

Among the initial problems faced by APEC were whether socialist economies, such as the People's Republic of China (PRC) and North Korea, should be invited to join and what to do about the "other two Chinas"—Taiwan and Hong Kong. At the July 1990 conclave, APEC agreed to explore arrangements that would permit all three Chinas to become members. The PRC views Taiwan as a province, while Hong Kong will revert to China in 1997. Both Hong Kong and Taiwan are among the most dynamic economies in the world. APEC also agreed to promote technology transfer from its industrial members to the less developed when foreign investment is made.

During APEC discussions, ASEAN criticized the hesitancy the developed states displayed over lowering trade barriers to tropical products and complained about quotas on textile trade. Although intra-Asian trade amounts to about 40% of the region's total world trade, an exclusive Asian trading bloc is unthinkable.

Security Issues. Despite the waning of the Cold War, several security issues continued to dominate regional diplomacy. The U.S. Seventh Fleet was deploying 107 warships and 51 submarines in the western Pacific along with 120,000 U.S. army forces in Japan and South Korea. Total U.S. forces were to be cut by 10% in 1991–92 because of U.S. fiscal constraints.

The Soviet Union was maintaining a Pacific Fleet of 77 ships and 120 submarines, with about 500,000 forces deployed along the Chinese border and another 10,000 on the islands north of Japan. U.S. ships and aircraft were deployed throughout the western Pacific and Indian Ocean, while 90% of the Soviet fleet remained within 200 mi (321 km) of its home base of Vladivostok for coastal defense and to protect its strategic submarines in the Sea of Okhotsk. The Soviets promised to withdraw 120,000 troops from the Asian portion of the USSR and Mongolia by January 1991 and stated they would close their air and naval facilities in Vietnam by the end of the 1990s at the latest.

Diplomatic Initiatives. On the Korean peninsula, post-Cold War politics already were in evidence as both Washington and Moscow urged their respective allies to engage in direct negotiations to promote tension reduction. In late 1990 the Soviets established diplomatic relations with South Korea (ROK). Annual two-way trade between the ROK and Soviet Union is about $1 billion. (PRC-South Korean trade is $3 billion, although political relations have not warmed as rapidly as they have with the USSR.) The United States has resumed discussions with North Korean diplomats in Beijing and has permitted North Korean scholars to enter the United States for conferences. Diplomatic pressures on Pyongyang, its mounting international debt, declining productivity, and indications that the Soviet Union soon would demand hard currency for its oil and high technology have resulted in signs of a new North Korean foreign policy. This was dramatized in the September 1990 unprecedented meeting of the prime ministers of the two Koreas in Seoul.

In the North Pacific, President Mikhail Gorbachev was scheduled to become the first Soviet leader to visit Tokyo in April 1991. The thorny issue of the return of the four islands north of Hokkaido occupied by the USSR at the end of World War II was expected to be high on the discussion agenda.

In Southeast Asia, progress also was achieved in resolving the decade-long Cambodian conflict. In August 1990 the five permanent members of the UN Security Council reached an agreement on a plan that would create a UN interim administration for Cambodia. (*See also* CAMBODIA.)

Oil Embargo. In the final quarter of the year, an international embargo on Iraq-Kuwait oil had a varied impact on Asia. In addition to the negative effects of oil-price escalation, the region's poorest countries, including Bangladesh, Pakistan, and the Philippines, were losing millions of dollars in remittances from hundreds of thousands of their nationals who were working in both countries.

SHELDON W. SIMON
Arizona State University

ASTRONOMY

In 1990 an unprecedented number of new space-based astronomical observatories probed the universe, began their voyages, or were queued on the launchpad. This cosmic fleet was all the more remarkable in that it could—for the first time—simultaneously explore the spectrum from high-energy gamma rays to low-energy infrared rays. The year's most successful spacecraft dramatically broadened man's knowledge, but others caused profound frustration and disappointment. Truly shattering for the science was the discovery that the primary mirror of the Hubble Space Telescope (HST) had been ground to the wrong shape, prohibiting it from forming sharp images (*see* special report, page 130).

COBE. In January astronomers announced that the Cosmic Background Explorer satellite (COBE) had made spectacular measurements of the farthest depths of space. The temperature of this so-called cosmic background radiation—the cooled remnant of the Big Bang event, which is believed to have created our universe—was determined to be 2.735° above absolute zero. COBE also showed that the background is a perfect emitter and absorber of radiation. Both results are in excellent agreement with the Big Bang model.

But COBE also caused problems for cosmologists by finding that the cosmic background seems to be precisely the same in every direction and at every angular scale. This result suggests that matter and radiation a few hundred thousand years after the beginning of time were distributed with incredible uniformity. In fact, such homogeneity precludes both the formation of galaxies and their eventual coalescence into the large-scale structures that have been discovered recently.

Evidence supporting those structures has never been more robust. In 1990 a survey of 2 million galaxies confirmed that they form mainly on the surfaces of bubbles hundreds of millions of light-years across. The largest coherent structure known in the universe, a "wall" involving thousands of galaxies stretching across 500 million light-years of space, had been discovered in 1989.

Most astronomers invoke unseen "cold dark matter"—which may comprise 99% of the universe but whose existence rests only on circumstantial evidence—as providing the "seeds" for the gravitational collapse of galaxies. But COBE did not see evidence of such seeds. If this finding is confirmed, along with the frothy nature of the universe, the foundations of modern cosmology will be shaken.

Galileo. In February the Galileo spacecraft glided past Venus at an altitude of 11,800 mi (19 000 km). While in that planet's vicinity, it took some 80 images of Venus' cloud-covered atmosphere that revealed details as small as 25 mi (40 km) across. This close encounter also gave Galileo a gravity-assisted boost toward Jupiter, its primary target, which the probe is scheduled to reach in 1995.

Magellan. After a 15-month voyage from Earth, this planetary probe began routine mapping of Venus' surface on September 15. This program will require 1,200 scans, each covering a 12-mi (20-km) swath, over 243 days as Venus makes one rotation beneath Magellan. Using so-called synthetic-aperture radar to pierce Venus' clouds, Magellan has recorded features as small as 390 ft (120 m) across, ten times finer than those mapped by two Soviet probes in the mid-1980s.

Among Magellan's early findings were volcanic calderas, rift valleys, and lava flows with many small fractures that suggest Venus has been volcanically more active in recent geological time than previously believed. Regions deformed by troughs and ridges indicate pervasive crustal movement, and mountain belts suggest compressional forces. An area half the size of California is scarred by two systems of cracks spaced a few miles apart, which implies homogeneous surface material. Fortunately, erosion seems to be minimal; thus scientists are seeing a fresh planetary surface. In fact, the paucity of meteorite-impact craters indicates that Venus' surface solidified only during the past few hundred million years.

Rosat. On June 16 an Earth-orbiting satellite called Rosat began surveying the sky for some of nature's most violent objects, such as black holes and the remnants of exploded stars. The most energetic ones, with temperatures up to 100 million° Kelvin, are recorded by the spacecraft's X-ray detectors. Slightly more benign objects are seen by a detector sensitive to extreme-ultraviolet light; it reveals a universe never censused before. With an anticipated lifetime of at least one and a half years, Rosat should record 100,000 X-ray sources and expose their features with unprecedented clarity.

Ulysses. Another astronomical space voyage began October 6 when Ulysses was launched from space shuttle *Discovery* on a five-year journey to the Sun. To get there, this probe first will have to pass near the planet Jupiter in February 1992. This encounter will flip Ulysses into an orbit that will carry it over the solar polar regions in 1994 and again in 1995.

Never before has our star been seen from such a vantage. By viewing the Sun's high latitudes from directly above, astronomers hope to improve their understanding of how the solar wind—which continually bathes the Earth in a torrent of atomic nuclei—escapes through holes in the solar magnetic field. While in transit, the nine instruments aboard Ulysses will make a variety of measurements of Jupiter, the gas and dust that pervade interplanetary space, and gamma rays.

The Hubble Space Telescope

Photos, NASA

Although the Hubble Space Telescope, left, which was lifted into Earth orbit in April, was unable to perform many of the planned programs, it transmitted some spectacular photos, including a color image of Saturn, above, and a close-up of one of the first images of Supernova 1987A.

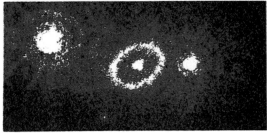

On April 24, 1990, the Hubble Space Telescope (HST) was lofted into a 381-mi (614-km) Earth orbit by the space shuttle *Discovery*. This launch culminated more than four decades of design, political lobbying, and construction to create an astronomical discovery machine with unrivaled capabilities.

The excitement generated by the launch of this powerful observation tool quickly was overshadowed by major disappointment when a significant flaw was discovered in the primary mirror of the telescope, compromising the performance of all of its instruments.

The Background. HST is named after Edwin P. Hubble, who proved that galaxies are star systems just like our Milky Way and that our universe is growing larger. By ground-based standards, HST is a relatively small telescope, since its primary mirror is only 94.5 inches (2.4 m) in diameter. HST gets its edge because it views the universe from outside Earth's blurring and light-absorbing atmosphere. Of boxcar size and weighing 13 tons (11 600 kg), and with a price tag of $1.55 billion, HST is the heaviest and most expensive scientific spacecraft yet lifted into orbit. HST cost about three times more than estimated when it was funded initially in 1977 and was launched six years later than planned.

Two months after launch HST made unwanted headlines when the National Aeronautics and Space Administration (NASA), builder of the telescope with the European Space Agency, announced that it could not form sharp images. Through oversight, its primary mirror had been ground to the wrong shape. The culprit was the principal testing device, which had been set up incorrectly.

To form an image, light from HST's primary mirror is reflected to a secondary mirror 12 inches (31 cm) in diameter and 16 ft (4.9 m) away, which returns the converging beam through a hole in the center of the primary mirror. Both mirrors had to be shaped as precise hyperboloids, curved concave for the primary and convex for the secondary mirror.

HST also suffers from another major problem. The spacecraft's "wings," 39 ft (12 m) long and tiled with solar cells to provide the telescope with power, flex whenever HST goes into or out of sunlight. This causes the telescope to wiggle, and for 15–20% of every 97-minute orbit it may take blurred images or lose its target altogether.

Accomplishments and Assessment. Although unable to carry out about half the scientific programs originally scheduled, HST is still a unique and powerful tool for astronomical research. For example, by late summer it began to deliver spectacular pictures, thanks largely to sophisticated computer techniques that can sharpen fuzzy images. Yet a question that dogs NASA is: What would those images have looked like, and what more could we have learned, had the telescope been made properly? A deeper question asks: Will HST ever justify its enormous cost?

Perhaps HST's present performance best can be gauged by assessing the telescope's ability to complete three "key" projects. These were deemed to be so important that they were given priority observing time in case HST should fail prematurely. The first was to determine the distance scale of the universe to 10% accuracy. The second was to take 50 or so pictures of random sky areas to see what surprises might turn up among faint objects never before recorded. Neither of these is now possible. What can be done successfully is to record the ultraviolet spectra of very distant and ancient quasars. This program not only will search for clues telling how these celestial powerhouses work but also will study matter along the vast tracts of space probed by the quasars' light en route to Earth.

All of HST's instruments have been compromised, either in the type of science they can do or the time required to make an observation. Most affected are two devices that take pictures. The Wide Field and Planetary Camera, intended to be the most versatile instrument aboard, also was to act as a pathfinder for the other instruments. The second device is the Faint Object Camera, which was designed to detect the most distant objects ever seen in the universe, such as the long-sought primordial galaxies, and to exploit HST's highest resolution in search for planets around other stars.

Less diminished are the capabilities of two instruments that can determine an object's temperature, motion, and chemical composition. Both the High Resolution Spectrograph and the Faint Object Spectrograph should be able to accomplish most of their intended programs, particularly at little-studied ultraviolet wavelengths. Similarly preserved are many targets for the High Speed Photometer, which was designed to measure the intensity of starlight up to 100,000 times a second. Yet, because of HST's blurred vision, all of these instruments will acquire data at dramatically slower rates than intended and will not be able to exploit regions of sky where targets are crowded together.

The Future. Fortunately, HST is repairable, though not before 1993 when plans call for one or more of its present, telephone-booth-size instruments to be replaced. By outfitting these new devices with optics that act like corrective eyeglasses, the telescope's light should be focused as originally intended.

HST is the first in a long-standing program called the Great Observatories, four Earth-orbiting satellites to scrutinize the universe at all wavelengths except radio. The second, the Gamma-ray Observatory, is scheduled to leave Earth in 1991, and the partially funded Advanced X-ray Astrophysics Facility is scheduled for launch sometime during 1997. Still undergoing study is the Space Infrared Telescope Facility.

Whether all these observatories are completed depends on how the U.S. government reacts to the oversights that led to HST's flawed mirror, to the telescope's performance now and during its 15-year anticipated lifetime, and to assessments of NASA's ability to manage so-called megaprojects. The denouement of these programs well may be HST's most lasting legacy.

LEIF J. ROBINSON

Other Missions. Two observatories were scheduled to be lifted into space in 1990. The Astro, postponed several times as a result of the 1986 *Challenger* explosion, was launched on December 2 aboard the space shuttle *Columbia*. Although not widely publicized, Astro is a powerful observatory with a quartet of telescopes. Three of the telescopes were to explore ultraviolet wavelengths intermediate between those accessible to the Hubble and Rosat; the other would probe X rays at energies higher than Rosat can detect.

The Gamma-ray Observatory (GRO), following HST as the second in a proposed series of four "Great Observatories," was to have flown in November, but problems with the shuttle prevented launch. Weighing 17 tons, it will be the shuttle's heaviest scientific payload. With an anticipated lifetime of ten years, GRO first will survey the highest-energy sources known in the universe and then will spend the next eight years taking a closer look at promising objects.

LEIF J. ROBINSON, *"Sky & Telescope"*

AUSTRALIA

In a year of deepening recession for Australia, concerns over the economy shared attention with environmental issues as green politics began to bite. A federal election in March returned the Australian Labor Party (ALP) with a reduced majority to give Robert J. Hawke a fourth term and make him Australia's second-longest-serving prime minister. Treasurer Paul Keating became deputy prime minister. The government held to a tight monetary policy in spite of increasing concern over the national drift with its massive business failures, rising unemployment (7.5%), and continuing balance-of-payments deficits.

National Economy. As the year progressed, inflation fluctuated at about 7% and wage pressure continued, with sporadic strikes settled only with acceptance of the union demands. The stock market showed nervousness and edged lower. Carmakers reported poor sales against import competition; building activity declined further. Export income was depressed by a decline in the price of gold and a drop in the sale of wool abroad. With the year's economic growth estimated at 2%, the government's budget strategy continued to provide for a large surplus (A$8 billion).

"Restructuring"—aimed essentially at raising productivity while holding wages in check—was slower than promised; the Commonwealth Bank, in urging faster microeconomic reform to promote productive capacity, found that "demand management and macroeconomic stabilization policy alone" were incapable of bringing the structural changes necessary to redress the external imbalances.

As a delayed outcome of the 1987 stock market crash, corporate failures on a grand scale and an increasing trail of bad debts emerged in 1990 as liquidity problems and led to a serious collapse in asset values. Lending institutions (including the banks and some savings associations) were seen to have been too eager to provide funds for undertakings without due regard to underlying profitability or sound asset backing. Excesses in the real-estate market based on easy credit, and in particular a vastly ambitious downtown building boom in Melbourne, produced an outcome reminiscent of the 1890 crash after a similar bout of euphoric expansion. The resulting 1990 financial collapses were interwoven with excessive pump-priming by lending bodies backed by Victoria's and Western Australia's state Labor governments; in August the State Bank of Victoria was rescued through a takeover by the federally owned Commonwealth Bank.

Increasingly commentators were drawing attention both to imbalances within the economy due to the high cost structure and to a serious dichotomy: the government's perception of continuing prosperity while a recession was occurring in the real world of business.

The Rural Sector. Faced with high operating costs and an adverse exchange rate at a time of falling markets, the entire farm and pastoral sector faced a deepening credit crisis, marked by widespread financial hardship and insolvency.

A major reason was the collapse of the world market for wool, a leading export commodity. With the wool stockpile reaching monumental proportions, the growers' option to sell to the grower-funded Australian Wool Corporation at A$8.70 per kilogram was revised at midyear; however, the new floor price of A$7 per kilo failed to result in sufficient sales to user buyers, and the stockpile continued to grow. With the aim of cutting sheep numbers by 20% from the 180 million level, a producer levy of 20% on wool sales was introduced and plans advanced to shoot tens of millions of sheep. Wheat growers also faced a slump in the world market and an end of sales to Iraq.

Politics. The March election (called prematurely) was fought against a muted background of long-evident economic malaise; more was made of the quality of leadership displayed by Andrew Peacock as a potential prime minister heading a Liberal/National Party coalition. In the campaign, Hawke and Keating promised support for a $50-per-week all-round wage rise for unionists, and for "green" (environmentalist) measures. However, the polls showed many voters were disillusioned with Labor, with a solid drift in traditional strongholds. The result turned on ALP-targeted electorates where distribution of preferences from candidates espousing "green" or other causes favored Labor candidates ahead of the Liberals.

The Liberals' main vote was strengthened and the party gained seats, especially in Victoria; however, the swing was insufficient for victory in view of declining support for the rural-based Nationals and inroads made by the

---

AUSTRALIA • Information Highlights

Official Name: Commonwealth of Australia.
Location: Southwestern Pacific Ocean.
Area: 2,967,896 sq mi (7 686 850 km²).
Population (mid-1990 est.): 17,100,000.
Chief Cities (June 30, 1986, provisional): Canberra, the capital, 285,800; Sydney, 3,430,600; Melbourne, 2,942,000; Brisbane, 1,171,300.
Government: *Head of state,* Elizabeth II, queen; represented by Bill Hayden, governor-general (took office February 1989). *Head of government,* Robert Hawke, prime minister (took office March 11, 1983). *Legislature*—Parliament: Senate and House of Representatives.
Monetary Unit: Australian dollar (1.2948 A$ equal U.S.$1, Nov. 29, 1990).
Gross National Product (1989 est. U.S.$): $240,800,-000,000.
Economic Indexes (1989): *Consumer Prices* (1980 = 100), all items, 203.3; food, 195.8. *Industrial Production* (1988, 1980 = 100), 129.
Foreign Trade (1989 U.S.$): *Imports,* $40,030,-000,000; *exports,* $36,923,000,000.

minor parties in sensitive close-fought seats. The Democrats failed to enter the House of Representatives but continued to hold the balance in the Senate.

After the election the Liberal parliamentary leadership passed from Peacock to Dr. John Hewson, an economist, while the Nationals chose Tim Fisher, a farmer, as their new leader.

In September the ALP broke with tradition and accepted Hawke's plan to sell off government-owned Australian Airlines and partially privatize Qantas; competition for government-owned Telecom also was approved.

By now differences on environmental policy were evident among members of the government; Hawke chose a middle way (in headline parlance, "pale green politics"), with acceptance of an interim planning target of 20% reduction in greenhouse gases by 2005 and some relaxation of an earlier stringency on forest logging. Indications were that green politics in the future would be based on compromise, balance, and more detailed scientific and economic assessment.

The Gulf Crisis. Following the Iraqi invasion of Kuwait in August, Australia backed UN-sponsored sanctions against Iraq, and sent two destroyers and a supply ship to augment the international force in the Persian Gulf.

Transition. The Australian Securities Commission, with stricter enforcement guidelines, replaced the National Companies & Securities Commission, which had been unable to curb the free-wheeling activities of company entrepreneurs in the 1980s.

In October, London-born Patrick White, 78, Nobel Prize winner and Australia's most celebrated writer, died. White immigrated to Australia as a boy. The first of his novels to gain major attention were *The Tree of Man* (1955), a saga of pioneering just beyond the outskirts of Sydney, and *Voss* (1957), based on a tragic inland journey of exploration.

R. M. YOUNGER
Author, "Australia and the Australians"

AUSTRIA

In 1990, Austria held parliamentary elections that resulted in a continuation of the Socialist-People's Party coalition government; the nation also solidified its ties with the European Community and with the new non-Communist regimes emerging in Eastern Europe.

Government. The parliamentary elections held on October 7 aroused only moderate interest, with 83.2% of the electorate participating in contrast to 90% four years earlier. Under a new law it was the first election in which Austrian citizens living abroad were permitted to vote. The Socialists led with 80 seats, the same

as in 1986; the People's Party had 60 seats, a loss of 17; the far right Freedom Party led by Joerg Haidler, 33 seats, a gain of 15; and the Greens ten, a gain of two. Socialist Franz Vranitzky continued as chancellor in his coalition with the People's Party, headed by Josef Riegler. The noticeable increase in the strength of the Freedom Party was attributed by some to its charge of government corruption and to its advocacy of stricter controls on immigration when the end of Communist rule in Eastern Europe led many legal and illegal refugees to flee to the West.

On July 29 former Chancellor Bruno Kreisky died. Elected to parliament in 1956, Kreisky was foreign minister (1959–66), and as chancellor led a Socialist government from 1970 to 1983. A state funeral was held on August 7.

Foreign Affairs. Austria applied for membership in the European Community (EC) in 1989, but action on its application was not expected before 1993. Meanwhile, the government was continuing to bring its trade regulations and laws into line with those of the EC. The hard-currency policy of linking the Austrian schilling to the German mark is an important step toward closer economic integration with the Community.

In 1990, Austria joined with Italy, Hungary, Czechoslovakia, and Yugoslavia in a new regional grouping known—because of its five members—as the Pentagonale. At meetings held in Bratislava, Czechoslovakia, in April and in Venice at the end of July, they reached agreement on a wide range of initiatives to spur regional economic development and improve transportation ties.

Attended by top military officials of 35 European and American countries, a seminar on East-West military doctrines met in the Hofburg Palace on January 16 for a three-week conference. Sponsored by the Conference on Security and Cooperation in Europe, the seminar provided an opportunity for the 16 North Atlantic Treaty Organization (NATO) members, the seven Warsaw Pact nations, and some nonaligned countries (Austria among them) to exchange views and discuss Europe's security.

Since being admitted to the United Nations on Dec. 14, 1945, Austria has taken an active part in its activities. Foreign Minister Alois Mock addressed the General Assembly on February 20 at a session on drug abuse. He addressed the Assembly again on September 28 when he condemned Iraq's aggression against Kuwait and said Austria would support the UN resolutions in the Persian Gulf crisis. Austria regularly provides troops for UN peacekeeping operations. More than 25,000 Austrian citizens have served under the UN flag, and 25 have lost their lives in the service of the world body.

In February, Chancellor Vranitzky visited the United States, where he consulted with

Austrians who had been stranded in Iraq and Kuwait following Iraq's invasion of Kuwait are delighted to return to their homeland in late August. They were allowed to leave Iraq following a Baghdad meeting between Iraq's President Saddam Hussein and Austria's President Kurt Waldheim.

© Langenhagen/Sipa

President Bush and numerous other officials. Although still banned from the United States, Austria's President Kurt Waldheim to some extent has broken the diplomatic isolation which was his lot after he had been accused of allegedly committing war crimes while serving as an intelligence officer with the German army. On Dec. 4–6, 1989, he went on an official visit to Tunisia at the invitation of the Tunisian government. Then, in January 1990, East Germany's Prime Minister Hans Modrow paid a one-day official visit to Vienna and was received by Waldheim.

Before he was elected president of Czechoslovakia, Václav Havel had been invited to open Austria's 1990 Salzburg Festival. Now, as president, he kept his engagement and in the company of West German President Richard von Weizsäcker he went to Salzburg where he met with President Waldheim on July 26. The Havel-Weizsäcker visit received much publicity and generally was considered a step toward Waldheim's rehabilitation. His position was enhanced when, accompanied by various officials, he flew to Baghdad, met with Iraqi leader Saddam Hussein on August 25, and was able to bring back some 80 Austrians who had been stranded in Iraq and Kuwait during the Persian Gulf crisis.

In February it was announced that the Austrian government had reached an accord with the Committee for Jewish Claims on Austria, by which Austria agreed to pay nearly $200 million to benefit Austrian Jews who suffered during the Nazi era. Most of the funds will provide social-insurance payments to those who would have been eligible had they continued to live in Austria; the rest will be used to assist homes for the aged in various countries.

Economy. The performance of the Austrian economy in 1989 and 1990 exceeded the Western European average. The forecast for the real growth of the gross domestic product (GDP) for 1990 was from 3.5% to 4%. The rate of unemployment was about 4.9%, with inflation at about 2.5%. The tax reform of 1989 generally was held to have stimulated production and purchases. A so-called "East-West Fund" of 5 billion schillings (about $425 million) has been established to help Austrian firms meet the financial risks of investments in Eastern Europe. More than 65% of Austria's imports and exports are with EC countries, about half of these with Germany; 9% are with East Europe; and 3.6% are with the United States. On Jan. 1, 1990, there was a substantial reduction of customs on industrial products and further reductions were envisaged.

ERNST C. HELMREICH, *Professor of History Emeritus, Bowdoin College*

AUSTRIA • Information Highlights

Official Name: Republic of Austria.
Location: Central Europe.
Area: 32,375 sq mi (83 850 km^2).
Population (mid-1990 est.): 7,600,000.
Chief Cities (1981 census): Vienna, the capital, 1,531,346; Graz, 243,166; Linz, 199,910; Salzburg, 139,426; Innsbruck, 117,287.
Government: *Head of state,* Kurt Waldheim, president (took office July 1986). *Head of government,* Franz Vranitzky, chancellor (took office June 16, 1986). *Legislature*—Federal Assembly: Federal Council and National Council.
Monetary Unit: Schilling (10.46 schillings equal U.S. $1, Nov. 29, 1990).
Gross Domestic Product (1989 est. U.S.$): $103,200,000,000.
Economic Indexes (1989): *Consumer Prices* (1980 = 100), all items, 136.8; food, 128.9. *Industrial Production* (1980 = 100), 123.
Foreign Trade (1989 U.S.$): *Imports,* $38,873,000,000; *exports,* $32,429,000,000.

AUTOMOBILES

An already sluggish 1990-model year suffered an unexpected blow in August 1990 when Iraq's takeover of Kuwait raised the prospect of the third U.S. fuel-supply crisis since 1974. Slowdowns in new-car and truck sales deepened in August and September for the Big Three U.S. producers—General Motors, Ford, and Chrysler Corp.—and reduced their share of year-to-date car deliveries to a modern-day low of 65.59%.

Sharply increased volume and market penetration, however, were reported for the same period by Japanese importers and their "transplant" U.S. assembly plants. Paced by Toyota and Honda, the Japanese share of the U.S. market advanced to a record 28.06% in the January-August period on a volume gain of nearly 7% from a year earlier, to 1,805,938 sales of new cars in the United States. This contrasted with a Big Three slide of 6.6% to 6,435,758 cars.

Overall, the economic slowdown which began in late 1989 cut U.S. sales in the first eight months of 1990 to 9,670,132 cars and trucks (including vans and utility vehicles). The falloff from the comparable period of 1989 was 5.2% for the year to date, but August's drop of nearly 20% was a portent of rising consumer uncertainties over the Iraq-Kuwait situation.

Although late model-year sales also were hurt by strike threats growing out of the Big Three's contract negotiations with the United Auto Workers (UAW), executives were disappointed by the failure of consumers to respond to the wave of incentive programs and early debuts of 1991 models. The Detroit-based producers, which rarely had held less than a two-thirds share of the U.S. new-car market, also admittedly were perplexed by the inroads of the Japanese manufacturers despite the general recession mood in the vehicle market and the Persian Gulf eruption.

In the January-August period of 1990, the pressures on the domestic manufacturers were highlighted by the fact that sales of both Honda and Toyota cars on the U.S. market were higher than those of Chrysler Corp. Honda, benefiting from its two U.S. transplant assembly plants and popular Acura upscale division, also sold more domestic cars than imports for

the first time. Toyota, seeking to raise its U.S. volume to 1.5 million units per year by 1995, announced plans late in the year to build a second assembly plant in the United States and to acquire the Fremont, CA, plant it shares with GM by 1996.

The Big Three, each of which has ties with Japanese automakers, were fighting hard to reverse the sales slide and to regain their previous market penetration levels. These comeback attempts for the domestic automakers, ushering in the final decade of the 20th century, were being directed by new chairmen and chief executive officers at GM and Ford. Also, Chrysler Chairman Lee A. Iacocca was scheduled to retire in late 1991. Robert C. Stempel took office as GM chairman on Aug. 1, 1990, succeeding Roger B. Smith, whose nine-and-one-half-year reign was the second-longest of any GM chairman. Harold A. (Red) Poling became Ford chairman April 1, replacing Donald E. Petersen, who served five years. At Chrysler, Iacocca's heir apparent, Vice-Chairman Gerald Greenwald, resigned suddenly in June to take charge of an employee-run bid for control of UAL, Inc. (United Air Lines).

The Number 1 U.S. automaker, GM, greeted the 1991-model year with an ambitious program to recover sales losses with introduction of cars more appealing to younger buyers. The new Saturn division of GM, a $3 billion investment in a project openly committed to winning back Japanese-car owners, finally was launched seven years after its initial announcement. Other GM divisions were stressing performance and youth-product themes, but there were fears that the Middle-East flareup would revive demand for "economy cars" with po-

Chrysler Corporation

Saturn Corporation

New Models for 1991. *The Saturn Sports Coupe, left, part of General Motors' Saturn division program to reduce Japan's share of the U.S. automobile market, was aimed at the younger car buyer. The Dodge Stealth, above, another sports coupe, was built by Chrysler's Mitsubishi partner.*

Mazda Motor of America

The Mazda Navajo, with five-speed manual or four-speed automatic overdrive transmission, was the first auto made by a U.S. producer for sale by an "import" network.

tential enactment of congressional bills raising corporate fuel average mandates from 27.5 to 35 and even 40 miles per gallon (44.2 to 56.3 to 64.3 km/g).

Ford, which steadily increased its sales volume and market share in the late 1980s, fell back substantially on both counts in 1990. A restyled Ford Escort, using the platform of Ford's Japanese partner Mazda, did not reach initial sales goals. But an instant hit in the truck segment was the new Ford Explorer utility vehicle, successor to the Bronco II. A version of the Explorer two-door, called the Navajo, was furnished to Mazda's U.S. dealers as the first

vehicle made by a domestic producer for sale by an "import" sales network.

Chrysler and GM also were relying on their Japanese partners for product assistance. Chrysler, whose domestic sales share plunged below 9% in 1990, began selling the Dodge Stealth, a sports coupe produced by its Mitsubishi partner, as the 3000GT. Chrysler and Mitsubishi already were sharing in a sports coupe built at their Diamond Star assembly plant in Normal, IL.

GM's Chevrolet division offset sales declines on several of its smaller models with cars marketed by its GEO division and produced by partners Isuzu and Suzuki or in association with Toyota. Ford and Nissan were developing a minivan, which Ford would produce at a new plant in Avon Lake, OH.

The 1991 Models. Wider availability of antilock brakes included their availability as an option on GM's 1991 Saturn and three other compacts—Buick Regal, Oldsmobile Calais, and Pontiac Grand Am. Fuel-efficient multivalve engines, using three or four valves per cylinders instead of two, also grew in number. Nissan's luxury Infiniti Q45 sedan became the first production car to offer an "active suspension" system, in which springs react to road conditions electronically.

Chrysler's highly successful front-wheel-drive minivan, long the leader in its segment, was face-lifted with rounded corners and brighter interior trim. New coupe entries ranged from the Korean automaker Hyundai's Scoupe fastback at the lower-price end to the $60,000, 270-horsepower performance roadster uncorked by Honda's upscale Acura division—the Acura NSX.

Oldsmobile, whose sales declined nearly 50% from 1986 to 1990, added the Bravada utility vehicle to its year-old Silhouette minivan in an effort to cultivate younger buyers. Chevrolet restyled its Caprice sedan, a six-passenger V-8 which Buick will adapt in 1991 with the recycled Roadmaster nameplate. Honda added a station wagon to its Accord line, now almost fully built in its Marysville, OH, plant.

The luxury segments of the market expanded in late 1989 with the addition of Toyota's Lexus and Nissan's Infiniti. Lexus met its first-year sales goal with 60,000 sales and planned to add coupes. Infiniti, slower to reach volume targets, unveiled the G20 subcompact in the fall in the $20,000 price range and added the M30 convertible. A traction control option was introduced by Mercedes-Benz.

Two venerable European automakers, Jaguar and Saab, were purchased by U.S. automakers in what was foreseen as a sign of future linkages across the industry. Ford bought Jaguar for $2.5 billion, and GM purchased Saab for $600 million.

MAYNARD M. GORDON
Detroit Editor, "Auto Age"

WORLD MOTOR VEHICLE DATA, 1989

Country	Passenger Car Production	Truck and Bus Production	Motor Vehicle Registrations
Argentina	107,597	20,227	5,680,000
Australia	330,492	27,772	9,221,100
Austria	6,638	5,026	3,457,794
Belgium	304,055	84,524	3,972,297
Brazil	731,013	280,970	12,916,553
Canada	1,001,588	937,914	15,860,000
China	21,568	467,907	4,325,000
Czechoslovakia	188,611	50,570	3,460,678
France	3,409,017	510,759	25,342,000
Germany, East	215,000	42,000	3,882,538*
Germany, West	4,563,673	287,974	30,036,440
Hungary	–	11,930	2,012,236
India	177,190	155,325	3,329,390
Italy	1,971,969	248,805	25,480,000
Japan	9,052,406	3,973,272	52,450,155
Korea, South	871,898	257,572	2,035,448
Mexico	439,538	202,241	7,795,000
The Netherlands	130,000	33,330	5,790,000
Poland	285,600	53,000	5,520,160
Spain	1,638,615	406,942	12,860,828
Sweden	384,206	81,670	3,764,043
USSR	1,200,000	900,000	24,674,700
United Kingdom	1,299,082	326,590	24,597,746
United States	6,823,097	4,038,958	184,396,732**
Yugoslavia	302,985	39,949	4,077,500
Total	35,455,838	13,435,227	539,789,621***

* Includes East Berlin. ** U.S. total does not include Puerto Rico, which has 1,518,544 vehicles. *** World total includes 412,907,178 cars and 126,882,443 trucks and buses, of which U.S. has 141,251,695 cars and 43,145,037 trucks and buses. Other countries with more than one million registrations are: Bulgaria, 1,128,400; Colombia, 1,200,000; Denmark, 1,897,784; Finland, 2,034,166; Greece, 2,215,923; Indonesia, 2,005,510; Malaysia, 1,706,572; New Zealand, 1,870,000; Nigeria, 1,379,000; Norway, 1,935,828; Portugal, 1,745,000; Saudi Arabia, 4,300,000; South Africa, 4,240,962; Switzerland, 3,207,421; Taiwan, 2,103,265; Thailand, 2,222,825; Turkey, 1,953,498; and Venezuela, 1,711,812. Source: Motor Vehicle Manufacturers Association of the United States, Inc.

BANGLADESH

The forced resignation of the government of President H.M. Ershad in December, as well as the Middle East crisis and reductions in aid, overshadowed bright prospects for food production and the discovery of new natural-gas reserves in Bangladesh in 1990.

Politics. Local subdistrict elections were held between March 12 and March 25 in which opposition parties participated. Although the ruling Jatiya Party (JP) won 155 of 400 contests, more were won by the Awami League (AL), Bangladesh Nationalist Party (BNP), and other parties together. Nonetheless, opposition leaders expressed concern that there had been widespread vote-rigging and suggested that Ershad had no interest in fair elections.

The JP's poor showing increased intraparty conflict. In May, Ershad reshuffled his cabinet for the 63d time in eight years and announced his candidacy early for the 1991 national elections.

Massive student protests led to the declaration of a state of emergency on November 27. Curfews were ignored and demonstrations continued, with the support of the army. On December 4, President Ershad announced his resignation, and the next day Chief Justice Shahabuddin Ahmed was named as caretaker president by opposition leaders. After what became known as the "revolution," the army was reshuffled to oust Ershad loyalists and, on December 12, Ershad and his wife were arrested. Other officials from Ershad's administration also were apprehended. Free elections were scheduled for February 1991.

In 1989 the government had enacted measures granting greater autonomy to local councils in the Chittagong Hill Tracts (CHT) in an effort to defuse long-standing ethnic conflict. The Chakma tribes, who are mostly Buddhist, felt these measures were cosmetic and by midyear violence again forced many tribespeople to cross the border into India. Bangladesh accused India of aiding tribal "rebels," while India said the conflict should be resolved internally and resented the nearly $5 million annual costs of maintaining refugee camps.

Although policy and law have not been changed since Islam became the state religion in 1989, one indication of increased fundamentalism was the rise of the Zaker Party—a movement dedicated to "safeguard" Islam. Party leaders claimed more than 20 million followers, including the president. The party's strength has shaken the more secular political establishment, including the AL and BNP, both of which are led by women.

Economics. The year 1990 began with bright forecasts: self-sufficiency in food for the first time in years and plans to end illiteracy by the year 2000. Most importantly, new natural-gas reserves discovered in the northeast held

---

BANGLADESH • Information Highlights

Official Name: People's Republic of Bangladesh.
Location: South Asia.
Area: 55,598 sq mi (144 000 km²).
Population (mid-1990 est.): 114,800,000.
Chief City (1981 census): Dhaka, the capital, 3,430,312.
Government: *Head of state and government,* Shahabuddin Ahmed, caretaker president (assumed power Dec. 5, 1990). *Legislature—*Parliament.
Monetary Unit: Taka (35.59 taka equal U.S.$1, August 1990).
Economic Indexes: *Consumer Prices* (Dhaka, 1989, 1980 = 100), all items, 255.9; food, 247.6.
Foreign Trade (1989 U.S.$): *Imports,* $3,524,000,000; *exports,* $1,305,000,000.

---

promise for turning Bangladesh into a surplus-energy state and increasing hard-currency reserves.

The Grameen Bank started by economist Muhammad Yunus to provide credit to the poorest was acclaimed as a prime example of self-help programs. By late 1990 it had 800,000 small loans outstanding and a repayment rate of 98%.

Worrisome to the economy was a decline in external aid of $400 million in 1989 to a total $1.8 billion from the World Bank consortium. Disbursements were withheld until fall in order to force the government to implement streamlining measures. Bangladesh feared that aid increasingly would be diverted to Eastern Europe, a policy that would be disastrous in Bangladesh as 90% of its development budget depends on outside aid.

The August 2 Iraqi invasion of Kuwait meant a shortfall of at least $200 million in foreign remittances; the expense of repatriating nationals, many of whom had crossed the border into Jordan; and a doubled oil bill. Inflation was expected to reach 14% during the year.

Foreign Relations. In support of United Nations resolutions, Bangladesh sent a 2,000-man force to Saudi Arabia. However, with changes in Eastern Europe and the conflict in the Middle East, the government was concerned that the needs of the poorest countries would be sidelined by the international community.

ARUNA NAYYAR MICHIE
Kansas State University

BANKING AND FINANCE

Problems in the thrift and banking industries spread in 1990. The slide of the thrift industry continued as the Resolution Trust Corporation (RTC) began an aggressive program of thrift closures. The RTC sold the assets of 154 thrifts in the first three quarters of 1990 and closed another 33 thrifts. This compares with 54 thrift sales and six closings in 1989, RTC's first year of operation. Most of the sales, however, did not represent the sale of entire institutions to either investors or to banks and thrifts. Instead the RTC sold deposits and branch offices, most often to commercial banks, and retained most of the assets of the failed thrifts for later sale. The charters of the failed thrift institutions were valueless.

Problems in the market for commercial real estate, which had profound effects on thrifts from 1987 to 1990, spread to commercial and savings banks, resulting in a decline in their earnings and concerns over the solvency of prominent institutions in the Northeast and of some large money-center institutions (extremely large commercial banks mostly located in New York and Chicago). As commercial banks and savings banks are insured by the Bank Insurance Fund (BIF) of the Federal Deposit Insurance Corporation (FDIC), attention in Congress began to shift toward the solvency of that fund and of the FDIC as an entity. Congress was likely to reconsider both the structure of the deposit-insurance system and the powers of commercial banks in 1991 as a result of these problems.

Thrifts. There has been a marked decline in the number of thrift institutions since 1980 when approximately 4,000 thrifts were in business. The number fell to 3,284 at the end of 1985 and was reduced further to 2,701 in June of 1990. Only 65% of those institutions were profitable. It was expected that between 700 and 800 additional thrifts would close before 1993, when statute requires that the Resolution Trust Corporation (RTC) stop accepting new thrifts for closure. The institutions that were expected to fail contain approximately $430 billion in deposits, or 45% of all current thrift deposits. The Savings Association Insurance Fund, the other branch of the FDIC, would resolve any thrift failures that occur after October 1992. The RTC was expected to remain in business to dispose of its assets until 1996.

As of June 1990 there were 1,655 profitable thrift institutions with capital-to-asset ratios that exceed 3%. These institutions most likely

would survive. Another 308 thrifts have capital-to-asset ratios exceeding 3% but lost money in the first quarter of 1990. A total of 213 thrifts made money in that quarter but had capital-to-asset ratios of between 0% and 3%. The existence of these institutions was in question and depended on the path of interest rates, the condition of their investments, and their ability both to make money and to boost their capital-to-asset ratios in a recession, which the United States apparently was facing late in 1990. This was a difficult challenge. There were 164 solvent thrifts with capital-to-asset ratios below 3% that lost money from March to June. They most likely would fail. The 112 thrifts that were insolvent and losing money in June were waiting for the RTC to take them over. As of Sept. 18, 1990, the RTC had 223 institutions in conservatorship.

Losses in the thrift industry increased as the year progressed and were expected to peak in the last quarter after regulators finished inspecting the books of thrifts. These inspections would result in the reclassification of an increased portion of the real-estate investments of troubled thrifts as "nonperforming" which, in the view of the regulatory agencies, means that they are worth less than the outstanding amount of the loans made on the properties and that the loans are unlikely to be repaid. The RTC would accelerate its takeover of troubled thrifts in 1991, in a move to stem part of these losses. It was taking over two institutions per week in 1990 and planned to increase this rate to seven per week in 1991.

A survey conducted by the *American Banker* in early October indicated that thrift resolutions by the RTC and Federal Home Loan Bank Board affected $172 billion of $500 billion in thrift assets requiring resolution. Forty percent of the assets that remained to be liquidated were from institutions located in Texas, California, or Florida. Most of the assets of the liquidated institutions remained in the possession of the RTC, however. As of

The cost of bailing out the faltering U.S. savings and loan industry in accord with 1989 federal legislation increased above original estimates throughout 1990, adding burdens to the nation's taxpayers.

L. William Seidman, chairman of the U.S. Federal Deposit Insurance Corporation, and Robert Litan, a Brookings Institution economist, chat during a break in mid-December 1990 hearings before a U.S. House banking subcommittee. Seidman testified that a $25 billion assessment on the commercial banking industry and an 18% increase in the contribution banks make to the U.S. insurance fund would be one way of strengthening the ailing banking industry.

AP/Wide World

September the book value of assets in the possession of the RTC was $165 billion.

The public riveted its attention on the thrift industry's problems in early 1990. U.S. Secretary of the Treasury Nicholas F. Brady acknowledged in testimony before the Senate Banking Committee on May 23 that the administration underestimated both the number of thrifts which need to be closed and the cost of those closures. This statement, coupled with extensive media attention on the condition of the thrift industry, focused the public's attention on the "thrift debacle."

The administration indicated in the spring of 1989, when the Financial Institutions Reform, Recovery and Enforcement Act (FIRREA) was being considered, that the cost of cleaning up thrift failures from 1989 until 1992 would be $50 billion, not including interest payments on the borrowing. The FIRREA also authorized the RTC to spend $40 billion to settle the costs incurred by the federal government when 207 thrifts were sold in 1988 and another 26 were closed. Both of these estimates proved to be low due to the depressed value of the assets held by failed thrifts, especially in the real-estate market.

L. William Seidman, the chairman of the FDIC and of the RTC, estimated in May that the funding for the 1988 resolutions was at least $12 billion short; this estimate was revised in September to a shortfall of $32 billion. The total cost of the 1988 closings now was placed at $71 billion. Appraisals from the Congressional Budget Office and the General Accounting Office indicated that funding for the post-1988 failures was between $75 to $90 billion short. The present value of the bailout, including the cost of the 1988 closures, would exceed $200 billion, again not including the interest cost on federal borrowing used to finance the payments. This estimate exceeded the budget authorization in FIRREA by at least $100 billion.

The RTC did not have much luck with its attempts to sell its assets. A major auction was scheduled for the fall but was canceled when the RTC and the auction company had a dispute over the amount of risk capital the auctioneer was to put forward. The RTC did hold a sale of single-family homes in Arizona in November. The houses sold for 20% less than the going market price, which represents a discount of 40% from their book value.

There were two major differences between solvent and insolvent thrifts. The first was their capital-to-asset ratios. Those thrifts that survived the 1980s were those that grew slowly. Well-capitalized thrifts also did not engage in overly risky lending practices and did not rely on expensive brokered deposits. The other major difference was in the composition of their loan portfolios. Solvent thrifts invest 65% of their assets in home mortgages; insolvent thrifts have 51.7% of their loans placed in home mortgages. Insolvent thrifts were invested more heavily in commercial real estate, construction and land-development loans, consumer lending, and commercial loans. They also were invested more heavily in below-investment-grade commercial bonds.

The threat to solvent thrifts lies with the impact of the recession on home sales. FIRREA requires that 70% of the assets of thrifts be invested in mortgages or mortgage-backed securities. Legally thrifts do not have the asset diversity to withstand a prolonged downturn in home sales due to their dependence on mortgages for their income. This might cause currently healthy thrifts to shrink if the recession is prolonged, due to their weak capital positions.

AP/Wide World

Neil Bush, the U.S. president's son, came under fire during 1990 for his role as a director of the failed Silverado Banking, Savings and Loan Association of Denver.

Banks. Real estate is the largest single category of lending for commercial banks and that was the reason for concern over the health of the commercial-banking industry in 1990 and for the BIF. Commercial banks have 40.4% of their lending portfolios in real-estate loans, versus 27.5% in commercial and industrial lending. Weakening markets in commercial real estate and large multifamily lending have had a profound impact on commercial banks. The large regional institutions in New England have been affected most dramatically. In addition, money-center banks and a few of the very large regional banks have invested heavily in loans to firms involved in corporate takeovers; this is the banking equivalent to "junk bonds" and is known as highly leveraged lending. These loans were endangered as the borrowers were finding repayment difficult.

Banks headquartered in Arizona had the highest portion of nonperforming real-estate loans (11.2%), followed by Massachusetts (9.4%), Rhode Island (8.6%), Connecticut (8.4%), New York (6.8%), New Hampshire (6.2%), Texas (6.0%), Louisiana (5.1%), New Jersey (5.1%), and Washington, DC (4.8%).

The single largest concern to bank regulators in 1990 was Boston-based Bank of New England. The bank, which failed due to making excessive mortgage loans to large condominium projects, was taken over by the U.S. government early in 1991. The bank had lost or sold 22.5% of its assets during the first half of 1990 and FDIC Chairman Seidman estimated

that it would have to declare $3 billion to $6 billion of its assets worthless. Seidman also said that the takeover would cost taxpayers $2.3 billion. Prior to the takeover the bank had fired employees and was negotiating to swap some of its bonded debt for equity.

Most large banks were cutting employment and other expenses in the face of declining earnings. In New York, Chase Manhattan announced an employment cutback of 5,000 in September; Manufacturers Hanover planned to cut 1,400; and Chemical Bank 1,100. These employment losses, coupled with major declines among Wall Street firms, contributed to massive projected budget deficits in New York City and New York state, due to losses in revenue from wage and income taxes. Similar cuts were announced by banks with more than $10 billion in assets throughout the United States.

Even though most commercial banks were profitable there was growing concern over the adequacy of the BIF. The BIF was increasing its insurance charge from 12 cents per $100 in deposits to 19.5 cents in January 1991. Yet this increase was not enough to recapitalize the fund fully. The fund itself was expected to pay out $4 billion to finance commercial bank failures in 1990, bringing it down to $9 billion.

The FDIC would consider ways to recapitalize the BIF early in 1991. A study released by the U.S. House of Representatives Financial Institutions subcommittee in mid-December was pessimistic about the solvency of the fund and indicated that many large banks were undercapitalized. The study suggested major reforms in ownership and powers. It should be noted that 36 of the nation's 48 largest banks were profitable in the third quarter of 1990.

The year 1991 would be a watershed one for the financial-services industry. Congress and the administration would have to consider the pricing of deposit insurance—not only how much to charge but also how to assess the risk of a particular institution. An international treaty has forced U.S. banks to increase their capital, and capitalization requirements differ from bank to bank depending on their mix of investments. A major political controversy about whether Congress should approve national branch banking (also known as interstate banking) or not was anticipated; as 1990 ended this was up to the states. Most importantly the powers and ownership of banks would be reexamined. Should nonfinancial companies be allowed to own banks as subsidiaries? Should banks with insured deposits be allowed to compete with investment banks in issuing stocks and bonds? Should banks be allowed to sell insurance? All of these issues would be raised and debated in 1991. The one certainty was that the banking and thrift industries would not be the same thereafter.

EDWARD W. HILL
Cleveland State University

BELGIUM

Political stability, significant legislation, and economic growth accented Belgium's domestic affairs in 1990. Adjustment and reactions to changes in Eastern Europe, rethinking of Cold War policies, renewed difficulties with Zaire, and response to the Kuwait crisis dominated external relations.

Legislation. The age of majority was lowered from 21 to 18, allowing 18-year-olds to purchase homes and marry without parental permission. The minimum age for divorce was dropped from 23 to 20. Steps were taken to abolish the death penalty except for major war crimes.

Rather than risk their governmental coalition with the Socialists, the Christian Democrats allowed deputies to vote their conscience on abortion. By 126 votes to 69, women "in distress" were granted the right to abortion during the first 12 weeks of pregnancy. After that, two doctors must certify that a woman's health is endangered or that her child will be born with incurable serious defects. Belgium's Roman Catholic bishops termed the legislation "tragic," and King Baudouin, a devout Roman Catholic, would not sign it. Yet the king did not wish to "block the proper functioning of democratic government." Solution was found in Article 82 of the constitution, which permits the cabinet to declare the king unable to reign. Intended for occasions of illness or incapacity, the article made it possible for the king to step aside while the bill became law on April 4. Parliament restored the king's powers the next day.

Criticism by Parliament of the inefficiency of the police and secret services in solving store bombings in the 1980s led to the resignation of the head of the secret service. The government announced it would supervise that service more closely and placed it under the interior rather than the defense ministry.

Economic Affairs. Belgium and Luxembourg ended the two-tier currency system in place since 1955. The currencies are at one-to-one parity, but the antiquated system of different rates for capital flows and trade transactions was contrary to efforts of the European Community (EC) to free capital movement. Withholding taxes on interest income were lowered as part of a modernizing effort to make the Belgian financial market more competitive.

The 1991 budget cut defense spending, as Belgium rejected pressure from the North Atlantic Treaty Organization (NATO) allies to increase its contribution to NATO defenses. The gross national product (GNP), along with wages and salaries, rose in the favorable economic climate of the first half of the year.

Foreign Affairs. In February accord was reached with Zaire by which the former colony would pay interest on commercial debt owed Belgium to a special fund for developmental projects in Zaire. Improvement in relations and planning for future cooperation was brief. The killing of students at Lubumbashi University, allegedly by local police and the Zairean elite guard, led Belgium to suspend a major loan and cancel a joint commission meeting. President Mobutu Sese Seko of Zaire retaliated by reducing the number of Belgian consulates and limiting Belgian flights to Zaire.

In Europe, Belgium backed Austria's application for membership in the EC. Prime Minister Wilfried Martens urged acceleration of the movement toward political and economic union, and Foreign Minister Mark Eyskens called for the granting of substantial executive power to the European Commission and new powers to the European Parliament. He also said that the EC should take over the defense coordination role of the Western European Union (a step resisted by neutral Ireland).

Within NATO, Belgium opposed modernization of short-range nuclear missiles and objected to an expensive plan for coordinating Western air defenses. Such plans were seen as obsolete given changes in Eastern Europe.

In late summer, Belgium froze Kuwaiti assets in Belgium and sent two mine hunters, a support ship, and a frigate to the Gulf of Oman during the Kuwait crisis. Although Belgium bought only 8.6% of its oil from Iraq and none from Kuwait in 1989, oil prices in Belgium rose.

Other. Damaging January storms took several lives. Farmers suffered destruction of hundreds of thousands of pigs to curb an outbreak of swine flu. A negotiated exchange of four Belgian hostages held by the Fatah Revolutionary Council for a Palestinian terrorist jailed ten years in Belgium collapsed in midsummer.

J. E. HELMREICH, *Allegheny College*

BELGIUM • Information Highlights

Official Name: Kingdom of Belgium.
Location: Northwestern Europe.
Area: 11,780 sq mi (30 510 km^2).
Population (mid-1990 est.): 9,900,000.
Chief Cities (Dec. 31, 1987): Brussels, the capital (incl. suburbs), 970,346; Antwerp (including suburbs), 476,044; Ghent, 232,620; Charleroi, 208,938; Liège, 200,312; Bruges, 117,857.
Government: *Head of state,* Baudouin I, king (acceded 1951). *Head of government,* Wilfried Martens, prime minister (formed new government Oct. 1985). *Legislature*—Parliament: Senate and Chamber of Representatives.
Monetary Unit: Franc (31.25 francs equal U.S.$1, Oct. 31, 1990).
Gross Domestic Product (1989 est. U.S.$): $136,000,000,000.
Economic Indexes (1989): *Consumer Prices* (1980 = 100), all items, 150.8; food, 147.2. *Industrial Production* (1980 = 100), 118.
Foreign Trade (1989 with Luxembourg, U.S.$): *Imports,* $99,675,000,000; *exports,* $101,261,000,000.

BIOCHEMISTRY

A U.S.-Canadian research team succeeded in 1989–90 in identifying the gene responsible for cystic fibrosis (CF) and its protein product. CF is an inherited disorder affecting one in 2,000 white children, and one in 20 Caucasians is a carrier. Afflicted individuals produce large amounts of thick mucus in their lungs, which leads to blockage of the airways and bacterial infection. Death, generally before the age of 30, usually results. Scientists believe that the CF patients have difficulty in moving salt and water in and out of cells.

The gene that is defective in CF encodes a protein of 1,480 amino acids. The protein is located in the cell membrane and is involved in the transport of ions, such as sodium and chloride, across the membrane. Although several mutations in the CF gene have been identified, most CF patients (68%) contain a mutant gene which directs the cells to produce a flawed protein with an amino acid, called phenylalanine, missing at a specific point in the molecule. This abnormality apparently interferes in the normal functions of the protein, so that ions cannot enter or leave cells. Scientists hoped to devise a genetic screening test for cystic fibrosis, including one for fetuses through the use of amniocentesis.

Protein Synthesis. Biochemists made striking progress during 1989–90 in elucidating a key step in protein synthesis (also called translation) that was elusive for 30 years, since the process first was discovered. Protein synthesis is under genetic control and involves the translation of mRNA, a molecule that is transcribed from the genetic information encoded in a stretch of DNA.

During translation tRNA molecules carrying specific amino acids "read" the mRNA and the protein molecule is assembled in a correct amino acid sequence. For correct assembly, a tRNA reads a codon of three bases in mRNA through its anticodon consisting also of three bases complementary to the codon and inserts the amino acid it carries. Thus, a key step in the accurate translation of genetic information is the reaction by which tRNA molecules are charged with appropriate amino acids, a reaction catalyzed by enzymes called aminoacyl-tRNA synthetases. Since there are 20 synthetases (one for each of the 20 amino acids), and 45 to 50 different tRNAs, each enzyme must recognize a particular amino acid and its cognate tRNA. What had been puzzling biochemists was how a given synthetase enzyme recognizes an amino acid and the tRNA, particularly since all the tRNAs are virtually alike and all are L-shaped.

Using the X-ray crystallographic technique, Thomas A. Steitz and his colleagues at Yale University showed for the first time the direct picture (image) of an intermediate in the charging of tRNA. These images showed that the enzyme has multiple contact points all along the tRNA "L." The tip of the long arm of the "L" fits snugly into a deep narrow pocket in the enzyme—an expected finding since this tip contains the tRNA's anticodon which already was known to be crucial for the recognition of the tRNA by its synthetase. However, the new data showed that the enzyme interacts mainly with two bases of the anticodon and only weakly with the third, which helps to explain how one synthetase can recognize two different tRNAs differing in the third base of the anticodon.

The image also showed that the tip of the short arm of the "L" is inserted into a gaping cavity in the enzyme; it is at this tip that the enzyme catalyzes the formation of the link between the amino acid and the tRNA. This linkage requires input of energy from a molecule called ATP, and the Yale group's image showed the presence of an ATP molecule in the cavity. Although these studies are a landmark, several points, including how a synthetase recognizes an amino acid and whether there is an editing step which ensures that a tRNA is not linked to the wrong amino acid, remained to be explained.

Herpesvirus Receptor. After almost two decades of effort, biochemists discovered how the herpesvirus that causes cold sores enters human cells. Herpes simplex I is a widespread virus affecting almost 90 million Americans. Most of those affected have had painful cold sores that the virus produces; no known treatment is available.

A new discovery by Dr. David P. Hajjar and his associates at Cornell Medical College showed that the virus first attaches to a hormone-like protein called fibroblast growth factor (FGF), which plays a role in wound healing and proliferation of blood vessels and arterial walls. In order for FGF to carry out these functions, it must enter a cell by binding to its receptor protein located on the outer surface of the cell membrane. Once bound to the receptor, FGF enters the cell and as it does it carries along, in a piggyback fashion, the herpes simplex I. That this is the mode by which herpes simplex I enters cells was confirmed by the finding that if cells normally lacking the FGF receptor are engineered genetically so that they acquire the receptor, they become susceptible to infection by the virus.

Identification of the FGF receptor as the entry point would make it possible to devise strategies to control herpes simplex I infection through interference with the virus-receptor interaction, either by utilizing a soluble form of the receptor as a decoy or by utilizing genetically engineered FGF so that it loses the ability to bind to the virus.

PREM P. BATRA
Wright State University

BIOGRAPHY

A selection of profiles of persons prominent in the news during 1990 appears on pages 143–57. The affiliation of the contributor is listed on pages 591–94; biographies that do not include a contributor's name were prepared by the staff. Included are profiles of:

© Damian Strohmeyer/Allsport USA

Jose Canseco

CANSECO, Jose

On June 27, 1990, one week before his 26th birthday, outfielder Jose Canseco of the Oakland Athletics signed a five-year, $23.5 million contract extension that made him the highest-paid player in baseball. Less than a week later, he learned that he had received 2,313,091 votes, the most by any player since Gary Carter in 1982, to start in the annual All-Star Game. The twin achievements reinforced the feeling of many baseball experts that Canseco is the best player in the game.

Once a scrawny high-school third baseman who could hit but not field, Canseco built himself into a 6′4″, 240-lb (1.9-m, 109-kg) slugger through ambitious weight training. The program resulted in an immediate home-run explosion that catapulted him to the majors. Joining the Oakland organization in the 1982 draft, he played on seven minor-league teams before making it to the majors and being named American League rookie of the year in 1986. Tutoring from Joe Rudi and Herm Fraser helped Canseco improve his outfield defense and running game.

Two years later he became the first player to hit 40 or more home runs and steal 40 or more bases in the same season. An extremely self-confident player, Canseco had predicted three weeks into the season that he could achieve the feat. He also managed to boost his batting average to a career-high .307 by adopting a conven-tional upright stance, and had 42 home runs and a club-record 124 runs batted in. He was the unanimous choice as the league's most valuable player. Canseco hit three homers, tying a league record, in the 1988 American League Championship Series, but slumped in the World Series after a game 1 grand slam.

A year later, after missing half the season with a bro-ken wrist, he climaxed his comeback with a titanic play-off home run at the Toronto SkyDome. In 1990 the Ath-letics took their third consecutive division title and their highly paid outfielder, who missed part of the season due to a back injury, had a .274 batting average, 37 home runs, and 101 runs batted in. Although his season home-run and runs-batted-in totals were among the league's leaders, his postseason play was below par. In the play-offs against Boston, Canseco got two hits in 11 times at bat and in the World Series the star outfielder had only one hit, a home run, in 12 times at bat as the Athletics were swept by the Cincinnati Reds in four straight games.

Background. Jose Canseco was born minutes after twin brother Osvaldo in Havana, Cuba, on July 2, 1964. He was the third child of Barbara and Jose Canseco, Sr., an Esso executive who lost his job, house, and car when Fidel Castro took power in 1959. After teaching English for $15 per month, the elder Canseco moved his family to Miami in late 1965. He worked day and night jobs before joining Amoco as an executive.

Young Jose hit .400 at Coral Park High and was signed by Oakland in June 1982 for a $15,000 bonus. After his mother died of a brain hemorrhage in 1984, Jose Canseco relied on his father, a perfectionist, as his mentor.

Canseco married Esther Haddad, a former Miss Miami, in 1988. His hobbies include weight-lifting, play-ing basketball, and collecting exotic cars.

DAN SCHLOSSBERG

CHAMORRO, Violeta Barrios de

On Feb. 25, 1990, Violeta Barrios de Chamorro won the presidency of Nicaragua in a stunning victory over the Sandinistas, capturing 57% of the vote to 41% for President Daniel Ortega. Chamorro was the candidate of the National Opposition Union (UNO), a loose multiparty coalition whose only unity lay in its opposition to the Sandinistas. She was inaugurated April 25. Lacking po-litical experience, Chamorro faced overwhelming prob-lems—the disastrous economy that helped bring Ortega down; the opposition of some members of her own party, including the vice-president; Sandinista control of the army and police; contras still spoiling for war with Sandinistas; laborers demanding huge raises; business expecting freer trade; and peasants needing and claim-ing land. Despite a pledge of help from the United States, promised aid stalled in Washington.

Despite much controversy, Chamorro boldly retained Gen. Humberto Ortega as head of the armed forces; together they brought about a cease-fire, began reducing the size of the military, and disarmed the contras by promising them free land. But terrible inflation caused serious strikes in midyear, one of them leading to street fighting and bloodshed. The land-reform program became a shambles as many factions ignored the courts and simply occupied debated properties. Sheer national exhaustion and the fear of war's resumption seemed all that made government possible in 1990.

Although an inexperienced and reluctant politician, Chamorro seemed determined to provide her people with good government. Whether she would succeed in this goal remained to be seen.

Background. Violeta Barrios was born on Oct. 18, 1929, in Rivas, Nicaragua, to an upper-class cattle-ranching family. She attended schools in the United States for three years. In 1950 she married Pedro Joaquín Chamorro Cardenal, heir to the nation's major newspaper and a member of perhaps Nicaragua's most distinguished family. The marriage thrust Violeta into the midst of the long struggle of the Chamorros against the dictatorships of the Somozas. In 1952, on the death of his father, young Pedro Joaquín became editor of *La Prensa*, often the only outspoken opposition to the governments of three different Somozas.

In the next two decades Chamorro raised four children and supported her husband in his precarious crusade: She brought food to him in jail, lived with him in exile, and mourned for him when he was assassinated in 1978. Anastasio Somoza Debayle may not have sought the assassination, but most Nicaraguans considered him responsible, and within months opposition united to overthrow him.

Violeta Chamorro became a loved symbol of freedom to Nicaraguans. She played no part in the rise of the Sandinistas, but they needed her name, and placed her in their five-member ruling junta when they overthrew Somoza in July 1979. Within less than a year she left the party, disillusioned and fearful of its Marxism, to return to publishing *La Prensa* as the voice of liberty in Nicaragua. She was chosen as the UNO's presidential candidate in September 1989.

Violeta Chamorro is a tall, striking woman, still family-oriented although two of her children opposed her election and remained devoted to the Sandinistas.

See also CENTRAL AMERICA.

THOMAS L. KARNES

CHRETIEN, Joseph-Jacques Jean

Jean Chrétien, longtime Canadian political figure and former deputy prime minister, was elected leader of the nation's Liberal Party at Calgary, Alta., on June 24, 1990. Ironically, in 1986, two years after being defeated soundly by fellow Liberal John Turner in a bid for the party post, the Quebec native had left politics to join a major law firm.

While claiming to have abandoned politics, Chrétien had kept his ambitions alive with his best-selling memoirs, *Straight from the Heart* (1985), frequent speeches, and a discreet organization. When Turner lost his second national election in 1988, Chrétien's turn as Liberal leader became inevitable. His first-ballot victory was achieved with little more than ringing insistence on his love for Canada. Attempts by rivals to smoke out specific policies and ideas failed.

Chrétien's popularity and long government experience were assets but critics insisted that he was "yesterday's man," bereft of ideas and policies. His support against Quebec's 1980 separatist referendum and his opposition to the Meech Lake proposal to recognize Quebec's distinctiveness left him little support in his native province, the former Liberal stronghold. Supporters insisted, however, that the self-styled "little guy from Shawinigan" could charm voters with his folksy, populist style.

Background. Joseph-Jacques Jean Chrétien was born in Shawinigan, Que., on Jan. 11, 1934, the 18th of 19 children of a paper-mill worker. He was educated at St. Joseph's Seminary in Trois-Rivières and was graduated in law from Laval University in 1957. In his early teens, Chrétien already was helping out in Liberal campaigns.

He first was elected to Parliament from Shawinigan in 1963, and only then learned to speak English. Chrétien's chance came in 1965 when Prime Minister Lester Pearson selected him as parliamentary secretary. He entered the government as a minister of state in 1967 and as minister of national revenue in January 1968. Pierre Elliott Trudeau, Pearson's successor, found Chrétien a loyal and popular subordinate and promoted him to Indian affairs and northern development in July 1968. In 1976, Chrétien became president of the Treasury Board (responsible for the civil service), and later that year minister of industry, trade and commerce; in 1977 he was appointed minister of finance.

In Trudeau's new government in 1980, Chrétien became minister of justice and led the "no" side to victory that year in Quebec's independence referendum. In 1982, as minister of energy, mines and resources, Chrétien took over the government's controversial National Energy Policy. When Trudeau announced his retirement from government in 1984, Chrétien challenged the favorite, John Turner, for Trudeau's succession. Embittered by his 1,862 to 1,368 ballot defeat, he did little to avert Turner's stunning defeat by Brian Mulroney's Conservatives three months later, despite having been appointed secretary of state for external affairs and deputy prime minister under Turner's leadership.

Chrétien has been married to the former Aline Chainé since 1957. The couple have three children.

DESMOND MORTON

COLLOR DE MELLO, Fernando Affonso

Fernando Collor emerged from political obscurity to become the first directly elected president of Brazil in 29 years, winning a Dec. 17, 1989, runoff with 53% of the ballots cast. On his way to election victory, he led a 22-candidate field in the first round before capturing the December runoff. In the latter contest, Collor defeated

Fernando Collor

Luís Inácio ("Lula") da Silva, a former labor leader who advocated increased welfare by a strong interventionist state.

In contrast, Collor pledged to reduce the state's economic role, privatize public enterprises, and rely on the free market to create wealth. He also promised to combat corruption, eliminate privileges enjoyed by high officials, and dismiss thousands of overpaid, redundant bureaucrats. These appeals reinforced Collor's reputation as a reformer gained as governor of Alagoas (1986–89). In this small, impoverished northeastern state, he slashed the salaries of elite government employees known as "maharajas."

Also contributing to the 40-year-old Collor's success was the attractive image that he projected on television. TV is the most important source of information in a nation of more than 145 million inhabitants, where illiteracy is high and more than half the population is under age 35. As president of his family's media group, Collor enjoyed close business ties to Brazil's dominant Globo TV network, which provided sympathetic coverage of his campaign.

At his March 15, 1990, inauguration, Collor reiterated his commitment to market forces, an attack on the soaring inflation rate, and revamping an inefficient national education system. He also vowed to advance social justice and environmental protection. Speaking before legislators and representatives from 100 countries, the new chief executive said that Brazil's $114 billion foreign debt could not be allowed to "starve" the economy.

The day after taking office Collor unveiled a "shock plan" that included a one-month price freeze, limits on bank withdrawals, sharply higher prices on publicly provided goods and services, and a floating exchange rate. He also abolished 13 government ministries and 24 state firms and foundations. He later announced a new industrial policy keyed on encouraging imports and requiring Brazilian companies to compete against foreign producers.

Background. Fernando Affonso Collor de Mello was born in Rio de Janeiro on Aug. 12, 1949. His father, a successful entrepreneur, served as governor of Alagoas state and later as a representative of Alagoas in the Senate. He moved the family to Brasília in 1963 after shooting a fellow senator and retiring from politics. In the capital, Collor studied economics and journalism at the University of Brasília. He enjoyed racing sports cars and competing in karate in his spare time. After college, he went to work for his family's media group in Alagoas, becoming president in 1978.

Brazil's military regime appointed Collor mayor of Alagoas' capital in 1979; three years later he was elected a federal deputy, and became governor in 1986. Collor has belonged to five political parties, including the National Reconstruction Party founded for his presidential campaign.

Divorced from his first wife in 1981, Collor married Rosane Malta in 1984. He has two sons from his first marriage.

GEORGE W. GRAYSON

CRUISE, Tom

Tom Cruise—his name is familiar to almost everyone, and his handsome face smiles out from, it seems, every magazine cover in the United States. Cruise, who began his career acting in typical "teenage" movies and gained a reputation as a member of the "brat pack" in the mid-1980s, has matured into an unusually talented and dedicated performer.

Since his 1981 film debut in *Endless Love*, Cruise has moved well beyond "teen idol" status. First winning widespread critical acclaim for his role as a pool-playing prodigy in *The Color of Money* (1986), in which he co-starred with Paul Newman, Cruise has been described as "exuding the spirit of human triumph." He is noted for his ability to change his personality and appearance and to make heroic, larger-than-life characters believ-

© Trapper/Sygma

Tom Cruise

able, and has gained a reputation as a perfectionist, preparing himself both physically and mentally for each role and immersing himself in it. He attended a Pennsylvania high school to play a high-school athlete in *All the Right Moves* (1983), flew in an F-14 jet in preparation for *Top Gun* (1986), learned to play pool for *The Color of Money* (1986), and raced stock cars for *Days of Thunder* (1990).

In the two roles for which he has won the most critical praise, Charlie Babbitt in *Rain Man* (1988) and Vietnam vet Ron Kovic in *Born on the Fourth of July* (1989), he did even more intense research. In preparation for the latter part, he got to know the real Ron Kovic well and impressed him so much that Kovic presented the actor with his Bronze Star when filming ended.

Cruise is known for being unusually considerate and polite, as well as for exerting extreme control over his career. He is happiest when working: " . . . if you can't create," Cruise has said, "you eventually start to destroy yourself."

Background. Thomas Cruise Mapother IV was born on July 3, 1962, in Syracuse, NY. He was the third of four children and the only son of Thomas Cruise Mapother III, an electrical engineer, and Mary Lee Mapother, a teacher of dyslexic children. The family moved frequently, and Cruise, who himself suffered from dyslexia, eventually attended eight grade schools and three high schools. His parents divorced when he was 11, with his mother remarrying five years later. Cruise enrolled at a Franciscan seminary at the age of 14, with the idea of becoming a priest, but eventually concluded that he "loved women too much."

Cruise decided to become an actor after playing a lead role in a high-school version of the musical *Guys and Dolls*. After graduation, he headed for New York City to find work. Within a few months, he landed a minor part in *Endless Love* (1981), which led to a major role in *Taps*, a story set in a military school, later the same year. Critics were impressed by Cruise's performance, and in 1983, he made his next major film, *The Outsiders*, accepting a minor role for the privilege of working with the director Francis Ford Coppola. Later in 1983, he starred in *Risky Business*, a teenage comedy which won critical approval and started Cruise on the way to mainstream success.

Tom Cruise, who enjoys racing cars and spending time with his mother and sisters in his limited spare time, is divorced from actress Mimi Rogers, whom he married in 1987.

DARMAN, Richard Gordon

With 1990 much ballyhooed as the year a significant plan would be put in place to reduce the federal deficit (estimated at $200 billion at the end of the 1990 fiscal year), Washington's eyes were focused on Richard G. Darman, director of the Office of Management and Budget in the Bush administration. But, despite a budget plan that ultimately took steps to reduce the deficit, 1990 was not to be the year of Darman's victory. Indeed, Darman's strong backroom lobbying angered Democrats and alienated some Republicans.

As the October 1 budget deadline approached, and with a sequester of federal funds threatened by the Gramm-Rudman-Hollings Act should a deficit-reducing budget accord not be reached, Darman had on the table a proposal paring the 1991 deficit by $50 million while still reinstituting a reduced tax rate on capital gains. Opponents, however, did not like where the necessary cuts would come from nor the way the wealthy seemed to be getting breaks at the expense of the middle class. The political maneuvering ended up—after the government declared a fiscal emergency and shut down all but essential services over the Columbus Day weekend—with Congress and the administration finally reaching a budget accord nearly a month late. The compromise bill, designed to reduce the deficit by $500 billion over the next five years, reduced Medicare spending, raised taxes on gasoline, liquor, and cigarettes, and increased the top marginal income-tax rate. By the time it reached that stage, however, Darman was keeping a low profile.

Background. Richard G. Darman was born in Charlotte, NC, on May 10, 1943, the oldest of four children of a wealthy textile manufacturer. He grew up in Woonsocket, RI, and Wellesley Hills, MA. After graduating with a bachelor of arts degree from Harvard in 1964 and from the Harvard Business School in 1967, he entered government service in 1970. He has remained there ever since, except for brief forays into consulting and lecturing during the final years of Richard Nixon's administration, the Democratic presidency of Jimmy Carter, and the last 20 months of the Reagan tenure during which he was managing director of Shearson Lehman Brothers, the investment bankers.

Darman's initial inspiration for public service was a predecessor at Harvard, John F. Kennedy, but he learned at the hands of such moderate Republicans as Elliot L. Richardson and James A. Baker. He followed

Richard Darman

© P.F. Gero/Sygma

Richardson from the Department of Health, Education, and Welfare to Defense, to Justice, and then out of the government when then Attorney General Richardson resigned rather than fire special prosecutor Archibald Cox at the height of the Watergate scandal. He rejoined the government during the Ford administration as an assistant secretary of commerce (1976–77). When Ronald Reagan was elected president, Baker brought Darman in as a key member of the transition team. He served on the White House staff (1981–85) and as deputy secretary of the treasury (1985–87).

A hard worker who prides himself on his strategic abilities, Darman played a key role in many Reagan initiatives, including tax reform in 1986. He and his wife Kathleen, a cultural historian and author, have two sons.

de KLERK, F(rederik) W(illem)

In a bold response to mounting domestic and international pressures, President F. W. de Klerk has set South Africa on a new political path. In early 1990 he lifted the ban on the country's black liberation movement, the African National Congress (ANC). He then released without conditions one of the movement's most prominent leaders, Nelson Mandela, who had been imprisoned for more than 27 years. De Klerk also promised to implement reforms that would lead to a more equitable sharing of political power.

P. W. Botha had relinquished the leadership of the ruling National Party (NP) and the party's caucus elected de Klerk, then minister of national education, as the new party leader in February 1989. On Aug. 14, 1989, Botha resigned as president after 11 years in power. One month later, de Klerk was elected formally the new president by the electoral college representing all three houses of the tricameral Parliament. The choice of de Klerk actually was made by the National Party's majority in the white Assembly. He was sworn in at a church ceremony in Pretoria six days later.

Meanwhile the ruling National Party, which had been in power since 1948, had emerged from Sept. 6, 1989, elections for the white Parliament with a reduced majority. De Klerk soon made it clear that he was committed to reforms and to initiating talks about a new constitution for a postapartheid society.

Background. F(rederik) W(illem) de Klerk was born in Johannesburg on March 18, 1936. He was the son of Sen. Jan de Klerk, a leading politician, who became a minister in the South African government. His brother Willem ("Wimpie") is a liberal newspaperman and one of the founders of the Democratic Party.

De Klerk was graduated with a law degree from Potchefstroom University in 1958, and then practiced law in Vereeniging in the Transvaal. In 1969 he married Marike Willemse, with whom he has two sons and a daughter. De Klerk was offered a professorship of administrative law at Potchefstroom in 1972, but he declined the post because he had been elected to Parliament as NP member for Vereeniging at the time.

In 1978, de Klerk was appointed to the cabinet by P. W. Botha, who had become prime minister in that year. He held a number of different cabinet portfolios, and in 1986 he was appointed leader of the House of Assembly. As minister of national education, de Klerk was a strong supporter of segregated universities, and as leader of the National Party in the Transvaal, he was not known to advocate reform. Therefore, it was surprising that in his first speech after assuming the party leadership he called for a nonracist South Africa and for negotiations about the country's future.

In decisive moves in 1989 and 1990, de Klerk responded to external and internal pressures for change. By lifting the ban on the ANC and releasing Nelson Mandela, he opened the way for the drafting of a new constitution for the country. His 1990 decision to open the National Party to all races indicated that he envisions a role for the party in a postapartheid South Africa.

PATRICK O'MEARA

Nick Faldo

© Dan Smith/Allsport USA

FALDO, Nicholas Alexander

His mother wanted him to be a model, or perhaps an actor. At one time on the professional golf scene he was known as El Foldo, thanks to his proclivity for letting tournament victories slip away. From this unlikely beginning, England's Nick Faldo had emerged at the end of 1990 as arguably the world's best golfer. Certainly he had been the dominant player in the major championships from 1987 to 1990. In the final 14 of those, starting with the 1987 British Open, he finished fourth or better eight times, winning four times and losing another in a play-off.

Faldo won only two tournaments worldwide in 1990, but they were big ones. In April, trailing Raymond Floyd by five strokes at the halfway point of the Masters, he closed with 66–69 to even the score, then won his second consecutive Masters title when Floyd found the water on the second play-off hole. In July in the British Open at St. Andrews, he won by five strokes with an immaculate display of shot-making. His 270 total, 18 under par, was five strokes better in relation to par than anybody ever had scored in the championship. "Winning at St. Andrews is the ultimate achievement in the ultimate setting," he said.

Although he played in only seven tournaments in the United States in 1990, winning $345,262, the two majors carried him to player of the year honors awarded by the U.S. Professional Golfers Association. He now was Number 1 in the Sony World Rankings and, at the age of 33, stood at the top of the golf world.

Background. Born in July 1957 into a working-class family in the London suburb of Hertfordshire, Faldo was an all-around good athlete as a youngster and, thanks to his mother, was exposed to culture and the arts as well. She once thought he would make a good model because "he had smashing legs."

Instead, he took up golf at the advanced age of 13 and quickly developed proficiency. He turned professional at the age of 21 and had mixed success for ten years. It was not until 1986, when he put himself under the care of teaching professional David Leadbetter, that he became a world-class player.

As the 1990 golf season ended, Faldo still had won only 24 tournaments around the world, but his emphasis was on the majors. He won the British Open in 1987, lost in a play-off to Curtis Strange in the U.S. Open in 1988, and captured the Masters in Augusta, GA, in 1989 when he shot 65 in the final round to catch Scott Hoch, then holed a lengthy birdie putt on the second play-off hole for the victory.

He has a rather mechanical swing, but he has supreme confidence in it. "He thinks he can win the Grand Slam," says Leadbetter.

Faldo and his second wife Gill have two children.

LARRY DENNIS

HAVEL, Václav

When Czechoslovakia's Communist regime began to fall apart in the fall of 1989, various dissident groups formed a Civic Forum to lead them in the last phase of the anti-Communist struggle. Internationally renowned playwright Václav Havel soon emerged as the Forum's main spokesperson and negotiator. Long serving as a political conscience to his compatriots, he now showed his practical, common-sense abilities. Havel's leadership and subtle but effective negotiating strategy contributed to his nation's surprisingly smooth transition from dictatorship to democracy, soon called the velvet revolution.

Because of Havel's tremendous popularity, his election as Czechoslovakia's interim president on Dec. 29, 1989, and his election to a two-year term as president by the newly elected Federal Assembly (parliament) on July 5, 1990, were foregone conclusions. A man of strong will, described as a philosopher king, he has avowed that he wants his fellow citizens to feel individually responsible for their destinies. In the early months of his presidency, many citizens criticized the Civic Forum, but not openly Havel, for being slow to dismantle the Communist Party and the secret police. Economic reforms were presented to parliament only after much debate.

President Havel was active in the diplomatic realm during his first year in office. He traveled to East Germany in early January, where he backed German reunification; addressed a joint session of the U.S. Congress in Washington in February; met with Soviet President Mikhail Gorbachev in Moscow in late February; conferred with British Prime Minister Margaret Thatcher in March; and went to Israel and Austria in April and July, respectively.

Background. Václav Havel was born to upper-middle-class parents on Oct. 5, 1936, in Prague. Because of his parents' background, he was denied education beyond elementary school. While working at a menial job

Václav Havel

© Schreider/Sipa

in a chemistry laboratory, he was able to study nights and pass secondary school. In 1955 he was admitted to Prague's Technical College and later to the Prague Academy of the Arts. After completing his two years of mandatory military service, Havel began working as a scenery technician in one of Prague's many theaters.

From then on he became linked inextricably with theater and writing plays. Even though the Communist regime prohibited the production of his plays and the publication of his literary works in Czechoslovakia, his plays were produced abroad and brought their author well-deserved international praise. His most famous works in the West include *The Garden Party* (1963), *The Memorandum* (1965), and *Letters from Olga* (1989).

During the 1960s and 1970s, Havel got involved increasingly in the growing dissident movement. He joined the editorial staff of the monthly *Tvář* ("The Face"), which was sharply critical of Communist repressive measures. The future president also served as chairman of the Club of Independent Writers and was a member of the Club of Engaged Non-Party Members and the Committee for the Protection of Unjustly Persecuted, all of which stood in strong opposition to the regime's dictatorial practices. When the Charter 77 human-rights movement was founded in 1977, Havel emerged as one of the movement's designated spokespersons and a most active worker. While many honors were conferred upon him abroad, Havel was subjected at home to continuous police harassment. He was forced to earn his living by menial jobs and spent a total of nearly five years in Communist jails and three years under house arrest.

President Havel has been married to Olga Šplíchalová since 1964. They have no children.

EDWARD TABORSKY

HNATYSHYN, Ramon John

On Jan. 29, 1990, Ray Hnatyshyn was installed as Canada's 24th governor-general, the representative of Queen Elizabeth II, Canada's titular head of state.

The selection of Hnatyshyn, a Progressive Conservative who served in Parliament for the western half of Saskatoon from 1974–88, by the Mulroney government on Oct. 6, 1989, was approved by all parties. The choice was welcomed particularly in the West and by Cana-

Ramon John Hnatyshyn

DND

dians of Ukrainian ancestry. (The new governor-general is of Ukrainian ancestry.) While Hnatyshyn's lack of knowledge of the French language might have been a problem in Quebec, criticism was muted by the awareness that his office was symbolic. He also won approval by promising that he and his wife, Gerda, known for their informal style, would humanize the office.

Background. Ramon John Hnatyshyn was born in Saskatoon, Sask., on March 16, 1934, to John Hnatyshyn, who later became a senator, and Helen Constance Pitts Hnatyshyn, a former president of the National Council of Women. He attended Saskatoon schools and received his law degree from the University of Saskatchewan in 1956. After being called to the bar in 1957, he practiced law in Saskatoon and lectured in law at the University of Saskatchewan from 1966–74.

After an interval in 1958–60 as assistant to the government leader in the Senate, Hnatyshyn's political career resumed in 1974 with his election to Parliament. He was reelected in 1979, 1980, and 1984.

In the short-lived government of Joe Clark (1979-80), Hnatyshyn was minister of energy, mines, and resources and minister of state for science and technology. Appointed as House leader in 1984 when the Conservatives were in opposition, he continued in this capacity after Brian Mulroney formed a new Progressive Conservative government later that year, and also was named president of the Queen's privy council.

In 1986 he was appointed to the special portfolio of minister responsible for regulatory affairs to spearhead the government's policy of deregulation. Hnatyshyn also became minister of justice in 1986, at a time when constitutional reform, application of the Canadian Charter of Rights and Freedoms, and the debate over abortion rights created tough choices. In both Conservative governments he was senior Saskatchewan minister.

In 1988, Hnatyshyn lost his seat to the New Democrats in a regional revolt against the Conservative government, largely because of its free-trade agreement with the United States. He took a job with a prominent Ottawa law firm, where he remained until his viceregal appointment.

Hnatyshyn married Karen Gerda Andreasen on Jan. 9, 1960. They are the parents of two sons. He is active in many community causes, including the YMCA, the Royal Canadian Air Force auxiliary, and the United Way.

DESMOND MORTON

HUSSEIN, Saddam

On Aug. 2, 1990, President Saddam Hussein of Iraq ordered the invasion of Kuwait, beginning the 1990 Gulf crisis that pitted the United States, the United Nations, Saudi Arabia, the exiled government of Kuwait, and many other countries against Iraq. The Iraqi leader hoped by annexing Kuwait to gain permanent control of its enormous oil wealth and also to achieve dominance over other countries in the region of the Middle East. As the world's attention turned to this first major crisis following the end of the Cold War between the United States and the Soviet Union, President Saddam Hussein's life and personality were crucial for the choice between war and peace.

Background. Saddam Hussein is a Sunni Muslim Arab who was born to a poor peasant family on April 28, 1937, in the small Iraqi town of Takrit. Since his father died before he was born, he was raised by his uncle, Khair Allah Talfah, a nationalistic Iraqi Army officer who fought the British in 1941. While attending secondary school in Baghdad in 1956, he began to take part in revolutionary politics; following his unsuccessful 1959 attempt to assassinate the leader of the new revolutionary government of Iraq, Hussein escaped to Syria.

Later, after two years of legal studies in Egypt, he returned to Baghdad in 1963 when the Baath Party seized power, but he soon was imprisoned by the party's enemies. In 1966 he escaped from prison and then became deputy secretary-general of the Iraqi section of the Baath Party. He married and had four children.

In July 1968 the Baath returned to power and Hussein was named deputy chairman of the Revolutionary Command Council. For ten years Saddam Hussein was responsible for maintaining the Baath in control. By means of military purges, ruthless intimidation of enemies and careful control of his party, he became the most powerful person in Iraq, succeeding to the presidency and headship of the Iraqi Baath Party on July 16, 1979.

Using the new wealth generated by higher world prices for Iraqi oil, Saddam Hussein in the 1970s and 1980s attempted to increase industrial production, reorganize government policy in agriculture, improve education, and change the status of women. At the same time he tried to retain all power in his own hands. Economic and social advances were put at risk when he chose to invade Iran on Sept. 22, 1980, hoping to gain control of Arab-inhabited areas and oil resources. The ensuing eight-year-long war between Iran and Iraq resulted in hundreds of thousands of dead and wounded soldiers and civilians and billions of dollars in damages.

The war with Iran was a disaster for Iraq, ending with a cease-fire on July 18, 1988. The task of national economic reconstruction only had begun when Saddam Hussein turned against his former benefactors by invading Kuwait and threatening Saudi Arabia.

See also feature articles, page 24.

WILLIAM OCHSENWALD

KENNEDY, Rose Fitzgerald

''. . . Rose Fitzgerald Kennedy has worked to advance the idea that strong and loving families, built on the rock of religious faith, are the foundation of a strong and caring society. By example in word and deed, she has encouraged her children—and, indeed, all Americans—to use their gifts for the benefit of their fellow man.'' Thus did President Bush describe one of the nation's most admired women, in a proclamation which declared July 22, 1990, as ''Rose Fitzgerald Kennedy Family Appreciation Day.''

The mother of several of the 20th century's best-known politicians, including one of its most popular presidents, celebrated her 100th birthday on that date. The presidential proclamation was only one of many celebrations held nationwide to honor Rose Kennedy.

Kennedy is characterized by those who know her well as a strong-willed, self-disciplined perfectionist who possesses great stores of humor and energy. Her children and grandchildren cite many ways in which she has inspired them, among them her tireless efforts on behalf of those with physical and mental disabilities.

Background. Rose Fitzgerald was born in Boston, MA, July 22, 1890, to John and Josephine Fitzgerald. Her father, known as ''Honey Fitz,'' was a congressman and twice served as mayor of Boston. A naturally talented politician herself, Rose often campaigned with her father and served as hostess at political functions. (Her son Teddy later stated that it was she who guided her sons toward the political spotlight.)

Rose was graduated from Manhattanville College, and in 1914 married Joseph Patrick Kennedy, a successful young businessman. The couple settled in Brookline, a Boston suburb. Their first child, Joseph, was born in 1915; eight more followed. Rosemary, the first daughter, was born mentally retarded, spurring Rose to lifelong involvement in causes benefiting the retarded.

Despite a life lived largely in the public eye, Kennedy managed to raise her nine children in a calm, stable atmosphere, nurturing each and never making them aware of the family's fame. At the same time, she devoted herself zealously to charity and politics.

President Franklin Roosevelt named Joseph Kennedy as ambassador to Great Britain in 1937, and the family resided in England until Kennedy resigned his post in 1940. After returning to the United States, the Kennedys eventually settled in Hyannis Port, MA.

Tragedy seemed to strike the Kennedy family again and again in later years. The couple's oldest son, a fighter pilot in World War II, was killed in a bombing run in 1944. A daughter, Kathleen, died in a plane crash in 1948. And then two sons—John, a U.S. president, and Robert, a senator running for the White House, were felled by assassins' bullets during the 1960s. Despite these calamities, Kennedy always maintained her serenity, holding the family together and rarely giving in to self-pity.

Now in fragile health, Kennedy still lives at the family compound in Hyannis Port, and is visited often by her family.

LeMOND, Gregory James

In 1990, Greg LeMond won bicycling's most difficult and celebrated race, the Tour de France, for the third time. In prevailing for the second consecutive year in the more than 2,000-mi (3 180-km) contest, LeMond triumphed over all manner of obstacles that many had considered insurmountable.

As the first American ever to win the Tour de France bicycle race, in 1986, LeMond had become an instant celebrity. At only 25 years of age, he just was entering his competitive prime, and was expected to dominate the sport of cycling for years to come. However, a series of tragic mishaps sidelined LeMond almost completely for two years; in 1989 he even considered retiring from the sport. His 1989 and 1990 back-to-back victories in the Tour de France demonstrated an indomitable spirit, as well as great athletic talent.

Background. Gregory James LeMond was born in Los Angeles, CA, on June 26, 1961, to Bertha and Robert LeMond. Growing up in Nevada, LeMond began cycling in 1975, mostly as a way to stay in shape during the off-season from skiing (his preferred sport at the time). However, he soon was entering cycling races and taking championships in his age group.

LeMond dropped out of high school to devote himself to cycling, later earning a diploma through correspondence courses. By 1979 he had become the first rider to win three medals (one each gold, silver, and bronze) in one world meet, at the junior world championship in Buenos Aires, Argentina. He had planned to compete in the 1980 Olympics, but was unable to do so because of the U.S. boycott of the games.

Turning professional in 1980, LeMond signed a contract with Renault and began to race in Europe. He made

Greg LeMond
© Gouverneur/Gamma-Liaison

his debut in the Tour de France in 1984, finishing in third place, a first for a non-European competitor.

A year after his first win of the Tour in 1986, LeMond's string of misfortunes began. In April 1987, during a hunting expedition in California, he was shot accidentally by his brother-in-law; several internal organs and his heart lining were pierced, and two ribs were broken. Although he was near death, all the damage was reparable. However, LeMond's recovery was set back continually by problems—an emergency appendectomy four months after the shooting, an infected shin tendon in 1988, a bout with severe anemia. LeMond, however, continued training, determined to return to competitive cycling.

Although LeMond himself was ready to quit just before the 1989 Tour de France, he somehow regained his physical and psychological edge, and ended up winning the race by a mere eight seconds—the narrowest margin in the race's history.

LeMond and his wife, the former Kathy Morris, were married in 1980, and have two sons and a daughter. They split their time between homes in Belgium and Minnesota. LeMond enjoys jogging, weight-lifting, and cross-country skiing during cycling's off-season.

MAJOR, John. *See* page 256.

MANDELA, Nelson Rolihahla

Nelson Mandela has become a symbol of black resistance to white rule in South Africa. In the 1940s, he helped to move the African National Congress (ANC) in new directions. In the 1960s, he was instrumental in setting up the more militant underground wing of the ANC. Today, after spending more than 27 years in South African prisons for his militant stand against apartheid, he has become the chief negotiator and spokesperson for the ANC movement.

Background. Nelson Rolihahla Mandela was born into the royal Tembu household in the Umtata district in the Transkei on July 18, 1918. Following the death of his father in 1930, he became the ward of his cousin, acting paramount chief of Tembuland, Jongintaba David Dalindyebo. Mandela was graduated from high school at Healdtown in the Ciskei and went on to Fort Hare University in 1938. Suspended from Fort Hare in 1941 for leading a student demonstration, he soon moved to Johannesburg where he worked as a mine policeman and eventually completed his studies at the University of Witwatersrand. He received his law degree from the University of South Africa in 1942.

In 1944, Mandela helped to found the ANC's Youth League (YL) with Oliver Tambo and Walter Sisulu. He married Evelyn Ntoko Mase, a nurse, in 1944. They had three children and were divorced in 1957. Mandela was elected national secretary of the YL in 1947 and became part of the ANC executive two years later. He emphasized nonviolence and mass mobilization at this time and served as "volunteer-in-chief" of the highly successful 1952 Defiance of Unjust Laws Campaign. In December 1952, Mandela and 19 others were charged under the Suppression of Communism Act. He was given a nine-month suspended sentence and was forbidden to leave the Johannesburg area or attend meetings. Despite the ban, he became deputy national president of the ANC, then under the leadership of Chief Albert Luthuli. Within the ANC, he was an advocate of the ideals of the 1955 Freedom Charter, which emphasized equality before the law and human rights for all.

On Dec. 5, 1956, Mandela and 155 other political leaders were arrested and charged with treason. The so-called "Treason Trial" continued until March 1961 and ended in acquittal for all of the accused. Because of the intransigence of the system, Mandela began to advocate a more militant approach. In November 1962, Mandela was convicted of charges of incitement and illegally leaving the country, for which he received a five-year prison sentence. However, in July 1963, he was brought from prison on Robben Island to stand trial as a member of the high command of the underground wing of the ANC. He was convicted of treason. Because of world pressure, Mandela was spared the death penalty, but on July 11, 1964, he received a life sentence. He spent the next 25-plus years in prison.

Responding to international pressures and the continuing crisis within South Africa, F.W. de Klerk, the nation's president since September 1989, released Mandela unconditionally from prison in February 1990. His release opened the way to negotiations on power sharing and a new constitution for the country. Mandela was elected deputy president of the ANC in early March. He remained committed to the ideals of a nonracial, just, and democratic South Africa.

New problems that began confronting Mandela in 1990 included increasing violence between supporters of the ANC and followers of Zulu leader Gatsha Mangosuthu Buthelezi. Mandela also was concerned with redressing social and economic imbalances in South Africa without crippling the economy.

Mandela married his second wife, Winnie Nomzamo Madzikela, a medical social worker, in 1958. They have two daughters.

PATRICK O'MEARA

Nelson Mandela
© P. Durand/Sygma

MASUR, Kurt

The year 1989–90 was a heady one for Kurt Masur, the conductor since 1970 of one of Europe's most venerable ensembles, the 247-year-old Gewandhaus Orchestra of Leipzig.

In the closing months of 1989, Masur had been a leader of the New Forum, a Leipzig opposition group that helped spark the demonstrations against the East German government that eventually drove the country's Communist leaders from power. Early in 1990 there was serious discussion of Masur running for his country's presidency. But he declared that his political objectives had been achieved and that he wanted to concentrate fully on music. In April, when it was clear that his political involvement would not necessarily tie him to his homeland, a delegation from the New York Philharmonic offered Masur the orchestra's music directorship, and he accepted.

Masur's appointment to the Philharmonic post, to begin with the 1991–92 season, followed a two-year search for a successor to Zubin Mehta, who would leave the orchestra in May 1991. Masur will remain music di-

© Michael Hirsch/Gamma-Liaison

Kurt Masur

rector in Leipzig as well, at least through the Gewand-haus Orchestra's 250th anniversary celebrations in 1993–94.

The administrators of the New York Philharmonic held their breath in May, however, when Masur was hospitalized in Frankfurt after suffering chest pains on a flight home to Leipzig from Tel Aviv, where he had been conducting the Israel Philharmonic. He was hospitalized for several days, but it was determined that he had not suffered a heart attack.

Background. Kurt Masur was born in Brieg, Silesia, on July 18, 1927, and began his musical studies in 1942 at the National Music School in Breslau. His instruments were the cello and the piano. In 1946 he enrolled at the Leipzig Conservatory as a piano, composition, and conducting student. Masur pursued the traditional Germanic route to the podium, beginning as a rehearsal pianist at the Halle National Theater in 1948. In the 1950s he moved on to conductorships and music directorships in small opera companies in Erfurt, Leipzig, and Schwerin. His first significant orchestral post was as director of the Dresden Philharmonic (1955–58 and 1967–72), and his first major operatic post was with the Komische Oper, Berlin (1960–64).

Masur has toured extensively in Europe and in the United States. He debuted as guest conductor with the New York Philharmonic in 1981. He has established a reputation for solid, straightforward interpretations of the central Germanic Romantic repertory, particularly the works of Beethoven, Strauss, Wagner, and Mendelssohn, as well as early 20th-century Russian music. He also has championed some East German composers—most notably Siegfried Matthus, whose work he has conducted in guest appearances with the New York Philharmonic. He has recorded fairly prolifically.

He said that he hopes to find his way with contemporary American music, using his dual podiums as a bridge over which new German and American works may cross.

ALLAN KOZINN

RAITT, Bonnie Lynn

After 20 years in the music business, Bonnie Raitt finally achieved mainstream fame in 1990 when she won four Grammy Awards: for album of the year, best pop vocal performance (female), best rock vocal performance (female), and best traditional blues recording (*I'm In the Mood* with John Lee Hooker). Her prizewin-

ning album, *Nick of Time*, combines her distinctive mix of rhythm and blues, folk, and rock styles with her reflections on growing older. It was a special triumph for Raitt, who had not released a complete album since 1983, and who had suffered through several years of serious personal and professional setbacks.

Raitt's success with *Nick of Time* also demonstrated the growing public interest in alternate forms of music like rhythm and blues, which usually are overshadowed by more commercially oriented pop music.

Background. Bonnie Lynn Raitt was born Nov. 8, 1949, in Burbank, CA. Her father, John, was a prominent actor and singer who was successful on Broadway. Her mother, Marjorie, was a piano accompanist. Raitt's early childhood was spent traveling between homes on each coast before the family settled in Los Angeles. Raitt became interested in music at an early age, and soon learned to play guitar in the folk and rhythm and blues styles. Her Quaker upbringing helped make her aware of social injustice, and she became an outspoken political and environmental activist.

After dropping out of Radcliffe in the late 1960s to pursue a musical career, Raitt attained a degree of popular success, befriending and performing with such legends of blues music as Fred McDowell and Junior Wells. Her albums, although never very successful commercially, were admired by critics. In 1977 her version of Del Shannon's song "Runaway" almost made the Top 40. During this period, Raitt helped organize and played at many benefit concerts for antinuclear and various political causes, and was a founder of Musicians United for Safe Energy (MUSE), rock's antinuclear organization.

In the late 1970s, the success of disco music caused Raitt's more blues-oriented style to lose its popularity. In 1983, Warner Brothers, with whom Raitt had been recording since 1971, dropped her from its label. In 1987, after conquering a longstanding drinking problem, Raitt began work on *Nick of Time*, her tenth album. Since her first nine records had not yielded a hit, Raitt decided to keep the tenth simple and straightforward, saying, "you might as well do something that's going to be artistically true to what you do." But the album, reflecting her more mature point of view and showcasing her flawless slide guitar playing, was received enthusiastically by critics and the public alike, and achieved gold status.

Raitt, who never has been married, lives in northern California, although she spends most of every year performing throughout the country.

Bonnie Raitt

© Joffett/Sipa

AP/Wide World
Ann Richards

RICHARDS, Ann

Ann Richards proved herself a formidable politician in 1990 as she won election to the Texas governorship, the second woman in Texas history to gain that office. Labeling her victory "sociologically significant," she said, "There are going to be a lot of little girls who open their history texts and see my picture, and they will say, 'If she can do it, so can I.'"

In her gubernatorial campaign she engaged in a bitter and costly battle with millionaire Republican candidate Clayton Williams, complete with mudslinging and some gaffes on the part of her opponent which apparently aided in her narrow victory. As a product of the progressive wing of the Texas Democratic Party, Richards and her type of liberalism have not been seen in Texas politicians in 25 years.

The governor-elect, a former teacher, immediately announced her plans to change school financing and comply with a court order to provide more equal financing to poor school districts. She also announced that she would demand greater federal-government financing for social-welfare policies mandated in Washington, but often paid for by the states—a political stance that echoed her often-repeated line, "If you can't fill the till, don't pass the bill."

Richards, the Texas state treasurer since 1983, first came to national attention in 1988 when she delivered the keynote address at the Democratic National Convention in Atlanta, GA. Her speech, sprinkled with one-liners, particularly her characterization of Republican candidate George Bush as "born with a silver foot in his mouth," was a memorable moment of the convention.

Background. Ann Willis Richards was born in Waco, TX, Sept. 3, 1933, a Depression-era baby and the only child of Cecil and Ona Willis. She was graduated from Baylor University (B.A., 1954) and did postgraduate work at the University of Texas (1957). At the age of 19 she married her university sweetheart, and from 1954 to 1969 she and her husband, a lawyer, were activists in liberal Democratic Party politics in Texas.

She was county commissioner, Travis County (1977–82), an elected position that allowed her to come into her own as a political figure. During that period, she also became more involved in the struggle for equal rights at both the local and national levels. Although she had

been treated for alcoholism (an issue that came up during her campaign for the governorship), she nonetheless was picked in 1982 to run for the statewide office of treasurer, an office that she won and in which she gained a reputation as a strict fiscal conservative. She won a second term in 1986.

Ann Richards, who is divorced, has four children.

RYAN, Lynn Nolan, Jr.

Although he turned 43 before the 1990 baseball season started, Nolan Ryan did not act like the oldest player in the game. On June 11 he threw a record sixth no-hitter, beating the Oakland Athletics, 5-0. Seven weeks later, on July 31, he beat the Milwaukee Brewers, 11-3, making him the 20th major-league pitcher with at least 300 career victories. The star right-hander of the Texas Rangers finished the season with a 13-9 record (302 career wins) and a 3.44 earned run average even though he was bothered by back spasms that forced him onto the disabled list in May.

Ryan had joined the Rangers via free agency in 1989 after previously pitching for the New York Mets, the California Angels, and the Houston Astros. He has led his league in strikeouts 11 times, winning his fourth consecutive crown in 1990 with 232, and has fanned 300 batters in a season six times. Although he is also the all-time strikeout king (Rickey Henderson became his 5,000th victim on Aug. 22, 1989), he never has won a Cy Young Award, given annually to the best pitcher in each league.

Early in his career, the hard-throwing Ryan intimidated both batters and catchers. He overcame bouts of wildness only after adopting a more compact pitching motion at the suggestion of California battery-mate Jeff Torborg, now the manager of the Chicago White Sox. In 1972, his first season with the Angels, Ryan won 19 games, had a 2.28 earned run average, and struck out 300 hitters. A year later, he fanned a record 383 and pitched his first two no-hitters. A student of pitching who adheres to a strict conditioning regimen, Ryan relishes the chance to pitch—even when he is hurting.

Background. Lynn Nolan Ryan, Jr., was born in Refugio, TX, on Jan. 31, 1947. The son of Mary Haneal and Lynn Nolan Ryan, an oil-field supervisor, Ryan was a star pitcher at Alvin High School. As a senior he appeared in 24 of 36 games played. Ryan attended Alvin Community College before the Mets selected him in the 1965 amateur free-agent draft.

Nolan Ryan married his childhood sweetheart, the former Ruth Elise Holdruff, on June 26, 1967. The oldest of their three children, 18-year-old Reid, started pitching at the University of Texas in September 1990.

A family man with a reputation for being polite to a fault, Ryan spends his winters running two south Texas cattle ranches and a small bank near his hometown of Alvin, 30 mi (48 km) south of Houston. He also serves as a spokesperson for the Special Olympics, Little League Baseball, and various other charities.

"He is very typical of what you expect from a frontier Texan," said George W. Bush, managing partner of the Rangers and son of the U.S. president. "Everybody everywhere admires the guy. He is by far the most popular figure in Texas."

DAN SCHLOSSBERG

SCOWCROFT, Brent

As the national security adviser to U.S. President George Bush, Brent Scowcroft played a key role in formulating U.S. policy and strategy toward the Persian Gulf after the Iraqi invasion of Kuwait in August 1990. Scowcroft, known as a team player who prefers to maintain a low profile, reportedly encouraged a careful, limited-objectives approach, urging the president to send troops into Saudi Arabia in a show of strength and to persuade allies to join in the effort. Within the National Security Council (NSC), he was said to have built a consensus for the pursuit of diplomatic and economic channels to oust Iraq from Kuwait and for use of military action only as a last resort. (See feature article, page 24.)

Highly qualified for his position and critical of the political infighting and covert activity of the NSC in the past, Scowcroft was named to the post by President-elect Bush in November 1988. He then assembled a high-powered staff of foreign-policy experts for the NSC, but restricted them to research, policy advice, and speech writing. As an East-West expert, he was instrumental in the 1989 nuclear-arms-control negotiations, and despite criticism regarding his initial caution toward the new Eastern European governments, he supported deep troop reductions in Western Europe.

Background. Born on March 19, 1925, in Ogden, UT, Brent Scowcroft began his military career by earning a B.S. degree in 1947 from the U.S. Military Academy, West Point, NY. He soon gained his Air Force fighter-pilot wings, but an injury caused him to redirect his goals. He continued his education at Columbia University (M.A., 1953; Ph.D., 1967) and embarked on a teaching career at the U.S. Military Academy (1953–57), where he taught Russian history. He later taught at the U.S. Air Force Academy in Colorado Springs (1962–64), and briefly at the National War College (1967–68) in Washington. In between his studies and teaching—he is a specialist in Slavic languages and received his doctorate in international relations, he held operational and administrative staff positions. In 1964 he was a staffer in the Air Force's long-range planning division in Washington. Beginning in 1968, Scowcroft held a number of national-security posts in the Defense Department.

Scowcroft, who has served every U.S. president since Richard Nixon, became Nixon's military aide in 1971, accompanying him on his initial trip to Communist China. From 1973 to 1975 he was his deputy assistant for national security affairs, serving under Henry Kissinger, who had been impressed by Scowcroft's ability as an administrator and by his direct and forceful manner. Under President Gerald Ford, Scowcroft resigned his commission as a lieutenant general to serve as national security adviser (1975–77). Later he served on Jimmy Carter's General Advisory Committee on Arms Control (1977–80), helping to formulate the SALT II treaty, and early on in the administration of Ronald Reagan.

From 1982 to 1988 as a vice-president of Kissinger Associates Inc. consulting firm, he was out of govern-

ment service, but in late 1986 he returned as part of the three-man Tower Commission, charged with investigating the NSC's role in the Iran-contra scandal.

A practicing Mormon who keeps physically fit through skiing, swimming, golf, tennis, and squash, Scowcroft is considered by many as the quiet tiger in President Bush's think tank.

He is married to the former Marian Horner. They are the parents of a daughter.

CAROLYN G. NUZZI

SINGH, Vishwanath Pratap

Although he had been an active politician in India for more than 20 years, V. P. Singh gained widespread recognition only in 1987, when he resigned as minister of defense in Rajiv Gandhi's Congress(I) government. Emerging as the leader of an opposition seven-party National Front (in which the party he headed, the Janata Dal, was the most important constituent), he led a successful fight against Gandhi and the Congress(I) in the ninth general election in November 1989. The Front won fewer seats in the Lok Sabha (the lower house of the Indian Parliament) than the Congress(I), but Singh was able to form a coalition government with the support of the Bharatiya Janata Party (BJP), a rightist pro-Hindu nationalist party, and the two main Communist parties. The coalition took office on Dec. 2, 1989.

During the initial months of 1990, Singh's government made some progress on the economic front and in improving relations with Sri Lanka and Nepal. Relations with Pakistan improved briefly, then took a turn for the worse. The situation in the troubled Punjab region worsened, and a major crisis developed in Jammu and Kashmir, India's only Muslim-majority state.

Because of serious divisions within the National Front and mounting internal problems, Singh's tenure as prime minister lasted only 11 months. On Nov. 7, 1990, he was defeated in a no-confidence vote in the Lok Sabha and immediately resigned. Singh, faced with a shaky coalition from the beginning, had been in political jeopardy throughout the year. He was succeeded by political rival Chandra Shekhar of the Janata Dal party, who had the initial support of the Congress (I) Party and the BJP.

Background. A Hindu of a princely family of the Rajput/Thakur (warrior or ruling) caste, Vishwanath Pratap Singh was born in Allahabad in the state of Uttar Pradesh on June 25, 1931. Despite his privileged background, Singh's childhood was difficult and lonely. He earned bachelor of arts, bachelor of science, and law (LL.B.) degrees from Allahabad and Poona universities. He never has practiced law, however.

Singh's active political career began in 1967, when he was elected to the legislative assembly of Uttar Pradesh. Four years later he became a member of the national parliament. During the period of 1974–77 he was successively deputy minister and minister of state in the ministry of commerce of the Congress(I) government headed by Indira Gandhi. With the return of Gandhi to power in 1980, he again became a member of the Lok Sabha. From 1980 to 1982 he served as chief minister of Uttar Pradesh. Between 1983 and 1987 he held important posts—minister of commerce, finance, and defense—in the cabinets of Indira Gandhi and her son, Rajiv. He was a member of the Rajya Sabha (the upper house of Parliament) from 1983 to 1988. Because of his efforts to investigate scandals in the government, especially in arms purchases abroad, he fell out of favor with Prime Minister Rajiv Gandhi. In April 1987 he resigned as minister of defense and three months later he was expelled from the Congress(I) Party.

Singh is regarded as a man of ability and integrity, and as a baffling and complex personality. He has been called "the Mona Lisa of Indian politics."

In 1955 Singh married Sita Kumari, also of princely descent. The couple have two sons.

NORMAN D. PALMER

Brent Scowcroft

© Walker/Gamma-Liaison

© Zoe Dominic

Maggie Smith

SMITH, Maggie

Dame Maggie Smith's return to Broadway in Peter Shaffer's *Lettice and Lovage*, which opened at the Ethel Barrymore Theater on March 25, 1990, was a personal triumph. For her performance, Dame Maggie, who already had scored a hit in the comedy in London's West End, was awarded a Tony Award as best actress in June.

Smith's adoring fans reveled once again in her stylistically singular brand of comedy—characterized by an unusually nasal voice, glassy stares, deliberately affected gestures, and an air of undefeated pessimism. While Dame Maggie is viewed as one of England's best classical actresses—she has been an active member of the august British National Theatre since 1963—it is her comedic skills, especially in the realm of caricature, that have brought her extraordinary acclaim and popularity.

Although Smith prefers the stage, she has done notable work in film as well. For her brilliant performance as the individualistic schoolteacher in *The Prime of Miss Jean Brodie*, she was chosen best actress of 1969 by the Academy of Motion Picture Arts and Sciences in Hollywood. Smith already had received an Oscar nomination for her riveting portrayal of Desdemona, playing opposite Sir Laurence Olivier, in the film *Othello* (1966). In Britain, she had won a best actress stage award for her performance in related one-act comedies *The Private Ear* and *The Public Eye* (1962), also by Peter Shaffer. Smith earned Tony nominations for best actress in Noel Coward's *Private Lives* (1975) and *Night and Day* by Tom Stoppard (1979). She also took a second Oscar for the film version of Neil Simon's play *California Suite* (1978).

For her contribution to the British theater, Maggie Smith was made a dame commander of the Order of British Empire in December 1989.

Background. Margaret Smith was born in Ilford, Essex, England, on Dec. 28, 1934, the youngest of three children, to Nathaniel Smith, a public-health pathologist, and Margaret Little (Hutton) Smith. The family moved to Oxford when she was five, where she attended the Oxford School for Girls. Her interest in theater surprised her family, and at 16 she started studying drama at the Oxford Playhouse School. Smith appeared in many Oxford University productions, predominantly revues, an art form suited to her comic flair.

In 1955, Leonard Sillman, the U.S. producer, saw her in *On The Fringe*, a small revue in London, and her per-

formance attracted his interest for Broadway's *New Faces of 1956*. The film world and Smith discovered one another in 1958 when she starred as a wealthy girl who befriends an escaped convict in *Nowhere to Go*. Accolades followed with roles in National Theatre productions, including *The Master Builder* (1964) and *Miss Julie* (1965). Also active in films in the 1960s, Smith appeared with Rex Harrison in *The Honey Pot* (1967).

Smith's marriage in 1967 to Robert Stephens, an actor, ended in divorce. They had two sons. In 1976 she married playwright Beverley Cross.

GLADYS HANDELMAN

SOUTER, David Hackett

President Bush waited barely 72 hours to name a replacement for Supreme Court Justice William J. Brennan after the court's leading liberal announced his retirement. Bush, with his first opportunity to fill a high-court vacancy, chose David Souter, an obscure judge from New Hampshire.

Picking a man with a limited record on major social and constitutional issues was designed to blunt the kind of liberal-led attack that spelled defeat in 1987 for President Ronald Reagan's nomination of Robert H. Bork to the high court. The strategy worked, with considerable help from Souter. In three days of testimony before the Senate Judiciary Committee, the nominee impressed his inquisitors with a low-key style, precise knowledge of the law, and an apparently moderate approach to judging.

Almost the only ones not convinced were women's-rights groups, who sought assurance Souter would not vote to overturn the court's 1973 ruling in *Roe v. Wade* that legalized abortion. Souter refused to be drawn into any discussion of the issue. But he did say he agreed that married women have a privacy right to practice contraception, thus lending support to an earlier high-court ruling that provided the foundation for the 1973 decision. Souter also said he had an open mind on whether *Roe v. Wade* should stand or fall.

The Senate wasted little time in confirming Souter to become the 105th justice in the high court's history. By a 90–9 vote, his nomination was approved on Oct. 2, 1990, just one day after the 1990–91 term began. Chief Justice William H. Rehnquist administered the oath of office to Justice Souter on October 9.

David H. Souter

© Bob McNeely/Sipa

Background. David Hackett Souter marked his 51st birthday on Sept. 17, 1990, as he concluded his Senate testimony. He has lived almost all his life in New Hampshire, where he practiced law and served as state attorney general, a state judge, and then a federal judge.

An only child, Souter is the son of the late Joseph Souter, a bank official, and Helen Hackett Souter. He was graduated from Harvard University, attended Oxford University as a Rhodes Scholar, and returned to Harvard to obtain his law degree. In the late 1970s he was attorney general under Gov. Meldrim Thomson of New Hampshire, at the time one of the most conservative governors in the nation. Souter spent five years as a state Superior Court judge and seven years as a state Supreme Court justice before President Bush named him a federal appeals-court judge in April 1990.

A bachelor with an ascetic life-style, Souter has continued to live in a weather-beaten farmhouse in Weare, NH, where he grew up. He is an avid reader of books and a mountain climber. Despite his interest in solitary pursuits, friends said he is warm and witty in their presence. His key supporters include two prominent New Hampshire Republicans with contrasting political reputations, conservative White House Chief of Staff John Sununu, a former governor, and moderate Sen. Warren Rudman.

JIM RUBIN

AP/Wide World

George M. Steinbrenner III

STEINBRENNER, George Michael, III

George Steinbrenner's tempestuous tenure as general partner of the New York Yankees ended abruptly Aug. 20, 1990, after Baseball Commissioner Fay Vincent forced him to resign the position.

Vincent, completing a four-month investigation spearheaded by John Dowd, ruled July 30 that Steinbrenner had acted contrary to "the best interests of baseball" in associating with gambler Howard Spira. After Steinbrenner refused Vincent's offer of a two-year suspension followed by a three-year probation, the commissioner effectively changed Steinbrenner's ownership interest from general partner to limited partner.

In an 11-page decision, Vincent ordered the owner to reduce his stock holdings in the team from 55% to less than 50% and to yield his position August 20. Although Steinbrenner and his family still controlled the majority of team stock, the former general partner is not allowed to participate in player personnel matters. He also agreed to acknowledge wrongdoing, forgo litigation, and accept a lifetime ban on discussing the Yankees with the new managing partner.

Vincent said two days of testimony from Steinbrenner revealed "a pattern of behavior that borders on the bizarre." He also rejected Steinbrenner's claims that he paid Spira $40,000 because he feared for the safety of his family. Spira said Steinbrenner paid him to provide information that could be used against Dave Winfield, a star outfielder whose battles with the club owner consumed most of his ten-year stay in the Bronx. Winfield, who was traded to the California Angels in May, once employed Spira at his David M. Winfield Foundation.

Although Steinbrenner agreed to yield his position, he handpicked Broadway producer Robert Nederlander as his immediate successor and indicated that he would like his sons and sons-in-law to run the team later on. Steinbrenner's resignation was greeted with jubilation by Yankee fans disenchanted with the turmoil that had plunged the once-proud franchise into last place. During a stormy stewardship that survived 17½ seasons, Steinbrenner changed managers 19 times.

He had bought the ball club from CBS for $10 million in 1973, three years before the advent of free agency. Willing to win at any cost, Steinbrenner spent lavishly to land such veteran stars as Catfish Hunter, Reggie Jackson, Goose Gossage, Tommy John, and Winfield. The team won its first flag in 12 years in 1976, then won consecutive World Championships in 1977–78. It produced another pennant during the split season of 1981 but went steadily downhill thereafter.

Steinbrenner's ego often interfered with his judgment. Desperate to compete with the crosstown Mets for newspaper space, he made more headlines than any previous owner. He had verbal wars with Jackson, Winfield, and the late Billy Martin, who was hired and fired as Yankee manager a record five times.

Background. George Michael Steinbrenner III, the son of Henry G. and Rita Haley Steinbrenner, was born in Rocky River, OH, on July 4, 1930. Young George earned pocket money delivering eggs in a Cleveland suburb before becoming an all-around athlete at Culver (IN) Military Academy. He was a track star and glee-club president at Williams College before joining the U.S. Air Force as a second lieutenant. In 1957 he joined Kinsman Marine Transit, the original family business. It later became a subsidiary of American Shipbuilding, a firm that made Steinbrenner president after he purchased a large block of its stock.

He and his wife, the former Elizabeth Joan Zieg, have two sons and two daughters. The Steinbrenners live in Tampa, FL, where American Shipbuilding has a facility. George Steinbrenner holds four honorary degrees and is involved in civic and community causes.

DAN SCHLOSSBERG

SUNUNU, John Henry

Although President Bush has become known as a "hands-on" chief executive, his chief of staff, John H. Sununu, continued to be considered the White House power center during 1990. In the words of House Minority Whip Newt Gingrich, "no person since Harry Hopkins [President Franklin Roosevelt's principal aide] has been able to cover as many different topics with the president's approval" as Sununu. Of his position and power, the former New Hampshire governor, a conservative Republican, noted that "what happens in the White House is what the president of the United States wants to happen in the White House. The policy that comes out of here is the policy of the president of the United States. And the president is very active in dealing with the details of the formulation of policy, not just the checking off of boxes at the end. He likes to hear about things as early as possible. I do my best to make sure he hears about it as things are being formulated."

In late August 1990 the White House chief of staff was in Moscow to tutor the Soviet leaders on the workings of a presidential system of government.

John H. Sununu

Background. John Henry Sununu was born on July 2, 1939, in Havana, Cuba, while his parents were on a business trip. His father was descended from Lebanese and Greek immigrants and his mother, the former Victoria Daly, was born in El Salvador to a Greek family. He grew up in the Forest Hills section of Queens, NY, and was graduated from Massachusetts Institute of Technology (MIT) with a degree in mechanical engineering in 1961. He then worked as the chief engineer for Astro Dynamics, a company he had founded in 1960, earned his doctorate from MIT in 1966, established the consulting firms of JHS Engineering Company in 1966 and Thermal Research in 1968, and began teaching at Tufts University in 1966. From 1968 to 1973 he served as associate dean of Tufts' College of Engineering.

In 1969 he and his wife, the former Nancy Hayes, and their young family moved from Massachusetts to New Hampshire, where Sununu began developing an interest in Republican politics. He was elected to the New Hampshire House of Representatives for a two-year term in 1972. Following unsuccessful campaigns for the state Senate, the state executive council, and the U.S. Senate and after serving as a member of the Governor's Energy Council (1973–78), Sununu was elected governor of New Hampshire in 1982. He won reelection in 1984 and 1986. As governor, he turned a budget deficit into a surplus and was a strong supporter of the Seabrook nuclear power plant. He also was active in various governors' associations.

After being given much of the credit for George Bush's victory in New Hampshire's Republican presidential primary in February 1988 and serving as a national director of the Bush campaign, he was named White House chief of staff by the president-elect on Nov. 17, 1988.

John Sununu is a computer enthusiast, baseball-card collector, and skiing and softball buff. He and his wife are the parents of eight children.

WILDER, L(awrence) Douglas

Under a bright winter sun amid a cold breeze, Jan. 13, 1990, L. Douglas Wilder, the 58-year-old grandson of slaves, was inaugurated as governor of Virginia. On Nov. 7, 1989, then Lieutenant Governor Wilder, a Democrat, had scored a narrow election victory over former state Attorney General J. Marshall Coleman, becoming the first black to be elected chief executive of a U.S. state. His election victory was considered remarkable in that not only was Virginia the capital of the old Confederacy but the state's current population is less than 20% black. More than 80% of those who voted for Wilder in 1989 were white. Many credited his victory to his pro-choice stance on abortion.

In his inaugural address the new governor declared that "we mark today not a victory of party or the accomplishments of an individual but the triumph of an idea, an idea as old as America, as old as the God who looks out for us all." The governor also noted that although Virginia had enjoyed more than a decade of economic prosperity, tough economic times were ahead. In establishing his new administration, Wilder sought a middle-of-the-road approach, selecting officials who represented the state's political mainstream. He said that he "won the governorship by appealing to a cross section of the state" and that he "intended to keep on that track."

On August 16 the governor presented his plan for reducing Virginia's budget deficit, which included freezing the salaries of state employees.

Background. L. Douglas Wilder was born on Jan. 17, 1931, in Richmond, VA, the seventh of eight children of an insurance salesman and a maid. His paternal grandparents were slaves at the time of their marriage. From an early age he was encouraged by his mother toward educational pursuits. After attending grammar and high schools in Richmond, he was graduated from Virginia Union College in 1951. While serving in the Korean War he was awarded the Bronze Star for bravery.

In 1959 he was graduated from Howard Law School in Washington, DC, and returned to Virginia to practice law. Ten years later he became the first black since Reconstruction to be elected to the Virginia legislature. His first legislative proposal was to recommend the declassification of *Carry Me Back to Old Virginia* as the state song. During his 16 years in the state Senate he advocated fair-housing legislation, labor-union rights for public employees, and greater minority hiring in public business. During this time he also became famous for his Afro hairstyle, colorful shirts, and flamboyance. In 1985 he adopted a more conservative approach to politics and ran successfully for the state lieutenant governorship.

The divorced governor is the father of two daughters and a son. He enjoys barbecuing and an occasional Greek or Roman classic.

L. Douglas Wilder

WILSON, August

In 1990, U.S. playwright August Wilson won his second Pulitzer Prize and his fourth New York Drama Critics Circle Award for *The Piano Lesson*. Wilson thus became one of seven American playwrights to receive at least two Pulitzer Prizes. He had won the prize in 1987 for *Fences*.

The Piano Lesson is set in the 1930s and centers on an ancient, carved piano that embodies a black family's history in America. The play asks whether the piano should be sold to buy the land the family once farmed as slaves or kept as a sign of their heritage—whether it is a burden or a promise, a symbol of degradation or pride. Wilson's earlier Pulitzer winner, *Fences*, which also took a Drama Circle Award and a Tony Award as best play, occurs in a northern city in the 1950s. The unresolved frustrations of its powerful central character lead him to destroy his relationship with his wife and son. With *Fences*, Wilson was praised for his perceptions about the deep and cruel effects of racial prejudice and his understanding of family dynamics.

Background. August Wilson was born in 1945 in Pittsburgh, PA, and grew up in a family of six children in a black slum community of the city. When he was 15, persecution by white students drove him from school, and he quit another school when the high quality of his work brought an unjust accusation of plagiarism. In the 1960s the Black Power movement led Wilson to stage various dramas. He also studied and wrote poetry.

Wilson's interest in writing a cycle of plays on the black experience in America brought him to the attention of Lloyd Richards, dean of Yale's drama school, who has been involved in all his stage productions. The playwright came to public attention with *Ma Rainey's Black Bottom*, which opened on Broadway in October 1984. The play takes place in a recording studio in Chicago in the late 1920s and dramatizes the tension between talented black musicians and white studio owners who exploit their work. Wilson was celebrated not only for his treatment of an important theme but also for his creation of vital characters who spoke with poetry and humor. He took his first Drama Critics Circle Award for the work.

Following the successful *Fences*, Wilson's *Joe Turner's Come and Gone* appeared on Broadway in 1988. Its setting is a boarding house in Pittsburgh in 1911, where a number of characters whose lives have been fractured in various ways tell their stories. The title comes from the true story of Joe Turner, a Tennessee plantation owner who would trick former slaves into a sort of peonage that would last for years. Though the work was recognized for its poetry and ambition, many critics felt it to be too diffuse. The New York Drama Critics Circle, however, voted it the season's best play.

A dramatist for a relatively short period of time, August Wilson already has been compared with Eugene O'Neill and is considered one of the most promising present-day playwrights. His latest work, *Two Trains Running*, an account of black street life in the late 1960s, began its debut run at the Yale Repertory Theater in the spring of 1990.

JEROME STERN

YELTSIN, Boris Nikolayevich

The Soviet politician Boris Yeltsin, who had been in political disgrace in 1987, completed his comeback in 1990 by becoming president of the Russian Republic and the archrival of Soviet president Mikhail Gorbachev. A consummate practitioner of the new Soviet politics, Yeltsin, who was elected to the Congress of People's Deputies in 1989, published a campaign autobiography, *Against the Grain*, early in 1990, and in June stood for election as president of the Supreme Soviet of the Russian Republic. He prevailed despite strong opposition orchestrated by Gorbachev, and it was recognized quickly that his popularity with the Soviet public had

© F. Hibon/Sygma

Boris Yeltsin

eclipsed Gorbachev's. In July, Yeltsin stunned the country by dramatically resigning from the Communist Party at the 28th party congress.

Free of the party and with his own power base, President Yeltsin set up a young, pro-reform government that proclaimed the sovereignty of the Russian Republic. Open challenges to Gorbachev followed—on Lithuania's drive for independence, and over control of banking and natural resources on Russian territory. In late summer, Yeltsin set off on a long barnstorming tour of his vast new domain, from the Volga River in the west to Vladivostok in the Far East. Everywhere he drew enormous, enthusiastic crowds as he began his campaign for the first direct, popular election for the Russian presidency, scheduled for 1991.

He spoke of the need to confederate the USSR, privatize property, and rapidly create a free-market economy. Back in Moscow, Yeltsin embraced the radical, 500-day Shatalin Plan for conversion to a market system, forcing Gorbachev on the defensive in the midst of a seriously deteriorating economic situation. Late in 1990 his stance in opposition to Gorbachev continued as he rejected the Soviet president's proposal for a national governmental system in which the 15 republics would have a far more active role in decisions than their current advisory position afforded. Yeltsin, however, left the possibility of compromise in place, conditioned upon the central government's recognition of the 15 republics' full sovereignty.

Background. Boris Nikolayevich Yeltsin was born on Feb. 1, 1931, to a poor Siberian peasant family in Sverdlovsk Province. Educated as a civil engineer, he advanced rapidly in his profession. He joined the Communist Party and eventually was drawn into professional party work. Yeltsin came to national attention with his 1976 appointment as first secretary of the Sverdlovsk Regional Party Committee, which carried with it membership in the All-Union Central Committee in Moscow. He became known for his executive ability and for having the courage of his convictions.

Yeltsin was called to Moscow by Gorbachev in 1986 to head the Moscow party organization, and soon was elevated to the Politburo. However, his party career came to an abrupt end late in 1987, when he criticized Gorbachev over the slow pace of reform. Stripped of his posts, he remained in disgrace until his landslide election as a deputy early in 1989, and his subsequent emergence as a leading figure in the opposition.

ROBERT SHARLET

BIOTECHNOLOGY

The year 1990 brought further advances in the fields of medicine, food production, and waste disposal through biotechnology.

Aiding the Aging. Children who suffer from a deficiency of growth hormone (pituitary gland) must receive weekly injections of it if they are to grow to more than 4 ft (1.2 m) in height. Since 1982 human-growth hormone has been available from genetically engineered bacteria, carrying the gene for this hormone.

Among many individuals who as children produced normal levels of growth hormone, one finds that the production of this hormone tapers off after age 40. Accompanying this decrease in growth hormone is an increased fat deposition, decreased muscle mass, and thinner skin. Dr. Daniel Rudman of the Medical College of Wisconsin took a group of 12 men aged 61 to 81 who had low levels of growth hormone in their blood and had them give themselves injections of the hormone. A control group of nine men, matched for age and blood-hormone level, received no treatment. After six months, the treated group showed an 8.8% increase in lean body mass, a 14.4% decrease in fatty tissue, and a 7.1% increase in skin thickness. The control group did not exhibit any such changes. The group studied was quite small, and the recentness of the study precluded any evaluation of long-term effects. However, if the results are confirmed, it would mean that human-growth hormone also benefits the aging.

Antibody-Producing Plants. Antibodies, bacteria-binding proteins, are produced by the B-cell lymphocytes of an animal's immune system. Antibodies consist of pairs of identical heavy chains and light chains which are encoded by different genes.

Dr. A. Hiatt and colleagues at the Research Institute of Scripps Clinic in La Jolla, CA, have isolated the genes for heavy and light antibody chains and transferred them separately into different tobacco-plant cells, where each became attached to one of the plant's 48 chromosomes (24 pair). These cells then were grown, initially in tissue culture and later in soil, into mature tobacco plants that produced, respectively, heavy and light antibody chains. Heavy chain-making plants were crossed with light chain-making plants. As expected, based on meiosis and subsequent chance gametic fusions, one quarter of the resulting offspring plants contained both types of genes in all its cells and, as a result, produced complete antibodies. This was the first time that the production of an important medical product resulted from such a transfer of genes.

Pesticide Protection in Corn Plants. U.S. farmers spend about $50 million annually on chemicals to fight the corn borer, *Pyrausta nubilalis*, a moth whose larvae bore into the stems of corn plants and kill the plants. It is known that the bacterium *Bacillus thuringiensis* produces spores that contain an endotoxin which, upon ingestion, is released into the digestive tract of an insect, killing the animal. Another bacterium, *Clavibacter xyli*, not found normally in corn plants, can be made to infect a corn plant where it lives only in the plant's xylem (a type of conducting cell), does not appear to injure the plant, does not leave the plant, and is not transmitted in the seed. When the plant dies, the bacterium dies.

Scientists at the biotechnology company Crop Genetics International in Hanover, MD, transferred the endotoxin-producing gene from *B. thuringiensis* into *C. xyli*. The *C. xyli* then were introduced into corn plants where they multiplied and were distributed throughout the plant. When corn borers began to feed on the stalks, they ingested some of the bacteria and their spores and were killed by the endotoxin within the spores.

In providing for the commercial distribution of the genetically engineered bacteria, the bacteria are to be forced into the tissues of dried corn seeds through the use of high pressure. When the seed is planted and begins to germinate, the bacteria will proliferate within the plant as it grows. Thus the corn borers will be killed by bacteria living within the tissues of the corn plant.

Monitoring Microbial Biodegradative Activity. It is known that bacteria can be used to break down environmental pollutants. However, prior to 1990, there was no simple system to monitor the efficiency of such catabolic processes. Dr. J. M. H. King and colleagues at the University of Tennessee have reported on their work using bioluminescence, the production of light by living organisms, to monitor biodegradative activity.

Bioluminescence is characteristic of such diverse organisms as the firefly and the bacteria *Photobacterium* and *Vibrio*. In each case the enzyme involved in light production is luciferase. In the reported experiment, the bacterial gene for luciferase was transferred from *Vibrio fischeri* to *Pseudomonas fluorescens*, a soil bacterium known for its biodegradative activity, which contains naphthalene catabolic enzymes. Naphthalene is an undesirable compound present in artificially manufactured soils. When genetically engineered *P. fluorescens* were placed in a soil suspension containing naphthalene, the luciferase and naphthalene catabolic enzymes were activated and it was found that the amount of light produced was proportional to the amount of biodegradative activity of the bacteria. The luciferase gene now is to be transferred to those bacteria that are involved in the breakdown of other organic contaminants in soils and waters.

LOUIS LEVINE
City College of New York

BOLIVIA

For Bolivia, 1990 marked the fourth consecutive year of positive economic growth and modest inflation. High unemployment and persistent poverty, however, continued to plague the country, keeping political unrest and labor discontent at high levels.

Austerity. Jaime Paz Zamora had assumed the presidency of Bolivia in August of 1989, pledging to continue the austerity measures adopted under the New Economic Policy (NEP) of his predecessor. By adhering to the NEP guidelines, the government held inflation to a rate of 12% in 1990, the lowest in South America, and achieved an economic growth of 2.5%, compared with negative growth rates in the first half of the 1980s and hyperinflation that exceeded 14,000% in 1985, the year the NEP went into effect. The government also tightened its tax system, collecting 14% of the gross domestic product (GDP) in taxes in 1990, compared with just 1% in 1985.

Foreign Investment. Paz Zamora traveled widely during 1990, seeking foreign assistance for his country's economic recovery and new sources of foreign investment. In September the Bolivian legislature moved to reduce restrictions on foreign corporations and permit easier repatriation of profits in mining, agriculture, and tourism.

In April the government concluded negotiations with the ten largest industrial countries, which reduced the country's foreign-debt-service load and extended more concessional terms on its debt balance. A new agreement with Argentina provided for payment of Bolivian natural-gas exports to Argentina to be made in convertible currencies.

In May the United States and Bolivia signed a bilateral trade and investment agreement, a first step toward liberalized trade arrangements between the two countries. Trade between the United States and Bolivia totaled $265 million in 1989, with Bolivia in deficit by $25 million.

Drugs. International drug trafficking remained a point of contention in relations between Bolivia and the United States in 1990. Along with Peru, Bolivia is one of the principal sources of coca leaf, from which cocaine is refined. According to official estimates, Bolivian coca farmers produce 150,000 metric tons of coca each year, valued at some $500 million. Most of the processing of cocaine is done in Colombia.

Since 1986 the U.S. Drug Enforcement Agency (DEA) has provided assistance and training in antinarcotics tactics to Bolivia and Peru under a program known as "Operation Snowcap." In 1990 the U.S. government attempted to expand its efforts to include direct military assistance if the Andean countries would commit their armed forces to the drug war. The offer met resistance both in Peru and in Bolivia, where President Paz Zamora was accused by the political opposition of abetting "U.S. imperialism." In September a DEA agent was wounded in Bolivia when a joint U.S.-Bolivian antinarcotics patrol was ambushed by heavily armed drug traffickers; he was the first U.S. drug agent to be hit by hostile fire since Operation Snowcap began.

Andean Initiative. The Bush administration did not rely solely on military strategies in the drug war, however. In February, President Bush met with the presidents of Bolivia, Peru, and Colombia to discuss proposals for trade concessions to the Andean countries. The Latin leaders endorsed the so-called "Andean initiative," and called for additional U.S. assistance. In September the White House sent to the Congress a proposed Andean Trade Preference Act, which would authorize duty-free entry to the U.S. market for ten years for a number of exports from countries of the region that cooperate in antidrug efforts.

RICHARD C. SCHROEDER, *Consultant to the Organization of American States*

BOLIVIA · Information Highlights

Official Name: Republic of Bolivia.
Location: West-central South America.
Area: 424,162 sq mi (1 098 580 km²).
Population (mid-1990 est.): 7,300,000.
Chief Cities (mid-1988 est.): Sucre, the legal capital, 95,635; La Paz, the actual capital, 1,049,800; Santa Cruz de la Sierra, 615,122; Cochabamba, 377,259.
Government: *Head of state and government,* Jaime Paz Zamora, president (took office Aug. 5, 1989). *Legislature*—Congress: Senate and Chamber of Deputies.
Monetary Unit: Boliviano (3.180 bolivianos equal U.S.$1, July 1990).
Gross National Product (1988 U.S.$): $4,600,-000,000.
Economic Index (1989): *Consumer Prices* (La Paz, 1983 = 100), all items, 943,192.9; food, 852,215.3.
Foreign Trade (1989 U.S.$): *Imports,* $615,000,000; *exports,* $817,000,000.

BOSTON

Crime was on the minds of many Bostonians during 1990 as the city faced one of the most violent periods in its long history. With more than 110 murders by the end of September, police estimated that a record number of more than 150 persons would be killed by the end of the year. The number of murders was linked by police to conflicts in the drug trade.

A most startling killing had occurred on Oct. 23, 1989, but continued to reverberate throughout Boston and the nation for many months. On that date Charles Stuart and his wife Carol, seven months pregnant, were on their way home from a prenatal class at a local hospital. According to Charles Stuart, the couple were accosted by a black man who forced them to drive to a neighborhood known as Mis-

Construction is under way on wastewater treatment facilities on Deer Island in Boston's harbor. The work is part of the Massachusetts Water Resources Authority's $6.1 billion, 11-year project to clean up the well-publicized waterway.

sion Hill, where the Stuarts were shot—Carol, fatally. The Stuarts' prematurely born son died 17 days later. The crime shocked and angered the entire city and state and was reported nationally. A black man, William Bennett, was arrested and identified by Stuart in a police lineup.

Suddenly, on Jan. 4, 1990, Charles Stuart, apparently fearing that his story was unraveling under continuing police investigations, jumped from the Tobin Bridge 145 ft (44.2 m) to the Mystic River. The previous evening, Stuart's brother Matthew had confessed to Boston police that he had received a revolver and Carol Stuart's purse and engagement ring from Charles at a meeting on the deserted street where the Stuarts' car was found. The gun and purse were dropped into a river north of Boston, where police later recovered them.

The bizarre Stuart case continued to captivate many during 1990. A motive for Charles Stuart's brutal act had not been determined. None of the Stuart family were charged as accessories, although authorities mulled over the issue for many months. The Stuart family, along with Carol's family, the DiMaitis, set up a trust to help people in the Mission Hill neighborhood, and family members attended meetings and church services designed to heal the scars that the murder had created.

Schools. Boston's school system, troubled since the mid-1970s when court-ordered desegregation began, saw continued problems begin-

ning in February 1990, as the 13-member School Committee, dividing along racial lines, fired black Superintendent Laval Wilson. The action led to demands for change in the structure of the committee, which is elected directly. A proposal supported by Mayor Raymond L. Flynn creating a smaller committee of appointed and elected members failed to gain inclusion on the November ballot. In December the City Council voted to abolish the School Committee. The mayor signed the legislation, but it remained at year's end subject to final approval by the state legislature and the governor.

Major Projects. Three large public-works projects slowly advanced during the year. A plan to clean up the polluted Boston harbor, the subject of controversy for more than a decade and an issue in the 1988 presidential election, moved forward. With the federal courts insisting on rapid implementation of the plan, a key decision about the siting of contaminated grit and sludge landfill still remained to be made. A plan to build a third vehicle and rail tunnel under the harbor also inched toward reality. The tunnel would connect the downtown area with Logan International Airport across the harbor. Finally, a multibillion-dollar plan to place the Central Artery, an elevated highway that bisects the business district, underground moved ahead. The three projects were expected to aid in reviving Boston's sagging construction trades.

HARVEY BOULAY, *Rogerson House*

BRAZIL

Taking advantage of the honeymoon following his mid-March 1990 inauguration, Brazil's President Fernando Collor de Mello (*see* BI-OGRAPHY) emphasized the magic of the marketplace in crafting comprehensive economic reforms. But even as inflation declined, charges of corruption diminished the standing of Brazil's new chief executive.

Politics and Government. Immediately after taking office, Collor announced plans to restructure the nation's hugely statist, inflation-plagued economy along free-market lines. He promised to combat soaring prices, privatize inefficient public enterprises, trim the bloated federal bureaucracy, and eliminate privileges enjoyed by high officials. He also pledged to provide incentives to the business community and to tumble sky-high protectionist walls both to stimulate international trade and to encourage competition.

In the October 3 congressional elections voters favored conservative and centrist candidates sympathetic to Collor's reformist policies. All told, his supporters won about half of the 503 seats in the Chamber of Deputies, as well as a similar portion of 31 contested Senate seats. The president was delighted by the strong showing of the Liberal Front Party, which enthusiastically endorses his policies.

Old-line politicians known as "wrinklies" fared extremely well in the 27 gubernatorial elections also held on October 3. For example, five ministers from the discredited administration of former President José Sarney captured governorships. In addition, such veteran politicians as Paulo Maluf of São Paulo, Leonel Brizola of Rio de Janeiro, and Nelson Marchezan of Rio Grande do Sul made it into the November 25 runoffs for governor of their respective states. These men were accustomed to the old politics of trading support for favors, which Collor had vowed to fight. In the 15 states where gubernatorial runoffs were held, opposition candidates swept the major races.

One quarter to one third of the ballots cast in the legislative and gubernatorial elections were blank or spoiled. Several factors—complicated ballots, disdain for compulsory voting, numerous elections in recent years, and disenchantment with political mudslinging—helped explain this outcome. To distance himself from the electoral process, Collor traveled abroad during the final two weeks of the campaign.

Allegations of wrongdoing tarnished the image of Collor, who had won election on a strong anticorruption platform. In mid-October, Justice Minister Bernardo Cabral, 58, a married father of two, resigned because of a highly publicized romance with Economy Minister Zélia Cardoso de Mello, 37. Even more serious were charges by Luis Otávio da Motta Veiga that he was forced from the helm of Pe-

© Gregg Newton/Sipa

Coal miners in Brazil demonstrate for reform, mirroring the dissatisfactions of many Brazilians with problems relating to inflation, unemployment, and higher interest rates.

trobrás, the state oil company, because of his refusal to loan public funds to a well-connected businessman. According to Motta Veiga, presidential confidants such as Collor's brother-in-law urged him to release monies from Petrobrás. To restore his reputation, Collor called for an investigation of the Petrobrás accusations.

Economy. On March 15, Collor unveiled plans to slash inflation, which was running at an 84.3% rate that month, and to eliminate a $31 billion federal deficit. These measures embraced a wage and price freeze, high wealth and capital-gains taxes, the replacement of the *cruzado* with a free floating *cruzeiro* currency, the closure of 24 government enterprises, a boost in utility rates, and the privatization of state firms. This "shock" plan, which chilled economic growth, slowed price increases to 3.3% in April before they rose to 14.2% in October. Several factors combined to thwart achievement of zero inflation: Companies circumvented the freeze on bank deposits; credit purchases were resumed; and pensioners drove up demand by withdrawing funds from savings.

Collor's efforts to slash 360,000 jobs from the nation's 1.6-million-member bureaucracy ran into administrative inertia and judicial hostility. By June 18, the date that the president had set for meeting his target, senior officials had found only 100,000 jobs that could be eliminated. Meanwhile, the Supreme Court ruled that full salaries would have to be paid to government workers placed in the state of "availability." The president had hoped to pay such laid-off civil servants a reduced salary based on their years of service.

Also complicating economic reforms were elevated energy prices in a country that imports half of the 1.2 million barrels of oil it consumes each day. In November, in response to higher world prices, the government raised the cost of consumer fuels, electricity, and mass transit by between 25% and 30%.

Collor took bold steps to open the Brazilian economy. In late June he announced a sharp tariff reduction to boost efficiency in the industrial sector, one of the most protected in the world. By 1994, Brazil was to cut average duties from 35% to 20%, with maximum tariffs to be lowered from 105% to 40% in 1991. On July 1 the country eliminated the 20% tariffs on raw materials, fibers, machinery and parts, and cloth and clothing. During a transition period, duties of 40% to 85% were imposed on automobiles, chemicals, kitchen appliances, toys, and electronic equipment—items previously subjected to an import ban. To mitigate the consequences of liberalization, the government offered incentives to domestic companies that adopt new technology. It also promoted a new anti-dumping law aimed at foreign competitors, while guaranteeing businessmen "active participation" in formulating future industrial policy.

In an attempt to win friends in Washington, Collor promised that by March 1991 he would sponsor legislation to safeguard the intellectual property of foreign firms. U.S. Special Trade Representative Carla A. Hills responded to this pledge by stating her readiness to lift tariffs on Brazilian imports. Since 1988 Washington had imposed 100% duties on paper products, consumer electronics, and drugs in retaliation for Brazil's failure to provide patent protection for U.S. pharmaceuticals.

An influx of imports, higher oil charges, and lower prices for such commodities as orange juice, cocoa, soybeans, and coffee diminished export earnings. The trade surplus, originally projected at $15 billion, only approximated $9.5 billion in 1990.

International Relations. The International Monetary Fund (IMF) looked approvingly at Collor's austerity initiatives. In principle, it agreed to grant a $2 billion standby loan to Brazil, whose $112.7 billion external debt is the Third World's biggest. As part of its September 13 letter of intent to the IMF, Brazil outlined rather ambitious economic goals for 1991: reducing inflation to 25%, wiping out its $2 billion arrearage with major creditor countries, and eliminating the deficit of state-owned companies (2.5% of gross national product, GNP, in 1989). Brazil continued to encounter creditor coolness because of its refusal to make even a

---

BRAZIL · Information Highlights

Official Name: Federative Republic of Brazil.
Location: Eastern South America.
Area: 3,286,473 sq mi (8 511 965 km²).
Population (mid-1990 est.): 150,400,000.
Chief Cities (mid-1987 est.): Brasília, the capital, 1,567,709; Sao Paulo, 10,063,110; Rio de Janeiro, 5,603,388; Belo Horizonte, 2,114,429.
Government: Head of state and government, Fernando Collor de Mello, president (took office March 15, 1990). Legislature—National Congress: Senate and Chamber of Deputies.
Monetary Unit: Cruzeiro (157.1 cruzeiros equal U.S.$1, Dec. 31, 1990).
Gross Domestic Product (1989 est. U.S.$): $377,000,-000,000.
Economic Indexes (1989): Consumer Prices (Sao Paulo, 1980 = 100), all items, 47,328.1; food, 59,973.2. Industrial Production (1980 = 100), 111.
Foreign Trade (1989 U.S.$): Imports, $18,281,-000,000; exports, $34,392,000,000.

---

token payment toward $8 billion in overdue interest on its foreign commercial-bank debt. Collor insisted that domestic creditors should be paid before international ones, and that official and multilateral lenders enjoy preference over private creditors.

Science and Technology Minister José Goldemberg reported that ranchers and farmers had burned 11,600 sq mi (30 052 km²) of the Amazonian rain forest in 1989 compared with an annual average of 9,230 sq mi (23 912 km²) since 1978. All told, 8% of the rain forest has been destroyed. This mounting destruction convinced Collor to back protection of fragile areas in exchange for foreign-debt forgiveness. Former President Sarney decried such "debt-for-nature" swaps as a threat to national sovereignty.

Even before Saddam Hussein's takeover of Kuwait in August, Brazil had reduced its arm sales and energy ventures with Iraq. Still, some 500 Brazilians found themselves in Iraq at the time of the invasion. Negotiations by a high-level team obtained the release of most of the hostages. In return for their freedom the foreign ministry guaranteed that contracts signed with Iraq by private Brazilian firms would be completed once the crisis was over. High officials stressed that Brazil neither had made a secret deal with Iraq nor promised compensation in the event of noncompliance of contracts between Brazilian companies and Iraqi state enterprises. Brazil remained active in the Middle East, agreeing to supply $3 billion in arms to Saudi Arabia and other countries.

Brazil's foreign debt, the U.S. sale of a high-performance supercomputer to Brazil, and the Persian Gulf situation were among items discussed during George Bush's early December visit to Brazil. The U.S. chief executive lobbied in behalf of his Enterprise for the Americas Initiative, a plan to establish free trade throughout North and South America.

GEORGE W. GRAYSON
College of William and Mary

BRITISH COLUMBIA

A sixth successive by-election loss in December 1989 led to speculation that British Columbia's Premier William Vander Zalm of the Social Credit Party might retire, but in a January televised address, he announced that he would not step aside. Controversy over the premier's ownership and sale of a biblical theme park also made news during 1990.

Budget. In the 1990–91 budget, the provincial general-fund expenditure was estimated at C$15,260,000,000, with a projected deficit offset by a transfer of $684 million from the budget-stabilization fund. Two special funds—sustainable-environment and science and technology—were created, and tax relief was provided to homeowners through a supplement to the homeowners' grant and a new block funding system for primary and secondary schools.

Legislation. Bills passed during the sitting of the legislative assembly (April 5-July 27) included a Members Conflict of Interest Act, a Referendum Act, and (following Alberta's example) a Senatorial Selection Act. An attempt was made in the Carmanah Pacific Park Act to balance logging and environmental interests, and a new provincial university was to be established at Prince George. A Royal Commission on Health Care and Costs was appointed, and a 31-member "round table" group on the environment and the economy was formed.

Intergovernmental Relations. Premier Vander Zalm's five-point, constitutional-reform plan to resolve difficulties surrounding the Meech Lake accord found little support. The province's challenge to the federal government's capping of payments under the Canada Assistance Plan was successful in the B.C. Court of Appeal, and challenges also were joined against the federal goods and services tax, scheduled to take effect in January 1991, and the 1990 Senate appointments. During the

summer, native peoples resorted to roadblocks to draw attention to their land claims, and one blockade by Mount Currie Indians continued until early November. In October, for the first time, the provincial government agreed to take part in federal land-claim talks.

Cabinet. Resignations from the provincial cabinet grew to ten. The minister of social services resigned in May. On July 12, amid controversy surrounding a decision not to proceed with criminal charges against the former provincial secretary, Attorney General Stuart (Bud) Smith resigned. Tape recordings of his car-telephone conversations made by a reporter had been tabled in the legislature by the opposition, but subsequent investigations found no evidence of political interference in the administration of justice. In December the minister of environment resigned in a disagreement with the premier over pulp-mill emissions. A mini cabinet shuffle brought three backbenchers in along with Bud Smith, returning as minister of regional and economic development. In December efforts were launched among Social Credit constituency associations for a convention to review party leadership.

Economy. A strong Canadian dollar, high interest rates, and slow growth in North American markets resulted in slower economic growth than in the previous three years. Manufacturing shipments, particularly of forest products, fell significantly, and employment in the goods-producing sector declined steadily in the first six months of 1990. Growth in more diversified overseas markets, however, offered some reassurance.

NORMAN J. RUFF, *University of Victoria*

BULGARIA

Throughout 1990 the Bulgarian Communist Party (BCP) responded slowly to the pressure for liberalization and the demands of an opposition coalition. Finally, at year's end, it was forced to surrender control of Bulgaria.

Domestic Affairs. Following the resignation of Todor Zhivkov, leader for 35 years of the BCP, in late 1989, the BCP, under General Secretary Petar Mladenov, announced its intent to transform Bulgaria into "a modern democratic and law-governed state." Soon afterward, however, some 16 unauthorized anticommunist organizations formed a coalition, the Union of Democratic Forces (UDF), and demanded the introduction of a multiparty political system, a free-market economy, religious toleration, and a new constitution.

The beleaguered BCP initially responded by purging some notable hardliners, rehabilitating some dismissed reformers, and yielding some access to the communications media. In January 1990 the Grand National Assembly (parliament) formally enacted legislation to liberalize

AP/Wide World

In a time of greater political openness, Bulgarians sign a petition calling for the return of King Simeon, who had fled Bulgaria after a 1946 plebiscite abolished the monarchy.

the penal code, grant amnesty and rehabilitation to persons formerly convicted of political crimes, and lift the ban on establishing new political parties. On January 15 it amended the Bulgarian constitution, lifting the BCP's monopoly on political power.

The Communists, however, tried doggedly to salvage whatever power they could, but in late January, under renewed street pressures, they surrendered control of the army and police. On February 1, facing heavy censure over a lagging economy, Premier Georgi Atanasov and his entire cabinet resigned. A week later a new all-Communist cabinet was formed, headed by Andrei Lukanov, but by that time,

---

BULGARIA • Information Highlights

Official Name: People's Republic of Bulgaria.
Location: Southeastern Europe.
Area: 42,823 sq mi (110 910 km²).
Population (mid-1990 est.): 8,900,000.
Chief Cities (Dec. 31, 1987 est.): Sofia, the capital, 1,128,859; Plovdiv, 356,596; Varna, 305,891.
Government: *Head of state,* Zhelyu Zhelev, president (took office August 1990). *Head of government,* Dimitar Popov, premier (took office December 1990). *Legislature*—Grand National Assembly.
Monetary Unit: Lev (1.73 leva equal U.S.$1, July 1989).
Gross National Product (1989 est. U.S.$): $51,200,-000,000.
Economic Index (1989): *Industrial Production* (1980 = 100), 149.
Foreign Trade (1988 U.S.$): *Imports,* $16,582,-000,000; *exports,* $17,223,000,000.

---

party cohesion had begun to erode rapidly. An emergency party congress elected a new general secretary, Aleksandur Lilov, on February 2; nonetheless, on February 11, 30 reformist members split off to form an "Alternative Socialist Party." During April the BCP renamed itself the Bulgarian Socialist Party (BSP), and parliament enacted legislation for multiparty June elections. It also unanimously elected Mladenov as interim president.

June election results were surprising. The new BSP won 211 of the 400 seats in the assembly; the UDF 144. Charging fraud, intimidation, and bribery, the anticommunist parties refused to join a governmental coalition, leaving the BSP and Premier Lukanov to face Bulgaria's economic problems alone. In July, Mladenov resigned and was replaced on August 1 by Zhelyu Zhelev, former head of the UDF.

August polls indicated that 57% of Bulgarians wanted the UDF to take over the government, and later in the month the headquarters of the old BCP was ransacked and burned. On November 29, after two weeks of street demonstrations in the capital and a paralyzing nationwide four-day general strike affecting perhaps 1 million workers, Premier Lukanov also resigned. The next month leaders of the main political parties agreed to form a transitional government, headed by Dimitar Popov, a politically independent judge. New elections were scheduled for the summer of 1991.

Hallowed Communist symbols disappeared in 1990. In July the body of Bulgaria's revered Communist hero, Georgi Dimitrov, which had lain in state in Sofia since 1949, was removed and cremated. One of the first reforms that followed the fall of Zhivkov had been the ending of his six-year campaign to force the assimilation of Bulgaria's large ethnic Turkish minority. Ironically, that produced a passionate backlash among the country's predominantly Slavic population. By year's end, Zhivkov, imprisoned in Sofia, awaited trial.

Foreign Affairs. Meetings dealing with regional concerns occurred during 1990, beginning with talks early in the year between representatives of Bulgaria and Greece aimed at dealing with their resurgent ethnic Turkish minorities. In October, Bulgaria participated in a meeting of the foreign ministers of the six Balkan nations in Tiranë, Albania. During the year, Bulgaria restored diplomatic relations with Israel and the Vatican.

To aid Bulgaria's ailing economy, the Group of 24, consisting of the world's leading industrial nations, promised a restructuring of the nation's $11 billion foreign debt.

JOSEPH FREDERICK ZACEK
State University of New York at Albany

BURMA. *See* MYANMAR.

BUSINESS AND CORPORATE AFFAIRS

The financial excesses of the 1980s caught up with U.S. business in 1990, dealing a mortal blow to companies small and large, the most publicized being in finance, banking, real estate, housing, and securities. A U.S. economy that barely skirted recession through most of the year was only part of the reason why; underlying many of the problems was a burden of debt that no longer could be supported by individuals, businesses, and governments.

Business Failures. After three straight years in which business failures declined, Dun & Bradstreet reported a 14.5% rise to 43,836 in the first nine months of 1990. Collapses in finance, insurance, and real estate rose 31%. For manufacturers, the increase was 20%. Standard & Poor's Corp. said corporations defaulted on more publicly held debt than in any other year. Through October nonfinancial companies had defaulted on more than $11 billion of bonds, far more than 1989's total of $3.1 billion.

And more businesses were hurtling toward insolvency. Eastern Airlines, already in bankruptcy reorganization, was threatened with dissolution by creditors. Pan Am sought to sell routes and Continental found itself in bankruptcy court as 1990 drew to a close. Two years before, the airline industry profited by $1.7 billion; in 1990 it faced a loss of $1.2 billion in just the fourth quarter.

Debt. Corporate earnings fell for five straight quarters, including the final two of 1989. Those thought to have had the most financial acumen—bankers, brokers, insurers, and financiers—were among those most hurt. In banking and finance alone, the layoffs numbered more than 75,000. Manufacturers too were hurt; nearly 800,000 factory jobs were lost since January 1989. Some individuals and companies that had risen swiftly on borrowed money in the 1980s shrank for the same reason in 1990, unable to meet interest payments. What once was thought to be their financial daring now was called financial folly.

How extensive was corporate debt? In the 20 years before 1990, the ratio of interest expense to corporate earnings more than doubled; nonfinancial corporate borrowing as a percentage of gross national product (GNP) rose from 47% to 67%. And in the late 1980s, one half of all funds raised by nonfinancial corporations came from debt issues, the rest from equity offerings. As recently as the 1970s, the average was only 24% debt.

Downfalls. Asked why he was considering sales of assets, entrepreneur Donald Trump declared "cash is king," but he did not have it when needed. His assets were estimated to be less than liabilities, and he was spared official bankruptcy only by ceding much of his operational control to lenders. Japan's Matsushita Electric Industrial Company, in contrast, used its ample cash to purchase MCA Inc. for about $6.1 billion, the largest such purchase ever by a Japanese company in the United States.

Michael Milken, the financier whose promotion of high-risk, high-interest bonds personified the reckless money methods of the 1980s, was sentenced to ten years in jail after tearfully pleading guilty to charges of fraud, and accepting a $600 million fine. A broken man, he conceded he knew his actions were illegal. Drexel Burnham Lambert, the firm for which he worked—and earned as much as $550 million per year—collapsed and was dissolved.

Photos, AP/Wide World

Two major newsmakers of the 1990 business year were Gerald Greenwald (far left), vice chairman of Chrysler Corporation until his resignation in May, and real-estate magnate Donald Trump, who ran into business reverses that made his shaky financial empire increasingly susceptible to control by bankers and bondholders.

(*See also* STOCKS AND BONDS—*Junk Bonds.*) Charles Keating, whom the government said looted San Diego's Lincoln Savings & Loan, was in jail, unable to raise $5 million in bail, although just a few years earlier his personal fortune was estimated at about $100 million.

Retirements. It was hard to say whether William Jovanovich was victim or perpetrator. As head of an old-line publishing house to which he added his own name, making it Harcourt Brace Jovanovich, he successfully fought off a hostile takeover attempt. To do so, he borrowed an astounding $3 billion, but the victory was costly. With the company sinking under the heavy load of interest payments that forced him to sell off assets, and facing a grim future, Jovanovich retired at age 70. Former U.S. Treasury Secretary W. Michael Blumenthal also retired. In 1986 he had engineered the merger of Burrough and Sperry into the Unisys Corp., the better, he said, to make the two big computer makers competitive in world markets. But he too had relied on borrowed money. When he left the company it was burdened with $2.6 billion of borrowed money, a third-quarter loss of $357 million, a stock price that was a mere fraction of what it had been two years earlier, and had plans to eliminate 5,000 jobs, or 6% of its work force.

There were successful retirements, too. Peter Lynch, 46, sometimes called the Babe Ruth of mutual-fund management, retired as head of Fidelity's Magellan Fund, leaving those who invested with him in 1977 about 19 times richer. Roger Smith, 65, retired after ten years as General Motors chairman, replaced by engineer Robert C. Stempel. Critics pointed to an eight-percentage-point decline to 36% of the domestic car market share during his tenure, but supporters said he left the company, still the world's largest manufacturer, far more efficient and able to compete. Lee Iacocca, also 65, surprised many people, including his heir apparent, Gerald Greenwald, when he chose to continue as chairman at Chrysler. Greenwald left to lead a union effort to buy the parent company of United Airlines.

Areas of Gain. Not all businesses, industries, and geographic areas felt the pinch equally. Farmers did better than in previous years and the Midwest "rust belt" performed with strength through much of the year. Health-care costs continued out of control but many new companies were formed to monitor hospital stays, arrange at-home care, and handle insurance claims (*see* page 351). Soaring oil prices spurred wildcat drillers; late in the year close to 1,000 rigs were operating, up from 858 units in 1989. And, while the falling value of the U.S. dollar reflected some loss of prestige, it enabled exporters to compete aggressively abroad. McDonald's invaded the USSR with its largest-ever restaurant. General Motors earned more abroad than domestically.

New Times Ahead. Analysts often said the year 1990 might have been a turning point for U.S. companies. They were more export-oriented than ever before, intent on recapturing all those dollars sent abroad during the 1980s, and trying to reduce debt to carry out that mission more ably. It was a contrast to the 1980s, when credit was cool. Now debt was dumb.

JOHN CUNNIFF, *The Associated Press*

CALIFORNIA

A race for governor attracted less voter interest than either candidate desired, while an avalanche of ballot propositions confronted those who did go to the polls. A budget impasse, drought, devastating brush fires, and a December cold snap also were news in California in 1990.

Election. The primary turnout was the lowest in 30 years, despite a vigorous contest for the Democratic nomination. The winner of the Democratic primary, former San Francisco Mayor Dianne Feinstein, was defeated by U.S. Sen. Pete Wilson in the general election. Turnout was again low—59% of registered voters—despite Republican efforts to encourage the use of absentee votes. An unusually large number of important ballot propositions attracted attention. Most of them were defeated, including a wide-ranging environmental-protection proposition known as "Big Green." It was attacked as being too vague and uncertain in effect. Almost all the $3.3 billion in construction bonds submitted by the legislature were rejected. Voters approved a proposal limiting the number of terms that can be served by legislators and state officials.

The legislature remained heavily Democratic. It will apportion new Congressional districts in 1992, when California gains seven seats in the U.S. House of Representatives. The new total of 52 members would be the largest delegation from a single state in the nation's history and results from California's 23.7% population increase during the 1980s. With an official 1990 population of 29,839,250, one in eight U.S. residents now lives in California.

Budget. The final state budget was a record 43 days late, a victim of long-standing disagreements between the governor and legislative leaders. Gov. George Deukmejian presented a $53.7 billion budget, with nearly a $2 billion revenue gap, in January. By mid-May it was clear that the deficit would be about $3.6 billion, a result of smaller-than-expected tax collections, swelling mandatory appropriations, and increased service demands by the state's growing population. Months of compromise efforts followed over how to handle the shortfall. Legislative leaders favored more taxes, but the governor said he would veto any general tax increase. He favored cuts, mostly in welfare

© Sam Mircovich/Sipa

California U.S. Sen. Pete Wilson (center), flanked by his wife and outgoing Gov. George Deukmejian, defeated the Democratic former mayor of San Francisco, Dianne Feinstein, in November elections to win the state's gubernatorial race.

areas. The result was a reduction in social and educational programs, with some tax increases.

Spurred by the 1989 Alaskan oil spill, the legislature created a plan to deal with coastal oil spills, one of which occurred in February off Huntington Beach. Lawmakers failed to break the impasse on auto insurance premium rates or on medical insurance for those not now covered.

Corruption. In February, State Sen. Joseph B. Montoya was convicted in federal court on seven counts of extortion, racketeering, and money laundering. He was California's first legislator in 35 years to be convicted on corruption charges while in office. He resigned and

was sentenced to six and a half years in prison. Former Sen. Paul Carpenter was convicted on similar charges in September. The FBI investigation of other state officials continued.

Weather. California, in its fourth year of a drought, with the Sierra snowpack at 50% of normal, was increasingly susceptible to fires. Especially hard hit was the Santa Barbara area, where a fire in June caused $50 million in damages, including the loss of at least 25 homes. In Glendale, 64 homes were destroyed or damaged, including more than 20 in a canyon left unprotected so equipment could be deployed at the front of the fire. Losses totaled about $19 million. Several other serious fires were made worse by the dry conditions.

In December southern California was hit by unusual below-freezing temperatures that caused extensive damage to the state's citrus, vegetable, and flower crops. The damage, estimated in the hundreds of millions of dollars, probably would bring higher prices for supermarket fruits and vegetables.

Nixon Library. The Richard Nixon presidential library and museum, delayed for years, was opened in July at Yorba Linda, the former president's boyhood home. Unlike other presidential libraries, it was built and would be run entirely with private funds. Its $21 million cost made it the most expensive such library to date. (*See* page 89.)

Universities. The University of California, Berkeley, which had been accused of unfairness in admissions of Asian-Americans, named Chang-Lin Tien as its chancellor in February. Tien, who was born in China, was a mechanical

---

CALIFORNIA • Information Highlights

Area: 158,706 sq mi (411 049 km²).
Population (1990 census prelim.): 29,279,000.
Chief Cities (July 1, 1988 est.): Sacramento, the capital, 338,220; Los Angeles, 3,352,710; San Diego, 1,070,310; San Francisco, 731,600; San Jose, 738,420; Long Beach, 415,040; Oakland, 356,860.
Government (1990): *Chief Officers*—governor, George Deukmejian (R); lt. gov., Leo McCarthy (D). *Legislature*—Senate, 40 members; Assembly, 80 members.
State Finances (fiscal year 1989): *Revenue,* $81,708,000,000; *expenditure,* $72,583,000,000.
Personal Income (1989): $579,189,000,000; per capita, $19,929.
Labor Force (June 1990): *Civilian labor force,* 14,852,900; *unemployed,* 742,600 (5.0% of total force).
Education: *Enrollment* (fall 1988)—public elementary schools, 3,317,194; public secondary, 1,300,926; colleges and universities, 1,753,564. *Public school expenditures* (1989–90), $22,308,738,000.

engineer and a vice-chancellor at the university's Irvine campus. W. Ann Reynolds, chancellor of the state university and college system since 1982, resigned in April after legislators objected to large salary increases (21% to 43%) given in secret to her and other top officers and to extensive improvements to her state-owned home. The raises were rescinded and a search begun for a successor.

CHARLES R. ADRIAN
University of California, Riverside

CAMBODIA

In 1990, after 20 years of bitter factional warfare in which many foreign powers took part, Cambodia finally moved closer to peace.

The four Cambodian factions and their foreign supporters are: the government of Hun Sen, based in Phnom Penh, which was installed by Vietnam and supported by Moscow; the Communist Khmer Rouge, aided by China; and two non-Communist groups, led by Prince Norodom Sihanouk and Son Sann, a former prime minister. The latter groups were aided by the United States, but Hun Sen and the Khmer Rouge were more powerful militarily.

Peace Plans. In 1989, Australia proposed that the United Nations be given a mandate to police a cease-fire in Cambodia, organize elections, and run the country until a freely elected government was in place. The first sign that this might be acceptable to the warring factions came at a conference organized by Japan in June 1990. At the Tokyo conference, Prince Sihanouk and Hun Sen agreed to the creation of a Supreme National Council (SNC), which would provide a degree of Cambodian influence over the transition period, when the country would be largely under UN control.

Under the formula agreed to in Tokyo, Hun Sen would be assigned six seats on the SNC, while the other three factions each would have two seats. Several factions later raised objections to this formula, but they seemed to be moving toward agreement by year's end.

Meanwhile, in July the United States announced it no longer would support the claim of the three Cambodian resistance groups (led by the Khmer Rouge, Sihanouk, and Son Sann)

to Cambodia's UN seat. Moreover, the United States would open a dialogue with Vietnam to seek an end to the Cambodian conflict. The main reason for this was that the U.S. Congress was unwilling to provide any further support to the Khmer Rouge, who had killed as many as 1 million Cambodians when they ruled the country in the 1970s.

The new U.S. policy seemed to stimulate further conciliatory moves by other countries. In August the Soviet and Chinese foreign ministers agreed to stop arming Hun Sen's group and the Khmer Rouge. And China and Vietnam, which long had been at odds over Cambodia, began to discuss normalizing their relations.

The Agreement. Finally, on August 28 the five permanent members of the UN Security Council (Britain, China, France, the Soviet Union, and the United States) agreed on the concept of placing Cambodia under UN control until an elected government was in place. Their plan also spelled out how a UN force would supervise a truce during the transition period, conduct free elections, protect human rights, and provide guarantees for Cambodia's future neutrality.

Although the agreement was signed by the main foreign supporters of the Cambodian factions (China, the USSR, and the United States) it could not be implemented unless the Cambodians themselves accepted it. In early September, Indonesia and France hosted a meeting of the faction leaders in Jakarta. On September 10 the Cambodian faction leaders announced they had accepted the plan to place Cambodia under UN administration while elections were being organized. The Cambodians also agreed to set up the SNC to embody Cambodian sovereignty during the transition. It was decided to hold another meeting in Paris to develop concrete plans to implement this agreement.

Another meeting at Jakarta in November failed to resolve fully the question of who would serve on the SNC. While all the Cambodian and outside parties seemed committed to moving ahead, it looked as if it would be sometime in 1991 before the UN peacekeeping and administrative body could be put in place.

The UN program was similar in some respects to ones that have been carried out recently by the UN in Nicaragua and Namibia. It reflected the growing cooperation between the United States and the USSR to resolve regional conflicts. The program in Cambodia was expected to involve up to 10,000 peacekeeping troops and an equal number of civilian administrators. It might take several years to implement and cost as much as $10 billion before the operation is complete. Under UN rules, Washington will be required to pay one quarter of the costs.

PETER A. POOLE
Author, "Eight Presidents and Indochina"

CAMBODIA • Information Highlights

Official Name: Cambodia.
Location: Southeast Asia.
Area: 69,900 sq mi (181 040 km²).
Population (mid-1990 est.): 7,000,000.
Chief City (1989 est.): Phnom Penh, the capital, 800,000.
Government: *Head of state,* Heng Samrin (took office 1979). *Head of government,* Hun Sen, prime minister (took office Jan. 1985).
Monetary Unit: Riel (218 riels equal U.S.$1, November 1989).

Attention was focused on the Canadian Senate as Prime Minister Brian Mulroney used an arcane constitutional clause to appoint eight additional Conservatives to the body in an effort to pass a goods and services tax.

CANADA

The year 1990 saw the failure of the Meech Lake compromise, which was supposed to have reconciled Quebec to the 1982 constitution. In addition, Indian land claims led to violence, a summer-long standoff near Montreal, and a national crisis of conscience. Attempts to impose a new national consumption tax led to a further standoff between the government and the Canadian Senate. By no coincidence, the Mulroney government fell to a record low in opinion polls.

Meech Lake. Since 1985 the federal government in Ottawa, and Quebec and the other nine provinces had worked to heal the 1982 rift created by Quebec's refusal to accept former Prime Minister Pierre Elliott Trudeau's constitutional reforms. In June 1987 a complex compromise was adopted by all 11 first ministers, subject to legislative ratification. Christened for the government conference center where it was conceived, the Meech Lake accord recognized Quebec's special role in immigration policy and its status as the expression of a "distinct [French-speaking] society." It gave all provinces a voice in the selection of members of the Senate and the Supreme Court and fiscal compensation if Ottawa introduced national policies in areas of provincial jurisdiction such as health, education, or welfare. Unanimity would be needed to introduce new provinces.

The 1987 unanimity soon shredded away. Former Prime Minister Trudeau attacked a deal that, in his view, surrendered too much to the provinces and gave Quebec an open-ended right to go its own way. Quebec's Bill 178, adopted in 1989, restored most of the former ban on English-language signs. That helped fuel an antibilingualism backlash in Ontario (where 50 municipalities voted to be English-only) and in the West. Voters in three provinces defeated governments that had backed the Meech Lake compromise. New Brunswick's Premier Frank McKenna demanded a fresh compromise. Manitoba's Gary Filmon, a Conservative, had favored the accord but held power only with support from Liberals and New Democrats who opposed it. Neither province had ratified the deal. In March 1990, Newfoundland's Clyde Wells, a former Trudeau aide, rescinded his province's former support. Outside Quebec, where the deal was supported by all but hard-core separatists, support for Meech faded with the popularity of the Mulroney government. Still, most observers assumed that, somehow, the prime minister's negotiating skills would pull the deal through.

It would not be easy. Having made compromises to get provincial unanimity in 1987, Quebec's Premier Robert Bourassa flatly refused any further concessions. A resurgence of the separatist Parti Québécois—which won 40% of the vote in Quebec's 1989 election—left him no room to maneuver. Yet McKenna, Filmon, and Wells demanded change. Feminists insisted that the Meech Lake accord gave nothing to women. Furious that first ministers could agree about Quebec but not about defining aboriginal rights, Indian groups added their protests. Specifically, they noted, the unanimity rule about new provinces would make it more difficult for northern territories, where Indians predominate, to achieve provincial status. Faced with discord and a ratification deadline of June 23, a parliamentary task force under Jean Charest toured the country seeking compromise. When it reported, suggesting changes acceptable at least to New Brunswick, Mulroney's Quebec lieutenant and close friend Lucien Bouchard resigned from the government in protest.

The Meech accord had been born in two marathon all-night sessions in 1987; hoping it

---

THE CANADIAN MINISTRY

M. Brian Mulroney, prime minister
Harvie Andre, minister of state and leader of the government in the House of Commons
Perrin Beatty, minister of national health and welfare
Pierre Blais, minister of consumer and corporate affairs and minister of state for agriculture
Benoit Bouchard, minister of industry, science, and technology
Pierre H. Cadieux, solicitor general of Canada
Kim Campbell, minister of justice and attorney general of Canada
Joe Clark, secretary of state for external affairs
Mary Collins, associate minister of national defense and minister responsible for the status of women
Jean Corbeil, minister of labor and minister of state for transport
John C. Crosbie, minister for international trade
Marcel Danis, minister of state for youth, minister of state for fitness and amateur sports, and deputy leader for the government in the House of Commons
Robert R. De Cotret, minister for the environment
Paul Dick, minister of supply and services
Jake Epp, minister of energy, mines, and resources
Tom Hockin, minister of state for small business and tourism
Otto J. Jelinek, minister of national revenue
Monique Landry, minister for external relations
Doug Lewis, minister of transport
Gilles Loiselle, minister of state for finance and president of the Treasury Board
Elmer M. MacKay, minister of public works and minister for the purposes of the Atlantic Canada Opportunities Agency Act
Shirley Martin, minister of state for Indian affairs and northern development
Marcel Masse, minister of communications
Charles J. Mayer, minister of western economic diversification and minister of state for grains and oilseeds
Donald F. Mazankowski, deputy prime minister, president of Queen's Privy Council for Canada, and minister of agriculture
John McDermid, minister of state for privatization and regulatory affairs
Barbara J. McDougall, minister of employment and immigration
William H. McKnight, minister of national defense
Gerald S. Merrithew, minister of veterans affairs
Lowell Murray, leader of the government in the Senate and minister of state for federal-provincial relations
Frank Oberle, minister of forestry
Alan Redway, minister of state for housing
Thomas E. Siddon, minister of Indian affairs and northern development
Bernard Valcourt, minister of fisheries and oceans
Monique Vézina, minister of state for employment and immigration, and minister of state for seniors
Gerald Weiner, secretary of state of Canada and minister of state for multiculturalism and citizenship
Michael H. Wilson, minister of finance
William Winegard, minister of science

---

could be saved the same way, and using the imminent deadline to raise the stakes, Mulroney summoned all ten provincial premiers to Ottawa on June 3. A dinner meeting turned into a weeklong marathon for 11 men and their advisers. Moods rose and fell. At one point Bourassa withdrew rather than discuss compromises. At another point Clyde Wells' walkout was blocked physically by Alberta Premier Don Getty, a former football player. Ontario's Premier David Peterson broke the logjam by promising to give up some of his province's 24 Senate seats to provinces with only six seats. Just in time for late-night television on Saturday, June 9, a shaky "companion agreement" appeared to open up Senate reform, promised to protect legal equality of the sexes, offered a legal opinion minimizing the constitutional significance of the "distinct society" clause, and promised a vote in the dissenting legislatures by June 23.

It did not happen. Meech Lake critics denounced decisions made by "11 middle-class white males" and scorned the companion agreement. Premier Wells, fundamentally unreconciled, became a national hero to the anti-Meech majority in English-speaking Canada. So did an unexpected figure, Elijah Harper, a Cree chief and New Democrat member of the Manitoba legislature. Though Filmon and the two other party leaders had yielded to the Ottawa compromise, Harper was free to use the rules of the Manitoba legislature to stall discussion and a vote. Indian leaders ignored federal promises and blandishments. Despite frenzied efforts by Ottawa to get a decision from Newfoundland, Wells cheerfully left it to Harper to kill the accord. When the Manitoba legislature adjourned without a vote on June 22, Meech Lake was dead.

With it, something died in the Confederation, too. For a second time Quebec was excluded from Canada's constitution, this time despite the best efforts of its most pro-federalist leaders. Quebeckers celebrated St. Jean-Baptiste Day, their national holiday, with what most observers described as "serene certainty" that their independence was now inevitable. Bourassa announced that Quebec henceforth would negotiate unilaterally with Ottawa and that a commission representative of all viewpoints would explore constitutional futures. While some Meech opponents claimed that English Canada would emerge from the crisis with a new unity, four western premiers met in Lloydminster in July to plan a "partnership for prosperity" and to announce that they would be as bilateral as Quebec in future negotiations with Ottawa. Ontario's David Peterson, who had worked hard to bridge the differences with Quebec, was voted out of office on September 6. On November 1, Prime Minister Mulroney announced the formation of a 12-member commission, headed by former

© Raffi Kirdi/PonoPresse Internationale

Mohawk Indians living near Oka, Que., 19 mi (30 km) west of Montreal, blocked a local road to reinforce a claim to land proposed for a golf course. A long clash between the Indians and police aided by government troops resulted.

Official Languages Commissioner Keith Spicer, to listen to Canadians' views about the future of Canada.

First Nations. For an Indian politician to change Canada's constitutional history fitted a year when "first nation" issues dominated national news as seldom before. Canadians had to address Indian frustration over unresolved land claims, unfulfilled treaty promises, and a vaguer insistence on sovereignty. Indian demands overlay the widespread poverty and despair of 466,000 people on more than 2,200 reserves, and another million Métis (mixed-bloods), Innu, and "nonstatus Indians" off reserves. Damning statistics reminded Canadians that Indian life expectancy was eight years under the national average, infant mortality was up to double the white average, and most reserve residents were unemployed chronically.

In the spring, claims settlements for 7,000 Yukon Indians, 13,000 Déné and Métis of the Mackenzie Valley, and 17,000 Inuit of the Eastern Arctic seemed to set the stage for a year of overdue progress. Supreme Court decisions recognized almost unlimited hunting and fishing for Nova Scotia and British Columbia Indians. A $7 million Nova Scotia inquiry recommended a full apology and $965,000 in compensation for Donald Marshall, a Micmac who had served 11 years in prison for a murder he had not committed. In Manitoba an official inquiry showed how the justice system failed Indian communities. A solution was Indian self-government and an Indian justice system.

Yet at Akwasasne, a Mohawk reserve straddling Quebec, Ontario, and New York state, a dispute over gambling casinos led to two deaths and anger that white authorities had failed to intervene when Indian policing collapsed.

Indian land claims remained a dominant issue, especially in British Columbia and Alberta, and in Quebec, where Mohawks set up a roadblock near their settlement of Kanesatake outside the village of Oka to reinforce a 250-sq-mi (648-km²) claim that included land proposed for a golf course. The courts were unsympathetic and an injunction was issued to end the disruption. At dawn on July 11, 100 police advanced on the Mohawks, who were armed with automatic weapons. In the fusillade that followed, an officer died and the police withdrew, leaving several patrol cars to be added to the roadblock. At Kahnewake, near Montreal, Mohawks immediately blockaded the Mercier Bridge, closing a major commuter route to the south shore of the St. Lawrence. Police isolated the area. Outside Quebec, Indian sympathizers blocked the major transcontinental rail lines, barricaded highways, and toppled a few electricity pylons.

Indians and civil-rights activists condemned the police for violence and the Mulroney government for failing to negotiate. The federal government, responsible for Indian affairs, bought the disputed golf-course land and announced that it would negotiate when the Mohawks laid down their arms. Residents of Oka, cut off by the Mohawk and police lines, abandoned their homes. Chateauguay commuters, faced with extra hours of driving to get to work, burned effigies of Mohawks, wrestled with police, and demanded action. Since most Indians were English-speaking and won overwhelming sympathy from media and civil-liberties groups outside Quebec, the dispute added to French-English friction.

The affair provided Canadian and foreign media with a major summer-long story. On August 17, after carloads of women, children, and elderly Mohawks were stoned by angry whites, the Bourassa government called in troops to assist the police. Soldiers of the Royal 22e Regiment won a public-relations battle by calmly enduring abuse and threats and, on August 29, patiently pushing the well-armed Indians and their allies back from their barricades. The Kanesatake Mohawks gave up on September 26, insisting that they had done all they could to bring Indian rights to the top of the Canadian agenda.

Politics. Underlying public response to both Meech Lake and the Mohawk standoff was the deep unpopularity of the Mulroney government. By September the Conservatives had reached a record low of 15% in the opinion polls. A deepening economic recession, job losses blamed on the Canada-U.S. Free Trade agreement, and a new goods and services tax (GST) to take effect on Jan. 1, 1991, were reasons enough.

As a replacement for a 13.5% manufacturers' sales tax, Finance Minister Michael Wilson insisted that the 7% GST would be "revenue neutral," but Canadians faced with their first-ever tax on haircuts, parking fees, and postage stamps did not believe him. Exemptions, ranging from groceries to stocks and bonds, added enormously to the complications and administrative costs. By the time the House of Commons passed the new tax, 74% of Canadians claimed to be opposed. Two Alberta Conservative members of Parliament (MPs) who opposed it were suspended promptly by their party and one of them, David Kilgour, later joined the Liberals. As for free trade, its potential blessings were hidden largely in the shadow of the deepening continent-wide recession and by the loss of 100,000 manufacturing jobs in Ontario alone.

Faced with the problem of how to prevent the Liberal majority in the Senate from killing the GST, Mulroney filled 11 available vacan-

---

CANADA · Information Highlights

Official Name: Canada.
Location: Northern North America.
Area: 3,851,792 sq mi (9 976 140 km²).
Population (mid-1990 est.): 26,600,000.
Chief Cities (1986 census): Ottawa, the capital, 300,763; Montreal, 1,015,420; Toronto, 612,289.
Government: *Head of state,* Elizabeth II, queen; represented by Ray Hnatyshyn, governor-general (took office January 1990). *Head of government,* M. Brian Mulroney, prime minister (took office Sept. 17, 1984). *Legislature*—Parliament: Senate and House of Commons.
Monetary Unit: Canadian dollar (1.1597 dollars equal U.S.$1, Nov. 23, 1990).
Gross Domestic Product (1989 est. U.S.$): $513,600,000,000.
Economic Index: *Consumer Prices* (1989, 1980 = 100), all items, 169.9; food, 157.0.
Foreign Trade (1989 U.S.$): *Imports,* $113,975,000,000; *exports,* $116,013,000,000.

---

cies in the upper house with loyal Tories; then, over a cacophony of political protests and court challenges, he used a prerogative allowed to him by section 26 of the Constitution Act to add eight more, giving the Conservatives a two-vote edge. The outnumbered Liberals used procedure tricks and a filibuster to delay a vote on the tax, which passed in mid-December.

It was a good time for the opposition parties. The New Democratic Party (NDP) won its first-ever Quebec seat in a federal by-election when Phil Edmonston, the U.S.-born founder of the Automobile Protection Association, won in Chambly. Liberals soared in the polls as candidates vied for the party leadership. Of the aspirants, rookie MP Paul Martin, former head of Canada Steamship Lines, favored Meech Lake; so did Hamilton MP Sheila Copps. Tom Wappel, a Toronto MP, ran as a pro-life candidate as did John Nunziata. All were eclipsed by

Canada's Liberal Party selected Joseph-Jacques Jean Chrétien, 56-year-old longtime party activist, as its tenth leader at its June convention in Calgary. In December, Chrétien was elected to the House of Commons from a New Brunswick riding.

© Brian Willer/"Maclean's"

the veteran Trudeau cabinet minister, 56-year-old Jean Chrétien (*see* BIOGRAPHY), who had opposed Meech but covertly supported attempts at a last-minute compromise. On June 23, at the end of a four-day convention in Calgary, Chrétien emerged as the new leader of the Liberal Party, having received nearly 60% of the delegates' votes.

Chrétien's Meech Lake stand, exploited by Martin and Copps, hurt him in his native Quebec and led him to seek election in Beauséjour, a seemingly safe seat in the Acadian region of New Brunswick. Failure in two summer by-elections, defeats in Ontario and Manitoba provincial elections, and a sharp fall in the opinion polls, especially in Quebec, told nervous Liberals that their new leader was no guarantee of victory, even against Brian Mulroney. The NDP's new leader, Audrey McLaughlin, dismissed by many in the media as a disappointment, could point to two by-election victories (including Oshawa in August), an unexpected NDP win in Ontario and a second-place finish in Manitoba, and a narrow national lead of 34% in the polls in late November.

Labor. The Canadian Labour Congress reelected Shirley Carr as president, although 30% of the delegates favored Alberta's Dave Werlin, a far more radical choice. Union membership kept rising, but more slowly than the work force. Unionists blamed wage increases lower than inflation and a lack of militancy that cut strikes to one quarter the rate in the 1970s. Though unions learned that their right to strike was not protected by the Charter of Rights and Freedoms, it was a militant year with serious strikes in the steel and construction industries and a short but successful battle by the Canadian Auto Workers against the big three automakers for better compensation in the event of plant closure. Major steel strikes were longer and more crippling; union victories were offset by long-term layoffs.

External Affairs. If domestic affairs were rancorous in 1990, Canada's relations with the rest of the world began hopefully. A February meeting between North Atlantic Treaty Organization (NATO) and Warsaw Pact representatives allowed Canada and Hungary to lead discussions on open-skies proposals. In Ottawa officials sought ways to produce a peace dividend from Canada's C$12 billion defense budget. Canada's reward for supporting the United States at the seven industrialized democracies' summit in Houston in July was a promise of U.S.-Canadian negotiations on an acid-rain accord. However, Canadian farmers, about to harvest a bumper crop and desperate at the U.S.-Europe grain price war, received no definite relief.

Then came Iraq's invasion of Kuwait. Canada refitted two destroyers, the 18-year-old *Athabaskan* and the 31-year-old *Terra Nova*, and the supply ship *Protecteur*, and dispatched

© Peter Bregg/"Maclean's"
U.S. President Bush joined Prime Minister Mulroney and his son Mark at the SkyDome for the Toronto Blue Jays' home opener. The two leaders consulted frequently during 1990.

them to the Persian Gulf. A squadron of CF-18 aircraft from Canada's NATO contingent went to Qatar in October. Opposition critics complained that the government's haste suggested that the United States, not the United Nations, had given the orders, but Canadians did not seem much concerned.

People and Society. Though few Canadians noticed, Canada's 24th governor-general since confederation, Ramon Hnatyshyn (*see* BIOGRAPHY), took office. A predecessor, Georges Vanier, was being considered for canonization by the Roman Catholic church. As convention dictated, when Chief Justice Brian Dickson retired, his successor was a French-Canadian, Justice Antonio Lamer, a former Montreal criminal lawyer appointed to the bench by the Trudeau government in 1980. Other vacancies were filled by more conventionally Conservative appointments.

In a year of bruising controversy, the government hoped to cool one hot issue in a second attempt to provide an acceptable abortion law. The new law made abortion available at any stage if the physical, mental, or psychological health of the mother was in danger. Kim Campbell, a new, ostensibly pro-choice minister of justice, backed the law; pro-choice and antiabortion groups did not. It passed by 140–131 votes with 13 Conservatives joining the opposition. Campbell assured doctors that they would not be victimized by pro-life prosecutions, but many practitioners announced that they would not run the risk.

In 1990 as the government's Green Plan emerged for environmentalists, Benoit Bouchard's resignation from the environment ministry undermined the government's campaign. The hottest controversy broke over whether Bouchard's successor, Robert De Cotret, had assented in Saskatchewan's decision to ignore federal court rulings requiring review and to complete the Rafferty and Alameda dams on the Souris River.

In the year of Meech, Oka, and the GST, some observers wondered what had happened to the Canadian self-image of tolerance and compromise. In the West posters and buttons spread hatred of visible minorities and the Alberta government professed itself powerless when the Aryan Nation held a camp at Provost. When the government agreed to let Sikhs wear turbans with their Royal Canadian Mounted Police uniforms, a Calgary Mountie tabled 125,000 hostile signatures.

On a lighter side, the interminable hockey season ended with the Boston Bruins at the head of the National Hockey League, only to collapse in the play-offs against the Edmonton Oilers. Toronto's Blue Jays again frustrated local baseball fans by fading in the final stretch. Kurt Browning won his second world figure-skating championship. Justice Charles Dubin reported on the use of drugs by athletes and urged that Ben Johnson, the sprinter whose 1988 Olympic disqualification had exposed the scandal, should be allowed to run again for Canada. Sports officials, anxious for a box-office drawing card, agreed.

DESMOND MORTON
Erindale College, University of Toronto

The Economy

The year 1990 led Canadians into an economic recession. Massive layoffs in the manufacturing sector, dwindling housing starts, and low retail sales were producing a rippling effect through all sectors of the Canadian economy. In August the value of factory shipments and new orders for the manufacturing sector fell by 1.4% and 1.1%, respectively. The sector had been experiencing significant structural shifts as companies endeavored to improve their competitive position by shifting resources from plant to plant and country to country. These shifts caused a permanent loss of jobs in the auto-parts, tire-production, and meat-packing industries.

More serious was the collapse of consumers' confidence in the economy due to expected further deterioration in the job market. Consequently, demand for consumer loans at the major Canadian banks was flagging as the 1990 forecast of a 12% rise in loans was clipped to 5%. Seasonally adjusted sales of expensive items, such as appliances and household furniture, for the year ended September 1990 dwindled 10.3%, while vehicle purchases were off 5.7%. Even grocery-store and supermarket sales grew by less than the rate of inflation. The sluggishness in consumer spending was rectified partially by an increase in government ex-

© Chris Schwartz/"Maclean's"

Torontonians express their opposition to the proposed goods and services tax. Sentiment against the 7% GST, which would replace a 13.5% manufacturers' sales tax, was high.

penditure by 2.6% during the second quarter of 1990. But the whopping C$350 billion of public debt, which continued to grow at an annual rate of C$30 million, eliminated any possibility of further expansion in government expenditure during the remainder of 1990.

Again the housing market, with sales of existing homes plummeting 31% for the year ended September 1990, experienced the worst hit since the 1981–82 recession. This lulled residential construction activity. The housing starts in September dropped to 15,416, creating an annualized rate of 144,000—the lowest in 5½ years. In addition, firms' enthusiasm to invest in their plants was dampened by weak domestic demand, dwindling after-tax profits, uncertainty caused by the Persian Gulf crisis, and controversy surrounding the imposition of the goods and services tax.

Business capital spending was down 2.2% in the second quarter, leaving it 3.8% below its level a year earlier. In the international-trade sector, the high value of the Canadian dollar sharply reduced the competitiveness of several export industries. The second-quarter rise in exports by 4.9% was just an aberration attributed to a temporary surge in auto exports in June. Overall the value of exports for the year, even after taking account of a 32% gain in grain exports, was expected to rise by a meager 1.4% to C$144 billion.

The Canadian inflation rate remained steady at 4.1% for the first eight months of the year. In September gasoline prices were up 1.7%, pushing up transportation and home-heating costs. Wage increases were showing no signs of softening as annual wages rose in the third quarter by 6.5%, up from 5.4% in the second quarter. Hence while the specter of inflation continued to haunt the system, Canada's seasonally adjusted jobless rate in November touched 9.1%, the highest jobless level since September 1987.

R. P. SETH, *Mount Saint Vincent University*

The Arts

The Canadian Broadcasting Corporation (CBC), the country's largest employer of artistic talent, again faced tough budget controls which would see C$240 million cut over six years. (In 1989 it had been ordered to cut C$140 million over five years.) CBC also faced prospects of federal legislation that would change it radically by ending its mandate to foster national unity. There would be separate English and French programs. CBC president Gérard Veilleux and CBC chairman Patrick Watson opposed both plans.

The CBC's 24-hour news and information service, *CBC Newsworld*, completed its first year without a break but had stringent budget limitations. Increasing CBC's advertising revenue was a daunting prospect as the economy faced uncertain times that made national advertising less attractive than cheaper local advertising. The Vancouver, B.C., outlet of CBC, which previously had lost much of its production time, received a big increase in productions in the fall TV schedule. The CBC's once highly popular TV series *The Beachcombers* was canceled after appearing weekly for 19 years. A low-key story about log-salvage workers on British Columbia's Sunshine Coast, it was canceled due to low ratings. It starred Bruno Gerussi as Nick and Robert Clothier as Relic.

Meanwhile CBC radio took three gold medals at New York's International Radio Festival in competition with 15 other countries. CBC won in the history category for *Lost Innocence: The Children of World War II*, in sports for *The Tragedy of Birgid Russell*, and in writing for *Suffering Fools*.

Visual Arts. The National Gallery of Art in Ottawa exhibited 180 works by famed Victoria, B.C., artist Emily Carr, whose blazing oils depicted nature and Northwest Indian themes. The show was assembled by Doris Shadbolt. Since Carr's death in 1945 her popularity and prices have increased enormously. At the Art Gallery of Ontario, "Towards a Lyrical Abstraction" showed the powerful nature scenes of the late L.A.C. Panton. The Gallery also presented "Lucius R. O'Brien: Visions of Victorian Canada," showing the landscapes of Canada's leading painter of the 1870s. The Montreal Museum of Fine Arts treated the public to a magnificent show, "The Passionate Eye: Impressionist and Other Master Paintings," from the collection of Emil G. Buehrle. It comprised 85 works by Renoir, Degas, Van Gogh, Manet, Monet, and others.

"Voice of Fire," a painting which the late U.S. abstract expressionist Barnett Newman did for Expo 67, became the most celebrated picture in Canada. The huge painting, 18 ft (5.5 m) tall by 8 ft (2.4 m) wide, consists of three equal-sized vertical stripes: a bright red stripe

National Gallery of Canada, Ottawa
Reproduced courtesy of Annalee Newman
Barnett Newman's "Voice of Fire," which was purchased for C$1.76 million by the National Gallery of Canada, was Canada's most viewed and discussed painting of 1990.

bordered on either side by a dark blue stripe. The furor started with the announcement that the National Gallery of Canada in Ottawa had bought it for C$1.76 million (U.S.$1.5 million), more than half of the gallery's annual acquisition budget. Felix Holtmann, chairman of the House of Commons cultural committee, criticized the gallery for spending so much on a U.S. painting rather than for Canadian ones. Indignant letters flooded the newspapers, saying in essence that the work could be duplicated in ten minutes with two cans of paint and a brush. Artists rallying to the other side pointed out that copying was a lot easier than creating and that Newman was an important figure. In its own defense, the gallery explained that the money came from the non-Canadian share of the acquisition fund so that it could not have bought Canadian paintings with it.

Shirley L. Thompson, director of the National Gallery, told members of the Commons cultural committee that "'Voice of Fire' is a dramatic witness to Newman's uncontested place in the history of painting and a priceless record of a key moment in the evolution of art in North America." A gallery official stated that gallery attendance increased due to all the publicity about the picture.

The Shaw Festival at Niagara-on-the-Lake opened its 1990 season with a well-received version of George Bernard Shaw's 1910 play "Misalliance," starring (l-r) Sharry Flett, Simon Bradbury, and Barry MacGregor.

Performing Arts. The Stratford (Ont.) Festival opened its 38th season with Shakespeare's *Macbeth*, directed by David William and Robert Beard and with Brian Bedford as Macbeth and Goldie Semple as Lady Macbeth. These two principals were praised as were Scott Wentworth's Macduff and the directing, which was clear and forceful and emphasized the essential darkness of the play. Shakespeare's *As You Like It* had the forest scenes staged in rural Quebec of 1678. Glamorous Lucy Peacock as Rosalind was as pleasing as the set's bright autumn leaves. Director Richard Monette and designer Debra Hanson drew loud applause. An interesting and successful novelty was a Canadian play, *Forever Yours, Mary Lou* by Montreal's Michel Tremblay. Winning the most praise from audiences and critics was Eugene O'Neill's *Ah, Wilderness!* It featured a show-stopping performance by Douglas Rain as the drunken Sid.

The Shaw Festival at Niagara-on-the-Lake, Ont., opened its season with a pleasing version of Shaw's *Misalliance*, directed by Christopher Newton, the festival's artistic director. It starred Sharry Flett, Barry MacGregor, Jennifer Phipps, and Helen Taylor. Emlyn Williams' thriller, *Night Must Fall*, was among other productions, as was Cole Porter's musical, *Nymph Errant*. The latter was considered too daring when it opened in 1933 because it traces the attempts of Evangeline to lose her virginity. It raised no eyebrows this season or last when the festival first presented it. Charlotte Moore played Evangeline; the railway station set was by Christine Plunkett; and Bob Ainslie was the choreographer. Shaw's *Mrs. Warren's Profession*, directed by Glynis Leyshon, cast Joan Orenstein as the prostitute, Mrs. Warren, and Tracey Ferenz as her daughter, Vivie. The play was a triumph for both actresses.

Peter Moss announced his retirement at the end of the season from his ten-year post as artistic director of the Young People's Theatre in Toronto, Ont. Also in Toronto, Guy Sprung, Canadian Stage's artistic director, and Lyn Osmond, its general manager, were asked by a review committee of the company's board to step down. Three of its originally slated plays were canceled. In Edmonton, Alta., the annual Sterling Awards saw Fraser's suspense play *Unidentified Human Remains* win the drama award. Jim Guedo won the award for best director, David Fox for best actor, and Tantoo Cardinal for best actress.

Because of "irreconcilable differences," the board of Ballet B.C. asked artistic director Patricia Neary to resign after less than one year's employment. English dancer Barry Ingham, ballet master of the Frankfurt Opera Ballet, became interim artistic director. The Royal Winnipeg Ballet, under new artistic director John Meehan, presented Dutch choreographer Rudi van Dantzig's well-received *Romeo and Juliet*. In Toronto the National Ballet of Canada celebrated its 40th season with tours of Quebec and Atlantic Canada and with the commissioning of three new ballets.

See also LITERATURE—*Canadian.*

DAVID SAVAGE, *Free-lance Writer*

CARIBBEAN

Moves toward economic integration continued in the Caribbean in 1990. During a summit meeting in Kingston, Jamaica, in August, the heads of state of the 13-member Caribbean Community and Common Market (CARICOM) gave final approval to the installation of a common external tariff (CET) and rules of origin governing regional trade, to go into effect on Jan. 1, 1991.

Introduction of the tariff, a package of duties on goods imported by CARICOM members from countries outside the region, is the first step in the creation of a single CARICOM market of 5.5 million people by Jan. 1, 1994. To ensure effective implementation of the integration process, a CARICOM commissioner was appointed, to take office on October 1. Beginning on Jan. 1, 1991, the region's three stock exchanges—in Barbados, Jamaica, and Trinidad and Tobago—would be integrated via cross-listing and cross-trading of securities. The heads of state also eased rules on interisland travel by nationals of member states and approved an "industrial programming scheme" to eliminate trade barriers between Community countries by July 1, 1991.

Observer status in CARICOM was granted to Mexico, Puerto Rico, and Venezuela. Mexican President Carlos Salinas de Gortari attended the Kingston summit; it was the first time that CARICOM leaders met as a body

Dominican Republic's President Joaquín Balaguer votes in the May 16 presidential election. The 83-year-old incumbent was declared the winner of the close race in June.
AP/Wide World

with a Mexican chief of state. CARICOM and Mexican officials signed an Agreement on Technical Cooperation and Trade Promotion, covering joint ventures, trade finance, export insurance, and exchanges of trade missions. The agreement was expected to help increase CARICOM exports to Mexico.

Caribbean Basin Initiative. Caribbean trade prospects were enhanced further in August, when the U.S. Congress passed the Customs and Trade Act of 1990. Among other provisions, the act repealed the scheduled 1995 termination date of the U.S. Caribbean Basin Initiative (CBI). The CBI provides duty-free entry to the United States for an array of exports from the Caribbean and Central America.

The act effectively made the CBI a permanent feature of U.S. trade policy. It maintained present exclusions from duty-free treatment of textiles and apparel, canned tuna, petroleum and petroleum products, leather goods, and certain watches, but expanded an existing program for duty-free imports of some products assembled from U.S. components. The law also reduced tariffs by 20% over five years (effective Jan. 1, 1992) on handbags, flat goods, work gloves, and leather apparel.

U.S. officials said that making the CBI permanent would make the Caribbean more attractive to foreign investors. Enthusiasm within the region was tempered, however, by the release in September of a report by the U.S. International Trade Commission (ITC), which said that most of the new investment in the region is for production of goods and services that are ineligible for duty-free access to the United States under the CBI.

The report showed that, for the third year in a row, the United States enjoyed a substantial trade surplus of nearly $1.5 billion with CBI countries in 1989. Imports from the CBI region that actually benefited from the duty-free program amounted to only 0.1% of U.S. imports.

Foreign Aid. If there was disappointment in the Caribbean with the limited results of the CBI, there was actual anger when the United States during the year cut its economic assistance to the region by two thirds, from a planned $60 million to a little more than $20 million. The region had received $82 million in U.S. economic aid as recently as 1987. The reduction reflected, in part, a tighter U.S. foreign-aid budget, and in part, shifting U.S. priorities in the Caribbean Basin as the threat of Soviet and Cuban encroachment receded.

Partly offsetting the U.S. aid cut, Canada announced in April that it was forgiving $182 million in outstanding official development debt owed to it by the Commonwealth Caribbean countries. Canada has provided $963 million in development assistance to the region since 1957. According to the announcement, Canada is the first country to forgive development debt in the Caribbean.

Demanding the resignation of Prime Minister Arthur N.R. Robinson, some 100 members of a black Muslim sect staged an unsuccessful coup attempt in Trinidad and Tobago in July. Thirty people were killed in the five-day disturbance.

Drugs. Drug trafficking continued to be a matter of serious concern for Caribbean governments, as well as for the United States. A report issued by the Caribbean Drug Money Laundering Conference, held in Aruba in June, stated that "there is strong belief that the drug trade now owns or influences a considerable number of commercial transport companies and financial institutions, and has the financial power not only to corrupt but to destabilize governments in the region." The conference issued 61 recommendations for action by governments participating in the conference and scheduled a follow-up meeting for the end of the year.

Trinidad and Tobago. A violent coup attempt by some 100 members of the Jamaat al-Muslimeen, a Black Muslim sect, erupted in Port of Spain, the capital of Trinidad and Tobago, in July. The rebels, said to be fed up with austerity measures and government corruption, stormed the national parliament building on July 27, seizing Prime Minister Arthur N.R. Robinson and half his cabinet. Robinson and two of his colleagues were shot. In all, 30 people were killed and as many as 300 injured, including looters who broke into stores in the downtown area while police were busy with the hostage situation. Losses from theft and arson were estimated at $70 million.

The rebels, led by a former policeman, Yasim Abu Bakr, demanded Robinson's resignation and immediate national elections. After five days, they surrendered when government officials signed a document acceding to their demands, including an amnesty and the installation of an interim government. The 113 armed rebels freed 46 hostages and were taken into custody. The government then denounced the document as "completely invalid," and said it was signed "under duress." The rebels were charged with treason and murder.

Dominican Republic. National elections in the Dominican Republic in May pitted two octogenarians and longtime political rivals against each other. Four-time incumbent President Joaquín Balaguer, 83, defeated former President Juan Bosch Gavino, 80, by a slim 25,000 votes out of a total of 1.9 million votes cast. The elections were monitored by 34 international observers, including former U.S. President Jimmy Carter, who said the vote had been "orderly, peaceful, and honest." Bosch, however, pronounced the result a "massive electoral fraud," and in July his Dominican Liberation Party (PLD) organized a 48-hour period of "national mourning."

Balaguer was inaugurated, nonetheless, on August 16, but his Social Christian Reformist Party (PRSC) did not control the national legislature. Bosch's PLD won 44 seats in the House of Deputies, while the PRSC took 41. In the Senate, the PRSC held 16 seats and the PLD had 12. The balance of power was held by the Dominican Revolutionary Party (PRD) with 33 seats in the House and two in the Senate. The PRD is led by former Santo Domingo Mayor José Francisco Peña Gómez, a onetime Bosch political ally, who finished third in the presidential contest. Coalition politics seemed in store for the Dominican Republic for the next four years, as the nation faced serious problems of inflation, unemployment, labor strikes, and other civil unrest.

See also CUBA, HAITI, JAMAICA, PUERTO RICO.

RICHARD C. SCHROEDER, *Consultant to the Organization of American States*

© Jeremy Bigwood/Gamma-Liaison

At the June 1990 Central American Conference in Antigua, Guatemala, leaders of six Central American independent states met to discuss regional economic integration and the need to minimize tensions and weaknesses.

CENTRAL AMERICA

Events in 1990 once again demonstrated how readily Central America can drop out of the news and out of the minds of North Americans. In the first few months of the year, startling changes in Nicaragua and continuing civil disturbances in El Salvador, Guatemala, and Panama provided a steady diet for the U.S. public, press, and government. Then Iraq invaded Kuwait, and Central American news was no longer front-page material. Yet, in fact, Central American conditions had improved little and warranted the interest and concern of North Americans.

Before the Mideast explosion, U.S. President George Bush had requested aid for Nicaragua and Panama (the amount for the latter nearly halved by Congress). But in October he reduced his request for 1991 by about 30%, declaring that trade, not aid, would mark his program.

In June the Central American presidents convened in Antigua, Guatemala, to promote regional integration and perhaps minimize some of the tensions and weaknesses of the states. They reported that in the past decade about 120,000 Central Americans had been killed in civil strife, billions had been spent on the military, and some 60% of the citizens lived in "extreme poverty." El Salvador still faced 33% unemployment, and half of the peoples of Guatemala and Honduras remained illiterate.

The presidents sought to enlarge their economies, not redistribute the wealth; thus land reform and population control were not on the agenda. The approach resembled that of the Alliance for Progress and the Caribbean Basin Initiative of years gone by, plus a revival of the Central American Common Market, so buffeted by recent civil wars. But the excessive military establishments and the almost total stagnation of the 1980s discouraged optimism. Trade among the five nations had declined from $1.1 billion in 1981 to $600 million in 1989; U.S. aid had been reduced from $702 million in 1989 to $565 million projected for 1990.

Belize

Defense. As a member of the British Commonwealth, Belize has retained some ties to Great Britain, including a crown-appointed head of state who serves as governor-general. It took another step toward full sovereignty in 1990 when a Belizean officer assumed command of the Belize Defense Force (BDF). The state's southern border continued to be guarded jointly by British and Belize forces, but all British troops were removed from the western boundary and the waterfront. After the change, Her Majesty's government confirmed its intention to protect Belize if needed.

Immigration. Belize, with only about 200,000 people in an area the size of Massachusetts, actively sought immigration. Currently, perhaps 15,000 Central American refugees make their homes there, and about 6,000 Mennonites reside along the Guatemalan border. Most of these people received free agricultural land.

The Environment and the Economy. Although residing in a poor and underdeveloped state, Belizeans have exhibited considerable concern for their environment. Current programs include those to preserve the invaluable Mayan and other Indian buildings and artifacts, to clean the waterfront of Belize City, and to save the forests that cover nearly three fourths of the land. Coca-Cola Foods recently gave 42,000 acres (16 997 ha) in northern Belize to the government to hold in trust.

The nation's proximity to the United States, its clear coastal waters, and its remains of ancient civilizations made it an obvious site for a future in tourism. A giant step in that direction included the construction in 1990 of a 120-room Ramada Hotel. Facing the waterfront of Belize City and the distant barrier reef, the longest in the world except for Australia's, the hotel is Belize's largest and the first operated by a major chain.

The Caribbean Basin Initiative was designed by the United States to benefit small states such as Belize by giving access to the large U.S. markets, but so far Belize has continued to import more than it exports. The major export is sugar, whose producers enjoyed a record crop in 1990. Unemployment was at 14%, but inflation was held in the moderate 2%-3% range.

An undesirable export surfaced in the late 1980s when farmers, hurting from a low sugar income, shifted to marijuana for a cash crop. Although police and outside pressure nearly wiped out the marijuana trade, little ultimately was accomplished because Colombian cocaine entrepreneurs quickly stepped in to fill the vacuum. Belizeans in outlying regions of the north, paid in cocaine as well as ready cash, have assumed the tasks of refueling the Colombian planes or off-loading the drug to skiffs that rendezvous with seaplanes or larger ships destined for the United States. It is believed that 20 to 30 planes per month land in Belize; one that crashed carried $20 million in cocaine, the easy availability of which has created many addicts in Belize and made money laundering a thriving industry.

Costa Rica

Election. On February 4 the nation held an election to replace President Oscar Arias Sánchez, who was not eligible for immediate reelection. The candidate of Arias' National Liberation Party (PLN), Carlos Manuel Castillo, was handicapped by his party affiliation and the drug scandals of the Arias regime, and he gained little from Arias' great personal popularity as a peacemaker. The PLN also suffered from its failure to solve the nation's continuing economic problems.

The challenger was Rafael Angel Calderón Fournier, son of former President Rafael Calderón Guardia, who had been forced into exile in 1948. The younger Calderón, leader of the Social Christian Unity Party (PUSC), in fact had been born in 1949 in Nicaragua during that exile. A former foreign minister, he ran unsuccessfully for the presidency in 1982 and 1986. Also up for consideration were the 57 seats in the National Assembly and about 1,000 municipal offices. Calderón Fournier triumphed by 52% to 48%, and his PUSC took 29 seats in the Assembly to 25 for the PLN. He was inaugurated May 8 in Costa Rica's tenth consecutive peaceful administration change.

Economy. At his inaugural President Calderón warned that the nation faced two years of the worst fiscal crisis in its history. As a portion of his program to combat the crisis, he pledged an extensive welfare program, including 160,000 low-income housing units and 6,000 mi (9 656 km) of paved rural roads. The nation's deficit was more than 3% of the gross domestic product (GDP), twice the austerity goal set by the International Monetary Fund, which tried to help in Costa Rica's solvency recovery. Nearly $2 billion was owed to commercial banks, and the debt service was about $325 million in arrears. During a November trip to east Asia, Calderón was promised nearly $1 billion in aid and trade.

Along with Mexico and the Philippines, Costa Rica began receiving benefits from special debt packages designed by U. S. Secretary of the Treasury Nicholas Brady. It appeared that Costa Rica would save about $150 million per year in interest from these arrangements. Some stabilization of conditions seemed to result from personal and corporate income-tax reforms and certain credit restrictions imposed by international lending agencies.

Death of Figueres. On June 8, José Figueres Ferrer died of a heart attack in his home near San José. Ill for several years, the successful rancher personified the "democratic left" movement of Latin America, and during the 1950s and 1960s was at the same time the most popular Latin American figure in Washington and its most responsible critic. Figueres served as provisional president following the 1948 rev-

CENTRAL AMERICA · Information Highlights

Nation	Population (in Millions)	Area (sq mi)	(km²)	Capital	Head of State and Government
Belize	0.2	8,865	22 960	Belmopan	Minita Gordon, governor-general George Price, prime minister
Costa Rica	3.0	19,730	51 100	San José	Rafael Angel Calderón Fournier, president
El Salvador	5.1	8,124	21 040	San Salvador	Alfredo Cristiani, president
Guatemala	8.9	42,042	108 890	Guatemala City	Marco Vinicio Cerezo Arévalo, president
Honduras	5.0	43,278	112 090	Tegucigalpa	Rafael Leonardo Callejas, president
Nicaragua	3.5	49,998	129 494	Managua	Violeta Barrios de Chamorro, president
Panama	2.4	30,193	78 200	Panama City	Guillermo Endara, president

olution and was elected president for two later terms. (*See* OBITUARIES.)

El Salvador

Criminal Proceedings. More than a year had elapsed since the murder in November 1989 of six Jesuit priests and two women; the case appeared to be no nearer settlement. Under great pressure from the U.S. government and even more from some individual congressmen and church groups, the administration of President Alfredo Cristiani conducted an investigation and made some arrests, but few persons believed the case had been solved. The military was upset greatly at the arrest of Col. Guillermo Alfredo Benavides Moreno, but soon thereafter crucial evidence in the case disappeared. Other problems related to the case involved a judge questioning the wrong soldiers, witnesses vanishing before giving testimony, and the transferring of military officers from place to place in order to make the court's task more difficult. The unwillingness of the army to cooperate caused U.S. Ambassador William Walker to declare his discouragement, and the embassy withheld $2 million designed for legal-aid seminars.

Testimony did reveal that members of the army unit accused of the murders had searched several houses before the killings, even warning neighbors that fighting might take place in the area, which appeared to suggest a concerted plan. Two other cases against human-rights violators were dismissed when judges declared a lack of evidence; one instance involved the murder of ten peasants and the other concerned a right-wing kidnapping ring. No Salvadoran officer yet has been convicted of a human-rights violation.

Peace Talks. These events and the bogged-down peace talks proved so troublesome to the United States that cuts in overall aid to El Salvador seemed inevitable. In October, Congress rebuked the Salvadoran military by voting to withhold half the projected military assistance, estimated to be $85 million, for 1991. The entire package could be scrapped if El Salvador failed to pursue the murder investigations or withdrew from peace talks with the rebel Farabundo Martí National Liberation Front (FMLN). On the other hand, the aid could be reinstated if the administration found that the rebels were not serious about the talks. Not surprisingly, the Cristiani government still talked of the threat of communism, in spite of its death elsewhere. Nor was it surprising that the military reportedly was stockpiling equipment.

The peace talks, meanwhile, made little progress in 1990. The war, which has been blamed for 70,000 deaths in ten years, continued unabated, while long series of discussions took place. The failure of communism in Eu-

© Miguel Solis/Sygma

President Alfredo Cristiani of El Salvador conducted an investigation in 1990 into some military power abuses, but greater reform along those lines was considered unlikely.

rope and Nicaragua, presaging a reexamination of the U.S. aid program, probably forced both sides to the bargaining table. The United Nations also attempted to pressure the factions into meeting. Talks were held in Caracas, Venezuela, in May; in Mexico in June; and in San José, Costa Rica, several weeks in July, August, and September—a total of six rounds since November 1989.

Differences were narrowed little; the parties merely seemed more willing to talk. The rebels insisted upon agrarian reforms, the total demobilization of the army, and the punishment of officers guilty of human-rights violations. The government would agree to some military reforms and reductions in troop strength, but little more. It sought a cease-fire and an end to the rebellion. The parties did agree to create a human-rights monitoring agency, but only after a cease-fire.

The Military. The contumacy of the military was based as much upon fear of losing its position as the possible punishment of high-ranking officers. In ten years it had received $1 billion in U.S. aid, giving it great political power. Most officers graduated from the same military academy and formed a loyal, tightly knit group.

President Cristiani, in his efforts to contain the military, held on in spite of cashiering a few officers, and he did not roll back the ten-year-old agrarian law. Nonetheless it did not appear likely that he would be able to move further in the direction of reform, nor was it likely that he could win the civil war. The awful consequences of the war were an estimated one half of the nation's children under age 5 being undernourished and one third suffering from diarrhea. Outside agencies, in attempting to reduce the harm, created "Days of Tranquility," during which their representatives went into the

Voters waited their turns at the polls during the November presidential election in Guatemala City. Twelve candidates ran for the presidency, but none received a large enough vote to avoid a January 1991 runoff.

war zones for first aid, dental care, and vaccinations in order to prevent the destruction of the generation. Additional help came from Salvadoran migrants in the United States who contributed some $350 million per year to their families back home.

Guatemala

Human Rights. For about two years after the government of President Marco Vinicio Cerezo Arévalo took over in 1986, it achieved a fair civil-rights record. Then it deteriorated badly, and during 1990 Cerezo began receiving significant outside pressure to curb the many human-rights violations in Guatemala. The first sign of urgency came from Washington, with the State Department sharply criticizing the Cerezo government's failure to prosecute members of the armed forces for the "recent surge of killing and abductions." Next, the United Nations branded Guatemala as one of the worst violators of human rights. Then, in the strongest action taken since that of Jimmy Carter in 1977, the Agency for International Development suspended $16 million in health assistance because millions of dollars in Guatemalan medical-aid funds were missing. In December the U.S. State Department suspended its $2.8 million military-aid program because of Guatemala's failure to address human-rights abuses.

Civil War. Blame for these crimes generally was placed at the door of the military, based on the presumption that it never had ceased to rule. But the army's authority and independence did not appear to extend to the battlefield. Small groups of rebels frequently and easily occupied villages without firing a shot, then wandered off before the arrival of government troops, who rarely pursued them. Morale among the largely conscripted army dropped as the audacity of the rebels increased. After nearly 30 years of Central America's oldest and

most violent war, the Cerezo government, although it took sharp criticism, was in no danger of being overthrown. Early in the 1980s the rebels had controlled nearly the entire countryside, but the army fought back with total war, slaughtering tens of thousands of peasants and nearly ending the civil war. The brutality, however, was unacceptable to most Guatemalans, and the rebels would not quit, resulting more recently in the ambush of patrols and the sabotage of more than half the provinces. Something of a mystery was the rebels' continued ability to obtain arms even after the fall of Nicaragua's Sandinistas.

In Madrid, May peace talks—a consequence of the 1987 efforts of Costa Rica's President Arias—took place among the rebels and several political parties in an effort to end the war. Led by Guatemalan Archbishop Rodolfo Quesado and a council, the opposing groups spent several days talking peace. The parties agreed to participate in the drafting of a new constitution in 1991, to greater civilian control of the armed forces, the disbanding of paramilitary civil patrols, and rebel noninterference in the November elections. But they did not agree upon a cease-fire. Another round of talks took place in October in Metepec, Mexico. Participation was very broad, but accomplishments again were few, for the army continued to insist upon the disarming of the guerrillas before carrying out any of the terms.

The military picture in fact changed little. President Cerezo did agree to replace his defense minister, but the successor appeared to be less moderate, and the appointment may have been designed to mollify young right-wing officers. Twice the army had saved Cerezo from rebellion, and in return it received a free hand from him in running the government television station and building the roads.

Two unfortunate groups were caught in the midst of the civil war with little prospect of winning anything. Thousands of homeless children were on the streets, begging, stealing, and sniffing glue. Soldiers often abused them, and the government wanted merely to hide them from foreigners. A second group, the Indians, remained a target of both rebels and the army, the former making them grow food and the latter bombing their crops. Several hundred thousand still lived in Guatemala, even though the large numbers who fled to Mexico seemed better off because of United Nations help.

Elections. The turbulence in Guatemala brought about calls for the return of former President Efraín Ríos Montt, who bragged of the sturdy rectitude of his administration. Ríos Montt, however, was constitutionally ineligible to run because of his part in the 1982 military coup. Nonetheless the fundamentalist "law and order" candidate exhibited surprising public support, perhaps indicating a popular disillusionment with democracy. Indians were frightened at the prospect, for he had treated them brutally. Ríos Montt pursued various legal means to get his name on the ballot; all failed. He made vague threats of a coup, but none occurred.

At least 15 political figures were murdered during the campaign, including nine candidates for office, but violence at the polls on November 11 was slight. Twelve candidates ran for the presidency and 19 parties contended for 116 congressional and 300 mayoral seats. Three contenders took most of the votes. Coming in third was the former mayor of Guatemala City, who pulled enough votes to force a runoff between the two leaders, each of whom received about 25% of the vote. The two finalists in the January 1991 runoff were Jorge Carpio Nicolle, a publisher, and Jorge Antonio Serrano Elias, an associate of Ríos Montt. Businessmen who never had held public office, they both favored free markets, privatization of many government businesses, the pursuit of peace talks, and the granting of blanket amnesties. The campaign failed to touch on the tougher issues of land reform, human rights, and control of the military, and since neither man campaigned for military reform, it seemed likely that the election would make little change in Guatemala.

Honduras

Elections. Rafael Leonardo Callejas, age 46, won the presidency in November 1989, and was inaugurated in January 1990. This was the nation's first transfer of power to an opposition party through the ballot in 57 years. A member of a landed family who received his education in the United States, Callejas inherited as president the usual economic problems.

Economy. In 1989 the nation failed to carry out certain austerity steps dictated by the International Monetary Fund, resulting in the withholding of about two thirds of that source's aid.

In March, under a similar threat for 1990, the new administration passed a number of sweeping economic reforms: Tariffs were to be cut from a high of 135% to 20% in a period of two years, income and corporate taxes reduced, a value-added tax initiated, and certain excise taxes increased. Hundreds of special subsidies and tax exemptions for many businesses were to be abolished, and a shift to realistic exchange rates was planned. The international financial agencies forced these measures because of Honduras' critical financial condition. Immediately, many unions, larger businesses, and the military protested.

President Callejas, plagued by labor unrest virtually since his inauguration, faced the threat of a general strike often during the year. In June approximately 10,000 banana workers of the Chiquita Brands multinational corporation struck for a 55% raise. Most of the banana workers earned about $10 to $15 per day, and compared with the nation's per-capita income of perhaps $20 per week, the banana workers seemed well off. They protested, however, that there had been no increase since 1984, and that their cost of living had increased about 50% each year. The strike dragged on into August, never quite broadening into the general strike desired by so many. Some 2,000 Texaco oil-refinery workers struck briefly, as did some smaller unions. About 4,000 Castle and Cooke banana workers threatened to strike, but that came to little. The army was ordered to La Lima, the company town, and Chiquita sent strikebreakers to pressure the workers.

UN peacekeeping forces inspect surrendered weapons at a Nicaraguan contra camp in Honduras after an agreement between the contras and the new Nicaraguan government.

© Nancy McGirr/JB Pictures

Closing the 24 Chiquita plantations proved to be the costliest labor feud in more than 30 years. The company is Honduras' largest employer, and its shutdown threatened chaos to the nation's economy. President Callejas declared that the nation lost $18.5 million in export receipts and taxes and that he had to devalue the lempira and raise taxes to restore the nation's international credit.

The strike ended August 6, as the workers had failed to get sufficient support for a general strike. They averaged a 17% increase in wages, far below their initial demand.

Ending one strike did not mean ending the state's serious economic problems, however. The decade of the 1980s had been disastrous to Honduras, with a drop in real per-capita income from $980 in 1978 to scarcely $600 projected for 1990. While Honduras did receive aid for permitting the Nicaraguan contras to take refuge there, their presence proved very costly. The destitute Nicaraguans added little to the economy and greatly increased the nation's social burdens and costs. Their presence ruined valuable rain forests, for example, and the capital city of Tegucigalpa was largely a slum, where all services were overburdened. The poor even were forced to buy their water from street vendors. According to Callejas, 70% of his people were in absolute poverty. For the first time in a decade defense costs were cut (10% for 1990), but a bill to end the draft failed to pass the assembly. And the United States, now seeing less threat in Central America, provided $21 million in aid for 1990, compared with a peak of $81 million in 1986.

Nicaragua

Elections. In a stunning upset Violeta Barrios de Chamorro (*see* BIOGRAPHY) defeated the incumbent, Daniel Ortega Saavedra, for the presidency of Nicaragua on Feb. 25, 1990. Representing a loose coalition of parties called the National Opposition Union (UNO), she won by a clear margin of about 55% to 41%. Partly because of some confused polling, most people, especially the Sandinistas, were surprised greatly by the vote, but it appears that a failing economy and heavy U.S. financial aid had set the stage for their defeat. The UNO also won a majority of seats in the National Assembly. Chamorro received courteous congratulations from Ortega, who made no coup threats.

Of itself the election provided a study in modern politics. Of the 1.75 million eligible voters, more than 90% participated; about 2,000 foreigners, led by former U.S. President Carter and representatives of the United Nations and the Organization of American States (OAS), monitored the polling, and about 1,000 journalists covered it. Substantial fraud did not come about. Chamorro was inaugurated April 25.

Chamorro, who never had held elected office, was born in 1929 to a rural upper-class family. She received some education in the United States and in 1950 married the distinguished Nicaraguan journalist Pedro Joaquín Chamorro, a leading opponent of the several Somoza regimes, who was assassinated in 1978. His martyrdom thrust her into the limelight, and with the victory of the Sandinistas in 1979, she was invited to become a member of the ruling junta. Within less than a year, she became disenchanted by their policies and resigned. She assumed her husband's role as the major media critic of the government and the logical candidate against Ortega when the 1990 election was scheduled.

The New Government. In office Chamorro's problems could prove overwhelming. Looming above all was a national and perhaps regional exhaustion caused by years of civil wars. At the top of her agenda were bringing about a cease-fire between the Sandinista army and the rebel contras, and convincing the contras to give up their rebellion and weapons, move out of Honduras, and accept the promise of free land back home. Emotional wounds also had to be healed. (Two of her own children supported her; two did not.) And too, the years of war and the U.S.-sponsored embargo simply had destroyed the elements of a normal economy.

Working closely with Humberto Ortega, brother of the former president and the head of the Sandinista army, she concluded a cease-fire and arranged for the contras to move into five large "secure" zones separate from the equally wary Sandinista forces. A most startling decision was her appointment of Humberto Ortega as head of the armed forces; he helped her begin a reduction of Nicaragua's army to about one half what she had inherited from the Sandinistas. In June about 100 contra commanders surrendered their troops' weapons, evidence that the nine-year-old civil war had ended. The draft was abolished on inauguration day.

The Ortega appointment worried many of President Chamorro's followers, and they became more fretful in September when it was learned that a Sandinista law, apparently passed prior to the elections and never debated, removed all civilian control over Ortega's budget, troop size, and many other matters. But as the months passed her problems with the army appeared more manageable than the economy.

Economy. The nation was clearly bankrupt. President Chamorro urgently sought the help of the United States, but Congress stalled on a $300 million aid bill. In May a Sandinista union of public employees went on strike for a few days as a consequence of the devaluation of the córdoba. Some workers got as much as a 100% raise. The strike raised another bitter issue; in 11 years the Sandinista regime had permitted no strikes. Now it seemed that the party's lead-

Violeta Barrios de Chamorro (right), who became president of Nicaragua in April after defeating the incumbent Sandinista leader Daniel Ortega in February elections, surprised and worried many of her followers when she appointed Humberto Ortega (left), the former president's brother and head of the Sandinista army, as head of Nicaragua's army.

© Arturo Robles/JB Pictures

ership used its position to encourage them. Reports circulated that the government might resign over the massive problems of finance and the fear of resurging Sandinista power.

A broader and more dangerous strike broke out in July and lasted ten days. Tens of thousands struck, not just over wages, but over the very nature of the government's economic program. Violence between the mostly Sandinista unions and the government brought to the front the question of police and army—mostly Sandinistas—loyalties. The president ordered the police to break up road blockades and force workers out of government offices; it appeared that they neither defied her orders nor did much to break the strike. Street fighting led to six deaths and much destruction of government services and property.

Perhaps the more serious matter was the use of Sandinista power; unquestionably the party could do much harm, and perhaps bring down the government. The public blamed them for the strike, yet Daniel Ortega helped settle it. Chamorro also faced a threat from the right wing of her own party, which placed its trust in Vice-President Virgilio Godoy Reyes, an angry and jealous leader who wanted the destruction of the Sandinista movement.

Beginning in May a new currency, the gold córdoba, gradually was introduced into the economic system. Linked to the U.S. dollar, it had the effect of imposing an economic straitjacket, but supporters indicated that the ultimate effect would be positive. During the last few weeks of the year the nation's problems changed little, and the continuing survival of the government represented as much a miracle as its election. More strikes were followed by raises, which often became meaningless in the face of inflation—1,800% in 1990—and currency devaluation—34 adjustments since the inauguration. Unemployment exceeded 40%,

and food and transportation subsidies disappeared. Most of the late aid from Washington went to repay bank loans. The foreign debt exceeded $1 billion. Land-reform and rain-forest-preservation programs seemed to be on hold, awaiting better times.

Panama

Noriega and the U.S. Invasion Aftermath. Manuel Noriega no longer ruled Panama or even lived there, but his shadow hung ominously over the land. U.S. forces, which had invaded Panama in December 1989, flushed him from hiding, taking him captive in January 1990, when he left the Vatican Embassy. He was flown to Miami for imprisonment and trial on various drug-related charges. The new Panama government also wanted to try him for murder, racketeering, theft, and fraud against his people. At the end of 1990 he remained in a U.S. prison.

In a matter of days the 1989 assault had brought more than 20,000 Americans into combat. The shooting was over in eight hours, and several U.S. and Noriega soldiers were killed and many wounded, but hundreds—or thousands, depending upon the source—of Panamanian civilians lost their lives. Within months charges were raised, even in the U.S. Congress, of a scandalous cover-up of mass burials of these persons. The brief invasion did vast physical damage to the nation as well. A number of Panamanians sought an investigation by the OAS of "indiscriminate killing," and brought suit for $250 million for property damages. The United States responded that it had not violated international law but did bring charges of murder against three U.S. soldiers, one of whom was acquitted in August.

The Noriega trial did not go smoothly. In June defense attorneys, threatening to with-

© Charlyn Zlotnik/Sipa-Press

Panama in 1990 did not see the hoped-for recovery following the 1989 U.S. invasion that ousted Manuel Noriega and brought in its wake millions of dollars of property damage, unemployment, looting, and governmental nepotism.

draw from the case, forced the unfreezing of some of Noriega's millions of dollars in assets so that they could be paid. They also sought to force the release of classified documents about past payments Noriega received from the United States, but the U.S. government insisted their release would violate national security. Then in November, CNN cable news revealed that it had copies of tapes made by federal prison authorities of conversations between Noriega and his lawyers, and the station aired brief excerpts. The matter went before the Supreme Court, as apparently both the 1st and 6th constitutional amendments were involved, and the Noriega trial perhaps was jeopardized. The court upheld a ban (lifted in late November) while the tapes were viewed by authorities.

Reconstruction. Against this background, President Guillermo Endara's government in February froze more than 200 bank accounts allegedly linked to the Colombian drug cartel as well as to Noriega. The rebuilding of the army and police forces proved difficult without relying excessively on men who had supported General Noriega. Anarchy briefly followed the invasion, and the crime rate soared; police morale was also low as the force faced high unemployment and widespread gun ownership.

Strains showed when the two vice presidents, who are of different parties, sharply disagreed over the issue of free markets and government intervention. Banking, because of its rather loose governance by the central administration, often has been Panama's major industry. Now this rather casual policy was

being thwarted by the United States, whose antidrug policy required close supervision of accounts to prevent money laundering. The United States sought a Mutual Legal Assistance Accord, which required the swapping of banking information by the two governments, but President Endara protested his intention to cooperate on all but fiscal crimes. Other new restrictions on investment put thousands of bank jobs at risk, and hundreds of thousands of anonymous stockholders faced disclosure if Panama gave in to U.S. pressure, which came in the form of delays in the sending of aid dollars.

Recovery from the excesses of the Noriega era and the war that brought it to an end did not seem to be in sight. Unemployment exceeded 30%, police feared the superior weapons of the criminals, the administration suffered from runaway nepotism and cronyism, while looting and physical damage from the invasion forced thousands of citizens to live in airplane hangars. In October and November protests took place almost daily over issues such as privatization, labor codes, and instability. An unsuccessful December coup, staged by a former national police chief, was quelled quickly with help from U.S. troops in Panama.

The installation of a Panamanian—Fernando Manfredo—as acting Panama Canal administrator was a positive note of 1990. The transition, stipulated in the 1977 canal treaties, took place January 1. U.S. President Bush in April announced the nomination of Gilberto Guardia Fabrega for the post.

THOMAS L. KARNES, *Arizona State University*

CHEMISTRY

Developments in chemistry in 1990 included the creation of new and better diamonds, the first experimental observation of ultrafast molecular motions, and a combination of theory and experiment in understanding the simplest chemical reaction. Debate over the risks of chemicals continued as the 10 millionth registered chemical compound was announced.

Diamonds. Diamonds have unique properties that make them popular in industry and commerce. A form of pure carbon, diamond is the hardest substance known, has the highest thermal conductivity, acts as an electrical insulator, and is extremely resistant to chemical reaction. Synthetic diamonds traditionally have been produced from graphite and other carbonaceous materials using very high temperatures and enormous pressures, feeding a $500 million-dollar annual need for abrasive materials.

Advances announced in 1990 will allow the production of super-hard diamond coatings for a variety of specialty materials. The technique, chemical vapor deposition, has been under development for a number of years. It involves first heating a mixture of hydrogen and a carbon-containing gas, such as methane, to high temperature at a relatively low pressure. When properly done, the carbon atoms deposit on enclosed surfaces as diamond films. In particular these films have the valuable property of soaking away heat from hot spots, which should make them extremely useful as coatings for delicate electronic components.

In July scientists from General Electric Co. reported that they had created diamonds with properties superior to nature's own. Natural diamonds are mixtures of two carbon isotopes: They contain about 99% carbon-12 and 1% carbon-13. The GE scientists reported that they had produced one-carat synthetic diamonds with greatly reduced amounts of C-13. Theory had predicted that such diamonds should have slightly better properties than their natural cousins. The scientists were surprised to find that the artificial gems in fact conducted heat 50% better than natural diamonds and were ten times more resistant to damage from powerful laser beams.

Ultrafast Chemistry. For many purposes molecules can be considered as collections of balls (atoms) connected by springs (bonds). The balls are in continuous motion, vibrating and rotating in characteristic patterns. The motions are very fast—a typical vibration might take just 300 femtoseconds (a femtosecond is 10^{-15} second) and a typical rotation takes 1,000 times longer. Scientists normally follow these motions indirectly by observing transitions between the allowed "quantum" levels as lines in infrared and microwave spectra.

In February a team of chemists from the California Institute of Technology reported the first direct observation of these motions. They used a technique that they had employed earlier to study chemical reactions, consisting of two extremely short laser pulses. The technique works in much the same way that flashes from a stroboscope "freeze" the motions of athletes and machinery, except that the time scale for the molecular events is roughly 1 billion times shorter. The CalTech team of chemists used their precision methods to follow the motions of iodine molecules, which they found to be consistent with prevailing theoretical ideas.

The CalTech group also reported ultrafast observations of the breakup of a compound following absorption of short pulses of laser light. They studied the breakup of the compound $C_2F_4I_2$, which loses two iodine atoms after being zapped. The first I atom comes off rapidly, within less than 1 trillionth of a second. The second I atom is lost more slowly, they reported, coming off only after about 30–150 trillionths of a second. These studies should help in the understanding of how these bond-breaking reactions take place.

Simplest Reaction. To chemists the simplest chemical reaction is the "exchange" of a hydrogen atom between two hydrogen partners, as indicated by the scheme $H + H_2 \rightarrow H_2 + H$. In 1990 theory and experiment finally were melded into agreement on the details of this reaction. The theoretical analysis, involving complicated quantum mechanical calculations, was contributed by workers at the University of California, Berkeley, and the University of Minnesota. The precision experiments, which focused on the rotational states of the products, were carried out at Stanford University. Final agreement on this basic reaction brought pleasure to both camps and confirmed the ultimate quantum mechanical nature of events on the molecular level.

Chemicals, Risks. In February, Chemical Abstracts Service in Columbus, OH, announced that it had entered the 10 millionth chemical into its 25-year-old computer registry system. The chemical, a moderate-sized organic compound, was synthesized by a group of Japanese chemists.

At the same time debate picked up over how to estimate the risks that chemicals in the environment, such as pesticides, pose to humans. In animal tests for carcinogenicity, for example, many chemicals test positive—too many, say some critics. In fact, the positive results may be due merely to the very high doses of the chemicals administered to the test animals. The high doses alone can cause cell injury, which in turn may lead to tumor formation. This could give an exaggerated impression of the risks of lower doses, say some scientists.

PAUL G. SEYBOLD
Wright State University

CHICAGO

Someone was murdered in Chicago about once every ten hours in 1990, giving the city its highest incidence of violence since the record-setting year of 1974. Homicides were up 21% in the first nine months of the year. The increase was higher than equally alarming rises in bloodshed in New York City, Los Angeles, and Washington, DC. Each day, according to the Chicago Police Department, there was an average of 36 shootings, 28 stabbings, and 45 serious assaults with other weapons. Of 517 murder victims during the first nine months, 82.5% were male, 73% were black, and 68% of them died as a result of gunfire. The violence brought demands by aldermen and Mayor Richard M. Daley that additional policemen be hired through a tax on Illinois lottery tickets.

The Mayor. Polls showed that Mayor Daley remained immensely popular after a year and a half in office. In that short time Daley diffused the racial politics that polarized the city and the mayor's office in the 1980s. The mayor named 15 members to the new Chicago Board of Education that included members from most of Chicago's large ethnic groups, although some blacks complained that they were underrepresented. Late in November the Illinois Supreme Court declared the city's year-old school-decentralization plan unconstitutional.

Electrical Power. Commonwealth Edison Co. agreed to a one-year extension of its electrical franchise, which was to expire at the end of 1990. That extension, if ultimately approved by the City Council, could remove a complicated issue that would be troublesome in the 1991 election. Edison had three major power failures in the city's mostly black West Side. The most serious one brought sporadic looting of retail shops. Some political leaders charged that Edison did not maintain its equipment properly in the city's minority neighborhoods. The assertion refueled demands by some aldermen that taxpayers purchase some or all of the company's facilities.

Redevelopment. Mayor Daley's proposal that a third major airport be sited on the city's southeast side brought protests from residents in the largely blue-collar industrial area. They did not want their homes and neighborhoods leveled for a 21st-century airport. Tax revenue is another problem area. Chicago's real-estate tax base continued to erode as the city is populated more and more by poor minorities.

Also during 1990 the Chicago White Sox played their last baseball game at historic Comiskey Park and architect Cesar Pelli was designing a major new office building for the city. A new stadium would replace the torn-down Comiskey Park in the same area, and the new Pelli edifice would be the world's tallest.

Census. Preliminary Bureau of Census figures showed that Chicago's population declined by 279,000 or 9.3% in the 1980s. Chicago claimed a census undercount. Local demographers insisted that the city's population rose to 3,020,000 in the 1980s, or 15,000 more than the official 1980 census of 3,005,072.

ROBERT ENSTAD
"Chicago Tribune"

CHILE

The installation of Patricio Aylwin as president of Chile on March 11, 1990, eliminated South America's last remaining military dictatorship and restored the country to civilian rule. The events of 1990 showed, nonetheless, that a full transition to democracy would be slow and difficult, as tensions persisted between the military and the new government.

Inauguration. Aylwin, 71, a former senator and the leader of Chile's Christian Democrat Party, had been chosen president as the nominee of a 17-party opposition coalition in nationwide balloting Dec. 14, 1989. He decisively defeated a candidate backed by Chilean dictator Gen. Augusto Pinochet, receiving more than 52% of the vote in a three-man race.

He took office in a solemn ceremony in the newly completed Congress building in the Pacific port city of Valparaiso, becoming the country's first popularly elected civilian chief in nearly 17 years. Pinochet attended the oath-taking and then withdrew to let Aylwin swear in his 20-member cabinet. In his inaugural statement, Aylwin stressed that "Chile doesn't want violence or war; it wants peace."

Limitations. Upon assuming the presidency, Aylwin quickly found himself hampered by numerous constitutional barriers erected in the closing days of the Pinochet rule. Although Aylwin's *Concertación por la Democracia* coalition won control of the national legislature, Pinochet was able to appoint nine senators as a bulwark against changes by the civilian government. In addition, Aylwin has had to negotiate, rather than mandate, monetary policy because Pinochet made the Central Bank autonomous.

Civilian-military relations became the most serious problem facing the new government. Only ten days after the transfer of power from Pinochet to Aylwin, a former member of the military junta, Gen. Gustavo Leigh, was shot by gunmen in his Santiago office. The Manuel Rodriguez Patriotic Front, an arm of the Chilean Communist Party, claimed responsibility, saying the attack (from which Leigh recovered) was a response to the delay by Chilean courts in prosecuting those responsible for human-rights violations under the military government. Other former junta members reported receiving threats against their lives.

Aylwin was unable to hold the armed forces accountable for human-rights crimes committed during the dictatorship because of an amnesty law imposed by Pinochet. The law bars prosecutions for acts committed between 1973 and 1978, the period when most human-rights violations occurred, and was upheld by the Chilean Supreme Court. In addition, Aylwin could not remove Pinochet or any other top military commander. Pinochet could remain as head of the army for nearly eight more years. The military draws up its own budget and the relatively high level of military spending drew money away from social programs that Aylwin would like to implement.

Rights Commissions. In June, Aylwin appointed a nine-member Truth and Reconciliation Commission to gather evidence on political killings and disappearances during the military rule. The work of the commission was hampered by the amnesty law, which was interpreted by the military as barring investigation as well as prosecution.

Popular feelings on the human-rights issue were inflamed by the finding of several mass graves where the military buried suspected leftists who were executed following the 1973 coup that ousted Socialist President Salvador Allende. Human-rights groups claimed that as many as 2,000 Chileans were killed during and after the military takeover in 1973. To avoid a clash with the military, Aylwin assured Pinochet that he would resist public pressure to repeal the amnesty. But discovery of the graves raised the possibility that they might contain the remains of persons who disappeared after 1978. Defense Minister Patricio Rojas announced in June that, "If it is discovered that high-ranking military officers are involved, they will have to answer for their actions. All Chileans are equal before the law and they will have to appear when summoned by the proper courts."

The Truth and Reconciliation Commission was scheduled to issue a report to the president by the end of 1990. Due to the potentially explosive nature of the report, its contents were not expected to be released to the public.

Allende Reburied. The body of President Salvador Allende, who died in the 1973 military coup, was exhumed from an unmarked tomb in the resort city of Viña del Mar and reburied in Santiago, the Chilean capital, on September 4. The reburial ceremony was attended by Allende's family and several government officials, and tens of thousands of Chileans turned out to see the funeral procession. The Chilean military took no note of the ceremony, however, and Pinochet said, "People are exploiting the issue for political purposes. . . . The Armed Forces will not take part."

One week later, on September 11, the anniversary of the 1973 coup, thousands of demonstrators marched through Santiago to Allende's tomb. The crowd threw stones and bricks at police, who responded with tear gas. Thirteen people were injured in the melee.

The Chilean military in previous years celebrated the anniversary by staging a large-scale military parade through the city. In 1990, though, the army held a low-key religious ceremony at which Pinochet spoke. "If the circumstances [of 1973] were to repeat themselves," Pinochet declared, "I would not hesitate for a moment to act in the same way."

Economy. Under Pinochet, the Chilean economy was among the strongest in Latin America. Even before taking office, Aylwin committed his government to maintaining the military government's free-market and open-trading-system policies. As a result, economic growth remained strong during the first half of 1990, but as the inflation index began creeping up, nearing 35% on an annual basis, the Aylwin government worked with the Central Bank to dampen the growth surge with more stringent monetary measures. The growth rate, which reached 10% in 1989, was estimated to be only 2% in 1990, and inflation would be held below 25%. Nonetheless, according to Finance Minister Alejandro Foxley, Chile was "entering a phase of sustained growth."

During the year the Chilean government negotiated with the United States for the restoration of duty-free trade benefits under the U.S. Generalized System of Preferences (GSP), which were suspended in 1987 for alleged violations of workers' rights by the Pinochet government. The Chilean request for reinstatement was supported by the U.S. labor movement, which had demanded the removal of Chile from the GSP three years earlier.

In October the United States and Chile signed a framework trade agreement as the first step in negotiating a liberalized trade arrangement between the two countries. The framework pact established a joint council on trade and investment that would monitor binational commercial and financial relations, pursue the goal of open markets, and negotiate additional agreements where appropriate.

RICHARD C. SCHROEDER
Consultant to the Organization of American States

CHILE • Information Highlights

Official Name: Republic of Chile.
Location: Southwestern coast of South America.
Area: 292,259 sq mi (756 950 km²).
Population (mid-1990 est.): 13,200,000.
Chief Cities (June 30, 1985): Santiago, the capital, 4,318,305; Viña del Mar, 315,947.
Government: *Head of state and government,* Patricio Aylwin, president (took office March 1990). *Legislature*—Congress (dissolved Sept. 1973).
Monetary Unit: Peso (323.16 pesos equal U.S.$1, official rate Dec. 10, 1990).
Gross Domestic Product (1989 U.S.$): $25,300,000,000.
Economic Index (Santiago, 1989): *Consumer Prices* (1980 = 100), all items, 504.2; food, 486.3.
Foreign Trade (1989 U.S.$): *Imports,* $6,535,000,000; *exports,* $8,190,000,000.

AP/Wide World

In April 1990, Li Peng became the first Chinese premier to visit the USSR since 1964. During his visit he conferred with Soviet Premier Ryzhkov (right). The two nations agreed to reduce the number of troops stationed along their border.

CHINA, PEOPLE'S REPUBLIC OF

In many respects China appeared to be in a state of suspended animation for much of 1990. The aging and conservative leaders who were responsible for the brutal suppression of the democracy movement in June 1989 continued to exert a commanding influence on the political system from behind the scenes. So long as they remained in power there was little possibility of positive change.

The Gerontocracy. China's aging leadership, the "Gang of Elders" as they are disrespectfully known by many disaffected Chinese people, is composed of Deng Xiaoping, 86, economist Chen Yun, 84, former National People's Congress Chairman Peng Zhen, 88, former national President Li Xiannian, 81, and Wang Zhen, 82, who, as vice-president, is the only one of the five who continues to hold an office in the government. Those accustomed to seeing Chinese politics as a perpetual conflict between two opposing camps of shifting composition portrayed the 1990 scene as a conflict between a relatively more reform-oriented group headed by Deng Xiaoping and a group headed by Chen Yun that opposes the renewal of political and economic reforms. The future direction of Chinese politics, according to this interpretation, depends on which of these two elderly men dies first.

An academic symposium was held late in the fall on the topic of "Chen Yun Thought." Much of his thought was shaped in the 1950s, when China fell most completely under the influence of the Soviet Union. Chen's ideas are encapsulated in an analogy: he likened market forces in a socialist system to a bird, and central planning to a bird cage. The bird is free to fly, but only within the narrow confines of its cage.

Pessimists believe that, were Chen to outlive Deng, economic and political reform would suffer a further setback, and that China would cut itself off from the outside world and return to the autarkic economic policies of the 1960s. Optimists argue that, since Chen played no public role in the events of April, May, and June 1989, his ascendancy could result in a reassessment of those events and a return to a moderate program of reform.

Mindful of the ouster and execution of Romania's dictator Nicolae Ceauşescu in Romania in late 1989, the Gang of Elders was concerned about the loyalty of the People's Liberation Army. During the spring some 400 officers and 1,600 enlisted men were dismissed from the army, accused of having resisted orders in Beijing in June 1989. In a reshuffling of six of the seven regional military commanders during the summer, officers known for their loyalty in having supported the imposition of martial law and the clearing of Tiananmen Square were selected to replace those deemed to have wavered in their support.

Economic Consequences. China's conservative leaders were equally anxious to avoid a renewed outbreak of the worker discontent that fueled demonstrations in most of China's cities in the spring of 1989. As a result, they authorized economic measures that, while effective in the short run, may have negative consequences for the economy in the longer term. During the first three quarters of 1990, the government pumped more than $30 billion into the economy, most of it directed toward state-owned industries. The state sector thus was able to raise wages and avoid layoffs, thereby allaying worker dissatisfaction. The government took this step despite the deplorable condition of the state economy. One third of state-owned enterprises were operating at a deficit. Losses during the first nine months of 1990 totaled more than $4 billion and profits were down 58% from the same period in 1989. Meanwhile, the more efficient and productive collective and private sectors were deprived of needed capital.

Despite these steps unemployment in urban areas reached 5%, according to unofficial statistics. This meant that 7 million workers of an urban work force of 150 million were jobless. The problem was exacerbated by the fact that during 1990 there were jobs for only about one half of the 12 million young people entering the work force. Although the leaders focused their attention on the potentially explosive situation in China's cities, conditions continued to be much worse in the countryside, where efforts to curb the runaway growth of rural collective industries in 1988 and 1989 have resulted in an unemployment rate of close to 40%. That translates into 120 million rural workers out of work or, at best, underemployed.

Effective measures to solve these problems would mean a return to full-scale, market-oriented economic reform, and that is politically unacceptable to the elderly conservatives. This conundrum is clearly unsatisfactory to China's regional leaders. At two conferences of provincial and municipal political leaders in Beijing during the year, participants voiced their dissatisfaction with the central leaders and their policies. Manifestations of economic regionalism became more frequent and more pronounced as the year wore on. Provincial governments enacted informal regulations preventing the transfer of key producer goods across provincial borders. Municipally owned department stores refused to stock goods manufactured outside of the local region. Mayors and governors took to paying lip service or to ignoring entirely central regulations that worked to the economic disadvantage of their constituents.

There were some bright spots in the economy. Inflation, which in 1988–89 had reached rates as high as 30%, was brought under control. In June it sunk below 3% and was very likely to be no higher than 5% when figures for the year were calculated. Grain production, too, was up, with record harvests in both spring and fall.

People and Pollution. Seven million census workers fanned out across the country during ten days in early summer to complete the first enumeration of the Chinese population since 1982. The results, when published in October, showed the population at 1.13 billion. This figure exceeded the Chinese government's projection by some 13 million, but came very close to estimates by United Nations experts.

While the government claimed success for its birth-control policies, the census revealed 20 million births above the target figure for 1990 set by population planners when the "one child" policy was initiated a decade earlier. Although widely observed in China's cities, the one-child policy is much less effective in the countryside. Births nationwide between 1980 and 1987 averaged 2.47 per family. Of particular concern is the very large number of women of childbearing age who are themselves the product of an earlier "baby boom." These women now constitute more than one quarter of the population. They are giving birth to 17 million babies per year, nine million of whom are "illegal" in that they are not first births. Given this situation, it is highly likely that the target population figure of 1.25 billion in 2000 will be exceeded.

The census also showed that illiteracy fell from 23% of the population to 16% since 1982, while the proportion of the population living in

China completed the most thorough census in its history during 1990. The final results revealed a July 1 population of 1,133,682,501 and an annual growth rate of 1.47%.

urban areas has increased from 21% to 26% since the previous census. Environmental experts took note of this latter statistic with some concern. They observed that 18 of the world's 30 "megacities"—cities with populations in excess of 4 million—are located in Asia. In China, 90% of the country's cities fail to meet their government's own standards for air quality, and those standards are among the world's least stringent. Qu Geping, head of China's Environmental Protection Agency, acknowledged the seriousness of the country's pollution problems and promised that spending on environmental protection would increase in 1991 from 0.7% of China's gross national product (GNP) to 1%.

Studies conducted in 1990 showed improvements in the quality of rural health care in China. One of the achievements of the Maoist era most frequently called to the attention of foreigners was the improvement of rural health-care delivery through the recruitment of "barefoot doctors." Many of these rural health workers abandoned medicine to engage in the more lucrative pursuits of farming or rural collective industry. Statistics showed that rural health-care workers decreased in number from more than 1 million in 1980 to 873,000 in 1990. On the other hand, efforts at improving the quality of these workers was paying off, with almost all rural clinicians now having three years of medical training.

Basic health care in China's cities is provided at no cost to workers in state enterprises. This is not true for rural workers who, although they are enjoying better-quality health care, also are paying higher rates for it. Nationwide expenditures on health care are up in absolute terms, but are down from 3% to 2.7% as a proportion of the national budget as compared with a decade ago.

China and the Outside World. In their dealings with the outside world, China's conservative leaders were faced with unpalatable choices. Indulging in what, for many Chinese people, is a natural reaction, they fixed the blame for 1989's democracy movement on foreign influences. The United States, Europe, and Japan were at fault for having exerted a "bourgeois liberal" influence on those Chinese who had dealings with the outside world. The Soviet Union and Eastern Europe, too, added fuel to the fires of discontent in China by their abandonment of socialist orthodoxy.

Given their interpretation of events, conservatives' instinct was to cut off contact with the outside world and go it alone, as China often had done in the past. But China's most recent opening to the outside world, begun with Deng Xiaoping's accession to power in 1978, could not be abandoned so easily even were the leadership unanimously behind such a move. First, there is more than $40 billion in foreign debt that must be serviced and eventually repaid. Second, foreign trade nearly trebled between 1978 and 1990 from about 10% of GNP to more than 27%. Closing China's open door would cut its economy off from needed capital, markets, and raw materials.

Given this situation, China found itself taking steps it would not otherwise have chosen to take. Perhaps the most difficult of these was the agreement in late May to allow leading dissident Fang Lizhi to leave his refuge in the U.S. embassy in Beijing and, accompanied by his wife and their son, to emigrate to England. Earlier there had been stringent preconditions attached to his release: The United States was to resume military sales to China and was to exert its influence on the World Bank to resume its program of lending. Although these conditions were not met, U.S. President George Bush agreed to extend most-favored-nation status to China for another year despite considerable opposition to the move in Congress.

© Mary Beth Camp/Matrix/China

Chinese women in the southern province of Guangdong help manufacture stuffed animals, a high percentage of which would be exported to the United States. An effort by some members of the United States Congress to remove China's most-favored-nation trade status failed.

CHINA · Information Highlights

Official Name: People's Republic of China.
Location: Central-eastern Asia.
Area: 3,705,390 sq mi (9 596 960 km²).
Population (1990 census): 1,133,682,501.
Chief Cities (Dec. 31, 1987 est.): Beijing (Peking), the capital, 6,710,000; Shanghai, 7,220,000; Tianjin, 5,540,000.
Government: *General Secretary of the Chinese Communist Party,* Jiang Zemin (chosen June 1989); *Head of government:* Li Peng, premier (took office Nov. 1987); *Head of state:* Yang Shangkun, president (took office March 1988). *Legislature* (unicameral)—National People's Congress.
Monetary Unit: Yuan (4.722 yuan equal U.S.$1, official rate, August 1990).
Gross National Product (1988 U.S.$): $350,000,-000,000.
Foreign Trade (1989 U.S.$): *Imports,* $58,561,-000,000; *exports,* $51,631,000,000.

In addition to agreeing to Fang's departure, the Chinese government released from jail more than 300 dissidents held since their arrest in the aftermath of the events of June 4, 1989. The government's announcements of these releases named only a few of the more prominent individuals among those freed, and noted that an equal number remained in custody. Human-rights organizations outside of China, while expressing their satisfaction at the release of these prisoners, called for the publication of a complete list of names including both those released and those remaining in prison.

Responding to these releases, the Japanese government announced at a meeting of the "Group of Seven" nations in Houston in June that it was resuming a $5.2 billion program of loans to China. Later in the summer the World Bank agreed to resume lending to China as well.

Unlike government agencies, private traders and investors attended less to the morality of doing business with China and more to its potential for profit. In this respect they found China a significantly less promising partner than it had seemed five or ten years earlier. New contracts for joint ventures were down by some 40% in the early months of 1990. Earlier interest in hotels and office complexes waned as occupancy rates remained well below 50% and project managers had difficulty in servicing their outstanding debt.

A delegation of Chinese mayors visited the United States in midsummer. The group was led by Shanghai Mayor Zhu Rongji, who pushed hard for U.S. investment in the projected multibillion-dollar Pudong industrial region in the eastern part of his city. A second delegation of 300 representatives of corporations interested in foreign trade and state-owned enterprises visited the United States in October with plans to spend more than $200 million on U.S. goods and equipment. This shopping expedition was designed to offset somewhat a projected $10 billion surplus in China's favor in Sino-U.S. trade in 1990.

Taiwan and Hong Kong continued to be major players in China's economic interaction with the outside world. The lure of low labor costs continued to draw Taiwan to projects in China's coastal province of Fujian. The fact that Taiwan investment in China fell somewhat short of the 1990 projected figure of $1 billion had more to do with the slowdown of the Taiwan economy than it did with the lack of enthusiasm for economic ties across the Taiwan Straits.

China's leaders had hoped the publicity surrounding the holding of the Asian Games in Beijing in September would help rebuild their reputation. Although the games took place without incident, thanks to the imposition of tight security in the capital, they proved to be less than the economic and propaganda success that had been hoped. Nonetheless, it was a year of considerable diplomatic success for China in the Asian region. Premier Li Peng traveled to Southeast Asia during the summer. During return visits to Beijing by Indonesian President Suharto and Singapore's Prime Minister Lee Kuan Yew, both nations announced the establishment of diplomatic ties with China. Meanwhile, economic ties with South Korea continued to expand, outstripping those between China and North Korea.

More than these positive developments, it was the Iraqi invasion of Kuwait that proved to be the most important contributing factor in China's reemergence into the world community. China's decision to go along with United Nations sanctions against Iraq and to avoid blocking the Security Council resolution authorizing the use of force in the Gulf crisis served to realign its foreign policy with that of the major powers. It was clear that Beijing intended to exact concessions in exchange for its acquiescence. Such concessions would take the form of an easing of sanctions imposed upon China in June 1989.

Despite the leveraging effect of China's agreement to go along with the Western powers in opposing Iraqi aggression, China remained on the periphery rather than at the center of great power politics in 1990. With friendly relations between the United States and the Soviet Union at a post-World War II zenith, China found that it had lost its role as the key player in a "strategic triangle." Whereas events in Beijing in the spring and summer of 1989 rendered the nation an international pariah, a year later China found itself less spurned than ignored—a position that China's leaders who had spent 12 years dedicated to increasing China's potential as a great power must have found particularly galling.

See also TAIWAN.

JOHN BRYAN STARR
Yale-China Association

CITIES AND URBAN AFFAIRS

The year 1990 was especially important for U.S. cities because a decennial census was conducted that would have far-reaching consequences for cities and their residents for years to come. Because the census count determines the distribution of important federal and state grants and the apportionment of congressional, state, and county legislative seats, it was watched closely.

The 1990 Census. In 1990 the census was carried out in a fishbowl atmosphere of media scrutiny and public controversy. Many urban leaders and social-welfare workers were convinced that the homeless and the urban underclass would be undercounted systematically. Whereas in previous censuses the people living in such facilities as flophouses and missions were tallied through the "casual count," on March 20–21, 1990, census workers fanned out in cities across the United States on S-Night (Streets and Shelters Night) in search of the homeless. Intense scrutiny by local media and protests in some cities focused attention on the census as never before. The focus was intensified a few weeks later when it was reported that by census day, April 1, more than one third of the 100 million census forms sent by mail had not been returned. There was speculation that high rates of noncooperation among minorities and illegal immigrants might exaggerate the undercounting problems in some cities.

The Census Bureau had devised such new procedures as "S-Night" in an attempt to avoid a repeat of the controversy involving its alleged undercounting of urban populations ten years earlier. As a result of litigation and the threats of still more court battles, the bureau would be pressured to make statistical adjustments for undercounting—but any such adjustments hardly would avoid controversy, especially since official census figures would influence grant decisions and determine legislative apportionment for years to come.

For many cities, the news would be bad enough even without undercounting. Preliminary figures showed that Baltimore, Cleveland, Detroit, Pittsburgh, St. Louis, and several other older cities in the Frostbelt continued to lose population in the 1980s, though at a slower rate than before. For example, the population of St. Louis dropped about 13% in the 1980s, compared with 27% in the previous decade. However, several metropolitan areas reversed their population declines; indeed, most of those with more than 1 million residents showed clear signs of revival. In the 1970s the New York, Philadelphia, and St. Louis metropolitan areas were stagnant or declining, but all of them gained population in the 1980s. Metropolitan areas with less than 1 million population grew more slowly than in the previous decade. It appeared that the northern metropolitan areas that were hit hard by industrial restructuring and job losses had diversified their local economies so that several now were benefiting from the national economic trends favoring the service, high-tech, and recreational sectors.

Over several decades the cities have lost political clout because of the movement of population to the suburbs and to the Sunbelt states. Projections showed that congressional and state legislative reapportionment reflecting the 1990 census would continue this trend. New York would lose three to four congressional seats, and Pennsylvania, Illinois, Ohio, and Michigan at least two each. Altogether, the states in the Northeast and the Midwest would lose at least 15 congressional seats. These lost congressional seats would be reapportioned to states in the South and West. As shown by the differences between central city and metropolitan-area growth rates, several big cities would be smaller players in Congress, and their states and regions as well.

The Emerging Agenda. For a decade urban officials have been preoccupied with issues of local economic growth, an agenda that was forced upon them by economic restructuring (especially in areas dependent on manufacturing) and by the withdrawal of federal grant programs. In 1990, however, there were clear indications that social issues had become vitally important in local politics.

Problems of crime, drug abuse, family disorders, health care, and homelessness had become impossible to ignore. In a Ford Foundation program that recognizes outstanding innovations by state and local governments, six of the ten annual awards in 1990 recognized social programs; four of the programs were aimed at helping children. In an era when cities must rely mainly on their own resources, cities have learned to experiment with public-private partnerships to build housing and provide medical care, and nonprofit institutions are expected to assume responsibilities once financed by government.

Most urban experts doubt that cities, using only their own resources, are in a position to make much headway in solving problems that are actually national in scope. For a decade state and local governments have been increasing tax rates and finding new revenue sources in an attempt to make up for cuts in federal grants. In 1980 federal aid to cities accounted for about 26% of local budgets. By 1988 this proportion had declined to 7.5%. States and localities have been scrambling to make up for the withdrawal of federal funds. In 1988 state and local governments collected 53% of revenues collected by all governments in the United States, a far cry from days in the mid-1960s when the national government raised two thirds of all revenues. In the decade up to the 1987–88 fiscal year, state and local revenues increased at twice the national inflation rate.

A National League of Cities survey of 576 municipalities showed that in 1989–90, 76% of them had increased user fees and other charges and 41% had increased property-tax rates. The search for revenues was becoming increasingly difficult. Fiscal default was a real possibility for Philadelphia, which faced a budget shortfall of more than $200 million. The League's survey found that two thirds of the cities responding would find it harder to balance budgets in the 1990–91 fiscal year than one year earlier. Because of their declining political influence, the cities could not expect a new round of financial assistance. During 1990 a prolonged impasse over the national budget deficit dominated the news for weeks. And though some state legislators were sympathetic, most states were not in a position to increase urban aid appreciably. Only 16 states ended fiscal 1989 with budget balances of 5% or more of expenditures—the minimum recommended by budget officers. Many states, like their cities, would find it difficult to find resources for new programs.

DENNIS R. JUDD
University of Missouri-St. Louis

COINS AND COIN COLLECTING

The year 1990 was an evolutionary one for numismatics. No longer a casual pastime, coin collecting has become a serious business for many. According to an independent survey, coins ranked fourth in one-year appreciation among 14 different investments. Several Wall Street brokers—among them Kidder-Peabody and Merrill Lynch, Pierce, Fenner & Smith—entered the numismatic market with the introduction of rare-coin portfolios.

Independent, third-party grading and authentication services, which sprang up several years ago in response to widespread ignorance and abuse of coin-grading standards, have hastened the transition from hobby to industry with the encapsulation of valuable coins in sonically sealed plastic holders. In turn, these holders, or "slabs," have opened the way for computerized trading of "sight-unseen" coins.

On May 14, 1990, the California-based Professional Coin Grading Service made computerized grading of coins a reality. Using state-of-the-art technology, the computer examines coins for flaws, luster, and quality of strike. Coin collectors remained skeptical, however, despite the developers' claims that computerized grading would ensure greater consistency and objectivity.

The year in numismatics witnessed a number of record sale prices for rare coins. A brilliant proof 1894-S dime was sold at auction by Stack's of New York for $275,000 on January 16, and two months later was traded privately for a reported $400,000. Believed to be the finest known specimen of the 1894-S dime, the

coin last had appeared at auction in 1947, when it brought $1,050.

The King of Siam proof set, assembled in 1834 as a diplomatic gift for the sovereign of the Southeast Asian country, brought an astounding $2.9 million at an auction conducted by Superior Galleries on May 28. A 1907 $20 gold piece shattered the price barrier when it sold on July 9 for $1.5 million. The ultra-high relief Saint-Gaudens "double eagle" with the date represented by Roman numerals is one of 13 to 15 known surviving specimens.

Front-page news was made when the wreck of the S.S. *Central America*, a 19th-century steamship, was discovered 160 mi (257 km) off North Carolina's Cape Hatteras in 1986. Laden with more than three tons of gold, including a delivery of coins from the San Francisco Mint and an estimated $1.25 million in payments to banks and private firms, the ship sank in a storm on Sept. 12, 1857. The numismatic artifacts recovered from the wreck, most of which are in mint-state condition, constitute one of the most important finds in U.S. history and are likely to have an immense impact on the hobby and the marketplace in the years to come.

Collectors were rewarded with two noteworthy releases from the U.S. Mint in 1990. In honor of the 100th anniversary of the birth of President Dwight D. Eisenhower, the Mint struck a $1 coin showing the late president's Gettysburg, PA, home and an unusual dual portrait of Eisenhower as five-star general and as president.

In August the Mint's 1990 proof and "Prestige" sets, each comprised of five proof versions of U.S. circulating coins plus a proof specimen of the 1990 Eisenhower commemorative dollar, created excitement in the collecting community when it was found that an estimated 3,555 sets contained San Francisco-minted cents lacking the "S" mintmark. Within weeks of the discovery, sets containing the error were selling for as much as $1,400.

BARBARA H. GREGORY
American Numismatic Association

COLOMBIA

The seemingly interminable mix of violence, politics, and economic growth continued in Colombia in 1990. The year saw municipal elections in March and the election of a new president. The presidential election campaign was punctuated by the assassination of three candidates by the Medellín narcotics syndicate. While most of the violence came from the Medellín cartel, two leftist guerrilla groups continued to struggle against the government, while right-wing paramilitary groups attacked politicians on the left. A much-heralded "drug summit," in Cartagena on February 15, had no real effect on the government's antidrug war.

Politics. Liberal Party candidate César Gaviria was elected president with 48% of the vote. The Conservative Party split into two camps: one led by defecting party leader Alvaro Gomez Hurtado, who received 24% of the vote, and the other by traditional Conservative Rodrigo Lloreda, who took 12%. The election surprise was Antonio Navarro Wolff of the M-19, who had joined the race only a month before, after the assassination of M-19 candidate Carlos Pizarro. Navarro actually came in third with 13% of the vote, leading some analysts to sound the death knell for Colombia's formerly strong two-party system. The continuing wave of terrorism did not appear to intimidate Colombian voters, and the abstention rate of 58% was no higher than usual.

Gaviria was inaugurated on August 7 amid elaborate security precautions. In his inaugural address the new president backed away slightly from former President Barco's tough stance against the drug cartels, stating that he would use extradition to the United States only as a last resort. He also called for privatization and internationalization of the economy.

The president's new cabinet contained a majority of Liberals but also had representatives from the Social Conservatives, the M-19, and the army. In September, Gaviria began implementing his new economic doctrine by reducing government controls and subsidies on agricultural products and by allowing private competition with TELECOM, the government-owned communications monopoly. The president also visited the United States in September, addressing the United Nations and meeting with President Bush and other U.S. officials.

Terrorism. Bombings, killings, and kidnappings continued unabated. On March 22, Bernardo Jaramillo, candidate of the leftist Patriotic Union (UP), was gunned down at Bogotá airport by a 16-year-old contract killer. The Medellín cartel, which claimed responsibility for the killing, also engineered the assassination on April 26 of Carlos Pizarro. His M-19 Movement had agreed to reenter the political arena in 1989. A third candidate, Luís Carlos Galán of the Liberal Party, had been killed by the drug gangs in August 1989. By mid-1990 the drug lords appeared to have changed tactics, as random bombings decreased and kidnappings of journalists escalated. By late October seven well-known journalists, including Francisco Santos, deputy editor of *El Tiempo*, Colombia's most respected newspaper, had been kidnapped.

Economy. President Gaviria's plan to privatize and internationalize the Colombian economy got off to a shaky start. Inflation through August was 21.26%, up from 18.53% during the same period of 1989. Although the International Coffee Agreement had been renewed in February, no quotas were assigned to the producing countries. Although the gross domestic product had increased by 3.2% in 1989, it appeared doubtful that the 1990 figure would surpass 3% and fears of a severe recession were voiced.

Foreign Affairs. President Gaviria's pleas for more assistance from the international community, including the United States, to aid in the drug war produced little but frustration for the Colombian government. Perhaps even more frustrating and (to judge from editorial comment) enraging, was the virtual acquittal in August of District of Columbia Mayor Marion Barry on drug charges. Colombia also expressed its resentment at the refusal of the United States to implement fully the International Coffee Agreement and a U.S. threat to invoke antidumping regulations against cut flowers, one of Colombia's major exports to the United States.

ERNEST A. DUFF
Randolph-Macon Woman's College

COLOMBIA · Information Highlights

Official Name: Republic of Colombia.
Location: Northwest South America.
Area: 439,734 sq mi (1 138 910 km²).
Population (mid-1990 est.): 31,800,000.
Chief City (Oct. 15, 1985): Bogotá, the capital, 3,982,941.
Government: *Head of state and government,* César Gaviria Trujillo, president (took office Aug. 1990). *Legislature*—Parliament: Senate and House of Representatives.
Monetary Unit: Peso (523.00 pesos equal U.S.$1, Dec. 31, 1990).
Gross Domestic Product (1988 U.S. $): $35,400,-000,000.
Economic Index (Bogotá, 1989): *Consumer Prices* (1988 = 100), all items, 115.8; food, 114.4.
Foreign Trade (1989 U.S.$): *Imports,* $5,010,000,000; *exports,* $5,478,000,000.

COLORADO

While Colorado voters in 1990 enthusiastically embraced the idea of limiting the terms of elected officials, they also returned most incumbents who sought reelection.

Aspen, CO, Mayor Bill Stirling casts his ballot in a February motion to ban fur sales in the ski resort. The mayor, a proponent of the ban (which was defeated), later survived a recall attempt.

AP/Wide World

The Election. In passing term-limiting Amendment 5, Colorado joined several other states in limiting the terms of its state officeholders and became the only state to limit the terms of its congressional delegation as well. State officeholders are limited to eight consecutive years in the same office, while Colorado's members of the U.S. Congress are limited to 12 consecutive years in the same position. The limits are not retroactive and apply only to terms filled in the 1990 election and thereafter.

Ironically, with Amendment 5 getting 71% of the vote, or 705,494 votes, all five of Colorado's incumbent U.S. representatives who sought reelection won easily. The sixth—five-term Republican Hank Brown—kept the U.S. Senate seat of retiring Republican Bill Armstrong in GOP hands by downing Democratic candidate Josie Heath. Republican State Sen. Wayne Allard moved up to Brown's old congressional district seat by defeating Democratic State Rep. Dick Bond with 88,450 votes to Bond's 75,451. That was the closest congressional race as incumbents Patricia Schroeder (D-1st), David Skaggs (D-2d), Ben Nighthorse Campbell (D-3d), Joel Hefley (R-5th), and Dan Schaeffer (R-6th) won easily. Incumbent Dem-

ocratic Gov. Roy Romer, incumbent Democratic State Treasurer Gail Schoettler, and incumbent Republican Secretary of State Natalie Meyer also won reelection.

Attorney General Duane Woodard was the only statewide incumbent to lose, as challenger Gale Norton (R) became the first woman elected to Colorado's top legal position.

Only five incumbents lost in the 83 legislative races. Democrats picked up one seat in the 65-member House and another in the 35-member Senate, but Republicans still controlled the House 38–27 and the Senate 23-12. A record 31 of the 100 legislators were women, up from 29 women elected in 1988.

Voters also authorized gambling in three old mining towns—Central City, Black Hawk, and Cripple Creek, and narrowly rejected a tax-limitation plan. Although it was the eighth such rejection since 1966, the narrow margin prompted officials to commission a $300,000 study of the state's tax system.

Disasters. A "monster" hailstorm hit the Denver area on July 11, causing more than $400 million worth of damage. Ironically, the resulting flood of insurance payments for damaged homes and automobiles gave a substantial stimulus to the region's economy.

Denver was the site of another disaster on the Sunday after Thanksgiving when a fire erupted near Stapleton Airport, the nation's sixth-busiest airport. Fed by more than 2 million gallons (7.6 million l) of jet fuel, the blaze, which occurred at a fuel depot owned by United Airlines, burned for two days. United's flights were delayed but not those of the other 19 airlines at the airport.

Other News. Attempts to resume plutonium processing at the Rocky Flats nuclear-weapons plant received a setback when a federal district judge in Denver ruled that the thousands of barrels of plutonium-laced material being stored there were subject to regulation by the state and therefore were being stored illegally. In Aspen voters in February defeated a well-publicized attempt to ban fur sales.

BOB EWEGEN, *"The Denver Post"*

COLORADO • Information Highlights

Area: 104,091 sq mi (269 596 km²).
Population (1990 census prelim.): 3,272,000.
Chief Cities (July 1, 1988 est.): Denver, the capital, 492,200; Colorado Springs, 283,110; Aurora, 218,720; Lakewood, 119,340.
Government (1990): *Chief Officers*—governor, Roy Romer (D); lt. gov., Michael Callihan (D). *General Assembly*—Senate, 35 members; House of Representatives, 65 members.
State Finances (fiscal year 1989): *Revenue,* $6,967,000,000; *expenditure,* $5,878,000,000.
Personal Income (1989): $58,221,000,000; per capita, $17,553.
Labor Force (June 1990): *Civilian labor force,* 1,770,800; *unemployed,* 93,200 (5.3% of total force).
Education: *Enrollment* (fall 1988)—public elementary schools, 399,853; public secondary, 160,228; colleges and universities, 186,288. *Public school expenditures* (1989–90), $2,744,309,000.

COMMUNICATION TECHNOLOGY

In 1990 fiber-optic technology was applied widely to increase the speed and capability of communication channels, signal processors, and the facilities used in such communication systems as local area networks (LANS) and high-speed computer networks. Interpersonal computing, which links people and information resources, grew at an annual rate of nearly 40%.

The Integrated Services Digital Network (ISDN) now is the basis for a growing number of applications and is expected to be in use in most countries by 1993. In the United States, AT&T committed itself to making all of its services digital by the end of 1990. Several companies disclosed plans for new systems for worldwide, satellite-aided person-to-person calling in which small, low-power, pocket-sized telephones could be used for inexpensive local, national, and international connections.

It became increasingly evident in 1990 that associated software (computer programs and documentation) is an ever-growing component in the cost of developing and producing telecommunications equipment. Software is responsible for much of the versatility, performance, and maintainability of these large complex systems. A leading communication company in the United States estimated that more than 60% of its research and development (R&D) employees were involved in the production of software. Many communication companies were initiating programs to increase the productivity and quality of their software development.

Transmission and Switching Technology. A new high-capacity optical-fiber data transmission system has been developed jointly by AT&T and Japan's Nippon Telegraph and Telephone (NTT). It is capable of data rates up to 622 megabits per second. The system consists of a set of optical transmitting, receiving, multiplexing, and repeater equipment designed in accordance with a new universal communications standard termed the Synchronous Optical Network (SONET).

In early 1990 the National Science Foundation announced a plan for development of an advanced high-speed national computer network by a group of private companies, including IBM and AT&T, U.S. government agencies and laboratories, and such leading universities as MIT, Caltech, and the University of Pennsylvania. The network will transmit data, images, and voice signals at speeds 700 times faster than is presently possible, achieving a rate of one billion bits per second.

A fiber-optic underseas cable system with potentially ten times the capacity and one tenth the cost of present systems was undergoing research at AT&T Bell Laboratories. The system is based on a new type of glass fiber containing erbium, a rare earth element, and on pump lasers which generate low-resistance waves called solitons. The cable has a capacity of 700,000 simultaneous telephone calls or the equivalent data rate of 5 billion bits per second, compared with 80,000 calls and a 560-megabit rate for the latest of the current designs. Development and field trials would continue during the early 1990s.

Australia's next generation of communication satellites, AUSSAT B, are to be built by the Hughes Corporation. They will be more powerful than the present designs and will provide Australia with direct-television broadcasts and worldwide mobile communications. It is expected that their high power level of 3 kilowatts will permit the use of receiving antennas of very small aperture (hence, small size), a great inducement to use in moving vehicles and for television reception in the home. The first satellite is scheduled to be launched in late 1991.

More than six U.S. equipment manufacturers and communication companies active in personal cellular mobile radio and radio paging businesses have proposed plans for new systems based on low-power, low-cost satellite technology usable by truck fleets, ships, and other vehicles. One of the proposed systems will use 20 satellites in low orbits of 600 mi (966 km), permitting rudimentary two-way communications requiring far less power than the conventional satellites which are in orbits 22,300 mi (35 887 km) above the Earth. Cost of a suitable ground-based terminal is estimated to be $200, compared with about $10,000 for present designs.

Motorola Inc. proposed the building of a worldwide pocket-radio telephone system using 77 low-orbiting satellites. Each satellite will cover 37 cells on the surface of the Earth, and each cell will be 400 mi (644 km) across with a capacity of 336 simultaneous conversations. Launching of the satellites is to begin in 1994. The promoters of the new system believe that it might have 5 million subscribers by the year 2000.

In mid-1990, Hitachi Ltd. announced the development of a memory chip that can store 64 million bits of information, roughly the equivalent of at least six good-size books. The chips contain 140 million semiconductor devices on an area about the size of a fingernail. This 64-megabit chip will increase greatly the capabilities of small desktop and portable battery-operated computers. A new multifunction processor chip capable of processing 66 million instructions per second was made available by the Intel Corporation. It will be used in communication equipment and in such imaging apparatus as laser printers and facsimile machines.

M. D. FAGEN
Formerly, AT&T Bell Laboratories

COMPUTERS

Research on national networks, optical computers, and other new technologies that hold promise for the future highlighted computer developments in 1990. The year also saw the introduction of numerous new computers.

Networking. Networks have become an integral part of computing. "The era of personal computers has ended. The 1990s will be the era of interpersonal computing," commented Steve Jobs, a founder of Apple Computer and, more recently, the founder of NeXT.

Local area networks (LANs) are now common within buildings, and equipment that connects LANs to each other or to wider telecommunications networks is essential to business, education, research, and government organizations. Data traffic is heavy and increasing at a phenomenal rate on these networks and on the international "umbrella," Internet, that connects some 2,000 networks in 35 countries. For example, data traffic on Internet's main pathway, NSFnet, increased at a monthly rate of 25% during 1990.

In June the National Science Foundation announced that a group of corporations, universities, and federal agencies would work together to begin development of a high-speed national network, or "data highway," that one day may connect every home in the United States. The network, using fiber-optic cables, would allow computer data to be transmitted at speeds almost 700 times faster than is possible over existing networks. Movie-like image and sound quality were planned, and the system would allow users to change data displayed on their computer screens and almost instantaneously send such data to other users. Similar development programs were under way in Japan and France.

A vivid reminder of how dependent on computers and computer networks the world has become—and how easily computer failures can cause havoc—occurred in January, when a programming error led to a nine-hour breakdown of AT&T's long-distance telephone network. Only 50% of the approximately 148 million long-distance and 800-number calls placed with AT&T that day were completed, costing AT&T up to $75 million in lost revenues and also resulting in lost business for hotels, car-rental companies, telemarketing firms, and other businesses.

New Computers. IBM introduced its System/390 generation of mainframe computers, which are designed to function in decentralized computer environments where numerous large and small computers must communicate and share information. The company also launched a new line of home computers called the PS/1.

Among the entries in the rapidly growing notebook-size computer category was Sharp Electronics' PC-6220. Weighing only 4 lbs (1.81 kg) including its battery, the powerful computer was the first of the category to use video graphics array (VGA), a high-resolution video system that makes graphics sharp and easy to read. The screen also uses the new triple-supertwist technology to improve brightness and contrast.

Sony and Canon began selling battery-operated notebook-size computers nicknamed "pen computers" and "smart paper." A user writes on the machine's touch-sensitive screen with a pen; software recognizes the letters or the complex ideographs of the Japanese language and converts them into computer type. A major drawback is that the systems depend on all users writing each letter or ideograph in a uniform manner.

Scientists at AT&T's Bell Laboratories unveiled an experimental computer that uses photons, the fundamental particles of light, rather than electronic signals to process data. When perfected, such an optical computer could work at speeds 1,000 times faster than today's most powerful machines. Unlike electrons, which react with one another and thus must be confined to wires, photons can move in free space, crossing through one another without interference. This gives optical computers the potential of carrying out millions of tasks simultaneously. Backers of the technology expected optical computers to be available commercially within the next few decades. Skeptics, however, questioned whether such a device ever would be practical.

Chips. Currently, most computers are being made with one- or four-megabit memory chips; computers with 16-megabit chips were expected within the next year or two. In June, Hitachi announced a working prototype of the world's first 64-megabit memory chip—a capacity sufficient to store the text of several novels. The thumbnail-sized chip has 140 million electronic devices, with circuits only 0.3 micron wide. Because the chip uses very little power, it will be suitable for battery-operated machines, thus allowing for the development of such products as hand-held computers that do not require heavy disk drives for data storage.

Another area that was receiving much attention from Japanese companies is X-ray lithography, a technology that many scientists were predicting will replace today's optical method of making chips. More than a dozen programs to develop the technology were under way in Japan, whereas the United States had only one major program in 1990, at IBM. X-ray lithography, which was expected to begin making chips in the mid-1990s, uses X-ray beams instead of light to wire the electronic circuits on a chip. It allows many more circuits to be packed on a chip—a necessity if companies are to produce 64-megabit and other super chips.

JENNY TESAR, *Free-lance Science Writer*

CONNECTICUT

The political scene dominated 1990 events in Connecticut.

Politics. Lowell P. Weicker, Jr., running as A Connecticut Party candidate, was elected the state's 85th governor on Nov. 6, 1990, defeating Republican John G. Rowland, Democrat Bruce A. Morrison, and Concerned Citizens Party nominee Joseph A. Zdonczyk. The victory was a political resurrection for Weicker. In 1988, Weicker, who at that time ran on the Republican ticket, narrowly lost the U.S. Senate seat he had held for 18 years to Democrat Joseph I. Lieberman.

Weicker, who always dealt with the Republican Party's leadership from a distance when he was in office, made a clean break with the party in his quest for the governorship. He formed his own party—A Connecticut Party—and was nominated by petition. Weicker repeatedly labeled his Democratic and Republican opponents as politicians and pictured himself as free of any political baggage. He led in all the polls during the campaign, although his margin of victory was slimmer than the pollsters had predicted. Weicker was the first third-party candidate in 135 years to be elected governor. He would succeed Democrat Gov. William A. O'Neill, who had been in office since 1981. O'Neill, beset by opposition in his own party and a budget deficit caused by lower-than-predicted tax revenues, did not seek reelection.

The governor-elect, however, would have to deal with a General Assembly made up of Democrats and Republicans. The Democrats retained control of the legislature. In other balloting, Weicker's running mate, attorney Eunice S. Groark, became the first woman ever elected lieutenant governor in Connecticut and Richard Blumenthal, a Democratic state senator from Stanford, was elected attorney general.

© Mara Lavitt/"New Haven Register"/Gamma-Liaison

Waterbury Alderman Gary Franks, 37, won election to the U.S. House in November, the first black Republican elected to that body in more than 50 years.

In another political first, Republican Gary Franks, a real-estate developer and basketball-team captain when he attended Yale University, became the first black elected to Congress from Connecticut. He was elected to the 5th District seat that had been held by Rowland, defeating former Congressman Toby Moffett. Reelected in other congressional races were Democrat Barbara B. Kennelly in the 1st District, Democrat Sam Gejdenson in the 2d District, Republican Christopher Shays in the 4th District, and Republican Nancy L. Johnson in the 6th District. In the 3d District, Democrat Rosa DeLauro was elected to the seat that Bruce Morrison gave up to run for governor.

Legislation. The 1990 session of the General Assembly enacted a law that opened Connecticut to nationwide banking. Previously, only New England banks could merge with or acquire Connecticut banks. Connecticut also became the first state to enact legislation making abortion a legal right under state law, rather than merely outlining the conditions under which it is permitted. A bill restricting the sale of military-style assault rifles died on the final day of the session.

Business. The 680-store Ames Department Stores Inc. in Rocky Hill sought protection from creditors in April by filing a Chapter 11 petition under the U.S. Bankruptcy Code. Part of the problem at Ames was attributed to debt it took on when it acquired the Zayre discount

---

CONNECTICUT • Information Highlights

Area: 5,018 sq mi (12 997 km²).

Population (1990 census prelim.): 3,227,000.

Chief Cities (July 1, 1988 est.): Hartford, the capital, 131,300; Bridgeport, 139,770; New Haven, 123,840; Waterbury, 104,520.

Government (1990): *Chief Officers*—governor, William A. O'Neill (D); lt. gov., Joseph J. Fauliso (D). *General Assembly*—Senate, 36 members; House of Representatives, 151 members.

State Finances (fiscal year 1989): *Revenue,* $9,045,000,000; *expenditure,* $8,972,000,000.

Personal Income (1989): $79,936,000,000; per capita, $24,683.

Labor Force (June 1990): *Civilian labor force,* 1,834,500; *unemployed,* 92,700 (5.1% of total force).

Education: *Enrollment* (fall 1988)—public elementary schools, 331,397; public secondary, 132,091; colleges and universities, 165,677. *Public school expenditures* (1989–90), $3,110,000,000.

stores chain in 1988. Colonial Realty Co. of West Hartford, a nationwide real-estate syndicator, whose limited partnerships in real estate were popular investments, was forced into bankruptcy proceedings in September. Adding to the syndicator's problems were allegations by bankers that company officials transferred company funds to personal accounts.

Court Cases. A Superior Court jury in June acquitted 19-year-old Karin Aparo of Glastonbury of being an accessory to the 1987 murder of her mother. Aparo's boyfriend was sentenced to 34 years in prison for the crime. Because the jury deadlocked over a charge of conspiracy to commit murder, Aparo was scheduled to be retried on that charge.

Former Democratic Mayor James E. Dyer of Danbury was acquitted on six counts and convicted on one count of filing a false income-tax return in a federal corruption trial. On appeal, the conviction was overturned, and a new trial was ordered.

Education. University of Connecticut President John T. Casteen III resigned after being appointed president of the University of Virginia in March. Professor Harry Hartley took over as interim president.

ROBERT F. MURPHY, *"The Hartford Courant"*

CONSUMER AFFAIRS

The conflict between the individual's right to privacy and the benefits of a consumer society continued to be a major issue in 1990. "Consumers want it all," according to Alan F. Westin, a Columbia University professor who conducted a consumer survey for Louis Harris & Associates. Westin's survey found that 70% of those questioned were either very concerned or somewhat concerned about threats to their personal privacy. A large majority said that privacy should be considered a fundamental right, and 30% said they had decided against applying for a job, credit, or insurance because they did not want to provide certain kinds of information about themselves.

"All too often, consumers are left out of the decision-making process on how personal information about them will be used," according to Bonnie Guiton, who stepped down as director of the U.S. Office of Consumer Affairs in late 1990.

Oil Prices and Inflation. The crisis in the Persian Gulf created havoc with gasoline and home-heating-oil prices during the second half of 1990. Toward the end of the year, the Consumer Price Index was increasing at an annual rate of 9.6%. Gasoline prices had risen 16.1% by the end of the third quarter, and petroleum price increases accounted for slightly more than 40% of the increase in the index. There was debate about whether the Bush administration should begin releasing oil from the Strate-

gic Petroleum Reserve, where 590 billion barrels of petroleum have been stored. In September, with prices soaring, President Bush authorized the release of 5 million barrels of oil from the reserve, less than 1% of the total reserve. (*See also* ENERGY.)

Time-Share Consumer Frauds. Many time-share vacation plans lure prospective buyers to hear their sales pitches with a variety of enticing gifts of actual minimal value. In many cases, the buyers find that after they have purchased their time-share they wish to sell the plan. In one time-share plan, 40% of the owners actively were attempting to sell their plans. Responding to these frustrated would-be sellers is a new type of business: one that claims to help time-share owners resell their vacation plans—for a fee. The Federal Trade Commission (FTC) reported, however, that in many cases these businesses have taken up-front money and failed to do anything to assist the time-share plan owner.

Telephone Settlement. A consumer settlement in Pennsylvania in 1990 ordered the Bell Telephone Company to refund $35.2 million and contribute $5 million to a telecommunications education fund. The settlement resulted from a consumer complaint focusing on deceptive marketing practices used to sell Touch-Tone and various custom-calling services. The complaint stated that Bell representatives assigned the services without advising customers they were optional and without regard to phone habits or ability to pay.

Secret Car Warranties. Automobile manufacturers periodically issue "product campaign bulletins" to their dealers about a vehicle defect for which the dealer would be reimbursed for making the needed repair. The car owner is not always informed of this warranty, however, and may or may not be reimbursed. Some of the secret warranties apply even after the vehicle's warranty has expired. The owner with a problem can protect himself by asking the dealer if there is a secret warranty for the repair.

Bank Deposits and Preapproved Credit Cards. Effective Aug. 31, 1990, Americans were guaranteed quicker access to their bank deposits. A new federal rule reduced the maximum time that banks, savings and loan associations, and credit unions can hold most deposited checks before crediting them to an account. Local checks can be held for no longer than two business days and nonlocal checks for no more than five business days.

As of May 1990, creditors who prescreen applicants, such as companies that send out "preapproved" credit-card solicitations, must be prepared to grant credit to all consumers on the prescreened list. The lender no longer may "postscreen" the applicant to see if the customer's credit status is still acceptable.

STEWART M. LEE, *Geneva College*

AP/Wide World

In Brooklyn, NY, demonstrators react to the news that Joseph Fama, a 19-year-old white, was found guilty of the second-degree murder of Yusuf Hawkins, 16, a black.

CRIME

The U.S. focus on crime during 1990 continued to be centered around illicit drugs. Much of the nation's crime, especially that of a violent nature in the urban centers, was attributed to drug-related activities.

The national drug problem took on a foreign-policy flavor with the U.S. military invasion of Panama in late 1989 and subsequent arrest of its dictator, Manuel Antonio Noriega. The military operation against Noriega was predicated significantly upon claims of Noriega's involvement in international drug smuggling and money-laundering operations against the United States.

Another political leader and his involvement with illicit drugs became the focus of national attention during 1990. Marion Barry, the mayor of Washington, DC, was caught in an FBI "sting operation" in which Barry was videotaped smoking crack cocaine. The nation's response to Barry's arrest and subsequent trial often was polarized along racial lines. Ultimately, Barry was found guilty of only one misdemeanor count of possessing cocaine while the jury was deadlocked on 12 other counts, including three felony charges of lying to a grand jury. Mayor Barry's trial highlighted the drug problem in the nation's capital. (*See also* DRUGS AND ALCOHOL.)

Famous Crimes of 1990. The crimes that made the nation's headlines in 1990 again illustrated the continued problem with violence. One of the year's most publicized crimes was the work of a serial murderer in the vicinity of the campus of the University of Florida in Gainesville. This discovery of five murder victims within 40 hours during late August threw the university and the surrounding community into a panic. The crimes were reminiscent of the serial killings of coeds at the nearby Florida State University campus. After a local student was arrested on an unrelated charge, there were no additional homicides, but law-enforcement authorities were unsure as to whether they had the murderer in custody.

The city of New York continued to be plagued with a reputation as one of the nation's most violent cities. The murder of a tourist in a New York subway by a local street gang grabbed national headlines. Young Brian Watkins, on vacation with his family, was stabbed when he came to the aid of his mother when she was assaulted by a gang member during a robbery. Much of the nation's outcry about the crime centered around the alleged motive: The gang allegedly committed the crime to get funds to get into a local nightclub. In a separate incident, an argument between a nightclub employee and her former boyfriend eventually resulted in the deaths of 87 people. Julio Gonzalez, 36, was ordered to leave the Happy Land Social Club in New York after he began arguing with his estranged girlfriend. Gonzalez later returned to the club with a container of gasoline and set the front door aflame.

Three suspects in the 1989 "wilding" incident were tried in 1990 for the brutal assault and rape of a young woman who was jogging through Central Park. Yusef Salaam, Antron McCray, and Raymond Santana were found guilty of their roles in the attack and sentenced to prison terms. Two other defendants in the case—Kevin Richardson and Kharey Wise—later were found guilty of attempted murder and rape and of sexual abuse and assault, respectively. A sixth defendant, Steven Lopez, was to go on trial in the case early in 1991.

Another publicized 1989 crime story took on a bizarre conclusion during 1990. In the latter part of 1989, the alleged shooting of a pregnant attorney and her husband by a black armed robber touched off an intense manhunt and investigation in Boston. Carol Stuart and her prematurely born son died as a result of the incident, while her husband, Charles, was hospitalized with a gunshot wound in the abdomen. Early in 1990 evidence began to surface that the entire incident was a hoax and that Charles Stuart, a prosperous businessman, had murdered his wife, fabricating the robbery story to cover his crime. Charles Stuart committed suicide before he could be questioned about the new evidence.

AP/Wide World

In July a mistrial was declared in the second trial of Raymond Buckey, ending the long McMartin child-molestation case in Los Angeles. He was acquitted in his first trial.

The year 1990 also saw the conclusion of the longest and one of the most expensive criminal trials in U.S. history. The McMartin Preschool trial, lasting almost three years, ended with the acquittal of Peggy McMartin Buckey and her son Raymond Buckey on 52 counts of child sexual abuse. The jury was hung on 13 other charges. A jury later was deadlocked on eight remaining charges against Raymond Buckey. Much of the inability of the prosecution to win this case was attributed to interview techniques utilized with the child victims, as well as the extended length of the investigation and trial. The McMartin investigation and trial highlighted the problems associated with child sexual-abuse cases, the reporting of which has increased significantly since the mid-1970s. Overall the case cost the state some $15 million.

Hate Crimes. In the final days of 1989, two mail bombs killed a federal judge in Alabama and a black civil-rights lawyer in Georgia. During the same period, two more parcel bombs were discovered in Florida and in Georgia, but were disarmed by law-enforcement authorities. The bombings became the focus of a major investigation by the Federal Bureau of Investigation (FBI) and in November, Walter Leroy Moody, a 56-year-old Georgian, was charged with murder in the case. The incidents also prompted the passage of a federal "Hate Crimes Act," which mandates reporting of racially motivated events to law enforcement authorities.

Crime Rates. The FBI released its compilation of crime statistics for 1989 in August. The Crime Index rose 2% from 1988 to 143 million offenses in 1989. These 1989 figures were 15% higher than in 1985 and 6% above the 1980 level. The biggest gain in the crime rate concerned violent crime, which increased 5% from 1988. All violent crimes registered an increase, including murder (4%) and forcible rape (2%). Property crime was up 2% during the same time period. Increases in property crime were reported in two categories: motor-vehicle theft (9%) and larceny-theft (2%). Property crime declined, however, for the offenses of burglary (down 2%) and arson (down 1%).

Preliminary reports indicated that 1990 may have been a record year for murder in the United States. A study by the Senate Judiciary Committee found an 8% increase in the nation's murder count during the first six months of 1990. If that trend continued, an estimated 23,220 Americans would be slain in 1990. That number would surpass the previous record of 23,040 homicide victims who died in 1980. During the first six months of 1990, violent offenses increased overall by 10%, twice the increase registered in the same category for 1989.

Crime Legislation and Gun Control. The major crime legislation of 1990 was the Comprehensive Crime Control Act, which was enacted just prior to congressional adjournment. Among the many provisions of the act, which was a watered-down version of the original crime package, were new penalties for child abuse, bank fraud, and certain drug offenses. The act also contained provisions for funding increases for law enforcement and prison alternatives. Senate-House conferees were unable to agree on provisions regarding the death penalty, appeals by condemned prisoners, and gun control.

The accessibility and availability of guns continued to be a controversial topic in 1990. Fueled by several "spree" killings (where an individual randomly shoots people in a public place or business), the focus of 1990 gun-control legislative and media battles was the enactment of "waiting periods" for handgun purchases. Such legislation also would require prospective handgun buyers to undergo a background check by law-enforcement authorities before being allowed to purchase a handgun. The purpose of such waiting periods, therefore, would be to force an angry and potentially violent citizen to "cool off" before buying a handgun, while also permitting police to determine if the individual has factors in his background that might preclude him from owning a firearm (i.e., a felony conviction). Proposals of this nature were the focus of federal and state gun-control bills.

In years past, the primary opponents and lobbyists battling over this issue were the pro-gun National Rifle Association (NRA) and the

On Feb. 9, 1990, John Gotti, the reputed head of the Gambino crime family, was acquitted in State Supreme Court in New York City of assault and conspiracy charges.

gun-control advocacy group Handgun Control. Much of the efforts of these opposing groups has concerned a national seven-day waiting period supported by Handgun Control. The Brady bill, named after Jim Brady, a gunshot victim of John Hinckley during the 1981 assassination attempt on President Ronald Reagan, is the primary legislative agenda of Brady's wife, Sarah, the head of Handgun Control. Sarah Brady argues that the national waiting period would reduce violence related to handguns and would ensure that guns would not fall into the hands of such persons as convicted felons and the mentally disturbed. The NRA has attacked the Brady bill as a harassment of honest citizens and argues that criminals only would continue to resort to obtaining guns through illegal means. Congress again failed to enact the Brady bill in 1990.

The Death Penalty. Since the death penalty was reinstated in the landmark 1976 case of *Gregg v. Georgia*, the populations of the nation's "death rows" have continued to grow, while actual executions have continued to be relatively infrequent. About 300 prisoners are condemned every year, but fewer than 20 are executed, and the death-row population in 1990 exceeded 2,300 in the 37 states that sanction capital punishment. Much of the delay in executions is attributed to appeals based on writs of habeas corpus, which permit prisoners to

challenge how they were arrested and convicted. The U.S. Supreme Court attempted to limit these appeals in a 1990 ruling concerning a South Carolina death-row inmate. The court held that a condemned inmate cannot base habeas-corpus challenges on rulings announced by courts after his case has gone through a first round of appeals. This decision, therefore, substantially diminished the potential length of the appeal process by omitting the amount of appeals to the federal court system. As a result of this new ruling, executions of death-row inmates were expected to increase significantly in the coming years.

The question of the death penalty also grew as a political issue in the 1990 election year. With a majority of Americans now favoring capital punishment, many politicians adopted the death penalty as part of their campaign platform. Though the use of capital punishment usually has been associated with a conservative/Republican philosophy, 1990 was the year that saw the death penalty being endorsed also by more liberal, Democratic politicians. Among the new "converts" to the death penalty were Andrew Young in his unsuccessful bid for the governorship of Georgia and Dianne Feinstein, the former mayor of San Francisco who lost the gubernatorial race in California.

Organized Crime. The FBI continued its targeting of traditional organized-crime syndicates belonging to the Mafia or "La Cosa Nostra." In February 1990 the Justice Department filed a massive civil-racketeering lawsuit against top officers of the International Longshoremen's Association, several dockworker employers, and dozens of suspected organized-crime figures for an alleged takeover of New York and New Jersey waterfronts. In March, Attorney General Dick Thornburgh announced three indictments in Boston charging virtually the entire active leadership and membership of the Raymond Patriarca family of La Cosa Nostra with criminal activities, including murder, conspiracy to commit murder, extortion, kidnapping, drug trafficking, gambling, and obstruction of justice. Twenty-one defendants would face 113 counts of alleged criminal activity.

White-Collar Crime. The major white-collar-crime issues of 1990 continued to be investigations concerning the savings-and-loan controversy, one of the biggest financial scandals in U.S. history (*see* BANKING AND FINANCE). In another white-collar case, baseball great and former Cincinnati Reds manager Pete Rose was sentenced to prison for two felony counts of tax evasion. Rose, whose gambling activities while manager of the Reds resulted in his lifetime suspension from baseball, was serving his sentence in federal prison.

JACK ENTER, *Program Director*
Criminal Justice Coordinating Council
Atlanta, GA

Cuba under Fidel Castro (right) was one of the few nations to reject the growing tide toward democracy and remain steadfast toward the Communist system.

AP/Wide World

CUBA

Serious economic difficulties, endemic in Cuba virtually since it fell under the rule of Fidel Castro three decades ago, worsened precipitously in 1990 and prospects were for an even deeper decline in 1991. At the same time, the country was the only member of the former Communist bloc in which no reforms took place, and in which none were contemplated.

Politics. The Castro regime continued to proclaim its unwavering faith in Marxist-Leninist doctrine. Havana denounced, often in bitter terms, changes in the Soviet Union and its former allies, and the criticisms of Cuba that appear in those nations' media now that they are free from state censorship. Rather than liberalizing the economy, President Castro stated, "we must progressively socialize more." The ruling Communist Party of Cuba, though nominally in charge of the country's life, was becoming more irrelevant. In 1990 the size of its apparatus, and thus its power base, was cut by 50%. Its position was reduced to being a vehicle for constant adulation of Castro.

Economy. Cuba's economic problems were basically twofold: Domestic production decreased in most sectors, as did the already low productivity; and the annual $5 billion Soviet subsidy, which for years practically has kept the country afloat, diminished substantially. There were frequent delays in the arrival of vital products, among them on one occasion flour, which resulted in a severe monthlong shortage of bread in Cuba. The economic aid was expected to disappear in 1991. By then, Moscow's trade with Havana, which in 1990 represented 75% of Cuba's total, would begin to be based on hard-currency exchanges of goods rather than on the present system of subsidized pricing which heavily favored Cuban exports, principally sugar, and undervalued So-

viet imports, notably petroleum. But despite Moscow's rapid movement toward a market economy, its trade with Cuba was expected to continue, Soviet officials declared in Havana. Cuba still supplies the USSR with 30% of its sugar consumption and 50% of its citrus fruit.

Cuba's once substantial and also subsidized trade with East European countries practically disappeared in 1990. The Soviet Union also reportedly notified Cuba in April that beginning in 1995, it would have to begin repaying in dollars its accumulated trade-imbalance debt, estimated at $20 billion. Even though the government announced that the 1990 harvest of sugar, the country's main export, was 8.04 million metric tons, just below the 1989 total of 8.1 million, Havana said there were serious delays in the sugarcane planting for the 1991 harvest. For the first time in 50 years, because of an oil shortage, oxen and other animals were used in large numbers in Cuban agriculture.

Preparing the population for a period of severe economic hardships, the government put into effect a new, stringent rationing of food and energy. In September it added 28 food items to its ration list, as well as other goods such as shoes, clothes, textiles, hygiene products, and toys. Many other products disap-

---

CUBA • Information Highlights

Official Name: Republic of Cuba.
Location: Caribbean.
Area: 42,803 sq mi (110 860 km²).
Population (mid-1990 est.): 10,600,000.
Chief Cities (Dec. 31, 1987 est.): Havana, the capital, 2,059,223; Santiago de Cuba, 389,654; Camagöey, 274,974; Holguín, 218,148.
Government: *Head of state and government,* Fidel Castro Ruz, president (took office under a new constitution, Dec. 1976). *Legislature* (unicameral) —National Assembly of People's Power.
Foreign Trade (1988 U.S.$): *Imports,* $7,579,000,000; *exports,* $5,518,000,000.

peared from Cuban shops. Deliveries of oil and gas were cut to industries, and families were told to reduce their electricity consumption by at least 10%. The government imported 500,000 bicycles, giving them to workers in order to save fuel used by public transportation in the cities. Because of the shortage of Soviet-supplied newsprint, Havana closed several major publications; *Granma*, Cuba's only national newspaper, was reduced to eight pages.

More important, some large and many medium-size industries were shut down, and the workday was cut in others to save energy. President Castro himself announced the shutdown of the Moa nickel plant, one of Cuba's largest industrial installations, stoppage of work at the large Cienfuegos oil refinery, and a construction slowdown at a nuclear-power plant. Castro also warned that other industries might suffer the same fate and indicated that workers, who he said would continue to be paid, would be sent to work in agriculture.

But despite growing shortages of all consumer goods and political stagnation, the 64-year-old Castro appeared to be in firm control. He seemed to have the complete support of the army and the huge security apparatus, both of which were purged in 1989 of real and potential advocates of *perestroika* and *glasnost*. There were no signs of dissidence on the streets, where the Committees for the Defense of the Revolution (government-sponsored vigilante groups) were able to thwart any attempts by Cubans to express their views on the way the Castro regime was ruling the country.

Foreign Affairs. Cuba condemned the Iraqi invasion of Kuwait and voted at the UN Security Council to demand that Iraq withdraw its forces to reestablish the sovereignty of Kuwait, although it abstained on the embargo resolution. In November the Cuban UN delegation voted against a U.S.-sponsored resolution authorizing the use of force against Iraq, despite a meeting between U.S. Secretary of State James Baker and Cuba's Foreign Minister Isidoro Malmierca in which Baker made a vain attempt to gain Cuban support. The meeting was the highest-level contact between the two countries since 1981.

Cuban troops continued to be withdrawn from Angola, where they had been stationed since 1975, and Havana announced that the remaining soldiers would be brought home by the middle of 1991, thus ending the last of the Castro government's military interventions in foreign conflicts. On the propaganda-war front, Havana scored a victory of sorts by effectively jamming transmissions of TV Marti, an anti-Castro station based in Florida. The legality of this $33 million propaganda project, produced under the aegis of the U.S. Information Agency, was disputed under the 1982 International Telecommunication Convention.

GEORGE VOLSKY, *University of Miami*

CYPRUS

The year 1990 marked the 30th anniversary of Cyprus' independence from Great Britain as well as the 16th year since the island-country had been cut in two by a Turkish invasion in support of the minority Turkish Cypriots. The northern territories that had been grabbed by Turkey in 1974 had been proclaimed unilaterally as the "Turkish Republic of Northern Cyprus" in 1983. Except for Turkey, this political entity was not recognized by the international community. Nonetheless a Turkish Cypriot, Rauf Denktas, was reelected president in the north on April 22. The unoccupied part of the island was led by Greek Cypriot George Vassiliou, president of the internationally recognized Republic of Cyprus. Vassiliou steadfastly refused to recognize Denktas' position as legitimate.

Attempts to find a solution to the division were complicated by the presence of large numbers of Turkish troops in the north, the influx of an estimated 65,000 to 80,000 emigrants from mainland Turkey, the inability of the 200,000 Greek Cypriot refugees to return to the northern homes and businesses they fled during the 1974 invasion, and the continued question of the fate of more than 1,500 Greek Cypriots missing since 1974. In 1990 the mandate of the UN peacekeeping force once again was renewed. These troops had been stationed on Cyprus since 1964, after the first outbreak of intercommunal fighting between Greek and Turkish Cypriots in 1963.

Search for a Solution. Formal talks between Vassiliou and Denktas, sponsored by UN Secretary-General Javier Pérez de Cuéllar, broke down in early 1990, although he made continuing efforts to revive them. U.S. Ambassador Nelson Ledsky, special Cyprus coordinator at the State Department, also made several trips to Greece, Turkey, and Cyprus to discuss the impasse.

Cyprus and the Kuwaiti Crisis. The government of President Vassiliou, ruling in a state where about 37% of the territory was under

---

CYPRUS · Information Highlights

Official Name: Republic of Cyprus.
Location: Eastern Mediterranean.
Area: 3,571 sq mi (9 250 km²).
Population (mid-1990 est.): 700,000.
Chief Cities (1982 est.): Nicosia, the capital, 149,100; Limassol, 107,200.
Government: *Head of state and government,* George Vassiliou, president (took office Feb. 1988). *Legislature*—House of Representatives.
Monetary Unit: Pound (0.452 pound equals U.S.$1, July 1990).
Gross Domestic Product (1988 est. U.S.$): $4,200,-000,000.
Economic Index (1989): *Consumer Prices* (1980 = 100), all items, 154.0; food, 164.5.
Foreign Trade (1989 U.S.$): *Imports,* $2,281,000,000; *exports,* $810,000,000.

foreign occupation by Turkey, quickly condemned Iraq for invading Kuwait. Vassiliou also pointed out that prior UN resolutions in 1974 dealing with the occupation of Cyprus had been disregarded by Turkey. The Turkish government, in turn, resisted any efforts to link the Cyprus situation with what was transpiring in Kuwait.

Under the terms of Cypriot independence in 1960, Great Britain retained complete control over its Sovereign Base Area totaling about 3% of the island's territory. This area took on added importance as the crisis over Kuwait escalated.

Economy. The Republic of Cyprus, an associate member of the European Community (EC), applied for full membership on July 4. The Greek government applauded the move, but Denktas, backed by Turkey, objected to the admission of unoccupied Cyprus into the economic alliance.

Despite the occupation in the north, the rest of Cyprus continued to enjoy a strong economy in 1990, including a tourism industry that contributed substantially to the foreign exchange earnings.

Art Treasures. The Cyprus Antiquities Department in unoccupied Cyprus deplored the destruction of the beautifully frescoed 14th-century monastery church of the Panagia Avgasidas in the Turkish-occupied village of Aloa. In October the U.S. Court of Appeals for the Seventh Circuit in Chicago upheld a Federal District Court decision of August 1989 which returned to the Greek Orthodox Church of Cyprus ownership of four priceless, 6th-century mosaics that had been looted from the Panagia Kanakaria church in the north after the 1974 invasion.

GEORGE J. MARCOPOULOS, *Tufts University*

CZECHOSLOVAKIA

In 1990, Czechoslovakia experienced its first year of freedom from Communist rule, and tried to deal with the difficult problems resulting from the change in regime.

Politics. On June 8 and 9 elections were held for the Federal Assembly as well as for the Czech and Slovak National Councils, the legislatures of federated Czechoslovakia's two states. These were the first free elections since 1946. Voter participation reached an impressive 96% of the electorate. Some 23 political parties and groupings took part, but most of them did not win any seats, since they failed to get the required minimum 5% of the vote. As had been expected, the big winners were the Czech Civic Forum and the Slovak Public Against Violence, the twin anticommunist groups which spearheaded the movement that toppled the Communist dictatorship in the fall of 1989. Together they obtained 47% of the

vote, which netted them 87 of the 150 seats in the Federal Assembly's House of the People and 83 of the 150 seats of the House of Nations. The Civic Forum also won 127 of the 200 seats in the Czech National Council and the Public Against Violence won 48 of the 160 seats of the Slovak National Council. The reconstituted Communist Party took second place with 14% of the vote; the Christian Democratic Coalition was third with 12%.

The new Federal Assembly reelected Alexander Dubček as its chairman and Václav Havel (*see* BIOGRAPHY) as president of the republic, both for two-year terms; former Communist Marian Čalfa continued as prime minister.

On November 23–24 the voters went to the polls again to elect new organs of local government to replace the Communist-controlled national committees. In the Czech Republic voters elected communal assemblies which then chose the community's council and mayor. In the Slovak Republic voters elected the communal assembly and mayor separately.

The Economy. The government's first task was to restructure the stagnant economy and make it more competitive in world markets. In the first six months of 1990, as compared with 1989, industrial production fell by 2% and construction by 5%; 26.6% fewer apartments were built. The average wage rose by 2.5%, but labor productivity remained at the same level. Disproportions between supply and demand were said to have "deepened." Although foreign trade with free-market countries rose by 6.1%, the trade deficit remained at about $87 million. About the only good economic news was a very good grain harvest.

After a lengthy debate about how best to achieve the desired transition to a predominantly privatized, market-oriented economy, the Federal Assembly passed a number of laws designed to facilitate this change. By the end of 1990 some 70,000 smaller publicly owned enterprises, such as restaurants, shops, and other services, were to be sold at auction to the high-

---

CZECHOSLOVAKIA • Information Highlights

Official Name: Czech and Slovak Federative Republic.
Location: East-central Europe.
Area: 49,371 sq mi (127 870 km²).
Population (mid-1990 est.): 15,700,000.
Chief Cities (Jan. 1, 1989 est.): Prague, the capital, 1,211,207; Bratislava, 435,710; Brno, 389,789.
Government: *Head of state,* Václav Havel, president (elected June 1990). *Head of government,* Marian Calfa, premier (took office Dec. 10, 1989). *Legislature*—Federal Assembly.
Gross National Product (1989 est. U.S.$): $123,200,000,000.
Economic Indexes (1989): *Consumer Prices* (1980 = 100), all items, 112.7; food, 114.1. *Industrial Production* (1980 = 100), 124.
Foreign Trade (1989 U.S.$): *Imports,* $14,277,000,000; *exports,* $14,455,000,000.

Czechoslovakia's new President Václav Havel welcomed Pope John Paul II to a windy Prague on April 21, 1990. Two days earlier, Czechoslovakia and the Vatican had reestablished diplomatic relations.

AP/Wide World

est bidder. Most of the larger enterprises would be converted into joint-stock companies and their shares sold to the public, with priority given to their respective employees. State subsidies were to be reduced gradually, state expenditures drastically cut, a new tax system enacted, and prices gradually decontrolled. Import restrictions were being liberalized and foreign investments encouraged. Private entrepreneurs had the right to establish their own businesses with no limit on the number of employees they could hire. By the end of 1990 there were some 224,000 private entrepreneurs in Czechoslovakia, compared with 86,000 in December 1989. The majority, however, still were operating only on a part-time basis. Members of agricultural cooperatives now could reclaim their land or be paid fair compensation for it. If all went as hoped, Czechoslovakia's currency would become convertible.

These changes would not be accomplished easily. As government subsidies are reduced, prices will rise, and living standards will suffer. Unemployment will increase as poor and superfluous workers are laid off and unprofitable enterprises are closed. With hardly any oil of its own, Czechoslovakia also will be hurt badly by reduced shipments of Soviet oil, and the Soviet decision to trade only for hard currencies beginning in January 1991. All these difficulties are made even worse by the huge expense the country will face when coping with the rampant pollution caused by decades of disregard for the environment.

Growing Disillusion. People's unhappiness about falling living standards was compounded further by increasing skepticism about the government's ability to handle the situation. There were widespread complaints about Communist bureaucrats still clinging to their offices, and about official procrastination and amateurism. Although President Havel himself remained popular, the Civic Forum, his main political power base, was weakened by dissension among its heterogeneous segments.

Power-Sharing Crisis. The freedom of expression that resulted from the "velvet revolution" of 1989 opened up a channel for the Slovaks to press for more powers to be transferred from federal authorities to the Slovak republic. In response to Slovak wishes the name of Czechoslovakia was changed to Czech and Slovak Federal Republic. In December, however, a dispute arose over a power-sharing agreement between the federal government and the two republics. Slovak Premier Vladimir Meciar declared that if Prague did not meet Slovak demands, his government would "proclaim the supremacy of its laws over the laws of the Federal Assembly." President Havel charged that this would mean "the beginning of Czechoslovakia's disintegration as a state," and asked the Federal Assembly for "special powers" to deal with the situation. On December 12 parliament enacted legislation clearly outlining the powers of the Czech and Slovak regional governments.

International Relations. A tremendous increase occurred in contacts with the Western world. High-level Czech and Slovak representatives paid visits to a long list of countries. President Havel traveled to Washington, where he addressed a joint session of the U.S. Congress. Prague too became a favorite destination for Western dignitaries. Pope John Paul II visited Czechoslovakia in April, and U.S. President George Bush went in November.

Czechoslovakia was granted most-favored-nation status in a U.S.-Czechoslovak trade agreement concluded in April. An agreement signed with France provided for cultural and educational exchanges. Czechoslovakia became a member of the World Bank and the International Monetary Fund. Negotiations began with the European Commission about Czechoslovakia's association with the European Community.

See also EUROPE feature, page 36.

EDWARD TABORSKY
University of Texas, Austin

DANCE

Change in many aspects colored the U.S. dance scene in 1990. Financial uncertainties, internal disputes, and retirements affected major ballet companies. New choreographers came to the fore. U.S. audiences welcomed an influx of folk dancing and for the first time, regional ballet troupes attracted the kind of national attention usually reserved for companies based in New York.

Ballet. American Ballet Theatre (ABT) underwent an important administrative change with artistic implications during the year when the company named Jane Hermann and Oliver Smith as codirectors to succeed Mikhail Baryshnikov, who had resigned suddenly in September 1989 after a clash with executive director Hermann and the company board. Smith, a scenic designer, served previously as director with Lucia Chase from 1945 to 1980, but it was assumed that in the near future Hermann would make the artistic decisions.

On January 14, Ballet Theatre celebrated its 50th anniversary with a gala performance at New York's Metropolitan Opera House. Many company alumni returned, but Baryshnikov was absent. Celebrations continued during the year in New York and in various other cities. Among the presentations during the jubilee season, from January through July, were Frederick Ashton's 1956 *Birthday Offering* and the premieres *Brief Fling* by Twyla Tharp and *Elegy* by Vladimir Vassiliev, the former Bolshoi star who also performed in ABT's *Giselle* with his wife Yekaterina Maksimova. Faruk Ruzimatov of the Kirov joined ABT for the spring season.

Jerome Robbins already had announced his retirement as codirector (with Peter Martins) of the New York City Ballet but supervised the rehearsal of 28 of his works. When City Ballet closed its two-week *Festival of Jerome Robbins' Ballets* on June 17, it became clear that the choreographer was bidding farewell to the company with which he had been associated since 1949. While the Robbins festival included no new pieces, City Ballet celebrated the originality that is Robbins' signature. The City Ballet season included premieres by others: *Prague Symphony* by Richard Tanner; *Missa Sicca* by Robert LaFosse and Peter Martins; and *Fearful Symmetries* by Martins.

A bitter dispute within the Joffrey Ballet made national headlines. Gerald Arpino, who founded the troupe in 1956 with Robert Joffrey (who died in 1988), defeated what he called a takeover attempt from a faction on the Joffrey board. It was disclosed that the management had not paid $800,000 in withholding taxes. When the board appointed a committee whose power would supersede Arpino's as artistic director, he resigned and withdrew performance rights to his ballets. In the wake of support from his dancers and the public, Arpino returned and the company's cochairmen, Anthony Bliss and David Murdock, resigned. The Joffrey survived the crisis but, like other U.S. dance troupes, faced financial difficulties.

The Dance Theatre of Harlem announced an unexpected six-month layoff and a projected deficit of $1.7 million. New grants enabled the dancers to resume rehearsals in the fall.

Eliot Feld was prolific during the year, creating *Ah Scarlatti*, *Contra Pose*, *Charmed Lives*, and *Mother Nature* for Feld Ballets/NY.

On an artistic level the ballet world was changing to include a surge toward national recognition by troupes outside New York City. The San Francisco Ballet's artistic director, Helgi Tomasson, staged a new version of *The Sleeping Beauty*, placing the action in Russia rather than in France. When the company performed at the Kennedy Center in Washington, Tomasson was acclaimed for raising the dancers' classical technique to a new standard.

The Boston Ballet gained attention with an unusually staged *Swan Lake*. Each cast featured a star from either the Soviet Bolshoi or Kirov Ballets and a partner from the Boston Ballet. The straightforward production by Konstantin Sergeyev of the Kirov was welcomed after recent untraditional versions.

Despite the mounting of such classics, there were fewer revivals than in the past. The accent was on new works. Ballet Chicago, directed by Daniel Duell, was another regional group to win notice. It introduced a promising new choreographer in Gordon Piece Schmidt, whose ballet, *By Django*, displayed a fresh but assured neoclassical style.

Among ballet troupes to visit the United States in 1990 were the Australian Ballet and, from France, the Ballet Theater of Nancy and the National Ballet of Marseilles. French superstar Patrick Dupond, who in February succeeded Rudolf Nureyev as artistic director of the Paris Opera Ballet, appeared in both.

Soviet dancers were ubiquitous, either as guests (Lyudmila Semenyaka danced with Ballet Theatre) or with their own companies. The Bolshoi Ballet, in New York and at Wolf Trap Farm Park in Virginia, did not have the impact of the past in Yuri Grigorovich's ballets, but dancers like Nina Ananiashvili and Aleksei Fadeyechev stood out. A touring contingent from the Kirov Ballet revealed talented newcomers such as Igor Zelensky. Young talent was seen in the Russian Ballet, directed by Vyacheslav Gordeyev, and in *The Nutcracker*, as performed by a troupe formed by the Bolshoi Ballet director and known as the Bolshoi Ballet Grigorovich Company.

Modern Dance. The most original premieres of the dance year were in the area of modern dance. Mark Morris, whose company is based in Brussels, presented new works in New York, Boston, and at the Jacob's Pillow Dance

One of the most talked-about premieres of the dance year was Bill T. Jones' "The Last Supper at Uncle Tom's Cabin/The Promised Land," an experimental piece using dance and drama that dealt with love, loss, faith, betrayal, and race.

Festival in Becket, MA. Baryshnikov also formed a modern-dance troupe, the White Oak Dance Project (named after the White Oak Plantation in Jacksonville, FL, the rehearsal site), that performed only Morris works, including *Pas de Poisson* and *Motorcade*.

Morris' style was captured better by his own Monnaie Dance Group/Mark Morris, whose big success was *L'Allegro, il Penseroso ed il Moderato*, with its inventive view of Handel's music. Morris' work was considered uneven, but his association with Baryshnikov attracted a new following. *Behemoth*, *Going Away Party*, *Wonderland*, *Love Song Waltzes*, *Prelude and Prelude*, and *Tamil Film Songs in Stereo* were the other premieres.

Two experimental works stimulated wide interest. In *The Last Supper at Uncle Tom's Cabin/The Promised Land*, choreographer Bill T. Jones asked questions about faith and freedom, using dance, drama, speech, and spectacle, and ending with an all-nude cast. In *Contenders*, Susan Marshall explored athletic partnering and used a sports metaphor to describe emotional relationships.

Among other modern-dance premieres were *August Pace*, *Inventions*, and *Polarity* by Merce Cunningham; *Maple Leaf Rag* by Martha Graham; *The Sorcerer's Sofa* and *Of Bright & Blue Birds & the Gala Sun* by Paul Taylor; *Fandango* and *From Paris to Jupiter* by Lar Lubovitch; and *Shaman II*, *Infinity*, and *Inner Circle* by Laura Dean. The Alvin Ailey American Dance Theater, under its new director, Judith Jamison, offered Pearl Primus' *Impinyuza* and Donald McKayle's *Games*.

Ethnic Dance. There were visits to the United States from foreign companies performing in various dance idioms, with a rise in folk ensembles. The most outstanding were the Hungarian State Folk Ensemble and Soviet groups—the Don Cossacks, the Georgian State Dancers, the Rustavi Dance Company of Georgia, and Lezginka from Daghestan.

The start of the yearlong Indonesia Festival introduced the Court Art of Java. Other groups with an ethnic flavor included Cumbre Flamenco from Spain, Ballet Folklórico from Mexico, and the Classical Dance Company of Cambodia.

Other News. A major event that focused on U.S. dance took place in France at the Biennale Internationale de la Danse in Lyons, which presented works by 23 U.S. troupes or choreographers. Ralph Lemon, a rising star on the experimental scene, Karole Armitage, and Lucinda Childs created works to music by Frank Zappa for the Lyons Opera Ballet as part of the festival. A pall was cast at the beginning of the Biennale when Steve Condos, a tap virtuoso, died of a heart attack following his performance.

Other deaths in 1990 included Hermes Pan, one of Hollywood's best choreographers; Ian Horvath, cofounder of the Cleveland Ballet; and Norbert Vesak, a former director of the Metropolitan Opera Ballet.

Twyla Tharp received the Samuel Scripps-American Dance Festival Award and Jacques d'Amboise received the Capezio Dance Award.

Anna Kisselgoff, *"The New York Times"*

As chairman of the U.S. Senate Judiciary Committee, Delaware's Sen. Joseph Biden presided over the hearings into the nomination of David H. Souter to the U.S. Supreme Court. In November the 48-year-old Democrat was reelected to a fourth Senate term.

© Bob McNeely/Sipa

DELAWARE

Politics dominated events in Delaware during 1990.

Elections. Vindication was a theme sounded on election night in Delaware. Sen. Joseph Biden (D) was returned to office with 62% of the vote over his opponent M. Jane Brady. Biden, who chairs the Senate Judiciary Committee, had run for the 1988 Democratic presidential nomination but had dropped out amid charges that he plagiarized some of his speeches and former schoolwork. He also had recovered from a life-threatening illness. Brady attempted to make his character a major issue, but his resounding reelection enhanced his prominence as one of the Senate's leading Democrats and a possible presidential aspirant.

Also emerging with new political clout was U.S. Rep. Tom Carper (D), who defeated his opponent Ralph O. Williams with 66% of the vote to capture a fourth term. Carper, who overcame a bitter primary challenge, emerged as a likely person to succeed Gov. Michael Castle, who is forbidden by law from seeking a third term in 1992.

In state legislative elections, the Democrats strengthened their majority in the state Senate by two votes and the Republicans, who controlled the state House, increased their lead by one vote. Two of Delaware's county councils changed hands politically as Kent went Republican and Sussex returned to majority control by the Democrats. New Castle County remained under the control of the Democrats.

Legislative Session. The onset of fiscal stress did not daunt Governor Castle and legislative leaders from proclaiming the 135th General Assembly the most successful in recent memory. Legislators were forced to cope with revenue projections which had declined from those used to build the governor's original budget proposal. Although the budget was passed with relative ease, the continuing decline in projected revenues precipitated additional expenditure cuts in the 1991 budget.

Significant legislation passed during 1990 included a new statewide paramedic program, a law permitting state-chartered banks to sell insurance, and the creation of a new state "superfund" law to finance the cleanup of hazardous-waste sites. Legislation also was passed to expand the acquisition of environmentally sensitive lands for public use. A new program to set up "greenways" (natural corridors or trails) in the state was created. Lawmakers considered a number of recycling proposals, but passed only one program establishing voluntary recycling centers.

DELAWARE • Information Highlights

Area: 2,045 sq mi (5 295 km²).
Population (1990 census prelim.): 658,000.
Chief Cities (1980 census): Dover, the capital, 23,512; Wilmington, 70,195; Newark, 25,247; Elsmere, 6,493.
Government (1990): *Chief Officers*—governor, Michael N. Castle (R); lt. gov., Dale E. Wolf (R). *General Assembly*—Senate, 21 members; House of Representatives, 41 members.
State Finances (fiscal year 1989): *Revenue,* $2,257,000,000: *expenditure,* $1,929,000,000.
Personal Income (1989): $12,437,000,000; per capita, $18,483.
Labor Force (June 1990): *Civilian labor force,* 367,600; *unemployed,* 12,800 (3.5% of total force).
Education: *Enrollment* (fall 1988)—public elementary schools, 68,886; public secondary, 27,792; colleges and universities, 38,260. *Public school expenditures* (1989–90), $478,763,000.

Along with New Jersey, Delaware approved legislation to expand the powers of the bistate Delaware River and Bay Authority, which operates the Delaware Memorial Bridge and the Cape May to Lewes Ferry. The legislation authorizes the authority to enter into environmental and economic development projects around the river's shoreline. Some revenue enhancements, including a local option to increase the real-estate-transfer tax and increases in the tax on liquor, cigarettes, and gasoline, were passed.

The Economy. Recession came into view in the second half of 1990 as Delaware joined neighboring states in registering declining job growth, higher unemployment, and declining state revenues. Unemployment stood at 5.4% in October 1990, compared with 3.6% one year earlier, bringing the rate up to the level of the national average. As 1990 came to a close economists expected that the downturn in the state would be shorter and milder than that being experienced elsewhere in the nation.

JEROME R. LEWIS
University of Delaware

DENMARK

A number of changes in Denmark's cabinet as well as a series of local elections in late 1989 helped set the nation off on a fairly steady course in 1990.

Political Affairs. Upon the resignation of Finance Minister Palle Simonsen on Oct. 30, 1989, Prime Minister Poul Schlüter appointed Henning Dyremose in his place. The latter was succeeded as minister of labor by Knud Erik Kirkegaard. Minister of Industries Niels Wilhjelm also resigned and was succeeded by Anne Birgitte Lundholt. All departing and incoming ministers were members of Schlüter's Conservative Party. As of late 1990 the Danish coalition government, strongly opposed by the Social Democrats and its allies, consisted of nine Conservatives, seven Liberals, and five Radical Liberals.

Local and provincial elections, held on Nov. 21, 1989, had shown some decline in the national support of the Conservative Party, with the Progressives and the Liberals (Venstre) registering certain gains.

The advances made by democracy in East Europe vis-à-vis the Communists served as an example for the Danish Communist Party, which succeeded in depriving the Stalinist old guard of its power. At an extraordinary congress of the party, the Stalinists kept only five members on the Central Committee while the reformers won 30 mandates. In the future the Communist Party would participate in national elections as a partner on a single ticket with the Left Socialists and the Socialist Workers' Party.

The Economy. The Danish economy had been somewhat depressed in the late 1980s, but a spring 1990 economic report by the economic secretariat of the government pointed out various favorable aspects. Included were rising production, increasing exports, growing investments, increasing consumption, 38,000 new jobs in the private sector, lower taxes to the tune of 2%, and lower prices.

A report by the Organization of Economic Cooperation and Development (OECD) issued early in the year stated that the government's intervention in the economy has not been sufficiently effective and such problems as unemployment and the deficit still were unsolved. It held that Denmark's annual economic growth stood at 10%, lower than the average among the OECD countries.

The Faroe Islands. Economic difficulties continued to put their stamp on daily life in the Faroe Islands, with growing unemployment being a serious problem. The islands, which unlike Denmark are not a member of the European Community (EC), entered into a fisheries agreement with the Community in the spring.

A Royal Birthday. On the 50th birthday of popular Queen Margrethe II, April 17, 50,000 Copenhageners paid tribute to her at Amalienborg Palace. The royal birthday coincided with the 50th anniversary of Denmark's occupation by Nazi Germany.

Bridging the Belt and the Sound. Two giant bridges—one to span the Great Belt separating Denmark's two largest islands, Zealand and Fyn, the other bridging Øresund (The Sound) between Denmark and Sweden—reached their final planning stages. The Great Belt bridge, slated to be Denmark's biggest industrial undertaking ever, is scheduled to open in 1996. Costing about $4.8 billion, it will consist of two bridges for automobiles and trains, in addition to a tunnel for trains only.

ERIK J. FRIIS
"The Scandinavian-American Bulletin"

DENMARK • Information Highlights

Official Name: Kingdom of Denmark.
Location: Northwest Europe.
Area: 16,629 sq mi (43 070 km²).
Population (mid-1990 est.): 5,100,000.
Chief Cities (Jan. 1, 1986 est.): Copenhagen, the capital, 1,351,999 (incl. suburbs); Århus, 195,152; Odense, 137,286.
Government: *Head of state,* Margrethe II, queen (acceded Jan. 1972). *Head of government,* Poul Schlüter, prime minister (took office Sept. 1982). *Legislature* (unicameral)—Folketing.
Monetary Unit: Krone (5.90 kroner equal U.S.$1, Dec. 31, 1990).
Gross Domestic Product (1989 est. U.S.$): $73,700,-000,000.
Economic Indexes (1989): *Consumer Prices* (1980 = 100), all items, 172.9; food, 164.0. *Industrial Production* (1980 = 100), 130.
Foreign Trade (1989 U.S.$): *Imports,* $27,744,-000,000; *exports,* $26,913,000,000.

DRUGS AND ALCOHOL

In 1990 there was some positive news in the U.S. fight against the importation, sale, and use of cocaine, heroin, marijuana, and other illegal drugs, but there also was a discouraging side. On the positive side, surveys released during the year indicated that the price of cocaine was up sharply across the United States (a sign that interdiction efforts were paying off), that the number of cocaine-related hospital emergencies was down, and that the number of people reporting "casual" use of cocaine and marijuana had declined. Those statistics were "clear signs of progress" in the war against drugs, U.S. President George Bush said at a September 5 press conference, marking the first anniversary of his call for an expanded federal antidrug strategy that stressed increased law-enforcement activity against drug traffickers. Balancing the progress, however, were reports of an inner-city "crack-baby" epidemic, as well as a marked increase in drug-related violent crime.

William Bennett, the first director of the National Office of Drug Control Policy in the Bush administration, announced his resignation on November 8. President Bush later named Florida Gov. Bob Martinez, who had been defeated for reelection, to the post.

Pricing and Use. The State Department's annual report on world drug production, released in March, estimated that international production of coca was up 12% in 1989 compared with 1988, and that the production of opium (heroin's base) increased 47%. Nevertheless, throughout 1990 the price of cocaine in the United States rose significantly. The U.S. Drug Enforcement Administration reported in July that during the first half of 1990 the wholesale price of cocaine increased up to 50%, to as much as $35,000 per kilogram. Officials attributed the increases—the largest in a decade—to intensified antidrug activities in Latin America, especially in Colombia, where about 80% of the world's cocaine is processed and distributed.

That positive news was accompanied by reports issued in May and August by the National Institute on Drug Abuse that the number of cocaine-related hospital emergency-room visits declined 24% in the fourth quarter of 1989, compared with the previous three-month period, and by 4% in the first three months of 1990.

Drug consumption was also down. National surveys released in 1990 indicated that casual drug use among Americans in general declined in 1989, the last year for which complete statistics were available. The annual survey of high-school seniors done for the federal government by the University of Michigan's Institute for Social Research is one example. The 1990 study found that 19.7% of the seniors interviewed reported using some illicit drug during the preceding month, compared with 21.3% in 1988. Marijuana use was reported by 16.7% of the seniors—down markedly from 40% in 1979. Some 2.8% said they had used cocaine, compared with 6.7% five years earlier. Overall, 50.9% of the seniors said that they had used an illicit drug at least once during the previous year, compared with 53.9% in 1988 and 56.6% in 1987.

Drug Babies and Crime. Experts believed that about 10% of all newborns, some 375,000 per year, were born to mothers who used illegal drugs during pregnancy. Federal statistics indicated that 100,000 of those newborns had been exposed to crack—the relatively inexpensive smokable form of cocaine that often leads to premature births, birth defects, neurological problems, and an increase in Sudden Infant Death Syndrome.

With relation to crime, August Federal Bureau of Investigation statistics showed 21,500 homicides in 1989, making that year the most violent in the decade, and preliminary figures for 1990 suggested that the number would increase again. In some cities, such as Washington, DC, homicide rates were at record levels in 1989 and 1990. Law-enforcement officials blamed the increase in violent crimes primarily on drugs.

A federal study, released in January, estimated the overall cost of illicit drugs to U.S. society to be $60 billion annually, an increase of more than $10 billion compared with 1985.

Alcohol Abuse. Although alcohol is not an illicit substance for adults, many health officials consider it to be the nation's most abused drug. Federal statistics indicated that some 15.1 million Americans suffered from alcoholism or alcohol dependence, that alcohol contributed to the deaths of more than 105,000 people annually, and that about two thirds of the 1.7 million people who seek treatment in substance-abuse programs each year report that alcohol is their main problem. There also was concern about widespread alcohol abuse among high-school and college students.

Alcohol abuse was a big problem on the highways. Government statistics indicated that in 1988 nearly 40% of the estimated 47,000 people killed in car crashes were legally drunk. The National Transportation Safety Board, in the first survey of its kind, reported in February that 12.5% of truck drivers killed on the highway had used alcohol.

In the air, three former Northwest Airline pilots were convicted of being intoxicated while flying a Boeing 727 passenger flight from Fargo, ND, to Minneapolis. The pilots—who lost their jobs and had their licenses revoked by the Federal Aviation Administration following the March 8 incident—were sentenced to 12- and 16-month prison terms by a federal judge in Minneapolis in October.

MARC LEEPSON, *Free-lance Writer*

ECUADOR

As Rodrigo Borja completed his second year as Ecuador's president, the nation's economy began to respond positively to his program of gradual economic liberalization. The political response, however, was increasingly negative, and the combination of discontent over economic policy with the new problems of Indian nationalism and drug trafficking posed serious challenges to the government.

The Economy. The government's greatest economic success was the renegotiation of the country's $11.7 billion foreign debt, announced in August. After becoming current with its obligations to multilateral lending agencies, Ecuador was promised $1.7 billion in new lending over the next three years, mostly from the World Bank. The government also hoped to reach an agreement by the end of the year that would reduce both principal and interest based on a more realistic assessment of the country's ability to pay.

The foreign-exchange situation also showed substantial improvement by July, with the realization of a small positive balance in foreign-exchange reserves and considerable narrowing of the gap between official and parallel exchange rates. Inflation, however, remained high (in the 40–60% range), and economic growth for the year was expected to be positive but sluggish. The small oil-exporting nation was expected to benefit relatively little from the higher oil prices during the Persian Gulf crisis, since it had little oil in storage to sell on the spot market. Approximately 88% of its oil exports were tied up in long-term contracts.

The Government's Program. Borja tried to convince the Ecuadorian population that the only alternative to his gradual approach would be a more drastic shock program, but some important sectors, including the labor unions, remained unconvinced and rebellious. Incensed by weekly devaluations of the sucre and constant price increases for gasoline and public services, the *Frente Unitario de Trabajadores* (FUT) staged its third general strike since November 1988 with the backing of both the national teachers' union and the Confederation of Indigenous Nationalities (CONAIE).

As one would expect, a president from the Democratic Left Party (*Izquierda Democrática*, or ID) could not pursue a program that pleased the business community and antagonized the labor movement without losing some political support. Popular discontent cost the Democratic Left Party half of its seats in the June legislative elections. Averroes Bucaram, leader of the opposition *Concentración de Fuerzas Populares* (CFP), later was elected president of the Legislative Assembly.

These two major defeats for the administration contributed to frequent disputes between the president and the congress over government policy and personnel. In July, Abelardo Pachano, president of the Monetary Board and designer of Ecuador's gradualist economic policies, resigned along with Central Bank Manager José Murillo. In September the legislature voted to dismiss Borja's Superintendent of Banks, Fernando Guerrero. It also served summonses on the government's present ministers of energy, education, and public works.

The Indians and the Guerrilla War. Borja also was challenged by increased protests among the Indian populations, represented by CONAIE. In the hope of obtaining greater regional autonomy and property rights over oil and other natural resources on Indian lands, CONAIE launched a national uprising in March in which it took 12 military hostages. The dispute was settled after three days of negotiations during which the government promised to hold talks with the Indians. However, these talks broke down in August when the government insisted that some of the Indians' demands were incompatible with the sovereignty of the national government. CONAIE threatened to organize another uprising.

Although it appeared in June that the *¡Alfaro Vive Carajo!* (AVC) guerrilla group was on the verge of surrendering its weapons in return for recognition as a legitimate political party, the AVC announced in August that it had suspended these talks as a result of the government's delay in establishing a dialogue.

Drug Trade. After the Barco government in Colombia cracked down on the Medellín and Cali cartels and the United States exposed money-laundering operations in Miami, the cartels relocated some of their operations in Ecuador, where they bought up large areas of land as sites for cocaine-processing plants. Ecuador's bank-secrecy laws and its lack of strict controls on chemical imports made it an ideal transshipment and money-laundering point for the Colombian drug trade.

MICHAEL COPPEDGE
Johns Hopkins University

ECUADOR • Information Highlights

Official Name: Republic of Ecuador.
Location: Northwest South America.
Area: 109,483 sq mi (283 560 km²).
Population (mid-1990 est.): 10,700,000.
Chief Cities (mid-1986 est.): Quito, the capital, 1,093,278; Guayaquil, 1,509,108; Cuenca, 193,012.
Government: *Head of state and government,* Rodrigo Borja Cevallos, president (took office August 1988). *Legislature* (unicameral)—Chamber of Representatives.
Monetary Unit: Sucre (856.0 sucres equal U.S.$1, floating rate, Oct. 31, 1990).
Gross Domestic Product (1989 U.S.$): $9,800,-000,000.
Economic Index (1989): *Consumer Prices* (1981 = 100), all items, 1,283.6; food, 1,827.8.
Foreign Trade (1988 U.S.$): *Imports,* $1,714,000,000; *exports,* $2,165,000,000.

EDUCATION

Public elementary and secondary education began the last decade of the century by looking toward the end of it, adopting policies and starting initiatives aimed at long-range goals.

National Goals. The national educational goals agreed to by the White House and the National Governors' Association in fall 1989 were spelled out in objectives released by the governors in summer 1990. At that time, a group to assess progress on the goals was established, but not without some controversy. And as reports of student achievement levels accumulated during 1990, it became obvious that these goals for the year 2000 were ambitious, indeed. If any one message came out of the year's activities, it was that education reform was much more complex than had been admitted previously.

As the year ended, it was not clear exactly how the monitoring of the national goals would be structured. The White House and the National Governors' Association agreed on the composition of a monitoring group. However, the process left out Congress; some members introduced legislation to create a structure that would include Congress and the education community.

Less controversial but probably with more potential for providing useful data was another monitoring initiative—the new longitudinal study of students. Termed NELS:88 (for the National Educational Longitudinal Survey conducted in 1988), this survey recorded a great deal of data about eighth graders in 1988, which were released in the spring of 1990. The students would be followed by surveys every two years as long as funding continued.

Assessment Reform. As governors and their staffs attempted to set objectives for the national goals, they realized that the issue of assessment would have to be addressed first. Traditionally reliant on standardized test scores as an indicator for public policy-making, the governors ran head-on into the problems inherent in these tests when they tackled the very first goal—that all children should start school ready to learn. What does "ready" mean? And how is that to be determined?

Their dilemma was being felt also by education, parent, and research groups across the country. A three-year study funded by the Ford Foundation, released in May with the endorsement of major education groups, called for a "restructuring" of testing policy in the United States, although not for the complete elimination of standardized multiple-choice testing. The National Commission on Testing and Public Policy recommended that:

• Testing policies and practices be reoriented to promote development of all human talent;

AP/Wide World

Commenting on U.S. academic achievement, Secretary of Education Cavazos on May 2 called for "a total commitment to the reform and restructuring" of the school system.

• Testing programs shift from a reliance on multiple-choice tests to alternative forms of testing;

• Test scores be used only when they differentiate on the basis of characteristics relevant to the opportunities afforded students to learn;

• The need is greater for tests to measure such characteristics when test scores disproportionately deny opportunities to minorities;

• Test scores not be used alone to make important decisions about individuals, groups, or institutions;

• Use of more effective assessment strategies to make institutions accountable, greater public accountability for testing, and more investment in testing research.

This important statement came at a time when testing policies seemed to be going in opposite directions. During 1990 the governing board for the National Assessment of Educational Progress (NAEP) took steps to put "teeth" into assessment results by proposing levels of proficiency in achievement results. Instead of reporting average student performance, the results, to be tried with the math assessments due to be released in June 1991, would tell what percentage of students achieved basic, proficient, or advanced levels. The math assessment also would be the first to report results state-by-state.

As 1990 ended, voices began to be heard from business, political, and some education circles favoring a national test. The Commission on Skills of the American Workforce had broken the ice on the subject in June when its report, "High Skills or Low Wages," jolted educators. It recommended young people be "certified" by the age of 16 as having achieved mastery of essential skills; after that, they would be free to choose further education, leading directly to the work force or to higher education.

The President's Advisory Committee on Education Policy was set to endorse the idea of a national testing program in late fall, recommending that development begin and testing instruments be ready within five years.

A slightly different tack was proposed by Marshall Smith, dean of the School of Education at Stanford University. He told the American Educational Research Association annual meeting that a national curriculum for elementary and secondary schools should be used to set standards for students, guide teacher education, and hold teachers accountable for student learning. With national goals in place, new frameworks being set for different subjects, and new research on what teachers should know and do, a national view of a common curriculum is the next logical step, he said.

On the other hand, federal and state support for the designing of alternative assessment strategies are beginning to bear fruit. Vermont, for example, went from the experimental to the statewide stage in its development of student portfolios, to be tried in writing as a beginning. Connecticut heads a multistate effort to design hands-on science tests and those which require group work. The Educational Testing Service is working with Connecticut on several other projects, including the NAEP, to create "intelligent" assessments, which would require students to think about relationships among the

pieces of knowledge they have in order to answer questions. For example, students might be asked to describe what happens when water drops on different materials or to design an experiment to measure the effects of exercise on the heart rate. The NAEP governing board also announced that the reading and writing tests to be administered in 1992 would shift 40% of the test items to open-ended ones, double the number from past tests. The American Federation of Teachers also approved a resolution calling for "phasing out standardized, multiple-choice tests and replacing them with reliable, valid and educationally appropriate alternatives."

In November the College Board, which sponsors the Scholastic Aptitude Test (SAT), announced substantial revisions to the test. The changes would put more emphasis on reading skills, allow the use of calculators, and move away from multiple-choice answers and toward individual thinking. The name of the test also would be altered, to Scholastic Assessment Test. The Board stopped short of more sweeping changes that had been considered. Critics charged the changes were little more than cosmetic, and that they would not eliminate the bias against women and minorities they claimed was inherent in the test. The revised SAT was to be given first in 1994.

Student Achievement. The assessments which were available in 1990, particularly NAEP, continued to be disillusioning to education reformers. After seven years of increasing requirements and other traditional strategies to improve academic performance, the Scholastic Aptitude Test and American College Test (ACT) scores reported in 1990 showed that achievement was static or even had slipped in some areas.

NAEP released reports on geography and history/civics achievement during the year, both of which fueled demands for a major overhaul of what is taught in schools. The geography results showed that students could not perform well in applying the concepts of geographic knowledge. Similarly, the history/civics assessment demonstrated that students know basic facts but do not have understanding of contexts or concepts.

In a review of 20 years of the national assessment, the Educational Testing Service (ETS) concluded that overall achievement levels "are little different entering the 1990s than they were two decades ago." And those levels are far below what could be considered competent in challenging subjects, such as English, math, science, history, and geography. ETS' report also said that:

• Few students show that they can use their minds well. Basic skills seem to be improving, but fewer students are able to demonstrate higher-level application of those skills.

• The differences between white and minority students remains "unacceptably large."

U.S. Public and Private Schools

	1990–91	1989–90
Enrollment		
Kindergarten through Grade 8	33,765,000	33,309,000
High school	12,427,000	12,654,000
Higher education	13,558,000	13,419,000
Total	59,750,000	59,382,000
Number of Teachers		
Elementary and secondary	2,785,000	2,737,000
Higher	762,000	755,000
Total	3,547,000	3,492,000
Graduates		
Public and private high school	2,522,000	2,701,000
Bachelor's degrees	1,024,000	1,017,000
First professional degrees	67,000	68,000
Master's degrees	322,000	320,000
Doctor's degrees	36,000	36,000
Expenditures		
Public elementary-secondary school	$212,900,000,000	$198,600,000,000
Private elementary-secondary	18,100,000,000	16,900,000,000
Public higher	98,200,000,000	92,200,000,000
Private higher	54,300,000,000	51,000,000,000
Total	$383,500,000,000	$358,700,000,000

Likewise, there has been no movement to reduce the gender differences, shown by higher performance of males in science and math and of females in writing.

• Little has changed in how students are taught, with instruction still dominated by textbooks, lectures, and short-answer worksheets.

The report also noted that data and research provide information about strategies which would produce higher achievement. Parental involvement in children's learning is a critical component. So are reinforcement of school-work through homework and outside reading and the use of hands-on learning activities.

© Eric Sander/Gamma-Liaison

TV News in the Classroom

Although schools now are relying more on instructional television to help meet curricular needs, the recent entry of communications and cable-television companies into the educational market has resulted in fierce debate over the role and nature of television programming in the classroom.

"Channel One." At the forefront of the debate is Whittier Communication's Educational Network. This three-channel network attempts to meet a variety of instructional needs by providing general educational programming, in-service-related programming for teachers, and a special news program, *Channel One*. The latter is designed to address the growing cultural and current-events illiteracy of junior- and senior-high-school students.

In exchange for a three-year agreement requiring that *Channel One* be shown during 90% of the academic year, participating schools are given all necessary equipment to receive the programming, at an approximate value of $20,000. However, unlike other educational television programming, *Channel One* carries two minutes of commercials. The revenue from such ads is used for the equipment. As of early 1990, 1,050 U.S. schools were subscribing to the network.

Critics charge that schools should not be promoting specific products and that by having the relatively captive classroom audience exposed to advertising, education is supporting commercialism. Moreover, critics contend that although *Channel One*, which features international and U.S. news, special features, and cultural trivia, is technically of high quality, the content of the program is incomplete and overly abridged. Generally, the rapid presentation style, flashy graphics, and loud pop music do not help maintain student attention to program content. Supporters emphasize the value of the equipment, especially since few school systems have such technology, and the need for instruction in the news area.

Content problems notwithstanding, it is the presence of commercials that has caused the greatest concern among educators and has led the New York State Board of Regents to ban the Educational Network in the state. In addition, California's Board of Education has informed schools that they will lose state aid in an amount commensurate to the current rate for two minutes of advertising if they subscribe to *Channel One*.

Turner and Others. In contrast with Educational Network are a spate of educational programs being produced by cable television companies. The most prominent is Turner Broadcasting Company's *Cable News Network (CNN) Newsroom*, a 15-minute, commercial-free broadcast developed in cooperation with the National School Boards Association. *CNN Newsroom* is available to subscribers who have paid cable-access charges and who have television and VCR equipment. Program content focuses on business, arts, and science news presented by young correspondents in a manner appropriate for junior-and senior-high-school students. As of early 1990, 4,000 schools had subscribed to *CNN Newsroom*. In June 1990 it was given an award for quality by the Action for Children's Television.

In addition to these two new programs, other networks, including the Discovery Channel and Arts & Entertainment Network, have developed various educational offerings. All equipment purchases are the responsibility of the individual school district. As has been the case with earlier forms of instructional television, the ultimate impact of these new programs will be determined by the availability of the receiving equipment and the educational soundness of the various programs.

DEBRA A. MATHINOS

The Teaching of Science

Science teaching, like other areas of U.S. education, is undergoing drastic, badly needed reforms. The myriad problems in science education and the relationship of education to the economic viability of the United States provide a complex situation.

Elementary Level. The situation can be described as monumental in the elementary school. There are approximately 1.3 million U.S. elementary-school teachers, who somehow are expected to teach all subjects. Fewer than 300,000 have any subject-matter training in science. Because secondary-school science preparation also is weak, most of these teachers never have studied a physical science. It is not surprising that such teachers do not understand the difference between teaching science as reading and teaching science for the kind of real understanding that comes from hands-on experience with scientific phenomena.

The role of hands-on experience is to provide direct, concrete experience with science phenomena before terms, words, and symbols are used. Often at the elementary level, hands-on teaching is simply paper-and-pencil activities, often analogies, in the form of games or simulations. Although the latter can be useful sometimes, they never should substitute for experience with the phenomena of science.

When teachers lack subject-matter knowledge, they have great difficulty motivating children to learn science. After all, the teachers themselves never were motivated to do so. This limitation often leads to attempts to make the science "relevant" in order to stimulate interest. Such efforts lead to so-called science technology society topics—complex social or societal problems or issues with a scientific component. But treating such problems without any knowledge of basic science provides little understanding of either science or its applications.

In an attempt to overcome these difficulties, significant reforms are under way in the

© Tom Stack/Tom Stack & Associates

United States. They involve two major components. First, science-content coverage is being reduced greatly, with much of the meaningless abstraction removed. In its place are scientific topics taught with much greater depth in ways that help children understand the material. Secondly, hands-on activities involving actual scientific phenomena are being emphasized, creating a repertoire of concrete experiences that are needed to understand concepts to be developed later in more quantitative terms. The fundamental technique of teaching science concepts at successively higher levels of abstraction, always experiencing phenomena before terminology, provides the necessary foundation for understanding science at the elementary-school level. Applications of science should be limited to solving personal problems. Societal problems having scientific components can be examined when children reach secondary school.

Secondary Level. In the secondary school, science teaching can be separated roughly into middle level (grades six-nine) and high school (grades 10–12). At the middle level, science in most schools traditionally has been one or two years of general life science, environmental science, or earth science. Usually at the middle level, there has been no other physical science. Some middle-level teachers have been educated in one or more science fields. Others come from the elementary school and lack significant science preparation. The mix of children going through the trauma of puberty with those who have not started it and with those who have completed the change leads to a most challenging situation for science teachers. The consensus appears to be that some sort of integrated science taught by teams of teachers who get to know the children is best. Science made relevant to the immediate concerns of such children, with an opportunity to develop individual interests, offers the greatest promise.

High-school science teaching is the most seriously deficient because in its usual form it simply offers nothing to most students. The layer-cake curriculum, first set down by the National Education Association's Committee of Ten in 1893, dominates high-school science in the United States. This approach offers biology in grade ten, chemistry in grade 11, and physics in grade 12. The United States is the only industrialized nation to offer such a pattern. The consequences are serious.

Most students take biology, about half go on to study chemistry, and less than 20% enroll in physics. With a high-school dropout rate of 30%, this provides a citizenry with essentially no knowledge of the physical sciences. The enrollment of women and minorities in the physical sciences is much lower, depriving the nation of technically trained personnel that are essential. Another negative aspect of high-school science is that in each course abstractions and terminology begin immediately. The pace is intense, with all of that particular science covered during the year. No effort is made to introduce experience first and then symbols and abstractions. Not enough time is provided to understand the science.

The major program being advanced to reform high-school science is the Scope, Sequence, and Coordination Project, coordinated by the National Science Teachers Association and funded at more than $10 million by the National Science Foundation and the U.S. Department of Education. This nationwide project calls for the teaching of science in four subjects—physics, chemistry, biology, and earth-space science—over six years. The learning is spaced carefully over six years in each subject. At the middle level, the science is integrated. At the high-school level, it is coordinated, with different teachers in each of the four sciences. The changes required of the reform involve having a subject such as physics for two or three hours per week, rather than every day. The student then moves slowly from concrete to empirical to theoretical and abstract over several years. Teachers get to know students well, and there are opportunities for students to do special projects in the summers.

The major obstacle to such reform is the erroneous attitude that if someone studies several years of science that person is going to become a scientist or engineer. All citizens need such instruction for a complete education. When this reform has spread and is in place throughout the United States, citizens will understand better their technological world and far more minority students and women will become scientists and engineers. At all levels, science-education reforms require competent teachers. With shortages of scientifically trained personnel for business and industry, the need for good science teachers will be hard to meet. The education of science teachers is the major challenge of the 1990s.

The United States faces severe economic competition from the European Community and Japan. Its huge reserve of natural resources will not be sufficient to meet that competition. The United States must produce the human resources needed for the 21st century. Those resources must have as a fundamental core education in the sciences. National and global problems increasingly are connected to scientific and technological solutions. Innovation requires knowledge in the workplace and in management of science and technology. The reforms now being put into place in U.S. science education, hopefully, will prepare U.S. citizens for these challenges.

BILL G. ALDRIDGE

Editor's Note: Bill G. Aldridge is executive director of the National Science Teachers Association. A former physics teacher and author of two textbooks, he is a leading proponent of the reform of science teaching.

Eliminating Tracking. A much more radical change in educational policy gained considerable momentum in 1990—the elimination of tracking and ability grouping. A number of factors converged to make this a crucially important development that most likely will come to have a greater influence over schooling in the 1990s than any other element of restructuring or reform. With more than 30% of school-age children now from minority groups and the number rising every year, the preponderance of minority students in remedial or low-track classes is especially troublesome to educators and policymakers.

At the same time, business leaders and others have been telling educators that more demanding workplaces require all entering workers to have the problem-solving and computation skills once considered important only for the top achievers in school. So, it is not surprising that efforts to restructure the nation's schools eventually would turn to higher expectations for *all* students.

The criticism of tracking practices, present but muted for many years, first surfaced in discussions about education in the middle grades. A Boston, MA, children's advocacy group issued a scathing report on tracking in middle schools in that city; and a publication about urban middle-grades education, *High Strides*, published many viewpoints on the subject, as well as descriptions of school programs trying to reduce tracking.

Research reviews by Johns Hopkins University's center on the study of disadvantaged children revealed no substantive benefits to tracking, but did show detrimental effects on those in the low tracks. The center's researchers prepared a report for the National Education Association (NEA), used as the basis for an NEA statement that said tracking does more harm than good. It did not go so far as to suggest the immediate elimination of tracking, but held that out as the ultimate goal. Meanwhile, tracking could be beneficial under certain well-controlled circumstances, according to the NEA statement, such as grouping only for specific skills and frequent reassessments.

A few weeks later, the National Governors' Association issued its objectives for the national goals, among them the elimination of tracking. That was followed by a College Board publication on equal access to knowledge containing several essays with direct or oblique references to the negative effects of tracking. Finally, University of California/Los Angeles education researcher Jeannie Oakes added a new study to several she has conducted on tracking, which documented its effect on poor and minority students' opportunities to learn math and science. She said tracking persists because of deeply held beliefs about differences in abilities. And those differences are seen to relate to social class.

Meanwhile, several school districts moved to begin doing away with tracking practices. Pittsburgh, PA, for example, reduced all programs to only two streams—vocational and academic. San Diego, CA, was phasing in a "no fail" policy combined with the elimination of rigid tracking. The Massachusetts State Department of Education took statewide action by disseminating research to all districts about the effects of tracking.

School-Funding Equity. Tracking reappeared as an issue in another form—the unequal distribution of wealth among school districts which condemns the poorest districts to poor-quality programs. Financial equity suits were hot again in 1990. Anticipating that the New Jersey Supreme Court would call for greater equity to poor and middle-class districts (which it did), newly elected Gov. Jim Florio moved swiftly to have a more equitable school-funding bill passed by the legislature. The controversial measure reduced state support for wealthy districts and increased support for districts with large numbers of at-risk students. Texas, on the other hand, dealt with its state court order for more equitable funding over protracted legislative sessions, finally coming up with a formula which was used for the 1990–91 school year but was in jeopardy because the court declared it inadequate. School finance equity suits were pending in 1990 in Alabama, Nebraska, Minnesota, and North Dakota, and were being considered in several other states. Meanwhile, Kentucky entered the first year of its massive reorganization plan, brought about by a state court mandate to

reform financing. In doing so, the court threw out the entire structure for the public schools. The rebuilt system emphasizes outcomes by setting standards and reducing state regulation, focuses resources on early childhood and primary programs, and provides a limited form of choice. Parents whose children are in schools which do not show sufficient progress over a three-year period may transfer their children to schools of their choice.

Long criticized for the poor showing of U.S. students in international assessments, public schools came up short in another global comparison, this one on the issue of funding. Refuting a decade of statements by federal administration officials who argued that public education was receiving sufficient funding, the Economic Policy Institute set off another round of debate with the release of its study on school funding in 16 countries. The United States ranked third from the bottom, according to the study. To bring spending up to the average level for elementary education in the other countries, the United States would have to spend annually about $25 billion more on schools, it said.

Higher Education. As the higher-education community geared up for renewal of the Higher Education Act, two issues began to emerge. One was the experience of minority students on college campuses. Not only was there concern about the large number of minority students who never complete college, but the rise in incidences of racial prejudice toward minority students at four-year campuses alarmed college officials. Hispanics represent only 5.2% and blacks 8.7% of college enrollment. Only 15% of Hispanic and 14% of black high-school graduates receive an undergraduate degree. A related concern was the unpopularity of teaching careers among minorities. Only 10% of present elementary and secondary teachers are from minority groups, and projections of enrollments and supply indicated that figure would drop to 5% by the end of the 1990s—this during a time when the minority enrollment in schools was expected to increase dramatically. As 1990 ended, various studies and groups were addressing all of these concerns.

Another issue facing the higher-education community was that of the cost of obtaining a postsecondary education. During the 1980s the rise in college tuition levels was twice the rate of inflation. This happened during a time when income inequality in the United States spread, making it even more difficult for young people from poor families to afford a college education. Compounding the problem were the inability of federal student aid from all sources to keep pace with inflation, and the drop in the federal share of student aid from 83% to 73% during the decade.

ANNE C. LEWIS
Education Policy Writer

EGYPT

Egypt's economic problems were intensified greatly by Iraq's invasion of Kuwait on Aug. 2, 1990. While political unrest marked by outbreaks of sectarian violence continued, President Hosni Mubarak's foreign policy and his contacts at the international level helped reestablish Egypt's central role as a dominant factor in inter-Arab politics.

Economic Problems. With an additional 1 million people added to its population of 55 million every eight months, the country faced prospects of food shortages by the end of 1990. Unable to cope with its foreign debt of some $50 billion, Egypt also began talks with the International Monetary Fund (IMF) in June to seek relief. Despite the government's concessions to raise prices on cooking gas, wheat, flour, cigarettes, kerosene, and gasoline, no agreement was reached with the IMF on reforming the economy. Until August, U.S. aid to Egypt was jeopardized by Cairo's inability to pay the interest due on previous U.S. loans. However, following Egypt's cooperation in the international efforts to contain Iraq, President George Bush asked Congress to forgive some $7 billion owed for military purchases.

The deleterious economic impact of the Iraq-Kuwait crisis outweighed the benefits gained when the United States and the IMF relaxed their pressures on Egypt. In a report submitted to the World Bank, Egypt estimated that the invasion would cost it approximately $9 billion, a sum almost equivalent to half the country's gross domestic product (GDP). Included in the $9 billion estimate was the loss of money sent home by the 1.5 million Egyptians who had worked in the Persian Gulf before the crisis, along with the additional expense required to create jobs for 600,000 returning war refugees. Also included were decreases in revenues from the Suez Canal oil-tanker shipments, declining tourism, and declining revenues from Kuwaiti development organizations, air traffic, and trade with Iraq. Assistance from Saudi Arabia, the Kuwaiti government in exile, Japan, and various Western countries was insufficient to make up the losses.

Deteriorating economic conditions were a major factor contributing to continued domestic unrest. At least 40% of the population were living below the poverty line and unemployment exceeded 20%. Annual inflation was running at more than 25%. Official figures put the number of drug users at more than 1 million. The most severely impacted were youths and those living on "starvation salaries."

Violence. Throughout the year there were periodic eruptions of sectarian violence by Islamic fundamentalist factions attacking Coptic and other Christian groups. Militant Palestinians also were involved in terrorist attacks on both government and civilian targets. In March, Islamic fundamentalists attacked two Coptic churches in Minya province; in April they burned Christian property and bombed a church. Some Muslim attacks were sparked by a leaflet, *Wipe Out the Disgrace, O Muslims!*, which charged that Christians were seducing Muslim girls and forcing them to act in pornographic films. During October a group of Palestinian and other Arab terrorists was caught entering the country, reportedly with plans for "assassination and destabilization of Egypt's security." On October 12, Rifaat al Maghoub, the speaker of Egypt's parliament, and the country's second-ranking official after the president, was assassinated by gunmen believed to be associated with either Islamic fundamentalists or terrorists.

The government continued its "carrot and stick" approach to the problem. On one hand, the Egyptian Organization for Human Rights maintained that officials were using torture on political prisoners, with Islamic fundamentalists the primary victims. At the same time the government encouraged the recognized Islamic establishment to extend its network of hospitals, schools, and clinics; hours of religious programming on government TV and radio also were increased. In addition, the number of new mosques nearly had doubled in the last few years. In January, Interior Minister Zaki Mustafa Ali Badr was replaced. He had been accused by fundamentalist and other dissidents of using harsh and illegal methods to cope with unrest.

Politics. Domination of the political system by Mubarak's National Democratic Party (NDP) was weakened in 1990 by the intervention of the courts. In April the Political Parties Tribunal legalized three formerly banned parties—the Greens, Democratic Unionists, and Young Egypt—but did not lift the ban on the Nasserite Party. In May the Constitutional Court ruled that the 1986 election law tailored to ensure control by the NDP was unconstitutional, invalidating the results of the 1987 par-

---

EGYPT • Information Highlights

Official Name: Arab Republic of Egypt.
Location: Northeastern Africa.
Area: 386,660 sq mi (1 001 450 km²).
Population (mid-1990 est.): 54,700,000.
Capital: Cairo.
Government: *Head of state,* Mohammed Hosni Mubarak, president (took office Oct. 1981). *Head of government,* Atef Sedki, prime minister (took office November 1986). *Legislature* (unicameral)—People's Assembly.
Monetary Unit: Pound (2.8736 pounds equal U.S.$1, free-market rate, Dec. 31, 1990).
Gross Domestic Product (1989 est. U.S.$): $38,300,-000,000.
Economic Index (1989): *Consumer Prices* (1980 = 100), all items, 408.6; food, 473.1.
Foreign Trade (1989 U.S.$): *Imports,* $23,527,000,-000; *exports,* $8,150,000,000.

liamentary election. A referendum in October called for new elections to be held before the end of the year for the 458-member National Assembly.

In the December 2 election, President Mubarak's National Democratic Party won some 80% of the 444 contested seats. Because the three main opposition parties boycotted the election, most remaining seats were captured by independents. However, the small left-wing National Unionist Progressives won enough votes to become the parliamentary opposition. Figures on participation by the country's 16 million eligible voters ranged from 44% to 70%. A major task of the new parliament was to elect a new speaker.

Diplomacy. President Mubarak's shuttle diplomacy, and efforts to present Egypt as a mediator in international crises, brought Cairo again to the forefront of Middle East affairs. In March the Arab League decided to move the headquarters of the organization back to Cairo, ten years after it relocated to Tunis in protest against Egypt's relations with Israel. Normal relations with Syria were reestablished and the presidents of each country visited the other's capital, the first such exchange in 13 years. During April, Foreign Minister Ismat Abd al-Magid asked the UN Security Council to call for the abolition of all "weapons of mass destruction" in the Middle East to check possibilities of both nuclear and chemical warfare there. Egypt played a moderating role in the newly formed Arab Cooperation Council (Egypt, Jordan, Iraq, Yemen) and in the Arab League when militant anti-U.S. and anti-Israel resolutions were introduced. Until the outbreak of the Gulf crisis in August, President Mubarak continued his role as principal intermediary between the Palestine Liberation Organization (PLO), the United States, and Israel.

In June he met in Cairo with Israel's former Prime Minister Shimon Peres, in an unsuccessful attempt to break the impasse in the Arab-Israel conflict. Another indication of Mubarak's attempts to improve relations with Israel was the reestablishment of direct contact with Prime Minister Yitzhak Shamir in February. After Palestinian terrorists killed nine Israelis on a tourist bus near Cairo, Mubarak abandoned his long-standing refusal to speak to Shamir and called the Israeli leader to express shock and revulsion at the attack.

As tensions between Iraq and Kuwait mounted in their dispute over oil production during July, Mubarak tried to persuade the two countries to negotiate their differences. However, when Iraq invaded Kuwait on August 2, Egypt unequivocally condemned Saddam Hussein, and supported the measures to censure him that followed, both in the Arab League and in the UN. In the split that occurred among the 21 Arab states over the invasion, Egypt stood with the 12 that called for immediate withdrawal by Iraq. While Mubarak continued his efforts to persuade Saddam Hussein to settle his differences with Kuwait peacefully, he placed Egypt firmly behind U.S. and UN actions, including the economic blockade and military buildup in Saudi Arabia. Despite Egypt's difficult economic situation, which was exacerbated by the crisis, President Mubarak pledged to send 20,000 troops to support the U.S.-led military buildup. (*See* feature articles, page 24.)

DON PERETZ
State University of New York, Binghamton

ENERGY

The energy trends of the last half of the 1980s continued through the first seven months of 1990 drawing little attention from most people. The amount of crude oil and petroleum products imported into the United States in relation to the amount consumed passed the 50% mark with only brief notice in the press. Some experts predicted only a slow increase in the price of crude oil internationally. Others predicted random increases and still others admitted they did not know. The nuclear-energy industry operated quietly and without incident in the United States and continued a slow expansion elsewhere. Gasoline and electricity remained relatively inexpensive and the United States was experiencing little hardship due to energy-related factors.

The sudden and unexpected Iraqi invasion of Kuwait in early August had a dramatic impact on the oil industry and indirectly affected other energy sources because of the limited interchangeability of fuels. The complex relationships between energy, economics, politics, and eventually environmental matters surfaced in profound ways that undoubtedly will be the subject of many future studies.

Oil Exploration and Research. While the price of crude oil both in the United States and internationally was high enough to support some exploration, no giant fields were found outside the Middle East and possibly the USSR in the first half of 1990. U.S. domestic exploration really was not needed in the first half of the year and most international exploration was politically and economically inaccessible. The natural and inevitable decline of the production of domestic oil fields was not counterbalanced by more enhanced oil recovery (EOR) applications because the price of the additional oil produced did not justify the cost and imported oil was less expensive. The number of drilling rigs operating declined from 4,500 in the early 1980s to 1,500 by 1990. The near demise of what had been a great U.S. industry was apparent to many associated with the oil industry.

Drilling crews were disbanded and parts of the United States highly dependent on oil production, such as Texas and Louisiana, became economically depressed. Enrollment in petroleum engineering curriculums declined precipitously because there were few career opportunities in domestic work for graduates in this field. There were, however, two technical developments that produced prosperity in limited geographic areas. These developments were horizontal drilling of oil wells and what is known as coal-bed methane.

Since rotary drilling started at the turn of the century, much has been learned about controlling the direction of drilling. Oil wells can be deviated to all points of the compass and also can be kept essentially vertical when needed. New developments in drilling techniques allow wells to be deviated economically from the vertical gradually to the horizontal, while drilling continues for thousands of feet. This new technique will increase greatly production rates from some kinds of oil-bearing reservoir rocks which have naturally occurring vertical fractures, such as the Austin chalk of Texas. Horizontal wells cross the fractures, and the oil flows through them into the wells rather than through the small intergranular pores in the rock.

Many coal beds contain methane gas either adsorbed on the organic surface of the coal or in the water filling the coal pores or fractures. In ordinary shaft and tunnel mining, this methane had been the source of many fires and explosions which have led to loss of life. New research has developed methods to recover this methane economically by using wells drilled vertically through the beds similar to ordinary oil or natural-gas wells. The water then is pumped rapidly off the coal through the wells until the evolved methane flows up the wells from its own expansion. This growing source of methane will supplement that already obtained from ordinary natural-gas fields or produced along with crude oil.

Oil Crisis. The international embargo of Iraqi and hence Kuwaiti crude oil, imposed in August, decreased the crude oil available to the rest of the world by about 4.2 million barrels per day, but in absolute terms this was well under 10% of total consumption. In a matter of a few months, this shortfall was replaced by increased production from other countries, particularly from the nations of the Organization of Petroleum Exporting Countries (OPEC) with additional capacity that could not be utilized previously because of OPEC restrictions designed to keep up the price of oil.

Even though there was not a significant shortage of oil, speculators and some oil companies increased the price of oil from well under $20 per barrel to more than $40 per barrel over several months' time. Gasoline marketers also increased their prices by about 40%, not by a conspiracy, but rather because others were doing it and they could get away with it. Marketers tried to justify this increase by saying they used an accounting practice known as LIFO (last in, first out) rather than FIFO (first in, first out), which has the potential for greater profit for them. The intricate relationship between energy supply and economics as well as politics was exceedingly apparent by the end of 1990.

Estimates of crude oil and product stocks reported in September 1990 revealed that the world had enough crude oil, plus products in storage tanks above ground, to last almost 100 days. The strategic petroleum reserve (SPR) of the United States had underground storage of almost 600 million barrels, which could last for almost two years. Many other industrialized countries also had SPRs whose capacities were not advertised for political or strategic reasons.

The interrelationships between energy, economics, and politics also were demonstrated earlier in the year when the Baltic republics of the USSR tried to assert their independence from the central government in Moscow (*see* feature article, page 44). The Soviet Union then reduced and briefly cut off the supply of oil and natural gas, principally to Lithuania, which had to modify its schedule for full independence. Western Europe also is highly dependent on Soviet natural gas, but the USSR's need for hard currency and its diminishing oil exports helped stabilize this situation.

Oil and the Environment. Energy-related environmental trends of the 1980s continued in 1990. The *Exxon Valdez* disaster of 1989 was cleaned up almost completely during 1990 at great expense that gradually was passed on to consumers. Other tanker, pipeline, and refinery spills were contained more rapidly because of better contingency planning and the realization of the expense of less expedient action. At the urging of environmentalists, Congress tried to legislate the use of double-hulled tankers, despite their expense and the other hazards they may introduce. Some major tanker operators discontinued service to U.S. ports because of new laws that subject them to unlimited liability in the event of oil spills. In time this will lead to greater costs to the consumer because of increasing insurance costs and diminishing transportation options.

Gasoline and its combustion products generally are considered to be a major source of air pollution, particularly in urban areas. Some gasoline marketers sold reformulated gasolines which they claim to be less polluting. A growing number of marketers also offered pumps dispensing methanol. Ethanol made from fermentation of grain also is blended with gasoline to make ''gasohol'' but significant tax incentives are necessary to make this economical.

Prior to 1990 the California Energy Commission began assembling a test fleet of 500

Fords and 2,200 General Motors vehicles which use either pure methanol, pure gasoline, or any blends of these two miscible liquids. The goal was to test both the reliability of the cars and any reduction in air pollution experienced during operation, mainly in the Los Angeles area. The preliminary test results were very encouraging and may lead to some state government requirements mandating this approach in the future.

Smoke from the exhaust pipes of large trucks and buses has been a long-standing environmental concern. In 1990 the Environmental Protection Agency (EPA) ordered a change in the composition and properties of diesel fuel to reduce this exhaust pollution significantly. Tests also began on the use of methanol as a diesel-engine fuel.

Natural Gas. U.S. natural-gas reserves continued to decrease through consumption during 1990, but encouraging exploration success slowed the rate of depletion. About 20% of domestic reserves were locked up in the North Slope of Alaska because of the lack of an economical way of transporting them to market. Various groups continued to promote a natural-gas pipeline through Canada or paralleling the oil pipeline to the southern coast of Alaska, where it would be liquified for tanker transport to Japan. However, the basic economics remained no more favorable in 1990 than they were a decade before.

Japan remained the largest importer of liquified natural gas (LNG) in 1990. Its sources of natural gas in the East Indies and offshore Australia are less costly than the North Slope gas would be. For more than two decades, Japan also has imported relatively small amounts of LNG from small fields along the southern coast of Alaska. These sources are economical because they do not bear the burden of the cost of a major pipeline.

A small fraction of North Slope natural gas produced along with crude oil is used for oil-field operation, but most is reinjected into the oil reservoirs at high pressures and at considerable expense. By law, it cannot be burned or flared for safe disposal. From older reservoirs, the total rate of gas production is increasing with time, while oil production is decreasing with time. Because newer oil reservoirs have an increasing production rate with time, the total oil-production rate during the 1990s is expected to be fairly constant. However, total oil production will be restrained by gas production unless the no-flaring regulations are changed.

In 1990 the USSR demonstrated an airplane it had developed which had one engine operating on LNG and two others using jet fuel. The Soviets' goal is to have interchangeable use of these fuels in all of the engines and thereby use more of the country's natural-gas reserves.

The natural-gas industry emphasized in 1990 that natural gas contributes less to the so-called greenhouse effect and has lower oxides of sulfur emissions than does either fuel oil or coal. This advantage is due to the ease of removal of sulfur compounds from natural gas and by its favorable ratio of oxides of carbon produced per unit of combustible energy. The difficulties and costs of transporting natural gas as LNG or CNG (compressed natural gas) may encourage the alternate use of manufacturing methanol in so-called "chemical liquifaction."

Nuclear Energy. In 1990 nuclear power produced about 20% of the electricity in the United States, while the percentage was much higher in other industrialized parts of the world. For example, France produces 74% of its power from nuclear energy. While many countries continue to construct more nuclear-power plants, the United States canceled the construction of all plants ordered since 1974 because of public opposition to this form of energy. Antinuclear groups cite the accidents at Three Mile Island and Chernobyl in raising health and safety concerns about the use of nuclear power. Nuclear proponents, however, continued to point out the benefits of the technology as a clean-burning, almost inexhaustible energy resource and the advantages of advanced reactors developed during the 1980s that are safer and can be built at a fraction of the cost of existing plants.

Despite the opposition of antinuclear groups, a national survey reported in 1990 that 80% of Americans believe that nuclear energy will be important in meeting the energy needs of the future. A two-year study by the National Cancer Institute also found no evidence that the use of nuclear power leads to high cancer rates.

In March the Nuclear Regulatory Commission voted to give a full-power operating license to the Seabrook nuclear reactor. Many experts consider this New Hampshire plant to be the most controversial nuclear project in the United States. Opponents of the plant, including the neighboring state of Massachusetts, planned to appeal the decision. Should the appeals fail, Seabrook would become the 110th commercial reactor in the United States. Only four more projects are in the pipeline: Comanche Peak 1, in Somervell County, TX, received a test license in February; Comanche Peak 2 and Watts Bar 1 and 2 in Spring City, TN, were under construction in 1990. The Shoreham reactor on Long Island is finished, but under an agreement with the state of New York, never will operate.

The crisis in the Middle East demonstrated the energy dependence of the United States on an inherently unstable part of the world. The nation continues to need a greater variety of energy sources that are safe, economical, and most appropriate for each of its sections.

SULLIVAN S. MARSDEN, JR.
Stanford University

ENGINEERING, CIVIL

The field of civil engineering continued to lead the way in the design and construction of tall buildings, deep tunnels, and long highways and bridges. The first months of 1990, however, were spent deepening the civil engineer's involvement in disaster protection and in analyzing the damage from two late 1989 natural disasters: California's Bay Area earthquake, and Hurricane *Hugo*, which struck the eastern seaboard of the United States.

Disaster Protection. The earthquake caused major damage and loss of life, but when compared with the Armenia earthquake of late 1988, it became clear that seismic construction codes work. Although the two earthquakes were similar in magnitude, about seven on the Richter scale, nearly 400 times as many people died in Armenia in buildings that were not built to seismic specifications. San Francisco's downtown skyscrapers, built to code, were affected minimally. Unreinforced masonry buildings, however, collapsed as did the Bay Bridge, the Embarcadero Freeway, and the double-decked Nimitz Freeway in Oakland, proving the need for more seismic retrofitting in the state.

Some retrofitting of California's bridges and highways had begun in 1971, after another earthquake damaged area highways in the San Fernando Valley. Lack of funds, however, had slowed Caltrans, the state's transportation agency, from implementing most retrofit projects. In the aftermath of the 1989 earthquake, retrofit of bridges and highways was made a priority for the agency and $80 million in funds was allotted, with about $5 million set aside for research in seismic analysis and design.

Hurricane *Hugo* caused more than $10 billion in damages along the East Coast, the highest amount for a single hurricane in U.S. history. In Charleston, SC, the city that took the brunt of the 135 mph (217 km/hr) winds and the waves that crested at 12 ft (4 m) above sea level, the new municipal pier, then under construction, along with an 800-ft- (244-m-) long seawall, helped to protect the city's immediate coastline. The ends of the T-shaped pier had been designed to break away in a hurricane rather than force a tearing of the pier's 32-ft- (10-m-) wide main area that extends 400 ft (122 m) into Charleston Harbor. The entire pier survived, however, even though it moved about 3 inches (8 cm) horizontally.

U.S. Transportation Policy. Meanwhile, "Moving America: New Directions, New Opportunities," a U.S. transportation policy for the 1990s, was presented by President Bush and Secretary of Transportation Samuel Skinner. The plan stressed less federal participation in transit matters, with more funding responsibility shifted to state and local governments through tolls and user fees.

© Durgut/Sipa

Ataturk Dam, Turkey. *Stretching across the Euphrates River, the $1.5 billion Ataturk Dam was activated by Turkey's President Turgut Ozal in January 1990. The dam, which would begin turning out electricity in 1991, will irrigate some 46,000 acres (18 616 ha) of arid land in southeastern Turkey. It is part of the $21 billion, 21-dam Southeastern Anatolia Project. Since Iraq and Syria also depend heavily on the Euphrates for their water supply, an international water-sharing agreement is required before the entire project is completed.*

Most areas already had begun moving in this direction. In 1990, Houston opened its $868 million Harris County Toll Road, comprised of two tollways, each more than 20 mi (32 km) long, and financed with voter-approved bonds. The two roadways comprise the world's largest system of lanes devoted to high-occupancy vehicles. A $2.5 billion, 15-mi (24-km) system of tollways was approved in 1990 for southern California. It would be the first toll road in that state.

The Department of Transportation, in its report, estimated that it would take $26 billion per year to maintain the U.S. transportation system, with $3 trillion needed to restore it completely. Within the 1990s, according to the report, about 30 airports will experience more than 20,000 hours of flight delays each year and annual highway delays will reach more than two billion hours. The report also said that 11% of the principal highways were deficient as were 42% of highway bridges.

To offset some of these problems, research was continuing with high-speed rail and intelligent vehicle-highway systems. Work also was continuing on mass-transportation systems. The first leg of Los Angeles' Metro Rail opened in July with a 22-mi (35-km) stretch of light rail connecting Long Beach to downtown Los Angeles. Work continued on the first 4.4 mi (7 km) of subway that will transverse downtown Los Angeles and open in 1993. The entire system will contain 17 mi (27 km) of subway and be finished by 2000.

Given 1990's emphasis on moving U.S. traffic, it is not surprising that the top civil-engineering projects were transportation-related. A privately financed California to Nevada Super Speed Train was being planned for the 1990s, as were high-speed rail projects between Houston and Dallas, TX, and in Florida between the cities of Miami, Orlando, and Tampa.

Airports in many cities, including St. Louis, Philadelphia, and New York, continued to be expanded to meet the nation's needs. A new $95 million international terminal opened in Houston. In the state of Washington, a 1.3-mi (2.1-km) downtown bus tunnel, part of a $450 million Downtown Seattle Transit Project, that would enable commuters to travel through the city's downtown area three times faster than before began operating. The diesel-powered buses enter the tunnel and then switch to electric power.

In addition to Seattle's electric buses, the city's Mount Baker Ridge Tunnel began moving three levels of traffic through the the Seattle portion of I-90, also providing landscaped recreational areas on top of the tunnel's lidded approaches. The 3,500-ft (1 066-m) tunnel and lid complex was named the Outstanding Civil Engineering Achievement of 1990 by the American Society of Civil Engineers. The project, cost $1.4 billion, 90% of which was federal funds. The top level is a 15-ft- (4.5-km-) wide bicycle and pedestrian concourse. The second level carries six lanes of regular traffic, while the lowest level allows buses and car pools to travel along a reversible roadway that eventually may be converted to light rail. It takes only one person to operate and monitor the entire complex. This is possible because one computer console controls such systems as video cameras, detectors embedded in the roadway to track traffic blockage, variable message signs, ventilation fans, mechanical-electrical rooms, a rebroadcast system with emergency frequencies as well as AM and FM

radio stations, and the largest foam sprinkler system in North America.

In Jacksonville, FL, a major transportation gap between the city's north and south areas was solved with the opening of the $72 million Napolean B. Broward Bridge. The six-lane bridge has a 1,300-ft (396-km) main span and two 650-ft (198-km) flanking spans, making it the longest cable-stayed structure in the nation of either concrete or steel and the longest span in the Western Hemisphere of concrete. A record for pouring concrete was set twice during construction. One involved pouring 9,260 cu yds (7 085 m³) in a continuous 35-hour schedule, setting a mass pour record in the southern United States. The record was broken when 18,970 cu yds (14 514 m³) of concrete were poured for the north pier during a continuous 47-hour cycle.

Other Projects. Work continued on the $3.6 billion Central Arizona Project, begun in 1974 by the U.S. Bureau of Reclamation to divert billions of gallons of water annually from the Colorado River to the arid regions of Phoenix and Tucson, AZ. The entire project, which will be finished in the 1990s, becomes more important as the western U.S. need for water reaches critical proportions. One of the most ambitious capital-improvement programs of the 20th century, it is made up of 15 separate projects, including construction of several hundred miles of main and arterial canals, modification of two existing dams, and the construction of a new dam near Phoenix.

The world's newest tallest building moved a few steps toward reality in 1990. Chicago's planning commission approved and ground was broken on the 1,999.9-ft- (610-m-) tall Miglin-Beitler Tower, estimated to cost $500 million. At 125 stories it will offer 1.4 million sq ft (130 060 m²) of office space.

An engineering study, with photographic mapping, began on South Dakota's Mount Rushmore. A private organization hoped to raise $40 million for an engineering facelift before the memorial's 50th anniversary in 1991.

Computers and specially designed engineering software continued to influence every aspect of a project. Portable computers are found on-site, which allows design changes to be made immediately. Complex project management software, able to manage the scheduling and financing of a project, once was used on large mainframes for one specific project. Now the software can run off personal computers and organize entire government agencies. Many state departments of transportation have begun putting complex multiproject capital improvement programs on-line. While more than half of these state transportation agencies now require contractors to use computer-assisted design packages, many also are requiring the use of program management software.

TERESA AUSTIN, *Free-lance Writer*

ENVIRONMENT

Environmentalists saw April 22, 1990, the 20th anniversary of the original Earth Day, as an opportunity to reassess the status of the Earth. *See* feature section, pages 54–71.

ESPIONAGE

Superpower rivalry between the United States and the USSR dwindled in 1990 as the Cold War ended. Spying continued, but the focus shifted to other nations. Iraq was the flash point.

Spies Over Iraq. While there apparently were no human spies who warned about Iraqi President Saddam Hussein's invasion of Kuwait on August 2, the subsequent situation was ideal for technological espionage. The desert terrain made concealment virtually impossible and enabled the United States to gather details about Hussein's military operations. U.S. television cameras on satellites orbiting over Iraq noted troop movements on the ground. Listening devices recorded phone messages between Iraqi commanders. High-flying planes returned with photos of Iraqi airfields, tank formations, and mobile rockets. The United States hoped that the use of technology for the purpose of military espionage would convince Hussein that he could not win a war against Operation Desert Shield, the multinational forces arrayed against him in Saudi Arabia.

Candidate from the KGB. The career of Oleg Kalugin offered evidence of the dramatic changes occurring within the Soviet Union. After Kalugin was forced out of the KGB (Soviet civil intelligence) for revealing some of its secrets, he ran successfully for the Supreme Soviet on an anti-KGB platform, taking a stand for democracy and capitalism. During his political campaign, Kalugin indicated that while he was a KGB officer, he directed the Walker spy ring in the United States, winning a medal for his activities. (John Walker, his son Michael, and Jerry Whitworth stole secrets from the U.S. Navy for 18 years.) U.S. counterespionage broke up the ring in 1985.

Panic Among Spies. German reunification on October 3 caused disarray in the espionage agencies of the former Soviet bloc. Hardest hit was the Stasi, once the intelligence arm of the Communist regime in East Germany. Some former spies fled to Moscow. Others were arrested. The opening of Stasi files in East Berlin unmasked hundreds of spies who had worked in West Germany. One Stasi agent was Gabriele Gast, an aide to West German Chancellor Helmut Kohl. Another, Klaus Kuron, a senior West German counterintelligence officer, added to the panic among spies when he turned himself in on October 7, and identified those who he knew also had been Stasi operatives. The new Germany faced the problem of punishing some former spies as criminals, and extending amnesty to others.

Echoes of the Past. Despite the changes in East-West relations, old espionage cases continued to make headlines. On June 7, Roderick Ramsay, who had been a U.S. Army sergeant in West Germany, was arrested in Tampa, FL, and charged with revealing classified information to agents of East Germany. Evidence gathered in the Ramsay case led to Clyde Conrad, also a U.S. sergeant in West Germany. Ramsay alleged that he was recruited by Conrad to spy for the East Germans. Condemned by a German court, Conrad received a life sentence just one day before Ramsay was arrested.

Former Federal Bureau of Investigation (FBI) agent Richard Miller faced his third trial in 1990 and was found guilty in October of spying for the Soviet Union. Meanwhile the U.S. Air Force dropped its prosecution of Captain John Hirsch, finding no proof that he had spied for the Soviets while serving in West Berlin.

An agent known to the U.S Central Intelligence Agency (CIA) as Top Hat was captured in Moscow. He had reported to U.S. intelligence for nearly 30 years. The Communist Party newspaper *Pravda* reported in January that he had been sentenced to death. It then became known that Top Hat was General Dmitri Polyakov of the GRU (Soviet military intelligence). A *New York Times* report cast some doubt on parts of the Soviet news release, indicating that Polyakov already was dead.

The Bloch Affair. On July 5, Felix Bloch tried to resign from the U.S. State Department. His superiors refused to let him, and on November 5, he was fired instead. It was the latest phase in a bizarre affair that began in 1989, when it became known that Bloch was suspected of spying for the USSR when he was at the U.S. embassy in Vienna. FBI agents shadowed him in case he attempted to escape to Moscow, and the news media followed him for weeks. The FBI remained unsure whether Bloch had been a spy.

Mossad Furor. A former Israeli espionage officer created a furor with his book *By Way of Deception*. Victor Ostrovsky said that the Mossad (Israel's civil intelligence) acted free of government control and claimed that it spied on friendly countries, including the United States. His most sensational statement was that the Mossad knew of the planned terrorist truck attack in Lebanon in 1983 that killed 241 U.S. Marines, and that it concealed this information from Washington. The Israeli government tried unsuccessfully to prevent publication of the book in the United States.

Khrushchev Remembered. A memoir of Nikita Khrushchev, premier of the USSR from 1958 to 1964, written by his son solved one mystery of the Cold War. The memoir indicated that the KGB had assured Khrushchev in

1962 that his missiles in Cuba were concealed from air surveillance. He was startled when U.S. President John Kennedy publicized photos of the missiles taken from U.S. spy planes.

Khrushchev also said that the Americans Julius and Ethel Rosenberg gave the Russians U.S. atomic secrets that helped Soviet scientists build a nuclear bomb. The Rosenbergs were convicted and executed as spies in 1953.

VINCENT BURANELLI
Coauthor, "Spy/Counterspy"

ETHIOPIA

During 1990 the Ethiopian government lost control of virtually the entire northern part of the country to rebel troops, while the Soviet Union withdrew half its advisers and indicated that Soviet military aid would be halted in 1991. While Israel initiated a military-aid program, the United States and the USSR made it clear they would work in tandem to resolve the Ethiopian civil wars and to prevent another famine. Ethiopia also announced that it was abandoning its commitment to Marxist economics.

Civil War. In February 1990 one rebel group, the Eritrean People's Liberation Front (EPLF), captured Ethiopia's vital Red Sea port of Massawa, a key staging point for the distribution of emergency food shipments to the famine-stricken country; by midyear EPLF forces also had surrounded Asmara, Eritrea's provincial capital. At the same time troops of the Tigrean People's Liberation Front (TPLF) struck deep into the heart of Wollo and Gonder regions and penetrated Shoa region; by fall 1990 they were less than 75 mi (121 km) north of the national capital, Addis Ababa.

In May, President Mengistu Haile-Mariam, acting in the midst of these military setbacks, announced the execution of 12 generals accused of having been involved in an abortive coup in 1989. Their deaths were meant as a warning to the military to stand their ground.

Eastern Europe and Soviet Withdrawal. With the Soviet pullout and the simultaneous collapse of Communist governments throughout Eastern Europe, Ethiopia lost its primary military allies. Czechoslovakia and East Germany also ended arms shipments to Ethiopia in 1990. In June the United States and the USSR agreed to seek a nonmilitary resolution to the civil war, and to cooperate on delivering food aid.

Israel and Ethiopia. At the same time, however, Israel came forward as a new source of aid for Ethiopian President Mengistu Haile-Mariam. In late 1989, Ethiopia and Israel reestablished diplomatic relations after a 16-year break. In February and March 1990 several hundred Israeli military advisers arrived, along with large supplies of small arms. U.S. officials claimed that Israel also sent 100 cluster bombs to Ethiopia.

ETHIOPIA • Information Highlights

Official Name: People's Democratic Republic of Ethiopia.
Location: Eastern Africa.
Area: 471,776 sq mi (1 221 900 km²).
Population (mid-1990 est.): 51,700,000.
Chief Cities (1984 census): Addis Ababa, the capital, 1,412,577; Asmara, 275,385; Dire Dawa, 98,104.
Government: *Head of state,* Mengistu Haile-Mariam, president (took office Sept. 10, 1987). Legislature —Parliament (National Shengo, established Sept. 9, 1987).
Monetary Unit: Birr (2.07 birr equal U.S.$1, July 1990).
Gross Domestic Product (1989 est. U.S. $): $6,600,000,000.
Economic Index (Addis Ababa, 1989): *Consumer Prices* (1980 = 100), all items, 146.4; food, 142.1.
Foreign Trade (1988 U.S.$): *Imports,* $1,075,000,000; *exports,* $448,000,000.

There were two motives behind Israel's actions. Meir Joffe, Israel's ambassador to Ethiopia, maintained that Israel does not want to see the EPLF turn the "Red Sea into the Arab Sea." Secondly, in return for the aid, Mengistu agreed to allow the 17,000 Ethiopian Jews left in Ethiopia to immigrate to Israel. During the early part of the year 500 Ethiopian Jews emigrated each month. Later Mengistu halted the flow in an effort to increase Israeli aid, making a secret trip to Tel Aviv for renegotiations.

Domestic Affairs. Trying to win support from an increasingly disenchanted populace, Mengistu scrapped Ethiopia's Soviet-style economic system, replacing it with a mixed economy. The right to own a private business was restored, state-owned industry would operate on a profit basis, private ownership of land was legalized, and apartments and office buildings could be rented or sold. In essence the theoretical and political basis for the 1974 revolution was tossed aside.

Famine. The civil war added to the miseries of those millions suffering from malnutrition and starvation. After the U.S.-Soviet agreement in June, Ethiopia was forced to permit food aid to be shipped to the starving in the north. But the EPLF prevented the docking of ships carrying emergency food supplies at Massawa, insisting that first the UN must recognize Eritrea as an independent nation. The UN refused. With 4.4 million people threatened with starvation, the United States dealt directly with the rebels in an effort to deliver food.

The United Nations Food and Agriculture Organization appealed for additional donations of food and money, despite the fact that vast supplies of food were rotting on ships and warehouses in Massawa. In July, at the heads of state conference of the Organization of African Unity, Ethiopia, along with Somalia, Sudan, Kenya, Uganda, and Djibouti, signed an accord pledging to seek peaceful means to end regional conflicts.

PETER SCHWAB
State University of New York at Purchase

ETHNIC GROUPS

The federal census of 1990 reminded Americans of the ethnic mix and distribution of the United States. Preliminary census returns indicated an increased separation of races since 1980, with minorities becoming more concentrated in cities and whites in suburbs. The returns also recorded substantial population gains for Asians and Hispanics in the Sunbelt and a continuing black remigration to the South. Hispanics made up about 10% of the U.S. population and were the nation's fastest-growing ethnic group.

California officials estimated that between 1 million and 3 million illegal alien residents, mostly Hispanic, did not show up in the census count. Leaders of all the major ethnic groups charged the Census Bureau with undercounting minority populations in inner cities, and black mayors in such cities as Detroit and Atlanta filed suit to have recounts. Sensitive to the nation's more pronounced minority demographic profile, Congress in 1990 passed the first comprehensive reform of immigration laws since 1965. (*See* REFUGEES AND IMMIGRATION.)

Although the number of Asian Americans entering colleges continued to rise in 1990, Hispanics and Native Americans in college remained underrepresented. The overall number of blacks in colleges crept up in 1990, but the percentage of eligible black males enrolled full-time in college continued to decline. Despite such trends, the U.S. Department of Education said in December it would prohibit colleges and universities that receive federal funds from offering scholarships designated solely for minority students. An assistant education secretary said that "race-exclusive" scholarships were discriminatory and therefore illegal. After much furor from civil-rights activists and educators the administration ruled that colleges could award racially based scholarships as long as the money came from private donors or federal funds designated to aid minority students.

Responding to criticism that college-admissions tests discriminated against minorities, the College Board in 1990 approved revisions in its Scholastic Aptitude Test (SAT), with a new emphasis on critical reading over vocabulary and on data interpretation and applied mathematical questions.

In October, President Bush vetoed the 1990 civil-rights bill on the grounds that it forced employers to adopt race- and sex-based hiring quotas to avoid lawsuits. The bill was intended to reverse five 1989 Supreme Court decisions that made it more difficult for women and minorities to win job-discrimination suits. Supporters planned to reintroduce similar legislation in Congress in 1991. In February the president named Arthur A. Fletcher as chairman of the Civil Rights Commission.

In reviewing two Federal Communications Commission (FCC) programs designed to boost minority-group ownership of broadcast licenses, the U.S. Supreme Court upheld the power of Congress to enact affirmative-action programs favoring minorities. The court also ruled that local taxes may be used to undo state-created discrimination.

Blacks. For blacks, the year opened with the inauguration of Virginia Gov. L. Douglas Wilder (*see* BIOGRAPHY) as the nation's first elected black governor and of David Dinkins as the first black mayor of New York City. In June, South African antiapartheid leader Nelson Mandela made a triumphant eight-city tour of the United States. There were few political gains for blacks in 1990. Two new faces on the political scene were Sharon Pratt Dixon, who was elected as mayor of Washington, DC, to become the first black woman mayor of a major U.S. city, and Connecticut's Gary Franks, who

AP/Wide World

Hilary Waukau, Sr., an elder of the Menominee tribe, smokes a symbolic peace pipe after signing an international treaty, pledging the tribes of the United States and Canada to protect their tribal rights.

became the first black Republican elected to the U.S. House since 1935. Jesse Jackson won his first election—as one of two "shadow" U.S. senators from Washington, DC.

Gone was Marion Barry, Jr., who did not seek reelection as mayor of Washington, DC, following his conviction in federal court of a misdemeanor drug-possession charge. He also lost in a run for an at-large seat on the Washington, DC, city council. Beaten in Georgia's Democratic runoff primary for governor was Andrew Young, who seemed to ignore his black supporters while unsuccessfully trying to woo rural whites. In the Louisiana senatorial primary, former Ku Klux Klansman David Duke garnered 44% of the vote by trading on white resentment toward affirmative action and welfare. In North Carolina, Republican Sen. Jesse Helms overcame a 20-point gap in opinion polls to beat former Charlotte Mayor Harvey Gantt, a black liberal Democrat, in a bitter campaign.

Many blacks continued to live in desperate conditions in the United States, with black unemployment exceeding that of any group in the nation. A disproportionate number of young black males were in prison or on parole. The infant-mortality rates of blacks were twice those of whites. Dr. Louis Sullivan, U.S. secretary of health and human services, reported in March that the life-expectancy rate for blacks was only 69.5 years, compared with 75.5 years for whites. He attributed the lower rate to patterns of living among blacks, including poor diet and heavy cigarette smoking as well as inadequate medical care.

The 25-year-old Freedom National Bank in New York City's Harlem, the fourth-largest black-owned bank in the United States, failed.

Hispanic Americans. In 1990 both major political parties campaigned vigorously for Hispanic votes and urged Hispanic Americans to demand redrawing of voting districts to comply with the 1982 voting-rights amendment. Republicans made inroads among Hispanic-American voters, winning 31% of their vote in the November 6 elections, compared with 24% in 1988. In Florida, Republican U.S. Rep. Ileana Ros-Lehtinen, a Cuban American, was reelected on the strength of Hispanic votes, but Republican Gov. Bob Martinez failed in his reelection bid. In California, Hispanic voters reelected Democrats Matthew Martinez, Jr., and Esteban Torres to the U.S. House, and Texas U.S. Congressmen Albert Bustamante (D) and Henry Gonzalez (D) also were reelected.

A major controversy about the direction of educational programs for Hispanic Americans erupted in April, when U.S. Secretary of Education Lauro F. Cavazos blamed Hispanic parents for the 40% dropout rate among Hispanic students. Cavazos, who resigned his cabinet post in December, urged an "attitudinal change" among Hispanics to counter low levels of Hispanic student performance. Critics argued that Hispanics have supported increased educational spending in many states.

Native Americans. Peter MacDonald, chairman of the 180,000-member Navajo Nation for 13 years and an advocate of modernizing the Navajos' reservation, was convicted of bribery and conspiracy by a tribal court in 1990. The court's assertion of jurisdiction reaffirmed Navajo sovereignty and fed a movement for increased tribal autonomy. The Navajo tribal council meanwhile declared MacDonald ineligible for reelection and Peterson Zah was elected chairman in November.

In several states, Indians levied taxes on nontribal residents of reservations. Various tribes also claimed rights to fishing, timber, water use, minerals, and even gambling operations as provisions of treaties. They also filed suits to regain artifacts from museums and collectors. Rivalries continued to exist between "traditionalists" who want to return to "the old ways" and "modernists" who want to exploit their resources for profit. In April the U.S. Supreme Court ruled that states may ban the use of peyote, a hallucinogen used for religious purposes by several tribes. Courts also refused to block oil drilling on Blackfoot reservation land with tribal religious significance.

In 1990 almost 50 Indians were serving in state legislatures, and many more on school boards and county offices. In Idaho a Pawnee, Larry Echohawk, made a strong bid for state attorney general. Colorado's U.S. Rep. Ben Nighthorse Campbell, the only native American in the U.S. Congress, was reelected easily. Native Americans also fielded all-Indian slates of candidates to consolidate Indian voting blocs in far Western and Plains states.

Asian Americans. In 1990, Asian Americans vigorously challenged ethnic slurs and stereotyping. Three Asian-American organizations demanded in May that New York's *Newsday* fire columnist Jimmy Breslin for disparaging remarks he made about a Korean-American colleague. Breslin apologized but was suspended for two weeks when he made light of the incident on a radio talk show. More important was the attempt by Asian actors, through Actors Equity, to prevent a British actor from playing the lead role of a Eurasian in an upcoming Broadway production of *Miss Saigon*. The show's producer pulled the production, threatening numerous jobs for Asian-American actors in minor roles, and Actors Equity conceded the producer's right to bring in a celebrated British actor.

Asian Americans generally continued to lack political cohesion in 1990. On the local level black boycotts against Korean merchants in black neighborhoods in New York City and Philadelphia were dominant news items.

RANDALL M. MILLER
St. Joseph's University, Philadelphia

EUROPE

With Germany undergoing reunification and Eastern bloc nations becoming more democratic, 1990 was a historic year for the European continent. (*See* feature article, page 36.)

FAMILY

The plight of the world's children was the focus of 70 world leaders who met at the United Nations in September 1990. The summit meeting directed the world's attention to the millions of children who suffer from malnutrition, disease, infant mortality, illiteracy, and homelessness: 150 million children under the age of 5 suffer from malnutrition, 30 million live in the streets, and 7 million are driven from their homes by war and famine.

Leaders at the meeting endorsed a ten-year plan to reduce mortality rates and poverty among children and improve access to immunizations and education. The World Bank and other international lenders pledged to increase lending for primary education and health care in poor countries by $500 million per year in the coming decade, support which could save the lives of 1 million children annually.

U.S. Children at Peril. As international attention focused on the plight of children around the world, hundreds of thousands of U.S. children faced their own set of perils relating to poverty, prenatal and neonatal care, and abuse, as the 1990s began. The National Commission on Children reported that more than one in five U.S. children live in poverty, putting them at risk for poor health, school failure, teenage pregnancy, crime, and drug abuse. Nearly 25% of U.S. children live in single-parent households, a contributing factor to children living in poverty, performing poorly in school, and becoming themselves single parents. Census Bureau data, part of a report issued by the House of Representatives' Select Committee on Children, Youth, and Families, found that children in the United States are more likely than children in 11 other industrialized countries to live in poverty, to live with only one parent, or to be killed by the age of 25.

The infant mortality rate in the United States reached its lowest level in 1989 but, at a level of 9.7 per 1,000 live births, remained higher than the mortality rates in most industrialized nations. Federal health officials indicated that there was little likelihood that the United States would achieve its goal of reducing its infant mortality rate to 9 per 1,000 live births by the early 1990s. Toward that effort, a White House task force called for spending an additional $500 million annually for maternal health resources and neonatal intensive care.

A report by the U.S. Advisory Board on Child Abuse and Neglect said that at least 900,000 children in the United States were abused physically or sexually in 1989. While the number of incidents of child abuse rose, resources to protect children and help families diminished. One bright spot was a 1990 U.S. Supreme Court decision, ruling that children no longer would be required to testify in front of the persons accused of mistreating them.

The rising number of "parentless" families and the shortage of foster-care homes has led to a return of orphanages. Although there were 125,000 foster homes in the United States in 1990, 500,000 children required out-of-home placement, and the number of children requiring placement was expected to increase to 840,000 by 1995. Most child-care experts agree that private foster homes remain the most beneficial option for children needing placement. However, newer institutional facilities can provide small-group care along with a range of services—from intensive therapy for emotionally disturbed children to short-term placement for children who later would be returned to their families or adopted.

In 1990 the Department of Labor began a crackdown on the growing violations of child-labor laws in a program called Operation Child Watch. The government reported that child-labor violations increased from 8,877 in 1984 to 22,508 in 1989. Underage workers included undocumented immigrants, impoverished urban youths, and middle-class teenagers supplementing their allowances. (*See also* LABOR.)

Legislation. Congress and the administration of President George Bush continued to struggle with legislation that would ease the burdens of working parents and low-income families through guaranteed parental leave for births or family illnesses and expanded tax credits and grants for child care.

A family-leave bill passed the Congress only to be vetoed by President Bush in June. The president argued on that occasion that mandated leave would take away employers' flexibility and possibly lead them to cut other benefits. Supporters of a mandatory national family-leave policy have argued that the country is overdue in adopting federal minimum requirements to bring business in line with the changing demographics of the workplace.

In addition, a 1990 study by the National Academy of Sciences concluded that the nation's child-care services were inadequate and called on the government to allocate an additional $5 billion to $10 billion per year for improvements. Addressing some of the issues was child-care legislation passed by Congress in the fall that provided grants to states to subsidize child-care programs, expanded the existing tax credit for low-income families with children, and established a new tax credit relating to health-care coverage for children of low-income families.

ELIZABETH MCNALLY, *Free-lance Writer*

Photos, © Barthelemy/Sipa

The styles of the 1960s impacted the fashion world in 1990 with a strong return to rising hemlines, colorful and glossy fabrics, the "tent" silhouette (left), *and updated versions of psychedelic prints* (right).

FASHION

The year in fashion began on an upbeat creative note, but by the end of 1990 as the worldwide economic picture worsened, fashion retreated into a nostalgic replay of 1960s themes and looks from "mod madness" to the cool Camelot style epitomized by that era.

Trends in Apparel. Evoking the mini, skirts were shorter than ever. Pencil-slim versions were in leathers or hard-finished, firm fabrics such as gabardine, twill, linen, or pique while softer flared or pleated types floated in jerseys or chiffon-like fabrics. Most were topped with tunic-length jackets, sweaters, or overblouses, some only inches shorter than the skirts themselves. For modesty's sake, some designers provided matching panties or shorts as part of the ensemble, but more often leggings or tights were the major accessory for the shorter skirts. Mainly opaque and textured in ribbed, herringbone, or lacy patterns, they were newest in wildly printed fabrics or brilliant colorations that often contrasted vividly with the clothes they accompanied. For evening, there were glittery metallic versions or those in luster yarns that gave a high gloss to legs. Another look showed miniskirts with thigh-high boots in suedes or kid leathers.

The dress also was an important item as easy, relaxed shapes were resurrected. The chemise, slip dress, A-line, and tee dress, with their higher hemlines, were a throwback to the 1960s, but lent themselves to a variety of fabrics from soft, drapable crepes and jerseys to crisper flannels, piques, or shantung. Dresses were shown both for daytime and evening, and every designer had his or her distinctive versions. There was Sonia Rykiels' pink velour slip dress and Marc Jacobs' rainbow-striped sequin version. Calvin Klein scored with his pale suede tank dresses, his simple silk georgette shifts, and his white silk slip dress covered with tiny pearls, and Bill Blass did elegant little A-shapes in double-faced wools or firm silks.

The new coats were short and swingy tents or trapeze shapes in high-voltage colors. Classic trench coats, long and short, also were important especially when done in unusual fabrics.

Another fashion item popular during the year was the "catsuit," a form-fitting unitard that was the novelty running through all the collections. At its most dramatic it was seen in wildly colored psychedelic or Pucci-inspired prints in stretch jersey, in brilliant or metallic luster knits, lavishly beaded top to toe, as at Versace, or in vinyl at Thierry Mugler; at its most wearable, it was seen at all price levels in stretch velvets, velours, or knits in black or charcoal gray. Bell-bottom pants were another déjà vu item from the 1960s that was popular.

Courtesy, Revlon

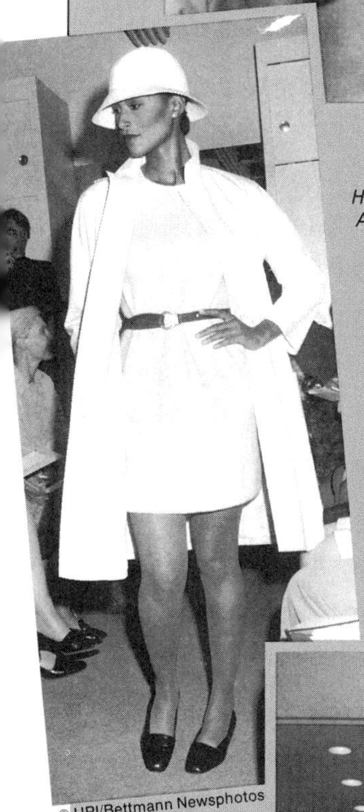

Halston (above), who died of AIDS in March 1990, was the first American designer to gain international celebrity, putting his stamp on 1970s style and influencing the fashion of succeeding decades.

© UPI/Bettmann Newsphotos

AP/Wide World

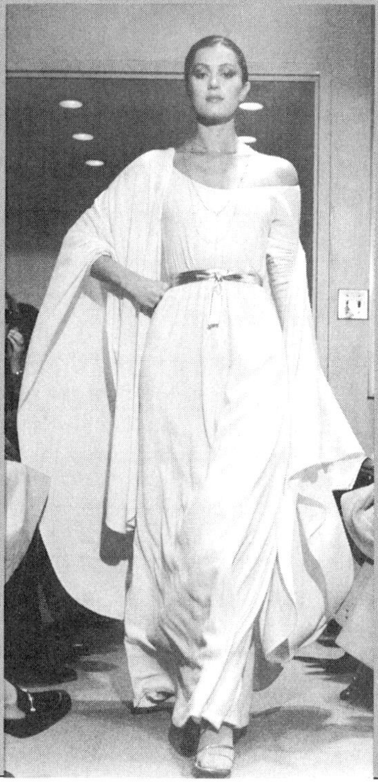

The Halston Legacy

From the trend-setting pillbox hats worn by Jacqueline Kennedy to the use of luxurious fabrics and the relaxed approach to the clothes of the 1980s and early 1990s, the international fashion world was influenced profoundly by the classic designs of Halston. When he died on March 26, 1990, Halston left a legacy as the creator of U.S. style, an international star whose designs symbolized taste and timeless fashion. With his death from AIDS, Halston joined a growing list of fashion luminaries who have succumbed to this devastating illness.

Background. Roy Halston Frowick was born in Des Moines, IA, on April 23, 1932, and began his career in Chicago in 1953, designing hats. He soon moved to New York to work for famed milliner Lilly Daché. By 1958 he was in charge of custom millinery at Bergdorf Goodman. In 1961 he was catapulted to fame when he designed the pillbox hat Jacqueline Kennedy wore to her husband's inauguration as president. With this success, he soon began to produce and sell his own clothing designs. In 1968 he left Bergdorf's to start his own company, Halston Enterprises, and he quickly acquired a star-studded clientele.

The 1960s were the days of "fun fashion" and flamboyance, full of miniskirts, vinyl boots, hippie beads, psychedelic prints, and ethnic fashion. Halston's first show was a bombshell: It was minimalist, classic, sophisticated, and all-American. His Ultrasuede shirtdresses, cashmere twin sweater sets, jersey pantsuits, chiffon caftans, and gracefully draped strapless gowns were serenely elegant, timeless, and tasteful. It was modern dressing and it changed fashion. It also raised the status of U.S. design worldwide.

Halston often had said that he wanted to dress America and in 1983 he contracted to produce inexpensive fashion for mass merchandiser J.C. Penney. In a move that shocked him, upscale retailers such as Bergdorf Goodman dropped his haute couture, ready-to-wear, and perfume lines. In 1973 he sold his company to Norton Simon to concentrate on designing, but by 1983 the company had changed hands six times and he suddenly found that he was barred from creating anything under his name: It belonged to others. Depressed and discouraged, he stopped designing professionally in 1984. However, up until the time of his death, he continued to battle to regain the use of his name. At the same time, however, his international influence in the relaxed, sportswear approach to fashion and the use of luxurious fabrics continued.

ANN M. ELKINS

Fabric and Color Trends. Shine and stretch were the year's fabric trends. Glossy patent leather and vinyl were strong in both accessories and apparel. Michael Kors did short swingy coats and sleek catsuits in black patent; Ungaro showed miniskirts in bright-colored vinyls; and Marc Jacobs had clear plastic redingotes over bright silk shifts in his collection for Perry Ellis. Thierry Mugler in his modernistic collection used vinyl in every apparel category. Stretch fabrics went beyond the knits and jerseys used for bodysuits and tights. Stretch piques, flannels, and gabardines added a comfort factor to suits and dresses while clingy velvets and velours with spandex were sexy after-five dress fabrics. Jeans in stretch denim and poplin were promoted heavily.

Texture was present in the form of crisp, crunchy lace and fuzzy chenille that moved from the beds to the backs of trendy consumers. Quilting was another fabric look that lost its homespun attitude when done in suede, silk, or velvet for anoraks and jackets.

Color was important in 1990 not only for the variety of bright shades but in the way they were mixed in glaring pop- and op-art prints, in color blocking on garments, or coordinated in ensembles. Typical were the layered looks in mixed colors from Bill Blass and Isaac Mizrahi, Ungaro's brilliant fantasy florals, and the many psychedelic prints patterned after those of Pucci and Peter Max from the 1960s. Black served as a minor relief to the vibrant color, but white replaced black as the major color for evening.

Footwear and Other Accessories. Boots were the important accessory in every collection. At Lacroix and St. Laurent, many were adorned with stitching, embroidery, appliqué, or studded with gemstones to give them a lavish ethnic tone that echoed those designers' fashions. The Western boot, still strong, was updated with the use of exotic leathers and skins, elaborate colorations, or fringe trims; and a cutoff, demi-boot version was a trendy, popular innovation. Other important boot

© John Mantel/Sipa

The Fur-Coat Debate

Animal-rights groups protesting the wearing of fur had a year of vociferous activity in 1990. A growing and emotional anti-fur media blitz had celebrities renouncing furs and supporting animal rights or displaying disturbingly graphic photographs of trapped or battered animals. Leaflets describing the "atrocities" suffered by animals used for coats were distributed and aggressive tactics at demonstrations and rallies were designed to shame or chastise buyers or wearers of fur.

There even were reports of "guerrilla" tactics, such as the smoke bombing of fur salons and the slashing or spray painting of fur coats.

Fur-industry representatives banded together and countered with their own emotional campaign attempting to tap the public's resentment of what they considered harassment and bullying by anti-fur activists. They also focused on the ever-growing list of demands set forth by activists that were designed to provide animals with rights equal to human rights. Referring to the agenda of animal-rights groups, ads read: "today fur, tomorrow leather, then wool, then meat. . . ." Others stressed the warmth, durability, and beauty of fur to consumers and the industry's dedication to conservation as well as responsible and humane wildlife management and fur ranching.

The fur industry had been experiencing difficulties for a number of years prior to 1990. Designers, reacting to anti-fur pressure, deserted. Major retailers and furriers went bankrupt, and sales growth flattened. Activists claimed credit for the shrinking fur market, but the industry cited other reasons, including overbreeding, warmer-than-usual winters, a new, strong fashion look—shearlings, and a generally weak economy. Rising unit sales, however, indicated that more women were choosing to wear fur and lower prices were making fur more affordable than ever. Not all of the major designers stopped offering fur and many younger designers began to do fur lines in response to customer requests. Furriers pointed to these facts as indicators of a healthy revival of the industry.

ANN M. ELKINS

Photos, © Barthelemy/Sipa

The timeless Chanel suit (left) and the 1960s A-line silhouette (right) were updated in 1990 with the use of bright, bold color and lace, both representative of popular and innovative trends of the fashion year.

styles were sleek, polished-leather riding boots, the short jodhpur type, and the field boot with lacing at the instep. Hiking boots, chukkas, and desert boots were part of the many outdoor looks shown, and Ralph Lauren even added "Wellies" and angler's hip boots.

Suede and velvety nubuck were 1990's most popular fashion materials in footwear and were colored in a multitude of hues that ranged from soft pastels through hot brights to lush Renaissance darks. They also often were crushed or draped for an elegant feminine softness. Polished leathers were a close second choice, mainly in more basic colors and in utilitarian footwear. Flats were styled as ballerina slippers, moccasins, or skimmers with embroidery or braid trims, while mannish oxfords sported ghillie ties, wing tips, or monk straps. Popular chunky square or curved mid-heel pumps featured high throats, squared or boxed toes, and button, braid, or jeweled ornamentation, while stiletto-heeled shoes with needle toes appeared in many European showings as T-straps, slings, or slides for evening. Many were ornate and studded, beaded, or sequinned.

In jewelry, pearls got bigger, and chokers or necklaces of baroque nuggets were wrapped high around the throat. Metal in sculptured form or studded with gemstones hung from the neck as pendants or wrapped the wrist in wide cuff bracelets usually worn in pairs—one to each arm. Belts were chunky chains draped around the hips or tailored leather classics. Long mufflers and scarves of wool or silk, patterned or plain, were knotted or wrapped at the throat. The beret and wide headbands were favorite headgear.

Handbags came in sporty styles like backpacks, and belt bags were done in everything from quilted leathers to alligator, velvet, or metallic materials. Oversized drawstring bags and totes stood out in suede and lizard, and structured hard-cased bags like miniature luggage came in luxurious leathers and skins.

Menswear. The news in menswear was in the softening of the silhouette. In suits there was less tailoring and an emphasis on comfort and mobility. Jackets were softer, looser, and longer, often unconstructed and unlined, and sporting an easy shawl collar. Trousers were comfortably wider, with waist pleating; shirts were unfitted and boxier with softer, wider collars. Coats took on military airs that owed more to a private than an officer or were modeled on outdoor looks such as the drover's coat, anorak, or field jacket.

There was also a lighter approach to the way clothes were combined; business and weekend clothes mixed. Sportswear items like mock turtlenecks or chambray work shirts were worn under more formal blazers; an anorak or slicker was tossed over a business suit, and conventional wardrobes were spiced with offbeat accessories or unusual color mixes. Tapestry vests, the aviator's watch, bright-colored rain gear, or a wide tie in a bold and unusual print were the route to adventurous dressing.

ANN ELKINS
"Good Housekeeping"

FINLAND

The question of whether Finland should become a member of an enlarged European Community (EC) was a dominant concern during 1990. At first opposed to such a move, the government wanted the issue to be debated widely. A continued linkup with the European Free Trade Association (EFTA) and possible EC membership through the creation of a European Economic Area were suggested. At year's end it was hoped that firm arrangements could be entered into by 1992, the year in which the EC is to be reconstituted.

Political Affairs. The coalition government of Harri Holkeri of the National Coalition Party underwent changes early in the year. Ole Norrback was elected chairman of the Social Democratic Party and was transferred from the ministry of defense to the ministry of education. The newly named minister of defense was Elisabeth Rehn, 55, of the Swedish People's Party, who became the first woman ever to hold the post. Paavo Väyrynen, a former government minister, resigned as chairman of the Center Party on March 29, but continued to represent his party in parliament. On June 17 he was succeeded in the party post by Esko Aho. In March, Minister of Finance Erkki Liikanen was succeeded by Minister of Justice Matti Louekoski. Two women moved into the open positions: Tarja Halonen went to the Justice Department and Tuulikki Hämäläinen to the Department of Social Affairs.

At the end of August, Prime Minister Holkeri pressured Raimo Vistbacka, minister of transportation, the only cabinet minister representing the Finnish Rural Party, to resign, the main reason being his party's refusal to approve the latest state budget. At its 22d party congress on February 25, the Communist Party resolved that the party as such virtually would cease to exist. Its political activities were transferred to a so-called Union of the Left, founded in April.

Foreign Affairs. On August 28–30, Prime Minister Holkeri hosted the visit by British Prime Minister Margaret Thatcher, during which she met with President Mauno Koivisto. Helsinki was the scene for the second 1990 summit meeting between Presidents George Bush and Mikhail Gorbachev, September 8–9. Held at the Finlandia House, the meeting between the U.S. and USSR leaders focused on the Middle East and other world problems. The visiting presidents also conferred with President Koivisto.

At the United Nations the Finnish representative on the Security Council voted in favor of all motions concerning an economic blockade of Iraq.

The Economy. In the 1980s the growth of the gross national product (GNP) averaged 4% but reached 5% in 1989. For 1990, however, it was

FINLAND • Information Highlights

Official Name: Republic of Finland.
Location: Northern Europe.
Area: 130,127 sq mi (337 030 km²).
Population (mid-1990 est.): 5,000,000.
Chief Cities (Dec. 31, 1988 est.): Helsinki, the capital, 489,965; Tampere, 171,068.
Government: *Head of state,* Mauno Koivisto, president (took office Jan. 27, 1982). *Head of government,* Harri Holkeri, prime minister (took office April 30, 1987). *Legislature* (unicameral)—Eduskunta.
Monetary Unit: Markka (3.56 markkaa equal U.S.$1, Dec. 12, 1990).
Gross Domestic Product: (1989 est. U.S.$): $74,400,-000,000.
Economic Indexes (1989): *Consumer Prices* (1980 = 100), all items, 180.7; food, 176.2. *Industrial Production* (1980 = 100), 132.
Foreign Trade (1989 U.S.$): *Imports,* $24,570,-000,000; *exports,* $23,289,000,000.

expected that the figure would hover around 2%. The year 1990 was characterized by continued high inflation, reaching 6.2% at midyear. With moderate unemployment, about 3.5%, the growth of exports in 1990 was expected to be between 2% and 3% in volume. The annual trade balance had worsened since 1984; in 1990 the trade deficit was held at $4 million and the deficit on current account was expected to rise to $6.4 billion. Some harm to the economy was inflicted by a one-month strike by all bank employees, from February 1 to March 4.

ERIK J. FRIIS
"The Scandinavian-American Bulletin"

FLORIDA

As one of the nation's largest and most heterogeneous states, Florida made news on many fronts in 1990, including a heated race for the statehouse between the incumbent governor and a political legend.

Politics. Lawton Chiles, who had served 18 years in the U.S. Senate before stepping down in 1989, reentered the political arena in 1990 as the Democratic candidate for governor of Florida. Following an easy victory in the primary, Chiles defeated Republican Gov. Bob Martinez in the general election by a decisive margin. Chiles' victory gave Democrats control over congressional redistricting in a state expected to gain four seats in the U.S. House of Representatives as a result of spiraling population growth. Preliminary census figures indicated that Florida's population had grown to 12.8 million, an increase of 31% since 1980.

President George Bush later named Martinez to succeed William Bennett as director of the Office of National Drug Control Policy.

The Economy. Florida felt the shock waves from a devastating freeze and the failure of several major businesses and institutions during 1990. President Bush declared part of the state a major disaster area in January following a Christmas 1989 freeze that destroyed citrus and other crops. Some industry officials placed the value of crop losses in excess of $100 million.

In February federal regulators seized the Centrust Bank, Florida's largest thrift, declaring it insolvent. Centrust operated 75 branch banks in the state and held $5 billion in deposits. In April, General Development Corporation, a developer based in Miami, filed for bankruptcy protection. Three weeks earlier, the company admitted that it had sold Florida real estate at inflated prices, intending to defraud.

Orlando gained another tourist attraction when Universal Studios opened its largest working film studio outside of Hollywood.

The Environment. Florida again suffered from an extended drought, compelling state officials to declare a water emergency and restrict water use in parts of the state. The Florida legislature passed a law restricting development activities in environmentally sensitive areas. In June, President Bush blocked new oil and gas drilling off the coasts of Florida until the year 2000. Environmentalist Marjory Stone Douglas, a champion of the Everglades, used the occasion of her 100th birthday to campaign for additional protection for the state's fragile environment.

Florida experienced its largest outbreak of St. Louis encephalitis since 1977. More than 100 people were afflicted with the mosquito-related disease.

Crime. James Edward Pugh, a disgruntled customer, opened fire on a finance company in Jacksonville, killing ten people before turning his gun on himself.

In June, U.S. District Judge Jose Gonzalez ruled that *As Nasty As They Wanna Be*, an album by the Florida rap group 2 Live Crew, was obscene under state law. Several days later members of the group were arrested on obscenity charges after performing at a Hollywood nightclub. They later were acquitted.

© Chris Brown/Sipa

Democrat Lawton Chiles, a former U.S. senator, won Florida's November gubernatorial election, supporting abortion rights and the limiting of campaign contributions.

Gainesville, the home of the University of Florida, was rocked by the murders of five college students in September. The case remained unsolved at the end of the year. By July more than 30 investigations of corruption by local, state, and federal officials in southern Florida were under way.

December riots in Miami's mostly Hispanic Wynwood section brought the year in crime to a close. The upheaval at the hands of Puerto Rican teenagers followed the acquittal of six policemen charged with the beating death of a Puerto Rican man, a suspected drug dealer.

People. In January, Panamanian dictator Manuel Noriega surrendered to U.S. authorities and was arraigned in federal district court in Miami. He remained incarcerated in Florida at year's end. Nelson Mandela, leader of South Africa's African National Congress, visited Miami in June as part of his U.S. tour. But he was snubbed by the community's Cuban-American political leaders because of his support of Fidel Castro.

In June, Leander Shaw became the first black to serve as chief justice of the Florida Supreme Court. Shaw later survived a campaign to oust him after he wrote a decision striking down Florida's law requiring parental permission for a minor to obtain an abortion.

PAUL S. GEORGE
University of Miami

FLORIDA • Information Highlights

Area: 58,664 sq mi (151 939 km²).
Population (1990 census prelim.): 12,775,000.
Chief Cities (July 1, 1988 est.): Tallahassee, the capital, 125,640; Jacksonville, 635,430; Miami, 371,100; Tampa, 281,790; St. Petersburg, 235,450.
Government (1990): *Chief Officers*—governor, Bob Martinez (R); lt. gov., Bobby Brantley (R). *Legislature*—Senate, 40 members; House of Representatives, 120 members.
State Finances (fiscal year 1989): *Revenue,* $22,160,000,000; *expenditure,* $19,977,000,000.
Personal Income (1989): $223,609,000,000; per capita, $17,647.
Labor Force (June 1990): *Civilian labor force,* 6,362,200; *unemployed,* 419,900 (6.6% of total force).
Education: *Enrollment* (fall 1988)—public elementary schools, 1,232,007; public secondary, 488,923; colleges and universities, 515,590. *Public school expenditures* (1989–90), $7,763,614,000.

FOOD

Developments in the food industry in 1990 included the introduction of new low-fat products, an increased emphasis on food safety, and efforts to improve food-assistance programs. With publicity about the diet-health link, more U.S. consumers sought low-fat, low-cholesterol foods, fruits, and vegetables. Global food supplies increased at a rate slightly greater than the world population.

For the first time U.S. chicken-meat consumption exceeded that of pork and beef. The trend toward poultry reflected growing consumer preference for low-fat meat, as well as cost considerations and ease of preparation. Fish consumption also rose in 1990.

The U.S. Congress passed and President Bush signed legislation requiring comprehensive nutrition labels on most packaged food and restricting food manufacturers from making health or nutrition claims about their products.

New Products. The 1990 *Surgeon General's Report on Nutrition and Health* and the National Research Council's Committee on Diet

The worst cold spell in more than 50 years was devastating California's $8 billion fruit and vegetable industry as 1990 ended. Prices were expected to increase as a result.

AP/Wide World

and Health recommended that Americans reduce total fat and saturated-fat consumption. About half of the typical U.S. consumer's fat consumption comes from spreads, salad dressings, cooking oils, and related products. Another 31% is from meat, with 14.5% from dairy products. Dairy products vary in fat content, ranging from zero for skim milk to 10% to 15% for ice cream, and 30% or more for some cheeses.

The Nutrasweet Company of Deerfield, IL, in 1990 introduced a fat substitute called Simplesse. The product is used to replace milk fat in frozen desserts. It is made from egg whites and milk proteins, and through a complex blending and heating process takes on a taste and texture similar to milk fat. Simplesse has potential applications in yogurt, cheese, sour cream, dips, salad dressings, and mayonnaise. However, it is not suited for baking or frying since heat takes away its creamy consistency. When replacing milk fat in ice cream, Simplesse can reduce calories by 50% to 80%, while greatly reducing the cholesterol content.

Simplesse may be the first of a new generation of fat substitutes. Several other products, all intended to replace dietary fat, were in the research, testing, or regulatory approval stages in 1990. Products not yet on the market were based on dried egg whites, whey protein, fatty acids, sucrose, or oat fiber. The end products are either low in calories and cholesterol or have no calories. One product in the development stage achieves zero calories by being undigestible. Other prospective fat substitutes may replace shortening and cooking oils. These products could have substantial dietary impact.

Food-Safety Concerns. According to the U.S. Food and Drug Administration's (FDA's) annual report on residues in food, the U.S. food supply is the safest in the world. Ninety-nine percent of domestic food supplies and 96% of the imported foods tested had no pesticide residues above allowable limits. Even so, pesticide use is a concern of both private citizens and public officials. In California legislation created a pesticide-research center to develop alternatives to use of chemicals in agriculture.

Growing consumer demand expanded the limited market for products grown without pesticides. Products being sold with a "natural" or "organic" label included meat, cereals, fruits, and vegetables. "Nest eggs," which come from chickens fed in an outdoor environment with a chemical-free diet, joined this list in 1990 in at least ten Eastern and Midwestern states.

Food-Assistance Programs. Assistance to low-income persons under the U.S. Food Stamp program was increased about 10% in fiscal 1989–90 to offset rising food costs. A five-year pilot project was begun in a Baltimore, MD, suburb allowing participants to buy food with plastic cards resembling credit cards instead of food stamps. If successful, the program may lead to nationwide use, with increased efficiency, cost savings, and greater convenience for those being assisted. To encourage consumption of fruits and vegetables, U.S. Department of Agriculture rules were changed to let program participants use food stamps at several thousand farmer markets.

Other domestic food-assistance programs reauthorized during the year included the Special Supplemental Food Program for Women, Infants, and Children, Commodity Distribution, and School Breakfast programs. Nearly 40 million people or 16% of the U.S. population are served by these and related programs.

The United States also provides food aid to low-income developing countries through PL-480 Food For Peace Programs. PL-480 reduces the cost of products such as wheat, rice, and vegetable oil to consumers in Africa, parts of Asia, and Latin America. Lower grain prices allowed PL-480 recipients to purchase at a lower cost than in the previous two years.

World Supplies. A large increase in 1990 world wheat production due to good weather was expected to increase slightly world reserve stocks to offset the sharp drawdown of the previous three years. World grain stocks by mid-1990 had fallen slightly below minimum food-security levels.

Several studies cited better weather as the main cause of recently improved food supplies in sub-Saharan Africa. Despite temporarily increased supplies, Africa has major long-term food challenges due to desertification, inadequate credit to buy fertilizer, lack of crop research, and agricultural policy disincentives. It has the world's most serious food problems, although chronically inadequate food supplies also are a problem in parts of Latin America and Asia.

ROBERT WISNER, *Iowa State University*

FOREIGN AID

As the world's richest nation, the United States also has been the most generous donor of aid to poorer nations for most of the post-World War II period. U.S. leadership in this field diminished, however, as Japan and the countries of Western Europe prospered and in turn provided more assistance at a time when the mounting U.S. federal budget deficit prompted lawmakers to cut the foreign-aid budget. Since the years immediately following World War II, the portion of U.S. economic output dedicated to foreign aid has shrunk from 3% to less than 0.3%. By 1989, Japan was the world's leading donor of aid.

U.S. Foreign Aid. U.S foreign aid was a subject of prolonged congressional debate in 1990. Reflecting their desire to reduce spending, lawmakers appropriated $15.4 billion in the 1991 foreign-aid bill (HR 5114), $129 million less than the George Bush administration had requested and $165 million less than the amount appropriated in fiscal 1990. The bill appropriated less military aid and economic assistance to military-aid recipients, while it granted more than the administration had requested for development in sub-Saharan Africa, agriculture, health, and AIDS prevention. Congress also appropriated more money for population programs than was requested, but rejected a proposal to overturn policy set up by the Ronald Reagan administration that denies U.S. aid to international family-planning organizations that provide abortions. Budget concerns were evident in the increase in "tied-aid credits," funds that recipients are required to spend for U.S. products and services.

USSR and Eastern Europe. Several events specific to 1990 caused additional changes in the U.S. approach to foreign aid. The year began with calls for assistance from the Soviet Union and East European nations, trying to integrate their economies into the world trading community. *Perestroika*, Soviet President Mikhail Gorbachev's campaign of "economic restructuring" at home, spread to other East European countries that during 1989–90 had replaced Communist regimes with democratic governments. The economic upheaval caused by the transformation from a state-controlled economic system to one based more firmly on free-market principles, however, left these countries in desperate need of aid.

Several West European nations, especially Germany, France, and Italy, extended generous offers of assistance to their neighbors to the East. While the Bush administration welcomed the thaw in U.S.-Soviet relations that the democratic transition brought, it balked at providing more than technical assistance to the Soviet Union until it adopts more sweeping and irreversible moves toward a market economy. The administration was more willing, however, to provide direct assistance to foster the democratic transformation in Eastern Europe. The 1991 foreign-aid bill set aside $369.7 million in direct aid for these countries. It also contributed $70 million to the European Bank for Reconstruction and Development, set up in May by the United States and 39 other nations.

U.S. participation in the European Development Bank marked a shift in official attitude toward multilateral institutions, which include the International Monetary Fund, the World Bank, and several regional development banks. Criticized by the Reagan administration, these institutions found favor once again as a less expensive means of extending financial assistance to needy countries through their provisions mainly in the form of loans rather than outright grants and generally conditioned on recipient countries' willingness to undertake painful economic reforms.

Japanese food supplies are prepared for emergency shipment to the Soviet Union, the victim of a severe food shortage.

AP/Wide World

Third World. As the leading aid donors turned their attention toward Eastern Europe, the poorest nations feared their own needs, fueled by deteriorating living conditions in much of the Third World, would be ignored. At the second United Nations Conference on the Least Developed Countries in September, the 42 poorest nations said they would need $36 billion in aid by the year 2000 to make a perceptible improvement in their standard of living. By contrast the industrial world, which includes the United States, Western Europe, Japan, Canada, Australia, and New Zealand, gave these countries $12 billion in 1989. Their request for a pledge from the industrial world to double the current level of aid went unsatisfied when the United States refused to promise to commit a fixed percentage of gross national product for that purpose. The Netherlands, Norway, Denmark, and Sweden already exceeded the requested aid level. Instead the United States and Japan, the two biggest donors in absolute terms, promised to increase aid by an unspecified amount.

While the end of the Cold War increased the need for aid by the Soviet Union and its allies, it reduced the willingness of the United States to continue funneling aid to anticommunist governments and rebel forces in the Third World. The fiscal 1991 intelligence authorization bill (S 2834) limited covert aid programs provided to non-Communist forces in Afghanistan, Angola, and Cambodia, where longstanding civil conflicts were the object of diplomatic negotiations in 1990. The law also required the president to keep Congress better informed of intelligence activities.

Central America, which received more than $9 billion in U.S. economic and military aid during the Reagan administration, saw funding drop precipitously with the thaw in U.S.-Soviet relations. Aid to the region peaked in 1985, the year Gorbachev came to power, and has fallen almost steadily ever since. Aid recipients who received unquestioning support from the Reagan administration for geopolitical reasons came under closer scrutiny for their policies as well as for alleged human-rights violations. Despite strong Republican opposition, the 1991 foreign-aid bill required the withholding of military aid to El Salvador pending completion of an investigation into the 1989 murders of six Jesuit priests.

Major U.S. Aid Recipients. While lawmakers cut back on military aid to most parts of the world, Iraq's invasion of Kuwait on August 2 prompted new infusions of both military and economic assistance to the Middle East. Israel and Egypt long have been the two biggest recipients of U.S. aid, and 1990 was no exception, as Congress appropriated $3 billion to Israel and $2.15 billion to Egypt in military assistance. In return for its support of the U.S.-led deployment of forces to Saudi Arabia, the United States forgave Egypt's $6.7 billion military debt. The bill also made it possible for Israel to gain access to an additional $1 billion worth of U.S. military equipment.

Pakistan, another important ally in the region and the third-largest recipient of U.S. foreign aid, was denied assistance for 1991 because of mounting evidence that it was developing nuclear weapons. Allied with the United States in supporting anticommunist forces in Afghanistan, Pakistan received $582 million in military and economic aid in 1990. But the Bush administration, which had requested $438 million in economic and military aid for 1991, was unable to certify that the country was not pursuing a nuclear capability, a condition to aid for Pakistan required by a 1985 amendment to the Foreign Assistance Act aimed at curbing nuclear proliferation.

One innovative feature of the 1991 foreign aid bill, debt forgiveness (provided for Egypt and Poland), may set an important precedent at a time when budgetary constraints limit more traditional types of foreign aid.

MARY H. COOPER
"Editorial Research Reports"

French President François Mitterrand told the biennial French-African summit meeting in La Baule in June 1990 that French aid would flow "more enthusiastically" to those former colonies that took steps toward democracy.

FRANCE

The year following the bicentennial of the French Revolution proved to be a particularly challenging one for France.

The emergence of a unified German nation that was prepared to develop a political stature to match its economic might changed Europe's post-World War II order—and France's place in it. Despite President François Mitterrand's public support for unification, the event threw off the balance of the German-French partnership and created fears that France's international diplomatic role would be overshadowed progressively.

The year also shook French relations with traditional allies in Africa and the Middle East. Prodemocracy movements throughout Africa, and notably in a number of former French colonies, spelled trouble for a paternalistic approach to Africa that dated from the post-colonial era of President Charles de Gaulle. Deepening economic difficulties in the former colonies also convinced France that it was time to begin requiring democratic and economic reforms in exchange for continued aid.

In the Middle East, France saw its "special relationship" with Lebanon crumble in acrimony under the defeat of renegade Christian General Michel Aoun in mid-October. But Iraq's August invasion of Kuwait pierced the very heart of France's Middle East policy, which had been built around close political and commercial ties to Iraq.

In November, Paris served as host to a three-day meeting of the 35-nation Conference on Security and Cooperation in Europe (CSCE), where historic Conventional Forces in Europe (CFE) accords were signed. Soviet President Mikhail Gorbachev's concept of a "common European house" and President Mitterrand's idea for a European "confederation" also were discussed. In June the French president hosted leaders from 33 African countries—ten from French-speaking Africa—for three days of talks in the Atlantic resort city of La Baule. And in a speech before the United Nations in September, Mitterrand endorsed the idea for an international conference to address the full panoply of issues facing the Middle East.

Despite these high-profile initiatives, however, France in 1990 was uncharacteristically a country forced by world events to search for new foreign-policy bearings.

Party Politics. In March the ruling Socialist Party held a four-day party congress whose deep divisions suggested the beginning of the end of the Mitterrand dominance. After a particularly raucous debate, none of the proposed party platforms—each identified by the rising party leader whose name it carried—was capable of commanding a majority of the delegates' votes.

A furious President Mitterrand, who had expressed a characteristic ambiguity about his platform preference before the congress, informed party leaders privately that a compromise had to be reached for the party's good. National legislative elections would not take place until March 1993, but Mitterrand, whose mandate runs until 1995, wished to avoid at all costs a conservative legislative victory that would force him to name a prime minister from the right and thus relive the so-called "cohabitation" of 1986-88.

It was not until the week following the congress that an agreement was reached, retaining former Prime Minister Pierre Mauroy at the party's helm. But the hard-won compromise appeared to be temporary, and suggested that Socialist power struggles only had begun.

Other political parties experienced their share of dissension and upheaval over the year. To the Socialists' left, the French Communist Party was torn by challenges to its leader, Georges Marchais, who was attacked by dissident party leaders for maintaining a Stalinist approach to party governance. Despite some embarrassment over his close ties to Romania's deposed Ceauşescu regime, Marchais weathered the storms preceding the party's congress in December.

On the right, Gaullist leader and Paris Mayor Jacques Chirac confronted a lively challenge from within his Rally for the Republic (RPR), but ultimately held on to party reins at a party congress in February. In June the opposition's two principal parties, the RPR and former president Valery Giscard d'Estaing's Union for French Democracy, agreed to create a confederation called "Union for France." The union's chief target was the presidency, and to that end the two parties agreed to place one candidate on the 1995 presidential ballot following a primary vote.

Domestic Affairs. The country was shaken in early May by the desecration of a small Jewish cemetery in the southeast village of Carpentras. Repugnance toward the vandalism of 34 graves became horror with the revelation that the body of a recently buried man had been exhumed and mutilated. President Mitterrand, placing the vandalism in the context of recent racist and anti-Semitic acts, called on the French people to "gain control" of themselves. On May 14 thousands of people paraded through the streets of Paris to express their "refusal of racism and anti-Semitism." Among political parties, only the far-right National Front, criticized by many for encouraging racism in France, was absent from the march.

On July 14, Bastille Day and traditionally a day for commemorating France's military preparedness and independence, President Mitterrand announced a reduction in the country's

FRANCE • Information Highlights

Official Name: French Republic.
Location: Western Europe.
Area: 211,208 sq mi (547 030 km²).
Population (mid-1990 est.): 56,400,000.
Chief City (1982 est.): Paris, the capital, 8,706,963.
Government: *Head of state,* François Mitterrand, president (took office May 1981). *Chief minister,* Michel Rocard, prime minister (took office May 1988). *Legislature*—Parliament: Senate and National Assembly.
Monetary Unit: Franc (5.061 francs equal U.S. $1, Dec. 7, 1990).
Gross Domestic Product (1989 est. U.S.$): $819,600,-000,000.
Economic Indexes (1989): *Consumer Prices* (1980 = 100), all items, 178.0; food, 177.2. *Industrial Production* (1980 = 100), 113.
Foreign Trade (1989 U.S.$): *Imports,* $192,484,-000,000; *exports,* $178,846,000,000.

obligatory military service from 12 to ten months, beginning in 1992. He also said, at a Franco-German summit in September, that the 46,000 French troops stationed in Germany would be reduced by 20,000 within two years.

In August protests erupted from Avignon south to Nice against the proposed southeast lines for France's technological showpiece, the *Train à Grand Vitesse,* or TGV. Earlier protests against the TGV generally had come from cities that were not on the train's proposed lines, and which feared relegation to France's economic backwater. In France's celebrated Provence region, however, protesters who blocked train tracks at the height of tourist season said they feared the super-fast trains would ruin their quiet, rural life-style.

The worst urban riots in France in nearly a decade occurred in the Lyon suburb of Vaulx-en-Vélin in early October, after a passenger on a motorcycle whose driver was trying to evade police was killed in a crash. Youths, primarily French Arabs, stoned police and pillaged one of the city's commercial centers before burning it to the ground. President Mitterrand linked

© Boccon Gioud/Sipa

Some 80,000 persons, including the French president, marched in Paris on May 14 to protest racism and anti-Semitism. Earlier in the month Jewish graves at a cemetery in Carpentras and in two other French locales were found to have been desecrated.

the disorder to the barrenness and "grayness" of France's urban periphery, but other experts blamed the youths' malaise on high unemployment and discrimination.

The riots were partly responsible for a renewed debate in France on urban safety and growing violence. In tune with that debate, high-school students in Paris and several provincial cities demonstrated in the streets to protest lack of security and crumbling conditions in the nation's high schools. In response, Prime Minister Michel Rocard pledged to hire 1,000 additional personnel to patrol the schools.

In October, Mitterrand reshuffled the Rocard government's ministers. The retirement of one minister and the voluntary departure of Edith Cresson, minister of European affairs, appeared to reinforce Rocard's hold on the prime ministry. Known for her protectionist stance toward French and European industry —especially regarding Japanese pressure to enter the European car market—Cresson was unhappy with the lack of government support for her crusade. In November, Rocard survived a tough vote of confidence in the National Assembly over a new social-security tax.

In Paris, Mayor Jacques Chirac in January unveiled a five-year plan for refurbishing the capital's most famous street, the Avenue des Champs-Elysées. Lamenting that uncontrolled commercialization, a mushrooming of fast-food restaurants, and the departure of elegant hotels and restaurants had damaged the famous avenue, Chirac promised the multimillion-dollar plan would return the street's beleaguered walkways to pedestrians and allow the "Champs" to reclaim its title as "the most beautiful street in the world."

Economy. A bright picture through the summer months was dimmed by the repercussions of the Persian Gulf crisis. Finance Minister Pierre Beregovoy in August declared his determination to "preserve our economic growth and avoid a return of inflation," but by October the economy was feeling the effects of higher oil prices and growing international fears of a worldwide downturn.

Still, most indicators remained positive. The country's growth rate hovered at an annual 2.5% by the end of summer, and inflation at a 4% annual rate gave France one of the best performances for an industrialized country, after Japan and Germany. More than 760,000 jobs were created in three years, although this was not enough to put a large dent in an unemployment rate that floated around 10%.

Not so bright, however, was France's trade performance, whose monthly deficits took a big jump in September, to $2 billion for the one month. The government laid the blame for the increase at the feet of Saddam Hussein, after the energy deficit rocketed to $1.96 billion, a nearly one-third rise over previous months. But economists noted a worsening of France's manufactured-goods deficit and a shrinking of the agriculture surplus—regarded as a traditional strength in French trade performance— and suggested that the country's economy could slow further.

Throughout the summer the French witnessed heated and often violent protests by farmers unhappy over what they considered insufficient government protection against drought and growing meat imports from cheaper producers—notably in Eastern Europe. The climate of discontent discouraged the government from agreeing to any European Community position to present to the General Agreement on Tariffs and Trade (GATT) negotiations on reducing farm subsidies.

Also during the year, the French economy witnessed several important mergers and joint ventures, as businesses continued to prepare for the European Community's single market, scheduled to take full effect at the end of 1992. Air France took control of UTA airlines, making it the seventh-largest airline in the world and the second-largest in Europe. In February the nationalized auto manufacturer Renault announced an industrial and financial accord with Volvo, the Swedish carmaker. The government said the agreement did not alter Mitterrand's 1988 campaign pledge against either further nationalizations or denationalizations during his tenure.

Foreign Affairs. The issue of permanently fixing the border between Poland and Germany (the former German Democratic Republic) became a thorn in the side of French-German relations early in 1990. France could not accept German Chancellor Helmut Kohl's unwillingness, for electoral reasons, to commit to fixing the border on the "Oder-Neisse" line, which has defined the Polish-East German border since World War II. Germany was irritated by France's call, during a Polish state visit to Paris, for an "international act" establishing the border before reunification. Mitterrand and Kohl attempted to lay misunderstandings between the two countries to rest by jointly declaring April 28 for accelerated "political union" of the European Community.

On April 10 a French woman, Jacqueline Valente, her Belgian companion, and their infant daughter were released in Beirut by the terrorist group Abu Nidal. The couple had been held hostage since 1986. President Mitterrand personally thanked Libyan leader Muammar el-Qaddafi for his role in their release, and Foreign Minister Roland Dumas referred to Qaddafi's "elevated and humanitarian gesture." Their words caused a flurry of criticism in the French and European press, especially following speculation that Valente originally was taken hostage by Libyan terrorists.

France and the Gulf Crisis. Partly because of its close relationship with Iraq over the previous 15 years and partly because of its repu-

In late October, 282 French hostages caught in Iraq and Kuwait by the Persian Gulf crisis were freed and allowed to return home. Prior to their departure from Baghdad they were addressed by the French ambassador to Iraq, above.

tation for having put pragmatic considerations above Western solidarity during earlier oil shocks, France found itself facing recurring suspicions among its Western allies—and even to some extent at home—as it responded to the major international crisis of 1990.

From the outset of Iraq's invasion of Kuwait in August, France, one of the five permanent members of the United Nations Security Council, stood solidly behind UN sanctions to enforce international law and force Iraq's unconditional retreat. But France's engagement remained largely diplomatic—until Iraqi soldiers stormed the French ambassador's residence in Kuwait on September 14 and took three hostages.

In August, Mitterrand said at a press conference that the Iraqi position had placed the world in "the logic of war," but he also sent out a dozen political personalities, including members of the opposition, to explain the French position to the country's allies—notably Arab nations. But Iraq's violation of diplomatic immunity set Mitterrand in action: In addition to an aircraft carrier already deployed to the Gulf, he sent more than 4,000 ground troops, with helicopters, tanks, and fighter planes to Saudi Arabia. The decision gave France the second-largest Western presence in the Gulf and constituted the country's largest military deployment since the Algerian war. By November the number of French ground troops had increased to 5,500, bringing the French presence in the Gulf to more than 11,000.

Also in September, France called on the UN Security Council to extend the embargo against Iraq to air traffic. At home, more than 40 Iraqis, including 11 diplomats, were ordered to leave the country.

Still, questions about France's position in the crisis resurfaced following Mitterrand's September 24 speech to the UN General As-

sembly, in which he stated that his "logic is one of peace." The president confused world leaders and diplomats by stating, "let Iraq affirm its intention to evacuate its troops, let it free the hostages, and everything becomes possible." Iraq quickly hailed what it considered to be the "nonaggressive" tone of the speech, and seized on Mitterrand's words as a departure point for what soon became a very apparent campaign to drive wedges in the international front arrayed against it. In part as an attempt to rectify any misconceptions about France's firmness, Mitterrand took a two-day trip to Saudi Arabia and the United Arab Emirates.

France faced the double emotions of joy and embarrassment when Iraq announced on October 23 that it would free all French hostages held there and in Kuwait. Foreign Minister Roland Dumas insisted that "no negotiation preceded the decision taken unilaterally by President Saddam Hussein," and Mitterrand reiterated those words several days later. In commenting on the planned hostage release, Iraqi Foreign Minister Tariq Aziz said, "France is undertaking declared and undeclared efforts in the search for a peaceful settlement," but France assured its allies that it remained intransigent on the issue of Kuwait's independence and freedom for all hostages.

On October 29, 262 French hostages arrived home on board an Iraqi Airways jet. The government, hoping to keep the return personal and low-key, sent no high-ranking official to the airport to greet the former hostages, and kept press coverage to the periphery. The former hostages who did speak with the press expressed solidarity with the remaining 4,000 hostages, and many spoke of harrowing conditions during nearly three months of captivity.

HOWARD LaFRANCHI, *Paris Bureau*
"The Christian Science Monitor"

244

Expo '90, Osaka

The colorful and diverse Valley of Flowers exhibit, with the Statue of Life in the background, was a focal point of Expo '90, an international garden and greenery exposition held in Osaka, Japan, April through September 1990.

GARDENING AND HORTICULTURE

The International Garden and Greenery Exposition (Expo '90), a display of millions of trees, plants, and shrubs from throughout the world, was held on a 346-acre (140-ha) site near Osaka, Japan, April 1 to Sept. 30, 1990. The fair included exhibits from more than 80 nations and 55 international organizations and attracted some 23 million visitors. Its purpose was to "explore the relationship between gardens and greenery and human life . . . with the goal of creating an environment where people and nature live in harmony."

More than 70 million households or 75% of the 92 million households in the United States participated in at least one indoor or outdoor gardening activity in 1989, according to the *National Gardening Survey* published in 1990 by the National Gardening Association. The number of households involved in herb-gardening activities increased from 5 million in 1988 to 6 million in 1989.

Award Winners. The 1989 Florens Debevoise Medal was awarded to James E. Cross of Catchogue, NY, plant breeder and nurseryman, for his cultivation of exotic dwarf daphne and compact broad-leaved evergreens, including very tiny English and Japanese hollies. The medal is presented by the Garden Club of America (GCA) to nonmembers for horticultural achievement with preference to plant material suitable for rock gardens.

The All-America Selections (AAS) announced seven flower and three vegetable winners for the 1991 AAS Awards. The AAS Awards are selected from the 33 flower and 20 vegetable trial sites across North America. Gaillardia pulchella "Red Plume," Geranium F1 "Freckles," Vincas "Pretty in Rose," "Pretty in Pink," and "Parasol," and pansies "Maxim Marina" F1 and "Padparadja" were given the AAS Flower Awards. The AAS Vegetable Awards were presented to a pole bean "Kentucky Blue," a vegetable spaghetti squash "Trivoli" F1, and a watermelon "Golden Crown" F1.

The All-America Rose Selections Awards (AARS) for 1991 included four new introductions: two hybrid tea roses, "Sheer Elegance" and "Perfect Moment," one grandiflora, "Shining Hour," and one everblooming landscape rose, "Carefree Wonder." "Sheer Elegance," hybridized by amateur Jerry Twomey of Leucadia, CA, was recognized for being highly disease-resistant with show quality, soft pink with salmon-colored edge blossoms on long, stiff florist-quality stems. "Perfect Moment," hybridized by Reimer Kordes of Sparrieshoop, West Germany, features a unique yellow-based bloom with red tips and dark green, leather-like foliage.

The AARS award-winning "Shining Hour," rated extremely floriferous with high-centered yellow blossoms of approximately 35 petals, was hybridized by William A. Warner, retired, of Jackson and Perkins Co., Medford, OR. Warner is responsible for more AARS winners than any other hybridizer. The AARS everblooming landscape rose category winner, "Carefree Wonder," hybridized by Selection Meilland, Antibes, France, requires low maintenance and is very hardy in winter and summer.

Publications. *The National Arboretum Book of Outstanding Garden Plants* by Jacqueline Heriteau with Dr. Marc Cathey, director of the U.S. National Arboretum, and other staff members and consultants was published by Simon and Schuster in 1990. It is an authoritative guide to more than 1,700 garden plants in North America.

A revised *USDA Plant Hardiness Map of the United States* was released by the U.S. Department of Agriculture in 1990.

RALPH L. SNODSMITH
Ornamental Horticulturist

GENETICS

The year 1990 saw important advances in the understanding of the role of genes in human disease, plant development, and evolution.

Genetics of Lyme Disease-Induced Arthritis. Lyme disease is caused by the bacterium *Borrelia burgdorferi* which is transmitted to humans when they are bitten by an infected tick. The disease may produce flu-like symptoms which disappear in most patients after several weeks. However, about 10% of the patients develop a chronic arthritis of the knee two to three years after contracting the disease. This condition may be relatively mild and last about a year or it may be long-term and crippling. The chronic arthritis rarely develops if antibiotics are taken in the first six weeks after infection.

It has been known for some time that certain diseases, for reasons not understood, are associated with particular genetically determined antigenic properties of the person's body cells. An increasing number of cases of disease-antigen association have been found to involve the HLA (human leukocyte antigens) locus on chromosome #6. Drs. A. C. Steere and R. Winchester led a research team that found that 89% of Lyme disease arthritic patients had either the antigen called HLA DR4 or HLA DR2, whereas only 27% of other arthritic patients had these antigens. Those tick-bitten persons who have either of the above genetic traits must be given antibiotics.

Genetic Uniformity and Species Decline. Genetic studies of cheetahs and other endangered animal species have revealed that, in many cases, the species are homozygous at a much greater number of their loci than closely related but nonendangered species. In general, a species with more variability in its genome is considered better able to survive sharply changing environmental challenges than a comparable species that is genetically more uniform.

Drs. D. H. DeHayes and G. J. Hawley of the University of Vermont have reported that genetic uniformity also characterizes a declining species of plants. They examined 42 gene loci of the red spruce of eastern North America and found that an average of only 8% of the genes were heterozygous. This is approximately one third to one half the heterozygosity of other temperate-zone tree species. Increased homozygosity of both plant and animal species results from inbreeding which increases as individual populations become smaller and more isolated.

Touch-Induced Genes in Plants. Tactile stimulation of growing plants, whether by rain, wind, or human touch, results in shorter, stockier plants than those protected from such environmental stimuli. This phenomenon, which has been found in 80% of tested plant species and called *thigmomorphogenesis*, is defined as the developmental growth alterations that result as a response to noninjurious mechanical stimulation.

Drs. J. Braam and R. W. Davis of Stanford University, working with *Arabidopsis* (a plant in the mustard family), discovered that touching of the plant results in the activation of at least four genes. These so-called "touch genes" encode calmodulin and calmodulin-related proteins that bind to calcium, forming compounds that regulate a variety of cellular processes, leading to the observed altered growth patterns.

Paternal Inheritance of Extranuclear DNA in Plants. It has been a long-held tenet that extranuclear genomes, whether of mitochondrial or chloroplast origin, would follow a strict maternal line of inheritance. This expectation followed from the fact that egg cells contribute most of the cytoplasm of the zygote whereas sperm cells were considered little more than flagellated nuclei.

However, Dr. D. B. Wagner and colleagues have found that paternal inheritance of chloroplasts was the rule rather than the exception in the conifer jack pine (*Pinus banksiana Lamb*). Further evidence of paternal inheritance of extranuclear genomes was found by Dr. D. B. Neale and colleagues who studied mitochondrial inheritance in another conifer, the redwood tree (*Sequoia sempervirens*).

Genetics and Paleontology. One of the problems in the study of fossils is to establish the degree of evolutionary relationship between the extinct organisms and modern-day species. Quite clearly, genetic comparisons between fossil and living forms could clarify the evolutionary lineages of many species. Unfortunately, most fossils do not contain DNA because they have been mineralized completely. However, under a particular set of circumstances, an organism or part of an organism can be preserved virtually intact with a minimum amount of decomposition or mineralization. Such a situation apparently occurred about 20 million years ago in a dying lake at what now is called the Miocene Clarkia shale deposit near Moscow, ID.

Among the many preserved specimens was a leaf of a prehistoric magnolia tree. Of great importance was the presence, intact, of some of its DNA. Dr. E. M. Golenberg and colleagues succeeded in isolating and analyzing a piece of DNA which contained a gene called *rbcL*, which is involved in photosynthesis. They then compared the nucleotide sequence of that gene with that of a modern magnolia plant and found that only 17 of 820 base pairs were different. Whether this small amount of evolutionary change also characterizes other genes requires further study. This investigation marked the first genetic comparison between organisms that lived 20 million years ago and those alive today.

Louis Levine, *City College of New York*

Alaska's Mount Redoubt volcano, southwest of Anchorage, became active in late 1989 after a 25-year period of dormancy and continued to erupt sporadically in early 1990.

AP/Wide World

GEOLOGY

Significant 1990 geological events included a deadly earthquake in northern Iran, fossil findings about the dinosaurs and other ancient creatures, new information about the planet's lithospheric plates, and an important report on the threat of global climate change.

Earthquakes. The world's most deadly earthquake in more than 13 years rocked Iran on June 21, killing as many as 50,000 people in the northwestern section of the country. Measuring 7.7 on the Richter scale, the quake originated on a fault underneath the Caspian Sea near Iran's border with Azerbaijan. This geologically unstable region of the world has spawned many severe earthquakes in the past, including a devastating magnitude 6.9 shock in Armenia in 1988 and a magnitude 7.7 temblor in eastern Iran in 1978. Quakes occur in this area because it sits in a geologic vise, where two of Earth's tectonic plates are colliding.

A month after the Iranian disaster, on July 16, a magnitude 7.8 shock struck Luzon Island in the Philippines, killing more than 1,600 people and causing severe damage. In Peru, 135 people died after a magnitude 6.4 tremor rocked the northern section of the country on May 30. It occurred on the eastern flank of the Andes mountain range. On the same day a magnitude 6.7 quake rattled northern Romania and nearby countries, killing nine.

In the United States, a magnitude 5.5 tremor struck southern California near the town of Upland on February 28. The temblor injured 38 people and wreaked more than $10 million in damage. A moderate earthquake struck northern California in October.

Seismologists significantly increased their estimates of the chance San Francisco will experience a major earthquake in the near future. After studying new scientific information on the three major faults in the Bay area, a federal panel reported that this region stands a 67% chance of suffering a major quake within 30 years. Such a tremor centered in the metropolitan region likely would cause more damage than the October 1989 quake, which originated in the unpopulated Santa Cruz mountains about 60 mi (96 km) south of San Francisco. The eastern and central states also face quake risks, according to seismologists who reported there is a 40% to 60% chance that a damaging shock will hit the area east of the Rocky Mountains within the next 30 years.

Volcanoes. Mount Redoubt in Alaska erupted sporadically through late 1989 and early 1990. While the activity caused no major damage, ash clouds fouled air traffic to Anchorage and sparked one near disaster when a plane flew through the ash and temporarily lost engine power. The eruption also threatened an oil installation on the Cook Inlet.

The volcano Kelut on the Indonesian island of Java erupted on February 10, reportedly killing more than 30 people and causing the evacuation of 60,000 from the nearby area. On Hawaii lava from the volcano Kilauea leveled more than 100 homes between April and August, prompting President Bush to declare the area a federal disaster zone. The outpouring is part of a continuing eruption since 1983.

Fossils and Extinctions. The ongoing debate about the death of the dinosaurs took on a Caribbean flavor. For the last decade, scientists have argued whether a huge meteorite, volcanic eruptions, or slow climate change killed off the dinosaurs and many other forms of life 65 million years ago. In recent years, evidence of an impact has grown and geologists have searched eagerly for a crater left by the crash. Several researchers in 1990 reported finding signs that the meteorite landed in the Caribbean Sea. Some suggested the object splashed down just north of Colombia, while others proposed it hit off the coast of Cuba.

When scientists first raised the meteorite hypothesis in 1980, they suggested the impact would have kicked up a dust cloud that blocked out sunlight, thereby killing off plants and animals. New studies have raised other possible deadly side effects of a huge meteorite impact. From research on fossil plants, one paleobotanist concluded that the climate grew suddenly moist and warm after the impact, a change that would have killed many species. Other scientists theorize that the impact would have caused massive wildfires and acidic rain.

The dinosaur *Tyrannosaurus Rex* has received a new image, according to paleontologists who suggest this animal was better armed than previously thought. Traditional paintings have featured this knife-toothed carnivore with puny forelimbs. But studies of the most complete known arm bones indicate *T. rex* had strong forelimbs bearing nasty claws.

Fossils from Greenland have revealed that the oldest known amphibians had extra toes. Living about 360 million years ago, these creatures belonged to the first wave of vertebrates making the transition from life in the water to life on land. Paleontologists long had assumed these early amphibians had five digits on their hind limbs and forelimbs, but the Greenland fossils show species with seven-toed hind feet and eight-toed front feet, indicating a flexible early limb-development pattern.

From Egyptian rocks, paleontologists have unearthed fossils of a 40-million-year-old whale with feet, revealing a critical step in the evolutionary history of these marine mammals. Scientists believe whales evolved from four-legged land mammals, but they never before have found evidence of functional hind limbs on ancient whale remains.

Fossils from Antarctica show that a different whale species living 40 million years ago had notched teeth, which may represent the evolutionary forerunner of baleen. These teeth were apparently too fragile for gripping or tearing prey. Instead, the whale may have used the notches in the teeth as a filter for catching fish and shrimp-sized invertebrates.

Plate Tectonics and Inner Earth. New findings are revealing important details about Earth's lithospheric plates. The lithosphere is the hard outer shell of the planet that covers a hotter, softer region called the mantle. Using sound waves generated by air guns, geophysicists have probed down to the base of the lithosphere for the first time. In an ocean experiment south of Norway, researchers shot off sound waves and recorded waves that reflected off geologic structures at the bottom of the lithosphere, about 65 mi (105 km) below the ocean floor. Using this technique, scientists can study what happens at the base of plates involved in tectonic collisions.

The most violent plate collision on the modern Earth is one between India and Asia. Over the last 40 million years, India has moved northward and pushed its way deeply into Asian territory. Geologists studying Chinese rocks have found evidence that the colossal collision has squeezed Tibet and forced this high plateau to slide out of the way to the East.

Among the ancient rocks of northwestern Canada, geologists have gathered evidence suggesting Earth's plates were much different 1.9 billion years ago. The researchers suspect the lithosphere of the ancestral Canadian plate extended to a depth of about 31 mi (50 km), only half the present thickness of continental plates around the globe. The Canadian rocks also reveal clues about what lay underneath the primeval plates. While modern continents overlay thick "roots" of cold mantle material, the Canadian plate apparently lacked a root 1.9 billion years ago. The findings should heat up a long-standing debate concerning how continental roots formed.

Researchers studying rocks from a South African diamond mine have discovered some of the deepest known material to come out of the planet's interior. The rocks originated in the Earth's upper mantle, some 186–250 mi (300-400 km) below ground, and were carried to the surface long ago through ancient volcanic conduits. The fragments support a controversial theory that Earth's upper mantle and lower mantle do not mix.

Climate Change. An international panel of top climate experts provided government leaders with a unified message concerning the threat of global climate change. The scientists reported they were certain that Earth's surface will warm in response to increasing atmospheric concentrations of greenhouse gases such as carbon dioxide, methane, chlorofluorocarbons, and nitrogen oxide. The panel members agreed that because of numerous uncertainties, it is difficult to predict how fast the climate will warm and how those changes will affect individual regions around the globe. But the best available information suggests the average global temperature will rise about 1°C by 2025 and 3°C before 2100. They also predict the global sea level will swell 8 inches (20 cm) by 2030.

RICHARD MONASTERSKY, *"Science News"*

GEORGIA

The selection of Atlanta to host the 1996 Olympic Games and the November elections led the news in Georgia in 1990.

GEORGIA • Information Highlights

Area: 58,910 sq mi (152 576 km²).
Population (1990 census prelim.): 6,387,000.
Chief Cities (July 1, 1988 est.): Atlanta, the capital, 420,220; Columbus, 177,680; Savannah, 145,980.
Government (1990): *Chief Officers*—governor, Joe Frank Harris (D); lt. gov., Zell Miller (D). *General Assembly*—Senate, 56 members; House of Representatives, 180 members.
State Finances (fiscal year 1989): *Revenue,* $11,898,000,000; *expenditure,* $10,835,000,000.
Personal Income (1989): $103,313,000,000; per capita, $16,053.
Labor Force (June 1990): *Civilian labor force,* 3,231,700; *unemployed,* 190,500 (5.9% of total force).
Education: *Enrollment* (fall 1988)—public elementary schools, 807,864; public secondary, 300,130; colleges and universities, 230,762. *Public school expenditures* (1989–90), $3,502,136,000.

U.S. Rep. Newt Gingrich, the House minority whip and Georgia's only Republican congressman, took a stand against the initial White House-congressional leaders budget plan. He barely won reelection in November.

© Martin Simon/Saba

1996 Olympics. Newspaper headlines proclaimed, "It's Atlanta!" as strangers turned to each other muttering just the word, "Incredible." The dream came true on Sept. 18, 1990, as Atlanta was chosen to host the 1996 Olympic Games. Winning out over the sentimental favorite, Athens, Greece, and other strong contenders such as Toronto, Canada, and Melbourne, Australia, had required a relentless three-year effort by the Atlanta Organizing Committee, especially by members Billy Payne and Andrew Young. Following a ticker-tape parade down Peachtree Street, planning got under way for construction of the necessary facilities, which would include a $160 million Olympic village where the athletes will live and a $145 million domed stadium which will be occupied by the Atlanta Braves and the Falcons after the games. The stadium is to be used prior to the Olympics in 1994 when Atlanta hosts the Super Bowl. (*See* page 87.)

Elections. In the realm of politics, as in sports, Georgians watched several candidates emerge as uncontested winners. Former Atlanta Mayor Maynard Jackson was elected without opposition to the post after his only challenger, Michael Lomax, chairman of the Fulton County Commission, dropped out of the race months before the election. Jackson had been elected in 1974 as Atlanta's first black mayor, and in 1990, after Andrew Young's two terms as mayor, Jackson was chosen again.

The gubernatorial campaign resulted in a clear victory for Zell Miller, first in the Democratic primary, then in the runoff against Andrew Young, and finally in the defeat of Republican Johnny Issakson in the general election. Analysis of the win focused upon the fact that Miller's name was attached to a popular proposal for a statewide lottery to raise funds for public programs and on voters' dissatisfaction with the Republican administration of George Bush. In addition to garnering traditional Republican votes in suburban Atlanta, Miller received more than half of the female votes and 92% of the black vote.

The struggling Georgia Republican Party suffered a setback in 1990. Along with witnessing the defeat of its gubernatorial candidate, who received campaign visits from President Bush and Vice-President Dan Quayle, the Republican Party also watched as Democrats reelected nine congressmen, won the races for lieutenant governor and insurance commissioner, and gained three seats in the state House. The state's one Republican U.S. congressman, Newt Gingrich, defeated his Democratic challenger, David Worley, by less than 1,000 votes.

Legislation. Ethics reform and an overhaul of the child-welfare system were major accomplishments of the General Assembly. The ethics bill requires extensive disclosure of candidates' personal finances and limits campaign contributions for the first time in the state's history. In other legislation, antidrug bills were passed in order to punish those convicted of drug use with the loss of their jobs, the opportunity for an education at state-supported schools, and their retirement benefits.

The Assembly approved a $7.79 billion budget which allocated funds mainly for prisons, education, the university system, and programs for children.

Court Ruling. In early December the Georgia Supreme Court ruled that the state has the right to prohibit the wearing of hoods and masks by the Ku Klux Klan. The 6–1 decision overturned a lower-court ruling that struck down Georgia's 39-year-old antimask law.

Economic Development. Metropolitan Atlanta was expected to require more new office space than any other U.S. city in the 1990s. Construction was started in 1990 on 85% of the planned additional office space.

KAY BECK, *Georgia State University*

Some 1 million people gathered at midnight, Oct. 3, 1990, at the Reichstag in Berlin as East Germany and West Germany were reunited. The raising of a black, red, and gold flag and the ringing of a liberty bell marked the historic event.

GERMANY

The year 1990 was the most momentous in German history since the end of World War II. On October 3, less than a year after the fall of the Berlin Wall, the German Democratic Republic (GDR) or East Germany ceased to exist as an independent state and joined the Federal Republic of Germany (FRG) or West Germany. Europe's almost 80 million Germans were united once again in a single state. Unlike the unified Germany of the Bismarckian Reich (1871–1918) or Hitler's Third Reich (1933–1945), German unity in 1990 was achieved without violence and with the full support of its neighbors in East and West, indeed of the entire international community.

Unification. The celebrations on October 3, the official Unity Day that is now the new national holiday, were preceded by a complicated series of treaties and agreements between the two German states and the World War II allies —the United States, the Soviet Union, Great Britain, and France—that had defeated Nazi Germany in 1945; the four allied powers still held residual occupation rights in Germany and controlled Berlin, the former capital of the Reich. In addition, separate treaties were concluded between unified Germany and the Soviet Union and Poland.

In a series of elections held during 1990, the great majority of East Germans left little doubt that they wanted unification with the West as quickly as possible. In March the GDR held its first-ever free, democratic parliamentary elec-
tion. The big winner was the Alliance for Germany, a group of three parties largely organized by the West German Christian Democratic Union (CDU), which received almost 50% of the vote. The East German Social Democrats, also committed to unity, secured more than 20%, while various liberal and regional parties were supported by about 10% of East German voters. Thus more than 80% of East Germans voted for parties that promised unity with the West. The first (and last) freely elected East German government was led by Lothar De Maizière, a lawyer who had defended dissidents under the Communist regime and was the leader of the CDU in East Germany.

In May the two German states concluded a treaty that unified their monetary, economic, and social-security systems. On July 1 the West German deutsche mark (DM) became the sole legal currency for all of Germany. This unprecedented currency union allowed every East German to exchange GDR currency, which had little value outside the Communist bloc, for West German marks at generous rates ranging from complete parity (one to one) for most private savings to one to three for larger accounts held by business enterprises.

The second and final inter-German agreement was completed in August. This massive, 1,000-page document regulated the merger of the two states' educational, military, legal, transportation, cultural, and communications systems. Prior to the dissolution of the GDR, the country was reorganized into the five states representing its traditional regions—Brandenburg, Mecklenburg-Vorpommern, Saxony,

Saxony-Anhalt, and Thuringia—which had been abolished by the Communists in 1952. On October 3 these states then joined the 11 West German states in the Federal Republic of Germany. The pact also set December 2 as the date for the first free all-German election since 1932.

The December Election. Unification was the central theme of the election campaign. The ruling coalition of the CDU, the Bavarian Christian Social Union (CSU), and the Free Democrats (FDP), led by Chancellor Helmut Kohl of the CDU, emphasized that it had fulfilled the aim set forth in West Germany's 1949 Constitution: the reunification of the country in peace and freedom, a goal that had eluded 15 previous governments during the previous 40 years. The Christian Democrats stressed that Kohl's leadership had secured widespread international support for unity and accelerated the pace at which the entire process was completed. The Free Democrats claimed that the lion's share of the credit belonged to their leader, Foreign Minister Hans-Dietrich Genscher.

The major opposition party, the Social Democrats (SPD), countered by charging that the government had rushed into unity without considering its economic and social costs, and that it largely had ignored the legitimate right of East Germans to be more involved in the process. The SPD leader, Oskar LaFontaine, the young minister-president of the Saar, was slow to grasp the significance of unification for the 1990 campaign. He belongs to a generation that had known only a divided Germany, and he assumed that unification was not an issue with broad electoral appeal. Early in the campaign, LaFontaine was stabbed in the neck by a mentally deranged woman. The attack had no political significance, but the candidate was unable to resume the campaign for almost two months.

The other opposition party, the Greens, were even more skeptical about unification than the Social Democrats. The party's relatively young electorate was concerned less about "Germany" than were voters of the older parties. The Greens wanted the indigenous East German revolutionary groups to have more time to find a "third way" between the Stalinism of the old GDR regime and what they considered the anti-environmentalist capitalism of the West.

Opinion polls throughout the campaign showed the governing parties with a commanding lead. After a year of unprecedented political developments, many Germans were tired of politics and the campaign was generally routine, if not dull. As expected, Chancellor Kohl's government was returned with an increased majority. In the new parliament, which had about 160 additional seats because of unification, the government enjoyed a solid majority of 134. Within the coalition the big winner

was the Free Democratic Party, which achieved the third-best result (11%) in its history. This vote was largely a personal tribute to Foreign Minister Genscher for his achievements in the unification process.

The parties on the left of the political spectrum were the big losers. The Social Democrats, with only 33.5% of the vote, dropped to their lowest level since 1957. In the new East German states the party received less than one fourth of the vote—a reaction to LaFontaine's lukewarm attitude toward unification. SPD losses were also especially heavy among middle-class voters, including skilled manual workers, the traditional core of the party's electorate. The big surprise of the election was the failure of the West German Greens to return to parliament. With only 3.9% of the vote, down from 8.3% in 1987, the party failed to clear the 5% minimum necessary for representation in the legislature. Low turnout among Green voters and losses to the Social Democrats were the major factors in the party's decline.

In the East the former Communist Party, now named the Party of Democratic Socialism (PDS), did secure enough votes under special provisions of the electoral law to enter the new parliament. East German parties needed only to secure at least 5% of the vote in the former territory of the GDR to enter parliament. With about 10% in the East, but only 2.4% nationwide, the PDS cleared this hurdle as did a coalition of East German Greens and former GDR dissidents ("Alliance 90"). In the future, however, all parties must receive a minimum of 5% nationwide.

The Economy. Fueled by strong demand from East Germany for consumer goods and high levels of capital investment, the West German economy in 1990 grew for the eighth straight year, a post-World War II record. In

With reunification, the East German flag and military uniform were retired throughout the Democratic Republic (below). The GDR had left the Warsaw Pact in September.

© Gilles Saussier/Gamma-Liaison

© Patrick Piel/Gamma-Liaison

On Dec. 2, 1990, Chancellor Helmut Kohl casts his ballot in the first all-German election in 58 years. The chancellor's Christian Democratic Union won an easy victory.

the first three quarters real growth reached 5.5%, the highest level since 1976. With East German figures included for the fourth quarter, the growth rate dropped slightly to 4.0% for all of 1990. Inflation remained relatively low at 3%, in spite of a surge in oil prices following the Iraqi invasion of Kuwait. In the West, unemployment also dropped to less than 7%, the lowest level since 1981.

In the East, however, economic conditions deteriorated rapidly following the July 1 currency union. With open borders and hard currency in their pockets, citizens of the old GDR preferred Western products to their own goods; demand for many East German products collapsed. In addition many East German industries, deprived of state subsidies, could not compete in a free, competitive market. Thus in 1990 the East German gross national product dropped by more than 14%, and unemployment, which had been practically nonexistent, soared to more than 6%, with another 20% of the work force on short-time.

The rebuilding of the economy was the major problem facing the new government. Many of the 8,000 enterprises in the former GDR must either be closed or extensively modernized. Only about 25–30% of these firms could compete in a free market. Through a Trusteeship Authority, which now was the nominal owner of all former state-run firms in the old GDR, the Kohl government hoped to privatize these competitive firms and use the proceeds to modernize those companies which could be saved. But the process was proceed-

ing slowly and the plan would require additional subsidies from Bonn. The cost estimates of bringing the new regions up to West German levels ranged from $600 billion to $1 trillion over the next decade. The Kohl government proposed to finance this operation through budget cuts in defense and other programs, private investment, and borrowing. It ruled out any increase in taxes, but by the end of the year the head of the country's powerful Bundesbank was calling for reduced deficits and some increase in revenue to avoid excessive inflation and a drop in the value of the mark.

In 1990 the costs of unification, including the currency union and subsidies to unemployed and retired East Germans, increased the government's deficits to $66 billion, as compared with only $13 billion in 1989. In 1991 the deficit would jump to a record-high $100 billion.

The Communist Legacy: The Environment. After unification it became apparent that large regions of the former East Germany were environmental disaster areas. The damage was severe particularly in the southeastern section of the country where the GDR's chemical and mining industries were located. In the area around Leipzig smog was constant during the fall and winter. During smog alarms the death rate for the elderly and sick increased by 30%. Almost half of the former GDR's population was living in regions in which sulfur-dioxide emissions exceeded the legal limits.

The primary source of the extensive water, air, and ground pollution was the brown coal, or lignite, that supplied almost 70% of East Germany's energy requirements. The coal was being used not only for heating but also in the chemical industry. Fuels, lubricants, fertilizers, pesticides, and even medicines were manufactured from lignite; even the plastic body of the Trabant, East Germany's two-cylinder car, originated from brown coal.

With unification many of the most obsolete and dirtiest chemical plants simply were shut down. These closures alone reduced water pollution in the Leipzig-Bitterfeld area by 20% and air pollution by 15%. The strip mining of lignite also was curtailed greatly.

In the north of the country five Soviet-built reactors, similar to those at Chernobyl, were shut down in December. The most polluted area outside of the coal and chemical region was the uranium-mining district around the city of Wismar. This mining operation, which employed almost 31,000 workers, was owned jointly by East Germany and the Soviet Union Since 1946 more than 220,000 tons of uranium for the nuclear-power industry and weapons had been sent to the Soviet Union. The mining operation had left huge water-filled craters with depths of more than 200 ft (61 m) laden with radioactive waste. In the mining shafts radioactive material was seeping into the groundwater. In residential areas near the mines, more than one half of all homes had dangerous levels of radioactivity.

There was also an urgent need for sewage-treatment facilities throughout old East Germany. In Dresden, a city of 600,000, residential and industrial sewage had been discharged untreated into the Elbe since 1987, when the city's 80-year-old sewage-treatment facility stopped operating because of a flood. Some cities such as Wittenberg never had sewage-treatment plants. Experts estimated that a cleanup of the former East Germany would take at least 20 years with a total cost of more than $200 billion.

The "Stasi" State. The collapse of the Communist system and unification also brought new revelations about the activities of the GDR's hated "Stasi," or state security ministry, a mammoth secret-police apparatus that employed almost 500,000 official and "unofficial" (informants) workers. The Stasi maintained files on more than 5 million East Germans and also conducted a wide-ranging surveillance and spy network in West Germany. Its sophisticated electronic eavesdropping equipment enabled it to tap some 25,000 West German telephones. During 1990 numerous West German government officials were arrested on charges of spying for the old GDR. As 1990 ended, however, no major West German political leader had been implicated in any Stasi activities.

On the other hand, several of the new democratic leaders in East Germany, including the CDU leader Lothar de Maizière, were accused of collaboration with the Stasi. In late December, de Maizière resigned his position in the Kohl government in the face of allegations that he regularly supplied the Stasi with information about dissidents he was defending. De Maizière denied the charges, but stepped down to avoid further embarrassment to the government. The former leader of East Germany's Social Democrats also resigned his post because of alleged Stasi connections.

In June it also was revealed that the Stasi, with the knowledge and approval of Communist leaders, harbored eight West German terrorists for more than ten years. The terrorists had been sought worldwide by West German authorities for murders and bombings dating from the late 1970s. The GDR also provided new identities and protection for several international terrorist organizations, including the Abu Nidal group.

In December former GDR leader Erich Honecker was indicted as an accessory to murder for his issuance of a "shoot-to-kill" order in the 1970s for East Germans trying to breach the Berlin Wall. Honecker, who at the time was in a Soviet military hospital near Berlin, rejected the charges. Soviet authorities declined to turn him over to German police.

© R. Bossu/Sygma

The guard hut at the Western-controlled Checkpoint Charlie crossing point between West Berlin and East Berlin was removed in June. It was to be displayed in a museum.

Foreign Policy. Germany's relations with the Soviet Union reached new levels of cooperation in 1990. At the beginning of the year, Soviet President Mikhail Gorbachev still opposed any unification of the two German states. Under the press of events in East Germany, however, the Soviet position steadily changed. By spring Moscow was advocating a unified German state that would be neutral and demilitarized. This position was rejected by Bonn and its Western allies. Then in July, Kohl and Gorbachev achieved a major breakthrough in a summit meeting at the Soviet leader's summer retreat in the Caucasus. In exchange for German economic aid, a sharp reduction in the number of German troops, and a comprehensive treaty regulating the two nations' future economic, technical, and political relations, Gorbachev agreed that a unified Germany could remain in the North Atlantic Treaty Organization (NATO) and pledged that all of the Soviet Union's 400,000 troops in East Germany would leave by 1994. The price tag for Germany was almost $10 billion in addition to additional billions in loans. The treaty, which made Germany the Soviet Union's closest European ally, was signed formally in November.

In late November, as economic conditions in the Soviet Union continued to worsen, Bonn responded with additional aid. An emergency

GERMANY • Information Highlights

Official Name: Federal Republic of Germany.
Location: North-central Europe.
Area: 137,931 sq mi (357 241 km²).
Population (1990 est.): 78,700,000.
Chief Cities (Dec. 31, 1987 est.): Berlin, the capital, (1990 est.), 3,400,000; Hamburg, 1,594,190; Munich, 1,201,479, Leipzig, 547,309; Dresden, 519,527.
Government: *Head of state,* Richard von Weizsäcker, president (took office July 1, 1984). *Head of government,* Helmut Kohl, chancellor (took office Oct. 1982). *Legislature*—Parliament: Bundesrat and Bundestag.
Monetary Unit: Deutsche mark (1.4975 D. marks equal U.S.$1, Dec. 31, 1990).

program of food supplies, the largest foreign-aid program in the history of modern Germany, was begun with both public and private funds. German generosity reflected both a lingering guilt for the crimes committed in the Soviet Union by Nazi armies in World War II and gratitude for Gorbachev's decisive role in the unification process. But sending food and other economic aid to the East was also an attempt to prevent a massive migration of Soviet citizens to the West. By year's end many Germans feared that their country could become a magnet for refugees from Eastern Europe.

In 1990, Bonn also improved its relations with Poland, the country that had suffered the highest casualties per capita at the hands of the Nazis. At the negotiations between the two German states and the four World War II powers (the ''2 plus 4 talks''), Poland was given a special seat when the question of its Western border with Germany was discussed. The Kohl government, in spite of strong pressure from its Western European neighbors, refused to recognize the validity of the border until after unification. Finally, in November the Kohl government completed a treaty with Warsaw recognizing the current border between the two nations. The pact also contains a comprehensive economic-aid package. Negotiations for a similar treaty with Czechoslovakia were begun in 1990.

Throughout the year, Bonn continued to assure its fellow members of the European Community (EC) that it had not become preoccupied with unification and Eastern Europe to the detriment of its Western European responsibilities. Plans for a European Central Bank, a common currency, and eventual political union continued with strong German support. In December a draft statute or constitution for a Central Bank was approved in Rome.

The Gulf Crisis. Germany was quick to condemn the Iraqi invasion of Kuwait and gave its full support to the UN resolutions calling for sanctions and the eventual use of force to remove Iraqi troops from Kuwait. Later, after some diplomatic prodding by the Bush administration, the Kohl government agreed to contribute about $1 billion toward the costs of Operation Desert Shield. Under current law, however, Bonn was prohibited from deploying any troops outside the NATO region. Chancellor Kohl pledged to change that law, citing Germany's responsibilities as a member of the UN. There was little public support for any use of German troops in the Gulf.

Berlin. At the stroke of midnight on Oct. 3, 1990, Berlin once again became a single city. Four Power control, which had existed since

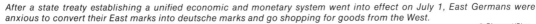

After a state treaty establishing a unified economic and monetary system went into effect on July 1, East Germans were anxious to convert their East marks into deutsche marks and go shopping for goods from the West.

© Chesnot/Sipa

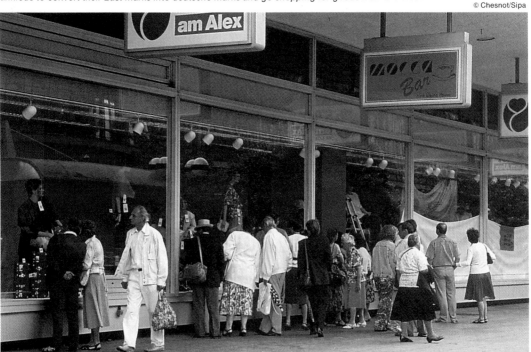

the Nazi capitulation in May 1945, came to an end. There were no longer any military sectors, 4,000 Allied laws and decrees were no longer valid, and of course, the Wall was gone. Also ended was Berlin's status as a demilitarized city, which had meant that younger citizens were not subject to the German draft. Beginning in 1992, Berliners could be drafted into the German armed forces.

In the first citywide election since 1946, Berlin voters replaced the Social Democratic government of Lord Mayor Walter Momper with a grand coalition led by the Christian Democrats. The new mayor was Eberhard Diepgen. The Momper government was damaged by its unsuccessful coalition with the Greens, which collapsed shortly before the election.

According to the Unity Treaty, Berlin is once again Germany's official capital. But it was by no means certain that the national government would move from Bonn. A lively debate began in 1990 over this "capital city" question. A growing number of political leaders from other states and cities in Germany contended that the post-World War II federal system would be weakened by moving all government offices from Bonn to Berlin. Also the costs, estimated at more than $15 billion, precluded any move in the near future. Some Germans also see Berlin as a symbol of Germany's militaristic, authoritarian, and totalitarian past—the Prussian Kaisers and Hitler all waged war from Berlin. Bonn, its supporters argued, is a small provincial city on the Rhine associated with West Germany's postwar transformation into a stable democracy and a model member of the Western community of nations.

Supporters of Berlin countered that it is unfair to blame an entire city for the acts of a few individuals many years ago. They also pointed to Berlin's steadfast commitment to Western values during the darkest days of the Cold War. The city also needed the economic boost that the government would bring. Because of its geographic position, the city would be the ideal bridge between Eastern and Western Europe.

Regardless of how this question is resolved, Berlin once again would become a cultural center for Eastern Germany and Europe and a major economic link to the developing economies of Eastern Europe and the Soviet Union. In 1990, Berlin began what many observers believed would be an extended period of rapid economic growth. A record construction boom already was under way. Real-estate prices jumped by 30% since the opening of the Wall. The market for lawyers, accountants, tax experts, managers, and financial experts was very strong. Berliners hoped that in a few years their city again would rival London, Paris, and Rome as one of Europe's great cities.

DAVID P. CONRADT, *University of Florida*

© K. Harvey/Sipa

The era of Margaret Thatcher as Britain's Conservative Party leader and prime minister came to a sudden end in November 1990. She had been prime minister since May 4, 1979.

GREAT BRITAIN

No one would have or could have predicted that 1990 would close with a new prime minister, John Major (*see* page 257), in residence at No. 10 Downing Street. But on November 22, bowing to political pressure, Prime Minister Margaret Thatcher stepped down after 11½ years. The longest-serving British prime minister in the 20th century, the country's first-ever woman prime minister, and a leader who lent her name to a political revolution, Thatcher, on deciding to resign, said simply: "It's a funny old world."

Domestic Politics. For Thatcher and her Conservative Party, 1990 had been a funny old year. It opened ominously with a near mutiny against Thatcher by Conservatives opposed to her plan to replace property taxes for local government services with a "community charge." More commonly known as the "poll tax," the tax was to be paid at a flat rate, determined by individual local councils, by every adult member of a household (with some allowances for people on low incomes). Around the country, people took to the streets in protest as councils set their community charges. On March 30, 40,000 people joined an anti-poll-tax march in central London. According to the police, riots broke out after demonstrators attempted to charge the security gates at No. 10 Downing Street. Luxury cars were set afire, restaurant and store windows were shattered, and fires were set in Trafalgar Square. More than 340 people were arrested and more than 130 injured. Politicians and the police blamed "rent-a-mob" anarchists for the violence. Others, such as John Benyon, director of the Center for the Study of Public Order at the University of Leicester, claimed the violence had roots in

Thatcherism itself. "What we find in Britain under the Thatcher regime is that about 70% of the population have done very well indeed but we are left behind with 30% who are not benefiting, but falling further behind," Benyon told *The New York Times*. By the autumn one in five Londoners reportedly was not paying.

Electorally, Thatcher's party suffered, too, losing unexpectedly to the centrist Liberal Democrats in a parliamentary election in October that was held to fill the Eastbourne seat of Ian Gow, a Conservative member of Parliament killed by the Irish Republican Army (IRA).

Sir Geoffrey Howe, deputy prime minister, dealt Thatcher a major political blow when he resigned on November 1. The last remaining member of Thatcher's original cabinet and a chief architect of Thatcherism, Howe said in his resignation letter that he was "deeply anxious" at the mood struck by Thatcher on the issue of European unity. Howe's resignation immediately sparked speculation that there would be a challenge to Thatcher's party leadership, which came in mid-November with the challenge mounted by former cabinet member Michael Heseltine. Also a pro-European figure, Heseltine earlier had issued an "open letter" declaring that the Thatcher government was facing a "crisis of confidence" and at risk of losing to Labour in the next election.

The heat on Thatcher increased following Howe's resignation. In a blunt speech that shocked many in the House of Commons,

Howe had said he no longer could resolve the conflict between his loyalty to Britain and his loyalty to Thatcher, whose "nightmare vision" of Europe he did not share.

On November 20, Conservatives voted to decide if Thatcher should remain party leader (and thus prime minister) or if the mantle of leadership should transfer to Heseltine. Thatcher won the vote, but only by four votes, not enough to prevent a second ballot. Amid calls for her to step down, Thatcher remained defiant, declaring, "I fight on, I fight to win." But on November 22, to the joy of some, the despair of others, and the surprise of nearly all, she resigned when her cabinet members urged her to do so. Among those who regretted her exit was U.S. President George Bush, who said he would miss her "counsel and wisdom." She had been, Bush said, "an outstanding ally for the United States."

A week after Thatcher's resignation, her chancellor of the exchequer and favored successor, John Major, defeated Heseltine and Foreign Minister Douglas Hurd to become, at age 47, Britain's youngest prime minister for a century. Prime Minister Major called for the creation in Britain of a "classless society," in which citizens could advance, no matter what their backgrounds. To his cabinet he appointed Heseltine, who was charged with the task of reviewing the unpopular poll tax. Heseltine's appointment as environment minister won approval from Conservatives, who saw it as a positive step toward restoring party unity. Ma-

John Major

On Nov. 28, 1990, 47-year-old John Major, billed by the press as "the poor boy who made good," succeeded Margaret Thatcher as Britain's prime minister.

Major, whose father was once a circus acrobat, was born in London on March 29, 1943. From the time he was 11, his family lived in a two-room flat in the working-class neighborhood of Brixton. Not a brilliant student, he left school at 16, working as a concrete mixer and an insurance-company clerk before going into the banking business, where he made his mark. He eventually became an aide to Anthony Barber, chairman of the Standard Charter Bank, who served in the cabinet of Prime Minister Edward Heath. Major ran unsuccessfully for Parliament in 1974 and was elected as a Conservative in 1979. A loyal party worker, he became a protégé of Prime Minister Thatcher, under whom he served as a junior minister of social security (1986-87), chief treasury secretary (1987–89), foreign secretary (1989), and chancellor of the exchequer (1989–90).

© Cherrualt/Sipa

Major's wife, the former Norma Johnson, whom she married in 1970, is the author of a biography of opera star Joan Sutherland. They have a 16-year-old son and a 19-year-old daughter.

jor's omission of women from his cabinet, however, won him criticism from women members of Parliament in both his party and the opposition Labour Party.

As the Conservative Party returned to regular business in December, many still were marveling at the quick, if somewhat brutal, ease with which one leader had been replaced with another. For the Labour Party, the appointment of a new Conservative leader spelled bad news. Having enjoyed, thanks largely to Thatcher's domestic unpopularity, a comfortable lead in the opinion polls over the Conservatives for months, Labour fell behind the Conservatives in a major poll conducted for a British newspaper by National Market Research in early December. Labour's chances of defeating the Conservatives in the next general election would improve, said the poll, if party leader Neil Kinnock were to be replaced by John Smith, Labour's shadow chancellor.

Out of the running entirely was the Social Democratic Party, which was folded in June by its leader, Dr. David Owen.

Economy. As the interest rate soared and then Chancellor of the Exchequer Major resisted calls to bring it down, saying that it was his best weapon against inflation, the clamor grew for Britain's entry into the European Community's Exchange Rate Mechanism (ERM), which would peg the pound sterling to other European currencies. Thatcher had agreed in 1989 to join the ERM, but not until Britain's high level of inflation was on a par with that of other member countries. By September inflation in Britain was at 10.6% and the base interest rate at 15%. In October the clamor turned into cautious cheers as the Conservative government announced Britain's entry into the ERM and Major announced a 1% cut in interest rates.

In mid-October the Confederation of British Industry announced that the country was in a "very serious recession." A confederation survey was the bleakest in nearly a decade, noting plummeting business confidence and the biggest drop in demand and output since early 1981. At a late October European Community (EC) summit in Rome, the other 11 members ignored Thatcher's objections and set a timetable for the adoption of a single currency. In November, British economists said a war in the Persian Gulf could mean a deepening of the recession at home.

Northern Ireland. The year began with the reemergence of what has come to be known simply as "the Stalker affair." In 1984 a British detective named John Stalker was appointed to lead an inquiry to determine if Northern Ireland's police were operating a "shoot-to-kill" policy against terrorists. In what Stalker said was a cover-up and conspiracy, he was removed in 1986 from the inquiry, and criminal links were alleged against him. In January he

GREAT BRITAIN · Information Highlights

Official Name: United Kingdom of Great Britain and Northern Ireland.
Location: Island, western Europe.
Area: 94,525 sq mi (244 820 km²).
Population (mid-1990 est.): 57,400,000.
Chief Cities (mid-1988 est.): London, the capital, 6,735,400; Birmingham, 993,700; Leeds, 709,600; Glasgow, 703,200; Sheffield, 528,300.
Government: *Head of state,* Elizabeth II, queen (acceded Feb. 1952). *Head of government,* John Major, prime minister and First Lord of the Treasury (took office November 1990). *Legislature—* Parliament: House of Lords and House of Commons.
Monetary Unit: Pound (0.5260 pound equals U.S.$1, Dec. 20, 1990).
Gross Domestic Product (1989 est. U.S.$): $818,000,-000,000.
Economic Indexes (1989): *Consumer Prices* (1980 = 100), all items, 172.3; food, 152.9. *Industrial Production* (1980 = 100), 119.
Foreign Trade (1989 U.S.$): *Imports,* $197,728,-000,000; *exports,* $152,447,000,000.

announced that he had a document that proved that senior Cabinet and Home Office civil servants were involved in his removal, but the government denied his claims. Later in the month the government was forced to admit that "Clockwork Orange," a disinformation campaign waged by security forces against the Provisional Irish Republican Army (IRA) in the 1970s, indeed had taken place and Colin Wallace, a former Army information officer involved in the operation, was granted an inquiry into his claim of unfair dismissal. Wallace, ostensibly dismissed for leaking a classified document to a journalist, believes he was dismissed because he wanted to get out of covert operations. He also maintained that Clockwork Orange sought to destabilize Harold Wilson's government and smear politicians interested in negotiating with the IRA. In September, Wallace won compensation for unfair dismissal, but the government continued to deny his claims about Clockwork Orange.

Northern Ireland Secretary Peter Brooke worked throughout the year to establish talks on Northern Irish self-rule, but his initiatives were resisted by Unionists still smarting from the 1985 Anglo-Irish Agreement, which gave the Irish government a say in the running of the province.

A Granada television program in March gave the names of four IRA men that the program makers asserted were responsible for the 1974 bombings of two Birmingham pubs in which 21 people were killed and 162 injured. In August the government sent the case of the Birmingham Six, the men convicted for the bombings, to the Court of Appeal for the second time. In June the director of public prosecutions ruled "unsafe and unsatisfactory" the convictions of the Maguire Seven, seven people alleged to have run a bomb factory for the IRA in the 1970s.

A police report released in May concluded that the Northern Irish police and army had passed information about alleged IRA members to Protestant extremists. It came as little surprise to the province's Catholic nationalist community, which long has alleged collusion between the security forces and Protestant extremists.

Nelson Mandela, a leader of the African National Congress (ANC) and an unfamiliar figure on the Northern Irish political scene, incurred the anger of British politicians when, in Dublin in July, he said in response to a question about the IRA that "people are slaughtering one another when they could sit down and address the problems in a peaceful manner." Mandela, who insisted that he was misunderstood, was accused of urging the British government to negotiate with the IRA while the IRA continued to embrace violence.

During the summer the IRA stepped up its campaign of violence on the British mainland by bombing the Carlton Club, a Conservative club in London, and the London Stock Exchange. In July an IRA car bomb killed Ian Gow, a longtime Unionist supporter and close friend of the prime minister, outside his East Sussex home; and in September the IRA shot and seriously wounded Sir Peter Terry, former governor of Gibraltar, at his Staffordshire home, in apparent retaliation for the killing of three IRA guerrillas in Gibraltar in 1988. In October the IRA was condemned widely for forcing three civilians to drive bombs to military sites in Northern Ireland by holding their families hostage. Six soldiers and one civilian died when two bombs exploded.

Foreign Affairs. At the start of 1990, Parliament debated a government plan to offer full British citizenship to the families of 50,000 key Hong Kong Chinese before China takes over the crown colony in 1997. The opposition Labour Party called the plan elitist, while right-wing Conservatives warned that an influx of Hong Kong Chinese into Britain would exacerbate racial tensions. The plan eventually was passed with a large majority.

In March, Thatcher hosted two days of talks with the West German Chancellor Helmut Kohl. Both leaders agreed that a united Germany should remain in the North Atlantic Treaty Organization (NATO), but Thatcher disagreed with Kohl that the pace of European economic and political unity should accelerate. In July speculation about Thatcher's views on German dominance in Europe heightened when cabinet member Nicholas Ridley told *The Spectator*, a British magazine, that European unity was "a German racket designed to take over the whole of Europe." Ridley resigned in the ensuing uproar. At a meeting in Brussels in December, Foreign Minister Hurd said Britain might favor giving the European Community a legal role in security and foreign-policy issues.

Other ministers welcomed the announcement, interpreting it as a signal that the new Major government might look more positively on European union than had the Thatcher government.

In July, NATO leaders held a historic two-day summit in London at which they agreed to invite Soviet President Mikhail Gorbachev to meet with them. They also declared their intention to ask Warsaw Pact members to recognize with them that the Cold War was officially over. And, despite opposition from Britain and France, they declared that nuclear weapons would be used only as a "last resort." At the summit's closing press conference, Thatcher maintained a hard-line stance, emphasizing that the new "last resort" formula had not weakened the alliance's doctrine of deterrence. Thatcher also met with ANC leader Nelson Mandela in July and although he failed to convince her of the continued necessity of sanctions against South Africa, he pronounced her "a woman I can do business with."

In August, Britain's attention turned to the Persian Gulf after Iraqi President Saddam Hussein ordered his troops to invade Kuwait. Relations with Hussein had been tense throughout the year. In March he ignored international pleas for clemency for Farzad Bazoft, a British-based journalist sentenced to death for alleged spying. In the same month, British and U.S. customs officials foiled an international

Late in 1990 a Brit and a Frenchman join together to mark the completion of the first stage of the Eurotunnel, which will connect the two nations across the English Channel.

© P.Durand/Sygma

plot to send triggering devices for nuclear weapons to Iraq, and in April, British Customs impounded massive steel tubes that were believed to have been components for an Iraqi "supergun." Calling him a "dictator, a despot, and a tyrant," Thatcher ruled out negotiation with Hussein and ordered into Saudi Arabia Britain's largest deployment of heavy armored forces since World War II. In December, Prime Minister Major upheld Thatcher's hard-line stance against Iraq.

As the situation in the Gulf intensified, former Conservative Prime Minister Edward Heath, calling for a diplomatic solution to the crisis, traveled to Iraq to meet with Hussein in an effort to win the release of elderly and ill British hostages held by the Iraqis. He returned to Britain with 33. In December, Hussein announced that he would release all foreigners held hostage.

In September, Britain and Iran restored diplomatic links, raising hopes for other British hostages in the Middle East. Diplomatic ties were restored with Syria in November.

The Royal Family. Controversy was a frequent, if unwelcome, guest of the British royal family in 1990. In June the writer A.N. Wilson broke with standard practice and recorded in *The Spectator* his conversation with the Queen Mother at a private dinner party. According to Wilson, she spoke candidly, and somewhat flippantly, about her private financial arrangements and politics. Royal commentators were shocked at Wilson's breach of protocol. In July a book titled *Courting Disaster*, coauthored by a former Buckingham Palace employee, was banned by the British High Court at the request of Queen Elizabeth's lawyers. In October the Institute of Economic Affairs, a free-market think tank, proposed that the queen's remaining political powers should be removed. And a book titled *Secrets of the Royals* claimed that Queen Mary's death in 1953 was quickened so as not to interfere with Queen Elizabeth II's coronation. Royal historians emphatically denied the claim.

On a brighter note, the Queen Mother marked her 90th birthday in 1990. In August in the grand finale of five months of birthday parties, 4,000 people gathered along The Mall in London to cheer the woman one banner described as "The Grandmother of England."

The year 1990 was a more trying one for Prince Charles. After breaking his arm playing polo in June, he was reported in the British press to have plunged into depression when the fracture led to an operation and a long recuperative spell. He bowed out of his official duties for four months, during which time his wife, Diana, the princess of Wales, was seen to work tirelessly on his behalf.

In October, Princess Anne was charged with speeding and was banned from driving for one month and fined about $300. Also in October the Duke and Duchess of York, who became parents for the second time in March, moved into their new, approximately $9.9 million home at Sunninghill Park near Ascot, celebrating the move with a party for 200 people.

Other News. In the latest in a spate of food scares over the past couple of years, British consumers were faced first with the specter of bovine spongiform encephalopathy (BSE), known more commonly as "mad cow disease," and then with listeriosis, a sometimes fatal infection carried in store-bought "cookchill" meals, soft cheeses, and pâté. Consumer activists called on the government to establish a food ministry, separate from the agriculture ministry, to oversee food standards.

Prison overcrowding and poor conditions were deemed to have triggered several serious instances of prison unrest in 1990. The worst riots took place at Strangeways Prison in Manchester where inmates staged a siege in April that lasted nearly a month, the longest such siege in British penal history.

At a London meeting in June on the Montreal Protocol on Substances That Deplete the Ozone Layer, Thatcher called on nations to curb quickly production of ozone-destroying chemicals. Later in the year, however, her government's proposals for cleaning up Britain were panned by environmentalists, who had hoped for, but did not get, new taxes on polluters.

Bishop George Carey was named in July to succeed Archbishop Robert Runcie as the archbishop of Canterbury, spiritual leader of the Church of England and 70 million Anglicans around the world. A darker aspect of spiritualism revealed itself in Nottingham, where social workers and foster parents claimed that children were being abused ritually by members of satanic cults. The police said no evidence for such abuse existed.

In October in an effort to win back the support of those who felt it had gone too far in trimming social spending, the government introduced a new form of child benefit, which had been frozen for three years, and announced the formation of a new child-support agency that would pursue absent parents who fail to pay child maintenance. In November the Law Commission proposed that "no-fault" divorce be allowed in Britain. It also suggested that couples seeking a divorce be required to undergo a 12-month "reflection period," during which they would have to resolve practical matters that would result from their divorce. In December, Britain met France under the English Channel as the first stage of the $14.5 billion Eurotunnel was completed. For the first time since the Ice Age, Britain was linked to the European continent.

SUZANNE CASSIDY
Researcher, London Bureau
"The New York Times"

Dame Margot Fonteyn (center), one of Britain's luminaries of the international ballet world, was honored in May at a gala performance of "Romeo and Juliet" at the Royal Opera House. In attendance were Princess Margaret (right) and the Princess of Wales, as well as stars of the opera and dance worlds.

© Donald Southern

The Arts

Arguably the most exciting events of 1990 on the British arts scene took place north of the English border, as Glasgow celebrated its year as the European Culture Capital with a tartan flourish. Elsewhere in Britain, the controversy over arts funding raged, as the opposition Labour Party warned that one third of the nation's performing companies were on the verge of insolvency. According to a study by the liberal Policy Studies Institute, Britain was second from the bottom in a league table of seven countries' direct expenditure per head on arts and museums by local and central government.

Theater. An 11% increase in government funding was not enough for the flagship Royal Shakespeare Company, which made the dramatic announcement in February that its two London theaters would have to close for four months beginning in November because of a deficit of more than £3 million (about $5.3 million). In April the company announced that associate director Adrian Noble would succeed Terry Hands as artistic director. Michael Attenborough, son of Sir Richard Attenborough, was appointed executive producer. Later in the year, The Young Vic, one of Britain's foremost fringe theaters, announced that it would close permanently if it did not raise £100,000 (about $175,000) by the end of September. In June, Prince Edward resigned as production assistant with Andrew Lloyd Webber's Really Useful Group to form a new production company led by Biddy Hayward, a Lloyd Webber executive who was said to be displeased by Lloyd Web-

ber's plans to diversify away from theater into film. In October 80 professionals, including Sir Peter Hall and Vanessa Redgrave, called on the Conservative government to give more cash to Britain's subsidized theater.

On stage, U.S. plays dominated 1990, both in the West End and at the Royal National Theatre. The National staged two Arthur Miller plays, *The Crucible* and *After the Fall*, as well as Stephen Sondheim's *Sunday in the Park with George*. Another Sondheim musical, *Into the Woods*, opened in the West End, along with Lanford Wilson's *Burn This* and August Wilson's *Fences*. Far less successful was *King*, a musical about the Rev. Dr. Martin Luther King, Jr., which closed after less than two months.

Other notable plays included a revival of Noel Coward's *Private Lives*, with Joan Collins; David Hare's *Racing Demon*; Peter Flannery's *Singer*; Brian Friel's *Dancing at Lughnasa*; and Tariq Ali and Howard Brenton's *Moscow Gold*, a play about Mikhail Gorbachev and *perestroika*.

Music. The last night of the Proms, a series of annual summer concerts at the Albert Hall, is, with its profusion of Union Jacks, a tradition that Britons hold dear. So the uproar was considerable when Mark Elder, the English National Opera music director who was to conduct the last-night concert, announced that he might drop the patriotic songs ("Land of Hope and Glory" and "Rule Britannia") that mark the concert's end. After telling an English newspaper that the songs' lyrics "come from an age that was able and happy to celebrate

Britain's irresistible march across the world," Elder was fired immediately. Controversy also visited the Glyndebourne Festival when Sir Peter Hall resigned as artistic director because, he said, he had not been consulted about U.S. director Peter Sellars' decision to omit all of the spoken dialogue from Sellars' production of *The Magic Flute*.

Notable music events in 1990 included Japanese pianist Mitsuko Uchida playing Mozart with Jeffrey Tate and the English Chamber Orchestra; a performance by the Soviet Union's Bolshoi Symphony Orchestra, as part of the Barbican Centre's "Great Orchestras of the World" series; and the Royal Opera's production of Puccini's *Turandot*.

Visual Arts. The exhibition of the year was without a doubt "Monet in the '90s: The Series Paintings," which went to the Royal Academy of Arts from the United States. (*See also* page 123.) Other notable exhibitions included "Picasso, Leger, de Chirico and the New Classicism" at the Tate Gallery and "Futurism in Flight" at the Accademia Italiana delle Arti. The Museums and Galleries Commission, the government's advisory body, reported that export control procedures were failing to prevent the hemorrhage of important art treasures. The National Campaign for the Arts, among other bodies, called for tighter controls.

At the Tate Gallery, the first major rehang in more than 20 years was completed in January, with paintings laid out in a chronological order that traced the development of British art from 1550 to Impressionism. It then examined the relationship of British art to American and European art in the 20th century. At the National Gallery, it was announced in May that Heinz Berggruen, a U.S. art dealer, had tendered a five-year loan of 72 paintings by Cézanne, Picasso, Braque, Seurat, and Miró. Also in May the Courtauld Institute reopened at its new home at Somerset House on The Strand in London.

Dance. The Royal Ballet opened the year with the announcement that it was abandoning its planned U.S. tour because it could not obtain adequate financing. That was followed by a threat of industrial action by the company's dancers. At the English National Ballet, artistic director Peter Schaufuss was fired by the company's directors. In his five years with the ballet, the Danish-born former dancer won acclaim for his innovative work. He was replaced by Hungarian Ivan Nagy, who had his work cut out for him after Schaufuss took about a dozen of the company's dancers with him to the Deutsche Oper Ballet in Berlin.

In May, Dame Margot Fonteyn was honored at a gala performance of "Romeo and Juliet" at the Royal Opera House. Placido Domingo opened the tribute with a serenade to the 71-year-old Dame Margot, and Rudolf Nureyev, who was once Romeo to her Juliet,

© Gordon Rainsford/The Young Vic

Drawing attention to the financial plight of The Young Vic theater was actor Richard Harris, who took to the London streets to collect money for the theater.

danced the part of Mercutio. In June the Bolshoi's Irek Mukhamedov, regarded by many as the world's most exciting ballet dancer, joined the Royal Ballet as a principal dancer. In October it was announced that American Robert Hill also would join as a principal dancer.

Film and Television. As in the other arts, the color of money was the biggest film story in 1990. With British-film production reaching its lowest level since 1981, Prime Minister Margaret Thatcher met in June with 25 leading filmmakers, including David Puttnam, John Boorman, and Sir Richard Attenborough, and agreed to give £5 million (about $8.8 million) in government funds over the next three years to the industry. Major films of the year included Peter Medak's *The Krays* and David Leland's *The Big Man*.

On television, viewers saw *The Portrait of a Marriage*, a miniseries about the unusual marriage of writer Vita Sackville-West and diplomat Harold Nicolson. Author Salman Rushdie also made his first television appearance since he went into hiding in February 1989.

Suzanne Cassidy

GREECE

Greece began 1990 with an unstable political situation after two general elections in 1989 had left no party with an absolute majority in Parliament. Contending for power in early 1990 were three main parties: the conservative New Democracy party headed by Constantine Mitsotakis, the Panhellenic Socialist Movement (PASOK) headed by former prime minister Andreas Papandreou, and the Communist-dominated Coalition of the Left and Progress under Harilaos Florakis.

Parliamentary Elections. General elections were held on April 8. New Democracy won 150 seats and joined a coalition with the one elected deputy of the otherwise insignificant Democratic Renewal party to gain the 151 seats needed for an absolute majority in the 300-seat chamber. PASOK won 123 seats; the Coalition of Left and Progress, 19; while the eight remaining seats were distributed among four Independents, two Muslims, one Ecologist, and the one Democratic Renewal deputy.

Constantine Mitsotakis, 72, was sworn in as prime minister on April 11, and he immediately tried to strengthen the country internally and externally. He embarked on a series of visits to various capitals including London, Madrid, Dublin, and Washington where he conferred with U.S. President George Bush. In an effort to ensure stronger parliamentary majorities for ruling political parties in the future, Parliament on November 9 enacted legislation changing the electoral system that had resulted in three general elections between June 1989 and April 1990. Parliament elected Greece's most eminent post-World War II statesman, 83-year-old Constantine Karamanlis, to a five-year term as president of the Hellenic Republic on May 4. Sworn in on May 5, Karamanlis returned to the post he had held from 1980 to 1985. Before that, he had served as prime minister from 1955 to 1963 and again from 1974 to 1980. He also has been recognized universally as the restorer of democracy to Greece and the founder of the current Hellenic Republic in 1974 after a seven-year period of disastrous military rule.

Greek Bases Accord. The Mitsotakis government signed an eight-year Defense Cooperation Agreement (DCA) with the United States on July 8. The two countries agreed on plans to close two major U.S. bases and several minor installations in Greece. The July defense agreement provided for the continued presence of some U.S. installations, including two located on the island of Crete, which are bases of immense strategic importance in the Mediterranean. In return for the continued U.S. armed presence, the United States agreed to supply Greece with arms and military credits. Included in the accord was a provision, open to various interpretations, that the United States would help prevent or oppose any attack on Greece.

The Economy and Labor Unrest. Faced with recurrent strikes and economic problems that included a public debt close to $100 billion, the Mitsotakis government embarked on an ambitious economic policy. Among its goals were reforms of the taxation laws, privatization of publicly owned business organizations, and the eventual reduction of the rate of inflation from its 20%-per-year average. But measures such as increases in excise taxes, dismissing workers in state-controlled positions, and a new social-security law met stiff resistance from civil servants and others, plunging Greece into widespread public-sector strikes. To add to the nation's woes, a prolonged drought caused crop losses, weakening the economy's important agricultural sector.

Greece and the Kuwaiti Crisis. Greece condemned Iraq's invasion of Kuwait, joined the other European Community countries in imposing sanctions on Iraq, supported the UN Security Council's decisions against Iraq, and sent a frigate to participate in the multinational force. The Greek government also drew parallels between Iraq's invasion of Kuwait and the continued military occupation by Turkey of about 37% of Cyprus' territory since 1974.

Municipal Elections. Municipal elections were held in two stages: the first on October 14, followed by run-off elections on October 21. New Democracy adherents won Athens and Thessaloniki, the largest cities in the country, but a candidate supported by PASOK and the Coalition of the Left and Progress won Piraeus, the country's third-largest city. The final tally showed that out of 359 municipalities and rural centers, New Democracy took 136; PASOK, 166; Coalition of the Left and Progress, 47; and Independents, 10.

Allegations of Corruption. Investigations continued in 1990 regarding allegations of corruption and misconduct during PASOK leader Andreas Papandreou's rule as prime minister from 1981 to 1989. Sensational charges contin-

---

GREECE • Information Highlights

Official Name: Hellenic Republic.
Location: Southeastern Europe.
Area: 50,942 sq mi (131 940 km²).
Population (mid-1990 est.): 10,100,000.
Chief Cities (1981 census): Athens, the capital, 885,737; Salonika, 406,413; Piraeus, 196,389.
Government: *Head of state*, Constantine Karamanlis, president (took office May 1990). *Head of government*, Constantine Mitsotakis, prime minister (took office April 1990). *Legislature*—Parliament.
Monetary Unit: Drachma (158.7 drachmas equal U.S.$1, Dec. 31, 1990).
Gross Domestic Product (1989 est. U.S.$): $56,300,-000,000.
Economic Indexes (1989): *Consumer Prices* (1980 = 100), all items, 473.0; food, 467.4. *Industrial Production* (1980 = 100), 113.
Foreign Trade (1988 U.S.$): *Imports*, $12,015,-000,000; *exports*, $5,307,000,000.

ued to link former members of Papandreou's PASOK government with the Bank of Crete scandal. Two former high-ranking officials in the Papandreou government, Agamemnon Koutsogeorgas and George Petsos, also were arrested in 1990.

An Olympic Blow. Greeks reacted with bitter disappointment when the International Olympics Committee passed over Athens in favor of Atlanta as the site of the 1996 games. The games will mark the 100th anniversary of the modern revival of the Olympics, held in 1896 in Athens.

GEORGE J. MARCOPOULOS, *Tufts University*

HAITI

Haiti surprised itself and the world in 1990 by holding an honest and relatively peaceful national election for president on December 16. But whether the winner, Jean-Bertrand Aristide, would be permitted to take office on Feb. 7, 1991, as scheduled was questionable at the end of 1990.

Aristide, 37, a fiery Roman Catholic priest who had been expelled from the Salesian order, won as much as 80% of the vote. Results still were being tabulated late in December. Known as "Titid," Aristide is a folk hero to the Haitian masses but anathema to the army and the remaining elements of the Duvalier dictatorship that collapsed in 1986. He has survived at least three assassination attempts, including one at church in 1988 when gunmen sprayed the pulpit and the congregation with machine-gun fire. The perpetrators of the attack, in which 12 people died, were believed to be members of the Tonton Macoutes, the dreaded Duvalier paramilitary squads that were disbanded but not disarmed after Jean-Claude "Baby Doc" Duvalier fled the country in 1986.

The Tonton Macoutes vowed to prevent Aristide from assuming the presidency. Roger Lafontant, a former defense minister and head of the Tonton Macoutes, who was disqualified from running for president in December, told

AP/Wide World

Jean-Bertrand Aristide, a 37-year-old expelled Salesian priest, was to assume the presidency of Haiti on Feb. 7, 1991, following his victory in December's democratic elections.

the foreign press in Port-au-Prince that he forcibly would bar Aristide. Another onetime leader of the goon squads, Zacharie Delva, said, "It's impossible. There will be no Aristide tomorrow."

Turbulent Year. The way to the December 16 election was opened when Lt. Gen. Prosper Avril, the head of an 18-month military regime, resigned and fled the country on March 10 in the face of mounting public protest and violence. He was replaced three days later by a provisional government headed by Ertha Pascal-Trouillot, the only woman sitting on Haiti's 12-member Supreme Court.

The presidential election was scheduled originally for October 17, then postponed until November 4, and finally rescheduled for December 16. A previous presidential election on Nov. 29, 1987, was disrupted when roving bands of armed men opened fire on polling places, killing at least 34 people and wounding another 60. Security in the 1990 election was assured by the presence of some 700 foreign observers.

The election result represented the first time in Haiti's 186 years of independence that the voters had given an overwhelming and unchallenged popular mandate in free voting. Aristide has been bitterly critical of U.S. policy toward his impoverished country. Yet, paradoxically, most observers agreed that he could take office only with heavy pressure from Washington on the army and the Duvalierist elements to respect Aristide's mandate.

RICHARD C. SCHROEDER, *Consultant Organization of American States*

HAITI · Information Highlights

Official Name: Republic of Haiti.
Location: Caribbean.
Area: 10,714 sq mi (27 750 km²).
Population: (mid-1990 est.): 6,500,000.
Chief City (mid-1984 est.): Port-au-Prince, the capital, 738,342 (incl. suburbs).
Government: *Head of state and government,* Ertha Pascal-Trouillot, provisional president (took power March 1990). *Legislature*—suspended.
Monetary Unit: Gourde (5.0 gourdes equal U.S.$1, buying rate, August 1990).
Gross Domestic Product (1988 est. U.S.$): $2,400,000,000.
Economic Index (1989): *Consumer Prices* (1980 = 100), all items, 158.1; food, 144.4.
Foreign Trade (1988 U.S.$): *Imports,* $344,000,000; *exports,* $200,000,000.

HAWAII

A political landslide, the discovery on the ocean floor of the missing door from a United Airlines plane involved in a 1989 crash, and an acquittal for Imelda Marcos highlighted the news in Hawaii during 1990.

Politics. When Democratic U.S. Sen. Spark Matsunaga (D) died of cancer in April, it opened up a political scramble that brought campaigning to a frenzy. Democratic Rep. Daniel K. Akaka was appointed to the seat by Gov. John Waihee to serve until the fall elections. Republican Rep. Patricia Saiki decided to run against Akaka, opening the way not only for a hotly contested Senate race, but also for the two House seats. Two veteran Democratic campaigners, Patsy Mink, a former member of the U.S. House of Representatives who was chosen in a special election to fill the remaining months of Saiki's House term, and Neil Abercrombie, ran against Republicans Andrew Poepoe and Michael Liu, respectively, in November for two-year House terms. The Akaka-Saiki contest was close up to the general election, but Mink and Abercrombie held comfortable leads throughout the campaign. When the results were tallied, all three seats in Washington went to the Democrats, who also reelected Waihee and his running mate, Lt. Gov. Benjamin Cayetano. The Democrats also retained overwhelming majorities in the state House (45-6) and Senate (22-3).

The Economy. A Bank of Hawaii economist confirmed what most residents suspected: The cost of living in Hawaii accelerated between 1989 and 1990. By mid-1990 it was 33% higher than on the U.S. mainland. The average cost of a three-bedroom home was $363,000 in June, up 41% from the previous year.

Chemical Arms Disposal. Governor Waihee joined Pacific Island leaders in calling for the United States to cease destroying chemical arms on Johnston Island, 700 mi (1 126 km) southwest of Honolulu. The projectiles, shipped from Germany, contained deadly nerve gas and other chemicals. President Bush met with the leaders of the Pacific Islands in a minisummit October 27 in Honolulu and promised them that all precautions were being taken to protect the Pacific environment. Waihee was not invited to the one-day conference but met separately with island leaders.

Underwater Search. Navy crewmen aboard the minisub *Sea Cliff* located the missing door of a United Airlines plane that had opened during a Feb. 9, 1989, flight from Honolulu to Auckland, New Zealand, taking the lives of nine persons. The Navy submersible, making the second-deepest dive of any similar craft—some 14,000 ft (4 267 m) below the surface of the Pacific—located the door in two sections and brought them to the surface. Federal aviation experts then examined them in hopes of discovering the cause of the midair accident.

Marcos Acquittal. Sometime Honolulu resident Imelda Marcos, widow of the late Philippine President Ferdinand Marcos, returned to Hawaii following her acquittal July 2 in New York City on charges of helping her husband defraud their homeland of $200 million. Philippine President Corazon Aquino continued to deny Mrs. Marcos permission to bring home the body of her husband, which lies in a crypt on the windward side of the island of Oahu.

Lava. Lava from the Kilauea volcano eruption continued to pour relentlessly on the Puna coast of the island of Hawaii. Most of the houses and buildings in the Kalapana Gardens community were destroyed, including a landmark church and a National Parks structure.

CHARLES TURNER
Free-lance Writer, Honolulu

HONG KONG

In 1990, Hong Kong began preparing for the first direct elections to its 60-member Legislative Council (Legco), scheduled for 1991. On April 4, 1990, China adopted the Basic Law of the Hong Kong Special Administrative Region (HKSAR), which will regulate Hong Kong's status when it passes from British to Chinese control in 1997.

Political Affairs. In March 1990, Hong Kong announced the introduction of a more directly representative system of government: For the first time, 18 Legco members will be chosen in September 1991 by universal suffrage. Hong Kong will be divided into nine constituencies, each comprising populations ranging from 300,000 to 600,000 voters. Two candidates from each constituency polling the highest number of votes will be elected. By August 1990, 1.6 million people had registered, out of a total of 3.7 million eligible to vote.

Several political parties have been organized. The United Democrats of Hong Kong,

---

HAWAII · Information Highlights

Area: 6,471 sq mi (16 759 km²).
Population (1990 census prelim.): 1,095,000.
Chief Cities (1980 census): Honolulu, the capital (1988 est.), 376,110; Pearl City, 42,575; Kailua, 35,812; Hilo, 35,269.
Government (1990): *Chief Officers*—governor, John D. Waihee III (D); lt. gov., Benjamin J. Cayetano (D). *Legislature*—Senate, 25 members; House of Representatives, 51 members.
State Finances (fiscal year 1989): *Revenue,* $4,041,000,000; *expenditure,* $3,184,000,000.
Personal Income (1989): $20,543,000,000; per capita, $18,472.
Labor Force (June 1990): *Civilian labor force,* 541,300; *unemployed,* 15,600 (2.9% of total force).
Education: *Enrollment* (fall 1988)—public elementary schools, 118,648; public secondary, 48,840; colleges and universities, 52,297. *Public school expenditures* (1989–90), $703,920,000.

led by Legco member Martin Lee, was formed by a prodemocracy lobby that includes members of the Hong Kong Alliance in Support of the Patriotic Democratic Movement in China, a group branded counterrevolutionary by Beijing. Professionals and businessmen, led by Legco members Jimmy McGregor and Leong Che-hung, established the Hong Kong Democratic Foundation. Other probusiness political groups include the Liberal Democratic Federation, supported by business tycoons; the Group of 89, headed by businessman Vincent Lo; the Hongkong Foundation, headed by Legco member Stephen Cheong; and the Progressive Hong Kong Society, headed by Legco member Maria Tam. The Association For a Better Hong Kong was formed by advocates of Sino-Hong Kong cooperation who believe that Hong Kong may have to learn to live with a system run by businessmen and professionals who are Beijing surrogates.

The announcement of the Basic Law did not help stem emigration, which had increased from 20,000 in 1986 to more than 45,000 in 1989, with estimates running as high as 60,000 for 1990. On July 23, 1990, Britain's Parliament adopted the British Nationality (Hong Kong) Act, under which 50,000 key personnel in the government and private sector and their families would be given full British citizenship without having to reside in Britain. This law, together with a bill of rights passed by the Hong Kong legislature, was intended to shore up the confidence of the population. Both measures were opposed by China.

Economy. Despite 1989's slow (2.5%) rate of growth (compared with 14% in 1987), public investment was increasing. This included the $16.3 billion Port and Replacement Airport Development Project at Chek Lap Kok, a multimillion-dollar expansion of the city's container port, and a new 7,000-student University of Science and Technology.

The port of Hong Kong maintained its position as the world's busiest container port for the third consecutive year. In 1990, Hong Kong set up an independent shipping register and started issuing certificates in the name of "Hong Kong, China."

The 70-story Bank of China Building, 1,204 ft (367 m) high, was opened officially on May 17, 1990; it is the tallest building in Asia and ranks fifth in the world.

DAVID CHUENYAN LAI
University of Victoria, British Columbia

HOUSING

The year 1990 was one of contraction for the U.S. housing market, extending a downward trend that began in 1987. Total housing starts fell to 1.2 million units, down 13% from 1989 and one third below the 1986 peak. Starts of single-family housing units slid to 900,000 units, 9% below 1989 and off nearly one fourth from 1986. Multifamily starts plunged to 300,000 units, down 23% from 1989 and more than 50% below the highs of the mid-1980s.

Downslide. The downslide in housing-market activity in 1990 was part and parcel of a broader economic slowdown in the United States that degenerated into economic recession by the fourth quarter of the year. Indeed, the housing sector was the weakest component of the U.S. economy in 1990, performing a typical "leading" role in the economic downswing. High interest rates, weakened household income, and faltering job growth all contributed to the downslide in housing activity. The August invasion of Kuwait by Iraq and the associated surge in oil prices also were telling factors in U.S. housing markets. These developments placed heavy hits on consumer purchasing power, interest rates, and consumer sentiment. Prospective home buyers moved to the sidelines in droves late in the year.

Several other special factors depressed housing activity in 1990. The multifamily sector, already reeling from high vacancy rates and from adverse impacts of the Tax Reform Act of 1986 on investment incentives for rental real estate, was disadvantaged further by new rules relating to the accessibility of newly produced multifamily units to handicapped persons. Tremendous confusion about the new requirements was created when the U.S. Department of Housing and Urban Development (HUD) failed to finalize the rules by the end of the year. It also appeared that final HUD rules would be costly for builders to comply with, aggravating affordability problems already being faced by renter households.

The housing sector also was beset by a special "credit crunch." This crunch took the form of a shortfall in the availability of credit for housing production, i.e., for land acquisition, land development, and construction.

Some areas of the country were in deep recession condition, while others showed stable or increasing activity in 1990. In the weakest markets, house-price declines emerged, further weakening consumer sentiment and contributing to the cumulative contraction in consumer spending and overall economic activity. The Federal Reserve Board (the U.S. central bank) eased monetary policy aggressively toward the end of 1990 in an effort to bolster the sagging economy and the interest-sensitive housing sector.

The Credit Crunch. The year brought a new type of credit crunch to the U.S. housing market. For the first time in history, the producers of housing faced a serious credit crunch, while credit generally remained available to the ultimate buyers of housing. For many years, virtually all of the housing-production credit in the United States was supplied by thrift institu-

On many blocks in towns and cities across the United States, a house for sale sign was a common sight. Weakened personal income, high interest rates, as well as fear of war in the Persian Gulf contributed to the downward trend in U.S. housing.

© Shawn Henry/Saba

tions and commercial banks—in roughly equal proportions. The credit crunch of 1990 involved sharp contractions in the supply of such credit at both thrifts and banks.

The thrift side of the credit crunch began to develop when thrift-reform legislation became law in 1989. Tough new "core" capital requirements ensured the shrinkage of the thrift industry, in terms of both numbers of institutions and total industry assets. A new set of risk-based capital requirements biased the shrinking thrift industry toward certain assets and away from others; these rules created a strong bias against housing-production loans by placing these assets in the highest risk category. And the amount that an adequately capitalized thrift institution can lend to a single borrower was reduced from 100% of total capital to 15% of unimpaired capital, disrupting many long-standing arrangements between builders and thrifts.

In the early stages of the 1990 credit crunch at thrift institutions, many builders/developers established alternative credit arrangements at commercial banks. But then the crunch spread to banks as well, for several reasons. First, banks began to adjust to impending risk-based capital rules (implemented at year's end) that will place housing-production loans in the highest risk category. Second, alarms sounded by bank regulators cast a deep chill on lending by the banks. In February the federal regulator of national banks circulated an advisory letter stressing the potential risks of real-estate development and construction loans, and teams of examiners descended on banks throughout the country to scour their real-estate-loan portfolios. As a result, banks became part of the credit-crunch problem rather than a solution for borrowers shunned by thrift institutions.

The shortfall in supply of housing-production credit at thrifts and banks was not made up by new entrants to the market in 1990. There was no federally related safety valve in place, since such credit has not been on the

menu of the Federal Housing Administration (FHA), Ginnie Mae, Fannie Mae, or Freddie Mac. Lack of standardization of housing-production loans, and inadequate understanding of risk and other characteristics of these loans, created barriers to the entry of other private sources of capital, such as pension funds, life-insurance companies, and foreign investors. As the year ended, efforts were under way on many fronts to broaden the sources of credit supply to enable builders and developers to gear up for an anticipated upswing in housing and the economy in 1991.

Home Prices. During 1989–90 there was a proliferation of media reports touting an impending collapse of house prices in the United States. These stories became particularly destructive in 1990, when an economic downswing commenced and consumer sentiment was sent reeling for a variety of reasons.

There is no doubt that house-price appreciation slowed markedly on a national basis during 1990 and downward price adjustments were recorded in a significant number of market areas. House-price increases ran well below the overall rate of consumer-price inflation on a national basis, and year-to-date declines in median prices of existing homes sold were evident in about 25 metropolitan areas. These declines were concentrated in areas where price appreciation had been very rapid a few years earlier and where changes in market fundamentals made downward price adjustments virtually inevitable. Most of these adjustments occurred in New England, New Jersey, New York, California, and a few spots in the "oil patch."

Throughout the rest of the country, house prices continued to rise in 1990, and prices climbed by 5% or more in about 35 metro areas. As a rule, steady price appreciation continued in markets that had not become unbalanced earlier—including most of the Midwest and South as well as interior portions of the West and Northeast. Very rapid (and probably unsustainable) price increases occurred in a few hot markets during 1990, including Honolulu, Seattle, and Sacramento.

Forecasts of a widespread downward spiral in house prices focus on recent price declines in some areas and argue two points: First, when prices start to go down in specific areas, a downward momentum develops in these areas; second, price declines in some areas quickly spread to other areas, producing the widespread downward spiral that gets projected in the headlines. Neither of those points is correct. History clearly shows that downward price adjustments in specific markets do not deteriorate into a price rout within these markets. The key reason is that homes are where people live, and are not like financial assets that get shifted around in portfolios of investors in response to short-term price movements. The vision of Americans "dumping" their homes and shifting to stocks, bonds, or commodities is unrealistic. That is why prices in local markets seldom fall below the levels that prevailed before some unsustainable pressure drove them upward.

Arguments that falling house prices in a given area inevitably will spread to other areas also lack foundation. Most people do not sell houses in a strong or stable market in order to move to an area where house prices have fallen. Jobs, schools, and a host of other connections to a local area limit such shifts, and price data clearly show that downward price adjustments tend to be restricted to those areas where prior overheating leads to a cooling-off process.

National Policy. There were major changes in U.S. housing policy in 1990. The Cranston-Gonzalez National Affordable Housing Act was signed into law late in the year. This act established three new vehicles to provide housing assistance for lower-income, first-time home buyers, as well as for lower-income renters. The act also made substantive changes to the home-mortgage-insurance program of the FHA, and addressed the problem of prepayments of mortgages on privately owned, federally assisted rental properties. Many of these properties are in danger of being lost from the stock of rental housing reserved for lower-income people in the United States.

The three new programs contained in the Cranston-Gonzalez housing act were dubbed HOME, HOPE, and the National Homeownership Trust. The HOME program involves federal block grants to state and local governments that can be used for several types of housing support, including rehabilitation of substandard rental housing, construction of new rental housing, direct rental-assistance payments to eligible households, and second-mortgage assistance for first-time home buyers. The state and local sponsors are required to provide matching funds, and the required contribution varies with the type of housing assistance provided. For new construction of rental housing, the sponsors must match half of every federal dollar received.

The HOPE program allows low-income families to buy government-owned housing, an approach that was pioneered in England. The program is designed to spur homeownership among low-income tenants living in public-housing projects as well as other government-owned multifamily or single-family rental properties. Planning and financial assistance are provided through grants for architectural and engineering work, rehabilitation of public housing units, counseling and training of prospective home buyers and homeowners, and legal fees. Financing of eligible home buyers may involve federally insured mortgage loans and, in case of borrower default, lenders must give the public-housing agency or other appropriate entity an opportunity to cure the default.

The National Homeownership Trust provides assistance for low- and moderate-income, first-time home buyers. Assistance takes the form of interest-rate buydowns or down-payment assistance; the interest rate paid by the home buyer can be no higher than 6% and the down payment can be reduced to 1%. Home buyers using this program must certify that they have made a good-faith effort to obtain a market-rate mortgage and have been denied a loan because of inadequate income. Furthermore, assistance must be repaid to the federal government upon sale of the properties, as long as sufficient homeowner equity is available upon sale. The repaid assistance flows back into a revolving fund, bolstering resources available for assistance to additional first-time home buyers.

The Cranston-Gonzalez housing act authorized the HOME, HOPE, and the National Homeownership Trust programs, but funding must be provided through separate congressional appropriations. Thus, these programs would remain inactive unless Congress approves a supplemental appropriations bill or a reprogramming of funds appropriated for other programs of the Department of Housing and Urban Development.

KENT W. COLTON and DAVID F. SEIDERS
National Association of Home Builders

HUNGARY

In 1990 under close international monitoring, Hungary made slow, steady, and sometimes painful progress toward multiparty democracy and a free-market economic system.

Domestic Affairs. In March, Hungary held its first free parliamentary elections in more than 40 years. During the preceding months, more than 50 political parties registered and participated in the electoral campaign. The internal-security forces were accused of spying on the opposition parties, and anti-Semitic smears were common during the campaign. Leading contenders were the center-right and nationalist Hungarian Democratic Forum, the liberal and pro-Western Alliance of Free Democrats, the farmers' Independent Smallholders Party, the Christian Democratic People's Party, and the "reformed" version of the old Communist Party—the Hungarian Socialist Party. A group of 64 observers from 16 countries, including the United States, declared the election of March 25 and the runoff elections of April 8 essentially orderly and honest. No party polled a majority of the 386 parliamentary seats. The Democratic Forum gained 165 seats, the Free Democrats 92, the Smallholders 43, the Socialists 33, and the Christian Democrats 21.

In early May the two leading parties agreed to support Árpád Goncz, the 68-year-old author-playwright and former political prisoner, as interim president of Hungary. (He was reelected to a regular five-year term in August.) Goncz promptly appointed the leader of the Democratic Forum, Jozsef Antall, prime minister and asked him to form a new government. Antall put together a coalition of his own party with the Smallholders and the Christian Democrats that controlled a 229-seat majority in the National Assembly. In subsequent months, there was a great deal of squabbling between the governing coalition and the opposition led by the Free Democrats and the League of Young Democrats, much of it over the pace of privatization and the degree of Hungary's pro-Western alignment. In local elections held in September-October, the opposition, benefiting from growing popular dissatisfaction, won in 733 electoral districts, the government parties in only 385.

From the start of the year, Hungary faced a severe economic crisis, with high and growing inflation (23%), unemployment (10%), and numbers of homeless people (swelled by thousands of amnestied prisoners and ethnic Magyars fleeing from Romania); falling industrial production; and a foreign debt of more than $20 billion. Under strong pressure from its international creditors, the government adopted an austerity budget and took tough measures to end centralized economic controls and begin the transition to a free-market economy. Taxes were raised and subsidies to unprofitable state enterprises stopped. Unprofitable trade between Hungary and the Soviet Union and the other COMECON countries of Eastern Europe (with which Hungary already had accumulated a surplus of 1.5 billion nonconvertible rubles or about $2.5 billion) was reoriented toward the West, especially Germany. In the summer and fall, the government set the terms for the privatization and sell-off to domestic and foreign purchasers of all state-owned farms and agricultural cooperatives, and also of tens of thousands of industrial and commercial enterprises, including such major ones as IBUSZ, the national travel agency, and MALEV, the national airline. Such hardheaded decisions brought Hungary several billion dollars in loans and financial credits from the International Monetary Fund, the World Bank, the European Investment Bank, and the "Group of 24" (including the leading industrial nations of the world), as well as economic-aid packages from the United States, Germany, and Japan.

Generous new laws on taxation and the repatriation of profits also attracted more foreign investment to Hungary than to any other East European country. Some 2,000 international joint ventures included companies from Austria, Germany, Japan (Suzuki), and some 100 U.S. firms, including General Electric, General Motors, Ford, Kodak, Schwinn, Digital Equipment, and Levi Strauss. In other areas of legislation, the National Assembly established freedom of conscience and religion and approved financial compensation for persons who had been jailed or suffered economic discrimination for political reasons during the period 1945–63.

The anti-Soviet uprising of 1956 was declared officially to have been "a revolutionary struggle for freedom" and October 23, the date of the uprising, was designated a national holiday. In its annual report on the status of human rights throughout the world, the U.S. State Department praised Hungary for respecting them and for moving so rapidly toward multiparty democracy. Although Hungary's 80,000 Jews faced growing expressions of popular anti-Semitism, the government dedicated a monument to the 600,000 Hungarian Jews who had been murdered in World War II.

Foreign Affairs. In February, after extended negotiations, Hungary and the Soviet Union reached agreement on the removal of more than 50,000 Soviet troops from Hungarian soil

---

HUNGARY · Information Highlights

Official Name: Republic of Hungary.
Location: East-central Europe.
Area: 35,919 sq mi (93 030 km²).
Population (mid-1990 est.): 10,600,000.
Chief Cities (Jan. 1, 1989): Budapest, the capital, 2,113,645; Debrecen, 219,251; Miskolc, 207,826.
Government: *Head of state,* Arpád Goncz, president (elected August 1990). *Head of government,* Jozsef Antall, prime minister (took office May 1990). *Legislature* (unicameral)—National Assembly.
Monetary Unit: Forint (62.222 forints equal U.S.$1, August 1990).
Gross National Product (1989 est. U.S.$): $64,600,000,000.
Economic Indexes (1989): *Consumer Prices* (1980 = 100), all items, 215.5; food, 206.6. *Industrial Production* (1980 = 100), 111.
Foreign Trade (1989 U.S.$): *Imports,* $8,803,000,000; *exports,* $9,584,000,000.

by July 1991. In June, Hungarian armed forces were removed from the joint military command and maneuvers of the Warsaw Pact. Hungary also became the first post-Communist regime to announce its imminent withdrawal from the Warsaw Pact (by the end of 1991). In February, Foreign Minister Gyula Horn even suggested that Hungary was interested in a nonmilitary role in the North Atlantic Treaty Organization (NATO). Also in February, after the government eased restrictions on Roman Catholics, Hungary and the Vatican reestablished diplomatic relations, severed since 1945.

Throughout the year, Hungary reaffirmed and pursued its ultimate goal of integration with the European Community through participation in the meetings of smaller like-minded regional organizations, such as the summit of the five "Pentagon" nations (i.e., Hungary, Czechoslovakia, Austria, Yugoslavia, and Italy) in Venice in July and August. In November the Council of Europe admitted Hungary as its 24th member nation, the first former Warsaw Pact member to be accepted.

Continued violence against and other alleged mistreatment of the 2 million ethnic Hungarians in Romania brought diplomatic protests and a call for UN intervention from Hungary, and mass demonstrations in Budapest. Hungary also revived dual citizenship for Romanians of Hungarian descent, abolished in 1979. Hungary and Czechoslovakia agreed on fair and humane treatment for their ethnic Slovak and Magyar minorities.

JOSEPH FREDERICK ZACEK
State University of New York at Albany

ICELAND

The year 1990 in Iceland was marked by the development of closer ties to the European Community (EC) and by efforts to diversify the country's economy.

Prime Minister Steingrímur Hermannsson, leading a trade mission to Cairo, Egypt, in March, made a special trip to Tunis, Tunisia, to meet with Palestinian leader Yasir Arafat, and urged Western nations to take prompt steps toward resolving the Israeli-Palestinian conflict. Both Hermannsson and Foreign Minister Jón Baldvin Hannibalsson expressed support for the independence efforts of Latvia, Lithuania, and Estonia, and suggested they be admitted to international organizations such as the Nordic Council as soon as possible.

EC Contacts. The year 1990 was designated officially as European Travel Year, and Iceland's President Vigdís Finnbogadóttir was asked to preside over numerous congresses, trade fairs, and other events. In June she welcomed Britain's Queen Elizabeth II to Iceland. Although relations between Britain and Iceland were strained in the 1960s and 1970s by the

---

ICELAND • Information Highlights

Official Name: Republic of Iceland.
Location: North Atlantic Ocean.
Area: 39,768 sq mi (103 000 km²).
Population (mid-1990 est.): 300,000.
Chief Cities (Dec. 1, 1987): Reykjavík, the capital, 93,425; Akureyri, 13,856.
Government: *Head of state,* Vigdís Finnbogadóttir, president (took office Aug. 1980). *Head of government,* Steingrímur Hermannsson, prime minister (took office Sept. 1988). *Legislature*—Althing: Upper House and Lower House.
Monetary Unit: Króna (56.580 krónur equal U.S.$1, selling rate, August 1990).
Gross Domestic Product (1989 est. U.S.$): $4,000,-000,000.
Foreign Trade (1989 U.S.$): *Imports,* $1,396,000,000; *exports,* $1,409,000,000.

"Cod Wars" (disputes over fishing rights in Icelandic waters), Britain is now the largest single export market for Iceland's fishing industry.

French President François Mitterrand visited Iceland in September, signing agreements for extensive cultural exchanges between Iceland and France, and holding discussions with Icelandic leaders on Iceland's growing trade contacts with the EC.

Economy. A significant reduction in the inflation rate was achieved after representatives of the government, employers, and unions reached a new wage settlement in February. The gross domestic product (GDP) rose by only 1%, while foreign-currency earnings dropped by almost 3%, only a slight improvement after the repeated decreases of the previous two years. Major fish stocks such as cod and capelin were reportedly on a downswing, according to the Marine Research Institute, and there was little prospect for increased catch quotas. Fish-farming production increased by some 250%, but dropping world market prices for salmon and trout forced several of the largest enterprises into bankruptcy.

New liberalizing legislation on banking and capital movements passed by the government in the spring will remove all restrictions on Icelandic investment abroad and open the way for foreign investment in Iceland in stages during 1990–92.

Faced with a surplus of hydroelectric power when the new Blanda power project comes into full swing in 1991 and 1992, the Icelandic government signed an interim agreement for a new aluminum smelter after three years of negotiations with Atlantal, a consortium of three aluminum producers: Alumax of the United States, Gränges of Sweden, and Hoogovens of the Netherlands. Construction of the new 200-ton-capacity smelter using 350 megawatts of electricity was scheduled to begin in the spring of 1991.

KENEVA KUNZ
BBC Foreign Correspondent, Reykjavik

IDAHO

Idaho made national news during its centennial year when its legislature passed what would have been the nation's most restrictive law regulating abortions. Gov. Cecil Andrus (D) turned off the spotlight by vetoing the bill eight days later. Andrus went on to win a fourth term in a landslide victory that also saw Democrats capture both of the state's seats in the U.S. House of Representatives and tie with Republicans for control of the state Senate.

Legislature. State legislators convened in January with an extra $125 million in surplus revenue to spend, and a general-fund budget request from Governor Andrus totaling $1 billion. But the yearly battle of the budget took a back seat to the drive to outlaw all abortions other than those required to save the life of the mother or terminating pregnancies resulting from rape or incest.

Andrus, long a vocal opponent of legal abortion, on March 30 vetoed legislation approved by the Republican-controlled legislature, saying he found it poorly written and unable to withstand constitutional challenge. Pro-life forces branded the governor a traitor and vowed to unseat him.

Elections. Republicans found themselves unable to enlist a strong opponent to Andrus, who enjoyed high popularity as he basked in the limelight of a series of centennial celebrations throughout the state. Republican Roger Fairchild, former majority leader of the state Senate, claimed only 34% of the vote, leaving Andrus with an overwhelming mandate for what he said would be his final term.

The U.S. Senate seat vacated by Republican James McClure was captured easily by 1st District Rep. Larry Craig (R), who inherited much of McClure's campaign organization. But Republican state Sen. Skip Smyser was unable to claim Craig's House seat, losing a bitterly fought contest to Democratic Boise stockbroker Larry LaRocco, a former aide to the late Sen. Frank Church. Democratic Rep. Richard Stallings easily won reelection in the 2d District.

Larry EchoHawk, 42, a full-blooded Pawnee Indian, returned the attorney general's office to Democratic hands. And Democratic legislative candidates unseated enough Republicans—including some responsible for the abortion bill earlier in the year—to leave leadership of the tied Senate in doubt, although Republican Lt. Gov. Butch Otter remained in office to break the tie in party-line votes.

Environment. In late January, Governor Andrus abandoned his support of the federal legislation he had written with Senator McClure that would establish 1.4 million acres (566 000 ha) of additional Idaho wilderness.

Battles raged in neighboring Washington and Oregon during the year over efforts to save the northern spotted owl from loss of its habitat to logging of old-growth forests. The potential for similar protection to restore depleted salmon runs in dam-choked rivers in and downstream from Idaho in other states loomed on the horizon as the year ended.

JIM FISHER
"Lewiston Morning Tribune"

ILLINOIS

Illinois elected its first new governor in 14 years as Jim Edgar, a protégé of outgoing Republican Gov. James R. Thompson, won a narrow victory over Democrat Neil Hartigan.

The Elections. The hardfisted gubernatorial campaign ended with Republican Edgar, the Illinois secretary of state, winning just 51% of the vote. He said his victory proved that politicians who "level with voters about taxes before the election" can win. Hartigan, the state's attorney general, had promised to trim state spending and roll back the Illinois income-tax surcharge. The temporary surcharge provides about $370 million annually for schools. Edgar refused to promise he would cut taxes or abate the surcharge if elected governor.

The election of Edgar ended the 14-year reign in Springfield of "Big Jim" Thompson, the state's longest-serving governor. Thompson's dreams of national office faded in 1988, and in his last year as governor, he drew wide criticism for his frequent and costly foreign-trade missions at taxpayers' expense. The critics charged Thompson seldom brought back many economic benefits for Illinois from his globe-trotting.

Meanwhile, U.S. Sen. Paul Simon, a liberal Democrat, easily won reelection over U.S. Rep. Lynn Martin of Rockford. Simon said his 30% margin over Martin would not tempt him to try for the presidency in 1992, as he did in 1988. "If I had decided to become a presiden-

Republican Jim Edgar, Illinois' secretary of state and a protégé of outgoing Gov. James Thompson, narrowly defeated state Attorney General Neil Hartigan, the Democratic candidate, in the Illinois gubernatorial race.

Office of the Governor-Elect

tial candidate I would not have run for reelection,'' Simon said after his November victory. ''That's the simple reality.'' Simon also said his big win proved that legislators with liberal and populist agendas still can win elections. In the race for the U.S. House of Representatives in the 16th District, the seat vacated by Lynn Martin, county prosecutor John Cox scored a major win. He would be the first Democrat to represent the district in 135 years. Otherwise, incumbent members of the U.S. House were reelected. In December, President Bush named Representative Martin to succeed Elizabeth Dole as secretary of labor.

In other significant Illinois elections, Charles Freeman, an appellate-court judge in Chicago, became the first black to be elected to the Illinois Supreme Court. Another Democrat, Dawn Clark Netsch of Chicago, was elected state comptroller to become the first woman to win statewide office in Illinois.

Tornadoes. A cluster of tornadoes that came without warning roared through Will County, near Chicago, on August 28, killing 29 people and injuring hundreds. In Plainfield, the midafternoon disaster leveled the local high school and the St. Mary Immaculate Catholic Church and its rectory, gymnasium, and school. Three persons died at Plainfield High School and three died at the St. Mary's School. The twisters grew out of some thunderstorms passing over northeast Illinois and spread across 12 mi (19 km) from Oswego to Joliet.

McDome. Illinois legislators wrestled with proposals for the $1.4 billion expansion of McCormick Place in Chicago. McDome, as the project is called, would expand convention space at McCormick Place and provide a domed stadium for concerts and the Chicago Bears football games. But it was a political hot potato for the legislators, who were asked to approve an $80 million-per-year financing plan for McDome. The tax package was defeated early in the year, as lawmakers feared a voter backlash in the November elections, and again after the election at a special legislative session.

Neither Mayor Richard M. Daley of Chicago nor Governor-elect Edgar were backing McDome with much enthusiasm. Daley was facing reelection in 1991 and apparently did not want to take a political gamble, and Edgar was reluctant to back a proposal raising taxes in his first year in office. However, backers of McDome argued that the expansion was necessary if Chicago is to compete with new convention centers and domed arenas in other cities. They maintained the new facility would create 14,000 new jobs, $100 million annually in new tax revenue, and generate $2 billion more each year in new economic activity for Illinois. Opponents said the money could be better spent on education, social welfare programs, better highways, and other Illinois needs.

See also CHICAGO.

ROBERT ENSTAD, *"Chicago Tribune"*

ILLINOIS • Information Highlights

Area: 56,345 sq mi (145 934 km²).
Population (1990 census prelim.): 11,325,000.
Chief Cities (July 1, 1988 est.): Springfield, the capital (1986 est.), 100,290; Chicago, 2,977,520; Rockford, 134,500.
Government (1990): *Chief Officers*—governor, James R. Thompson (R); lt. gov., George H. Ryan (R). *General Assembly*—Senate, 59 members; House of Representatives, 118 members.
State Finances (fiscal year 1989): *Revenue,* $22,243,000,000; *expenditure,* $20,346,000,000.
Personal Income (1989): $219,448,000,000; per capita, $18,824.
Labor Force (June 1990): *Civilian labor force,* 6,058,600; *unemployed,* 369,600 (6.1% of total force).
Education: *Enrollment* (fall 1988)—public elementary schools, 1,259,124; public secondary 535,792; colleges and universities, 688,974. *Public school expenditures* (1989–90), $7,560,057,000.

AP/Wide World

Just sworn in as India's new prime minister, Chandra Shekhar (left) *is congratulated by his predecessor and political rival V.P. Singh. The Singh government lasted 11 months.*

INDIA

India's political and social scene became increasingly chaotic in 1990. After decisively defeating Rajiv Gandhi and the Congress(I) party in the ninth general elections in November 1989, Vishwanath Pratap Singh (*see* BIOGRAPHY) and the National Front government, allied with the Bharatiya Janata party (BJP) and two Communist parties, encountered increasing difficulties. Among the problems were divisions in the National Front, the alienation of the BJP, growing crises in Kashmir and Punjab, a caste war over the government's decision to extend special reservations of government jobs to lower castes, and a communal-cum-religious struggle precipitated by demands of Hindu fundamentalists. On November 7, after a vote of no confidence in the Lok Sabha (India's lower house of parliament), Singh resigned. His successor was his main political rival, Chandra Shekhar, leader of a breakaway faction of the Janata Dal party, who had the support, at least temporarily, of the Congress(I) and the BJP.

State Elections. Elections on February 27 in eight states and one union territory temporarily strengthened the National Front government and further weakened the Congress(I) party.

The Congress, which had controlled all of these states, was able to get a majority in only one—Arunachal Pradesh. In Maharashtra it was still the largest party, and with the help of independents was able to form a government. The BJP won majorities in Himachal Pradesh and Madhya Pradesh, and V. P. Singh's Janata Dal, the main party in the National Front, won 123 of 147 seats in Orissa. The BJP and Janata Dal formed coalition governments in Bihar, Gujarat, and Rajasthan.

Two aspects of the February 27 elections, aside from the Congress(I) reverses, were particularly noteworthy. Between 80 and 100 people were killed and hundreds were injured in the worst violence in any Indian election. The election results called attention to the growing influence of the BJP, a development that created continuing problems for V. P. Singh and further violence during the year.

Crises in Kashmir and Punjab. That escalating political and social violence would be a major feature of the troubled year was indicated even before the February 27 elections. In January the deepening crisis in Kashmir flared up into large-scale confrontations between Kashmiri separatists and Indian security forces. Some separatists sought a higher degree of autonomy within the Indian union. Others, who gradually won widespread support, demanded separation from India, and either union with Pakistan or an independent state.

On January 19, Farooq Abdullah—son of Sheikh Abdullah, the longtime "Lion of Kashmir"—who had become chief minister with the support of the Congress(I), resigned. The central government appointed a new governor, Jagmohan, who took a tough stance on the conflict in Kashmir. Before the end of the year, 150,000 Indian army troops and paramilitary forces were sent to Kashmir, mainly to Srinagar, the capital and center of the conflict.

In late January six foreign journalists were expelled, and thereafter access to the state by foreigners was forbidden almost completely. In spite—or perhaps because—of the stern policies of Governor Jagmohan and the central Indian government, large demonstrations, usually accompanied by violence and often by deaths, were frequent. Acts of violence and protest marches were set off by the assassination of the vice-chancellor of the University of Kashmir on April 8 and of the imam of the largest mosque in Srinagar on May 21. A week after the imam's murder, Jagmohan resigned and was replaced by Girish Saxena. On July 18, Kashmir was placed under direct rule by the central government. All of these developments failed to quell the upsurge of violence in Kashmir. By early October it was reported that some 1,500 people had died in the conflict.

The deteriorating situation was a particularly severe blow to Prime Minister Singh, who had pledged to restore law and order in Kashmir and Punjab. He and other government officials and the Indian press accused Pakistan of aiding and abetting the Kashmiri separatists—charges that Pakistan denied, while also expressing sympathy for the separatists' cause in the Indian-held part of Kashmir.

Among the many unfortunate results of the disturbances were the increasing tensions between India and Pakistan, the growth of anti-India sentiment in Kashmir, a widening gap between Hindus and Muslims, and the exodus of some 100,000 Hindus from the state.

In Punjab the violence and agitation had equally tragic consequences. V. P. Singh had hoped to reverse the disaffection that had been recurrent in this major state ever since June 1984, when Indian troops stormed the Golden Temple complex in Amritsar—the holiest of Sikh shrines—to oust Sikh extremists. Unlike Rajiv Gandhi, Singh made several visits to Punjab, with minimum security, and made significant concessions to the Sikh dissidents. He promised to hold long-delayed elections in Punjab, but due to the continued conflict, emergency rule, already in effect for many months, was extended for an additional six months in April. In July killings by Sikh extremists in Punjab reached an all-time high of 300. By late September it was reported that nearly 2,000 people had been killed.

Caste and Religious Conflict. Two other episodes in 1990—one that might be described as a caste war, the other a product of Hindu-Muslim tensions—created serious social and communal conflict and contributed to the growing difficulties of V. P. Singh and his National Front government. These were the reservation issue and the Ayodhya controversy.

On August 7, Prime Minister Singh announced that his government would reserve 27% of all central government jobs for members of the "socially and educationally backward classes." This would be in addition to the 22.5% of government jobs and university places already reserved for "scheduled castes" and "scheduled tribes." Protests against this decision were immediate, widespread, and vehement, mainly by young members of middle and higher castes for whom, in a period of high unemployment, government jobs would be even more difficult to obtain. In a few weeks more than 80 young men tried to commit protest suicides by soaking their clothes with kerosene and setting themselves on fire, or by taking poison. Thirty died and about 40 others were killed in clashes with police. Even though his new reservationist policy was a belated attempt to implement a decade-old recommendation of a high-level government commission, Singh was criticized harshly for it, even by some members of his own party; but he adhered adamantly to the policy at great political and personal cost.

The Ayodhya crisis also had serious social and political repercussions in 1990. For some months militant Hindu fundamentalists had demanded the right to tear down a mosque in the holy city of Ayodhya in the state of Uttar Pradesh and to construct a Hindu temple on the site. The mosque was built in the 16th century, during the reign of the Mogul emperor Babar. Devout Hindus believe that the god Rama was born in what is now Ayodhya, perhaps on the site where the mosque is located.

Demands to replace the mosque with a temple reached a climax in October and early November. V. P. Singh's government warned that the mosque's destruction would not be permitted, but the BJP supported the demands of the Hindu fundamentalists. When the leader of the BJP, L. K. Advani, joined demonstrators on their way to Ayodhya, he was arrested promptly. This led the BJP to withdraw its support of the National Front, leaving the Front

AP/Wide World

Implementing the decade-old recommendations of the Mandal Commission, Prime Minister Singh in August said that his government would reserve a percentage of central government jobs for "socially and educationally backward classes." The decision led to widespread protests and civil disorder.

without a majority in the Indian parliament and thereby precipitating the fall of the government. Thus a major Hindu-Muslim dispute led to a political crisis in India, and to at least 300 deaths and the arrest of more than 100,000 demonstrators. Some Indians felt that these developments threatened the secular foundations of the Indian state.

Political Crises. Before V. P. Singh became a political victim of this religious-cum-communal conflict, he already was experiencing difficulties in holding his shaky coalition together. On March 16 about two and one-half weeks after the strong showing of the National Front and the BJP in the February 27 state elections, a major split developed in the top leadership of the Front. Deputy Prime Minister Devi Lal came under attack both from the party and the public and resigned on March 16. Although he was persuaded by V. P. Singh to withdraw his resignation two days later, the episode revealed the deep fissures in the shaky coalition that Singh headed. In July, Devi Lal came under further attack for engineering the return of his son, Om Prakash Chautala, as chief minister of the state of Haryana. Chautala had taken over as chief minister when his father resigned the post to join the National Front government, on Dec. 2, 1989, but the son had been forced to resign on May 22. Thirteen ministers resigned from the National Front government in July and Chautala once again resigned as chief minister of Haryana. The next day Singh himself, stating that he had lost the confidence of some of the Front's top leaders, wrote a letter of resignation to the president of his party, but he soon yielded to demands that he remain in office. On August 1 he dismissed Devi Lal, causing another political crisis.

In August, Singh found himself embroiled in the protests over his new reservations policy and in October in the crisis over the mosque-temple dispute in Ayodhya. These crises proved to be his political undoing—or at least they were the climax of political troubles that had been building up since he took office in December 1989.

Singh resigned on November 7, following a decisive defeat on a no-confidence resolution in the Lok Sabha. The president of India, Ramaswamy Venkataraman, asked Rajiv Gandhi, leader of the major opposition party, to try to form a coalition government. Gandhi declined but offered to give "outside support" to Chandra Shekhar, leader of a dissident faction in the Janata Dal, called the Janata Dal-Socialist. This veteran socialist leader was sworn in as prime minister on November 10, but his continued stay in office was dependent on the continued "outside support" of the Congress(I) and the BJP. Rajiv Gandhi again became the most powerful figure in Indian politics, without assuming the burden of office at a very troubled period in India's political history.

The Economy. Among the most disturbing negative aspects of the economic situation were the budget and trade deficits, declining foreign-exchange reserves, increasing external debt (about $70 billion to $80 billion, making it the fourth-largest in the world), the adverse impact of the Persian Gulf crisis, an increase in inflation to about 10%, a sharp rise in prices, and increasing unemployment. Encouraging aspects included a rise in exports, record foodgrain production of about 180 million tons—thanks largely to excellent monsoons for the third year in a row, and an overall growth rate of about 5% with 8% to 8.5% growth in the industrial sector.

An ambitious new five-year plan (the eighth) was launched. There was some improvement in the investment climate, but foreign investment remained quite low. Prospective investors complained about India's heavily planned and protected economy, and the innumerable barriers to foreign investment and enterprises. While continuing to recommend and coordinate substantial aid for India, the World Bank urged the Indian government to move more rapidly toward economic liberalization, and to halt the growth of government bureaucracy. In June the World Bank warned that India's economy was "at a crossroads."

The budget for 1990–91, presented to parliament by Finance Minister Madhu Dandavate on March 16, showed a marked rural bias, with special emphasis on agriculture and rural development and employment projects. Another announced objective was "to restrain the budgetary deficit and contain the inflationary pressures." Both direct and indirect taxes were increased, with heavier levies on the more affluent, and with some relief for low-and medium-income groups. Total expenditures for 1990–91 were estimated at about $55.6 billion and total revenues at $51.4 billion, leaving a deficit of approximately $4.2 billion. (For 1989–

INDIA • Information Highlights

Official Name: Republic of India.
Location: South Asia.
Area: 1,269,340 sq mi (3 287 590 km²).
Population (mid-1990 est.): 853,400,000.
Chief Cities (1981 census): New Delhi, the capital, 273,036; Bombay, 8,243,405; Calcutta, 3,305,006.
Government: *Head of state,* Ramaswamy Venkataraman, president (took office July 25, 1987). *Head of government,* Chandra Shekhar, prime minister (took office Nov. 10, 1990). *Legislature*—Parliament: Rajya Sabha (Council of States) and Lok Sabha (House of the People).
Monetary Unit: Rupee (18.181 rupees equal U.S.$1, official rate, Dec. 20, 1990).
Gross National Product (1989 est. U.S.$): $333,000,000,000.
Economic Indexes (1989): *Consumer Prices* (1980 = 100), all items, 216.2; food, 214.7. *Industrial Production* (1980 = 100), 188.
Foreign Trade (1989 U.S.$): *Imports,* $18,998,000,000; *exports,* $15,982,000,000.

90 the deficit was about $5.65 billion.) Defense expenditures were projected at $8.25 billion, a substantial increase from $7.6 billion in 1989–90. Nearly half of the total expenditures was allotted to interest payments, the new five-year plan, and defense. It was estimated that 64% of the receipts would come from internal borrowing and excise and customs taxes.

Iraq's invasion and annexation of Kuwait in August had many adverse effects on India. Financial costs alone in 1990 were estimated at between $2.5 billion and $4 billion. The social dislocation, disruption of the economy, added political problems, and an increase in regional tensions were perhaps even more serious. Between 180,000 and 185,000 Indian workers were stranded in Iraq and Kuwait. The Indian government was faced with major financial, logistical, and political problems—to get food and medical supplies to its citizens in Kuwait and Iraq, to repatriate them as quickly as possible, and to provide for their resettlement and employment on their return to India. The loss of remittances from Indian workers in the two Gulf countries, which had been a major source of family support and foreign exchange, was another financial blow. India also was affected adversely by the rise in oil prices and the abrupt termination of supply from Iraq and Kuwait, which had supplied nearly 50% of its imports of crude oil and petroleum products.

Foreign Policy. Internal and external conditions led to increasingly nationalistic orientations in foreign policy and to increasing attention to relations with the neighboring countries of South Asia. India feared that it no longer could depend as heavily as it had in recent years on the Soviet Union for economic, political, and military support. The nation began to reexamine even its long-standing orientation toward nonalignment, giving this orientation a new meaning and new directions without abandoning it.

Both V. P. Singh and Pakistan Prime Minister Benazir Bhutto had pledged to do their utmost to improve relations between the two countries. For a time in late 1989 and early 1990, they seemed to be moving toward an easing of tensions and greater cooperation; but soon their difficulties in maintaining political support within their own countries made it virtually impossible for them to take the "high road" in Indo-Pakistan relations. Before the end of the year both had fallen from power. Their successors seemed to be catering to strong nationalist and fundamentalist groups and pressures in their own countries, and to be taking a more belligerent line in foreign as well as domestic affairs.

The fact is that Indo-Pakistan relations in 1990 plummeted to one of the lowest levels in recent years. Tensions became so great that many observers in both countries openly talked of a possible fourth war. Punjab continued to be one focus of strained relations. India accused Pakistan of encouraging the Sikh extremists and of allowing arms and other aid to enter Punjab through Pakistan. Tensions reached a near breaking point because of the escalating crisis in the Indian-occupied part of Kashmir, and Pakistan's alleged role in encouraging and assisting the Muslim separatists there. The BJP, a nominal ally of the National Front government until October, long had taken a militant stand toward Pakistan. The BJP embarrassed the government by calling for military strikes into the Pakistan-occupied part of Kashmir. After the fall of both Benazir Bhutto and V. P. Singh, the danger of another Indo-Pakistan war seemed to be greater than ever.

Relations with Sri Lanka improved after representatives of the two countries, in January, agreed to sign a treaty of friendship to replace the controversial India-Sri Lanka accord of 1987, and after the withdrawal in March of the last of the Indian peacekeeping forces. (The Indian army had been sent to the northern and eastern provinces of Sri Lanka to assist the Sri Lankan government in disarming the Liberation Tigers of Tamil Eelam.) Indo-Sri Lankan relations continued to be complicated by the presence in India, mainly in Tamil Nadu, of many thousands of Sri Lankan refugees, mostly Tamils and Muslims. The flood of refugees became even greater after the withdrawal of Indian troops.

After two days of talks in July with the prime minister of Nepal, Krishna Prasad Bhattarai, Singh agreed to lift the 15-month embargo on trade, to reopen the border posts, and to enter into negotiations for new trade and transit treaties. This ended a prolonged period of tension between the two countries.

During 1990 the United States frequently expressed its concern over the mounting tensions between India and Pakistan. In late April the U.S. trade representative, Carla Hills, announced that India would remain on the list of "unfair trading partners," while the only other countries so designated in 1989–90, Brazil and Japan, no longer would be listed. This created considerable resentment in India, somewhat mitigated by President George Bush's subsequent decision not to impose higher tariffs on Indian imports. The United States is India's leading trading partner, with a considerable trade deficit in its trade with India. In January, Dr. Karan Singh resigned as India's ambassador to the United States. His successor was Dr. Abid Hussain.

In July, Prime Minister Singh led a large delegation on an official visit to Moscow. External Affairs Minister K. J. Gujral was particularly active in international diplomacy. In August he visited Bangladesh, Jordan, the Soviet Union, and the United States.

NORMAN D. PALMER, *Professor Emeritus*
University of Pennsylvania

INDIANA

Off-year election results reaffirmed the resurgence of the Democratic Party in Indiana in 1990 and attested to the increasing political strength of Democratic Gov. B. Evan Bayh. The General Assembly's 30-day, alternate-year short session produced significant legislation. Natural disasters and an economic downturn also headlined events in 1990.

Election. Even as Republican Sen. Dan Coats, appointed in 1988 to fill the vacated seat of Vice-President J. Danforth Quayle, defeated challenger Baron Hill by more than 100,000 votes to retain his seat for the remaining two years of Quayle's original term, Democratic gains in Indiana overshadowed Republican victories in key senatorial and state-office races. Incumbent Republicans also won two of four contested state offices by substantial margins, but in a historic race for secretary of state, Democrat Joseph H. Hogsett, Governor Bayh's campaign manager in 1986 and 1988, captured 52% of the vote to stun four-time Indianapolis Mayor William H. Hudnut III, whom the GOP had touted as their standard-bearer for the 1992 gubernatorial race. Dwayne M. Brown (D), another Bayh supporter, was elected clerk of the Indiana Supreme Court and Court of Appeals, becoming the first black to hold a state office in Indiana. Republicans held the remainder of the uncontested state offices.

For the first time since 1977–78, party control was split in the General Assembly. Republicans retained their 26–24 advantage in the state Senate; Democrats, with four of the seats contested, claimed the House by a margin of 53–47, their first outright control in 14 years. With political districts' reapportionment scheduled for the 1991 session, a partisan fight could

develop. The defeat of incumbent Republican Rep. John Hiler in the 3d District increased the number of Indiana Democrats in the U.S. House to eight of ten.

Legislature. Amid partisan bickering and boycotts that threatened a legislative breakdown, the Indiana General Assembly reduced the state's hated motor-vehicle excise tax by as much as 30%; enacted a series of antidrug laws; and provided environmental legislation that sets recycling goals, regulates out-of-state waste dumped in Indiana, and establishes solid-waste planning districts for handling trash disposal. Legislators also enacted the administration's 21st Century Scholars program that provides money for college for underprivileged teenagers who fulfill certain pledges, including avoiding illegal drugs.

Educational funding dominated the supplemental budget debate. In a reversal of roles, Republicans favored larger expenditures than

AP/Wide World

In early June tornadoes touched down in several parts of southern Indiana. A major twister struck the town of Petersburg (left), where six persons were killed, two thirds of the town was damaged or destroyed, and hundreds were left homeless.

Democratic legislators and Governor Bayh, whose insistence on no tax increases was popular with Hoosier voters. The compromise $213.6 million budget was passed at the last minute under a rare rules suspension. Democrats accepted the administration's lower $9.3 million figure for tuition support for local schools only after Bayh agreed to cut $4 million from his economic-development package. Also included in the budget were $8 million for faculty salaries at state universities; $6.4 million for the educational Prime Time program; $33 million to replace cutbacks in federal catastrophic health care; and $56 million for the construction of a new prison, plus $10 million for other correctional facilities and $2.5 million for child-welfare caseworkers.

Other. In the worst spring-tornado activity in 16 years, 50 funnels killed seven Hoosiers, injured 125, and inflicted extensive damage in 27 of Indiana's 92 counties. Nonetheless, agricultural production neared record levels. Depressed prices and an overall downswing in business, however, made 1990 less than a banner economic year for Indiana.

LORNA LUTES SYLVESTER
Indiana University, Bloomington

INDONESIA

In 1990, Indonesia continued to expand its role as an economic and political power in Southeast Asia.

Domestic Politics. For the first time there was open discussion about who would succeed President Suharto—the military man who has ruled the country since 1967, and is expected to retire in 1993. Parliamentary elections would precede the end of Suharto's term and, as the parliament elects the president, it was just possible that there might be a multiparty slate for the presidency. Among the potential candidates who already seemed to be campaigning discreetly were Home Affairs Minister Rudini, Vice-President Sudharmono, and Defense Minister Benny Murdani. Of course, everything would depend on Suharto's willingness to step down, and he himself has been ambiguous in his public statements about the matter.

The president's family business interests also became a topic of limited public discussion, but when the *International Herald Tribune* published an article on the subject, the issues carrying the article were banned and the journalist who wrote it was forbidden to enter the country.

Economy. Indonesia now was classified officially as a "middle-income country" by international institutions, and also was considered a potential newly industrializing country (NIC) by many market analysts. Encouraged by the country's economic growth and confident about its own ability to deal with it, the govern-

INDONESIA • Information Highlights

Official Name: Republic of Indonesia.
Location: Southeast Asia.
Area: 741,097 sq mi (1 919 440 km²).
Population (mid-1990 est.): 189,400,000.
Chief Cities (Dec. 31, 1983 est.): Jakarta, the capital, 7,347,800; Surabaya, 2,223,600; Medan, 1,805,500; Bandung, 1,566,700.
Government: *Head of state and government,* Suharto, president (took office for fifth five-year term March 1988). *Legislature* (unicameral)—House of Representatives.
Monetary Unit: Rupiah (1,889.0 rupiahs equal U.S.$1, Dec. 31, 1990).
Gross National Product (1989 est. U.S.$): $80,000,-000,000.
Economic Index (1989): *Consumer Prices* (1980 = 100), all items, 211.3; food, 219.5.
Foreign Trade (1988 U.S.$): *Imports,* $13,249,-000,000; *exports,* $19,218,000,000.

ment not only privatized the banking sector but also allowed private companies to move into television broadcasting, highway building, petrochemicals, and telecommunications. More industries were set to be turned over to the private sector in the near future.

While nearly 80% of Indonesia's population was living under very dense conditions in the islands of Java, Bali, and Sumatra, thousands of outlying islands remained undeveloped and very thinly populated. To correct this imbalance the government embarked on a number of projects in the other islands, particularly projects aimed at improving ports and communication facilities, and building new power plants.

Government statistics showed that foreign investment in the first half of 1990 was $4.6 billion, only a little less than the figure recorded for the same period in 1989. Exports in the latest period increased by 7.4%, to $11.2 billion.

An industrial park on Batam island, which was being developed jointly by Indonesia and Singapore, was expected to be in operation by the end of 1991. The space would be occupied by about 30 companies, most of them multinationals relocating from high-cost areas such as Singapore.

Foreign Affairs. The most important foreign-affairs event in 1990 was the reestablishment of full diplomatic relations between Indonesia and China for the first time in more than 20 years. China's Prime Minister Li Peng visited Indonesia in August and Suharto visited China in November. Relations with China would allow Indonesia to play a more active mediating role in regional affairs, particularly in the effort to resolve the conflict between competing factions in Cambodia, which continued in 1990, and in disputes over the exploration of mineral resources in the South China Sea. In late 1989, Indonesia concluded the "Timor Gap Treaty" with Australia, an agreement on sharing the mineral wealth of the Timor Sea.

N. BALAKRISHNAN
"The Far Eastern Economic Review"

© Courtesy, Sun Hill Industries

Sun Hill Industries of Stamford, CT, introduced an entire line of Stuff-A-Pumpkins. The plastic bags that can be filled with lawn rakings were a Halloween 1990 success story.

INDUSTRIAL PRODUCTION

The 1990 economic slowdown in the United States had a telling effect on industrial production. While West Germany, the Netherlands, Belgium, Austria, Japan, and Switzerland were among industrial countries posting respectable gains, joining the United States in lackluster performance were Great Britain, Canada, Australia, Sweden, Spain, and Italy. The command economies such as the USSR and the East European countries struggling to switch over to market-oriented economics experienced severe declines in industrial output.

U.S. industrial production in the final stretch of 1990 declined for four months in a row, posting some of the steepest drops since the recession year 1982. Still, industrial production for all of 1990 posted a 1.3% gain, after gaining 2.6% in 1989. The Federal Reserve Board's (FRB's) index was revised and the base period was moved to 1987, the most recent year of the census of business.

Transportation. The U.S. transportation group reflected both brisk demand from abroad and a domestic slump. While the automotive sector posted declines of 5%, the aircraft industry racked up gains of similar magnitude. As for U.S. auto assemblies, the total for 1989 was 7.104 million, and that was 4% fewer than in 1988. For 1990 the drop was 10%. About 1.25 million of the cars assembled in the United States were produced in Japanese transplant facilities. Truck production held up a little better: Some 3.6 million were assembled in 1990, down 6% from 1989.

Orders for large commercial aircraft boosted the fortunes of Boeing and McDonnell Douglas. They delivered a total of 540 large commercial airplanes in 1990, a 45% advance from 1989. The industry's total shipments rose 15.5% to $108 billion. While the large civil-transport business boomed, the military and general aviation production did not do so well. The number of military planes delivered declined 4% to about 980, and general aviation deliveries dropped 20% to about 1,200. The number of military-airframe makers was likely to drop as a result of federal budget cuts. There also was new competition for military export markets. The USSR actively was seeking export sales for its newest technology aircraft, such as the MiG-27 and the MiG-29. Taiwan tested its Indigenous Defense Fighter developed to replace its aging U.S.-made fleet. India planned to build a new fighter, and Embraer of Brazil was developing a fighter-bomber designed in partnership with Italian firms.

Steel. The U.S. steel industry showed surprising resilience in 1990 despite slowing U.S. economic activity. Steelmakers poured 97.9 million tons of raw metal in 1989 and shipped 84.1 million tons of mill products. They matched that record in 1990. The amount of steel shipped equaled that of ten years earlier, and it was done with only half the work force of 1980, a result of successful efforts to raise productivity.

Nonferrous Metals. Facing intense competition in both domestic and international markets, U.S. companies have emerged as competitive producers of primary aluminum. They increased exports of ingots by nearly 50% in 1990, while imports were unchanged. Total shipments, however, did drop by 6.5% to 6.8 million tons. The industry increasingly relies on value-added products such as composite materials, fiber-aluminum laminates for the aerospace industry, and metal-matrix composites where aluminum is the matrix metal.

U.S. copper production was changed little from the 1.9 million tons of primary and secondary refined metal turned out in 1989. Fiber-optic telecommunications cable, sometimes cited as a competitive threat to copper consumption, actually may create additional demand for the metal: Fiber-optic cable cannot be used yet to transmit electricity needed to generate light for the signal.

The U.S. nonferrous industry as a group registered a 3.4% increase on the FRB production index in 1989, but dropped 1.3% for 1990.

Fuels. Despite the crisis in the Persian Gulf caused by Iraq's invasion of Kuwait, no physical shortages of petroleum occurred, although war fears sporadically drove prices to record levels. Although production by the Organization of the Petroleum Exporting Countries (OPEC) hit a low for the year in August, pumping 20 million barrels per day, output by members other than Iraq and Kuwait was boosted quickly to a daily rate of some 23 million barrels. U.S. coal production, the traditional beneficiary of crises in the Middle East, reached the 1-billion-ton mark, after turning out 980 million tons in 1989. U.S. coal accounts for 35% of the world's proven reserves.

Construction. U.S. building activity slowed considerably in 1990. New construction accounted for 8% of the gross national product (GNP) compared with 11.9% in 1986, the post-World War II peak. U.S. housing starts dropped 12% to 1.2 million, the lowest level since the recession year of 1982. While starts of single-family homes declined 9%, apartment starts plummeted by more than 20%. Although new construction of residential buildings declined, repair and remodeling work grew briskly, helping to limit the decline in U.S. residential construction to 5%. Reflecting overbuilding in the 1980s, U.S. office construction dropped 12% and commercial-building activity declined 5%. Public construction advanced 6% in volume, with educational structures up by 14%. Other substantial increases were recorded for the construction of hospitals, water-supply facilities, and other public buildings, including prisons and general administrative buildings.

Capital Spending. After increasing investment in new plant and equipment by 11.4% in 1989 to a total $507.4 billion, U.S. industries reduced the rate of investment growth to 5.3%

in 1990. A few industries stepped up capital spending considerably: The air-transportation industry boosted outlays by 37%, after a 19.5% increase in 1989; electrical-machinery producers posted a 10% growth, after cutting new investment by 1.8% in 1989. Nonferrous-metals producers raised investment by 9.3%, following a 5.2% increase. The communications group's investment grew by 9.3%, after a 7.0% gain.

U.S. manufacturing as a group showed a 5.3% increase in spending on new plant and equipment, a slowdown from the 12.5% advance in 1989. The slowdown was most pronounced in the nondurables group where the overall increase was 7%, compared with 17.2% in 1989. The paper industry, which had increased spending by 42.7% in 1989, expanded by 12.9% in 1990. The food and beverage industry's advance shrank to 7.8%, compared with 12.3%. Textiles registered a 5.1% decline in contrast with a 3.2% gain shown for 1989. Chemicals reduced the rate of increase to 2.6%, following an 11.1% investment increase in the preceding year. Petroleum industry's investment advanced by 10%, following a gain of 15%. Rubber and plastics producers cut spending by 3%, following a 16.3% increase in 1989.

U.S. durable-goods producers increased capital spending by 3%, after posting a 7.2% addition in 1989. The stone, clay, and glass group reversed direction with a 15.5% reduc-

U.S. Industrial Production			
	Percent Change 1988 to 1989	Index (1987=100) 1990 level	Percent* Change 1989 to 1990
Total Production	2.6	108.1	1.3
Mining	−1.3	100.5	1.7
Utilities	2.9	107.0	1.4
Manufacturing	2.9	108.9	1.2
Consumer Goods	2.6	106.7	0.8
Business Equipment	6.6	119.7	3.4
Defense and Space Equipment	−0.6	97.4	−0.1
Durable Goods Manufacturing	3.1	110.9	1.1
Lumber and products	−1.5	103.1	−1.3
Furniture and fixtures	1.6	105.3	1.7
Primary metals	−1.0	109.2	0.0
Fabricated metal products	1.0	107.2	−0.7
Nonelectrical machinery	7.0	121.8	4.4
Electrical machinery	2.9	109.5	2.2
Transportation equipment	1.9	107.2	−0.6
Nondurable Goods Manufacturing	2.7	106.4	1.3
Foods	2.6	105.5	1.5
Tobacco products	−1.7	99.6	−2.4
Textile mill products	2.1	101.9	−0.4
Apparel products	2.0	104.3	−4.4
Paper and paper products	0.3	103.2	1.3
Printing and publishing	4.8	108.5	2.8
Chemicals and products	3.0	108.5	1.8
Petroleum and products	2.5	106.1	2.9
Rubber and plastic products	2.8	108.9	2.1
Leather and products	4.2	103.7	−0.6

* Preliminary Estimate
Source: Board of Governors of the Federal Reserve System

Value of New Construction Put in Place in the United States (Billions of 1987 dollars)			
	1989	1990*	Percent Change
Total new construction	399.9	394.8	−1
Private construction	308.7	297.8	−3.5
Residential buildings	182.0	172.9	−5
Nonresidential buildings	126.7	124.9	−1
Industrial	17.2	18.9	10
Office	26.6	23.4	−12
Hotels and motels	7.1	7.5	5
Other commercial	28.6	27.2	−5
Religious	2.8	2.8	0
Educational	3.1	3.3	6
Hospital and institutional	7.0	7.4	5
Miscellaneous buildings[1]	3.7	3.6	−3
Telecommunications	8.2	8.5	4
All other private[2]	2.7	2.7	0
Public construction	91.4	97.0	6
Housing and redevelopment	3.5	3.6	1
Industrial	1.2	1.3	7
Educational	15.5	17.7	14
Hospital	2.3	2.5	10
Other public buildings[3]	13.8	15.2	10
Highways and streets	27.4	27.7	1
Military facilities	3.3	3.6	10
Conservation and development	4.6	4.7	2
Sewer systems	8.5	8.9	5
Water supply facilities	3.7	4.1	10
Miscellaneous public[4]	7.6	7.7	1

Source: Bureau of the Census   * Preliminary Estimate
[1] Includes amusement and recreational buildings, bus and airline terminals, animal hospitals, and shelters, etc.   [2] Includes privately owned streets and bridges, parking areas, sewer and water facilities, parks and playgrounds, golf courses, airfields, etc.   [3] Includes general administrative buildings, prisons, police and fire stations, courthouses, civic centers, passenger terminals, postal facilities.   [4] Includes open amusement and recreational facilities, power generating facilities, transit systems, airfields, open parking facilities, etc.

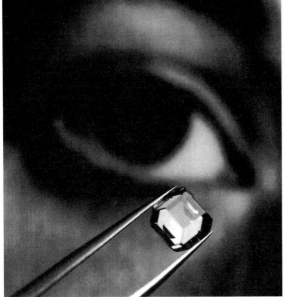
AP/Wide World

General Electric announced a new method of producing gem-quality diamonds for industrial use. The one-carat crystal conducts heat more efficiently than the natural diamond.

tion that followed a 10.2% gain. Transportation-equipment producers as a group swung investment into a 0.5% decline, following an 18.7% increase. Steelmakers cut the rate of increase to 2.4% from 12.3%. Fabricated metals were just about unchanged, compared with the 6.6% increase in 1989. Nonelectrical machinery posted a 1.3% advance, compared with 6.4%.

In U.S. nonmanufacturing, railroads, unlike airlines, reduced capital spending by 5%, after an increase of 13.4% in 1989. In mining, plant and equipment investment increased 7% after a 0.5% cutback in 1989. Trade and services showed a 5.7% increase, following a 12.4% expansion. Public utilities showed no overall change, after an increase of 9.8% in 1989. However, electric utilities reduced outlays by 1.7%, after a 9.6% advance. Gas utilities showed a moderate increase of 3.7%, following a 10.3% expansion in 1989.

International. While unification of Germany set off a boom in the West, with industrial production at year's end up about 6%, the former German Democratic Republic saw the production of its industry plummet by as much as 40% from the preceding year. Low productivity, as small as one third of that in West Germany, obsolete plants and equipment, and dated designs combined to render industry in the East uncompetitive. Much the same problems plagued industry in Poland, Czechoslovakia, Romania, and the other former Soviet-bloc nations, including the USSR itself.

U.S. industrial production at year's end was about 1% lower than the year before. Canada lagged by more than 4%; Great Britain and Spain were behind by more than 2% and 4%, respectively; and Sweden's output at year's end 1990 was 1% below 1989. In addition to

booming Germany, Japan saw its production at year's end up 7%, the Netherlands' output was up by 6%, and Belgium enjoyed a 5% gain.

New Products. Literally the biggest "new product" introduced in 1990 was *Crystal Harmony*, a 49,000-ton luxury passenger ship completed at the Nagasaki shipyard. An end to a 15-year depression in the Japanese shipbuilding industry came about thanks to Japan's appetite for new status symbols. Several smaller luxury ships were under construction. On a smaller scale, Sony introduced an electronic book system. Aiming to create an entirely new market, Sony's Data Discman player has a screen that displays text recorded on compact discs (CDs). Each CD stores 100,000 pages of text, just about equal to 300 paperbacks. The machines went on the market in Japan for about $350. This latest microelectronic gadget, touted as a paperless book, rang up 200,000 sales in the year it was introduced in Japan.

In keeping with Japan's custom of introducing new products in the domestic market first, Sony Corp. also introduced a television set capable of handling high-definition broadcasts (HDTV). The price, about $18,000, and the fact that there is no regular HDTV broadcasting,

Employees on Nonagricultural Payrolls (in thousands)			
	1989	1990*	Percent Change
Good-producing industries	25,326	25,030	-1.2
Mining	700	735	5.0
Construction	5,200	5,216	0.3
Manufacturing	19,426	19,096	-1.7
Durable goods	11,422	11,148	-2.4
Lumber and wood products	758	741	-2.2
Furniture and fixtures	526	512	-2.7
Stone, clay, and glass products	569	555	-2.5
Primary metal industries	772	715	-2.4
Fabricated metal products	1,446	1,412	-2.3
Machinery, except electrical	2,132	2,102	-1.4
Electrical and electronic equip.	1,753	1,692	-3.5
Transportation equipment	2,054	1,992	3.0
Instruments and related products	1,026	998	-2.7
Miscellaneous mfg. industries	386	385	-0.2
Nondurable goods	8,004	7,948	-0.7
Food and kindred products	1,645	1,650	0.3
Tobacco manufactures	49	47	-6.6
Textile mill products	724	701	-3.2
Apparel and other textile goods	1,074	1,030	-4.1
Paper and allied products	697	698	0.2
Printing and publishing	1,564	1,547	-1.0
Chemicals and allied products	1,074	1,085	1.1
Petroleum and coal products	157	160	1.8
Rubber and misc. plastics products	884	869	-1.7
Leather and leather products	136	127	-6.9

* Preliminary Estimate
Source: Bureau of Labor Statistics

Industrial Production: International Overview 1985 = 100						
	1984	1985	1986	1987	1988	1989	1990*
Industrial Countries	97	100	101	104	110	114	115
Australia	96	100	105	101	105	111	110
Austria	96	100	101	102	106	113	120
Belgium	99	100	101	104	109	114	116
Canada	91	100	100	106	112	113	112
Denmark	96	100	108	104	106	108	110
Finland	96	100	101	106	110	113	113
France	99	100	101	103	107	111	113
Germany	96	100	102	102	106	111	117
Ireland	97	100	103	115	128	144	145
Italy	99	100	104	108	114	117	120
Japan	96	100	100	103	113	120	125
Luxembourg	94	100	103	103	115	125	124
Netherlands	96	100	100	101	101	106	108
Norway	96	100	103	111	117	136	138
Spain	98	100	102	107	111	117	115
Sweden	98	100	100	104	106	107	105
Switzerland	95	100	104	104	112	117	125
United Kingdom	95	100	102	106	110	110	109
United States	98	100	101	105	110	113	114

*Preliminary Estimate
Source: International Monetary Fund

will limit the appeal of that product. Another electronic wonder aimed at the consumer is a satellite-navigation system for passenger cars. Coming, too, is a new generation of portable telephones, costing far less than cellular phones, that are just about the size of a wallet and require special transmitter-receiver units to be placed in the area served by the new system.

Meanwhile, in the United States, the General Electric Company created a new form of diamond with an enhanced ability to transmit heat and light. Able to conduct heat 50% better than natural diamond, up to now the best heat conductor, the new diamond also can absorb ten times more laser light than a natural diamond. The new synthetic should come in handy in microelectronic signal boosters in optical-fiber transoceanic communication cables and in developing more powerful and faster computers. It would help make laser cutting tools more efficient and laser measurement devices more accurate. Another U.S. first was Intel Corp.'s development of a tiny microprocessor—80386SL—chip that will enable a new generation of laptop computers to run complicated programs. The new chip's circuitry contains 855,000 transistors in an unusually tight package.

AGO AMBRE
U.S. Department of Commerce

INSURANCE, LIABILITY

The liability-insurance crisis of the mid-1980s continued to abate in 1990. For much of the 1980s, doctors and other professionals, as well as manufacturers, day-care centers, and local governments, were faced with premium hikes and cancellations of policies to cover claims of injury caused by their products or services. While many lines of liability insurance remained hard to obtain in 1990, doctors saw their medical-malpractice premiums fall in many states for the first time since the mid-1980s.

The fall in premiums came in the wake of new state laws aimed at containing what insurers and their supporters say has been a rash of frivolous and unfair lawsuits since the early 1980s. Many states have passed laws restricting punitive damages, limiting lawyers' fees, and encouraging out-of-court settlement of cases involving liability. Another reason for the fall in insurance premiums was suggested by new data that showed that juries were beginning to decide more frequently than in the past in favor of defendants and their insurers in malpractice and product-liability cases.

The good news for liability policyholders and their insurers was offset in large part by the industry's spreading financial woes. Insurance companies count on profits from their investments to cover the payments they make to customers for claims. Like the savings and loan industry, insurers suffered in 1990 from declining values in real estate and junk bonds, both of which account for much of the industry's investments. Following the failure in 1989 of 23 property and casualty insurers, 11 more companies had failed by mid-1990, continuing the high insolvency rate that began in the mid-1980s. Because there are about 900 property and casualty companies in the United States, the insolvency rate among insurers does not pose a serious financial threat yet. State guaranty funds, underwritten by solvent insurance companies, have been able to absorb the industry's losses. Proposals to create national standards governing the state guaranty funds or to establish a separate federal bureaucracy to handle insurance insolvencies have gained support in Congress.

Measures that would increase the federal government's control over the insurance industry met with little success in 1990, however. A bill that would end the industry's exemption from federal antitrust laws gained support for the first time from the House Judiciary Committee but failed to come to a vote. The McCarran-Ferguson Act of 1945 exempts insurance companies from antitrust laws on the grounds that they need to compare actuarial data to set accurate premiums. The bill's supporters claim that the industry has used the exemption unlawfully to set premiums above their fair value.

In September property and casualty insurers and their policyholders turned to the Supreme Court to resolve a case involving punitive damages, an issue that long has pitted them against consumer advocates and attorneys. The court was expected to decide in early 1991 whether the Constitution requires limits on punitive damages.

MARY H. COOPER
"Editorial Research Reports"

INTERIOR DESIGN

Starting what has been called optimistically "the decade of the home," Americans began the 1990s with a continuing interest in making their homes more livable. With concerns about the global environment heightened, the idea of home represented a sheltering, nurturing haven from a threatening world. The home also presented the opportunity to express—through a knowledge of interior design—one's personal style.

In August, however, a slowing U.S. economy was hit by a crisis in the Middle East, resulting in weakened consumer confidence. Economic concerns led to a decline in furniture purchases—generally regarded as postponable. The exceptions were immediately decorative, and usually low-cost, accessories as well as upholstered furniture.

Although 1990 saw the demise of Kittinger Furniture, Baker Furniture of Grand Rapids, MI, celebrated 100 years of continual operation by reissuing 13 representative and unrelated pieces in its distinctive Centennial Collection.

Overall Trends. In an increasingly sluggish market, home furnishings that did sell offered pleasing esthetics over equally well-made products of conventional design. This preference was true even among less affluent buyers. Manufacturers of high-style interior designer collections, including those by Ralph Lauren, Mario Buatta for John Widdicomb, Mark Hampton for Hickory Chair, and Jay Spectre for Century Furniture, continued to develop, introduce, and find markets for new products. Such manufacturers as Baker and Henredon participated in licensed historic-reproduction programs.

Traditional style, incorporating American country, English 18th century, and Colonial, remained the most popular. American country lost steam during the year, although other classic rural themes, such as English, Scandinavian, and French styles, continued to be major influences in interior design. Thanks to *glasnost*, opulent, pre-Revolutionary Russian style began to appear in furniture, textiles, accessories, and tabletop items—imparting an unexpected richness to interiors. Continuing its preeminence in upholstered goods, contemporary styling was expected to make considerable gains in all home-furnishing areas.

Comfort and Quality. No matter how striking a room's styling, however, its furniture had to be comfortable. Designers faced the fact that relaxing at home in the evening is the way of life for millions of tired two-income households. For example, comfort was so important that even on traditional-style upholstery shown at the 1990 International Home Furnishings Market, shapes frequently deviated from historically accurate proportions to deliver deeper seating and increased fill over previous years. Ottomans continued their popularity.

Quality also became a critical factor in the decision to buy in 1990. Unlike the more trend-driven consumer of the 1980s, people bought fewer things less often, but they bought investment quality. Some areas of the United States became particularly cautious in 1990. Century Furniture's representatives reported that in the formerly high-spending Northeast market—when indeed anything was bought at all—there was a desire for furniture that would last.

Eclecticism and Natural Allure. The mixing of furnishings and accessories from various cultures and periods to give a personal twist to a room was a strong interior-design force in 1990. Matched suites in furnishings began to look dated and unimaginative. Following the lead of the apparel industry—a trend already more widespread in the tabletop and linen industries—furniture manufacturers began to offer an artfully ready-made eclectic look in a few of their collections, encouraging the buyer to mix the pieces confidently in unexpected and expressive ways. Drexel Heritage's accessory collection—laden with exotic imports and introduced in 1990—heralded the trend.

The pull of nature was particularly strong in 1990, showing up unmistakably in upholstery fabrics, accessories, tabletops, and furniture. Print fabrics ran the gamut from florals to animals and animal skins. Inspired by the film *Out of Africa*, faded cabbage-rose-printed linens appeared on sofas and chairs in several showrooms at the April International Home Furnishing Market. Exotic bird prints and Near Eastern-inspired designs appeared in October.

Important new accessories included bird cages and urns. Ivy led the garden motifs. Animal motifs appeared wrapped around mirrors, matted in frames, and glazed on porcelains. Fake animal-skin textures enlivened decorative tabletop objects and furniture.

Jewel Tones. A notable selection of upholstered home furnishings was presented in deep, rich jewel tones—particularly at the top end of the market. Multiple shades of green, followed by yellow, appeared everywhere. Colors for the year overall were strong and clear. The dusty, subdued, grayed, and musty tones were deleted from the designer palette.

Finishes. In 1990 furnishing materials continued to be mixed; that is, wood was mixed with stone, wood or rattan with iron, and wood with wicker. Woods done in lighter washed finishes entered the mainstream. Once accepted only in Sunbelt markets and on contemporary stylings, white, washed, and translucent finishes appeared on some traditional and neo-traditional designs at several high-end furniture manufacturers. The North Carolina company Henredon launched Charisma, a major contemporary collection surfaced in a pale two-tone stripling finish, at the April International Home Furnishings Market.

CARLA BREER HOWARD, *"Traditional Home"*

INTERNATIONAL TRADE AND FINANCE

When the International Monetary Fund (IMF) and the World Bank held their joint annual meeting in Washington, DC, in late September 1990, a delegation of Soviet observers was in attendance for the first time, signaling a start to the inclusion of the Soviet Union in the Western world of finance and trade.

Overall Trends. That was just one of the astonishing events of 1990. There also was a major hike in oil prices after Iraq invaded Kuwait. The U.S. Congress raised taxes and President George Bush did not veto the measure despite his "read-my-lips" 1988 campaign pledge to block tax hikes. Mexico decided to negotiate a free-trade agreement with the United States. East and West Germany unified politically and economically. Britain decided to join the European Monetary System. The nations of Eastern Europe launched multiple reforms aimed at converting from communism into a free-market system.

The end of the Cold War prompted President Bush, at the July 9 opening of the economic summit of the largest seven economic democracies in Houston, to state: "A new world of freedom lies before us: hopeful, confident; a world where peace endures, where commerce has conscience, and where all that seems possible is possible." The seven leaders were obviously keen on shaping a post-Marxist world.

Thus it was a disappointment when less than a month later, on August 2, Iraq's Saddam Hussein ordered his tanks and troops into Kuwait. The average spot price of oil, which had slipped to $16.40 per barrel in July, soared $3 to $22 per barrel in frenzied trading in London that invasion day. In the following six weeks, this average price fluctuated between $23 and $33 a barrel, reflecting market fears that war might break out and disrupt the flow of oil from Saudi Arabia and other Persian Gulf producers.

By late October extra production of oil by member nations of the Organization of Petroleum Exporting Countries (OPEC), particularly by Saudi Arabia, the United Arab Emirates, and Venezuela, made up for more than 3 million of the 4 million barrels per day lost as a result of the Iraq-Kuwait crisis. But the higher oil price was damaging the economies of many oil-consuming nations. The United States, which imports about half its oil, saw a jump in inflation and by mid-November, most economists reckoned the country was either already in a recession or about to enter one.

Despite the rise in the cost of imported oil, the U.S. trade balance was improving in 1990. For the first nine months, the trade deficit was running at a seasonally adjusted annual rate of $99.13 billion, compared with $109.4 billion in 1989, $118.5 billion in 1988, and a record $152

AP/Wide World

World Bank President Barber Conable and the IMF's Michel Camdessus (left) confer prior to a May meeting of the world's leading industrial nations (the Group of 24).

billion in 1987. Despite the improvement, the deficits did add to the nation's international debt. On a net basis, these debts amounted to $620 billion by the end of 1989. This Department of Commerce number, however, probably exaggerates the real U.S. position because it uses book value for investments in plant and equipment. Since many U.S. direct investments were made years or even decades ago, they likely are worth much more today.

Seeing signs of an economic slowdown with its accompanying rise in unemployment, the Federal Reserve System's (the Fed's) policy-making body, the Open Market Committee, gradually lowered short-term interest rates in 1990. By mid-November, the 7.5% federal funds rate—the interest commercial banks charge each other on overnight loans—was down more than two full percentage points from the spring of 1989. The 30-year Treasury bond yield, however, was slower to move down. It was still around 8.5% in mid-November, down from 9% and 9¼% in March 1989. Bond investors were still skeptical about the prospects for lower inflation. Consumer prices climbed during the first ten months of 1990 at an annual rate of 6.7%, compared with 4.7% during the comparable 1989 period.

The Fed stepped up its move toward easing its monetary policy after Congress and President Bush reached a deal to trim the deficit by

Most-Favored-Nation Status

There was considerable debate in the United States, especially in the House of Representatives, in 1990 over whether to take away China's "most-favored-nation" (MFN) trade status. It was not a trivial matter.

Since China has MFN privilege, its exports to the United States pay according to the MFN duty, which averages about 5%. If China did not have MFN status, its exports would face the Smoot-Hawley tariffs established in 1930, which average about 50%. A study by the U.S.-China Business Council calculated that the loss of MFN status would have boosted tariffs on China's exports to the United States an average 40%.

Although the U.S. House voted 247 to 174 on October 18 to deny China MFN status as a protest to the continued restrictions on political dissent in that nation, the bill never was voted on in the Senate and thus died when Congress adjourned. The vote was largely symbolic, since President George Bush had promised to veto the measure and there did not appear to be the two-thirds-majority vote in Congress necessary to overcome such a veto.

History. The 1990 incident indicates the importance of the MFN principle to world trade. MFN was one of the rules established under the General Agreement on Tariffs and Trade (GATT) that was signed by 23 countries in 1947 as part of the post-World War II international economic system. It requires each country to extend to other countries the lowest tariff it charges on imports from any country that is a signatory of GATT. Thereby it prevents trade discrimination. One country cannot single out some other nation for higher tariffs or other trade obstacles.

Without the MFN clause, large industrial nations would find it easier to discriminate against small industrial nations or developing countries when it suited their political or economic convenience.

As might be expected, there are some exceptions to the MFN rule. The British Commonwealth arrangements were at one time of some importance. The United States has had a preferential trade agreement with the Philippines. More recently the United States has applied so-called "Super 301" provisions of a 1988 trade law to nations it considered not dealing fairly in trade. That provision calls for the administration to take trade action against nations that do not reduce their trade barriers to U.S. goods. Under GATT rules a group of nations can join together in a free-trade area (with each member nation retaining its individual tariff structures against nonmembers) or a common market (a unified tariff structure facing outsiders) if these eliminate most trade barriers between members. Examples include the 12-nation European Community (EC), the European Free Trade Association (EFTA), and the Canada-U.S. Free Trade Agreement that was launched at the start of 1989. The United States and Mexico planned to start negotiating a free-trade agreement in 1991, which also could embrace Canada.

The Current Situation. Then there is trade discrimination against Communist countries, including some that were abandoning the philosophy in 1990. Of these, Romania, Bulgaria, Albania, Cuba, Laos, Cambodia, Vietnam, Afghanistan, Mongolia, North Korea, the Soviet Union and its republics of Estonia, Latvia, and Lithuania still were denied MFN status by the United States late in 1990. Thus they faced Smoot-Hawley tariffs. In June 1990, President Bush and Soviet President Mikhail Gorbachev signed a historic trade agreement, which included the granting of MFN to the USSR. President Bush indicated, however, that he would not submit the agreement for congressional ratification until the Soviet Union enacted a law removing barriers to emigration. The USSR then would qualify for a waiver to the so-called Jackson-Vanik amendment, which bars MFN status for countries that prevent the free emigration of their citizens. China has been granted a yearly waiver to the Jackson-Vanik measure since 1980. It was this status that the House sought to revoke in 1990.

East Germany won MFN status with the United States when it joined West Germany to become united Germany on Oct. 3, 1990. Poland has had MFN status since 1960, a status withheld during the time when the country was under martial law. Hungary got MFN status in 1978, subject to annual review. In 1989 it was granted permanent MFN status. The U.S. Congress voted Czechoslovakia MFN status in October 1990. Bulgaria was working toward MFN status as 1990 was moving to a close, having reached a trade agreement with the United States on October 5.

The Uruguay Round of trade negotiations under GATT, which was suspended without agreement in December 1990, sought to maintain MFN status in general. But there was some discussion of whether new exceptions might be permitted in some areas where agreement among the more than 100 GATT members might prove impossible.

DAVID R. FRANCIS

nearly $500 billion over the succeeding five fiscal years.

The U.S. Budget Battle. The budget measure, passed October 28, was surprising in its modest shift of some of the tax burden onto the rich. This was a major change from the Reagan era, which was marked by cutting tax rates (especially for the affluent) and counting on the formation of new enterprises and new jobs to trickle revenue down to middle-income and poor families. With a jump in stock prices, higher interest rates, and soaring property values, the 1980s saw the richest families obtain a greater share of both the nation's income and wealth. The Democrats, in the midterm elections, used this trend to accuse the Republicans of being the party of the privileged. They pointed to Bush's efforts to win a cut in the capital-gains tax that most would have benefited the affluent.

The final package established a new 31% marginal tax bracket. It set the top capital-gains-tax rate at 28%, a little below the previous maximum rate of 33% but not low enough to encourage new tax shelters greatly. By disallowing specific amounts of deductions and personal exemptions, the package boosted slightly the real tax burden for those with adjusted gross incomes of more than $100,000. Despite this package, the budget deficit in the fiscal year ending Sept. 30, 1991, was projected by White House Budget Director Richard Darman at between $250 billion and $300 billion.

Trade. The value of world merchandise trade rose perhaps 5% in 1990, slower than the 7.5% increase in 1989 when it reached a new record of $3.1 trillion. (The value of world trade was below $2 trillion as recently as 1985.) In 1989 the United States once again had moved ahead of West Germany as the world's largest exporter. U.S. exports were worth $364 billion, versus $341 billion for West Germany and $275 billion for Japan.

During 1990 the Uruguay Round of trade negotiations under the General Agreement on Tariffs and Trade (GATT) moved toward a climax. By mid-November, a logjam over agricultural subsidies threatened the talks. U.S. Agricultural Secretary Clayton Yeutter emerged from talks with the 12-nation European Community (EC) saying he was "very pessimistic." Launched in 1986 at Punta del Este in Uruguay, the round was scheduled for completion at a session of trade ministers starting on December 3 in Brussels. This ambitious round sought not only lower tariffs, but major reductions in nontariff barriers such as subsidies, national licensing requirements in service areas, and quotas. The negotiations covered a huge range of topics—textiles and clothing, tropical products, a review of the GATT articles of agreement, multilateral codes regarding such areas as standards, antidumping procedures, import licensing, and customs values,

AP/Wide World

In April, U.S. Trade Negotiator Carla Hills explained the Bush administration's decision not to reidentify Japan and Brazil as unfair trading partners under 1988 legislation.

"safeguard" measures against imports, subsidies and countervailing duties, intellectual property rights and trade in counterfeit goods, trade-related investment measures, trade in services, and dispute-settlement procedures. The failure of the United States and the EC to overcome their deadlock over the issue of reducing subsidies to farmers led to the collapse of the Uruguay Round in Brussels on December 7. The talks' chairman expressed the hope that the discussion would resume early in 1991.

In the farm-goods area, the United States had sought a 75% or larger reduction in government subsidies to European farmers. The EC had offered reductions of only 30%. With 11 million farmers still on the land, EC politicians were reluctant to slash deeply its high subsidies. The Paris-based Organization for Economic Cooperation and Development estimated that its membership of industrial nations altogether spend around $250 billion on farm subsidies.

Mexico-U.S. Free Trade. Mexican President Carlos Salinas de Gortari made his request for talks on a bilateral free-trade agreement official in early September, thereby staking Mexico's economic future on closer integration with the United States; but the negotiations, expected to start before the middle of 1991, could take two years. The goal is the full phased elimination of import tariffs, reductions in nontariff trade barriers such as import quotas, licenses, and technical obstacles, and the establishment of binding protection for intellectual property rights.

Mexico follows Canada and Japan as the third-biggest trading partner of the United States. It had a $2 billion trade surplus with the United States in 1989. It imported $2.7 billion in farm products from the United States. The two countries trade about $52 billion worth of goods per year.

Canada has said it would like to join the negotiations for a free-trade area with Mexico. If the talks are successful, the agreement would bring all of North America with its 363 million people into a single market free of tariffs and many other trade barriers. Canada and the United States began a ten-year schedule of dismantling trade obstacles at the start of 1989.

International Stock Markets. It was a relatively calm year for world stock markets, though prices mostly declined. By mid-November, U.S. stock prices were down about 10% from the start of the year. In terms of U.S. dollars, Japanese stock prices dropped 36%, while Britain's were up 2.5%. Canadian stock prices were down 17.8%; Australia down 18.5%; France down 10.1%; Germany down 5.1%; and Italy down 19%. Swiss stock prices were off only 2.9%, and Hong Kong prices were up 4.5%. The Japanese were much concerned that their lower stock prices also might depress their inflated real-estate prices.

The U.S. Dollar. The dollar fell sharply against other major currencies during 1990. By mid-November it was down about 20% against the Japanese yen from its high for the year of 160 yen to the dollar on April 2. At 128 yen the dollar was nearing its all-time low of 120 yen set in January of 1988. The dollar had plunged about 13% to 1.48 German marks, the lowest level in the post-World War II era. However, the dollar's weakness caused little alarm among the Group of Seven industrial powers, perhaps with the exception of France. French Finance Minister Pierre Beregovoy said in the autumn that the Seven should get together to do something about the dollar's decline.

Despite the sounding of war drums in the Persian Gulf, there was no major flight of foreign investment into the United States. But there was such a high demand for actual greenbacks that the demand had the Bureau of Engraving and Printing working three shifts a day, seven days a week. Fueled by the demand for paper currency in such places as inflation-ridden Argentina, the Middle East, and East Europe, the outstanding amount of U.S. currency rose from $221.9 billion at the end of 1989 to $241.5 billion at the end of September 1990, an increase of almost $20 billion. That compared with about $10 billion growth in all of 1989. It meant that the government was getting twice as much seigniorage as usual, and was not having to finance as much debt as it otherwise would have had to.

Global Economic Picture. The IMF projected a growth of global economic activity of 2% in 1990. Growth weakened in both the industrial countries and the developing countries. In East European nations and the Soviet Union, output was contracting sharply as the switch to a free-enterprise system was launched. The IMF expected 3.9% real growth in West Germany, 3.1% in France, 3.7% in Italy, 1.4% in Britain, 1.1% in Canada (which had fallen into a recession by year's end), 5.1% in Japan, and 1.3% in the United States.

The Asian region was enjoying about a 5% growth rate, while in much of Latin America output was declining as several nations fought —with some success—to lower high inflation rates.

At the annual meeting of the IMF and World Bank, September 25–27, most of the governors, representing 154 member countries, joined in promising to assist both the frontline states in the Middle East crisis and the developing countries that especially are harmed by higher oil prices, a loss of workers' remittances, and disruptions and costs of reabsorbing workers from that region. Saudi Arabia, Kuwait, and the United Arab Emirates did provide billions of dollars of relief to the frontline states, as well as paying for most of the out-of-pocket expenses of U.S. armed forces in the area. The IMF and the Bank also were pledged to step up lending in the region.

The Pound Joins European ERM. Britain announced October 5 that the pound sterling would become the tenth currency to join the exchange-rate mechanism of the European Monetary System. Prime Minister Margaret Thatcher's government also noted that the bank base rate would be cut by one percentage point to 14%. But the pound was given a margin for fluctuation of up to 6% on either side of a central parity. By this action, Britain hoped gradually to lower its high inflation rate toward that of Germany. Thatcher refused to consider a single European currency or a single central bank of Europe. She suggested she might put this issue to voters in a national referendum. Her opinions were criticized widely as anti-European, adding to her political difficulties. On November 20 at a Conservative Party conference, she failed to win a large enough majority to defeat a challenge to her party leadership on the first ballot, and later decided to resign her leadership position, ending her 11½-year reign as prime minister. Some observers felt that her successor, John Major, might be more amenable to the unified European financial system.

DAVID R. FRANCIS
"The Christian Science Monitor"

IOWA

Iowans made state history in the 1990 elections when they reelected a Democrat to the U.S. Senate for the first time. Sen. Tom Harkin defeated U.S. Rep. Tom Tauke by 529,003-448,182 votes. With the two candidates spending more than $10 million, it proved to be the most expensive political campaign in the state's history.

Elections. Meanwhile, Republican Gov. Terry Branstad was reelected to a third four-year term over Democratic House Speaker Don Avenson by a margin of 588,362-377,390. Branstad outspent Avenson by a margin of four to one. Democrat Bonnie Campbell became the first woman elected as Iowa's attorney general when she defeated Ed Kelly, a former Jefferson County attorney. Other Democrats reelected to their positions were state Treasurer Michael Fitzgerald, Secretary of State Elaine Baxter, and Secretary of Agriculture Dale Cochran. Also reelected was Republican Richard Johnson as state auditor.

The Democrats continued to control both houses of the Iowa General Assembly but their margin in each house was reduced. Under a new constitutional amendment, the senate would elect from its own members its presiding officer, as the lieutenant governor was to serve strictly in the administrative branch of the state government.

In the 2d District, Republican Jim Nussle defeated Democrat Eric Tabor for the seat vacated by former Rep. Tom Tauke in one of the most heated contests on the ballot. All other incumbent members of Congress were reelected.

Legislature. The 1990 session of the Iowa General Assembly was one of the shortest in recent years. Governor Branstad's record budget of more than $5.2 billion was increased by the Democratic legislature by several million dollars. As a result, the governor exercised a record number of vetoes, none of which was

AP/Wide World

Tom Harkin, 51-year-old former five-term U.S. representative, became Iowa's first Democrat to win reelection to the U.S. Senate. He defeated U.S. Rep. Tom Tauke, 54% to 46%.

overturned by the General Assembly. No new taxes or increases were enacted.

Population Changes. The 1990 census showed that for the first time since 1920, the state's population decreased in the 1980s. The drop was listed at 126,384, with 92 of the state's 99 counties suffering population declines. The state would lose one seat in Congress with the reapportionment.

However, public-school enrollments increased slightly in both the 1988–89 and 1989–90 school years, reversing 20 years of declines. Northern Iowa University registered a record number of 12,500 students in 1990–91.

The Economy. Unemployment in Iowa continued to be low with fewer than 3.9% on the unemployment rolls. More Iowans were employed in nonagricultural jobs than ever before in history. The state revenues continued to run at record rates, increasing each month by nearly 10% over the previous year.

Iowa received above-normal rainfall in 1990, after two years of drought. The corn yield as well as soybean crops were near record highs.

Disasters. More than 80 people were injured in April when seven cars of a 19-car Amtrak train derailed in the southeastern Iowan town of Batavia. United Airlines was determined to have missed finding a defective engine part that caused the 1989 crash of Flight 232 in Sioux City and the resultant loss of 112 lives.

RUSSELL M. ROSS, *University of Iowa*

IOWA • Information Highlights

Area: 56,275 sq mi (145 753 km²).
Population (1990 census prelim.): 2,767,000.
Chief Cities (July 1, 1988 est.): Des Moines, the capital, 192,910; Cedar Rapids, 110,300.
Government (1990): *Chief Officers*—governor, Terry E. Branstad (R); lt. gov., Jo Ann Zimmerman (D). *General Assembly*—Senate, 50 members; House of Representatives, 100 members.
State Finances (fiscal year 1989): *Revenue,* $6,441,000,000; *expenditure,* $5,892,000,000.
Personal Income (1989): $43,978,000,000; per capita, $15,487.
Labor Force (June 1990): *Civilian labor force,* 1,512,600; *unemployed,* 58,300 (3.9% of total force).
Education: *Enrollment* (fall 1988)—public elementary schools, 333,988; public secondary, 144,212; colleges and universities, 161,174. *Public school expenditures* (1989–90), $2,129,524,000.

IRAN

Iran in 1990 still was existing in the aftermath of the Khomeini era—a decade that had been a period of extraordinary intensity and strain. After the fall of the Shah, the Ayatollah Khomeini, through his dominant personality, had imposed a regime of rigid Shiite Islam that had permeated every level of public and private life and that had dictated a violently anti-Western, and particularly anti-U.S., foreign policy. Iran's difficulties were compounded by the eight-year (1980–88) war with Iraq, which Iran had not sought, but which Khomeini prolonged unnecessarily for years.

The Khomeini revolution had gone sour long before the ayatollah's death in June 1989. The seemingly endless war dragged on, with Iran suffering far higher casualties than Iraq. Islamic fundamentalism, expected to spread like wildfire to neighboring countries, in fact never did spread. Khomeini, who had criticized the Shah for cruelty and corruption, headed a government that was itself incompetent, corrupt, economically disastrous, and far more cruel than the Shah's regime ever had been.

"Dekhomeinization." The new phase in Iran in 1990 was described by some observers as one of "dekhomeinization." The two most powerful men in Iran—Hashemi Rafsanjani, who was elected president by an overwhelming majority in August 1989, and Seyyed Ali Khamenei, whom the Assembly of Experts chose in June 1989 to be Khomeini's successor as the nation's spiritual leader—usually were considered pragmatists or moderates, but this merely meant that they are what passes for moderate in the Iranian context—an important qualification. Rafsanjani usually was considered to be more of a moderate than Khamenei. However, Rafsanjani was for years Khomeini's closest confidant, perhaps his only close confidant. Khamenei came to power when Khomeini, in one of the last important acts of his life, deposed the Ayatollah Hussein Ali Montazeri from the position of designated heir to Iran's spiritual leadership. Montazeri had been elected to that position in 1985 by the Assembly of Experts, but he was dismissed summarily by Khomeini in March 1989 because he had dared to criticize official actions, including the handling of the *Satanic Verses* affair.

Satanic Verses Controversy. The ambiguities in the views of leading figures, and the limited extent to which "moderation" is to be expected even in the early 1990s, was illustrated neatly by the continuing issue of the condemnation of Salman Rushdie, Indian-born British citizen and author of *The Satanic Verses*. Khomeini's decree (*fatwa*) formally sentencing to death the author of a book held to be offensive to Islam was issued on Feb. 9, 1989. Khamenei suggested Rushdie might be

AP/Wide World

Behind a large portrait of the late Ayatollah Khomeini, President Rafsanjani opened ceremonies marking the 11th anniversary of Iran's Islamic revolution in February 1990.

pardoned if he repented but, after being rebuked by Khomeini, said he had made a mistake. Montazeri, however, strongly had opposed the *fatwa*, and had upheld the proposal for forgiveness.

While Rushdie remained under a death sentence, there were some signs of moderation in Iran. In an address to the diplomatic corps in Tehran on February 7, Rafsanjani spoke of Iran's desire to renounce "all forms of warmongering, military adventurism, crises, convulsions, and unjust confrontations everywhere in the world." Other remarks of his also were thought to demonstrate a readiness to introduce far-reaching reforms. Rafsanjani's moderation, however, was hobbled by strong opposition forces, including a more or less hostile majority in the *Majlis* (parliament) led by Ali Akbar Mohtashemi. In the second half of 1990, with things going well for the president, there was speculation that he soon might dissolve the *Majlis* and hold another election.

Meanwhile, Montazeri was essentially powerless. He was held under house arrest in the holy city of Qum, where demonstrations against him were organized by Khamenei. However, there also were demonstrations in his favor in the provinces, and his supporters among the younger clergy argued that most Iranian spiritual leaders regard him, not Khamenei, as Khomeini's legitimate successor.

Assembly of Experts Election. The position of Khamenei and Rafsanjani was much strengthened by the nationwide election on October 8 of a new Assembly of Experts, the body that elects the supreme spiritual leader. Security forces were on alert to prevent possible disturbances by anti-Western fundamentalists, who had hoped to win the election and depose Khamenei. They were outraged—and defeated —by the adroit move of Khamenei (supported by Rafsanjani) in requiring all candidates for the Assembly to prove to the Council of Guardians their suitability as candidates and their knowledge of Islamic law. Many candidates, including Mohtashemi, were rejected. Khamenei commanded a comfortable majority in what was a stunning defeat for the hard-liners.

Human-Rights Issues. Iran continued to be criticized for human-rights violations, but at least some investigation of these matters was possible. An envoy of the UN Human Rights Commission made a weeklong visit to Iran in January and on March 8, Iran announced its readiness to investigate accusations of torture and executions. There could be little doubt that executions, though less numerous than under Khomeini, continued on a fairly large scale. On October 11 in Khorasan province, 37 people were executed for drug dealing. On October 28 the official news agency announced the public execution of 27 "armed bandits" at Zabol in eastern Iran, as well as 19 executions in Mashhad for drug smuggling. There were more than 200 such executions in the second half of the year.

However, even if the loosening of rigid controls in Iran was sporadic and still precarious, some loosening indeed had occurred. People still may have been arrested sometimes for "breaches of morals," but political comment had become surprisingly free. Even Westernized Iranians seemed less fearful in 1990.

Economic Questions. The Iranian economy continued to be in poor shape in 1990. It was estimated to be working at less than half capacity, despite a great need to rebuild after the war. Foreign banks were ready to lend, because Iran (unlike Iraq) came out of its recent war with practically no foreign debt. Some of the clergy were adamantly, but vainly, opposed to the creation of debt, or to dealings with the outside world in general. However, a trickle of foreign investment did begin early in 1990 and was increasing. On January 29, West Germany announced it was giving Iran a credit line worth $270 million for long-term economic development. The same day, Iran announced it was to spend $6.2 billion on the reconstruction of its commercial and fishing ports. In October the government announced it had arranged a $300 million loan from the World Bank. That same month, Roger Fauroux, French minister of industry, headed an economic delegation to Iran which concluded several deals, including one to assemble Renault cars in Iran.

A great, and fundamental, difficulty of Iran's economic situation is the very high rate of population growth, one of the highest in the world. In 1980 the Iranian population was some 38 million; in 1990 it was estimated at 53 million. Official policy on this issue has changed in recent years. Earlier, the official line opposed any restrictions on population growth, but in 1990 the government with UN assistance embarked on a program of encouraging birth control.

Disaster. A major earthquake measuring 7.7 on the Richter scale struck northern Iran on June 21, causing more than 40,000 deaths. The government on the whole responded efficiently and the Rafsanjani administration enhanced its prestige through its handling of the disaster.

Foreign Relations. Events of 1990 enabled Iran to improve greatly the climate of its foreign relations. This was especially true after the Iraqi conquest of Kuwait on August 2, which moved Iran from a position of isolation to being an object of courtship. Still, the improvement began earlier. On July 3 under UN auspices the foreign ministers of Iran and Iraq held the first direct talks since the war, and in speeches on July 17 both nations' presidents expressed optimism about the prospects. However, the dramatic breakthrough came with an Iraqi offer on August 14 of three major concessions: to accept the 1975 agreement on the Shatt al-Arab, which Iraq had repudiated in 1980; to withdraw all Iraqi troops from Iranian territory they occupied; and to commence repatriation of some 30,000 prisoners of war. The offer was accepted enthusiastically the next day by Iran. It amounted, in fact, to Iraq's giving up everything it had gained in eight years of war. Normal diplomatic relations were reestablished, and ambassadors were exchanged on October 20.

IRAN • Information Highlights

Official Name: Islamic Republic of Iran.
Location: Southwest Asia.
Area: 636,293 sq mi (1 648 000 km²).
Population (mid-1990 est.): 55,600,000.
Chief City (1986 census): Tehran, the capital, 5,770,000.
Government: *Head of state and government,* Ali Akbar Hashemi Rafsanjani, president (took office August 1989). *Legislature* (unicameral)—Islamic Consultative Assembly (*Majlis*).
Monetary Unit: Rial (66.297 rials equal U.S.$1, August 1990).
Gross National Product (1989 U.S.$): $97,600,-000,000.
Foreign Trade (1986 est. U.S.$): *Imports,* $10,000,-000,000; *exports,* $7,800,000,000.

Already good relations with China and the Soviet Union were improved further, while the long association with Syria, Iran's sole Arab supporter during the war, strengthened. Relations with Great Britain had been broken off in March 1989 over *The Satanic Verses* affair but their immediate resumption was announced in New York on September 27 by the foreign ministers of the two countries.

Iran and the Kuwait Crisis. If Iraq had hoped that its great concessions to Iran, made in order to free its troops on the Iranian front for deployment elsewhere, would gain Iranian support in the international crisis over Kuwait, it was mistaken. Iran's reaction to the events of August remained consistent throughout the year. Iran's policy had three aspects: welcoming formal peace with Iraq; condemnation of the Iraqi invasion and take-over of Kuwait; strong opposition to the presence of U.S. and other Western forces in Saudi Arabia and in the Persian Gulf.

ARTHUR CAMPBELL TURNER
University of California, Riverside

IRAQ

At the beginning of 1990 the armistice that ended Iraq's eight-year war with Iran was only a year and a half old. In these circumstances, the normal expectation is that a country would be preoccupied with licking its wounds, would eschew at least for the time foreign adventures, and would concentrate on the problems of reconstruction. These expectations were belied in the case of Iraq.

Arms Buildup and Defiances. On April 2, in a speech to the armed forces, Saddam Hussein (*see* BIOGRAPHY) asserted that the West was searching for some pretext for another Israeli attack on Iraq (a reference to the Israeli preemptive strike of 1981 against an Iraqi atomic-research establishment), "but, by God, we will make fire eat up half of Israel if it tries to do anything against Iraq." He also said that Iraq did not need a nuclear device, because it already had binary chemical weapons. This speech was branded by the U.S. State Department "inflammatory, irresponsible, and outrageous." There was, indeed, no doubt that Iraq had made great strides in its capacity to build rockets, chemical weapons, and long-range missiles. *The New York Times* reported on March 29 that Iraq for the first time now possessed fixed launchers for missiles in western Iraq, within range of Tel Aviv (Israel) and Damascus (Syria).

Baghdad Summit. An emergency Arab summit held in Baghdad (May 28–30) provided an ideal occasion for Saddam Hussein to put himself forward as the champion of the Arab world. In violent language he reiterated his threats of retaliation against Israel, but went beyond this in fierce criticisms that linked the United States with Israel in his denunciations. This conference in the Iraqi capital did enhance Saddam Hussein's prestige among many elements in the Arab world. He was able to secure final conference resolutions which held the United States responsible for Israeli policies of "aggression, terrorism, and expansion," and reasserted Iraq's claim to the whole of the Shatt Al-Arab waterway; but his success was not unqualified. Syria (another aspirant to the role of pan-Arab leader) did not attend the Baghdad conference and however pleasing the final resolutions might be to Jordan and the Palestine Liberation Organization (PLO), they were less so to Egypt and Saudi Arabia, which opposed the criticisms of the United States and succeeded in toning them down.

Supposed Arms Shipments Intercepted. Western anxieties about an Iraqi arms buildup were the motivation of a whole series of incidents in the spring. On March 28, British authorities, in the culmination of an elaborate "sting" operation, arrested five people who were accused of trying to smuggle to Iraq electronic devices that could be used to trigger nuclear weapons. In a still more curious case, British customs officials on April 11 seized a consignment of eight steel tubes about to be loaded onto a ship bound for Iraq. It was claimed that they were intended to be components of an artillery piece of larger caliber than any ever made. On April 20, Greek and Turkish officials seized trucks supposedly laden with parts for this giant gun. The "supergun" theory was not accepted universally, and the Iraqi government protested that the hardware was entirely innocent, and the whole thing a U.S.-British-Israeli plot to denigrate Iraq. The whole affair remained somewhat obscure, all the more so since it was linked somehow to the mysterious murder on March 22 of Gerald Bull, a Canadian-born scientist and entrepreneur who had assisted the Iraqi military in the development of long-range artillery. He had founded a Brussels company that possibly had worked on arms for Iraq, and when discovered murdered outside his Brussels apartment he had $20,000 in cash in his pockets.

On May 12 the Italian authorities seized steel castings bound for Jordan; these were said to have been intended for use as parts of the "supergun." Also in May reports surfaced that authorities at Frankfurt airport had confiscated other supergun parts, and that German, Belgian, and Swiss firms were implicated. Both Belgian and British governments began investigations into the whole imbroglio.

Executions. On March 15, Iraq executed by hanging Farzad Bazoft, 31, a correspondent for the London *Observer*, despite an international chorus of pleas for clemency. Bazoft had been arrested on Sept. 19, 1989, along with Daphne Parish, 53, a British nurse. Their arrest followed a huge explosion in August at a military complex 45 mi (72 km) south of Baghdad, which the Iraqi government had played down but which may have cost hundreds of lives. Bazoft had gone there with the nurse and, apparently employing some degree of deception, actually had gained admission and taken photographs. The military court in March had sentenced Bazoft to death for espionage and Parish to 15 years' imprisonment. Parish was freed unexpectedly by Iraq on July 16 as the result of a personal plea by President Kenneth Kaunda of Zambia.

In a somewhat similar case, an Iraqi-born Swedish citizen, Jali Mehdi al Neamy, was hanged on July 11. He had been sentenced to death for spying on Palestinian refugees in Iraq on behalf of Israel. Sweden withdrew its ambassador on July 12.

Military Cooperation with Jordan. The Jordanian government announced in February that a joint squadron of pilots and planes from both the Iraqi and Jordanian air forces was to be formed. This was followed shortly by another announcement that a joint Iraqi-Jordanian army brigade was to be formed, and possibly another later, which would be stationed on their common border. The announcements seemed to indicate a new military policy spearheaded at Israel. Israel long had known that Iraq was the most determined, ruthless, and powerful of its enemies. The two states, however, have no common border; Jordan is between them. Israel and Jordan had developed a tacit, tolerable, *modus vivendi*, though this had shown recent signs of strain. Now the policy of Jordan, a convenient buffer state, came into question.

Kuwait. Iraqi discontent about Kuwait existed at two levels. One was the underlying belief that Kuwait ought not to exist at all, that it should be part of Iraq—though Kuwait is the far older political entity. More immediate grievances arose out of Iraq's enormous economic difficulties stemming from the recent war with Iran, which left Iraq with an economy to rebuild and some $40 billion in debts to non-Arab creditors. Iraq claimed that Kuwait had been robbing their joint Rumaila oil field, but the greater grievance was the overproduction of oil (beyond the Organization of the Petroleum Exporting Countries—OPEC—quotas) by Kuwait and other Gulf states. Since this overproduction reduced the price obtainable for oil, Iraq thought of itself as being robbed of many millions of dollars weekly.

Even if it were conceded there was something in Iraq's charges, they formed a somewhat slender excuse for its invasion of Kuwait, a neighboring sovereign state, on August 2. On August 28, Kuwait, which was conquered easily, was absorbed formally into Iraq, becoming its 19th *liwa* (governorate). On September 15, Ali Hasan Majid, former Iraqi chief of security and a cousin of Saddam Hussein, was made governor. The same day, citizens of Kuwait were given until October 1 to apply for Iraqi citizenship. From August on, Iraqi actions and intentions became the prime focus of the world's attention. (*See* feature articles, page 24.)

Iran. In late August, Saddam Hussein agreed to withdraw his troops from Iranian territory, gave up his claim to exclusive control of the Shatt Al-Arab waterway, and consented to the repatriation of prisoners of war. On this basis negotiations rapidly progressed toward a definitive peace to replace the mere armistice of 1988, and ambassadors were exchanged. The Iraqi president in this way ensured at least a somewhat more friendly Iran, and by an abrupt change of course cleared the decks in order to deal with the Kuwait crisis.

New Constitution. A new national constitution, under discussion for about a year, was drawn up by the ruling Revolutionary Command Council (RCC) headed by Saddam Hussein. It was approved on July 18 by the 250-member National Assembly and was published on July 30 before its ratification. It provided for the election of the president for an eight-year renewable term. The Assembly had recommended that Saddam Hussein should be elected president for life, but this did not form part of the draft as issued. The draft also proposed the replacement of the RCC by a 50-member Consultative Council, half to be appointed by the president and half by direct, secret ballot. New political parties would be allowed, but only the ruling Baath party might have branches in the nation's armed forces and police.

In mid-October, Saddam Hussein dismissed his military chief of staff, Lt. Gen. Nazir al-Khazraji, replacing him with a war hero, Lt. Gen. Hussein Rashid. On December 12, Defense Minister Abdel Jabbar Khalil Shanshal, 70, was replaced by 40-year-old Lt. Gen. Saadi Tuma Abbas, a commander in the war with Iran.

See also MIDDLE EAST.

ARTHUR CAMPBELL TURNER
University of California, Riverside

IRAQ • Information Highlights

Official Name: Republic of Iraq.
Location: Southwest Asia.
Area: 167,923 sq mi (434 920 km²).
Population (mid-1990 est.): 18,800,000.
Chief City (1987 census): Baghdad, the capital, 3,844,608.
Government: *Head of state and government,* Saddam Hussein, president (took office July 1979).
Monetary Unit: Dinar (0.311 dinar equals U.S.$1, selling rate, August 1990).
Gross National Product (1989 est. U.S.$): $35,000,-000,000.
Foreign Trade (1986 est. U.S.$): *Imports,* $9,500,-000,000; *exports,* $7,450,000,000.

IRELAND

Ireland's membership in the European Community (EC) made 1990 a memorable year, as the country hosted meetings and conferences of the 12-nation consortium.

European Community (EC). The foreign ministers of the EC nations met in Dublin on February 20 and took up such issues as race relations in South Africa and the desire of British Prime Minister Margaret Thatcher to lift some of the sanctions imposed upon that country. Ireland's Foreign Minister Gerard Collins warned about the disruptive effect this unilateral move would have on the Community's consensual foreign policy.

The foreign ministers also approved the reunification of Germany. On April 28 the leaders of the 12 countries met in Dublin to consider ways of enhancing Community cooperation once East and West Germany had merged. On June 25–26 the EC leaders returned to Dublin for another summit conference and resolved to provide both "short-term credits" and advice to the USSR in order to stimulate its economy.

Foreign Affairs and Northern Ireland. On May 16 several Iranian and European officials met in Dublin to discuss the hostages still held in Lebanon as well as the sentence of death on the head of Salman Rushdie for having written *The Satanic Verses.* On August 24, Brian Keenan, the Belfast teacher who holds both a British and Irish passport, flew into Dublin after being held hostage in Beirut for more than four years.

Anglo-Irish relations were dominated by the familiar issues of security measures to combat terrorism and the extradition of suspects charged with guerrilla activities. After British soldiers disguised as civilians killed three men trying to rob a betting shop in Belfast on January 13, Premier Haughey and Foreign Minister Collins joined with the Rt. Rev. Cahal Daly, the Catholic bishop of Down and Connor, to demand a full-scale inquiry into the shootings. But Britain's Secretary of State for Northern Ireland Peter Brooke replied that he trusted the Royal Ulster Constabulary to investigate the shootings. Such incidents did not help Brooke's efforts to promote the cause of devolution through multiparty talks aimed at the limited transfer of power in local affairs from Westminster to Northern Ireland. In late January, Haughey cautiously expressed his hope that relations between Britain and Northern Ireland would improve, but negotiations ended in stalemate in late October.

The Irish Supreme Court refused on March 13 to approve the extradition to England of Dermot Finucane and James Pius Clarke, convicted members of the Provisional Irish Republican Army (IRA), who had escaped from the Maze prison near Belfast in 1983. The judges based their decision on the presumed danger

IRELAND · Information Highlights

Official Name: Republic of Ireland.
Location: Island in the eastern North Atlantic Ocean.
Area: 27,135 sq mi (70 280 km²).
Population (mid-1990 est.): 3,500,000.
Chief Cities (1986 census): Dublin, the capital, 920,956 (incl. suburbs); Cork, 173,694; Limerick, 76,557.
Government: *Head of state,* Mary Robinson, president (took office Dec. 3, 1990). *Head of government,* Charles Haughey, prime minister (took office March 1987). *Legislature*—Parliament: House of Representatives (Dail Eireann) and Senate (Seanad Eireann).
Monetary Unit: Pound (0.5543 pound equals U.S.$1, Dec. 10, 1990).
Gross Domestic Product (1989 est. U.S.$): $31,400,-000,000.
Economic Indexes (1989): *Consumer Prices* (1980 = 100), all items, 203.0; food, 184.9. *Industrial Production* (1980 = 100), 184.
Foreign Trade (1989 U.S.$): *Imports,* $17,564,-000,000; *exports,* $20,974,000,000.

the two men would face if they had to reenter a British-controlled prison. Northern Irish Secretary Brooke called the verdict, which set the men free, "an unacceptable slur"; Prime Minister Thatcher insisted that this "grossly unfair" ruling would encourage terrorists to regard the Irish Republic as a "safe haven."

Three weeks later the Supreme Court refused to extradite Owen Carron, a Sinn Fein supporter and a former member of the British Parliament, who was wanted by the authorities on a firearms charge. Haughey defended this decision on legalistic grounds. But others called for reform of the law in such cases.

As president of the European Council, Haughey paid an official visit to Belfast on April 11. No Irish premier had visited the north for some 25 years. Haughey stressed that the Irish and British governments were committed to suppressing terrorism.

In Dublin on July 2, African National Congress leader Nelson Mandela called on the British government to begin talks with the Provisional IRA about a peaceful resolution of the struggle over Northern Ireland. The comment caused much controversy.

Domestic Affairs and Other News. On October 31, Premier Haughey barely survived a vote of confidence in the Dail over his dismissal of Brian Lenihan, an old friend and deputy prime minister. The action followed charges that Lenihan had not told the truth about a 1982 political deal. Despite the crisis, Lenihan ran a strong race for the presidency of the republic. However, his chief rival, Sen. Mary Robinson, the Labour candidate, won a stunning victory in the runoff elections on November 9 to become Ireland's first woman president.

The Irish treasury announced that during 1989 government borrowing fell to 2.4% of gross national product (GNP), the lowest such figure in 40 years.

L. PERRY CURTIS, JR., *Brown University*

AP/Wide World

Following the collapse of Israel's National Unity Government of the Labor and Likud parties in March 1990, Yitzhak Shamir successfully formed a new right-of-center coalition government three months later.

ISRAEL

The Arab-Israel conflict overshadowed both domestic and foreign affairs in Israel during 1990, leading to collapse of the National Unity Government (NUG) formed in 1988. The conflict converged with a new Persian Gulf crisis caused by Iraq's invasion of Kuwait on August 2, when riots in Jerusalem became the principal item on the agenda of the UN Security Council during October. The unexpected arrival of about 200,000 new Jewish immigrants from the Soviet Union had a major impact on the country's economy, adding to severe unemployment and housing shortages.

Domestic Affairs. By September some 165,000 Israelis, about 10% of the work force, were unemployed. The finance ministry estimated that the figure would exceed 200,000 by 1994 and that for the next five years the unemployment rate would be at least 10%. Despite promises by the right-wing Likud Party to privatize the economy, the government consumed more than 60% of the gross national product (GNP), and one third of the work force was in the public sector. Output per capita was estimated to be one half of that in other Western countries. Although 56% of earned income was taxed, tax evasion was estimated at $3 billion per year with a "black" economy running at 30% of GNP. Debts of public-sector institutions such as *kibbutzim* (collective settlements) and *moshavin* (cooperative settlements) totaled $4 billion; Koor, the country's largest industrial conglomerate, needed a large government bailout to avoid bankruptcy. The health and education systems also seemed to be on the verge of collapse. As a result of the large influx of new immigrants, foreign debt was expected to rise by $4 billion in the next four years.

In 1990 some 200,000 new immigrants arrived in Israel, the largest number since the early days of the state. Some estimates were that immigration from Eastern Europe might exceed 1 million by the mid-1990s. This unanticipated influx resulted from the political turmoil in Eastern Europe: on one hand travel restrictions and emigration controls were relaxed; on the other there was a resurgence of anti-Semitism, especially in the Soviet Union.

The sudden arrival of tens of thousands of new immigrants caught the government unprepared. The already existing housing shortage was exacerbated greatly. Furthermore, the economy was unable to absorb the huge numbers of new scientists, engineers, musicians, doctors, academicians, and other such professionals. While there was an oversupply of the highly skilled, shortages of labor were such that Arabs from the occupied territories continued to be employed in construction, agriculture, and unskilled labor.

As the cost of housing escalated many Israelis were unable to afford the new high rents, and were forced to leave their homes to make way for the new arrivals from the Soviet Union whose accommodations were paid for by the state or public institutions. By midyear tent encampments of Israeli homeless began to spring up throughout the country; in several places their protest demonstrations led to altercations with the police. By October the absorption minister told the cabinet that the housing crisis fast was approaching the "zero hour" and that soon there would be no alternative but to put new immigrants in tents and army bases.

As population increased, Israel, like its neighbors, also was faced with a growing water shortage. Engineers warned that unless immediate steps were taken to solve the country's water problems, Israel would face rationing and diminishing agricultural activity within five years. Proposals were introduced for desalination, recycling of sewage, flood catchments, and higher water prices to encourage water conservation.

New Government. Domestic unrest caused by clashes between Jews and Arabs intensified during 1990. Violence in Jerusalem, Israel's capital, was the worst since the 1967 war. Labor and Likud, the two principal parties in the NUG, continued to disagree over policy toward the Palestinians throughout the year. Leaders of the Labor Party were willing to accept compromise proposals offered by the United States and Egypt for negotiations between Israel and the Palestinians. However, the prime minister, Likud leader Yitzhak Shamir, maintained his opposition to negotiations involving the Palestine Liberation Organization (PLO). Even so, Shamir was attacked at a meeting of the Likud Central Committee in February by Minister of Trade and Industry Ariel Sharon for proposing elections in the West Bank and Gaza. Sharon, charging that the plan would lead to a Palestinian state, resigned from the cabinet and threatened to form a new faction of his own.

A few days later the Labor Party gave Shamir an ultimatum demanding acceptance of a compromise with the United States. This led to Shamir's firing of Deputy Prime Minister Shimon Peres, leader of the Labor Party, in March. The other Labor members of the cabinet then resigned and the Knesset voted 60 to 55 to dissolve the NUG because of Shamir's refusal to accept a U.S. framework for talks with the Palestinians.

It took three months until a new government could be formed in June by Shamir. The new coalition excluded Labor; it was a right-of-center, nationalist government with support from the religious bloc. Fifteen of the new cabinet's 23 members were from Likud. Other parties represented were the militantly nationalist Tzomet and Tehiya, and the orthodox National Religious Party and Shas. Shamir remained prime minister; important new appointments were David Levy as deputy prime minister and

minister of foreign affairs, Moshe Arens as minister of defense, Yitzhak Modai as finance minister, and Sharon returning to the cabinet as minister of construction and housing.

Foreign Relations. As a result of the new government's adamant position against negotiations with Palestinians from Jerusalem or any of those affiliated with the PLO, the peace process was stalled and relations with the United States continued to deteriorate rapidly; U.S. Secretary of State James Baker threatened to break off U.S. efforts to mediate the conflict. Several incidents that led to altercations between Israelis and Palestinians in the occupied territories further worsened U.S.-Israeli relations. Among the more provocative were two in Jerusalem. In April, 150 orthodox Jewish settlers moved into several buildings belonging to the Greek Orthodox Church near the Holy Sepulchre. The move touched off riots by Arab protesters, created divisions within the Jewish community, and jeopardized Israel's request from the United States for guarantees of $400 million in housing loans. A few days after the incident, Israel's High Court ordered the settlers to leave the occupied buildings.

In October another riot between Jews and Palestinians in Jerusalem thrust the Arab-Israel conflict to the forefront of international attention, briefly displacing the Iraq-Kuwait crisis as the number-one issue before the UN Security Council. The incident was sparked by rumors that Jewish zealots were about to invade the Haram es-Sherif (Temple Mount), Islam's third-most holy site, to lay the cornerstone for a new Jewish temple. Muslim protesters began to stone Jews who were worshipping at the Wailing Wall that adjoins the Temple Mount, considered Israel's most sacred place. Israeli security and police forces called to suppress the rioting fired into the crowd of Muslims, killing at least 18 and wounding more than 100. Israel's handling of the outbreak was debated for several days at the Security Council and by November two resolutions were passed condemning Israel. They were the first UN condemnations of Israel supported by the United States since the invasion of Lebanon in 1982, and only the third time in UN history that the United States had taken such a step.

A major consequence of the Jerusalem outbreak in October was that the Arab-Israel conflict remained one of the two major issues before the Security Council for the rest of the year. This led to increasing diplomatic isolation of Israel. Despite attempts by the United States to persuade the new Israeli government to modify its position, Israel continued to resist provisions of the Security Council resolution calling for an international investigation of the Jerusalem melee.

See MIDDLE EAST.

DON PERETZ
State University of New York, Binghamton

ISRAEL • Information Highlights

Official Name: State of Israel.
Location: Southwest Asia.
Area: 8,019 sq mi (20 770 km²).
Population (mid-1990 est.): 4,600,000.
Chief Cities (Dec. 31, 1985 est.): Jerusalem, the capital, 457,700 (including East Jerusalem); Tel Aviv-Jaffa, 322,800; Haifa, 224,600.
Government: *Head of state,* Chaim Herzog, president (took office May 1983). *Head of government,* Yitzhak Shamir, prime minister (took office October 1986). *Legislature* (unicameral)—Knesset.
Monetary Unit: Shekel (2.0283 shekels equal U.S.$1, Dec. 31, 1990).
Gross National Product (1989 U.S.$): $38,000,-000,000.
Economic Indexes (1989): *Consumer Prices* (1980 = 100), all items, 55,832.6. *Industrial Production* (1980 = 100), 124.
Foreign Trade (1989 U.S.$): *Imports,* $12,706,-000,000; *exports,* $10,318,000,000.

ITALY

Italy sought to play a larger role in the European Community and world affairs in 1990. At home, the country's Communist Party, its power diminished, changed its name and tried to change its image in an attempt to find a new place for itself in Italian political life. North-South sectionalism, always strong in Italy, took on political form as regional parties won support from northern voters. As in other European countries, an influx of Third World immigrants provoked a backlash among the population.

Coalition Government. Italy started the year with a shaky coalition government, headed since July 1989 by Giulio Andreotti, a right-wing Christian Democrat who displaced Ciriaco De Mita, leader of the party's left wing. The five-party *(pentapartito)* government consisted of Christian Democrats, Socialists, Social Democrats, Republicans, and Liberals. The members of the coalition jealously divided up the patronage available to them in the huge state-controlled industrial and banking sectors of the economy.

Andreotti's government survived two revolts launched by De Mita in March and July. In the latter crisis, five ministers loyal to De Mita resigned from the cabinet. At issue was a proposed law to limit commercials on television, a move aimed at Silvio Berlusconi, the king of Italian private television and a major financial supporter of Bettino Craxi's Socialist Party, the principal rival to the Christian Democrats. The survival of his wobbly government enabled Premier Andreotti to remain in control of the presidency of the European Community during the last half of 1990 when Italy assumed this rotating office.

The Political Left. The anti-Communist earthquake in Eastern Europe in 1989–90 also rattled the hammer and sickle in Italy. Achille Occhetto, leader of the Italian Communist Party, quickly sought to promote a new role for his 1.5-million-member party by dropping its old image and changing its name. For several months, many of the faithful referred to their party as simply *La Cosa* (The Thing). By October 1990, after long debate, the party leadership recommended that it rename itself the *Partito Democratico della Sinistra* (Democratic Party of the Left) and adopt a social democratic stance that would emphasize such issues as feminism and the environment. The new party banner would be a tree with spreading branches, to show the hoped-for spread of support. At the foot of this symbolic tree would be the old initials (PCI) and the hammer and sickle, albeit much reduced in size.

Though there was some resistance from Pietro Ingrao and others in the party's "old guard," these changes probably would be approved at the party's conference in January

AP/Wide World

In March, Italy's Premier Giulio Andreotti addressed a joint session of the U.S. Congress, with House Speaker Thomas Foley (left) and Sen. Robert Byrd presiding.

1991. Occhetto also expressed the desire to have his party join the Socialist International, but this seemed out of his reach for the present.

Meanwhile, the rival Italian Socialist Party also assumed a new name in October, in a move taken by its ambitious leader, former Prime Minister Bettino Craxi. With no warning, he announced that henceforth it would be known as the Party of Socialist Unity. This was seen as an open invitation to everyone on the left who remained unimpressed by the Communists' change of labels. Behind the Socialists' name change lay a struggle for control of an eventual left-wing alternative to the Italian governments that since World War II either have been led or dominated by the Christian Democrats.

The Communist Party still was in second place but slipping, dropping from 34% of the popular vote in the 1976 parliamentary elections to 24% in nationwide local elections held in May 1990. Craxi's Socialists, in third place, had grown steadily, polling 15% of the vote in these elections. While they continued, pragmatically, to join the Christian Democratic coalition governments, they aspired to close the gap with the Communists and become the undisputed leader of the left. This would enable them to offer a viable "democratic alternative" to the Christian Democrats.

Environmental Issues. In a nationwide referendum in June, three measures that effectively would have banned hunting and greatly restricted the use of pesticides in farming won

92% support from those who voted. But because less than the requisite one half of eligible voters bothered to show up, the results had no validity. This was the first time since World War II that a referendum failed to attract the required number of voters. As such, it raised questions about the future of this much-used political device, which in the past has made possible the legalization of divorces and abortions in this Roman Catholic land.

North-South Regional Split. One of the most surprising results of the nationwide local elections in May was the strong showing of the new Lombard League in the area around Milan, Italy's most industrialized and populous region. The league had become the second-biggest party in Lombardy, winning nearly 20% of the vote. Nationally, the league now ranked fourth, with 5% of the vote, ahead of both the Republicans, a member of the government coalition, and the fast-declining neo-fascist Italian Social Movement (MSI). Similar leagues in the prosperous northern regions of Piedmont, Veneto, and Liguria also did well.

These new regional political forces in the North voiced loud opposition to continuation of the post-World War II pattern of "wasteful" subsidization of the economically backward South. The northern leagues contended that the area of Italy that lies south of a line extending from Ancona across the peninsula to Rome is a hopeless economic bog. They complained that the Mafia and other crime syndicates have penetrated the ruling Christian Democratic Party in the South and gained control of the northern subsidies. The last thing the feudal-minded Mafia wants is modernization, these critics asserted, and they pointed out that 66% of the homicides in Italy take place in three regions of the deep South: Sicily, Calabria, and Campania (Naples). Some even voiced regret that Giuseppe Garibaldi brought these areas into the unified state in 1860.

The Lombard League would prefer to reconstruct Italy into a confederation, like Switzerland, with a self-governing North separate from the center and the South. After Italy's President Francesco Cossiga sadly conceded on national television in October that "materially and morally an iron curtain runs through our own people," some observers wondered if Italy was coming apart at its regional seams at the very time the European Community was moving toward political federation.

Economy. Despite the great disparity between North and South, and the vast social problem of organized crime, Italy was better off than many countries. Its economy was the fifth-largest in the world and it had a healthy balance of trade. Its inflation rate (6.6%) was lower than Britain's, and its people were richer. In April the country ended its last controls on the movement of capital abroad. Italy was investing heavily in east-central Europe, and in November extended more than $6 billion in loans and export credits to the Soviet Union, at President Mikhail Gorbachev's urgent request. Although the economy was growing less spectacularly in 1990 than it did in the 1980s, Italy's prosperity was not in doubt. Nevertheless, huge economic and social problems faced the country. Tax evasion was common. Many inefficiencies existed in the oversized bureaucracy, the banks, and the public sector of industry. The public debt, aggravated by the high cost of pensions and public health services, also was gigantic. As a percentage of gross domestic product (GDP), this public debt was 11%, which was proportionately about five times the size of that of the United States. As a result, interest rates were very high. The national rate of unemployment was 11.7%, but it was double this figure in the South.

Traditionally, Italy has been a country of emigration; but recently it has become one of immigration. With limited visa requirements, Italy has been an easy point of entry to the European Community, especially for Africans. As a result, perhaps 1.5 million such immigrants now live in Italy. They often start out as farm workers in the South. As soon as they learn a bit of Italian, they drift north and work in small factories or become traders in the streets of big cities, or perhaps drug pushers. Growing hostility toward this underclass erupted into violence in Florence in March, where clashes led to the resignation of the mayor. As a consequence, the government imposed tighter controls on non-EC immigration, while granting an amnesty to those who arrived prior to 1990.

Foreign Affairs. Following the collapse of the Berlin Wall, Italy had misgivings about German unification and was unhappy at being left out of the "two plus four" talks. But Premier Andreotti and Foreign Minister Gianni De Michelis soon agreed that German unification was inevitable. In De Michelis' words, it was "the only possible way to prevent Central Europe from becoming even more destabilized than it is now." Insisting that an enlarged Germany must be anchored firmly in the European Community and the North Atlantic Treaty Organization (NATO), Premier Andreotti also urged the United States and Canada to keep troops in Europe in order to maintain stability.

De Michelis, an unconventional diplomat who comes from Venetia (once a part of the Habsburg Empire), repeatedly urged creation of a "Mitteleuropa" economic bloc in which Italy could play a profitable role with Austria, Hungary, Czechoslovakia, and Yugoslavia. Ethnically divided Yugoslavia showed less interest than the others in the suggestion.

In July, Italy arranged for the evacuation to Brindisi of thousands of Albanian anti-Communists who had taken asylum in the foreign embassies in Tiranë, the Albanian capital. Many later were resettled elsewhere.

From July until year's end, Italy held the rotating presidency of the European Community. Italy was an enthusiastic advocate of the removal of all remaining barriers to the free movement of capital, goods, and labor within the Community.

At a summit meeting in Rome in October, Premier Andreotti persuaded all the Community leaders, except Margaret Thatcher of Britain, to begin the second stage of Economic and Monetary Union on Jan. 1, 1994. That stage includes the establishment of a European central bank, followed by creation of a single currency.

In the wake of Iraq's invasion of Kuwait in August, Foreign Minister De Michelis managed to get Italy's fractious political parties to rise above their often equivocal stance toward Middle Eastern problems and to lend full support to UN economic sanctions against Iraq. Although public opinion, particularly on the political left, prevented Italy from sending ground forces, the government did respond to Washington's call for "burden sharing" by dispatching four warships and eight Tornado fighter planes to the Persian Gulf. Italy also tried to get the EC to speak with one voice in dealing with the Gulf crisis. To this end, De Michelis advocated revitalization of WEU (the Western European military alliance which preceded NATO)—without much success. Hoping to split the UN bloc, Iraq permitted many Italian hostages to go home.

In October, De Michelis invited representatives from several countries bordering the Mediterranean and Black seas to come to Rome for talks. He proposed establishment of a permanent Conference on Security and Cooperation in the Mediterranean (CSCM), to be modeled on the Conference on Security and Cooperation in Europe (CSCE). How inclusive such a body would be and what its role might be remained unclear.

Gladio. Also in October, Premier Andreotti revealed the existence of Gladio, a secret anti-

AP/Wide World

The Leaning Tower of Pisa, in danger of toppling, was closed in January so that university and oil-industry experts could begin work to make the famous landmark safe.

Communist guerrilla organization whose existence in Italy dates back to the 1950s. The group, operating within the framework of NATO, consisted of several hundred "resistance fighters" with access to arms caches hidden in different parts of the country, to be used in the event of a Soviet invasion. Government critics suggested a connection between Gladio and right-wing terrorist groups active in Italy during the 1970s. Andreotti's disclosures were followed by reports of similar networks in other NATO countries. With Cold War tension easing, it was revealed late in 1990 that Gladio was disbanding.

World Cup. Italy was the host country for the summer 1990 World Cup soccer competition. In the semifinals in Naples on July 3, Italy was eliminated by Argentina on penalty kicks. In the finals played in Rome, West Germany defeated Argentina to win the cup.

Obituaries. The year 1990 marked the passing of some of Italy's most prominent citizens. These included 93-year-old Sandro Pertini, a former president of the republic (1978–85) who as an anti-Fascist resister had spent many years in Mussolini's prisons; Mariano Rumor, a five-time Christian Democratic premier during the tumultuous 1960s and 1970s, who died in Vicenza at the age of 74; and Alberto Moravia, one of Italy's most famous novelists, who died at 82 in his beloved Rome.

CHARLES F. DELZELL, *Vanderbilt University*

ITALY • Information Highlights

Official Name: Italian Republic.
Location: Southern Europe.
Area: 116,305 sq mi (301 230 km²).
Population (mid-1990 est.): 57,700,000.
Chief Cities (Dec. 31, 1988): Rome, the capital, 2,816,474; Milan, 1,464,127; Naples, 1,202,582.
Government: *Head of state,* Francesco Cossiga, president (took office July 1985). *Head of government,* Giulio Andreotti, prime minister (sworn in July 10, 1989). *Legislature*—Parliament: Senate and Chamber of Deputies.
Monetary Unit: Lira (1,122.75 lire equal U.S.$1, Dec. 6, 1990).
Gross Domestic Product (1989 est. U.S.$): $803,300,000,000.
Economic Indexes (1989): *Consumer Prices* (1980 = 100), all items, 235.6; food, 219.1. *Industrial Production* (1980 = 100), 113.
Foreign Trade (1989 U.S.$): *Imports,* $152,913,-000,000; *exports,* $138,503,000,000.

Japan's Prime Minister Toshiki Kaifu is greeted by Prince Abdul Aziz Al-Saud of Saudi Arabia during Kaifu's October tour of the Mideast, after which Japan agreed to provide a $2 billion aid package to "front-line nations" in their struggle to end the Iraqi occupation of Kuwait.

AP/Wide World

JAPAN

Despite the "Iraq shock," soaring crude oil prices, a volatile Tokyo Stock Exchange (TSE), and an increase in the official discount rate by the Bank of Japan, the Japanese economy continued to expand in 1990. The Economic Planning Agency (EPA) projected that the economy would surpass the 4% growth-rate target for the fiscal year ending in March 1991, while private economists projected a real growth rate of 4.5% to 5%. Japan also remained the world's largest creditor nation with a 1989 net balance of assets totaling $293.2 billion.

At the same time, Japan faced uncertainty over its role in the world community. There were obstacles in translating economic clout into political power abroad. Public opinion at home was ambivalent over the suggested dispatch of Japan's defense forces to the Middle East. Moreover, the nation's international legal status on fielding troops outside Japan remained in limbo. In October at the 45th session of the United Nations General Assembly, Foreign Minister Taro Nakayama recommended amending provisions of the UN Charter, which in 1945 defined Japan as an "enemy state." Revision would require the consent of the five permanent members of the Security Council—the United States, Great Britain, the Soviet Union, France, and China—and two thirds of the members of the General Assembly.

Domestic Affairs

In July 1989 the ruling Liberal-Democratic Party (LDP) lost control of a Diet chamber for the first time since the party's formation in 1955. In an election for half of the (upper) House of Councillors, the LDP won only 36 seats. Combined with the 73 LDP seats not up for reelection, the total (109) was well below a simple majority (127). The Japan Socialist Party (JSP) won ten more new seats (46) than the LDP. With 20 seats not up during the election, the JSP had a total of 66 seats. Allied with other opposition parties—the Komeito, the Japan Communist Party (JCP), the Democratic Socialist Party (DSP), and independents—the JSP could outvote the LDP in the 252-seat house.

Although Takako Doi, chairwoman of the JSP and leader of the opposition, had been nominated to be prime minister in the upper house in August 1989, the LDP majority in the (lower) House of Representatives took precedence. As a result, LDP President Toshiki Kaifu was reelected as prime minister, pending a general election for the lower house in February 1990.

Party Politics. Prime Minister Kaifu had a weak power base within his party but moved with determination to rid the LDP of stains remaining from the so-called Recruit influence-buying scandal of 1988–89. "Money politics" had swept out of office his predecessors, Noboru Takeshita and Sousuke Uno. Moreover, his principal rivals within the LDP—former Foreign Minister Shintaro Abe, former Finance Minister Kiichi Miyazawa, and party leader Michio Watanabe—also had been tainted in the Recruit affair.

In the campaign for the general election, Kaifu faced several difficult issues: "money politics"; election reform; a 3% consumption tax, which was implemented in 1989; and international demands for liberalization of Japan's domestic rice market. The rice issue struck at one of the cores of perennial LDP support, represented by the Central Union of Agricultural Cooperatives (Renchu), which insisted on rice self-sufficiency for Japan.

In the election held February 18, the LDP won a slim victory by capturing a little less than half of the popular vote. The 512 seats in the lower house were distributed as follows: LDP-275, JSP-136, Komeito-45, JCP-16, DSP-14, independents-26. When 11 successful independents joined its party caucus in the Diet, the LDP party commanded 286 seats. The total was enough to control deliberations in all of the standing committees.

Again the JSP made dramatic gains, increasing representation from 89 to 139 seats (including three independents). The increases were, however, at the expense of other opposition parties, which lost seats. Nonetheless, as an *Asahi Shimbun* editorial put it, Socialist success was "an indication of strong dissatisfaction with LDP politics."

Prime Minister Kaifu acted promptly to offset the negative image. In forming a new cabinet, he relied on traditional LDP factions: his own, inherited from Toshio Komoto; and two identified with former prime ministers, Yasuhiro Nakasone and Takeshita. He, however, did pass over party figures who had been involved deeply in the Recruit scandal. He chose Nakayama to be foreign minister and Ryutaro Hashimoto, finance minister. A possible rival in the future, Ichiro Ozawa, took the strategic post of secretary-general of the LDP.

Opposition strength soon produced gridlock in Diet deliberations. Led by the JSP, opposition parties boycotted budget hearings, demanding reconsideration of the 3% consumption tax. The government was forced to adopt a stopgap budget to cover April and May. Early in June, for the first time, the House of Councillors rejected a government budget by a vote of 131–110. Having been endorsed by the LDP-controlled House of Representatives in May, however, the budget became law on June 9. Here again, under the national constitution, the decision of the lower house took precedence.

The fiscal 1990 budget provided for expenditures of 66.3 trillion yen (about $442 billion). It represented a 9.7% increase over the original budget for the previous year, boosting social welfare, defense, and official development assistance.

After the budget battle, Diet proceedings subsided into a spirit of cooperation. By the end of the ordinary session on June 26, some 90% of government bills had been passed. The ruling party agreed to postpone consideration of tax matters, including the controversial consumption levy. The LDP and the opposition formed joint committees of the two houses to seek a compromise in a special fall session. "The JSP took a realistic approach as a responsible party and did not boycott Diet business," an LDP spokesman said.

In their 55th regular convention held in Tokyo in March, the Socialists had affirmed the reappointment of Doi as head of the JSP for a third term. The party revised its program to support movement toward social democracy in Japan, dropping the more radical goal of social revolution.

Meanwhile, the Kaifu administration faced the delicate issue of reform of election constituencies. In a May 10 news conference, the prime minister appealed for public support, pledging that he would "stake the life of my government" on election reform. He referred to a report submitted by a panel of advisers on April 26. After more than a year of deliberations, the committee recommended replacement of the lower House's multiseat constituency system with a scheme in which 60% of voting districts would be allotted only one seat each. Representation in the remaining 40% would be determined on a proportional basis. The total number of representatives also would be reduced from 512 to 500.

On May 11, Kaifu appeared before five LDP faction heads in a televised meeting, encountering complaints that incumbents would find it more difficult to be elected in such a system. The prime minister also promised to talk with leaders of three opposition parties, the JSP, the DSP, and Komeito. There seemed little doubt that the new electoral plan, if adopted, would reduce sharply the influence of "money politics."

Economy. On March 31, the end of fiscal 1989, the EPA estimated inflation-adjusted growth for the year at 5%. For calendar 1989 the gross national product (GNP) totaled 347 trillion yen (about $2.67 trillion).

In May 1990 the seasonally adjusted unemployment rate stood at 2.1%, the lowest level since 1981. Japan had practically full employment. Indeed, in September the labor ministry

---

JAPAN • Information Highlights

Official Name: Japan.
Location: East Asia.
Area: 145,882 sq mi (377 835 km²).
Population (mid-1990 est.): 123,600,000.
Chief Cities (March 31, 1988 est.): Tokyo, the capital, 8,155,781; Yokohama, 3,121,601; Osaka, 2,543,520; Nagoya, 2,099,564.
Government: *Head of state*, Akihito, emperor (acceded Jan. 9, 1989). *Head of government*, Toshiki Kaifu, prime minister (took office Aug. 9, 1989). *Legislature*—Diet: House of Councillors and House of Representatives.
Monetary Unit: Yen (133.17 yen equal U.S.$1, Dec. 17, 1990).
Gross National Product (1989 est. U.S.$): $2,670,000,-000,000.
Economic Indexes (1989): *Consumer Prices* (1980 = 100), all items, 118.8; food, 116.9. *Industrial Production* (1980 = 100), 142.
Foreign Trade (1989 U.S.$): *Imports*, $210,840,-000,000; *exports*, $275,173,000,000.

announced a labor shortage of almost 2 million skilled workers, especially in construction and information processing. This shortage was accompanied by immigration of unskilled laborers, with many job seekers coming to Japan illegally.

Among advanced industrial nations, Japan recently has had a relatively modest inflation rate. The consumer price index stood at 107.1 in May, compared with 104.2 in May 1989, and 100 in May 1985. Implementation of the 3% consumption tax in 1989 put pressure on prices, as did soaring crude-oil costs after August. In any case, on March 20, Governor Yasushi Mieno of the Bank of Japan moved against the threat of inflation by raising the official discount rate to 5.25%. On August 30 he raised the prime rate again to a nine-year high of 6%. The governor also was influenced by wild fluctuations on the TSE.

In December 1989 the 225-issue Nikkei stock average on the TSE had peaked at an all-time high of 38,915 yen. On March 22, even before Iraq's invasion of Kuwait and the resulting Persian Gulf crisis, the average plunged below the 30,000-yen level. It soon rebounded to 31,841 yen but the market remained under pressure, a result of the Gulf crisis.

Imperial Family. As the new emperor, Akihito, prepared for his formal accession to the throne in Tokyo, public debate swirled around the ancient rituals. A number of groups protested the celebrations as violations of the constitutional separation of church and state. From the beginning of planning, the government carefully distinguished the *Soku no rei* (enthronement ceremony, November 12) as a "public affair"; and the *Daijosai* (great food offering, November 22–23) as a "private ceremony." The former was attended by as many foreign dignitaries as witnessed the funeral of the Showa Emperor, Hirohito, in 1989. The latter was a time-honored Shinto rite, carried out in a temporary shrine in the precincts of the Imperial Palace.

Perhaps the Japanese public paid more attention to another imperial ceremony: the wedding of the emperor's 24-year-old second son, Aya (Prince Akishino) and his commoner classmate, Kiko Kawashima. Kiko-chan, or "Little Kiko" as she is known in the media, is the daughter of an economics professor, and she had lived in Philadelphia for six years mastering English. The prince also had studied abroad at Oxford University. The young couple seemed to offer the Japanese a modern image. (*See* page 86.)

Foreign Affairs

During the year the fad in Tokyo was to speak of the "internationalization" *(kokusaika)* of Japan. The campaign to make the nation less insular, less parochial, had been launched by former Prime Minister Nakasone, perhaps the Japanese leader best known abroad.

The TSE had been opened up so that foreign firms held seats on the exchange. Education was reworked to instill cosmopolitan values, while at the same time continuing to emphasize traditional Japanese culture. More than 1 million Japanese tourists went abroad in August, serving to reduce the current account surplus by more than $2 billion. Trade disputes continued and were worrisome, but they too tended to link Japan with the world. And finally, the crisis in the Middle East raised a variety of new questions about Japan's status in the world.

U.S. Relations. Although the trade surplus with the United States fell 12.7% to about $43 billion in fiscal 1989, trade issues continued to dominate negotiations between Tokyo and Washington. One of the most sensitive problems arose from constant U.S. pressure on Japan to liberalize its market to allow rice imports. According to a General Agreements on Tariffs and Trade (GATT) report, Japan's government has been paying 600% more for rice than the corresponding world price. To many —including Japanese consumers—rice has become a key issue in the campaign for internationalization.

During the February election campaign, candidates of both the LDP and opposition parties chorused that "not a single grain of rice" ever should be imported. The LDP in particular feared loss of support from a traditional constituency, the nation's rice farmers, and even retaliation by the Federation of Agricultural Cooperatives.

In June, Komeito, the second-largest opposition party, broke the political taboo by urging partial liberalization. A former prime minister, Noboru Takeshita, praised the Komeito posture as "courageous." On July 13, Toshio Yamaguchi, head of an LDP panel, proposed that rice imports should account for 5% of the nation's annual demand of 10 million tons. Deputy Cabinet Secretary Nobuo Ishihara then restated the LDP's opposition to the importing of rice.

On July 7, on the eve of the Houston summit meeting of advanced industrial democracies, U.S. President George Bush stressed to Prime Minister Kaifu the importance of rice liberalization. At the summit, the matter of rice imports was put off to be considered among agricultural issues at the GATT Uruguay Round talks, scheduled for Geneva in December. Back in Japan, the media predicted that the LDP would move to ease restrictions after local elections in April 1991.

At the same time, Tokyo and Washington entered a realm of unprecedented trade negotiations. The U.S. side, led by Linn Williams, the deputy trade representative, called the talks the "Structural Impediments Initiative"

(SII). The Japanese, led by Deputy Foreign Minister Koji Watanabe, made no reference to "impediments," referring to the talks instead as a "Structure Conference." The Americans and Japanese proceeded to bore into the respective economies and indeed into the very hearts of the two societies.

The United States urged Japan to *increase* spending and, therefore, imports; Japan argued that Americans should *decrease* spending, specifically, the excessive use of credit cards. The Tokyo team proposed that the United States *increase* its savings rate and balance its own budget; the Americans responded that Japanese should *decrease* their savings. Japanese officials were startled most by the request that they pledge a specific ratio (10%) of GNP for public expenditures on infrastructure. Watanabe remarked that this demand could be viewed as "tantamount to meddling in Japan's domestic affairs."

U.S. negotiators criticized Japanese exclusionary business practices, specifically affiliated businesses known as *keiretsu*. Seizing on an even more delicate issue, the U.S. team urged revision of a retail stores law, which protected neighborhood shops against intrusion by large-scale chains (including foreign firms). The Japanese lashed back with criticism of the United States for its lack of an overall industrial policy and its permitting business to concentrate on short-term profits rather than long-term gains.

Although acerbic comments had been exchanged in the SII talks, the Japanese public remained calm. In fact, many editorials supported structural reforms as favorable to consumers. On June 28, Tokyo announced tentative agreement in the marathon negotiations. Despite the fact that Japan's public-service investment (fiscal 1988, 8.7% of GNP) exceeded that of the United States (calendar 1988, 4.3% of GNP), the Kaifu government pledged to undertake a ten-year package of public-works projects worth almost $3 billion. Tokyo also agreed to monitor price patterns and domestic business practices. Trade tension declined somewhat, but many observers on both sides of the Pacific feared that scars remained to irritate the 30-year-old alliance. The Gulf crisis did little to improve relations.

The Middle East. Prior to August 2, when Iraq invaded Kuwait, Japan had imported 12% of its crude oil from the two countries and about 70% of its supplies from the Middle East as a whole. Some thought that Prime Minister Kaifu acted with courage on August 6 by imposing a ban on Iraqi oil and by freezing aid to Baghdad. Tokyo was uneasy with criticism, especially comments voiced by U.S. Ambassador Michael Armacost, that Tokyo's actions were unimpressive.

After a tour of the capitals of Iraq's neighbors in October, Kaifu unveiled a $2 billion aid package to "front-line nations"; he pledged an additional $2 billion to the multinational forces facing Iraq. The prime minister remained opposed, however, to revision of constitutional limitations on sending the nation's Self-Defense Forces (SDF) overseas.

When the prime minister did propose a so-called United Nations peace cooperation bill to use the SDF and other Japanese personnel in noncombat roles overseas, he encountered stiff public opposition in his homeland. Unfortunately, in Tokyo's view, Washington linked Japan's "free ride" in defense with an obligation by Japan to cover total costs of U.S. forces based in Nippon. In an informal news conference, defense chief Yozo Ishikawa remarked, "We did not ask for the stationing of U.S. forces here. We will have to say, 'Please return the forces home.' "

Soviet Relations. Tokyo had normalized relations with Moscow in 1956, but a formal post-World War II peace treaty remained hung up on a territorial issue. It involved what the Japanese call the "northern territories," small islands in the Kuriles occupied by Soviet forces since 1945. In September, Soviet Foreign Minister Eduard Shevardnadze visited Tokyo and a joint statement was issued calling on Iraq to withdraw from Kuwait. The Japanese-Soviet territorial debate was postponed, pending a visit to Japan by Soviet President Gorbachev, scheduled for April 1991.

Northeast Asia. In June an LDP figure, Michio Watanabe, met with Chinese Premier Li Peng in Beijing. He carried assurances of restoring a $5 billion loan package, suspended for a year after the Chinese crackdown on students in Tiananmen Square. Japan had been providing 70% of China's foreign aid prior to the crackdown.

In late May, President Roh Tae Woo of the Republic of (South) Korea was in Tokyo to receive a historic apology from Emperor Akihito. The emperor expressed regret for the suffering of Koreans caused by Japan's occupation of the peninsula from 1910 to 1945. The apology also opened up the possibility of normalization of relations with the Democratic People's Republic of (North) Korea, with which Tokyo has had no formal relations. Although Seoul was uneasy over this rapprochement, an LDP delegation led by Shin Kanemaru visited Pyongyang on September 24 and promised official talks as "soon as possible."

Southeast Asia. In June, Japan hosted peace talks on the Cambodian civil war. Representatives of the Vietnam-backed government and two of three resistance groups were brought together in Tokyo. However, the Khmer Rouge, who are radical Communists and former rulers of the country, boycotted the meeting.

ARDATH W. BURKS, *Rutgers University*

JORDAN

In Jordan interest centered for the first seven months of 1990 on domestic issues, and in the last five on external matters. It was, in general, an extremely difficult year. Added to the internal stresses that had been testing the country's institutions severely for several years was a whole new Himalayan range of problems for the monarchy arising out of the Iraq-Kuwait crisis. But that supreme survivor, the adroit, civilized, British-educated King Hussein, 37 years on the throne, had survived once again—no minor achievement. (*See* feature articles, page 24.)

Toward Parliamentary Democracy. The political changes in Jordan toward the end of 1989 and in 1990 were as interesting, and very nearly as far-reaching, as those in Eastern Europe. The ruling Hashemite family is Bedouin, and its traditional support is found in Jordan's Bedouin population; but Bedouins now are outnumbered slightly by Palestinian residents. Thus the Palestinian problem as a whole has come to seem for Jordan the one supremely important question in the Middle East.

To allay popular discontent the monarchy has embarked on a significant, and probably irreversible, series of steps toward democracy in the form of a parliamentary constitutional monarchy. The general election of November 1989, which was conducted with complete fairness, was the first in 22 years, and the first ever

in which women were able to vote. Candidates ran as individuals, political parties having been banned in 1957, but the Muslim Brotherhood, allowed to register as a charitable body, in effect functioned as a party. It won 20 seats in the 80-seat house, and together with 14 allies controlled 34 seats, easily the largest bloc. The new lower house, though not overtly antimonarchical, has sought a much more important role for itself.

A new prime minister, Mudar Badran, took office in December 1989; he had been prime minister from 1979 until 1984, and in the 1970s was head of the intelligence organization *(mukhaharat)*. Badran won a vote of confidence for confirmation on the first day of the new year, by 65 votes to nine. However, success came only after three bruising days of debate. Badran skillfully had split or conciliated potential opposition forces by a well-chosen set of cabinet appointments. He also had brought about at the turn of the year a number of significant reforms, and had promised others. Under the reforms, three newspapers taken over in 1988 were returned to their former owners. Banned journalists were allowed to write again, and the Writers' Association was allowed to function. Of more general impact, the lifting of restrictions on travel was promised. The prime minister also promised to suspend martial law and to cooperate in exposing corruption.

The first half of the year saw the government moving gradually to implement these re-

Shortly after Iraq's invasion of Kuwait in August 1990, Jordan's King Hussein (left) conferred in Kennebunkport, ME, with President Bush, Secretary of State James Baker (right), and National Security Council Adviser Brent Scowcroft (center).
AP/Wide World

JORDAN • Information Highlights

Official Name: Hashemite Kingdom of Jordan.
Location: Southwest Asia.
Area: 35,475 sq mi (91 880 km²).
Population (mid-1990 est.): 4,100,000.
Chief Cities (Dec. 1986): Amman, the capital, 972,000; Zarqa, 392,220; Irbid, 271,000.
Government: *Head of state,* Hussein I, king (acceded Aug. 1952). *Head of government,* Mudar Badran, prime minister (took office Dec. 4, 1989). *Legislature*—Parliament: House of Representatives and Senate.
Monetary Unit: Dinar (.64090 dinar equals U.S.$1, Dec. 31, 1990).
Gross National Product (1989 U.S.$): $5,200,000,000.
Economic Index (1989): *Consumer Prices* (1980 = 100), all items, 174.0; food, 154.2.
Foreign Trade (1989 U.S.$): *Imports,* $2,119,000,000; *exports,* $926,000,000.

forms. The king, early in April, appointed an advisory commission to draw up a "national charter to regulate political parties," to ensure that any newly authorized parties would not be manipulated from outside Jordan. The 60-member body was widely representative and included members of the Communist Party, the Jordanian branch of the Popular Front for the Liberation of Palestine, and the Muslim Brotherhood.

In March parliament decided to refer to the judiciary a number of cases of alleged corruption involving prominent Jordanians. Also in March the political left scored sweeping victories in professional-organization and trade-union elections. On the other hand, Islamic fundamentalists won a number of local elections in May.

Foreign Relations. Jordanian support for Saddam Hussein of Iraq, so prominent in the latter part of 1990, was already noticeable in the year's first half. The motivation appeared to be to bolster Jordanian security. Jordan feared that the increased immigration of Russian Jews into Israel would lead to an ousting of Palestinians there, and to an attempt by Israel to turn Jordan into the "Palestinian homeland." If this was an increasing nightmare for Jordan, the Jordanian response—military cooperation with Iraq in the form of joint air squadrons and joint ground-troop units—was a nightmare for Israel. It was also a striking departure from the tacit "live and let live" policy mutually followed by Jordan and Israel for decades.

The Kuwait crisis placed Jordan in an extremely vulnerable position militarily, economically, and politically. In August the king assumed, and maintained constantly thereafter, the role of the responsible statesman interested above all in maintaining peace. However, this was perceived in the West as a good deal less than was expected from the supposedly pro-Western king. While King Hussein opposed the annexation of Kuwait by Iraq, and continued to recognize the emir as Kuwait's legitimate ruler, Jordan voted against the Arab League's condemnation of Iraq, and strongly opposed the deployment into Saudi Arabia of international forces. In his role of peacemaker the king, especially in the first two months of the crisis, pursued energetic but fruitless diplomatic efforts. The king was caught between the adamant refusal of the dictator in Baghdad to leave Kuwait and the determination of the U.S.-led coalition to get him out. Relations with Cairo, London, Paris, and Washington were chilled. In September, Saudi Arabia expelled Jordan's diplomats, cut off its oil supply, and forbade trade. However, King Hussein rode an unprecedented wave of popularity at home as he refused to line up against Iraq. The king's popularity with Palestinians was enhanced further by his permitting the convocation in Amman on September 15 of a three-day anti-U.S. conference of Arab militants and Muslim radicals.

Refugees and Economic Hardships. Jordan had been under great economic stress for at least two years before the crisis erupted; it had been striving to meet International Monetary Fund conditions for economic aid since 1989. All the difficulties were exacerbated immensely in August by the flood of refugees that began to pour across the desert into Jordan from Iraq and Kuwait. Most of the refugees were displaced foreign workers from Egypt, but many also were originally from India, Pakistan, Bangladesh, or other nations. Most were making their way home, but transportation could not keep up with the flow of an estimated 700,000 refugees. Jordan faced the problem resolutely with limited resources, housing the refugees in transit camps at a cost of approximately $50 million. Another grievous burden was compliance with UN sanctions against Iraq. At the cost of bringing its economy (in the words of Crown Prince Hassan) "virtually to a standstill," Jordan was observing the sanctions fully by the end of September. It, however, was receiving Iraqi oil in payment against Iraqi debts.

By the end of November the immediate crisis at least had passed. Refugee camps were virtually empty, the rains had come, and Saddam Hussein posters were rarer.

ARTHUR CAMPBELL TURNER
University of California, Riverside

KANSAS

Kansans elected their first woman governor in 1990 and the most heated issue in the Kansas legislature concerned increased property taxes. The state's economy remained sluggish although agricultural production increased. Early in 1990 oil production hit a ten-year low, but began to increase as oil prices later rose. The state experienced several destructive thunderstorms and tornadoes.

Kansas joined the nation in marking the 100th birthday of its former resident, Dwight D. Eisenhower. (*See* special report, page 553.)

Elections. Primary and general election campaigns resulted in the defeat of a former and an incumbent governor. Incumbent Republican Gov. Mike Hayden survived a tough primary challenge only to be defeated by State Treasurer Joan Finney in the general election by approximately 48,000 votes. Finney, who would be the first woman governor of Kansas, had defeated former Gov. John Carlin in the August primary. Finney billed herself as the "people's candidate," while the Hayden campaign was hampered by the unpopularity of increased property taxes.

In other statewide races, Nancy Kassebaum (R) was elected to her third term in the U.S. Senate, Bill Graves (R) was reelected secretary of state, Robert Stephan (R) won a fourth term as attorney general, and political newcomer Sally Thompson (D) was elected state treasurer. Four of the state's incumbent U.S. representatives—Pat Roberts (R), Jim Slattery (D), Jan Meyers (R), and Dan Glickman (D)—were reelected and Republican Dick

© Nathan Ham, Topeka

Joan Finney

Joan Finney was born in Topeka, Feb. 12, 1925, and received a bachelor's degree from Washburn University. A former Republican turned Democrat, she was a member of the staff of former U.S. Sen. Frank Carlson. She also served as administrative assistant to the mayor of Topeka. Prior to her election as governor of Kansas in 1990, Finney had served for 16 years as the state's treasurer. A Roman Catholic, she is the mother of three children.

KANSAS · Information Highlights

Area: 82,277 sq mi (213 098 km²).
Population (1990 census prelim.): 2,467,000.
Chief Cities (July 1, 1988 est.): Topeka, the capital, 122,360; Wichita, 295,320; Kansas City, 160,630.
Government (1990): *Chief Officers*—governor, Mike Hayden (R); lt. gov., Jack D. Walker (R). *Legislature*—Senate, 40 members; House of Representatives, 125 members.
State Finances (fiscal year 1989): *Revenue,* $4,630,000,000; *expenditure,* $4,206,000,000.
Personal Income (1989): $41,454,000,000; per capita, $16,498.
Labor Force (June 1990): *Civilian labor force,* 1,342,000; *unemployed,* 50,600 (3.8% of total force).
Education: *Enrollment* (fall 1988)—public elementary schools, 306,751; public secondary, 119,845; colleges and universities, 152,847. *Public school expenditures* (1989–90), $1,761,851,000.

Nichols won the 5th District seat vacated by Bob Whittaker (R). The Democrats gained a slim majority in the Kansas House of Representatives. No elections were held for the state Senate, which maintained its GOP majority.

Legislation. The 1990 Kansas legislature struggled with financial issues, primarily the public's demand for property-tax relief. Property taxes, imposed and collected by Kansas counties, had increased greatly due to statewide reappraisal and the implementation of a classification system based on property use. In some instances, tax assessments increased 200%-300%. In most counties the bulk of property-tax money goes to support local school districts and, thus, property-tax relief is tied to finding additional sources of funding for education. Debate was complicated by shrinking state reserves as actual state revenue was lower than estimated for most of the year.

A drive to reinstate the death penalty failed, but a law imposing a minimum 40-year sentence for first-degree murder was passed. Other legislation set a cap on health costs in worker-compensation cases and strengthened penalties for drug possession, sale, and use.

Agriculture. The 1990 Kansas wheat crop was the highest on record, totaling 472 million bushels and surpassing the previous record in 1983 by 3%. The average yield was 40 bushels per acre, an increase of 16 bushels per acre over the drought-damaged 1989 crop.

Kansas once again led the nation in sorghum production with an estimated harvest of 184.8 million bushels, although total production decreased by about 7% due to a 25% decrease in harvested acreage. The 1990 corn crop was the state's largest since 1906, totaling 188.5 million bushels. Production of barley, rye, and hay crops was up, but oat, soybean, and sunflower production decreased. Income from livestock remained one of the leading cash producers in Kansas agriculture.

PATRICIA A. MICHAELIS
Kansas State Historical Society

KENTUCKY

Highlighting 1990 news in Kentucky was historic legislation passed by the General Assembly which totally revamped the state school system and placed Kentucky among the nation's leaders in educational reform. Politics also was a dominant issue, with the 1990 elections and maneuvering already under way for the 1991 gubernatorial election and probable reapportionment in 1992.

School Reform. The Kentucky Education Reform Act (KERA), which resulted in substantial changes in the governance, curriculum, and financing of Kentucky's public schools, came about because of a 1989 Kentucky Supreme Court ruling that declared the state's entire public-school system unconstitutional. Beginning in 1991 the state's school system will be headed by an appointed commissioner of education rather than an elected superintendent of public instruction. The Department of Education will be revamped and new state agencies will be formed to oversee education. At the local level, there will be a reduction in the power of local school boards through the formation of local school councils, composed of three teachers, two parents, and the school principal.

A major curriculum change is the introduction of an ungraded primary-education program which replaces grades one through three and sets more general performance-based standards and learning goals. Financing changes generally give substantially more funding to most school systems through increases in almost all state and local taxes. At the state level, a controversial $1.3 billion tax increase was passed. Most of the money came from individual-income-tax hikes and a 1% sales-tax increase.

Elections and Politics. The major statewide election contest was the U.S. Senate race, in which incumbent Mitch McConnell (R) de-

feated challenger Harvey Sloane (R) to win a second term with 52% of the vote despite strong Democratic registration and an anti-incumbency mood among the electorate. This mood nearly defeated 7th District Congressman Carl Perkins (D), who squeaked by with a 2,000-vote margin over William Scott, and did defeat a higher-than-usual proportion of incumbents in state legislative races.

Gubernatorial politics heated up as a number of candidates announced their intention to run for governor in 1991. Included was Martha Wilkinson (D), wife of incumbent Gov. Wallace Wilkinson, who unsuccessfully had sought a constitutional amendment allowing him to run for a second term. On the other side, Republicans were encouraged when 6th District Congressman Larry Hopkins joined the race, giving the GOP what many thought was its best chance for the governor's seat since 1967 when Louie B. Nunn was elected.

The 1990 General Assembly passed several important measures, particularly in health care. Included were a comprehensive health-care reform act, which targets poor and rural areas for increased medical support, and a bill allowing terminally ill persons to write "living wills," expressing their desires concerning the use of extraordinary measures to keep them alive.

Census. Preliminary 1990 census data showed Kentucky's population growth lagging behind the national average, which made it likely that the state would lose a congressional seat and experience strong political maneuvering during 1992's reapportionment.

PAUL BLANCHARD
Eastern Kentucky University

KENYA

During 1990 growing domestic and international opposition to President Daniel arap Moi's one-party rule led to greater restrictions on political dissent in Kenya, and international condemnation of Moi's policies threatened the country's sources of economic aid.

Domestic Unrest. In February, Foreign Minister Robert Ouko disappeared and was found murdered three days later. Ouko's funeral was accompanied by popular demonstrations expressing opposition to Moi and his Kenya African National Union (KANU). This prompted the president, who had come under heavy fire for human-rights violations during a recent visit to the United States, to ban all public meetings. Moi also sacked his minister of information, Waruru Kanja, after Kanja charged that Ouko's murder had been motivated politically and that it was linked to the government—an allegation later upheld during an investigation by Britain's Scotland Yard requested by Moi himself.

KENTUCKY • Information Highlights

Area: 40,410 sq mi (104 660 km²).
Population (1990 census prelim.): 3,665,000.
Chief Cities (July 1, 1988 est.): Frankfort, the capital (1980 census), 25,973; Louisville, 281,880; Lexington-Fayette, 225,700.
Government (1990): *Chief Officers*—governor, Wallace Wilkinson (D); lt. gov., Brereton Jones (D). *General Assembly*—Senate, 38 members; House of Representatives, 100 members.
State Finances (fiscal year 1989): *Revenue,* $8,028,000,000; *expenditure,* $7,401,000,000.
Personal Income (1989): $51,214,000,000; per capita, $13,743.
Labor Force (June 1990): *Civilian labor force,* 1,811,500; *unemployed,* 107,200 (5.9% of total force).
Education: *Enrollment* (fall 1988)—public elementary schools, 451,805; public secondary, 185,822; colleges and universities, 159,868. *Public school expenditures* (1989–90), $1,882,066,000.

Demonstrations in Kenya against President Daniel arap Moi and his one-party rule were sparked in February by the murder of Foreign Minister Robert Ouko. Moi retaliated by banning all public meetings and firing his minister of information.

© Joe Bernsen/Gamma-Liaison

Four months after Ouko's death, the home of opposition leader Kenneth Matiba was ransacked and his family severely beaten. Matiba, a powerful businessman and former government minister, had called for a public meeting to discuss multiparty democracy. Following Moi's ban on such events, Matiba and co-organizer Charles Rubia were placed (July 4) under indefinite detention. This move sparked Mwakenya, the underground movement led by novelist Ngugi wa Thong'o, to organize massive demonstrations throughout the country. While opposition to Moi and support for Mwakenya were thought to have deep roots among Kenya's educated middle class, feelings at the grass roots were more difficult to determine.

On July 10, Moi hurriedly returned from Ethiopia, where he had been preparing for a summit meeting of the Organization of African Unity. Following pledges of support from the military, Moi began arresting those advocates of multiparty elections, including a Presbyterian minister who was accused of having made "subversive" entries into his personal datebook.

International Aid. Moi's actions were criticized by international donors, who threatened to reconsider their aid, and by church leaders. Anglican Bishop Henry Okullu called for Moi's resignation to end Kenya's "dictatorship," and the nation's Roman Catholic bishops issued a pastoral letter voicing their concern.

In the U.S. Congress, pressure mounted to freeze U.S. assistance, and the Scandinavian countries issued a direct ultimatum: Improve human rights or lose more than $100 million in aid per year.

While the Kenyan economy registered its fifth consecutive year of 5% growth, both its balance of payments and its domestic budget registered substantial deficits. Imports grew by 26% while exports increased by just more than 7%; this was due in part to the collapse of international coffee prices. To remedy the situation, Kenya's Vice-President and Minister of Finance George Saitoti emphasized the need for continued concessionary assistance and expanded production for export in all sectors. Diversifying and expanding exports would require massive new investment, 34% of which currently was generated externally. Thus, Kenya's economic prospects were highly dependent upon its ability to generate international support—a task made all the more difficult by its political unrest.

WILLIAM CYRUS REED, *Wabash College*

KENYA • Information Highlights

Official Name: Republic of Kenya.
Location: East Coast of Africa.
Area: 224,961 sq mi (582 650 km²).
Population (mid-1990 est.): 24,600,000.
Chief Cities (1985 est.): Nairobi, the capital, 1,162,189; Mombasa, 442,369.
Government: *Head of state and government,* Daniel T. arap Moi, president (took office Oct. 1978). *Legislature* (unicameral)—National Assembly, 188 elected members, 12 appointed by the president.
Monetary Unit: Kenya shilling (23.232 shillings equal U.S.$1, August 1990).
Gross Domestic Product (1989 est. U.S.$): $8,500,-000,000.
Economic Index (1989): *Consumer Prices,* (Nairobi, 1980 = 100), all items, 289.5; food, 236.8.
Foreign Trade (1988 U.S.$): *Imports,* $1,993,000,000; *exports,* $1,071,000,000.

KOREA

The year 1990 in Korea saw a high level of uncertainty and tension over the political future of both halves of the divided peninsula and over the relationship between them.

Republic of Korea (South Korea)

Politics and Government. A major problem facing South Korea's President Roh Tae Woo and his ruling Democratic Justice Party (DJP) was their lack of a majority in the National Assembly. To remedy this, the DJP in January amalgamated with two of the three major opposition parties—Kim Young Sam's Reunification Democratic Party and former Premier Kim Jong Pil's New Democratic Republican Party—to form the new Democratic Liberal Party. This step was very controversial in the eyes of both of the radical opposition, which demonstrated against it, and the parliamentary opposition. The main figure in the latter category, Kim Dae Jung, leader of the Party for Peace and Democracy, began to fear isolation and in October carried his opposition to the point of a fast. He demanded that the government and the ruling party give up their plan to shift to a parliamentary from a presidential form of government, carry out their promise to make local governments elective rather than appointive, implement economic reforms, and stop surveillance of civilians by military intelligence agencies.

The popularity of Roh Tae Woo's government, which had stood fairly high over the previous two years, declined after the January merger, on account of these issues and others, such as brutality on the part of the riot police. Many felt that the liberalizing trend of Roh's first two years in office was being reversed on the pretext that a stronger hand was needed to stave off chaos. To protest the government's railroading of legislation through the National Assembly, the parliamentary opposition began a boycott of the assembly in July.

Roh's increasingly negative image was not helped by two further developments during the year: A cabinet reshuffle in March left few posts under the control of the two former opposition parties that had merged with the DJP; in October a scandal arising from revelations that the army had been spying on members of the public in the name of national security led Roh to sack Defense Minister Lee Sang Hoon, and the chief of army intelligence, Lee Jong Koo. Roh shuffled his cabinet again as 1990 ended, naming Ro Jai Bong as prime minister.

Drastic action by riot police was fairly effective in containing the rising level of student and labor discontent in 1990. In April and May demonstrations were held to commemorate the anniversaries of the overthrow of the dictatorial President Syngman Rhee in 1960, and the

© Steve Lehman/Saba

South Korean students favoring reunification with North Korea rally in Seoul in front of a poster of a student in custody in 1990 for traveling to the North.

bloody repression by the army of a protest march in the southwestern city of Kwangju in 1980. The 1990 demonstrations included actions against the U.S. embassy in Seoul and various U.S. installations in other cities by those who blamed the United States for propping up the Roh government and preventing the unification of the country by its armed presence in South Korea. Among the penalties applied to radical demonstrators was blacklisting for jobs and other benefits. Opposition figures, some of them prominent, who visited North Korea without Seoul's official authorization generally were prosecuted and jailed.

Economy. After three years of exuberant growth (at about 12% per year), the economy slowed in 1989 to a still respectable rate of about 6% in real terms. This slowdown was attributable to a variety of factors, including insufficient investment and wage increases in excess of gains in labor productivity. Consumption, including housing construction, was on a long-overdue rise, with potentially revolutionary effects on the economy as a whole, including the foreign-trade balance. The inflation rate was in the neighborhood of 5%; unemployment stood at approximately 2.5%.

In the first half of 1990, growth picked up again, to about 10%, in spite of serious flooding in the Seoul area. The inflation rate crept upward, to roughly 7%. Increased consumer demand appeared to be the main factor responsible for these trends.

In 1989 the current-account surplus fell from $14 billion (in 1988) to $5 billion. Imports rose nearly ten times as fast as exports. The government nevertheless declined to make more than minor adjustments in the exchange rate with the dollar. Electronics and textiles were the two main export categories; automobiles declined as a result of reduced demand in the United States. The most dynamic import category was raw materials to be processed into goods for the domestic market. An interesting component of South Korea's foreign trade, one with political implications, was the $3.2 billion trade (both ways) with the People's Republic of China. Foreign investment in South Korea declined about 20% from 1988 as a result of a drop in hotel construction after the 1988 Seoul Olympic Games, labor disputes, and problems connected with tax laws and the exchange rate. South Korean investment abroad, however, rose some 85%, the main areas involved being Southeast Asia (where labor costs were low) and North America.

In the first half of 1990, exports declined slightly, while imports continued to rise briskly; the trade and current-account balances

AP/Wide World Photos

South Korea's President Roh Tae Woo meets the press after a June meeting in San Francisco with Soviet President Mikhail Gorbachev.

appeared likely to be in deficit for the year as a whole; trade with the United States was still in surplus, but the surplus was smaller than in previous years. In March the government began to allow the won to fluctuate (downward) with respect to the dollar at a somewhat faster rate than before. Overall, the economy was sufficiently vigorous so that its foreign debt ($29 billion gross, $4.4 billion net) was not a problem in the eyes of the international banking community, which still was willing to lend to South Korea. Foreign investment in South Korea grew (after a decline in 1989), as did South Korean investment abroad.

Foreign Affairs. South Korea's international image and influence, which had been growing for about ten years, continued to improve, partly as a result of the 1988 Seoul Olympics.

For the past few years, a central feature of Seoul's foreign policy had been its so-called Nordpolitik, aimed at establishing commercial and, if possible, diplomatic relations with the Communist states, the ultimate goal being a viable relationship with North Korea. Considerable progress along these lines was made in 1990, largely because of the attractiveness of the dynamic South Korean economy. By early 1990 four East European countries (Hungary, Yugoslavia, Poland, and Bulgaria) had established diplomatic relations with South Korea.

In December 1989, South Korea and the USSR exchanged trade offices. Roh met with Soviet President Mikhail Gorbachev in San Francisco in June, and at the end of September the two countries announced the establishment of diplomatic relations ("normalization"). A dispute soon arose, however, over the former czarist Russian legation property in central Seoul, which Moscow wanted for its embassy site but which the South Korean government was reluctant to concede. South Korea exchanged trade offices with China in October.

SOUTH KOREA • Information Highlights

Official Name: Republic of Korea.
Location: Northeastern Asia.
Area: 38,023 sq mi (98 480 km²).
Population (mid-1990 est.): 42,800,000.
Chief City (1985 census): Seoul, the capital, 9,639,110.
Government: *Head of state,* Roh Tae Woo, president (formally inaugurated February 1988). *Head of government,* Ro Jai Bong, prime minister (appointed Dec. 27, 1990). *Legislature*—National Assembly.
Monetary Unit: Won (714 won equal U.S.$1, August 1990).
Gross National Product (1989 U.S.$): $200,000,-000,000.
Economic Indexes (1989): *Consumer Prices* (1980 = 100), all items, 169.1; food, 173.4. *Industrial Production* (1980 = 100), 275.
Foreign Trade (1989 U.S.$): *Imports,* $61,448,-000,000; *exports,* $62,375,000,000.

South Korea's basically touchy relations with Japan eased somewhat in 1990. The legal status of the large Korean minority in Japan, which had suffered considerable discrimination, was improved. During a visit by President Roh in May, Emperor Akihito expressed regret for Japan's heavy-handed colonial domination of Korea for about half a century prior to 1945, a matter about which many Koreans still feel strongly.

Largely for budgetary reasons, and also by way of a concession to South Korean nationalism, the United States was beginning to reduce its military profile in South Korea by withdrawing some noncombat troops, evacuating the large U.S. military complex in downtown Seoul (Yongsan), and lowering the level of the annual joint military exercises (Team Spirit). Since it was understood that these moves involved no weakening of the U.S. commitment to the security of South Korea, Seoul raised no serious objection to the first and welcomed the other two. On the economic front, the United States continued to be dissatisfied with the pace of South Korea's liberalization of its various import restrictions but refrained from taking retaliatory action.

Democratic People's Republic of Korea (North Korea)

Despite some small signs of possible mellowing, North Korea remained perhaps the most nearly totalitarian state in the world, one in which the central political fact was the dictatorship of President Kim Il Sung and his determination to bequeath his power to his son Kim Jong Il.

Domestic Affairs. The thrust toward dictatorship in North Korea seemed to be intensified, if anything, by developments in the other direction in the Soviet Union and Eastern Europe, including Soviet recognition of South Korea. It generally was assumed outside North Korea, however, that in the long run Pyongyang would find it necessary to fall into line with the trend toward economic and political liberalization in most of the Communist states.

NORTH KOREA · Information Highlights

Official Name: Democratic People's Republic of Korea.
Location: Northeastern Asia.
Area: 46,540 sq mi (120 540 km²).
Population (mid-1990 est.): 21,300,000.
Chief Cities (1986 est.): Pyongyang, the capital, 2,000,000; Hamhung, 670,000.
Government: *Head of state,* Kim Il Sung, president (nominally since Dec. 1972; actually in power since May 1948). *Head of government,* Yon Hyong Muk, premier (appointed Dec. 1988). *Legislature* (unicameral)—Supreme People's Assembly. The Korea Workers' (Communist) Party: General Secretary, Kim Il Sung.
Gross National Product (1989 U.S.$): $28,000,-000,000.

In the near term, there were few grounds for optimism. One was a somewhat reduced "cult of personality" for Kim Il Sung in the North Korean media around the time of his 78th birthday (April 15, 1990). Another was the cautious emergence of some signs of political opposition for the first time in decades. The North Korean economy continued to be controlled strictly, with only very slight touches of liberalization. Efforts to promote foreign trade and foreign tourism had little effect.

Foreign Affairs. Pyongyang was disturbed clearly and profoundly, not so much by its general international isolation as by the gestures by its two allies, the Soviet Union and China, toward South Korea. There was evidence that Moscow had not informed its North Korean allies in advance of the Gorbachev-Roh summit. Kim Il Sung reportedly paid a secret visit to China in an unsuccessful effort to talk Beijing out of establishing a trade office in Seoul. Moscow and Beijing clearly wanted Pyongyang to begin reforming its economy, and their attitude may have been responsible partly for the resumption by Pyongyang, early in 1990, of interest payments on its foreign loans after a lapse of several years.

The establishment of commercial and diplomatic relations between the Soviet Union and South Korea helped to increase North Korean interest in an opening to Japan. North Korea is the only significant country in the world with which Tokyo enjoys no official relations. In September, Shin Kanemaru, an elder statesman of Japan's ruling Liberal Democratic Party, visited Pyongyang. He got a cordial reception, and the two sides agreed to open talks on the establishment of diplomatic relations. Compensation for the period of Japanese colonial rule also was promised. It appeared, however, that Kanemaru was not necessarily speaking for the Japanese government, and that Tokyo had not yet reached a firm decision on its policy toward North Korea.

North Korean-U.S. relations were still far from the level of full mutual recognition. Talks did occur between officials of their embassies in Beijing, and there were a limited number of private contacts. In May, North Korea turned over to a U.S. congressional delegation the remains of five U.S. servicemen killed in the Korean War, an unprecedented if not especially magnanimous gesture. On the other hand, and much to Pyongyang's annoyance, the United States continued officially to classify North Korea as a terrorist state because of its demonstrated involvement in acts of international terrorism.

The Two Koreas

As for years past, the relationship between North Korea and South Korea in 1990 displayed elements of both confrontation and con-

North Korean Prime Minister Yon Hyong Muk (right) greets South Korean Unification Minister Hong Sung-chul at the border village of Panmunjom during a September meeting.

tact, and it was unclear which component would turn out to be the wave of the future.

Continuing Confrontation. There was widespread fear in South Korea, and elsewhere, that North Korea's sense of isolation and the prospective accession of the unstable Kim Jong Il might lead to an outburst of its aggressive tendencies. Its million-man armed forces, largely deployed near the Demilitarized Zone, were clearly capable of an offensive. In addition, Pyongyang was believed, in spite of predictable official denials, to be trying to develop a nuclear-weapons capability based on a reactor at Yongbyon, north of the capital. It was certain that Pyongyang was testing surface-to-surface missiles with a range of about 300 mi (480 km), and capable of delivering either chemical or nuclear warheads.

One of the many bizarre aspects of North Korean behavior has been the construction, since the early 1970s, of an estimated 20 large tunnels under the Demilitarized Zone. The fourth of these was discovered by the South Korean military in March.

Political Contacts. For years, North Korea and South Korea each have claimed to favor unification, accused the other of obstructing it, and made proposals known in advance to be unacceptable to the other side. Pressures from the international community, as well as the strong support for unification from the South Korean public, seem to have accounted for the fact that in 1990 there was more progress, or apparent progress, than usual.

Since 1980 Seoul has been proposing, without much hope of success, a summit meeting between the two presidents. In 1988, Seoul further proposed the creation of a Korean "community," which would have a joint council at each of three levels—the presidential, the cabinet, and the parliamentary.

North Korea has not made a clear response to these proposals and apparently was having difficulty making up its mind about them for a variety of reasons: fear that its regime might be overthrown if it embarks on a course of domestic reform combined with contact with the South; a lingering hope that the South itself may collapse in the course of democratization; and a belief that the United States may be about to create a long-awaited opening by withdrawing its troops from South Korea.

Despite these reservations, there was important progress in 1990. In July the two sides agreed that the two premiers would meet in September in Seoul, and that there should be a second such meeting the following month, in Pyongyang. Probably the most important aspect of this agreement was the fact that for the first time Pyongyang gave the appearance of recognizing the legitimacy of the Seoul government and was prepared to negotiate with it. At the September meeting the North as usual demanded a U.S. troop withdrawal from the South, while the South proposed a nonaggression pact. There was disagreement on a number of other matters, mostly relating to specific types of North-South contact. President Roh received the North Korean delegation and repeated his call for a summit. The October meeting went no better, except that at his reception for the South Korean delegation Kim Il Sung agreed to meet with Roh if the two premiers' talks, a third round of which was scheduled for December, made some progress.

Meanwhile in July the two sides had tried and failed to agree on procedures for opening their common border to travel in both directions. Radicals in the South long had been trying to pressure Seoul into a more permissive attitude on this issue. The two sides were also unable to agree on a joint team for the September 1990 Asian Games in Beijing.

There was further disagreement over South Korea's desire to enter the United Nations as a full member, rather than being a mere observer. The North seemed to favor the idea of a joint membership and delegation, an idea that Seoul found impractical.

HAROLD C. HINTON
The George Washington University

KUWAIT

On Aug. 2, 1990, the Persian Gulf state of Kuwait was invaded and occupied by Iraq. Kuwait's emir took up residence in Saudi Arabia, and many Kuwaiti citizens fled to other Arab countries in the wake of much pillage. The United States led an international effort to stop Iraqi aggression and return Kuwait's sovereignty. (*See* feature, page 24.)

LABOR

An economic downturn pushed up unemployment in the United States and several other industrial countries in the last half of 1990. On the global labor scene, the bright spot was that Poland's Solidarity trade union no longer stood alone in its part of the world as a genuine trade union freed of the combined yoke of the state and the Communist Party.

United States

After hovering around the 5.3% mark for nearly two years, the U.S. civilian unemployment rate rose to 5.6% in the third quarter, and climbed to 5.9% in November. The number of jobless persons totaled 7.4 million in November, a three-year high. Only about one third of those unemployed received unemployment benefits (which vary from state to state, averaging $152 a week nationally in 1989), compared with about one half in the 1982 recession.

Unskilled and semiskilled factory and construction workers made up about one quarter of the unemployed. However, since those blue-collar workers comprise only 10% of the labor force, the new unemployment came largely from other occupations. In fact, about three fourths of the numbers added to the jobless totals over the year came from the much larger ranks of managerial, professional, technical, administrative, and clerical staffs.

The civilian employment total—which normally grows as the population grows—actually shrank by 400,000 from the second to the third quarter of the year. Over four quarters, employment grew sluggishly, by only 368,000 (*see* table), compared with 2.3 million over the comparable 1988–89 time frame. The percentage of adult women working outside the home (not counting those in the armed forces) reached a historic peak of 55.5% in May and June before dropping back a full percentage point by November. The great majority (75%) of those women were holding full-time jobs.

Earnings. By practically every measure, incomes from employment declined over the year in real (inflation-adjusted) terms. Average real weekly earnings of production workers in the

U.S. Employment and Unemployment (Armed Forces excluded)

	1989	1990
Labor Force	124,035,000	124,798,000
Participation rate	66.5%	66.3%
Employed	117,468,000	117,836,000
Unemployed	6,567,000	6,962,000
Unemployment rate	5.3%	5.6%
Adult men	4.6%	5.0%
Adult women	4.7%	4.8%
Teenagers	15.0%	16.2%

N.B.: Figures above, compiled by the Bureau of Labor Statistics, are seasonally adjusted averages for the third quarter of each year. The participation rate is the number of persons in the labor market, whether employed or unemployed, as a percentage of the civilian noninstitutional population.

private sector (excluding agriculture) decreased by 3.5% between October 1989 and October 1990. Counting both wage and salary workers, but only those working full time, the average real earnings per week dipped 2% from the third quarter of 1989 to the same quarter of 1990. Over the same period, the actual weekly earnings of families, including those with two or more jobholders, rose by 4.1% on the average, but the Consumer Price Index rose even more, 5.5%. In the case of married couples, weekly income during the third quarter averaged $517 when only the husband had a job; $850 when both husband and wife did.

The long-term stagnation in earnings underwent widespread critical scrutiny in 1990. In a survey of U.S. living-standards trends since 1973, the weekly *Economist* concluded that "the American dream is at risk" because of the near-stagnant real incomes of the country's middle class. A best-selling book, *The Politics of Rich and Poor*, by Kevin Phillips, a noted Republican, analyzed the long-term trend as producing a major redistribution of wealth because of widening income inequalities: For example, according to data collected by *Business Week*, the average corporate chief executive officer (CEO) in 1979 made 29 times the income of the average factory worker; in 1988 he or she made 93 times more.

Legislation. The number of foreign workers allowed to immigrate legally into the United States rises sharply under new legislation that President George Bush signed on November 29 and hailed as the "most comprehensive reform of our immigration laws in 66 years." As part of an overall increase in legal immigration from 540,000 to 700,000 per year in fiscal years 1992–94, the new law expands from 54,000 to 140,000 the quota of visas to be granted annually to foreigners specifically on the basis of their job skills. Only 40,000 of that quota will require the formal certification of the U.S. Department of Labor that no qualified Americans are available for the jobs to be filled by the immigrants.

In other legislative actions, the president vetoed a number of bills that passed Congress with strong labor backing. The major vetoed bills would have:

• increased sharply limits on imports of textiles, wearing apparel, and footwear.

• required employers to give workers up to three months' unpaid leave to care for newborn babies or seriously ill parents or spouses.

• restored the full range of legal remedies for employment discrimination that recent decisions of the Supreme Court had narrowed down in accordance with its interpretation of existing civil-rights laws.

Health Care. Meanwhile the 14-million-member American Federation of Labor and Congress of Industrial Organizations (AFL-CIO) launched a major campaign to make national health legislation a high priority for the

On the U.S. labor scene during 1990, United Auto Workers (UAW) President Owen Bieber (left) marched in a spontaneous demonstration during the union's special collective-bargaining convention in Kansas City in May; Labor Secretary Elizabeth Dole (below left) and Assistant Secretary of Labor for Employment Standards William Brooks announced the findings of an investigation of violations of the nation's child-labor laws; and President Bush named outgoing Rep. Lynn Martin (below center) to replace Dole, who resigned, as labor secretary. (At the same time the president introduced his new education secretary, Lamar Alexander.)

1991 session of Congress. In addition to earmarking $4 million to publicize the issue on television, the AFL-CIO held well-attended regional hearings in eight cities, at which 86 witnesses gave testimony on how gaps in the present health-care system hurt them personally.

In line with a trend in other industries, managements at Chrysler, Ford, and General Motors formally agreed to join the United Auto Workers (UAW) in working toward what UAW President Owen Bieber called "a new national approach to health-care delivery." A major reason for such joint labor-management initiatives, according to AFL-CIO President Lane Kirkland, is that employers, union workers, and others who have health-insurance coverage "are forced to pay for the 37 million working Americans who have no benefits because their employers are freeloading on the rest of us."

U.S. Labor Department. After nearly two years as secretary of labor in the Bush cabinet, Elizabeth Dole announced her resignation in October to accept the presidency of the American Red Cross. More so than her predecessors in the 1980s, she took personal leadership in the Labor Department's enforcement of federal labor laws, particularly those affecting child labor (*see* sidebar) and occupational safety and health. As part of a job-safety campaign, she persuaded the Big Three automakers to redesign jobs to reduce repetitive-motion injuries, which nationally now account for more than one half of all occupational illnesses. Reversing a previous hands-off policy on labor disputes, she waded into the long and bitter strike of the United Mine Workers against the Pittston Coal Group and won plaudits from both sides when they announced a settlement on New Year's Day 1990.

Danger: Children at Work

The rapid growth in the illegal employment of children in U.S. stores, factories, and farms during the last half of the 1980s is "a national disgrace," according to an investigative report published in April 1990 by *The Boston Globe*. "A half century after child-labor laws were enacted, millions of children are working long and frequently illegal hours across America," wrote Bruce D. Butterfield, author of the five-part series. Although most violations of child-labor laws involve teenagers, Butterfield's nationwide investigation uncovered examples of younger boys and girls working in urban sweatshops and on large commercial farms.

In April 1990 the General Accounting Office (GAO), Congress' watchdog agency, also reported that the number of detected violations of federal child-labor laws had increased by 150% in six years. In addition, an uncounted number of violations had gone undetected. As the GAO pointed out, the U.S. Labor Department's inspections staff, with fewer than 1,000 persons to monitor 2.6 million business establishments for compliance with all 51 features of the U.S. Fair Labor Standards Act, in recent years has spent less than 5% of its time on checking child-labor violations. Moreover, their child-labor inspections rarely were made unannounced without a specific complaint.

The Labor Department changed that routine in 1990. Four times during the year, "strike forces," involving at least 500 persons each, made unannounced visits to fast-food outlets, garment factories, and other workplaces. The first strike force found a 51% violation rate in March; the fourth, in September, rechecked practices of the places inspected in March and found a 12% violation rate. "The cop is on the beat," said then U.S. Secretary of Labor Elizabeth Dole. "Violations, whether motivated by greed or ignorance, will not be tolerated."

Although federal law sets a general minimum working age of 16 in nonagricultural industries, it allows 14- and 15-year-olds to work in specific occupations in food outlets, retail stores, and certain other fields. However, the law does place limitations on the youngsters' working hours. They may work no more than eight hours per day, 40 hours per week, during school-vacation periods, and no more than three hours during a school day or 18 hours during a school week. Further, they may not work before 7 A.M. or after 7 P.M., or 9 P.M. during the summer. The most numerous violations involve illegal working hours; the most serious ones involve employing children under 18 in hazardous occupations, such as coal mining, logging, and animal slaughtering.

Until 1990 employers caught at child-labor violations paid fines averaging $165. Of the many reforms proposed by Congressman Don Pease (D-OH) and the Child Labor Coalition, Congress adopted only one. Buried in the budget reconciliation package approved in October was an item raising the maximum civil penalty for a child-labor violation from $1,000 to $10,000.

ROBERT A. SENSER

In mid-December the White House announced the selection of Lynn Martin, 50-year-old U.S. congresswoman from Illinois and Bush loyalist who had made an unsuccessful bid for Paul Simon's Senate seat in November, as Dole's successor.

International

Other industrial nations besides the United States experienced growth in unemployment during the year. The sharpest increases came in Canada, with a jobless rate of 8.2% in the third quarter compared with 7.4% a year earlier, and Australia, with a rate of 7.2% compared with 6.1% a year earlier. Sweden's rate remained at its traditionally low level, but edged up from 1.3% in May to 1.6% in September. Japan's rate stayed at about the same low level as in 1989, 2.1%, as its industries reported a shortage of almost 2 million skilled workers. Meanwhile, the third-quarter rates of France (9.5%) and of the United Kingdom (6.4%), while high, were marginally lower than in 1989. Germany's jobless statistics (a rate of about 5.2% in the West) did not reflect unification with the East yet, where the unemployment rate jumped to 6.1% in October, a year after it officially stood at zero while the Communist regime still clung to power. (Some of these figures differ from rates announced in individual countries since they were adjusted by the U.S. Bureau of Labor Statistics to U.S. jobless definitions.)

Many developing countries in Asia and Africa, already plagued with widespread unemployment and underemployment, were hard-hit by the sudden return home of persons fleeing the crisis in Iraq and Kuwait. The countries with the largest number of their nationals working in the area—Bangladesh, India, Pakistan, the Philippines, Sri Lanka, Jordan, Egypt, and Vietnam—also were flooded with returnees.

Solidarity in Poland. From its very beginnings a decade ago, Poland's Solidarity trade union and its leader, Lech Walesa, campaigned fervently for "pluralism" in the country—meaning a flowering of nongovernmental organizations to replace the Communist Party's institutional monopoly in factories, offices, and politics. In 1990, though, Walesa faced pluralism aplenty, much more than he had bargained for, especially in parliament, where many former Solidarity officials lined up against him, and in the rancorous multiparty campaign for the Polish presidency, which he won in a runoff on December 9. Solidarity was to hold an extraordinary congress in early 1991 to choose Walesa's successor as the union's leader.

With about 2.5 million members in a union structure still being reorganized, Solidarity was competing against a renamed Communist labor organization, OPZZ, which claimed a membership of 5 million and was benefiting from buildings and income-producing assets bestowed by the old Communist regime. OPZZ leaders, who under Communist rule were meekly compliant, under a democratic government were enjoying the luxury of militancy in an opposition role that criticizes the decline in living standards (down 50% since the late 1980s) and mounting unemployment (about 6% in October).

Trade Unionism Elsewhere. There were breakthroughs for free-trade unionism in various corners of the world. A minor one occurred in Indonesia, for example, when leaders of a human-rights organization in November announced the formation of the Solidarity Free Trade Union, which government officials promptly denounced as illegal. The most important development, however, was that Poland's Solidarity lost its uniqueness in its own part of the world. The largest new union center in Eastern Europe now is the 6-million-member Czech and Slovak Confederation of Trade Unions (CKOS). It was created in March 1990 out of strike committees formed in 1989 in defiance of the Communist labor apparatus, now dissolved. Smaller non-Communist unions also took root in Hungary, Bulgaria, and Romania. Meanwhile, in the former East Germany, members of the Communist labor structure, minus their old leaders, gradually were absorbed into the German Trade Union Federation (DGB), headquartered in Dusseldorf.

In Moscow, USSR President Mikhail Gorbachev and Prime Minister Nikolai Ryzhkov personally participated in the 19th congress of the Soviet Party's worker arm, the All-Union Central Council of Trade Unions, in October. The 2,500 delegates voted unanimously to disband the council and to substitute a new party mass organization, the General Confederation of Soviet Trade Unions, which supposedly would have some independence from central party control. Affiliates in Estonia, Latvia, Lithuania, and Georgia exercised their independence by staying away. More significantly, during the same week in October, 900 coal miners from throughout the USSR, meeting in the Ukrainian industrial city of Donetsk, voted to create the Soviet Union's first national independent labor union. With a potential of 2 million members, the new miners' union could become the rallying point for a truly independent national labor movement for workers in all sectors.

Global Rivalry. The Brussels-based International Confederation of Free Trade Unions (ICFTU) and some of its affiliates, especially the AFL-CIO, were highly active, giving moral and financial support to the struggling new non-Communist unions in Eastern Europe and the Soviet Union. In May the Czechoslovak CKOS became the first East European labor movement to affiliate with the ICFTU since Solidarity did so in 1986.

Meanwhile, the ICFTU's rival, the Communist-dominated World Federation of Trade Unions (WFTU), based in Prague, lost much ground. Since CKOS withdrew from the WFTU before it joined the ICFTU, the WFTU no longer has an affiliate in the country in which it has its headquarters. Its main affiliate in Eastern Europe is now the OPZZ of Poland. Nevertheless, the WFTU is far from dead. In Moscow in November delegates from more than 100 countries attended its 12th world congress, which opened with a speech by President Gorbachev. For the first time in the 45-year history of the organization, a Soviet citizen, Alexander Zharikov, was named to the key WFTU leadership post of general secretary, replacing Ibrahim Zakaria of Sudan, who became the new president.

ILO. At its annual conference in Geneva in June, the International Labor Organization (ILO), a UN agency, adopted two new conventions, which would be submitted to its 139 member states for ratification. One, updating a 1948 convention that prohibited night work by women in industry, regulates night work so as to apply its restrictions to all workers regardless of sex. The other, dealing with occupational health and safety, requires countries that outlaw a hazardous chemical in their workplaces to disclose this decision to any country importing the chemical.

In June, U.S. Labor Secretary Dole was able to give the ILO formal notification that the United States had ratified the ILO convention on labor statistics. By late 1990 the United States had ratified only ten (all fairly minor) of the 171 conventions adopted by the ILO. Over the years, U.S. employer groups usually have objected to the use of the treaty-ratification procedures to deal with U.S. labor standards. However, in 1990 consultations with labor and management produced a breakthrough consensus supporting the important ILO convention against forced labor, which President Bush was scheduled to send to the Senate for approval in early 1991.

ROBERT A. SENSER, *Free-lance Labor Writer*

LAOS

In Laos the Communist Lao People's Revolutionary Party remained firmly in control of the government. Party leaders sought to attract Western investment, but they seemed unwilling to allow multiparty democracy.

Politics. In a February 1990 speech, Party Chief and Premier Kaysone Phomvihan urged the Supreme People's Assembly, which his party controls, to "develop democracy" in Laos. But he called the recent changes in Eastern Europe "confusing" and said democracy without party leadership becomes anarchy.

Kaysone visited China shortly after the pro-democracy movement was crushed there in 1989, and his philosophy is like that of China's rulers. He has cited Laos' new criminal code and judicial system as examples of his efforts to introduce democracy, but these institutions seem designed mainly to reassure foreign investors.

Economics. After three years of economic reform, the towns along the Mekong River were active in trade with Thailand. There was a modest building boom in Vientiane, and foreign tourists again were visiting Laos. But per capita income in the upland villages was about $180, among the lowest in the world.

Lao exports of wood products and electricity pay for less than half of the country's imports. Foreign aid makes up the difference. The USSR has been the main aid donor, supplying 250 million rubles (officially $410.8 million), during the period 1986–90.

Foreign Relations. With Soviet aid due to fall, the Lao were turning to the West. They signed 82 foreign-investment contracts worth $70 million. A U.S. and European consortium will explore for oil in southern Laos. The West also was providing government aid. Australia will build the first bridge over the Mekong River and a ground satellite station to expand overseas telephone service.

The United States began work on an $8.7 million rural development project meant to encourage hill tribesmen to substitute cash crops for opium. Laos has been cooperating with the United States in suppressing drug trafficking and in the search for Americans missing in action.

PETER A. POOLE
Author, "Eight Presidents and Indochina"

LAOS · Information Highlights

Official Name: Lao People's Democratic Republic.
Location: Southeast Asia.
Area: 91,430 sq mi (236 800 km²).
Population (mid-1990 est.): 4,000,000.
Chief City (1985 census): Vientiane, the capital, 377,409.
Government: *Head of state*, Phoumi Vongvichit, acting president; *Head of government*, Kaysone Phomvihan, chairman. *Legislature* (unicameral) —national Congress of People's Representatives.

LATIN AMERICA

Democracy moved ahead steadily in Latin America in 1990 and the region's chronic foreign-debt problems eased somewhat. The news that drew the biggest response in Latin America, however, came out of Washington—a proposal by U.S. President George Bush for a Western Hemisphere free-trade zone.

Bush Plan. On June 27, President Bush summoned diplomats to the White House to outline a new plan to stimulate economic growth and recovery in Latin America and the Caribbean. The Bush proposal, called the "Enterprise for the Americas Initiative," had four parts:

• Negotiations leading eventually to a free-trade agreement between the United States, Latin America, and the Caribbean;

• Reduction of part of the $12 billion official debt owed to the U.S. government;

• An enhanced program to stimulate private investment in the region; and

• A stronger emphasis on environmental protection in the hemisphere.

The Latin American reaction to the Bush initiative was immediate and positive.

In September the White House sent to the Congress a legislative package to implement the investment, debt, and environmental aspects of the Enterprise Initiative. Included in the proposals was the creation of a new $1.5 billion multilateral investment fund to be administered by the Inter-American Development Bank (IDB), with the United States contributing $500 million over five years.

The proposed legislation did not contain provisions on free trade, but in his message to the Congress, President Bush indicated that it remained his "ultimate goal." Despite a heavy session-ending schedule, both houses of Congress approved parts of the bill in late October, but eliminated provision for the multilateral fund.

Integration. In presenting his initiative, Bush indicated that the United States would encourage Latin American and Caribbean countries to form regional trading blocs as a first step toward negotiating free-trade arrangements with Washington. In fact, the pace of regional and subregional economic integration —long a goal of hemisphere leaders—accelerated during 1990. Among the major developments:

• Mexico and the United States agreed to begin formal negotiations on trade liberalization in 1991. Canada said it would join the talks. Canada and the United States already have a free-trade agreement and both countries have preliminary trade pacts with Mexico.

• In June five of the six Central American countries (excluding Panama) drew up a regional integration plan to revitalize the Central American Common Market and to eliminate all protectionist barriers by 1992.

In Colombia, César Gaviria Trujillo, 43-year-old Liberal Party member, former newspaperman, and government minister, was installed as president following his victory in the May 27 election. In his inaugural he promised to fight the drug cartel.

AP/Wide World

• Brazil and Argentina agreed to establish a common market by the end of 1994. Chile, Uruguay, and Paraguay indicated interest in joining a Southern Cone market.

• In the Andean region, Bolivia, Colombia, and Ecuador signed pacts with the United States creating binational trade councils.

• ALADI, the 11-member Latin American Integration Association, announced in August it was reducing by 50% the tariffs on trade among its member nations. ALADI includes Mexico and ten South American nations.

Economy. Trade liberalization and integration movements were accompanied during the year by continuing structural adjustment efforts, designed to reduce public-sector spending, cut government deficits, and privatize numerous state-owned entities. The process was painful and many countries showed negative economic results during 1990. An assessment issued by the United Nations Economic Commission for Latin America and the Caribbean (ECLAC) estimated that regional output would fall by nearly 1% and per-capita gross domestic product (GDP) by some 3%. The ECLAC statement also predicted a slight increase in the region's external debt, but indicated that interest due in 1990 would go down because of the drop in interest rates, the modest reduction in commercial bank debt, and the cuts in interest rates forming part of the agreements signed with the creditor banks by Costa Rica, Mexico, and Venezuela.

Politics. The democratic tide continued to surge in Latin America in 1990, most notably in Nicaragua, where the National Opposition Union (UNO), led by newspaper publisher Violeta Chamorro, scored a stunning electoral victory over the Marxist Sandinista government of Daniel Ortega on February 25.

A civilian government was inaugurated in Chile in March, ending nearly 17 years of military rule. Newly elected governments also assumed power in Brazil, Colombia, Costa Rica, the Dominican Republic, Peru, and Uruguay during the year. In Panama a civilian government was installed during the U.S. invasion in December 1989, replacing the dictatorship of Gen. Manuel Noriega, who was arrested by U.S. troops and remained in U.S. custody.

From the U.S. standpoint, one of the most significant political developments of the year was the waning of Soviet influence in the Western Hemisphere, as the Cold War drew to a close. Soviet support for Marxist-led guerrillas in Central America dried up, and Moscow's assistance to Cuba dwindled sharply.

International drug trafficking remained high on the inter-American agenda. Bolivia, Colombia, and Peru turned down U.S. offers of military aid to combat drug merchants, but actively pursued a White House plan for trade concessions designed to provide alternative sources of foreign-exchange income to reduce the lure of cocaine profits. President Bush attended a summit meeting with Andean presidents in Cartagena, Colombia, in February, and in September sent proposed legislation to the Congress, giving trade preferences to the Andean countries in return for cooperation in the war against drugs.

International. Canada became a full member of the Organization of American States (OAS) on January 1 and at the organization's annual General Assembly in June agreed to contribute a substantial portion of the OAS budget. OAS Secretariat officials, along with United Nations personnel, served during most of the year as members of the International Commission for Support and Verification (CIAV) in Nicaragua. The OAS monitored the country's electoral process and participated in disarming and relocating the former "contra" rebels who had fought the Sandinista government during much of the 1980s. Later in the year, the OAS and the IDB became involved in promoting President Bush's Americas Initiative proposal.

RICHARD C. SCHROEDER, *Consultant to the Organization of American States*

Following the resignation of Justice William Brennan, David Souter (center) joined (l-r) Justices Rehnquist, Scalia, O'Connor, Marshall, Kennedy, Blackmun, Stevens, and White (not in photograph) on the U.S. Supreme Court.

LAW

In a dramatic conclusion to a year in which conservatives further solidified their control of the U.S. Supreme Court, Justice William J. Brennan, Jr., announced his retirement because of failing health. The 84-year-old jurist had been the anchor of the high court's liberal wing for some 34 years. His departure led quickly to the nomination by President Bush of David H. Souter, a little-known judge from New Hampshire. After spending the summer preparing, Souter spent three days testifying before the Senate Judiciary Committee. His appointment was confirmed by a 90–9 Senate vote, and Justice Souter took his seat on the court on October 9. (*See also* BIOGRAPHY.)

As for the 1989–90 high-court term, it seemed to bear out a comment Justice Harry A. Blackmun made to an interviewer. Conservatives "have control of the court completely and are making the most of it," said Blackmun, one of the remaining more-liberal justices. In the closely divided and most newsworthy decisions, liberals most often found themselves in the minority. The conservative dominance had been established in 1988 after Justice Anthony M. Kennedy became Ronald Reagan's third appointee on the high court. Justices Sandra Day O'Connor and Antonin Scalia were the others. The former president also elevated William H. Rehnquist from associate justice to chief justice.

Justice Byron R. White, appointed by President John F. Kennedy in 1962, often was the fifth vote for a conservative outcome. But on occasion in significant rulings, one or more of the conservatives lined up with the more liberal justices—Brennan, Blackmun, Thurgood Marshall, and John Paul Stevens. Some commentators said the court's jurisprudence reflected a reluctance to supplant legislative and presidential initiatives with the will of judges. An absence of such judicial activism was underscored by key 1989–90 rulings in such areas as abortion, the "right to die," the rights of criminal suspects, and police powers to conduct searches.

In the lower U.S. courts, cases that made news included a California court ruling on ownership of bodily tissue used in scientific research and a Mississippi verdict in favor of neglected nursing-home patients. The mayor of the nation's capital was tried on drug and perjury charges; a former governor of West Virginia was convicted of fraud and related charges; and there were developments in the Iran-contra case.

Issues involving Panama's Manuel Noriega, the Iraqi invasion of Kuwait, and Iran during the 1980s were dominant in international law.

United States

Supreme Court. The work load was down and the number of cases decided by a single vote was up in the court's 1989–90 term. The court issued 129 signed majority opinions, the lowest total of the decade. The justices had issued as many as 151 signed decisions in some recent years. The number of 5–4 rulings in the 1989–90 term rose to 37, six more than in the previous term. About two thirds of those closely divided cases produced a conservative result. The court's deep divisions also were reflected by a declining number of unanimous rulings: 30% compared with nearly 38% the previous year and nearly 42% in 1987-88.

"In nearly every case that divides the court ideologically, there are now five justices for a conservative result," said Professor Walter Dellinger of the Duke University Law School. The conservative trend was nowhere more apparent than in the field of criminal law and police powers. The justices buttressed the fight against drunken drivers by ruling that police may stop motorists at roadside checkpoints and examine them for possible intoxication. Police need not have any grounds for suspecting motorists of inebriation before stopping them, the court said (*Michigan v. Sitz*).

The court also held that a videotape of a drunken-driving suspect being questioned at a police station may be introduced as evidence even if the suspect was not warned of his right to remain silent or have the help of a lawyer (*Pennsylvania v. Muniz*). But the court expanded double jeopardy protection for some suspects, ruling that someone who has pleaded guilty to drunken driving may not be prosecuted for homicide in a death caused by the same accident (*Grady v. Corbin*).

Efforts to stem child abuse figured prominently on the court's agenda. The justices ruled that a parent who is under a court's supervision for previously abusing a child may not rely on the right against self-incrimination to conceal from authorities the whereabouts of the child (*Baltimore v. Bouknight*). The court also said that children may testify on closed-circuit television to avoid possible trauma that might come from a court confrontation with those accused of child abuse (*Maryland v. Craig*). But the court said there is no reason automatically to permit doctors or other adults who have interviewed a young abuse victim to testify at trial about the interviews (*Idaho v. Wright*).

The court gave federal crime fighters broad power to search property abroad owned by foreign citizens, ruling they do not need a search warrant to hunt for drugs or other contraband (*U.S. v. Verdugo-Urquídez*).

The court's death-penalty cases generally reflected the court's hostility to permitting unlimited delays in carrying out capital punishment. The justices sharply restricted the power of federal judges to overturn death sentences based on retroactive application of Supreme Court rulings handed down after an inmate's conviction (*Butler v. McKellar*). The high court also said a jury may impose a death sentence if it finds unanimously that a convicted murderer's mitigating evidence is outweighed by the "aggravating circumstances" of the murder (*Blystone v. Pennsylvania*).

In one of the most dramatic cases of the term, the court barred family members from asserting a "right to die" for a permanently comatose relative unless there is clear evidence of the patient's wishes, such as a living will or the designation in writing of the power of attorney for the family member (*Cruzan v. Missouri*). Thousands of Americans in coma-like conditions are being kept alive by life-sustaining treatment.

Regarding Medicaid, the court ruled that health-care workers may challenge the adequacy of Medicaid reimbursements (*Wilder v. Virginia Hospital Association*).

In a pair of rulings, the court upheld state laws prohibiting unmarried teenage girls from obtaining abortions unless they notify their parents. But the court said states must give the teenager a chance to bypass parental notification by getting a judge's permission for the abortion (*Hodgson v. Minnesota* and *Ohio v. Akron Center for Reproductive Health*). The court, which a year earlier had broadened the power of states to limit abortions, once again did not decide whether the constitutional right to abortion established by *Roe v. Wade* in 1973 should be overturned.

In a case involving the privacy of prison inmates, the court said prison officials may force mentally ill inmates to take anti-psychotic drugs without first seeking court approval (*Washington v. Harper*).

The justices handed down important rulings on religious freedom and free expression. The justices upheld a 1984 federal law requiring public high schools to give religious and political clubs the same access to school facilities as other extracurricular activities (*Westside Board of Education v. Mergens*). The court also said governments may prosecute those who use illegal drugs as part of religious rituals (*Employment Division v. Smith*). The ruling was a defeat for American Indians who use peyote in religious ceremonies. The court ruled unanimously that the sale of religious items may be taxed by states just like any other merchandise (*Swaggart Ministries v. California*).

The court once again ruled that laws against flag burning or desecration violate freedom of expression. A year after striking down a similar Texas law, the justices ruled that a federal law to protect the Stars and Stripes was unconstitutional (*U.S. v. Eichman* and *U.S. v. Haggerty*). The decision triggered a move to amend the Constitution and permit prosecution of flag burners. But the drive failed in Congress.

The court upheld the right of federal and state governments to restrict the involvement of corporations in political campaigns. It ruled that states may require corporations to make their political expenditures through separate political-action committees (*Austin v. Michigan State Chamber of Commerce*).

In a libel case that could have wide-ranging impact, the court said the Constitution does not shield automatically expressions of opinion from being found libelous. But the court said

Community Service

During the last 20 to 30 years, "community service," requiring offenders to perform unpaid labor, has become a common and increasingly publicized practice in the criminal courts of the United States, Canada, and Great Britain. Community service orders (CSOs) range in length from a few to several thousand hours. They vary from highly individualized tasks capitalizing on an offender's particular skills—such as having a safecracker give crime-prevention talks to executives in the safe industry—to far more typical and mundane tasks of picking up litter from highways or menial work in hospitals, parks, soup kitchens, and recreational facilities for charitable or governmental organizations.

The Celebrity Sanction?. Much recent attention to the CSO is due to its association with a handful of high-profile cases involving well-known individuals. Zsa Zsa Gabor and Pete Rose both were sentenced to perform community service in connection with their clashes with the California Highway Patrol and the Internal Revenue Service (IRS), respectively. This, coupled with the more general imposition of CSOs upon many of the offenders convicted in federal courts of such offenses as fraud, corruption, and embezzlement, has contributed to a widespread misperception that community service is a penalty reserved exclusively or mostly for better-off, white-collar criminals.

In reality, community service is imposed more typically upon the lower-class, often minority offenders whose convictions for theft, burglary, assault, and other "street-crimes," not "suite-crimes," constitute the vast majority of criminal prosecutions in state and local courts in the United States. In addition, the CSO most recently has become the sanction of choice in many states for the thousands of offenders convicted annually of driving under the influence of alcohol.

Usually imposed as a condition of probation, or more rarely as a condition of parole following an offender's release from prison, the CSO may be used as an alternative or add-on to a fine, incarceration, or most other statutory forms of punishment. Offenders may be assigned individually to such work sites as youth centers and homes for the elderly, where maintenance and janitorial services commonly are provided; alternatively, they may be required to discharge their CSO as part of a work crew engaged in such tasks as cleaning the highways or washing police cars. In the former case, on-site supervision of the offender to verify punctual and satisfactory performance to the court is the responsibility of the agency benefiting from the offender's labor. Work crews, on the other hand, more often are supervised directly by staff of the probation department or sheriff, not wholly unlike the chain gangs of earlier days.

Benefits and Drawbacks. If used as an alternative to incarceration, the CSO offers a less expensive, less repressive, and more constructive way of inflicting retribution on offenders than imprisonment in institutions that frequently are overcrowded and expensive to build, staff, and maintain. And although there is little research evidence to suggest that requiring offenders to perform community service will prevent them from committing subsequent crimes, there is equally little cause for optimism that time spent behind bars, especially in local jails from which the inmate will be returning to the community after a short time anyway, does any better.

Most research evidence suggests that the CSO is not used often in lieu of incarceration, but that it simply is added to "toughen" the conditions of probation for offenders whose offenses ordinarily would not lead to a custodial sentence. In such cases, cost savings over incarceration cannot be claimed, and the additional costs of the CSO to the system render its growing popularity far more questionable than its superficial appeal to society's retributive emotions.

Community service by offenders is not, as many believe, a free source of labor. Insurance premiums and compensation claims must be met to cover injuries sustained by offenders while performing their tasks and, more alarmingly, for injuries inflicted by offenders on fellow workers and other third parties at the work site. Criminal-justice employees who must locate, inspect, and monitor suitable work sites, as well as place and supervise offenders, and perhaps revoke them to incarceration if they fail to comply with the community service orders, are a costly resource. Their time, skills, and salaries often might be directed more justifiably to services and supervision practices projected to make a more direct and measurable contribution to the most pressing challenge of the criminal-justice professions, i.e., reducing the chances of crime and reoffending.

ALAN T. HARLAND and STEPHEN SMITH
Temple University

expressions of opinion would continue to receive full constitutional protection as long as they do not contain "a provably false factual connotation" (*Milkovich v. Lorain Journal*).

In a case pitting free expression against political patronage, the court said the Constitution prohibits use of partisan political consideration in hiring, promoting, or transferring most public employees (*Rutan v. Republican Party of Illinois*).

The court also let states make it a crime to possess pornographic photographs of children, even in the privacy of one's home (*Osborne v. Ohio*). The court in the past held that people may not be prosecuted for looking at obscene material, if they are not buying or selling it.

Liberals won a pair of important victories in the area of civil rights, a surprise since the previous term was regarded by civil-rights activists as a low point in recent years. The court said Congress has sweeping power to enact affirmative-action programs that give special benefits to minorities. The justices upheld Federal Communications Commission (FCC) policies that favor minorities seeking broadcast licenses (*Metro Broadcasting v. FCC*).

The court also ruled that federal judges may order local governments to increase taxes to pay for programs to eliminate school segregation (*Missouri v. Jenkins*). But the court in another case overturned contempt fines a federal judge imposed against four Yonkers, NY, city councilmen who voted against legislation needed to carry out a court-ordered plan to ease housing segregation (*Spallone v. U.S.*).

The court also said universities accused of discriminating in tenure decisions must make personnel files available to federal investigators. The justices rejected arguments that such disclosure violates academic freedom (*University of Pennsylvania v. EEOC*). The justices headed off a crisis in the federal regulation of pensions. The court said the federal agency that protects the pensions of more than 30 million U.S. workers may order employers to restore terminated pensions (*Pension Benefit Guaranty Corp. v. LTV Corp.*).

Local Law. The California Supreme Court ruled that individuals do not retain property rights over body tissues used to develop new drugs or medicines. But the state court said physicians may be sued if they fail to tell patients that researchers have an economic or personal interest in using or studying the tissues. The case was watched closely by those in genetic engineering and related fields since it was the first to set legal principles for those who use human tissue for commercial purposes. The case involved a doctor said to have made $3 million by selling the rights to a blood-cell line developed from the blood of a patient operated on for cancer.

In Mississippi a federal jury ruled that the families of nursing-home patients are entitled to damages because the patients were neglected. The verdict could have broad impact because it means that nursing-home chains could be forced to pay when residents suffer from what nursing-home critics describe as routine practices. In the past, multimillion-dollar damages have been awarded only for isolated acts of gross negligence.

In Washington, DC, Mayor Marion Barry was convicted on a single drug charge and acquitted on another as the jury deadlocked on 12 other counts, including perjury charges. It was a stunning end to a six-week trial that featured an FBI videotape of the mayor smoking crack cocaine with a former girlfriend who invited him to her hotel room in a federal sting operation.

In West Virginia former Gov. Arch A. Moore Jr., pleaded guilty to mail fraud, extortion, filing false income taxes, and obstruction of justice. He was sentenced to five years and ten months in prison and fined $170,000. The three-term Republican governor was charged with crimes involving his 1984 campaign and his 1985–89 term in office. Moore admitted extorting $573,000 from a coal operator in return for a $2.1 million refund from a state fund that provides benefits to coal miners suffering from black-lung disease.

In Washington, DC, a federal-appeals court upset Oliver North's Iran-contra convictions. The appeals court said the former National Security Council aide did not receive a fair trial because of the possible impact on grand jurors and others of North's immunized testimony before nationally televised congressional hearings. North had been convicted of obstructing Congress in its probe of weapons sales to Iran and diversion of the money to Nicaraguan rebels. He had been sentenced to probation and 1,200 hours of community service.

The notorious child-abuse case involving the McMartin school in Los Angeles finally came to an end. Child-molesting charges were dismissed against the remaining defendant, Raymond Buckey, after the jury deadlocked in his retrial on eight charges. The McMartin case started with seven defendants, consumed seven years of court time, and cost Los Angeles County more than $13.5 million. The first trial ended earlier in 1990 with the acquittal of Buckey's mother and a deadlock on some of the charges against her son. Charges against the other defendants had been dropped.

In two separate New York City trials, five youths were convicted in the 1989 rape and beating of a woman jogging in Central Park. The woman, an investment-banking executive, testified that she had no recollection of the gang attack. Three young men were convicted in August and two in December; one more defendant was to be tried early in 1991. The unusually brutal case had brought nationwide publicity.

JIM RUBIN, *The Associated Press*

International Law

International law was under great pressure during 1990, a year dominated by much change.

Panama Invasion. The U.S. invasion of Panama, which commenced on Dec. 20, 1989, was justified on four grounds before the Organization of American States (OAS) and the United Nations (UN) early in the new year. Washington's strongest claim was that of self-defense, based on the allegation that a U.S. serviceman had been murdered by forces loyal to Panama's leader Gen. Manuel Noriega. In addition, Washington relied on the so-called declaration of war by the Panamanian National Assembly of Dec. 15, 1989, the right to protect the Panama Canal under the 1977 treaty, and the endorsement given to the intervention by the newly installed Endara government and large segments of the local population.

All of these arguments overwhelmingly were rejected at the OAS and the UN General Assembly. A condemnation from the Security Council could only be averted through the use of the veto by the Western powers.

The Noriega Trial. General Noriega surrendered from his refuge in the Vatican embassy to U.S. forces in Panama in early January. With certain other former Panamanian officials, he was transported immediately to the United States, where he faced indictments on multiple counts of narcotics trafficking and related offenses. Noriega's defense team claimed prisoner of war status on his behalf.

Legally, this assertion was unassailable under the universally accepted 1949 Geneva Convention on the subject. The U.S. attorney general's office was informed by the Department of State on January 31 that General Noriega indeed would be treated as if he were a prisoner of war, although he would not be granted that status formally.

The Federal District Court in Miami took note of this decision and postponed further hearings until at least January 1991. The court not only would have to address the question of whether or not prisoners of war may be tried for criminal offenses committed abroad before the beginning of hostilities, but it also would have to review the controversial *Kerr-Frisbie* rule. Under that doctrine, it is immaterial whether an individual was brought into the jurisdiction of the U.S. courts in violation of his or her rights and of international law. In the meantime a controversy developed over whether Noriega's rights under the 6th Amendment of the U.S. Constitution had been violated after a TV station obtained tapes of conversations between Noriega and his attorneys.

Bryan Case. In an unrelated decision, a U.S. court-martial acquitted 1st Sgt. Roberto Enrique Bryan on a charge of premeditated murder in connection with the slaying of an unidentified Panamanian man during *Operation Just Cause*. Sergeant Bryan had been accused of shooting the Panamanian at close range without justification. The court found that the action was covered by a presumption of hostile intent, as the man allegedly had made suspicious moves while lying on the ground.

Kuwait Invasion. On the morning of August 2 the UN Security Council found that that day's Iraqi invasion of Kuwait constituted a breach of the peace and called for an immediate and unconditional withdrawal in Resolution 660 (1990). Baghdad's assertion that it had acted upon the invitation of a "free revolutionary provisional government" was rejected unanimously in the Council, which instituted comprehensive economic sanctions.

While the U.S. decision to send troops to the Persian Gulf for the defense of Saudi Arabia undoubtedly was covered by Article 51 of the UN Charter on self-defense, it was debated whether the naval blockage, or "interdiction," instituted by Washington and London at the request of the emir of Kuwait was justified fully. The issue was resolved when the United States and Great Britain went back to the Council to obtain a mandate for that operation, so as not to endanger the unprecedented consensus characterized by the UN response.

The annexation of Kuwait as Iraq's 19th province also was rejected formally by the Council in Resolution 662 (1990). States were urged not to undertake any measures that might indicate acceptance of the annexation, and in response a number of diplomatic missions were kept open in Kuwait City. The taking of foreign nationals as hostages by Iraq also was condemned, as it constituted a violation of the most fundamental principles of international law. In addition, the Iraqi authorities were warned formally that any action constituting a "grave breach" of the Geneva law-of-war convention well could be tried before a Nuremberg-style, war-crimes tribunal at the end of hostilities. Under the Geneva law, individuals who are involved in grave breaches can be held individually accountable. The Security Council also contemplated serving notice on Iraq that it would be required to pay reparations for damage caused as a result of the invasion.

Other Developments. Iran filed its memorial before the International Court of Justice in the case concerning the shooting down of an Iranian civilian airliner by the USS *Vincennes* in the Persian Gulf in 1988. A U.S. offer of $250,000 in *ex gratia* payments to each of the bereaved families was rejected.

Proceedings at the U.S.-Iran Claims Tribunal, which has been adjudicating claims arising out of the turmoil that prevailed in Iran after the 1979 revolution, continued. In June the first major settlement was reached as Iran agreed to pay claims totaling $600,000 to a U.S. oil company.

MARC WELLER, *University of Cambridge*

More than 750 persons reportedly were killed on Oct. 13, 1990, as Syrian military forces, above, overthrew Maj. Gen. Michel Aoun, the Christian army commander who had refused to back the Elias Hrawi government in Lebanon.

LEBANON

Internal and external violence continued to beset Lebanon throughout 1990, but the military end of the mutiny in one Christian district opened vistas of hope for an orderly transition to a "second republic" under the Taif reform agreement, which called for equal sharing of power between Christians and Muslims.

From Internal Reform to Internal Conflict. The reforms agreed to by Lebanese representatives meeting in Taif, Saudi Arabia, and ratified by the Lebanese parliament in November 1989 remained a dead letter for most of 1990 because Gen. Michel Aoun refused to surrender the presidential palace and the defense ministry to the new national government under President Elias Hrawi. Aoun rejected the Taif accord because it failed to provide a timetable for the withdrawal of Syrian forces from Lebanon, and continued to regard himself as the country's legal prime minister. The Lebanese Forces (LF), the principal Christian militia group—led by Samir Geagea—took no public position on Taif, but the Kataeb Party, which they controlled, supported the agreement.

At the end of January, General Aoun demanded that the LF disarm, which would have left him in control of the eastern area of Lebanon. When they refused, his followers attacked LF positions, initiating the bloodiest and most destructive phase the eastern area had experienced in 15 years of violence. This time the LF was better prepared to resist Aoun than they had been in 1989. They immediately launched counterattacks in the north, where their pre-

dominance was clear. After the first week of hostilities, the LF had effective control of Jubayl and Kesruan, the two northern districts of the Christian area, and remained firmly entrenched in their Ashrafiyeh and Karantina strongholds in East Beirut. Aoun's forces seized the small town of Dbayeh, which resulted in cutting the land links between the northern LF positions and Beirut. However, repeated assaults on Ashrafiyeh failed. The fighting between the two Christian factions lasted intermittently through May. When it was over, approximately 1,000 had been killed and more than two thirds of the area was under LF control. Aoun was cut off from the sea, and therefore from all sources of foreign support—except from his old nemesis, Syria.

Beginning in the spring, Syrian forces allowed supplies to cross their lines to reach Aoun's area. In return, Aoun permitted two Syrian-controlled groups—the militias of Elie Hobeika and the Syrian Social Nationalist Party—to operate freely in his sphere. By the summer, the crossing points to Syria were completely open, and many Christians began traveling into and out of Lebanon via Damascus. Abandoning his hostility to the Syrians, Aoun went so far as to describe himself as "in the same trench" with them, fighting Israel and its agents (by which he meant the LF).

A further result of the "war of the brothers" in the Christian area was to force many Christians to return to homes they had fled in search of security in earlier years. Some returned to the Shouf, others to West Beirut. However, tens of thousands fled Lebanon entirely, a further demographic hemorrhage of skilled and educated people that profoundly threatened the country's future potential.

The War Among the Shi'a and Palestinian Intervention. Lebanon's Christians were not alone in engaging in brutal internecine warfare; the Amal and Hezbollah factions also intensified their long and bloody struggle for supremacy within the Shi'a Muslim community. After many small outbreaks of fighting in Beirut and the Iqlim at-Tuffah area southeast of Sidon, a large-scale conflict erupted in the Iqlim in mid-July. Hezbollah seized a mountaintop village, and Amal, unable to dislodge its rival, in turn captured another village closer to the sea. Little further change occurred, but the intensity of the fighting served as a pretext for intervention by Yasir Arafat's Fatah faction of the Palestine Liberation Organization (PLO), which itself seized positions in the Iqlim on the very edge of the Israeli-established "security zone" in southern Lebanon.

The PLO's involvement in Lebanese factional fighting reflected the restoration of its military power in Lebanon, temporarily destroyed by the Israeli invasion of 1982. Since then several thousand guerrillas have infiltrated back into Lebanon, and additional numbers have been recruited, producing a total of about 10,000 fighters, approximately half of them Fatah loyalists. Under pressure from pro-Syrian factions, the Arafat loyalists in the PLO were forced out of their bases in northern and central Lebanon, but during 1990 were able to consolidate their positions in the south around Sidon and Tyre, despite resistance from PLO groups aligned with Abu Nidal.

The Gulf Conflict Helps the Government. Following a year without visible progress after the Taif accord, the Iraqi invasion of Kuwait in August 1990 accelerated the collapse of General Aoun's rebellion. Syria agreed to send troops to Saudi Arabia to counter Iraq's invasion and to bolster the U.S.-led coalition against Iraq. Both the United States and Saudi Arabia urged Syria to facilitate the assertion of Lebanese government authority by cutting off supplies to Aoun. The Syrian government soon redeployed its forces in Lebanon, then turned control of its checkpoints over to the Lebanese army. That army in turn set up a blockade of the areas held by Aoun. By the time the Lebanese government officially asked for Syrian military support, the planning already was completed and the operation ready for implementation.

Early on the morning of October 13, elements of the Lebanese and Syrian armies, accompanied by various militia units and supported by Syrian aircraft, moved against Aoun's forces. Despite his promise to "fight to the death," the general abandoned the presidential palace in the first half hour and was granted asylum in the French embassy. In the

ensuing fighting, as many as 750 people are believed to have been killed, making it the deadliest single day of the 15-year civil war.

The Government Consolidates. Following the collapse of the mutiny, most of Aoun's followers were reintegrated quickly into the Lebanese army, but commanders of units that continued to resist after Aoun's flight were singled out for punishment. Meanwhile, the area Aoun had controlled, the Metn, witnessed a resurgence of pro-Syrian militias, which abducted their enemies and carried out other acts of violence in the immediate aftermath of the fighting. Dany Chamoun (son of former President Camille Chamoun), his wife, and his two sons were murdered in their home during this period.

At the national level, a plan for establishing security in greater Beirut was negotiated and implemented in November, and all militias had left the city officially by early December, although most left some individual militiamen behind with hidden weapons. The U.S. ambassador returned to the U.S. embassy for the first time since diplomats evacuated it in September 1989. A heavily pro-Syrian national unity government in which all factions were represented was announced at the end of December, but there were strong indications that neither the LF nor the Kataeb would participate in the new government on the grounds that it was a Syrian puppet.

The major opposition to the Syrian-dominated framework for peace in Lebanon remained the PLO and Hezbollah. However, the relationship between Iran and Syria offered sufficient common ground to effect a cease-fire between Amal (supported by Syria) and Hezbollah (supported by Iran) in November, and both agreed to cooperate with the greater Beirut security plan. Iran and Syria also made some effort to persuade Hezbollah to release its foreign hostages, and in fact several European and American hostages were released during the year. The PLO insisted on keeping its newly taken positions in the Iqlim, and demanded negotiations with the new government on an agreement defining the group's status in Lebanon.

LEBANON • Information Highlights

Official Name: Republic of Lebanon.
Location: Southwest Asia.
Area: 4,015 sq mi (10 400 km²).
Population (mid-1990 est.): 3,300,000.
Chief Cities (1980 est.): Beirut, the capital, 702,000; Tripoli, 175,000.
Government: *President,* Elias Hrawi (took office November 1989); *prime minister,* Salim al-Hoss (took office November 1989). *Legislature* (unicameral) —National Assembly.
Monetary Unit: Lebanese pound (850 pounds equal U.S.$1, Dec. 31, 1990).
Foreign Trade (1985 U.S.$): *Imports,* $2,200,000,000; *exports,* $482,000,000.

Prospects for Peace and Prosperity. In spite of the acquiescence of all major groups in the greater Beirut plan at the end of the year, the Taif reforms enjoyed very little public support. The Shi'a and Druze overwhelmingly rejected the accord as irrelevant to their basic needs and vital interests, and the Christians were divided. Only the weak Sunni Muslim community was enthusiastic about the agreement. This basic lack of consensus among the country's divided religious communities formed an ominous backdrop to the undeniable progress made in restoring security.

As in the past, Lebanese economic indicators served as a barometer of public confidence rather than a measure of economic productivity. Throughout 1990 the state continued to pay salaries and make other expenditures without significant sources of revenue. The official budget, which showed the deficit to be 65% of total expenditures, probably underestimated its magnitude. Debt service now was twice the size of any other outlay. The public internal debt doubled between 1989 and 1990, while the Lebanese pound declined rapidly in value from about 500 to the dollar at the beginning of the year to more than 1,000 to 1 on the eve of Aoun's defeat. Central bank reserves have been affected adversely by efforts to halt the depreciation of the pound. Amid the optimism that followed the end of the mutiny it regained some of its lost value, but the exchange rate continued to hover around 750 to 1 at the end of the year.

RONALD D. McLAURIN,
Abbott Associates, Inc.

LIBERIA

The corrupt and oppressive rule of President Samuel Doe ended in 1990. Doe, who himself had come to power in a bloody coup in 1980, was murdered by rebels as civil war engulfed Liberia.

Doe's rule first was challenged in December 1989 by a small cadre of dissidents led by Charles Taylor, a former Liberian government official who had been educated in the United States. Taylor's National Patriotic Front of Liberia (NPLF) by midyear had grown into an ill-trained, but successful, 10,000-man army.

The uprising became more complicated as Prince Yeduo Johnson broke with Taylor and formed his own guerrilla army. By July the two rebel armies, working independently and sometimes fighting each other, had gained control of most of the country. Doe's forces, meanwhile, had a tenuous hold on the capital, Monrovia.

The civil war renewed old tribal antagonisms and the undisciplined combatants on all sides murdered, raped, and looted. Government troops targeted Gio and Mano ethnic groups, while rebels slaughtered Mandingos and Doe's tribesmen, the Krahn. As rebel forces closed in on the capital, the atrocities multiplied. One of the worst examples was the murder of 600 Gio and Mano civilians in a church compound in August.

Despite the authoritarian nature of Doe's regime, the numerous human-rights violations, and economic mismanagement, the United States had continued to support the government financially. However, the United States refused to aid Doe's forces in fighting the rebels, and in June dispatched Marines to evacuate Americans.

Johnson's forces outflanked Taylor's rebels in the bid to take control of Monrovia from the government. At the same time, Doe's government troops were reduced to barricading themselves around Government House, the executive mansion.

In an attempt to end the civil war, Gambian President Dauda Jawara convened a meeting of the Economic Commission of West African States (ECOWAS). Subsequently, a peacekeeping force made up of troops from five West African nations was sent to Liberia.

When Doe left the sanctuary of the executive mansion on September 9 to attend a meeting with the peacekeeping force, he was ambushed, wounded, and captured by Johnson's rebels. He later died amid reports of torture. Doe's death did not end the civil war, although a tenuous cease-fire was signed by the various factions in November. A new Liberian government backed by ECOWAS was formed in Sierra Leone with Amos Sawyer as interim president, but Taylor, who controlled most of the country, refused to recognize it. Meanwhile, the 9,000-man West African force attempted to demilitarize Monrovia by keeping Johnson's forces and the remnants of Doe's army apart.

More than 10,000 people had died in the civil war; more than 500,000 Liberians had become homeless; the economy had been wrecked; and widespread starvation threatened Monrovia.

HARRY A. GAILEY, *San Jose State University*

LIBERIA • Information Highlights

Official Name: Republic of Liberia.
Location: West Africa.
Area: 43,000 sq mi (111 370 km²).
Population (mid-1990 est.): 2,600,000.
Chief City (1984 census): Monrovia, the capital, 421,058.
Government: *Head of state,* Amos Sawyer, interim president-in-exile (selected 1990).
Monetary Unit: Liberian dollar (1.0 dollar equals U.S. $1, August 1990).
Gross Domestic Product (1988 U.S.$): $988,-000,000.
Economic Index (1988): *Consumer Prices* (Monrovia, 1980 = 100), all items, 141.8; food, 128.8.
Foreign Trade (1989 U.S.$): *Imports,* $335,-000,000; *exports,* $550,000,000.

LIBRARIES

Concerns over library education were at the forefront of issues confronting librarians, library trustees, and library educators in 1990. This intense focusing of attention was brought on by the announcement by Columbia University's Board of Trustees of their intention to phase out the University's School of Library Service over the next several years.

The closing had a particularly strong impact because the school at Columbia was the first library school in the United States, having been founded by Melvil Dewey in 1887. Following the announcement, Robert Wedgeworth, dean of the School of Library Service at Columbia, called on the American Library Association (ALA) to create a "blue-ribbon" panel to "review all reports and events and to look directly at the school." ALA answered that call and planned to convene the panel, to be composed of representatives of distinguished scholarly and professional organizations. The panel would examine the whole issue of education for library and information science as well as research in the field.

Federal Activities. Following the resignation of Susan K. Martin as executive director of the National Commission on Libraries and Information Services (NCLIS), Commission Chairman Charles Reid announced the appointment of Peter R. Young to the post. Young, formerly director of academic information services at the Faxon Company, previously held posts at CLSI, a library vendor, and at the Library of Congress, where he served for eight years.

Preparation for the Second White House Conference on Library and Information Services (WHCLIS) began taking on a sense of urgency. The conference, scheduled for July 9–13, 1991, would focus on the provision of library and information services for literacy, productivity, and democracy. Linda Resnick was appointed executive director of the conference in late January 1990, but resigned in August. Following her resignation, Peter Young announced that he would serve as executive director of both WHCLIS and NCLIS. (Administration of WHCLIS is handled under the auspices of NCLIS.)

In order to help educate the expected 900 WHCLIS delegates and the thousands of delegates to state governor's conferences in preparation for the national conference, the ALA published *Issues and Challenges for America's Libraries*, a compilation of position papers on the major issues confronting U.S. libraries. More than 20 states and territories held governor's conferences in 1990 to elect their delegates to and pass resolutions for the national conference.

Academic Libraries. The Association of College and Research Libraries, another ALA division, commissioned a survey to discover the

LIBRARY AWARDS FOR 1990

Beta Phi Mu Award for distinguished service to education for librarianship: Robert D. Stueart, dean, Graduate School of Library and Information Science, Simmons College, Boston

Randolph J. Caldecott Medal for the most distinguished picture book for children: Ed Young, *Lon Po Po: A Red Riding Hood Story from China*

Melvil Dewey Award for recent creative professional achievement of a high order: to Helen F. Schmierer, library systems/planning analyst, Rockefeller Library, Brown University, Providence, RI

Grolier Award for unique contributions to the stimulation and guidance of reading by children and young people: Patricia B. Holt, book review editor, *San Francisco Chronicle*

Joseph W. Lippincott Award for distinguished service to the profession of librarianship: Alphonse F. Trezza, professor, School of Library and Information Studies, Florida State University

John Newbery Medal for the most distinguished contribution to literature for children: Lois Lowry, *Number the Stars*

most critical issues of concern to academic librarians. Rising journal prices, providing access to information, preservation of library materials, recruitment and retention of library staff, and maintaining the safety of both collection and users were the five issues cited most frequently.

Preservation. Librarians began having a great deal of success in calling the nation's attention to the fact that the world's written history and knowledge is eroding swiftly on library shelves. Paper used since 1850 to publish books and records has been predominantly acidic; this paper deteriorates swiftly. Research is under way to find economical methods for mass deacidification of the paper, and millions of dollars have been spent microfilming those materials beyond restoration. It remains to be seen, however, whether enough research can be accomplished before the national situation is beyond repair.

Associations. A record-breaking 19,982 people attended the 109th ALA annual conference, held in Chicago, IL, June 23–28, and presided over by Patricia Wilson Berger. Dr. Richard M. Dougherty of the University of Michigan was inaugurated as president at the end of the conference and Patricia Glass Schuman, president of Neal-Schuman Publishers, was welcomed as president-elect. The ALA celebrated the induction of its 50,000th member, Wendy Sinnott, a library-school student at Long Island University.

The Canadian Library Association (CLA) held its 45th annual conference in Ottawa, June 13-17, with the theme "Libraries: Exploring the Myth, Rediscovering the Magic." CLA President Ernie Ingles presided, and Marnie Swanson, university librarian at the University of Victoria, was welcomed as first vice-president/president-elect. In early July, CLA Executive Director Sharon Henry resigned.

CHARLES HARMON
American Library Association

© Cheryl Hatch/Sipa

Libya's Muammar el-Qaddafi (right), who depicts himself as a champion of Arab unity, met with Egypt's President Mubarak (left) in February. In March, Libya arranged a rapprochement meeting between Mubarak and Syrian President Assad.

LIBYA

Reports of a destructive fire at a chemical factory allegedly producing poison gases and other similar weapons lay at the heart of a complex controversy that involved Libya, the United States, and several European nations early in 1990. Later in the year, relations with Italy, the former colonizer, were strained by Libyan demands for compensation for injustices dating to the colonial era. In the spring, months of negotiations intended to settle differences with Chad ended amid accusations of Libyan interference in the internal affairs of its southern neighbor. Throughout 1990, Col. Muammar el-Qaddafi continued to depict himself as a champion of Arab unity, although in August, Libya was one of the few nations to support the Iraqi invasion of Kuwait.

Relations with the West. A series of related international events began to unfold early in March when Qaddafi announced to the General People's Congress, Libya's parliament, that France had agreed to return three Libyan fighter planes it had held for more than three years. The French authorities had cited a European Community ban on arms exports to Libya as the justification for their detention of the French-built aircraft that had been sent back to France for repairs in 1986. In the following month, Libya played a role in negotiations that led to the release of France's last three remaining hostages in Lebanon.

Some observers attributed the improvement in Franco-Libyan relations to the tempering, since the start of the year, of Qaddafi's criticisms of the West and his invitation to the European countries with which Libya was at odds to open dialogue. This more moderate stance on the part of Colonel Qaddafi also pleased Libya's partners in the Arab Maghreb Union (Tunisia, Algeria, Morocco, and Mauritania), since they believed it would facilitate the negotiation of trade agreements between the Union and the European Community (EC), enabling them to cope more effectively with the anticipated consolidation of the European market in 1992. While the return of the planes represented an improving relationship between the governments of Libya and France, French newspapers criticized the agreement, as did newspapers in Great Britain.

Almost concurrently with France's return of the Libyan planes, U.S. intelligence officials made public an assessment of activity at the Rabta chemical plant near Tripoli which also may have been aimed at pressuring France to review its lenient policies toward Libya. Disputing Libya's assertion that Rabta produced only pharmaceutical products, the U.S. report maintained that the factory already was turning out small quantities of chemical weapons and was being expanded to increase its capacity. Before further investigations could be undertaken, however, Libya reported that a fire, which it described as sabotage, destroyed much of the plant on March 14. U.S. officials confirmed that the factory had sustained serious damages, but vigorously denied any complicity in the blaze. In the aftermath of the fire, Qaddafi abandoned his conciliatory tactics and resumed his vigorous denunciations of the West.

Because several of its citizens had figured prominently in the design and construction of the Rabta plant, West Germany found itself squarely at the center of a controversy that strained its relations with both the United States and Libya. The latter accused German businessmen of providing information about the factory to the United States, imposing economic sanctions on West Germany immediately after the U.S. charges were leveled. In an apparent effort to smooth relations with Libya, West Germany publicly opposed the U.S. demand that Libya dismantle the factory and, instead, advocated securing Libyan consent for the visit of an international inspection team to Rabta.

The Rabta incident concluded with a bizarre twist late in March when information gleaned from satellite photographs strongly suggested that the fire had been a hoax designed to give the appearance that the plant had been destroyed, divert international attention from its activities, and secure Libya support and sympathy from Arab, and other, opponents of the West.

Chad. In 1989, when the withdrawal of Libyan forces from Chad brought the hostilities between the two countries to an end, they agreed to submit their dispute over sovereignty in the contested Aouzou Strip along their frontier to international arbitration if they could not reach an agreement through bilateral negotiations within a year. Such talks quickly reached a stalemate and, by the spring of 1990, renewed clashes between Libyan and Chadian soldiers threatened to derail the peace process altogether.

In May, Chadian troops searching for antigovernment forces operating from sanctuaries inside western Sudan intercepted and seized a Libyan convoy believed to be carrying supplies to the rebels. Both Libya and Sudan denounced the seizure. The Chadian authorities countered that the Libyan Islamic Legion, a mercenary force maintained by Qaddafi, was aiding the Chadian rebels in an effort to undermine a government with which it was making no headway in negotiations. Shortly after this incident, the deadline for reaching a negotiated settlement passed and the dispute was turned over to the International Court of Justice. If, as was probable, the Court's deliberations were time-consuming, conflicts between Libyan and Chadian forces were likely to flare up.

Arab Affairs. In keeping with the theme of Arab unity that has characterized its regional policies for more than two decades, Libya arranged talks between Egyptian President Hosni Mubarak and Syrian President Hafez al-Assad in Tripoli in March. The meeting was the first rapprochement between the two influential Arab leaders whose frequently conflicting policies had led them to shun each other for more than a decade. Also in March, Libya signed an agreement to merge with Sudan. In the autumn, Sudanese officials voiced their approval in principle of a Libyan-style system of government, but took no other immediate steps to implement the union. In another example of Libya's improving relations with other Arab countries, Jordan reestablished its diplomatic links with the country for the first time in more than six years and sent an ambassador to Tripoli.

When Iraqi forces invaded and occupied Kuwait in August, Qaddafi was one of the few Arab leaders to support the Iraqi offensive. Although Libya criticized the subsequent buildup of international forces in the Persian Gulf and threatened to provide Iraq with military assistance to force them out, no concrete steps in this direction were taken. Indeed, like most countries with economies dependent upon oil exports, Libya benefited from the increase in crude-oil prices that accompanied the cessation of shipments from Kuwait after its occupation and from Iraq after the imposition of international trade sanctions in the fall.

Anniversary. On October 26, Libya observed the anniversary of the 1911 Italian invasion that opened more than 30 years of colonial rule. The national day of mourning was marked by a 12-hour break in transportation and communication links with the outside world, along with the issuing of demands that Italy compensate those Libyans (believed to number about 5,000), or their heirs, deported from the colony between 1911 and 1942. Libya also sought information on the burial sites of deportees who perished in Italy. The Italian government has insisted that a 1.4 billion lira payment to Libya in 1956 closed the matter of colonial-era compensation.

KENNETH J. PERKINS
University of South Carolina

LIBYA • Information Highlights

Official Name: Socialist People's Libyan Arab Jamahiriya ("state of the masses").
Location: North Africa.
Area: 679,359 sq mi (1 759 540 km²).
Population (mid-1990 est.): 4,200,000.
Chief Cities (1984 census): Tripoli, the capital, 990,697; Benghazi, 485,386.
Government: *Head of state,* Muammar el-Qaddafi (took office 1969). *Legislature*—General People's Congress (met initially Nov. 1976).
Monetary Unit: Dinar (0.277 dinar equals U.S. $1, August 1990).
Gross National Product (1988 est. U.S.$): $20,000,-000,000.
Foreign Trade (1988 est. U.S.$): *Imports,* $5,000,-000,000; *exports,* $6,100,000,000.

LITERATURE

Overview

Political activism among men and women of the world of letters long has been an acceptable endeavor, and in 1990 the term took on new meaning as two internationally renowned writers found themselves in the brightest of political spotlights. Václav Havel, a well-known Czech playwright as well as a prominent political dissident, had become president of Czechoslovakia in December 1989 and was reelected to a two-year term in July 1990. Peruvian writer Mario Vargas Llosa, whose work has made him a world literary figure, similarly was a candidate for president of Peru in 1990, although he ultimately was defeated in a runoff election. Both Havel, with a series of his interviews and commentaries—*Disturbing the Peace*, and Vargas Llosa, with his latest novel—*In Praise of the Stepmother*, also made literary news in 1990. Hungary, too, had a president who is a writer and dissident.

Even the 1990 Nobel laureate, Mexico's Octavio Paz, had a diplomatic career, serving as Mexico's ambassador to France, Switzerland, Japan, and India before resigning from service in 1968. Perhaps the idea of poets as "unacknowledged legislators of the world," put forth by 19th-century British poet Percy

Octavio Paz

© Fred R. Conrad/NYT Pictures

Shelley, should be broadened to include the more overt political role played by some writers in this last decade of the 20th century.

Prizewinners. Literature's most prestigious award, the Nobel Prize, was won in 1990 by Octavio Paz of Mexico. The 76-year-old Paz, who in Latin America long has held status as a literary, intellectual, and political celebrity, is a poet of surrealistic verse and a writer of social essays. He published his first collection of poems as a teenager and remains active as a writer and critic. Major contributions among his more than 25 books of poetry and prose (which have been translated into many languages) are the long poem *Sunstone* (1957), inspired by an Aztec calendar stone, and *The Labyrinth of Solitude* (1950), a prose analysis of modern Mexico and the Mexican personality. Paz had received the Cervantes Prize in 1981 and the Neustadt Prize in 1982.

Oscar Hijuelos, an American of Cuban parentage, won the 1990 Pulitzer Prize in fiction for his second novel, *The Mambo Kings Play Songs of Love*, about two Cuban musicians who journey from Havana to New York in the late 1940s. Among other major literary prizes was the $25,000 biannual Neustadt Prize, which in 1990 went to the poet Tomas Transtömer of Sweden. The Library of Congress awarded a national poetry prize in 1990, its first since 1948 when Congress banned library prize-giving after the controversial Ezra Pound was honored. The $10,000 biannual Bobbitt National Prize for poetry was won by James Merrill.

Other News. The year marked the 100th anniversary of the birth of British mystery writer Agatha Christie, prompting several celebrations and a new biography. Christie remains one of the world's most widely read authors; her books are outsold only by the Bible and Shakespeare.

Two treasured manuscripts with jewel-encrusted gold and silver bindings, that belonged to a cathedral in Quedlinburg, Germany, and had disappeared from a place of safekeeping in a nearby mine shaft shortly after U.S. forces occupied the town in 1945, were recovered during 1990. One, a Carolingian manuscript of the four Gospels, was returned in May after a West German cultural foundation paid a portion of a "finder's fee" of $3 million, an amount which the foundation sought later to recover through legal action in Texas, where the manuscripts had been taken. No money was exchanged for a second, 16th-century manuscript, recovered in October.

Mark Strand—poet, translator of Spanish literature, and short-story writer—became the fourth poet laureate of the United States in 1990. James Billington, the librarian of Congress, appointed Strand, a professor of English at the University of Utah, in May.

SAUNDRA FRANCE

© Benjamin Ford/Courtesy, Atlantic Monthly Press

Courtesy, Atlantic Monthly Press

Ron Chernow, 41-year-old former director of financial studies for the 20th Century Fund, won the 1990 National Book Award for nonfiction for his "The House of Morgan: An American Banking Dynasty and the Rise of Modern Finance."

American Literature

An old saying holds that U.S. writers "have no second act," the belief being that while writers from other countries have long and fruitful careers, Americans have initial success and then burn out. This generalization, based on a few spectacular examples, never had much validity, but today's writers disprove it even more markedly.

John Updike provides the most conspicuous example. His novels, stories, essays, and poems are marked by a growing understanding of U.S. culture and human nature. In his 1960 novel *Rabbit Run*, he introduced Harry "Rabbit" Angstrom, a young man prematurely trapped into family responsibilities and financial obligations in the 1950s. In *Rabbit Redux* (1971), Rabbit is puzzled by the rapidly changing 1960s and a new generation that looks upon him as an older man who never really has lived. *Rabbit Is Rich* (1981) depicts Rabbit in a country basking in its unevenly distributed wealth but losing its sense of direction; Rabbit, while gratified by his success in business, still is baffled by life. In *Rabbit at Rest*, Updike's 1990 work, the processes of aging and loss predominate. Politics, money, and love become a background for the eternal struggle of life against death. With the brilliantly created character of Rabbit, destined to become a permanent part of American literature, Updike relentlessly has chronicled the last half of the 20th century.

Philip Roth's *Goodbye Columbus* (1959) marked his debut as an important writer. He followed with *Portnoy's Complaint* (1969), and with *The Ghost Writer* (1979) began a series of insightful stories about Zuckerman, a writer who seemed very much like Roth. His *Deception* (1990) is a tour de force written entirely as

talk between a writer, his mistress, and other characters. Roth's character speaks of creating Zuckerman, and the dialogue suggests that *Deception* is both fiction and a real transcript of conversations, demonstrating again Roth's mastery of form and language.

As a contemporary satirist Kurt Vonnegut faces the problem of avoiding despair, didacticism, or simple trivialization. *Player Piano* (1952), which warned of a dehumanized future, brought him critical attention. Then with such classics as *Cat's Cradle* (1963), *God Bless You, Mr. Rosewater* (1965), and *Slaughterhouse Five* (1969), Vonnegut became a cultural icon for a zany irreverence that disguised his deep concern for human survival. Though he continued to do interesting work in the 1970s and 1980s, he received less attention. In his latest novel, *Hocus Pocus*, Vonnegut regains his title as the master of the philosophical position that can retain a sense of humor in the face of the stupidities and cruelties of the world.

Tom Robbins received enormous attention with *Another Roadside Attraction* (1971) and *Even Cowgirls Get the Blues* (1976). He deconstructed conventional narrative with his mixture of zany characters, wild plots, and digressive discourses on history, biology, and culture. *Skinny Legs and All* (1990) shows no flagging of energy. Buoyant with life, the story of an exotic dancer and activities in a nightclub near the United Nations building in New York transforms itself into a satirical disquisition on art, politics, and love.

Joyce Carol Oates suffers the peculiar fate of not receiving appropriate critical attention, despite the quality of her work, because she is so prolific. Hardly a year has gone by since *Garden of Earthly Delights* (1967) when she has not produced a novel, a collection of stories, and often a book of poetry or essays as

AMERICAN LITERATURE: | 1990
MAJOR WORKS

NOVELS

Auster, Paul, *The Music of Chance*
Barthelme, Donald, *The King*
Barthelme, Frederick, *Natural Selection*
Batchelor, John Calvin, *Gordon Liddy Is My Muse: By Tommy "Tip" Paine*
Beattie, Ann, *Picturing Will*
Bell, Christine, *The Pérez Family*
Blount, Roy, Jr., *First Hubby*
Bottoms, David, *Easter Weekend*
Boyle, T. Coraghessan, *East Is East*
Busch, Frederick, *Harry and Catherine*
Crews, Harry, *Body*
Cunningham, Michael, *A Home at the End of the World*
Epstein, Leslie, *Pinto and Sons*
Ford, Richard, *Wildlife*
Garrett, George, *Entered from the Sun*
Gifford, Barry, *Wild at Heart*
Hagedorn, Jessica, *Dogeaters*
Hegi, Ursula, *Floating in My Mother's Palm*
Hoffman, Alice, *Seventh Heaven*
Johnson, Charles, *Middle Passage*
Jong, Erica, *Any Woman's Blues*
King, Stephen, *The Stand*
Kingsolver, Barbara, *Animal Dreams*
Leffland, Ella, *The Knight, Death and the Devil*
McFarland, Dennis, *The Music Room*
Matthiessen, Peter, *Killing Mister Watson*
Miller, Sue, *Family Pictures*
Morgan, Seth, *Homeboy*
Naumoff, Lawrence, *Rootie Kazootie*
Oates, Joyce Carol, *Because It Is Bitter, and Because It Is My Heart*
O'Brien, Tim, *The Things They Carried*
Olson, Toby, *Dorit in Lesbos*
Parini, Jay, *The Last Station: A Novel of Tolstoy's Last Year*
Price, Reynolds, *The Tongues of Angels*
Pynchon, Thomas, *Vineland*
Robbins, Tom, *Skinny Legs and All*
Roth, Philip, *Deception*
Thurm, Marian, *Henry in Love*
Turow, Scott, *The Burden of Proof*
Updike, John, *Rabbit at Rest*
Vidal, Gore, *Hollywood: A Novel of America in the 1920s*
Vonnegut, Kurt, *Hocus Pocus*
Wideman, John Edgar, *Philadelphia Fire*
Wolff, Geoffrey, *The Final Club*

SHORT STORIES

Bausch, Richard, *The Fireman's Wife and Other Stories*
Baxter, Charles, *A Relative Stranger*
Bell, Madison Smartt, *Barking Man and Other Stories*
Davenport, Guy, *The Drummer of the Eleventh North Devonshire Fusiliers*
Hempel, Amy, *At the Gates of the Animal Kingdom*
Kotzwinkle, William, *The Hot Jazz Trio*
Leavitt, David, *A Place I've Never Been*
L'Heureux, John, *Comedians*
Michaels, Leonard, *Shuffle*
Millhauser, Steven, *The Barnum Museum*
Moore, Lorrie, *Like Life*
Smith, Lee, *Me and My Baby View the Eclipse*
Stegner, Wallace, *Collected Stories of Wallace Stegner*
Tilghman, Christopher, *In a Father's Place*
Williams, Joy, *Escapes*

POETRY

Alexander, Elizabeth, *The Venus Hottentot*
Angelou, Maya, *I Shall Not Be Moved*
Baxter, Charles, *Imaginary Paintings and Other Poems*
Clampitt, Amy, *Westward*
Gerstler, Amy, *Bitter Angel*
Gluck, Louise, *Ararat*
Hacker, Marilyn, *Going Back to the River*
Hall, Donald, *Old and New Poems*
Jones, Rodney, *Transparent Gestures*
Sheck, Laurie, *Io at Night*
Simic, Charles, *The Book of Gods and Devils*
Simpson, Louis, *In the Room We Share*
Smith, Dave, *Cuba Night*
Soto, Gary, *Who Will Know Us?*

HISTORY AND BIOGRAPHY

Bayley, Isabel, ed., *Letters of Katherine Anne Porter*
Bergreen, Laurence, *As Thousands Cheer: The Life of Irving Berlin*

HarperCollins

Braude, Ann, *Radical Spirits: Spiritualism and Women's Rights in Nineteenth-Century America*
Caro, Robert A., *The Years of Lyndon Johnson: Means of Ascent*
Cassady, Carolyn, *Off the Road: My Years With Cassady, Kerouac, and Ginsberg*
Fast, Howard, *Being Red*
Franklin, John Hope, *Race and History: Selected Essays, 1938–1988*
Kurth, Peter, *American Cassandra: The Life of Dorothy Thompson*
Lane, Ann J., *To "Herland" and Beyond: The Life and Work of Charlotte Perkins Gilman*
Lingeman, Richard, *Theodore Dreiser: An American Journey 1908–1945*
MacAdams, William, *Ben Hecht: A Biography*
Mariani, Paul, *Dream Song: The Life of John Berryman*
Millett, Kate, *The Loony-Bin Trip*
Molesworth, Charles, *Marianne Moore: A Literary Life*
Naifeh, Steven, and Smith, Gregory White, *Jackson Pollock: An American Saga*
Nixon, Richard, *In the Arena: A Memoir of Victory, Defeat, and Renewal*
Noonan, Peggy, *What I Saw at the Revolution: A Political Life in the Reagan Era*
O'Toole, Patricia, *The Five of Hearts: An Intimate Portrait of Henry Adams and His Friends, 1880–1918*
Pritchard, William H., *Randall Jarrell: A Literary Life*
Reagan, Ronald, *An American Life*
Rhodes, Richard, *A Hole in the World*
St. Just, Maria, *Five O'Clock Angel: Letters of Tennessee Williams to Maria St. Just, 1948–1982*
Smith, Sally Bedell, *In All His Glory: The Life of William S. Paley: The Legendary Tycoon and His Brilliant Circle*
Stampp, Kenneth, *America in 1857: A Nation on the Brink*
Styron, William, *Darkness Visible: A Memoir of Madness*

CULTURE AND CRITICISM

Ackerman, Diane, *A Natural History of the Senses*
Bloom, Allan, *Giants and Dwarfs: Essays 1960–1990*
Bloom, Harold, *The Book of J* (translated by David Rosenberg)
Ehrenreich, Barbara, *The Worst Years of Our Lives: Irreverent Notes from a Decade of Greed*
Hitchens, Christopher, *Blood, Class, and Nostalgia: Anglo American Ironies*
Kernan, Alvin, *The Death of Literature*
Kimball, Roger, *Tenured Radicals: How Politics Has Corrupted Higher Education*
Kline, David, *Great Possessions: An Amish Farmer's Journal*
Lhamon, W.T., Jr., *Deliberate Speed: The Origins of a Cultural Style in the American 1950s*
Malcolm, Janet, *The Journalist and the Murderer*
Paglia, Camille, *Sexual Personae: Art and Decadence from Nefertiti to Emily Dickinson*
Petroski, Henry, *The Pencil: A History of Design and Circumstance*
Tannen, Deborah, *You Just Don't Understand: Talk Between the Sexes*
Will, George F., *Men at Work: The Craft of Baseball*
Wills, Garry, *Under God: Religion and American Politics*

© Susan Pierce/Courtesy, HarperCollins

Barbara Kingsolver's books continued to be well-received. The narrator of her 1990 novel "Animal Dreams" is committed to saving her hometown despite the changing times.

well. In 1990 two novels were published: *I Lock My Door Upon Myself* and *Because It Is Bitter, and Because It Is My Heart*. Both proved that her volume of work does not diminish her individual offerings.

Several other recognized talents also have maintained their creative powers over time. Reynolds Price became famous in 1962 with *A Long and Happy Life*. Although he was struck with paralysis in 1984 that confined him to a wheelchair, he has continued to work. *The Tongues of Angels*, his eighth novel, telling of a tragic incident in a boys' summer camp, demonstrates the maturation of his artistic powers and intense exploration of human relations and moral responsibility. Tim O'Brien, known for his massively successful *Going After Cacciato* (1978), does a fine job of describing the lives of Vietnam veterans after the war in *The Things They Carried*. In *The Knight, Death and the Devil* Ella Leffland, whose *Rumors of Peace* (1979) brought her so much attention, daringly addresses the life of the notorious Nazi leader Hermann Goering. Barbara Kingsolver's highly praised first novel, *The Bean Trees* (1988), was followed by *Homeland* (1989), a fine collection of short stories. She shows continued growth with *Animal Dreams*.

On the other hand, despite its lively virtues, Thomas Pynchon's *Vineland* did not satisfy a public waiting for a novel as spectacular as *Gravity's Rainbow* (1973), and Erica Jong's *Fear of Flying* (1973) remains her most striking book despite the emotional revelations of *Any Woman's Blues*.

Some of the most interesting novels of 1990 violated the conventional rules of narrative. Nicholson Baker's *Room Temperature* brilliantly focuses an entire novel on a 20-minute bottle feeding of the narrator's infant daughter. Charles Johnson's *Middle Passage* tells a lyrical and compelling story of the slave trade in 1830 through the eyes of a stowaway with a distinctly 20th-century point of view. Harry Crews' *Body* mixes low farce and violence. Toby Olson's *Dorit in Lesbos* meditates upon itself like a book-length poem. Lawrence Naumoff's *Rootie Kazootie* makes us sympathize with a difficult woman who does not play by the rules. Christine Bell's *The Pérez Family* treats the plight of immigrants to Florida as satiric comedy. George Garrett's successful *Entered from the Sun* takes place in Elizabethan England, telling the story of Christopher Marlowe and completing a trilogy begun with his novel about Sir Walter Raleigh, *Death of the Fox* (1971), and continued in *The Succession* (1983).

Short Stories. Short-story collections in 1990 demonstrated high quality and a healthy range of subjects and styles. Charles Baxter's *A Relative Stranger* shows a wry sensitivity to the incongruities and surprises of contemporary life. The title story tells of a long-lost brother who crashes into the narrator's world, creating a strange bond despite their blatantly different personalities. "The Old Fascist in Retirement" sensitively recreates an Ezra Pound-like figure.

Richard Bausch's *The Fireman's Wife and Other Stories* exemplifies the continued power of traditional narrative dealing with ordinary lives. Lorrie Moore's *Like Life* is populated with more urbane characters, but the stories

Peggy Noonan speaks of her experiences and observations as a speechwriter in the Reagan White House in "What I Saw at the Revolution: A Political Life in the Reagan Era."

© Diana Walker/Courtesy, Random House

In "Men at Work: The Craft of Baseball," George F. Will leaves his familiar political base for a "nonromantic look at a game that brings out the romantic in the best of its fans."

show a similar direction. Leonard Michaels' *Shuffle* is startlingly direct. The first part, "Journal," is composed of brief autobiographical vignettes, some only a single line. The stories that follow, with titles like "My Father," appear equally revealing.

Successful metaphysical fiction also continued with Steven Millhauser's *The Barnum Museum* and Guy Davenport's *The Drummer of the Eleventh North Devonshire Fusiliers*.

Poetry. In 1990 a number of poets spoke through historical characters and mythic figures. "Persona poetry," as it is called, allows the poet to transcend the limits of individual experience and autobiography. In Elizabeth Alexander's *The Venus Hottentot*, the voices of the scientist Cuvier and the tragic African woman, the "Venus Hottentot," who became a circus attraction in Europe, are heard. Laurie Sheck's *Io at Night* has the classical gods speak. Amy Gerstler's *Bitter Angel* revives the dramatic monologue.

Louise Gluck's *Ararat*, with its poems about family trauma and tensions, proves that personal poetry still can have great power, but a surprising number of poets in 1990 wrote about politics and the inadequacies of society. Rodney Jones' *Transparent Gestures* starts with "Who Runs the Country," in which Sen. Jesse Helms is mentioned specifically. A beautifully ironic poem, "Winter Retreat: Homage to Martin Luther King, Jr.," describes a conference of well-meaning educators. Gary Soto's *Who Will Know Us?* describes field workers, job injuries, and the hardships of poverty. Charles Simic's *The Book of Gods and Devils* expresses the urban landscape. The

major piece from Dave Smith's *Cuba Night* ponders race relations in the rural South.

History and Biography. Despite the enormous influence of the entertainment industry in shaping U.S. culture, its important figures rarely have been the subject of serious biographies. In 1990 several works suggested a new depth of interest. Sally Bedell Smith's *In All His Glory* not only tells the life of William S. Paley, the energetic power that ruled the Columbia Broadcasting System (CBS), but also recreates the history of the development of network radio and television. Laurence Bergreen's *As Thousands Cheer* shows both the enormous contribution and the dark side of the prolific songwriter Irving Berlin. William MacAdams' *Ben Hecht* reveals the complex personality of one of our best screenwriters. Peter Kurth's *American Cassandra* traces the life of journalist Dorothy Thompson.

Although the memoirs of elected politicians, such as Richard Nixon's *In the Arena*, tend not to reveal major secrets, Reagan speechwriter Peggy Noonan's *What I Saw at the Revolution* does make clear how much of Ronald Reagan was a manufactured image, while Noonan defends her own record at the White House. Authors who value honesty over privacy can evoke an intimacy that gives a deeper insight into the writer and society. Richard Rhodes' *A Hole in the World* tells of the cruel treatment he suffered as a child at the hands of his stepmother. William Styron's *Darkness Visible* recounts his intense bouts with depression. Kate Millett's *The Loony-Bin Trip* shows how the psychiatric treatment she received only drove her further from sanity.

Culture and Criticism. The national debate about education continued in 1990. Allan Bloom's *Giants and Dwarfs* maintains his attacks on contemporary efforts to make non-Western literature part of the college curriculum. Roger Kimball's *Tenured Radicals* argues that feminism and Marxism have destroyed liberal-arts studies. Alvin Kernan's *The Death of Literature* shows how the electronic media and contemporary criticism have combined to make traditional culture irrelevant.

Other culture critics were similarly scathing. Barbara Ehrenreich's *The Worst Years of Our Lives* focuses on the self-centered greed of the 1980s. Christopher Hitchens' *Blood, Class, and Nostalgia* traces many U.S. policy mistakes to a foolish Anglophilia that allowed the nation to be misled by everything British.

The most memorable books, however, were not so much polemical as physically specific. These included Henry Petroski's *The Pencil* and Diane Ackerman's *A Natural History of the Senses*, which creates the emotions and sensations of smell, touch, taste, hearing, and vision through language that is as richly informative as it is movingly poetic.

JEROME STERN, *Florida State University*

Children's Literature

The health of the children's book market continued to be reflected in 1990 by an increase in the number of new titles, some of which were accounted for by publishers adding entirely new lines to their roster of offerings. Classroom trends such as an increased reliance on literature-based curriculums were perhaps key reasons underlying this boom; teachers were helping create an appreciation of good writing for children.

The year's Caldecott Medal for outstanding illustration was awarded to Ed Young for *Lon Po Po: A Red-Riding Hood Story from China*. The Newbery Medal went to popular author Lois Lowry for *Number the Stars*, a story of courage and resistance set against the German occupation of Denmark during World War II.

Distinguished Offerings. The venerable Theodor S. Geisel, otherwise known as Dr. Seuss, presented a new book, *Oh, the Places You'll Go!*, an energetically illustrated parable on keeping a positive attitude through life's ups and downs. Other distinguished authors with new titles included Mary Stolz with *Bartholomew Fair*, a lively tale of 16th-century England; and Newbery medalists Sid Fleischman with an economically told ghost story entitled *The Midnight Horse*, and Jean Craighead George with a sequel to her award-winning *My Side of the Mountain* entitled *On the Far Side of the Mountain*.

Picture Books. Picture books continued to be a platform for distinguished bookmaking. Among the year's best were Lois Ehlert's *Fish Eyes* and Barbara Cooney's *Hattie and the Wild Waves*. A particularly distinguished retelling of the Christmas story could be found in Madeleine L'Engle's *The Glorious Impossible*, illustrated with Giotto's handsomely reproduced frescoes from the Scrovegni chapel.

Picture books for older readers remained a significant trend. William Hooks' conjure tale, *The Ballad of Belle Dorcas*, outstandingly illustrated by Brian Pinkney, is a striking, bittersweet love story of a black couple circumventing the bonds of slavery. Allen Say's *El Chino*, a startling biography of a Chinese-American who became a bullfighter in Spain, is illustrated exquisitely and carries a remarkably stated message of self-acceptance. Also in the picture-book category but definitely for middle-grade to junior-high-school-age children was Sheila Hamanaka's *The Journey*, a powerful commemoration of the achievements of Japanese-Americans in the face of racial prejudice.

Middle-Grade Books. There also was a fine sampling of stories for middle-grade readers in 1990. Betsy Byars' *Bingo Brown, Gypsy Lover* followed up Bingo Brown's previous adventures with great hilarity. Virginia Hamilton's *Cousins* is a compelling story with considerable

Cover from the book *Number the Stars,* published by Houghton Mifflin Company, Boston. © 1989 by Lois Lowry. Reprinted by permission.

Illustration by Ed Young is reprinted by permission of Philomel Books from *Lon Po Po, A Red-Riding Hood Story from China,* © 1989 by Ed Young.

appeal, and there is pure fun in Barbara Parks' schoolyard tale, *Maxie, Rosie, and Earl—Partners in Grime*.

Paul Yee's *Tales from Gold Mountain* is a vivid collection of original stories celebrating the experiences of Chinese settlers in America, and Bruce Brooks presented a fine story in *Everywhere*.

Junior High and Young Adult. Junior high school readers could find thoughtful reading in nonfiction such as Milton Meltzer's *Crime in America* and Susan Terkel's *Should Drugs Be Legalized?*.

Meaty fiction could be found in Paul Fleischman's *Saturnalia* and Rosemary Sut-

SELECTED BOOKS FOR CHILDREN

Picture Books
Bunting, Eve, *The Wall*
Burningham, John, *Hey! Get Off Our Train*
Gross, Ruth Belov, *What's On My Plate?*
Hest, Amy, *Fancy Aunt Jess*
Joyce, William, *A Day with Wilbur Robinson*
Kuklan, Susan, *Going to My Nursery School*
Lyon, George Ella, *Come a Tide*
Munro, Roxie, *The Inside-Outside Book of London*
Pillar, Marjorie, *Pizza Man*
Robbins, Ken, *A Flower Grows*
Shott, Stephen, photog., *Baby's World*

The Middle Grades
Parks, Van Dyke, *Jump On Over*
Ancona, George, *Riverkeeper*
Boedecker, Cecil, *Mary of Nazareth*
Cooper, Ilene, *Choosing Sides*
DeFelice, Cynthia, *Weasel*
Ekoomiak, Normee, *Arctic Memories*
Fisher, Leonard Everett, *The Oregon Trail*
Foley, Patricia, *John and the Fiddler*
George, Jean Craighead, *One Day in the Tropical Rain Forest*
Goor, Ron and Nancy, *Insect Metamorphosis*
Hurwitz, Johanna, *Aldo Peanut Butter*
Johnson, Rebecca L., *The Greenhouse Effect*
Lasky, Kathryn, *Dinosaur Dig*
Pringle, Laurence, *Global Warming*
Ventura, Piero, *Great Composers*

Junior High
Adler, David, *We Remember the Holocaust*
Browne, Anthony, and Strauss, Gwen, *Trail of Stones*
Conrad, Pam, *Stonewords: A Ghost Story*
Freedman, Russell, *Franklin Delano Roosevelt*
Giblin, James Cross, *The Riddle of the Rosetta Stone*
Gilmore, Kate, *Enter Three Witches*
Holman, Felice, *Secret City, U.S.A.*
Howe, James, *Dew Drop Dead*
Lasky, Kathryn, *Traces of Life*
Lester, Julius, *Further Tales of Uncle Remus*
Martin, Katherine, *Night Riding*
Reeder, Carolyn, *Shades of Gray*
Thesman, Jean, *Rachel Chance*
Warren, James A., *Portrait of a Tragedy: America and the Vietnam War*

cliff's *The Shining Company*; and peer relationships—a topic of special interest to adolescents—were at the heart of Norma Fox Mazer's *Babyface* and Jan Slepian's *Risks and Roses*.

DENISE MURCKO WILMS
Free-lance Children's Book Reviewer

Canadian Literature: English

Although worried about a possible tax increase that would have the effect of raising book prices, Canadian writers and publishers nonetheless produced a record number of volumes in 1990.

Nonfiction. The 17th book of Canada's most popular writer, Pierre Berton, is *The Great Depression, 1929–1939*. Meticulously researched, the book documents some tragic stories of suffering, and accuses then prime ministers R.B. Bennett and Mackenzie King of failing to grasp the Depression's impact on millions of ordinary Canadians, and hence also failing to take desperately needed steps. *Margaret Atwood: Conversations*, edited by Earl G. Ingersoll, records 21 interviews with the celebrated author. Inevitably, the quality of the interviews is as varied as the interviewers, but some are excellent.

The biggest-ever venture in Canadian printing and publishing is publisher Mel Hurtig's C$12.5 million five-volume *Junior Encyclopedia of Canada*. Aimed at children aged 8 to 15, it took scores of researchers five years to produce. *Canadian Essays 1990*, edited by Doug Fetherling, is an entertaining collection that includes essays by Mordecai Richler, Michael Ignatieff, and John Mills. *Mysterious Encounters* by John Robert Colombo consists of 72 reports of strange encounters and strange people, all of them in Canada.

Conservation of the Earth's dwindling resources inspired numerous books, among them Farley Mowat's *Rescue the Earth! Conversations with the Green Crusaders*; *Planet under Stress: The Challenge of Global Changes*, edited by Constance Mangall and Digby McLaren; *The Redesigned Forest* by Brian Fawcett; and *2 Minutes a Day to a Greener Planet* by Marjorie Lamb.

Among biographical works were *A Life on the Fringe: The Memoirs of Eugene Forsey*. Senator Forsey says of former Prime Minister Pierre Trudeau that he kept Quebec in Canada when no one else could have done it. *Pirouette, Pierre Trudeau and Foreign Policy* by J.L. Granatstein and Robert Bothwell says that, although Trudeau always fascinated Canadians with his ventures on the world stage, he nevertheless failed to alter basic Canadian foreign and defense policies.

Poetry. Al Purdy's latest volume is *Woman on the Shore*. Gary Geddes' *Light of Burning Towers: Poems New and Selected* spans 20 years of his poetry. *Winter* by Patrick Lane is 45 poems about the chill, stark season that typifies most of Canada. Fred Cogswell's *Black and White Tapestry* has poems in the demanding form of the sestina, and received critical praise. The poems in *Being on the Moon* by native Indian Marie Annharte Baker are influenced by her belief in native women's capability to heal themselves. *The Complete Works of A.M. Klein* is edited by Zailig Pollock. Don Kerr's *Talkin' Basie* is about New Orleans, LA, and the famous Count Basie band. Tony Cosier's *Landsinger* praises the Canadian landscape and nature.

Thelma Poirer's *Grasslands* has poems set in the south Saskatchewan Badlands. *Positions to Pray In* by Barry Dempster contains spare, well-crafted poetry of a high order. Harold Fenisch's *A Delicate Fire* has some pleasing poems by a man who knows and loves the land. *New Cowboy Poetry*, edited by Hal Cannon, is interesting and unusual. Dave Margoshes' *Northwest Passage* deals realistically with everyday life.

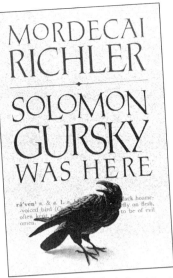

Jacket illustration by Gerard Gauci.
Jacket design by David Wyman. © Alfred A. Knopf.

Doubleday

Fiction. *The Evening News*, Arthur Hailey's first novel in six years, is an exciting story about TV newsmen pursuing the big news of a prominent American kidnapped in Peru. Hailey's passion for research makes the tale ring with authenticity. Brian Moore's *Lies of Silence* is a suspenseful story of violence in Northern Ireland. *Solomon Gursky Was Here*, Mordecai Richler's first novel in ten years, follows four generations of a rags-to-riches family.

Rosamunde Pilcher's *September* is a fast-moving story about two families in a Scottish village. Leslie Hall Pinder's *On Double Tracks* is about a judge and a lawyer involved in a land-claim case. Poet Dorothy Livesay's *The Husband* is an epistolary novel, told in a wife's letters to intimate friends. The wife, whose husband is an elderly invalid, falls in love with their young boarder. George Bowering's *Har-*

ry's *Fragments* breaks the standard mold of spy stories into interesting fragments. Anita Brookner's *Lewis Perry* concerns a man's painful growth through youth and middle age to a final maturity. *Sexing the Cherry* is the unusual title of Jeanette Winterton's skilled and imaginative third novel, set in 17th-century England.

Short-story collections were unusually numerous. Alice Munro, who writes about ordinary people extraordinarily well, added to her international reputation with *Friend of My Youth*. Impressive is Audrey Thomas' *The Wild Blue Yonder*. Other volumes include Clare Rothman's *Salad Days*, William Trevor's *Family Sins*, and W.D. Valgardson's *In the Couch*.

DAVID SAVAGE
Free-lance Writer

English Literature

During 1990, British nonfiction provided the most exciting offerings among literary works, although several important novelists brought out new works during the year. From hiding, Salman Rushdie, who in 1989 had been subjected to threats from Iranian fundamentalists, published *Haroun and the Sea of Stories*.

Fiction. Many other distinguished novelists also produced new works. Ian McEwan's *The Innocent*, set in West Berlin in 1955, was accomplished and shocking, though perhaps a little knowing. Muriel Spark's *Symposium*, a latter-day examination of good and evil at a London dinner party, was found to be witty. Noteworthy, too, were William Boyd's *Brazzaville Beach*, set in West Africa; Fay Weldon's *Darcy's Utopia*, set in a fantasy world; and Alice Thomas Ellis' *The Inn at the Edge of the World*, exploring bourgeois unease. *The Folks That Live on the Hill* by Kingsley Amis pleased his admirers. *Brief Lives*, from Anita Brookner, continued her examination of despair and survival. A. N. Wilson's *A Bottle in the Smoke*, set in hard-drinking Soho circles, entertained. A novel of religious intensity on the subject of the Resurrection, *On the Third Day*, was contributed by Piers Paul Read.

An oddity, *Dwarfs*, appeared from Harold Pinter. The book, his only novel written in the 1950s, until now was unpublished. The atmosphere of menace in the work was thought to be recognizable Pinter, although the dialogue was felt to be the most skillful aspect of the work.

The comic novel of the year was *Temples of Delight* by Barbara Trapido, a work that confirmed her growing reputation. A lively new talent, that of Hanif Kureishi, well-known for his film script for *My Beautiful Laundrette*, was seen in *The Buddha of Suburbia*, depicting the world of a young Pakistani growing up in south London.

POSSESSION
A ROMANCE

A. S. BYATT

Reprinted by permission of Random House, Inc.

Booker Prize selections for the shortlist of the six best novels of the year were: *An Awfully Big Adventure* by Beryl Bainbridge, set in the theater world of Liverpool in the 1950s; *The Gate of Angels* by Penelope Fitzgerald, the 1979 winner of the prize who made her fourth appearance on the shortlist; John McGahern's *Amongst Women*, recounting the end of an Irish patriarch; Brian Moore's *Lies of Silence*, set in the urban terror of Belfast; Canadian author Mordecai Richler's *Solomon Gursky Was Here*, published after a ten-year silence, recounting the eccentric saga of a Canadian Jewish family; and the year's Booker Prize winner, *Possession* by A. S. Byatt. Byatt is a novelist and academic with a great love of the Victorian age, who in the work threw in her own vivid pastiche of the poetry written by the Victorian protagonists.

Nonfiction. The year saw especially rich nonfiction offerings. Among literary biographies, two large-scale works concentrated on the lives of great Victorian writers. *Dickens* by Peter Ackroyd attracted praise and controversy, while *Anthony Trollope: A Victorian in His World* by Richard Mullen was welcomed and illuminating. *Proust* by Ronald Hayman took advantage of the French writer's recently published correspondence. The centenary of the birth of the Russian poet and novelist Boris Pasternak saw many translations of his work and appreciations, also a zestful biography from Peter Levi and the first volume of a biography by Christopher Barnes.

James Joyce and the Politics of Desire by Suzette A. Henke showed Joyce as an instinctive feminist, while *Charles Darwin: A New Life* by John Bowlby, the eminent child psychi-

atrist, provided a fascinating look at the springs of Darwin's creativity. *Paul Scott: A Life* by Hilary Spurling was a first account of the author of *The Raj Quartet. Robert Graves: The Years with Laura* by Richard Perceval Graves was an account of the poet's life with a demanding muse. A. N. Wilson contributed *C. S. Lewis: A Biography*, and Hugh and Mirabel Cecil, a lively account of two of the mentors of Bloomsbury in *Clever Hearts: Desmond and Molly MacCarthy*.

Among the publication of letters, *Henry James and Edith Wharton: Letters 1900–1915*, edited by Lyall H. Powers, provided great interest; also the *Letters of Leonard Woolf*, edited by Frances Donaldson, laid bare the solemn personality behind the scintillating style. A further volume of diaries, *Hanging On —Diaries December 1960 to August 1963* by Frances Partridge, added to Bloomsbury records from the oldest living member of that group.

Noel Annan's *Our Age: Portrait of a Generation* provided a fascinating overview of the cultural and intellectual achievements of those who were born between 1900 and 1925 and who "went up" to Oxford and Cambridge between 1919 and 1950—a narrow but infinitely influential elite in the recent past.

Among political works, *Conflicts of Interest* by Tony Benn pursued the author's account of contemporary British politics. *Blood, Class and Nostalgia: Anglo-American Ironies* by Christopher Hitchens provided a look at Anglo-American understandings and misunderstandings.

A number of interesting collections appeared, including *As the Story Was Told: Uncollected and Late Prose* by Samuel Beckett; *Reflections* by Graham Greene; and *As It Was* by Sybille Bedford. In the compilation *The State of the Language*, edited by Christopher Ricks and Leonard Michaels, modern English in all its variety and utility was examined. The conclusion was that the language never can be in danger.

Poetry. The Arvon International Poetry Competition was won in 1990 by Sheldon Flory, a U.S. poet, but the runners-up included a host of new voices from both sides of the Atlantic. Among established poets of 1990, Seamus Heaney published *New Selected Poems, 1966-1987*, and Ciaran Carson's new collection was *Belfast Confetti*.

The new young poet Andrew Gregg's *The Order of the Day* was much appreciated, as was *Tale of the Mayor's Son* by Glyn Maxwell. The established poets Eavan Bolan and Vikram Seth brought out *Outside History* and *All You Who Sleep Tonight*, respectively. All of the four poets' works were selected as Poetry Book Society choices throughout 1990.

MAUREEN GREEN
Free-lance Writer, London

World Literature*

Reverberations from the sociopolitical upheavals of 1989, particularly in Central Europe and China, began leaving their mark on world literature in 1990. This influence resulted in part from the greater artistic freedom now allowed in many areas and in part as a direct response to or description of those events. Three prime examples were new works by Christa Wolf of East Germany (GDR), Václav Havel of Czechoslovakia, and Liu Xinwu of China. This literary impact of political change was not the only story of the year, however, as world literature also saw the appearance of a wealth of first-rate new works by writers both well established and previously little known.

The year also saw Mexico's poet, critic, and humanist Octavio Paz win the Nobel Prize for Literature. (*See* page 328.)

German. Christa Wolf, long a revered beacon of courage and integrity as well as an outstanding prose writer, drew an unexpectedly ferocious firestorm of criticism for her autobiographical novella *What Remains*. Written in 1979, the book recounts the story of a noted woman writer whose life suddenly is altered when, for reasons unknown, she is placed under 24-hour surveillance by anonymous men in ever-changing anonymous automobiles outside her home. Charges of a past failure of nerve amounting to tacit complicity in police-state repression and of present opportunism in publishing the work only after the demise of the Erich Honecker government have shaken Wolf badly. However, her many admirers—including several writers who suffered imprisonment/exile and were treated far worse by the East German regime—have begun belatedly speaking out more vociferously in her defense. Among these supporters were the bad-boy poet-balladeer Wolf Biermann and the subtle poet and prose writer Günter Kunert. Both writers, now resident in the West for more than a decade, also brought out new titles of their own in 1990: Biermann his collected songs of 30 years (*All the Songs, 1960–1990*) and Kunert a new collection of verse, *A Stranger in One's Own Land.*

Max von der Grün's complex modern-day thriller, *Spring Flood*, led a rather lackluster year in West German letters. A stronger showing from Austria included two major new books: *Another Child* by Barbara Frischmuth struggled with huge questions of memory, forgetfulness, despair, and hopeful determination; and the novelette *Attempt about a Jukebox* by Peter Handke carried the autobiographical narrator to a sleepy Spanish town, where he hoped to write in peace about a fondly recalled superjukebox from his youth, only to find his intended essay/excursus slowly metamorphosing into a fictional metanarrative. The gifted Swiss writer Silvio Blatter weighed in with *The Blue House*, a picaresque chronicle covering three generations of the Zinn (Tin) family's colorful patriarch Johann and his scions.

Slavic Languages. Václav Havel (*see* BIOGRAPHY), the dissident playwright turned president, became better known as a thinker and artist in 1990 through the international success of *Disturbing the Peace*, a series of interviews, conversations, and commentaries dating from 1986 and touching on such topics as power, reticence, and the absurdist tradition that forms the basis of his political and philosophic outlook. His countryman Ivan Klíma provided a finely crafted and provocative look at the 1980s in his homeland with *Love and Garbage*, the multilayered story of the life, loves, and literary efforts of a novelist and sanitation worker.

Polish literature continued its active resurgence of the 1980s with the publication of several new works both at home and abroad, including the novels *Rondo* by Kazimierz Brandys, *Bohin Manor* by the prodigiously talented Tadeusz Konwicki, and *The Beautiful Mrs. Seidenmann* by the exile-turned-senator Andrzej Szczypiorski. The self-proclaimed masterwork of Albanian novelist Ismail Kadare, the epic Kafkaesque fantasy *The Palace of Dreams*, became available to Westerners in French translation; and the prizewinning Belorussian novelist Vasil Bykov (actually Bykau) was reintroduced to the West through an English edition of his 1986 novel *Sign of Misfortune*, a moving tale of survival and complicity in Nazi-occupied Belorussia during World War II. The war as seen from exile in Paris provides the backdrop for three novellas by the Russian Nina Berberova, issued together in a single volume titled *Three Novels*. And *Goodnight!* by Abram Tertz (Andrei Sinyavsky) moves backward and forward in time as it weaves an amalgam of fantasy, memories, and history into a fictionalized autobiography that illuminates the author's emergence in the 1960s as a writer and dissident.

Asia. Liu Xinwu, a prominent and acerbic chronicler of Chinese society in the 1980s who was removed as editor of the influential journal *People's Literature* following the June 4, 1989, crackdown, was introduced to English readers with the story collection *Black Walls*. It contains works from 1980 to the protests of 1989. Wang Meng, China's minister of culture from 1986 until his ouster in September 1989, likewise debuted in the West in 1990; his *Bolshevik Salute*, billed as the first Chinese modernist novel to appear in English translation, covers 35 years in the life of a dedicated Communist trapped between self-knowledge and party dictates. Li Cunhao's *Wreath at the Foot of the Mountain* created a sensation upon first publication in 1982 for its realistic portrayal of the 1979 China-Vietnam conflict. Bei Dao's novel *Waves* and Ah Cheng's three-novella collection *King of Children* record the painful years of the

Cultural Revolution, while the stories of Ai Bei's *Red Ivy, Green Earth Mother* present the frankest depiction yet of the lives of women in contemporary China.

Japan's acclaimed novelist Kenzaburô Oe delved into science fiction with *The Healing Tower*, about a 21st-century resettlement effort on a "new Earth" in a faraway galaxy following the total devastation of our own planet. Western readers got a first look at Satoko Kizaki and a second glimpse of Saiichi Maruya in the fine short-story collections *The Phoenix Tree* and *Rain in the Wind*, respectively.

India's venerable R.K. Narayan presented readers with another delightful tale from the mythical town of Malgudi in *The World of Nagaraj*. This time he focuses on the idle, uninvolved life of the rich but resolutely unambitious title character and his desultory efforts at writing the biography of an obscure sage. Khushwant Singh, a proponent of realism and humor in Indian writing, offered *Delhi*, retelling the history of the city through the eyes of an aging reprobate. The cause of the banned Indonesian novelist Pramoedya Ananta Toer doubtless was helped by the English-language publication of his slender, poetic new novel *The Fugitive*, a story of treachery and deceit set amid the Japanese occupation at the end of World War II.

Africa. The outstanding and prolific South African writer Nadine Gordimer gave us *My Son's Story* in 1990, weaving a charged and psychologically complex tale of a township family caught up in both their own private affairs and the political struggles and changes currently going on in their troubled nation. The noted Nigerian author Amos Tutuola offered *The Village Witch Doctor*, an extraordinary collection of traditional and original stories drawing heavily on Yoruba legend and folklore. Tutuola also produced a definitive reworked version of his 1948 novel manuscript *The Wild Hunter in the Bush of Ghosts*, previously published only in a limited scholarly edition in 1982. Henri Lopes of Zaire brought out his first novel in nearly a decade, *In Search of Africa*, recounting in alternating sequences the two worlds of its African-European protagonist. From North Africa came ambitious and first-rate new French-language works of fiction by Tahar Ben Jelloun of Morocco (*Days of Silence in Tangiers*) and Chantal Chawaf of Algeria (*Clearing Skies*).

Near East. The 1988 Nobel laureate Naguib Mahfouz's most highly acclaimed work, the 1,500-page *Cairo Trilogy*, became available to Western readers, at least in part, with the publication of the English translation of volume 1, *Palace Walk*. It chronicles two years in the life of a respectable middle-class Cairo family caught up in the sociopolitical changes occurring in Egypt in the aftermath of World War I. Israel's Aharon Appelfeld brought out *The Healer*, a powerfully original novel set in pre-war Central Europe (like many of his earlier books) and examining the plague of anti-Semitism that haunted both individuals and entire populations (here it is Vienna) during that period. His countryman David Grossman, critically hailed for 1989's *See Under: Love*, enjoyed the first English publication of his 1983 novel *The Smile of the Lamb*, about the erosion of values caused by Israel's subjugation of Palestinians on the West Bank. From Iran came first English versions of works by both the popular prerevolutionary woman writer Simin Daneshvar (*Savushun*) and the pseudonymous "Manuchehr Irani" (*King of the Benighted*), considered by his peers as the finest contemporary Persian short-story writer.

France. An otherwise uninspiring year in French literature was brightened considerably by the dazzling verbal artistry of Hélène Cixous, whose "novel" *Days of the Year* incorporates such disparate elements as anniversaries (both imaginary and real) for various dates, meditations on death and the irresistibility of night, and fantasized voyages across the Styx in the company of the deceased authors Clarice Lispector and Thomas Bernhard. In Patrick Modiano's novel *Honeymoon*, the narrator tries to come to terms with his longstanding guilt and remorse over his young bride's suicide 40 years ago and also over his current companion's sudden abandonment of him. Other works of note from France included Patrick Grainville's fictionalized autobiography of his childhood and youth, *The Orgy, the Snow*; Julien Green's journal from the 1980s, *The Expatriate*; and the complete poems of Edmond Jabès, *The Threshold, the Sand*, covering the years 1943-88.

Other. The outstanding Dutch-language author Hugo Claus' lengthy but riveting and lively novel *The Sorrow of Belgium* chronicles the events and effects of World War II in one corner of one small country as filtered through the eyes and pen of an obnoxious young artist in the making. *Fado Alexandrino* by Portugal's António Lobo Antunes covers some of the same post-Angolan war terrain treated in the author's much-praised earlier novel, *South of Nowhere*. This time he focuses more expansively and in more complex fashion on the crisscrossed fates of four failed Portuguese combatants in the ten years after the troops returned home from Angola. And lastly, the gifted Romanian author Paul Goma made his debut in English with the publication of *My Childhood at the Gate of Unrest*, a Proustian exploration of memory and experience, centering on a remote Moldavian village that survives the war only to be swallowed up in Stalin's Russia.

WILLIAM RIGGAN
World Literature Today

The first ceremonial train of the Los Angeles Blue Line, a light-rail trolley that will connect the city's downtown with Long Beach, approaches Pico Station in mid-July.

AP/Wide World

LOS ANGELES

Among the chief news items in Los Angeles in 1990 were Mayor Tom Bradley's efforts to regain the public's confidence, the city council's struggle to secure a pay increase, and the county board's attempt to settle an apportionment dispute.

Local Government. Mayor Bradley tried hard to put 1989's scandals behind him and had considerable success, but he failed to gain support for his personal policy agenda and clearly had lost his leadership momentum.

After much indecision, the city council submitted to a vote a proposal to increase members' pay, already the highest in the nation, to $86,157—a 40% rise. Pay for elective officers and retirement benefits also would be increased. To make the proposal more acceptable, a rider was added to restrict gifts and outside pay. However, despite fearing rejection of its proposal, the council would not submit a more comprehensive ethics bill proposed by an advisory group.

A federal district court ruled in June that the districting of the Los Angeles county board of supervisors violated the U.S. Voting Rights Act by drawing district boundaries so as to dilute Latino voting power. The circuit court held on appeal that the case involved too many issues to be settled immediately. An election was postponed indefinitely until all questions could be settled, which might take a year or more. Among the troublesome issues was the fact that, since there were only five supervisors for nearly 10 million people in the county, districting tended to divide up suburban cities, weakening their representation.

In a carryover from the political scandals of 1989, City Treasurer Leonard Rothenberg resigned when faced with removal for lack of management capacity, although he still was considered to be a fine investments officer.

In February the Los Angeles school board voted to establish a year-round schedule in all district schools by the 1991–92 school year.

Budget. The mayor's $3.68 billion budget was adopted amidst conditions of tight state funds, declining revenue projections, rising litigation awards, and higher medical costs. The council increased the business tax by 10% and added a new 10% surcharge on the use of parking lots and structures. Trash-collection fees were doubled to pay for a new recycling program, but despite the increases, service levels were cut.

Transportation. The 6.8-mi (10.9-km) second leg of the Metro Rail project was approved by federal authorities in March. However, in July a cave-in resulting from a two-day tunnel fire caused further delays and added costs to the project.

The light-rail trolley between Long Beach and downtown was opened at a cost of $877 million, the first leg of a 150-mi (240-km) system to be built over 20 years. Some critics doubted the new line would attract predicted passenger levels, however, because the route passes through areas of violent youth gangs.

Water. The city was enduring its fourth year of drought in 1990. With the Sierra snowpack at 50% of normal, the council avoided mandatory water rationing but adopted a voluntary routine. Its goals were being met successfully.

Crime. In what was said to be the most expensive and longest criminal trial (three years) in U.S. history, the McMartin Preschool child-molestation case ended with a whimper in July with a jury deadlocked on eight remaining charges against Raymond Buckey, 32. In January, Buckey and his mother, Peggy McMartin Buckey, 63, former director of the school, had been acquitted on 52 charges, with a hung jury on 13 others.

In the first three months of 1990, 1,302 gang-related violent felonies were reported, an 18% increase over the same period in 1989. Gangs of youths from Southeast Asian ethnic groups became evident additions to the brutality during the year.

CHARLES R. ADRIAN
University of California, Riverside

Louisiana Democratic Sen. J. Bennett Johnston was returned to Washington for a fourth term after defeating controversial challenger David Duke, a state representative and a former leader of the Ku Klux Klan, in the state's October 6 open primary. No runoff was necessary as Johnston won more than 50% of the vote.

AP/Wide World

LOUISIANA

A chaotic state legislative session and the challenge of former Klansman David Duke for the seat of U.S. Sen. J. Bennett Johnston attracted national attention to Louisiana politics in 1990.

Elections. Duke, a controversial former Ku Klux Klan leader and American Nazi Party member, was elected to the state House in 1989 from an almost all-white suburban New Orleans district. He was given little chance to defeat Johnston, who first won election to the Senate in 1972. But Duke won 60% of the white vote and gave the veteran senator a tougher race than expected. Duke ran as a Republican, although several national Republican figures endorsed the Democratic Johnston. The regular Republican candidate, state Sen. Ben Bagert of New Orleans, withdrew the week of the election.

Following Duke's defeat, New Orleans voters elected state Sen. William Jefferson as the state's first black congressman since Reconstruction. Jefferson defeated attorney Marc Morial, son of New Orleans' first black mayor, in a bitter campaign. The race was to fill the seat of U.S. Rep. Lindy Boggs, who retired after serving in Congress since 1973. Six other U.S. congressmen—Robert Livingston (R) of Metairie, Billy Tauzin (D) of Thibodaux, James McCrery (R) of Shreveport, Jerry Huckaby (D) of Ringgold, James A. Hayes (D) of Lafayette, and Clyde Holloway (R) of Forest Hill—won reelection in the first primary and the seventh, Richard Baker (R) of Baton Rouge, was unopposed.

The preliminary 1990 census showed a drop in the state's population, which could result in the loss of one of its eight House seats. However, state officials were hoping that a recount would find enough residents to allow Louisiana to keep all eight seats.

Legislation. The legislative session was a tumultuous one, even by Louisiana standards. It began with the state Senate's ouster of Gov. Charles E. (Buddy) Roemer's choice as Senate president, Allen Bares (D) of Lafayette. He was replaced by Samuel B. Nunez (D) of Chalmette, who had been ousted by Roemer forces in 1988. Never in recent history had a presiding officer of either legislative house been removed in midsession.

Both houses passed the nation's toughest abortion bill, which would have allowed the procedure only in cases where the mother's life was in danger. Roemer vetoed the bill and the legislature then passed an only slightly less restrictive version, which the governor also vetoed. National feminist groups had threatened to boycott Louisiana products and tourism if the bill became law.

LOUISIANA • Information Highlights

Area: 47,752 sq mi (123 677 km²).
Population (1990 census prelim.): 4,181,000.
Chief Cities (July 1, 1988 est.): Baton Rouge, the capital, 235,270; New Orleans, 531,700; Shreveport, 218,010.
Government (1990): *Chief Officers*—governor, Charles E. Roemer (D); lt. gov., Paul Hardy (R). *Legislature*—Senate, 39 members; House of Representatives, 105 members.
State Finances (fiscal year 1989): *Revenue,* $9,558,000,000; *expenditure,* $8,734,000,000.
Personal Income (1989): $56,615,000,000; per capita, $12,921.
Labor Force (June 1990): *Civilian labor force,* 1,921,600; *unemployed,* 134,400 (7.0% of total force).
Education: *Enrollment* (fall 1988)—public elementary schools, 581,095; public secondary, 205,588; colleges and universities, 176,031. *Public school expenditures* (1989–90), $2,435,304,000.

Another bill passed by the legislature that brought threats of boycott by national music groups was a measure to require warning labels on records and tapes with possibly obscene lyrics. Roemer also vetoed that bill.

The legislature defeated a bill that would have fined a person only $25 for assaulting someone who burned the U.S. flag. A bill sponsored by David Duke to weaken state affirmative-action programs also was voted down. A bill outlawing spousal rape was passed, but only after derogatory remarks by some lawmakers about women brought more adverse attention to the legislature.

State Insurance Commissioner Doug Green was indicted by a federal grand jury for allegedly using his office to benefit Champion Insurance Company and accepting financial benefits from Champion's owners.

The year ended on an upbeat note when state budget officials predicted a $400 million surplus for fiscal 1990–91. The windfall was caused by higher oil and gas prices, resulting in higher royalties, severance taxes, and sales taxes.

JOSEPH W. DARBY III
"The Times Picayune," New Orleans

MAINE

Maine's troubled economy was a major campaign issue in the 1990 November election, but incumbent Republican Gov. John R. McKernan survived a challenge from former two-term Democratic Gov. Joseph E. Brennan, who left his 1st District congressional seat to make the gubernatorial race. With a record 57.4% of Maine's registered voters casting ballots on a wet and windy day, McKernan's final totals were 233,233 to Brennan's 220,150. Independent candidate Andrew Adam got 46,616 votes. Several postelection analysts speculated that Adam's anti-Washington campaign theme contributed to Brennan's defeat.

In the U.S. Senate race, GOP incumbent William R. Cohen easily defeated his Democratic opponent, Neil Rolde. Democrat Thomas Andrews of Portland, running for Brennan's congressional seat, won what amounted to a landslide victory in his race against Republican David E. Emery of Rockland. In Maine's other U.S. congressional contest, 2d District Republican incumbent Olympia J. Snowe was reelected in an unexpectedly close race against Democrat Patrick K. McGowan.

The statehouse balance of power remained essentially unchanged as Democrats retained control of both the Maine House and Senate. The 1990 elections failed to shift existing party balances in any major posts. Maine continued to have a Republican governor who would work with a Democratic legislature. And in

---

MAINE • Information Highlights

Area: 33,265 sq mi (86 156 km^2).
Population (1990 census prelim.): 1,218,000.
Chief Cities (1980 census): Augusta, the capital, 21,819; Portland, 61,572; Lewiston, 40,481; Bangor, 31,643.
Government (1990): *Chief Officers—governor,* John R. McKernan, Jr. (R); secretary of state, G. William Diamond (D). *Legislature—*Senate, 33 members; House of Representatives, 151 members.
State Finances (fiscal year 1989): *Revenue,* $3,164,000,000; *expenditure,* $2,837,000,000.
Personal Income (1989): $19,860,000,000; per capita, $16,248.
Labor Force (June 1990): *Civilian labor force,* 640,200; *unemployed,* 26,000 (4.1% of total force).
Education: *Enrollment* (fall 1988)—public elementary schools, 148,904; public secondary, 63,998; colleges and universities, 47,903. *Public school expenditures* (1989–90), $1,018,702,000.

Washington, the two parties held equal shares of the two Senate and two House seats.

Shopping patterns in Maine were expected to change as a result of the election's referendum to repeal the state's regulations that prohibit most major retailers from opening on Sunday. One of just two states to maintain so-called blue laws, Maine dropped from the ranks as 53% of the voters decided to allow stores to do business on Sunday. Voters approved a bond issue to improve rail transportation and school maintenance but turned down plans to increase spending for public lands, prison improvements, and the preservation of historic sites.

One site that could be selected for historic preservation in the future is the mansion that serves as President George Bush's summer White House at Walker Point in Kennebunkport. Many government officials traveled to meet with the president in Maine during the first weeks after Saddam Hussein's Iraqi forces invaded Kuwait in August.

Economy. For the first time in a decade, there was little or no increase in the state's economic index. Housing sales and retail sales both dropped from 1989 totals.

There were, however, plenty of lobsters to be caught, so many that the price dropped below levels lobstermen considered acceptable and more than half kept their boats at the dock until the numbers improved.

Education. The Maine Common Core of Learning, a proposal emphasizing a more integrated approach to teaching and learning, was introduced in the state schools in the fall. Intended to reduce the school dropout rate and help meet the needs of the state's work force, the new concept teaches the "essence of what it means to be human." It involves four categories: communication, reasoning and problem solving, the human record, and personal and global stewardship.

JOHN N. COLE
Cofounder,"Maine Times"

MALAYSIA

Major elections, high economic growth, and various diplomatic activity highlighted 1990 events in Malaysia.

Elections. Malaysia's eighth general elections in October 1990 saw the ruling coalition of 11 parties comprising the National Front, led by Prime Minister Mahathir bin Mohamad, returned to power. The National Front secured 127 of 180 seats in the national parliament, giving it the two-thirds majority needed to make constitutional changes.

The opposition parties had grouped around Razaleigh Hamzah, the former finance minister under Mahathir and the leader of the Somangat '46 (Spirit of '46) party. This was the first time that a multiracial coalition of parties had confronted the ruling multiracial National Front. The ruling alliance is dominated by the United Malays National Organization (UMNO), while in the past the opposition had tended to be dominated by the Chinese parties, primarily the Democratic Action Party.

Razaleigh's party did not do particularly well at the polls, securing only eight of the 61 seats it contested and less than the 12 it had held in the previous parliament. However, in state elections held at the same time, Razaleigh's home state of Kenlantan as well as the East Malaysian state of Sabah were captured by the opposition. The best gain by the opposition was made by the Islamic fundamentalist Parti Islam (PAS), which won seven seats in parliament—compared with one previously. It also captured the Kelantan state government. However, analysts pointed out the PAS essentially is a regional phenomenon, rooted in the poor state of Kelantan. It is unlikely to make any inroads in mainstream Malaysian politics, which are based on free enterprise and secularism—though the official religion of the state is Islam.

Although the inability to win the Malay heartland states, such as Kelantan, was a setback for Mahathir, he got his desired two-thirds majority in parliament. The fact that Malaysia's economy was booming at the highest level in more than a decade as well as the fact that there was little ideological difference between Mahathir and Razaleigh contributed to Mahathir's election success. A team of 12 observers from the British Commonwealth pronounced the elections "free in accordance with Malaysian law and circumstances," though they noted some minor imperfections.

The Economy. The Malaysian government continued to cope with an economy growing at too rapid a rate. Its growth rate was expected to reach 10% by the end of the year and was one of the highest in Asia. The growth was due mainly to the dynamism of the export-oriented manufacturing sector, which in recent years had replaced such traditional commodities as palm oil, tin, and rubber as the basis for the expansion.

Japanese, U.S., and Taiwanese investments continued to pour into Malaysia in search of lower labor costs and a developed infrastructure in which best to export operations to the United States and Japan. Malaysia's wages were lower than those in Taiwan, Korea, Singapore, or Hong Kong. The Malaysia Industrial Development Authority reported that investments approved in the first half of 1990 came to M$18.3 billion (about U.S.$7 billion), a 50% increase from the same period a year earlier.

To boost domestic economic activity, Malaysia was engaged in a massive $6 billion infrastructure-development program, which included the building of highways, as well as the expansion of ports and railway tracks.

As an oil producer and a net exporter of oil, Malaysia actually was expected to benefit from the crisis in the Persian Gulf caused by Iraq's invasion of Kuwait in August. Government officials estimated that for every increase of U.S.$1 in the price of oil, Malaysian government revenues would increase by about M$100 million (about U.S.$40 million).

Foreign Affairs. In June representatives of 15 developing (G-15 group) nations, including India, Zimbabwe, and several large Latin American nations, gathered in Malaysia. African National Congress leader Nelson Mandela visited Malaysia in October and was promised M$13.5 million (about U.S.$5.2 million) in Malaysian aid.

As a member of the United Nations Security Council, Malaysia cosponsored the resolution that demanded the withdrawal of Iraqi troops from Kuwait. However, Malaysia did not send its own troops to the Persian Gulf and said it would reconsider that decision only if the UN was involved directly in commanding the troops.

N. BALAKRISHNAN
"The Far Eastern Economic Review"

MALAYSIA • Information Highlights

Official Name: Malaysia.
Location: Southeast Asia.
Area: 127,317 sq mi (329 750 km²).
Population (mid-1990 est.): 17,900,000.
Chief City (1980 census): Kuala Lumpur, the capital, 919,610.
Government: *Head of state*, Sultan Azlan Shah, king (elected March 1989). *Head of government*, Mahathir bin Mohamad, prime minister (took office July 1981). *Legislature*—Parliament: Dewan Negara (Senate) and Dewan Ra'ayat (House of Representatives).
Monetary Unit: Ringgit (Malaysian dollar) (2.688 ringgits equal U.S.$1, August 1990).
Economic Indexes (1989): *Consumer Prices* (1980 = 100), all items, 133.7; food, 131.1. *Industrial Production* (1980 = 100), 205.
Foreign Trade (1989 U.S.$): *Imports,* $22,558,-000,000; exports, $25,080,000.

MANITOBA

Major 1990 events in Manitoba were centered on the Meech Lake accord discussions and a provincial election. The Manitoba economy showed slight improvement. On a lighter note, the Winnipeg Blue Bombers defeated the Edmonton Eskimos, 50-11, for the Canadian Football League's Grey Cup championship in November.

Meech Lake Accord. In June 1990 a major Canadian constitutional amendment was defeated in the Manitoba legislature by a single vote, cast by a backbench opposition member.

The 1988 provincial election had left Manitoba with a minority Progressive Conservative (PC) government. Just before that election, the legislature was considering the Meech Lake constitutional accord; the accord needed the support of each provincial legislature to become law. During 1989 the accord went before a series of public hearings in different parts of Manitoba; the hearings showed strong opposition to the proposed constitutional changes. The Liberal leader, Sharon Carstairs, particularly was opposed to Meech Lake.

In 1990, however, after lengthy discussion in the Manitoba legislature and a constitutional conference in Ottawa in June, the three Manitoba party leaders agreed to introduce the accord in the provincial legislature. Carstairs apparently yielded on the issue following intense pressure from her party.

The accord had an approval deadline of June 23, 1990. The legislative timetable required immediate passage, which in turn required unanimous consent of the members of the legislature to introduce it. One member, Elijah Harper, a Cree, refused this consent until June 20, saying that the accord benefited Quebec, but not the aboriginal population of Canada. Harper's delaying tactics virtually killed the accord, although it was not destroyed officially until the Newfoundland legislature re-

scinded its previous approval. Harper's actions foreshadowed a series of native protests across Canada during the summer of 1990.

Election. In September 1990 the government called an election. Premier Gary Filmon ran independently of the national PC organization, frequently coming out against Prime Minister Brian Mulroney. This proved to be a winning formula, especially given Mulroney's abysmal approval rating, and the PCs gained six seats from the Liberals. The New Democratic Party (NDP) gained seven seats from the Liberals and one from the PCs, thus giving the PCs a slim overall majority. The Liberals lost their status as the official opposition party to the New Democrats of Gary Doer. The percentage votes for the three major parties were: PC 42% (up 4% from 1988), NDP 29% (up 2%), and Liberals 28% (down 7%).

Economy. For several years, Manitoba farmers had faced drought. There was more than adequate rainfall in 1990, but because of depressed international grain prices, net farm income dropped by 21%, to C$295 million. Other sectors of the Manitoba economy were more prosperous, and the real gross domestic product of the province was up by 3.1%, compared with the Canada-wide average increase of 2.9%.

This slight improvement in Manitoba's economy allowed the finance minister to introduce a postelection budget showing no significant tax increases.

MICHAEL KINNEAR, *University of Manitoba*

MANITOBA • Information Highlights

Area: 250,946 sq mi (649 950 km²).
Population (September 1990): 1,090,700.
Chief Cities (1986 census): Winnipeg, the capital, 594,551; Brandon, 38,708; Thompson, 14,701.
Government (1990): *Chief Officers*—lt. gov., George Johnson; premier, Gary Filmon (Progressive Conservative). *Legislature*—Legislative Assembly, 57 members.
Provincial Finances (1990–91 fiscal year budget): *Revenues,* $4,797,809,600; *expenditures,* $5,081,-163,600.
Personal Income (average weekly earnings, July 1990): $462.09.
Labor Force (September 1990, seasonally adjusted): *Employed* workers, 15 years of age and over, 505,000; *Unemployed,* 7.0%.
Education (1990–91): *Enrollment*—elementary and secondary schools, 218,200 pupils; postsecondary—universities, 20,520; community colleges, 3,940.
(All monetary figures are in Canadian dollars.)

MARYLAND

After four years of huge state budget surpluses, Maryland was confronted in 1990 with a budget crunch and a possible recession. Warnings came early in the year, when fiscal experts forecast drops in tax revenue. Meanwhile costs for social programs increased 10% and anti-property-tax protests swept the state's largest counties. During the summer, Gov. William Donald Schaefer ordered cuts in expenses and imposed a hiring freeze, but by winter experts had forecast a fiscal 1991 deficit of $423 million. A state commission recommended increasing taxes to bring $807 million in additional revenue, most of which would be earmarked for education. The General Assembly would consider the tax proposal in 1991.

Elections. The Democratic Party continued to dominate the state following 1990 elections, despite the loss of ten seats in the House of Delegates. Governor Schaefer, seeking a second term, defeated Republican challenger William Seth Shepard by a 60% to 40% margin. In U.S. congressional elections incumbents were reelected save one, Roy Dyson, a Democrat who was unseated by Wayne Gilchrest. There were signs that the Democratic Party was beginning to lose its huge majority, a trend most noticeable in the growing suburban counties bordering Baltimore and Washington, DC.

Government and Legislation. The biggest issue in the 1990 Maryland General Assembly was abortion. It led thousands of activists on both sides to Annapolis, sparked an eight-day filibuster in the legislature, and had a major effect on later elections. The showdown occurred when pro-choice legislators in the Senate sought to codify and liberalize Maryland's abortion laws in case the U.S. Supreme Court should overturn *Roe v. Wade*, while pro-life legislators introduced restrictive abortion legislation. The pro-life bills were killed, but 16 pro-life senators blocked passage of the pro-choice legislation via a filibuster. Eight days later, on March 22, the warring sides reached an unusual compromise in which both bills were to be put to referendum. The next day, however, the House of Delegates killed the compromise, and no legislation was enacted. While there were no clear winners, there were some losers: four veteran pro-life senators lost primary elections in September to pro-choice challengers.

The legislature was stymied in its effort to preserve and plant trees through a reforestation bill, widely supported in both the House and Senate. House Speaker R. Clayton Mitchell, Jr., quashed its passage with a last-minute parliamentary maneuver that sparked a state investigation.

For the first time since 1985, the fishery for the endangered striped bass, one of the Chesapeake Bay's most popular game fish, was opened in 1990 on a limited basis. The state made a commitment to fund fully a program for purchasing of woodlands and open spaces.

The Economy. Fueled by energy-price hikes, inflation jumped to 5.6% in October, a 1.2% increase over 1989. Unemployment in the state grew faster than the national average, up .8% over October 1989 totals to 4.4%, but below the national average of 5.6%. The number of new jobs posted increased by 1% by mid-1990, less than half the 1989 growth rate.

Education. The state Board of Education in 1990 recommended that the public-school year be extended by 20 days. The General Assembly was to take up the proposal in 1991.

The U.S. Naval Academy in Annapolis was accused of sexism on campus. A female midshipman resigned from the academy after it failed to discipline several male midshipmen who assaulted and humiliated her in a dormitory bathroom in December 1989. The academy downplayed the incident as a college prank, but a citizens' board that investigated did not agree. Neither did Congress, which threatened to reduce the academy's $100 million budget by 5% if changes were not made.

DAN CASEY, *"The Annapolis Capital"*

MASSACHUSETTS

The Republican Party regained a foothold in the Bay State in a tumultuous November election. Democrats had dominated the state for so long that elections only rarely provided real two-party competition. This was not so in 1990. Republicans won the governor's and treasurer's offices and made significant gains in the state Senate.

Elections. In the governor's race, William Weld was the first Republican to be elected governor in the state since Francis W. Sargent in 1970. Weld won a narrow victory over Boston University President John R. Silber, who waged one of the most combative and controversial campaigns in recent memory. A central issue in the governor's race was which candidate could cope best with the rapidly declining condition of the Massachusetts economy, which resulted in huge state budget deficits and unemployment levels which had not been seen in many years.

Weld was the head of the U.S. Justice Department's Criminal Investigation Division until he resigned in 1988 after disagreements with U.S. Attorney General Edwin Meese. Presenting himself as a fiscal conservative with liberal views on many social issues such as abortion and gay rights, Weld stressed his career as a prosecutor who could deal with what he termed waste and corruption in state government. He became the GOP candidate after defeating state House Minority Leader Stephen Pierce in the primary election.

Silber, who took a leave of absence from Boston University to run for governor, had never before held political office. Signs of his unusual approach became evident in his subsequent primary campaign against former state Attorney General Francis Bellotti, a widely known and popular figure, who was favored heavily by preprimary polls. Silber won atten-

---

MARYLAND · Information Highlights

Area: 10,460 sq mi (27 092 km²).
Population (1990 census prelim.): 4,733,000.
Chief Cities (1980 census): Annapolis, the capital, 31,740; Baltimore (July 1, 1988 est.), 751,400; Rockville, 43,811.
Government (1990): *Chief Officers*—governor, Donald Schaefer (D); lt. gov., Melvin A. Steinberg (D). *General Assembly*—Senate, 47 members; House of Delegates, 141 members.
State Finances (fiscal year 1989): *Revenue,* $11,501,000,000; *expenditure,* $10,117,000,000.
Personal Income (1989): $98,630,000,000; per capita $21,013.
Labor Force (June 1990): *Civilian labor force,* 2,551,700; *unemployed,* 100,700 (3.9% of total force).
Education: *Enrollment* (fall 1988)—public elementary schools, 489,115; public secondary, 199,832; colleges and universities, 249,079. *Public school expenditures* (1989–90), $3,728,000,000.

© Rick Friedman/Black Star

Republican William Weld (left), formerly with the U.S. Justice Department, and Democrat John Silber, president of Boston University, prepare to debate during their Massachusetts governorship race. Weld emerged the victor on November 6.

tion by criticizing certain racial and ethnic groups in what the press came to call "Silber shockers." He went on to defeat Bellotti handily in the primary.

The election campaign was a colorful one with Silber calling the red-haired Weld a "carrot-topped WASP" and Weld arguing that Silber's brisk manner made him "temperamentally unsuited to be governor." Postelection analysis indicated that Weld's view prevailed; Silber's continually harsh judgments and aggressive style led many normally Democratic voters to switch to Weld.

Democrats still outnumbered Republicans in both houses of the legislature as well as in party registration, so Weld would have to build a coalition in order to govern successfully. However, in a major change, Republicans picked up seven seats in the 40-member state Senate, raising their number from nine to 16, more than enough to sustain a veto by the new governor. In the House, Republicans had a net gain of six seats and would begin the new legislative year with 37 of the chamber's 160 seats. As governor-elect, Weld called for repeal of a 5% tax on service industries.

In other races, Joseph Malone became the first Republican to win the treasurer's office in 40 years. District Attorney Scott Harshbarger, a Democrat, easily won the attorney general's office. In a hotly contested race for the U.S. Senate, Democratic incumbent John Kerry defeated political newcomer James Rappaport, 57%-43%. In congressional races, all incumbents won, keeping the state's delegation at one Republican and ten Democrats.

Initiatives. The 1990 elections also were notable for three ballot questions. Question Two would have limited sharply the state's use of consultants in favor of regular employees. It was defeated. Question Three would have rolled back certain state taxes to 1988 levels. Promoted by the state's high-technology council and by a coalition of conservative forces which previously had succeeded in limiting taxing powers at the local level, the question was defeated resoundingly. Question Five mandated that 40% of state revenues must be distributed among the cities and towns. This question passed, creating a crisis because existing state programs would have to be cut.

HARVEY BOULAY, *Rogerson House*

MASSACHUSETTS • Information Highlights

Area: 8,284 sq mi (21 456 km²).
Population (1990 census prelim.): 5,928,000.
Chief Cities (July 1, 1988 est.): Boston, the capital, 577,830; Worcester, 156,190; Springfield, 150,320.
Government (1990): *Chief Officer*—governor, Michael S. Dukakis (D); lt. gov., Evelyn F. Murphy (D). *Legislature*—Senate, 40 members; House of Representatives, 160 members.
State Finances (fiscal year 1989): *Revenue,* $16,000,000,000; *expenditure,* $17,320,000,000.
Personal Income (1989): $131,118,000,000; per capita, $22,174.
Labor Force (June 1990): *Civilian labor force,* 3,232,900; *unemployed,* 189,000 (5.8% of total force).
Education: *Enrollment* (fall 1988)—public elementary schools, 577,795; public secondary, 245,633; colleges and universities, 426,620. *Public school expenditures* (1989–90), $4,495,161,000.

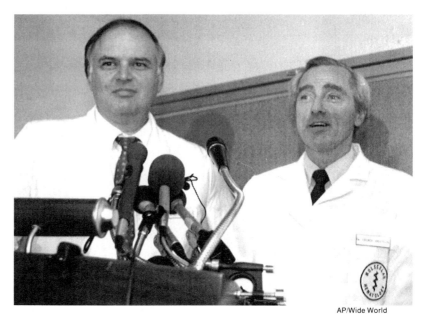

In September 1990 a 4-year-old girl became the first person to receive human-gene therapy. Dr. W. French Anderson (right) of the National Heart, Lung, and Blood Institute, who developed the experimental procedure with Dr. R. Michael Blaese (left) of the National Cancer Institute and others, believes that "gene therapy is potentially a major medical option."

AP/Wide World

MEDICINE AND HEALTH

History was made in 1990 when gene therapy was used for the first time as a treatment for a hereditary disease and major surgery was performed successfully on a fetus. The year also saw progress in the battles against osteoporosis, gum disease, and bladder cancer. The news was less encouraging on other medical fronts, however. The incidence of cancer and AIDS continued to grow, and there was a resurgence of tuberculosis and other diseases once thought to be on the road to extinction.

Gene Therapy. In September a 4-year-old girl became the first person ever to receive gene therapy. The girl suffered from a rare inherited disease called ADA deficiency. Children with this disease are born without the gene needed to produce the enzyme adenosine deaminase, or ADA, which is essential for normal functioning of the immune system.

The procedure involved removing white-blood cells called T-lymphocytes from the patient's blood and culturing them in test tubes to produce billions of copies. Separately, ADA genes were inserted into the genetic material of harmless viruses. The viruses then were used to infect the cultured T-lymphocytes. In this manner the ADA gene entered the genetic matter of the T-lymphocytes, which then were transfused into the patient's blood. Researchers should know within a year if the gene has caused the T-lymphocytes to make ADA, enabling the girl to build resistance to disease. If the procedure is successful, it will offer hope to people suffering from a broad range of hereditary diseases.

Among these diseases is cystic fibrosis. In this disorder a defective gene produces an ab-normal protein. As a result the lungs and other organs become clogged with a thick mucus. Using genetically engineered viruses, researchers led by James M. Wilson of the University of Michigan in Ann Arbor inserted healthy copies of the cystic-fibrosis gene into respiratory tract and pancreas cells in test tubes. Once inside the cells, the genes produced normal proteins. If promising results continue, clinical use of gene therapy to treat cystic-fibrosis patients may be possible in several years.

AIDS. Acquired Immune Deficiency Syndrome (AIDS), a disease caused by HIV viruses, continued its rapid spread. Hardest hit is Africa, which accounts for more than half of an estimated worldwide total of 8 million to 10 million virus carriers. In cities such as Lusaka, Zambia, and Kampala, Uganda, more than 20% of the adults are infected. By the end of September 1990, 93,775 Americans had died of AIDS since the first deaths were recorded in the late 1970s. An estimated 1 million are infected with the virus.

Pregnant women infected with the HIV virus have a 30% chance of passing the disease to their fetuses. In September the World Health Organization (WHO) reported that many more children than previously thought are being infected with HIV viruses. WHO estimates that a total of 25 million to 30 million people will be infected by the year 2000; of these some 10 million will be children.

While there are no known cures for AIDS, drugs are available to delay the onset of symptoms and to prolong the lives of patients. Treatment is costly, however, making it inaccessible even to some AIDS patients in developed nations. By one estimate, early AIDS treatment for every American who needs it could cost $3 billion per year.

Cancer. Cancer deaths among people 55 and older have soared since the early 1970s. Especially rapid increases have occurred in the rates of deaths from brain cancer and multiple myeloma, a cancer of the bone marrow. Cancer experts could not explain the increases. One controversial theory suggests that electromagnetic fields from power lines, power stations, and appliances promote the growth of brain tumors. New evidence supporting this theory came from a University of North Carolina study that found that children whose mothers used electric blankets during pregnancy developed 2.5 times more brain tumors than children in a control group whose mothers did not use such blankets. The children also showed a 70% higher incidence of leukemia and a 30% higher incidence of all cancers.

In a study conducted at the M.D. Anderson Cancer Center of the University of Texas, Houston, high doses of the acne drug Accutane appeared to block the growth of new tumors in patients who had been treated successfully for mouth or throat cancer. Fifty patients took the drug for a year. After more than three years, only 4% of them had developed a second cancer, in contrast to 24% in a control group.

The U.S. Food and Drug Administration (FDA) approved an unusual new treatment for some kinds of bladder cancer—use of a weakened strain of a bacterium that causes tuberculosis in cows. When a preparation of the germ known as BCG (for bacille Calmette-Guerin) is introduced into the bladder, it causes an infection that usually—but not always—remains localized within the bladder. The patient's immune system responds by producing antibodies that help to kill the cancerous cells. In some studies 82% of the patients became free of the disease. On average patients treated with BCG remained in remission eight times longer than patients treated with chemotherapy.

Resurgence of Infectious Diseases. There has been a global explosion of tuberculosis (TB), triggered primarily by the spread of the AIDS virus, which makes people unusually susceptible to TB. Tuberculosis now infects an estimated 1.7 billion people—almost one third of the world's population. It is the world's single biggest bacterial killer, causing 3 million deaths annually. The problem is greatest in the developing world, with sub-Saharan Africa especially hard-hit. In the United States public-health experts had predicted that TB would be eliminated almost entirely by the end of the century. Instead the number of new cases has begun to rise, particularly in cities such as Newark (NJ), Miami, Atlanta, and New York.

Measles cases in the United States rose to a nine-year high during 1989, with 17,850 cases,

Generic Drugs

In 1980 generic drugs—drugs that contain the same active ingredients as their brand-name counterparts but sell at a fraction of the cost—comprised about 11% of the $10.7 billion prescription drug market in the United States. As the 1990s began, the total market was $33.2 billion a year, of which $8.3 billion—about 24%—was spent on generics. But this does not tell the entire story of the rising popularity of generics. When viewed in terms of number of new prescriptions being filled, generics accounted for about 33% of the total. And when only prescriptions for which generics are available are considered, the number is about 45%.

Several factors contribute to the growth of generics. First, new legislation in the 1980s facilitated marketing of generics. For example, prior to 1982, physicians had to specifically request the generic; now they can indicate on the prescription form that a generic is permissible. Second, many popular products came off patents in the mid-1980s, encouraging competition. And third, escalating drug prices combined with cost-cutting pressures favored the switch. Some 9,000 generic drugs have been approved by the Food and Drug Administration (FDA) as bioequivalent to brand-name counterparts.

Brand-name manufacturers have used a variety of tactics to slow the growing use of generics. They have challenged generics' safety and efficacy and spoken of instances where switching from a brand-name to a generic resulted in severe harm to the patient. But such charges have failed to be proven. True, the FDA has recalled some generic drugs, but it has recalled branded drugs, too. For example, the arthritis drug Oraflex was pulled off the market within three months of its introduction after it was linked to 72 deaths in the United States and Great Britain. Dr. Sidney Wolfe of the Public Citizen Health Research Group has pointed out that "the major drug disasters [in the United States] all involve brand-name drugs that have come on the market recently."

Though brand-name manufacturers decry generics, about 60% of all generics are made or distributed by subsidiaries of brand-name companies. However, since the brand-name drugs have higher profit margins, they are more important to the companies than the generics. Nevertheless the future of generics seems positive. Between 1991 and 1995, patents are scheduled to expire on brand-name drugs with an estimated $10 billion in annual sales. This should encourage even greater competition between brand-name and generic drugs.

JENNY TESAR

including 45 deaths, reported to the Centers for Disease Control. Indications were that 1990 cases would surpass these figures. The resurgence of the disease was blamed on the failure of many parents to have their children immunized. A study conducted in South Africa found that vitamin A supplements can reduce significantly the risk of death, pneumonia, and other severe complications in children afflicted with measles.

There also has been a large increase in the number of cases of whooping cough among U.S. children. Many parents have refused to have their children vaccinated for this disease because of reports of severe reactions to the vaccine. However, such reactions are few—less than 40 babies of the 3.5 million vaccinated each year experience problems.

Osteoporosis. Some 24 million Americans, most of them women over 50, suffer from osteoporosis, a crippling disease marked by the progressive loss of bone. Osteoporosis causes 1.3 million fractures a year, and these fractures are one of the leading causes of death in elderly people. According to the Osteoporosis Foundation, the cost of caring for the fractures may exceed $10 billion annually—a figure that is predicted to triple over the next 30 years.

Research conducted at Tufts University confirmed the value of dietary calcium in slowing bone loss. Bess Dawson-Hughes, the project's principal investigator, recommended that all healthy postmenopausal women consume a diet that provides the Recommended Dietary Allowance for calcium of 800 milligrams per day. Government surveys show that most U.S. women consume far less calcium than that.

Currently, osteoporosis generally is treated with the hormones calcitonin and estrogen. Nelson B. Watts of Emory University headed a study of more than 400 postmenopausal women that found that treatment using calcium and the drug etidronate may be superior, both in building bone mass and in reducing fractures. Participants took etidronate for 14 days; then they took calcium for 76 days, either in foods or as a supplement. The etidronate slowed the process of bone loss, and the calcium helped build new bone tissue.

Alzheimer's Disease. Alzheimer's disease is the most common type of dementia, a progressive state marked by memory loss, confusion, and other signs of mental decline. About 4 million Americans are believed to have Alzheimer's; in 1987 (the latest year for which figures are available) the disease was the underlying cause of death for 11,311 people in the United States.

The vast majority of Alzheimer's patients are over age 65. The only medication approved by the FDA for treating Alzheimer's is Hydrogine, but a study at the University of Colorado Medical School found that patients who took this drug deteriorated faster than those who

AP/Wide World

Dr. Shyan Sun is director of neonatology at the Children's Hospital in Newark, NJ. The importance of neonatal care continues to receive greater emphasis in medical circles.

were given dummy pills. Another drug that had been viewed as a promising treatment for Alzheimer's is tetrahydroaminocrydine (THA). It, too, lost luster after scientists at Montreal's McGill Center for Studies in Aging found that patients given the drug failed to show improvement. Serge Gauthier, who led the study, also pointed out that THA was toxic to the liver; patients had to be monitored closely to prevent liver disease.

Researchers at the Albert Einstein College of Medicine of Yeshiva University in New York spent ten years studying 442 men and women to determine what factors might increase the risk of dementia. They found that elderly women who had had heart attacks were five times more likely to develop dementia than other women of the same age. Surprisingly, however, a similar connection between heart attacks and dementia was not seen among men in the study.

Pregnancy. A new technique enables a woman who has gone through menopause to become pregnant, though not as the genetic parent of the child. Eggs from a healthy donor are fertilized with sperm in a laboratory dish, then implanted into the older woman's uterus. Prior to and following implantation, the woman is given hormones for several months.

Norplant, a birth-control method involving an implantation under the woman's skin that provides for the release of progestin, was introduced in the United States in December. It had been used in parts of Europe.

At the University of California in San Francisco, successful surgery was performed on a fetus with a hernia in the diaphragm. The fetus' stomach, spleen, and intestines had moved through the hole into the chest cavity, preventing the lungs from growing. Without surgery to close the hole, the baby probably would have died at birth. The surgeons partially removed the fetus from the womb, rearranged the organs, and returned it to the womb. Seven weeks later, the baby was born in good health.

Smoking. Disease and death due to tobacco smoking continue to increase. According to WHO more than 2.5 million people died worldwide in 1990 of tobacco-related diseases. In the United States, 390,000 people die every year from diseases caused by smoking. Cigarette consumption among adult Americans has fallen, but according to U.S. Surgeon General Antonia Novello, more than 3,000 teenagers become regular smokers each day. "Because only a very small percentage of smokers begin smoking as adults, efforts at prevention must focus on children," she said.

Evidence of the dangers of passive smoking —the inhalation of smoke by nonsmokers— continued to mount. The U.S. Environmental Protection Agency concluded that passive smoking causes 3,800 U.S. lung-cancer deaths per year, plus numerous other ailments, and in mid-1990 listed secondhand smoke as a known carcinogen. Stanton A. Glantz of the University of California at San Francisco reported that nonsmokers who live with smokers have a 20% to 30% greater risk of dying from heart disease than do other nonsmokers. According to Glantz, "the heart-disease deaths combined with the cancer deaths make passive smoking the third leading cause of preventable death, behind smoking and alcohol."

A study directed by Dwight T. Janerich of the Yale University School of Medicine estimated that 17% of all lung cancer in the United States among people who never smoked results from their exposure to smokers while growing up. The researchers determined each person's "smoker-years"—that is, the number of years they lived in a home multiplied by the number of smokers there. For example, a person who lived at home for 18 years with two smoking parents had an exposure of 36 smoker-years. The researchers found that exposure to 25 or more smoker-years during childhood and adolescence doubled the risk of lung cancer.

Two Swedish physicians, Bengt Haglund and Sven Cnattingius, analyzed 190 cases of sudden infant death syndrome (SIDS). These are deaths with no known cause in infants less than six months old. They found that pregnant women who smoked from one to nine cigarettes daily were twice as likely as nonsmokers to lose their infants to SIDS. Women who smoked ten or more cigarettes a day tripled the risk of SIDS. Smokers who quit realize "major and immediate" benefits, according to Surgeon General Novello. Their risks of heart disease, cancer, and other health problems caused by smoking decline steadily for 15 years following cessation, until the risk of death returns almost to that of people who never smoked. Women who stop smoking before pregnancy reduce their risk of having low-birth-weight babies to that of women who never smoked; women who stop smoking during their first months of preg-

Giving the annual report on smoking, U.S. Surgeon General Antonia Coello Novello tells Americans that it is never too late to give up the habit. Dr. Novello is the first woman and the first Hispanic to serve as surgeon general.

AP/Wide World

nancy have babies with higher birth weights than do women who smoke throughout their pregnancy.

Nutrition and Dieting. In February the FDA approved the first low-calorie fat substitute. Named Simplesse, it was developed by the NutraSweet Company. Made of proteins from egg white and milk, it has one to two calories per gram. In contrast, fats have about nine calories per gram. Other food manufacturers also were developing fat substitutes.

For years hundreds of thousands of dieters took the food supplement L-tryptophan, an amino acid that occurs naturally in many high-protein foods. In March, following the outbreak of 1,411 cases of eosinophilia myalgia syndrome (EMS) and 19 deaths in the United States, plus a number of cases in Europe, the FDA recalled almost all supplies of L-tryptophan, which had been linked to the crippling and sometimes fatal blood disorder. A month later it was reported that all of the EMS cases that could be traced reliably were linked with an L-tryptophan product that came wholly or in part from a single company, Showa Denko of Japan. The cause of the epidemic was believed to be a contaminant in the product.

In October the FDA announced a proposed ban on 111 ingredients in nonprescription diet drugs. Most ingredients were to be banned because they had not been proven effective. But one, said the FDA, is a safety hazard. Guar gum, which is extracted from plant matter, is a soluble, nontoxic fiber that is used safely as a commercial thickening agent in ice cream and other foods. When consumed in concentrated form without adequate liquid, however, it can swell by absorbing moisture from the digestive tract, causing an obstruction of the throat or esophagus. Earlier in the year the FDA asked Health Care Products to recall Cal-Ban 3000, a guar-gum-based product.

Dentistry. The FDA approved the first laser designed for general dentistry. The instrument, owned and marketed by American Dental Laser, was already in use in Canada and Europe. The intense beam of laser light instantly vaporizes infected gum tissue, kills bacteria, and cauterizes blood vessels. Treatment with it is much more precise than scalpels and other instruments, and is marked by a reduction in bleeding and in the use of anesthesia. The laser is expected to be helpful in providing treatment to the millions of people who totally avoid dental care for fear of pain. It also may have an impact on the treatment of gum disease, which has emerged as a major unsolved U.S. dental problem.

Francis A. L'Esperance, a New York City surgeon, received a patent for a laser-use method to reverse gum disease by exposing the gums to two beams of low-powered laser pulses, transmitted at either different angles or with different timing. Preliminary tests indicated that the technique stimulates the growth of fresh gum tissue and might be effective in fighting receding gums, a common dental problem among older people.

Another new tool for dentists is a tiny video camera about the size of a finger. Mountable on a dental mirror, it can focus as close as 0.2 inch (5 mm) from a tooth. It sends a magnified image to a color monitor, allowing both the dentist and the patient to view areas of decay and other problems. In addition to being a diagnostic and educational tool, dentists find that the camera enables them to work more efficiently on rear teeth and other difficult areas.

Cosmetic dentistry is becoming an increasingly important part of dentists' workloads, as new techniques and materials enable them to improve dramatically the appearance of teeth. Recent additions to this field include whitening agents designed to bleach teeth, particularly those darkened by aging or stained from smoking. The dentist prepares a retainer-like arch to fit over the patient's teeth. At home the patient pours a bleaching solution into the retainer that he or she then wears for several hours at a time. Noticeable improvements usually are apparent within a week or two. There also are numerous nonprescription whiteners that can be purchased in pharmacies and other stores. The treatments are not recommended for everyone, and the American Dental Association cautioned that ''much about the long-term safety of tooth whitening agents appears to be unknown at this time.'' The possibility that the whiteners may damage the gums and other soft mouth tissues is a concern.

JENNY TESAR
Free-lance Science Writer

NutraSweet Co. officials sample Simple Pleasures, the first food product to be made from a fat substitute. It was approved by the U.S. Food and Drug Administration in 1990.

AP/Wide World

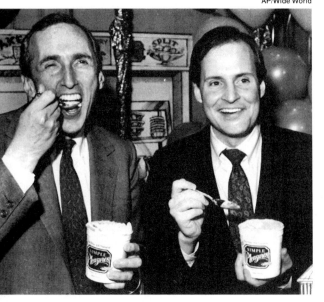

AP/Wide World

Health Care in the 1990s

CHANGES IN CONSUMER PRICES[1], 1980-90

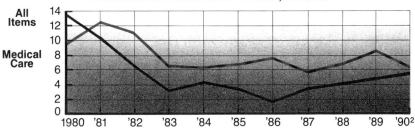

¹All Urban Consumers. ²August Estimate. Source: Bureau of Labor Statistics.

By 1990 nearly everyone agreed that the U.S. health-care system was sick.

Among the symptoms were:

• An estimated 32 million Americans under age 65 without any health insurance.

• Skyrocketing medical inflation, with health-care costs rising almost twice as fast since 1960 as prices for other goods and services.

• A public health-care system for the poor that reached fewer than half of those officially deemed to be living in poverty.

• A public health-care system for the elderly that left them completely uncovered for expenses involving long-term care, the most common health need for those over age 65.

• A medical-malpractice crisis of such magnitude that in many areas of the country, no doctor was willing to deliver babies for fear of being sued.

While the diagnosis was straightforward, the "doctors" who oversee the nation's health-care system remained far apart on how to treat the ailment.

Some favored conservative treatment—band-aid approaches like expanding the federal-state Medicaid program for the poor and encouraging the development of private insurance policies to help the elderly pay the costs of long-term care.

Others called for radical surgery—eliminating the existing system by which most Americans received health insurance through their employers and moving to a system of national health insurance funded and/or run by the federal government.

The standoff was such that the preliminary report unveiled in March by the Pepper Commission—a 15-member bipartisan group named for its founder and first chairman, the late Rep. Claude Pepper (D-FL)—was shot down almost immediately. The commission had been created as part of the 1988 Medicare Catastrophic Coverage Act, which later was re-

pealed, and charged with coming up with a prescription for how to improve the system. The commission's plan, which sought to guarantee health insurance for all as well as cost protection for long-term care, would cost the federal government an estimated $69.6 billion per year. The proposal to solve the problem of the uninsured barely was accepted, as the commission split 8–7, and while the long-term-care proposal was approved by 11–4, commission members and outsiders complained that the group had failed in its task by sidestepping the most sensitive issue in health-care reform —who would have to pay for it.

The Pepper Commission was far from the only informal government group searching for a solution. Also seeking common ground between the interests of health-care providers, insurance companies, employers, and patients were a working group within the Department of Health and Human Services and yet another administration task force, charged by President George Bush in his State of the Union message with reviewing recommendations "on the quality, accessibility and cost of our nation's health-care system."

Also seeking a solution was an independent commission that convenes every four years to study programs under the auspices of the Social Security Act, which include Medicare—the federal health program for the elderly and disabled—and Medicaid. The 1990 version of the commission was headed by Deborah Steelman, who had been a health-budget official under President Ronald Reagan and who had directed domestic policy during Bush's 1988 presidential campaign. That commission struggled as well, announcing in October that it would not issue an interim report as originally planned.

Health-Care Reform: Historical Data. Efforts to reform the nation's health-care system date as far back as the administration of President Harry S. Truman (1945–53), who issued the first call for system-wide reform. It was not until 1965, however, that Congress finally answered Truman's call and Lyndon B. Johnson signed into law legislation creating Medicare and Medicaid.

Medicare, which in 1990 provided an estimated 30 million elderly and 3 million disabled Americans with limited coverage of hospital, doctor, and other health costs associated with acute illnesses, was considered by most as primarily a health-care plan for the elderly. It, however, did not pay most of the costs associated with long-term care needed for such common chronic conditions as Alzheimer's disease, which afflicts an estimated 4 million adults.

Medicaid, a joint federal-state program (the federal government pays an average of 55% of costs) that provides all types of health-care services to the very poor, did pay for long-term care, but only after a person had "spent down" all income and assets and had become impoverished and therefore eligible.

Congress' next major effort to reshape the health-care system did not come until more than 20 years later, in 1988, when it passed overwhelmingly the ill-fated law to provide "catastrophic coverage" through Medicare. The law capped the amount of hospital and doctor bills that beneficiaries could be forced to underwrite, expanded the program's limited coverage of home-health and nursing-home care, and extended Medicare coverage for the first time for outpatient prescription drugs.

What proved problematic in the plan was that in an era of burgeoning federal-budget deficits it also required Medicare beneficiaries to cover all the new costs—an estimated $33 billion over five years—themselves. For the first time ever in a Social Security program, it required those financially better off to pay more than those of more modest means in order to receive the same benefits. The novel financing scheme backfired, and after a fierce backlash from affluent Medicare beneficiaries, Congress repealed the law in late 1989.

The catastrophic debacle, as it came to be known on Capitol Hill, taught health policymakers an important lesson. The U.S. public desperately wanted more access to health care, but they did not want to pay for it.

Health Care Today. In the meantime, however, health-care problems in the United States continued to worsen.

The key culprit was the inexorable rise in medical costs. By 1989 the nation's annual health-care bill topped $600 billion; by the year 2000, health care was expected to consume 15% of the entire gross national product. The Pepper Commission found that since 1965 health-care spending as a share of government revenues and business receipts had tripled.

The rising costs were due to a variety of factors—expensive new technology; a demographically older, and sicker, population; and so-called "defensive medicine," in which doctors perform tests or procedures not because they think the patient needs them, but to provide legal protection in case of lawsuit.

The predictable result of rising prices was that fewer Americans were able to obtain the care they needed. Faced with rapidly rising premiums, many employers sought to have their employees share the costs of health-insurance coverage or dropped plans altogether.

At the same time, states who saw their Medicaid budgets ballooning sought to cut back as well. Because states set Medicaid eligibility requirements, they vary widely, and in many states a person had to have an income well below the poverty line in order to qualify. As a result, by 1987 Medicaid was reaching only 42% of officially impoverished Americans. Also occurring was the aging of the U.S. population, leaving a larger and larger share of the population at risk for needing expensive long-term-care services—and no organized way to pay for them.

The first major attempt in the 1990s to address the combined problems of rising costs and an aging population came from the Pepper Commission, which released a health-care plan in September that took a two-pronged approach. To address the problem of the uninsured, the commission recommended requiring employers with more than 100 workers to offer their workers health coverage, and called for a new program to replace Medicaid in providing coverage for the unemployed and those for whom insurance was not otherwise available. The commission called for long-term-care coverage through a new federal plan to help pay for the first three months of nursing-home care as well as care in the home or community, and a joint federal-state plan to help those who need extended institutional care. Its failure to agree on where the money to pay for the plan would come from helped ensure its initial failure.

Complained commission vice-chairman Rep. Bill Gradison (R-OH) after the virtually identical preliminary plan was announced in March, "It begs the question that's been hampering us all along and that's financing."

Nevertheless, Sen. John D. Rockefeller IV (D-WV), who succeeded Pepper as chairman of the commission, continued to insist that a plan of the sort the Pepper Commission envisioned ultimately would be adopted. "The cost of inaction is overwhelming in health care," said Rockefeller after the commission released its final report in September. "This is inevitable. The country will force us to do this."

JULIE ROVNER

Mental Health

Mental-health researchers made significant new discoveries about the brain during 1990—the first year of the Decade of the Brain.

Decade of the Brain. In July 1990 more than 1,000 scientists and members of the interested public gathered at the Institute of Medicine (IOM) in Washington, DC, for a symposium on new horizons in brain research. The symposium was sponsored by the National Institute of Mental Health (NIMH) and the IOM. It marked the beginning of the Decade of the Brain, which will extend until 2000. During the decade, brain researchers are expected to build on the recent progress in the neurosciences and make new discoveries that will improve the treatment of mental disorders and advance scientific understanding of the brain.

Brain Abnormalities in Schizophrenia. Sets of genetically identical twins in which one twin has schizophrenia and the other does not have provided brain researchers with an excellent opportunity to identify key factors associated with the disease. In a study of 15 such twin pairs, NIMH researchers found that in 14 of them, the twin with schizophrenia had smaller brain volume than the healthy twin. In a related study, scientists supported by the NIMH also found abnormalities in the circuitry connecting key brain structures in people with schizophrenia. Mental-health professionals long have speculated that such mental illnesses as schizophrenia were linked to specific brain abnormalities. This important finding offers irrefutable evidence that schizophrenia is a deep-rooted brain disease.

Cell Research. Scientists at the NIMH have succeeded in isolating the marijuana receptor—the tiny structure on the surface of some brain cells that interacts with the active ingredients of marijuana and allows the drug to exert its effect on the brain. Now that this receptor can be studied in detail, it may be possible to devise drugs that have some of marijuana's useful effects—such as controlling nausea—but are not harmful to the user. Another receptor that has been isolated recently is the second of the two main types of receptors that interact with the important brain chemical dopamine. This advance will help scientists to learn more about the actions of dopamine in the brain and eventually understand its role in such mental illnesses as schizophrenia and depression. These and other brain-research projects will be facilitated by the recent discovery of a way to keep human-brain cells growing in culture in the laboratory, so that they can be used for a variety of much-needed studies.

Child and Adolescent Mental Health. A mental-health study concluded in 1990 found that the onset of many serious mental disorders can be traced to childhood and adolescence. The study found that adolescence is an important period for the development of major depression, manic-depressive illness (bipolar disorder), and phobias. In some individuals these disorders emerge even before the teenage years, the study found. Much more research is needed on these and other serious mental disorders of adolescence and childhood, which affect about 7.5 million U.S. youngsters. Under the sponsorship of the NIMH, a national plan for research in improving diagnosis, prevention, and treatment of child and adolescent mental health was completed in 1990.

In a related effort, a national hearing on child and adolescent mental health was held in Los Angeles. The hearing was sponsored by the National Advisory Mental Health Council and the National Mental Health Leadership Forum and planned by the NIMH. The information that emerged from the hearing will help to guide federal efforts to conduct research and disseminate information relevant to the needs of mentally ill children and adolescents.

Panic Disorder. Almost 2 million Americans have panic disorder, a condition in which a person experiences episodes of intense fear called panic attacks. The condition can be as disabling as a major medical illness. Unfortunately, only one in five persons with panic disorder receives appropriate treatment. In 1990, NIMH began planning a campaign to encourage treatment. The importance of this effort was underscored by reports that people with panic disorder compare similarly with those suffering from major depression in low quality of life and high probability of attempting suicide.

Alzheimer's Disease. A group of scientists have devised a biochemical test that promises to be the most reliable method yet for determining which elderly patients have Alzheimer's disease. The test reveals whether the patient's brain cells have a specific protein that is found only in people with the disease. This test will make it much easier for patients with superficially similar, but more treatable conditions, such as depression, to be identified and receive appropriate care.

Impact of Mental Illnesses. An economic study completed in 1990 showed that mental illnesses are more costly to the United States than previously believed. The total annual cost of mental illnesses, including direct costs for treatment and indirect costs for lost productivity, was estimated at more than $100 billion. A survey of public attitudes showed that Americans are acutely aware of the impact of mental illnesses: Nine in ten people described mental illness as a serious problem in society today; 60% said they should know more about mental illness; and 14% describe themselves or someone close to them as currently having a mental illness.

LEWIS L. JUDD, M.D., *Director*
National Institute of Mental Health

© Le Progrès/Sipa

The Rhône-Alpes region of France (above) was hit by a massive December snowstorm. The storm, which covered much of Europe, resulted in at least 12 deaths, closed roads and schools, snarled traffic, and left thousands without electricity.

METEOROLOGY

Long-term human effects on the climate prodded governmental action in 1990 even as scientists worked to narrow uncertainties.

Environmental Policy. During the year the United States adopted a new, far-reaching version of the 1970 Clean Air Act, the first revision since 1977. Some aspects represented updates on previous issues, including reducing automotive hydrocarbon emission by 40% and automotive nitrogen-oxide emission by 60%, beginning with 1994 model cars, as well as mandating improved automotive emission-control equipment, requiring cleaner fuels, setting new targets for smog control, and expanding regulations on various toxic pollutants.

Other aspects of the act addressed new topics not considered in 1977, including stratospheric-ozone-layer protection. Carbon tetrachloride, chlorofluorocarbons (CFCs), and methyl chloroform were to be phased out between 2000 and 2002, while hydrochlorofluorocarbons (HCFCs) would not be banned until 2030. Another addition was control of the sulfur dioxide and nitrogen oxides that lead to acid rain. The goal was to halve industrial emissions of these pollutants by the years 2000 and 1997, respectively. It was estimated that these measures would raise the cost of generating electricity some $4 billion per year by 2005.

The act did not address the issue of carbon-dioxide emission, despite pressure from numerous domestic and international sources. In contrast, during late 1990, Japan adopted the goal of holding per-capita emissions of carbon dioxide at the 1990 level. The policy was the result of 18 months of study, and depended on reducing oil use, boosting mass transit, developing hydrogen fuel, and mandating higher automotive fuel efficiency.

Ozone Depletion. The ozone depletion over Antarctica in 1990 matched the record depletions in 1987 and 1989, except the 1990 hole appeared one week earlier than in 1989. The depletion in each of these years essentially represented total elimination of ozone in the middle and lower stratosphere, so deeper holes were not likely. However, future holes might be longer-lasting or cover a larger area. Meanwhile, continued analysis of data from the 1989 Airborne Arctic Stratospheric Experiment indicated more ozone depletion in the Arctic spring than previously thought. At some levels in the lower stratosphere the depletion was observed to be around 17%.

Vessel Icing. Ships operating in polar regions are liable to icing, when seawater (usually in the form of spray) freezes onto exposed surfaces. In extreme cases the additional, unanticipated weight can capsize and sink the ship. Recent research has provided the tools to make useful forecasts as much as 36 hours before the event, advance time that is crucial since vessels operate many hours of travel time from the nearest port. Forecasting depends on meteorological factors (air and water temperatures, wind), sea state (ocean spray, wave height and length), and the ship's configuration (length, hull shape, direction and speed of travel). In addition, the individual forecaster and the vessel operator bear significant responsibility for applying the results of the icing computation.

Observing Systems. Modernization of observing systems continued to be a major focus for U.S. governmental agencies in 1990. The Air Force, Federal Aviation Administration (FAA), National Weather Service (NWS), and Navy each were developing computerized data and forecasting systems. Despite a variety of missions, each agency was responding to the need to harness effectively and unlock the information flowing from the increasing number of sensors and numerical models.

One new observing system was the next-generation radar (NEXRAD), now given the model identifier WSR-88D. After years of development work, the first operational unit was installed in Oklahoma in December. Sites in Virginia and Florida were to be brought up in early 1991. In the next five years, the NWS was to install 137 WSR-88D units and the Department of Defense and the FAA another 38.

Satellites. The next generation of Geostationary Operational Environmental Satellites (GOES) continued to experience problems in 1990. Most notably, engineers discovered that the 12-by-20 inch (30-by-51 cm) primary mirrors, used to reflect views of the Earth to the satellite's instruments, were five times more sensitive to temperature changes than previously thought. Such changes occurred as the mirror alternately warmed in sunlit conditions and cooled in shaded conditions. A launch, scheduled for February 1992, might be delayed to allow time for resolving this and other problems. NWS officials estimated that the single functional GOES currently in orbit had a 90% chance of functioning through 1992.

Climate. A vigorous debate continued on whether and when the climate might show signs of change resulting from the large quantities of carbon dioxide and other "radiatively active trace gases" put into the atmosphere by human activity. Increasingly detailed research on global warming uncovered new subtleties in the climate-regulating relationships between the oceans, atmosphere, and land surface. For example, the current state of knowledge was not sufficient to explain the observed quantities of carbon in its various forms (including carbon dioxide as a gas, carbon dioxide dissolved in seawater, fossil fuels, and plant material).

Also, some phenomena that might appear to be related closely to climatic change have turned out to be independent of it. For example, sudden collapses of the West Antarctic ice sheet, which are suggested by data on prehistoric sea levels, were not correlated well with previous warm (interglacial) epochs. Instead, the collapse seemed to be driven by internal processes. In the same vein, the U.S. drought of 1988 was thought more likely a result of La Niña (the opposite of El Niño), characterized by stronger trade winds and cooler than average sea-surface temperatures in the eastern and central Pacific Ocean, than a result of global warming.

Lacking a definitive answer on the future course of the climate, policymakers were forced to act (or not) on the basis of various, sometimes conflicting estimates. The different courses taken by the governments of Japan and the United States illustrate diverse 1990 responses to the problem.

Weather Highlights. Much of the United States had above-average temperatures in 1990. The eastern two thirds of the country experienced very warm conditions in January and February, a fact made all the more remarkable by the dramatic reversal from the bitterly cold conditions of November and December 1989. Large parts of the western and southern Soviet Union also experienced warm conditions for much of the winter, causing springtime growth to begin four to six weeks early in many locations. Heat waves in late June (primarily across the southern tier of the United States) and late August (focused in the Central Plains) helped make the U.S. summer the 15th-warmest on record, comparable to the 1950s but short of summers in the 1930s. For the globe as a whole 1990 was the warmest year ever.

Moisture conditions across most of the United States were favorable or overly wet, with drought confined to portions of the Rocky Mountains and southern Florida.

Localized floods occurred in several parts of the mid-Mississippi Valley and Ozark Mountains during the spring and early summer. In late April parts of eastern Texas received as much as 17 inches (43 cm) of rain in one day. The single worst event occurred in early June when the watershed above Shadyside, OH, received more than 5 inches (13 cm) of rain in three hours, touching off a flash flood that killed 26 people. Western Washington state endured persistent flood conditions due to storms in October and November.

The Atlantic hurricane season was considerably more active than usual, with 14 named storms of which eight became hurricanes. The most extreme event for the U.S. mainland occurred in mid-October, when the Southeast and East Coast were drenched successively by the remnants of hurricane *Klaus*, the remnants of tropical storm *Marco*, and hurricane *Lili*.

Following the trend of 1989, tornadoes were more numerous than average, totaling more than 60% above the yearly average of 786, while tornado-related deaths continued to be about one half of the average of 88. The single worst outbreak occurred on June 2, when the Midwest saw more than 100 twisters, of which 54 occurred in Indiana in five hours. The most lethal event was the Plainfield, IL, tornado of August 28, when 28 died.

GEORGE J. HUFFMAN
University of Maryland

A free-trade agreement between Mexico and the United States as well as the use of force in the Persian Gulf were issues discussed by President Carlos Salinas de Gortari and President Bush in Monterrey, Mexico, Nov. 26–27, 1990.

AP/Wide World

MEXICO

Efforts to reorient Mexico toward a market economy continued in 1990 as President Carlos Salinas pushed privatization of state enterprises and sought free-trade agreements with other nations. More striking, however, were his efforts to turn Mexico away from one-party, authoritarian rule and toward a truly competitive, democratic political system. Both the economic and political changes provoked serious debate and the emerging new political order was marked by violence in some states. Although relations between Mexico and the United States remained warm, U.S. involvement in a kidnapping brought strong protests from all sectors of Mexican society.

Economic Policy. President Salinas sought to stimulate economic growth by forcing Mexican producers to compete in both national and international markets. Salinas argued that Mexico no longer could afford inefficient state enterprises but needed funds to repair the economic infrastructure and meet social needs. In May the Mexican Congress amended the constitution to allow reprivatization of the banking system, which had been nationalized in 1982. To pacify nationalists and prevent takeovers by international banks, foreign stock ownership was limited to 30% of equity. The move was intended to produce between $3 billion and $5 billion in government income. Salinas also sold off the government's 56% interest in Telmex, the national telephone company. Foreign investors can own the majority share of stock, but daily operations would be controlled by Mexicans owning 20% of the equity. To encourage capital investment, the government also reduced the top marginal tax rate to 35%, making it competitive with the United States' rate.

Economy. Economic indicators gave mixed signals about the direction of the economy. The gross national product (GNP) was expected to grow about 3% in 1990, outstripping the population growth rate for the first time since 1982. The inflation rate was projected to be 25%, down significantly from the triple-digit levels of the past years. Retail sales in the first five months of 1990 dropped 22.8% compared with the same period of 1989. Non-oil exports, which account for 65% of Mexico's export income, rose only 4% in the first half of the year. It was hoped that the current-account deficit, originally projected at $5 billion, might be offset by billions of dollars in unanticipated oil income created by the Iraq invasion of Kuwait and the resulting Persian Gulf crisis. The government extended the price freeze on basic commodities until Jan. 31, 1991, to offset the effects of inflation.

In February, Mexico and 15 foreign banks used the plan of U.S. Secretary of the Treasury

---

MEXICO • Information Highlights

Official Name: United Mexican States.
Location: Southern North America.
Area: 761,602 sq mi (1 972 550 km²).
Population (mid-1990 est.): 88,600,000.
Chief Cities (1980 census): Mexico City (Federal District), the capital (1983 est.), 9,663,360; Guadalajara, 1,626,152; Monterrey, 1,090,009.
Government: *Head of state and government,* Carlos Salinas de Gortari, president (took office Dec. 1988). *Legislature*—National Congress: Senate and Federal Chamber of Deputies.
Monetary Unit: Peso (2,940 pesos equal U.S.$1, floating rate, Dec. 13, 1990).
Gross Domestic Product (1989 U.S.$): $187,000,-000,000.
Economic Indexes: *Consumer Prices* (1989, 1980 = 100), all items, 11,888.1; food, 11,190.4. *Industrial Production* (1988, 1980 = 100), 109.
Foreign Trade (1989 U.S.$): *Imports,* $23,633,-000,000; *exports,* $22,819,000,000.

Nicholas Brady to reduce Mexico's foreign debt from $95 billion to $80 billion, thereby saving $1.6 billion per year in interest payments between 1990–94.

The Persian Gulf crisis provided a much-needed income boost but also created problems. Although Mexico is the world's fifth-largest oil producer, the uncertain level of long-term prices and the adverse effect of high prices on the United States made Mexican officials cautious, since a U.S. economic recession would damage the Mexican economy. Mexico agreed to increase its oil production by 100,000 barrels per day but could not expand production enough to make a significant dent in the amount of oil taken off the world market by the blockade of Iraq. Mexico has not had the necessary income to invest in its oil industry in recent years. The government adopted a $50 billion five-year energy-expansion plan, financing the project with public and private funds.

President Salinas ardently sought free-trade agreements with the United States, Canada, and some Latin American nations—a policy reversal for Mexico, which in past years had rebuffed the concept of a North American free-trade zone. This new policy emerged in reaction to the likely increase in economic competition resulting from the rapid liberalization of Eastern European economies, German reunification, and a general Latin American trend toward free trade. In September, U.S. President George Bush asked congressional approval to speed free-trade negotiations. Salinas indicated that he wanted agreement by 1993. Canada, which had signed a free-trade agreement with the United States in 1988 on the assumption that Mexico would not be a party, moved quickly to establish a strong bilateral agreement to ensure independent Canadian access to the Mexican economy.

In spite of the problems seen by some observers, a North American free-trade zone could compete more effectively with the European Community (EC), Eastern Europe, and the Asian economic dynamos because it would combine cheap Mexican labor, U.S. high technology, and Canadian natural resources. Both U.S. and Canadian labor unions, however, feared that jobs would be lost to Mexico.

President Salinas also sought additional markets for Mexican exports and additional sources of capital investment in other parts of the world. His trip early in the year to Portugal, the United Kingdom, Belgium, Germany, and Switzerland to lobby with European Community officials for increased trade and investment achieved little, for the EC was more concerned about Eastern Europe. He then went to Australia, Singapore, and Japan in June to seek expanded trade. In October he traveled to Honduras, Bolivia, Uruguay, Brazil, and Venezuela to start negotiations for bilateral free-trade agreements.

Politics. Encouraged by President Salinas' very narrow and disputed victory in 1988, the slim majority of the ruling Institutional Revolutionary Party (PRI) in Congress, and the government's willingness to recognize some opposition victories, opposition parties contested the government's actions both in local elections and in the Congress. Most active was the leftist Democratic Revolutionary Party (PRD).

In the early months of 1990, leftist political-party activists used protests and violence in unsuccessful efforts to reverse official election returns which they believed fraudulent. Confrontations between PRD partisans and public-security forces in Guerrero resulted in ten deaths. In Michoacán, home of PRD leader and former presidential candidate Cuauhtémoc Cárdenas, activists who had occupied 21 city halls in December 1989 were dislodged forcibly by the army from 17 of them in April 1990. In Puebla ten died in a dispute between PRI and Workers' Revolutionary Party supporters over the outcome of a mayoralty contest.

In April the opposition parties PRD, the National Action Party (PAN), the Authentic Party of the Mexican Revolution, and the Independent Group boycotted Congress to protest the PRI's refusal to investigate the bankruptcy of the national fisheries bank. PAN broke with the other opposition parties to cooperate with PRI to pass legislation to reprivatize the banks.

Ernesto Ruffo, the PAN governor of North Baja California state, revealed that his PRI predecessor illegally had used state funds to support the PRI gubernatorial candidate. Opposition politicians long had asserted that the government and PRI regularly engaged in such illegal practices but had been unable to gain access to the public records to prove the charges until Ruffo assumed office as the first opposition governor in Mexico in more than 70 years.

Rising opposition to the government encouraged President Salinas to accelerate the democratization of the political system by beginning to restructure both the government and the PRI. Public support for PRI has declined steadily in recent decades but dropped precipitously when the economy plunged into recession in 1982 and the government adopted austerity policies. Although PRI claims to be the world's largest political party with 20 million members, Salinas only received 9 million votes in 1988. Throughout its history, PRI has been controlled by national political bosses in Mexico City; the bosses chose the candidates at all levels and the PRI machinery, backed by the government, ensured that those candidates took office.

In preparation for PRI's national meeting in September, party leaders were ordered to allow 70% of the delegates to be elected in mu-

AP/Wide World

Pope John Paul II met privately with President Salinas during his eight-day visit to Mexico in May. Mexico last had diplomatic relations with the Vatican in 1857.

nicipal assemblies instead of being appointed by state governors. For the first time, former national presidents were not invited to attend the meeting. When party conservatives showed signs of resisting these democratic changes, Salinas floated the trial balloon that he might create a new party called Solidarity. At the national meeting, PRI adopted rules which might make the party more democratic. In most states, the system was changed so that the party would use primary elections to select gubernatorial and senatorial candidates. Delegates to the party's national council now would be elected by direct, secret ballot, instead of being appointed from Mexico City. The party's presidential candidate would be selected by majority vote of the council members. The new rules allow individuals to join the PRI; previously party membership had depended upon membership in a PRI-allied union or organization controlled by political bosses.

Foreign Policy. Mexico grew in importance as a battleground in the U.S. crusade against illicit drugs. Narcotics experts estimated that the bulk of the cocaine entering the United States crosses the Mexican border. Mexico has cooperated with U.S. drug-control efforts but an incident involving Mexico's national sovereignty severely strained that cooperation. In early April the role of the U.S. government in the kidnapping of Dr. Humberto Alvarez from Guadalajara to California outraged Mexico. Alvarez was accused of aiding drug traffickers in the torture and eventual murder of Enrique Ca-

marena, an agent of the U.S. Drug Enforcement Administration (DEA). U.S. authorities reportedly paid a Mexican criminal to arrange the abduction but denied that any DEA agents in Mexico participated. Angered, Mexico protested and demanded that it be allowed to station Mexican policemen inside the United States on the same basis that the United States stations policemen in Mexico. Mexican views were vindicated in August when a federal judge in California freed Alvarez and allowed him to return to Mexico because of the means by which he was abducted.

The state visit in May of Pope John Paul II temporarily reopened issues of church-state relations in this officially anticlerical nation. The papal visit renewed demands by some to remove the anticlerical provisions of the constitution—something the pope wants. Instead he chose to condemn abortion, divorce, and materialism during his stay in Mexico. In spite of speculation that this papal visit was a prelude to Mexico establishing diplomatic relations with the Vatican, President Salinas only agreed to send a personal representative.

In August, Mexico imposed sanctions on Iraq and agreed to send troops to the Persian Gulf in support of UN resolutions. Since Mexico had not sent troops abroad since World War II, the decision represented a reversal of foreign policy in the effort to integrate itself more fully into the Western community.

DONALD J. MABRY
Mississippi State University

MICHIGAN

Politics and Detroit's fight to maintain an official population of more than 1 million were major 1990 news events in Michigan.

Election. Republican challenger John Engler, 42, upset incumbent Gov. James J. Blanchard by 19,134 votes in Michigan's closest statewide race in 40 years. With Republicans maintaining control of the state Senate, Engler's November 6 victory gave the GOP the upper hand in Lansing for the first time since 1970, in a period when legislative districts were to be redrawn following the 1990 census.

The stunning loss by Blanchard, who had led Engler by more than 20 percentage points earlier in the campaign, was attributed to low voter turnout in heavily Democratic Detroit, along with Engler's promises of tax reforms. Blanchard also was hurt by Engler's television ads which portrayed him as an "imperial" governor who traveled on state-owned helicopters and planes. Negative publicity also stemmed from Blanchard's spat with Lt. Gov. Martha Griffiths, whom Blanchard dropped from the ticket in favor of a younger running mate.

U.S. Sen. Carl Levin (D) was reelected, as were 16 of the state's 18 members of the U.S.

AP/Wide World

Detroit Mayor Coleman A. Young was sworn in for a fifth term January 11. Debate over the census count and a damaging book helped make 1990 a difficult year for the city.

MICHIGAN • Information Highlights

Area: 58,527 sq mi (151 586 km²).
Population (1990 census prelim.): 9,179,000.
Chief Cities (July 1, 1988 est.): Lansing, the capital, 124,960; Detroit, 1,035,920; Grand Rapids, 185,370; Warren, 145,410; Flint, 141,620; Sterling Heights, 114,720.
Government (1990): *Chief Officers*—governor, James J. Blanchard (D); lt. gov., Martha W. Griffiths (D). *Legislature*—Senate, 38 members; House of Representatives, 110 members.
State Finances (fiscal year 1989): *Revenue,* $22,707,000,000; *expenditure,* $20,881,000,000.
Personal Income (1989): $161,764,000,000; per capita, $17,444.
Labor Force (June 1990): *Civilian labor force,* 4,664,500; *unemployed,* 349,400 (7.5% of total force).
Education: *Enrollment* (fall 1988)—public elementary schools, 1,113,595; public secondary, 469,190; colleges and universities, 542,580. *Public school expenditures* (1989–90), $7,648,551,000.

House. In Michigan's 10th District state Rep. Dave Camp was elected to succeed Bill Schuette, who ran against Levin, and in the 13th District, Barbara Rose Collins was chosen to replace George Crockett, Jr., who retired.

Abortion. The Michigan legislature on September 12 overwhelmingly approved an abortion bill that requires unmarried teenagers to obtain the permission of a parent or a judge before having an abortion. Because the bill was initiated by a citizens' petition drive, it automatically became law in April 1990 without requiring the signature of Governor Blanchard, who vetoed a similar measure earlier in the year. The law was the second successful effort to restrict abortions in Michigan. In 1988 voters banned Medicaid-funded abortions.

Abortion was a factor in the race for governor with the incumbent Blanchard billing himself as "pro-choice," while Engler voiced opposition to abortion in most cases.

Euthanasia Case. In early December, Jack Kevorkian, a Michigan doctor and advocate of euthanasia, was charged with the murder of a 54-year-old woman suffering from Alzheimer's disease. In the spring, Kevorkian had connected Janet Adkins of Portland, OR, to a homemade suicide device and watched as she pushed a button and died. A Michigan district judge later threw out the murder charges against Kevorkian. Pointing out that Michigan has no specific law against suicide, the judge urged the legislature to consider the matter.

Detroit. Preliminary census figures in August placed Detroit's population at 970,156, prompting city officials to protest an undercount and sparking an intensive two-month search by the city and the Census Bureau to find residents missed by the count. On November 20, U.S. Census Director Barbara Bryant said that as a result of the extra effort, the city's population was officially more than 1 million. More than a dozen state laws, including those allowing Detroit to levy utility and income taxes, are written specifically for cities with a population exceeding 1 million.

Detroit's national image was battered by the publication of the book *Devil's Night and Other True Tales of Detroit,* which was excerpted in *The New York Times Magazine* and became the focus of a segment on the nationally televised program *Prime Time Live.* Mayor Coleman A. Young and other civic leaders objected that the portrayals were unfair.

A federal grand jury in Detroit investigated allegations that the Young administration misused a secret police-department fund. The grand jury probed the spending of what court documents described as a $2.4 million fund received from drug forfeitures and designed to fight drug trafficking. City officials claimed that disclosure of how the money was spent would impede investigations and endanger undercover officers.

Opposition arose in Detroit to a proposal to raze the publicly owned Ford Auditorium on the Detroit riverfront and sell the property to Comerica, a major bank, which said it would build a high-rise headquarters building on the site. A citizens' group started a petition drive to force a citywide vote on the proposal.

Bishop Adam J. Maida of Green Bay, WI, succeeded Cardinal Edmund C. Szoka, who was named head of the Prefecture for Economic Affairs of the Holy See at the Vatican, as archbishop of Detroit. The Detroit *News* and Detroit *Free Press,* which merged their business operations in late 1989, suffered losses in total circulation and advertising.

CHARLES W. THEISEN, *"The Detroit News"*

MICROBIOLOGY

The year 1990 brought new information on and increased understanding of ways to combat infectious diseases.

Group A Streptococcal Infections. There are 25–35 million cases of group A streptococcal infections diagnosed in the United States annually. The virulence of these bacteria can be attributed primarily to a surface protein (the M protein), which gives the organism the ability to resist phagocytic attack. The M protein consists of a conserved (fixed) end and a variable end. People who become resistant to streptococcal infection have produced antibodies that are specific for the variable end of the M molecule of the infecting bacterium. Unfortunately, more than 80 different variable ends have been identified, making it unlikely that a vaccine against the organism could be made using the variable ends.

Using a different approach, Dr. V. A. Fischetti and associates transferred the gene fragment of the fixed end of the M protein to the vaccinia (cowpox) virus. The recombinant vaccinia virus was used to immunize a group of mice. After four weeks, attempts were made to infect the mice with streptococcal bacteria. The mice were found to be resistant to the bacteria. Experiments were planned to test whether this type of cross-protection is possible for other pathogens.

Gene-for-Gene Relationship. Soybean plants may be infected by the bacterium *Pseudomonas syringae*, which invades the leaves of susceptible host plants and begins to multiply in the intercellular fluid. The bacteria spread in the leaves, producing water-soaked chlorotic lesions (*bacterial blight*). In a resistant soybean plant, resistance is expressed by a *hypersensitive reaction* (HR) in which the leaf cells around the infection collapse to produce a desiccated necrotic lesion which inhibits bacterial multiplication.

To be resistant to *P. syringae* infection, soybean plants must carry the dominant resistance gene *Rpgl*. However, this gene is activated only by those *P. syringae* strains that carry the avirulence gene *avrB*, whose protein gene product induces the hypersensitive reaction. (Avirulent is HR-inducing.) This interaction between *avrB* and *Rpgl* is designated a *gene-for-gene relationship*.

Dr. T. V. Huynh and colleagues have found that the soybean resistance gene *Rpgl* does not control the expression of the bacterial pathogen gene *avrB*, which is expressed in resistant and susceptible strains of the soybean plant. They also found that the hypersensitive reaction occurs rapidly after infection, implying that even before the *avrB* gene is expressed, a resistant plant is primed for action. This indicates an evolutionary relationship between host and parasite.

Mad Cow Disease. Bovine spongiform encephalopathy (BSE), or mad cow disease, is a neurologic disease in cattle that results in a degeneration of brain tissue, making the brain appear spongy and full of holes. The disease's symptoms include an increased sensitivity of the animals to sound and touch, a swaying gait, and kicking during milking. No pathogen has been isolated from diseased animals but a virus-like infectious agent is suspected. BSE resembles the neurologic disease of sheep called scrapie and the human Creutzfeldt-Jakob disease.

BSE cases have increased dramatically among British herds, which until recently had sheep meat included in their feed. Although the British have banned the inclusion of sheep meat in cattle feed, uncertainty remains not only over whether the disease could have been transmitted from an infected cow to her calves, but also whether the disease could have been transmitted to humans through the eating of infected meat. Unfortunately, with a four-to-five-year incubation period between infection and symptoms in cattle, the human consequences of this epidemic will not be evident for some time.

Viral Mimicry of Host Genes. Immune responses to infectious organisms tend to be very complex, involving systems of inhibitory immunoreactive cells. One important example of this in the mouse involves the T-cell clones T_H1 and T_H2. T_H1 cells secrete, among other compounds, interferon-gamma, which is an antiviral and possibly anticancer compound. T_H2 cells secrete, among other compounds, *cytokine synthesis inhibitory factor* (CSIF), which inhibits synthesis of interferon-gamma by stimulated T_H1 cells.

Dr. K. W. Moore and colleagues have studied the nucleotide sequence of the chromosome of the Epstein-Barr virus, a DNA virus of the herpes group, which is associated with Burkitt's lymphoma, a cancer affecting the jaw and adjacent facial bones. They found that a gene of the virus known as BCRF1 shows about 70% nucleotide sequence identity with CSIF of the mouse. Subsequently, it also was discovered that human T cells produce CSIF which is very similar to that of the mouse.

Infection of either mouse or human by the Epstein-Barr virus, followed by activation of its BCRF1, would result in a blocking of the synthesis of interferon-gamma, thereby promoting survival of the virus. In effect the viral gene would be mimicking a host immunoregulatory gene. These findings suggest that the BCRF1 gene might represent an ancestral, cellular CSIF gene captured by the virus from a host (mouse, human, etc.). This might represent an evolutionary strategy used by a variety of pathogens to suppress a host's immune reaction to their presence.

Louis Levine, *City College of New York*

MIDDLE EAST

Many of the Middle East's long-term problems were simply on "hold" in 1990, as more pressing events, particularly Iraq's invasion and occupation of Kuwait in August, called for instant responses and adjustments. (*See* feature articles, page 24.)

Palestinians. No kind of resolution of the Palestinian problem appeared to be in the offing or even likely. The *intifada* or uprising against Israel in the West Bank and Gaza Strip reached its third anniversary in December, and the opinion of most analysts was that it had accomplished little. Control of the movement by the Palestine Liberation Organization (PLO) was slipping manifestly as it was challenged by the activities of Islamic fundamentalist groups. The chief effect of the uprising has been to afford tempting opportunities for the settling of private grudges. In all, by late 1990 more than 600 Palestinians had been killed by Israelis, mostly by troops restoring order in riots and demonstrations, a few by civilians. But more than 250 Arabs have died at the hands of other Arabs, a rapidly growing total.

Events in Israel made it less likely that the occupying power in the West Bank and Gaza would adopt conciliatory policies. The political crisis in Israel in the spring brought to an end six years of Likud-Labor coalitions. The crisis ended in June when a coalition with a very narrow majority brought into being a government comprising Likud and an array of religious and far-right nationalist parties.

Nor, in its international context, did the Palestinian movement fare better. The attempted, but abortive, speedboat raid on an Israeli beach on May 30 led to U.S. President Bush's suspension on June 30 of the U.S.-PLO "dialogue" initiated 18 months before, the reason being the PLO's failure to condemn the raid. Tentative U.S. plans to resume the talks again came to nothing because of PLO leader Yasir Arafat's reaction to the Iraqi conquest of Kuwait, which at first he supported. Later he reneged when he realized the dimensions of his error.

Israel's international position was strengthened by a growing rapprochement between Israel and the Soviet Union. In Washington in early December, Israeli Prime Minister Yitzhak Shamir met Soviet Foreign Minister Eduard Shevardnadze—an unprecedented and fairly cordial event. A few days later the Soviet Union dropped, as a condition for the restoration of diplomatic relations, Israeli consent to an international conference on the Middle East.

All Arab governments pay lip service to the Palestinian cause, and the oil-rich Gulf states, remote from Palestine, have bankrolled the PLO handsomely. For many of them, perhaps, these things were no more than a politically

© Kevin McKiernan/Sipa

Portraits of Jordan's King Hussein and Iraq's President Saddam Hussein are on sale in a street of Amman, Jordan's capital. Despite Hussein's aggressive actions against Kuwait, many Arabs consider him the champion of their cause.

necessary obeisance, or a useful stick with which to beat Israel. The question began to assume more urgency in 1990, however, with the prospects of a large-scale immigration into Israel of Soviet Jews, which already had begun. What outraged Arab opinion was their assumption that the incoming Jews would be settled on the West Bank, known to Israel as Judea and Samaria, changing the demographic character of the area. The Arabs then would be forced into Jordan, with Jordan becoming the Palestinian homeland sought in recent years. This is a nightmare for Jordan, since King Hussein's realm already has a majority of Palestinians—a people with no particular loyalty to the Hashemite house. Israel denied such plans.

Arab Unity and Lebanon. Arabs no longer could count on the Soviet Union to be a reliable counterweight to U.S. policy in the Middle East. They thus welcomed the strenuous denunciations of Israel and the United States voiced by Iraq's President Saddam Hussein

The Yemens Merge

The merger of the Yemen Arab Republic (North Yemen) and the People's Democratic Republic of Yemen (South Yemen) on May 22, 1990, meant the emergence of a new state—the Republic of Yemen—with at least the potentiality to be an important player in Middle East politics.

Located in the southwest corner of Arabia, the Yemen area has an abundance of fertile soil and adequate rainfall. Most of the population live in the highlands, where there is a more intensive pattern of agriculture than in any other part of Arabia. Several towns exhibit a unique local architecture of multistory adobe structures. Yemen also has been set apart by its poverty. Limited amounts of oil were discovered only in the early 1980s.

The merger might be described as "reunification" more truly than "unification," because at some points in its history Yemen had been one country. It generally is thought that Yemen was the realm of the Queen of Sheba. In the first millennium B.C., it was a prosperous trading state. Changing trade routes and political chaos ruined Yemen. The population was converted to Islam in the 7th century.

Temporarily unified in the 17th century under a strong ruler, Yemen broke again into North and South in 1728. The Ottoman sultan in Constantinople maintained an ineffective claim to suzerainty over the region. The British in 1839 took Aden, on the strait of Bab el Mandeb (the narrow southern entry to the Red Sea) as a supply point on the sea route to India, and turned it into a great port. An oil refinery was built in the 1950s. Britain also established protectorates over Aden's hinterland.

North Yemen remained isolated until 1962, when the ancient Rassid dynasty was deposed and the Yemen Arab Republic was proclaimed. In the south, British withdrawal from Aden in 1967 led to the setting up of the People's Democratic Republic of Yemen (PDRY), a state which attempted to combine Islam with Marxism.

Thus from 1967 until 1990 there were two Yemens with contrasting regimes. North Yemen saw a series of governments. After two presidential assassinations, Lt. Col. Ali Abdullah Saleh became president in 1979. He played the nonalignment game skillfully, accepting aid from both the United States and the USSR. The Communist regime based in Aden, closed to the West, invited in thousands of East Bloc advisers, and made the large offshore island of Socotra available to the Soviet Union as a base. Economically the regime was a disaster.

For 23 years the two countries have alternated between fighting and talk of union. Various plans for union came to nought. The two nations fought a border war in 1979, and the south was ravaged by a civil war in 1986. The 1990 merger pact was approved on April 22 and ratified by both legislatures on May 21.

San'a became the new capital, but Aden was recognized as the economic capital. Saleh, the North Yemen president, was promoted to general, became president of the new republic, and was named head of the five-man transitional council. South Yemen's President Haydar Abu Bakr al-Attas became premier. United Yemen sent a single delegation to the Arab League summit in late May and assumed a single seat at the United Nations. (*See also* page 583.)

ARTHUR CAMPBELL TURNER

(*see* BIOGRAPHY) throughout the spring. Even if linked to an evident paranoia and aggressiveness, he figured as the Arab champion, not afraid to "take on" the United States. This was the persona Saddam Hussein presented at the emergency Arab summit held in Baghdad, May 28–30. It was a forceful bid for the leadership of the Arab world. Jordan's King Hussein fully approved and veered more and more toward outright alignment with Iraq—the only savior in sight for Jordan. It was Saddam Hussein himself who unraveled this achievement by his conquest of Kuwait.

One of the Middle East's chronic problems can be said in some fashion to have ended with the final defeat of Maj. Gen. Michel Aoun in Lebanon in October and the virtual takeover of Lebanon by President Hafiz al-Assad of Syria. It seemed that Lebanon would become, for all practical purposes, a Syrian protectorate. The Israelis, however, still occupied a "security zone," a strip of territory north of the Israeli-Lebanese border. Life in Beirut and the whole of Lebanon rapidly became more peaceful, and commercial activity speedily resumed. The new Lebanon, however, would not be the same constitutional state that existed before the civil war began in 1975. The cynical may observe fascinating parallels between President Assad of Syria and Saddam Hussein. Both detest Israel's existence. Both aspire to lead the Arab world. In 1990, Saddam Hussein took over Kuwait on the march to a greater Iraq. Assad took over Lebanon, which Syrians always have regarded as properly part of Syria. The Kuwait crisis was a great boon to Syria. No protests met Syria's actions in Lebanon; Assad was able to establish, with Egypt's President Hosni Mubarak, a new Syria-Egypt axis, and to assume a mantle of respectability in the eyes of the United States.

See also articles on individual nations.

ARTHUR CAMPBELL TURNER
University of California, Riverside

MILITARY AFFAIRS

Frequent statements in 1990 by U.S. President George Bush and Soviet President Mikhail Gorbachev that the Cold War was over set the stage for both the United States and the USSR to restructure their massive military establishments to reflect newly emerging political realities. The most impressive changes were seen in the Soviet-sponsored Warsaw Pact and the West's North Atlantic Treaty Organization (NATO).

The Warsaw Pact. A collection of East European states which had been forced since 1955 to participate in the Soviet alliance built to counter NATO, the Warsaw Pact virtually collapsed in the months after the Nov. 9, 1989 opening of the Berlin Wall. As the Eastern European nations cast off their Communist governments, pressure mounted for the departure of the Soviet troops which for 40 years had propped up the detested Communist regimes. The most remarkable change occurred in East Germany, which was united with West Germany in October. Part of that arrangement, accepted by the Soviet Union, was that Soviet troops would remain in the former East Zone, but would be withdrawn by 1994. Late in the year the Bundestag of the united Germany approved a treaty with the USSR which changed the status of the 380,000 Soviet troops from de facto occupation forces to invited guests. The change meant that henceforth Soviet soldiers and their dependents would be subject to German laws and regulations, much as had been the case with British, French, and U.S. forces stationed in the former West Germany. The German government also agreed to provide $9 billion to finance the return of the Soviet forces and their dependents to the USSR. Soviet military forces were supposed to leave Czechoslovakia and Hungary by July 1991. Yet to be announced was Moscow's timetable for the departure of Soviet troops from Poland. The last joint military maneuvers for Warsaw Pact nations were held in December 1989.

The imminent departure of the Soviet military and the disintegration of communism in Eastern Europe did present some problems. Tension developed between Soviet soldiers and the populations among whom they were stationed. In mid-August a Soviet colonel was shot to death in East Berlin. Later in the fall two Soviet enlisted men were found beaten to death on a back road in Hungary. A growing problem for Soviet commanders was the desire of some troops to defect to the West rather than return home to a failing economy and the potential dismemberment of the Soviet Union.

The North Atlantic Treaty Organization. In July, NATO leaders assembled in London toasted "the most successful defensive alliance in history." However, after 41 years of marshalling Western military might against the Soviet Union, it now was said jokingly that NATO might be threatened more in the 1990s by the breakup of the Soviets' Eastern European empire than it ever was by the Red Army.

Looking forward to the future, and wondering how the alliance could justify its continuation, NATO leaders adopted four guidelines which, it was claimed, would help shape the organization as it prepared to enter the era of post-Cold War relationships. Called the "Four M Principles"—minimum nuclear deterrence, mobility, mobilization of conventional forces, and multinational forces—the guidelines were much easier to state on paper than they were realizable in practice.

A major question facing NATO concerned the nature of future U.S. participation in the alliance. A possibility that had considerable support in Washington is that U.S. troops could be part of a new framework for security in Europe, to be worked out by the Conference on Security and Cooperation in Europe (CSCE), which began a series of meetings in Paris late in November. The United States, Canada, and all European nations except Albania were represented at the negotiations. (*See* feature article, page 36.)

How Much Military Strength is Enough? As the Soviet Union began wrestling with adjusting its military establishment to the new international realities, the United States also sought to redefine its future military role and the forces needed to support its military objectives. Although a definitive doctrine for the future was not developed fully in 1990, Secretary of Defense Dick Cheney pointed toward the general direction of U.S. policy when he announced that U.S. military strength would be reduced by approximately 25% by 1995. Plans also were disclosed to shut down some military bases, and to disband some Reserve Officer Training Corps (ROTC) units at colleges and universities.

The move toward a leaner U.S. military was stalled to some extent by the August 2 Iraqi invasion of Kuwait, and the resultant U.S. military buildup in the Persian Gulf area (*see* feature articles, page 24). The Persian Gulf crisis also soaked up, at least for the time being, funds that had been referred to as the "peace dividend." This was to have been monies released by the downturn in defense spending made possible because of the reduction in the Soviet threat. Prior to Iraq's invasion of Kuwait numerous proposals had been made on how the savings from defense activities could be utilized by nonmilitary entities within the government, or by tax reductions. Many of those plans were shelved by the end of the year.

Strategic Nuclear Forces. A substantial debate developed over the question of whether, given the altered U.S.-USSR relationship, it still was necessary to deploy major weapons that had been developed during the period of intense Cold War rivalry between Moscow and Washington. By year's end it appeared that the ten-warhead, rail-mobile, MX ICBM probably would not be deployed; nor would the off-road mobile Midgetman ICBM be built. Congress decided that the production of B-2 Stealth bombers would be held for the time being at 15 aircraft. The defense against nuclear-missile attack officially termed the Strategic Defense Initiative (SDI—called "Star Wars" by its detractors), continued to be funded, but at a lower rate than before. SDI research continued to shift from the early emphasis upon exotic beam weapons such as lasers, to small rockets which would disable incoming warheads by the kinetic force of mutual impact. This concept is called brilliant pebbles.

For its part, the USSR, aware of concern that ethnic strife in some Soviet republics could place nuclear weapons in jeopardy, made several announcements to calm Western concerns. Specifically the Ministry of Defense stated that nuclear weapons were being guarded well by elite troops at depots within the Russian Republic.

Both nations awaited the outcome of the START (Strategic Arms Reductions Talks), which would establish limits on the numbers of strategic weapons that could be deployed in the 1990s (*see* ARMS CONTROL AND DISARMAMENT).

The Greening of the Pentagon. A singular result of the warming relations between the United States and the USSR was seen in an unusual speech delivered by the chairman of the Senate Armed Services Committee, Sen. Sam Nunn (D-GA). Nunn suggested that in the future the Department of Defense employ its far-flung forces, such as planes, submarines, surface ships, and satellites, to gather scientific information regarding potential environmental change, and that the Pentagon use its advanced technologies to develop new means of cleaning up the environment. Citing the reduction in the Soviet threat, Nunn called worldwide environmental destruction "a growing national security threat." Some cynics suggested that Nunn, generally perceived as a friend of the Pentagon, was interested more in finding reasons to maintain Pentagon appropriations than he was interested in the environment. Still, it was pointed out that the Department of Defense does have both physical and fiscal resources that could be used for environmental purposes.

The Proliferation of Nuclear Weapons. While the United States and the Soviet Union moved away from the Cold War confrontation, other nations engaged in military activities which were troubling to Moscow and Washington. Paramount was the movement by some countries toward the development of nuclear-weapons technology, and correlative delivery systems. Foremost among the nations considered by the West, and the Soviet Union, as nearing nuclear weapon status were Pakistan, Iraq, and Brazil.

The technological potential for the development of atomic weapons in Pakistan became so serious that in the fall Congress suspended future aid to the Islamabad government in order to demonstrate Washington's displeasure.

In 1981 the Israeli air force bombed the French-built Osirak nuclear-power plant near Baghdad, Iraq, which ostensibly was being constructed to produce electricity. The justification for the raid was Israel's concern that once the reactor in the plant went critical and started producing the artificial element plutonium, which is a primary atomic-bomb ingredient, the Iraqis would fabricate nuclear weapons. Although that particular nuclear plant has not been rebuilt, rumors abound that the Iraqis are working on the construction of atomic bombs in a series of dispersed facilities whose locations are not known. The crisis in the Persian Gulf served to intensify worry about Iraq's nuclear ambitions.

Late in the year a startling story broke in Brazil. According to government authorities the Brazilian military had been working on atomic-bomb research clandestinely since 1975. An investigation of the secret activity revealed that the military was perhaps two years away from obtaining the 20 to 30 lbs (9 to 13.6 kg) of enriched uranium necessary for construction of a bomb similar to the one dropped by the United States against the Japanese city of Hiroshima in World War II. In an effort to reassure the world about Brazil's intentions, Brazilian President Fernando Collor de Mello, speaking before the United Nations General Assembly in September, said that "Brazil today rejects the idea of any test that implies nuclear explosives, even for peaceful ends." In a related move, Brazil and its neighbor Argentina, another nation believed to have nuclear-weapons potential, began negotiations on a system of mutual inspections of each other's atomic facilities.

Dismissal of a U.S. General. In September, Secretary of Defense Cheney fired the Air Force Chief of Staff, Gen. Michael Dugan, after the four-star general publicly discussed sensitive plans to kill Iraqi President Saddam Hussein and destroy critical Iraqi targets with bombing raids. It was the first time a top U.S. commander had been removed since the Korean War, when President Harry Truman relieved Gen. Douglas A. MacArthur as commander of United Nations forces. General Dugan was replaced by Gen. Merrill A. McPeak, who at the time of his appointment was commander of the Pacific Air Force based in Hawaii.

ROBERT LAWRENCE
Colorado State University

Minnesota State Auditor Arne Carlson, the gubernatorial nominee of the Independent-Republican Party for just nine days, and his running mate Joanell Drystad, were pleased with the results on election night.

AP/Wide World

MINNESOTA

The election of Democrat-Farmer-Laborite (DFL) Paul Wellstone to the U.S. Senate in an upset victory over Independent-Republican (IR) Rudy Boschwitz and the defeat of incumbent Gov. Rudy Perpich capped a bizarre political year in Minnesota.

Wellstone, 46, a political-science professor at Carleton College, was viewed as a certain loser when endorsed by the DFL in March. He had meager financing with which to challenge Boschwitz, 60, who had an estimated campaign fund of $7 million. A strong advocate of liberal policies, Wellstone was regarded by many as outside the mainstream. But with an army of volunteers and television spots spiced with humor he confounded everyone, capturing 52% of the vote. In the final days of the campaign a letter from Boschwitz supporters to Jewish voters claiming Boschwitz was more deserving of Jewish support than Wellstone (both are Jewish) was regarded as extremely harmful to Boschwitz for suggesting a religious test for holding office. After the election, Boschwitz apologized for the letter.

Meanwhile, the race for governor was tumultuous. The IR convention, controlled by the party's right wing, endorsed Jon Grunseth, a Twin Cities businessman, but polls gave the better-known State Auditor Arne Carlson—who did not seek endorsement—a big lead and his nomination seemed assured. But pro-life Grunseth, aided by aggressive support from antiabortionists, upset pro-choice Carlson in the IR primary. The reelection of DFL Rudy Perpich at that point seemed likely. But in October the Grunseth campaign was derailed by allegations of sexual misconduct. After three weeks of turmoil within IR circles, Grunseth withdrew. Nine days before the election, Carlson became the IR nominee.

Despite the brief campaign, Carlson, aided by crossover DFL pro-choice supporters, defeated pro-life Perpich with 51% of the vote, ending Perpich's ten-year tenure (December 1976–79, 1983–91) as governor, longest in the state's history.

The DFL won an additional U.S. congressional seat, strengthened its control of the legislature, and retained other constitutional offices. The congressional gain was due in part to another offbeat development. Arlan Stangeland (R), seeking an eighth term from the rural 7th District, was hurt by the revelation that he had made 400 phone calls at public expense to a woman in the Washington area. The revelation was viewed as contributing to his defeat and he lost to former state legislator Collin Peterson.

MINNESOTA • Information Highlights

Area: 84,402 sq mi (218 601 km²).

Population (1990 census prelim.): 4,359,000.

Chief Cities (July 1, 1988 est.): St. Paul, the capital, 259,110; Minneapolis, 344,670; Duluth (1980 census), 92,811.

Government (1990): *Chief Officers*—governor, Rudy Perpich (DFL); lt. gov., Marlene Johnson (DFL). *Legislature*—Senate, 67 members; House of Representatives, 134 members.

State Finances (fiscal year 1989): *Revenue,* $12,390,000,000; *expenditure,* $10,584,000,000.

Personal Income (1989): $76,861,000,000; per capita, $17,657.

Labor Force (June 1990): *Civilian labor force,* 2,403,200; *unemployed,* 101,000 (4.2% of total force).

Education: *Enrollment* (fall 1988)—public elementary schools, 511,279; public secondary, 215,671; colleges and universities, 244,706. *Public school expenditures* (1989–90), $3,315,000,000.

Voters approved a constitutional amendment dedicating 40% of the earnings from the new state-supported lottery to an environmental trust fund. Property-tax referenda in 53 school districts were divided almost evenly between winners and losers.

Earlier in the year, Minnesota's other U.S. senator, Dave Durenberger (IR), was denounced by his colleagues following a lengthy investigation for a series of unethical acts.

Entering the 1991 legislative session, state finances and worker-compensation reform would be top issues. IR leaders claimed the state would face a $1 billion shortfall, but DFLers insisted the state had a big surplus.

ARTHUR NAFTALIN, *Professor Emeritus*
University of Minnesota

MISSISSIPPI

Disagreement between Gov. Ray Mabus and the state legislature over how to fund education reform and how to cope with a growing budget shortfall held center stage in Mississippi in 1990. Congressional elections generated little voter interest and produced no surprises.

Legislative Activity. The regular legislative session was extended from 90 to 95 days, cost taxpayers an estimated $9 million, and was marked more by bickering between the two houses and with the governor over education reform than it was by the passage of major legislation. While legislators eventually approved a compromise reform package, they were unable to reach a consensus on how the package should be funded. The Senate refused to approve the governor's call for a lottery to finance improvements, and the governor remained adamant in his opposition to increased sales and/or income taxes.

Despite its refusal to submit a lottery amendment to the electorate, the legislature authorized gambling aboard riverboats on the

Mississippi River and liberalized gambling on cruise ships in the Mississippi Sound. Other significant actions included establishing a process to site a state commercial hazardous-waste management facility and approval of a $69.5 million bond program for state building improvements.

On June 18 legislators were called into special session to fund the education-reform package they had approved in April with the understanding that it would self-destruct if action was not taken by July 1. After a stormy 13 days and an expenditure of more than $350,000, lawmakers adjourned June 30 without reaching agreement. Hope for educational improvements was kept alive, however, when Attorney General Mike Moore ruled that the education-reform bill would become law even though its provisions could not go into effect until the legislature appropriated money for them.

Elections. Mississippi's senior U.S. senator, Thad Cochran (R), and 3d District U.S. Representative G.V. Montgomery (D), were unopposed in the November 6 general election. The four remaining congressmen—Jamie Whitten (D), Mike Espy (D), Mike Parker (D), and Gene Taylor (D)—won easy victories over Republican challengers. Eight outright wins in the June primaries, coupled with two victories in the November general election, brought to ten the number of black circuit-and chancery-court judges within the state. This number, 10% of the total judgeships, represented the most significant showing for black judges in Mississippi since Reconstruction.

In other balloting, voters approved six "cleanup" amendments to the Mississippi constitution. They refused, however, to authorize removal of the constitutional requirement that counties be divided into five districts.

Budget Woes. A projected budget shortfall in excess of $100 million (fueled primarily by slack corporate-income-tax collections reflecting a slow-growth economy) forced Governor Mabus to cut selected agency programs in both August and November. The first cut totaled $8.2 million and affected 42 agencies; the second amounted to $20 million and was felt by about a dozen agencies. The governor refused to call a special legislative session to deal with the situation, setting the stage for across-the-board cuts if a quick solution was not found in the regular session beginning in January 1991.

1990 Census. Preliminary 1990 census figures showed that Mississippi had increased its number of inhabitants only slightly during the 1980s. Fearing the loss of a congressional seat, the state challenged the count.

Other. During the year considerable attention was focused on court actions questioning the legality of bingo operations and the status of initiative and referendum provisions ruled unconstitutional in 1922.

DANA B. BRAMMER, *University of Mississippi*

MISSISSIPPI • Information Highlights

Area: 47,689 sq mi (123 515 km²).

Population (1990 census prelim.): 2,535,000.

Chief Cities (1980 census): Jackson, the capital (July 1, 1988 est.), 201,250; Biloxi, 49,311; Meridian, 46,577.

Government (1990): *Chief Officers*—governor, Raymond Mabus, Jr. (D); lt. gov., Brad Dye (D). *Legislature*—Senate, 52 members; House of Representatives, 122 members.

State Finances (fiscal year 1989): *Revenue,* $5,055,000,000; *expenditure,* $4,528,000,000.

Personal Income (1989): $30,732,000,000; per capita, $11,724.

Labor Force (June 1990): *Civilian labor force,* 1,201,100; *unemployed,* 98,400 (8.2% of total force).

Education: *Enrollment* (fall 1988)—public elementary schools, 367,593; public secondary, 135,733; colleges and universities, 112,872. *Public school expenditures* (1989–90), $1,342,869,000.

MISSOURI

In 1990 the Missouri legislature enacted a major recycling bill, state lawmakers were tried for misbehavior, and earthquake predictions spread panic among the population.

Elections. In November 6 elections, Republican Jack Buechner was the only Missouri congressional incumbent ousted, losing a close race to Democrat Joan Kelly Horn. The state's two biggest counties elected new executives after bitter campaigns. George "Buzz" Westfall became the first Democrat in 30 years to win the highest post in St. Louis County. He defeated Republican incumbent H.C. Milford. Marsha Murphy won after upsetting incumbent Bill Waris in the Democratic primary for Jackson County executive.

Three attempted statewide citizen initiatives fell short of receiving voter approval. Promoters failed to gather enough signatures to force a vote on a proposal to protect abortion rights and roll back the 1986 abortion law that was upheld by the U.S. Supreme Court in 1989. In a setback for Republican Gov. John Ashcroft, the courts threw out a ballot proposal that would have created a state ethics commission and overhauled the General Assembly. The one measure that succeeded in making the November ballot, designed to protect scenic streams from development, lost by a three-to-one margin.

Press. One venerable metropolitan newspaper and one still in its infancy folded. The 121-year-old morning *Kansas City Times* merged with the afternoon *Kansas City Star* on March 1. The surviving morning paper was called the *Kansas City Star*. The *St. Louis Sun*, launched with great fanfare in September 1989, died suddenly April 25, 1990, when editor and owner Ralph Ingersoll II gave up on his effort to take on the long-established *St. Louis Post-Dispatch*.

AP/Wide World

The 25th anniversary of the St. Louis Gateway Arch, designed by Eero Saarinen as a symbol of the city's role in the U.S. movement westward, was marked in October 1990.

Courts. In a landmark right-to-die case, the U.S. Supreme Court ruled that the state could prevent the parents of Nancy Cruzan from having feeding tubes disconnected from their comatose daughter. The court said the state could require clear and convincing evidence that Cruzan, unconscious since a 1983 car accident, would not have wanted to live that way. After a hearing a probate judge in Missouri's Jasper County ruled on December 14 that the feeding tube could be disconnected. The tube was removed and the 33-year-old woman died 12 days later.

The U.S. Supreme Court also upheld the authority of federal judge Russell Clark to order property-tax increases to pay for desegregation of the Kansas City schools.

Legislature. The General Assembly's most notable legislation was a bill designed to cut the state's trash burden by encouraging recycling and banning yard waste and tires from landfills.

State Rep. Dewey Crump (D) of St. Louis County was convicted of selling cocaine and amphetamines. His trial included testimony about a sexual encounter with a teenage girl in his capitol office. State Rep. E. J. "Lucky" Cantrell, a St. Louis County Democrat, was convicted with Kansas City labor leader Sam

---

MISSOURI • Information Highlights

Area: 69,697 sq mi (180 516 km²).

Population (1990 census prelim.): 5,079,000.

Chief Cities (July 1, 1988 est.): Jefferson City, the capital (1980 census), 33,619; Kansas City, 438,950; St. Louis, 403,700; Springfield, 142,690; Independence, 115,090.

Government (1990): *Chief Officers*—governor, John Ashcroft (R); lt. gov., Mel Carahan (D). *General Assembly*—Senate, 34 members; House of Representatives, 163 members.

State Finances (fiscal year 1989): *Revenue,* $8,703,000,000; *expenditure,* $7,738,000,000.

Personal Income (1989): $84,053,000,000; per capita, $16,292.

Labor Force (June 1990): *Civilian labor force,* 2,678,100; *unemployed,* 136,600 (5.1% of total force).

Education: *Enrollment* (fall 1988)—public elementary schools, 567,860; public secondary, 238,779; colleges and universities, 261,667. *Public school expenditures* (1989–90), $3,073,069,000.

Long of conspiring to steal union funds. State Sen. Ed Quick of Kansas City was acquitted of conspiring with Long and Cantrell.

Earthquake. Iben Browning, a New Mexico climatologist, forecast that a major earthquake was likely to occur about December 3 along the New Madrid Fault, which runs through the Missouri Bootheel. A few minor quakes in the fall fed a panic that swept eastern Missouri. Although school was canceled and the news media flocked to New Madrid, the appointed day passed uneventfully.

STEPHEN BUTTRY
"The Kansas City Star"

MONGOLIA

Both the democracy movement and nationalism gained strength in Mongolia in 1990 and led to a complete change in the nation's leadership.

Politics. Ulan Bator, the capital, was the scene of frequent demonstrations by Mongolians demanding that the ruling Communist party, known as the Mongolian People's Revolutionary Party (MPRP), accept major political and economic reforms. The people also demanded a reduction in the Soviet Union's influence in Mongolia and criticized the Communist government's mismanagement of the economy.

In March the party responded by removing its top leaders and surrendering its monopoly of power. Gombojavyn Ochirbat replaced Jambyn Batmonh as general secretary, or head, of the MPRP. The 61-year-old Ochirbat had returned only recently from Czechoslovakia. At a session of the People's Great Hural, or as-

---

MONGOLIA · Information Highlights

Official Name: Mongolian People's Republic.
Location: East Asia.
Area: 604,247 sq mi (1 565 000 km²).
Population (mid-1990 est.): 2,200,000.
Chief Cities (January 1989): Ulan Bator, the capital, 548,400; Darhan, 85,800.
Government: *Head of state,* Punsalmaagiyn Ochirbat, president (elected September 1990). *Head of government,* Sharavyn Gungaadorj (chosen March 1990). *Legislature*—People's Great Hural.

---

sembly, held soon after, Punsalmaagiyn Ochirbat, 47, was chosen as the new chairman of the Presidium (head of state). A lower-ranking Communist, he had been a minister of trade and author of a new policy promoting trade with the West. Sharavyn Gungaadorj was named chairman of the Council of Ministers, or premier. The Great Hural also deleted references in the constitution to the MPRP as the country's "guiding force."

In July the country's first multiparty elections since the Communist takeover in 1921 were held. The voter turnout was high. The election procedures were said to be generally fair, as the Communists won a majority of seats in the Great Hural. In the Hural's first session, in September, it elected Punsalmaagiyn Ochirbat to the newly created office of president. The office of chairman of the Presidium was abolished.

Economics. While Soviet aid declined in 1990, there remained some 50,000 Soviet specialists (including dependents) in Mongolia. There were reports of truck drivers and coal miners striking to protest layoffs of Mongolian staff by Soviet managers at various enterprises.

© L. Zylberman/Sygma

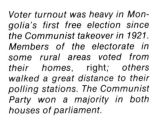

Voter turnout was heavy in Mongolia's first free election since the Communist takeover in 1921. Members of the electorate in some rural areas voted from their homes, right; others walked a great distance to their polling stations. The Communist Party won a majority in both houses of parliament.

With the work force growing by 3.4% annually, unemployment was becoming a major problem. The government reportedly was considering shortening the workweek to five days, creating small enterprises in rural areas, and exporting labor abroad, mainly to the USSR. In July the government was reported to have applied for membership in the International Monetary Fund (IMF).

Foreign Relations. Mongolia's head of government visited Japan in February to promote increased trade and investment. Japan accounts for nearly half of Mongolia's trade with the non-Communist world. Although the volume was small—only about $30 million in 1988 —it was growing rapidly.

In August, U.S. Secretary of State James Baker made an official visit to Mongolia, the first by a U.S. secretary of state. The two countries signed a consular convention and a commercial agreement. Baker promised U.S. aid of about $1 million and consideration of most-favored-nation status for Mongolia.

Closer to home, China had reason to be concerned about the movement for democracy and nationalism spreading south, with its 6 million Mongolians as well as many other unassimilated minorities.

PETER A. POOLE
Author, "Eight Presidents and Indochina"

MONTANA

Montana voters reelected two U.S. congressmen and a senator in 1990's elections and gave their property- and income-tax systems a vote of confidence. A declining population, however, was expected to reduce the state's number of congressional seats to one in 1992.

Elections. Democratic Max Baucus easily defeated Republican Lt. Gov. Allen Kolstad to retain his seat in the U.S. Senate. Republican Rep. Ron Marlenee and Democratic Rep. Larry Williams each beat out nominal competition to retain their seats.

A proposal to replace all existing state and local taxes in Montana with a 1% tax on all financial transactions was defeated by a 3–1 margin. The proposal was pitched as a protest against increases in all taxes and left the details of tax collection and administration up to the state legislature. Voters also defeated a proposed tobacco tax designed to fund antismoking campaigns.

Democrats gained control of both houses of the state legislature for the first time since 1977.

Census. The 1990 census revealed a steady drop in the number of people in Montana since 1985. The result apparently would mean one fewer congressman after the 1992 election. Preliminary census figures showed that Montana had about 794,000 people, about 6,000 shy of that needed for a second person in the U.S. House of Representatives. With the change in 1992, Montana's sole congressman would represent more people than any other person in the House.

Economy. Tourist numbers hit a new high in the major national parks in and around Montana in 1990. Special events, such as a re-enactment of Custer's Last Stand, gave tourism one of its best years ever.

The agricultural economy suffered, however, under a third year of drought in eastern Montana, accompanied by higher fuel prices and flat grain prices. Strong beef prices and a warm fall benefited cattle rangers and irrigated-sugar-beet farmers.

A nationwide sag in the demand for lumber forced layoffs and business failures throughout the western Montana logging and wood-products industries. Environmental concerns and controversy over the endangered spotted owl prompted concern about the future financial health of the industry.

Religion. Followers of the Church Universal and Triumphant spent the first few months of the year stocking massive underground bomb shelters at the sect's headquarters along the northern border of Yellowstone National Park. In March many of the followers went into the shelters, coinciding with a prediction by the sect's leader, Ruth Clair Prophet, that nuclear war would destroy the world at that time. Followers left the shelters after a short stay and spent much of the rest of the year excavating underground diesel-fuel tanks that had leaked into nearby streams.

Education. The presidents of both state universities resigned in 1990 amid complaints of inadequate funding and faculty pay.

Funding for public education received a substantive boost from court-mandated legislation requiring all property owners to pay nearly the same amount to the state, which divides it among schools based on the number of students.

ROBERT C. GIBSON
"The Billings Gazette"

MONTANA • Information Highlights

Area: 147,046 sq mi (380 848 km²).

Population (1990 census prelim.): 794,000.

Chief Cities (1980 census): Helena, the capital, 23,938; Billings, 66,798; Great Falls, 56,725.

Government (1990): *Chief Officers*—governor, Stan Stephens (R); lt. gov., Allen Kolstad (R). *Legislature*—Senate, 50 members; House of Representatives, 100 members.

State Finances (fiscal year 1989): *Revenue,* $2,087,000,000; *expenditure,* $1,880,000,000.

Personal Income (1989): $11,342,000,000; per capita, $14,078.

Labor Force (June 1990): *Civilian labor force,* 410,700; *unemployed,* 22,800 (5.5% of total force).

Education: *Enrollment* (fall 1988)—public elementary schools, 109,526; public secondary, 42,665; colleges and universities, 35,772. *Public school expenditures* (1989–90), $584,323,000.

MOROCCO

While Moroccan leaders were concerned about the possibility of a fundamentalist Islamic upheaval, the most serious domestic disturbance in 1990 was sparked instead by economic conditions.

On the international front, the kingdom stood firmly with the West and most Arab countries in opposing Iraq's August invasion of Kuwait. A major oil spill threatened the coast as the year began.

Domestic Affairs. Concern over the growth of Islamic fundamentalism was heightened by the legalization of the Islamic Salvation Front (FIS) in neighboring Algeria and by the party's strong showing there in June elections. Fundamentalist sentiment was already on the rise in Morocco, and a large protest rally in Rabat the month before culminated in the arrest of 2,000 protesters. In a conciliatory move, however, King Hassan II soon released most of those arrested and announced the formation of a 37-member council for human rights.

Far more serious were the riots that grew out of a December nationwide strike called to protest economic conditions. The riots first erupted in the city of Fez and then spread to several other Moroccan cities.

The Fez riot reportedly started when youths threw stones at policemen and soldiers who had been pressed into service to drive buses during the strike. Thousands of Moroccans took part, looting stores and setting fires. The government, in turn, was criticized for the alleged brutality with which it put down the unrest. Hundreds of injuries were reported, and more than 30 people were killed.

The economic hardships that led to the worst riots in seven years included a high unemployment rate and a per-capita-income level of $880 per year. In the aftermath the government promised to raise the minimum wage and to increase social benefits. A committee also was set up to examine the underlying causes of the disturbances. However, nearly 200 Moroccans who were arrested during the riots remained slated for trials.

Meanwhile, the Polisario Front continued its fight for the independence of the western Sahara in a conflict ongoing since Spain ceded the region to Morocco in 1975. While a cease-fire was called during the holy month of Ramadan, the diplomatic battle continued. United Nations Secretary-General Javier Pérez de Cuéllar worked during the year to bring the two sides together. The UN Security Council endorsement in June of a 1988 peace plan paved the way for a possible future deployment of a UN peacekeeping force, but by year's end no final agreement had been reached. The conflict was also a potentially divisive issue for the Arab Maghreb Union—the economic alliance of Morocco, Algeria, Tunisia, Mauritania, and Libya formed in February, 1989. Although Algeria's relations with Morocco recently had been cordial, it continued to side with the Polisario rebels.

Foreign Affairs. Even before the invasion of Kuwait by Iraq, Morocco had demonstrated a moderate stance in foreign relations. King Hassan, along with a number of other Arab leaders, boycotted a special Arab League summit held in Baghdad on May 28–30. Iraq's Saddam Hussein had called the summit to protest Israeli immigration and West Bank settlement policies and Western efforts to deny Baghdad sophisticated weapons of mass destruction.

After the August 2 invasion, Morocco denounced Iraq and was one of 16 Arab countries that supported UN sanctions against Saddam Hussein. The kingdom also sent a contingent of troops to link up with Egyptian units for the defense of Saudi Arabia. In September the World Bank named Morocco as one of the ten nations most likely to be hurt economically by the continuing conflict. (*See* feature articles, page 24.)

Environmental Disaster. At the beginning of the year, a major oil spill threatened the coastline off Rabat, following an explosion and fire in December 1989 on an Iranian tanker. An estimated 19 million gal (71.9 million l)—nearly twice the amount of the 1989 *Exxon Valdez* spill off Alaska—spewed into the ocean, creating a 100-sq-mi (259-km^2) oil slick. The leak was capped after two weeks, and ocean currents dispersed the slick before it could wreak havoc on Morocco's coast.

Moroccan officials also expressed environmental concerns over the future of Fez. A booming population in recent years has caused the ancient city to decay, and in 1990 officials announced plans to relocate 100,000 residents. A total of 25,000 apartment units were to be built in nearby towns over a five-year period.

JERRY STOREY
Free-lance Writer/Editor

MOROCCO · Information Highlights

Official Name: Kingdom of Morocco.
Location: Northwest Africa.
Area: 172,413 sq mi (446 550 km²).
Population (mid-1990 est.): 25,600,000.
Chief Cities (mid-1987 est., incl. suburbs): Rabat, the capital, 1,287,000; Casablanca, 2,904,000; Fez, 933,000; Marrakech, 1,425,000.
Government: *Head of state,* Hassan II, king (acceded 1961). *Head of government,* Azzedine Laraki, prime minister (appointed Sept. 30, 1986). *Legislature* (unicameral)—Chamber of Representatives.
Monetary Unit: Dirham (8.240 dirhams equal U.S.$1, August 1990).
Gross Domestic Product (1989 est. U.S.$): $21,900,000,000.
Economic Indexes (1989): *Consumer Prices* (1980 = 100), all items, 188.6; food, 186.8. *Industrial Production* (1980 = 100), 123.
Foreign Trade (1989 U.S.$): *Imports,* $5,492,000,000; *exports,* $3,307,000,000.

"Dick Tracy," a hit of the summer season, continued the trend of bringing cartoon characters to the screen in big-budget, commercial films. The all-star cast included, in the title role, director, producer, and star Warren Beatty (right), Charlie Korsmo, and Glenne Heady (left), as well as Madonna and several stars in character roles.

© Photofest

MOTION PICTURES

The most dramatic change in the movie-rating system since its inception in 1968 broadened the distribution potential for films judged suitable only for adults. In response to mounting pressure from filmmakers and producers, the Motion Picture Association of America (MPAA), which administers the ratings, reluctantly abandoned its long-disputed X. In its place came a new NC-17 designation which, like the X, specifies that no one under 17 can be admitted. Unlike the X, it does not carry the stigma of pornography. Jack Valenti, president of the MPAA, often had asserted that the X was meant merely to signify adult fare and not to be pejorative, but apart from the argument of those who oppose any enforceable restrictions, the letter X connotes something to be crossed out. Seriously intended adult movies were hindered by the X rating because many newspapers refused to accept advertising and many theaters refused to play such films. In making the change, the hope was that the more neutral-sounding NC-17 would enable adult films to find acceptance for what they are and not be lumped with hard-core pornography. The MPAA also decided to explain the reasons for the R rating (no one under 17 admitted unless accompanied by an adult) in each specific case.

The first film to obtain the new NC-17 rating was the steamy *Henry and June*, Philip Kaufman's drama based on the diaries of Anaïs Nin and concerning her relationship with author Henry Miller and his wife June, released by Universal Pictures. Although the MPAA denied that Universal's influence led to the new rating designation, it would appear that a major studio had more power than the many independent producers who often charged that their films were subject to harsher ratings. Another

apparent contributor to X's demise was a court decision criticizing the rating system while upholding the legal right of the MPAA to rate Spanish director Pedro Almodovar's *Tie Me Up! Tie Me Down!* with an X.

Henry and June was shown widely, although some limited opposition did develop. A theater in Massachusetts declined to play it, and two newspapers, one in California and another in Alabama, refused advertising. There were some charges that by whatever label, frank sex and excessive violence were objectionable. On balance, however, the rating alteration reflected changing attitudes that can be traced from the strictness of the old Hollywood code through the contemporary rating system that itself has broadened standards.

Love or Death. Despite the saturation of violent movies, there were signs at the box office that the public heartily welcomed films concerned with human relations. True, violence continued to be a big money-maker. *Total Recall*, with Arnold Schwarzenegger demolishing his opponents, and *Die Hard 2*, starring Bruce Willis as the lethal man of action disposing of terrorists, were blockbusters grossing more than $100 million each. "Movies today are bloodier and more brutal than ever," wrote critic Vincent Canby in *The New York Times*, and to prove it, he cited 264 violent deaths (including victims of a blown-up airliner) in *Die Hard 2*.

Running counter to the taste for brutality, however, *Pretty Woman* became a surprise hit. The Cinderella-like romantic comedy (teaming Julia Roberts and Richard Gere) about a prostitute rescued from the streets by her "Prince Charming" businessman topped $175 million at the box office. The other surprise was *Ghost*, a supernatural love story in which a murdered husband (Patrick Swayze) returns to solve the crime. It also starred Demi Moore and Whoopi

Goldberg. *Ghost*'s box office receipts quickly zoomed to $163 million.

Avalon, written and directed by Barry Levinson (*Rain Man*, 1988) was yet another picture with heart. Set in Levinson's home city of Baltimore, the film drew on his own family history in telling of immigrants who struggled to realize the American dream. With a touching performance by Armin Mueller-Stahl at its center, it featured superb ensemble acting, especially from Lou Jacobi as a resentful immigrant brother. In *Mermaids*, directed by Richard Benjamin, the relationship between a mother and daughter (Cher and Winona Ryder) is explored. Another mother-daughter relationship was at the core of *Postcards from the Edge*, written by Carrie Fisher from her novel and directed by Mike Nichols. Shirley MacLaine gave a colorful performance as a controlling mother, with Meryl Streep as the drug-addicted daughter. The bond between artist Vincent Van Gogh and his brother was the basis for *Vincent and Theo*, a new work by director Robert Altman.

Weighty Subjects. Moviegoers eager for entertainment with substance had a variety of finely crafted films from which to choose. *GoodFellas*, one of the year's best, reflected director Martin Scorsese in top form. The disturbing crime film, which Scorsese coscripted with Nicholas Pileggi from Pileggi's book *Wiseguy*, energetically and brilliantly depicted the crass, deadly world of New York mobsters. Another effective gangster film was *Miller's Crossing*. Part thriller, part comedy, it looked satirically at 1930s petty mobsters pursuing their own warped version of the American dream. The sly, stylized film was the work of talented brothers Joel and Ethan Coen. In addition, Francis Ford Coppola's *The Godfather, Part III* finally made it to the screen.

Director Barbet Schroeder had a bemused take on the controversial case of Claus von Bulow in *Reversal of Fortune*. Jeremy Irons played von Bulow and Ron Silver portrayed Alan Dershowitz, von Bulow's actual lawyer on whose book the drama is based. Tom

---

The National Film Registry

The Library of Congress for the second year in 1990 named 25 American films to the National Film Registry. The films are listed in accordance with a 1988 law, specifying that none can be altered without a designation to that effect.

The 1990 designated films, classified as "culturally, historically, or esthetically significant," were: *All About Eve* (1950), *All Quiet on the Western Front* (1930), *Bringing Up Baby* (1938), *Dodsworth* (1936), *Duck Soup* (1933), *Fantasia* (1940), *The Freshman* (1925), *The Godfather* (1972), *The Great Train Robbery* (1903), *Harlan County, U.S.A.* (1976), *How Green Was My Valley* (1941), *It's a Wonderful Life* (1946), *Killer of Sheep* (1977), *Love Me Tonight* (1932), *Meshes of the Afternoon* (1943), *Ninotchka* (1939), *Primary* (1960), *Raging Bull* (1980), *Rebel Without a Cause* (1955), *Red River* (1948), *The River* (1937), *Sullivan's Travels* (1941), *Top Hat* (1935), *The Treasure of the Sierra Madre* (1948), and *A Woman Under the Influence* (1974).

Wolfe's best-seller *Bonfire of the Vanities* became a movie, as did Scott Turow's *Presumed Innocent*.

The days of the bus boycott in Alabama during the 1950s were recalled in *The Long Walk Home*, starring Sissy Spacek and Whoopi Goldberg and directed by Richard Pearce. Another movie that reached into history was *Come See the Paradise*, Alan Parker's drama about the fate of Japanese-Americans who were interned during World War II. Actor Kevin Costner made his bid as a director by dramatizing injustice to American Indians after the Civil War in his *Dance with Wolves*. Tom Stoppard provided a screen adaptation of his play *Rosencrantz and Guildenstern Are Dead*.

In the documentary category, Barbara Kopple (*Harlan County, U.S.A*, 1976) unveiled *American Dream* at the New York Film Festival, the culmination of five years of work. Other thought-provoking documentaries included Al Reinert's *For All Mankind* and Nina Rosenblum's *Through the Wire*.

Numerous foreign-language films also dealt with challenging subjects. Attempts in France to minimize casualties in World War I provided the setting for *Life and Nothing But*, directed by Bertrand Tavernier and starring Philippe Noiret. A town's Nazi past was uncovered in *The Nasty Girl*, a German film that was a hit at the Berlin International Film Festival. Hungarian writer-director Ildiko Enyedi made a stunning debut with *My 20th Century*.

Regrettably, the market for foreign films in the United States continued to be limited, but a major contribution to the existing scene was the restoration of the 1934 French classic *L'Atalante*, directed by Jean Vigo before his death at the age of 28. The film was a highlight of film festivals in Toronto and New York.

Outstanding Talent. Actors, well-known and relative newcomers, and directors, proven and novice, merited special attention. Marlon Brando delightfully spoofed his *Godfather* character in a light gangster comedy, *The Freshman*. Joe Pesci will be remembered for his portrayal of a vicious, psychotic killer in *GoodFellas*. Denzel Washington, who won a best supporting actor Oscar for *Glory* (1989), demonstrated his leading-man potential playing a musician in Spike Lee's *Mo' Better Blues*. Veteran Peter Falk was outrageously funny as the egotistical soap-opera author in *Tune in Tomorrow*, while French actor Gérard Depardieu gave a tour-de-force performance in *Cyrano de Bergerac*. Warren Beatty deserved to be remembered for *Dick Tracy*; his low-key title performance and direction were admirable despite his detractors.

Winona Ryder established herself as a young actress to watch in *Mermaids* and *Welcome Home Roxy Carmichael*. James Spader (*sex, lies, and videotape*, 1989) added another notch to his career as the young man in love

Two major films of 1990 were "Postcards from the Edge," Carrie Fisher's screenplay of her novel that provides an insider's view of the Hollywood scene and stars Meryl Streep (left) and Shirley MacLaine, and "Pretty Woman," with Richard Gere and Julia Roberts, a spring mega-hit.

© Columbia Pictures

MOTION PICTURES | 1990

THE ADVENTURES OF FORD FAIRLANE. Director, Renny Harlin; screenplay by Daniel Waters, James Cappe, and David Arnott. With Andrew Dice Clay.

AFTER DARK, MY SWEET. Director, James Foley; screenplay by Robert Redlin and Mr. Foley, based on the novel by Jim Thompson. With Jason Patric, Rachel Ward, Bruce Dern.

AKIRA KUROSAWA'S DREAMS. Written and directed by Akira Kurosawa. With Akira Terao, Martin Scorsese.

ALICE. Written and directed by Woody Allen. With Mia Farrow, Joe Montegna, William Hurt, Keye Luke, Blythe Danner, Alec Baldwin.

ANOTHER 48 HOURS. Director, Walter Hill; screenplay by John Fasano, Jeb Stuart, and Larry Gross. With Eddie Murphy, Nick Nolte.

ARACHNOPHOBIA. Director, Frank Marshall; screenplay by Don Jakoby and Wesley Strick. With Jeff Daniels.

AVALON. Written and directed by Barry Levinson. With Aidan Quinn, Armin Mueller-Stahl, Joan Plowright, Eve Gordon, Elizabeth Perkins, Lou Jacobi.

AWAKENINGS. Director, Penny Marshall; screenplay by Steven Zaillian, based on the book by Oliver Sacks. With Robert De Niro, Robin Williams, Julie Kavner.

BACK TO THE FUTURE, PART III. Director, Robert Zemeckis; screenplay by Bob Gale. With Michael J. Fox, Christopher Lloyd, Mary Steenburgen.

BAD INFLUENCE. Director, Curtis Hanson; screenplay by David Koepp. With Rob Lowe, James Spader.

BETSY'S WEDDING. Written and directed by Alan Alda. With Alan Alda, Molly Ringwald.

BIRD ON A WIRE. Director, John Badham; screenplay by David Seltzer, Louis Venosta, and Eric Lerner, based on a story by Mr. Venosta and Mr. Lerner. With Mel Gibson, Goldie Hawn, David Carradine.

THE BONFIRE OF THE VANITIES. Director, Brian De Palma; screenplay by Michael Cristofer, based on the novel by Tom Wolfe. With Tom Hanks, Bruce Willis, Melanie Griffith.

CADILLAC MAN. Director, Roger Donaldson; screenplay by Ken Friedman. With Robin Williams, Tim Robbins.

CINEMA PARADISO. Written and directed by Giuseppe Tornatore. With Philippe Noiret, Jacques Perrin.

COME SEE THE PARADISE. Written and directed by Alan Parker. With Dennis Quaid, Tamlyn Tomita.

THE COOK, THE THIEF, HIS WIFE, AND HER LOVER. Written and directed by Peter Greenaway. With Richard Bohringer, Michael Gambon, Helen Mirren, Alan Howard.

CRY-BABY. Written and directed by John Waters. With Johnny Depp, Traci Lords, Troy Donahue.

CYRANO DE BERGERAC. Director, Jean-Paul Rappeneau; screenplay and adaptation of the Edmond Rostand

© Gamma-Liaison

play by Mr. Rappeneau and Jean-Claude Carrière. With Gérard Depardieu.

DANCES WITH WOLVES. Director, Kevin Costner; screenplay by Michael Blake, based on his novel. With Kevin Costner.

DAYS OF THUNDER. Director, Tony Scott; screenplay by Robert Towne. With Tom Cruise, Robert Duvall.

DESPERATE HOURS. Director, Michael Cimino; screenplay by Lawrence Konner, Mark Rosenthal, and Joseph Hayes, based on the novel and Broadway play by Mr. Hayes. With Mickey Rourke, Anthony Hopkins.

DICK TRACY. Director, Warren Beatty; screenplay by Jim Cash and Jack Epps, Jr., based on characters created by Chester Gould for the "Dick Tracy" comic strip. With Warren Beatty, Madonna, Al Pacino, Dustin Hoffman, Charlie Korsmo, Glenne Headly.

DIE HARD 2. Director, Renny Harlin; screenplay by Steven E. de Souza and Doug Richardson. With Bruce Willis, Bonnie Bedelia, William Atherton.

EDWARD SCISSORHANDS. Director, Tim Burton; screenplay by Caroline Thompson. With Johnny Depp, Winona Ryder, Dianne Wiest.

EVERYBODY WINS. Director, Karel Reisz; screenplay by Arthur Miller. With Debra Winger, Nick Nolte.

THE FRESHMAN. Written and directed by Andrew Bergman. With Marlon Brando, Matthew Broderick.

GHOST. Director, Jerry Zucker; screenplay by Bruce Joel Rubin. With Patrick Swayze, Demi Moore, Whoopi Goldberg.

GHOST DAD. Director, Sidney Poitier; screenplay by Chris Reese, Brent Maddock, and S. S. Wilson. With Bill Cosby.

THE GODFATHER PART III. Director, Francis Ford Coppola; screenplay by Mario Puzo and Mr. Coppola. With Al Pacino, Diane Keaton, Talia Shire, Andy Garcia.

GOODFELLAS. Director, Martin Scorsese; screenplay by Nicholas Pileggi and Mr. Scorsese, based on the book

Wise Guy by Mr. Pileggi. With Robert De Niro, Ray Liotta, Joe Pesci, Paul Sorvino.

GREEN CARD. Written and directed by Peter Weir. With Gérard Depardieu, Andie MacDowell.

THE GRIFTERS. Director, Stephen Frears; screenplay by Donald Westlake, based on the novel by Jim Thompson. With Anjelica Huston, John Cusack, Annette Bening.

HAMLET. Director, Franco Zeffirelli; screenplay by Christopher De Vore and Mr. Zeffirelli, adapted from the play by William Shakespeare. With Mel Gibson, Glenn Close.

THE HANDMAID'S TALE. Director, Volker Schlöndorff; screenplay by Harold Pinter, based on the novel by Margaret Atwood. With Natasha Richardson, Faye Dunaway, Elizabeth McGovern, Victoria Tennant.

HAVANA. Director, Sydney Pollack; screenplay by Judith Rascoe and David Rayfiel. With Robert Redford, Lena Olin, Alan Arkin.

HENRY AND JUNE. Director, Philip Kaufman; screenplay by Mr. Kaufman and Rose Kaufman, based on the book by Anaïs Nin. With Fred Ward, Uma Thurman, Maria de Medeiros.

HOME ALONE. Director, Chris Columbus; screenplay by John Hughes. With Macaulay Culkin.

HOUSE PARTY. Written and directed by Reginald Hudlin. With Christopher Reid, Robin Harris, Tisha Campbell.

THE HUNT FOR RED OCTOBER. Director, John McTiernan; screenplay by Larry Ferguson and Donald Stewart, based on the novel by Tom Clancy. With Sean Connery, Alec Baldwin, Scott Glenn, James Earl Jones.

I LOVE YOU TO DEATH. Director, Lawrence Kasdan; screenplay by John Kostmayer. With Kevin Kline, Tracey Ullman, Joan Plowright, William Hurt.

JACOB'S LADDER. Director, Adrian Lyne; screenplay by Bruce Joel Rubin. With Tim Robbins, Elizabeth Peña.

JESUS OF MONTREAL. Written and directed by Denys Arcand. With Lothaire Bluteau.

JOE VERSUS THE VOLCANO. Written and directed by John Patrick Shanley. With Tom Hanks, Meg Ryan.

KINDERGARTEN COP. Director, Ivan Reitman; screenplay by Murray Salem, Timothy Harro, Herschel Weingrod. With Arnold Schwarzenegger.

THE KRAYS. Director, Peter Medak; screenplay by Philip Ridley. With Gary Kemp, Martin Kemp, Billie Whitelaw.

LONGTIME COMPANION. Director, Norman René; script by Craig Lucas. With Stephen Caffrey, Patrick Cassidy, Bruce Davison.

LOOK WHO'S TALKING TOO. Director, Amy Heckerling; screenplay by Miss Heckerling and Neal Israel. With John Travolta, Kirstie Alley, and voices of Bruce Willis, Roseanne Barr, Damon Wayans.

LOVE AT LARGE. Written and directed by Alan Rudolph. With Tom Berenger, Elizabeth Perkins, Anne Archer, Kate Capshaw, Annette O'Toole, Kevin J. O'Connor.

MEN DON'T LEAVE. Director, Paul Brickman; screenplay by Barbara Benedek and Mr. Brickman. With Jessica Lange, Chris O'Donnell, Charlie Korsmo.

MERMAIDS. Director, Richard Benjamin; screenplay by June Roberts, based on the novel by Patty Dann. With Cher, Winona Ryder, Bob Hoskins, Christina Ricci.

METROPOLITAN. Written and directed by Whit Stillman. With Edward Clements, Christopher Eigman, Carolyn Farina, Taylor Nichols.

MILLER'S CROSSING. Director, Joel Coen; screenplay by Mr. Coen and Ethan Coen. With Gabriel Byrne, Albert Finney, Jon Polito.

MISERY. Director, Rob Reiner; screenplay by William Goldman, based on the novel by Stephen King. With James Caan, Kathy Bates, Lauren Bacall.

MO' BETTER BLUES. Written and directed by Spike Lee. With Denzel Washington, Spike Lee, Joie Lee, Cynda Williams.

MR. AND MRS. BRIDGE. Director, James Ivory; screenplay by Ruth Prawer Jhabvala, based on the novels *Mr. Bridge* and *Mrs. Bridge* by Evan Connell. With Paul Newman, Joanne Woodward, Blythe Danner.

MY TWENTIETH CENTURY. Written and directed by Ildiko Enyedi. With Dorotha Segda.

THE NASTY GIRL. Written and directed by Michael Verhoeven. With Lena Stolze.

NIGHT OF THE LIVING DEAD. Director, Tom Savini; screenplay by George A. Romero, based on the original screenplay by John Russo and Mr. Romero. With Tony Todd, Patricia Tallman.

PACIFIC HEIGHTS. Director, John Schlesinger; screenplay by Daniel Pyne. With Melanie Griffith, Matthew Modine, Michael Keaton, Tippi Hedren.

POSTCARDS FROM THE EDGE. Director, Mike Nichols; screenplay by Carrie Fisher, based on her novel. With Meryl Streep, Shirley MacLaine.

PRESUMED INNOCENT. Director, Alan J. Pakula; screenplay by Frank Pierson and Mr. Pakula. With Harrison Ford, Raul Julia, Bonnie Bedelia, Paul Winfield.

PRETTY WOMAN. Director, Garry Marshall; screenplay by J. F. Lawton. With Richard Gere, Julia Roberts.

PUMP UP THE VOLUME. Written and directed by Allan Moyle. With Christian Slater.

Q AND A. Written and directed by Sidney Lumet, based on the novel by Edwin Torres. With Nick Nolte, Timothy Hutton.

REVERSAL OF FORTUNE. Director, Barbet Schroeder; screenplay by Nicholas Kazan, based on the book by Alan M. Dershowitz. With Glenn Close, Jeremy Irons, Ron Silver.

ROCKY V. Director, John G. Avildsen; screenplay by Sylvester Stallone. With Sylvester Stallone.

THE RUSSIA HOUSE. Director, Fred Schepisi; screenplay by Tom Stoppard, based on the novel by John le Carré. With Sean Connery, Michelle Pfeiffer, Roy Scheider.

THE SHELTERING SKY. Directed by Bernardo Bertolucci; screenplay by Mark Peploe, based on the book by Paul Bowles. With Debra Winger, John Malkovich.

A SHOCK TO THE SYSTEM. Director, Jan Egleson; screenplay by Andrew Klavan, based on the novel by Simon Brett. With Michael Caine, Elizabeth McGovern, Swoosie Kurtz, Peter Riegert, Will Patton.

STANLEY AND IRIS. Director, Martin Ritt; screenplay by Harriet Frank, Jr., and Irving Ravetch. With Jane Fonda, Robert De Niro.

STATE OF GRACE. Director, Phil Joanou; screenplay by Dennis McIntyre. With Sean Penn, Ed Harris.

STELLA. Director, John Erman; screenplay by Robert Getchell. With Bette Midler, Trini Alvarado.

THE TALL GUY. Director, Mel Smith; screenplay by Richard Curtis. With Jeff Goldblum.

TEEN-AGE MUTANT NINJA TURTLES. Director, Steve Barron; screenplay by Todd W. Langen and Bobby Herbeck. With Elias Koteas, Judith Hoag, Josh Pais, Michelan Sisti, Leif Tilden, David Forman.

TEXASVILLE. Director, Peter Bogdanovich; screenplay by Mr. Bogdanovich, based on the novel by Larry McMurtry. With Jeff Bridges, Cybill Shepherd.

THREE MEN AND A LITTLE LADY. Director, Emile Ardolino; screenplay by Charlie Peters, Josann McGibbon, and Sara Pariott. With Tom Selleck, Steve Guttenberg, Ted Danson, Robin Weisman, Nancy Travis.

TIE ME UP! TIE ME DOWN! Written and directed by Pedro Almodovar. With Victoria Abril, Antonio Banderas.

TOTAL RECALL. Director, Paul Verhoeven; screenplay by Ronald Shusett, Dan O'Bannon and Gary Goldman. With Arnold Schwarzenegger.

TUNE IN TOMORROW. Director, Jon Amiel; screenplay by William Boyd, based on the novel *Aunt Julia and the Scriptwriter* by Mario Vargas Llosa. With Barbara Hershey, Peter Falk.

THE TWO JAKES. Director, Jack Nicholson; screenplay by Robert Towne. With Jack Nicholson, Harvey Keitel.

VINCENT AND THEO. Director, Robert Altman; screenplay by Julian Mitchell. With Tim Roth, Paul Rhys.

WAITING FOR THE LIGHT. Written and directed by Christopher Monger. With Shirley MacLaine, Teri Garr.

WHITE HUNTER, BLACK HEART. Director, Clint Eastwood; screenplay by Peter Viertel, James Bridges, and Burt Kennedy, based on the novel by Mr. Viertel. With Clint Eastwood, Marisa Berenson.

WHITE PALACE. Director, Luis Mandoki; screenplay by Ted Tally and Alvin Sargent. With Susan Sarandon, James Spader.

WILD AT HEART. Written and directed by David Lynch, based on the novel by Barry Gifford. With Nicolas Cage, Laura Dern, Diane Ladd, Willem Dafoe.

THE WITCHES. Director, Nicholas Roeg; screenplay by Allan Scott, based on a novel by Roald Dahl. With Anjelica Huston.

WITHOUT YOU I'M NOTHING. Director, John Boskovich; screenplay by Sandra Bernhard and Mr. Boskovich. With Sandra Bernhard.

YOUNG GUNS II. Director, Geoff Murphy; screenplay by John Fusco. With Emilio Estevez, Kiefer Sutherland.

with an older woman in *White Palace*, while veteran actress Susan Sarandon gave one of her best performances as the woman. Although David Lynch's *Wild at Heart* drew mixed response, it was a good vehicle for Laura Dern and Nicolas Cage.

Among directors, while attention inevitably was drawn to such old hands as Martin Scorsese (*GoodFellas*) and Woody Allen, with his latest, *Alice*, several newcomers commanded applause. In his debut Whit Stillman won praise for *Metropolitan*. Allan Moyle's *Pump Up the Volume* was praised extensively, as was Hal Hartley's *The Unbelievable Truth*.

No year is complete without a film arousing a measure of anger, and that designation went to British director Peter Greenaway's brazen but satirical *The Cook, the Thief, His Wife & Her Lover,* a brilliantly executed assault on taste that won fans and prompted walkouts. At the other end of the spectrum was *Teenage Mutant Ninja Turtles*, a popular film with children that became a huge money-maker.

Business. Movie companies sought to take advantage of the expanding market in the USSR and East Europe as a result of movement toward a free-market economy. Hollywood was shaken by the agreement for the purchase of MCA Inc., including Universal Pictures, by Matsushita of Japan for $6.13 billion. With this development, in addition to the earlier purchase of Columbia Pictures by Sony and of MGM/UA by an Italian investor, it seemed the U.S. film industry was losing its domestic base of control.

A hot Hollywood topic was columnist Art Buchwald's lawsuit against Paramount. He was awarded $250,000 and a 19% share of the *net* profits from *Coming to America* after a judge ruled that the film was based on his idea. But an old Hollywood joke is that there never is any net, and with Paramount claiming there was no money to which Buchwald was entitled, an intricate, closely watched court process of digging into accounting procedures began.

WILLIAM WOLF, *New York University*

MOZAMBIQUE

Two of the biggest problems facing the government of Mozambique's President Joaquím Chissano were solved partially in 1990. Continuing dialogue with South Africa resulted in some economic aid. More importantly, South Africa's President F. W. de Klerk denounced the Mozambique National Resistance (Renamo). This removed a major source of support for the rebels. Direct discussions with Renamo representatives in Rome in July held out hope for eventual settlement of the decade-old war.

Political Reform. In January, Chissano, attempting to move Mozambique away from its one-party Marxist system, issued a draft con-

---

MOZAMBIQUE • Information Highlights

Official Name: People's Republic of Mozambique.
Location: Southeastern coast of Africa.
Area: 309,494 sq mi (801 590 km²).
Population (mid-1990 est.): 15,700,000.
Chief City (1987 est.): Maputo, the capital, 1,006,765.
Government: *Head of state,* Joaquím A. Chissano, president (took office November 1986). *Head of government,* Mário da Graça Machungo, prime minister (took office July 1986). *Legislature* (unicameral)—People's Assembly.
Gross Domestic Product (1988 U.S.$): $1,600,000,000.

---

approved, the constitution would provide for a multiparty political system with direct elections for the legislature and president by means of a secret ballot. A judiciary independent from party politics also was promised. In July the president further elaborated on the proposed reforms, which would make the ruling Mozambique Liberation Party (Frelimo) only one of the recognized parties contesting for power in free elections.

The Civil War. The military struggle with Renamo, which has claimed an estimated 1 million lives, continued while negotiations proceeded in Rome. Despite outside assistance, the performance of the Mozambique army was generally poor. Its best units were posted near the main cities or along the rail lines. The ill-trained army units in the rural areas struggled with Renamo for scarce food and supplies and proved in many cases as rapacious as their enemy. The road system almost was destroyed, most schools were closed, and the towns and cities were crowded with refugees. An estimated 2.9 million displaced persons were within the country and an additional 1.3 million had fled to neighboring states. Most refugees were kept alive by foreign relief.

Economic Developments. The economy, damaged by Marxist experimentation, corruption, and the murderous civil war, has been sustained by large-scale foreign private investment and direct government aid. Engineers from the Netherlands were reconstructing the port of Beira, a Finnish group aided in rebuilding the damaged railway between Malawi and Ncala, and British contractors, protected by troops from Zimbabwe, continued work on the Limpopo line to Maputo. Italian agricultural experts were involved deeply in resettlement and development in Zambezia province.

Despite such aid, inflation and unemployment increased dramatically. Attempts to control inflation by curbing wage increases led to a series of strikes early in the year. Settled without violence, they indicated how tenuous support for the government was in the cities. Uncertainty over the future combined with inflation caused an increase in the numbers of persons involved in corrupt practices.

HARRY A. GAILEY
San Jose State University

© James Pozarik/Gamma-Liaison

Australia's Dame Joan Sutherland, one of the leading coloratura sopranos of the 20th century, gave her farewell performance in "Les Huguenots" at the Sydney Opera House in October. Her final curtain call lasted for nearly 45 minutes.

MUSIC

A major highlight of the 1990 music year was the opening, after six years, of the Bastille Opera in Paris. The spacious glass-and-tile structure was judged a success, although during its construction, the project had been immersed in various controversies. A controversy of a different sort arose when obscenity charges were leveled against the popular rap group 2 Live Crew in Florida. The group was acquitted in October, but the issue of obscenity and the arts promised to remain problematic in the 1990s.

The emergence of a younger generation of U.S. divas was noted during the year. Prominent among the group were Carol Vaness, Dawn Upshaw, and Harolyn Blackwell. The young baritone Dmitri Khvorostovsky also was a hit. Other musical milestones included the performances in a joint benefit concert in Rome of the world's three leading tenors—José Carreras, Placido Domingo, and Luciano Pavarotti —with Zubin Mehta conducting; 75th-birthday celebrations for Ol' Blue Eyes, Frank Sinatra; the retirement of Australian soprano Dame Joan Sutherland; and the loss of a giant, Leonard Bernstein, on October 14.

Classical

On Christmas Day 1989, Leonard Bernstein had been in Berlin and with the flair and flamboyance typical of him, celebrated the fall of the Berlin Wall with a performance of Beetho-

ven's Ninth Symphony with a truly international ensemble that included orchestras and choruses from East and West Germany, the Soviet Union, France, Britain, and the United States. The concert was broadcast live around the world, and Bernstein looked vigorous and energized, although it had been known for some time that he was suffering from emphysema. A few months later, in late May, he withdrew from the Spoleto Festival U.S.A., in Charleston, SC, where he had planned to conduct the opening gala. Although he conducted some of his concerts at the three-week Pacific Music Festival in Japan, which began in late June, poor health forced him to withdraw from his others.

Bernstein made his annual appearance at Tanglewood, the Boston Symphony's summer home, where on August 19 he gave what proved to be his final concert. On the program were Britten's *Four Sea Interludes*; his own *Arias and Barcarolles*, which at the last minute he decided not to conduct, leaving the task to Carl St. Clair, a Boston Symphony assistant conductor; and what turned out to be a luminous performance of the Beethoven Seventh. On October 9, on his doctor's advice, he announced his retirement from performing, intending to devote himself fully to composition and his memoirs. Five days later, he died suddenly of a heart attack. For the two generations of Americans who grew up under the spell of the 72-year-old conductor's magic—not only from his performances, but his books, lectures, and television programs, not to mention such works as the Broadway musical *West Side*

Story and the film score for *On the Waterfront* —it was the end of an era. (*See also* OBITU-ARIES.)

Orchestral Appointments. The New York Philharmonic—of which Bernstein had been music director (1958–69)—had some good news earlier in 1990. The search for a new music director to replace Zubin Mehta, the Philharmonic's current director, who had announced late in 1988 that he would be leaving the New York Philharmonic at the end of the 1990–91 season, finally ended in April when Kurt Masur (*see* BIOGRAPHY), the director of the Gewandhaus Orchestra of Leipzig, accepted the post.

A similar passing of the baton took place at the Philadelphia Orchestra, although the process moved more quickly there. In March the Italian conductor Riccardo Muti, the orchestra's director since 1980, said that he wanted to spend more time working in Europe after 1992. Within a few months the orchestra's search for a successor ended as West German conductor Wolfgang Sawallisch, director of the Bavarian State Opera, was appointed (as of 1993) in September.

There were some other notable appointments. Sir Georg Solti, who would conduct his final performance as music director of the Chicago Symphony in April 1991, is slated to become the director of the Salzburg Easter Festival in 1992. Sir Georg, who will be succeeded by Daniel Barenboim at the Chicago post, is filling a post left vacant by the death in 1989 of Herbert von Karajan, who founded the festival in 1967. That completes the post-Karajan Salzburg; in August 1989 the Belgian director Gerard Mortier was appointed director of Salzburg's summer festival.

Musicians. The 19-year-old Soviet pianist Yevgeny Kissin, known to Western record collectors for surprisingly mature and technically astonishing performances of works by Rachmaninoff, Shostakovich, and Tchaikovsky, made his U.S. concerto and recital debuts in New York in September. For the most part, his Chopin First Concerto with the New York Philharmonic and the Schumann and Prokofiev works he played at his recital left listeners with the impression that Kissin indeed had measured up to his reputation: a technical wizard with a Romantic interpretive temperament, a rarity in today's musical world.

Another Soviet who astonished many was Dmitri Khvorostovsky, a 27-year-old baritone from Krasnoyarsk, Siberia. Word of the baritone's power and rich vocal tone spread after he won the Singer of the World competition in Cardiff, Wales, in 1989. By March, when he made his New York recital debut, he had a sizable following, as well as a major-label (Philips) recording contract.

The East-West artistic migrations have worked the other way, too. The cellist and con-

© Laski/Sipa

Mstislav Rostropovich returned to his native USSR for the first time in 16 years in February. The National Symphony Orchestra under his direction toured the Soviet Union.

ductor Mstislav Rostropovich and his wife, the soprano Galina Vishnevskaya, left the Soviet Union in 1974 and were stripped of their Soviet citizenship four years later. Rostropovich, who flourished in the West, is music director of the National Symphony Orchestra in Washington, DC, and remains one of the world's greatest cellists. In January the Soviet Union reinstated Rostropovich's and Vishnevskaya's citizenships, and the following month, Rostropovich toured the Soviet Union with his U.S. orchestra.

Opera. In the world of opera, there was little in the way of innovation or controversy in 1990. Such controversy as there was took place at Glyndebourne, the summer opera festival in England, where the young avant-garde U.S. director Peter Sellars staged Mozart's *Die Zauberflöte* ("The Magic Flute"). As he has done in his other Mozart productions, Sellars updated the work to modern times and overlaid the work's own imagery with images from contemporary culture. In this production, set in Los Angeles, Mozart's Masonic elements are tied to Southern California cultism. Unusual, too, was Sellars' decision to drop the spoken dialogue in favor of illuminated messages—an element some critics felt was a miscalculation. As in the United States, Sellars had his supporters and detractors. One of the latter was Sir Peter Hall, who soon resigned as Glyndebourne's director.

In Paris the $400 million Bastille Opera opened with Hector Berlioz's *Les Troyens* in March and was deemed to have overcome its problems of 1989, when Daniel Barenboim was fired as the company's artistic director. Myung-Whun Chung, the young South Korean

With William Pell, a Denver-born tenor, singing the title role, Wagner's "Parsifal" had its U.S. premiere at the Spoleto Festival U.S.A. in the spring.

© William Struhs

conductor who stepped in, faced a formidable task in overcoming the bad feelings in the vocal world left by Barenboim's dismissal, but the house's opening was received as a triumph.

In the United States the Metropolitan Opera did not vary from its diet of conservative offerings in productions that were straightforward, expensive, and glitzy. The hope that it might branch out into adventurous programming was dashed early in the year when a planned collaboration between the company and the Brooklyn Academy of Music was canceled. As it was, the high point of the Met's season was the return of the complete Wagner *Der Ring des Nibelungen*, but that production was not trouble-free. During one of the early performances of *Götterdämmerung*, the company's Brunnhilde, Hildegard Behrens, was injured by falling scenery and was unable to appear in subsequent performances. This was a problem as the company not only was completing its recordings of the cycle, but was videotaping its performances for public-television broadcast and home-video release. Fortunately, the company was able to use an early performance in its video series, the summer broadcast of which drew a large national audience.

At the New York City Opera, Christopher Keene belatedly embarked on his first season as general director; his actual first year (1989) was canceled due to an orchestra strike. Among 1990's new productions were two 20th-century works—Leos Janacek's *House of the Dead*, in its U.S. premiere, and Arnold Schoenberg's *Moses und Aron*, in its New York stage premiere. On the lighter side was Stephen Sondheim's *A Little Night Music*.

The start of the San Francisco Opera's 1990–91 season fell prey to a strike in September. Elsewhere in the West, some lively and impressive stagings were offered during the year. The Seattle Opera's season included an interesting approach to Strauss' *Ariadne auf Naxos*, in which the tragedians sang in German and the *comedia dell'arte* troupe sang in English, a device that further separated the notions of high and low art. The company's most ambitious offering, however, was a $2 million July production of Sergei Prokofiev's mammoth *War and Peace*, a production the company videotaped for eventual showing on high-definition television. The Santa Fe Opera's *Judith* was an Expressionistic look at the Biblical tale by the contemporary East German composer Siegfried Matthus. The University of California at Berkeley provided a West Coast response to the biannual Boston Early Music Festival and Exhibition, presenting Niccolo Jommelli's *La Schiava Liberata*, an antecedent from 1768 of Mozart's *Entführung aus dem Serail* ("Abduction from the Seraglio").

New Music. In the world of new composition, the battles among atonality, Minimalism, and neo-Romanticism continued, with each field scoring its victories. Mel Powell, a 12-tone composer, won a Pulitzer Prize for his *Duplicates*, a labyrinthine concerto for two pianos. Philip Glass, one of Minimalism's founders, had his trilogy of operas about historical figures —*Einstein on the Beach*, *Satyagraha* (about Gandhi), and *Akhnaten*—performed as a cycle in Stuttgart, while a new collaboration with the poet Allen Ginsburg, *The Hydrogen Jukebox*, had premieres at the American Music Theater Festival in Philadelphia and the Spoleto Festival U.S.A. in Charleston. Among the neo-Romantic compositions, John Corigliano's Symphony No. 1 was reckoned a powerful, emotionally direct addition to the literature when Daniel Barenboim led the Chicago Symphony in its premiere in March.

Obituaries. Besides Leonard Bernstein, other figures of the musical world who died in 1990 were Cuban-born pianist Jorge Bolet, the Italian avant-garde composer Luigi Nono, and John Dexter, the English stage director.

ALLAN KOZINN, *"The New York Times"*

The youthful group New Kids on the Block found a huge audience in 1990, especially among preteenage girls, despite criticism of their lack of originality. Their performances featured energetic dance routines and positive social messages.

Popular and Jazz

The biggest stories in popular music in 1990 did not take place in concert halls and recording studios, but in courtrooms and state legislatures. The issues, involving uniform warning labels on recordings, 1st Amendment rights, and whether the sale of some recordings should be restricted or made illegal, were pushed into the spotlight mainly by rap-music lyrics considered by some to be obscene or demeaning to women. The rap group 2 Live Crew was in the center of the furor—their album *As Nasty As They Wanna Be* was ruled obscene by a Florida judge. A Florida retailer later was convicted for selling the banned record.

The controversy renewed the argument over the issue of labeling records, which had been in public debate since the mid-1980s. By mid-1990, in fact, the National Association of Record Merchandisers, representing virtually all the major labels, agreed to a standard warning label to be placed on records containing foul language or excessive references to violence or sex. (*See also* ARTS, THE—*The Issue of Obscenity*).

Rap. The ability of rap to inflame controversy paralleled its rising popularity. The decade-old, principally black musical style has found increasing mainstream acceptance. Far and away the most popular rap artist of the year, however, was also the most benign. M.C. Hammer spent a good portion of 1990 at the top of the album charts with *Please Hammer Don't Hurt 'Em*, which sold more than 4 million copies to become the best-selling rap record in history. By year's end, Hammer, whose usually nontopical music is mostly about dancing and self-glorification, was appearing in Pepsi commercials.

Not so Public Enemy, the most critically praised rap group; it nearly disintegrated in 1990 due to a prolonged controversy regarding anti-Semitic statements made by a group member. Nonetheless, Public Enemy's third album, *Fear of a Black Planet*, sold 1 million copies within weeks of its release.

The black-power anthems of Public Enemy, however, seem mild next to the songs of performers who play so-called "gangster rap." Rappers like Ice Cube and groups like N.W.A. use their music to tell tales of violence, decay, and desperation in the black inner city. Though such songs do not get much exposure on media outlets like MTV, gangster rap made the news in 1990. Geffen Records, which distributes recordings made by the Def America label, refused to ship an album by the Geto Boys which included graphic sex, violence, and even necrophilia. Ultimately, Geffen and Def America severed their business relationship, and the Geto Boys album was distributed by a division of the giant WEA conglomerate.

All this was small potatoes compared to the furor raised by 2 Live Crew. During the year, group members were arrested for performing an adults-only concert including controversial material from *As Nasty As They Wanna Be*. Not surprisingly, the turmoil sold a lot of 2 Live Crew albums, and the group's follow-up record, *Banned in the U.S.A.*, composed around the central musical figure from Bruce Springsteen's "Born in the U.S.A.," was distributed by Atlantic Records.

Two of the most successful popular musicians of 1990 were women with very different styles. Dancer/singer Janet Jackson, left, mounted her first headline tour, and Sinéad O'Connor, right, made waves with her powerful voice and unique persona.

Dance Music. A decade ago, pundits declared that disco was dead, but the beat-heavy music that defined the late 1970s really just changed its name to dance music. In the past few years, music designed for the dance floor and promoted by highly choreographed videos has proven very popular.

Janet Jackson's Rhythm Nation 1814 confirmed that Michael Jackson's younger sister was the Jackson clan's second blockbuster solo act. She mounted a successful concert tour during the year, as did Madonna, the queen of '80s dance music, who also garnered good reviews for her performance in the film *Dick Tracy*.

A scandal arose late in the year when it was revealed that the male dance duo Milli Vanilli, winners of the Grammy Award for best new artist, did not sing on their hit album, *Girl You Know It's True*. The singing actually was done by three other men, two of whom were credited as background singers on the album. In a first, the National Academy of Recording Arts and Sciences rescinded Milli Vanilli's Grammy Award on November 19. The duo's label, Arista Records, claimed it had not known of the deception, but Milli Vanilli and their former manager claimed Arista had known all along. The performers had been criticized earlier for using canned vocals during concerts.

England exported a number of successful dance-oriented acts in 1990, including Soul II Soul, which not only incorporated elements of rap and reggae into its music, but packaged itself as a fashion statement. Lisa Stansfield's successful debut, *Affection*, drew heavily upon the smooth, Philadelphia style of soul that was popular in the early 1970s.

Kid Power. The group New Kids on the Block enjoyed the financial windfall of the year, with its *Hangin' Tough* album reviving the sales of earlier efforts, and young girls gobbling up concert tickets and souvenirs at an astounding rate. The success of the New Kids underscored the value of savvy marketing. Their mentor, Maurice Starr, had found similar success in the early 1980s with another youthful group, New Edition. Just as New Edition was modeled on the Jackson 5, so the New Kids were fashioned after New Edition.

Speaking of kids, one of the most successful debut albums of the year was the self-titled effort by Wilson Phillips, a female trio consisting of Wendy and Carnie Wilson, the daughters of Brian Wilson of the Beach Boys, and Chynna Phillips, the daughter of John and Michelle Phillips of the Mamas and the Papas. Where their parents were '60s groundbreakers, the trio was emblematic of the trend toward young performers who feature a carefully manicured style. The singer Mariah Carey, whose successful debut covered the dance-and-ballad territory of Whitney Houston, was another case in point.

Two Independent Women. Two of the year's most heartening success stories involved extremely independent women. Sinead O'Connor is a young woman from Ireland with a shaved head and a voice as powerfully arresting as her highly personal songs. Her interpretation of a song written by Prince, "Nothing Compares 2 U," made her second album, *I Do Not Want What I Haven't Got*, one of 1990's biggest hits, and O'Connor one of the decade's newest stars.

Bonnie Raitt has been making fine, blues-based music for two decades, but it was not until she walked away with four Grammy Awards in 1990 that the mass audience caught wind of what her fans have known for years. Her album of the year award for *Nick of Time* sent the record to the top of the charts after it had reached an earlier peak of Number 22. Raitt's sweeping victory, at age 40, was sweet vindication for the artist, and for an older audience which knows that pop music is not just for the very young. (*See also* BIOGRAPHY.)

Deaths. The rock world mourned the loss of Stevie Ray Vaughan, a fiery 36-year-old blues-rock guitarist, who died in an August helicopter crash hours after appearing in concert with two of his instrumental peers, Eric Clapton and Robert Cray. Veteran rock singer Del Shannon, known from such early '60s hits as "Runaway" and "Hats Off to Larry," took his own life at the age of 50.

And Sammy Davis, Jr., who died at age 64, though famous for doing a bit of everything, included 19 chart singles in his resume. (*See also* OBITUARIES.)

Country. Lyle Lovett and k.d. lang won Grammys for male and female country vocals. What was unusual was that, while both artists have won an audience among sophisticated pop fans, they are considered commercial underachievers within the country genre. Unlike Lovett and lang, with their hipster attitudes, the new stars of Nashville cut a much more familiar figure.

Pundits call them "the hats"—male singers who have come in the wake of Randy Travis and George Strait and perform similarly traditional songs about the enduring themes of love won and love lost. Artists like Garth Brooks, Travis Tritt, and Alan Jackson fit this mold, but the biggest new star of them all is Clint Black, whose debut album, *Killin' Time*, spent most of the year at the top of the country charts. The title tune, about an abandoned lover bellying up to the bar, sounded like a country classic the day it was released.

Jazz. In the past few years, the major story in jazz has been the studied classicism of younger players like trumpeter Wynton Marsalis and his saxophone-playing brother, Branford. For much of the previous two decades, young players had been drawn to various jazz-rock fusion styles. By contrast, the new breed of neotraditionalist is steeped in the history of jazz, from its flowering in New Orleans to its explosive growth in the hands of bebop masters like Charlie Parker and Dizzy Gillespie.

Now the jazz world is bursting with youthful talent, with many new players making names for themselves. One of these is pianist Marcus Roberts. Blind since age 4, he played with Wynton Marsalis from 1985 until 1989, when he formed his own group. Roberts' latest album, titled *Deep in the Shed*, hit number 1 on the Billboard jazz chart in 1990.

A pair of alto saxophonists, Wessell Anderson and Christopher Hollyday, also were making themselves known in the jazz world. Hollyday, only 20 years old, has been playing publicly since he was 13. At first patterning himself after such greats as Charlie Parker, Hollyday now is developing his own distinctive style.

Another budding talent is guitarist Mark Whitfield. George Benson, impressed with Whitfield's playing and his potential, helped him get a record contract, and Whitfield released his debut album, *The Marksman*, to good reviews.

New Orleans-born Harry Connick, Jr., 23, at first primarily a pianist, has found success as a singer and bandleader as well.

Although these musicians generally have failed as yet to make innovative artistic statements, their already seasoned chops have given them an essential leg up on becoming truly original artists.

Jazz lost two great voices in 1990. Sarah Vaughan, one of the greatest vocalists jazz ever has known, died at age 66. Known to friends and fans as "Sass," she had a voice fit for opera, an improvisatory ability perfect for jazz, and a melodic sensibility that made her a benchmark interpreter of standards.

Dexter Gordon, a tenor saxophonist known for his hearty inflection and headlong rhythms, died at 67. Gordon, who bridged the eras of Charlie Parker and John Coltrane, gained some mainstream attention after starring in the film *'Round Midnight*, a tale of the jazz life that was based loosely on his life story.

The jazz world also was saddened by the death at age 71 of drummer and bandleader Art Blakey. Blakey, leader of the Jazz Messengers since the late 1940s, had a tremendous influence on the way modern jazz is played, and has been called a one-man university for young jazz players. Among the musicians he hired and influenced were Woody Shaw, Wayne Shorter, Bobby Timmons, and Wynton and Branford Marsalis.

JOHN MILWARD
Free-lance Writer and Critic

MYANMAR

There is a surreal quality to reporting on Burma. It changed its name to Myanmar, but few call it anything but Burma. It changed its official leadership several times in the period 1988–90, but most Burmese specialists considered that Gen. U Ne Win, who "retired" in 1988, still was making the decisions for the military government of Saw Maung in 1990. It changed its economic system from isolationism to one welcoming foreign investment, but its repressive politics made most governments reluctant to trade or invest in the country. Finally, the nation had a remarkably free election on May 27, its first multiparty election in three decades. At least the voting was fair, even if the number one opposition leader Aung Sang Suu Kyi and 400 supporters remained under arrest. The opposition parties won a landslide victory of 392 of the 485 seats. But by late 1990, the victors still were without power, their leader still was arrested, and the military was firmly in power.

Clearly the military was astounded by the winning appeal of the National League for Democracy (NLD) to the electorate. Preelection activities had been muted. Silent protests had consisted of wearing the NLD's symbol of the bamboo hat while tying rice sheaves (symbol of the military-endorsed National Unity Party) to one's feet.

The ruling State Law and Order Restoration Council (SLORC) could not deny that the opposition had won the election. But it then proceeded to define "victory." In July the SLORC announced its sequence of political conditions. A new constitution must precede any new government. The National Assembly just elected would have as its only role the submission of a draft constitution for SLORC approval. That draft was to be based on guidelines from a SLORC convention. A referendum on the new constitution then would follow. Other military accounts suggested different scenarios—each without a timetable. The whole process could take years.

The NLD and another opposition party, the United Nationalities League for Democracy, were working on a coalition agreement, but both seemed unwilling to risk the bloodshed that might accompany a more activist stance. Students and other elements of the opposition might force their hand. U.S. Secretary of State James Baker and Australian Foreign Minister Gareth Evans also called on the government to transfer power.

The government probably was concerned more about the reliability of the armed forces, particularly the naval forces, since the opposition won easily even in some military containment areas. The enormous public-works program initiated before the election did not appear to have impressed the citizenry. As September 18, the second anniversary of the military crackdown, approached, more NLD leaders were arrested and student rebels protested in Mandalay. The massed presence of the army kept the situation under control.

Ethnic Unrest. Sporadic fighting against nearly a dozen minority groups that have held de facto control of nearly half of the nation's territory for 45 years continued. The ethnic minorities reportedly have financed their war against the Burman majority through the opium trade. In 1990 the government had considerable military success with Thailand's cooperation against the ethnic Karens.

The Economy. Myanmar continued the economic slide of the previous two years despite a record level of contracts with foreign businesses. The regime rejected the discredited Burmese Way to Socialism and embraced the theory if not the reality of economic interdependence. Ironically, Myanmar's change of economic direction in 1988 was accompanied almost immediately by a vicious crackdown on the nation's fledgling prodemocracy movement. The human-rights abuses that followed led to the cessation of aid and reduction of contacts between Western governments and the new regime. Gradually some nations, especially Thailand, Japan, China, and South Korea, began doing business with the government, but there was more trade than foreign investment.

Moreover, Myanmar oil, timber, fishing rights, and other resources have been sold at fire-sale prices to keep the nearly bankrupt government afloat. Draconian controls on prices for rice and gas led to hoarding, while at the same time the government had to allow the black market to operate with relative impunity if the economy was to function. The official 1990 exchange rate was six to seven kyats for U.S.$1. The unofficial black-market rate was more than 55 per U.S.$1. The government made tourism a priority and now allowed closely monitored visits of up to two weeks. About 42,000 tourists visited in 1989.

LINDA K. RICHTER, *Kansas State University*

MYANMAR • Information Highlights

Official Name: Union of Myanmar.
Location: Southeast Asia.
Area: 261,969 sq mi (678 500 km²).
Population (mid-1990 est.): 41,300,000.
Chief Cities (1983 est.): Yangon (Rangoon), the capital, 2,458,712; Mandalay, 532,895.
Government: *Head of government,* Gen. Saw Maung (took power Sept. 18, 1988). *Legislature* (unicameral)—National Assembly.
Monetary Unit: Kyat (6.331 kyats equal U.S.$1, July 1990).
Gross Domestic Product (1988 est. U.S.$): $11,000,-000,000.
Economic Index (Rangoon, July 1989): *Consumer Prices* (1980 = 100), all items, 279.1; food, 302.8.
Foreign Trade (1989 U.S.$): *Imports,* $191,000,000; *exports,* $215,000,000.

© J. Isaac/UN Photo

South Africa's President F. W. de Klerk (right) congratulates Sam Nujoma, the president of the new Republic of Namibia. A crowd of 20,000 people, including representatives from some 70 nations, witnessed the March 21, 1990 ceremonies.

NAMIBIA

At midnight on March 21, 1990, delegations from many of the world's nations witnessed the formal transfer of political power from South Africa to the newly independent Republic of Namibia. As the South African flag was lowered and the red, blue, and green flag of Namibia raised, South Africa's President F.W. de Klerk formally relinquished control of the region after 75 years of South African domination. Sam Nujoma, leader of the South West African People's Organization (SWAPO), was sworn in as the country's first president by United Nations Security General Javier Pérez de Cuéllar. Africa's last colony had been liberated.

The Road to Independence. The process leading to this momentous day had been complicated and drawn out. Between Nov. 7–11, 1989, elections were held for a Namibian constituent assembly, which was to draft a constitution and set the date for independence. In the elections, SWAPO received more than 57% of the votes cast, winning 41 of the 72 seats in the assembly, just short of the two-thirds majority needed to enable it to have a free hand in writing the country's constitution. The constituent assembly was convened for the first time in November 1989. The constitution was adopted unanimously on Feb. 9, 1990.

The Government. Namibia's constitution established it as a multiparty democracy: a re-public with a voting system based on proportional representation, a bill of fundamental human rights, and an independent judiciary. The executive president serves as head of state and governs with the aid of a council of ministers or cabinet. Presidents are restricted to two five-year terms of office. The legislative body, the National Assembly, comprises former members of the constituent assembly.

The government sought to allay the fears of Namibia's 11 major ethnic groups, as well as its 80,000 whites, and to reconcile the various factions by naming to the first cabinet individuals of different ethnic backgrounds, including opposition-party leaders. To ease further the fears of whites, who still controlled most of the economy, President Nujoma on February 9 named a white businessman, Gert Hanekon, minister of agriculture.

The Economy. Namibia continued to be dependent on South Africa for much of its food and investment. In keeping with SWAPO's pragmatic approach, Finance Minister Otto Herrigel announced on February 8 that Namibia would remain in the South African Customs Union (SACU) and that the South African currency, the rand, would remain legal tender for at least two years after independence.

During the independence celebrations, President Nujoma invited foreign investment in Namibia. "We are committed to a mixed economy," he stated. "In this regard, we look forward to a good partnership between the state

NAMIBIA • Information Highlights

Official Name: Republic of Namibia.
Location: Southwestern coast of Africa.
Area: 318,259 sq mi (824 290 km²).
Population (mid-1990 est.): 1,500,000.
Chief City (December 1988): Windhoek, the capital, 114,500.
Government: *Head of state and head of government,* Sam Nujoma, president (sworn in March 1990). *Legislature*—National Assembly.
Monetary Unit: South African rand (2.5725 rands equal U.S.$1, Dec. 31, 1990).
Gross National Product (1987 U.S.$): $1,540,000,-000.

and the private sectors, because only through working together will our economy prosper." It was considered significant that President Nujoma made no reference to nationalization of industries or to land redistribution, two policies that SWAPO originally had endorsed. The new nation inherited a budget deficit of more than $200 million and even larger debts were owed to South Africa. Furthermore, South Africa withdrew its annual 200-million-rand (about $80 million) subsidy. Namibia received pledges in excess of $300 million in development assistance from foreign donors. But with high unemployment (estimated at 30%) and average per-capita income barely more than $1,000 per year, the new nation faced serious economic problems.

Total exports from Namibia in 1988 were $850 million, but the processing of such important products as diamonds, beef, lamb pelts, and fish all took place outside the country. The president, in his independence speech, emphasized that the country now would have to start processing the raw materials that it previously had exported directly.

The Future. Nujoma and his government must address demands by Namibians for better health services (made worse by years of war), land resettlement (85% of the land remains in white hands), and reform of an educational system where a majority of the teachers are underqualified. It would take all of the political skills he and his government could muster.

PATRICK O'MEARA
and N. BRIAN WINCHESTER
Indiana University

NEBRASKA

Tax issues and the 1990 election created one of the most controversial political seasons in Nebraska in recent years.

Finances. In April the legislature passed a bill to increase state school support by raising the sales tax 25% and the income tax 17.5%, with the understanding that local property taxes then would be lowered. Gov. Kay Orr vetoed the bill, arguing that it did not guarantee property-tax relief, but the legislature overrode the veto. A group opposing the bill then mounted a petition drive for repeal; in the November election, however, the voters decided by a 56% to 44% margin to retain the new school-financing method.

An even more controversial issue was a proposal, also on the ballot by petition, to limit annual state and local government budget increases to 2%. Citizens' groups joined business, labor, and government leaders to arouse the public to the consequences of so stringent a limit, and the voters rejected the lid by a vote of more than two to one.

Governor's Race. The year's most hotly contested election was that for governor. Incumbent Kay Orr won the Republican primary against only one challenger, but the Democrats had seven candidates in their primary, with a near tie between the top two. A month of recounts revealed the closest primary race in the state's history: Ben Nelson had defeated Bill Hoppner by 42 votes out of more than 89,000 cast.

The fall campaign was criticized widely for its negative character; even the candidates agreed that the campaign was one of the nastiest in their state's history—though each claimed the other was responsible. President George Bush, former President Ronald Reagan, and Vice-President Dan Quayle all campaigned for Kay Orr's reelection, and a series of TV debates heightened the tension. When the votes were in, the race proved to be another squeaker, and for three days there was talk of a recount. Nelson finally was named the winner when absentee ballots gave him a lead of barely more than 1% over Governor Orr.

Republican Concerns. With the reelection of Democratic Sen. J.J. Exon, Jr., Nebraska Republicans had to face the fact of a serious decline in their fortunes in a state which long has been considered a Republican stronghold. The Democrats now held four of the six state offices, both U.S. Senate seats, and one of the three seats in the U.S. House of Representatives. Two Republicans—Congressman Doug

NEBRASKA • Information Highlights

Area: 77,355 sq mi (200 350 km²).
Population (1990 census prelim.): 1,573,000.
Chief Cities (July 1, 1988 est.): Lincoln, the capital, 187,890; Omaha, 353,170.
Government (1990): *Chief Officers*—governor, Kay Orr (R); lt. gov., William E. Nichol (R). *Legislature* (unicameral)—49 members (nonpartisan).
State Finances (fiscal year 1989): *Revenue,* $2,864,000,000; *expenditure,* $2,559,000,000.
Personal Income (1989): $24,885,000,000; per capita, $15,446.
Labor Force (June 1990): *Civilian labor force,* 858,500; *unemployed,* 17,300 (2.0% of total force).
Education: *Enrollment* (fall 1988)—public elementary schools, 191,302; public secondary, 78,132; colleges and universities, 104,617. *Public school expenditures* (1989–90), $1,137,142,000.

Bereuter, who won reelection with 65% of the vote, and Omaha Mayor P. J. Morgan—promptly called for the Republican Party to chart a more moderate course and announced their intent to provide leadership in that direction. On the positive side for the GOP, Bill Barrett, speaker of the state legislature, was chosen to succeed retiring U.S. Rep. Virginia Smith (R) in the 3d District.

Economy. The economic recovery of the late 1980s continued. Although the prolonged drought clearly was not ended, rain was more abundant than in the preceding two years. Crops were good, farmland values continued to rise, and Nebraska's unemployment rate of 2.3% was one of the lowest in the nation. Conservationists and environmentalists were heartened by news that plans for the controversial Two Forks Dam in Colorado, which would threaten wildlife on the Platte River, had been vetoed by the U.S. Environmental Protection Agency.

WILLIAM E. CHRISTENSEN
Midland Lutheran College

NEPAL

The mountainous kingdom of Nepal underwent dramatic political changes during 1990. King Birendra Bir Bikram Shah Dev relinquished near-absolute executive powers in response to sustained popular protest. The remarkably rapid transformation was accompanied by major economic as well as political challenges.

Political Developments. Protests against the monarch began in January, precipitated by the perceived mishandling of negotiations regarding trade and transit agreements with India, but complaints included palace involvement in politics, corruption, and the 30-year ban on political parties. Following six weeks of intense protest and the deaths of an estimated 500 demonstrators, King Birendra made several positive responses to the various demands of the movement.

On April 6 he dismissed Prime Minister Marich Man Singh Shrestha, lifted the ban on political parties, and opened negotiations with the leaders of the protest. On April 8 he agreed to the elimination of the *panchayat* system, the structure of nonparty councils through which he and his father had run the country since 1960. Press censorship was lifted, a multiparty committee was formed to write a new constitution, and popular elections were promised. K.P. Bhattarai, acting president of the Nepali Congress, was sworn in as prime minister of a new coalition government on April 18.

A draft constitution was issued in September, providing for a multiparty system and a bicameral parliament, as well as an independent judiciary, civilian control of the army,

---

NEPAL • Information Highlights

Official Name: Kingdom of Nepal.
Location: South Asia.
Area: 54,363 sq mi (140 800 km²).
Population (mid-1990 est.): 19,100,000.
Chief City (1981 census): Kathmandu, the capital, 235,160.
Government: *Head of state,* Birendra Bir Bikram Shah Dev, king (acceded Jan. 31, 1972); *Head of government,* K.P. Bhattarai, prime minister (sworn in April 18, 1990). *Legislature*—National Assembly.
Monetary Unit: Rupee (29.4 rupees equal U.S.$1, buying rate, August 1990).
Gross Domestic Product (1989 U.S.$): $2,900,000,-000.
Foreign Trade (1989 U.S.$): *Imports,* $580,-000,000; *exports,* $156,000,000.

---

freedom of the press, and universal suffrage over age 18. Parliamentary elections for a House of Representatives of 175 members were scheduled for April 1991.

Foreign Relations. Nepal's internal crisis was intertwined heavily with its relations with its neighbor, India. In recent years, Nepal sought to balance India's presence by cultivating relations with the country's other giant neighbor, the People's Republic of China. After negotiations with India to renew existing trade and transit agreements failed, India closed all but two of Nepal's land outlets to the south, virtually blockading the landlocked country. Indian politicians also participated in rallies in Nepal to focus on the rising discontent with the monarchy.

In June, Prime Minister Bhattarai and India's Prime Minister V. P. Singh agreed to restore the previous trade and transit arrangements, pending wider negotiations on relations between the two countries. India's claims to a "special relationship" with Nepal were expected to continue to clash with Nepali aspirations to national sovereignty.

The United States and other foreign countries largely welcomed Nepal's moves toward democratization, although the Chinese appeared somewhat wary about the implications for rival India's influence in the region.

The Economy. One of the world's poorest nations, Nepal suffered additional economic hardships as a result of its political problems. Growth slowed and inflation soared, to as much as 25% in the Kathmandu Valley. Halting the import of heating oil from India led to further environmental degradation. Deforestation and damage to the environment reached crisis proportions. Tourism, the country's largest foreign-exchange earner, also suffered in the wake of the violence and instability. Carpets, however, remained a strong export item and remittances from workers abroad were a solid asset.

WILLIAM L. RICHTER
Kansas State University

NETHERLANDS, THE

The year 1990 was an unusually calm one for the Netherlands. The end of the Cold War and the startling changes in Eastern Europe and the Soviet Union removed the principal subject of disagreement among the Dutch on foreign policy: the question of how to maintain peace without stumbling into nuclear war.

Politics. The new cabinet formed in 1989 by a coalition of the Christian Democratic Party (CDA) and the Labor Party (PvdA) continued under the leadership of Rudolf (Ruud) Lubbers of the CDA, who has been prime minister of the Netherlands since 1982. Lubbers' collaboration with his new vice-premier and finance minister, PvdA leader Willem Kok, ran smoothly, as Kok, a former trade-union official, guided Dutch finances with a cautious hand. A wage conflict with hospital nurses was settled by modest pay increases. Local elections in March, with a low turnout of voters, showed a significant shift from the Labor Party to the "Democrats '66," a progressive party not linked to the labor movement.

Economic Affairs. Farmers demonstrated against government attempts to hold down subsidies for agriculture in line with European Community (EC) policy; the government responded with a commitment to spend an additional 100 million guilders (about $53 million) to support agriculture in 1991. Agriculture and Fisheries Minister Gerrit Braks resigned after seven years in that post when it was discovered that his department had falsified figures on the fish catch.

Industry in general prepared for increased competition when the planned unification of the EC market takes place in 1992. The biggest firm in the country, Philips, world-famous for such innovative products as the audiotape cassette and the video camera, abandoned its efforts to become an effective producer of electronic chips. Philips already had sold off its European market in household appliances, and began to reduce its work force. Both agriculture and industry had to cope with increasingly stringent efforts to reduce environmental pollution, especially excessive use of fertilizers and pesticides in farming and waste storage in industry.

Nonetheless overall unemployment, which had been rising toward the figure of 1 million, dropped during the year by about 10%. A surprise development was the discovery that a much larger percentage of Dutch workers, who have a relatively high level of benefits, took sick leave or retirement than workers in other European countries.

Drug Policy. Premier Lubbers voiced concern over criminality linked in particular to drug addiction and the difficulties of immigrant populations. Many reports indicate, however, that the problem of drug-related crime has declined in the Netherlands, and this decline has been linked to the national policy on narcotics control. "Soft" drugs such as marijuana are available freely, and drug addiction in general is considered to be more of a medical than a legal problem. Dutch authorities argue that this permissive policy reduces incentives for criminal behavior by drug users.

Other. Differences developed between the Christian Democrats and the Labor Party over proposals to break the link between wages in the private sector and government entitlement payments. The restructuring of higher education continued, with further limitations upon government subsidies for university students. A proposed measure to introduce English as a language of instruction in the universities reflected anxieties in the country over the status of the national language, which is limited almost totally to the Dutch and their Flemish neighbors in Belgium.

HERBERT H. ROWEN, *Rutgers University*

NEVADA

The election of acting Gov. Bob Miller (D) to a full term, the passage of an initiative to protect Nevada's abortion law, and continued rapid growth in the state's economy and population dominated the news in 1990.

Politics. Bob Miller, who became acting governor in January 1989 when Gov. Richard Bryan moved to the U.S. Senate, was elected to a full term with 65% of the vote, defeating Republican Jim Gallaway. Women were elected to three of the six state offices. Republicans Sue Wagner and Cheryl Lau were elected lieutenant governor and secretary of state, respectively, while Democrat Frankie Sue Del Papa won the attorney general's race. Democrats gained control of the state Senate by an 11-to-10 margin, while retaining control of the Assembly (22–20). The 1989 legislature had a 13-to-8 GOP majority in the Senate, while Democrats controlled 30 to 12 in the Assembly.

Incumbents from both parties did poorly in Clark County where the local newspapers had made a continued issue out of the 300% pension increase the legislature voted itself over Governor Miller's veto during the 1989 session and subsequently rescinded during a 1989 special session of the legislature. Nevada's two U.S. representatives, James Bilbray (D) and Barbara Vucanovich (R), were reelected easily.

Initiatives and Referendums. After a divisive campaign, voters overwhelmingly passed a referendum supporting the state's law allowing abortion for any reason during the first two trimesters of pregnancy. The legislature now may not change the laws on abortion without another vote of the people. The possibility of new taxes did not fare so well. An initiative amendment to the state constitution forbidding a personal income tax won with 72% of the vote and a corporate income tax was defeated. A state lottery for charitable purposes received the first of two required votes of approval.

Economy. The state continued its economic boom. During the third quarter of 1990, Nevada led the nation with a tax-revenue increase of 26.3%. Gross gaming revenue was up 15.45% in June, while taxable sales increased by 13.61%. In July the unemployment rate dropped to 4.6%.

The state budget surplus for the 1989–91 biennium was projected at $150 million, dampening the likelihood that a general tax increase would be needed during the 1991 legislative session.

Other Issues. The impact of growth was in the forefront as Nevada led the nation with 49% population growth during the 1980s and a 6.56% growth rate from July 1988 to July 1989. The Clark County school district, which includes Las Vegas, was bursting at the seams and hired more than 1,000 new teachers for the 1990–91 school year.

Water also was an issue as Las Vegas planned to import water from scarcely populated counties to its north and Congress passed

legislation finally settling a 100-year-old water dispute in the north. The legislation divided the water of the Truckee and Carson Rivers and Lake Tahoe between California and Nevada, while still providing preservation safeguards for Pyramid Lake.

TIMOTHY G. HALLER
Western Nevada Community College

NEW BRUNSWICK

Fallout from the collapse of the Meech Lake accord, which was aimed at bringing Quebec into the Canadian constitutional fold, dominated much of New Brunswick news in 1990. Government fiscal policies largely were shaped by the looming recession.

Post-Meech Options. Premier Frank McKenna announced on September 10 the establishment of a nine-member commission to study New Brunswick's constitutional options. He said that New Brunswick could not be left behind while Quebec and other provinces were launching their post-Meech strategies. McKenna had been the first provincial premier to raise objections to the accord—soon after he was elected in 1987—but joined the federal government in a futile attempt to save it in 1990.

On September 12, McKenna suggested a form of common market for the three Maritime provinces as a further hedge against future uncertainties. "It is my conclusion that the Maritimes must begin to operate on the basis of a single economic unit," he told a meeting of businessmen in Moncton. The time had come to create a single integrated market of more than 1.5 million people, "and coordinate our strategic objectives so that we speak with a single voice at national and international levels."

The early response to his proposal from Nova Scotia and Prince Edward Island was a massive silence.

Cautious Budget. Finance Minister Allan Maher presented a hold-the-line budget to the legislature March 27, proposing no major tax increases. The budget projected expenditures of C$3.7 billion—up 6.5% from the previous year—and a tiny operating surplus of less than C$4 million. However, five months after the unveiling of the budget, government figures projected a C$19.6 million deficit. Maher blamed the economic slowdown, resulting in reduced tax revenues, for much of the sudden slippage.

Health-Care Costs Reduced. One month after Maher's budget was presented, Health Minister Ray Frenette launched a campaign to pare the billion-dollar cost of New Brunswick's health-care programs. Fees would be cut for highly-paid doctors and for new doctors settling in cities; total Medicare payments to physicians would be capped; and about 300 beds

---

NEVADA · Information Highlights

Area: 110,561 sq mi (286 352 km²).
Population (1990 census prelim.): 1,193,000.
Chief Cities (July 1, 1988 est.): Carson City, the capital (1980 census), 32,022; Las Vegas, 210,620; Reno, 115,130.
Government (1990): *Chief Officer*—governor, Robert J. Miller (D). *Legislature*—Senate, 21 members; Assembly, 42 members.
State Finances (fiscal year 1989): *Revenue,* $2,784,000,000; *expenditure,* $2,532,000,000.
Personal Income (1989): $21,403,000,000; per capita, $19,269.
Labor Force (June 1990): *Civilian labor force,* 624,800; *unemployed,* 30,600 (4.9% of total force).
Education: *Enrollment* (fall 1988)—public elementary schools, 127,414; public secondary, 49,060; colleges and universities, 48,832. *Public school expenditures* (1989–90), $681,492,000.

would be removed from hospitals over a five-year period as more community-based programs are put in place.

Help for Northeast. The federal and provincial governments signed a C$36 million, five-year economic diversification agreement at Shippegan, on New Brunswick's depressed northeast shore, on August 16. Most of the money—C$28 million—was earmarked for the so-called Acadian Peninsula, where Shippegan, Caraquet, and other economically distressed fishing towns are located.

Star-Kist Closes. Star-Kist Canada announced May 17 that it was closing its trouble-plagued tuna plant at St. Andrews. About 250 people were thrown out of work. Slumping world tuna prices were given as the reason for the closing. The plant never had recovered fully from the so-called tainted tuna scandal in 1985, which had forced it to close for three years.

JOHN BEST, *"Canada World News"*

NEWFOUNDLAND

The Canadian constitution and provincial fish and oil industries dominated the political and economic life of Newfoundland in 1990.

Meech Lake Accord. The Meech Lake accord constitutional amendment, seen as the culmination of the "Quebec Round" which would grant Quebec special status, had to be ratified by all ten provinces by June 23, 1990. But in April, Newfoundland's one-year-old Progressive Conservative government, led by Premier Clyde Wells, fulfilled an election promise by rescinding the province's previous approval of the accord. In doing so, Wells became the unofficial spokesman for those holding anti-Meech positions.

The resulting controversy culminated in the establishment of a parliamentary committee to consider amendments to the accord, followed in early June by an informal meeting between Prime Minister Brian Mulroney and the provincial premiers in an attempt to reach agreement.

At the end of these meetings, Wells announced a "free vote" in the provincial legislature whereby members, freed of party whips, could vote their conscience on the issue. However, the vote never was taken. The resulting failure of the Meech Lake accord meant that Canada had entered into a new and difficult period of English-French relations. Wells was blamed by some for his outspoken opposition to the accord.

Fishing Industry. During 1990 serious problems occurred in the Atlantic fishing industry; these hit Newfoundland particularly hard due to the overwhelming importance of fishing to the province's economy. In January the federal minister of fisheries announced overall cuts in the quantity of fish that safely could be caught. The quota for northern cod was cut to 197,000 metric tons from 235,000, and there were fishery biologists who recommended a quota of only 125,000 metric tons. Such levels had a devastating effect throughout the region as processors announced either the closing of plants or considerable downtime for both trawlers and plant workers.

In May the federal government announced a package of relief proposals amounting to C$584 million over five years, aimed at reducing the provincial economy's dependence on the fisheries. But the unemployment-insurance program did not change its rules to accommodate fishermen until October.

One of the largest processors in the region, National Sea Products Ltd., in July announced the closing of plants in Burgeo, Nfld., and Canso, N.S., affecting two towns completely dependent on the fishery. The plants were sold to a new company whose economic health was encouraged by the transfer to it of thousands of tons of "underutilized" Canadian fish for bartering purposes with Soviet trawlers.

Hibernia Oil Field. The story of the long-delayed Hibernia oil field was climaxed on September 15 with the signing of detailed contracts allowing the multibillion-dollar project to go ahead. Earlier in the year it had been feared that both the Hibernia project and hydro projects in Labrador would be stalled by the failure of the Meech Lake accord. In fact, in July the federal government had withdrawn consideration of legislation regarding Hibernia financing when Quebec members of Parliament (MPs) threatened to obstruct the bill's passage. But by September cooler tempers and the promise of "spin-off" industrial impacts in both Ontario and Quebec had persuaded governments and consortium members that the project could go ahead.

There was considerable doubt in both government and academic circles, however, that Hibernia would be a positive development for Newfoundland. The 6,000 jobs in the province associated with the platform construction would do much to relieve unemployment, but some thought the financial and tax arrangements would not aid Newfoundland in becoming a more prosperous province.

SUSAN MCCORQUODALE
Memorial University of Newfoundland

NEW HAMPSHIRE

During 1990 the overriding concern in New Hampshire was recession. An unemployment rate that had gained the envy of the nation when it was as low as 3% escalated from 4.5% in January to a seven-year high of 6.1% in June, before dropping to 5.3% in August. Elsewhere, too, it was obvious that the boom years of the 1980s were ended. There were increases in individual and business bankruptcies, real-estate auctions, and a glut of homes for sale. New construction had declined and in late October one of the state's largest bank-holding companies, BankEast Corp., filed for bankruptcy.

State Shortfall. The economic downturn brought an estimated $160 million shortfall in state revenues forcing layoffs for 250 state workers, reductions in state spending, and, despite its unpopularity, an increase in taxes for cigarettes, beer, telecommunications, and hotel rooms and meals. Despite the new tax, as well as reductions in spending, the state still ended the fiscal year with an estimated $25 million deficit.

Tax Debates and Elections. These economic issues became the focus of much of the debate among the candidates for state and national office. In the governor's race, J. Joseph Grandmaison (D) called for tax reform, while Gov. Judd Gregg (R) pledged not to consider any broad-based tax. Dramatic increases in local property taxes resulted in taxpayer revolts in cities such as Franklin and Laconia. The cutback in state funding placed more burden on the towns and cities, prompting some candi-

---

NEW HAMPSHIRE • Information Highlights

Area: 9,279 sq mi (24 032 km²).
Population (1990 census prelim.): 1,103,000.
Chief Cities (1980 census): Concord, the capital, 30,400; Manchester, 90,936; Nashua, 67,865.
Government (1990): *Chief Officer*—governor, Judd Gregg (R). *General Court*—Senate, 24 members; House of Representatives, 400 members.
State Finances (fiscal year 1989): *Revenue,* $1,840,000,000; *expenditure,* $1,851,000,000.
Personal Income (1989): $22,441,000,000; per capita, $20,267.
Labor Force (June 1990): *Civilian labor force,* 635,600; *unemployed,* 38,900 (6.1% of total force).
Education: *Enrollment* (fall 1988)—public elementary schools, 119,785; public secondary, 49,628; colleges and universities, 55,334. *Public school expenditures* (1989–90), $896,420,000.

dates to question the fairness of relying so heavily on the property tax.

Despite the gloomy economic news, political pundits predicted a solid Republican victory in the elections, but voters sent a mixed message. As predicted, Gregg won reelection easily, capturing 63% of the vote. Incumbent U.S. Rep. Robert Smith (R), running for the U.S. Senate seat being vacated by Gordon Humphrey (R), also was victorious, with 67% of the vote. In the races for the U.S. House of Representatives, however, the pundits fared badly. The supposedly close race between Bill Zeliff (R) and Joseph F. Keefe (D) turned into an easy ten-point victory for Zeliff, and in the race between conservative incumbent Chuck Douglas (R) and newcomer Dick Swett (D), Swett won with 53% of the vote in a district that last elected a Democrat in 1912. Potentially more meaningful were Democratic gains in the state Senate. The Republican margin of 16–8 was reduced to 13 Republicans and 11 Democrats. Many of the new senators favor tax reform.

Other News. Several other items captured the headlines but none was more surprising than the nomination and confirmation of former New Hampshire Supreme Court Judge David Souter to the U.S. Supreme Court (*see* BIOGRAPHY). The Seabrook nuclear-power plant was still in the news, finally getting an operating license in March and reaching full generating capacity on July 19, a decade later than originally projected.

Planning for the future of Pease Air Force Base continued with the Pease Development Authority voting in November to apply for the transfer of the base at no cost to the state, an agreement that would require the state to continue operating the airport.

And finally, the largest attendance at any sporting event in the state's history occurred when 45,000 fans attended a national stock-car event at the refurbished New Hampshire International Speedway in Louden.

WILLIAM L. TAYLOR
Plymouth State College

Antitax sentiment was common throughout New Jersey during 1990 as the state's new governor, James J. Florio, proposed and the legislature narrowly passed major tax increases.

© Bradley Grois/"The Times," Trenton

NEW JERSEY

The activities of the new administration of Gov. James J. Florio, popular discontent with Florio's tax policies, and the autumn elections were dominant 1990 themes in New Jersey.

Governor Florio. Florio, a Democrat, was elected in 1989 by a substantial margin over his Republican opponent, Congressman James Courter. A congressman himself, Florio had for many years represented the 1st District, centered in Camden, and was known primarily for expertise on environmental issues. Unlike many politicians assuming a new position, Florio allowed himself no "honeymoon" period.

Illustrative of his approach was the way he dealt with New Jersey's automobile insurance problem. Over the years, a $3 billion debt had been incurred by the Joint Underwriting Association (J.U.A.), the state agency established to insure high-risk drivers. Shortly after his in-

auguration, Florio sent to the legislature a proposal that would reduce the debt by taxing the insurance companies and eliminate the $212 million annual payment made by drivers to support the J.U.A. The bill was enacted despite a lawsuit against New Jersey by Allstate Insurance. By accusing the big insurance companies of "ripping off" the public, Florio positioned himself as a foe of big business. Similarly, he berated Exxon Corporation for being environmentally irresponsible because of oil spills in the Arthur Kill.

Taxes. Beyond a doubt, Florio's most controversial moves involved taxation. To a large extent his tax program was devised as a response to existing budgetary problems and the growing gap in the quality of life between the wealthy suburbs and the blighted inner cities. The $500 million deficit in state spending had to be eliminated, since the New Jersey constitution mandates a balanced budget. Furthermore, a tax increase was made necessary by the state Supreme Court's decision in the case of *Abbott v. Burke*, which invalidated the property tax as a means of support for public schools and ordered equal funding for all school districts.

Florio and State Treasurer Douglas Berman sent to the legislature an austerity budget of $12.4 billion, replete with cutbacks in spending for education, welfare, and drug enforcement. At the same time, dramatic tax increases were called for, notably a doubling of the highest income-tax bracket, from 3.5% to 7% by 1992, and a 1% rise in the sales tax. The new taxes would yield $2.8 billion and would be used to subsidize less affluent school districts and eliminate property-tax increases for homeowners making less than $65,000. The measures were passed narrowly by both houses in June.

The new state taxes, combined with increased local property taxes necessitated by

---

NEW JERSEY • Information Highlights

Area: 7,787 sq mi (20 169 km^2).
Population (1990 census prelim.): 7,617,000.
Chief Cities (July 1, 1988 est.): Trenton, the capital (1980 census), 92,124; Newark, 313,800; Jersey City, 217,630; Paterson, 138,620; Elizabeth, 105,150.
Government (1990): *Chief Officers*—governor, James J. Florio (D); secretary of state, Joan Haberle (R). *Legislature*—Senate, 40 members; General Assembly, 80 members.
State Finances (fiscal year 1989): *Revenue,* $21,869,000,000; *expenditure,* $20,812,000,000.
Personal Income (1989): $183,943,000,000; per capita, $23,778.
Labor Force (June 1990): *Civilian labor force,* 4,082,900; *unemployed,* 191,400 (4.7% of total force).
Education: *Enrollment* (fall 1988)—public elementary schools, 755,073; public secondary, 325,798; colleges and universities, 302,640. *Public school expenditures* (1989–90), $7,868,000,000.

state cutbacks, were universally unpopular. Florio, who while campaigning for the governorship had said there was no need for new taxes, saw his approval rating drop to about 20%.

The Elections. At stake in the 1990 elections were Bill Bradley's U.S. Senate seat, the state's 14 congressional seats, and a few state Senate seats. With Florio's record the unspoken issue in all races, the Republicans seemed to have the advantage, but much of that was lost after President Bush accepted tax increases in the national budget. Even so, Bradley's Republican opponent, Christine Todd Whitman, chided him throughout the campaign for avoiding discussion of the tax question. Other Democratic candidates tried to disassociate themselves from the governor.

Election results, while favorable to incumbents, showed voter discontent with increased taxes. Bradley defeated Whitman by an unexpectedly narrow margin, and the postmortems held that voters were casting ballots against Florio indirectly. All 12 congressional incumbents won, and there was no party change in the 1st and 12th districts, held previously by Florio and Courter.

HERMANN K. PLATT, *St. Peter's College*

NEW MEXICO

Democrats fared well in the Nov. 6, 1990, elections in New Mexico. The party was victorious in the gubernatorial race, won one congressional seat, captured all the statewide executive offices, knocked a Republican off the state Supreme Court, and tightened its control in both legislative chambers.

Elections. Democrat Bruce King became the state's first governor to hold office in three decades with his victory over Republican Frank Bond. King, a rancher and businessman, first was elected governor in 1970 and again was chosen for the post in 1978. As 1990 drew to a close he was preparing for his third four-year term as chief executive. Because of a state constitutional change, he is eligible to seek another term in 1994.

In the state legislature, Democrats strengthened their hold by picking up one Senate seat and four in the House. Democrats hold a 26–16 advantage in the Senate and outnumber Republicans 49–21 in the House. However, Republicans held their edge in the state's U.S. congressional delegation with Republican Sen. Pete Domenici winning a fourth term and Joe Skeen and Steve Schiff remaining as Republican congressmen from the state. Rep. Bill Richardson gave the Democrats their only victory in the congressional races.

For the first time, voters were asked to rule on whether judges should keep their seats. Two Court of Appeals judges and 50 judicial district judges made the cut. Voters rejected five of the six bond issues on the ballot, including one to provide $45.7 million for a variety of construction projects at public schools and colleges. The only bond issue that passed gave $1.9 million for senior citizens' facilities statewide. Voters turned down four proposals to change the state constitution, including a measure that would have paid state lawmakers a salary.

In May, Democrats from New Mexico, Colorado, Arizona, Nevada, and Utah met to plan a 1992 regional presidential primary similar to the South's Super Tuesday.

The Environment. Environmentalists and their opponents clashed on several occasions in the state during 1990. Advocates for the Mexican gray wolf challenged the U.S. Fish and Wildlife Service to reintroduce the lobo to New Mexico. Opponents maintain the wolf kills livestock. In Taos environmentalists opposed a proposed disposal site for waste from a molybdenum mine, which has provided relatively high-paying jobs for several generations of Hispanic workers in an area of the state where the unemployment level exceeds 15%. In Los Ojos federal and state agencies, along with environmental and hunting groups, formed an unlikely alliance in opposing ranchers who sought to graze their sheep in an area where they would be competing for forage with more than 100 species of wildlife.

S&L Losses. In October, New Mexico savings and loans associations reported a collective second-quarter loss of $79.3 million and a total debt of nearly $1 billion. Losses for the first half of 1990 totaled more than $150 million —$130 million of that accounted for by five thrifts taken over by the government.

Billy the Kid. In June, Gov. Garrey Carruthers rejected a writer's request that Billy the Kid be pardoned for his role in the 1878 shooting death of Sheriff William Brady. Billy the Kid camped in New Mexico and was killed in a shoot-out in Lincoln County.

DORRAINE M. HARRIS, *Free-lance Writer*

NEW MEXICO • Information Highlights

Area: 121,593 sq mi (314 925 km²).

Population (1990 census prelim.): 1,490,000.

Chief Cities (1980 census): Santa Fe, the capital, 48,953; Albuquerque (July 1, 1988 est.): 378,480; Las Cruces, 45,086.

Government (1990): *Chief Officers*—governor, Garrey Carruthers (R); lt. gov., Jack L. Stahl (R). *Legislature*—Senate, 42 members; House of Representatives, 70 members.

State Finances (fiscal year 1989): *Revenue,* $4,596,000,000; *expenditure,* $3,962,000,000.

Personal Income (1989): $20,080,000,000; per capita, $13,140.

Labor Force (June 1990): *Civilian labor force,* 712,900; *unemployed,* 53,000 (7.4% of total force).

Education: *Enrollment* (fall 1988)—public elementary schools, 200,129; public secondary, 92,296; colleges and universities, 79,450. *Public school expenditures* (1989–90), $949,734,000.

NEW YORK

An economic decline in New York state, part of a downturn that affected other northeastern states, upended state fiscal policy and colored the politics of the Empire State in 1990. Despite the state's fiscal problems, voters in November reelected 98.9% of the state legislators on the ballot and gave Gov. Mario Cuomo a third term. Although not as large as some projected, Cuomo's victory led to continued speculation that he would emerge as the Democratic candidate for president in 1992.

Legislation. The state's economic travails were clear as Cuomo presented his $51.3 billion budget proposal for 1990–91 in January. Warning that economic forecasters saw declining tax revenues on the horizon, Cuomo proposed only a 4.5% increase in spending raised from state taxes and fees. With limited resources to spend, debate over spending priorities was intense among leaders of the Democrat-dominated Assembly and the Republican-led Senate. Arguments stalled budget action long past the April 1 start of the fiscal year. Finally, 49 days into the new fiscal year, lawmakers enacted a state budget. But the budget was balanced only after Cuomo and legislators approved $1.4 billion in new taxes and postponed a scheduled $400 million cut in the personal income tax. The $1.8 billion tax-hike package was the largest in state history; coming atop a $1.2 billion tax increase the year before, it seemed sure to provoke voters' anger.

Once the budget was approved, however, lawmakers set out to write a legislative record for the year that might win praise from constituent groups. They approved job-training programs, strengthened work requirements for able-bodied welfare recipients, and increased benefits for injured workers. They approved a health-care proxy bill, giving individuals the right to designate someone to make life-sustaining decisions for them in the event they are incapacitated. They created a new health-insurance program for poor children and capped the fees that physicians can charge elderly patients. Several other issues were debated but failed to win legislative support. Proposals to expand insurance available for AIDS victims were killed. A bill to ban assault rifles and enact tougher penalties for bias-related crime died in the Senate. Lawmakers also rejected bills to establish no-fault divorce and to require businesses to set family medical leave policies, and failed for the eighth straight year to override Cuomo's veto of the death penalty.

Politics. Despite the tax hikes, opinion polls showed that Cuomo was all but sure to win reelection. After more than a dozen better-known Republicans rejected the offer of the gubernatorial nomination, millionaire businessman and economist Pierre Rinfret agreed to challenge Cuomo. Rinfret, a 66-year-old Canadian-born Manhattanite, launched an unorthodox campaign that angered many longtime Republican stalwarts. He attacked GOP legislative leaders as strenuously as he did Cuomo and advocated a number of controversial steps, including selling New York City's subways and airports to private investors, arming 100,000 "vigilantes" to keep order in city streets, and chemically castrating rapists.

In the November 6 election, Rinfret polled the lowest percentage of votes of a Republican candidate in state history, garnering only 22% to Cuomo's 53.6%. Herbert London, a New York University dean who was the candidate of the small Conservative Party, drew 21% of the vote. Cuomo's margin, considerably diminished from the 65% of the vote he drew to win reelection in 1986, was enough to make him the first Democrat ever to win a third four-year term as governor of New York.

Voters overwhelmingly reelected Attorney General Robert Abrams, a Democrat, to a fourth term. Republican state Comptroller Edward Regan edged former New York City Council President Carol Bellamy by three percentage points to win his fourth term. Opposition upstate led to narrow rejection of an environmental bond proposal endorsed by Cuomo and the state legislative leadership, which would have allowed the state to borrow $1.975 billion to acquire environmentally fragile land and cope with the state's mounting garbage problem.

REX SMITH, *Albany Bureau Chief, "Newsday"*

NEW YORK · Information Highlights

Area: 49,108 sq mi (127 190 km²).
Population (1990 census prelim.): 17,627,000.
Chief Cities (July 1, 1988 est.): Albany, the capital, 101,727 (1980 census); New York, 7,352,700; Buffalo, 313,570; Rochester, 229,780; Yonkers, 183,080; Syracuse, 153,610.
Government (1990): *Chief Officers*—governor, Mario M. Cuomo (D); lt. gov., Stan Lundine (D). *Legislature*—Senate, 61 members; Assembly, 150 members.
State Finances (fiscal year 1989): *Revenue,* $60,678,000,000; *expenditure,* $54,073,000,000.
Personal Income (1989): $378,273,000,000; per capita, $21,073.
Labor Force (June 1990): *Civilian labor force,* 8,808,200; *unemployed,* 413,400 (4.7% of total force).
Education: *Enrollment* (fall 1988)—public elementary schools, 1,760,596; public secondary, 813,119; colleges and universities, 1,007,411. *Public school expenditures* (1989–90), $18,402,-000,000.

NEW YORK CITY

Crime and money wait for no mayor, at least they did not in New York City in 1990. On January 1, David N. Dinkins was inaugurated triumphally as the city's 106th mayor and the first black to hold that post, but two days

New York City's Mayor David N. Dinkins (center) inspects the scene of a Bronx, NY, social-club fire that killed 87 persons in March. During his inaugural year in office, the city's first black mayor faced severe problems related to an economic downturn and a high crime rate.

AP/Wide World

after he promised to be New York's "toughest mayor on crime," financial realities intruded—prompting Dinkins to delay the scheduled hiring of 1,848 police officers. Skeptics hailed the mayor for being fiscally prudent, but his responses to crime and to the consequences of an economic downturn would haunt him throughout his first year in office.

Crime. Events during 1990 made New York's preoccupation with crime seem well-founded, particularly: the deaths of 87 people in a Bronx social-club fire—the worst in the city since 1911—allegedly started by an ejected patron; a string of shootings laid to a gunman who called himself Zodiac and who appeared to single out targets by their astrological signs; the deaths of more than one dozen bystanders —many under the age of 16—in the crossfire of drug dealers; the fatal stabbing of a 22-year-old Utah tourist as he fought off youths who had robbed and attacked his mother; the November fatal shooting of an Israeli militant, Rabbi Meir Kahane; and a level of violence, much of it drug-related, that sent the number of murders verging toward a record of more than 2,000.

At the same time, New Yorkers attempted to put behind them two shocking 1989 crimes. In May a 19-year-old white man was convicted of second-degree murder in the racial killing of Yusuf K. Hawkins, a 16-year-old black youth who had gone to a white neighborhood in Brooklyn to help a teenage friend shop for a used car. A second youth was found guilty of lesser charges. In later 1990 trials relating to the case, two other defendants also were convicted of lesser charges, and one defendant was acquitted. At year's end, three defendants remained to be tried. In Manhattan an investment banker known to the public only as the Central Park jogger testified in the trial of three youths accused of brutally attacking her; they were convicted of rape and assault in August. A second trial against two other youths began in the fall and resulted in the conviction of one defendant of attempted murder, rape, and lesser charges and the conviction of a second defendant of sexual abuse, assault, and a lesser charge. A sixth defendant was to go on trial early in 1991. The Hawkins case successfully tested Mayor Dinkins' reputation as a conciliator, as both sides were displeased by the verdict. He was less successful, though, in resolving a boycott by blacks of two Brooklyn grocery stores owned by Korean immigrants that began in January.

Governmental Affairs. Nelson Mandela, the symbol of resistance to South African apartheid, received an emotional New York welcome in June. Mayor Dinkins snared the 1992 Democratic national convention for New York City. And he balanced a budget by imposing a record tax increase—nearly $900 million—with barely a whimper from prospective taxpayers or from the city council, which held new power under a revised city charter that abolished the city's other governing body, the board of estimate.

The euphoria, however, was short-lived as city officials came under increasing pressure to institute measures to deal with crime. More police were deployed, and Dinkins promised in August to hire 1,058 additional officers by early 1991. In October he unveiled an ambitious plan to expand the force to a record 31,944 officers, coupled with social-service, education, and drug-treatment programs. Since he had just agreed to grant teachers a 5.5% raise in his first contract negotiation with municipal unions and with city officials projecting a more than $1 billion budget gap, it appeared doubtful that the public-safety plan would survive intact or, at least, on schedule.

Declining tax revenue and a real-estate slump were a consequence, in part, of a regional slowdown. Diverse neighborhoods, meanwhile, were being revitalized by an influx of new immigrants. As Ellis Island reopened as an immigration museum celebrating the influx of the past (see page 90), many modern immigrants may have been missed in the 1990 census, which placed the city's population at slightly more than 7 million—at least 600,000 fewer than city planners estimated.

People. Also in New York, Imelda Marcos, widow of the former Philippine president, was acquitted of charges that she raided her country's treasury. Father Bruce Ritter stepped aside as head of Covenant House, the nation's largest shelter for runaways, in an inquiry into allegations of sexual misconduct. Real-estate magnate Donald Trump and his wife, Ivana, separated and were divorced.

SAM ROBERTS, *"The New York Times"*

NEW ZEALAND

At the end of a year of consistently depressing economic indicators, the National Party won a decisive victory over Labour in the general election on Oct. 27, 1990. In March the National Party had announced its support for New Zealand's ban on visits by foreign naval vessels with a nuclear capability.

Politics and the Election. Prime Minister Geoffrey Palmer was replaced by Mike Moore, the minister of external relations and trade, just a few weeks before the nation went to the polls. An estimated 85% of the 2.2 million electors cast a vote, 48% of them for National, 35% for Labour, 7% for the Greens, and 5% for New Labour. The swing of nearly 12% against La-

bour was the biggest in 50 years; the party's representation was cut in half to 29 seats. By contrast, National gained its best-ever result, 67 seats. A referendum proposal to extend parliament from three to four years was rejected.

Jim Bolger, the new prime minister, was a 55-year-old farmer from the middle of the North Island. The father of nine children, he had been a member of parliament since 1972, and had served as minister of labor. He became the National Party leader in 1986.

The Economy. Economists were unanimous that New Zealand was in the grip of a serious recession. In January the unemployment rate stood at nearly 15% of the work force; by October 200,000 people were unemployed—the highest number since the Great Depression of the 1930s. The New Zealand dollar, which had slipped 5% against the U.S. dollar in 1989, continued its downward path and inflation rose to 5%. Estimates of the economy's annual growth rate ranged from complete stagnation to 3%.

In July an extension of the protocols of the Closer Economic Relations Agreement with Australia marked a further step in the nonpolitical integration of the two nations. Later, an "agreement for growth" compact was clinched with the trade union movement whereby, in return for annual wage settlements not exceeding 2%, the government would cut its spending and seek to reduce interest rates.

The Budget. The biggest single transaction in the government's privatization program occurred in June when Telecom, the public telephone-communications corporation, was sold to the United States giants of U.S. Bell Atlantic and Ameritech. The yield of NZ$4.25 billion (about $2.5 billion) was greater than the combined returns on all previous asset sales and was used partly to pay for normal state spending. This allowed the July budget to record a nominal surplus, but there was still a NZ$2.2 billion (about $1.3 billion) deficit forecast.

The budget marked a return to more classic Labour lines, with family support for the low paid, higher spending on education and health, and a cut in the defense vote. Land tax and excise duty on new cars were abolished.

Domestic Events. In late January the 14th Commonwealth Games were held in Auckland. They were opened by Queen Elizabeth II in the course of her eighth royal tour, which was principally to celebrate the 150th anniversary of the signing of the Treaty of Waitangi by which New Zealand became a British colony. During her visit the Queen announced the appointment of Dame Catherine Tizard, the mayor of Auckland since 1983, as the next and first woman governor-general.

In November the nation's worst massacre of the 20th century occurred in Aramoana, near Dunedin, when a man killed 13 people with a semiautomatic rifle. The police later killed him.

GRAHAM BUSH, *University of Auckland*

NEW ZEALAND • Information Highlights

Official Name: New Zealand.
Location: Southwest Pacific Ocean.
Area: 103,737 sq mi (268 680 km²).
Population (mid-1990 est.): 3,300,000.
Chief Cities (March 31, 1988 est.): Wellington, the capital, 325,200; Auckland, 841,700; Christchurch, 300,700; Napier-Hastings, 107,500.
Government: *Head of state,* Elizabeth II, queen, represented by Dame Catherine Tizard, governor-general (took office November 1990). *Head of government,* James Bolger, prime minister (took office November 1990). *Legislature* (unicameral) —House of Representatives.
Monetary Unit: New Zealand dollar (1.7109 N.Z. dollars equal U.S.$1, Dec. 31, 1990).
Gross Domestic Product (1989 est. U.S. $): $39,100,-000,000.
Economic Index (1989): *Consumer Prices* (1980 = 100), all items, 259.6; food, 241.6.
Foreign Trade (1989 U.S.$): *Imports,* $8,776,000,000; *exports,* $8,867,000,000.

NIGERIA

The 30th year of independence and the fifth year of military rule directed by Gen. Ibrahim Babangida witnessed a moribund economy, continued religious strife, north-south conflicts, and a growing disenchantment with the government which led in April to an unsuccessful coup attempt by younger army officers. Despite political and economic woes, the Armed Forces Ruling Council (AFRC) continued with plans to hold local elections in December.

Domestic Developments. The deep divisions within the army and nation concerning the economy, corruption, and the concentration of power in the president's office sparked a move to overthrow the government on April 22. A small band of soldiers loyal to Maj. Gideon Orka seized the radio station and gained access to Dodan Barracks in Lagos. The plotters announced their reasons to the nation. Chief among these were the fear that Babangida would not turn over power to a civilian regime, disgust with escalating corruption, the government's austerity measures, and its pro-Muslim stance. Orka proposed to excise five of the northern states with Muslim majorities until they met certain conditions. Fighting went on in Lagos for 12 hours until the threat had passed. Fourteen officers and 200 lower-rank soldiers were arrested. In July, 42 of the conspirators were executed publicly; in September an additional 27 were shot.

On August 30, Babangida reconstructed the AFRC and appointed ten new state governors. In preparation for a return to civilian rule in 1992, he scrapped the office of the chief of general staff, created the office of vice-president, and appointed 21 civilian deputy governors. The AFRC gave approval for two political parties, the Social Democratic Party (SDP) and the National Republican Convention (NRC), to campaign for the projected December 8 local government elections.

Economy. Babangida's January budget message indicated that there would be no divergence from the Structural Adjustment Program

(SAP) adopted in 1986. This blueprint was welcomed by Western creditors because it held hope for ultimate repayment of Nigeria's $33 billion debt. Unemployment decreased during the year and the inflation rate was a manageable 3.4%. Petroleum production, which provided 84% of total revenue, increased 11% in volume over the previous year, but still did not meet projected earnings.

The budget deficit was projected at $1.8 billion. The Persian Gulf crisis, which caused a sharp increase in the price of oil, promised to recoup a portion of this loss. Babangida unilaterally informed the commercial creditors in April that there would be a reduction in interest payments beginning with $5.4 billion due in May. This followed a rejection by the creditor banks of his suggestion that interest be lowered from nearly 10% to 3%. In October the European Community provided $45 million for programmed assistance and a further $31 million to assist SAP.

Foreign Affairs. Babangida's major 1990 foreign-policy effort again concerned the problem of the country's foreign debt. Nigeria also cooperated with efforts by the West African states to end the civil war in Liberia, and contributed troops to the peacekeeping forces there. In May the nation welcomed a visit by South African antiapartheid leader Nelson Mandela.

HARRY A. GAILEY
San Jose State University

NORTH CAROLINA

Politics, the economy, and hazardous waste provided North Carolina's lead stories during the year 1990.

Politics. Former Charlotte Mayor Harvey B. Gantt made history as the first black to win the Democratic nomination for the U.S. Senate from the state. However, veteran Republican Sen. Jesse A. Helms won reelection to a fourth term following a bitter campaign that drew national attention with its racial appeals and heavy out-of state financing by both sides. The Republicans also picked up one seat in the U.S. House, narrowing the Democrats' majority in the state delegation to seven to four. The General Assembly remained safely Democratic, but bitterness lingered from the 1989 overthrow of veteran Speaker Liston Ramsey by a coalition of Republicans and disgruntled Democrats.

The legislative session featured sharp disagreements between the two houses and the administration of Gov. James G. Martin as the delegates sought to adjust the state budget to a revenue shortfall of about $350,000. Teachers and state employees were given the equivalent of a 6% salary increase, but other appropriations for state agencies and institutions were

---

NIGERIA · Information Highlights

Official Name: Federal Republic of Nigeria.
Location: West Africa.
Area: 356,668 sq mi (923 770 km²).
Population (mid-1990 est.): 118,800,000.
Chief City (1987 est.): Lagos, the capital, 1,213,000.
Government: *Head of state and government,* Maj. Gen. Ibrahim Babangida, president, federal military government (took office Aug. 27, 1985). *Legislature*—Armed Forces Ruling Council; National Council of Ministers and National Council of States.
Monetary Unit: Naira (7.955 naira equal U.S.$1, July 1990).
Economic Index (1989): *Consumer Prices* (1980 = 100), all items, 534.1; food, 578.0.
Foreign Trade (1987 U.S.$): *Imports,* $3,917,000,000; *exports,* $7,383,000,000.

U.S. Sen. Jesse Helms, a Republican of North Carolina, won reelection in November, defeating his black Democratic challenger, Harvey B. Gantt, a former Charlotte mayor.

© Ralf-Finn Hestoft/Saba

slashed. Only a few increases were authorized, including programs for basic education, infant mortality, handicapped children, drug education and treatment, and alternatives to imprisonment.

Faced with rising crime and violence, the voters in November narrowly approved the issuance of $200 million in bonds for prison construction. A proposed gubernatorial veto again failed to pass, and North Carolina remained the only U.S. state whose governor is without that power.

The Economy. While North Carolina continued to lead the United States in site selections for new research and development plants, precipitately falling tax revenues and rising unemployment provided sobering reminders of the threat of a recession. Even as the state legislature struggled to cut spending, the crisis in the Middle East aggravated the shortfall by increasing oil prices, which in turn affected other costs. A number of industries closed or reduced their work force, and unemployment rose to 4.6% in October. Average wages remained among the lowest in the nation. Despite antismoking campaigns, tobacco continued to produce about as much income as all other crops combined.

Hazardous Waste. Six years after the state sought to locate and build a hazardous-waste-treatment facility, the effort still was thwarted by legislative and legal intrusions and "not-in-my-backyard" groups, some of whom disrupted public meetings. Meanwhile, states to which waste had been shipped in the past twice closed their facilities to North Carolina. Thus the state faced the prospect of being deprived of adequate disposal capability either within or outside its boundaries.

The Census. Preliminary census figures put the state's population at more than 6.5 million, giving North Carolina one additional congressional seat. For the first time the urban population outnumbered rural residents. The number of migrant workers in North Carolina grew and only California, Florida, Texas, and Washington employed more nonresident workers.

Other. In October residents of Hatteras Island were left without surface connection to the mainland as the Bonner Bridge collapsed. Duke University student Marjorie Judith Vincent was crowned Miss America.

H.G. JONES
University of North Carolina

NORTH CAROLINA • Information Highlights

Area: 52,669 sq mi (136 413 km²).
Population (1990 census prelim.): 6,553,000.
Chief Cities (July 1, 1988 est.): Raleigh, the capital, 186,720; Charlotte, 367,860; Greensboro, 181,970; Winston-Salem, 148,690; Durham, 115,430.
Government (1990): *Chief Officers*—governor, James G. Martin (R); lt. gov., Jim Gardner (R). *General Assembly*—Senate, 50 members; House of Representatives, 120 members.
State Finances (fiscal year 1989): *Revenue,* $13,533,000,000; *expenditure,* $12,366,000,000.
Personal Income (1989): $99,863,000,000; per capita, $15,198.
Labor Force (June 1990): *Civilian labor force,* 3,471,000; *unemployed,* 131,700 (3.8% of total force).
Education: *Enrollment* (fall 1988)—public elementary schools, 761,069; public secondary, 322,087; colleges and universities, 332,521. *Public school expenditures* (1989–90), $3,861,762,000.

NORTH DAKOTA

The elections of 1990 reflected a growing public pessimism in North Dakota as voters defeated nearly one dozen referred or initiated ballot measures, including a sales-tax increase and several attempts to expand the state's gambling industry. Crop production jumped in the state, but commodity prices plummeted.

Agriculture. Normal precipitation returned in 1990, boosting grain production to near-record levels. But huge harvests worldwide left farmers with the lowest crop prices in three years. The state produced 278 million bushels of spring wheat, 104 million bushels of durum wheat, 133 million bushels of barley, 31 million bushels of oats, and 10 million bushels of soybeans. A fall survey conducted by a university agency showed a plurality of rural North Dakotans were pessimistic about the long-term economic outlook for farming communities.

Politics. Eight ballot measures were defeated in the November general election, including proposals to allow insurance agents to offer rebates and to put the state auditor's office under the control of the legislature. In June voters defeated a proposal to impose a one-year, 1% sales tax to raise more money for education.

Two popular incumbents won reelection in November, despite apparent voter unrest. U.S. Rep. Byron Dorgan defeated Republican Ed Schafer. Public Service Commissioner Dale Sandstrom, a Republican, defeated challenger Floyd Stromme. Republican Craig Hagen became the state's new labor commissioner by defeating S.F. Hoffner. Insurance Commissioner Byron Knutson, a Democrat, was eliminated from the race in the June primary after Gov. George Sinner and other Democratic leaders accused him of mismanagement and called on him to resign.

Democrat Byron L. Dorgan, the state's U.S. representative at large, easily won reelection to a sixth term.

NORTH DAKOTA · Information Highlights

Area: 70,702 sq mi (183 119 km²).
Population (1990 census): 641,364.
Chief Cities (1980 census): Bismarck, the capital, 44,485; Fargo, 61,383; Grand Forks, 43,765; Minot, 32,843.
Government (1990): *Chief Officers*—governor, George A. Sinner (D); lt. gov., Lloyd Omdahl (D). *Legislative Assembly*—Senate, 53 members; House of Representatives, 106 members.
State Finances (fiscal year 1989): *Revenue,* $1,756,000,000; *expenditure,* $1,725,000,000.
Personal Income (1989): $8,953,000,000; per capita, $13,563.
Labor Force (June 1990): *Civilian labor force,* 335,300; *unemployed,* 13,800 (4.1% of total force).
Education: *Enrollment* (fall 1988)—public elementary schools, 85,182; public secondary, 33,627; colleges and universities, 38,293. *Public school expenditures* (1989–90), $387,145,000.

Census. The 1990 census revealed that North Dakota was one of just five states to shrink in population in the 1980s. The state's population was tabulated at 641,364, down almost 2% from 1980. For the first time, more North Dakotans lived in the state's larger cities than on farms and in small towns.

Business. A task force of business and government leaders recommended the state streamline government, plow more money into public education, provide new funding for start-up companies, and expand gambling to diversify its economy. Lawmakers added off-track betting to the games offered by the state's charitable gaming industry, and North Dakotans wagered more than $1 million on the ponies in the first six weeks. But voters in November soundly rejected three measures that would have allowed for-profit businesses to join the industry.

The state Chamber of Commerce and 16 businesses went to court to challenge the constitutionality of North Dakota's Sunday closing laws—the toughest in the nation. But the state Supreme Court ruled that the blue laws, which keep nearly all retail businesses closed on Sundays, were legal.

Other. A Northwest Airlines flight crew was sentenced in the nation's first-ever drunk-flying conviction after piloting a flight from Fargo, ND, to Minneapolis with blood-alcohol levels exceeding federal limits.

JIM NEUMANN
Grand Forks, ND

NORTHWEST TERRITORIES

During 1990 boundary disputes and rethinking by some native leadership in the west slowed down the process of settling land claims that had been proceeding relatively rapidly over the previous two years in the Northwest Territories (NWT).

Aboriginal Land Claims. The Inuit in the Arctic regions and the Déné Indians of the western sub-Arctic could not reach agreement on a boundary defining their claim areas and potentially two separate territories. Mediation efforts were under way and discussions continued at year's end. The Tungavik Federation of Nunavut (representing the Inuit) and the government of the Northwest Territories did reach agreement on a process for planning a new Nunavut Territory. Public involvement through a plebiscite, federal-government commitments on financing, and eventually, federal legislation would be key elements of the process. The ratification of the Déné/Métis land claim was halted by demands that the clause extinguishing aboriginal rights be removed. Tribal councils in the Mackenzie Delta area began separate discussions with the federal government in pursuit of smaller regional settlements.

NORTHWEST TERRITORIES
· Information Highlights

Area: 1,304,903 sq mi (3 379 700 km²).
Population (July 1990): 54,000.
Chief Cities (1986 census): Yellowknife, the capital, 11,753; Inuvik, 3,389; Hay River, 2,964.
Government (1990): *Chief Officers*—commissioner, Daniel L. Norris; government leader, Dennis Patterson. *Legislature*—Legislative Assembly, 24 elected members.
Public Finances (1988–89 fiscal year): *Revenues,* $876,761,000; *expenditures,* $858,041,000.
Education (1990–91): *Enrollment*—elementary and secondary schools, 13,910 pupils. *Public school expenditures* (1988–89), $146,539,000.
(All monetary figures are in Canadian dollars.)

Justice Reviews. The judicial system in the NWT was under public scrutiny in 1990 as complaints arose over the fairness of the courts in decisions related to native people, particularly native women. A formal inquiry was held into the performance of one judge who made remarks that led many to believe he did not consider the rape of native women in the North to be as serious a matter as rape in other parts of Canada; the judge later regretted his remarks. The inquiry found that his remarks did not constitute misconduct and that he should not be disciplined. The minister of justice established a gender-equality review and an advisory commission on aboriginal justice.

Economy. The downturn in the economy was reflected in the NWT as elsewhere in the country. With the cost of living already higher than anywhere else in Canada, individuals and business people were fearful of the impact that higher taxes would have on prices and the cost of operating both private enterprises and government programs.

ROSS M. HARVEY, *Television Northern Canada*

NORWAY

Norway's possible membership in the European Community (EC) was discussed throughout 1990 and became the contention over which the coalition government broke up on October 30. The Nobel Committee of Norway's Parliament awarded the 1990 peace prize to Soviet President Mikhail Gorbachev.

Political Affairs. The coalition government, headed by Jan P. Syse and consisting of members of the Conservative Party, the Center Party, and the Christian People's Party, which took office in October 1989, faced numerous problems in 1990. One was the fluctuating economic situation, with a fairly high unemployment, and a growing number of layoffs and bankruptcies in private business. The prime minister's position also was shaken by allegations of his having mishandled his private financial affairs. Another Conservative Party leader, Oslo Mayor Albert Nordengen, was forced to resign after many years in office for allegedly having made business decisions favorable to companies of which he and other city council members were part owners.

Having turned down membership in the EC in 1972, Norway, along with its fellow members of the European Free Trade Association (EFTA), was involved in negotiations with the EC about the possibility of creating a European Economic Area, which would consist of ten EC and EFTA members. In late October, Syse's coalition fell when it failed to support the prime minister's stand on negotiations with the EC and EFTA on establishing such a joint trade bloc. A new coalition, headed by Gro Harlem Brundtland of the Labor Party, took office on November 3. Brundtland, a Harvard-educated public-health specialist who twice had served as prime minister, had not voiced her opinion on EC membership.

A constitutional amendment passed during the summer makes it possible for a woman to ascend to the throne of Norway and become queen. The only exception involved members of the royal family born before 1990. This means that Prince Haakon Magnus would succeed his father Crown Prince Harald, even though he is younger than his sister, Princess Märtha Louise.

Foreign Affairs. Following a spring visit by Lithuania's Premier Kazimiera Prunskiene, Norway confirmed its support of full independence for the Soviet republic. Never having recognized the annexation of the three Baltic countries by the Soviet Union, Norway on several occasions appealed to the USSR to end its economic sanctions against Lithuania.

Norway also gave its full support to the UN resolution on an economic blockade of Iraq following its invasion of Kuwait. The Norwegian Council of State decided to send a coast guard vessel to the Persian Gulf area and contribute $20 million to help refugees in the area. Norway already had 1,000 soldiers participating in the UN peacekeeping force in Lebanon.

NORWAY · Information Highlights

Official Name: Kingdom of Norway.
Location: Northern Europe.
Area: 125,182 sq mi (324 220 km²).
Population (mid-1990 est.): 4,200,000.
Chief Cities (Jan. 1, 1989): Oslo, the capital, 456,124; Bergen, 211,095; Trondheim, 136,601.
Government: *Head of state,* Olav V, king (acceded Sept. 1957). *Head of government,* Gro Harlem Brundtland, prime minister (took office November 1990). *Legislature*—Storting: Lagting and Odelsting.
Monetary Unit: Krone (6.01 kroner equal U.S.$1, Dec. 31, 1990).
Gross Domestic Product (1989 est. U.S.$): $75,800,-000,000.
Economic Indexes: *Consumer Prices* (1989, 1980 = 100), all items, 200.2; food, 210.7. *Industrial Production* (August 1990, 1980 = 100), 162.
Foreign Trade (1989 U.S.$): *Imports,* $23,676,-000,000; *exports,* $27,061,000,000.

In mid-October, Norway broke diplomatic relations with Kenya. Reports of killings, torture, and imprisonment of opposition leaders in Kenya were responsible for Norway's action. Kenya, in turn, accused Norway of supporting rebel forces and interfering in Kenya's internal affairs.

Conferences. Some 4,500 delegates from throughout the world attended a major environmental conference in Bergen, May 8–16. Seventy participants from 29 nations attended a conference entitled "Anatomy of Hate: Resolving Conflicts Through Dialogues and Democracy" in Oslo, August 26–29.

ERIK J. FRIIS
The Scandinavian-American Bulletin

NOVA SCOTIA

During 1990, Nova Scotians witnessed the unfolding of political scandals and gloomy prospects of an economic recession.

Government. The Conservative-led provincial government was punctuated by political scandal. The center of controversy was Premier John Buchanan, who was accused by his former deputy minister, Michael Zareski, of misdirecting government funds by awarding contracts to friends in return for monetary kickbacks. The controversy reached its climax in September when the premier resigned from provincial politics, accepting a federal appointment to the Canadian Senate. In the meantime, Health Minister David Nantes was forced to resign for divulging confidential medical information related to Zareski's mental health.

Roger Bacon, a former minister of agriculture in Buchanan's government, was appointed caretaker premier until an expected February 1991 election. Zareski was the first to announce his candidacy for the premiership.

Despite the controversy, the government enacted 60 laws in its 1990 session. Legislative highlights were the establishment of a provincial health council for forming government strategy on health issues, the streamlining of mining legislation, a provision for private tax-shelter funds to clean up the environment, extension of the coverage of pay-equity legislation, and reforms to protect both children and parents in cases of suspected abuse. A trade office in Boston was opened.

Economy. In 1990 the Nova Scotian economy remained sluggish against the backdrop of a slowing Canadian economy, a rising interest rate, and the pending imposition of the goods and services tax. During the first half of 1990 the value of manufacturing shipments grew by a meager 2.4%, compared with 6.8% growth during the same period in 1989.

Fish landings were down, and lobster fishing was hampered by U.S.-imposed conservation measures. Employment in the industry

---

NOVA SCOTIA · Information Highlights

Area: 21,425 sq mi (55 491 km²).
Population (September 1990): 892,000.
Chief Cities (1986 census): Halifax, the capital, 113,577; Dartmouth, 65,243; Sydney, 27,754.
Government (1990): *Chief Officers*—lt. gov., Lloyd R. Crouse; premier, Roger S. Bacon (Progressive Conservative). *Legislature*—Legislative Assembly, 52 members.
Provincial Finances (1990–91 fiscal year budget): *Revenues,* $3,639,014,000; *expenditures,* $4,010,-313,000.
Personal Income (average weekly earnings, July 1990): $461.87.
Labor Force (September 1990, seasonally adjusted): *Employed* workers, 15 years of age and over, 379,000; *Unemployed,* 11.0%.
Education (1990–91): *Enrollment*—elementary and secondary schools, 167,880 pupils; postsecondary—universities, 30,150; community colleges, 2,830.
(All monetary figures are in Canadian dollars.)

---

dwindled as plants closed in response to falling quotas.

Signs of growth in the coal-mining sector, where output grew by 125% to the end of April 1990, were negated by a sharp dip in construction activity. The value of building permits during the first half of 1990 was down by 9%.

In the international-trade sector, exports fell due to a sharp upturn in the foreign-exchange value of the Canadian dollar. Overall investment activity also was expected to post only a moderate increase, despite the launching of capital projects such as the Michelin tire plant expansion and a C$600 million installation of pollution-abatement equipment at power plants throughout the province. Moreover, lower federal spending accentuated the pace of economic slowdown by curtailing municipal and provincial programs. Consequently, the rate of job creation fell sharply during the first half of 1990. This labor-market slack was expected to reduce retail sales during the second half of the year. The provincial gross domestic product (GDP) was expected to decline from 1989's growth rate of 3.4% to 2.1%.

Energy. Interest in the Nova Scotia oil and gas industry was renewed by plans to develop the Panuke/Cohasset oil fields. The two fields were expected to produce 36 million barrels of oil.

The launching of a controversial C$436 million Point Aconi thermal-power plant by Nova Scotia Power Corporation would increase provincial capacity for generating electricity by 150 megawatts. The plant was started at the government's behest without addressing fully environmentalists' concern about its impact on carbon-dioxide emissions in the province. Moreover, Nova Scotians were denied the opportunity for evaluating the economic viability of the plant, as public debate was cut off by the PUB-Point Aconi Bill.

R. P. SETH
Mount Saint Vincent University, Halifax

OBITUARIES

© Jack Manning/NYT Pictures

BETTELHEIM, Bruno

Naturalized-American psychologist and educator: b. Vienna, Austria, Aug. 28, 1903; d. Silver Springs, MD, March 13, 1990.

Considered one of the great figures in the field of child psychology, Bruno Bettelheim committed suicide at a Silver Springs nursing home on March 13, 1990. Devastated by the death of his wife of 43 years in 1984 and the victim of a stroke in 1987, he reportedly could not adjust to the loss of independence that nursing-home living meant.

Bettelheim's contribution to child psychology was outstanding because he was not just a respected practitioner but also a "historian and essayist of high quality." He had spent nearly 30 years at the Sonia Shankman Orthogenic School at the University of Chicago caring for

Culver Pictures, Inc.

AP/Wide World

GARBO, Greta

Motion-picture actress: b. Stockholm, Sweden, Sept. 18, 1905; d. New York City, April 15, 1990.

She never won an Oscar as best actress, had appeared in less than 30 films, had not made one in nearly 50 years, and constantly had shunned publicity, but at the time of her death, Easter Sunday, April 15, 1990, she was considered by many as the finest and most popular movie actress of all time. Such was the legacy of Greta Garbo.

As one critic noted, Greta Garbo "has an almost mythical status among movie buffs and casual filmgoers alike. . . . Her gifts have withstood the journey from cinema to video as impressively as her acting persona withstood the change from silents to talkies." And in the

DAVIS, Sammy, Jr.

U.S. entertainer: b. New York, NY, Dec. 8, 1925; d. Los Angeles, CA, May 16, 1990.

Sammy Davis, Jr., who sang and danced his way into the hearts of audiences for more than 60 years, was a complete entertainer. His wide-ranging talents enabled him to sing, tap dance, act, mimic, and play four musical instruments. He triumphed in film, theater, nightclubs, recordings, and television, becoming one of the first black performers to achieve mainstream success.

Davis was inducted into the Hall of Fame of the National Association of Colored People and was awarded Kennedy Center honors for lifetime career achievement (1987). With Jane and Burt Boyar, Davis wrote *Yes I Can* (1965) and *Why Me* (1989).

disturbed children who had been considered hopeless. At the school Doctor Bettelheim sought to understand the reasons for the behavior of the disturbed child, not just to modify it.

The Austrian-born psychologist also developed his own theories regarding the rearing and schooling of children. He did not believe that children should be told that learning is easy. Rather they should be told that a particular subject ''is difficult, but if you work hard, you can learn it.'' In his best-known and prizewinning book, *The Uses of Enchantment* (1976), he defended the violence prevalent in many fairy tales. He believed that such violence taught the child ''clear-cut lines between right and wrong.'' Bettelheim also felt that children should have a teacher for more than one year and criticized textbooks in which beautiful illustration hides dull writing.

Background. Bruno Bettelheim was born of middle-class Jewish parents. He trained as a psychologist, focusing on autism, at the University of Vienna and just had finished his doctorate and studies with Sigmund Freud when Nazi Germany entered Austria. After spending a year in the Dachau and Buchenwald concentration camps, he went to the United States in 1939. He taught at Rockford College in Rockford, IL, before serving on the University of Chicago faculty (1944–73).

Doctor Bettelheim's many writings include commentaries on social problems, studies of the concentration camp—*The Informed Heart* (1960) and *Surviving, and Other Essays* (1979) —and prolific works in his field, such as *Love Is Not Enough* (1950), *Truants from Life* (1955), and *A Good Enough Parent* (1987).

He and his wife had two daughters and a son.

---

words of Vincent Canby of *The New York Times*, her beauty was ''so formidable that it always comes as a discovery to recognize that Garbo was an actress in complete command of what introspective theater people call their 'instrument'.'' She became the norm which others tried to imitate and be judged by. She also had a strong influence on women's fashion.

Background. As a young teenager, Greta Louisa Gustafsson, the daughter of an unskilled laborer of peasant stock, won a scholarship to Stockholm's Royal Dramatic Theater Academy. While there she was discovered by director Mauritz Stiller. He changed her name to Garbo and took her to the United States in 1925. She appeared in her first MGM film, *The Torrent*, in 1926 and became an overnight success. Her other silent-film hits included *Flesh and the Devil* (1927), *Love* (1927), and *A Woman of Affairs* (1929).

Her first talking picture was an adaptation of Eugene O'Neill's *Anna Christie* in 1930. The film was advertised with the slogan ''Garbo Talks!.'' She then starred in *Mata Hari* (1931), *Grand Hotel* (1932), *Queen Christina* (1933), *Anna Karenina* (1935), *Camille* (1936), and the comedy *Ninotchka* (1939). Her last role was in a comedy, *Two Faced Woman* (1941). Although Garbo had hoped to return to acting, such arrangements never were finalized. In 1955 the movie idol was awarded a special Oscar for a ''series of luminous and unforgettable performances.''

For some 40 years she lived in a New York City apartment, traveled regularly, and continued to protect her privacy. As a newsman noted, ''by dodging publicity she [became] one of the most publicized women of the world.'' Linked romantically with several men, she reportedly never married.

Background. Sammy Davis, Jr., was the son of vaudevillians Elvera (Sanchez) Davis and Sammy Davis, Sr. When Sammy, Jr., was two his parents divorced, and his father took custody of him. As young as three, Davis performed with his father and the avuncular Will Mastin. He never attended school, but his father pacified truant officers by finding someone to tutor him wherever they worked. Davis was confronted with bigotry in the army when he was drafted at 18. Transferred to Special Services, he performed on bases nationwide.

On Broadway, Davis starred in three musicals. His personal notices in *Mr. Wonderful* (1956), which was created for him, were excellent. For his role in a refocused version of *Golden Boy* (1964), *Cue* magazine named him Entertainer of the Year. In 1978, Davis sang and danced his way through a revival of *Stop the World, I Want to Get Off.* Davis also ap-

peared in numerous films, several with fellow ''Rat Pack'' members, including Frank Sinatra and Dean Martin. Some of their films were *Ocean's 11* (1960) and *Johnny Cool* (1963).

In 1954, Davis lost his left eye in an auto crash. Following his convalescence, he converted to Judaism. By 1989, after a lifetime of heavy smoking, he developed the throat cancer which caused his death.

Davis' first marriage to Loray White, a black dancer, ended after a few months in 1960. In the same year he married a white Swedish actress, May Britt, which generated considerable hate mail. They had a daughter and adopted two boys. Britt divorced him in 1968. In 1970, Davis married Altovise Gore, a black dancer, and they adopted a boy.

GLADYS HANDELMAN

Editor's Note: Special obituaries are arranged chronologically by date of death. Unsigned obituaries were written by the staff.

© Walter Scott/Boston Symphony Orchestra

BERNSTEIN, Leonard

American conductor, composer, and pianist: b. Lawrence, MA, Aug. 25, 1918; d. New York City, Oct. 14, 1990.

A whirlwind of musical talent, the charismatic and versatile Leonard Bernstein had a phenomenally successful career in diverse areas of music. An acclaimed conductor, he also was an accomplished pianist and a gifted composer for the concert hall, musical theater, ballet, and film. An inspired teacher as well, he enthralled millions of television viewers with his insightful lectures on both the cultural series *Omnibus* (1952–59) and the New York Philharmonic's *Young People's Concerts* (1958-71). Although friends urged him to focus on one genre, Bernstein rejected the notion of limiting himself.

Bernstein was made lifetime laureate conductor of the New York Philharmonic in 1969, when he resigned as its full-time musical director to devote himself to composition and conducting major orchestras in the United States and abroad. Even critics of his highly animated, expressive conducting style conceded that he was gifted. His baton could evoke supremely sensitive interpretations of Mahler's Romantic music, of which he was a leading exponent; yet, musically speaking, he also could walk the mean streets of a big city and create the pulsating rhythms of *West Side Story*, a major Broadway musical created in 1957.

Among Bernstein's numerous honors and awards were an Emmy for his *Young People's Concerts* (1960), Kennedy Center Honors (1980), Lifetime Achievement Grammy Award (1985), and British Royal Philharmonic Society Gold Medal (1987). For his 70th birthday, a glit-

tering four-day gala was held at Tanglewood (formerly Berkshire) Music Center in Lenox, MA, the locale of many early triumphs, in August 1988, with the maestro on the podium for the final concert. In 1990, Bernstein was part of the Pacific Music Festival in Japan.

Also an author, Bernstein wrote *The Joy of Music* (1959), *The Infinite Variety of Music* (1966), and *The Unanswered Question* (1976). He also was active in liberal causes.

Background. Leonard Bernstein was the son of Russian immigrants, Samuel Joseph and Jennie (Resnick) Bernstein. He began studying the piano at age 10, after a relative stored an old upright in the family home. Bernstein attended Boston Latin School and then Harvard, with the intent of becoming a pianist. After graduating in 1939, his focus shifted to conducting, which he studied along with piano for two years at the Curtis Institute of Music.

During the summers of 1940–41, Bernstein continued his studies at Tanglewood with Serge Koussevitzky, the Boston Symphony's music director, who became his mentor and who engaged Bernstein as an assistant in 1942. From 1948 to 1955, Bernstein was a faculty member at Tanglewood, succeeding Koussevitzky as head of its conducting department (1951-55). Concurrently, he was professor of music at Brandeis (1951–56).

In 1943, Artur Rodzinski, music director of the New York Philharmonic, asked him to be assistant conductor, and on November 14 of that year, Bernstein at age 25 got his big break when he replaced an indisposed Bruno Walter. In 1947, Bernstein first conducted the Israel Philharmonic; he served as its music adviser (1948–49) and became laureate conductor in 1988. By 1953 he was the first U.S.-born conductor to mount the podium at Milan's La Scala, and in 1958, Bernstein became the New York Philharmonic's youngest music director.

Classical works composed by Bernstein include *Jeremiah* (Symphony No. 1, 1944) and *Age of Anxiety* (Symphony No. 2, 1949); *Trouble in Tahiti* (1952), a one-act opera; *Kaddish* (Symphony No. 3, 1963); the *Chichester Psalms* (1965); and *Mass* (1971). The latter opened Washington's Kennedy Center in 1971. He wrote the scores for the ballets *Fancy Free* (1944) and *Dybbuk* (1974) and the music for the film *On the Waterfront* (1954). His Broadway shows include *On the Town* (1944), *Wonderful Town* (1953), *Candide* (1956), and *West Side Story* (1957).

In 1951, Bernstein married the Chilean-born actress Felicia Montealegre Cohn, who died in 1978. They had three children. Bernstein and his music were remembered at a private concert at New York's Carnegie Hall in November and at a memorial, which was opened to the public, at New York's Majestic Theater in December.

GLADYS HANDELMAN

PALEY, William S.

U.S. broadcasting magnate: b. Chicago, IL, Sept. 28, 1901; d. New York, NY, Oct. 26, 1990.

A broadcasting executive with an instinctive sense for programming, William S. Paley largely was responsible for building the Columbia Broadcasting System (CBS) from a handful of radio stations into a giant communications network through his early recognition of the power of the airwaves and the television screen. He made household names of such entertainers as Lucille Ball, Jack Benny, George Burns and Gracie Allen, as well as broadcast journalists Edward R. Murrow and Walter Cronkite. Under his direction, CBS expanded into records (introducing the long-playing record in 1948), magazines, and filmmaking; and it became the premier television network, often referred to as the "Tiffany Network."

Background. William S. Paley was the oldest son of Samuel and Goldie Paley, Jewish Ukrainian immigrants who made their fortune making cigars in Chicago and later Philadelphia. The middle initial "S" was added to his name when Paley was 12 years old but stood for nothing. He was graduated from the University of Pennsylvania in 1922, and in 1928, at age 26, he became president of the Columbia Phonographic Broadcasting System, a small radio network that included a Philadelphia affiliate through which the Paley family advertised their cigars. He quickly expanded the network, increasing network program hours and setting peak listening hours as the time for network broadcasts of commercially sponsored programs. He also signed on the then unknown talents of Bing Crosby, Kate Smith, and the Mills Brothers. In the 1940s he wooed other well-known stars from the rival National Broadcasting Company (NBC). As television moved to the forefront of broadcasting, CBS brought audiences such critically acclaimed shows as *All in the Family*, *The Mary Tyler Moore Show*, and *M*A*S*H*.

Paley was a philanthropist and art collector who liked the high life. His two marriages were to beautiful and socially accomplished women, but while his charm with women was well-known, he was described as cold and aloof with his own children. A man who had a hard time letting go of his empire, he refused to retire at age 65, even though he later forced a longtime associate, Frank Stanton, to do so. With CBS' preeminence declining in the 1980s, Paley took the title of founder chairman in 1983, only to resume the position of chairman in 1987 when Laurence A. Tisch took over. He was survived by four children, two stepchildren, and eight grandchildren. Late in 1990 a critical biography by Sally Bedell Smith, *In All His Glory*, received much publicity.

MARTIN, MARY

American actress: b. Weatherford, TX, Dec. 1, 1913; d. Rancho Mirage, CA, Nov. 3, 1990.

Mary Martin, the impish star of some of Broadway's greatest musicals, gained an enduring place in the American theater with such outstanding characterizations as Nellie Forbush in *South Pacific* (1949), as the title character in *Peter Pan* (1954), and as Maria von Trapp in *The Sound of Music* (1959). The cheerful, exuberant star, who more than most of her colleagues, was in reality as she appeared on the stage, identified perhaps most with the eternal child embodied in Peter Pan, her favorite stage role. She expressed an affinity for flying, an art she learned for the aerial ballet she performed in the show, and in her autobiography *My Heart Belongs* (1976), she wrote that "Neverland is the way I'd like real life to be: timeless, free, mischievous, filled with gaiety, tenderness, and magic."

Background. Mary Virginia Martin, born on Dec. 1, 1913, was the daughter of Preston Martin, a lawyer, and Juanita (Pressly) Martin, a violin teacher. She was educated at the Ward-Belmont School, a finishing school in Nashville, TN, and as a young person, sang in churches and clubs and appeared in amateur theatricals. At age 16 she entered into a short-lived marriage with Benjamin Hagman. They had a son Larry, who later became famous in television's *Dallas*. Two years later, along with Mildred Woods, she opened the Mary Hagman School of Dance in Weatherford. For some years she went back and forth between Texas and California, teaching and performing. The school eventually burned down, and hoping to gain success as a performer, she returned to Hollywood.

Her first major break came when she was singing at a talent show at the Trocadero nightclub in Los Angeles. As a result of the appearance she won a small role on Broadway in the Cole Porter musical *Leave It to Me* (1938), where she stole the spotlight with "My Heart Belongs to Daddy," which became her signature song. Hollywood soon beckoned, and her first film, *The Great Victor Herbert* (1939), was followed by several forgettable releases of the early 1940s. She returned to New York for her first Broadway starring role in *One Touch of Venus* (1944), which began a succession of musical successes that brought the actress three Tony Awards—in 1950, 1955, and 1960. In 1955 she also won an Emmy award for her performance in the TV production of *Peter Pan*.

Mary Martin was married for the second time in 1940 to Richard Halliday, who died in 1973. They had a daughter. With regard to her famous son, she once joked, "I'm the legend. He's a passing fad."

AP/Wide World

COPLAND, Aaron

U.S. composer: b. Brooklyn, NY, Nov. 14, 1900; d. North Tarrytown, NY., Dec. 2, 1990.

Aaron Copland, a composer of orchestra, chamber, and vocal music, as well as music for dance and film, emerged early in his career as the central figure in the evolution of 20th-century U.S. music. Successful in his combination of the serious and the popular, he gave musical integrity to compositions such as the ballets *Billy the Kid* (1938), *Rodeo* (1942), and *Appalachian Spring* (1944), which combined folk songs and cowboy tunes with original themes; and he took musical risks with his later 12-tone compositions.

A strong advocate of the music of others, Copland founded, along with composer Roger Sessions, the Copland-Sessions Concerts in the late 1920s as a means of introducing New York audiences to important composers. He also served for many years with New York's League of Composers, spent 25 years on the faculty at the Berkshire (now Tanglewood) Music Center in Lenox, MA, lectured at Harvard, and was a figure in the early careers of such composers as Leonard Bernstein, Lukas Foss, David Diamond, Toru Takemitsu, and David Del Tredici.

Background. Aaron Copland, the youngest of five children, first studied music with an older sister who was an amateur pianist. He composed his first song at age 14 and began study at age 16 with Rubin Goldmark in Brooklyn. In 1920 he was the first student accepted to a new French summer music school for Americans at the palace of Fontainbleau. There he met and studied with the famed instructor Nadia Boulanger. She in 1923 introduced Copland to Serge Koussevitsky, the music director of the Boston Symphony Orchestra, who became one of Copland's strongest supporters. In 1925, Copland's Organ Symphony, written for Boulanger, was premiered by the New York Symphony Society, and his career was launched.

His early works in the 1920s incorporated elements of jazz, but by the 1930s and early 1940s he was in a populist phase, striving for simplicity in his music. *Appalachian Spring*, which won the Pulitzer Prize for Composition (1945), was commissioned by choreographer Martha Graham and included country fiddlers and a Shaker melody. He stopped composing but continued conducting and lecturing in the early 1970s after his highly structured 12-tone compositions, including *Inscape* (1967), were rejected by young composers.

Over the years, in addition to his Pulitzer Prize, he won a Presidential Medal of Freedom (1964), the Guggenheim Foundation's first music fellowship (1925), and an Academy Award (1949). He wrote several books on music and a two-volume autobiography. A lifelong bachelor, he was survived by a niece and two nephews.

The following is a selected list of prominent persons who died during 1990.
Articles on major figures appear in the preceding pages.

Abdul Rahman, Tunku (87), first prime minister of Malaysia (1957–70): d. Kuala Lumpur, Malaysia, Dec. 6.

Abernathy, Ralph David (64), U.S. civil-rights activist and Baptist minister; a trusted confidant of the Rev. Martin Luther King, Jr., with whom he worked for black civil rights beginning with a bus boycott in Montgomery, AL, in 1955. He became head of the Southern Christian Leadership Conference in 1968 after the assassination of King and served until 1977. He was pastor of a Baptist church in Atlanta from 1961 until his death. His autobiography, *And the Walls Came Tumbling Down* (1989), created controversy because of its revelations regarding Dr. King: d. Atlanta, GA, April 17.

Adler, Isidore (73), senior scientist with Goddard Space Flight Center of the National Aeronautics and Space Administration and professor at the University of Maryland (1974–86); was among the first to map the chemical composition of the back of the moon. He was codirector of "The World of Chemistry," a series for national public and cable television: d. Silver Spring, MD, March 26.

Allen, George (72), football coach; was known for his knack of making winners out of losing teams. After coaching for a number of seasons with the National Football League's Los Angeles Rams (1966-70) and Washington Redskins (1971–77), he coached briefly in the 1980s with the now defunct United States Football League and then in December 1989 ended a five-year retirement to coach the college level Long Beach State team. During his years with the Rams and the Redskins, he had the most wins of any coach in the histories of those teams: d. Palos Verdes Estates, CA, Dec. 31.

Alonso, Damaso (91), Spanish poet and scholar; was director of the Royal Academy of the Spanish Language (1968–82) and a member of the so-called "Generation of 1927." He received the Miguel de Cervantes Prize, the highest literary prize for Spanish-language writers, in 1978: d. Madrid, Spain, Jan. 24.

Althusser, Louis (72), French Marxist philosopher: d. near Paris, France, Oct. 22.

Arden, Eve (born Eunice Quedens) (83), film and television comedienne; probably best known for her role as the school-

Ralph Abernathy   Pearl Bailey

teacher in the radio and television series *Our Miss Brooks* (1948–57). She also appeared as a featured player in numerous movies and won an Academy Award nomination as best supporting actress in *Mildred Pierce* (1945): d. Beverly Hills, CA, Nov. 12.

Arenas, Reinaldo (47), Cuban novelist; his books included *Singing from the Well*, *Hallucinations*, and *Farewell to the Sea*. He came to the United States in 1980 during the Mariel exodus from Cuba: d. New York City, Dec. 7.

Arevalo, Bermejo Juan José (86), president of Guatemala (1945–51): d. Guatemala City, Oct. 6.

Auld, Georgie (70), Canadian-born saxophonist of the 1930s and 1940s: d. Palm Springs, CA, Jan. 8.

Bacon, Ernst (91), pianist, composer, conductor, teacher, and author; composed two symphonies, two piano concertos, and two operas, as well as orchestral suites and chamber music. He toured as a concert pianist in the United States and Europe before joining the faculty of the Eastman School of Music in Rochester, NY, and becoming conductor of the Rochester Opera Company: d. Orinda, CA, March 16.

Bailey, Pearl (72), singer; noted for her cabaret songs and her renditions of Broadway show tunes from *Hello, Dolly!*, in which she appeared from 1967 to 1969, and from her earlier shows *House of Flowers* and *St. Louis Woman*, among others. She also was noted for her film appearances in *Carmen Jones* (1954) and *Porgy and Bess* (1959). Among her best-known songs were *Tired*, *Takes Two to Tango*, *Birth of the Blues*, *Toot Toot Tootsie, Goodbye*, *That's Good Enough for Me*, and *Fifteen Years*: d. Philadelphia, PA, Aug. 17.

Balin, Ina (52), film and stage actress; made her film debut in *The Black Orchid* (1959); other films included *From the Terrace* (1960) and *The Greatest Story Ever Told* (1965): d. New Haven, CT, June 20.

Ballard, Harold (86), owner of the Toronto [Canada] Maple Leafs, a National Hockey League team. He had acquired the team in 1972: d. Toronto, Canada, April 11.

Baxley, Barbara (63), stage, film, and television actress; she received a Tony nomination for her performance in *Period of Adjustment* (1960): d. New York City, June 7.

Beech, Keyes (76), foreign correspondent in Asia; won a Pulitzer Prize in 1951 for his reporting on the Korean War: d. Washington, DC, Feb. 15.

Bennett, Joan (80), film actress of the 1930s and 1940s who began in movies in ingénue roles and later portrayed brunette femme fatales. Her leading mentor was her third husband, producer Walter Wanger, whose 1951 shooting of Miss Bennett's agent created a major Hollywood scandal. Among her films were *Disraeli* (1929), *Me and My Gal* (1932), *Man Hunt* (1941), *The Woman at the Window* (1944), *Woman on the Beach* (1947), and *Reckless Moment* (1949). She also appeared in the television series *Dark Shadows*, which ran from 1966 to 1971: d. Scarsdale, NY, Dec. 7.

Blakey, Art (also known as Abdullah Ibn Buhaina) (71), jazz-music drummer and bandleader; among the most influential figures in jazz music over a 40-year period. He integrated drums into small-group arrangements that became examples of hard bop: d. New York City, Oct. 16.

Boggs, Phil (40), Olympic Games gold medalist for diving in 1976: d. July 4.

Bolet, Jorge (75), Cuban-born pianist; specialized in Romantic-era music: d. Mountain View, CA, Oct. 16.

Boston, Lucy (97), British author of children's fiction; noted for her "Green Knowe" books: d. Huntingdonshire, England, May 25.

Bowles, Edward L. (92), electrical engineer; he played an important role in developing radar during World War II. He also had taught at the Massachusetts Institute of Technology for many years: d. Weston, MA, Sept. 5.

Bowman, Sister Thea (52), member of the Franciscan Sisters of Perpetual Adoration, the group's only black member, and a nationally active black educator who urged the Roman Catholic Church to embrace the culture of African Americans. In 1988 she released an album of 15 spirituals, *Sister Thea: Songs of My People*: d. Canton, MS, March 30.

Bridges, Alfred Renton Byrant (Harry) (88), Australian-born U.S. labor leader and a leading figure of the U.S. 20th-century labor movement. He organized the West Coast longshoremen in the 1930s, first in the International Longshoremen's Association and later in the International Longshoremen's and Warehousemen's Union, which he headed until 1977. He was accused by some of being a Communist, although he denied ever joining the Communist Party: d. San Francisco, CA, March 30.

Brown, Archie (79), former West Coast leader of the International Longshoremen's and Warehousemen's Union. He won a landmark Supreme Court ruling in 1965, when the court upheld the right of Communists to serve as union officials: d. San Francisco, CA, Nov. 23.

Bunshaft, Gordon (81), architect, among the most influential of the 20th century; was a partner in the firm Skidmore, Owings & Merrill, which he joined in 1937. He built modernist skyscrapers, museums, and libraries. He received the Pritzker Prize in 1988: d. New York City, Aug. 6.

Callaghan, Morley (87), Canadian writer who spent time in the 1920s living in Paris and associating with Ernest Hemingway and F. Scott Fitzgerald. His books included *Strange Fugitive* (1928), *A Many-Colored Coat* (1960), *A Time for Judas* (1983), and the memoir *That Summer in Paris* (1963) that contained Callaghan's view of a famous boxing match between him and Hemingway: d. Toronto, Canada, Aug. 25.

Caples, John (90), retired advertising executive; wrote in 1926 one of advertising's most famous headlines—"They Laughed When I Sat Down at the Piano, but When I Started to Play!"—and its accompanying text. The ad was an instant success and often copied: d. New York City, June 10.

Capucine (born Germaine Lefebvre) (57), French-born actress; appeared in movies during the 1960s, including *Song Without End*, *The Pink Panther*, *What's New, Pussycat?*, and *A Walk on the Wild Side*: d. Lausanne, Switzerland, March 17.

Carney, Robert B. (95), U.S. naval admiral; was chief of Naval Operations (1953–55) and commander in chief of the North Atlantic Treaty Organization forces in Southern Europe (1951–53): d. Washington, DC, June 25.

Carruthers, Jimmy (61), world bantamweight boxing champion (1952–54), the first Australian boxer in any weight class to win a world title: d. Sydney, Australia, Aug. 16.

Carvel, Tom (born Thomas Carvelas) (84), inventor of a machine to make soft ice cream and founder of a major U.S. chain of ice-cream stores: d. Pine Plains, NY, Oct. 21.

Casiraghi, Stefano (30), Italian financier and sportsman; the husband of Princess Caroline of Monaco: d. French Riviera (Monaco), Oct. 3.

Chapel, Alain (53), French chef, considered one of his nation's finest; owned a restaurant near Lyon: d. Avignon, France, July 10.

Charleson, Ian (40), British actor; gained international fame for his portrayal of the Presbyterian missionary in the Academy Award-winning film *Chariots of Fire* (1981): d. London, Jan. 6.

Childs, Marquis W. (87), foreign correspondent, columnist, author; was with the St. Louis *Post-Dispatch* from 1926 to 1974, when he retired, although he continued to write commentary occasionally. He won the Pulitzer Prize for distinguished commentary in 1970: d. San Francisco, CA, June 30.

Clark, Joseph S. (88), U.S. senator (D-PA, 1957-69); he earlier had been mayor of Philadelphia (elected in 1951), the first Democratic mayor in Philadelphia in 67 years: d. Philadelphia, PA, Jan. 12.

Clifton, Nat (Sweetwater) (65), basketball star of the New York Knicks (1950–57) and Detroit Pistons (1957–58), one of the first black players in the National Basketball Association: d. Chicago, IL, Aug. 31.

Clive, John (65), German-born professor of history; joined the faculty at Harvard University in 1948. He left to teach at the University of Chicago in 1960, but returned to Harvard in 1965. He won a National Book Award in 1974 for his biography of Scottish historian Thomas Babington Macaulay: d. Massachusetts, Jan. 7.

Collbohm, Franklin R. (83), pioneering aviation engineer and founding president of the Rand Corporation in 1946: d. Palm Desert, CA, Feb. 12.

Collins, Allen (37), an original member of the rock group Lynyrd Skynyrd: d. Jacksonville, FL, Jan. 23.

Conigliaro, Anthony Richard (Tony) (45), baseball player; former Boston Red Sox outfielder. In 1965 he led the American League with 32 home runs and in 1967 became the youngest major-league player to hit 100 career home runs. He was hit in the face by a ball in 1967 and suffered vision problems for some time: d. Feb. 24.

Costakis, George (77), Russian-born Greek art collector; owned what is considered the largest private collection of Soviet avant-garde art: d. Athens, Greece, March 9.

Norman Cousins   Bill Cullen

Cousins, Norman (75), editor in chief of *The Saturday Review*; he had joined the magazine in 1940 and was editor from 1942 to 1971 and again from 1973 until his retirement in 1977. He gained later fame with his best-selling book *Anatomy of an Illness* (1979), which presented the idea that a patient's attitude can combat illness. In all, he wrote or edited more than two dozen books; his last was *Head First: The Biology of Hope*: d. Los Angeles, CA, Nov. 30.

Cruzan, Nancy (33), comatose victim of an automotive accident whose family fought a long legal battle to have her feeding tube removed so that she might be allowed to die. The tube was removed in mid-December: d. Dec. 26.

Cugat, Xavier (90), Spanish-born bandleader; introduced many Latin American rhythms to North American audiences in the 1930s and the 1940s. His family moved to Cuba when he was 2 years old, and as a child he played with the Cuban Symphony. His band became successful during the big band era. He also appeared on radio, television, and in films: d. Barcelona, Spain, Oct. 27.

Cullen, William Lawrence (Bill) (70), television host and panelist on many game shows for more than 30 years. Early in his career he was an announcer for the Columbia Broadcasting System (CBS). Between 1953 and 1986 he was the host of *Give and Take*, *The Price Is Right*, *Place the Face*, *Name that Tune*, *$25,000 Pyramid*, and *The Joker's Wild*. He was a panelist on *Who's There*, *I've Got a Secret*, and *To Tell the Truth*: d. Los Angeles, CA, July 7.

Cummings, Robert (82), actor in dozens of motion pictures and in four television series—*My Hero* (1952–53), *Love That Bob* (1954–61), *The Bob Cummings Show* (1961–62), and *My Living Doll* (1964-65): d. Woodland Hills, CA, Dec. 2.

Dahl, Roald (74), British author; noted for his children's stories as well as books for adults and screenplays. He said that the key to his success was to conspire with children against adults. His juvenile fiction included *James and the Giant Peach* (1962), *Charlie and the Chocolate Factory* (1964; and the adapted screenplay *Willy Wonka and the Chocolate Factory*, film—1971), *Charlie and the Great Glass Elevator* (1972), and *The Witches* (1984). Adult short-story collections included *Someone Like You* (1953) and *Kiss Kiss* (1960). His screenplays included the James Bond film *You Only Live Twice* (1967) and *Chitty Chitty Bang Bang* (1968): d. Oxford, England, Nov. 23.

Danaher, John Anthony (91), U.S. senator (R-CT, 1939–45); later was a federal judge: d. West Hartford, CT, Sept. 22.

Davis, Walter, Jr. (57), jazz bebop pianist and composer: d. New York City, June 2.

de Mestral, Georges (82), Swiss inventor of the Velcro fastener in 1948: d. Commugny, Switzerland, Feb. 8.

Demy, Jacques (59), French director of musical comedy films: d. Paris, Oct. 27.

Dexter, John (64), British director of theater and opera; served for seven years as an associate director of Britain's National Theatre (1963–70). In the United States he received Tony Awards for directing *Equus* in 1975 and *M. Butterfly* in 1988. He also directed productions for the Metropolitan Opera (1974–81): d. London, March 23.

Doe, Samuel Kanyon (38–40?), president of Liberia (1980–90); killed by rebel forces: d. Monrovia, Liberia, Sept. 10.

Donovan, Hedley (76), editor in chief of Time Inc. (1964–79); he served one year as a senior adviser to President Jimmy Carter. His biography *Right Places, Right Times* was published in 1989: d. New York City, Aug. 13.

Dovima (born Dorothy Virginia Margaret Juba) (63), famous model of the 1950s: d. Fort Lauderdale, FL, May 3.

Duarte Fuentes, José Napoleón (64), president of El Salvador (1980–82; 1984–89). He helped found the Christian Democratic Party in 1961: d. San Salvador, Feb. 23.

Duerrenmatt, Friedrich (69), Swiss playwright, novelist, and essayist; considered one of Switzerland's leading writers of the 20th century; best known for his play *The Visit* (1955): d. Neuchatel, Switzerland, Dec. 14.

Duff, Howard (76), actor; noted for character roles; played the detective Sam Spade on radio in the 1940s. He made his film debut in 1947 in *Brute Force*, and in 1948 appeared in *The Naked City*. In the 1950s and 1960s he was a regular in a few television series, and during the 1980s was in the series *Flamingo Road*. A later film was *Kramer vs. Kramer* (1979): d. Santa Barbara, CA, July 8.

Dunne, Irene (91), film star of the 1930s and 1940s; she was adept at comedy and drama, and also made a few musical films. She had an image on screen as a lady. She was five times nominated for an Academy Award, but never won. Among her more than 40 films were *Cimarron* (1931), *Showboat* (1936), *The Awful Truth* (1937), *My Favorite Wife* (1940), *A Guy Named Joe* (1943), *The White Cliffs of Dover* (1944), *Anna and the King of Siam* (1946), *Life with Father* (1947), and *I Remember Mama* (1948): d. Los Angeles, CA, Sept. 4.

Durrell, Lawrence (78), Indian-born British novelist and poet; his fiction was noted for its sensuous exotic qualities, especially *The Alexandria Quartet—Justine* (1957), *Balthazar* (1958), *Mountolive* (1958), and *Clea* (1960). He indicated that these books were an investigation of modern love. His poetry volumes included *A Private Country* (1943), *Sappho* (a verse drama) (1950), *The Red Limbo Lingo* (1971), and *Collected Poems* (1979). Other prose included *The Black Book, an Agon* (1938), *Bitter Lemons* (1957), *The Avignon Quintet—Monsieur* (1975), *Livia* (1979), *Constance* (1983), *Sebastian* (1984), and *Quinx* (1985): d. Sommières, France, Nov. 7.

d'Usseau, Arnaud (73), playwright and screenplay writer; with James Gow, he wrote the plays *Tomorrow the World* (1943), *Deep Are the Roots* (1945), and *The Legend of Sarah* (1950). He collaborated with Dorothy Parker on *Ladies of the Corridor* (1953): d. New York City, Jan. 29.

Edgerton, Harold Eugene (86), inventor of the electronic flash or stroboscope that expanded the scope of photography, and professor of electrical measurements at the Massachusetts Institute of Technology, where he was a student and teacher for more than 50 years. He was also the inventor of many sonar and underwater photographic devices for ocean research. In 1973 he helped find the remains of the Civil War ironclad *Monitor* but failed in a 1976 expedition to locate and photograph Scotland's Loch Ness monster: d. Cambridge, MA, Jan. 4.

Edmondson, Ed (71), U.S. representative (D-OK, 1953-73): d. Muskogee, OK, Dec. 8.

Edwards, Douglas (73), radio and television newsman; was network television's first anchorman. He worked for CBS from 1942 to 1988: d. Sarasota, FL, Oct. 13.

Irene Dunne   Lawrence Durrell   Harold E. Edgerton   Ava Gardner

Elath, Eliahu (born Eliahu Epstein) (86), a Ukrainian-born journalist and ardent Zionist who helped found the state of Israel: d. Jerusalem, June 21.

Enriquez, Rene (56), television and film actor; appeared in the television series *Hill Street Blues* in the role of Lt. Ray Calletano: d. Tarzana, CA, March 23.

Erté (born Romain de Tirtoff) (97), Russian-born art designer; a master of the Art Deco style, known for his magazine covers and theatrical costumes. He gained recognition in Paris before World War I, but his first major success was as a stage designer in the 1920s and 1930s. In the 1970s and 1980s he did lithographs and serigraphs, and many of his works, including *The Alphabet* and *The Numbers* series, were sold as posters: d. Paris, April 21.

Evans, Ronald E. (56), U.S. astronaut; joined the space program in 1966 and was a pilot on the 1972 Apollo 17 mission, the last mission in the Apollo series: d. Scottsdale, AZ, April 7.

Fabrizi, Aldo (84), Italian character actor; achieved fame as the courageous priest executed by the Nazis in Roberto Rossellini's film *Open City* (1945): d. April 2.

Farrell, Charles (88), actor with a gentlemanly demeanor; had a career in movies and television spanning 40 years from silent movies to the 1950s television series *My Little Margie*: d. Palm Springs, CA, May 6.

Faulk, John Henry (76), radio and television humorist; was at the center of a famous trial on the blacklisting of entertainment personalities. Later he became a regular on television's *Hee Haw*, and in 1975 his book was dramatized in the television movie *Fear on Trial*: d. Austin, TX, April 9.

Figueres Ferrer, José (83), Costa Rican president in 1948 of a provisional junta that held power for 18 months. During that time, Figueres dissolved the country's army and placed Costa Rica on a democratic footing. He was elected president for two terms (1953–58; 1970–74). He had founded the National Liberation Party, a major force in Costa Rican politics, in 1953: d. San José, Costa Rica, June 8.

Fogerty, Tom (48), rhythm guitarist and cofounder with his brother of the rock group Creedence Clearwater Revival: d. Scottsdale, AZ, Sept. 6.

Forbes, Malcolm S. (70), chairman of Forbes Inc. and publisher of *Forbes* magazine: d. Far Hills, NJ, Feb. 24.

Franchi, Sergio (57), Italian-born tenor trained in opera who became a pop singer: d. Stonington, CT, May 1.

Frank, Ilya M. (81), Soviet physicist; shared the 1958 Nobel Prize in physics: d. USSR, June 22.

Frederick, Pauline (84), radio and television news analyst of world affairs and one of the first women to achieve prominence in the field. She was a National Broadcasting Company (NBC) correspondent at the United Nations for 21 years. After retiring from NBC in 1974, she was a foreign-affairs commentator for National Public Radio: d. Lake Forest, IL, May 9.

Freehof, Rabbi Solomon B. (97), a leader of the Reform Jewish movement and a world-renowned Jewish-law interpreter. He headed the Rodef Shalom Temple in Pittsburgh (1934–66): d. Pittsburgh, PA, June 12.

Fricker, Peter Racine (69), British composer; his major works include *The Vision of Judgement*, his Second Symphony, Viola Concerto, and Second Violin Concerto: d. Santa Barbara, CA, Feb. 1.

Lord Gardiner (born Gerald Gardiner) (89), Lord Chancellor of Britain (1964–70). A champion of human rights, he presided over the abolition in 1969 of the death penalty in Britain. In 1960 he successfully represented Penguin Books, which had been charged with obscenity for publishing the unexpurgated version of *Lady Chatterley's Lover*. In 1981 he was the target of a bomb attack by the Irish Republican Army: d. England, Jan. 7.

Gardner, Ava (67), motion-picture actress; well-known for her femme-fatale roles. Among her most famous films were *The Killers* (1946); *Show Boat* (1951); *Mogambo* (1953), for which she won an Academy Award nomination; *The Barefoot Contessa* (1954); *On the Beach* (1959); and *The Night of the Iguana* (1964): d. London, England, Jan. 25.

Gavin, James (82), U.S. Army lieutenant general; a World War II commander who went on to become a top Army administrator, diplomat, and management consultant. He was instrumental in developing the helicopter-borne forces so much in use in the Vietnam War. He retired in 1958, after which he became vice-president of Arthur D. Little Inc. and ambassador to France under President John Kennedy. He wrote several books, including *Airborne Warfare* (1947), *War and Peace in the Space Age* (1958), *Crisis Now* (1968), and his memoirs *On to Berlin* (1978): d. Baltimore, MD, Feb. 23.

Gilford, Jack (82), stage, film, and television actor and comedian, a veteran of the stage and film *A Funny Thing Happened on the Way to the Forum* and the stage *Cabaret*. Other of his films were *Catch 22*, *Save the Tiger*, and *Cocoon*: d. New York City, June 4.

Goddard, Paulette (born Marian Levy) (78), film actress of the 1930s, 1940s, and 1950s; adept at both comedy and melodrama. She was a former model and showgirl before her first major role in Charlie Chaplin's *Modern Times* (1936), the last silent comedy feature. Other films included *The Great Dictator* (1940), *Kitty* (1946), and *Unconquered* (1947). Known for her philanthropy, her extensive art collection, and her jewelry, she was married at one time to Charlie Chaplin and to the writer Erich Maria Remarque: d. Ronco, Switzerland, April 23.

Goldberg, Arthur J. (81), U.S. political and judicial figure; was secretary of labor under President John Kennedy (1961–62), U.S. Supreme Court justice (1962–65), and United Nations ambassador (1965–68). After 1968 he served as president of the American Jewish Committee, a nationwide human-rights organization; as a member of a New York law firm; and in the administration of President Jimmy Carter. He made an unsuccessful New York gubernatorial run in 1970. Earlier in his career he was a labor lawyer: d. Washington, DC, Jan. 19.

Goldfarb, David (71), Soviet geneticist; fought a seven-year battle to emigrate from the Soviet Union to the United States: d. Washington, DC, Feb. 24.

Goodall, Reginald (84), British opera conductor, especially of Wagner's repertoire; the high point of his career became the Ring cycle that he performed and recorded for the Sadler's Wells Opera: d. near Canterbury, England, May 5.

Gordon, Dexter (67), jazz tenor saxophonist, the first to play bebop; began his career in 1940 with Lionel Hampton's orchestra. He recently had made films, including *'Round Midnight* (1986). In 1943 he made his first recordings as a bandleader. A year later, he joined Billy Eckstine's orchestra, and it was with that band that he came to national prominence: d. Philadelphia, PA, April 25.

Goulding, Ray (68), humorist and satirist; part of the comedy team of Bob [Bob Elliott] and Ray that appeared on radio and television for more than 40 years and was noted for low-key humor and satire. In the early 1980s the team was on public radio doing an updated version of the original 1946 *Bob and Ray* show. They created several memorable characters, including Wally Ballou, Mary McGoon, and the Piel Brothers: d. Manhasset, NY, March 24.

Graziano, Rocky (born Thomas Rocco Barbella) (71), middleweight boxing champion (1947–48); he had a second career as an entertainer. His autobiography *Somebody Up There Likes Me* was made into a film in 1956: d. New York City, May 22.

Gucci, Aldo (84), last surviving son of the founder of the elite Italian fashion house; he once supervised Gucci's U.S. operations. In 1986 he pleaded guilty to U.S. tax evasion and served a year in jail: d. Rome, Jan. 19.

Hale, Alan, Jr. (71), actor; best known for his role as the Skipper in the television series *Gilligan's Island* (1964–67): d. Los Angeles, Jan. 2.

James M. Gavin

Arthur Goldberg

Dexter Gordon

Rocky Graziano

Armand Hammer   *Rex Harrison*

UPI/Bettmann

© Photofest

Halston (born Roy Halston Frowick) (57), fashion designer: d. San Francisco, CA, March 26. (*See* page 233.)

Hammer, Armand (92), industrialist and philanthropist; headed Occidental Petroleum Corporation (1957–90) and long was a spokesman for peace between the Soviet Union and the United States and active in the financial support of research toward a cure for cancer. He was trained as a physician but never practiced medicine, and at one time or another headed businesses in such diverse areas as art and bourbon whisky. A noted art collector, he had been involved in U.S.-Soviet trade for most of the time since 1921: d. Los Angeles, CA, Dec. 10.

Harmon, Thomas Dudley (Tom) (70), football all-America tailback at the University of Michigan in the late 1930s; he won the Heisman, Maxwell, and Walter Camp trophies. After World War II military service he played two seasons in professional football prior to becoming a sports broadcaster: d. Los Angeles, CA, March 15.

Harrison, Sir Rex (born Reginald Carey Harrison) (82), British-born film and stage actor; best known for his portrayal of Professor Henry Higgins in the Broadway and film versions of *My Fair Lady*, for which he won a Tony Award (1957) and an Academy Award (1964): d. New York City, June 1.

Hart, Marion R. (98), author and sportswoman; made seven solo flights across the Atlantic and earlier had sailed a ketch around the world: d. Berkeley, CA, July 2.

Henson, James M. (Jim). *See* page 519.

Herschler, Ed (71), former Wyoming governor; a Democrat, he was elected in 1974 and went on to serve a record three four-year terms: d. Cheyenne, WY, Feb. 5.

Hofstadter, Robert (75), physicist; won the Nobel Prize in 1961; taught at Stanford University (1950-85): d. Stanford, CA, Nov. 17.

Horvath, Ian (46), dancer, dance director, and choreographer; was a dancer with the Joffrey Ballet (1964–66) and the American Ballet Theatre (1967-72), after which he left to cofound the Cleveland Ballet (now the Cleveland-San José Ballet), where he was artistic director until 1983. He was also producing director of the José Limon Dance Foundation and had begun choreographing in 1974: d. New York City, Jan. 5.

Houghton, Arthur, Jr. (83), president of Steuben Glass for almost 40 years beginning in 1933; he was also an arts patron who had been chairman of New York's Metropolitan Museum of Art (1969–72) and the New York Philharmonic (1958–63). Although he remained president of Steuben Glass, he interrupted his tenure there, serving as curator of rare books at the Library of Congress (1940–42) and then in the Army Air Corps for three years: d. Venice, FL, April 3.

Huntley, Raymond (86), British actor; appeared in the television series *Upstairs, Downstairs*: d. London, June 15.

Hussein bin Dato Onn (68), prime minister of Malaysia (1976–81): d. Daly City, CA, May 28.

Ireland, Jill (54), actress who wrote of her long battle against breast cancer in *Life Wish* (1987). She also wrote *Life Lines* (1989). Married to actor Charles Bronson, she appeared in several films with him: d. Malibu, CA, May 18.

Jackson, Gordon (66), British actor; became known to millions of television viewers as Hudson the butler in the series *Upstairs, Downstairs*: d. London, Jan. 14.

Jacobi, Lotte (93), German-born photographer; noted for her photographs of scientists, statesmen, and people in the arts, as well as street scenes in New York, native scenes in New Hampshire, and people and scenes in the Soviet Union, Asia, and Germany: d. Concord, NH, May 6.

Janssen, Werner (91), composer and conductor; specialized in 20th-century music; was the first U.S.-born conductor appointed to lead the New York Philharmonic (in 1934): d. Stony Brook, NY, Sept. 19.

Karjalainen, Ahti (67), prime minister of Finland (1962–64; 1970–71): d. Finland, Sept. 7.

Keith, Lady Nancy (born Mary Raye Gross) (73), U.S.-born socialite of Britain and the United States. Her autobiography *Memories of a Rich and Imperfect Life* was published in 1990: d. New York City, April 6.

Keller, Charles E. (73), New York Yankees baseball outfielder in the 1940s; he played six full seasons with the Yankees beginning in 1939 and then played part-time (1947–49). He retired in 1952: d. Frederick, MD, May 23.

Kelly, Patrick (40), U.S.-born fashion designer; known for his snug-fitting shift dresses, covered with buttons: d. Paris, France, Jan. 1.

Kelman, Rabbi Wolfe (66), a leader of Conservative Judaism for 40 years; he helped pave the way for the ordination of women as rabbis: d. New York City, June 26.

Kennedy, Arthur (75), stage and motion-picture actor; appeared in more than 70 films and won a Tony Award in 1949 for his appearance on Broadway in the role of Biff in Arthur Miller's *Death of a Salesman*. In films he was in *Lawrence of Arabia*, *Elmer Gantry*, and many Westerns. He was nominated five times for Academy Awards—for *Bright Victory*, *Trial*, *Peyton Place*, *Champion*, and *Some Came Running*: d. Branford, CT, Jan. 5.

Keppel, Francis (73), U.S. commissioner of education (1962–66); he earlier had been dean of Harvard's Graduate School of Education for 14 years. Later he was vice-chairman of New York City's Board of Higher Education. A strong proponent of programs to improve learning opportunities for poor children, he worked for the passage of the Elementary and Secondary Education Act of 1965 and was involved with enforcement of the 1964 Civil Rights Act. He also had been a sculptor: d. Cambridge, MA, Feb. 19.

Kirilenko, Andrei (84), former high-ranking member of the Soviet Communist Party and member of the Politburo; was a close associate of Leonid Brezhnev: d. USSR, May 12.

Klassen, Elmer (81), U.S. postmaster general (1972-75); oversaw the post-office reorganization resulting from the 1970 act that made the postal service an independent agency of the federal government: d. Palm Harbor, FL, March 6.

Klein, Gene (69), owner of the San Diego Chargers of the National Football League (1966–84). After leaving pro football he went into thoroughbred racing, and his horse, *Winning Colors*, won the 1988 Kentucky Derby: d. La Jolla, CA, March 12.

Kliban, B[ernard] (55), cartoonist; famous for his drawings of striped, round-eyed cats. His first book, *Cat* (1975), was a best-seller: d. San Francisco, CA, Aug. 12.

Kreisky, Bruno (79), Austria's chancellor (1970-83). A Socialist, he first was elected to Parliament in 1956 and served as foreign minister (1959–66): d. Vienna, July 29.

Kuznetsov, Vasily V. (89), Soviet first vice-president (1977–86); was also first deputy foreign minister for 20 years and a former delegate to the United Nations: d. Moscow, June 5.

Landrum, Phillip Mitchell (81), U.S. representative (D-GA, 1953–77): d. Jasper, GA, Nov. 19.

Lanson, Snooky (76), singer; appeared on television in the 1950s on *Your Hit Parade* (1950–57); he later appeared in nightclubs: d. Nashville, TN, July 2.

Lasky, Victor (72), journalist and author; his anti-Communist views were the main focus of his writing and career. He began his newspaper career as a copyboy for *The New York Journal-American*. During World War II he was a correspondent with the *Stars and Stripes* and after the war joined *The New York World-Telegram*, where he assisted Frederick Woltman in writing a Pulitzer Prize-winning series on Communist infiltration in the United States. His coverage of the trial of Alger Hiss led to the book *Seeds of Treason*, written with Ralph de Toledano. In the early 1950s he became a screenwriter and in 1962 began writing a syndicated newspaper column: d. Washington, DC, Feb. 22.

Lehmann, Rosamond (89), British novelist; wrote of love, betrayal, and family rivalries. Her first book was *Dusty Answer* (1927), and she also wrote *Invitation to a Waltz* (1932), among several other books: d. London, March 12.

Leiris, Michel (89), French anthropologist and Surrealist writer; his early works included *Aurora*, *Manhood*, and *The Autobiographer as Torero*. Later publications were *Race and Culture* (1951), *Picasso and the Human Comedy* (1955), *Fibrilles* (1966), *African Art* (1968), and *Francis Bacon* (1983): d. Saint-Hilaire, France, Sept. 30.

LeMay, Curtis Emerson (83), four-star general of the U.S. Air Force; was chief of staff of the Air Force from 1961 to 1965, when he retired. He directed the U.S. bombing of Japan during World War II and in 1948 led the Berlin airlift. He was commander of the Strategic Air Command (1948–57). After retiring from the military, he was George Wallace's vice-presidential running mate during Wallace's unsuccessful 1968 campaign for the presidency: d. March Air Force Base, CA, Oct. 1.

Lewis, Mel (born Melvin Sokoloff) (60), jazz drummer and orchestra leader; made a name for himself in dance bands in the 1940s: d. New York City, Feb. 2.

Curtis LeMay   Karl Menninger   Lewis Mumford   Bronko Nagurski

Lewis, Richard (76), British international tenor star; achieved fame with his opera and concert performances: d. Eastbourne, England, Nov. 13.

Llera Camargo, Alberto (83), president of Colombia (1945–46; 1958–62); was the first secretary-general of the Organization of American States, serving from 1948 to 1954: d. Bogotá, Colombia, Jan. 4.

Lockwood, Margaret (73), Pakistan-born British actress; one of the most popular actresses in the late 1940s in British films. Her films included *The Lady Vanishes* (1938), *Night Train* (1940), and *The Stars Look Down* (1941). By 1957 she had appeared in more than 40 films: d. London, July 15.

Lovestone, Jay (91), Lithuanian-born head of the U.S. Communist Party in the 1920s and a figure in the U.S. labor movement. He had a confrontation with Joseph Stalin in 1929 that ended his career as a Communist, and he later became strongly anticommunist. He and his followers formed the Communist Party of the United States that later became the Independent Labor League of America; the members were known as Lovestonites. The group disbanded in 1940. He later was international-affairs director of the AFL-CIO. He retired in 1974: d. New York City, March 7.

Lund, Art (75), baritone band singer in the 1940s with the Benny Goodman orchestra: d. Holliday, UT, May 31.

Mack, Walter S. (94), head of Pepsi Cola (1938–51): d. New York City, March 18.

MacLennan, Hugh (83), Canadian novelist, essayist, and teacher; wrote seven novels. He wrote on English-Canadian colonialism, Canadian English/French relations, and Scottish-Canadian Calvinism. He received Canada's Governor-General's award several times. His novels included *Two Solitudes* (1945), *The Precipice* (1948), *Each Man's Son* (1951), *The Watch that Ends the Night* (1959), and *Return of the Sphinx* (1967). His nonfiction included *Scotchman's Return* (1960), a collection of essays; and *Seven Rivers of Canada* (1961). He taught at McGill University (1951–82): d. Montreal, Canada, Nov. 7.

Maitland, Lester J. (91), pioneer aviator who later became an Episcopal priest: d. Scottsdale, AZ, March 27.

Mannes, Marya (85), author, journalist, and social critic; she was a staff writer for the magazine *The Reporter* (1952–63) and also wrote for *The New Yorker*, *McCalls*, and *The New York Times*. She also wrote novels, poetry, a play, and an autobiography: d. San Francisco, CA, Sept. 13.

Marble, Alice (77), tennis player; a top player in women's tennis in the late 1930s: d. Palm Springs, CA, Dec. 13.

Martin, Graham (77), U. S. career diplomat; was the last U.S. ambassador to South Vietnam, where he served from 1973 to 1975: d. Winston-Salem, NC, March 13.

Matsunaga, Spark M. (73), U.S. representative (D-HI, 1963–77) and senator (1977–90): d. Toronto, Canada, April 15.

McCrea, Joel (84), actor; appeared in about 80 Hollywood films, many of them Westerns. Important roles were in the thriller *Foreign Correspondent* and *Sullivan's Travels*. Among his famous Western films were *Buffalo Bill*, *Wells Fargo*, and *Union Pacific*: d. Woodland Hills, CA, Oct. 20.

Medina, Harold (102), U.S. federal judge; served in a New York district court (1947–51) and with the U.S. Court of Appeals for the Second Circuit (1951-1980). He became well-known when he presided over a famous case in 1949 where 11 Communist leaders were charged under the Smith Act with conspiracy to teach and advocate the overthrow of the federal government by force: d. Westwood, NJ, March 14.

Menninger, Karl Augustus (96), psychiatrist and innovative and controversial figure in the field of mental health. Along with his father and brother, he helped found the Menninger Clinic and Foundation in Topeka, KS, in the 1920s, and to his practice he brought a humanist approach, emphasizing the creation of a human environment for patients. A graduate of the Harvard Medical School in 1917, he worked for a time at the Boston Psychopathic Hospital and taught at Harvard. He later returned to Topeka to practice with his father. He wrote 13 books and in his therapy emphasized the role of parents, particularly parental love: d. Topeka, KS, July 18.

Merrill, Gary (74), stage and film actor; worked in more than 40 films and was in the stage hit *Born Yesterday* (1945). He played in the films *Twelve O'Clock High* (1949) and *All About Eve* (1950), in which he starred with Bette Davis, whom he soon married. They divorced after ten years. He also appeared in the television series *Young Doctor Kildare*: d. Falmouth, ME, March 5.

Minshall, William Edward (79), U.S. representative (R-OH, 1955–74): d. Chevy Chase, MD, Oct. 15.

Mirowski, Michel (65), Polish-born professor of medicine at Johns Hopkins University and director of the Coronary Care Unit at Sinai Hospital in Baltimore; he was the principal developer of a device, known as an automatic implantable cardio-verter-defibrillator, that controls irregular heartbeats: d. Baltimore, MD, March 26.

Moravia, Alberto (born Alberto Pincherle) (82), Italian novelist; considered by many to be his country's best. His novels, which explored social alienation and obsessively focused on human sexuality, included *The Time of Indifference* (1929)—which was translated many years later—and *The Woman of Rome* (1949), *The Conformist* (1951), *Roman Tales* (1957), *Two Women* (1958), *Time of Desecration* (1980), and *The Voyeur* (1987). In addition he wrote plays, short stories, essays, and a memoir: d. Rome, Sept. 26.

Mothopeng, Zephania Lekoane (77), Pan-Africanist Congress president: d. Johannesburg, South Africa, Oct. 23.

Muenchinger, Karl (74), German conductor noted for his work with the Stuttgart Chamber Orchestra: d. March 13.

Muggeridge, Malcolm (87), British journalist, author, and social critic. He was a foreign correspondent for *The Guardian* (1932–33) and an editor for *The Daily Telegraph* (1946–52) and *Punch* magazine (1953–57). Later he was a television personality and lecturer. An admirer of the Soviet Union as a youngster, he traveled there in the 1930s and wrote the critical *Winter in Moscow* (1933). After an initial distrust of religion, he developed an attachment to nondenominational Christianity. His works included the play *Three Flats* (1931); a novel, *Autumnal Face* (1931); a 1936 biography of Samuel Butler; *In a Valley of This Restless Mind* (1938); and his religious-oriented works, including *Jesus Rediscovered* (1969), *Something Beautiful for God: Mother Teresa of Calcutta* (1971), *Jesus: The Man Who Lives* (1975), *A Third Testament* (1976), *Christ and the Media* (1977), and *Conversion: A Spiritual Journey* (1988): d. Sussex, England, Nov. 14.

Mumford, Lewis (94), social philosopher, literary critic, historian, and city planner; he fought the development of large-scale public works that he considered poorly planned. A moralist in some of his writings, he was accused of seeing science and the machine as evil, but he stressed that it was the "organized cult of machinery that was really evil." He wrote for *The New Yorker* magazine and authored more than 30 books, including the four-volume "Renewal of Life" series—*Technics and Civilization* (1934), *The Culture of Cities* (1938), *The Condition of Man* (1944), and *The Conduct of Life* (1951), as well as *The City in History, its Origins, its Transformations and its Prospects* (1961) and the two-volume *Myth of the Machine* that included *Human Development* (1967) and *The Pentagon of Power* (1971). In 1986 he received the National Medal of Arts: d. Amenia, NY, Jan. 26.

Mydland, Brent (37), keyboardist for the Grateful Dead rock group since 1979: d. Lafayette, CA, July 26.

Nagurski, Bronislau (Bronko) (81), Canadian-born U.S. football player; showed great strength as a running back and tackler. He won all-America recognition from 1927 to 1929 at the University of Minnesota. In 1930 he joined the Chicago Bears of the National Football League. He was voted All-Pro three times. He left the team when the team owner refused to pay him $6,000 for the 1938 season and became a professional wrestler, but returned in 1943 for one season. He became a charter member of the Pro Football Hall of Fame in 1963: d. International Falls, MN, Jan. 7.

Nakashima, George (85), famous woodworker and designer whose furniture was in high demand; he designed the Altar of Peace at New York's Cathedral of St. John the Divine: d. New Hope, PA, June 15.

Natwick, Myron (100), animator; created the cartoon character Betty Boop and also animated the character of Snow White in the Disney film: d. Santa Monica, CA, Oct. 7.

Nono, Luigi (66), Italian avant-garde composer, the most prominent of the post-World War II period; he made use of the 12-tone technique. He was a member of the Italian Communist Party and frequently based his works on Marxist and revolutionary writings: d. Venice, Italy, May 8.

Noyce, Robert N. (62), inventor of a computer chip that revolutionized the electronics industry; he developed a system of interconnecting transistors on a single silicon microchip known as integrated circuitry, for which he received a patent in 1959: d. Austin, TX, June 3.

O'Brien, Lawrence (73), Democratic political strategist; organized the senatorial and presidential campaigns of John F. Kennedy and was a special assistant for congressional relations in the Kennedy administration. He was postmaster general (1965–68) and Democratic national chairman (1968–69; 1970–72). He also served as commissioner of the National Basketball Association (1975–84): d. New York City, Sept. 28.

O'Fiaich, Cardinal Tomás (66), Roman Catholic primate of all Ireland since 1977; he became a cardinal in 1979: d. Toulouse, France, May 8.

Ohrbach, Jerome (82), president of Ohrbach apparel stores from 1948 until the store was sold to a Netherlands family in 1962: d. Los Angeles, CA, June 28.

Lord O'Neill (born Terence Marne O'Neill) (75), prime minister of Northern Ireland (1963–69): d. Hampshire, England, June 13.

Pan, Hermes (born Hermes Panagiotopulos) (79), choreographer who with dancer Fred Astaire created some of film's most memorable dances. He won an Academy Award in 1937 for *Damsel in Distress*: d. Beverly Hills, CA, Sept. 19.

Pandit, Vijaya Lakshmi (90), Indian independence fighter, diplomat, politician, and the sister of Nehru; she was the first woman to serve as president of the United Nations General Assembly (1953–54): d. Dehra Dun, India, Dec. 1.

Parkinson, Norman (born Ronald William Parkinson Smith) (76), British photographer; known for his portraits of royalty, stylish photos of women, and pictures of movie stars: d. Singapore, Feb. 15.

Percy, Walker (74), writer; wrote about modern man's search for faith and love in an absurd world. His novels, set in the modern South, included *The Moviegoer* (1961), *The Last Gentleman* (1966), *Love in the Ruins* (1971), *Lancelot* (1977), *The Second Coming* (1980), and *The Thanatos Syndrome* (1987). His two works of nonfiction were *The Message in the Bottle* (1975) and *Lost in the Cosmos* (1983). A Southerner, he was educated in medicine but never practiced. He became a Catholic in 1946 and was considered by some a great Catholic novelist: d. Covington, LA, May 10.

Perls, Laura (born Lore Posner) (84), German founder of the Gestalt school of psychotherapy, along with her husband Fritz. She headed the major Gestalt training institute in New York City for nearly 40 years: d. Pforzheim, West Germany, July 13.

Pertini, Alessandro (Sandro) (93), president of Italy (1978–85): d. Rome, Feb. 24.

Peter, Laurence J. (70), Canadian-born academic and writer; best known for the best-seller *The Peter Principle* (1969), which he wrote with Raymond Hull: d. Palos Verdes Estates, CA, Jan 12.

Phillips, Samuel C. (68), U.S. Air Force lieutenant general; beginning in 1964 he directed the Apollo space program through the lunar landing in 1969: d. Palos Verdes Estates, CA, Jan. 31.

Patriarch Pimen (Sergei Izvekov) (79), head of the Russian Orthodox Church, patriarch of Moscow and all Russia (1971–90); was the first patriarch educated under the Soviet system and was considered a compliant supporter of the Kremlin, which brought him under some criticism from church leaders late in his life: d. Moscow, May 3.

Porter, Eliot (88), photographer; noted for his color landscapes reproduced on Sierra Club posters and exhibited at New York's Metropolitan Museum of Art. His first love was photographing birds. His book *Birds of North America—A Personal Collection* (1972) is considered a classic: d. Santa Fe, NM, Nov. 2.

Poveda Burbano, Alfredo (64), military dictator of Ecuador (1976–79); his junta wrote a constitution in 1978: d. Miami, FL, June 7.

Powell, Michael (84), British film director, screenwriter, and producer of many films over a 50-year period. He had a long collaboration with screenwriter Emeric Pressburger. Among his best-known works were *The Edge of the World* (1937), *The Thief of Bagdad* (1940), *The 49th Parallel* (1941), *Black Narcissus* (1947), *The Red Shoes* (1948), *Tales of Hoffmann* (1951), and *The Boy Who Turned Yellow* (1972): d. Avening, Gloucestershire, England, Feb. 19.

Puig, Manuel (57), Argentine novelist; influenced by Hollywood films of the 1930s and 1940s. He wrote *Kiss of the Spider Woman* (1979), which was made into an award-winning film in 1985: d. Cuernavaca, Mexico, July 22.

Raborn, William F. (84), U.S. Navy vice admiral; led the development of the Polaris nuclear missile in the 1950s and later, under President Lyndon Johnson, headed the Central Intelligence Agency (1965–66): d. McLean, VA, March 7.

Rajneesh, Bhagwan Shree (born Chandra Mohan Jain) (58), Indian guru; set up a commune in Oregon in the early 1980s that attracted thousands of followers. He was deported from the United States in 1985: d. Poona, India, Jan. 19.

Rappaport, David (38), British-born actor; a dwarf, he was best known for his role on the television series *L.A. Law*: d. Los Angeles, CA, May 2.

Rashid bin Said al Maktum, Sheik (76), cofounder and vice president of the United Arab Emirates; ruler of the sheikdom of Dubai: d. Dubai, Oct. 7.

Ray, Johnnie (63), pop singer; created a sensation in 1951 with *Cry* and *The Little White Cloud That Cried*. Other hits were *Please Mr. Sun*, *Walkin' My Baby Back Home*, and *Just Walking in the Rain*: d. Los Angeles, Feb. 24.

Reischauer, Edwin (79), U.S. ambassador to Japan (1961–66) and a scholar on East Asian affairs at Harvard University. Two of his books, coauthored with others—*East Asia, the Great Tradition* and *East Asia, the Modern Transformation*—are classics in the field. Other of his books were *Japan, the Story of a Nation* and *The Japanese*: d. La Jolla, CA, Sept. 1.

Revere, Anne (87), film actress of the 1930s and 1940s; blacklisted for 20 years: d. Locust Valley, NY, Dec. 18.

Ritsos, Yannis (81), Greece's best-known poet; wrote more than 117 books of poetry, much of it inspired by his Communist ideology: d. Nov. 12.

Ritt, Martin (76), motion picture and television director; noted for his socially conscious films. His films included *Hud* (1963), *Sounder* (1972), *Norma Rae* (1979), and *The Front* (1976): d. Santa Monica, CA, Dec. 8.

Robbie, Joseph (73), a lawyer; became owner of the National Football League's Miami Dolphins in 1965: d. Jan. 7.

Roberts, Walter Orr (74), founder of the National Center for Atmospheric Research in 1960; was among the first scientists to warn that technology was changing the earth's climate: d. Boulder, CO, March 12.

Walker Percy

Laurence Peter

Eliot Porter

Johnnie Ray

| *Elliott Roosevelt* | *Irene Mayer Selznick* | *B. F. Skinner* | *William French Smith* |

Photos, AP/Wide World

Robles, Marco (84), president of Panama (1964–68): d. Miami, FL, April 14.

Rodale, Robert (60), head of a family publishing empire, Rodale Press in Emmaus, PA, whose magazines focused on such subjects as health and fitness: d. Moscow, USSR, Sept. 20.

Roman, Gilberto (29), Mexican superflyweight boxing champion (1986–87; 1988–89): d. near Chilpancingo, Mexico, June 27.

Roosevelt, Elliott (80), the second child of U.S. President Franklin D. Roosevelt; he was a breeder of Arabian horses and an author of mysteries. His books included *As He Saw It* (1946) and *An Untold Story* (1973): d. Scottsdale, AZ, Oct. 27.

Lord Rothchild (Nathaniel Mayer Victor) (79), member of the European banking family: d. March 20.

Rule, Elton H. (73), president of the American Broadcasting Company (ABC) (1972–83); he earlier had been head of ABC's television network: d. Beverly Hills, CA, May 5.

Rumor, Mariano (74), former prime minister of Italy and former head of the Christian Democratic Party; he formed five governments between 1968–70 and 1973-74: d. Vicenza, Italy, Jan. 22.

Sabicas (born Augustin Castellon) (78), Spanish-born gypsy solo guitarist. He was a concert artist who had played New York's Carnegie Hall: d. New York City, April 14.

Schrady, Frederick (82), sculptor; best known for his works on religious themes: d. Greenwich, CT, Jan. 20.

Selznick, Irene Mayer (83), producer of Broadway plays, including *A Streetcar Named Desire* (1947); she was the daughter of film mogul Louis B. Mayer: d. New York City, Oct. 10.

Seton, Anya (86), author of historic and biographical novels. Among her better-known books were *Dragonwyck* and *Foxfire*, both of which were made into motion pictures: d. Old Greenwich, CT, Nov. 8.

Sewell, Joe (91), baseball player; played 14 seasons (1920–33) with the Cleveland Indians and the New York Yankees. He set the fewest-strikeouts mark, having been struck out only 114 times over 14 years. He had a career batting average of .312 and was elected to the baseball Hall of Fame in 1977: d. Mobile, AL, March 6.

Shepherd, Lemuel Cornick, Jr. (94), commandant of the U.S. Marine Corps (1952–55); the first head of the Marines to serve as a member of the joint chiefs of staff: d. La Jolla, CA, Aug. 6.

Shero, Fred A. (65), coach of the National Hockey League's Philadelphia Flyers (1971–78); led the team to Stanley Cup championships in 1974 and 1975: d. Camden, NJ, Nov. 24.

Sigmund, Barbara Boggs (51), mayor of Princeton, NJ, elected in 1983, and a member of a well-known U.S. political family; she had run for the New Jersey governorship in 1989: d. Princeton, NJ, Oct. 10.

Singer, Arthur B. (72), naturalist and painter; he painted watercolors of birds of the 50 states that appeared on U.S. stamps during the 1980s: d. Jerico, NY, April 7.

Singher, Martial (85), French baritone; after 11 seasons with the Paris Opera he made his debut at New York's Metropolitan Opera in 1943, where he remained until 1959 when he gave up performing for health reasons. He then began a teaching career: d. Santa Barbara, CA, March 10.

Sitterly, Charlotte (91), astrophysicist; her analysis of sunlight first showed the existence in nature of the element technetium. During her career, she was with the Princeton University Observatory and the National Bureau of Standards: d. Washington, DC, March 3.

Skinner, B[urrhus] F[rederic] (86), pioneer behavioral psychologist and educator; studied human and animal behavior in unique experiments, including his so-called Skinner box, an experimental environment for rats and pigeons. After earning a Ph.D. from Harvard University in 1931, he taught at the University of Minnesota (1937–45) and Indiana University (1945–48) prior to returning permanently to Harvard in 1948. He retired in 1974, although he continued to go to his office there for many years. During his career he worked on teaching machines, utopian communities, warheads controlled by pigeons, temperature-controlled environments for infants, and education of the severely retarded. His most important achievement was his explication of the theory of operant behavior, which holds that any behavior is selected and reinforced by certain positive consequences in the environment. His books included *The Behavior of Organisms* (1938), *Walden Two* (1948), *Science and Human Behavior* (1953), *Verbal Behavior* (1957), *The Analysis of Behavior*, with J.G. Holland (1961), *The Technology of Teaching* (1968), and *Beyond Freedom and Dignity* (1971): d. Cambridge, MA, Aug. 18.

Smith, Stephen (62), financial analyst who became a political adviser to his brother-in-law, President John Kennedy: d. New York City, Aug. 19.

Smith, William French (73), lawyer and U.S. attorney general (1981–84): d. Los Angeles, CA, Oct. 29.

Snyder, Mitchell D. (46), advocate for the U.S. homeless, giving the movement a public voice in the 1980s. He was found hanged in an apparent suicide: d. Washington, DC, (found) July 5.

Soupault, Philippe (92), French writer and poet; one of the founders of the Surrealism movement in the early 1920s: d. Paris, March 11.

Soustelle, Jacques (78), anthropologist and a former French cabinet minister; was a leader of an underground movement that fought against Algerian independence from France. In 1955 he was appointed governor-general of Algeria, but was withdrawn in 1956. In 1962 he fled France and lived in exile for seven years: d. Neuilly-sur-Seine, France, Aug. 7.

Spackman, W[illiam] M[ode] (85), a classicist and writer; taught at New York University and at the University of Colorado. He was a radio writer and literary critic. Later in life, he began writing fiction. His first novel was *Heyday* (1953): d. Princeton, NJ, Aug. 3.

Spann, Gloria Carter (63), sister of former U.S. President Jimmy Carter: d. Americus, GA, March 5.

Spewack, Bella (91), Romanian-born coauthor along with her late husband Samuel of comedies for Broadway and film, including the Broadway hits *Boy Meets Girl* (1935) and *Kiss Me Kate* (1949): d. New York City, April 27.

Stanwyck, Barbara (born Ruby Stevens) (82), actress; noted for her roles in such movies as *Stella Dallas* (1937), *Ball of Fire* (1941), *Double Indemnity* (1944), and *Sorry, Wrong Number* (1948), all of which garnered her Academy Award nominations. Later she appeared on television, first in *The Barbara Stanwyck Show* (1960–61) and later in the popular Western series *The Big Valley* (1965–69), for which she won three Emmys: d. Santa Monica, CA, Jan. 20.

Steber, Eleanor (76), soprano with New York's Metropolitan Opera during the 1940s and 1950s; noted for her Mozart and Strauss roles: d. Langhorne, PA, Oct. 3.

Stoneham, Horace C. (86), principal owner and president of the New York and later San Francisco Giants baseball club (1936–76): d. Scottsdale, AZ, Jan. 7.

Stratton, Samuel S. (73), U.S. representative (D-NY, 1959–89): d. Gaithersburg, MD, Sept. 13.

Strout, Richard L. (92), journalist; wrote the "TRB From Washington" political column in *The New Republic* magazine for 40 years (1943–83) and was Washington correspondent for *The Christian Science Monitor* for 60 years: d. Washington, DC, Aug. 19.

Sulzberger, Iphigene Ochs (97), a member of the family that has controlled *The New York Times* newspaper since 1896. She was the mother of current *Times* publisher Arthur Ochs Sulzberger: d. Stamford, CT, Feb. 26.

Tayback, Vic (60), film, stage, and television actor; best known for the role of Mel, the diner owner, in the television series *Alice* (1976–85): d. Glendale, CA, May 25.

Taylor, Alan John Percivale (84), British historian; wrote more than two dozen books and had a reputation as a popularizer

Barbara Stanwyck

Terry-Thomas

An Wang

Ryan White

of history that was looked on with some disdain by a number of his colleagues. He taught at Oxford University for 25 years. His best-known work was *The Origins of the Second World War* (1961): d. Finchley, North London, England, Sept. 7.

Terry-Thomas (born Thomas Terry Hoar Stevens) (78), British comedian and character actor; satirized many types of Britons from the upper-class cad to crooks, dandies, and daredevils. His motion pictures included *Private's Progress, I'm All Right, Jack, School for Scoundrels, It's a Mad, Mad, Mad, Mad World, Those Magnificent Men in Their Flying Machines,* and *How to Murder Your Wife*: d. Godalming, Surrey, England, Jan. 8.

Tho, Le Duc (born Phan Dinh Khai) (79), chief North Vietnamese negotiator at the Paris peace talks that led to the 1973 Vietnam War cease-fire agreement. In 1973, along with U.S. Secretary of State Henry Kissinger, he was offered the Nobel Peace Prize, which he declined. A hard-line Communist, he was a member of Hanoi's Communist Party Politburo from 1955 to 1986, when he resigned in a party reshuffle: d. Hanoi, Vietnam, Oct. 13.

Titterton, Sir Ernest William (73), British nuclear scientist; helped build Britain's first atom bombs: d. Canberra, Australia, Feb. 8.

Tognazzi, Ugo (68), Italian actor; well-known for his role in the film *La Cage aux Folles* (1978): d. Rome, Oct. 27.

Turner, Dame Eva (98), British opera singer: d. London, June 16.

Ussachevsky, Vladimir (78), Manchurian-born composer; was a pioneer of electronic music: d. New York City, Jan. 4.

Van Heusen, Jimmy (born Edward Chester Babcock) (77), composer of popular music, including *Moonlight Becomes You, Call Me Irresponsible,* and *All the Way.* His longtime collaborators were first the lyricist Johnny Burke (1940–53) and then Sammy Cahn (starting in 1954). With them he composed some of the biggest song hits of Bing Crosby and Frank Sinatra. He also wrote the songs for six of the seven "Road" films of Bob Hope and Bing Crosby. He won four Academy Awards, and he and Cahn wrote several Broadway shows: d. Rancho Mirage, CA, Feb. 7.

Vaughan, Sarah (66), jazz singer; noted for her vocal leaps and swoops and her bebop improvisation and for singing theater songs with a symphony orchestra. In her nearly 50-year career she influenced countless others. As a child she studied piano and organ and at the age of 12 was a church organist. She began her professional career in 1943 and a career as a soloist in 1946. She had her first hit song in 1947 with *Tenderly,* and the next year she recorded *It's Magic.* Among her biggest successes were *Make Yourself Comfortable* (1954), *Whatever Lola Wants* (1955), *Mr. Wonderful* (1956), and *Broken-Hearted Melody* (1959). She appeared frequently in the 1980s at New

York's JVC Jazz Festival, often performing the show-stoppers *Misty* and *Send in the Clowns*: d. Los Angeles, CA, April 3.

Vaughan, Stevie Ray (35), guitarist of blues music; best known for his 1984 album *Couldn't Stand the Weather*: d. near East Troy, WI, Aug. 27.

Vishniac, Roman (92), Russian-born biologist and photographer of Jewish life in Eastern Europe shortly before the Holocaust and a practitioner of microphotography. He came to the United States in 1940 and was a professor at Pratt Institute and also had affiliations with Yeshiva University and the Albert Einstein College of Medicine: d. New York City, Jan. 22.

Vitez, Antoine (59), French actor, director, teacher; was director of the Comédie Française (1988–90) and a major figure in French cultural life: d. Paris, April 30.

Wallace, Irving (74), author of several best-selling novels as well as 17 nonfiction works. His books included *The Chapman Report* (1960), *The Prize* (1962), and *The Book of Lists* (1977), compiled with his son David Wallechinsky: d. Los Angeles, June 29.

Wang, An (70), Chinese-born founder, in 1951, of Wang Laboratories, which went from a small one-man operation to one of the world's major computer manufacturers. An inventor, he was the holder of 40 patents, including a ring of iron that served as the core of computer memory until the microchip became available. In recent years the Wang company has sustained various problems: d. Boston, MA, March 24.

Wayne, John Lewis (Johnny) (72), Canadian radio and television comedian of the 1930s and 1940s; was half of the Wayne and Shuster comedy team: d. Toronto, Canada, July 18.

Wheeler, Lyle (84), motion picture art director; won Academy Awards for art direction for the films *Gone With the Wind, Anna and the King of Siam, The Robe, The King and I,* and *The Diary of Anne Frank*: d. Woodland Hills, CA, Jan. 10.

White, Patrick (78), British-born Australian novelist; won the 1973 Nobel Prize in literature, the only Australian writer ever selected. He wrote more than a dozen novels and short stories, poetry, plays, and an autobiography. His novels included *Happy Valley* (1939), *The Tree of Man* (1955), *Voss* (1957), *A Fringe of Leaves* (1976), and *Memoirs of Many in One* (1986). His autobiography was *Flaws of Glass* (1982): d. near Sydney, Australia, Sept. 30.

White, Ryan (18), Indiana hemophiliac AIDs victim, who served as a leader in gaining greater understanding and compassion for victims of the disease: d. Indianapolis, IN, April 8.

Williams, Hope (92), stage actress of the 1920s and 1930s; starred in Philip Barry comedies: d. New York City, May 3.

Williams, William Appleman (68), historian; was the author of several revisionist books challenging traditional views of U.S. history. He was called the founder of the "New Left" school of American history: d. Newport, OR, March 5.

Wilson, Richard (55), Indian tribal head of the Oglala Sioux Indians at the time of the occupation of Wounded Knee, SD, in 1973. At the time he was a target of the dissident Indians who felt that he was too friendly with U.S. government officials: d. Rapid City, SD, Feb. 1.

Wynne, Paul (47), broadcast journalist who appeared on television in 1990 with *Paul Wynne's Journal,* an on-the-air diary of his battle with AIDS. He had been an entertainment reporter for three San Francisco television stations (1972–84): d. San Francisco, CA, July 5.

Xu Xiangqian, General (88), a leading Chinese military leader; was one of ten marshals of China's Red Army: d. Shanxi province, China, Sept. 21.

Young, Lois Moran (81), stage and film actress; made silent films in the 1920s and starred in *Stella Dallas* at the age of 15. In the 1930s she appeared in Broadway musicals. She retired in 1954 after costarring with Robert Preston in the television series *Waterfront*: d. Sedona, AZ, July 13.

Yun Po Sun (92), president of South Korea (1960-62): d. Seoul, South Korea, July 18.

Sarah Vaughan   *Irving Wallace*

OCEANOGRAPHY

GEOSAT, the geodetic and geophysical satellite launched in 1985, ended its useful life in 1990, after transmitting billions of bits of information on the size and shape of our planet, Earth. Its radar altimeter was capable of measuring the distance from the satellite's orbit to the ocean surface within 8 inches (20 cm) over most of the Earth's oceans.

GEOSAT data confirmed that because of the gravitational attraction of water to massive areas, such as mountainous regions, the surface of the ocean tends to mimic the shape of the ocean bottom. Ocean surface-wind speed, wave heights, and the sea-ice edge also were measured. From this data, a precise location of ocean fronts and eddies was available. Features such as the El Niño/Southern Oscillation in the Pacific Ocean, which causes changes in the Earth's climate, could be followed.

The Global Biosphere. A composite image of ocean chlorophyll concentrations has been produced from more than 30,000 views taken over four years by the Coastal Zone Color Scanner (CZCS), in combination with land-vegetation patterns derived from three years of daily images from visible and near infrared sensors on other satellites. This was the first truly global view of the Earth's biosphere. The ocean's biological productivity is reflected in the amount of pigments derived from living phytoplankton, single-celled plants at the base of marine-food chains. CZCS measurements of ocean color reveal the global variation in plant concentrations and the rate at which these plants carry out photosynthesis. CZCS images have been used to investigate the timing and duration of blooms in coastal waters at temperate latitudes and to delineate geographic and seasonal patterns for primary productivity.

Ocean Flux and Circulation Studies. An international fleet of research vessels followed the course of the spring phytoplankton bloom in the North Atlantic for the beginning of a Joint Global Ocean Flux Study (JGOFS) in 1990. Using satellite sensing with AVHRR (Advanced Very High Resolution Radiometer), U.S. and West German vessels observed physical circulation data over time at a fixed location. This information was compared with studies on a series of stations undertaken by Great Britain in a related Biochemical Ocean Flux Study (BOFS). Scientists from Canada, the Netherlands, and France participated.

The North Atlantic cruises represent the first large-scale study of the annual plant bloom in the oceans, which is believed to affect the cycling of carbon dioxide between the atmosphere and the oceans. JGOFS is part of a planned ten-year study known as the International Geosphere-Biosphere Program (IGBP), aimed at understanding the links between biogeochemical ocean cycles and exchanges that occur from the surface layer to both the atmosphere and the deep sea.

The World Ocean Circulation Experiment (WOCE) got under way in 1990. The study is to describe and understand the ocean circulation and its relationship to climate change. WOCE will employ satellites, ships, floats, and instruments to take a comprehensive global "snapshot" of the physical properties of the ocean. The data will be used in numerical models of the ocean circulation to be combined with models of the atmosphere for prediction of global climate change over long periods of time. The largest single part of the decade-long WOCE program, a hydrographic program for ships at sea, will focus on the Pacific Ocean, then the Indian Ocean, and later the Atlantic.

Ocean Drilling. A sample of what is believed to be the Earth's oldest ocean floor was extracted by drilling into the bottom of the Pacific beneath 18,652 ft (5 585 m) of water south of Japan. The ocean-drilling program, with its drill ship *Joides Resolution*, recovered the oldest known oceanic crust in sedimentary rocks which are estimated to be 170 million years old. The drill penetrated 15,522 ft (4 731 m) of sediment and 656 ft (200 m) of volcanic rock to reach the original ocean floor.

The age of the sample was determined from the known ages of the microscopic sea animals found in the rock and dating to the middle Jurassic period. Magnetic patterns on the seafloor indicated that the region south of Japan should be the oldest part of the world ocean. Most seafloor from this period is thought to have been lost to the Earth's interior at volcanic coasts and island arcs by the impact of new material spreading from mid-ocean ridges.

Hydrothermal Fields. A series of dives by the submersible *Alvin* at hydrothermal fields on the slow-spreading mid-Atlantic Ridge returned new information about the region's hydrothermal vents, massive sulfide deposits, and vent biota. Mapping and extensive mineral sampling were done at an active hydrothermal sulfide mound about 820 ft (250 m) in diameter and 131 ft (40 m) high, located at a depth of 12,041 ft (3 670 m) at the junction of the floor and east wall of the mid-Atlantic Ridge rift valley. Black smoker chimneys gave samples at 366°C (691°F). Clear solutions at 300°C (572°F) were taken from white smoker chimneys on the mound. Chemical processes produce high concentrations of gold in parts of the mound, up to 23 parts per million or nearly 1 oz (30 ml) per ton.

Chimney surfaces swarming with thousands of deep-sea shrimp were sampled to learn about the feeding behavior and food sources of this special fauna. The first living specimens of a form known only as a fossil of the Cretaceous age (70 million years ago) were collected.

DAVID A. MCGILL
U.S. Coast Guard Academy

Former Cleveland Mayor George Voinovich, a Republican, was elected governor of Ohio on Nov. 6, 1990. The 54-year-old attorney and former assistant attorney general said that the state must "work harder and smarter" to control costs.

AP/Wide World

OHIO

The election of a Republican governor, continuing problems for two scandal-plagued Ohioans, and a resounding World Series victory for the Cincinnati Reds highlighted news in Ohio in 1990.

Politics. Former Cleveland Mayor George V. Voinovich (R) defeated Ohio Attorney General Anthony J. Celebrezze, Jr., (D) to become the new governor of Ohio. Voinovich ran on a platform calling for no new taxes and better fiscal management. He succeeded Gov. Richard F. Celeste (D), whose two-term administration saw a major increase in the state's income tax, as well as several scandals in executive departments. Republican candidate Robert A. Taft II defeated incumbent Sherrod Brown in the race for Ohio secretary of state. The election of Voinovich and Taft gave the Republicans control of the state's reapportionment board for redistricting of legislative and congressional seats for the 1990s. Ohio was expected to lose two congressional seats by 1992 following the 1990 census.

In the U.S. congressional races, all 18 of the 21 incumbents who sought reelection were returned to office. Democrats and Republicans retained control of the state House and Senate, respectively. The voters also passed an amendment to the state constitution declaring housing to be a "public purpose," clearing the way for greater state involvement in construction of low-income housing. However, an amendment to allow the possibility of authorizing casino gambling in Lorain and other Ohio cities was defeated soundly.

Scandals. Donald E. (Buz) Lukens, a Republican congressman from Middletown, resigned suddenly in October, following new allegations of sexual impropriety. He had been convicted in 1989 of contributing to the unruliness of a minor and had been under investigation by the House Ethics Committee. In November, Republican John Boehner of West Chester was elected to fill Lukens' seat.

Former Cincinnati Reds manager Pete Rose, who had been banned from baseball in 1989 following betting allegations, began serving a prison term for income-tax violations.

Other. An ambitious downtown redevelopment project in Toledo, Portside, was closed for lack of retail business. Downtown commercial redevelopment enjoyed success in Columbus and Cleveland.

In December, Governor Celeste granted clemency to 25 women who had been convicted of killing or assaulting husbands or companions who the women said had abused them physically. In October the state's parental notification law for minors seeking

---

OHIO • Information Highlights

Area: 41,330 sq mi (107 044 km²).

Population (1990 census prelim.): 10,778,000.

Chief Cities (July 1, 1988 est.): Columbus, the capital, 569,570; Cleveland, 521,370; Cincinnati, 370,480; Toledo, 340,760; Akron, 221,510; Dayton, 178,000.

Government (1990): *Chief Officers*—governor, Richard F. Celeste (D); lt. gov., Paul R. Leonard (D). *General Assembly*—Senate, 33 members; House of Representatives, 99 members.

State Finances (fiscal year 1989): *Revenue,* $27,478,000,000; *expenditure,* $22,975,000,000.

Personal Income (1989): $178,583,000,000; per capita, $16,373.

Labor Force (June 1990): *Civilian labor force,* 5,480,700; *unemployed,* 301,500 (5.5% of total force).

Education: *Enrollment* (fall 1988)—public elementary schools, 1,229,384; public secondary, 549,160; colleges and universities, 541,737. *Public school expenditures* (1989–90), $7,250,000,000.

an abortion went into effect, having been declared constitutional by the U.S. Supreme Court. The law requires notification of a parent.

Major reforms and staffing changes were announced for the state's maximum-security prison at Lucasville, following the murders of an inmate and a teacher at the prison, along with allegations of mismanagement.

Ohio's ranking among the states in its resources for the care and treatment of the mentally retarded rose from 23d to 4th in the United States in 1990.

Torrential thunderstorms and flash flooding in June sent a "wall of water" through the Ohio River Valley town of Shadyside, killing at least 26 people and leaving dozens more missing and homeless. The governor declared a state of emergency and the National Guard was sent into the area.

Elaine Hairston became the first woman to hold the position of chancellor of the Ohio Board of Regents. She would oversee planning and budgeting for the state's public universities and colleges. Gordon Gee assumed the presidency of the Ohio State University in July.

JOHN B. WEAVER
Wright State University

OKLAHOMA

Oklahoma took the lead in the United States in two areas during 1990—passage of a term limit for state legislators and significant educational reform.

Elections. The most noteworthy election-year event in the state was the September 18 approval of a ballot proposition limiting the service of newly elected state legislators to a maximum 12 years. Current legislators would be allowed to serve 12 more years. Oklahoma was the first state in the nation to adopt such a term limit.

The state's November elections produced some surprises, although not necessarily in the

---

OKLAHOMA • Information Highlights

Area: 69,956 sq mi (181 186 km²).
Population (1990 census prelim.): 3,124,000.
Chief Cities (July 1, 1988 est.): Oklahoma City, the capital, 434,380; Tulsa, 368,330; Lawton (1980 census), 80,054.
Government (1990): *Chief Officers*—governor, Henry Bellmon (R); lt. gov., Robert S. Kerr III (D). *Legislature*—Senate, 48 members; House of Representatives, 101 members.
State Finances (fiscal year 1989): *Revenue,* $7,011,000,000; *expenditure,* $6,212,000,000.
Personal Income (1989): $45,638,000,000; per capita, $14,154.
Labor Force (June 1990): *Civilian labor force,* 1,577,100; *unemployed,* 76,200 (4.8% of total force).
Education: *Enrollment* (fall 1988)—public elementary schools, 413,656; public secondary, 166,770; colleges and universities, 176,307. *Public school expenditures* (1989–90), $1,760,000,000.

---

major contests. Democratic U.S. Sen. David Boren won reelection by a record margin of more than 80%. Five of the six members of the U.S. congressional delegation were reelected. In the 3d District in southeastern Oklahoma, Democrat Bill Brewster was chosen to replace the incumbent Rep. W. W. Watkins, who ran unsuccessfully in the Democratic gubernatorial primary. As in the previous session the state's congressional delegation would include four Democrats and two Republicans.

In contests for state office, Democrat David Walters won the gubernatorial race to replace the outgoing Republican Gov. Henry Bellmon. Democrats also won the other state offices with two prominent exceptions. Republican Claudette Henry defeated the incumbent Democratic state treasurer, who suffered from allegations of mishandling state funds. In the contest for a seat on the three-member Corporation Commission, Republican J.C. Watts defeated the incumbent Democrat to become the first black Republican to win a statewide contest. Departing Governor Bellmon hailed the victories of Henry and Watts as indications that Oklahoma was "becoming" a two-party state. Democrat Sandy Garrett was elected school superintendent. In legislative contests Democrats increased slightly their already large margin in the Senate and retained their large majority in the House.

Legislation. Education reform and its financing dominated the legislative scene in 1990. The 1989 session had deadlocked on a proposed education package and assigned to a commission the role of making reform recommendations. The commission's recommendations became the basis for new legislation taken up by the 1990 legislature. Both houses narrowly passed the education bill, which raised $230 million in taxes, chiefly through increases in the sales tax and the corporation and income taxes. The funds were to improve teacher salaries, extend early education, reduce class size, and improve curriculum. Reform measures funded consolidation of the state's many small school districts, abolished the office of county school superintendent, and altered provisions regarding teacher tenure. Advocates hailed the measure as putting Oklahoma in the forefront of education reform nationwide.

The 1990 session also passed $43 million for higher education, roughly $3 million for vocational-technical education, and $100,000 for a new special mathematics and science school.

Economy. Oklahoma's economy persisted in its pattern of sluggish growth in 1990. Midyear statistics showed a 1%-2% growth in employment over the previous year. The state's economy also began a gradual diversification away from its dependence on oil and gas. Census figures showed a population gain of 4.4% during the 1980s.

HARRY HOLLOWAY, *University of Oklahoma*

ONTARIO

The year 1990 was a surprising one in Ontario, which witnessed the election of its first-ever National Democratic Party (NDP) government. Early in the year, Premier David Peterson's Liberal government had seemed entrenched. The legislature adjourned in early summer after passing only three major pieces of legislation, overshadowed by the Meech Lake debate and a series of judicial decisions.

Court Decisions. In April the Supreme Court of Canada struck down a judicial inquiry into the activities of Patricia Starr, a former Liberal Party fund-raiser. Critics had seen the inquiry as a means of avoiding revelations embarrassing to the government. Charges subsequently were laid against Starr and others.

In June the courts invalidated the Retail Business Holidays Act, a major item of Liberal policy which had left the decision of Sunday store opening to municipalities. The new decision permitted Sunday opening and upset many municipalities eager to ban the practice.

In February the Ontario Supreme Court forbade religious instruction in schools.

Budget. The April 24 budget had better social programs and the environment as its themes. The only tax increases were on cigarettes (1¢ per cigarette) and tobacco; taxes were reduced for 115,000 low-income earners. A total of C$52 million was to be spent on long-term care for the elderly, C$1.3 billion was allocated over four years for hospitals and health facilities, and farmers were to receive C$48 million to help offset high interest rates. A sum of C$649 million was to be spent on the environment. Revenue, at C$44.53 billion, and expenditures, at C$44.5 billion, were expected to rise by 6.8%—giving a C$30 million surplus.

Provincial Election. The opposition, which had labeled the 1990 budget a preelection one,

were proved right when Premier Peterson called an election for September 6, claiming he needed a mandate to deal with the problems of confederation after the collapse of the Meech Lake accord. Only three years into its mandate, but with a more than 50% approval rating in the polls and no apparent major issues troubling the electorate, the Liberals expected an easy victory before the economy suffered a downturn and damaging revelations from the Starr affair occurred.

Voters reacted negatively to an "unnecessary election," responding more to Conservative leader Michael Harris' attack on high taxes and the NDP's charges of unfair taxation than to Premier Peterson's promise to cut the sales tax by 1% and last-minute attempt to paint the NDP as socialists who would destroy the economy.

In a stunning upset, the NDP won 74 seats, a gain of 55; the Liberals obtained 36, a loss of 57; and the Conservatives won 20, a gain of four. Premier Peterson lost his own seat by 8,000 votes and resigned as premier and party leader. The popular vote, however, was much closer: NDP 38%, Liberals 32%, Progressive Conservatives 23%, and other parties 7%.

New Premier Bob Rae (*see* page 18) found his plans constrained by an economic downturn. The new treasurer, Floyd Laughren, announced in October that the budget surplus of C$30 million announced by the former government in fact could be a deficit of C$2.5 billion. Premier Rae announced that Ontario would not "piggyback" the expected 7% federal goods and services tax (GST) on top of the provincial sales tax; he intended to fight the GST in the courts. He also made clear his opposition to the forthcoming free-trade talks between Mexico, Canada, and the United States and vowed not to let the U.S.-Canada free-trade agreement hinder efforts to help Ontario workers.

Unilingual Advocates. In January the town of Sault Sainte Marie voted itself unilingual English—the 27th town in the province to do so. The municipalities claimed their actions were not anti-French but fiscal. They were reacting to the provincial Language Services Act, which requires the provincial government to provide French-language services where warranted. Although the act does not apply to municipalities, they fear it will be extended to them. Many critics saw this as part of an anti-French backlash and opposition to the Meech Lake constitutional accord which Premier Peterson had supported strongly.

PETER J. KING, *Carleton University*

ONTARIO • Information Highlights

Area: 412,580 sq mi (1 068 580 km²).
Population (September 1990): 9,747,600.
Chief Cities (1986 census): Toronto, the provincial capital, 612,289; Ottawa, the federal capital, 300,763; Scarborough, 484,676; Mississauga, 374,005; Hamilton, 306,728; London, 269,140.
Government (1990): *Chief Officers*—lt. gov., Lincoln Alexander; premier, Robert Keith Rae (New Democrat). *Legislature*—Legislative Assembly, 130 members.
Provincial Finances (1990–91 fiscal year budget): *Revenues,* $44,530,000,000; *expenditures,* $44,-500,000,000.
Personal Income (average weekly earnings, July 1990): $538.57.
Labor Force (September 1990, seasonally adjusted): *Employed* workers, 15 years of age and over, 4,926,000; *Unemployed,* 6.4%.
Education (1990–91): *Enrollment*—elementary and secondary schools, 2,013,380 pupils; postsecondary—universities, 216,400; community colleges, 100,300.
(All monetary figures are in Canadian dollars.)

OREGON

Following one of Oregon's most bitter political campaigns, Barbara Roberts, a Democrat, was the first woman to be elected governor of

Loggers and their supporters jam Pioneer Courthouse Square in Portland, OR, to protest a possible cutback in logging in an effort to save the threatened northern spotted owl.

AP/Wide World

the state. Roberts, Oregon's secretary of state, entered the race in midsummer when Gov. Neil Goldschmidt declined to run for a second term. Attorney General Dave Frohnmayer was the Republican candidate. Independent Al Mobley, running as an antiabortion candidate, garnered 13% of the vote, and, according to some observers, cost Frohnmayer the election.

Republican Sen. Mark Hatfield was reelected in the toughest campaign of his career when he defeated Democrat Harry Lonsdale, a first-time office-seeker. Fifth District five-term congressman Denny Smith, a Republican, was defeated by Democrat Mike Kopetski, while the remaining four congressional seats were won by incumbents. The state Senate remained in Democratic control, but Republicans took charge of the lower chamber when five incumbent Democrats were defeated.

Eleven measures were brought before the voters on the November ballot. Approved was a property-tax reduction which over five years will roll back and cap the amount of property tax which can be collected for schools and non-school taxing entities. The measure required the state's general fund to replace the lost revenues, estimated to amount to more than $3 billion by 1995 when the limitations are phased in completely. Defeated was an abortion prohibition, a parental-notification requirement in cases of abortion for minors, and the shutdown of Trojan, the state's only nuclear-power plant.

The Economy. With the threat of recession looming over most of the nation in the waning months of 1990, forecasters were optimistic about Oregon's economic outlook. Although layoffs in lumber and retail industries pushed up unemployment, employment officials predicted that unexpected job growth in construction would prevent recession in the state.

Oregon's low birthrate was expected to keep wages high, preserving the state's status as a destination choice for many people seeking to relocate. The state's population grew by 53,000 during 1990. About two thirds of that growth was from net migration, mostly to the state's cities. Oregon was expected to continue to attract retirees from all over the country, especially from California. According to United Van Lines, Oregon was its top magnet state—having the highest ratio of in-moves to out-moves. Oregon was tied for second place among Allied Van Lines' magnet states.

The controversy over the northern spotted owl gathered intensity during 1990 when the owl was declared a threatened species. That designation required forestry agencies to consult with the U.S. Fish and Wildlife Service before doing anything that could affect the owl, including the selling of timber for logging. Timber-related interests decried the listing, predicting the loss of thousands of jobs and the demise of Oregon's logging and mill towns. Employment in logging and veneer and plywood mills stood at a record low for late autumn.

L. CARL and JoANN C. BRANDHORST
Western Oregon State College

OREGON • Information Highlights

Area: 97,073 sq mi (251 419 km²).
Population (1990 census prelim.): 2,828,000.
Chief Cities (July 1, 1988 est.): Salem, the capital (1980 census), 89,233; Portland, 418,470; Eugene, 108,030.
Government (1990): *Chief Officers*—governor, Neil Goldschmidt (D); secretary of state, Barbara Roberts (D); *Legislative Assembly*—Senate, 30 members; House of Representatives, 60 members.
State Finances (fiscal year 1989): *Revenue,* $6,767,000,000; *expenditure,* $5,686,000,000.
Personal Income (1989): $44,892,000,000; per capita, $15,919.
Labor Force (June 1990): *Civilian labor force,* 1,510,900; *unemployed,* 79,000 (5.2% of total force).
Education: *Enrollment* (fall 1988)—public elementary schools, 328,226; public secondary, 133,526; colleges and universities, 156,159. *Public school expenditures* (1989–90), $2,217,200,000.

OTTAWA

In 1990 education, development issues, and dreams of sports teams attracted the public's attention in Ottawa. Opposition forced the Ottawa Board of Education, in light of a declining school enrollment, to scale back a proposed tax increase from 23% to 7%. Ottawa's elementary-school teachers were on strike in the spring, and a strike by secondary teachers was averted on the eve of the fall term.

Sports. In June the city council agreed to a feasibility study for a C$21.2 million stadium for a Triple A baseball team. A 20-acre (8-ha) site and other lands were acquired from the federal government in return for a city commitment to maintain in perpetuity certain federal roadways, bridges, and parks in the capital area. The scheme and its vigorous supporter, Mayor Jim Durrell, came under fire because of the unknown costs of the city's commitment and uncertainty of obtaining a franchise. The hope of obtaining a National Hockey League franchise led to a proposal to build an arena-hotel complex in the suburb of Kanata.

Development. Opposition to a proposed bus tunnel under the city center and to downtown collector lanes to the major freeway was mounting on the grounds of cost and fear it would encourage greater traffic in the city core. The city itself came under attack from heritage groups for ignoring its own development freeze by pushing ahead with a social-housing and parking-garage complex in the old Byward market area. Regional chairman Andy Hayden proposed the creation of a 120,000-acre (48 582-ha) second greenbelt around the capital region.

Cooperation between the federal and provincial governments would give the city a new C$70 million, 454-bed geriatric hospital to replace an outdated chronic-care hospital and a veterans' home.

Government. Changes instigated by the provincial government in the structure of the Regional Council were contested by the city of Ottawa. In 1991 the council would be elected directly from newly formed regional wards. Previously it consisted of members of the municipal councils, some of whom thereby sat on two councils. The Ottawa aldermen, who automatically sat on the Regional Council, would have to choose which council to run for. Ottawa would lose its guaranteed majority and feared exploitation of its greater tax base by the suburbs. Membership of all local municipal councils was to be reduced to keep the total of elected councillors in the region the same.

Victoria Island. A dispute over ownership of Victoria Island, claimed by the National Capital Commission and a group of Algonquin Indians, ended with an agreement (subject to federal approval) to build a C$32 million aboriginal center on the island.

PETER J. KING, *Carleton University*

PAKISTAN

Pakistan underwent a major political shift in 1990. The Benazir Bhutto government, after 20 months in power, was dismissed by President Ghulam Ishaq Khan on August 6. Subsequent elections in October established new governments in Islamabad and the four provincial capitals. The new prime minister, Nawaz Sharif, promised improvements, but faced formidable political, economic, and foreign-policy challenges.

Political Developments. Several factors led to Bhutto's abrupt removal. Ishaq alleged unprecedented levels of corruption, loss of public confidence, breakdown in central-provincial relations, and an inability to maintain law and order. The ethnic crisis in Sindh province, lack of clear direction in foreign policy toward Afghanistan and Kashmir, and the failure to produce any meaningful legislation also were cited as precipitating factors. It was rumored widely that the Pakistan army leadership had told Ishaq to dismiss Bhutto by mid-August or face a possible coup.

After Ishaq dissolved the National Assembly and the provincial assemblies of Sindh and Northwest Frontier province (NWFP)—all led by Bhutto's Pakistan People's Party (PPP)—the non-PPP governments of the other two provinces, Punjab and Baluchistan, resigned in sympathy with the president's action. Interim governments were appointed. Although Ishaq argued his actions were needed to preserve Pakistan's democratic system, the move was controversial. The NWFP High Court declared the provincial government's dismissal invalid but was overruled later by the Supreme Court.

Equally controversial was the composition of the interim governments. Ghulam Mustafa Jatoi, opposition leader in the National Assembly, was named interim prime minister, and he appointed several ministers whose reputations were as questionable as those of the dismissed PPP leaders. The interim provincial govern-

---

PAKISTAN • Information Highlights

Official Name: Islamic Republic of Pakistan.
Location: South Asia.
Area: 310,402 sq mi (803 940 km^2).
Population (mid-1990 est.): 114,600,000.
Chief Cities (1981 census): Islamabad, the capital, 204,364; Karachi, 5,180,562.
Government: *Head of state,* Ghulam Ishaq Khan, president (elected Dec. 12, 1988). *Head of government,* Nawaz Sharif, prime minister (took office Nov. 6, 1990). *Legislature*—Parliament: Senate and National Assembly.
Monetary Unit: Rupee (21.72 rupees equal U.S.$1, Dec. 31, 1990).
Gross National Product (1989 fiscal year U.S.$): $43,200,000,000.
Economic Index (1989): *Consumer Prices* (1982 = 100), all items, 151.6; food, 156.1.
Foreign Trade (1989 U.S.$): *Imports,* $7,119,000,000; *exports,* $4,642,000,000.

Military personnel take a break while imposing a curfew in Karachi in February 1990. A general strike, called by the Mohajir National Movement to protest the policies of the Bhutto government, had paralyzed Pakistan's commercial center. Some 60 persons were killed and more than 100 persons were injured in the disturbance.

AP/Wide World

ments also included people unfriendly to Bhutto and the PPP. The president instituted "accountability" proceedings in specially appointed tribunals, in which only PPP politicians, including Bhutto and her husband, Asif Ali Zardari, were charged. Finally, the interim governments used the "advantage of incumbency" to bias public opinion. The media showcased interim leaders and publicized every corruption accusation against Bhutto, her relatives, and her party.

The Elections. The PPP joined with three other parties to form the Pakistan Democratic Alliance (PDA). Sharif's Islami Jamhoori Ittehad—often referred to internationally by its English equivalent, Islamic Democratic Alliance (IDA)—consisted of nine parties, the largest being the Pakistan Muslim League (PML). Through electoral alliances, the IJI managed to guarantee straight contests against the PPP-led PDA in many constituencies. The national elections resulted in an unexpectedly strong victory for the IJI and its allies. The IJI alone won 105 of the 207 contested seats, 91 of them in the giant province of Punjab. Among IJI's allies, the Mohajir Qaumi Movement (MQM) won 15 in Sindh, the Awami National Party (ANP) six in NWFP, and the Jamhoori Watan Party two in Baluchistan, to give the IJI a more comfortable parliamentary majority.

Nawaz Sharif was sworn in as prime minister along with an 18-member cabinet on November 6. The cabinet included veteran Foreign Minister Sahabzada Yaqub Khan, former Assembly Speaker Syed Fakhr Imam, and Mohammed Ijaz ul-Haq, son of the late military ruler Mohammed Zia ul-Haq. The PDA emerged from the elections with 45 National Assembly seats and Benazir Bhutto became leader of the parliamentary opposition. Provincial elections on October 27 produced similar results. In all four provinces governments led by the IJI or its allies were established.

Although an international observer team sponsored by the National Democratic Institute concluded that there was insufficient evidence to support the PDA charges of widespread "rigging," other observers suspected malpractice in the vote count.

The Economy. Pakistan's economic picture was mixed. The annual economic report indicated a 23% increase in exports, stable imports, a drop in inflation from 10.4% to 5.7%, and a 5.2% growth in gross domestic product (GDP). However, the population growth rate of 3.1%, one of the world's highest, reduced per-capita growth to about 2%. Pakistan was forced to make several structural adjustments, including cutbacks in budget deficits, to meet the conditions of a 1988 International Monetary Fund (IMF) loan inherited by Bhutto from the Zia regime. There was an attempt to put more emphasis on the private sector, but expenditures for education and military spending increased, too.

Official economic figures, however, were subject to dispute. The interim government in August claimed the deposed Bhutto regime left empty coffers, that Bhutto downplayed inflation rates, and that phenomenal sums had been squandered through corruption.

Two of Pakistan's areas of support declined. Worker remittances dropped and extensive foreign aid became a burden as well as a boon. In fiscal year 1989, debt repayments equaled 42.57% of total revenue, up from 27% a decade earlier. In October, U.S. aid was halted after President Bush decided not to submit to Congress the annual verification that Pakistan was not developing nuclear weapons.

As energy output grew, so did demand. The $1.1 billion Hub thermal-power project in Baluchistan was begun. It was financed with World Bank and other foreign support.

Foreign Affairs. Relations between India and Pakistan worsened. Bhutto and other Pakistani leaders expressed public sympathy for the Kashmiris' rights of self-determination, but denied India's claims that it instigated the separatist conflict. Diplomatic meetings helped to relieve tensions and assure both countries that neither wanted war.

The Afghan conflict continued on a lower scale and Pakistan's relations with the United States deteriorated. In February, French President François Mitterrand pledged to sell nuclear-power plants to Pakistan, despite U.S. opposition. Pakistan reiterated its intent to use the technology for power generation and its willingness to sign the nuclear nonproliferation treaty if India did.

After Bhutto's ouster the U.S. embassy issued assurances that the United States supported the democratic process, not any specific political leader, but Congress and the U.S. media were more critical. In October, U.S. Ambassador Robert Oakley gave a speech calling upon Ishaq to carry through with his pledge to hold fair elections. Oakley's speech was reported and criticized widely in the Pakistani press. The timing of the suspension of U.S. aid caused many Pakistanis to regard it as a further U.S. protest against Bhutto's ouster.

WILLIAM L. RICHTER
Kansas State University

PARAGUAY

In its second year under Gen. Andrés Rodríguez, Paraguay experienced economic growth and made further progress toward democratic government, but stood still on the question of land reform.

Politics and Government. A new electoral code approved by Congress in February provides that party leaders be chosen by direct vote, and excludes policemen and military men on active duty from party affiliation. Presidential contests in which no candidate wins an absolute majority in the first round are to be decided by runoff elections, and members of congress are to be elected by proportional representation. Juan Ramón Chaves, the longtime chairman of the ruling Colorado Party, resigned in a factional dispute on March 4. In August the entire cabinet resigned to facilitate the replacement of Foreign Minister Luis María Argaña, who was dismissed for having advocated that the Colorados remain in power indefinitely. He was replaced by Alexis Frutos Vaesken, who had been serving as minister of justice and labor.

President Rodríguez was hailed for his democratic decision to hold office for only one term, but his administration, despite its promises, showed no inclination to attack the nation's acute agricultural and financial problems. Col. Fernando Ugarte, head of the agrarian-reform commission, revealed in April that 120,000 peasant families were without land. But Rodríguez, himself a large landowner, refused to tolerate heightened activity by peasant organizations. In January government forces dispersed peasants who had occupied farmland illegally in central San Pedro department. Six of the protesters had to be evacuated to Asunción for treatment of bruises and broken bones. Meanwhile, an ongoing investigation of widespread corruption benefiting members of the regime of deposed President Alfredo Stroessner revealed that an agrarian-reform institute founded to distribute land to poor peasants had, instead, given 15 million acres (6.1 million ha) to Stroessner and his closest collaborators.

Economy. Central Bank President Crispiniano Sandoval reviewed the Paraguayan economy in February and found that, in the first year of Rodríguez' rule, the economy had grown by 6% and inflation had leveled off at 30%, while exports rose by 106% to just more than $1 billion. Foreign reserves more than doubled, approaching $300 million. Finance Minister Enzo Debernardi added that the Rodríguez administration had been able to reduce spending sharply and that the public-sector deficit had been eliminated entirely.

Foreign Relations. The Organization of American States (OAS) met in Asunción in June. On that occasion, heads of state from Argentina, Bolivia, Brazil, Suriname, and Uruguay were received by General Rodríguez. Paraguay was among the member-states whose human-rights record was condemned. An "American Declaration" was issued justifying the OAS' existence and calling for its renewal.

General Rodríguez visited the United States in mid-June to meet with U.S. President George Bush and potential investors in Paraguayan development. Rodríguez requested a resumption of U.S. trade benefits under the Generalized System of Preferences, suspended in 1986 because of abusive treatment of labor by the previous regime. The Bush administration promised greater cooperation with the Asunción government in its antidrug efforts.

LARRY L. PIPPIN, *University of the Pacific*

PARAGUAY · Information Highlights

Official Name: Republic of Paraguay.
Location: Central South America.
Area: 157,046 sq mi (406 750 km²).
Population (mid-1990 est.): 4,300,000.
Chief City (1982 census): Asunción, the capital, 455,517.
Government: *Head of state and government,* Gen. Andrés Rodríguez, president (took office 1989). *Legislature*—Congress: Senate and Chamber of Deputies.
Monetary Unit: Guaraní (1,205.0 guaraníes equal U.S.$1, selling rate, June 1990).
Gross Domestic Product (1989 est. U.S.$): $8,900,-000,000.
Foreign Trade (1988 U.S.$): *Imports,* $555,000,000; *exports,* $607,000,000.

PENNSYLVANIA

Elections dominated the news in Pennsylvania in 1990. As the year began, Democratic Party leaders were optimistic about capturing the state legislature and retaining the governorship behind popular incumbent Robert P. Casey. At stake was control of the state political redistricting following the 1990 census in which Pennsylvania's population decline resulted in a scheduled drop of two seats in the U.S. House of Representatives. Going into the fall election, the Democrats had a majority in the state House of 104 to 99 seats, while the Republicans controlled the state Senate by a 27-to-23 margin.

Opposing Governor Casey in the gubernatorial race was State Auditor General Barbara Hafer, who emphasized her opposition to Pennsylvania's stringent antiabortion statute that Casey had supported. She stated the election should be a referendum on the abortion issue. Instead, however, the election turned on questions of Hafer's judgment and Casey's performance. Shortly after defeating pro-life candidate Marguerite (Peg) Luksik to win the Republican primary on May 15, Hafer referred to Governor Casey as "a redneck Irishman from Scranton." This and other gaffes focused media attention on her judgment and sharply limited her ability to raise funds. The Casey campaign dominated television advertising with a positive message that Casey's leadership had made Pennsylvania "the rising new star of America" and resulted in his reelection with 68% of the vote.

Despite the Casey landslide, the Democrats were unable to capture the state legislature. Although they increased their advantage in the state House from 104 to 108 seats in the 203-seat assembly, the Republicans retained control of the Senate by 26 to 24 seats. In contests for the U.S. Congress, 22 of the 23 incumbents won—only an upset by Republican Rick San-

torum in a Pittsburgh district prevented an incumbent sweep. Incumbent victories were not always easy, however. Long-term incumbent Democratic Congressmen John P. Murtha and Joseph M. Gaydos easily defeated Republican challenges in the fall, but each had to fight off a difficult primary challenge in the spring.

Legislation. The major legislative initiative of the year was an antitakeover bill that Governor Casey signed on April 27. Supported by both business and labor, the intent of the legislation was to protect corporations from dismemberment in hostile takeovers by corporate raiders. The law provides for severance pay for workers who would lose their jobs; a prohibition against "greenmail" tactics by which a company buys its own stock at high prices; a requirement of shareholder approval of a sale by a single large "control shareholder"; and authority for boards of directors to make decisions with the interests of workers, the community, suppliers, and customers (as well as shareholders) in mind. The constitutionality of the law was challenged immediately on the grounds that it violated both property rights guaranteed by the Constitution and federal security laws.

Economy. Pennsylvania's stagnant economy appeared headed into a recession by year's end. By late fall, unemployment had risen to 6.1%, higher than the national average of 5.7%, and at the end of the year both Philadelphia and Scranton sought state help to deal with fiscal crises. A decline in manufacturing and construction jobs also continued, and the previously booming service sector failed to expand sufficiently to offset these losses. Western Pennsylvania faced declining populations and higher than average unemployment, and even in the prosperous counties of southeastern Pennsylvania outside Philadelphia, growth had slowed from the highs of the 1980s.

Other. On August 24, U.S. District Judge Daniel H. Huyett 3d struck down portions of the 1989 abortion law that required women to notify their husbands, mandated doctors to lecture women seeking abortions about the risks and benefits of abortion and childbirth, and established a 24-hour waiting period for women seeking abortions. The state appealed the judge's decision in a case expected eventually to reach the U.S. Supreme Court.

Environmental mishaps during the year involved two oil spills in the Pittsburgh area. In January, 10,000 gallons (37 800 l) spilled from a runaway barge into the Monongahela River 15 mi (24 km) south of Pittsburgh. In April an oil leak from a ruptured pipe leaked into the Allegheny River, disrupting water supplies in eight communities. In both cases the spills were controlled before contaminating Pittsburgh's water supplies.

ROBERT E. O'CONNOR
Pennsylvania State University

PENNSYLVANIA • Information Highlights

Area: 45,308 sq mi (117 348 km²).
Population (1990 census prelim.): 11,764,000.
Chief Cities (July 1, 1988 est.): Harrisburg, the capital (1980 census), 53,264; Philadelphia, 1,647,000; Pittsburgh, 375,230; Erie, 112,800; Allentown, 105,200.
Government (1990): *Chief Officers*—governor, Robert Casey (D); lt. gov., Mark Singel (D). *Legislature*—Senate, 50 members; House of Representatives, 203 members.
State Finances (fiscal year 1989): *Revenue,* $25,681,-000,000; *expenditure,* $22,987,000,000.
Personal Income (1989): $207,916,000,000; per capita, $17,269.
Labor Force (June 1990): *Civilian labor force,* 5,974,300; *unemployed,* 295,900 (5.0% of total force).
Education: *Enrollment* (fall 1988)—public elementary schools, 1,132,631; public secondary, 527,-083; colleges and universities, 573,927. *Public school expenditures* (1989–90), $8,792,816,000.

PERU

The central event of 1990 in Peru was the election of Alberto Fujimori as president. The 51-year-old son of Japanese immigrants was virtually unknown six weeks before the April 8 presidential elections, which neo-liberal novelist Mario Vargas Llosa had been expected to win handily. Riding on a wave of profound disillusionment with politicians, the agronomist with no previous experience as an elected official gained enough support to come in second and force a runoff election, which he won with 56% of the vote on June 10.

Fujimori's election was a reaction to the APRA government of Alan García, which destroyed confidence in the Peruvian economy, produced widespread unemployment and hunger, achieved an inflation rate of 2,700% in 1989, and failed to contain political violence, which claimed 3,198 lives in 1989. Fujimori succeeded in portraying himself as a candidate above politics. He pledged to liberalize the economy without the extreme shock measures promised by Vargas Llosa. He also benefited from being a nonwhite candidate in a nation with a predominantly Indian and mestizo population and from the support of evangelicals linked to the underground economy.

Economic-Adjustment Program. Ironically, shortly after taking office on July 28, President Fujimori announced that he would implement a drastic economic-adjustment program to attract foreign investment and enable Peru to resume servicing its $20 billion foreign debt. After renewing the state of emergency and putting the police and military on alert, Fujimori announced one of the most drastic economic-adjustment programs ever seen in Latin America. Removal of state subsidies raised basic food and transportation costs by 200–300%, and fuel costs by 3,000%. The "Fujishock" program reduced import tariffs and eliminated the official exchange rate in favor of a free float. Demand fell to a fraction of its preshock level in the next month as real wages declined by one quarter and uncertainty seized consumers.

Reacting to the program, more than 150,000 workers from the mining, banking, social-service, and government sectors organized strikes and demonstrations in August; 6,000 arrests were made and at least four protesters were killed. However, considering the extreme hardship that resulted, observers were surprised that the public reaction was not more violent.

The architect of the shock program was Prime Minister Juan Carlos Hurtado, a confidence-inspiring figure formerly associated with the Acción Popular Party. But the cabinet was a very eclectic one, with representatives from all major parties except APRA, the party of outgoing President García. Fujimori also made a point of replacing the commanders of the

AP/Wide World

Alberto Fujimori

Peru's new president, Alberto Fujimori, was born in Lima on July 28, 1938, to Japanese immigrants. After being awarded a master's degree in mathematics from the University of Wisconsin, he became an agronomist and was rector of National Agrarian University in Lima. He later was host of a television talk show on Peru's socioeconomic problems. Influenced by his Japanese background, he decided to enter Peruvian politics because of a belief that he personally could help solve Peru's many problems through technology and hard work. He speaks four languages.

navy and air force who had served under García. These dismissals were part of a new policy of cracking down on political corruption. They were followed by additional corruption charges made against 700 court employees and the dismissal of 350 police officers.

Law Enforcement. The *Sendero Luminoso* (Shining Path) guerrilla movement continued to pose a serious challenge to the government. No longer confined to the Andean highlands, *Sendero*'s armed membership was estimated to be about 5,000, scattered among all departments of the country and gaining strength among desperate youths in both rural and urban areas. During the April elections, *Sendero* assassinated dozens of candidates for local office, and in the climate of violence, one quarter of all electoral districts either reported a high rate of abstention or could not report results at all.

PERU · Information Highlights

Official Name: Republic of Peru.
Location: West coast of South America.
Area: 496,224 sq mi (1 285 220 km²).
Population (mid-1990 est.): 21,900,000.
Chief Cities (mid-1985 est.): Lima, the capital, 5,008,400; Arequipa, 531,829; Callao, 515,200.
Government: *Head of state,* Alberto Fujimori, president (took office July 28, 1990). *Head of government,* Juan Carlos Hurtado, prime minister (took office 1990). *Legislature*—Congress: Senate and Chamber of Deputies.
Monetary Unit: inti (547,945 intis equal U.S.$1, official rate, Dec. 31, 1990).
Gross Domestic Product (1989 est. U.S.$): $18,900,-000,000.
Economic Index (Lima, 1989): *Consumer Prices* (1980 = 100), all items, 2,991,466; food, 1,669,680.
Foreign Trade (1989 U.S.$): *Imports,* $1,798,000,000; *exports,* $3,491,000,000.

Drugs. The government also announced its intention to combat the problem of drug trafficking with economic development rather than with guns, on the grounds that peasants become coca growers only because of the lack of other means of subsistence, and because a military "war" against drugs strengthens the coal producers' dependence on *Sendero Luminoso* for protection. The drug trade provided Peru with an estimated $1.2 billion-$1.3 billion in 1990, making it the country's largest export earner. The United States proposed a $37.5 million military-aid package for Peru to be used to combat the drug trade. Fujimori rejected the aid because of its military emphasis.

MICHAEL COPPEDGE
Johns Hopkins University

PHILIPPINES

Corazon Aquino came so close to being overthrown in an early December 1989 coup that the Philippine president was forced to devote most of 1990 to damage control. Even as the threat to constitutional government from the Communist-led New People's Army (NPA) seemed to diminish, it became clear that armed opposition from military factions would continue. Reference to rebels no longer meant Communist forces in the field or their "sparrow" squads in Manila, but uniformed members of RAM (Reform the Armed Forces Movement) now identified as SFP (Soldiers of the Filipino People) or the newer YOU (Young Officers Union) faction. Mainly these rebels were elite graduates of the military academy, in their 30s or 40s.

Coup Attempts. On Dec. 1, 1989, hotels near Metro Manila's Makati business district had been seized, and many civilians entering the streets out of curiosity were wounded. The presidential palace itself was threatened until, at the government's request, U.S. Phantom jets from Clark Air Field overflew the area and prevented rebel air attacks. Eventually the insurgents negotiated what they refused to call a surrender and marched back to their barracks bearing their weapons and promising to rise again until a junta could occupy the presidency.

To prevent another coordinated uprising, Aquino ordered nearly 2,000 soldiers arrested early in 1990 and disbanded the First Scout Ranger Regiment that played a prominent role in the assault. Chief coup strategist Gen. Edgardo Abenina was captured in January, but two other important members of the rebels' provisional National Governing Council, Col. Gregorio Honasan and Gen. José Ma. Zumel, went underground. Rodolfo Aguinaldo, forced from the governorship of Cagayan province for supporting the coup, refused to surrender to Gen. Oscar Florendo early in March. During talks, Aguinaldo seized the general and held him hostage in a hotel in Tuguegarao. As the result of a four-hour gun battle, General Florendo and 13 others died. Aguinaldo escaped and went into hiding, with the government declaring he be shot on sight. On April 8 masked YOU commandos freed coup conspirator Col. Billy Bibit from prison in Manila while he was attending his jailor's birthday party. In August daily bombings by military terrorists began in metropolitan Manila.

The government struggled to restore civil order and public confidence. More than 500 captured rebel soldiers were held on three disabled ships in mined waters off Cavite; but because Honasan himself had bribed his way off just such a prison ship in 1988, which troops would remain loyal no longer could be predicted. Six officers who participated in a 1987 coup attempt began serving 20-year terms at hard labor in 1990. Yet major rebel leaders remained at large and Secretary of Defense Fidel Ramos asked that the 1987 constitution be amended to make rebellion a capital offense, subject to the death penalty. There was great concern that foreign investments would diminish as a result of the severity of the December coup attempt. Nearly half of the cabinet ministers were replaced and 22 senior generals and flag officers were retired to placate ambitious but frustrated younger officers. Still dissatisfied, insurgents raided an armory in Quezon City on September 9.

In October the seventh coup attempt was engineered on the southern island of Mindanao, by Col. Alexander Noble, the former deputy chief of the presidential security guard and a participant in the December attempt. Part of his force was drawn from right-wing Muslim secessionists of the Mindanao Independence Movement. Observers speculated that Noble was using these dissidents, along with hundreds of his own soldiers, to divert government attention from what he expected would be a nationwide uprising. No nationwide coup materialized; the Mindanao rebels were strafed by Philippine Air Force helicopters and within days surrendered to loyalist troops. No one, however, thought that the insurgency was over, for the army remained politicized. As Gen. Rodolfo Biazon, vice-chief of staff, explained: "We were appointed as governors and mayors" under former President Ferdinand Marcos. "So we ended up thinking we could do things other than soldiering."

If RAM rebels do not seize power before the May 1992 elections, they might join forces with political parties which still are undergoing realignment and, like the rebels, are without any clear agenda. The opposition Nacionalistas were trying to bring together such Marcos regulars as Eduardo Cojuangco, who reentered the country surreptitiously late in 1989, with such disaffected politicians as Vice-President Salvador Laurel, a former ally of Aquino who more recently had been trying to revive the UNIDA and UNA coalitions. The Nacionalistas also have had intermittent support from Sen. Ponce Enrile, onetime secretary of defense and long a favorite of RAM factions, who was indicted for assisting the December coup but was released in June for insufficient evidence. Less likely future partners with the military would be Senate President Jovito Salonga's Liberal-LDP coalition; the pro-Aquino PDP-LABAN; and leftist Partido ng Bayan.

Indicative of the political confusion in 1990 was the offer extended by the leftist NPA to form a common front with the right-wing RAM to campaign against an administration criticized as being unable to rule. The military dissidents, considering the NPA's diminishing importance, refused to share power with their old enemies. NPA numbers had decreased by several thousand, due to combat losses and their own "self-cleansing" purges. Party leader José Maria Sison was accused of counterfeiting in the Netherlands, and had to appeal the decision that he be declared persona non grata. Since Communist stalwart North Korea already had refused him asylum, his status was

perilous and his usefulness questionable. The Communist Party itself complained that Sison was spending funds on personal pleasures rather than on weapons or on raising the European consciousness to the plight of Philippine peasants.

Despite such volatility in loyalty, the one element in Philippine society that consistently has supported orderly process under the constitution, opposing revolution from both right and left, has been the general public. The average Filipinos still held the 1986 bloodless eviction of Marcos as the best model for change, a view encouraged by Church leader Cardinal Jaime Sin. However, increasingly they viewed that same event as a "restoration," not of democracy but of rule by the elite, and President Aquino as captive to her heritage as a landed aristocrat. The Cojuangcos' Hacienda Luisita, her family estate and the largest sugar plantation on Luzon, could have been a model of social justice extended to its tenant farmers. But critics charged the estate remained typical of those recalcitrant landlords who have obstructed implementation of the land reform bill of 1988. Aquino's popularity declined as her wavering leadership was blamed for continuing corruption in her administration.

Although the Presidential Commission on Good Government had recovered $1 billion of the $10 billion allegedly looted by Marcos cronies, too often the seized properties ended up in the hands of Aquino relatives at bargain prices. Even Secretary of Trade and Industry José Concepcion, Jr., enforcer of honest ballot counting in 1986, was accused of conflicts of interest. In addition, 22 Philippine Airlines officials were under investigation for plundering $87 million from the corporation. Philippine Assistance Plan (PAP) funds, from foreign nations, were suspended when the head of the Department of Agrarian Reform resigned amid charges of graft. Other PAP funds designated for aid to industry could not be absorbed quickly enough, for lack of clear programs. The pace of capital distribution decreased. At the same time, foreign investments paused as a result of the December 1989 coup attempt. The Asian Development Bank expressed less confidence in the Philippine economy than in other Southeast Asian countries because of the debt burden, the slow progress in infrastructure, and the failure both to control population growth and to implement agrarian reform. When complaints reached the president that vigilante groups were protecting the interests of large landowners rather than the rights of commoners from NPA incursions, she replied that "landlords have rights too."

The Economy. Cities had problems of their own, with recurring brownouts and water shortages contributing to a lowering of productivity just when the economy was growing at

---

PHILIPPINES • Information Highlights

Official Name: Republic of the Philippines.
Location: Southeast Asia.
Area: 115,830 sq mi (300 000 km²).
Population: (mid-1990 est.): 66,100,000.
Chief Cities (1984 est.): Manila, the capital, 1,728,441; Quezon City, 1,326,035; Davao, 552,155; Caloocan, 524,624.
Government: Head of state and government, Corazon C. Aquino, president (took office Feb. 25, 1986). Legislature (bicameral)—Senate and House of Representatives.
Monetary Unit: Peso (27.80 pesos equal U.S. $1, floating rate, Dec. 31, 1990).
Gross National Product (1989 U.S.$): $40,500,-000,000.
Economic Index (1989): Consumer Prices (1980 = 100), all items, 319.3; food, 323.2.
Foreign Trade (1989 U.S.$): Imports, $10,732,-000,000; exports, $7,747,000,000.

5.5%. During the first four years of the Aquino administration (1986–90), inflation had dropped from 10.6% to 8%, exports had increased 48%, the Cooperative Development Authority had been signed into law, the foreign debt had been renegotiated successfully, and the World Bank had signed a $390 million energy loan. Despite all these signs of an improving economy, concern remained in 1990 that if only the very wealthy were better off and most of the people remained in desperate poverty, the nation would continue on the edge of violence.

Natural disaster added to the troubles in the Philippines when a major earthquake struck the main island of Luzon on July 16, hitting the summer capital of Baguio particularly hard. Casualties totaling 1,600 were reported from the temblor which measured 7.8 on the Richter scale. The collapse of deluxe hotels and of the mountain roads also wreaked havoc on the tourist economy. In August typhoon floods inundated much of Metro Manila. That same month a disaster of a different sort affected the Philippines when Iraq invaded Kuwait. More than 100,000 Filipino workers in these countries were forced to flee. Although Saudi Arabia absorbed some of the refugees, the Philippine economy lost the millions of dollars normally sent home, and the thousands of returning Filipinos became a renewed burden to the nation.

Plans for the drilling of 16 oil wells off Palawan continued in 1990, but even if successful, could not bring immediate relief. The Philippines is the world's second-largest producer of geothermal energy, which provides 20% of the country's power needs; but an annual increase of 2.4% in the population overshadows this contribution. Gas was rationed late in 1990 and the peso devalued.

The United States. Not even traditional special relations with the United States alleviated the situation, as the U.S. Congress seemed intent on increasing aid to the new Eastern European democracies and limiting scarce funds ordinarily reserved for the Philippines. The treaty allowing U.S. air and naval bases in the Philippines ends in September 1991 and continuing bilateral negotiations over the bases indicated that a phased-out withdrawal was inevitable, although the exact terms remained undecided. The facilities are estimated to bring $1 billion into the Philippine economy annually, so that withdrawal is perceived as likely to be gradual. However, the very fact that the Aquino government had to rely on U.S. military support in order to survive has required, in the name of national honor, that it distance itself from further dependence and accede to the thousands of vehement antibase demonstrators. The U.S. State Department, in turn, temporarily removed all 261 Peace Corps volunteers from the islands as a sign of protest against disorder and waste in the Philippines.

Hazardous-duty pay also was assigned to overseas Defense and State personnel. A February report from the U.S. Congress had criticized Aquino for failing to curb extrajudicial killings, displacement of villagers by the military, arbitrary detention, and brutal treatment of prisoners. Many of these grievances matched the allegations made by RAM as motives for their coups.

Trials. Nor could Aquino find much personal consolation in the outcome of the trials of Imelda Marcos and of the persons accused of killing her husband Benigno Aquino. Despite an admittedly muddled defense by Mrs. Marcos' attorney, who claimed that kickbacks are a Filipino tradition, and uncontested evidence that Ferdinand Marcos illegally transferred millions of U.S. aid dollars and Philippine tax money to U.S. accounts, a New York City jury accepted her plea of noninvolvement in her husband's affairs in July. The acquittal was encouraged indirectly by Federal District Judge John Keenan's suggestion that the trial should have been held in Manila rather than New York, since Philippine interests rather were more at stake. Because of outstanding civil charges, however, Mrs. Marcos still was not free to return to Manila. Rafael Recto, her Manila attorney and son of the late distinguished senator Claro Recto, reacted to being removed from representing her island interests by threatening to press claims to his earned portion of the billions of dollars he described as Marcos wealth. The trial of those accused of killing Benigno Aquino in Manila ended on September 28 with a slightly more favorable result for President Aquino; one general and 15 soldiers were sentenced to life imprisonment. However, both President Aquino and the general public were disappointed that no irrefutable evidence identified which high government official ordered the slaying.

Other. In an effort to rekindle popular support, President Aquino inaugurated the Kabisig (arm-in-arm) movement on July 12. Deliberately bypassing the *trapos* (traditional politicians) of Congress, whom she implicitly blamed for obstructing progress, she announced that she would fund and direct unelected nongovernment organizations (NGOs) toward goals of socioeconomic justice. House Speaker Ramon Mitra, long an Aquino supporter, was alarmed by this indiscriminate attack on professional politicians and by the possibility that, despite her repeated denials, Aquino might organize a party of her own, should she choose to seek the presidency once again in 1992. He was expressing fears that Kabisig, described as a healing process, only might add to factionalism and divisiveness at a time that national unity had become more important than ever.

LEONARD CASPER, *Boston College*
GRETCHEN CASPER, *Texas A&M University*

PHOTOGRAPHY

In 1990 photography was truly at a crossroads. There were promises of great growth but also contradictions in the state of photographic art, commerce, journalism, and technology that presaged significant changes ahead.

Photography also was being used in the art world as never before. Controversial Post-Modernism, which arose in the 1980s, saw photographers using artificial-looking studio setups in decorator colors to evoke images from advertising and Hollywood's 1940s.

Photojournalism remained alive and well, especially with rapid political changes in Eastern Europe creating dramatic subject matter. Photo entrepreneurs worldwide were finding funds for long-term projects in videotape, exhibit, and, especially, book formats. The lines between journalism and commercialism, however, were blurred by advances in electronic imaging which made it easier to change a photograph's essence and harder to detect the process.

New Technologies and Photographic Uses. Portraiture abounded in unexpected ways: Former New York City Mayor Edward I. Koch broke with tradition by choosing a photographic portrait of himself for hanging at City Hall; 754 portraits went on display at the Flag of Faces exhibit at the new Museum of Immigration on Ellis Island; and the popular television program *America's Funniest Home Videos* offered humor in the mundane. In space exploration, the $1.5 billion Hubble Space Telescope made possible the first photograph of the solar system from beyond the planets.

Coming were technological changes that threatened to alter the definition of photography. "Fuzzy logic," a catch phrase among camera designers, was a major step in artificial intelligence enabling future cameras—rather than the photographers—to analyze a scene and make exposure and focusing decisions.

Hardware and Software. Among new 35mm single-lens-reflex cameras (SLRs), Chinon's Genesis III created excitement because of its dual autofocus systems (AF) and an extended concept of modes. It took advantage of the strong points of the active and passive AF systems and automatically switched between them as needed. From Canon came new EOS models, particularly, the innovative 700 for beginners and the multifeatured 10S. Several new AF models proved that there are differences among the plethora of such cameras: The EOS Rebel claimed to be the least expensive, smallest, lightest, full-featured AF SLR yet; Nikon's N6006 features spotmetering, autobracketing, and a versatile built-in flash; the incredibly compact Olympus IS-1 has a built-in zoom lens with a pop-up flash that reduces red eye. The Contax RTS III was the only new top-of-the-line nonautofocus SLR, while Minolta's X-

AP/Wide World

In a first step toward long-term cooperation between U.S. and Japanese companies, Polaroid allowed Minolta to market the Polaroid Spectra Pro as the Minolta Instant PRO.

370N was a good, old-fashioned SLR for the 15% of U.S. camera purchasers who prefer manual focus.

The strongest market was point-and-shoot cameras, with 7.5 million being sold annually. The 1990 trend in this category was weird design and ease in holding. For example, Canon's Photura looks like a cannon, and Minolta's Freedom 105i has a comfortable binocular grip.

Among the plentitude of disposable or single-use cameras, a war of the wides was shaping up between the pseudopanoramics. Fuji responded to the popularity of the 3.25-oz, 4.5-inch- (92-gram, 11-cm-) long Kodak Stretch 35 with a smaller camera for its home market—the Panoramic Hi with a 25-mm two-element lens and 24 Fujicolor HG 400 exposures. And Kodak introduced a flash version of its basic Fling—the Fun Saver 35. In instant photography, Polaroid broke its hold on the market by allowing Minolta to market the Polaroid Spectra Pro as the Minolta Instant PRO. And in rhythm with the blending of lines between art and technology, Polaroid's room-sized copy camera was used to print Old Master paintings, at up to $2,000 each.

Among filmless (or still-video) cameras, which electronically store and capture images, a slew of manufacturers brought out working prototypes at the annual Photo Marketing Association trade show in Las Vegas. Smaller camcorders, such as Panasonic's Palmcorder, also were seen. Kodak announced plans for a new system that would store photographs taken on conventional 35mm film on compact discs for display on TV sets and computers.

In software, slide films, which long had taken a backseat to color-negative films in popularity, were the big contenders. Fuji's super-saturated Velvia (ISO 50), with image quality fine enough to rival the Kodachrome 25, the industry standard, was pitted against Kodak's new Ektachrome 50 HC.

Exhibitions and Publications. The first exhibition to survey the medium since Beaumont Newhall's landmark "Photography: 1839–

1937'' opened in the same place, the Museum of Modern Art (MoMA) in New York City. ''Photography Until Now'' celebrated the medium's 150th birthday and the 50th anniversary of MoMA's photography department. At the Whitney Museum of Modern Art, ''The New American Pastoral: Landscape Photography in the Age of Questioning'' showed radical changes in the genre since Ansel Adams' time, with 90 images by eight photographers reflecting the effects of human degradation. At the International Center of Photography, ''A Coney Island of the Heart'' showed five decades of Harold Feinstein's humanistic work, while back at MoMA, Tina Barney's large-scale color images described ordinary daily rituals in intimate family settings on a grand and elegant scale. Events in Eastern Europe resulted in a Paris show by Patrick Herzog of a ten-year project documenting life on both sides

William Klein's "Moscow," top, and Dorothea Lang's "Migratory Cotton Picker, Eloy, Arizona" were part of the "Photography Until Now" exhibit at New York's Museum of Modern Art and later at the Cleveland Museum of Art.

Photos, Courtesy, The Cleveland Museum of Art

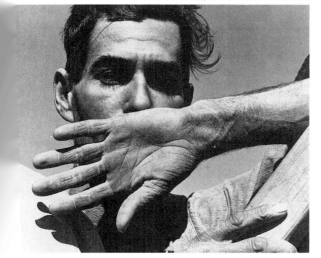

of the Berlin Wall. The book *The Berlin Wall* included more than 100 color images from 1984 to 1990 by Hermann Waldenburg of the 102-mi- (164-km-) long structure. And in Prague, Czechoslovakia, 30 art students roamed the streets daily shooting black-and-white photographs of the unfolding revolution, then exhibited them in a gallery near Wenceslas Square with *Life* publishing the best of them.

Anne Noggle's book *For God, Country, and the Thrill of It All* recorded the personal story of women Air Force service pilots in World War II. *The Power to Heal: Ancient and Modern Medicine* explored the connection between the two and included pictures of alternative healing processes. And in *In Our Own Image: The Coming Revolution in Photography*, author Fred Ritchin asked, ''What would happen if the photograph appeared to be a straightforward recording of physical reality, but could no longer be relied upon to depict actual people and events?''

See also Arts—*The Question of Obscenity.*

BARBARA LOBRON
Writer, Photographer, Editor

PHYSICS

Convincing evidence was presented in 1990 that the universe contains only three generations of particles, and preliminary results confirmed the solar neutrino deficit. The mounting cost of the Superconducting Super Collider was the subject of much discussion, while cold fusion seemed completely disproven.

Cold Fusion. The 1989 announcement by B. Stanley Pons of the University of Utah and Martin Fleischmann of the University of Southampton, England, that they had observed nuclear fusion at room temperature initiated an unparalleled series of attempts to reproduce the phenomenon. Although most attempts to reproduce the experiments failed, some partial confirmations were reported.

The experimental system consisted of an electrolytic cell—a palladium cathode surrounded by a bath of heavy water (D_2O). Palladium is known to absorb a large amount of hydrogen. The idea was to charge the palladium rods with deuterium, a heavy isotope of hydrogen, and force the deuterium nuclei together. When a voltage was applied, excess energy was released in such quantities that it seemed only nuclear processes could be responsible.

Nuclear fusion takes place when two deuterium nuclei combine to form helium plus a neutron or tritium plus a proton. In either case extra energy is released. Since deuterium can be extracted from water, the fuel supply is essentially limitless. However, overcoming electric repulsion and forcing the two nuclei together requires a temperature of millions of degrees. In nature, such temperatures are found only in stars. Thus the overwhelming interest in the purported inexpensive and inexhaustible source of power.

Efforts to reproduce cold fusion focused on the observation of the nuclear by-products. Claims for the direct observation of neutrons and gamma rays were withdrawn. The strongest remaining evidence seemed the reported observation by a number of scientists of tritium in their electrolytic cells.

Kevin Wolf of Texas A&M University performed a series of experiments designed to test for tritium contamination. He found that fresh palladium rods contained tritium, thus removing the evidence for cold fusion. Another blow to cold fusion was delivered by a team of researchers at Utah, who monitored Pons' and Fleischmann's own apparatus and found no signs of fusion. A distinguished panel of physicists and chemists established by the U.S. Department of Energy concluded that there is no "convincing evidence to associate the reported anomalous heat with a nuclear process."

Fundamental Particles. The new large electron-positron (LEP) storage ring at the European Laboratory for Particle Physics straddles the French-Swiss border and is the largest scientific instrument ever built. In LEP, circulating electron and positron beams are stored and collide again and again. The energy for each beam is 45 GeV (1 GeV equals 10^9 electron volts).

A great success of the standard model of particle physics was the observation in 1983 of the predicted Z and W bosons. The Z boson mediates the weak interaction just as the photon does for the electromagnetic interaction. In the standard model there are several families, each with two quarks, a lepton, and a neutrino. For example, the first family contains the up and down quarks (which make up the nucleons —neutron and proton), the electron, and the electron neutrino. Three families are known, but the standard model allows more.

From the lifetime of the Z particle the number of families can be determined. The problem was to measure the lifetime of the Z particle with sufficient precision. This is just what LEP can do very well, since it produces so many Z particles that it is sometimes called a Z factory. Early results indicate that the lifetime of the Z particle agrees very well with three families. Thus one of the fundamental open questions in the standard model has been answered.

Superconducting Super Collider. The status of LEP as the world's largest scientific instrument will last only until the Superconducting Super Collider (SSC) is built. The SSC, to be constructed at Waxahatchie, TX, will have a tunnel some 50 mi (80 km) long and have two 20-TeV (1 TeV = 10^{12} electron volts) colliding proton beams. The problem arises from the cost.

When the SSC was proposed, the estimated cost was \$4.5 billion. As design modifications occurred, the cost escalated rapidly. Estimates were between \$8 and \$9 billion in 1990. A reevaluation by the High-Energy Physics Advisory Panel recommended against reducing the scale of the SSC. Additional money may be provided by other countries and by the state of Texas. However, the other countries probably would participate by contributing finished materials and manufactured items, thus supplanting major U.S. high-technology manufacturers. Although the U.S. Congress in 1990 authorized a spending plan for the Super Collider and later approved President Bush's fiscal 1991 request for \$318 million toward construction of the project, a growing controversy was developing over the project's enormous cost in an era of budget restraints.

Solar Neutrinos. An enduring puzzle is the solar-neutrino deficit. Neutrinos are created in the nuclear-fusion processes which fuel the stars. Since the Earth's sun is a stable star in its simplest evolutionary stage, and the nuclear-fusion process is understood well, the apparent deficit in the number of neutrinos observed has been a puzzle for more than 20 years.

Detecting the neutrinos is extremely difficult, since neutrinos interact so weakly with matter. The first detector contained 100,000 gallons (378 540 l) of chlorine-rich cleaning fluid and was located in a mine in South Dakota. The few radioactive atoms produced by neutrino reactions were isolated chemically and counted. The number observed was much smaller than predicted. For more than 20 years, calculations and related measurements failed to remove the disagreement. A serious limitation in the original experiment was being sensitive only to higher-energy neutrinos. A new experiment called SAGE (Soviet-American Gallium Experiment) uses gallium rather than chlorine, and much lower-energy neutrinos can be detected. This new experiment, which uses 60 tons (54 metric tons) of gallium, is being conducted in the Soviet Union.

Preliminary results reported in 1990 strongly supported the previous measurements. How can the neutrinos be created in the sun, but not survive to reach the Earth? One explanation is the Mikheyev-Smirnov-Wolfenstein (MSW) effect, which assumes that neutrinos can change from one type to another. If the electron neutrinos changed into another type of neutrino, they could not be detected and the puzzle is resolved. However, such changes or oscillations can occur only if the neutrino has a mass. More data from the SAGE experiment, as well as from another new neutrino experiment in Italy, should provide conclusive evidence on the solar neutrino deficit.

GARY MITCHELL
North Carolina State University

AP/Wide World

In Warsaw, Feb. 27, 1990, Poland's Premier Mazowiecki (center), Foreign Minister Skubiszewski, and Israel's Foreign Minister Moshe Arens (left) congratulate one another after the two nations sign a protocol reestablishing diplomatic relations.

POLAND

For Poland, 1990 was a year of tumultuous change. The country continued to shed its Communist legacy and struggled to adapt to a multiparty pluralistic democracy and a market economy. It also was the year of Lech Walesa, as Poles elected the 47-year-old Solidarity leader and winner of the 1983 Nobel Peace Prize president.

Political Developments. In January parliament began consideration of measures confiscating the multimillion-dollar property holdings of the Communist Party, known as the Polish United Workers' Party (PUWP). Popular demonstrations supported confiscation, but former Communists alleged a vendetta against them.

On January 27 the Polish Communist Party held its 11th and final congress in Warsaw. The delegates voted to dissolve the party but split on the nature of its successor. A smaller faction, led by the relatively liberal former Gdansk party secretary, Tadeusz Fiszbach, created a new organization called the Social Democratic Union. The larger faction led by Aleksander Kwasniewski, another pragmatic reformer and former minister of youth and sports, created an entity called Social Democracy of the Polish Republic. At the time of dissolution, the Communist Party still claimed 1.8 million members but public opinion polls showed it with only about 2% of public support.

In a February 9 municipal election, the environmentalist Green Party's candidate Jerzy Rosciszewski defeated a Solidarity candidate for mayor of Krakow. The city had been impacted heavily by industrial pollution, and Rosciszewski's election was viewed as a watershed event ending decades of environmental degradation by the country's former Communist masters.

On February 18 in a Senate by-election in the Silesian region of Opole, Solidarity candidate Dorota Symonides defeated Henryk Krol, leader of the Silesian German Minority Cultural Association, by a 67% to 33% margin.

On May 27, Poland held its first multiparty local elections. More than 80 parties and organizations contested about 52,000 seats on some 2,300 local councils. The results showed plurality support for Solidarity candidates, who won about 41% of the seats. A majority of the vote, however, was scattered widely among a myriad of political parties and independent candidates. Only 42% of Poland's eligible voters participated in what was interpreted generally as a sign of discontent with the government's austerity policies.

In early July, Premier Tadeusz Mazowiecki fired three of the remaining four Communist ministers in his 24-member cabinet. Especially significant were the ousters of Gen. Florian Siwicki as defense minister and Gen. Czeslaw Kiszczak as interior minister. Both had been involved in repression against the Solidarity movement in the early 1980s. The changes were seen widely as Mazowiecki's response to accusations, frequently aired by Solidarity

Stanislaw Tyminski and his wife return to Canada after his unsuccessful presidential bid. Earlier he had posted a bond to assure his return to Poland to face charges that he slandered Premier Mazowiecki during the campaign.

leader Lech Walesa, among others, that the new regime favored former Communists instead of phasing them out.

On July 19, Gen. Wojciech Jaruzelski expressed his willingness to step down as Poland's president. Walesa had announced he would seek the presidency in early April.

Walesa's political platform was based on demands for faster reform toward a market economy, and a more radical break with the Communist past, reforms he insisted could be effected with minimal discomfort to the working population. Walesa also demanded prompt withdrawal of 40,000 Soviet troops from Poland, while Mazowiecki believed them to be a useful shield against a united Germany, at least until all border issues were settled. Many of his former Solidarity associates regarded Walesa as a populist demagogue unsuited to presidential responsibility and feared his allegedly authoritarian tendencies. The Polish Catholic Church arranged a private meeting between Walesa and Mazowiecki in July to mitigate the conflict between the two Polish leaders.

On July 16 the Solidarity supporters of Premier Mazowiecki founded the Citizens' Movement for Democratic Action. Many former trade union associates of Walesa were now his opponents. The new group endorsed what they perceived as Mazowiecki's more moderate and orderly reform program. In early October, Mazowiecki declared his candidacy for president, and the election was set for November 25.

Trade Union or Political Party. The Solidarity trade-union organization held a national conference in Gdansk in April, the first such national meeting since 1981. Differences among delegates on whether Solidarity should become a political party or remain a trade-union movement dominated discussions. The conference supported Mazowiecki's proposal that free elections to the Sejm, Poland's lower house of parliament, be held in early 1991. The delegates went beyond Mazowiecki's proposal, however, by simultaneously demanding the popular election of the president. The move was seen as expressing dissatisfaction with the pace of Mazowiecki's "de-communizing" reforms. Walesa was reelected chairman of Solidarity on April 22 by a majority of 362 out of 467 votes cast, or 77.5% of the total, a higher vote than his original 1981 majority of 55%.

Economy. Abandoning old Communist policies of subsidizing various staples, the government announced steep price increases on January 2. Coal prices were raised sixfold while gasoline, electricity, and natural-gas prices increased by about four times. Public-transportation costs doubled. The government also instituted a wage freeze, which in combination with the price increases, reduced real incomes by about one third.

Simultaneously, the government announced a devaluation of the zloty from a market rate of 6,500 to the U.S. dollar to 9,500. In February the International Monetary Fund (IMF) agreed to make substantial loans to Poland, beginning with $360 million in February, with more than $1 billion likely to follow. Poland was urged by the IMF to follow austerity policies to curb inflation and invigorate its economy. Premier Mazowiecki appealed to Western governments on February 9 to reschedule and/or reduce Poland's foreign debt, estimated at some $41 billion. Some rescheduling by Western nations, affecting about $9 billion, took place in mid-February.

Polish taxes and tariffs as well as interest rates were raised in the first half of 1990. The Mazowiecki government faced a miners' strike in February but appeals for a return to work ended it after four days. Considerable labor unrest and discontent prevailed throughout the year. At the end of June, unemployment was set at 3.8%, or about 500,000 workers. Further price increases were put into effect in July.

The government claimed great successes in converting Poland to a free-market economy; officials declared that inflation had been cut from 78% in January to 4% in May. They also declared that 90% of Polish prices now were determined by supply-demand relationships, and that in 1990 alone some 30,000 private companies had been founded in Poland.

In mid-July there were, however, widespread demonstrations and protests by Polish farmers who claimed that the new economy with its high costs and interest rates was squeezing them out. On July 13 the Sejm ap-

POLAND • Information Highlights

Official Name: Republic of Poland.
Location: Eastern Europe.
Area: 120,726 sq mi (312 680 km²).
Population (mid-1990 est.): 37,800,000.
Chief Cities (Dec. 31, 1988 est.): Warsaw, the capital, 1,651,200; Lodz, 851,500; Krakow, 743,700.
Government: *Head of state,* Lech Walesa, president (inaugurated Dec. 22, 1990). *Head of government,* Jan Krzysztof Bielecki, premier (appointed December 1990). *Legislature* (bicameral)—Sejm and Senate.
Monetary Unit: Zloty (9,500 zlotys equal U.S.$1, January 1990).
Gross National Product (1989 est. U.S.$): $172,400,000,000.
Economic Indexes (1989): *Consumer Prices* (1980 = 100), all items, 3,195.7; food, 3,901.4. *Industrial Production* (1980 = 100), 109.
Foreign Trade (1989 U.S.$): *Imports,* $10,085,000,000; *exports,* $13,155,000,000.

proved the most sweeping privatization legislation in Eastern Europe. It enabled all Polish citizens to buy stock in formerly state-owned companies. About 7,600 such enterprises, accounting for some 80% of the national output, were involved. By year's end, however, most enterprises had not been privatized, due to an apparent lack of investor interest.

In the latter part of the year, Poland was fairly successful at dealing with inflation, though at a cost of a substantial slowdown of the economy, unemployment of about 1 million, and severely lowered living standards. More than 40% of the population lived below an official poverty line; families which had spent about 30% of their budgets on food before 1989 were spending more than 60% in 1990.

Among the more visible and painful consequences of Polish reforms was a great upsurge in crime. According to official data there was a 69% increase in crimes during the first half of 1990 as compared with the same period in 1989. Crime in urban areas, especially Warsaw, rose even higher.

The Church. The Polish Catholic Church, headed by Cardinal Jozef Glemp, continued to exercise considerable influence in the country's political life. This was especially evident in the Walesa-Mazowiecki talks in July sponsored by Church leaders, and the open endorsement of Lech Walesa over Stanislaw Tyminski for president in December.

By agreement reached between the government and the Church on August 6, religious instruction in the Catholic faith was to be resumed in Polish public schools on a voluntary basis.

Presidential Elections. In the first round of voting on November 25, Lech Walesa led the field of six candidates with some 42% of the national vote. Since no one received the required majority, a runoff between the two leading candidates was held on December 9. To the surprise of most observers, Premier Mazowiecki was eliminated from the runoff. He finished third with only 18% of the vote behind a newcomer to Polish politics, 42-year-old Canadian and Peruvian businessman (with dual Canadian and Polish citizenship) Stanislaw Tyminski. Tyminski had not lived in Poland for about 20 years prior to the election. Nevertheless, he received 23% of the vote and appeared to be the beneficiary of widespread discontent with Mazowiecki's economic-austerity program.

While Walesa's criticism of Mazowiecki was relatively restrained, Tyminski harshly attacked the government. He charged Mazowiecki with, among other things, treason and sellout to foreign capitalists. Tyminski suggested that his own successful business experience would enable him to bring prosperity to Poland without the kind of suffering and reduction in living standards experienced so far. Tyminski was dubbed the "candidate from Mars" by the Polish media and wild rumors circulated about his largely unknown background.

Deeply hurt by his defeat, Mazowiecki immediately announced that he would resign as premier, but stayed on as a caretaker until a new government could be formed. In the December 9 runoff, Walesa defeated Tyminski by a three-to-one margin. Walesa's inauguration as president on December 22 was remarkable for its exclusion of outgoing President Jaruzelski and Walesa's pledge to lead Poland toward full independence and a complete break from its Communist past, economically and politically. On December 29, President Walesa announced the nomination of a 39-year-old businessman and economist, Jan Krzysztof Bielecki, as prime minister. Both actions indicated Walesa's commitment to a market economy based on private ownership.

Foreign Affairs. The year was a busy one for Polish diplomacy with many personal contacts among new and old partners. On January 16, Polish Deputy Prime Minister Jan Janowski visited Beijing to promote economic cooperation with the People's Republic of China. Almost simultaneously, Japanese Prime Minister Toshiki Kaifu pledged some $150 million in aid to Poland with prospects for $850 million more.

On January 25, President Václav Havel of Czechoslovakia visited Poland. In a speech to the Polish parliament, he called for close cooperation on foreign policy and economic development issues among Czechoslovakia, Poland, and Hungary. After a mid-February visit to Great Britain, Premier Mazowiecki demanded that Poland be allowed to participate in negotiations on German unification. On March 9 both Jaruzelski and Mazowiecki traveled to Paris where President François Mitterrand supported their demand for more specific and unequivocal German guarantees of the Polish frontiers.

On March 21, Premier Mazowiecki visited Washington, DC, for talks with President George Bush; he sought U.S. support for Poland's western frontiers and increased economic cooperation.

On April 13 during President Jaruzelski's visit to Moscow, the Soviet Union finally admitted responsibility for the mass murder of some 14,000 Polish officers captured during the Soviet invasion in 1939. Some of the graves with more than 4,000 bodies had been found at Katyn in 1943 by the Nazis.

West German President Richard von Weizsäcker visited Poland in early May, assuring his hosts that Germany would have no territorial claims on Poland in the future. U.S. Secretary of State James Baker went to Warsaw on May 6, inviting Poland to the German reunification talks in Paris.

France agreed on May 29 to reschedule Poland's $1.5 billion debt, calling for repayment over a 14-year period. The German Reunification Treaty, concluded on August 31, was seen in Poland as a major German commitment to the permanent nature of the current frontiers with Poland. This was followed by a Polish-German treaty on frontiers concluded October 31 in Warsaw.

On December 22, Poland announced its withdrawal from the Soviet-sponsored Council of Mutual Economic Assistance (COMECON).

See also EUROPE feature, page 36.

ALEXANDER J. GROTH
University of California, Davis

POLAR RESEARCH

Antarctic. Studies undertaken in 1990 provided more information on how increased exposure to ultraviolet (UV) radiation may affect marine ecosystems. Laboratory experiments on one-celled marine plants showed that many species can repair DNA damage caused by UV radiation, but survival and repair abilities among the species differ greatly. As part of the 1990–91 U.S. science program, 22 biologists were studying the ecosystem along the sea-ice edge—the most sensitive to increased UV exposure—to learn if this ecosystem is changing because of enhanced UV exposure. Their early reports suggested that the UV-radiation effects reach 3 ft (1 m) below the ocean surface.

The National Science Foundation, manager of the U.S. Antarctic Program (USAP), awarded a six-year grant for long-term study of how seasonal and yearly variations in the polar environment affect organisms and influence interactions in ecosystems. This research will identify natural variation in Antarctic ecosystems and contribute to a worldwide study of how global climatic change affects the biosphere. The Antarctic Peninsula site, encompassing an area 100 mi (63 km) in radius, also may help in identifying impacts from changes in ozone levels, temperature, ocean circulation, and sea-ice cover.

U.S., Soviet, and French glaciologists confirmed that atmospheric carbon dioxide rose before the end of the second-to-last ice age about 130,000 years ago. Air bubbles trapped in an Antarctic ice core, spanning 160,000 years, show a carbon-dioxide rise about 3,000 years before this ice age ended; the rise gradually warmed the atmosphere and spurred the retreat of ice sheets. Another study of the same ice core indicated that, while the amount of methane in the atmosphere doubled during warm periods between glacial ages, more methane at a faster rate has been emitted during the last 300 years. Researchers attributed the increase to human activities.

Scientists, measuring changes in the ozone layer above the continent, reported depletion levels similar to those recorded during 1987 when the lowest levels ever were recorded. In late October reports indicated that ozone levels were continuing to drop.

Responding to public opinion, France and Australia did not sign the controversial Wellington Convention to regulate Antarctic mineral activities, saying they wanted a complete ban on mining and drilling. Because these countries are original Antarctic Treaty signers and claim areas of Antarctica, they must approve the convention before it enters into force.

Arctic. In 1990 scientists confirmed for the first time that increasing levels of nitrates and sulfates in the atmosphere result from man-made emissions. Using high-resolution data from a southern Greenland ice core, they developed an atmospheric record extending back to the beginning of the industrial revolution. Although volcanoes, sea salts, and ocean plankton produce both compounds, the ice-core record showed a steady rise that could be correlated with industrial growth in North America and Europe. The most dramatic increases began in the 20th century.

In a controversial study, two Canadian researchers statistically linked sea-ice patterns and polar-bear migration with the 11-year sunspot cycle. They found the best link between the sea-ice and solar-cycle records when they added the quasi-biennial oscillation of equatorial winds. The solar cycle is believed to affect these winds, which change direction every one to one-and-a-half years. When the winds blow westward, ice conditions become more severe. The researchers suggested that periods of strong solar activity somehow create a high-pressure system over the Arctic and prevent sea ice from moving south. If this is true, polar bears would be able to move southward over the ice more easily during these times.

WINIFRED REUNING
National Science Foundation

PORTUGAL

An economic miracle sparked by Portugal's entry into the European Community (EC) has impelled democracy in a country once beset by authoritarianism and economic malaise.

Politics. Despite Prime Minister Aníbal Cavaco Silva's accomplishments, his Social Democratic Party (PSD) had lost ground in the July 1989 elections for the European Parliament and finished second to the Socialists (PSP) in the December 1989 municipal contests. In the latter balloting, blue-collar workers resented the failure to distribute equally the fruits of economic growth, while the feeling of being neglected drove some middle-class supporters of Cavaco Silva to the Socialist camp. The PSP also benefited from the candidacy of Jorge Sampaio, the party's secretary-general, who successfully sought the mayoralty of Lisbon.

Neither the Socialists nor the Social Democrats was expected to garner a plurality of the 230 Assembly seats in elections planned for July 1991. In contrast, President Alberto Mário Soares had only token opposition as he prepared to seek another five-year term in January 1991. As the campaigns neared, the Communists (PCP) suffered erosion of their electoral base. Financial distress forced the Communists to curtail publishing activities and liquidate assets. To avoid an intraparty squabble, Secretary-General Alvaro Cunhal endorsed Carlos Carvalhas as his deputy and probable successor.

Economics. EC membership has revitalized Portugal's economy. In the face of tough competition from Spain and Ireland, Lisbon has raised foreign investment from $156 million in 1986 to $1.3 billion in 1989—with the 1990 inflow anticipated to be even larger. Attractive to investors are cash grants, fiscal incentives, political stability, the vitality of Portugal's domestic market, and a highly regarded labor force that earns Western Europe's lowest wages and launches the fewest strikes. Portugal is an important beneficiary of the EC-aid program, designed to improve socioeconomic conditions.

A medley of factors—surging investment, mounting domestic demand, and accelerating exports—fostered four years of sustained economic growth. In 1989, Portugal's gross domestic product (GDP) expanded 5.4%—with somewhat slower growth projected for 1990. Industries operated at record levels of capacity and unemployment fell below 5%. Meanwhile, exports shot up 26% in 1989.

Still, the combination of unprecedented capital inflows, rising incomes, and heightened expectations fueled inflation. Exacerbating the situation were persistent budget deficits (7% of GDP) and a soaring public debt (70% of GDP). Through mid-1990, prices increased at an annual rate of 13.1%, up from 12.6% in 1989. The inflation rate dissuaded Cavaco Silva from seeking admission to the European Monetary Union in 1990. He feared that yielding control over the escudo's value vis-à-vis other currencies could threaten the country's export and growth levels on the eve of elections.

Rising prices sharpened demand for imports in 1989, and Portugal purchased $6.5 billion more goods from abroad than it exported. Earnings from tourists and remittances from the 4 million expatriate Portuguese helped to decrease the current account deficit to $550 million—an amount offset by capital inflows that elevated foreign reserves above $18 billion in 1990.

Cavaco Silva has privatized ever more firms nationalized in the mid-1970s. His administration, which moved cautiously at first, accelerated its pace in 1990. Under a more flexible law, the government sold its equity in shipping, cement, beer-making, and insurance companies.

Foreign Affairs. Portugal has sought to be the EC's interlocutor with sub-Saharan Africa. Lisbon hosted meetings between the Angolan government and the rebel Union for the Total Independence of Angola (UNITA), which is attempting to overthrow it. Portugal used its good offices less successfully to facilitate negotiations between the Mozambique government and a shadowy, right-wing resistance movement. Even as it integrates with Europe, Portugal prizes its special ties to the United States—a relationship cemented by military interests. The Lajes air base in the Azores constitutes the most conspicuous Luso-U.S. bond. The facility, important for projecting U.S. military power in Europe and the Middle East, is governed by an agreement that Cavaco Silva will seek to renegotiate in 1991. Portugal's cooperation with the United States amid Iraq's invasion of Kuwait in August should strengthen the prime minister's position.

GEORGE W. GRAYSON
College of William & Mary

PORTUGAL • Information Highlights

Official Name: Portuguese Republic.
Location: Southwestern Europe.
Area: 35,552 sq mi (92 080 km²).
Population (mid-1990 est.): 10,400,000.
Chief Cities (1981 census): Lisbon, the capital, 807,937; Oporto, 327,368; Amadora, 95,518.
Government: *Head of state,* Alberto Mário Soares, president (took office March 1986). *Head of government,* Aníbal Cavaco Silva, prime minister (took office November 1985). *Legislature* (unicameral)—Assembly of the Republic.
Monetary Unit: Escudo (131.4 escudos equal U.S.$1, Nov. 5, 1990).
Gross Domestic Product (1989 est. U.S.$): $72,100,000,000.
Economic Indexes (1989): *Consumer Prices* (1980 = 100), all items, 428.4. *Industrial Production* (1988, 1980 = 100), 136.
Foreign Trade (1989 U.S.$): *Imports,* $18,877,000,000; *exports,* $12,663,000,000.

U.S. Postmaster General Anthony M. Frank announces on March 6 that the Postal Service would seek a record 19% (five-cent) increase in the cost of a first-class stamp. The cost of second- and third-class postage also would rise under the proposal, which had to be approved by the Postal Rate Commission.

POSTAL SERVICE

Americans learned that the cost of mailing a letter might increase by five cents when the U.S. Postal Service (USPS) proposed a 19% increase in U.S. postal rates in March 1990. If approved, the proposed increase, which was scheduled to take place in February 1991, would raise the first-class rate for one ounce from 25 to 30 cents, with each additional ounce rising from 20 to 25 cents. The cost of mailing a postcard would move from 15 to 20 cents, with other rates and services increasing more or less proportionately.

The rate-change process, which was established by the Postal Reform Act of 1970, can be complicated. Nine months to a year before the USPS desires new rates to go into effect, it makes a proposal to the Postal Rate Commission (PRC). The USPS must justify its request in terms of costs, with the 1990 proposal document totaling 4,400 pages. The PRC reviews and checks the proposal, which it may accept, reject, or modify. If the USPS approves the result, it may put it into effect. If not, a unanimous decision by the USPS Board of Governors can override any decision of the PRC. If the governors cannot agree, they then reappeal to the PRC or seek relief through the courts. As 1991 began the PRC recommended a first-class rate of 29 cents for most letters and a rate of 19 cents for postcards, effective Feb. 3, 1991. The USPS Board of Governors was expected to accept the recommendations.

The USPS closed its fiscal year (FY) 1989 (ending September 30) with a $61 million surplus out of a nearly $40 billion budget. However, FY 1990 ended with a deficit of about $700 million. The agency's financial problems derived mainly from a decision by Congress in December 1987 to bring the formerly independent USPS on-budget and under the terms of the Gramm-Rudman deficit-reduction act.

After agreeing to exempt the USPS from Gramm-Rudman in the fall of 1989, Congress reneged. In effect, Congress assessed the agency several billion dollars between December 1987 and early November 1990. In its early November 1990 budget-reconciliation act, Congress assessed the USPS nearly $5.5 billion more over the next five years, with $710 million to be paid during FY 1991. Even with the aid of a prospective rate increase in early 1991, it was only barely possible that the service could balance its books by the end of FY 1991.

Meanwhile, though postal productivity was up 4%, more than double that expected, volume was leveling off, and important labor contracts were being negotiated. Discussions begun in late August were expected to conclude by Nov. 20, 1990, the expiration date of the existing contracts. However, contract talks broke down on November 20 over pay differences. The four main postal unions especially sought pay increases and job security against automation, while the USPS desired to hold down pay costs and to increase flexibility in using part-time workers. In view of the stalemate, the law provides for appointment of a fact-finding commission to report in 45 days. If the parties still do not reach agreement, the dispute goes to binding arbitration. A three-year contract had been at issue.

The one bright spot in Congress' indirect taxation of the USPS was its 1989 increase of $5 billion in the borrowing limit of the agency. Such authority is the key to a five-year capital improvement program established in 1989, and to plans to automate all mail by 1995. The proportion of automated letter mail grew during FY 1991 from 42% to 61%. "About 2,000 of the 10,000 pieces of equipment to be deployed by 1995 are now in place," said Postmaster General Anthony M. Frank. As a result of automation, postal employment was reduced by 27,000 workers by attrition during 1989–90.

A plan to lengthen delivery time for some first-class customers in order to provide a more consistent service desired by others was proposed in early 1990. Criticism of the plan as well as a desire to give mailers time to adjust caused USPS to delay start of the new standards until the summer.

Canada. The Canada Post (CPC) reported a surplus of $149 million for its FY 1990 (ending March 31). This and 1989's surplus of $96 million comprise the first profits seen for the Canadian postal system since 1957. The Canadian first-class rate of 39 cents went to 40 cents on Jan. 1, 1990. This was to be upped further when the specifics of a goods and service tax were agreed to.

PAUL P. VAN RIPER, *Texas A&M University*

PRINCE EDWARD ISLAND

The decades-old dream of a bridge connecting Prince Edward Island to the Canadian mainland faded some distance in 1990 when an environmental panel pronounced the project unsound. And Islanders were presented with a blueprint to preserve their rural heritage.

Bridge Unacceptable. Proponents of a "fixed link" to the mainland suffered a setback August 15 when a federal assessment panel found that a bridge across Northumberland Strait posed "unacceptable" environmental risks. The six-member panel, in a report released in Ottawa and Charlottetown, said that the proposed span between Prince Edward Island and New Brunswick would cause ice buildups that could threaten the Northumberland fishery. It also warned of possible damage to the marine environment during construction, and of possible spills of toxic material being transported across the bridge.

The panel added, however, that a bridge could be acceptable if a design ever were created that could overcome the problem of ice buildup. It also suggested that a tunnel might be acceptable, depending on whether it passed an environmental assessment.

In response to the panel's report, the federal public-works department said it believed the crossing project "could proceed" provided environmental and other concerns are addressed. A committee of ice experts was established to work out testing procedures. Premier Joe Ghiz stated that the idea of a fixed link was not dead, and that his government continued to support the concept.

Preserving Rural Heritage. Community Affairs Minister Leonce Bernard on September 26 outlined a government initiative to stem the tide of rural decay in Prince Edward Island. The minister said the government was determined to give effect to the findings of a cabinet committee on rural development which conducted provincewide inquiries in 1989. Among other things, the committee recommended the creation of a department of community development and of a rural-development board. In addition to these steps, said Bernard, a "community pride program" would be established to provide grants to local groups and businesses wishing to improve their community or commercial properties.

If present trends continued, Charlottetown and Summerside would grow and prosper at the expense of small communities. Rural Islanders wanted a strategy that would lead to alternative action, ". . . a vision that respects traditional rural values, prefers a diversified economy of smaller secondary enterprise coupled with our primary industry, and depends heavily upon a clean, healthy, and safe natural environment," stated Bernard.

Help for Summerside. Employment Minister Barbara McDougall announced on February 22 that Summerside had been approved as a designated area for the federal government's communities futures programs. The Summerside region could receive up to C$800,000 per year in spending authority to relieve the effects of the closure of Canadian Forces Base Summerside. More concrete help came May 3 when Prime Minister Brian Mulroney announced that Summerside would be the site of a processing center for the federal goods and services tax. The center would create up to 500 jobs.

Vice-Regal Appointment. Marion Reid, a former speaker of the legislature, was named lieutenant-governor of Prince Edward Island by Prime Minister Mulroney on July 29.

JOHN BEST, *"Canada World News"*

PRINCE EDWARD ISLAND
• Information Highlights

Area: 2,185 sq mi (5 660 km²).
Population (September 1990): 130,400.
Chief Cities (1986 census): Charlottetown, the capital, 15,776; Summerside, 8,020.
Government (1990): *Chief Officers*—lt. gov., Marion Reid; premier, Joe Ghiz (Liberal). *Legislature*—Legislative Assembly, 32 members.
Provincial Finances (1990–91 fiscal year budget): *Revenues,* $684,881,400; *expenditures,* $678,-679,000.
Personal Income (average weekly earnings, July 1990): $413.80.
Labor Force (September 1990, seasonally adjusted): *Employed* workers, 15 years of age and over, 57,000; *Unemployed,* 13.5%.
Education (1990–91): *Enrollment*—elementary and secondary schools, 24,720 pupils; postsecondary —universities, 2,470; community colleges, 1,000.
(All monetary figures are in Canadian dollars.)

PRISONS

As prison populations continued their upward spiral in 1990, increasing efforts were made to find new space and alleviate problems brought by overcrowding. Prison uprisings made the news in England and New York.

New Construction. The need for the vast prison-construction programs begun during the 1980s became evident in continuing annual increases in the prison population. More than 1 million Americans were behind bars on any given day during the year. Almost two thirds of these inmates were under long-term sentences in state or federal prisons.

Despite growing budget deficits, many states remained committed to completing projects begun years ago even though the costs of operating the prisons once they are built can triple in a few years' time. Connecticut, for example, sought a 50% increase in its budget for the state Department of Corrections, bringing the total to almost $350 million.

A trend occurring in state after state was a decrease in the amount of space allotted individual prisoners. Construction programs, in order to make the most space available, seldom were producing single, secure cells. Instead, prisoners were being placed in congregate settings, with many inmates sharing the same, large space. In New York City almost 800 new spaces for inmates were created by simply placing the beds closer together. State standards had called for 50 sq ft (4.6 m^2) of space for each prisoner, a 5' x 10' (1.5m x 3m) space. In October this requirement was reduced to 40 sq ft (3.7 m^2).

With 37 states under court order to ease overcrowding, efforts also were under way to find alternative penalties for nonviolent offenders, including house arrest, community service, and boot camps. (*See also* LAW—*Community Service.*)

Tensions. With the increasing numbers of prisoners in smaller spaces, tensions were high. In New York City, for example, 21,000 prisoners were in spaces that a decade earlier had housed less than 10,000 people. Additionally, 16-hour tours of duty were becoming common for correction officers in many states. Inmates sometimes were placed in less than ideal settings. This meant that minimum-security structures sometimes were holding maximum-security inmates.

Prison Riots. In England, on April 1, a riot broke out at the Strangeways prison in Manchester. Built in 1868, the facility was overcrowded and in poor condition. For several weeks, inmates held control of the top floors and riots, accompanied by fires and destruction, broke out in more than a dozen other correctional facilities in England and Wales. Officials estimated that renovations for the damaged prisons could cost the equivalent of more than $100 million.

Troubles also occurred at Rikers Island in New York City. There, nine separate prisons house more than 14,000 inmates. For several weeks in August it was the scene of violent confrontations between inmates and guards. On August 7 three inmates attacked Correction Officer Steven Narby, breaking his jaw and a rib. A week later, in an illegal job action, more than 600 correction officers, citing dangerous working conditions and angered that those accused of hurting the guard were not charged with attempted murder, blockaded the bridge which is the only route to the island. Food and visitors were prevented from entering the prisons and inmates scheduled for court hearings were prevented from leaving. Although reporters were barred from the prison, descriptions of brutal beatings of inmates were being phoned out from the prison. Ambulance workers called to treat inmates were threatened themselves by the guards. On August 14, according to witnesses, some 200 guards systematically began beating inmates. Nearly 150 inmates were injured with more than 50 requiring hospitalization.

Death Penalty. By July, there were 2,345 men and women on death row in the District of Columbia and 37 states with death-penalty provisions. During the year, some 20 people were executed. While most Americans polled favored the death penalty, events demonstrated that there are many difficulties in carrying out that ultimate sentence. Individual appeals can take more than eight years on average and, in many cases, cost the state millions of dollars. But efforts to speed up the process must take into account the fact that in one out of three cases, the court overturns the death penalty.

While 15 states do not have a death penalty at all, many of those that do are paying a very heavy price. In Florida, for example, which has more prisoners on death row than any other state, the courts spend more than one third of their time on death-penalty cases. The threat of the death penalty, however, has been found to be a help to prosecutors in getting admissions of guilt from recalcitrant suspects, including others charged with the same crime.

Drugs. By legal definition, drug use in the United States is criminal. Within the past decade, the fastest-rising category of crime for which people were sentenced was that related to drug use and sales. In the public mind, and in basic research, there is a strong connection between drug use and crime with studies showing that a high percentage of persons arrested test positive for recent drug use.

Changing Populations. Prison populations also are being composed increasingly of people from minority communities. One study, released in September by The Correctional Association of New York, a watchdog agency, noted that "on any given day, 11% of New York's black males between the age of 20–29 are confined in a state prison or local jail."

The U.S. Justice Department reported that the number of women in state and federal prisons grew 24.4% in 1989 versus 12.5% for men.

DONALD GOODMAN
John Jay College of Criminal Justice

PRIZES AND AWARDS

NOBEL PRIZES[1]

Chemistry: Elias James Corey, Harvard University, for developing a "comprehensive and varied assortment of methods [of synthesizing complex molecules] which, often showing the simplicity of genius, have become commonplace in the synthesizing laboratory"

Economics: Harry M. Markowitz, Baruch College of the City University of New York; Merton H. Miller, University of Chicago; William F. Sharpe, Stanford University; for work which provided new tools for weighing the risks and rewards of different investments and for determining the value of corporate stocks and bonds

Literature: Octavio Paz, Mexico, for lyric poetry exhibiting "impassioned writing with wide horizons, characterized by sensuous intelligence and humanistic integrity" (*See* page 328.)

Peace Prize: Mikhail S. Gorbachev, USSR, for "his leading role in the peace process which today characterizes important parts of the international community"

Physics: Jerome I. Friedman, Massachusetts Institute of Technology; Henry W. Kendall, Massachusetts Institute of Technology; Richard E. Taylor, Stanford University; for experiments achieving a "breakthrough in our understanding of matter"

Physiology or Medicine: Joseph Murray, Brigham and Women's Hospital, Boston, MA; E. Donnall Thomas, Fred Hutchinson Cancer Research Center, Seattle, WA; for discoveries "crucial for . . . severely ill patients who either can be cured or given a decent life when other treatment methods are without success"

[1] About $710,000 in each category.

ART

American Academy and Institute of Arts and Letters Awards
   Academy-Institute Awards ($5,000 ea.): art—Mel Bochner, Stephen De Staebler, Andrew Forge, Yvonne Jacquette, Catherine Murphy; music—Samuel Adler, Lee Goldstein (posthumous), Gerald Levinson, David Evan Thomas, Stanley Wolfe
   Award for Distinguished Service to the Arts: Paul Engle
   Arnold W. Brunner Memorial Prize in Architecture: Steven Holl
   Award of Merit for Sculpture: Joel Shapiro
   Jimmy Ernst Award: Milton Resnick
   Walter Hinrichson Award: John Downey
   Charles Ives Fellowship ($10,000): Lowell Leibermann
   Charles Ives Scholarships ($5,000 ea.): Jonathan Dawe, John Kennedy, Corinne Nordmann, Troy Peters, Russell Platt, William Waite
   Goddard Lieberson Fellowships ($10,000): Carolyn Steinberg, Frank Ticheli
   Gold Medal for Architecture: Kevin Roche
   Louise Nevelson Award in Art: Nell Blaine
   Richard and Hinda Rosenthal Foundation Award ($5,000): Bryn Jayes
Capezio Dance Award ($5,000): Jacques d'Amboise
Congressional Gold Medal: Andrew Wyeth
Grawemeyer Award for musical composition ($150,000): Joan Tower, *Silver Ladders*
John F. Kennedy Center Honors for career achievement in the performing arts: Dizzy Gillespie, Katharine Hepburn, Risë Stevens, Jule Styne, Billy Wilder
Edward MacDowell Medal: Louise Bourgeois
National Academy of Recordings Arts and Sciences Grammy Awards for excellence in phonograph records
   Album of the year: *Nick of Time*, Bonnie Raitt; Don Was, producer
   Classical album: *Bartok: Six String Quartets*, Emerson String Quartet; Wolf Erichson, producer
   Country music song: *After All This Time*, Rodney Crowell
   Jazz vocal performance: (female) *Blues on Broadway*, Ruth Brown; (male) *When Harry Met Sally*, Harry Connick, Jr.
   Record of the year: *Wind Beneath My Wings*, Bette Midler; Arif Mardin, producer
   Song of the year: *Wind Beneath My Wings*, Larry Henley and Jeff Silbar (songwriters)
National Medal of Arts: George Abbott, Jacob Armstead-Lawrence, Hume Cronyn, Merce Cunningham, Jasper

Johns, B.B. King, Ian McHarg, Beverly Sills-Greenough, Jessica Tandy
Praemium Imperiale for lifetime achievement in the arts ($100,000 ea.): Leonard Bernstein, United States (music); Federico Fellini, Italy (theater and film); Arnaldo Pomodoro, Italy (sculpture); James Stirling, Great Britain (architecture); Antoni Tàpies, Spain (painting)
Pritzker Architecture Prize ($100,000): Aldo Rossi, Italy
Pulitzer Prize for Music: Mel Powell, *Duplicates: A Concerto for Two Pianos and Orchestra*
Samuel H. Scripps/American Dance Festival Award ($25,000): Twyla Tharp
Richard Tucker Award in music ($25,000): Renee Fleming
Wolf Prize ($100,000): Anselm Kiefer, West Germany

JOURNALISM

Academy and Institute of Arts and Letters Award
   Medal for Spoken Language: Garrison Keillor
Maria Moors Cabot Prizes ($1,000 ea.): Richard Boudreaux, bureau chief, Managua, Nicaragua, *Los Angeles Times*; Marc Garcia and Elsie Etheart, coeditors and publishers, *Haïti en Marche*, Miami, FL; Alma Guillermoprieto, writer, Mexico City, Mexico, *The New Yorker*; Huáscar Cajías Kauffmann, founder, *Presencia*, La Paz, Bolivia
National Magazine Awards
   Design: *Esquire*
   Essays and criticism: *Vanity Fair*
   Feature writing: *The Washingtonian*
   Fiction: *The New Yorker*
   General excellence: *Sports Illustrated*, *Metropolitan Home*, *Texas Monthly*, *7 Days*
   Personal service: *Consumer Reports*
   Photography: *Texas Monthly*
   Public-interest: *Southern Exposure*
   Reporting: *The New Yorker*
   Single-topic issue: *National Geographic*
   Special-interest: *Art & Antiques*
Overseas Press Club Awards
   Business or economic news reporting from abroad: (magazines)—Saul Hansell, *Institutional Investor*; (newspapers and wire services)—Peter Gumbell, *The Wall Street Journal*
   Cartoon on foreign affairs: Mike Luckovich, *Atlanta Constitution*
   Daily newspaper or wire-service interpretation on foreign affairs: Jackson Diehl, *The Washington Post*
   Daily newspaper or wire-service reporting from abroad: Nicholas Kristoff and Sheryl WuDunn, *The New York Times*
   Magazine article on foreign affairs: Joel Millman, *The New York Times Magazine*
   Magazine reporting from abroad: Fred C. Shapiro, *The New Yorker*
   Photographic reporting from abroad: (magazines and books)—Peter Turnley, *Newsweek*; (newspapers and wire services)—anonymous, Associated Press
   Radio interpretation or documentary on foreign affairs: CBS Radio News
   Radio spot-news reporting from abroad: Gary Matsumoto, NBC Radio
   Television interpretation or documentary on foreign affairs: Ted Koppel, ABC News
   Television spot-news reporting from abroad (shared): Dan Rather, CBS News; Cable News Network and anchor Bernard Shaw
   Eric and Amy Burger Award (for entry dealing with human rights): Katherine Ellison, *The San Jose Mercury News*
   Robert Capa Gold Medal (photographic reporting from abroad requiring exceptional courage and enterprise): David Turnley, *Detroit Free Press*
   Madeline Dane Ross Award (for foreign correspondent showing concern for the human condition): Jeremy Iggers, *The Star Tribune*
George Polk Memorial Awards
   Career award: Fred M. Hechinger, The New York Times Company Foundation
   Foreign reporting: Nicholas D. Kristoff and Sheryl WuDunn, *The New York Times*
   International reporting: Stephen Engelberg and Michael R. Gordon, *The New York Times*
   Local reporting: *The Hartford Courant*
   Local television reporting: WCSC-TV, Charleston, SC
   Medical reporting: John M. Crewdson, *The Chicago Tribune*

National reporting: Rick Atkinson, *The Washington Post*
Network television reporting: CBS News
Political reporting: Andrew Melnykovych, *The Casper* (WY) *Star-Tribune*
Radio reporting: Robert Knight, senior producer, "Undercurrents," WBAI-FM, New York
Regional reporting: Miranda Ewell and David Schrieberg, *The San José* (CA) *Mercury News*
Television investigative reporting: Jonathan Kwitny, "The Kwitny Report," WNYC-TV, New York

Pulitzer Prizes
Commentary: Jim Murray, *Los Angeles Times*
Criticism: Allan Temko, *San Francisco Chronicle*
Editorial cartooning: Tom Toles, *Buffalo News*
Editorial writing: Thomas J. Hylton, *Pottstown* (PA) *Mercury*
Explanatory journalism: Steve Coll and David A. Vise, *Washington Post*
Feature photography: David C. Turnley, *Detroit Free Press*
Feature writing: Dave Curtin, *Colorado Springs Gazette Telegraph*
General-news reporting: *San José* (CA) *Mercury News*
International reporting: Nicholas D. Kristoff and Sheryl WuDunn, *The New York Times*
Investigative reporting: Lou Kilzer and Chris Ison, *Minneapolis-St. Paul Star Tribune*
National reporting: Ross Anderson, Bill Dietrich, Mary Ann Gwinn, and Eric Nalder, *Seattle Times*
Public service (two awards): *The Philadelphia Inquirer* and *Washington* (NC) *Daily News*
Specialized reporting: Tamar Stieber, *The Albuquerque* (NM) *Journal*
Spot news photography: *The Oakland* (CA) *Tribune*

Oscar winner Daniel Day-Lewis

LITERATURE

American Academy and Institute of Arts and Letters Awards
Academy-Institute Awards ($5,000 ea.): M.H. Abrams, Rick DeMarinis, Debora Greger, Rachel Hadas, Shelby Hearon, Maxine Hong Kingston, David Lehman, Edmund S. Morgan
Witter Bynner Prize for Poetry ($1,500): Jacqueline Osherow
E.M. Forster Award: Jeanette Winterson
Gold Medal for History: C. Vann Woodward
Howells Medal: E. L. Doctorow
Sue Kaufman Prize for First Fiction ($2,500): Allan Gurganus
Richard and Hinda Rosenthal Foundation Award ($5,000): Daniel Stern
Jean Stein Award ($5,000): Eva Hoffman
Harold D. Vursell Memorial Award ($5,000): Peter Brown
Morton Dauwen Zabel Award ($2,500): Paul Auster
Bobbitt National Prize for Poetry ($10,000): James Merrill
Canada's Governor-General Literary Awards ($10,000 ea.):
English-language awards
Drama—Judith Thompson, *The Other Side of the Dark*
Fiction—Paul Quarrington, *Whale Music*
Nonfiction—Robert Calder, *Willie: The Life of W. Somerset Maugham*
Poetry—Heather Spears, *The Word for Sand*
French-language awards
Drama—Michel Garneau, *Mademoiselle Rouge*
Fiction—Louis Hamelin, *La Rage*
Nonfiction—Lise Noel, *L'Intolerance*
Poetry—Pierre Desruisseaux, *Monème*
Ruth Lilly Poetry Prize ($25,000): Hayden Carruth
Mystery Writers of America/Edgar Allan Poe Awards
Novel: James Lee Burke, *Black Cherry Blues*
Critical/biographical work: Norman Sherry, *The Lives of Graham Greene, Volume 1: 1904–39*
Grandmaster award for lifetime achievement: Helen McCloy
National Book Awards ($10,000 ea.):
Fiction: Charles Johnson, *The Middle Passage*
Nonfiction: Ron Chernow, *The House of Morgan: An American Banking Dynasty and the Rise of Modern Finance*
National Book Critics Circle Awards
Biography/autobiography: Geoffrey C. Ward, *A First-Class Temperament: The Emergence of Franklin Roosevelt*
Criticism (posthumous): James Clive, *Not By Fact Alone: Essays On the Writing and Reading of History*
Fiction: E.L. Doctorow, *Billy Bathgate*

Nonfiction: Michael Dorris, *The Broken Cord*
Poetry: Rodney Jones, *Transparent Gestures*
Neustadt International Prize for Literature ($25,000): Tomas Tranströmer (Sweden)
PEN/Faulkner Award ($7,500): E.L. Doctorow, *Billy Bathgate*
Pulitzer Prizes
Biography: Sebastian de Grazia, *Machiavelli in Hell*
Fiction: Oscar Hijuelos, *The Mambo Kings Play Songs of Love*
General nonfiction: Dale Maharidge and Michael Williamson, *And Their Children After Them*
History: Stanley Karnow, *In Our Image: America's Empire in the Philippines*
Poetry: Charles Simic, *The World Doesn't End*
Rea Award for the Short Story ($25,000): Joyce Carol Oates

MOTION PICTURES

Academy of Motion Picture Arts and Sciences ("Oscar") Awards
Actor—leading: Daniel Day-Lewis, *My Left Foot*
Actor—supporting: Denzel Washington, *Glory*
Actress—leading: Jessica Tandy, *Driving Miss Daisy*
Actress—supporting: Brenda Fricker, *My Left Foot*
Cinematography: Freddie Francis, *Glory*
Costume design: Phyllis Dalton, *Henry V*
Director: Oliver Stone, *Born on the Fourth of July*
Film: *Driving Miss Daisy*
Foreign-language film: *Cinema Paradiso* (Italy)
Music—original score: Alan Menken, *The Little Mermaid*
Music—original song: Alan Menken and Howard Ashman, "Under the Sea" (from *The Little Mermaid*)
Screenplay—original: Tom Schulman, *Dead Poets Society*
Screenplay—adaptation: Alfred Uhry, *Driving Miss Daisy*
American Film Institute's Life Achievement Award: Kirk Douglas
Cannes Film Festival Awards
Golden Palm Award (best film): David Lynch, *Wild at Heart* (United States)
Grand Prix (shared): Idrissa Ouedraogo, *Tilai* (Burkina Faso); Kohei Oguri, *Shi No Toge* (Japan)
Best actor: Gérard Depardieu, *Cyrano de Bergerac* (France)
Best actress: Krystyna Janda, *The Interrogation* (Poland)
Best director: Pavel Lungin, *Taxi Blues* (USSR)
National Society of Film Critics Awards
Film: *Drugstore Cowboy*
Actor: Daniel Day-Lewis, *My Left Foot*

Actress: Michelle Pfeiffer, *The Fabulous Baker Boys*
Director: Gus Van Sant, Jr., *Drugstore Cowboy*

PUBLIC SERVICE

Charles A. Dana Foundation Awards for pioneering achievements in health and higher education ($50,000 ea.): David P. Billington, professor, Princeton University; John W. Farquhar, director, Stanford University School of Medicine Center for Research in Disease Prevention; Norbert Hirschhorn, vice-president, John Snow Inc., and lecturer, Harvard Medical School; David A. Micklos, director, DNA Learning Center, Cold Spring Harbor Laboratory
American Institute for Public Service Jefferson Awards
National Awards ($5,000 ea.): Jimmy Carter, Anne Donahue, Jaime Escalante, Gen. Colin Powell
Philadelphia Liberty Medal ($100,000): Jimmy Carter
Templeton Prize for Progress in Religion ($580,000 shared): L. Charles Birch, Australia, vice-chairman, World Council of Churches; Murlidhar Devidas Amte, India, lawyer
Harry S. Truman Public Service Award: C. Everett Koop
U.S. Presidential Citizens Medal: Tony Zale
U.S. President's Award for Distinguished Federal Civilian Service: Laurence Legere
World Food Prize ($200,000): Dr. John S. Niederhauser, U.S. plant breeder

SCIENCE

Bristol-Myers Squibb Award for distinguished achievement in cancer research ($50,000): Bert Vogelstein, Johns Hopkins University School of Medicine
Enrico Fermi Award ($100,000 ea.): George Cowan, head, Santa Fe Institute; Robley Evans, professor emeritus, Massachusetts Institute of Technology
Fields Medals in mathematics: Vladimir G. Drinfeld, Institute for Low Temperature Physics and Engineering, Kharkov, USSR; Vaughan F.R. Jones, University of California, Berkeley; Shigefumi Mori, Research Institute of Mathematical Sciences, Kyoto University, Japan; Edward Witten, Institute for Advanced Studies, Princeton, NJ
General Motors Cancer Research Foundation Awards ($130,000 ea.): Sir David Cox, Newffield College, Oxford, England; (shared) Webster K. Cavenee, Ludwig Institute for Cancer Research, Montreal, Que., and Raymond L. White, University of Utah School of Medicine and Howard Hughes Medical Institute, Salt Lake City, UT; Mark S. Ptashne, Harvard University
Louisa Gross Horwitz Prize for research in biology or biochemistry ($22,000 shared): Stephen C. Harrison, Harvard University; Michael G. Rossman, Purdue University; Don C. Wiley, Harvard University

TELEVISION AND RADIO

Academy of Television Arts and Sciences ("Emmy") Awards
Actor—comedy series: Ted Danson, *Cheers* (NBC)
Actor—drama series: Peter Falk, *Columbo* (ABC)
Actor—miniseries or a special: Hume Cronyn, *Age-Old Friends* (HBO)
Actress—comedy series: Candice Bergen, *Murphy Brown* (CBS)
Actress—drama series: Patricia Wettig, *thirtysomething* (ABC)
Actress—miniseries or a special: Barbara Hershey, *A Killing in a Small Town* (CBS)
Animated program: *The Simpsons* (Fox)
Cinematography—miniseries or a special: Donald M. Morgan, *Murder in Mississippi* (NBC)
Cinematography—series: Michael Watkins, *Quantum Leap* (NBC)
Comedy series: *Murphy Brown* (CBS)
Directing—comedy series: Michael Dinner, *The Wonder Years* (ABC)
Directing—drama series (shared): Thomas Carter, *Equal Justice* (ABC); Scott Winant, *thirtysomething* (ABC)
Directing—miniseries or a special: Joseph Sargent, "Caroline?", *Hallmark Hall of Fame* (CBS)
Directing—variety or music program: Dwight Hemion, *The Kennedy Center Honors: A Celebration of the Performing Arts* (CBS)
Drama series: *L.A. Law* (NBC)
Drama/comedy special (tied): "Caroline?", *Hallmark Hall of Fame* (CBS); "The Incident," *AT&T Presents* (CBS)
Miniseries: *Drug Wars: The Camarena Story* (NBC)

Supporting actor—comedy series: Alex Rocco, *The Famous Teddy Z* (CBS)
Supporting actor—drama series: Jimmy Smits, *L.A. Law* (NBC)
Supporting actor—miniseries or a special: Vincent Gardenia, *Age-Old Friends* (HBO)
Supporting actress—comedy series: Bebe Neuwirth, *Cheers* (NBC)
Supporting actress—drama series: Marg Helgenberger, *China Beach* (ABC)
Supporting actress—miniseries or a special: Eva Marie Saint, *People Like Us* (NBC)
Variety, music, or comedy series: *In Living Color* (Fox)
Variety, music, or comedy special: *Sammy Davis Jr.'s 60th Anniversary Celebration* (ABC)
George Foster Peabody Awards
Radio: KCBS-AM, San Francisco, *Earthquake '89*; CBS Radio, New York, *China in Crisis*; National Public Radio, Washington, DC, "Scott Simon's Radio Essays," *Weekend Edition Saturday*; The Canadian Broadcasting Corporation, Toronto, *Lost Innocence: The Children of World War II*; D. Roberts, independent producer, for American Public Radio's *Soundprint* series, "Mei Mei: A Daughter's Song"; Texaco, Inc., and the Metropolitan Opera Association, for 50 years of continuous Saturday afternoon radio broadcasts
Television: WCSC-TV, Charleston, SC, for "providing a lifeline for viewers" after Hurricane Hugo; KGO-TV, San Francisco, for public service after the 1989 earthquake; KING-TV, Seattle, *Project Home Team*; KRON-TV, San Francisco, *I Want to Go Home*; Cable News Network, Atlanta, for coverage of the China crisis; Central Independent Television, London, *Cambodia Year 10*; MTV, New York, *Decade*; CBS and Motown-Pangaea Productions, in association with Quintex Entertainment, *Lonesome Dove*; ABC and the Black-Marlens Company in association with New World Television, *The Wonder Years*; ABC and Sacret in association with Warner Brothers Television, *China Beach*, "Vets"; ABC, Lou Rudolph Films, Motown Productions, and Allarcom and Fries Entertainment, *Small Sacrifices*; Beyond International Group, Sydney, Australia, *The Great Wall of Iron*; HBO, New York, *Common Threads: Stories from the Quilt*; KCNC-TV, Denver, *Yellowstone: Four Seasons After Fire*; Public Affairs Television, New York, *The Public Mind*; WLOX-TV, Biloxi, MI, *Did They Die in Vain?*; Film News Now—The American Documentary, New York, *Who Killed Vincent Chin?*; Children's Television Workshop, New York, *Sesame Street*; NBC News, New York, *NBC News Special: To Be an American*; David Brinkley, ABC-TV, for "exceptional contributions to broadcasting"; J. Leonard Reinsch, "for a lifetime of outstanding service"

THEATER

Susan Smith Blackburn Prize ($5,000): Lucy Gannon, *Keeping Tom Nice*; runner-up ($1,000): Winsome Pinnock, *A Hero's Welcome*
New York Drama Critics Circle Awards
Best new play ($1,000): *The Piano Lesson*, by August Wilson
Best musical: *City of Angels*, by Larry Gelbart, Cy Coleman, and David Zippel
Antoinette Perry ("Tony") Awards
Actor—play: Robert Morse, *Tru*
Actor—musical: James Naughton, *City of Angels*
Actress—play: Maggie Smith, *Lettice and Lovage*
Actress—musical: Tyne Daly, *Gypsy*
Choreography: Tommy Tune, *Grand Hotel*
Director—play: Frank Galati, *The Grapes of Wrath*
Director—musical: Tommy Tune, *Grand Hotel*
Featured actor—play: Charles Durning, *Cat on a Hot Tin Roof*
Featured actor—musical: Michael Jeter, *Grand Hotel*
Featured actress—play: Margaret Tyzack, *Lettice and Lovage*
Featured actress—musical: Randy Graff, *City of Angels*
Musical: *City of Angels*
Musical—book: Larry Gelbart, *City of Angels*
Musical—score: Cy Coleman and David Zippel, *City of Angels*
Play: *The Grapes of Wrath*
Reproduction of a play or musical: *Gypsy*
Pulitzer Prize for Drama: August Wilson, *The Piano Lesson*

PUBLISHING

As the U.S. economy slowed during early and mid-1990, sectors of the publishing industry experienced serious problems. For example, dramatic signs of trouble appeared early in 1990 in the magazine industry, which boomed during the 1980s. Even in the traditionally recession-proof book industry, concern existed that many people who became book purchasers during the 1980s might stop buying in a dramatic slowdown. The Iraqi invasion of Kuwait in August only intensified recession fears. Economic forecasts suggesting that the situation would brighten by the end of 1991, however, provided some grounds for long-term optimism.

Books. For 1990 the U.S. Commerce Department forecast that total book sales would grow by about 3.5% above anticipated inflation. Even better growth was predicted through 1994. Final figures from the Association of American Publishers indicated that 1989 sales totaled $14.7 billion, an increase of 10.9% over 1988. Nonetheless, sectors of the industry, especially trade publishing, showed signs of weakening profit performance. Evidently re-

Chicago attorney Scott Turow, 41, is a successful author. His "The Burden of Proof" was a 1990 best-seller and his earlier "Presumed Innocent" was a Number 1 paperback.

© T. Westenberger/Sygma

flecting this, only 45,700 new titles appeared in 1989, down from more than 55,000 during 1988.

In early 1990 some observers suggested that the large media companies that had acquired so many book publishers eventually might unload them after realizing that books would not match the electronic and other media in profitability. Some of the problems were linked to large advances, often not recouped, that companies seeking a place in best-sellers lists paid to top authors. Losses often have resulted when publishers printed such large numbers of copies that bookstore chains returned many unsold. Expectations were widespread that the companies would moderate future advances. Nonetheless, in June, Dell purchased two unwritten books by best-selling English writer Ken Follett for $12.3 million.

In February the removal of André Schiffrin, longtime managing director of Pantheon Books, set off widespread protests among authors, editors, and agents. Observers said that Pantheon, part of S.I. Newhouse-owned Random House, lost much money during 1989 and that its future operations likely would be curtailed. Pantheon has a reputation as a respectable, serious publisher of works by authors such as Noam Chomsky, Jean-Paul Sartre, and Studs Terkel.

The impact of certain technological innovations became even more apparent. By 1990 audio books had become an estimated $250 million component of the industry, and authors saw audio royalties as an increasingly important part of their contracts. Some major authors commanded six-figure royalties for audio alone. Random House also experienced success marketing books scented with perfumes that complement their subject matter. Computer technology helped new mail-order book services to provide unprecedented ranges of book selections. Such operations, along with discount warehouse stores and some surviving large independent stores, provided increasing competition to the large chain stores, which enjoyed explosive growth during the 1980s.

Legal issues concerned the industry when a New York Supreme Court judge approved a request from Israel for a temporary restraining order on the U.S. publication of a book by Victor Ostrovsky, a former agent of Israel's Mossad intelligence service. Many publishers saw this as an unconstitutional form of prior restraint. Israel claimed that the book, *By Way of Deception: A Devastating Insider's Portrait of the Mossad*, threatened the safety of its agents. In September, however, the appellate division of the court lifted the ban. The book became one of the year's best-sellers.

Magazines. After an encouraging year during 1989, U.S. magazine publishers expected a more modest year in 1990. Advertising revenues for consumer titles included in Publishers Information Bureau data increased by about

10.9% during 1989, the largest such increase since 1984. Advertising pages were up by 3.5% for 1989. As the year opened, industry leader *Modern Maturity*, received by members of the American Association of Retired Persons, had a total circulation of about 21.43 million copies. Slightly more than 11,000 titles were being published.

In late April signs of crisis appeared. The bureau reported that ad pages decreased by almost 3.5% during the first three months of 1990, compared with the initial three months of 1989. Ad revenues increased about 1.5% during that period, but only because of significant rate increases. Some observers said the gloomy performance in early 1990 reflected the presence of too many magazines for available advertising. They predicted a major "shakeout," perhaps lasting two years, in which numerous weak titles would close, ultimately leaving those remaining in a stronger position. During the summer, advertising pages remained down, and the industry faced a possible 23% increase in second-class postal rates in early 1991. Nonetheless some signs of long-term optimism returned. The investment-banking firm of Veronis, Suhler & Associates, which specializes in communication industries, predicted that total spending on magazines will increase by an average of 7.5% annually through 1995. Because of the ad slump, listed prices for coated paper were predicted to remain flat through mid-1991. Evidence also suggested that the Kuwaiti crisis would have little adverse impact on publishing costs, at least initially.

In February the magazine field lost one of its most colorful figures when Malcolm Forbes, editor in chief of *Forbes* magazine, died. Forbes was known for his lavish parties and hot-air balloon trips as well as for his publishing and marketing geniuses. He was succeeded by his son Malcolm, Jr., and the privately held publishing operation remained under family ownership.

The rapid pace of mergers and acquisitions appeared to slow somewhat in 1990, evidently reflecting a softer market. In January the Reader's Digest Association purchased the million-circulation *American Health* magazine for $29.1 million. In February, 25 million nonvoting shares of common stock in the association, until then among the last privately held media companies, began selling at the New York Stock Exchange. The money raised in part was expected to help finance a planned international expansion that is to include books and magazines. In late March, Time Warner Inc. agreed to buy the Lane Publishing Co., publisher of *Sunset* magazine, for $225 million. During the late summer a new partnership gave a Japanese company its first major investment in a U.S. magazine venture. JICC, Inc. purchased 50% ownership of Owen Lipstein's New American Magazine Family Co., which

owns *Mother Earth News* and *Psychology Today*.

A number of visible titles underwent temporary publication halts and format overhauls during late 1989 and 1990. As the summer of 1990 ended, a new ad-free *Ms.* magazine, which had suspended publication almost a year earlier, appeared. *Psychology Today* also suspended its publication in April to make format changes. Technologically linked publishing innovations also continued during 1990. For example, *Life* magazine published in its August issue dramatic pictures of the beginning of human life in the womb.

The possibility of additional legal restrictions on alcohol and tobacco advertisements appeared once more with the introduction of several bills in the U.S. Congress. The Leadership Council on Advertising predicted that proposed bans on tobacco ads would kill 165 magazine titles and a ban on hard-liquor ads would finish off 84 more.

Newspapers. Initially 1990 was expected to be another rather mediocre year for U.S. newspapers. Forecasts predicted steady newspaper prices, a moderate 6% growth in advertising revenues, and flat daily and Sunday circulation. Advertising expenditures in newspapers grew by only 3.8% in 1989, the smallest in 20 years. As the general economy soured in 1990, however, the industry grew gloomier. For the first half of the year, advertising expenditures in newspapers ran only .1% ahead of the same period in 1989, and some newsprint suppliers raised their prices. Quarterly profits declined among most publicly owned newspaper companies during the second quarter of 1990. At midyear some hope appeared. Veronis, Suhler & Associates predicted that circulation and advertising spending would increase by an average of 6.7% annually through 1994. If these predictions are accurate, 1992 growth in newspaper spending will catch up with changes in the gross national product for the first time since 1987.

By the start of 1990 about 1,620 daily newspapers were published in the United States. Groups owned about 76% of these (1,233 or 14 fewer than a year earlier), which accounted for about 82% of total circulation (slightly down from 83% a year earlier). Total daily circulation was 62.6 million, off .1% for the year. Total weekly circulation rose about 2% to 55.2 million during 1989. As of late March, *The Wall Street Journal* led all U.S. newspapers in daily circulation, with a total of about 1,936,000 copies.

As 1990 advanced, several newspapers in cities with competing dailies stopped publishing, continuing a decades-old pattern. In late 1989 the *Los Angeles Herald-Examiner*, once the largest afternoon paper in the nation, ceased publication after 86 years. In April publisher Ralph Ingersoll II folded the *St. Louis*

© Jim Wilson/NYT Pictures

A SPORTS DAILY

On Jan. 31, 1990, *The National*, the first U.S. national sports daily, was launched by prizewinning sportswriter Frank Deford (*above*). The publishing venture was financed by Mexico's media tycoon Emilio Azcárraga Milmo, with Peter Price as the publisher. The new paper would be 32 to 48 pages in length, include news, opinion, and gossip, and be illustrated with full-color photos.

Although sports dailies thrive in Europe, *The National* was plagued with problems. Initially it was unable to provide late scores from West Coast games for publication in the East. The concept of local sports coverage did not sell, and in May the paper switched its focus to national results.

Sun, only seven months after its first issue appeared. The paper, designed as a color-splashed tabloid for "today's video world," failed in part because expected street sales did not materialize. Ingersoll, known for his success in dramatically lifting the profitability of family-owned newspapers that he acquired, then gave up his interests in U.S. newspapers to his business partner to concentrate on publications in Great Britain and in Ireland. In June the five-week-old *Kansas City Evening News* died. The paper had appeared two months after the afternoon *Kansas City Star* and the morning *Kansas City Times* merged to

form the morning *Star*. On the other hand, the threatened September death of the *New York Post* was averted when nine unions accepted massive staff and wage cutbacks. And the New York *Daily News* was hit by a costly strike involving nine craft unions. The walkout was continuing as the year ended.

Newspaper experiments with nontraditional information-delivery mechanisms such as facsimile transmission continued during 1990. For example, *The New York Times* began offering a six-page, fax synopsis of the paper to businesses and travelers in Japan. A number of newspapers also continued or introduced audiotex services, which allow the public to obtain information via telephone.

Although recent modest declines in capital expenditures were expected to intensify during 1990, some newspapers continued to invest heavily. For example, in March the *Los Angeles Times* opened a $230 million plant in downtown Los Angeles. Some new international investment in the U.S. industry occurred. In the spring, British media mogul Robert Maxwell bought three supermarket tabloids—the *Globe*, the *Sun*, and the *National Examiner*—for an estimated $100–150 million from Montreal's Globe International Publishing Inc.

Concerns about legal issues again were evident. A *presstime* magazine headline termed a June U.S. Supreme Court ruling the "worst libel decision in a decade." In reinstating for trial a suit filed by a high-school wrestling coach from Ohio, the court determined that no categorical exemption from libel action exists for statements of opinion that carry factual implications. The case arose after a sports columnist said he believed the coach lied under oath in an attempt to get his team, which had been suspended from competition following a brawl, reinstated. The coach sued, but the suit was dismissed prior to trial because of precedents protecting statements of opinion.

In July, Associate Justice William J. Brennan, Jr., one of only two dissenters in the Ohio case, retired from the U.S. Supreme Court, and some in the publishing industry worried that an increasingly conservative court might restrict further the scope of the 1st Amendment. Brennan had authored the majority opinion in the historic 1964 *New York Times v. Sullivan* case, which helped protect newspapers and other media from libel suits.

Many also complained about a growing number of state and local laws requiring that newspapers be printed in part with recycled paper. The laws have appeared in a number of areas because of rapidly filling solid-waste landfills. In response the American Newspaper Publishers Association set a goal to double the use of recycled stock to 28% of all newsprint by 1992.

DAVID K. PERRY
The University of Alabama

PUERTO RICO

Puerto Rico continued to grapple with its political identity in 1990.

Status Issue. During in the year, the U.S. House of Representatives passed a precedent-setting bill that called on the Puerto Rican electorate to choose the island's final political status in a 1991 plebiscite. The Senate, however, was unable to pass similar legislation before it adjourned for the year. Sen. J. Bennett Johnston, considered the driving force behind the plebiscite movement in Congress, proposed the vote be postponed to 1992, assuming Congress passes legislation for the special vote. (*See also* special report, page 554.)

While the pro-statehood and pro-independence parties generally favored the Johnston proposal, the ruling pro-commonwealth Popular Democratic Party (PDP) dissented. Congress would need a consensus among the three leading political parties on the island to make the plebiscite legitimate in the international community. On November 17 the PDP voted to give Congress until February 19 to approve legislation for a 1991 plebiscite or to postpone the vote until at least 1993. The PDP is opposed to holding a status referendum in 1992, a general-election year.

While the plebiscite made headlines in 1990, public-opinion polls showed a growing disenchantment with political leaders. Those polled were less concerned with the plebiscite and more concerned with increasing crime and other problems. The polls also gave statehood a narrow advantage as the preferred status of Puerto Ricans.

The status issue took another twist in 1990 with the filing of Commonwealth legislation to make Spanish the official government language of Puerto Rico. Although most local government business on the island is conducted in Spanish, the issue is politically sensitive to many Puerto Ricans because of a long-standing debate over whether the island would have to give up its language and culture to become a state. The Spanish-only legislation was passed in the Commonwealth House of Representatives but was not voted on in the Senate. The matter likely would be taken up again in 1991.

The Economy and Related Developments. Following a U.S. trend, the economy of Puerto Rico slowed down in 1990. Since the island imports almost everything it consumes, the cost

© Tony Pacheco/Sygma

Residents of Puerto Rico gather in San Juan for a pro-statehood demonstration. Puerto Rico's future political status continued to be debated on the island and in Washington.

of living in Puerto Rico tends to be more expensive than on the U.S. mainland, while island salaries are generally lower. The Persian Gulf crisis contributed to an increase in the costs of electricity, transportation, and consumer goods.

Puerto Rico had its own savings and loan scandal in 1990. Four local savings and loan presidents were removed by the federal Office of Thrift Management from office for improper behavior as banking officials.

The global wave of privatization hit Puerto Rico in 1990. Gov. Rafael Hernández Colón proposed selling the government-owned Puerto Rico Telephone Company, and using the proceeds to create two perpetual funds of $1 billion each to fund improvements in education and the public infrastructure. The announcement met resistance from the labor movement, which organized a massive one-day work stoppage of the government on March 28. By late 1990, the governor said that the Persian Gulf crisis had hurt efforts to sell the utility.

Deborah Ramirez, *"The San Juan Star"*

PUERTO RICO • Information Highlights

Area: 3,515 sq mi (9 104 km²).
Population (1990 census prelim.): 3,599,000.
Chief Cities (1980 census): San Juan, the capital, 434,849; Bayamon, 196,206; Ponce, 189,046.
Government (1990): *Chief Officer*—governor, Rafael Hernández Colón (Popular Democratic Party). *Legislature*—Senate, 27 members; House of Representatives, 51 members.

QUEBEC

Two stories dominated the Quebec scene in 1990. One was constitutional: the demise of the Meech Lake accord for bringing Quebec into the Canadian constitution. The other concerned native affairs: a confrontation between Mohawk Indians and Canadian security forces that kept the province on edge for 11 weeks.

Constitution. The Meech Lake accord, hammered out by Canada's 11 first ministers in June 1987, died a painful death in 1990. The accord collapsed when two of the ten provinces —Manitoba and Newfoundland—failed to ratify it by the midnight deadline on June 23. A set of desperate 11th-hour proposals by the federal government, aimed at winning over the two holdout provinces, failed to save the accord.

A variety of factors entered into the collapse, but they centered on a clause recognizing predominantly French-speaking Quebec as a "distinct society" within Canada. Many Quebecers—perhaps most—interpreted the defeat as a rejection of Quebec by English-speaking Canada. It thus imposed enormous new strains on national unity. Subsequent opinion polls showed a majority in the province supporting Quebec sovereignty.

Robert Bourassa, the Liberal premier, reacted by announcing that he no longer would attend federal-provincial conferences. Bourassa is a federalist but recently had talked a great deal about European-style "superstructures" as a model for Canada.

As the furor subsided, attention shifted to a legislative commission which the government, in cooperation with the avowedly separatist Parti Québecois, set up to study Quebec's constitutional options. The commission began holding public hearings toward year's end.

Defiant Mohawks. Mohawk Indian warriors and Quebec provincial police clashed at Oka, a town just west of Montreal, on July 11. The armed skirmish occurred when police attempted unsuccessfully to storm a road blockade the Indians had erected in a land dispute with municipal authorities. It left a police corporal dead and led to a protracted armed standoff between Mohawks and Canadian security forces.

The day of the battle, other Mohawks put up a road blockade at the southern end of the Mercier Bridge, which connects Montreal with suburbs on the St. Lawrence River's south shore. This caused an explosive buildup of tensions between the Indians and frustrated commuters.

When provincial police proved incapable of resolving the impasse, the Canadian army was called in with orders to open the bridge, get the Mohawks to lay down their arms, and dismantle networks of barricades the Indians had erected on a reserve close to the bridge and another on the fringes of Oka.

Eventually, this was accomplished without further bloodshed. The last, beleaguered band of Mohawks surrendered at Oka September 25. Meantime, however, native groups across Canada had been stirred into a new militancy by the display of Mohawk defiance. These developments seemed to portend more mini-insurrections unless land claims and other Indian grievances were dealt with expeditiously.

Politics. History of a kind was made August 13 when Gilles Duceppe cruised to an easy by-election victory in the federal riding of Montreal Laurier-Ste.-Marie. Duceppe was the first member of parliament (MP) elected under the banner of the Bloc Québecois, a group of independent MPs committed to work for Quebec sovereignty. The leader of the group is Lucien Bouchard, the former federal environment minister who quit Prime Minister Brian Mulroney's cabinet May 21 out of frustration with the handling of the Meech Lake accord.

An earlier political eruption occurred February 12 when, for the first time in history, a New Democratic Party candidate was elected to the House of Commons from Quebec. Phil Edmonston won in convincing style, polling 26,998 votes compared with only 7,000 for his nearest rival, Liberal Clifford Lincoln, in a by-election in Montreal-Chambly.

Budget. The Bourassa government gave Quebecers a holiday from personal-tax increases in its 1990–91 budget. However, it shifted part of its financial burden to the municipalities, allowing school boards to get a bigger bite of property taxes. The move was expected to cause a substantial increase in local taxes.

Finance Minister Gérard Levesque projected a deficit of C$1.75 billion, compared with C$1.6 billion in the previous fiscal year. Personal-income-tax exemptions, family allowances, and child-care deductions were indexed to inflation. The birth bonus was boosted from C$4,500 to C$6,000 for families having a third child, but stayed at C$1,000 for the second child and C$500 for the first.

Endangered Beluga. The federal and Quebec governments joined forces to try to save the endangered beluga whale. Under an agreement signed April 6, Ottawa and Quebec City would spend C$9.5 million to develop a marine park at the junction of the St. Lawrence and Saguenay rivers.

JOHN BEST, *"Canada World News"*

QUEBEC · Information Highlights

Area: 594,857 sq mi (1 540 680 km²).
Population (September 1990): 6,770,800.
Chief Cities (1986 census): Quebec, the capital, 164,580; Montreal, 1,015,420; Laval, 284,164.
Government (1990): *Chief Officers*—lt. gov., Gilles Lamontagne; premier, Robert Bourassa (Liberal). *Legislature*—National Assembly, 125 members.
Provincial Finances (1990–91 fiscal year budget): *Revenues,* $33,650,000,000; *expenditures,* $35,400,000,000.
Personal Income (average weekly earnings, July 1990): $502.34.
Labor Force (September 1990, seasonally adjusted): *Employed* workers, 15 years of age and over, 3,073,000; *Unemployed,* 10.5%.
Education (1990–91): *Enrollment*—elementary and secondary schools, 1,136,600 pupils; postsecondary—universities, 124,600; community colleges, 152,000.
(All monetary figures are in Canadian dollars.)

The digital audio tape (DAT) machine, capable of making distortion-free copies of recordings, was introduced to U.S. consumers in 1990. The Japanese-manufactured machines were resisted by U.S. record companies, which feared the DAT's recording capabilities would ruin the compact-disc business.

AP/Wide World

RECORDINGS

The U.S. recording industry sailed into 1990 on the strength of another bullish year, with 1989 sales of 800.7 million units generating $6.46 billion. The compact disc (CD) was the most profitable format, accounting for 30.1% of unit sales and $2.6 billion. Vinyl records, both the long-playing album (LP) and the single, continued on the road to extinction.

Industry Sales. Sales of LPs and 7-inch (18-cm) singles were both down more than 50% in 1989, but this was not just a matter of consumer choice, because increasingly, shoppers do not have the option to buy vinyl. In 1990 labels began to be much more selective about issuing new releases in the vinyl format, and sometimes declined to keep successful albums in print. Milli Vanilli's *Girl You Know It's True*, for instance, was the nation's Number 1 recording when Arista announced that it would no longer be available on vinyl. Similarly, when CBS released George Michael's *Listen Without Prejudice Vol. 1*, vinyl albums were available, but only on a no-return basis. A number of labels already have such a policy regarding 7-inch singles.

Industry statistics suggested that cassette sales were peaking, and were actually off about 1% in 1989. Meanwhile, compact-disc players were in only about 20% of U.S. households, but compact-disc sales were soaring because there was a core group of heavy buyers.

Digital Audio Tape (DAT). Digital audio tape machines reached the U.S. consumer market in 1990, following years of wrangling between Japanese electronic manufacturers and U.S. record companies who were afraid that the machines would ruin the CD market. As it happened, the machines arrived before Congress could agree on legislation protecting the interests of music copyright holders.

As DAT machines costing more than $1,000 each reached stores, other news in the electronics industry indicated that the new format's days may be numbered already. CD machines with recording capabilities were under development, while another manufacturer was working on a tape recorder that could accommodate both analog and digital tape. Also, the

U.S. record industry has maintained its resistance to marketing in the DAT format.

Conservation Efforts. In response to environmental concerns, the 6 x 12 inch (15.2 x 30.5 cm) longbox used to package CDs came under scrutiny. Major Canadian record companies already had stopped marketing discs in the throwaway packaging, as had some U.S. independents. Supporters of the packaging argued that retailers needed it to attract sales and discourage shoplifting. Many of today's longboxes are constructed from recyclable paper. Nonetheless, some predicted that as soon as some major artists refuse to have their CDs marketed in the longbox, the end will be near.

Label Sales. Continuing a trend of the past few years that has seen the larger independent record labels absorbed by the giants, David Geffen sold his Geffen Records to MCA in March 1990 for stock estimated to be worth $550 million. At about the same time, Geffen spun off a second label, DGR.

Irving Azoff, the former head of MCA Records, launched Giant Records with financing from the WEA group of labels. Disney also announced plans to enter the recording business with a label called Hollywood Records. CBS Records bought 50% of Important Records, whose affiliated labels specialize in heavy metal and rap music, a purchase reflecting a trend whereby the majors buy into independents that have the ability to respond quickly to musical trends. Earlier, Warner Brothers had purchased half of the rap-oriented Tommy Boy label with an option to buy the rest. Warner exercised that option, distributing some Tommy Boy records on its own, but marketing other releases via the company's own grassroots system.

Payola. A four-and-one-half-year Justice Department investigation of payola in the record industry led to a trial focusing on the operations of independent record promoter Joe Isgro. Isgro was one of a number of promoters who collected large fees from record companies to encourage radio stations to play the label's records by allegedly offering bribes. The case ultimately was thrown out of court.

JOHN MILWARD
Free-lance Writer and Critic

© Gamma-Liaison
Seeking permanent residence elsewhere, some 100,000 Vietnamese boat people continued to live in first-asylum locales, such as Hong Kong's Camp Shek Kong, above.

REFUGEES AND IMMIGRATION

The 1990s began with the emergence of new mass exoduses of refugees even as the prolonged refugee crises of the previous decade in Afghanistan, Central America, Indochina, the Horn of Africa, and Southern Africa remained unresolved.

New Emergencies. New emergencies uprooted hundreds of thousands more people, many of whom were assisted inadequately. More than 250,000 people, including 65,000 refugees, were uprooted by a crisis between Mauritania and Senegal; civil war in Liberia uprooted more than half of that country's population and more than 500,000 Liberians fled to Guinea, Sierra Leone, and the Ivory Coast; increased military activity in Myanmar (Burma) drove some 42,000 refugees into Thailand

where thousands were turned back forcibly by Thai border police; tens of thousands of Tamils arrived in southern India as a result of renewed violence and internal conflict in Sri Lanka; tension in Kosovo in Yugoslavia generated the exodus of thousands of Albanians to Western Europe; and the rise of Islamic fundamentalism in Kazakhstan in the Soviet Union drove large numbers of Christian Pontians to Greece.

The largest and most publicized displacement occurred in the Persian Gulf region as a direct result of Iraq's annexation of Kuwait. By mid-October more than 1 million Arabs and Asians had left, or found themselves stranded outside of Iraq and Kuwait. Many of these displaced people and refugees relied on their own resources or found help from governments in the region. But others, primarily Asians, required the assistance of the international community in order to be repatriated to their home countries—an operation which ran into the hundreds of millions of dollars. Repatriation might not be an option for people from refugee-producing countries, such as Sri Lanka, Vietnam, China, Romania, Sudan, Ethiopia, and Somalia, who had been working in the Gulf region but who might be unwilling to return home because of fear of persecution or conflict. The potential for further, even more massive, displacement of people was very real. Estimates of foreign nationals in Iraq and Kuwait in late 1990 ran as high as 2 million, and at least 400,000 of these people were displaced internally and poised to move into adjoining countries. In addition, there were more than 500,000 Kuwaitis still in their country. Thus a larger and more intractable refugee crisis was looming in the Middle East.

Old Groups and Those Omitted. While dealing with these largely unanticipated refugee emergencies, the international community also was confronted with the continuation of long-standing refugee problems. Even as the threat of war hung over the Middle East, more than 100,000 Soviet Jews moved to Israel during the year, causing serious housing shortages and escalating Arab-Israeli tensions. Some 150,000 to 250,000 Soviet Jews were expected to arrive in Israel during each of the next several years. At the same time, the doors began to close on the tens of thousands of Vietnamese boat people in Hong Kong, Malaysia, and Thailand despite the fact that the number of arrivals of refugees fell dramatically throughout the region by mid-year. The resolution of other long-standing refugee problems in Southern Africa, Afghanistan, Cambodia, Western Sahara, and Central America depended on the attainment of cease-fires and peaceful accords in those regions.

Certain refugee problems largely were ignored by the international community during 1990. The United Nations High Commission for Refugees (UNHCR) failed to receive sufficient funds from appeals it made to govern-

© A. Nouges/Sygma

Scores of thousands of non-Westerners, many from poor Asian nations, were forced to flee to refugee camps across the Jordan border as a result of Iraq's invasion and annexation of Kuwait in August 1990.

ments to assist Liberians in Guinea and the Ivory Coast, Somalis in Djibouti, Iraqi Kurds in Turkey, Burmese in Thailand, and Angolans wanting to return home from Zaire. Millions of internally displaced people in Sudan, Ethiopia, Angola, and Mozambique—to mention only a few places—essentially were left out of the international system for protecting and assisting uprooted people because they had not crossed an international border. As a result, millions of people were threatened by drought and war-induced famine in northern Ethiopia, southern Sudan, Angola, and Mozambique. By midyear, tens of thousands of people already had left their homes in search of food, and the number of people who might cross borders into neighboring countries if food did not become available soon could mushroom.

Asylum. The issue of asylum and refugee policy became more acute in public debate in Europe and North America. Most European countries experienced larger numbers of asylum requests from both Third World and Eastern European applicants during the first half of 1990. Progress was made toward harmonizing asylum policy within the European Community. The Schengen Treaty, signed in the Luxembourg village of Schengen in June 1990, abolished internal frontiers among France, Germany, Belgium, the Netherlands, and Luxembourg, reinforced external border controls, harmonized visa policies, and established a "one-chance" rule preventing the asylum seeker from exercising a right to choose his or her prospective country of asylum. A European Convention of Asylum, based on the Schengen Treaty, was signed by the European Community ministers. As numbers of asylum claims in North America also increased, new regulations were signed in the United States which established a specialized group of asy-

lum officers, using human rights information obtained from a newly established documentation center, within the Immigration and Naturalization Service to adjudicate asylum applications.

UNHCR. The UNHCR, the institution mandated to protect and assist refugees, experienced such severe financial difficulties that even basic, life-sustaining services to refugees were curtailed. During 1985–1990, for example, the number of refugees rose 50% but the UNHCR's budget rose only 25%. At the same time, U.S. contributions to UNHCR fell from 27% to 22%. As a result, the worldwide UNHCR budgets for food and water were cut by 25%, sanitation by 30%, and shelter and infrastructure by 35%.

U.S. Immigration Reform. Just prior to adjourning in late October, the U.S. Congress passed sweeping immigration reform. The act seeks to permit more immigration by Europeans and specially trained workers. It specifically increased the annual number of legal immigrants to 700,000 from 500,000 for the first three years of the act. After that, a permanent figure of 675,000 would be established. The totals do not include refugees or people seeking asylum due to persecution in their homelands. The new legislation calls for the admission of all immediate relatives of U.S. citizens without regard to allocation limits and provides 140,000 visas annually for people with a guaranteed job in the United States. The act also eliminates prohibitions of foreigners because of their political beliefs or sexual orientation and could ease restrictions on people with the AIDS virus. Sen. Edward M. Kennedy (D-MA) noted that with the new act the nation again would "open doors to those who no longer have immediate family ties in the United States."

GIL LOESCHER, *University of Notre Dame*

RELIGION

Overview

Increased religious freedom in the Soviet Union and in the nations of Eastern Europe highlighted 1990 religion news. A significant increase in the number of Soviet Jews allowed to immigrate to Israel and greater diplomatic activity between the Vatican and the USSR and the Eastern European nations were two offshoots of the new freedom.

The year also saw the appointment of a new archbishop of Canterbury; a new patriarch of Moscow; the continuing growth in the number of Muslims in the United States; the retirement of U.S. Archbishop Paul C. Marcinkus, a central figure in an Italian banking scandal in the early 1980s, after a 38-year career running the Vatican city-state; the Mormon Church undergo sweeping changes, including the elimination of the pledge of wifely obedience demanded of women; and two Christian Scientists being convicted of manslaughter because they had relied on prayer rather medical care in the treatment of their ill young son.

Australian ecologist L. Charles Birch shared the 1990 Templeton Prize for Progress in Religion with Murlidhar Devidas Amte, a lawyer who has worked with the poor and lepers in India.

Far Eastern

The Dalai Lama announced the International Year of Tibet in September 1990, dedicating 1990–91 to the preservation of his occupied nation's sacred ancient culture. At a news conference in New York, he said that after 40 years of Chinese occupation, more than 6,000 Buddhist monasteries had been razed and most of their works of religious art have been lost forever. The Dalai Lama's visit to the United States coincided with the publication of his autobiography, *Freedom in Exile*.

Osel Tendzin, leader of the Vajradhatu Buddhist Church and the first Westerner to head an international Tibetan Buddhist sect, died of an AIDS-related illness on Aug. 25, 1990, at the age of 47. Although he acknowledged that he had the illness in late 1988, he had resisted calls that he resign as leader of the church, which has 3,000 to 5,000 followers in the United States, Canada, and Europe. Born in New Jersey as Thomas Rich, he was tapped for leadership by Chogyam Trungpa Rinpoche, the founder of the sect, and in 1971 took the name Osel Tendzin, or "radiant holder of the teachings."

A bomb believed to have been set by Sikh radicals exploded in India's Punjab state during a Hindu religious procession April 3, killing at least 34 people. After the attack in the town of Batala, enraged Hindus went on a rampage in retaliation. At least 16 other persons were reported killed the same day in other incidents in Punjab, where Sikh extremists have been waging a violent campaign for a separate state for years. In addition, tensions between Hindus and Muslims led to serious social and communal difficulties in India throughout the year. (*See also* INDIA.)

A film biography of Tipu Sultan, an 18th-century Indian nationalist leader, stirred protests from Hindus who said the fervent Muslim was intolerant of other religious and ethnic minorities living in the kingdom of Mysore, which he ruled from 1782 to his death in 1790. Several Hindu organizations charged that Tipu Sultan forcibly had converted non-Muslims, and they threatened violence if the film was shown. The leader of one Hindu political party made a public appeal to the Indian government television network not to screen a film about a man he called "a traitor and a terrorist."

Kanshi Ram, a former government scientist in India, campaigned on behalf of a new political organization called the Bahujan Samaj, the party of the majority, to encompass the 650 million of India's 840 million people who exist outside the top three caste groupings of Hinduism. He said his party would field hundreds of candidates, "the majority of them Ph.D.s," in the next general election.

In Laos a revival of Buddhist life and culture was reported after 15 years of Communist rule.

An 87-ft (27-m) bronze Buddha was built by the monks of Po Lin Monastery on the island of Lantau in Hong Kong. The new statue, which was constructed to promote Buddhism, began to attract large crowds. According to Sik Chiwai, the monastery's director, "people from around the world will want to come to pay their respects to this Buddha."

DARRELL J. TURNER, *Religious News Service*

Islam

In the wake of major political upheavals during 1989, Muslim communities in several areas of Eastern Europe and the Soviet Union struggled to assert their distinctive identities during 1990.

Eastern Europe and USSR. In January the reformist leaders of Bulgaria's new government ordered the abandonment of policies restricting the religious rights of the country's minority Muslim Turkish population and forbidding Turks to use their Muslim names or speak their own language. Although some supporters of the previous regime resisted this reversal with strikes and demonstrations, government efforts to defuse ethnic tensions and assure Muslims of religious rights ultimately succeeded. Elsewhere in Eastern Europe at the start of the year, Muslims of Albanian origin, who constitute the majority of the population in the Yugoslav province of Kosovo, organized protests to demand a greater measure of autonomy that would enable them to adhere more closely to their religious and cultural traditions.

Unrest was also apparent among several Muslim nationalities within the Soviet Union. Communal strife between Azeri Turkish Muslims and Armenian Christians in the republic of Azerbaijan in January ended only with the dispatch of Soviet forces to the capital city of Baku. The repercussions of these events reached into the predominantly Muslim Central Asian republics of Tadzhikistan and Uzbekistan in the following month, as Armenians in those republics' leading cities of Dushanbe and Samarkand, some of them refugees from Azerbaijan, but others longtime residents, were subjected to attacks. These incidents reflected the conviction of many Soviet Muslims that economic and political programs drawn up in Moscow worked primarily to the advantage of other ethnic and religious groups.

Jammu and Kashmir. In January militant Kashmiri Muslims resumed a campaign to alter the political status of the primarily Muslim Indian state of Jammu and Kashmir. Bombings in the capital city of Srinagar were accompanied by demonstrations demanding a United Nations-sponsored plebiscite on the question of secession from India. India accused the Islamic Republic of Pakistan, which controls one third of the Kashmir region, and with which it has quarreled over sovereignty for more than 40 years, of abetting the Muslim separatists.

Pakistan, in turn, countered that Indian soldiers had wounded Pakistani civilians. Clashes between Pakistani and Indian military forces, and between Kashmiri separatists and those loyal to India, continued throughout the year. Although most Muslims in India did not support the demands of the militants in Kashmir, the escalating violence in the area created tensions between India's Muslim minority and its Hindu majority.

Algeria. Algeria witnessed a more peaceful assertion of Islamic identity in June. In the country's first free elections since winning independence from France in 1962, the Islamic Salvation Front captured more than half of the popular vote and won control over provincial administrations and the city councils of virtually every important urban center. The Front wishes to establish Islamic values as the guiding principles of state and society, but the fact that almost 40% of the electorate failed to participate in the vote left the extent of the Front's popular support unclear.

The Persian Gulf. Responding to the positioning of a multinational military force in the Gulf region after his country's August 2 invasion of Kuwait, Iraqi President Saddam Hussein appealed, with little success, to other Muslim nations to support a *jihad*, or struggle in defense of Islam, against the U.S.-led force. At a September meeting of the World League of Muslims, an international nongovernmental organization, Muslim scholars endorsed the decision of the Gulf states to seek the assistance of other governments in pressuring Iraq to evacuate Kuwait, saying that doing so was in conformity with Islamic principles. They also denounced Hussein's appeal as a distortion of the concept of *jihad*. (*See also* feature article, page 24.)

KENNETH J. PERKINS
University of South Carolina

Judaism

The attention of world Jewry in 1990 was riveted on the historic events taking place in the Soviet Union and Eastern Europe, events which had profound implications for Jews.

Soviet Jews are processed by Israeli authorities as they arrive in Tel Aviv. A significant increase in the number of Jews immigrating to Israel from the USSR in 1990 put additional stress on the Israeli economy. Worldwide Jewish philanthropic organizations were called upon for assistance.

Emigration and Anti-Semitism. After decades of barring Jewish emigration, the USSR implemented policies that allowed almost all Jews to leave the country. The constraints of U.S. immigration laws ensured that the great majority of those leaving the Soviet Union would go to Israel. The Jewish state, overjoyed to receive them, was unprepared economically for the task of absorption, and Jewish fund-raising agencies in the United States and elsewhere mobilized to help defray the costs.

On July 1 the Jewish Agency, which coordinates worldwide Jewish philanthropy for Israel, announced a $1 billion campaign over three years. While the level of giving in subsequent months was encouraging, some feared that this special campaign for Soviet Jewry resettlement might have a negative impact on fund-raising for other Jewish causes.

Jews also worried about the fate of their Soviet coreligionists who chose not to emigrate. The new freedom of expression made possible by the policy of *glasnost* facilitated the public expression of anti-Semitism which previously had been restricted by Soviet authorities. Extreme nationalist groups—*pamyat* was the best known—blamed Jews for the evils of communism and advocated their removal from positions of influence. While a rumored pogrom supposedly scheduled for May 5 did not materialize, there were sporadic reports of intimidation and harassment of Jews.

The historical legacy of anti-Semitism in several of the countries that had been Soviet satellites also raised the apprehensions of Jews. In Romania, Jews overwhelmingly supported the National Salvation Front which replaced the previous Communist dictatorship, fearing that the nationalist opposition might launch a wave of anti-Semitism. In Poland and Hungary, age-old religiously based suspicion of Jews, combined with the popular association of Jews with discredited communism, lay the groundwork for anti-Jewish propaganda. And the rapid sequence of events leading from the collapse of Communist East Germany to a united Germany raised the specter of a possible resurgence of German anti-Semitism—despite the reassurances of German leaders that this would not happen.

Court Ruling and Theological Disputes. A decision by the U.S. Supreme Court that seemed to place limits on religious freedom made many U.S. Jews uneasy. On April 17 the court ruled 6–3 that American Indians were bound by an Oregon law criminalizing the use of peyote, even though the drug is used for sacramental purposes in the Indian religion. Jewish organizations, recognizing that the ruling might endanger Jewish religious practices, rallied behind a proposal in Congress that would require a showing of "compelling government interest" before free exercise of religion could be overridden.

In 1990 the most liberal wing of Judaism took a major step away from the Jewish tradition, just as the most traditional elements within the religion distanced themselves further from any engagement with those outside their own group. On June 25 the Central Conference of American Rabbis—the rabbinical organization of Reform Judaism—voted to accept sexually active homosexuals into the rabbinate. Although the resolution adopted also noted that Jewish tradition viewed heterosexual marriage as "the ideal human relationship," the legitimation of homosexual rabbis marked a clear break from the more conservative branches of Judaism.

Meanwhile the Orthodox denomination—which adheres most closely to the tradition—became embroiled in an internal wrangle, as rabbis adamantly opposed to cooperative ventures together with the non-Orthodox sought influence over the policies of moderate Orthodox rabbinic, synagogal, and educational institutions that had maintained relationships with the other denominations. An attempt—which ultimately failed—to remove from the Rabbinical Council of America the member most involved in interdenominational activity showed the determination of the opposition to the moderates.

A sign of the new strength of the least modernized wing of Orthodoxy was the remarkable turnout and extraordinary publicity given to the gala completion—at Madison Square Garden in New York City—of a cycle of Talmud study. The Talmud, a vast compendium of Jewish law and lore, contains 2,711 folio pages. The extremely pious Jews who study a page a day complete the entire work in seven and one half years. About 20,000 of them attended the celebration, four times more than the number who turned out for the previous completion of the cycle in 1982.

LAWRENCE GROSSMAN
The American Jewish Committee

Orthodox Eastern

The Russian Orthodox Church in June 1990 chose 61-year-old Metropolitan Alexis Ridiger of Leningrad, for many years bishop of Tallinn in Estonia, as the patriarch of Moscow, succeeding Patriarch Pimen, who died in Moscow in May.

Alexis, chosen in a close election that was conducted for the first time since 1918 by secret ballot, is the first non-Slav in centuries to head the Russian Church. He was praised for his involvement in formulating the 1990 Soviet law that gives the Orthodox Church, and other religious groups, legal status, rights of ownership, a large measure of self-determination, and freedom to engage in educational and charitable activities.

In the Soviet Union in 1990, thousands of Orthodox churches reopened, and new parishes, dioceses, monasteries, and schools were founded or reestablished. Properties were returned to church control, and ancient monuments, including those in the Kremlin, were accessible for liturgical services. With the new freedoms, the "Russian Orthodox Church Outside Russia" also opened several communities in the USSR. This emigré group, which considers itself the authentic successor to the pre-revolutionary church, has a special appeal to right-wing Russian Orthodox nationalists, whom some associated with the September murder of Father Alexander Menn, an activist Moscow pastor of Jewish background.

The Ukraine. In 1990, Eastern-rite Catholics in the Ukrainian republic asserted their right to exist and to reclaim properties governed by the Moscow patriarchate since World War II. The patriarchate argued that Christians of this region, while under Polish-Lithuanian and Austro-Hungarian rule, were forced originally into union with Rome against their knowledge and will, with the retention of the Eastern rite employed as a type of deception. The fact that millions of these people now prefer to be Catholics has led to conflicts. In addition to the movement of millions of Eastern-rite Christians in the Ukraine to reunion with Rome, a group of several hundred clergy, including a small number of bishops, attempted to establish a Ukrainian Orthodox Church independent of the Moscow patriarchate.

Eastern Europe. In Czechoslovakia the properties of the Orthodox seminary in Presov were given to Eastern-rite Catholics, and the majority of Orthodox parishes in Slovakia chose to return to union with Rome. The election of Daniel Ciobotea, the Western-educated former director of the World Council of Churches' Ecumenical Institute in Switzerland, as metropolitan to the prestigious see in Moldavia, indicated important changes in the Romanian Orthodox Church. In Bulgaria and Yugoslavia, demands were heard for new directions, and in officially atheist Albania, Father Arthur Liolin of Boston celebrated the divine liturgy in a Tiranë hotel in the presence of government officials. In July, Dimitrios I, the ecumenical patriarch of Constantinople, visited the United States.

THOMAS HOPKO, *St. Vladimir's Seminary*

Protestantism

Questions concerning the ordination of homosexuals and women continued to be raised in several Protestant denominations during 1990. Bishop George Carey was selected to succeed Dr. Robert Runcie as the 103d archbishop of Canterbury and spiritual leader of 70 million Anglicans around the world.

A relative unknown, the 54-year-old Bishop Carey was described as an evangelical who has the confidence of Anglo-Catholics in the Church of England. He was slated to succeed Runcie in January 1991. The eighth triennial session of the Anglican Consultative Council drew 70 delegates from 36 nations to its mid-summer meeting in Cardiff, Wales. Runcie and other speakers stressed the challenge of maintaining communion without abandoning the principle of autonomy.

Ordinations. A disciplinary committee of the Evangelical Lutheran Church in America suspended two small congregations in San Francisco for five years for ordaining a lesbian couple and a gay man in January in defiance of church law. But while disciplining the congregations, the committee criticized the denomination for having "ignored homosexual people and the story of their faith," urged the two churches "to continue to be a voice and a witness," and encouraged the denomination to reconsider its policy.

The ordination of the Rev. Robert Williams, a practicing homosexual, by Episcopal Bishop John S. Spong of Newark, NJ, in December 1989 caused controversy, particularly after Williams made derogatory comments about

Bishop George Carey (left), 54-year-old bishop of the diocese of Bath and Wells in England, was selected to succeed Dr. Robert Runcie as the 103d archbishop of Canterbury.

monogamy and celibacy. Two investigating committees of the Newark diocese said there were no irregularities in the ordination, but in September the church's House of Bishops voted 78–74 to "disassociate" itself from the ordination and agreed with Presiding Bishop Edmond Browning and his Council of Advice in calling ordination of practicing homosexuals "inappropriate." In response, Spong accused his critics of hypocrisy and homophobia.

The General Council of the United Church of Canada reaffirmed its controversial stand that any of its members should be eligible for consideration for ordination as ministers, regardless of sexual orientation. The policy, adopted in 1988, had resulted in the departure of thousands of members and about 70 clergy from Canada's largest Protestant denomination. Those opposed to ordination of homosexuals formed a group called Community of Concern, which established chapters across Canada.

Ordination of women was an issue for the Christian Reformed Church (CRC) and the Seventh-day Adventist Church in 1990. The 314,000-member CRC overturned a century and a half of tradition in beginning the process of opening all church offices to women. Delegates to the denomination's synod in Grand Rapids, MI, voted 99–84 to "permit churches to use their discretion in utilizing the gifts of women members in all the offices of the church," although women cannot be ordained officially unless the changes are ratified in 1992.

In contrast, the ordination of women was turned down by the Seventh-day Adventist World Conference in Indianapolis by a vote of 1,173 to 377. A large number of the votes in favor of ordaining women came from North American delegates, but most Adventists from the rest of the world are opposed to women ministers. The church's division presidents reported that women's ordination is so unpopular that allowing it could cause a schism in the denomination of 6.2 million members.

The first two women to become Anglican Church ministers in Europe were ordained in the Church of Ireland.

The Baptists. Moderates in the Southern Baptist Convention (SBC) who are discontented with the direction the 14.9-million-member denomination has taken under fundamentalist leadership in the 1980s met in Atlanta in August and approved an alternative to the convention's $137 million Cooperative Program unified budget. The 2,700 people who attended the gathering declined to adopt a formal name for their movement and differed on whether they would stay in the SBC, leave to join other Baptist bodies, or form a new one. Conservatives continued to exercise their clout in the denomination by persuading the Southern Baptist Executive Committee to fire Al Shackleford and Dan Martin, the director and news editor of Baptist Press, following complaints that the official news agency had been biased against conservatives.

Other News. In the United States the governing board of the National Council of Churches (NCC) adopted a resolution calling into question the propriety of 1992 celebrations of the 500th anniversary of Christopher Columbus' arrival in the New World, saying the event led to "conquest and exploitation." The NCC also celebrated publication of the New Revised Standard Version of the Bible.

Delegates to a World Council of Churches (WCC) consultation in Seoul, South Korea, in March on "Justice, Peace and Integrity of Creation" added racism to a list of concerns but failed to adopt the theological section of a position paper called "Between the Flood and the Rainbow." Meeting in Geneva, the WCC Central Committee said it "regrets its mistaken judgment in failing to speak adequately" about repression in Romania under the Nicolae Ceauşescu regime.

The Rev. Allan Boesak, one of South Africa's leading foes of apartheid, left the presidency of the World Alliance of Reformed Churches.

DARRELL TURNER

Roman Catholicism

Throughout 1990, tension and hope marked Roman Catholicism as the post-Communist era opened in Eastern Europe. The Holy See established diplomatic relations with Czechoslovakia, Romania, and Hungary. Laws guaranteeing religious freedom in the Soviet Union, Czechoslovakia, and Hungary opened up new opportunities for practicing Roman Catholicism. In February new bishops were named in Czechoslovakia. The first meeting of Romanian Catholic bishops in 40 years was held in January.

World Politics. A joint Vatican-Russian Orthodox Commission met to resolve practical matters concerning church property and buildings in the USSR. In August, Roman Catholics took possession of the cathedral in Lvov but violence broke out in other communities as votes were taken over ownership. A September meeting of the joint commission ended without reaching an agreement.

In El Salvador the unsolved murders of six Jesuit priests and two laywomen in 1989 and the decade-old unsolved assassination of Salvadoran Archbishop Oscar Romero led 50 U.S. bishops to call for a cutoff of U.S. aid to the civil-war-torn country. Their request went unheeded, however, and the U.S. government continued to send more than $1 million per day to El Salvador. After the election of Violeta Chamorro as head of Nicaragua in February, relations between church and state improved.

Controversies. In July, Archbishop Eugene Marino, the first black U.S. archbishop, resigned as head of the Atlanta archdiocese after admitting to an ongoing intimate relationship with Vicki Long, a 27-year-old Atlanta singer. At year's end, Archbishop Marino was under supervision at a psychiatric hospital unit. Cleveland Auxiliary Bishop James P. Lyke, also a black, was named administrator of the Atlanta archdiocese.

George Stallings, a charismatic priest from Washington, was excommunicated in February for founding an Imani Temple for black Catholics in Washington and Baltimore. Accusations of sexual and financial improprieties hampered his efforts to expand his congregation.

Father Bruce Ritter, the founder of Covenant House, an outreach center for teenage runaways, resigned in February after accusations of sexual improprieties. Covenant House activities were curtailed by $10 million as contributions to the group dwindled. Daughter of Charity Sister Mary Rose McGeady took over as president in September.

In the archdiocese of Washington, two parish council members were fired from their posts after expressing ''pro-choice'' views on abortion during a political campaign. In April the bishops announced that they had retained the Hill and Knowlton public relations firm to develop a public campaign to change attitudes toward abortion in the United States.

Finances. Several U.S. dioceses announced budget cuts and closings because of shortages of personnel and money. The archdiocese of Chicago closed 13 parishes, six schools, and a seminary in January. Dioceses in Springfield, IL, Honolulu, and St. Louis announced budget cuts. Pittsburgh Bishop Donald Wuerl was reported ''joyful'' when his diocesan annual deficit came in at $741,000, not as bad as expected. The second annual collection to help fund the retirement needs of elderly nuns, priests, and brothers was $4 million less than the previous year. However, the Knights of Columbus announced that they had given $92 million in donations and 32 million hours of charitable service in 1989.

Teachings. Action on the U.S. bishops' proposed pastoral letter on women was delayed when it was sent to the Vatican for consultation. The letter, which had been through two drafts, had called sexism a sin but upheld church teaching on a male-only priesthood and diaconate. A world synod on the priestly formation was held at the Vatican in October. The final document defended priestly celibacy and called for spiritual training for priests. In June the Vatican issued a statement on theologians which asked them to ''reflect silently'' rather than dissent from church teaching in public. In September a Vatican statement on Catholic universities called for universities to establish a ''Catholic identity.'' The statement estab-

© Nusca/Gamma-Liaison

An ''identity crisis'' and ''burnout'' afflicting some Roman Catholic priests were to receive special attention as 238 bishops convened in Rome on September 30 for a synod.

lished norms that promote orthodoxy in teaching and affirm a strong Catholic perspective in education. A draft of the universal catechism, which is expected to shape the church for decades, received worldwide support, according to the Vatican.

The Pope and Other Leaders. Pope John Paul II traveled to western Africa in January, Czechoslovakia in April, Mexico and Malta in May, and parts of Africa in September.

The decade-long era of Archbishop Pio Laghi as papal ambassador to the United States came to an end. He was named head of the Vatican's Congregation for Catholic Education. Cardinal Edmund Szoka was named president of the Prefecture for the Economic Affairs of the Holy See. His post as archbishop of Detroit was filled by Archbishop Adam Maida, who had been bishop of Green Bay.

U.S. Archbishop Justin Rigali was named secretary of the college of cardinals. Archbishop Agostino Cacciavillan was named the 11th pronuncio to the United States in August. Mother Teresa resigned in April for health reasons but was reelected head of the Missionaries of Charity. Lutheran minister and theologian Richard Neuhaus converted to Catholicism. The Vatican reported that there were 900 million Catholics in the world, with 57 million in the United States.

DANIEL MEDINGER, *''The Catholic Review''*

A late 1989 going-out-of-business sale at New York City's B. Altman was indicative of the hard times facing the large U.S. department store. A landmark, Altman's was founded in 1865 and known for its crystal chandeliers, parquet floors, and decorations during the holiday season.

© John A. Giordano/SABA

RETAILING

U.S. retailing, ever sensitive to the rises and dips of the economy, had one of its most difficult years in more than a decade, only partly because of a dawning recession. Merger-created debt, divestitures, management shake-outs, and high people turnover combined with erratic sales turned 1990 into a year that retailers wished they could forget.

In January, Federated Department Stores and Allied Stores, both owned by the Campeau Corporation of Toronto, Canada, filed for voluntary bankruptcy. Separate Chapter 11 petitions were filed by the store divisions, including Bloomingdale's, Abraham & Straus, Burdine's, Jordan Marsh, and others. Earlier in 1989 the Hooker Corporation, the Australian developer with such subsidiaries as B. Altman, Bonwit Teller, and Sakowitz, had filed for bankruptcy.

These events shocked both the industry and the public, for these were some of the best-known, most-respected stores in the United States. More shocks developed quickly. B. Altman closed its six stores and Bonwit shuttered its 17 stores. Bloomingdale's, which Campeau had put up for sale in 1989 to raise cash, was pulled off the market because it did not draw any $1 billion bids, the price Campeau wanted.

More was to come. B.A.T. Industries, the British conglomerate, decided that it wanted to redeploy its assets and sold all its U.S. retail stores. So Marshall Field, Chicago, was bought for about $1.2 billion by the Dayton Hudson Corporation and Saks Fifth Avenue was sold for $1.5 billion to Investcorp, the Mideast financial firm. Dillard Department Stores also bought B.A.T.'s J.B. Ivey chain in the South.

Both financial pressures and eroding company focus hurt other companies. R. H. Macy & Company, grappling with a $5 billion debt created by a leveraged buyout and the purchase of the Bullock's and I. Magnin chains in California from Federated, produced several consecutive quarterly losses. And in what may have been the biggest shocker, Sears Roebuck & Company, the nation's biggest retailer, reacted to slippage in its huge retail business by demoting Michael Bozic, retailing chairman, and replacing him with Edward Brennan, corporate chairman and chief executive, who now wore two hats.

Even Wal-Mart Stores, the hottest, most successful retailer, which was expected to replace Sears soon in the top spot, suffered some decline in its same-store-sales, prompting Wall Street analysts to downgrade their recommendations on Wal-Mart. Menswear businesses, which had offset some of the decline in women's wear in 1987–89, saw a reverse in their fortunes and slumped. Analysts attributed the decline to men's awareness of difficult times and fear of job insecurity.

On a positive note, the May Department Stores Company and Dayton Hudson had strong years and The Limited and The Gap, two prime specialty-shop operators, recovered from their 1988–89 slumps. In food retailing, the big supermarket chains, such as the Great Atlantic & Pacific Tea Company, Safeway Stores, American Stores Company, and others appeared to weather the nonfood decline. The hypermarket trend grew, with Wal-Mart and K Mart Corporation pushing ahead with their opening of these food and nonfood stores. And the warehouse club stores, such as the Price Club, surmounted their sales and profit erosion and remained formidable, growing segments of the industry.

ISADORE BARMASH
"The New York Times"

The Department Store

A phenomenon the world over, the U.S. department store long has been the battlewagon of U.S. retailing. Often in landmark, prime locations, the huge emporiums can run to ten levels, sell 150,000 different items, attract as many as 300,000 customers daily in the holiday season, and during that time rack up daily sales of $1 million to $2 million.

But for a decade, pundits have predicted the demise of the big store as a dinosaur that could not adapt to change. Indeed, that seemed to have happened in the 1980s. Gimbels and Korvettes departed in that decade and in 1990 the B. Altman stores also closed. If one adds the large, more specialized stores such as Ohrbachs and Bonwit Teller that also disappeared, the predictions appeared sound.

The realities behind these demises were simple. Most of the stores operated at a loss because they could not sustain a clear focus to keep their customers. Despite its large size, the department store can be difficult to shop in, with too many dispersed departments and enclaves, disinterested salesclerks, and a habit of slashing prices to lure the shoppers. As William Dillard, Sr., the founder-chairman of Dillard Department Stores of Little Rock, AR, one of the most successful of U.S. retailers, put it, "If I sell a man a $400 suit and he sees it two weeks later for $300, he surely will not come back to my store. We try to have good prices every day and we rarely have sales."

But it took merger-created debt that led to such bankruptcies as those of Federated Department Stores and Allied Stores to create the greatest doubts about the species. First, after Campeau Corporation, the Canadian builder, bought Allied in 1986, the new owner sold or consolidated 17 of 22 store divisions. Then, in 1988, after Campeau acquired Federated, it sold the Bullock's stores in California to R. H. Macy, its Joske and Cain-Sloan stores in Texas, and its Foley's division in Houston.

Attempting to raise cash by selling Bloomingdale's, Campeau found bids insufficient and pulled Bloomie's off the market. Yet, when B.A.T. Industries, the British conglomerate, decided to sell Marshall Field and Saks Fifth Avenue, its U.S. retail assets, it received more than $1 billion for each. The reasons were that Field's had established itself as the dominant retailer in Chicago and the state of Illinois and Saks was deemed more adaptable as a national chain. Bloomingdale's, though it had opened stores in Chicago and the Southwest, was viewed as too much of a "New York" store.

Yet, the big store's demise really emerged as more of a metamorphosis from stores with everything for everyone into basically very large apparel stores. After surrendering such departments as major appliances, toys, sporting goods, pharmaceuticals, and others because of heavy pricing competition, the department store in recent years has concentrated mostly on apparel and other soft lines because that is where the big profits are. Hence, today, in the cities and suburbs, main floors present a vast array of cosmetics, women's sportswear, accessories, and dresses, while menswear and home furnishings are relegated to upper levels. And, as they sought to protect themselves from competition, management undertook aggressive programs of store or private labels that gave them exclusivity and higher markups than national brands. But, if customers buy store brands rather than national labels, they are insisting on distinct quality for a price.

Within the national department-store chains, strategic changes had to be made to sustain growth. J. C. Penney Company, after dropping all its home furnishings, sporting goods, and automotive departments, strove to become a national department-store chain selling only apparel and soft lines. Its management noted that it was one of the very few whose stores bore the same name everywhere. That also was true, of course, of Sears Roebuck & Company, but Sears was one of those that lost its focus and tried to remedy this with an "everyday low price policy." Meanwhile, Wal-Mart and K Mart, the two premier discounters, responded in kind and blunted Sears' effort.

The fact is that Sears must become more flexible and customer-responsive. As Heidi R. Steinberg, a retail analyst for Salomon Brothers, the New York investment bankers, put it, "The retailing industry today is mature, suffering from overcapacity and in the midst of a restructuring following the consolidation boom of the 1980s. The aging population and the bipolarization of income are two issues that retailers will need to address to survive. Older consumers will be interested in fewer high-quality items and superior service. The shrinking middle class will cause midmarket retailers such as Sears to suffer most. Consumers will want either top-quality merchandise (for which they would be willing to pay) or rock-bottom prices."

ISADORE BARMASH

RHODE ISLAND

The ailing state economy was a major concern in Rhode Island during 1990. It caused even more difficult budgetary problems than those of 1989, and was a key factor in the fall elections.

The Economy. Unemployment, low during the previous year, jumped above the national average to 6.6% in February. By July the rate was 7.1%, with marked declines in both the manufacturing and service sectors. Two months later, however, due largely to a rise in service-sector employment, it was down to 5.9%, only slightly above the national average. In November it was back up, to 7.3%.

The slowing real-estate market was another index of economic trouble. During the first quarter home prices fell, sales dropped, and inventories rose to record levels. There was some rebound in the spring, but by fall, home prices were down to 1988 levels and sales were the lowest since the 1982 recession.

In June the Peerless department store chain joined a number of other retail failures and announced that it was closing. Electric Boat, the submarine builder and one of the state's largest employers, announced nearly 600 layoffs and plans for an overall 5% cut in its Connecticut and Rhode Island work force of 23,000. Economists predicted a weak New England economy lasting at least two years.

Legislative Session. During much of the year the General Assembly wrestled with budgetary problems. January saw predictions of at least a $100 million revenue shortfall for the 1990 fiscal year. Having pledged not to raise taxes, Gov. Edward D. DiPrete (R) asked the Assembly to enact $71 million in "revenue enhancements." The requested auto-registration fee hikes, in particular, raised a storm of protest. In mid-March, after a long battle, the Assembly approved these proposals. Meanwhile the 1990–91 budget had been introduced calling for a small 2% increase for the year, achieved through severe program cuts and another package of fee and surcharge increases totalling $55 million. Without these measures, it was claimed, there would be a $200 million deficit.

As the session wore on, revenue projections worsened, and on May 21 the governor told a prime-time TV audience that he could not keep his no-tax-increase pledge and recommended a 1% sales-tax hike plus higher cigarette taxes. With these included, a budget was enacted in late June, with a 3.2% spending increase and $111 million in additional taxes.

The General Assembly also tightened gun-purchase regulations, overhauled the workers' compensation system, made available low-cost health insurance, and reorganized the Department of Environmental Management. Further regulation of abortion and of assault weapons failed to pass, as did mandatory auto-insurance legislation.

Elections. The Democrats won the governorship in November when challenger Bruce Sundlun overwhelmed DiPrete three to one. Other Democratic state candidates also were elected easily and the Democratic majority in the Assembly increased. U.S. Sen. Claiborne Pell (D) easily defeated U.S. Rep. Claudine Schneider (R), whose 2d District seat was won by John Reed (D). The only GOP win was U.S. Rep. Ronald Machtley's reelection in the 1st District. In Providence, Vincent Cianci (I) was returned to the mayoral seat.

ELMER E. CORNWELL, JR.
Brown University

ROMANIA

The year following the overthrow of Nicolae Ceauşescu in December 1989 was one of continuing strife and upheaval for Romania.

The Iliescu Regime. Almost immediately, the National Salvation Front, the provisional government that had replaced the executed Ceauşescu, came under sharp attack from its political foes, and faced mass demonstrations stirred up by student organizations and about 45 new political parties. Critics charged that the Front, led by Ion Iliescu, a former secretary of the Romanian Communist Party, was not representative of Romanian democratic forces, was permeated by former high-ranking Communists and members of the Securitate (the secret police), and was using "Stalinist" tactics in governing.

The Front, claiming to have been part of a long-term secret conspiracy preparing to overthrow Ceauşescu, declared itself in favor of free speech, press, emigration, and elections. It tried to diffuse popular dissatisfaction with a number of quick basic reforms. The Romanian Communist Party was outlawed and its vast properties and assets confiscated. The Securitate was disbanded. All Romanian citizens were granted ten-year passports, and all travel

---

RHODE ISLAND • Information Highlights

Area: 1,212 sq mi (3 140 km²).
Population (1990 census prelim.): 989,000.
Chief Cities (1980 census): Providence, the capital (July 1, 1988 est.): 156,160; Warwick, 87,123.
Government (1990): *Chief Officers*—governor, Edward D. DiPrete (R); lt. gov., Roger N. Begin (D). *General Assembly*—Senate, 50 members; House of Representatives, 100 members.
State Finances (fiscal year 1989): *Revenue,* $2,960,000,000; *expenditure,* $2,744,000,000.
Personal Income (1989): $17,919,000,000; per capita, $17,950.
Labor Force (June 1990): *Civilian labor force,* 524,900; *unemployed,* 34,100 (6.5% of total force).
Education: *Enrollment* (fall 1988)—public elementary schools, 95,285; public secondary, 39,062; colleges and universities, 74,839. *Public school expenditures* (1989–90), $807,471,000.

ROMANIA • Information Highlights

Official Name: Romania.
Location: Southeastern Europe.
Area: 91,699 sq mi (237 500 km²).
Population (mid-1990 est.): 23,300,000.
Chief Cities (July 1, 1986 est.): Bucharest, the capital, 1,989,823; Braşov, 351,493; Constanta, 327,676.
Government: *Head of state,* Ion Iliescu, president (took office December 1989). *Head of government,* Petre Roman, prime minister (took office December 1989). *Legislature* (unicameral)— Grand National Assembly.
Monetary Unit: Leu (19.770 lei equal U.S.$1, August 1990).
Gross National Product (1989 est. U.S.$): $79,800,-000,000.
Foreign Trade (1988 U.S.$): *Imports,* $8,750,-000,000; *exports,* $11,500,000,000.

restrictions were lifted. (During the year, an estimated 800,000 Romanians, ethnic Hungarians, ethnic Germans, gypsies, and Jews were reported to have left the country.) The death penalty was abolished, as were severe prohibitions against abortion and birth control. Farmers were permitted to own up to 1.5 acres (.6 ha) of land and to sell their produce on the open market. Private businesses employing up to 20 people were authorized. Senior figures in the Ceauşescu regime were prosecuted and sentenced to prison terms.

But the Front's enemies were not appeased. Tens of thousands expressed their opposition in an unending stream of street demonstrations during January and February, especially in the capital, Bucharest. The government responded by issuing tough laws against unauthorized demonstrations and by sponsoring its own counterdemonstrations. In February, fearing anarchy, the Front agreed to share some of its appropriated power with a coalition of representatives of about 30 other political groupings. The new interim government, called the Provisional Council for National Unity, was first expanded to 180, then to about 250 members. At the request of the opposition, it also was agreed that the upcoming presidential and parliamentary elections would be postponed from April to May.

Elections. About 80 new and revived political parties took part in the preelection campaign, which took place in an atmosphere of tumult, violence, and governmental intimidation. Candidates of the leading anticommunist parties, the National Liberal Party and the National Peasants Party, were harassed and beaten. The Front continued to control and exploit the media as well as the infrastructure and the financial resources and patronage of the old Communist Party. The elections, held on May 20—the first free elections in Romania in a half century—produced a landslide victory for Iliescu and the candidates supported by the Front. Iliescu won the presidency with 85% of the popular vote. The Front gained 67% of the

seats in the bicameral legislature. Some 500 foreign observers, including U.S. representatives, labeled the elections "flawed" but not "fraudulent." On May 22, Iliescu promised that Romania would be "an original type of democracy," with pluralism, the rule of law, and full recognition of individual and minority rights. He also promised slow, careful progress toward a free market and privatization. The new cabinet, under reappointed Premier Petre Roman, consisted largely of new, young, Western-oriented technocrats.

Protests and Repression. The electoral results provoked the worst wave of public violence since December 1989. During three bloody days, June 13–15, more than 500 people were injured, and a half dozen killed. Angered when police razed the tent city they had erected in Bucharest, university students went on a destructive rampage through the capital. Iliescu, apparently mistrusting the army, called about 10,000 miners from the countryside to Bucharest, "to save democracy from fascist rebellion." They, too, vandalized property and beat people indiscriminately, including foreign journalists. The government arrested several prominent opposition leaders as threats to public order and banned all further protests in central Bucharest. But nationwide demonstrations continued, swelled by strikes over food shortages and price increases. At year's end, a new opposition umbrella organization, the Civic Alliance, led tens of thousands in demanding the resignation of Iliescu and his government, elections for a new "government of national unity," and "a second revolution" to complete the one begun in December 1989. On December 25, King Michael, forced to abdicate in 1947, returned illegally to Romania from exile, but quickly was expelled from the country.

Economy. Romania suffered a sharp economic decline in 1990, with falling industrial production and exports, rising unemployment, and severe shortages of energy, food, and other staples. Initially, the United States, the Soviet Union, the European Community, and the Group of 24 (the world's most industrialized countries) extended millions of dollars in commodities and financial credits to the post-Ceauşescu government. The World Health Organization coordinated a worldwide effort against a pediatric AIDS epidemic in Romania. But growing doubt about the regime's commitment to democratic reforms and basic human rights cut off all "nonhumanitarian aid" later in the year.

Ethnic Unrest. Romania also continued to have minority problems with Hungary and the Soviet Union. On March 15 thousands of ethnic Magyars and their visiting kinsmen from Hungary celebrated Hungary's National Day in Transylvania, where they clashed with truckloads of armed Romanians sent in by the government. Hungary asked the UN to intervene to protect ethnic Hungarian civil and cultural rights in Transylvania. Romania charged that Hungary was trying to gain control of the area. In May and June more than 500,000 Romanians and inhabitants of the Soviet Union's Moldavian Republic met and called for the union of all "Romanian-inhabited territories." Moldavia, formerly Romanian Bessarabia, had been annexed by the USSR in 1940.

JOSEPH FREDERICK ZACEK
State University of New York at Albany

SASKATCHEWAN

A growing disenchantment with Premier Grant Devine's Progressive Conservative administration, the recovery of the provincial economy after several years of recession, and a major political scandal dominated Saskatchewan in 1990.

Politics. Premier Devine spent much of the year grappling with whether to call an election, as is traditional in a government's fourth year in office. Elected in 1982 and reelected in 1986 with a much-reduced majority, Devine had become increasingly unpopular. The voters were disillusioned with the government as the economy sank into a recession and the government continuously raised taxes although it was elected on tax-cutting promises. With every opinion poll showing the administration losing public support, and the socialist New Democrats likely to win a majority in an election, Devine finally put off an election until the fifth and final year of his term.

In a surprise move, Prime Minister Brian Mulroney appointed former Saskatchewan cabinet minister Eric Berntson to the Canadian Senate in Ottawa. Although there were no actual vacancies for a Saskatchewan appointment, Mulroney employed a never-before-used constitutional rule to add eight more senators. The move was taken after the Liberal majority

in the Senate vowed to block Progressive Conservative plans to reform the federal taxation system. The appointment was greeted with anger in Saskatchewan, since residents generally oppose the new tax policy.

Budget Deficit. Saskatchewan residents were shocked at reports that Finance Minister Lorne Hepworth had misjudged his budgetary projections and that there would be a 1990 deficit of C$548 million rather than the predicted C$363 million. Since the Devine government came to power in 1982 the accumulated deficit had climbed from zero to C$5 billion, an enormous sum for a province with fewer than 1 million residents.

Economy. After several years of decline due to low world commodity prices and an agricultural sector devastated by frequent droughts, the province's economy continued the recovery begun in 1989. The Conference Board of Canada predicted the province again would have the best economic growth rate in the nation, as it had in 1989. Ironically, however, low world agricultural prices meant farmers would continue to go deeper into debt despite record harvests. Regardless of rosy economic projections, the province still would be less buoyant economically than in the 1970s.

Scandals. The Progressive Conservative government had been plagued by allegations of patronage ever since it took power in 1982, and 1990 was no exception. In February the U.S. Federal Bureau of Investigation (FBI) arrested Donald Castle and Darrell Lowry, president and vice-president respectively of the Crown-owned Saskatchewan Transportation Company, while they were in Dallas, TX, negotiating to buy buses from a U.S. manufacturer. The two were charged with taking bribes and kickbacks. In September the Royal Canadian Mounted Police laid 22 charges against the pair and eight other individuals after wide-ranging investigations in Saskatchewan, Ontario, and the United States. There were allegations that the kickbacks were being funneled to the Progressive Conservative Party.

PAUL JACKSON, *"Saskatoon Star-Phoenix"*

SASKATCHEWAN • Information Highlights

Area: 251,865 sq mi (652 330 km²).
Population (June 1990): 1,000,400.
Chief Cities (1986 census): Regina, the capital, 175,064; Saskatoon, 177,641; Moose Jaw, 35,073.
Government (1990): *Chief Officers*—lt. gov., F. W. Johnson; premier, Grant Devine (Progressive Conservative). *Legislature*—Legislative Assembly, 64 members.
Provincial Finances (1990–91 fiscal year budget): *Revenues,* $4,280,000,000; *expenditures,* $4,640,-000,000.
Personal Income (average weekly earnings, June 1990): $445.03.
Labor Force (August 1990): *Employed* workers, 15 years of age and over, 452,000; *Unemployed,* 7.2%.
Education (1990–91): *Enrollment*—elementary and secondary schools, 211,120 pupils; postsecondary—universities, 21,710; community colleges, 3,340.
(All monetary figures are in Canadian dollars.)

SAUDI ARABIA

Saudi Arabia was affected deeply by the Aug. 2, 1990, Iraqi invasion of Kuwait and the subsequent international mobilization of forces against Iraq's aggression.

Before Kuwaiti Invasion. King Fahd of Saudi Arabia pursued a more active role in international affairs in late 1989 and early 1990. Saudi Arabia encouraged the Soviet Union and Afghan rebels to hold talks in Jidda in December 1989, and the Saudis gradually established warmer ties with China, eventually opening diplomatic relations on July 22, 1990. The union of the two Yemens on May 22 worried

© François Guenet/Odyssey-Matrix

Saudi Arabia's King Fahd (left) *listens to the grievances of a deputy governor. Iraq's invasion of Kuwait in August 1990, the subsequent threat of war, and military buildup in Saudi Arabia posed concerns for the king and his nation.*

the Saudi government as it threatened to upset the existing balance of power in southern Arabia. Close links to the United States were reinforced as Saudi Arabia agreed on July 9 to buy $3 billion worth of General Dynamics Corporation M-1 tanks. On July 2 a tragic accident in Mecca during the Muslim pilgrimage killed 1,426 people who apparently panicked as a result of crowd pressure in a tunnel.

Throughout early 1990, Saudi Arabia and the Organization of Petroleum Exporting Countries (OPEC) were concerned about oil production above existing OPEC quotas and the resulting low prices for crude oil. Saudi Arabia agreed to reduce its own production by 430,000 barrels per day as part of the May 3 OPEC agreement that was aimed primarily at mitigating excessive production by Kuwait and the United Arab Emirates. On July 11–12, Saudi Arabia and four other Persian Gulf oil states agreed at a meeting in Jidda to abide by the new production quotas. On July 27 in Geneva the Saudi government accepted Iraq's proposals to raise OPEC's official price from $18 to $21 per barrel, to set a new total OPEC production quota, and to control production rigorously.

The Invasion. King Fahd's conciliatory approach in oil policy was of no avail since President Saddam Hussein of Iraq rejected Saudi attempts to mediate his quarrel with Kuwait. In late July, Egypt's President Hosni Mubarak and King Hussein of Jordan met with King Fahd in Saudi Arabia to work out joint plans to deal with Iraq. Kuwaiti and Iraqi representa-

tives came to Jidda on July 31 but after one short meeting their talks broke off, and early the next day Iraq invaded Kuwait.

Jabir al-Ahmad Al Sabah, ruler of Kuwait, fled to Saudi Arabia where he established a government in exile at Taif. U.S. President George Bush condemned the Iraqi invasion and declared on August 3 that the integrity of Saudi Arabia is one of the "vital interests" of the United States. Bush later said that by defending Saudi Arabia against a potential Iraqi attack, "a line has been drawn in the sand. . . . " After some initial hesitation, the Saudis joined in the condemnation of the invasion. In a rare televised speech, King Fahd on August 9 called the Iraqi invasion of Kuwait "the most sinister aggression witnessed by the Arab nation in its modern history." He added

---

SAUDI ARABIA • Information Highlights

Official Name: Kingdom of Saudi Arabia.
Location: Arabian peninsula in southwest Asia.
Area: 829,996 sq mi (2 149 690 km²).
Population (mid-1990 est.): 15,000,000.
Capital (1981 est.): Riyadh, 1,000,000.
Government: *Head of state and government,* Fahd bin 'Abd al-'Aziz Al Sa'ud, king and prime minister (acceded June 1982).
Monetary Unit: Riyal (3.7495 riyals equal U.S.$1, Dec. 31, 1990).
Gross Domestic Product (1988 U.S.$): $73,000,-000,000.
Economic Index (1989): *Consumer Prices* (1980 = 100), all items, 96.2; food, 102.2.
Foreign Trade (1989 U.S.$): *Imports,* $21,153,-000,000; *exports,* $28,369,000,000.

that Saudi Arabia "declares its categorical rejection of all ensuing measures" taken by the Iraqis in Kuwait, while asserting that "Saudi Arabia will not be an easy victim for any aggressor . . . [since the Saudis] would all rather die than allow anyone to launch an aggression against a single inch of our territory."

Military and Diplomatic Response. U.S. Secretary of Defense Richard B. Cheney arrived in Saudi Arabia on August 6 and showed King Fahd evidence that Iraqi forces were massed to invade Saudi Arabia; in response the king invited the United States to help defend his country against Iraq. Only a few thousand U.S. troops were sent immediately, including paratroopers, an armored brigade, and jet fighters. After three weeks more U.S. troops had arrived than were in the entire 65,700-man Saudi military force. Saudi Arabia provided the Americans with transportation, bases, tents, water, and food. By the middle of November about 230,000 U.S. personnel were stationed in or near Saudi Arabia. After some transportation problems were solved, the United States also had placed about 1,600 tanks in the kingdom.

The United States kept command over U.S. forces stationed in Saudi Arabia, but it agreed in early November to coordinate its military actions with the Saudi government on general strategic issues. Other countries were slow to enter into arrangements for military cooperation although the British forces agreed to accept U.S. command in war. Saudi Gen. Khalid bin Sultan had at least theoretical command of Arab and other Muslim troops stationed in Saudi Arabia, but Syria and Egypt opposed the use of their forces outside Saudi Arabia in the event of war with Iraq.

Saudi Arabia soon began to expand its own military forces by adding recruits to its National Guard. By November the total of the kingdom's army, national guard, air force, and navy numbered about 120,000 men. The Saudis also wanted to purchase new weapons from abroad. In late August the United States agreed to sell the kingdom 24 F-15 fighters, 150 M-60 tanks, and 200 Stinger antiaircraft missiles. Additional sales worth $6 to $8 billion were planned for 1991 despite concerns by pro-Israeli U.S. legislators who feared that massive Saudi arms acquisitions might be used in the future against Israel.

Both the Saudis and Americans wished to broaden international participation in the defense of Saudi Arabia by including military forces from many other countries. This process began following the August 10 vote by 12 of the members of the Arab League to authorize sending troops. Forces from Arab League members Egypt, Syria, Morocco, and five Persian Gulf nations, as well as from Britain, France, Pakistan, Bangladesh, and several other nations ultimately were deployed.

Saudi Arabia eagerly sought diplomatic support for its own defense and against the Iraqi invasion of Kuwait. The Gulf Cooperation Council, the Organization of the Islamic Conference, and the Muslim World League endorsed Saudi goals and actions. Saudi Arabia and its Arab allies worked through the United Nations and the Arab League to gain additional backing, and the UN passed several resolutions condemning Iraq's actions. On September 17 the Soviet Union and Saudi Arabia established diplomatic relations for the first time in more than 50 years. To punish Yemen and Jordan for their sympathy with Iraq, Saudi Arabia expelled hundreds of thousands of Yemeni workers from the kingdom and ended oil shipments to Jordan. Saudi Arabia also joined in UN economic sanctions against Iraq, froze Kuwaiti and Iraqi assets in Saudi Arabia, and closed an Iraqi oil pipeline on Saudi territory that had been one of the chief conduits through which Iraq exported oil.

Invasion Consequences. The economic ramifications of the invasion were mixed. On the one hand, Saudi Arabia paid billions of dollars to the United States and other countries to help meet the costs of their assistance. More than 200,000 Kuwaiti refugees strained Saudi Arabia's hospitality. Foreign investors refused to risk money in Saudi Arabia. Mobilization of Saudis into the military was a drain on the civilian sector of the economy. On the other hand, as the price of oil doubled on world markets, Saudi revenue from petroleum sales dramatically increased. Saudi Arabian Oil Minister Hisham Nazer said on August 18 that production would be increased by 2 million barrels per day. Total Saudi production rose to 7.5 million barrels per day in September; in early November, Saudi production increased to 8.2 million barrels per day. At the same time, new discoveries of oil fields added as much as 20% to estimated reserves.

As the Kuwait crisis continued for months the international forces stationed in Saudi Arabia were reinforced while their future role came in for worldwide debate. President Bush ordered an additional 150,000 or more U.S. troops to the Persian Gulf on November 8 and he visited Saudi Arabia during the Thanksgiving holiday. When Bush met in Jidda with the leaders of the exiled Kuwaiti government and King Fahd he emphasized his desire to secure a UN resolution authorizing the use of force if needed to drive Iraq out of Kuwait. The measure passed resoundingly in the UN Security Council with only Cuba and Yemen voting against it, while China abstained.

Within Saudi Arabia a quiet debate took place in late 1990 about the implications of the presence of hundreds of thousands of foreign troops. A few Saudis favored a compromise peace with Iraq to secure the rapid withdrawal of foreign forces from both Kuwait and Saudi

Arabia. Many Saudis seemed to feel that only the overthrow of Saddam Hussein by the U.S.-led armies gathered in Saudi Arabia could ensure the future security of the region. On November 6 about 50 Saudi women demonstrated in Riyadh against the ban on their driving automobiles; the interior ministry subsequently outlawed all demonstrations by women. King Fahd also told Saudi newspaper editors in November that he was planning central and provincial consultative councils that would operate according to Islamic patterns.

See also feature articles, page 24.

WILLIAM OCHSENWALD
*Virginia Polytechnic Institute
and State University*

SINGAPORE

The year 1990 was marked by the official retirement of Singapore's longtime leader Lee Kuan Yew, an economic slowdown, and the development of closer ties to Malaysia and Indonesia.

Politics. In November, Lee Kuan Yew, who had been the country's prime minister since 1959, turned that post over to his colleague, Goh Chok Tong. However, because Lee would remain a senior cabinet minister and continue as secretary-general of the ruling People's Action Party (PAP), and because his son, Lee Hsien Loong, had been appointed deputy prime minister, it generally was believed that the former premier would continue to wield power from behind the scenes.

Parliament also passed a law transforming Singapore's presidency, now largely ceremonial in nature, into a directly elected office with wide-ranging executive powers, leading observers to speculate that Lee Kuan Yew himself would run for that post in 1991.

Foreign Affairs. In 1990, Singapore and China, which had enjoyed good relations for some time, finally established full diplomatic ties. Singapore also has good economic relations with Taiwan, but never has recognized

the Taiwan government's claim to sovereignty over the Chinese mainland. As a friendly gesture to the United States, Singapore invited that country to upgrade its naval facilities on the island, a process that would involve stationing U.S. personnel there. The move was said to be a symbolic one to help the United States in its negotiations with the Philippines.

Language Policy. On the cultural front, the Singapore government announced that in the future it would deemphasize the importance of English, currently the medium of instruction in all higher educational institutions and in most secondary schools, in favor of Mandarin Chinese. This prompted protests not only from the non-Chinese minorities who comprise about 22% of the population, but also from those Chinese whose first language is English, and who dominate the professional fields. Given the opposition to it, the pro-Mandarin policy cannot be expected to proceed very rapidly.

Economy. Signs of a slowdown were evident in Singapore's economy even before the Persian Gulf crisis started in August 1990, but in a country totally dependent on imported oil, the oil price increases triggered by the Gulf crisis significantly raised the cost of doing business. Because a high proportion of Singapore's export trade is with the United States, the recession in the U.S. economy also would have a dampening effect. With official external reserves that total about $25 billion and a government budget that shows a persistent surplus, Singapore was in a better position than most countries to weather the slowdown. Over the long term, however, the republic's stagnating population and declining productivity increase would make it difficult to sustain the rapid economic growth of recent decades into the 1990s.

The Growth Triangle. To overcome its labor and land constraints, Singapore was promoting itself as the center of an economic-growth triangle that also includes the Malaysian state of Johore in the north and the Indonesian island of Batam in the south. Johore has cheaper land and access to more abundant labor from Malaysia; Batam, though it lacks infrastructure, also has extremely cheap labor and land.

Although Singapore has been foremost in promoting the growth-triangle concept, the governments and business communities of Indonesia and Malaysia also have endorsed it as in the best interests of all the three countries. Singapore, whose population is more than three quarters Chinese with a substantial Malay minority, traditionally has had an uneasy if correct relationship with its two bigger neighbors, both of which have Malay majorities and Chinese minorities. Now, along with improved economic relations, political suspicions have receded as well.

N. BALAKRISHNAN
"The Far Eastern Economic Review"

SINGAPORE • Information Highlights

Official Name: Republic of Singapore.
Location: Southeast Asia.
Area: 244 sq mi (632.6 km²).
Population (mid-1990 est.): 2,700,000.
Capital: Singapore City.
Government: *Head of state,* Wee Kim Wee, president (took office September 1985). *Head of government,* Goh Chok Tong, prime minister (took office 1990). *Legislature* (unicameral)—Parliament.
Monetary Unit: Singapore dollar (1.75 S. dollars equal U.S. $1, Dec. 31, 1990).
Gross Domestic Product (1989 est. U.S.$): $27,500,-000,000.
Economic Index (1989): *Consumer Prices* (1980 = 100), all items, 120.9; food, 117.1.
Foreign Trade (1989 U.S.$): *Imports,* $49,676,-000,000; *exports,* $44,678,000,000.

The special interests of the U.S. elderly, including Medicare, were at the forefront as the U.S. Congress wrestled with the deficit and a budget package in October 1990. The elderly remain one of the nation's most powerful lobbies.

SOCIAL WELFARE

The U.S. economy's slide toward recession in 1990 affected all groups of society, but the economy's lack of growth—especially rising inflation and unemployment rates—was particularly unwelcome news for tens of millions of Americans at the low end of the economic scale. "If a deep recession sets in, [the poverty rate] could reach levels not seen in a quarter century," said Robert Greenstein, director of the private, nonprofit Center on Budget and Policy Priorities.

Poverty. The annual Census Bureau report on family income released in October found that in 1989 some 31.5 million Americans—about 12.8% of the population—lived below the poverty line, which was defined as a total cash income of $9,885 for a family of three and $12,675 for a family of four. The national poverty rate dropped by about 0.3% compared with 1988. The poverty rate among blacks decreased slightly to 30.7%; for whites the figure was 10%; for Hispanics, 26.2%.

The Census Bureau also reported that those on the bottom rung of the economic ladder were worse off economically than in previous years, while the richest Americans generally grew richer. Statistics showed that in 1969 the poorest one fifth of the population accounted for 4.1% of all household income; by 1989 the figure had decreased to 3.8%. During that same time period, the share of household income going to those in the top fifth of the income pyramid increased from 43% to 46.8%.

The Census Bureau data and other statistics released during 1990 strongly indicated that poverty remained a significant national problem. In August, for example, the U.S. Department of Agriculture reported that the number of Americans receiving food stamps increased by 1.3 million from May 1989 to May 1990. Increases were reported in at least 44 states during that time, as the national total of food-stamp recipients rose above 20 million.

The poverty picture with respect to children was disheartening. Nearly one of every four children less than 6 years old lived in families with incomes below the poverty line, according to a report issued in April by the Columbia University National Center for Children in Poverty. The report found that about half of all black children under 6 and some 40% of Hispanic children in that age group lived in poverty.

Among children of all ages, the poverty rate was about 20%, according to an interim report issued in April by the National Commission on Children, a congressional advisory group chaired by Sen. Jay Rockefeller (D-WV). The report found that 15% of white children, 45% of black children, and 39% of Hispanic children lived in families with incomes below the poverty line. The report also said that some 500,000 U.S. children suffered from malnutrition and about 100,000 were homeless.

The Homeless. The overall U.S. problem of homelessness continued in 1990. For the first time the Census Bureau attempted to count the nation's homeless. Some 15,000 bureau employees spent two days in March at homeless shelters in selected cities. The idea was not to gain an exact count of the number of homeless persons, which would be virtually impossible given the extremely transient nature of the homeless population. Instead, said bureau director Barbara Everitt Bryant, the goal was to determine "the order of magnitude" of the problem—to find out the ages, sexes, and races of the homeless population and to make a broad estimate about the number of homeless in the country. Previous estimates varied from about 600,000 to some 3 million.

Homeless advocates reported what they called a growing national backlash against the homeless among both government officials and the public at large in 1990. There were budget cuts in local homeless-aid programs, police crackdowns on homeless persons living in public places, and a growing antipathy among the public at street begging and homelessness in general. Mitch Snyder, the prominent homeless advocate who committed suicide in July, referred to the issue as "in recession."

Examples of the changed attitude toward the plight of the homeless included: the arresting of homeless persons for loitering, public drunkenness, and blocking traffic in Atlanta's downtown area; the banning by New York City's transit officials of panhandling on city subways; the weakening of a Washington, DC, ordinance that guaranteed shelter to any homeless person requesting it; and the posting of "no trespassing" signs by numerous downtown Phoenix businesses. A May *Washington Post*-ABC News poll indicated that fewer Americans believed that the homeless were victims of "circumstances beyond their control," and that fewer persons were willing to pay more taxes for homeless shelters.

One factor in the backlash against the homeless was the increasing number of mentally ill among the population. Experts believe that as many as 25% of the nation's homeless suffer persistent mental illness and that an additional 15% display some symptoms or have a history of mental illness. A report released in September by the Public Citizen Health Research Group and the National Alliance for the Mentally Ill claimed that the number of mentally ill living in the streets or incarcerated in prisons (more than 250,000) outnumbered those confined to mental hospitals (about 68,000). Deinstitutionalization—the movement that began in the mid-1950s to release mentally ill persons from psychiatric hospitals to halfway houses and clinics—"was a disaster," the report said.

There were some successes in the battle against homelessness. Citizens and religious groups and local officials in several cities— including Pittsburgh, PA, Portland, OR, and Sacramento, CA—put together innovative, effective community-based programs that helped find shelter, counseling, food, and job training for previously homeless persons.

Homeless advocates also set up dozens of successful food-distribution programs in cities across the country. One such program, called Share, began in 1983 and by 1990 was distributing weekly bags of groceries to poor and homeless persons in 15 cities. In more than 50 cities there were organized efforts to distribute perishable food from restaurants, bakeries, grocery stores, and hotels to homeless shelters, day-care centers for poor children, and other institutions that helped feed the homeless and others unable to afford to buy sufficient food. The Philabundance program in Philadelphia, for example, distributed some 500,000 lbs (226 800 kg) of food in 1989. "There is enough surplus food in every city to feed everyone in that city who is hungry," said Helen Ver-Duin Palit, who founded the New Haven Food Salvage Project in Connecticut and New York's City Harvest, which in 1989 distributed some 13 million meals.

The International Situation. U.S. social problems once again were dwarfed by those of hundreds of millions of others in Third World nations faced with hunger, disease, and starvation. More than 1 billion people—about one fifth of the world's population—lived on less than $370 per year, according to a report issued in July by the World Bank. Those conditions contributed to alarmingly high rates of infant and child mortality, short life expectancy, and severe problems with disease, malnutrition, and starvation. In sub-Saharan Africa, for example, life expectancy was 50 years. In South Asia, in which 51% of the population (some 520 million people) lived in poverty, the mortality rate for children under 5 was 172 per 1,000; in Sweden the rate was less than ten.

The direst situations in 1990 existed in Ethiopia, Angola, Mozambique, Malawi, and the Sudan, where drought and civil unrest led to severe food shortages, malnutrition, and potential starvation for millions. Severe social problems also existed in India and other parts of South Asia, in sections of the Middle East, and in Central and South America. In the Soviet Union and parts of Eastern and Central Europe, millions of persons faced shortages of food, apartments, medicine, and clothing.

Worldwide, the problems of hunger and disease were devastating particularly among children. That situation was highlighted September 30, when leaders of more than 70 nations went to the United Nations in New York for the first World Summit for Children. During the two-day summit, UN officials predicted that, annually, some 2,800 children would die from whooping cough, 8,000 from measles, 4,000 from tetanus, 5,500 from diarrhea, and 12,000 from pneumonia. Virtually all of those deaths were preventable. Summit leaders declared their intentions to step up efforts to fight infant deaths and malnutrition, reduce the number of women who die in childbirth, and provide clean water and primary education.

Health officials worldwide expressed concerns in 1990 about the rising spread of AIDS among women and children. The World Health Organization (WHO) reported in July that AIDS was the leading cause of death for women aged 20 to 40 in most big cities in North and South America, Western Europe, and sub-Saharan Africa. In September, WHO predicted that by the year 2000 some 10 million children would be infected with the HIV virus that causes AIDS. "The vast majority of these will have developed AIDS and died by the year 2000," said Dr. Michael Merson, director of WHO's AIDS program. WHO estimated that the overall number of AIDS patients could reach 30 million by the turn of the century.

MARC LEEPSON, *Free-lance Writer*

The Disabled

With the Jefferson Memorial as a backdrop, President George Bush signed into law the Americans With Disabilities Act on July 26, 1990. Both the Senate and House had approved the legislation overwhelmingly.

AP/Wide World

Some 43 million Americans have some type of physical, mental, or emotional disability that severely limits their capabilities. By far the biggest event that affected disabled Americans in 1990 came on July 26 when President George Bush—who in 1988 became the first presidential candidate to address directly the problems of the disabled—signed into law the Americans With Disabilities Act.

The new law, which experts said was comparable to the landmark 1964 Civil Rights Act, for the first time prohibited private employers from denying jobs on the basis of disability. Furthermore, the law obligated that beginning in 1991 all businesses that deal with the public make their facilities accessible to the disabled. The law also gave protection to the disabled from discrimination in public accommodations, transportation, and telecommunications. Sen. Tom Harkin (D-IA), one of the bill's chief sponsors, called it "the emancipation proclamation for disabled Americans."

First introduced in 1988, the bill was based on recommendations made by the National Council on the Handicapped, a commission set up by President Reagan. The new law mandated that beginning in 1992, businesses with 25 or more employees will be prohibited from discriminating against disabled workers in hiring and promotion. Those businesses, moreover, will be required to make "reasonable accommodations" for disabled workers to perform their jobs. In 1994 those provisions go into effect for all businesses with 15 or more workers; those firms with fewer than 15 employees are exempt from the law. Still, the law

will force thousands of employers across the country to install ramps, elevators, and other devices for disabled employees.

Business groups spoke out against the proposed law, focusing primarily on the expense involved in making physical changes in workplaces. The costs "would be enormous," said Zachary Fasman of the U.S. Chamber of Commerce, "and obviously could have a disastrous impact upon many small businesses struggling to survive." Others contended that the costs to businesses would be minimal and would pale in comparison with the estimated $170 billion to $200 billion a year that U.S. society currently spends supporting and subsidizing those with disabilities.

The 1990 legislation widely broadened the Rehabilitation Act of 1973, which barred discrimination against the disabled by the federal government as well as all public businesses that did business with the federal government. That law was one of many enacted during the 1970s and 1980s on the federal, state, and local levels, making buildings, education, and employment more accessible to the disabled. Those laws were passed following the alliance of disabled-rights groups and civil-rights and feminist organizations. "Standing alone, we could not have done that," said Pat Wright, executive director of the Disability Rights Education and Defense Fund. "But wrapped in the arms of the civil-rights community, we had a lot more power."

For the most part the disabled-rights laws enacted during the 1970s and 1980s were aimed at breaking down the societal barriers that denied disabled persons equal opportunities. They included statutes that mandated the elimination of physical barriers and the adoption of affirmative-action programs to hire and advance disabled persons, as well as a 1975 federal law (the Handicapped Children Act) that assured all disabled children the right to a free and appropriate public education in the least restrictive setting possible—what is known as "mainstreaming."

Technological Advances. Many recent technological and medical advances have helped unprecedented numbers of disabled persons move into society's mainstream. Computerized voice recognition devices, for example, help paralyzed persons use words to control their environments. These voice-activated machines enable users to dial telephones, turn fixtures on and off, and even write checks and letters. Optical character-recognition computers work similarly through written words and are used by those who are blind.

Other recent technological advances include: computerized devices that can read printed documents aloud; specially adapted "talking" computer terminals that enable blind persons to gain access to data banks; sip-and-puff air tubes that control the movements of motorized wheelchairs; computerized electronic grids attached to video cameras that translate eye movements into speech; and computerized electrical stimulation devices attached to nerves and joints to permit paralyzed persons to exercise their limbs.

One of the latest devices, still in the experimental stage, is a prosthetic foot containing a pressure-sensitive sensor that gives the sensation of feeling to amputees. The device, designed by John Sabolich of Sabolich Prosthetic & Research Center in Oklahoma City, has been in development since 1984.

Not all the new advances in helping disabled persons are of the technological variety. Many groups throughout the United States have set up volunteer-support programs to help disabled persons. These include the West Lafayette, IN, -based Breaking New Ground, which helps disabled farmers; the National Ocean Access Project in Newport, RI, which teaches disabled persons how to sail; and Boston-based Partners for Disabled Youth, which brings together disabled adult mentors with young disabled persons. The latter, formed in 1983, is based on the idea of exposing younger disabled persons to adults who are coping successfully with their disabilities.

In recent years there has been an increased use of specially trained guide dogs to help persons with many types of disabilities, not just blindness. The guide dogs—primarily golden and Labrador retrievers—are trained at several nonprofit schools. The dogs can help wheelchair-bound persons use light switches, retrieve food from refrigerators, open doors, and even pull wheelchairs. The dogs also make life easier for disabled persons in other, more subtle ways. "When handicapped people are out in public, many people don't feel comfortable approaching them," said George Kuhrts, southwest regional director of Canine Companions for Independence, a California-based consortium of dog-training organizations. "But when you have a beautiful golden retriever by your side, it's an icebreaker."

Role Models. Until relatively recently severely disabled persons were regarded widely with fear and suspicion. Often they were shut away in back rooms or committed to institutions. But in the last two decades there has been a shift in attitude that has led to new, more open, and productive patterns of living. One factor shaping this attitude change has been the fact that several severely handicapped persons have in recent years become successful and internationally famous writers, artists, scientists, and political activists—despite their disabilities.

Christopher Nolan, an Irish writer, for example, has been afflicted since birth with a severe neurological disorder. He cannot talk, walk, or chew food, and has no control of his arm or neck muscles. Yet, using a word processor that he activated with a rod strapped to his head, Nolan wrote a best-selling, critically acclaimed book of poems, short stories, and plays, *Dam-Burst of Dreams* (1981), as well as an autobiographical novel, *Under the Eye of the Clock* (1988).

Another role model for the disabled has been the physicist Stephen W. Hawking, who has been confined to a wheelchair for more than two decades with Lou Gehrig's disease. Since 1985, Hawking has been unable to speak. Today he communicates with a computerized speech synthesizer attached to his wheelchair. Hawking writes books, travels extensively, spends time with his family and is regarded as one of the preeminent physicists of the 20th century.

The stories of two severely disabled persons, Christy Brown and Ron Kovic, were made into two of the most critically acclaimed and popular movies of 1989–90, *My Left Foot* and *Born on the Fourth of July*. Brown, who died in 1981, was born in Dublin with cerebral palsy, but overcame his severe handicap and became a well-respected writer and painter using his left foot (the only body part which he could control) to write and paint. Kovic lost the use of both of his legs after he was wounded severely in the Vietnam war, and went on to become one of the best-known veteran-activists of the antiwar movement.

MARC LEEPSON

South Africa's President F.W. de Klerk and Nelson Mandela (front right) were joined by their advisers for a surprise meeting in Capetown June 2. De Klerk had ordered Mandela's release from prison in February.

SOUTH AFRICA

In an address before the South African parliament on Feb. 2, 1990, President F. W. de Klerk (*see* BIOGRAPHY) declared that the general election on Sept. 6, 1989, had given him the mandate to bring about political changes to avoid growing violence, tension, and conflict. He then lifted the 30-year-old ban on the African National Congress (ANC), on other black political parties such as the Pan Africanist Congress (PAC), and the South African Communist Party (SACP), and on 33 internal political organizations such as the United Democratic Front (UDF), to enable opposition leaders to participate in the drafting of a new constitution for the country. De Klerk announced that imprisoned ANC leader Nelson Mandela (*see* BIOGRAPHY) would be released from prison without conditions, as would 120 other political prisoners in South African jails. The emergency regulations that restricted activities of the media were rescinded and de Klerk promised that he would repeal the Separate Amenities Act which segregated public facilities.

A New Era. On Feb. 11, 1990, Nelson Mandela walked out of the Victor Verster prison accompanied by his wife Winnie. From there he drove to Cape Town where he spoke to a large crowd from the balcony of the City Hall saying, "I greet you all in the name of peace, democracy, and freedom for all." He thanked South African groups as well as the world community for campaigning for his release and said he hoped that there soon would be talks about a negotiated settlement. He also paid tribute to President de Klerk whom he maintained had

gone further than any other National Party (NP) leader to bring about change.

Talks were scheduled to take place between the ANC and the government on April 11, 1990, but were canceled by the ANC after an incident on March 26, when police fired on black protesters in Sebokeng, a township in the southern Transvaal province. At least 11 persons were killed in the ensuing violence and more than 400 were wounded, many by pellets from police shotguns. The talks were held subsequently in Cape Town, May 2–4. President de Klerk led a high-level negotiating team including Foreign Minister Roelof F. (Pik) Botha and Gerrit Viljoen, the minister of constitutional development whom de Klerk had designated to arrange negotiations for a new constitution. Members of the ANC delegation included Joe Slovo, general secretary of the South African Communist Party, and Alfred Nzo, general secretary of the African National Congress. As a result of the talks considerable progress was made in overcoming obstacles to broader negotiations for a new constitution. The ANC conceded that other organizations should be represented at future negotiations. During the meeting, President de Klerk made it clear that a Constitutional Assembly would not function in an interim government during the drafting of a new constitution as had been the case in neighboring Namibia. Instead he proposed a wide range of black and white leaders coming to the negotiating table. The government also continued to insist on guarantees being built into any new constitution to ensure that white political interests would not be dominated by blacks. The ANC insisted that the government abandon the concept of "group rights," which Africans perceived as a device to maintain white privileges.

In an apparently pragmatic move to widen its base of support, the NP proposed, in late August, to open its membership to all races. However, until the currently segregated parliamentary system itself is integrated this gesture is more symbolic than substantive.

Guerrilla War Suspended. On August 6, after a 15-hour negotiating session with the government, the ANC agreed to end nearly 30 years of armed struggle. Nelson Mandela announced that "No further armed actions and related activities by the ANC and its military wing *Umkhonto we Sizwe* will take place." The agreement, referred to as the Pretoria Minute, did not preclude mass actions such as boycotts and "stay-aways." It also set up joint working committees to monitor the return of about 22,000 exiles.

By the time of the agreement to suspend armed resistance, Mandela had become the effective head of the ANC. With ANC President Oliver Tambo in a clinic in Stockholm recovering from a stroke, Mandela was elected deputy president of the party in early March. His stature as a world leader was confirmed by the hero's welcome he received during his tours of Africa, Europe, and the United States. After its unbanning, the ANC moved its headquarters from Lusaka, Zambia, to Johannesburg.

Violence In Natal. Over the past several years Natal province continued to be devastated by the most intense violence experienced in the country since the mid-1980s with at least 2,500 deaths resulting from the internecine conflict. The violence reflected a fundamental difference between the ANC and its UDF ally, on the one hand, and the narrower ethnically based Zulu organization *Inkatha* led by Chief Mangosuthu Buthelezi of KwaZulu. The violence intensified after the February 2 address by President de Klerk to the South African parliament, in part because of *Inkatha*'s fear that it would be overshadowed and outmaneuvered by the ANC's increasing visibility and strength within South Africa. Appeals by Nelson Mandela and efforts by the South African government to curb the violence were ineffective. In a speech in Durban, Natal, on February 26, Nelson Mandela pleaded with the Zulu audience to "take your guns, your knives, and your pangas and throw them into the sea." For March the death toll resulting from the conflict was estimated to be more than 200, an average of nearly seven deaths per day. In April the South African government began deploying army troops in Natal. While Nelson Mandela expressed some misgivings over this move, his criticism was muted. A scheduled meeting toward the end of March between Mandela and Buthelezi was canceled as a result of pressure from colleagues within the African National Congress. Tragically, in August factional violence spread to Port Elizabeth, to Sebokeng, south of Johannesburg, and to the East Rand townships of Thokoza, Kathelong, and Vosloorus. In one week alone more than 200 died and several hundred were injured. By the end of October, because of the destructiveness of this internecine violence (which some alleged was promoted by white right-wing extremists opposed to reform), Mandela and Buthelezi agreed to meet. No date for such a meeting was set, however, and the violence continued.

A state of emergency remained in effect in Natal province as factional fighting between the Zulu organization "Inkatha" and a more radical Zulu group allied with the African National Congress (ANC) continued during the year.

© Balic/Sygma

Following a September White House meeting with F.W. de Klerk, President Bush declared that the United States believes that "the process of change in South Africa is irreversible." De Klerk was the first South African head of state in 45 years to visit Washington officially.

© Robert Trippett/Sipa-Press

SACP and ANC. In July the South African Communist Party (SACP) officially became a political party after operating underground and in exile for nearly 40 years. Strong ties between the ANC and the SACP remained. At least nine members of the SACP's Central Committee are also members of the ANC's national executive. The Communist Party also has a significant presence within the Congress of South African Trade Unions (COSATU), a close ally of the ANC. The SACP thus was expected to be an important actor at any constitutional negotiations.

The actual strength of the party is hard to gauge; the July 29 party rally in Soweto attended by 45,000 was not a true indicator of its strength since it was evident that large numbers of the spectators attended as ANC supporters or out of curiosity. Nelson Mandela has made an effort to emphasize that while the ANC and the SACP are linked, the ANC is a separate and independent entity with a different ideological stance and that the decision-making process within the ANC is not dominated by the SACP.

Lifting the State of Emergency. Early in June in a speech to parliament, President de Klerk said, "After thorough consideration of all the factors, I have decided to announce that there will no longer be a general country wide state of emergency, but that henceforth it will exist in Natal only." The ANC's Walter F. Sisulu described this move as a half measure and said that the ANC "never accepted that the [state of] emergency helped the situation in Natal." President de Klerk also announced that he was budgeting more than $380 million in additional funds to recruit and support policemen to combat such violence. The president said the extra money would be used to add 10,000 more policemen to the country's 60,000-member police force. Despite the lifting of the state of emergency, in effect since July 1985, the government retained broad powers to detain people

without trial, and to end political meetings and prohibit political activities.

Natal and Transvaal Elections. On June 6 in a by-election held in Umlazi constituency near Durban, the white electorate seemed to move further to the right. Although President de Klerk's ruling National Party won the by-election, it retained the seat with a much smaller vote margin than in recent elections because of right-wing gains. Evidence suggested that the seat would have been lost if it were not for members of the more liberal Democratic Party who voted for the NP to prevent the Conservative Party from winning.

The ruling party's margin of victory was far more decisive against a right-wing challenge in the Randburg election in the Transvaal in November. While the leader of the Conservative Party, Andries P. Treurnicht, claimed that his party's marginally better showing demonstrated voter approval of the right wing, Finance Minister Barend du Plessis, leader of the NP in the Transvaal, maintained that the CP's

---

SOUTH AFRICA • Information highlights

Official Name: Republic of South Africa.
Location: Southern tip of Africa.
Area: 471,444 sq mi (1 221 040 km²).
Population (mid-1990 est.): 39,600,000.
Chief Cities (1985 census, city proper): Pretoria, the administrative capital, 443,059; Cape Town, the legislative capital, 776,617; Durban, 634,301; Johannesburg, 632,369.
Government: *Head of state and government,* Frederik W. de Klerk, state president (took office Sept. 1989). *Legislature*—Parliament (tricameral): House of Assembly, House of Representatives (Coloured), and House of Delegates (Indians).
Monetary Unit: Rand (2.513 rands equal U.S. $1, Dec. 12, 1990).
Gross Domestic Product (1988 U.S.$): $83,500,-000,000.
Economic Index (1989): *Consumer Prices* (1980 = 100), all items, 343.0; food, 357.3.
Foreign Trade (1989 U.S.$): *Imports,* $16,952,-000,000; *exports,* excluding exports of gold, $11,509,000,000.

defeat should convince its leaders to reconsider their decision not to join multiracial negotiations on the country's future.

Death Squads. From March onward South Africans were shocked by allegations before the Harms Commission judicial inquiry that a powerful group of military and police commanders had authorized assassinations of government opponents. A special military unit, known as the Civil Cooperation Bureau (CCB), was established in 1985 which, from its inception, allegedly was involved in killings of political opponents. The hit squad was under the leadership of the commander of the defense force, Gen. Constant Viljoen. The star witness in the hearings was a former security policeman, Butana Nofomela, who on the day before he was scheduled to be hanged in October 1989 for the murder of a white farmer, confessed to the 1981 killing of Griffiths Mxenge, a prominent black lawyer with links to the ANC. He maintained that he had been paid by his police superiors to commit the murder and added that "I don't arrest anyone. I kidnap or assassinate them." Minister of Defense Magnus A. Malan and other high-ranking military personnel denied knowing anything about the Civil Cooperation Bureau, but opposition leaders in South Africa maintained that the military command and high-ranking politicians were fully aware of its activities.

The Winnie Mandela Affair. Late in May the chief bodyguard of Winnie Mandela, Gerry Musivuzi Richardson, was found guilty of murdering a 14-year-old boy, James (Stompie) Mokhetsi Seipei, who had been abducted to Mrs. Mandela's home in late 1988. Richardson had been coach of the Mandela United Football Club, a nominal soccer team whose principal activity had been to protect Mrs. Mandela. Richardson was sentenced to death in August for the murder. Judge Brian O'Donovan of the Rand Supreme Court ruled that Winnie Mandela had participated in the initial beating of the 14-year-old. In September the attorney general of the Witwatersrand announced that Mrs. Mandela and seven others would stand trial in February 1991 in the Rand Supreme Court on charges of kidnapping and assault.

Economy. Throughout the year, there was considerable discussion about the economic foundation of apartheid South Africa, including the hoped-for "postapartheid dividend" from the elimination of the military and policing costs associated with the apartheid system. Most controversial was the ANC's stated policy to nationalize mines, banks, and monopoly industries. However, in a meeting in late May attended by more than 300 business leaders and 40 members of the ANC and other antiapartheid groups, Mandela maintained that "the view that the only words in the economic vocabulary that the ANC knows are nationalization and redistribution is mistaken. There are many is-

sues we will have to consider as we discuss the question of the democratization and deracialization of economic power." Mandela allayed some business fears subsequent to the meeting when he maintained that the ANC had no blueprint for nationalization and that the issue might best be examined by a committee of economic experts. At the meeting both sides accepted in principle that taxation should be the basis for economic redistribution and that there should be affirmative action for black advancement. State and private-sector funds should be used to provide better housing, health, and education. Mandela also expressed concern that less than ten corporate conglomerates controlled almost 90% of the shares listed on the Johannesburg Stock Exchange and maintained that antitrust laws similar to those in the United States might have to be used to break up such a concentration of economic power.

Finance Minister Barend du Plessis' 1990-91 budget reflected the changing political climate of South Africa. There was a virtual freeze in the growth of defense spending and a number of budget priorities were redirected to improve black living conditions. According to du Plessis, higher priority would have to be given to alleviating problems of poverty, housing, inadequate education, illiteracy, and health needs. Total expenditures budgeted for 1990–91 amounted to $28 billion.

International Sanctions. After the repeal of significant portions of apartheid legislation, the government began calling for the removal of international sanctions against South Africa. The international debate throughout the year centered on when to end the economic sanctions and on what terms. In May, President de Klerk visited nine countries in Western Europe over 18 days. As a response to the changing conditions in South Africa he was well received by such world leaders as British Prime Minister Margaret Thatcher and French President François Mitterrand, as well as other leaders. Thatcher lifted her country's ban on new investment, but elsewhere there was a wait-and-see attitude, particularly after Mandela's highly successful visit to the United States in June during which he was adamant that sanctions should remain in place as a source of continuing leverage on the South African government. In September, de Klerk met with U.S. political leaders, including President George Bush, who said that while he felt that the reform process in South Africa was irreversible, the Comprehensive Antiapartheid Act of 1986 would remain in effect until all legal prerequisites had been met for its repeal. Nonetheless, these were important trips in South Africa's continuing efforts to normalize its relations with the major nations of the world.

PATRICK O'MEARA
and N. BRIAN WINCHESTER
Indiana University

SOUTH CAROLINA

A major scandal in the state legislature and the elections in November led the news in South Carolina in 1990.

Scandal. Eight state House members and one state senator were indicted on charges of violating the Hobbs Act, a federal anticorruption law that prohibits vote buying and extortion. One House member was charged with narcotics violations. Using a former legislator-turned-lobbyist who was avoiding drug charges as its agent, the Federal Bureau of Investigation (FBI) conducted a sting-type investigation. As the year ended six legislators had pleaded guilty, one had been convicted, and four awaited trial. More indictments were expected and ethical questions also surfaced about the actions of several state administrators and constitutional officers.

Politics and Government. Split voting dominated the November elections. Republican Carroll A. Campbell was reelected as governor with nearly 70% of the vote. He defeated Democrat Theo W. Mitchell, the first black to run for governor in the state. Despite Campbell's majority, Republicans failed to increase their number in the state House. Democratic Lt. Gov. Nick A. Theodore was reelected easily. For the first time in the 20th century, three Republicans defeated Democrats in statewide constitutional office elections—secretary of state, superintendent of education, and commissioner of agriculture. Democrats were reelected in the four other state offices. Republican U.S. Sen. J. Strom Thurmond was reelected to his seventh term and four Democrats and two Republicans were reelected to the U.S. Congress.

Voters defeated two constitutional amendments restricting the jurisdiction of the statewide grand jury. A referendum authorizing a local one-cent sales tax as a partial property-tax substitute won only in Charleston County and five rural counties.

The General Assembly borrowed $31 million to aid in the relief effort following 1989's Hurricane *Hugo*. It also reduced the amount of hazardous and infectious waste which can be processed; provided that state employees and teachers may retire after 25 years of service and upon reaching the age of 55; required that girls under the age of 17 receive permission from a parent or judge to have an abortion; approved the fingerprinting of applicants for teacher certificates; prohibited race discrimination in public facilities; and banned smoking in government buildings, schools, health facilities, and public transportation.

Education. School reform remained an issue in South Carolina and would face the newly elected Superintendent of Education Barbara Nielson. A Republican, Nielson defeated Charlie G. Williams (D), a 12-year veteran in the

AP/Wide World

South Carolina's Strom Thurmond (R) was reelected easily to the U.S. Senate on Nov. 6, 1990. The 88-year-old former Democrat has served continuously in the Senate since 1956.

post. Although the state's average scores on the Scholastic Aptitude Test (SAT) had improved more than 50 points over a ten-year period, the average ranked last in the nation in 1990. Students surpassed national norms in 13 of 15 categories on the California Test of Basic Skills (CTBS), but in only one category in the Stanford 8 test.

School-dropout rates continued to decline, and 125 high schools were permitted more local decision-making. High-school curriculums were expanded in languages, statistics, and economics in some schools. The high-school

---

SOUTH CAROLINA • Information Highlights

Area: 31,113 sq mi (80 582 km²).
Population (1990 census prelim.): 3,407,000.
Chief Cities (1980 census): Columbia, the capital (July 1, 1982 est.), 101,457; Charleston, 69,510; Greenville, 58,242.
Government (1990): *Chief Officers*—governor, Carroll A. Campbell, Jr. (R); lt. gov., Nick A. Theodore (D). *General Assembly*—Senate, 46 members; House of Representatives, 124 members.
State Finances (fiscal year 1989): *Revenue,* $8,061,000,000; *expenditure,* $6,958,000,000.
Personal Income (1989): $47,881,000,000; per capita, $13,634.
Labor Force (June 1990): *Civilian labor force,* 1,784,300; *unemployed,* 87,100 (4.9% of total force).
Education: *Enrollment* (fall 1988)—public elementary schools, 437,826; public secondary, 177,948; colleges and universities, 147,757. *Public school expenditures* (est. 1989–90), $2,191,892,000.

---

exit examination was passed by 94.4% of the tenth-graders in the state. Teachers' salaries ranked 34th nationally.

The Economy. Much of the destruction from Hurricane *Hugo* was overcome. Tourist business along the coast was good, but timber prices were down. Industrial investments were significant but did not reach the 1988 record. Economic diversification continued and major corporations chose South Carolina for their headquarters and facilities. Foreign investments increased for the third year in a row. While unemployment in the state was 5.2% in September, employment in service industries increased at a high rate.

Agriculture. Agriculture suffered from drought and freezes in the early season and excessive rain later in the year. The peach crop was reduced by two thirds; corn, soybean, and cotton yields were poor; and tobacco quality suffered. Heavy rains in October caused serious flooding, reductions in crop yields, and the loss of five lives.

ROBERT H. STOUDEMIRE
University of South Carolina

SOUTH DAKOTA

Republican election victories in 1990 did not threaten Democratic growth toward a partisan balance in South Dakota. Culturally and economically, South Dakota experienced trends common to western states. Relations between whites and native Americans remained tense as tribal leaders emphasized educational as well as economic growth.

Elections. Republican Gov. George Mickelson was reelected with 59% of the vote. Voters returned Republican Larry Pressler to the U.S. Senate with only 52% of the vote. Democrat Tim Johnson was reelected to the U.S. House of Representatives. A Republican majority was retained in both chambers of the state legislature. The GOP majority in the state House remained safe at 44 to 26, but was reduced to a single seat in the Senate (18R-17D). With two Democrats—Sen. Tom Daschle and Representative Johnson—in the three-member U.S. congressional delegation, growing power in the state legislature, and Senator Pressler's narrow victory, Democrats nearly restored the balance of partisan power they enjoyed throughout the 1970s. A growing urban population and an economic emphasis on service at the expense of agricultural industries was thought to account for the loss of the GOP's dominance in the state.

On environmental referenda, South Dakotans declined to restrict expansion in mining industries, but placed the new Lonetree landfill project under public supervision. Legislators were authorized to control the importation of solid waste for disposal in a sparsely settled

---

SOUTH DAKOTA · Information Highlights

Area: 77,116 sq mi (199 730 km²).
Population (1990 census prelim.): 693,000.
Chief Cities (1980 census): Pierre, the capital, 11,973; Sioux Falls, 81,343; Rapid City, 46,492.
Government (1990): *Chief Officers*—governor, George S. Mickelson (R); lt. gov., Walter D. Miller (R). *Legislature*—Senate, 35 members; House of Representatives, 70 members.
State Finances (fiscal year 1989): *Revenue*, $1,407,000,000; *expenditure*, $1,253,000,000.
Personal Income (1989): $9,784,000,000; per capita, $13,685.
Labor Force (June 1990): *Civilian labor force*, 365,500; *unemployed*, 14,400 (3.9% of total force).
Education: *Enrollment* (fall 1988)—public elementary schools, 92,556; public secondary, 34,354; colleges and universities, 31,460. *Public school expenditures* (1989–90 est.), $465,091,000.

---

southwestern district of the state. Voters rejected proposed amendments to the state constitution to restrict annual property-tax increases to 2% and to refer any legislation imposing an income tax to voter referendum. Aware that the state's constitution sharply limits its indebtedness, voters left to the governor and the legislature the freedom to pay for public facilities through taxation or revenue bonds.

Legislation. Legislators approved bonds up to a value of $15 million to expand and improve correctional facilities at both maximum-and minimum-security prisons in Sioux Falls and Springfield, respectively. They also established a lottery-operating fund, diversified the lottery system, and refined rules for license fees and gambling-revenue distributions. Legislators also authorized expenditures and rules for the readmission of high-school dropouts and opportunities for high-school juniors and seniors to enroll in higher-education courses.

The Economy. During the summer of 1990 unemployment in South Dakota declined by nearly one half of one percentage point to 3.7%, and personal income rose by 3% over the previous year. The major setback appeared in a decline of farm-property income by some 33% and of farm-product income by 20% due to a reduction in federal crop subsidies. Agricultural losses were offset by profits in the tourist, extractive, and service industries.

Tribal Affairs. Centennial observances of the tragic shooting of Sitting Bull and the killings at Wounded Knee gave occasion to a rhetorical "Year of Reconciliation." However, antipathies between Indians and whites were sustained by the resistance of state officials and federal courts to tribal jurisdictional authority and the unresolved Black Hills claim of western Sioux and neighboring tribes. The Flandreau Santee Sioux Tribe opened a major high-stakes gambling establishment on Indian lands. Tribally sponsored community colleges continued to grow in the state.

HERBERT T. HOOVER
University of South Dakota

SPACE EXPLORATION

Space exploration in 1990 moved forward dramatically with the shuttle deployments of the Hubble Space Telescope (HST) to low Earth orbit and the *Ulysses* spacecraft to Jupiter, and the Delta-II launch of the ROSAT satellite. Although a mirror-manufacturing error forced postponement of many of Hubble's objectives, the HST did provide a continuing stream of new pictures of the solar system, the galaxy, and of deep space. (*See* ASTRONOMY— *The Hubble Space Telescope*.) The most significant science advance of 1990 was the quality of radar data obtained by the *Magellan* planetary spacecraft (launched in 1989) from the surface of Venus. Other space news was less optimistic. The Space Exploration Initiative— establishment of a U.S. base on the moon and a manned expedition to Mars—received no congressional encouragement. Progress on the U.S. space station *Freedom* continued to be impaired. Even so, the National Aeronautics and Space Administration (NASA) received a 13.5% increase in its 1991 budget.

Shuttle Program. There were five shuttle flights during 1990, all by the United States. Eight U.S. flights were manifested for 1990, but unanticipated delays and technical problems took their toll. In February, Mission STS-36, carrying a Department of Defense (DoD) payload, became the first shuttle mission to be delayed, due to a crew health problem. On April 10 launch of the space shuttle *Discovery* was scrubbed at the T-4 second mark by a faulty auxiliary power unit. Major delays also occurred with the *Columbia* mission carrying the Astro-1 science payload. After extensive investigations of hydrogen leaks and four launch attempts, *Columbia* was rolled back from the launchpad to make way for the October *Discovery* mission which sent the NASA/European Space Agency (ESA) *Ulysses* probe on its journey to the sun. *Columbia* lifted off on December 2, the final 1990 mission.

The *Columbia* also had begun the shuttle-missions year with the STS-32 mission (January 9–20) that on January 12 deployed a communications satellite and retrieved the Long Duration Exposure Facility (LDEF), an experiment-laden satellite deployed by *Challenger* in 1984.

Mission STS-36 (February 22-March 4), a classified DoD mission, apparently deployed an advanced reconnaissance satellite, APF-731, for use by the Central Intelligence Agency (CIA) and the National Security Organization. Deployment utilized a new Shuttle Payload Deployment System, and this mission carried for the second time the "Phantom Head," a human skull that was to travel on three shuttle missions to study space-radiation effects.

The *Discovery* STS-31 mission, launched on April 24 with a crew of five, carried the HST

into orbit. The telescope, at an altitude of 331 nautical miles, was deployed as high as possible to put it above much of the Earth's atmosphere and to provide maximum time before shuttle reboosting. Thus, U.S. astronauts flew to the highest altitudes since the Apollo missions ended in 1972.

After more than five months without a shuttle launch, *Discovery* lifted off on October 6 on the four-day STS-41 mission, carrying the *Ulysses* spacecraft. The 814-lb (369-kg) European-built spacecraft was deployed from *Discovery*'s payload bay to begin a 500-million-mi (800-million-km) dash to Jupiter en route to survey the poles of the sun. *Ulysses* was to reach Jupiter in February 1992 and would pass under the sun's south pole in May 1994 and over its north pole in June 1995.

The STS-38 mission (November 15–20) lifted off from Cape Canaveral after long delays owing to repairs of a hydrogen leak. The *Atlantis* carried five military astronauts and a Pentagon spy satellite into orbit in NASA's last completely classified shuttle flight. Its secret payload was believed to have the capability of acquiring military information on Persian Gulf targets.

The last shuttle mission of 1990 was the December 2, STS-35 mission launch of *Columbia* that hauled into orbit a set of telescopes known as Astro.

Japan's first astronaut, Toyohiro Akiyama, was lifted into space by a Soviet Soyuz rocket, below, Dec. 2, 1990. He spent eight days aboard the Soviet space station "Mir."

© Vlastimir Shone/Gamma-Liaison

Space Station. At the Soviet *Mir* space station, Soviet cosmonaut Alexander Serebrov piloted the Soviet version of the Manned Maneuvering Unit on its first flight on February 1. In May the Kristall processing module, weighing 20 tons, was added to *Mir*. In July, Anatoly Solovyev and Alexander Balandin took a seven-hour space walk from *Mir*, the longest on record, to secure insulation blankets on the Soyuz TM-9 descent module that had been damaged when it docked with *Mir* in February. Later in July, Solovyev and Balandin forced an airlock closed on the Kvant-2 module, although a further attempt in November failed to repair the airlock seal. In August, Solovyev and Balandin were replaced by Lt. Col. Gennady Manakov and flight engineer Gennady Strekalov, who planned a 132-day mission. In December two other Soviet cosmonauts to replace Manakov and Strekalov and a Japanese journalist were sent to *Mir*. The journalist returned eight days later with Manakov and Strekalov.

Space Science. The shuttle mission STS-32 achieved success with the retrieval of LDEF. In orbit since 1984, the facility containing 57 scientific, technical, and applications experiments, designed for a ten-month duration in the environment of space, was delayed almost five years for a variety of reasons, most notably the *Challenger* accident. Greater solar activity and the resulting increased atmospheric drag on the satellite necessitated its retrieval before a fiery reentry destroyed it.

The NASA/ESA spacecraft *Ulysses* was deployed by the shuttle *Discovery* in October and was to travel faster than any other object of human origin in the solar system, with a maximum velocity of about 28 mi (45 km) per second, relative to the sun. *Ulysses'* major objective would be to study the solar environment, particularly our star's polar regions. *Ulysses* will pass as close as 120 million mi (193 million km) from the sun. The spacecraft's 11 instruments will obtain data on the physics of the inner and outer solar atmosphere, the origin and makeup of the solar wind, and the source of solar radio and X-ray emissions.

"Roentgensatellit," or ROSAT, a German observatory, rode into orbit atop a Delta 2 rocket from Cape Canaveral, FL, on June 1. ROSAT was designed to detect high-energy radiation, specifically X rays and ultraviolet radiation, which cannot penetrate through Earth's atmosphere. ROSAT's first mission would be a survey map of the sky, followed by study of specific high-energy radiation sources.

Although there were problems with the planetary explorer *Magellan*'s memory cells, results from the main mission agenda, the high-resolution radar mapping of the Venusian surface, astounded planetary scientists with the clarity and wealth of geologic information. The most Earth-like planet in terms of size and solar-system position, Venus hides its surface features under a visually impenetrable cloud of carbon dioxide, which causes a greenhouse effect and surface temperatures approaching 900°F (482°C). The new imagery, more detailed than existing radar pictures, eventually was to cover 70%-90% of the planet's surface. Although only a small percentage of the data was received at year's end, it rendered information of meteorite and asteroid impact craters, the most characteristic feature of the surfaces of the solid bodies of the solar system (except Earth, whose mobile crust and abundant surface water obliterates these features geologically quickly), reflecting Venus' dense atmosphere. Small meteorites ablate and disintegrate and thus leave no record as they would on the lunar surface. Larger craters, 20–30 mi (32–48 km) in diameter, appeared on an early *Magellan* mosaic and are brilliantly clear in their radar reflectivity. Other mosaics showed dense populations of long, linear fractures of the crust and may yield information on the stress-strain relations of the Venusian crust. Igneous domes, 15 mi (24 km) across and 2,500 ft (762 m) high, have topographic textures reminiscent of baked, cracked biscuits. Erosional and constructional features on Venus differ from similar features on Earth, owing in part to Venus' much greater atmospheric pressure. In a different mode *Magellan*'s instruments measured attributes of an unusual surface material that may be "fool's gold," or iron pyrite.

NASA's Cosmic Background Explorer satellite (COBE), launched late in 1989, provided initial and dramatic views of the entire Milky Way galaxy, first in near infrared and later in far infrared wavelengths. The earlier images reveal millions of stars in the galaxy; later images show cold, interstellar dust from which stars and planets are formed.

The amazing *Voyager* spacecraft continued to provide new information during the year. On February 13–14, *Voyager I* turned on its wide-angle camera system to take the first pictures of the entire solar system. This portrait, composed of a mosaic of 64 images, showed all planets except for Mercury, Mars, and Pluto. Data from *Voyager II* continued to be studied intensely, especially concerning Triton, the spectacular satellite of Neptune. The 5-mi- (8-km-) high plumes of gas and debris that rose through the icy body's atmosphere were a surprise. The earliest explanation, that the material was a kind of volcanic geyser, seemed difficult to reconcile with a lack of an adequate heat source. Continuing study provided alternative scenarios.

In September, *Pioneer 10*, launched in 1972, reached a distance of 50 AU (astronomical units) from the sun. The spacecraft has determined that the sun's heliosphere extends far beyond the orbit of Jupiter, as first believed. While searching for the boundary of the helio-

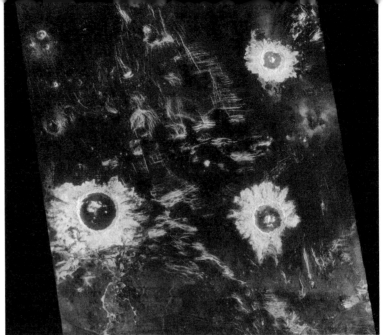

High-resolution radar mapping of the Venusian surface by the U.S. planetary explorer "Magellan" revealed in mid-September 1990 large impact craters with diameters from 23 mi (37 km) to 30 mi (50 km) in a region of fractured plains.

© Jet Propulsion Laboratory

sphere, *Pioneer 10* also was seeking evidence of a possible tenth planet.

In November the Hubble telescope collected striking images of a huge hurricane on Saturn.

Applications Satellites. On January 21 a second French SPOT remote sensing satellite was put into orbit by the Ariane V35 launcher. On January 24 the sixth U.S. Air Force Navstar Global Positioning satellite was launched on a Delta 2 rocket. (Additional launches to complete the planned 21-satellite system were scheduled every 60 to 90 days.) On that date, too, Japan became the third nation to launch an unmanned rocket to the moon, sending two satellites aloft. On April 3, Israel launched its second spacecraft, a technology-demonstration craft designated "Ofek 2" on a modified Jericho missile. The first Pegasus air-launched booster was deployed from a B-52 aircraft on April 5, putting a U.S. naval communications device and an atmospheric NASA satellite into orbit. Consort 3 was launched May 16 from New Mexico's White Sands Missile Range, carrying a microgravity experiment package. The launch vehicle was a Space Services Inc. Starfire rocket. A Titan 4 launch on June 8 was believed to carry four advanced surveillance spacecraft. The Chinese launched the first Long March 2E heavy-lift booster on July 16, carrying Pakistan's first satellite, Badr-1, an experimental scientific satellite, and a second simulated satellite. On July 25 the first commercial version of the General Dynamics Atlas Centaur carried the Air Force/NASA Combined Release and Radiation Effects satellite into a highly elliptical orbit on a 1–3 year mission to assess radiation effects on microelectronics and a vapor-release experiment for NASA. On September 3, China's second Feng Yun polar-orbiting weather satellite was launched on a Long March 4 booster from China's new Taiyuan launch site southwest of Beijing. On September 28 the Soviet Union launched a Meteor 3 class weather satellite. Earlier, during July and August, the Soviets launched three additional Cosmos surveillance and imaging reconnaissance satellites to monitor the Iraqi situation. October 2 marked the fifth Chinese satellite launch of 1990. The satellite, launched on a Long March 2 booster, was in orbit for eight days and carried animals and plants to study their reactions to space's weightless environment. An Air Force Titan 4 rocket was launched from Cape Canaveral on November 12, boosting into orbit what was believed to be an advanced early-warning satellite to detect missiles.

Communications Satellites. Two Japanese communications satellites were lost when their European-built Ariane rocket launcher blew up 100 seconds after the February 22 launch. As a result of the accident, Ariane launches were suspended until the July 24 launch of a French direct-broadcast satellite and a multipurpose telecommunications spacecraft for West Germany. On March 14 the Intelsat 6 spacecraft was stranded in a useless orbit by a malfunctioning Titan 3 booster. AsiaSat 1, the retrieved and refurbished Westar 6 deployed by a U.S. space shuttle in February 1984 and retrieved by a subsequent shuttle mission in November 1984, was launched in China on April 7. An Indonesian communications satellite, rescued during the same 1984 shuttle mission, was launched successfully on a Delta booster on April 13, the third commercial Delta launch of the year. On August 28 a Japanese television relay satellite was launched.

E. JULIUS and PATRICIA A. DASCH
National Aeronautics and Space Administration

SPAIN

During 1990, Spain's Prime Minister Felipe González increasingly focused on foreign affairs as critics, emboldened by lower economic growth and allegations of high-level corruption, stepped up their attacks on his free-enterprise-oriented government that remained Socialist in name only.

Politics and Government. On April 5, González won a vote of confidence in the newly formed Cortés (parliament), in which his Socialist Workers' Party (PSOE) held exactly half of the 350 seats. One hundred and seventy six members of parliament backed the prime minister and 130 members opposed him—with 37 abstentions.

During the debate, the conservative Popular Party (PP) demanded the resignation of Deputy Prime Minister Alfonso Guerra, to whom González had delegated domestic policy-making. Specifically, they alleged that Guerra's brother had used family connections to enrich himself. Similar charges about influence peddling had pervaded the 1989 parliamentary elections, in which the PSOE lost ground.

Alfonso Guerra's authoritarian behavior toward detractors sparked criticism at the PSOE's November 1990 party congress. Also discussed was the Socialist setback in October elections held in the violence-prone Basque region. The Socialists, who had governed the area as a junior coalition partner with the moderate Basque Nationalist Party (PNV), lost three of its 19 seats in the 75-member regional legislature. Another loser was Herri Batsuna, the radical separatist organization linked to the ETA terrorist group. The PSOE might reconstitute its coalition with the PNV, which gained five seats. Still, the most notable increase was achieved by the PP, which hoped eventually to gain a share of national political power.

Long before conservatives attain cabinet posts in Madrid, the 48-year-old González may seek the presidency of the European Community Commission, currently held by France's Jacques Delors. The next commission president would take office at the end of 1992.

Economics. Since joining the European Community (EC) in 1986, Spain had enjoyed robust economic growth—with 5% rates recorded in 1988 and 1989. In 1990 national income expanded by only 3.5%, as spiraling oil costs increased the overall price level more than 8%. Even so Spain still boasted one of the world's most dynamic economies.

Spain's high inflation rate encouraged Finance Minister Carlos Solchaga Catalán to advocate delaying until 1994 movement toward a single European currency. As EC integration advanced, Solchaga stressed the need for budget cuts to reduce Spain's inflation to 5% in 1991. The adroit finance minister also was assigned the task of peacemaker between the government and the nation's two large, combative trade unions.

The country's economic slowdown contributed to a $2 billion decline in government revenues. Another factor was evasion of the value added tax (VAT). This might prompt authorities to establish a Spanish version of the Internal Revenue Service to pursue wrongdoers.

Foreign Affairs. To emphasize Spain's role as a bridge to Latin America, González attended the inauguration of new presidents in Brazil and Chile. However, his government found itself at odds with Fidel Castro when, during the summer, 13 Cubans sought asylum in the Spanish embassy in Havana. The Cuban government excoriated Madrid for providing refuge to its citizens, and Spain condemned Cuba's disregard for diplomatic norms. At the end of the 58-day crisis, Spain suspended its $250 million assistance program and recalled its ambassador.

The end of the Cold War led the United States to announce that it would close 11 military installations in Spain, including the Torrejon air base that often has been the target of anti-U.S. demonstrations. Within the context of a Treaty on Conventional Forces in Europe, González unveiled plans to cut his country's artillery by 10% and its tank force by 20%. In addition, the length of compulsory military service, formerly 18 months, was lowered to 12 months in 1990—to be reduced to nine months in 1991.

In late October, Mikhail Gorbachev made a three-day visit to Spain. The Soviet president and González signed a dozen agreements designed to expand trade, increase Spanish investment in Russia, and improve bilateral relations. The most important accord involved a $1.5 billion Spanish credit to the USSR—half for products and services, half for food and other consumer goods.

GEORGE W. GRAYSON
College of William and Mary

SPAIN • Information Highlights

Official Name: Kingdom of Spain.
Location: Iberian Peninsula in southwestern Europe.
Area: 194,884 sq mi (504 750 km²).
Population (mid-1990 est.): 39,400,000.
Chief Cities (Jan. 1987 est.): Madrid, the capital, 3,100,507; Barcelona, 1,703,744; Valencia, 732,-491.
Government: *Head of state,* Juan Carlos I, king (took office Nov. 1975). *Head of government,* Felipe González Márquez, prime minister (took office Dec. 1982). *Legislature*—Cortés Generales: Senate and Congress of Deputies.
Monetary Unit: Peseta (98.9 pesetas equal U.S.$1, Dec. 31, 1990).
Gross National Product (1989 est. U.S.$): $398,700,-000,000.
Economic Indexes (1989): *Consumer Prices* (1980 = 100), all items, 228.3; food, 231.2. *Industrial Production* (1980 = 100), 120.
Foreign Trade (1989 U.S.$): *Imports,* $71,429,-000,000; *exports,* $44,424,000,000.

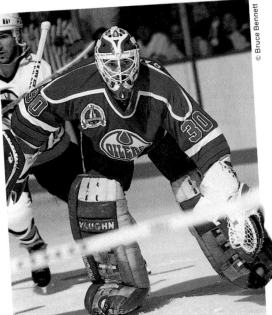

Overview

The underdog went to the winner's circle an unusual number of times during the 1990 sports year. In one of the biggest boxing upsets of all time, James (Buster) Douglas knocked out the previously undefeated Mike Tyson in the Tokyo Dome on February 11 (*below*); the top-ranked tennis stars of 1989, Steffi Graf and Ivan Lendl, each won only one 1990 Grand Slam singles title, as Andres Gomes and Monica Seles, and Pete Sampras and Gabriela Sabatini took their bows and the trophies at Paris and the U.S. Open, respectively; Cincinnati's baseball club, the Reds, overwhelmed the heavily

SPORTS

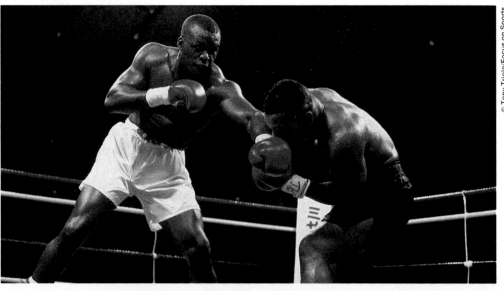

favored Oakland Athletics in the World Series; the colt Unbridled, a ten-to-one shot, took the 116th Kentucky Derby; and although Italy was a pretournament favorite, especially with the hometown crowd, highly regarded West Germany won soccer's World Cup.

Perhaps contradicting the upset trend, Bill Ranford (*page 476*) led the Edmonton Oilers to their first Stanley Cup without Wayne Gretzky; Pirmin Zurbriggen (*page 476*) became history's second skier to capture four World Cup overall titles; Greg LeMond crossed the finish line first for the second year in a row at the Tour de France bicycle race; and the Detroit Pistons won a second consecutive NBA crown.

Meanwhile the National Collegiate Athletic Association (NCAA) voted to allow all incoming athletes to receive financial aid based on their family income, even if their academic records do not meet those required for an athletic scholarship. The action was intended to ease the controversy arising over 1989's Proposition 42, which tied aid to academic standards. The NCAA also agreed to limit spring football practice, shorten the basketball season, require Division I and II schools to provide information on the graduation rates of athletes, and permit random, year-round testing of football players in major programs for performance-enhancing drugs.

The Goodwill Games

The 1990 Goodwill Games were held in Seattle and six other cities in Washington in late July and early August. More than 2,300 athletes from 58 countries participated in the athletic competition, first held in Moscow in 1986.

The games were created by Ted Turner, chairman of Turner Broadcasting System, Inc. (TBS), after Olympic boycotts in 1980 and 1984 prevented U.S. and Soviet athletes from competing against one another. Joining in the creation of the competition were the USSR State Committee for Physical Culture and Sport (Goskomsport) and the USSR State Committee for Television and Radio (Gosteleradio). Backers planned to hold the Goodwill Games every four years, alternating between the United States and the Soviet Union.

The 1990 Goodwill Games drew 780,000 spectators to events in 21 sports. An arts festival, exchange program, and series of conferences were held in conjunction with the games. In all, the events drew about 3,000 Soviet citizens to Washington, the largest visit ever to the United States by Soviets.

Soviet athletes led in the overall medal count with 188, including 66 gold medals; U.S. athletes came in second, winning 161 medals, 60 of them gold. Two world records were set during the 17 days of competition: American Mike Barrowman's time of 2:11.53 in the 200-m breaststroke and the Soviet Union's Nadezhda Ryashkina's 41:56.21 in the 10-km race-walk.

But these mini-Olympics fell short of some expectations. Several top athletes who had been expected to compete canceled, citing scheduling conflicts or insufficient prize money. The event also failed to produce the expected tourist boom for Seattle; many businesses said activity actually was down from the previous summer.

Disappointing cable-television ratings for the games compounded the financial losses incurred by TBS. The event drew an average

© Paul J. Sutton/Duomo

Janet Evans, winner of the Sullivan Award as the top U.S. amateur athlete and the NCAA's swimmer of the year, took three gold and two silver medals at the Goodwill Games.

prime-time rating of 2.6, representing an audience of only 2.6% of the approximately 40 million subscribers with access to the telecast. That figure was just over one half the rating Turner had promised to advertisers. As a result, about $18 million in free airtime was provided to advertisers, bringing TBS' losses to $44 million.

Overall costs of the event included $90 million from TBS, $68 million from the Seattle Organizing Committee, which contracted with TBS to organize and produce the games, and approximately $30 million from federal, state, and local governments. The expense and low ratings raised the question of whether the games would be held again, but in September, TBS directors voted unanimously to go ahead with plans to hold the 1994 games in Leningrad and Moscow. A key to the games' future was an agreement between TBS and ABC to let ABC air some of the 1994 events. Previously, Turner held exclusive U.S. broadcast rights.

JACK BROOM

© Vandystadt/Allsport

Brazil's Ayrton Senna and France's Alain Prost crash in the first lap of the Japanese Grand Prix. The resulting automatic elimination deprived Prost of any chance of winning another Formula One championship. The crown went to Senna.

Auto Racing

Ayrton Senna of Brazil won his second Formula One world driving championship in three years in 1990, wrapping up the title when he crashed with longtime adversary Alain Prost of France on the first lap of the Japanese Grand Prix. The accident eliminated both Senna and defending world champion Prost from the season's next-to-last event and wiped away any mathematical chance Prost had of winning his fourth title.

Senna won six races and seven pole positions in the 15-event schedule. Prost had five victories; the only other driver with multiple victories was Nelson Piquet, who won the last two races on the schedule.

Al Unser, Jr., son of a four-time winner of the Indianapolis 500, outdueled another second-generation driver, Michael Andretti, to win the Championship Auto Racing Teams (CART) Indy Car World Series. Unser, of Albuquerque, NM, won five of his 16 starts and outpointed Andretti, son of former Formula One champion Mario Andretti, 210-181. Rick Mears, Bobby Rahal, and defending champion Emerson Fittipaldi trailed the leaders. Unser had finished one point behind his father, Al Unser, Sr., in the 1985 CART points race.

Arie Luyendyk made the Indianapolis 500 his first Indy-car victory but then went winless the rest of the season in his first year with car owner Doug Shierson.

Dale Earnhardt of Kannapolis, NC, won a season-long duel with Mark Martin for the Winston Cup stock-car championship. Earnhardt forged ahead in the standings in the next-to-last race and clinched his fourth Winston Cup title by placing third in the season finale at Hampton, GA. Earnhardt had a six-point lead entering the final race and beat Martin 4,430-4,404. Only Richard Petty's seven championships exceeded Earnhardt's total.

The Daytona 500, stock-car racing's showcase event, had a surprise winner in Derrike Cope, who passed Earnhardt on the last lap when Earnhardt cut a tire and slowed to a fifth-place finish. In 67 previous Winston Cup races Cope never had finished as high as fifth.

STAN SUTTON
"Louisville Courier-Journal"

AUTO RACING

Major Race Winners, 1990

Indianapolis 500: Arie Luyendyk, United States
Marlboro 500: Al Unser, Jr., United States
Daytona 500: Derrike Cope, United States

1990 Champions

World Championship: Ayrton Senna, Brazil
CART: Al Unser, Jr.
NASCAR: Dale Earnhardt

Grand Prix for Formula One Cars, 1990

United States: Ayrton Senna, Brazil
Brazilian: Alain Prost, France
San Marino: Riccardo Patrese, Italy
Monaco: Senna
Canadian: Senna
Mexican: Prost
French: Prost
British: Prost
German: Senna
Hungarian: Thierry Boutsen, Belgium
Belgian: Senna
Italian: Senna
Portuguese: Nigel Mansell, Great Britain
Spanish: Prost
Japanese: Nelson Piquet, Brazil
Australian: Piquet

Baseball

For baseball 1990 was a year of agony and ecstasy. After a lockout delayed the season, nine starting pitchers threw no-hitters, a reliever carved a new record for saves, and a player hit 50 homers for the first time in 13 seasons. In addition, a team owner was banned from the game for life and a manager banned previously was sent to jail.

Play-offs and World Series. The Cincinnati Reds, beleaguered by the Pete Rose betting scandal in 1989, responded to new manager Lou Piniella by winning their first nine games and remaining on top in the National League (NL) West for the entire 162-game schedule—an unprecedented feat. The Pittsburgh Pirates became NL East champions four days before season's end but were favored to beat the Reds, who lost more than they won after the All-Star break. In the play-offs, however, Cincinnati's bullpen proved too powerful. After losing the opener at home, 4-3, the Reds took consecutive 2-1, 6-3, and 5-3 victories before Pittsburgh won again, 3-2. Cincinnati clinched the pennant with a 2-1 win in game 6. Superior pitching and defense proved decisive for the Reds, who held Pittsburgh to a composite .194 batting average. Cincinnati relievers Rob Dibble, Randy Myers, and Norm Charlton appeared four times each and posted a combined 0.57 ERA. Dibble and Myers shared play-off MVP honors.

In the American League (AL), the Oakland Athletics won 103 games to win their third straight AL West title. Oakland then made short work of the Boston Red Sox, whose two-game margin over Toronto was the smallest of any divisional champion. With two wins from play-off MVP Dave Stewart, the Athletics held the Red Sox hitters to a .183 average and swept the series, 9-1, 4-1, 4-1, and 3-1.

Although oddsmakers made Oakland prohibitive favorites in the World Series, the Reds had other ideas. Jose Rijo won the first and fourth games as the Reds swept the series, 7-0, 5-4 (10 innings), 8-3, and 2-1—the biggest October upset since the New York Giants swept the Cleveland Indians in 1954. Cincinnati's Billy Hatcher had a record seven straight hits en route to a .750 average, a World Series record, but Rijo was named Series MVP. Unexpectedly poor performances by Stewart, Dennis Eckersley, and star sluggers Jose Canseco (*see* BIOGRAPHY) and Mark McGwire contributed to the demise of the Athletics, whose three straight World Series showings included a 1989 sweep of the San Francisco Giants.

Regular Season. Baseball's seventh work shutdown in 18 years ended March 19 after 32 days—the second-longest stoppage in the stormy history of player-owner labor relations. The four-year agreement increased the minimum salary from $68,000 to $100,000, the own-

© Focus on Sports

Cincinnati's Jose Rijo was named the most valuable player of the 1990 World Series as he allowed Oakland only one run in 15⅓ innings. He won games one and four.

ers' annual contribution to the players' pension fund from $39 million to $55 million, and team rosters from 24 to 25 players, effective in 1991. It also included an agreement that the National League would add two expansion teams and changed salary arbitration eligibility to include the top 17% of players with between two and three years of service.

Because the labor stalemate had shortened spring training by one month, both sides agreed to postpone opening day one week to assure adequate training time. The players quickly proved they were ready. On April 11, two days after the delayed opener, free-agent signee Mark Langston, in his first game with the California Angels, teamed with Mike Witt to pitch the first of 1990's nine no-hitters, a single-season record. Others were pitched by Stewart, Randy Johnson (Seattle Mariners), Melido Perez (Chicago White Sox), Andy Hawkins (New York Yankees), Dave Stieb (Toronto Blue Jays), Fernando Valenzuela (Los Angeles Dodgers), Terry Mulholland (Philadelphia Phillies), and Nolan Ryan (Texas Rangers).

At age 43, Ryan (*see* BIOGRAPHY) not only pitched his record sixth no-hitter but led the American League with 232 strikeouts to win his 11th strikeout crown and second in the AL in succession. The star right-hander, who had led the NL in strikeouts in 1987 and 1988, also became the 20th pitcher to post 300 career victories. Dave Cone (New York Mets) led the majors with 233 strikeouts.

Six starters—three in each league—won 20 games, and three relievers—all in the American League—saved 40. Bob Welch (Athletics) won 27, most in the majors since Steve Carlton won that many in 1972, to win the AL's Cy Young Award for pitching excellence. Doug Drabek (Pirates) won the NL award with a league-high 22 wins in 28 decisions. Other 20-game winners were Stewart, Roger Clemens

(Red Sox), Ramon Martinez (Dodgers), and Frank Viola (Mets).

Bobby Thigpen (White Sox) saved 57 games, 11 more than Dave Righetti's 1986 record, to finish far ahead of Oakland's Dennis Eckersley, who converted 48 of 50 chances. Doug Jones (Cleveland Indians) saved 43, ten more than NL saves leader John Franco (Mets). Leaders in earned run average were Clemens (1.93) and the Houston Astros' Danny Darwin (2.21).

Pitching also prevailed in the All-Star Game, a 2-0 AL victory at Chicago's Wrigley Field on July 10. The key hit was a two-run, seventh-inning double by Julio Franco (Rangers) on Rob Dibble's third pitch after a 68-minute rain delay. The National League, held to two hits by six AL pitchers, now has lost four of the last five All-Star Games.

For most of the season, the hitters made their presence felt. The Detroit Tigers' Cecil Fielder, returning to the majors from the Japanese leagues, led the majors with 51 homers, 132 runs batted in (RBIs), and a .592 slugging percentage. Pittsburgh's Barry Bonds was named the National League's most valuable player (MVP) after hitting .301 with 33 homers, 114 RBIs, 52 stolen bases, 104 runs scored, and a league-best .565 slugging average. The only other 30/30 player in the majors was NL come-

BASEBALL

Professional—Major Leagues
Final Standings, 1990

AMERICAN LEAGUE

Eastern Division	W	L	Pct.	Western Division	W	L	Pct.
Boston	88	74	.543	Oakland	103	59	.636
Toronto	86	76	.531	Chicago	94	68	.580
Detroit	79	83	.488	Texas	83	79	.512
Cleveland	77	85	.475	California	80	82	.494
Baltimore	76	85	.472	Seattle	77	85	.475
Milwaukee	74	88	.457	Kansas City	75	86	.466
New York	67	95	.414	Minnesota	74	88	.457

NATIONAL LEAGUE

Eastern Division	W	L	Pct.	Western Division	W	L	Pct.
Pittsburgh	95	67	.586	Cincinnati	91	71	.562
New York	91	71	.562	Los Angeles	86	76	.531
Montreal	85	77	.525	San Francisco	85	77	.525
Chicago	77	85	.475	Houston	75	87	.463
Philadelphia	77	85	.475	San Diego	75	87	.466
St. Louis	70	92	.432	Atlanta	65	97	.401

Play-offs—American League: Oakland defeated Boston, 4 games to 0; National League: Cincinnati defeated Pittsburgh, 4 games to 2.

World Series—Cincinnati defeated Oakland, 4 games to 0. First Game (Riverfront Stadium, Oct. 16, attendance 55,830): Cincinnati 7, Oakland 0; Second Game (Riverfront Stadium, Oct. 17, attendance 55,832): Cincinnati 5, Oakland 4; Third Game (Oakland Coliseum, Oct. 19, attendance 48,269): Cincinnati 8, Oakland 3; Fourth Game (Oakland Coliseum, Oct. 20, attendance 48,613): Cincinnati 2, Oakland 1.

All-Star Game (Wrigley Field, Chicago, July 10, attendance 39,071): American League 2, National League 0.

Most Valuable Players—American League: Rickey Henderson, Oakland; National League: Barry Bonds, Pittsburgh

Cy Young Memorial Awards (outstanding pitchers)—American League: Bob Welch, Oakland; National League: Doug Drabek, Pittsburgh

Managers of the Year—American League: Jeff Torborg, Chicago; National League: Jim Leyland, Pittsburgh

Rookies of the Year—American League: Sandy Alomar, Jr., Cleveland; National League: Dave Justice, Atlanta

Leading Hitters—(Percentage) American League: George Brett, Kansas City, .329; National League: Willie McGee, St. Louis, .335. (Runs Batted In) American League: Cecil Fielder, Detroit, 132; National League: Matt Williams, San Francisco, 122. (Home Runs) American League: Fielder, 51; National League: Ryne Sandberg, Chicago, 40. (Hits) American League: Rafael Palmeiro, Texas, 191; National League: Brett Butler, San Francisco, 192. (Runs) American League: Rickey Henderson, Oakland, 119; National League: Sandberg, 116. (Slugging Percentage) American League: Fielder, .592; National League: Bobby Bonds, Pittsburgh, .565.

Leading Pitchers—(Earned Run Average) American League: Roger Clemens, Boston, 1.93; National League: Danny Darwin, Houston, 2.21. (Victories) American League: Bob Welch, Oakland, 27; National League: Doug Drabek, Pittsburgh, 22. (Strikeouts) American League: Nolan Ryan, Texas, 232; National League: David Cone, New York, 233. (Shutouts) American League: Clemens and Dave Stewart, Oakland, 4; National League: Bruce Hurst, San Diego, and Mike Morgan, Los Angeles, 4. (Saves) American League: Bobby Thigpen, Chicago, 57; National League: John Franco, New York, 33.

Professional—Minor Leagues, Class AAA

American Association: Omaha
International League: Rochester
Pacific Coast League: Albuquerque

Amateur

NCAA: University of Georgia
Little League World Series: Taiwan

Detroit's Cecil Fielder, who had spent 1989 hitting home runs in Japan, led the U.S. major leagues with 51 homers and 132 RBIs. He hit three homers in a game twice.

© Focus on Sports

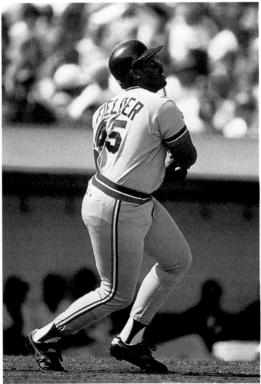

AP/Wide World

Like Father, Like Son

In August 1990, Ken Griffey, Sr., *(left)* and Ken Griffey, Jr., 21, became the first father-son pair to play for the same baseball team at the same time when Griffey, Sr., 40, was signed to the Seattle Mariners. In 1989, with Griffey, Sr., playing for the Cincinnati Reds and his son signed to the Mariners, the two had become the first father and son to play in the major leagues at the same time. Griffey, Sr., in his 18th major-league season, and his talented son, the youngest player in the majors, scored back-to-back home runs against the California Angels on September 14. Also, in a growing trend, 25 sons of former major-leaguers played in the majors during the 1990 season— the largest number ever in one year.

back player of the year Ron Gant (Atlanta Braves), who had 32 homers and 33 stolen bases.

Ryne Sandberg (Chicago Cubs) led the NL with 40 homers, 116 runs scored, and 344 total bases, while Matt Williams (Giants) led the league with 122 RBIs. Bonds, Eddie Murray (Dodgers), and Rickey Henderson (Athletics) were the only players in the majors to have a .300 batting average, .400 on-base average, and .500 slugging percentage. Henderson, who finished the season two shy of Lou Brock's career record of 938 stolen bases, won the AL MVP honors by leading the league with 65 steals, 119 runs scored, and a .439 on-base average. Vince Coleman (St. Louis Cardinals) led both leagues with 77 stolen bases.

Although Lenny Dykstra (Phillies) led the NL with a .418 on-base percentage and had a league-best 23-game hitting streak, he could not maintain the lead he held in the batting race when Willie McGee (Cardinals) was traded to Oakland on August 28. McGee, whose NL average was locked at .335, won his second NL crown when Dykstra faded in September. By leading the AL with a .329 mark, George Brett (Kansas City Royals) became the first man to win batting titles in three different decades. Brian Harper (Minnesota Twins) had a 25-game hitting streak, best in the majors. Dykstra and Brett Butler (Giants) shared the big-league lead with 192 hits, one more than AL leader Rafael Palmeiro (Rangers).

Rookies of the Year were Dave Justice, who hit .282 with 28 homers and 78 RBIs after replacing two-time MVP Dale Murphy (traded to Philadelphia) as Atlanta's right fielder, and Cleveland catcher Sandy Alomar, Jr., an All-Star starter who hit .290 with nine homers. After five consecutive years of increases, attendance at major-league games fell by .5%. The NL fell 3.1% to 24,540,121, while the AL registered a record 30,331,417.

Off the field, Baseball Commissioner Fay Vincent issued a lifetime suspension against Yankee owner George Steinbrenner (*see* BIOGRAPHY) on July 30. Eleven days earlier, former Cincinnati manager and career-hits leader Pete Rose, suspended for life on Aug. 24, 1989, had been slapped with a five-month prison term for income-tax evasion.

Another former Red—second baseman Joe Morgan—and former Baltimore pitcher Jim Palmer became the newest Hall of Famers on August 6.

The season ended on a bitter note for management when arbitrator George Nicolau ruled September 17 that the 26 club owners must pay players $102.5 million in lost salary for the 1987 and 1988 seasons. Those awards, added to $10.2 million in damages for 1986 previously awarded by arbitrator Thomas Roberts, were granted after the arbitrators found that the owners had colluded to restrict the movement and salaries of veteran free-agent players.

DAN SCHLOSSBERG, *Baseball Writer*

Basketball

The Detroit Pistons became only the third franchise in National Basketball Association (NBA) history to win back-to-back championships when they defeated the Portland Trail Blazers, four games to one, to take the 1990 title. The previous season, the Pistons had swept the Los Angeles Lakers in four games to capture the championship.

The National Collegiate Athletic Association (NCAA) men's basketball crown went to the University of Nevada-Las Vegas (UNLV), which set numerous records by trouncing Duke, 103–73, in the tournament's final game. UNLV had been the preseason favorite to finish Number 1. Unheralded Vanderbilt won the National Invitation Tournament (NIT), while Stanford took the women's NCAA championship. The college season, however, was marred by the tragic death of Hank Gathers, high-scoring and rebounding center for Loyola Mary-

mount. Gathers collapsed during a game against Portland in March and died a short time later.

The Professional Season

With the retirement of longtime center Kareem Abdul-Jabbar at the end of the 1988-89 season, the Los Angeles Lakers were expected to fall from among the elite of the NBA during the 1989–90 season. Instead, the Lakers surprised the rest of the league once again by finishing with the best regular-season record (63–19). Los Angeles wound up with its ninth straight Pacific Division title, but not before having to hold off Portland in the final months. Pat Riley, the Lakers coach, was voted coach of the year. He later resigned the post to become a television commentator.

Defending champion Detroit had been expected to dominate the league, but the Pistons had late-season injury problems, especially to

Detroit's Isiah Thomas (11) was the most valuable player as his Pistons defeated the Portland Trail Blazers in five games for their second consecutive NBA championship. Thomas averaged 27.6 points in the play-off finals.

© Focus on Sports

star guard Joe Dumars, and finished with a 59–23 record, the same as Portland. The Pistons barely held off fast-closing Chicago for the Central Division title. Still a transition of power continued in the NBA. Longtime champion Boston Celtics got off to a very slow start and never could catch Philadelphia in the Atlantic Division, losing by one game. Philadelphia enjoyed one of its most successful seasons since 1985–86 and produced one of the league's most entertaining players, Charles Barkley.

The Midwest Division featured a very close race, which finally was won in the last days of the schedule by the San Antonio Spurs, the most improved team in the league. The Spurs, who were led by rookie center David Robinson, improved by 35 games over the previous season, an NBA record. The Spurs held off Utah, winning by a game. Among the most disappointing teams were Atlanta, which had a 41–41 record; Seattle, which also finished 41–41; and Golden State, which was 37–45. Hawks coach Mike Fratello resigned after the season. An expansion team, the Minnesota Timberwolves, set an NBA home-attendance record in their first season, while the other new expansion franchise, the Orlando Magic, struggled with an 18–64 record. The league itself set an attendance record for the seventh straight season.

Chicago's Michael Jordan, the league's most prolific scorer since the retirement of Wilt Chamberlain, won his fourth straight scoring title. He averaged 33.6 points per game. Second was Utah forward Karl Malone (31.0) and third was New York Knicks center Patrick Ewing (28.6), who also was one of the league's most improved players. The season produced one of the closest races in recent years for the most-valuable-player award. Besides Jordan and Ewing, other top contenders were Magic Johnson of the Lakers, who was second in the league behind Utah guard John Stockton in assists (14.5 to 11.5); Barkley, who was sixth in scoring; Malone, who was both a dominant scorer and rebounder; Houston center Akeem Olajuwon, who led in rebounding (14.0) and was ninth in scoring; and Robinson, the prolific San Antonio center who was second in rebounding, tenth in scoring, and the league's rookie of the year. Johnson wound up winning the MVP trophy for the second straight year, edging out Barkley in the closest voting in the ten years that the balloting has been done by a media panel. Jordan was third, Malone fourth, and Ewing fifth.

Jordan, Johnson, Malone, Ewing, and Barkley made first-team All NBA, while Jordan joined Olajuwon, Dennis Rodman of Detroit, Buck Williams of Portland, and Dumars on the all-defensive team. Rodman, who is the Pistons' defensive specialist, was named the league's top defensive player. Stockton became the first player ever to have 1,000 assists for three straight years. His 1,134 assists in 1989–90 was a league record.

Play-offs. Based on the regular season, the Los Angeles Lakers and the Detroit Pistons were expected to meet in the final round of the play-offs for the championship, a repeat of the previous two seasons. But it did not work out that way.

PROFESSIONAL BASKETBALL

National Basketball Association
(Final Standings, 1989–90)
Eastern Conference

Atlantic Division	W	L	Pct.
*Philadelphia	53	29	.646
*Boston	52	30	.634
*New York	45	37	.549
Washington	31	51	.378
Miami	18	64	.220
New Jersey	17	65	.207
Central Division			
*Detroit	59	23	.720
*Chicago	55	27	.671
*Milwaukee	44	38	.537
*Cleveland	42	40	.512
*Indiana	42	40	.512
Atlanta	41	41	.500
Orlando	18	64	.220

Western Conference

Midwestern Division	W	L	Pct.
*San Antonio	56	26	.683
*Utah	55	27	.671
*Dallas	47	35	.573
*Denver	43	39	.524
*Houston	41	41	.500
Minnesota	22	60	.268
Charlotte	19	63	.232
Pacific Division			
*L.A. Lakers	63	19	.768
*Portland	59	23	.720
*Phoenix	54	28	.659
Seattle	41	41	.500
Golden State	37	45	.451
L.A. Clippers	30	52	.366
Sacramento	23	59	.280

*Made play-offs

Play-Offs
Eastern Conference

First Round	Chicago	3 games	Milwaukee	1
	Detroit	3 games	Indiana	0
	New York	3 games	Boston	2
	Philadelphia	3 games	Cleveland	2
Second Round	Chicago	4 games	Philadelphia	1
	Detroit	4 games	New York	1
Finals	Detroit	4 games	Chicago	3

Western Conference

First Round	Los Angeles	3 games	Houston	1
	Phoenix	3 games	Utah	2
	Portland	3 games	Dallas	0
	San Antonio	3 games	Denver	0
Second Round	Phoenix	4 games	Los Angeles	1
	Portland	4 games	San Antonio	3
Finals	Portland	4 games	Phoenix	2
Championship	Detroit	4 games	Portland	1
All-Star Game	East 130, West 113			

Individual Honors
Most Valuable Player: Magic Johnson, L.A. Lakers
Most Valuable Player (championship): Isiah Thomas, Detroit
Most Valuable Player (All-Star Game): Magic Johnson, L.A. Lakers
Rookie of the Year: David Robinson, San Antonio
Coach of the Year: Pat Riley, Los Angeles
Leader in Scoring: Michael Jordan, Chicago, 33.6 points per game
Leader in Assists: John Stockton, Utah, 14.5 per game
Leader in Rebounds: Akeem Olajuwon, Houston, 14.0 per game
Leader in Field Goal Percentage: Mark West, Phoenix, .625

The Lakers, who had finished strongly the last month of the season, had a difficult time in the play-offs. After struggling in the first round against Houston, Los Angeles could not handle quick Phoenix, which was led by the stellar guard play of Kevin Johnson. The Suns upset the Lakers, winning the series, four games to one. That advanced the Suns to the Western Conference finals against Portland. The Trail Blazers had survived a tough seven-game series against San Antonio, finally winning the last game on their home court. Portland then beat Phoenix in six games to advance to the finals against Detroit, which was pushed by Chicago to seven games in the Eastern Conference finals. Before meeting Chicago, the Pistons had lost just one of their eight previous play-off games.

The final series pitted Detroit's play-off experience against the youth and enthusiasm of Portland, which had six new players from the previous season and was not expected to last that long in the play-offs. The teams split the first two games in Detroit. The Trail Blazers led most of the way in the first contest only to see Piston guard Isiah Thomas score 16 points in the fourth quarter, including 12 of his team's final 16, to lead Detroit to a 105–99 win. But Portland was more fortunate in game two. The Trail Blazers forced an overtime and guard Clyde Drexler won the game by making two free throws with 2.1 seconds left.

The series switched to Portland for three games, where Detroit had not won in 20 contests, dating back to 1974. But the Pistons quickly ended that losing streak and regained control with a 121–106 triumph in game three. Dumars, the hero of the previous season's championship, scored 33 points and guard Vinnie Johnson added 21. Dumars learned after the game that his father had passed away that morning but he chose to continue playing. The last two games of the series were classics. In game four, Detroit lost a 16-point lead to fall behind by a point before two free throws from Thomas and a lay-up by Gerald Henderson salvaged a 112-109 win. In game five, Detroit's Johnson took over at the end. He scored seven points in the last 110 seconds, including the game winner with seven tenths of a second to go. It was the first time all season that Portland had lost three straight at home. Besides Detroit, the only other franchises to win back-to-back championships are the Boston Celtics and the Minneapolis-Los Angeles Lakers.

The College Season

The 1989–90 college-basketball season was overshadowed by the shocking death of Hank Gathers, center for Loyola Marymount and one of the leading scorers and rebounders in the United States. Gathers, who was considered a sure first-round professional-basketball draft

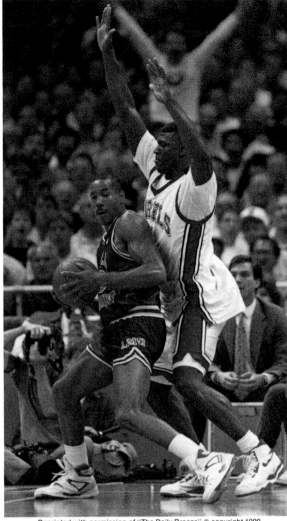

Reprinted with permission of ''The Daily Breeze'' © copyright 1990

Loyola Marymount, inspired by the death of their star Hank Gathers, advanced to the West Regionals of the NCAA tournament before losing to UNLV, 131-101. The Runnin' Rebels went on to take the NCAA crown.

choice, collapsed after a dunk during a March game against Portland. He struggled to his knees, fell back, and never regained consciousness. Gathers, who had led the nation in rebounding and scoring the previous season, suffered from cardiac arrhythmia or irregular heartbeat and was taking medication to treat the ailment. His death became an emotional rallying point for Loyola, the nation's top-scoring team, which advanced to the finals of the West Regionals of the NCAA tournament before losing to the University of Nevada-Las Vegas (UNLV). Most inspired by his death was close friend and teammate Bo Kimble, who led the nation in scoring and was especially brilliant in the postseason tournament.

UNLV was the preseason favorite to capture the national championship. But the Runnin' Rebels were certainly not a clear-cut choice. Syracuse, defending champion Michigan, and Louisiana State (LSU) all were considered very strong, as were Georgetown, Arkansas, Arizona, and North Carolina. But the surprise team turned out to be Oklahoma, which had suffered graduation losses and was not expected to be a championship contender. The Sooners, however, played very well in February and vaulted to the top spot in the polls. They finished the regular season ranked Number 1 and were a slim favorite to win the NCAA tournament. By then, other clear-cut contenders included UNLV, Big East champion Connecticut, Big Ten champ Michigan State, Kansas, and Syracuse. North Carolina and LSU, both of which made the tournament, still had disappointing seasons. The strongest conference was the Big Eight, from which Kansas, Missouri, and Oklahoma all were ranked Number 1 at some point during the regular season. Other talented leagues included the Big Ten and the Big East.

The best player in the United States was forward Lionel Simmons of La Salle. Simmons became the third all-time scorer and also was a consensus all-American. Another unanimous all-American was Georgia Tech's Dennis Scott, the nation's best three-point shooter. They were joined on most all-American teams by Larry Johnson of UNLV, Derrick Coleman of Syracuse, Gary Payton of Oregon State, Steve Smith of Michigan State, Kenny Anderson of Georgia Tech, and Chris Jackson of LSU. Jackson later decided to turn pro after his sophomore season.

Near the end of the season, reports of a possible controversy at North Carolina State eventually led to the resignation of coach Jim Valvano, who had led State to a national championship in 1983.

The Tournaments. Upstart Connecticut, which emerged as a national contender after years of basketball obscurity, joined UNLV, Michigan State, and Oklahoma as one of the top four seeds in the NCAA tournament. But as has been the case in recent years, the highly rated teams had a difficult time reaching the final four. While UNLV won the West Regional, Connecticut fell to Duke in the East Regional finals, Oklahoma lost in the early rounds of the Midwest Regionals, and Michigan State lost to Georgia Tech in the semifinals of the Southeast Regional. Eventually, Georgia Tech beat Minnesota to win the Southeast, while Arkansas defeated Southwest Conference rival Texas for the Midwest title.

In the final four at Denver's McNichols Arena, Duke met Arkansas in one semifinal and UNLV faced Georgia Tech in the other. Duke pulled away from the Razorbacks in the final six minutes of a fast-paced game and went on to win, 97–83. UNLV held high-scoring Georgia Tech to six points in the first ten minutes of the second half to break open a close

COLLEGE BASKETBALL

Conference Champions

Association of Mid-Continent: Northern Iowa
Atlantic Coast: Georgia Tech*
Atlantic-10: Temple*
Big East: Connecticut*
Big Eight: Oklahoma*
Big Sky: Idaho*
Big Ten: Michigan State
Big West: UNLV*
Colonial Athletic: Richmond*
East Coast: Towson State*
Ivy League: Princeton
Metro Athletic: Louisville*
Metro Atlantic Athletic: La Salle*
Mid-American: Ball State*
Mid-Eastern Athletic: Coppin State*
Midwestern: Dayton*
Missouri Valley: Illinois State*
North Atlantic: Boston University*
Northeast: Robert Morris*
Ohio Valley: Murray State*
Pacific-10: Arizona*
Southeastern: Alabama*
Southern: East Tennessee State*
Southland: Northeast Louisiana*
Southwest: Arkansas*
Southwestern Athletic: Texas Southern*
Sun Belt: South Florida*
Trans America Athletic: Arkansas-Little Rock
West Coast Athletic: Loyola Marymount (regular season champion; tournament canceled)
Western Athletic: UTEP*
*Won conference tournament

Tournaments

NCAA: UNLV
NCAA Division II: Kentucky Wesleyan
NCAA Division III: Rochester
NIT: Vanderbilt
NAIA: Birmingham-Southern
NCAA Division I (women): Stanford

game and pull away to a 90–81 win. That set up what was expected to be a terrific final between two closely matched teams. Instead Las Vegas won its first national championship by trouncing the Blue Devils, 103–73. Guard Anderson Hunt scored 29 and Johnson added 22 as the Rebels' 30-point victory margin was the largest of any tournament final. They also were the first team to break 100 points in a NCAA championship game. It was coach Jerry Tarkanian's first national title in 22 years of major college coaching. Tarkanian has had a long-running feud with the NCAA, including having programs at Long Beach State and UNLV placed on probation. Continuing its long case against Tarkanian, the NCAA in July 1990 banned UNLV from postseason play for one year, but lifted the ban later in 1990 after Tarkanian agreed to even stiffer penalties during 1991–92.

In the NIT, Vanderbilt was the surprise winner, beating St. Louis, 74–72, in the final on the strength of strong foul shooting in the last minutes. Vanderbilt had finished tied for eighth in the Southeastern Conference. Guard Scott Draud, who had 15 points in the final game, was named the tournament's MVP.

In the women's NCAA tournament, Auburn lost the championship game for the third straight season. The Tigers fell to Stanford, 88–81, on the strength of the Cardinals' three-point shooting. Guard Jennifer Azzi scored 17 points in the final and was named MVP.

PAUL ATTNER, *"The Sporting News"*

Boxing

One of the sport's greatest upsets marked the 1990 boxing calendar when Mike Tyson was knocked out in the tenth round of his heavyweight title defense by James (Buster) Douglas in Tokyo on February 11, a Sunday in Japan.

A Heavy Upset. Previously unbeaten and considered invincible by many boxing experts, the 23-year-old Tyson went into the fight weighing 220½ lbs (100 kg), 11 lbs (5 kg) lighter than Douglas. Tyson, a prohibitive 35–1 betting favorite, was stunned in the tenth round from a series of four savage punches by Douglas that sent him crumpling to the canvas for the first time in his professional career. A crushing left hook was the finishing blow and ended Tyson's four-year reign.

The bout, however, created controversy. Although Douglas dominated the fight, Tyson unleashed a flurry of blows in the eighth round and floored Douglas with a right uppercut. The referee was slow to pick up the count and Douglas remained on the canvas for at least 12 seconds, two more than a fighter is allowed. Tyson's camp claimed he thus had scored a legitimate knockout.

After the fight, the World Boxing Council (WBC) and the World Boxing Association (WBA), because of the "long count," were not ready to accept that Tyson had been dethroned. The International Boxing Federation (IBF), however, quickly recognized Douglas' victory. After a review, the outcome was upheld by all concerned.

The fact that Tyson's streak of 37 pro victories without a defeat came to an end at the hands of the 29-year-old Douglas, who turned pro in 1981, stunned boxing historians mostly because Douglas had a nondescript record and had earned a reputation for lacking "heart." They could not reconcile the picture of Iron Mike Tyson as a menacing, unstoppable mauler with 33 straight knockout victories and the picture created in an instant by Douglas of Tyson flipping over on the canvas, fumbling for his mouthpiece, inserting it backward, and helplessly staggering into the referee's arms.

Douglas had a chance in October to prove he was not an ersatz champion when he took on challenger Evander Holyfield in Las Vegas. Douglas was guaranteed more than $20 million for the defense, but he took his training for the fight very lightly and ballooned to 246 lbs (112 kg). Holyfield, who was a 7–5 favorite, weighed a trim 208 lbs (94.5 kg).

The end came at 1 minute 10 seconds of the third round, with Douglas flat on his back from a powerful right-hand punch that made the 28-year-old Holyfield the new champion. Douglas was criticized heavily for his lack of training, his poor showing in the ring, and for taking the defense of the title so lightly.

World Boxing Champions*

Heavyweight: World Boxing Council (WBC)—Evander Holyfield, United States, 1990; World Boxing Association (WBA)—Holyfield, 1990; International Boxing Federation (IBF)—Holyfield, 1990.
Cruiserweight: WBC—Massimiliano Duran, Italy, 1990; WBA—Robert Daniels, United States, 1989; IBF—Jeff Lampkin, United States, 1990.
Light Heavyweight: WBC—Dennis Andries, England, 1990; WBA—Virgil Hill, United States, 1987; IBF—Charles Williams, United States, 1987.
Super Middleweight: WBC—Marco Galvano, Italy, 1990; WBA—Christophe Tiozzo, France, 1990; IBF—Lindell Holmes, United States, 1990.
Middleweight: WBC—Julian Jackson, Virgin Islands, 1990; WBA—Mike McCallum, United States, 1989; IBF—Michael Nunn, United States, 1988.
Junior Middleweight: WBC—Terry Norris, United States, 1990; WBA—vacant; IBF—Gianfranco Rosi, Italy, 1989.
Welterweight: WBC—Maurice Blocker, United States, 1990; WBA—Aaron Davis, United States, 1990; IBF—Simon Brown, United States, 1988.
Junior Welterweight: WBC—Julio César Chávez, Mexico, 1989; WBA—Loreto Garza, United States, 1990; IBF—Chávez, 1990.
Lightweight: WBC—Pernell Whitaker, United States, 1989; WBA—Whitaker, 1990; IBF—Whitaker, 1989.
Junior Lightweight: WBC—Azumah Nelson, Ghana, 1988; WBA—Brian Mitchell, South Africa, 1986; IBF—Tony Lopez, United States, 1990.
Featherweight: WBC—Marcos Villasana, Mexico, 1990; WBA—Antonio Esparragoza, Venezuela, 1987; IBF—Jorge Paez, Mexico, 1988.
Junior Featherweight: WBC—Pedro Decima, Argentina, 1990; WBA—Luis Mendoza, Colombia, 1990; IBF—Welcome Ncita, South Africa, 1990.
Bantamweight: WBC—Raul Pérez, Mexico, 1988; WBA—Lusita Espinosa, Philippines, 1989; IBF—Orlando Canizales, United States, 1988.
Junior Bantamweight: WBC—Sunkil Moon, South Korea, 1990; WBA—Kaosai Galaxy, Thailand, 1984; IBF—Robert Quiroga, United States, 1990.
Flyweight: WBC—Sot Chitalada, Thailand, 1989; WBA—Yukihito Tamakuma, Japan, 1990; IBF—Dave McCauley, England, 1989.
Junior Flyweight: WBC—Humberto Gonzalez, Mexico, 1989; WBA—Woo-Yuh Myung, South Korea, 1985; IBF—Michael Carbajal, United States, 1990.
Strawweight: WBC—Ricardo Lopez, Mexico, 1990; WBA—Bong-jun-Kim, South Korea, 1989; IBF—Far-Lan Lookmingkwan, Thailand, 1990.

* As of Dec. 31, 1990; date indicates year title was won.

Other Divisions. There were outstanding battlers in the lighter divisions, too. Among them was Pernell Whitaker, who unified the lightweight division for the first time since 1978 when he knocked out Juan Nazario in the first round at Lake Tahoe, NV, in August to add the WBA crown to WBC and IBF titles he already held. He won the Edward J. Neil award as fighter of the year, given by the Boxing Writers of America. In May, Whitaker had scored a 12-round decision over Azumah Nelson of Ghana, the WBC junior lightweight champion, who was trying to move up in weight and win a title in a third different class.

Julio César Chávez, the junior welterweight champion of the WBC and the IBF, who popularly is considered this generation's best fighter "pound for pound," defended his WBC crown and added the IBF title in March by knocking out Meldrick Taylor in the last two seconds of a rugged and controversial 12-round bout in Las Vegas. Taylor led on points for 11 rounds, but with 35 seconds left in the fight, Chávez landed three big right-hand punches, followed by a left hook that sent Taylor down. It preserved Chávez' unbeaten record at 69–0, the longest in more than 75 years.

GEORGE DE GREGORIO, *"The New York Times"*

Football

For the National Football League (NFL), the 1990–91 season represented something very much expected and something very much new. The expected was the performance of the San Francisco 49ers, the two-time defending Super Bowl champions who compiled the best regular-season record in the league (14-2). The new was a revised play-off system, in which a wild-card team was added in each conference. That meant six wild-card teams in all and a full-fledged first round, which also included two division winners with the worst records. The season also saw two perennial powerhouses, the Denver Broncos and Cleveland Browns, collapse. The two teams had played for the American Football Conference title the year before; in 1990–91, neither came close to making the play-offs.

Super Bowl XXV was played before 78,813 fans in Tampa Stadium on Jan. 27, 1991. In a game that truly was superior, the New York Giants, who had deprived the 49ers of another Super Bowl appearance, defeated the Buffalo Bills, 20-19. A missed field goal by Buffalo's Scott Norwood in the final seconds allowed the Giants to clinch their second championship in five years. Giants running back Otis Anderson, who rushed for 102 yards and scored a touchdown, was the game's most valuable player.

In college competition, Colorado and Georgia Tech shared the mythical national title after both schools won their New Year's Day bowl games. Brigham Young quarterback Ty Detmer, who rewrote the National Collegiate Athletic Association (NCAA) record book, was selected Heisman Trophy winner as the nation's top college player.

In the Canadian Football League, two interceptions by linebacker Greg Battle helped the Winnipeg Blue Bombers to a 50-11 victory over the Edmonton Eskimos in the 78th Grey Cup.

The Professional Season

A new $3.6 billion television contract called for some changes in the 1990–91 National Football League (NFL) season. For the first time the schedule was extended to 17 weeks, with each team in the league receiving a week off sometime during the season. There also were more commercials during games and one more wild-card team in each conference was added to the play-offs, creating a four-game first round. The biggest question entering the season concerned the San Francisco 49ers. Could they win a third straight Super Bowl, making them the first team in history to accomplish that feat?

Regular Season. The 49ers gave no indication of a letdown during their regular-season schedule. They finished with a 14-2 record, best in the league, and won the National Foot-

AP/Wide World

With seconds remaining, Matt Bahr kicks the winning field goal as the New York Giants defeat the San Francisco 49ers, 15-13, for the National Football Conference title.

ball Conference (NFC) Western Division title. Their star player once again was Joe Montana, who was chosen by some organizations as the league's player of the year. Other groups selected Philadelphia quarterback Randall Cunningham, who had a spectacular season both as a runner and passer, making him the most versatile quarterback in the league. In fact, Cunningham beat out Montana for the Bert Bell Award as the league's player of the year, selected by the vote of NFL coaches, football writers, and fans. However, Cunningham's Eagles lost in the first round of the NFC's play-offs to the Washington Redskins, who featured top running back Earnest Byner.

The New York Giants, who lost to the 49ers in a Monday-night clash in early December, suffered a bad blow when starting quarterback Phil Simms hurt his foot in mid-December and missed the play-offs. However, Jeff Hostetler did an excellent job as Simms' backup and led the Giants to the Super Bowl. The Chicago Bears, who won the NFC Central Division crown, also lost their starting quarterback, Jim Harbaugh, for the play-offs. He suffered a dislocated shoulder. The New Orleans Saints were the sixth NFC team to make the play-offs.

The Buffalo Bills, who finished with a so-so 9-7 record in 1989, rebounded with a fine 13-3 mark to become the dominant team in the American Football Conference (AFC). The Bills took the AFC Eastern Division title as quarterback Jim Kelly led the league in passing efficiency and enjoyed the best season of his six-year NFL career. The Los Angeles Raiders, one of the most successful NFL teams in

PROFESSIONAL FOOTBALL

National Football League

Final Standings

AMERICAN CONFERENCE

Eastern Division	W	L	T	Pct.	Points For	Against
Buffalo	13	3	0	.813	428	263
Miami	12	4	0	.750	336	242
Indianapolis	7	9	0	.438	281	353
N.Y. Jets	6	10	0	.375	295	345
New England	1	15	0	.063	181	446
Central Division						
Cincinnati	9	7	0	.563	360	352
Houston	9	7	0	.563	405	307
Pittsburgh	9	7	0	.563	292	240
Cleveland	3	13	0	.188	228	462
Western Division						
L.A. Raiders	12	4	0	.750	337	268
Kansas City	11	5	0	.688	369	257
Seattle	9	7	0	.563	306	286
San Diego	6	10	0	.375	315	281
Denver	5	11	0	.313	331	374

PLAY-OFFS
Cincinnati 41, Houston 14
Miami 17, Kansas City 16
Los Angeles Raiders 20, Cincinnati 10
Buffalo 44, Miami 34
Buffalo 51, Los Angeles 3

NATIONAL CONFERENCE

Eastern Division	W	L	T	Pct.	Points For	Against
N.Y. Giants	13	3	0	.813	335	211
Philadelphia	10	6	0	.625	396	299
Washington	10	6	0	.625	381	301
Dallas	7	9	0	.438	244	308
Phoenix	5	11	0	.313	258	396
Central Division						
Chicago	11	5	0	.688	348	280
Tampa Bay	6	10	0	.375	264	367
Green Bay	6	10	0	.375	271	347
Detroit	6	10	0	.375	373	413
Minnesota	6	10	0	.375	351	326
Western Division						
San Francisco	14	2	0	.875	353	239
New Orleans	8	8	0	.500	274	275
L.A. Rams	5	11	0	.313	345	412
Atlanta	5	11	0	.313	348	365

PLAY-OFFS
Washington 20, Philadelphia 6
Chicago 16, New Orleans 6
New York 31, Chicago 3
San Francisco 28, Washington 10
New York 15, San Francisco 13

SUPER BOWL XXV: New York 20, Buffalo 19

the late 1970s and early 1980s, had not made the play-offs since 1985–86 before qualifying in 1990 by winning the AFC Western Division with a 12-4 record.

The AFC's Central Division championship went to the Cincinnati Bengals, who won it on the last day of the regular season when Houston beat Pittsburgh to create a three-way tie for first. The Oilers made the play-offs as a wild-card team even though quarterback Warren Moon, who enjoyed one of the greatest seasons in league history, was hurt and could not play in the play-offs. Moon led the NFL with 4,689 passing yards. In a game against Kansas City, he threw for the second-most yards in a game

in league history. The other AFC play-off wild-card teams were the Miami Dolphins and the Kansas City Chiefs.

The most disappointing teams were the Cleveland Browns and the Denver Broncos, who had met in the AFC title game the previous season. Cleveland finished with a 3-13 mark, worst in its history, while Denver fell to 5-11. Minnesota, thought to be a play-off contender in the NFC, limped to a 6-10 record. Dallas, which only won one game in 1989, almost made the play-offs, finishing at 7-9.

Individual Performances. Barry Sanders of Detroit won the league's rushing title on the last weekend of the season, finishing with 1,304 yards and nosing out Buffalo's Thurman Thomas, who gained 1,297 yards. San Francisco's Jerry Rice had the best season of an already fine career by pulling in 100 passes for 1,502 yards. Both marks were the best in the NFL. Although Montana was not the highest-rated passer, he still threw for the most yards in his career (3,944). Mike Horan of Denver was the best punter (44.4-yard average), while Nick Lowery of Kansas City led in scoring with 139 points. The best defensive player was Buffalo end Bruce Smith, who had 19½ sacks and was considered by some to be the league's most valuable player. Other standout defensive players included Reggie White of Philadelphia and linebacker Derrick Thomas of Kansas City.

Among coaches fired were Buddy Ryan of Philadelphia, Ray Perkins of Tampa, and Rod Rust of New England. Washington's Dexter Manley, who had been suspended for drug violations, was reinstated and then traded to Phoenix. Inducted into the Pro Football Hall of Fame were Pittsburgh's Jack Lambert and Franco Harris, San Francisco's Bob St. Clair, Dallas' Tom Landry, Ted Hendricks of Baltimore and the Los Angeles Raiders, Miami's Bob Griese, and Kansas City's Buch Buchanan.

Play-offs. In the opening round of the play-offs, Washington registered the biggest upset by defeating the Eagles in Philadelphia, 20-6, behind the sharp play of quarterback Mark Rypien. In the other NFC game, Chicago held off New Orleans, 16-6. In the AFC, Miami quarterback Dan Marino rallied his team for two fourth-quarter touchdowns and a 17-16 win over Kansas City, while Cincinnati overwhelmed Houston, 41-14, after jumping to a 20-0 halftime lead.

In the second round of the play-offs, Buffalo's Kelly, coming off a serious knee injury, threw for 339 yards as Buffalo beat Miami, 44-34. It was the second-highest-scoring play-off game in league history. The Raiders were too physical for Cincinnati and won the other AFC game, 20-10. Marcus Allen rushed for 140 yards. San Francisco jumped to a 21-10 halftime lead and came away with a 28-10 victory over Washington, which suffered from three interceptions in the second half, two inside the 49er 20-yard line. The Giants easily advanced to the NFC final as backup quarterback Hostetler directed them to a 31-3 romp over the Bears, who were playing with backup quarterback Mike Tomczak.

In the NFC title game, the Giants upset defending champions San Francisco, 15-13, when Matt Bahr kicked a 42-yard field goal on the last play of the game. New York was given the opportunity to score after 49er running back Roger Craig fumbled at the Giant 43 with less than three minutes remaining. The winning field goal was Bahr's fifth of the game. Earlier in the last period, defensive tackle Leonard Marshall smashed Montana from behind and the San Francisco quarterback suffered a broken bone in his right hand.

In the AFC championship contest, Buffalo's high-powered offense overwhelmed the Raiders, 51-3. Buffalo scored 41 points in the first half to set a play-off record. Los Angeles threw six interceptions and was unable to stop the Bills' no-huddle, hurry-up offense, which gained 502 yards.

The College Season

In what wound up being one of the most confusing and controversial seasons in history,

Brigham Young's quarterback Ty Detmer outpolled Notre Dame's Raghib Ismail for the Heisman Trophy. The 23-year-old junior set a NCAA season passing record of 5,188 yards.

© Mike Powell/Allsport

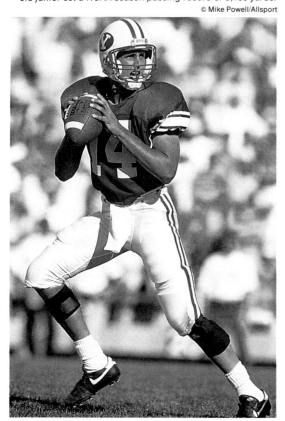

COLLEGE FOOTBALL

Conference Champions	Atlantic Coast—Georgia Tech Big Eight—Colorado Big Ten—(tie) Illinois, Iowa, Michigan, Michigan State Big West—San Jose State Ivy League—(tie) Cornell, Dartmouth Mid-American—Central Michigan Pacific Ten—Washington Southeastern—Tennessee Southwest—Texas Western Athletic—Brigham Young
NCAA Champions	Division I-AA—Georgia Southern Division II—North Dakota State Division III—Allegheny (PA)
NAIA Champions	Division I—Central State (OH) Division II—Peru State (NE)
Individual Honors	Heisman Trophy—Ty Detmer, Brigham Young Lombardi Award—Chris Zorich, Notre Dame Outland Trophy—Russell Maryland, Miami

Major Bowl Games

All-American Bowl (Birmingham, AL, Dec. 28)—North Carolina State 31, Southern Mississippi 27
Aloha Bowl (Honolulu, HI, Dec. 25)—Syracuse 28, Arizona 0
Blockbuster Bowl (Miami, FL, Dec. 28)—Florida State 24, Penn State 17
California Bowl (Fresno, CA, Dec. 8)—San Jose 48, Central Michigan 24
Copper Bowl (Tucson, AZ, Dec. 31)—California 17, Wyoming 15
Cotton Bowl (Dallas, Jan. 1)—Miami 46, Texas 3
Fiesta Bowl (Tempe, AZ, Jan. 1)—Louisville 34, Alabama 7
Freedom Bowl (Anaheim, CA, Dec. 29)—Colorado State 32, Oregon 31
Gator Bowl (Jacksonville, FL, Jan. 1)—Michigan 35, Mississippi 3
Hall of Fame Bowl (Tampa, FL, Jan. 1)—Clemson 30, Illinois 0
John Hancock Bowl (El Paso, TX, Dec. 31)—Michigan State 17, Southern California 16
Holiday Bowl (San Diego, CA, Dec. 29)—Texas A&M 65, Brigham Young 14
Hula Bowl (Honolulu, HI, Jan. 19)—East 23, West 10
Independence Bowl (Shreveport, LA, Dec. 15)—Maryland 34, Louisiana Tech 34
Liberty Bowl (Memphis, TN, Dec. 27)—Air Force 23, Ohio State 11
Orange Bowl (Miami, FL, Jan. 1)—Colorado 10, Notre Dame 9
Peach Bowl (Atlanta, GA, Dec. 29)—Auburn 27, Indiana 23
Rose Bowl (Pasadena, CA, Jan. 1)—Washington 46, Iowa 34
Sugar Bowl (New Orleans, LA, Jan. 1)—Tennessee 23, Virginia 22

any number of schools laid claim to the Number 1 spot in the polls during the regular schedule, including Notre Dame, Virginia, and Miami. Clearly, no team dominated, which became even more obvious with the results of the final ranking polls following the annual bowl games. In the Associated Press poll, where voting is done by broadcasters and sportswriters, the University of Colorado Buffaloes team was picked first. In the United Press International poll, where voting is done by a panel of coaches, Georgia Tech was selected first. Not since the 1978 season had two teams shared the national title.

Colorado (10-1-1) entered its Orange Bowl game against Notre Dame rated Number 1 in both polls. The Buffs had a similar ranking the previous year but had lost to Notre Dame in the same Orange Bowl to lose the national title. This time around, Colorado won the rematch, 10-9, but was not very convincing in doing so. Colorado trailed, 6-3, at halftime while also losing starting quarterback Darian Hagan with a knee injury. But his replacement, Charles Johnson, led the team to a third-quarter touchdown to give Colorado its winning margin. Notre Dame, however, almost pulled out the victory. With less than a minute to go, Colorado punted to Raghib (Rocket) Ismail, the most dangerous kick-return man in the college ranks. Ismail brought back the punt 91 yards for a touchdown, but the score was nullified by a clipping penalty. The Irish twice had been ranked Number 1 during the regular season but each time fell out of the top spot by losing, first to Stanford, then to Penn State.

Georgia Tech (11-0-1), the only undefeated team left, was ranked second entering the Citrus Bowl against Nebraska. There had been questions about the strength of Georgia Tech's schedule, but the Yellow Jackets proved a quality team by thrashing Nebraska, 45-21. Quarterback Shawn Jones passed for 277 yards and ran for another 41 to set a Citrus Bowl record with 318 total yards. He also passed for two touchdowns and ran for another. It was an impressive enough performance to help his team edge past Colorado in the UPI rankings.

Miami, which was ranked Number 4, took on Number 3 Texas in the Cotton Bowl. Texas had been one of the hottest teams in the nation but Miami was far superior, crushing the Longhorns, 46-3, despite a record 202 yards in penalties. Miami quarterback Craig Erickson passed for 272 yards and four touchdowns as the Hurricanes gained 339 total yards and held Texas, the Southwest Conference champion, to only 205. Miami had hoped that somehow a bowl win could earn it the Number 1 ranking but instead the Hurricanes had to settle for Number 3 in both polls. They also had been atop the regular-season poll but had lost to Notre Dame.

Tennessee rallied from a 16-point deficit to beat Virginia, 23-22, in the Sugar Bowl. It was a particularly heartbreaking loss for Virginia, which once had been ranked first but then lost four games at the end of the season to ruin what had been the greatest year in the school's history. In the Rose Bowl, Washington streaked to a 33-7 halftime lead over Iowa, then had to hold on against a strong Iowa rally. The Huskies finally won, 46-34.

Quarterback Ty Detmer of Brigham Young won the Heisman Trophy balloting, beating out Raghib Ismail of Notre Dame. Detmer, a junior, set or tied 34 college records during the season, including 5,188 passing yards. He will enter his senior year only 425 yards behind the all-time passing leader, Todd Santos of San Diego State. Detmer dislocated both shoulders in the postseason Holiday Bowl against Texas A&M. Ismail, also a junior, was the most dangerous all-purpose runner in the nation. In both of his team's regular-season losses, he was unable to play in the second half because of injuries. Third in the voting was Colorado running back Eric Bieniemy, who gained 1,628 rushing yards during the season.

The Outland Trophy, awarded to the top interior lineman, was won by Russell Maryland

of Miami. The Lombardi Award, for the top lineman or linebacker, went to Chris Zorich of Notre Dame, while Colorado's Alfred Williams was given the Butkus Award as the outstanding linebacker.

In NCAA Division I-AA competition, Georgia Southern overwhelmed Nevada-Reno, 36-13, to take the championship. Southern finished the year with a 12-3 record. In Division II, North Dakota completed an undefeated season by trouncing Indiana (PA), 51-11. In Division III, Allegheny edged out Lycoming, 21-14. Allegheny had a 13-0-1 record.

PAUL ATTNER
"The Sporting News"

Golf

Britain's Nick Faldo (*see* BIOGRAPHY) won two major championships and PGA player of the year honors. Australia's Greg Norman won the PGA tour money title. Beth Daniel dominated the LPGA and Lee Trevino devastated the Senior PGA tour. But the biggest story in U.S. golf in 1990 was Hale Irwin.

At the age of 45 and winless for five years, Irwin came from behind on the final day of the U.S. Open to tie Mike Donald, then came from behind again the next day to win his third Open championship in a 19-hole play-off. He became the oldest man to win the world's premier title. The next week he won again, at the Buick Classic in Westchester, NY, and went on to finish sixth on the money list with $838,249, the best year of his career.

Faldo won his second consecutive Masters title and his second British Open championship in four years with a walkaway at St. Andrews. That earned him the PGA's player of the year honors (he was the first non-American to win it), and the *Golf Digest* world player of the year award. Wayne Grady won the PGA Championship, the year's fourth major.

Norman, although he played in only 17 events on the U.S. Tour, won twice and earned $1,165,477 to top the money list. He also won the Vardon Trophy for lowest scoring average (69.10) and the *Golf Digest* performance award, both for the second time in a row.

Wayne Levi was the only man to win more than two tournaments on the PGA Tour. He won four times and earned $1,024,647 to finish second on the money list.

Robert Gamez, who won twice early in the year, was the rookie of the year, and Steve Elkington was named most improved professional by *Golf Digest*.

Trevino won seven times in his first season as a senior and amassed a record $1,190,518, which is more than Norman won on the regular PGA tour. Among his victories was the U.S. Senior Open in a duel with Jack Nicklaus, also a senior rookie. Nicklaus played in only four events, but he won two of them, including the Mazda Tournament Players Championship. Mike Hill won five tournaments and George Archer and Jim Dent each won four times on the Senior Tour.

LPGA Tour. Daniel won seven times on the LPGA Tour, including the LPGA Championship, her first major. She won the Vare Trophy for lowest scoring average (70.54) and the money title with $863,578. Her performance overshadowed a marvelous year by Patty Sheehan, who won five tournaments and finished

second five times in winning $732,618. Sheehan won the *Golf Digest* performance award, even though she lost the U.S. Open in the final round to Betsy King, who also won the Dinah Shore, another major, and was third on the money list.

Cathy Gerring, a three-time winner and Number 4 in winnings, was named most improved by *Golf Digest*, which also selected Japan's Hiromi Kobayashi as rookie of the year.

Amateurs. Left-hander Phil Mickelson won the U.S. men's Amateur and the individual NCAA title, was low amateur in the U.S.

GOLF

1990 PGA Tour

MONY Tournament of Champions: Paul Azinger (272)
Northern Telecom Tucson Open: Robert Gamez (270)
Bob Hope Chrysler Classic: Peter Jacobsen (339)
Phoenix Open: Tommy Armour III (267)
AT&T Pebble Beach National Pro-Am: Mark O'Meara (281)
Hawaiian Open: David Ishii (279)
Shearson Lehman Hutton Open: Dan Forsman (275)
Nissan Los Angeles Open: Fred Couples (266)
Doral Ryder Open: Greg Norman (273)
Honda Classic: John Huston (282)
The Players Championship: Jodie Mudd (278)
The Nestle Invitational: Robert Gamez (274)
Independent Insurance Agent Open: Tony Sills (204)
The Masters: Nick Faldo (278)
Deposit Guaranty Golf Classic: Gene Sauers (268)
MCI Heritage Classic: Payne Stewart (276)
K Mart Greater Greensboro Open: Steve Elkington (282)
USF&G Classic: David Frost (276)
GTE Byron Nelson Golf Classic: Payne Stewart (202)
Memorial Tournament: Greg Norman (216)
Southwestern Bell Colonial: Ben Crenshaw (272)
Bellsouth Atlanta Classic: Wayne Levi (275)
Kemper Open: Gil Morgan (274)
Centel Western Open: Wayne Levi (275)
U.S. Open: Hale Irwin (280)
Buick Classic: Hale Irwin (269)
Canon Greater Hartford Open: Wayne Levi (267)
Anheuser-Busch Golf Classic: Lanny Wadkins (266)
Bank of Boston Classic: Morris Hatalsky (266)
Buick Open: Chip Beck (272)
Federal Express St. Jude Classic: Tom Kite (269)
PGA Championship: Wayne Grady (282)
The International: Davis Love III (+14)
NEC World Series of Golf: Jose Maria Olazábal (262)
Chattanooga Classic: Peter Persons (260)
Greater Milwaukee Open: Jim Gallagher, Jr. (271)
Hardee's Golf Classic: Joey Sindelar (268)
Canadian Open: Wayne Levi (278)
B.C. Open: Nolan Henke (268)
Buick Southern Open: Kenny Knox (265)
H.E.B. Texas Open: Mark O'Meara (261)
Las Vegas Invitational: Bob Tway (334)
Walt Disney World/Oldsmobile Classic: Tim Simpson (264)
Nabisco Championships: Jodie Mudd (273)
Asahi Glass Four Tours WCOG: Australia/New Zealand
Isuzu Kapalua International: David Peoples (264)
RMCC Invitational: Fred Couples/Ray Floyd (182)
Skins Game: Curtis Strange
JC Penney Classic: Davis Love III/Beth Daniel (266)
Team Championship: Fred Couples/Mike Donald (254)

LPGA

The Jamaica Classic: Patty Sheehan (212)
Oldsmobile LPGA Classic: Pat Bradley (281)
Phar-Mor Inverrary Classic: Jane Crafter (209)
Orix Hawaiian Ladies Open: Beth Daniel (210)
Women's Kemper Open: Beth Daniel (283)
Desert Inn LPGA International: Maggie Will (214)
Circle K LPGA Tucson Open: Colleen Walker (276)
Standard Register Turquoise Classic: Pat Bradley (280)
Nabisco Dinah Shore: Betsy King (283)
Red Robin Kyocera Inamori Classic: Kris Monaghan (276)
Sara Lee Classic: Ayako Okamoto (210)
Crestar Classic: Dottie Mochrie (200)
Planters Pat Bradley International: Cindy Rarick (25 pts.)
LPGA Corning Classic: Pat Bradley (274)
JC Penney LPGA Skins Game: Jan Stephenson (6 skins)
Lady Keystone Open: Cathy Gerring (208)
McDonald's Championship: Patty Sheehan (275)
Atlantic City LPGA Classic: Chris Johnson (275)
Rochester International: Patty Sheehan (271)
du Maurier Ltd. Classic: Cathy Johnston (276)
Jamie Farr Toledo Classic: Tina Purtzer (205)
U.S. Women's Open: Betsy King (284)
The Phar-Mor in Youngstown Classic: Beth Daniel (207)
Mazda LPGA Championship: Beth Daniel (280)
Boston Five Classic: Barb Mucha (277)

Stratton Mountain LPGA Classic: Cathy Gerring (281)
The JAL Big Apple Classic: Betsy King (273)
Northgate LPGA Classic: Beth Daniel (203)
Rail Charity Golf Classic: Beth Daniel (203)
Ping-Cellular One LPGA Golf Championship: Patty Sheehan (208)
Safeco Classic: Patty Sheehan (270)
MBS LPGA Classic: Nancy Lopez (281)
Centel Classic: Beth Daniel (271)
Trophee Urban World Championship: Cathy Gerring (278)
Nichirei International: LPGA tour (22.50 pts.)
Mazda Japan Classic: Debbie Massey (133)

Senior PGA Tour

MONY Senior Tournament of Champions: George Archer (283)
Senior Skins Game: Arnold Palmer
Royal Caribbean Classic: Lee Trevino (206)
GTE Suncoast Classic: Mike Hill (207)
Aetna Challenge: Lee Trevino (200)
Chrysler Cup: United States
Vintage Chrysler Invitational: Lee Trevino (205)
Vantage at the Dominion: Jim Dent (205)
Fuji Electric Grand Slam: Bob Charles (214)
The Tradition at Desert Mountain: Jack Nicklaus (206)
PGA Seniors Championship: Gary Player (281)
Liberty Mutual Legends of Golf: Charles Coody/Dale Douglass (249)
Murata Reunion Pro-Am: Frank Beard (207)
Las Vegas Senior Classic: Chi Chi Rodriguez (204)
Southwestern Bell Classic: Jimmy Powell (208)
Doug Sanders Kingwood Celebrity Classic: Lee Trevino (203)
Bell Atlantic Classic: Dale Douglass (206)
The NYNEX Commemorative: Lee Trevino (199)
Mazda Senior TPC: Jack Nicklaus (261)
MONY Syracuse Senior Classic: Jim Dent (199)
Digital Seniors Classic: Bob Charles (203)
USGA Senior Open: Lee Trevino (267)
Northville Long Island Classic: George Archer (208)
Kroger Senior Classic: Jim Dent (133)
Ameritech Senior Open: Chi Chi Rodriguez (203)
Newport Cup: Al Kelley (134)
PaineWebber Invitational: Bruce Crampton (205)
Sunwest Bank/Charley Pride Senior Golf Classic: Chi Chi Rodriguez (205)
Showdown Classic: Rives McBee (202)
GTE Northwest Classic: George Archer (205)
GTE North Classic: Mike Hill (201)
Vantage Bank One Classic: Rives McBee (201)
Greater Grand Rapids Open: Don Massengale (134)
Crestar Classic: Jim Dent (202)
Fairfield Barnett Space Coast Classic: Mike Hill (200)
Vantage Championship: Charles Coody (202)
Gatlin Brothers Southwest Golf Classic: Bruce Crampton (204)
Transamerica Senior Golf Championship: Lee Trevino (205)
Gold Rush at Rancho Murieta: George Archer (204)
Security Pacific Senior Classic: Mike Hill (201)
Dupont Cup Japan v. USA Senior Golf Matches: U.S.A. Senior PGA Tour (20–12)
GTE Kaanapali Classic: Bob Charles (206)
The New York Life Champions: Mike Hill (201)

Other Tournaments

British Open: Nick Faldo (270)
World Match Play: Ian Woosnam
World Cup: Individual—Payne Stewart; Team—Germany
Solheim Cup: U.S. 11½; Europe 4½
U.S. Men's Amateur: Phil Mickelson
U.S. Women's Amateur: Pat Hurst
U.S. Men's Public Links: Michael Combs
U.S. Women's Public Links: Cathy Mockett
U.S. Mid-Amateur: Jim Stuart
U.S. Women's Mid-Amateur: Carol S. Thompson
U.S. Senior Men's Amateur: Jackie Cummings
U.S. Senior Women's Amateur: Anne Sander
U.S. Junior Boys: Mathew Todd
U.S. Junior Girls: Sandrine Mendiburu
Curtis Cup: U.S. 14, Great Britain 4
NCAA Men: Individual—Phil Mickelson; Team—Arizona State
NCAA Women: Individual—Susan Slaughter; Team—Arizona State

Open, and was named the nation's top male amateur by *Golf Digest*. Pat Hurst took the ladies' Amateur title.

LARRY DENNIS, *Creative Communications*

Horse Racing

The "sport of kings" endured a star-crossed year marked by the tragic deaths of three horses in the Breeders' Cup races Oct. 27, 1990, at Belmont Park in Elmont, NY, and the humane destruction of Alydar, Calumet Farm's 15-year-old chestnut famed for losing each of the 1978 Triple Crown races to Affirmed in classic stretch drives.

The Breeders' Cup. The 1990 Breeders' Cup, which was started in 1983 to showcase racing's best thoroughbreds on national television, instead displayed the dark side of the sport. Go for Wand broke her right foreleg dueling with Bayakoa in the $1 million Distaff, the third of the seven Cup races, and was given a lethal injection near the 16th pole. Go for Wand had won ten of her 13 races and the Argentine-bred won seven of nine starts during the year.

Earlier in the day, Mr. Nickerson died, apparently of a heart attack, during the Sprint and his jockey, Chris Antley, suffered a broken collarbone. Another horse, Shaker Knot, suffered injuries that necessitated his being destroyed humanely.

Alydar and Other Races. Alydar, one of racing's most preeminent sires, broke his right hind leg in a stall accident in Lexington, KY, November 13. Two days later, after Alydar had undergone surgery and rebroken the leg, the horse was put down. Besides winning 14 of 26 races, Alydar sired 30 graded stakes winners, including Alysheba and Easy Goer.

Unbridled won the $3 million Breeders' Cup Classic and the Kentucky Derby. Unbridled won the Classic by a length over English invader Ibn Bey and became the fourth Kentucky Derby champion also to win the Classic. Unbridled finished second to Summer Squall in the Preakness Stakes and Go and Go won the Belmont Stakes, the third leg of the Triple Crown. Sunday Silence was voted 1989 Horse of the Year after earning a one-year record of $4,578,454.

Harness Racing. Harmonious captured the 65th Hambletonian at East Rutherford, NJ, and Beach Towel won both the Little Brown Jug at Delaware, OH, and the Meadowlands Pace at East Rutherford, NJ. Beach Towel also won the three-year-old Colt Pace in the Breeders Crown races at Pompano Beach, FL, and became the first harness horse to win more than $2 million in one season. Peace Corps won the Breeders Crown Mare Trot by six lengths. She had raced in Europe since winning the Breeders Crown 3-year-old Filly Trot in 1989. Bay's Fellow won the Horse and Gelding Pace and returned $140.60, the largest payoff in the seven-year history of the Breeders Crown.

An administrative law judge declared Park Avenue Joe and Probe cowinners of the 1989 Hambletonian more than five months after the August 5 race. Track stewards had declared Park Avenue Joe the winner.

STAN SUTTON

HORSE RACING

Major U.S. Thoroughbred Races

Alabama Stakes: Go For Wand, $217,600 (total purse)
Arlington Million: Golden Pheasant, $1 million
Belmont Stakes: Go and Go, $686,000
Breeders' Cup Classic: Unbridled, $3 million
Breeders' Cup Distaff: Bayakoa, $1 million
Breeders' Cup Juvenile: Fly So Free, $1 million
Breeders' Cup Juvenile Fillies: Meadow Star, $1 million
Breeders' Cup Mile: Royal Academy, $1 million
Breeders' Cup Sprint: Safely Kept, $1 million
Breeders' Cup Turf: In The Wings, $2 million
Florida Derby: Unbridled, $500,000
Haskell Invitational Handicap: Restless Con, $500,000
Hollywood Gold Cup: Criminal Type, $1 million
Hollywood Invitational: Steinlen, $500,000
International: Fly Till Dawn, $750,000
Iselin Handicap: Beau Genius, $250,000
Jim Beam Stakes: Summer Squall, $500,000
Jockey Club Gold Cup: Flying Continental, $838,500
Kentucky Derby: Unbridled, $756,000
Kentucky Oaks: Seaside Attraction, $241,400
Man o' War Stakes: Defensive Play, $473,600
Metropolitan Handicap: Criminal Type, $597,000
Mother Goose: Go For Wand, $227,600
Pimlico Special: Criminal Type, $1 million
Preakness Stakes: Summer Squall, $686,000
Rothmans International: French Glory, $1,032,750
Ruffian Handicap: Quick Mischief, $240,800
Santa Anita Derby: Mr. Frisky, $500,000
Santa Anita Handicap: Ruhlmann, $1 million
Spinster Stakes: Bayakoa, $268,625
Strub Stakes: Flying Continental, $500,000
Suburban Handicap: Easy Goer, $399,000
Super Derby: Home at Last, $1 million
Travers Stakes: Rhythm, $1,178,500

Withers Stakes: Housebuster, $118,400
Wood Memorial: Thirty Six Red, $604,000
Whitney Handicap: Criminal Type, $234,400
Woodward Handicap: Dispersal, $590,000

Major North American Harness Races

Breeders Crown Mare Trot: Peace Corps, $203,458
Breeders Crown 3-year-old Colt Pace: Beach Towel, $366,933
Breeders Crown Horse and Gelding Pace: Bay's Fellow, $278,458
Breeders Crown Horse and Gelding Trot: No Sex Please, $221,458
Breeders Crown 3-year-old Colt and Gelding Trot: Embassy Lobell, $396,933
Breeders Crown 3-year-old Filly Trot: Me Maggie, $378,933
Breeders Crown Mare Pace: Caesars Jackpot, $200,000
Breeders Crown 3-year-old Filly Pace: Town Pro, $304,933
Breeders Crown 2-year-old Colt Pace: Artsplace, $605,870
Breeders Crown 2-year-old Filly Pace: Miss Easy, $514,870
Breeders Crown 2-year-old Colt Trot: Crysta's Best, $355,403
Breeders Crown 2-year-old Filly Trot: Jean Bi, $367,403
Cane Pace: Jake and Elwood, $486,550
Hambletonian: Harmonious, $1,346,000
Hambletonian Oaks: Working Gal, $441,555
Kentucky Futurity: Star Mystic, $180,000
Kentucky Pacing Derby: Tooter Scooter, $479,553
Little Brown Jug: Beach Towel, $468,610
Meadowlands Pace: Beach Towel, $1,153,500
Merrie Annabelle: Santa Royal, $464,750
Messenger Stake: Jake and Elwood, $444,371
Peter Haughton Memorial: Charlie Ten Hitch, $609,250
Sweetheart Pace: Miss Easy, $766,000
Woodrow Wilson Pace: Die Laughing, $1,043,500
World Trotting Derby: Harmonious, $600,000

Ice Hockey

The Edmonton Oilers capped a dream season in May 1990 by winning their first Stanley Cup without Wayne Gretzky. The Oilers whipped the Boston Bruins, who had won the regular-season point title with 101, in the playoff finals, winning four games to one. It was the Oilers' fifth National Hockey League (NHL) championship in seven years. The first four were spearheaded by Gretzky, who now was playing for the Los Angeles Kings. The Oilers, who had lost to Gretzky and company in the first round of postseason play in 1989, were within one game of being eliminated again in 1990. This time the Winnipeg Jets had the Oilers down, three games to one, in the best-of-seven opening-round series, only to falter.

Regular Season. The Bruins edged the 1989 Stanley Cup-champion Calgary Flames for the overall points championship, 101–99. Buffalo was third with 98 points. The Oilers rebounded from an 84-point season in 1989 to finish fifth with 90. The Bruins were the stingiest defensive team, giving up just 232 goals to win the Adams Division. The New York Rangers won their first Patrick Division title, while Chicago and Calgary took the Norris and Smythe divisions, respectively. The Flames had the number-one offense (348 goals).

Wayne Gretzky won his eighth Ross (scoring) Trophy with 142 points after a two-year absence. Oiler center Mark Messier, who was awarded his first Hart Trophy as the NHL's most valuable player, was second with 129. Detroit's Steve Yzerman was third with 127. Pittsburgh's center Mario Lemieux, who won the scoring crown in 1988 and 1989, was felled by a disc problem in his back and missed all but one game in the final seven weeks. Lemieux had a 46-game point streak, the second-longest in history before it ended on Valentine's Day —his last game until March 31. He finished with 123 points in 59 games.

In all, 13 players had at least 100 points. St. Louis winger Brett Hull became the sixth player to surpass 70 goals, leading the way with 72. He joined Gretzky, Lemieux, Jari Kurri, Phil Esposito, and Bernie Nicholls at that figure. Only eight players had 50 or more goals. Gretzky surpassed Gordie Howe as the all-time point leader on Oct. 15, 1989, with his 1,851st point. Ironically, the record-breaking point came against Edmonton.

Play-offs. Calgary's reign as NHL champions ended in the sixth game in the first round when Mike Krushelnyski scored in overtime to give the Kings a series win. The Kings had been 24 points behind Calgary in league play. The Oilers rallied to beat the Jets, four games to three, to stay alive, then crushed Los Angeles four straight in the Smythe Division final. In the Norris Division, Chicago outlasted Minnesota in seven games and St. Louis whipped

Toronto in five games. Chicago again went seven to squeeze past the Blues to advance to the final four.

In the Adams Division, Boston got a huge scare from Hartford but took the series, four games to three. The Canadiens, who lost to Calgary in the 1989 Stanley Cup final, got past Buffalo in six games. But they were whipped, four games to one, by Boston for the division title. In the Patrick Division, the Rangers got

ICE HOCKEY

National Hockey League
(Final Standings, 1989–90)

Wales Conference

Patrick Division	W	L	T	Pts.	Goals For	Goals Against
*N.Y. Rangers	36	31	13	85	279	267
*New Jersey	37	34	9	83	295	288
*Washington	36	38	6	78	284	275
*N.Y. Islanders	31	38	11	73	281	288
Pittsburgh	32	40	8	72	318	359
Philadelphia	30	39	11	71	290	297
Adams Division						
*Boston	46	25	9	101	289	232
*Buffalo	45	27	8	98	286	248
*Montreal	41	28	11	93	288	234
*Hartford	38	33	9	85	275	268
Quebec	12	61	7	31	240	407

Campbell Conference

Norris Division	W	L	T	Pts.	Goals For	Goals Against
*Chicago	41	33	6	88	316	294
*St. Louis	37	34	9	83	295	279
*Toronto	38	38	4	80	337	358
*Minnesota	36	40	4	76	284	291
Detroit	28	38	14	70	288	323
Smythe Division						
*Calgary	42	23	15	99	348	265
*Edmonton	38	28	14	90	315	283
*Winnipeg	37	32	11	85	298	290
*Los Angeles	34	39	7	75	338	337
Vancouver	25	41	14	64	245	306

*In play-offs

Stanley Cup Play-Offs
Wales Conference

First Round	Boston	4 games	Hartford	3
	Montreal	4 games	Buffalo	2
	N.Y. Rangers	4 games	N.Y. Islanders	1
	Washington	4 games	New Jersey	2
Semifinals	Boston	4 games	Montreal	1
	Washington	4 games	N.Y. Rangers	1
Finals	Boston	4 games	Washington	0

Campbell Conference

First Round	Chicago	4 games	Minnesota	3
	Edmonton	4 games	Winnipeg	3
	Los Angeles	4 games	Calgary	2
	St. Louis	4 games	Toronto	1
Semifinals	Chicago	4 games	St. Louis	3
	Edmonton	4 games	Los Angeles	0
Finals	Edmonton	4 games	Chicago	2

Stanley Cup Finals

Edmonton		4 games	Boston	1

Individual Honors

Hart Trophy (most valuable player): Mark Messier, Edmonton
Ross Trophy (leading scorer): Wayne Gretzky, Los Angeles
Vezina Trophy (top goaltender): Patrick Roy, Montreal
Norris Trophy (best defenseman): Ray Bourque, Boston
Selke Trophy (best defensive forward): Rick Meagher, St. Louis
Calder Trophy (rookie of the year): Sergei Makarov, Calgary
Lady Byng Trophy (sportsmanship): Brett Hull, St. Louis
Conn Smythe Trophy (most valuable in play-offs): Bill Ranford, Edmonton
Adams Trophy (coach of the year): Bob Murdoch, Winnipeg
King Clancy Trophy (humanitarian service): Kevin Lowe, Edmonton

NCAA: Wisconsin

past the rival New York Islanders, four games to one, and Washington beat the New Jersey Devils, four games to two. The Caps made the NHL semifinals for the first time, beating the Rangers, four games to one.

In the conference finals, the Oilers overcame a two-to-one series deficit to win three straight and get by Chicago—the fifth time in nine years the Hawks had lost the Campbell Conference final. In the Wales Conference, Boston swept an injured Caps team, setting up a rematch of the 1988 Oilers-Bruins finals.

The first two games of the play-off finals were in Boston. Game one was the longest finals game in history. It took 115 minutes and 13 seconds before Edmonton's Petr Klima beat Bruin goalie Andy Moog in the third overtime. The game ended at 1:23 A.M. after close to six periods of play. In game two, the Oilers scored six times on their first 11 shots on Moog and replacement Reggie Lemelin. Wing Jari Kurri had three goals, with the first breaking Gretzky's play-off goal record of 89.

In Edmonton, the Bruins surprised the Oilers, winning game three, 2–1. Rookie John Byce beat Oiler goalie Bill Ranford ten seconds into the game, tying Oiler Glenn Anderson for the fastest goal from the start of a game in finals history. Anderson and Craig Simpson had two goals and two assists to lead the Oilers to a 5–1 win in game four. In the fifth game in Boston, the Oilers got Simpson's play-off-leading 16th goal to take Boston, 4–1. Ranford, who gave up just eight goals in the finals, was named the play-offs' most valuable player.

Other. Wisconsin won its fifth National Collegiate Athletic Association (NCAA) crown since 1973, defeating Colgate, 7–3. The USSR retained the world championship. At the first women's world championship in Ottawa, Canada defeated the United States, 5–2, for the crown.

JIM MATHESON, *"Edmonton Journal"*

Ice Skating

Jill Trenary, 21, of Colorado Springs, CO, captured her first world figure-skating title in Halifax, N.S. Trenary's world title came on the heels of her third U.S. national championship in Salt Lake City, where she was overpowering in the final phase with five triple jumps and her first perfect 6.0.

In Halifax, Trenary's victory over defending champion Midori Ito of Japan was achieved on the strength of her compulsory figures early in the competition when she finished first and Ito was tenth. Ito won the long and short programs, but under the factored scoring system she could rise no higher than second. After 1990, compulsory figures, which had been worth 20% of the scoring, would be eliminated from world competition. The change would

© Vandystadt/Allsport

Jill Trenary skated beautifully in the free-skating competition in Halifax, N.S., to win her first world championship. Earlier she had captured her third U.S. national title.

pave the way for more open and creative freestyle skating.

Kurt Browning of Canada became the first male skater to repeat as world champion since Scott Hamilton of the United States won a fourth title in a row in 1984. The 23-year-old Browning, from Caroline, Alta., overtook Viktor Petrenko of the USSR, who wound up second. Christopher Bowman, who was unable to defend his U.S. title and had to withdraw at Salt Lake City with muscle spasms, finished third at Halifax. Soviet skaters retained their world titles in the pairs and ice dancing. Sergei Grinkov and Ekaterina Gordeyeva took the pairs and Sergei Ponomarenko and Marina Klimova won the dance.

Joining Trenary as a U.S. champion was 18-year-old Todd Eldredge of South Chatham, MA. Eldredge held off a brilliant bid by Paul Wylie in the men's free skating, where he earned four perfect 6.0s for style. Eldredge had built a lead big enough for victory in the compulsories and the original program. Kristi Yamaguchi and Rudi Galindo successfully defended their pairs title. Joseph Druar and Susan Wynne repeated in ice dancing.

Speed Skating. Bonnie Blair of Champaign, IL, the 1988 Olympics gold medalist, scored a sweep in World Cup races in Butte, MT, in February. She won the 500-, 1,000-, and 1,500-meter events on her way to a remarkable season. At the World Sprint Championships in Tromsoe, Norway, she lost out to Angela Hauck of East Germany by a fraction of a point as Hauck took the overall crown. But in Inzell, West Germany, Blair won the 500 meters and clinched a tie with Hauck for the overall World Cup title.

In the U.S. national sprint championships in Butte, Blair took her fifth overall title in a row. Dan Jansen of West Allis, WI, won his second straight U.S. title. Nick Thometz of Seattle set a U.S. record of 37.19 seconds for the 500 meters.

GEORGE DE GREGORIO

AP/Wide World

The Iditarod

On March 14, 1990, Susan Butcher, a 35-year-old owner of a dog kennel in Eureka, AK, won her fourth Iditarod Train Sled Dog Race in five years. Her time of 11 days, 1 hour, 53 minutes, and 23 seconds was a record and earned her $50,000 in prize money plus $25,000 from one of her sponsors. The 70 mushers (dogsled drivers), who began the 1,158-mi (1 864-km) race from Anchorage to Nome on March 3, had to fight the deepest snow in some 25 years, ash from Redoubt Volcano, some unusually warm weather, buffalo on the trail, and aggressive moose. Seven teams dropped out of the race and another was disqualified.

The popular event, named for an old supply route to the gold-mining districts of interior Alaska, was inspired by a relay of diphtheria serum from Nenana to Nome during a 1925 outbreak of the disease.

Skiing

Pirmin Zurbriggen, a 27-year-old Swiss, concluded his skiing career by becoming only the second man in history to win four World Cup overall titles, equaling the record set by Gustavo Theoni of Italy (1971–73, 1975). Zurbriggen, who had taken the title in 1984, 1987, and 1988, clinched his fourth championship in early March 1990 when he finished sixth in a slalom event in Veysonnaz, Switzerland, in his final race on home ground. Armin Bittner of West Germany, who won that race, captured season honors in the slalom.

A week after he took the title, Zurbriggen added another laurel to his star-studded season. He clinched the super giant slalom World Cup title in Hemsedal, Norway, in his last super giant appearance of the season to win that discipline for the first time.

The women's overall champion was Petra Kronberger, who became the first Austrian to win the title since Annemarie Moser-Proell in 1979. The downhill World Cup crowns went to Helmut Hoeflehner of Austria among the men and to Katrin Gutensohn-Knopf of West Germany among the women. Norway's Ole Christian Furuseth and Austria's Guenther Mader tied for the men's World Cup giant slalom. Austria's Anita Wachter captured the women's World Cup giant slalom and France's Carol Merle was first in the super giant slalom.

Two star skiers who were injured seriously late in the 1989 campaign returned to the circuit. The colorful and bombastic Alberto Tomba of Italy, who won nine World Cup events in 1988 but was beaten out by Zurbriggen for the overall crown that year, finished second in the slalom competition after he had been sidelined since December 1989 with a broken collarbone. Vreni Schneider of Switzerland, who broke Ingemar Stenmark's record of World Cup victories in one season in 1989, made a comeback after knee surgery in December 1989, taking the women's slalom title with a win in the season's last race in Are, Sweden.

A rare feat in skiing was achieved at the U.S. national cross-country championships in Anchorage, AK, in January. Audun Endestad, 36, of Fairbanks, AK, became the first male to sweep all four individual events, scoring in the 10-, 15-, 30-, and 50-kilometer races.

Vermont took its second straight National Collegiate Athletic Association (NCAA) title.

GEORGE DE GREGORIO

U.S. Alpine Championships

Men's Downhill: Skip Merrick
Men's Slalom: Felix McGrath
Men's Giant Slalom: Tommy Moe
Men's Super Giant Slalom: A.J. Kitt
Men's Combined: Kyle Wieche
Women's Downhill: Lucie Laroche
Women's Slalom: Monique Pelletier
Women's Giant Slalom: Kristi Terzian
Women's Super Giant Slalom: Krista Schmidinger
Women's Combined: Julie Parisien

© Duomo

Before 73,603 fans in Rome's Olympic Stadium on July 8, Andreas Brehme right-footed a shot to the right of Argentina's goaltender Sergio Goycoechea to capture soccer's 1990 World Cup for his West German team.

Soccer

The World Cup soccer tournament, which takes place every four years, was held throughout Italy in June and July 1990. The tournament, the most widely viewed television sporting event in the world, was scheduled for the United States in 1994.

World. Climaxing a monthlong tournament marred by erratic scoring, abundant penalties, and few highlights, West Germany needed a penalty kick in the 84th minute of the championship game to beat defending champion Argentina, 1-0, and win the World Cup in Rome. West Germany, which became only the third country to win the championship three times, had been one of the favorites, along with Italy and the Netherlands, to take the Cup. But after some brilliant games early on, the Germans fell into the same lethargic, defensive pattern that hindered the competition. In the final they outshot Argentina and its heralded captain, Diego Maradona, 16-1, but could not score until the final minutes, when Rudi Völler was fouled in the penalty area. West Germany was awarded a penalty kick and Andreas Brehme, kicking from 12 yds (11 m) in front of Argentina goalie Sergio Goycoechea, scored the winner.

The tournament had begun with 24 qualifying teams, including one from the United States —the first time a U.S. team had survived that far in 40 years. The Americans, however, lost all three of their first-round games and were eliminated.

The event, billed as Italia '90, wound up being very controversial. This was due in part to the high number of penalties (Argentina played the final without four players, who had been suspended for too many penalties), in part to the lack of offense, and in part to the penalty-kick situation. Under Cup rules, when teams finish regulation and then a 30-minute overtime and still are tied, the outcome is determined with a series of five penalty kicks for each club. Argentina won both its quarterfinal and semifinal games on penalty kicks, beating Yugoslavia and highly regarded Italy, respectively. The other semifinal, between West Germany and England, also was decided by an overtime penalty kick.

England had emerged as one of the overachievers of the tournament, along with Cameroon, the most successful African team in the event's history. The Cameroon team, the most exciting in the competition, beat Argentina in the round-robin phase of the tournament before losing to England (in overtime, of course). The Netherlands was a disappointment, falling to West Germany in the second round. Unlike 1986, when Maradona was easily the standout player, there was no true star of this Cup competition.

Besides lackluster play, the Cup also was hurt by the rowdiness of some visiting fans, especially those from England. Despite extraordinary security measures, there were repeated outbreaks of violence, and fans from England, West Germany, and the Netherlands, among others, were expelled from Italy.

United States. In U.S. soccer, the San Diego Sockers won the Major Indoor Soccer League title by defeating the Baltimore Blast in the championship series, four games to two. The Sockers finished the regular season with a 25-27 record and then became the first team with a losing record in the regular season to win the championship. Baltimore had the best regular-season record.

The Marlboro Cup, held in Miami, was won by Uruguay, which beat Costa Rica, 2-0. The U.S. team finished last in the four-nation field.

UCLA defeated Rutgers, 4-3, in the final of the NCAA Division I championship tournament. In an echo of the World Cup, the game was won with penalty kicks in overtime.

PAUL ATTNER

Swimming

Only two new world swimming records were set in 1990, both by Americans. Women were unable to lower a single world swimming standard.

Men's Records. One of the new world marks came in the U.S. swimming sprint championships at Nashville, TN, on March 24. The 50-m freestyle pitted Tom Jager against Matt Biondi in an exciting showdown between two of the world's fastest freestylers. Jager and Biondi, the Olympic gold medalist, advanced easily. In the semifinal round Jager lowered his world mark of 22.12 seconds with a clocking of 21.89, becoming the first to break the 22-second barrier; Biondi was also under the old record with 22.02. This set the stage for a historic final. On the line was $10,000 to the winner, $5,000 to the loser, and $2,000 bonus to whoever left the meet with the 50-m freestyle world record.

The final touch was close, but Jager came away with a time of 21.81 seconds for a new record and Biondi touched at 21.85. The two sprinters had made history—within the space of one hour they had broken the world record twice and turned in the four fastest 50-m freestyle swims in the annals of the sport.

At the Goodwill Games in Seattle, where U.S. swimmers were dominant, Mike Barrowman of Potomac, MD, covered the 200-m breaststroke in 2:11.53 on July 20 to shatter his own world record of 2:12.89 set in Tokyo in 1989. Second place wound up in a tie between Sergio Lopez of Spain and Kirk Stackle of the United States, who both were clocked in 2:12.24, a significant time in that it was faster than Barrowman's previous world mark. In the five-day competition, U.S. swimmers won 20 gold medals, 18 silver, and four bronze, and set three U.S. records.

The Women. Although female swimmers were unable to crack the world records, there were some outstanding performances. Janet Evans, the 18-year-old freestyler from Placentia, CA, was voted the nation's outstanding amateur athlete for 1989 when she received the James E. Sullivan Award on March 12, 1990, in Indianapolis. Evans was the first swimmer since Tracy Caulkins in 1978 to take the award. She showed her best form in 1990 in the NCAA championships in Austin, TX, when she registered a U.S.-record time of 4:34.39 on March 15 in the 500-yd freestyle final to topple Caulkins' 4:36.25, which had stood since 1979. Two days later she broke her own U.S. mark in the 1,650-yd event with 15:39.14. She was named the NCAA's swimmer of the year.

Texas won both the men's and women's NCAA titles. The men scored 506 points, 83 more than Southern California. The Longhorn women won the final event and beat out Stanford for the crown, 632 to 622.5.

GEORGE DE GREGORIO

Tennis

During the most splintered tennis season in nearly a quarter century, the eight major singles championships for men and women were won by eight different persons. That had not happened since 1966.

Although Germany's Steffi Graf, the Australian Open champ, and Sweden's Stefan Edberg, who won his second Wimbledon, occupied the Number 1 positions, as assessed by respective women's and men's pro computers at season's close, neither was a dominant figure. Graf did win ten tournaments, though, and Edberg took seven. Extremes ranged from Martina Navratilova of the United States, who turned 34 in October, seizing a record ninth Wimbledon title to Yugoslav's Monica Seles, 16, defeating Graf in the French Open final, 7-6, 6-4.

The year began uneventfully enough with Graf winning the Australian Open for a third straight year, 6-3, 6-4, over 18-year-old Ameri-

TENNIS

Davis Cup: United States
Federation Cup: United States
Wrightman Cup: suspended

Major Tournaments

Australian Open—men's singles: Ivan Lendl (Czechoslovakia); men's doubles: Pieter Aldrich (South Africa) and Danie Visser (South Africa); women's singles: Steffi Graf (West Germany); women's doubles: Helena Sukova (Czechoslovakia) and Jana Novotna (Czechoslovakia); mixed doubles: Jim Pugh and Natalia Zvereva (USSR).
International Players Championships—men's singles: Andre Agassi; men's doubles: Rick Leach and Jim Pugh; women's singles: Monica Seles (Yugoslavia); women's doubles: Helena Sukova (Czechoslovakia) and Jana Novotna (Czechoslovakia).
Italian Open—men's singles: Thomas Muster (Austria); men's doubles: Emilio Sanchez (Spain) and Sergio Casal (Spain); women's singles: Monica Seles (Yugoslavia); women's doubles: Monica Seles (Yugoslavia) and Helen Kelesi (Canada).
French Open—men's singles: Andres Gomez (Ecuador); men's doubles: Emilio Sanchez (Spain) and Sergio Casal (Spain); women's singles: Monica Seles (Yugoslavia); women's doubles: Jana Novotna (Czechoslovakia) and Helena Sukova (Czechoslovakia); mixed doubles: Arantxa Sanchez Vicario (Spain) and Jorge Lozano (Mexico).
Wimbledon—men's singles: Stefan Edberg (Sweden); men's doubles: Rick Leach and Jim Pugh; women's singles: Martina Navratilova; women's doubles: Jana Novotna (Czechoslovakia) and Helena Sukova (Czechoslovakia); mixed doubles: Rick Leach and Zina Garrison.
Player's International—singles: Michael Chang; doubles: Paul Annacone and David Wheaton.
Canadian Open—singles: Steffi Graf (West Germany); doubles: Betsy Nagelsen and Gabriela Sabatini (Argentina).
U.S. Open—men's singles: Pete Sampras; men's doubles: Pieter Aldrich (South Africa) and Danie Visser (South Africa); women's singles: Gabriela Sabatini (Argentina); women's doubles: Gigi Fernandez and Martina Navratilova; mixed doubles: Elizabeth Smylie (Australia) and Todd Woodbridge (Australia); senior men's singles: Alex Mayer; senior men's doubles: Tom Gullikson and Dick Stockton; senior women's doubles: Rosie Casals and Billie Jean King; boys' singles: Andrea Gaudenzi (Italy); boys' doubles: Martin Renstroem (Sweden) and Mikael Tillstroem (Sweden); girls' singles: Magdalena Maleeva (Bulgaria); girls' doubles: Kristin Godridge (Australia) and Kirrily Sharpe (Australia).
A.T.P. Finals—singles: Andre Agassi; doubles: Jakob Hlasek (Switzerland) and Guy Forget (France).
Virginia Slims Championship—singles: Monica Seles (Yugoslavia); doubles: Kathy Jordan and Elizabeth Smylie (Australia).
NCAA (Division I)—men's singles: Steve Bryan, Texas; men's team: Stanford; women's singles: Debbie Graham, Stanford; women's team: Stanford.

N.B. All players are from the United States unless otherwise noted.

With an all-powerful serve, Pete Sampras became the first American since 1984 to win the men's U.S. Open. He defeated fellow American Andre Agassi in the final, 6-4, 6-3, 6-2.

can Mary Jo Fernandez, and Czechoslovakia's Ivan Lendl retaining his title. An abdominal injury caused foe Edberg to quit the final, trailing 4-6, 7-6, 5-2.

But the windup of the Grand Slam events was possibly the most astounding of all U.S. Opens. Pete Sampras, 19 and seeded 12th, became the youngest male ever to win the U.S. Open. In a dynamite series he subdued fellow American Andre Agassi, 6-4, 6-3, 6-2. Startlingly, top-seeded favorite Edberg lost in the opening round, to the USSR's Aleksandr Volkov, as he had at the French, to Spain's Sergi Bruguers. Just as stunning as Sampras at Flushing Meadow was 20-year-old Argentine Gabriela Sabatini's 6-2, 7-6 title-round conquest of 1988–89 champ Graf. Ecuadorian lefty Andres Gomez also had played stunningly as he jolted Agassi in the French Open final, 6-3, 2-6, 6-4, 6-4.

Graf's bid for a third successive Wimbledon failed in the semifinals before American Zina Garrison. The first black woman to reach the final since Althea Gibson's 1958 triumph, Garrison could not make it all the way, losing to Navratilova, 6-4, 6-1. But she had opened the door for Navratilova to eclipse American Helen Wills Moody's record of eight Wimbledon singles titles (between 1927 and 1938). By adding the U.S. doubles title, her ninth (this time with American Gigi Fernandez) to a vast collection, Navratilova solidified her hold on second place among all-time women champions

at 54 majors (18 singles, 31 doubles, five mixed). She trailed Margaret Court's 62 (24-19-19).

German Boris Becker was the year's disappointment, relinquishing both his Wimbledon and U.S. titles. He squandered a 3-1 fifth-set lead and a spectacular comeback at Wimbledon against Edberg, 6-2, 6-2, 3-6, 3-6, 6-4. Agassi stopped him at the U.S. Open in the semis in four sets. In declining to play in the Davis Cup, Becker cost Germany—second-round loser to Argentina—a chance at a third successive win.

After an eight-year absence from the winners' circle, the United States won the Cup over Austria in the 42d renewal of the competition's foremost rivalry. Agassi and Michael Chang in singles and the doubles team of Rick Leach and Jim Pugh formed the winning combination in the final.

Yearlong publicity sensation Jennifer Capriati made her pro debut at 14 and achieved a number of "youngest" marks, including the youngest to play in a pro title match, youngest French Open semifinalist, and youngest to play for a Federation Cup winner. Capriati won all five Cup singles for the United States, complementing Zina Garrison, Gigi Fernandez, and Patty Fendick.

Despite losing his two major finals, Agassi finished strongly at tour's end, stopping Edberg in the ATP Masters final, 5-7, 7-6, 7-5, 6-2. Seles, whose French triumph made her the youngest major champ ever, also earned the accolade of youngest winner of the Virginia Slims Championship, the season climax in New York for the 16 top women.

BUD COLLINS, *"The Boston Globe"*

Track and Field

Athletes in the field events registered the eye-catching performances in the 1990 track and field season.

Field Events. One of the outstanding showings came in the shot-put when 23-year-old Randy Barnes of Charleston, WV, a 1988 Olympic silver medalist, unleashed a powerful put of 75'10¼" (23.12 m) at the Jack in the Box Invitational meet in Los Angeles in May and shattered the two-year-old world record of the German Ulf Timmermann by more than two inches. Barnes' performance was noteworthy for its all-round effort and for making him the first American to hold the shot-put world standard since 1976. The 6'4½" (1.93-m), 300-pounder (136-kg) set his mark on his second attempt, then rattled off four more puts that exceeded 73'3" (22.3 m). All told, he averaged 73'10¾" (22.5 m) for his entire series—the best series in shot-put history. He received a $50,000 check from the meet's promoter who offered it as a bonus for the athlete who set a world record in the shot-put.

There was also considerable activity in the javelin throw. Patrik Boden of Sweden set a world record in the javelin in Austin, TX, in March, registering a heave of 292'4″ (89.1 m). That tumbled the record set in 1987 by Jan Zelezny of Czechoslovakia by 4'9″ (1.4 m). But in July, Boden's mark came under attack from several quarters. First, Steve Backley of Britain bettered it with 293'11″ (89.58 m) at Stockholm. Then on July 14, Zelezny reclaimed it with 294'2″ (89.66 m) at Oslo, Norway. Later in the month Backley, on his home turf in London, reestablished his supremacy in the event with a throw of 298'6″ (90.98 m).

The world's top pole-vaulter, Sergei Bubka of the Soviet Union, who also holds the world outdoor record, broke his own indoor mark by soaring 19'10¼″ (6.05 m) in a meet in Donetsk, his hometown, in March.

Running Events. In the running events, world records were not so plentiful. The French team in the 400-m relay, however, broke a six-year-old standard set by the United States in the 1984 Olympics at Los Angeles. The French combine of Max Morinière, Daniel Sangouma, Jean-Charles Trouabal, and Bruno Marie Rose were timed in 37.79 seconds in the European championships at Split, Yugoslavia, in August. That bettered the previous mark by .04 second.

The winter season produced an abundance of indoor records. At Stuttgart, Germany, on February 4, Danny Everett, a third-place finisher in the event at the 1988 Olympics, broke a two-year-old mark in the 400-m, with a time of 45.04 seconds, shaving .01 of a second from Thomas Schönlebe's previous record. However, in May, Everett's mark was rejected by the International Amateur Athletic Federation because of an improper staggered start.

Doina Melinte of Romania broke her own indoor record in the mile at the Vitalis/Meadowlands Invitational in East Rutherford, NJ, with a time of 4:17.13 and enriched herself by $100,000 in bonus money.

Marathons. In the Boston Marathon, Italy's Gelindo Bordin, the 1988 Olympic marathon champion, emerged the victor in 2 hours, 8 minutes, 19 seconds. The top woman at Boston was Rosa Mota of Portugal, who took the event for a record third time. Her clocking was 2:25.23. Douglas Wakiihuri of Kenya, showing hardly any discomfort in the unseasonable 73°F (19°C) November temperature, set a methodical pace to win the New York City Marathon in 2 hours, 12 minutes, 39 seconds. The winner in the women's division was Wanda Panfil of Poland, who was timed in 2:30.45.

NCAA. For the second year in a row, the NCAA men's and women's outdoor championships went to Louisiana State. In the NCAA's indoor championships, Arkansas took the men's title and Texas captured the women's crown.

Steroids. Ben Johnson, who was stripped of his 1988 Olympic gold medal and world records in the 100-m dash and the 60-m indoor run after testing positive for steroids, was reinstated by the Canadian Olympic Association. He thus became eligible to participate in the 1992 Olympics in Barcelona, Spain. In November it was announced that shot-putter Randy Barnes and Butch Reynolds, the world-record holder in the 400-m, had tested positive for steroid use and faced a two-year ban from competition.

GEORGE DE GREGORIO

Yachting

After a three-year legal battle, the San Diego Yacht Club finally was awarded possession of the America's Cup by the New York Court of Appeals in April 1990.

Court rulings had shifted the possession of the cup three times between the Mercury Bay Boating Club of New Zealand and San Diego. By a 5–2 vote, a panel of seven Court of Appeals judges upheld a lower court ruling that ordered the New Zealand club to turn over the cup to San Diego. The Appeals Court majority opinion stated "nothing in the deed limits the design of the defending club's vessel" and refused to consider claims by New Zealand that using the catamaran created an unfair advantage for San Diego. It said questions of sportsmanship went beyond the court's purview and suggested that the yachting community resolve those matters.

On March 28, 1989, Justice Carmen Beauchamp Ciparick of the New York State Supreme Court had awarded the trophy to New Zealand on a forfeit, ruling that in September 1988 San Diego had sailed an unfair race against the Mercury Bay club by using a catamaran, a faster twin-hulled yacht, instead of a monohull. New Zealand was ordered to give back the cup, however, in a later ruling by the Appellate Division of the State Supreme Court.

New York courts hold jurisdiction over the cup under a century-old deed of gift, a document that governs the competition. The courts oversee the deed as a charitable trust through an agreement signed in 1887 by the New York Yacht Club. A defense of the cup by San Diego is scheduled for 1992.

Other Races. *Steinlager 2*, an 84-ft (25.6-m) ketch, skippered by Peter Blake of New Zealand, captured the Whitbread Round the World Race with a time of 128 days, 9 hours, 40 minutes, 30 seconds. In August the 70-ft (21-m) boat *Stripes*, captained by Bill Martin, took the Port Huron-to-Mackinac Island, MI, race. Also in August, Jurki Taiminen of Finland and Italy's Chiara Calligaris won the men's and women's world sailing championships, respectively, in Leghorn, Italy.

GEORGE DE GREGORIO

SPORTS SUMMARIES[1]

ARCHERY—World Champions: men: Ed Eliason, Stansbury Park, UT; women: Denise Parker, South Jordan, UT. **U.S. Indoor Champions:** men: Ed Eliason; women: Denise Parker.

BADMINTON—U.S. Champions: men's singles: Chris Jogis, Manhattan Beach, CA; women's singles: Linda Safarik-Tong, Berkeley, CA. **World Champions:** men's team: China; women's team: China.

BIATHLON—U.S. Champions: men: 10k: John Ingdal, Minneapolis, MN; 20k: Josh Thompson, Gunnison, CO; women: 7.5k: Mary Ostergren, Norwich, VT; 15k: Pam Nordheim, Bozeman, MT.

BILLIARDS—World Champions: men's 9-ball: E. Strickland, Greensboro, NC; women's 9-ball: Robin Bell, Costa Mesa, CA.

BOBSLEDDING—World Champions: world 2-man: Switzerland; world 4-man: Switzerland; World Cup 2-man: Germany; World Cup 4-man: Canada.

BOWLING—Professional Bowlers Association Tour: Firestone Tournament of Champions: Dave Ferraro, Kingston, NY; National Championship: Jim Pencak, Mayfield Heights, OH; Seagram's Coolers U.S. Open: Ron Palombi, Erie, PA; Touring Players Championship: Duane Fisher, Gloucester Township, NJ. **American Bowling Congress:** singles: Bob Hochrein, Dubuque, IA; doubles: Bob Ujvari and Mike Neumann, Tonawanda, NY; events: Mike Neumann; team all-events: Brunswick Rhinos, Tonawanda, NY; regular team: tie—Brunswick Rhinos and State Farm-Lou Magic Agency, Detroit, MI; Masters Tournament: Chris Warren, Dallas, TX.

CANOEING—U.S. Champions: canoe: 1,000 m: Stewart Carr, Indianapolis, IN; men's kayak: 1,000 m: Chris Ball, Irvine, CA; women's kayak: 500 m: Cathy Marino, Huntington Beach, CA.

COURT TENNIS—World: Wayne Davies, New York. **U.S. Open:** Wayne Davies; doubles: Peter Meares and Robert Faye, Australia. **U.S. Amateur:** M. Clothier, Philadelphia.

CRICKET—World Champion: The Ashes, Australia.

CROSS-COUNTRY—World Champions: men: Khalid Skah, Morocco; women: Lynn Jennings, Newmarket, NH. **U.S. Athletics Congress:** men: Robert Kempainen, Minnetonka, MN; women: Lynn Jennings.

CURLING—World Champions: men: Tommy Stjerne, Denmark; women: Dordi Nordby, Norway.

CYCLING—Tour de France: men: Greg LeMond, Wayzata, MN.

DOG SHOWS—Westminster: best-in-show: Ch. Wendessa Crown Prince, Pekingese, owned by Ed Jenner, Burlington, WI.

FENCING—U.S. Fencing Association: men's foil: Michael Marx, Michigan City, IN; men's épée: Robert Stull, San Antonio, TX; men's saber: Bob Cottingham, Orange, NJ; women's foil: Jennifer Yu, East Palo Alto, CA; women's épée: Donna Stone, Lincoln Park, NJ.

FIELD HOCKEY—NCAA Division 1: women: Old Dominion.

GYMNASTICS—U.S. Champions: men's all-around: John Roethlisberger, Minneapolis, MN; women's all-around: Kim Zmetskal, Houston, TX.

HANDBALL—U.S. Handball Association: men's one-wall: Joe Durso, Brooklyn, NY; men's four-wall: Naty Alvarado, Hesperia, CA.

HORSESHOE PITCHING—World Champions: men: Jim Knisely, Bremen, OH; women: Tari Powell, Rankin, IL.

HORSE SHOWS—U.S. Equestrian Team: dressage: Robert Dover, Lebanon, NJ, riding Walzertakt; three-day event: David O'Connor, Upperville, VA, riding Wilton Fair (spring) and Charles Plumb, Sherborn, MA, riding Landino (fall); show jumping: Michael Matz, Collegeville, PA, riding Heisman. **World Cup:** dressage: Sven Rothenberger, West Germany, riding Andiamo; show jumping: John Whitaker, Britain, riding Henderson Milton.

JUDO—U.S. Champions: men: heavyweight: Douglas Nelson, Englewood, NJ; open: Damon Keeve, San Francisco, CA; women: heavyweight: Carol Scheid, Nevado, ID; open: Grace Jividen, Colorado Springs, CO.

KARATE—U.S. Champions: men: Advanced Mandatory Kata: Joseph Talerico, Brooklyn, NY; Advanced Kata: Brian Hobson, Hampton, VA; 35 and over Advanced Kata: Chor Tan, Los Angeles, CA; 45 and over Advanced Kata: William Carlo, San Diego, CA; Advanced Weapons: Greg Scythes, Ironton, OH; 35 and over Advanced Weapons: Kimio Nelson, Warren, PA; 45 and over Advanced Weapons: Ronald L. Donahue, Milford Center, OH;

women: Advanced Mandatory Kata: Mimi Tang, Bellevue, WA; Advanced Kata: Stephanie Buckner, Hamilton, OH; 35 and over Advanced Kata: Hiroyo Ringler, Cardington, OH; 45 and over Advanced Kata: Jacqueline Long, Yorba Linda, CA; Advanced Weapons: Cheryl Suzuki, Santa Ana, CA; 35 and over Advanced Weapons: Hiroyo Ringler; 45 and over Advanced Weapons: Jacqueline Long.

LACROSSE—NCAA Division 1: men: Syracuse; women: Harvard.

LUGE—U.S. Champions: men: Jon Owen, Bethel, ME; women: Bonny Warner, CA. **World Champions:** men: Georg Hackl, West Germany; women: Susi Erdmann, East Germany; **World Cup:** men: Georg Hackl.

MODERN PENTATHLON—World Champions: men: Gianluca Tiberta, Italy; women: Eva Fjedllerup, Denmark; men's team: Soviet Union; women's team: Poland.

PADDLE TENNIS—U.S. Champions: men's singles: Scott Freedman, Venice, CA; women's singles: Ellie Comptman, Pacific Palisades, CA.

PLATFORM TENNIS—U.S. Champions: men's singles: Bob Kleinert, Franklin Lakes, NJ; men's doubles: Rich Maier, Scarsdale, NY, and Steve Baird, Harrison, NY; women's doubles: Sue Aery, Bedminster, NJ, and Gerri Viant, Nyack, NY; mixed doubles: David Ohlmuller, Montclair, NJ, and Patty Hogan, Summit, NJ.

POLO—World Champion: White Birch.

RACQUETBALL—U.S. Champions: men: Cliff Swain, Boston, MA; women: Lynn Adams, San Diego, CA.

RACQUETS—U.S. Open: singles: James Male, England; U.S. Pro: Wayne Davies, New York, NY; **U.S. Amateur:** William Maitby, England.

ROWING—U.S. Collegiate Champions: Varsity Eight: University of Wisconsin; women: Princeton. Intercollegiate Rowing Association: Wisconsin; Lightweight Eight: Yale; Eastern Spirit: Harvard; women: Princeton; Dad Vail Regatta: Temple; women: Virginia. **World Champions:** Men's Eights: West Germany; Women's Eights: Romania; Lightweight Eights: Italy.

SHOOTING—U.S. Champions: men's small-bore rifle, prone: T.R. Bishop, Lenoir, NC; men's small-bore rifle, three position: James Meredith; men's high-power rifle: Patrick McCann, Staunton, IL; men's all-round pistol: J. Lenardson.

SOFTBALL—U.S. Champions: men's fast pitch: Penn Corporation, Sioux City, IA; women's fast pitch: Raybestos Brakettes, Stratford, CT; men's major-slow pitch: New Construction, Shelbyville, IN; women's major-slow pitch: Anoka Spooks, Anoka, MN; men's super-slow pitch: Steele's Silver Bullets, Grafton, OH; U.S. college women: University of California, Los Angeles.

SQUASH TENNIS—U.S. Champion: men: Gary Squires, Darien, CT.

TEAM HANDBALL—U.S. Division 1: men: California Hedat, Hayward; women: University of Minnesota.

TRIATHLON—World Champions: men: Mark Allen, Cardiff, CA; women: Paula Newby-Fraser, Zimbabwe.

VOLLEYBALL—U.S. Open Champions: men: Nike, Carson, CA; women: Plymouth Californians, Hayward, CA. **NCAA:** men: USC; women: UCLA.

WATER POLO—U.S. Champions: men's outdoor: Harvard Foundation, Los Angeles, CA; women's outdoor: Beach, Long Beach, CA. **NCAA:** California at Irvine.

WATER SKIING—U.S. Overall: men: Carl Roberge, Orlando, FL; women: Deena Brush Mapple, Windermere, FL. **Masters Overall:** men: Mick Neville, Australia; women: Deena Brush Mapple.

WRESTLING—U.S. Open (freestyle): 48 kg: Rob Eiter, Tempe, AZ; 52 kg: Zeke Jones, Tempe, AZ; 57 kg: Joe Melchiore, Iowa City, IA; 62 kg: John Smith, Stillwater, OK; 68 kg: Nate Carr, Morgantown, WV; 74 kg: Rob Koll, Dryden, NY; 82 kg: Royce Alger, Iowa City, IA; 90 kg: Chris Campbell, Fayetteville, NY; 100 kg: Bill Scherr, Bloomington, IN; 130 kg: Bruce Baumgartner, Cambridge Springs, PA; (Greco-Roman): 48 kg: Lew Dorrance, Quantico, VA; 52 kg: Sam Henson, St. Charles, MO; 57 kg: Mark Pustelnik, Cedar Falls, IA; 62 kg: Ike Anderson, Albany, NY; 68 kg: Andy Seras, Schenectady, NY; 74 kg: David Butler, San Diego, CA; 82 kg: Derrick Waldroup, Ft. Campbell, KY; 90 kg: Randy Couture, Stillwater, OK; 100 kg: Chris Tironi, Albany, NY; 130 kg: Matt Ghaffari, Chandler, AZ. **U.S. Champions** (freestyle): super heavyweight: Bruce Baumgartner; (Greco-Roman): super heavyweight: Matt Ghaffari. **World Cup:** freestyle team champion: United States; Greco-Roman team champion: Soviet Union.

[1]Sports for which articles do not appear in pages 476–99.

SRI LANKA

Following a partial lull in the seven-year-old civil war in the first half of 1990, the conflict flared up again in even more savage form in the northern and eastern provinces after the Liberation Tigers of Tamil Eelam (LTTE) broke a 13-month truce in June. This provoked the worst internal crisis since Ranasinghe Premadasa became president in January 1989. The economy showed some signs of improvement prior to the new outburst of violence, but it continued to be affected adversely by the internal disorder and instability. The crisis in the Persian Gulf, beginning in early August, added new complications.

The Politics of Violence. At the beginning of the year the destructive conflict in the south between government forces and a revolutionary Sinhalese group, the Janatha Vimukthi Peramuna (JVP), seemed to be under control. The cease-fire between the government and the LTTE in the north and east was still in effect, with infrequent major violations. The Indian Peacekeeping Force (IPKF), which had been sent to the Tamil majority areas in 1987 to disarm the Tamil militants and supervise a peaceful election in these areas, was withdrawn in March. Although the IPKF did not achieve its missions, its withdrawal seemed to pave the way for some kind of coexistence, however uneasy, between the Sinhalese-dominated government and the dissident Tamils of the north and east.

These hopes were shattered in June, when the LTTE broke the cease-fire agreement, launched attacks on police stations in many parts of the eastern province, and brutally murdered many policemen. This led to retaliatory attacks on Tamils, even including some who were not involved in the LTTE assaults. In the following nine weeks, according to government sources, some 3,350 persons were killed, making this the deadliest phase of the seven-year war. Among the victims in the fighting were many Muslims, who constituted 35% of the population in the eastern province but only 7% of the population of the country. Several hundred thousand people moved to refugee camps in the area, and many others fled to India or elsewhere.

When the cease-fire was broken, the government declared all-out war against the LTTE, but its forces were unable to suppress the Tigers in the north and east.

The Economy. The renewal of large-scale violence, costing the government some $500,000 daily, had disastrous effects on Sri Lanka's already shaky economy and on the society. There were a loss of production, increased unemployment, a disruption of transportation, shortages of food, oil, and other items, and a rise in inflation. Exports declined precipitately, whereas imports increased, thus widening the trade and budget deficits. The nation's leading export, tea, declined in terms of production and price on the world markets. Foreign-exchange reserves also shrank to dangerously low levels.

The government incorporated a series of austerity measures in a five-year public-investment program. It had to rely on external assistance for some 65% of its development expenditures. Substantial assistance was forthcoming, especially from international financial institutions. In October the Sri Lankan aid consortium, meeting in Paris, pledged $785 million —a record amount.

Persian Gulf Crisis and Foreign Policy. The economic situation was made even bleaker by the crisis in the Persian Gulf caused by Iraq's Saddam Hussein's annexation of Kuwait. This brought an end to Sri Lanka's largest source of foreign exchange, the remittances from the approximately 135,000 Sri Lankans who were employed in Kuwait (100,000) and Iraq. These remittances amounted to about $75 million annually. The Sri Lankan government was faced with the problem of repatriating its citizens and of arranging for resettlement and employment upon their return. The great increase in oil prices following the invasion also added to the economic burdens of Sri Lanka, which had been importing 40% of its oil from Iraq and Kuwait. Moreover, Iraq was Sri Lanka's largest market for tea, and the loss of this revenue was another financial blow. The crisis also largely stopped the flow of arms to Sri Lanka, which were needed to maintain the operations against the Tamil rebels. Most of these arms had come from Persian Gulf states, most notably Iraq.

In March the government announced that it would break its diplomatic ties with Israel and would not resume them until Israel recognized the Palestine Liberation Organization (PLO). Meanwhile relations with India improved.

NORMAN D. PALMER, *Professor Emeritus*
University of Pennsylvania

SRI LANKA • Information Highlights

Official Name: Democratic Socialist Republic of Sri Lanka.
Location: South Asia.
Area: 25,332 sq mi (65 610 km²).
Population (mid-1990 est.): 17,200,000.
Chief Cities (mid-1988 est.): Colombo, the capital, 609,000; Dehiwala-Mount Lavinia, 190,000.
Government: *Head of state*, R. Premadasa, president (took office Jan. 1989). *Head of government*, D. B. Wijetunga, prime minister (appointed March 3, 1989). *Legislature* (unicameral)—Parliament.
Monetary Unit: Rupee (39.92 rupees equal U.S.$1, August 1990).
Gross Domestic Product (1988 U.S.$): $6,100,-000,000.
Economic Index (Colombo, 1989): *Consumer Prices* (1980 = 100), all items, 260.9; food, 260.4.
Foreign Trade (1989 U.S.$): *Imports*, $2,109,000,000; *exports*, $1,554,000,000.

STAMPS AND STAMP COLLECTING

"Something for everyone" was the theme of the 1990 U.S. Postal Service (USPS) stamp program. The USPS issuances commemorated a wide variety of people, places, and things.

In a gesture of *glasnost*, the United States and the USSR jointly issued four stamps featuring "Creatures of the Sea." This was the second U.S.-Soviet joint stamp issue. In 1975 the two nations released a pair of stamps honoring the historic Apollo-Soyuz space mission.

A block of four 25¢ stamps paid tribute to the 50th anniversary of the Academy Award-winning films *Gone With the Wind*, *Beau Geste*, *Stagecoach*, and *The Wizard of Oz*.

One sheet of five designs (25¢ each) hailed great U.S. Olympic gold-medal winners, while another depicted famous U.S. lighthouses. The circus came to town on a 5¢ stamp showing an early American wagon used to take circuses on the road.

Indian headdresses were displayed in a booklet of five designs in the Folk Art Series. Marianne Moore was featured in the Literary Arts Series. The U.S. Supreme Court received group honors in the Constitution Series. Luís Muñoz Marín of Puerto Rico was noted in the Great Americans Series, and Ida B. Wells was honored in the Black Heritage Series.

Statehood commemoratives were issued for Rhode Island, Wyoming, and Idaho. Two World War II heroes received postal acclaim. Gen. Claire Lee Chennault, leader of the famed "Flying Tigers," was honored on a 40-center, and Gen. Dwight D. Eisenhower was hailed with a 25¢ stamp commemorating the centennial of his birth.

U.S. Postal Service

Postal cards continued to provide colorful designs. Depicted on a 15¢ "America the Beautiful" card was a view of Niagara Falls. Stanford University's Quadrangle and the Daughters of the American Revolution (DAR) Memorial Continental/Constitution Hall were displayed as part of the Historic Preservation Series; a view of Isaac Royal House appeared on another card. To help promote the campaign to eradicate illiteracy, a 15¢ card was issued.

A plastic self-affixing flag stamp, part of an experimental program for stamp sales from automatic teller machines (ATMs) at some banks, was released on May 18. A $2 stamp portraying a bobcat was released in the Wildlife Series. This was the first issue in the conversion of high-value sheet stamps from the Great Americans Series to the colorful commemorative Wildlife Series.

An annual pair of Christmas stamps, one contemporary and one traditional in design, were issued near the end of the 1990 program. A joint issue with the Federated States of Micronesia and Marshall Islands honored these onetime U.S. trust territories in the Pacific.

The U.S. postal program would not be complete without a new design for the popular "Love" series. The 1990 stamp first was released in Romance, AR.

SYD KRONISH, *The Associated Press*

Selected U.S. Commemoratives 1990

Subject	Denomination	Date	Subject	Denomination	Date	Subject	Denomination	Date
			Marianne Moore	25¢	April 18	Niagara Falls	15¢	Sept. 14
Idaho Statehood	25¢	Jan. 6	Lighthouses (five)	25¢	April 26	Micronesia/Marshall Is.	25¢	Sept. 28
Love	25¢	Jan. 18	George C. Bingham	25¢	May 4	Stanford University	25¢	Sept. 30
Ida B. Wells	25¢	Feb. 1	ATM (plastic)	25¢	May 18	Creatures of Sea (four)	25¢	Oct. 3
U.S. Supreme Court	25¢	Feb. 2	Rhode Island Statehood	25¢	June 1	DAR Memorial	25¢	Oct. 11
Beach Umbrella	15¢	Feb. 3	Bobcat	$2.00	June 1	America Series	25¢	Oct. 12
Luís Muñoz Marín	5¢	Feb. 18	Isaac Royal House (card)	15¢	June 16	America Series	45¢	Oct. 12
Wyoming Statehood	25¢	Feb. 23	Olympians (five)	25¢	July 6	Dwight Eisenhower	25¢	Oct. 13
Paper Mill (card)	15¢	March 12	Indian Headdresses (five)	25¢	Aug. 17	Christmas (traditional)	25¢	Oct. 18
Literacy (card)	15¢	March 22	Circus Wagon	5¢	Aug. 31	Christmas (contemporary)	25¢	Oct. 18
Classic Films (four)	25¢	March 22	Gen. Chennault	40¢	Sept. 6	Orchestra Hall	15¢	Oct. 19

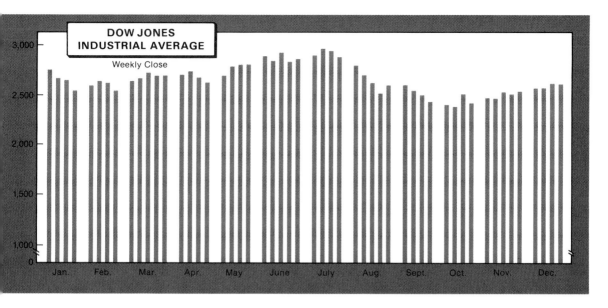

STOCKS AND BONDS

The first order of business for the U.S. financial markets in 1990 seemed to be to close the door for good on the Wall Street boom of the 1980s. In the stock market, banking, real estate, junk bonds, and the securities industry itself, the contrast was stark with the euphoric years just past.

A few weeks into the year, Drexel Burnham Lambert, the investment bank that had ridden the top of the wave in junk-bond finance, abruptly ran onto the financial rocks and sank from sight. Nine months later, in November, Drexel's foremost financier, Michael Milken, drew a ten-year prison sentence from a federal judge for six trading-related offenses to which he had pleaded guilty. (*See* special report, page 505.) The U.S. real-estate market, which had flourished all through the 1970s and 1980s, underwent a painful retrenchment that dimmed the stars of such deal-making legends as Donald Trump. The banking industry, already unsettled by shaky loans to Third World countries and high-risk corporate-takeover debt, suffered serious new woes in real-estate credit. The stocks of some of the biggest bank holding companies in the United States fell to their lowest prices in more than a decade.

A Bear Market. In keeping with the times, stocks in general lapsed into their first sustained bear market since 1981–82. The Dow Jones average of 30 industrials closed out the year at 2,633.66, down 119.54 points, or 4.34%, from the end of 1989. The bears of Wall Street tipped their hand early, sending the Dow down 9.5% in a four-week span during January as interest rates rose unexpectedly. The markets were unsettled by a rapid rise in overseas interest rates, most notably in Japan and West Germany. Confidence also was rattled by a steep decline in the Japanese stock market, which had entered the 1990s as the strongest of all the world's thriving arenas for corporate equities.

Over the next several months U.S. stocks gradually recovered from that early setback as foreign stock and credit markets showed signs of stabilizing. In July the Dow Jones industrials traded briefly above 3,000 for the first time. The average set a new closing high of 2,999.75 on July 16 and held at that same level the next day. But most broader market indicators were not faring as well. Indeed, indexes dominated by the great mass of smaller "secondary" stocks failed to surpass highs they had reached in 1989 or, in a few cases, 1987.

Both the Dow and the broader indexes soon were headed lower, as fears increased of an impending recession and a credit crunch induced by chastened lending practices in the banking industry. On August 2 anxieties about the economy intensified with Iraq's invasion and occupation of Kuwait. World oil prices more than doubled over the summer, from less than $20 per barrel to about $40 per barrel, in the crisis atmosphere that resulted from the showdown in the Persian Gulf.

On October 11 the Dow hit its closing low for the year of 2,365.10—down about 634 points, or 21.2%, from where it had stood less than three months earlier. With signals like that to go on, many analysts declared that the economy had entered a recession and was headed for rough going at least through the first quarter of 1991. The Federal Reserve Board (Fed), in its capacity as overseer of money and credit conditions, moved closer toward agreeing with that view. In late November, Alan Greenspan, the central bank's chairman, acknowledged "a meaningful downturn in aggregate output." By that time the Fed, which earlier in the year had been reluctant to relax its credit policy for fear of stirring up inflationary expectations, had begun a series of steps toward easier money.

This policy served as intended to push interest rates lower. Yields on long-term Treasury bonds fell to the 8.1%-8.2% range in December, compared with 9.2% in September. The drop in interest rates helped stock prices stage a partial rebound in the waning weeks of the year, by stimulating hopes for an eventual upturn in business activity and by reducing the relative appeal of bond and money-market investments that compete with stocks. Still, many analysts said it was far from certain that the worst was over for the stock market, especially if investors were underestimating the potential severity of the business slowdown.

Though just about everyone agreed that the oil shock induced by the crisis in the Middle East aggravated the U.S. economy's problems, a good many analysts argued that a recession probably would have loomed even without that influence. The United States, they said, was overdue for a period of withdrawal from years of debt excesses, especially for such unsustainable activities as deficit spending by the government and speculative financing of corporate takeovers. From 1980 through 1990, economists at Norwest Corp. in Minneapolis, MN, noted, the federal government increased its debt 325%; the U.S. consumer 253%, and business 243%.

Mutual Funds, Securities, and Investment Banking. Amid all the gloom, one segment of the financial world kept showing evidence of prosperity: the mutual-fund industry. Through the 1980s the fund business enjoyed explosive growth on many fronts, including bond funds, money-market funds, and both general and specialized stock funds. With the drop in the stock market in 1990, investors' long-term confidence in stock funds appeared to suffer no setback at all. Over the first ten months of the year, according to the Investment Company Institute, a mutual-fund trade association, stock funds rang up sales of new shares amounting to $56.2 billion, excluding shares bought with reinvested dividends. That exceeded the total for any previous year except 1987, when a record of $66.9 billion was set.

Aside from the business of money management, few things happened to relieve the pressures that had been bearing on the securities industry ever since the stock-market crash in 1987. The running total of job losses on Wall Street since that debacle neared 50,000 as cost-cutting and layoffs continued. The Value Line Investment Survey estimated that profit margins in a business once noted for its exceptional returns shrank to 2.8% in 1990, less than one half what they had been four years earlier. Industry leaders sought to assure their investors and customers that the Street merely was going through one of its periodic down cycles, and that better times were ahead. Some elements of the financial press were less sanguine, however. "Wall Street today has far more profound troubles than market cycles," asserted *Business Week* magazine. "It could well be headed toward an irreversible decline."

In investment banking, the traditionally lucrative business of raising capital for companies and governmental entities, Wall Street firms faced new competition from commercial bankers and from securities issuers themselves, who were developing new ways to save money by cutting out the middleman. At the same time, large investing institutions used new systems to bypass conventional brokers in buying and selling stocks and bonds for their portfolios. Even the storied stock-exchange floors looked threatened by obsolescence with the development of electronic systems for trading, and the emergence of worldwide competition to attract orders from investors. The magazine *Institutional Investor*, in a cover story titled "High Anxiety," said: "The illusions of the 1980s have been shattered. Left behind is a financial industry that isn't so much bearish as it is flat-out frightened."

In addition to its business problems, Wall Street had some damage to its image that needed repair. The collapse of Drexel and the sentencing of Milken climaxed a long series of scandals involving allegations of insider-trading offenses, stock-manipulation schemes, and other abuses. The feeling ran high that many elements of the financial community in the exuberant 1980s had put excessive emphasis on lining their own pockets, rather than fulfilling the role of promoting the progress of U.S. business and prosperity.

The World Scene. In the years ahead, the outlook for the U.S. markets and investment business seemed more closely linked to other world financial centers than ever before. Barring some sort of financial calamity, many observers expected the 1990s to produce, sooner or later, a truly around-the-world, around-the-clock system for raising and trading capital assets.

If it was any consolation to partisans of Wall Street, the U.S. stock market performed better than most of its foreign counterparts in 1990. Through the first 11 months of the year, it ranked second among 13 major markets tracked by Datastream International, measured by results calculated in local currencies and published in the *Wall Street Journal*. Number 1 was Hong Kong, up 4.53%. After the United States, down 7.03%, came Britain, down 11.28%; the Netherlands, down 16.62%; Germany, down 19.50%; France, down 19.79%; Australia, down 19.97%; Canada, down 20.63%; Spain, down 22.87%; Singapore, down 25.30%; Switzerland, down 25.36%; Italy, down 27.17%, and Japan, down 42.30%.

CHET CURRIER
The Associated Press

Junk Bonds

His body sagging in defeat, Michael Milken, 43, stood before federal judge Kimba Wood on April 24, 1990, and with tears in his eyes and a catch in his voice pleaded guilty to six criminal charges. He agreed to pay $200 million in fines and $400 million in restitution. "I am truly sorry," he said, reading from a statement in which he detailed his violations of the law, including counts of securities fraud, mail fraud, assisting in the filing of a false income-tax return, and conspiracy.

The Junk-Bond King. It was a sudden, stunning conclusion to the career of the "junk-bond king," who as head of Drexel Burnham Lambert's high-yield bond department financed some of the biggest corporate takeovers in business history, flooded corporate America with risky financing, and terrorized corporate managements with the threat of being dislodged by raiders. Milken, who at his peak in 1987 earned $550 million per year, was the last of an often arrogant cluster of crooked financiers who, said Richard Breeden, chairman of the Securities and Exchange Commission (SEC), "stood at the center of a network of manipulation, fraud, and deceit."

Until shortly before his April 24 plea bargaining, Milken had insisted on his innocence in speeches, media interviews, charity appearances, and statements issued through his lawyers. He reminded people that the financing technique he popularized, that of inducing lenders to buy bonds by offering interest rates far above the market, helped finance small but growing companies that otherwise had no access to the marketplace. He had many defenders who believed, as did Milken, that he had accomplished much good in turning the conservative investment business upside down.

Milken's protestations of innocence, however, could not undo the damage from admissions by those who had conducted business with him. Ivan Boesky and Dennis Levine, for example, had confessed to insider-trading schemes, served jail terms, and cooperated with prosecutors seeking a trail to Milken. And Milken's former employer, Drexel Burnham Lambert, already had admitted to guilt, paid a huge fine, and then, only weeks before, collapsed into bankruptcy.

In the statement read through reddened eyes, Milken said, "I realize that by my acts I have hurt those who are closest to me," but many Americans thought he should have expressed remorse for others too. A study by Salomon Brothers Inc., a securities firm, showed

AP/Wide World

A secretary and a junior analyst were among the thousands of employees dismissed by Drexel Burnham Lambert as the securities firm filed for bankruptcy in February 1990.

junk-bond defaults for 1990 through August 15 had risen to $9.4 billion, $600 million more than the total for all 1989. The cumulative total since January 1977, it said, was $27.8 billion. The measurements in non-dollar terms sounded even worse: ruined investors, weakened or collapsed companies, worker layoffs, towns left without industry, and a corporate-debt structure so tenuous it only could lead to more problems for years ahead.

The Junk-Bond Era. The junk-bond era which climaxed in scandals of almost incredible dimensions and excesses so preposterous it will take historians to place them in credible perspective, began quietly, almost innocently. High-yield, high-risk bonds had existed for years, a small but necessary part of the financing spectrum. Small companies and companies in financial difficulties found them necessary since it was impossible for them to compete for funds with the highly rated blue-chip corporations. If the best U.S. companies were paying 8% for funds borrowed through bonds, America's poorer and smaller companies had to pay perhaps 11% or 12%, take it or leave it. Offsetting the higher return for investors was the greater risk involved. Such bonds sometimes failed to perform; they became portfolio clutter, worthless junk.

Through aggressive selling, aided by promotions and publicity that declared such bonds to be much safer (and remunerative) than more highly rated bonds, Milken sought to make "junk" respectable in the portfolios of large individual investors, banks, insurance companies, and other lenders. Initial successes and some hard-nosed marketing by his firm, the otherwise undistinguished Drexel Burnham Lambert, caught the fancy of a marketplace already becoming attuned to a climate of easier money and fewer regulatory restraints. Competition helped do the rest; what institution could be happy with a mere 8% when its competitors might be earning 50% more?

The number of companies using high-cost or high-yield bonds grew. No longer was the junk-bond market solely for smaller companies; some of the United States' better companies were tempted to try the market on occasion. But the biggest thrust came from the use of junk in financing hostile takeovers, in which the funds so raised were used to buy a company's stocks; or in leveraged buyouts, in which groups of investors used junk bonds to purchase companies and retire the stock, hoping to pay off the newly acquired debt through higher production and sales or by selling off assets. Both techniques were used so widely that the 1980s became one of unparalleled debt.

The ultimate high-yield deal in terms of size was achieved in November 1988 with a $25 billion buyout of RJR Nabisco by the firm of Kohlberg Kravis Roberts, but size did not make it the most incredible deal. That dishonor had been achieved instead by the almost farcical purchase on April 1, 1988, of a large U.S. retailing chain, Federated Department Stores, by Robert Campeau for $6.5 billion. The self-made, highly successful Canadian builder, who dreamed not just of success but of empire, had purchased the Allied Stores Corp. in 1986 for $3.6 billion.

To own both Federated and Allied was considered a crown for Campeau, since all America knew of the retailers owned by the chains, and many had shopped in them—stores such as Jordan Marsh, Bloomingdale's, and Abraham & Straus. No matter that Allied alone was ten times larger than Campeau Corp. Bold dreams, financing wizardry, junk, and professional investors, including banks, insurers, and mutual funds, would overcome the total purchase price. Among the bag of financing tricks with which Campeau's investment advisers saddled him were two Federated junk-bond issues of 16% and 17.75%. Neither retail sales, which turned weak, nor sales of assets could overcome such a burden, and in January 1990 the empire crumbled into bankruptcy. It provoked *Fortune* magazine to comment in a June 18 cover story that "the overwhelming wonder of this affair is that so many supposedly shrewd lenders forked over so much money to a man whose instability would probably keep him from being hired as a Bloomingdale's salesclerk."

The Junk-Bond Collapse. The Campeau affair hurt all junk bonds, but the market was coming apart anyway. Debt was everywhere, and it was like sand in the foundation of the marketplace. To put the collapsed savings and loan industry on its feet probably would cost the U.S. government $130 billion; the commercial bank insurance fund was growing shaky; many insurers were loaded down with junk bonds whose value was falling steadily; Philadelphia, other municipalities, and states, too, were facing financial crises; the government's guaranteed student-loan program was plagued by $2 billion of defaults; and, of course, there was the perennial federal debt. It was impossible to say how much the junk-bond mentality contributed to the situation or, instead, reflected it. Whatever, there was no question at all that credit standards had deteriorated, and that junk-bond standards were an extreme example.

The collapse of Drexel Burnham Lambert came in February 1990. Unable to sell some of its junk-bond issues, the company was forced to buy them for its own portfolio, where they resided at face value. When the firm needed to raise cash, it could find nobody willing to buy. Wall Street old-timers said it was undone by its greed, by its very own product, whose values were probably unrealistic to begin with and certainly so in the end. In 1988, Drexel also had to pay the government $650 million to settle insider-trading charges. But Drexel Burnham Lambert was not the only company which owned large amounts of junk bonds. At one point during the year, Citicorp owned $8.7 billion of them, Chase Bank about $4.5 billion, Bank of Boston $5.3 billion, and Security Pacific $4.1 billion.

By some calculations, insurers held about $60 billion in face value, or close to 30% of the $200 billion of junk bonds outstanding. Conning & Co., a securities firm specializing in insurance stocks, estimated at midyear that Equitable Life by itself owned $13.9 billion of junk, representing 6% of its invested assets. That percentage was low compared with some others; a California insurer, for example, was said to have 51% of its invested assets in such securities. And, as might have been expected, the ill-fated savings and loan industry, many of whose units succumbed to mismanagement and fraud and were being dissolved by the Resolution Trust Company (RTC), once owned 7% of the total. The RTC itself inherited a big portfolio, estimated during the summer to have a face value of $4 billion. It loomed over the market. Moreover, the bill setting up the savings and loan bailout required thrifts to sell their junk by 1994. These and other factors inevitably would drive junk values even lower.

The Effects. The bad news persisted, and the decline fed on itself. Few sound investors wanted such securities, which some likened to costume jewelry amid cases of the real thing. By midyear the issuance of new high-yield bonds was down to an average of only $125 million a month, compared with almost 20 times that in 1989. Existing bonds were declining in price. Bonds of the Memorex Company, which raised $555 billion in July 1989 and then reported a 66% drop in operating earnings shortly afterward, declined to 50 cents on the dollar. An attempt was made to hold a weekly junk-bond auction to bring greater liquidity to the market, but for many bond issues the only buyers were the securities firms that were trying to sell them. Average interest rates that issuers had to pay kept growing, and by late summer the spread between U.S. treasury issues, the least risky of all investments, and junk bonds, the most risky, was well beyond 8%, a previously unheard-of premium.

As the statistics worsened they were fleshed out with drama. The personification of pride and financial success, Donald Trump, found that his net worth might be less than his debts, precipitating a sharp decline in the value of junk bonds supporting his Atlantic City hotel-casinos. Darling-Delaware Co., which paid a $179 million dividend to its prominent Texas and Connecticut investor-owners, told shareholders just 20 months later that it could not afford to pay interest on its junk. A memo that surfaced during the investigation of Charles Keating, Jr., head of the defunct Lincoln Savings & Loan, told bond salesmen to "always remember the weak, meek, and ignorant are always good targets." They and others were indeed good targets: The company sold $250 million worth of the bonds to 22,000 investors, most of them in Southern California. The salespeople took the memo to heart: The majority of customers were aged 60 years or more.

The market continued to fail, with prices dropping to their lowest point of the year in August. National Gypsum issues fell 33.3% to $23 during the month, and bonds of Burlington Industries dropped by 31.6% to $33.50. For the first time in several months withdrawals from junk-bond mutual funds rose. The fact that investor-speculator Carl Icahn showed interest in buying junk bonds, at a big discount of course, and the infusion of money into RJR Nabisco by its owners failed to generate much enthusiasm. Some junk-bond issuers took advantage of the situation and bought back their own bonds at a deep discount. An executive of R. H. Macy & Co. said the retailer had drafted plans to repurchase sizable amounts of its junk, at a deep discount of course, in an effort to cut its $600 million annual cash interest bill on $5.8 billion of debt. And there were hints from other issuers that they intended to do the same thing. After having financed leveraged buyouts by borrowing, they now would consider issuing stock to retire the bonded debt. The discounted prices for junk bonds, and the chance to get rid of the heavy burden of interest payments, made the idea attractive to them.

Many companies, however, were in no position to retire their costly bonds; had they even attempted to do so their efforts would have been rebuffed. Late in the year securities analysts issued grim warnings of further deterioration in the financial condition of such companies, especially in view of higher oil prices and the widely held opinion that the U.S. economy was headed into recession. Salomon Brothers issued a report saying that even the "good" junk bonds, those of top-tier companies that largely had escaped the battering taken by others, might face serious pressure in the immediate future. Federal Reserve Chairman Alan Greenspan did little to raise hopes that a recession could be averted, saying that oil-price increases simultaneously were weakening the economy and preventing the Fed from using the countermeasure of lowering interest rates. Moody's, the bond-rating firm, said that as much as 10% of the junk bonds outstanding, or about $20 billion worth, could fail before the year was out.

Late in the year no major new issues were being floated; only eight issues had been brought to market through August, and it was clear that the era of junk bonds was ending. Wall Street, which had earned nearly $600 million in junk-bond underwriting fees in the first eight months of 1989, had earned only $16.2 million in 1990, according to Securities Data Co. Nobody could say whether the finale would be an angry crash or simply a prolonged moan, but many of the participants were not waiting around to find out. Merrill Lynch, First Boston, Smith Barney, Harris Upham, Bear Stearns, and Paine-Webber all reduced their junk-bond departments. And in late November, Milken received a ten-year jail sentence.

JOHN CUNNIFF

Civil war, drought, and famine created a very bleak 1990 in the northeast African nation of the Sudan and led to an increasing number of persons—young and old—living in refugee camps, including the one outside Khartoum, right.

© Joe Bensen/Gamma-Liaison

SUDAN

Sudan continued to face the crises of civil war, economic weakness, and famine in 1990. The revolutionary government led by Omar Hassan Ahmed al-Bashir remained in power but made little progress in resolving the many challenges facing the country and its people.

Domestic Affairs. During 1990 the Bashir government became more clearly identified with the activist Islamic movement in the Sudan. Many nonfundamentalist officials and military officers were removed from their positions while Islamic activists became increasingly prominent. In December 1989 the government had begun implementation of the fundamentalist interpretation of Islamic law, a process first initiated by former leader Jaafar al Nemery in 1983 but suspended after he was overthrown in 1985.

Late in 1989 the government completed a National Dialogue Conference which brought together people representing a wide spectrum of views in an effort to end the civil war. The war involves a conflict between the ruling, Arab-speaking, Muslim majority in the north and the people in the southern third of the country, where the majority is neither Arab nor Muslim. The conference recommended a federal system of government which would recognize the diversity within the country, and the Bashir government formally accepted the federal principle.

The regime was not able to secure the agreement of the leading opposition movement, the Sudan People's Liberation Movement (SPLM), which had emerged in the early 1980s. Many of its leaders and most of its members were southerners, and the SPLM advocated regional autonomy. It also called for a revolutionary transformation of society as a whole and attracted some northern support. The SPLM insisted that government in Sudan must be secular and demanded the abrogation of the ordinances implementing Islamic law. The disagreement with the Bashir regime on this issue reflected the continuing inability of the SPLM and the government to reach a settlement and major fighting continued, especially in the southern region, throughout 1990.

The fighting was not restricted to the southern region. In the western provinces there also was a growing level of violence and local ethnic groups clashed. Some groups had received arms from previous governments and these local militias reportedly played a prominent role in massacres. Efforts to incorporate militias into governmental forces had failed and some observers spoke of the situation as resembling a large-scale repetition of conditions in Lebanon. The sense of instability was heightened by the continued reports of coup

---

SUDAN • Information Highlights

Official Name: Republic of the Sudan.
Location: Northeast Africa.
Area: 967,494 sq mi (2 505 810 km²).
Population (mid-1990 est.): 25,200,000.
Chief Cities (1983 census): Khartoum, the capital, 476,218; Omdurman, 526,287; Khartoum North, 341,146.
Government: *Head of government,* Omar Hassan Ahmed al-Bashir, prime minister (took over June 30, 1989). A 15-member Revolutionary Command Council of National Salvation serves as the supreme executive, legislative, and judicial body.
Monetary Unit: Pound (4.5 pounds equal U.S.$1, August 1990).
Foreign Trade (1988 U.S.$): *Imports,* $1,060,000,000; exports, $509,000,000.

attempts and conspiracies. Antiregime conspiracies were reported in March, June, and September; in April the government reported a major coup attempt and executed 28 military officers. By October an informal alliance made up of the members of banned political parties, dissident military officers, and the SPLM was formed. The government, however, was able to counter the challenges posed by this opposition and remain in power.

The Economy. The general instability in Sudan created difficult economic conditions. Civil war and local conflicts made transportation and production difficult and the number of refugees grew. By the end of 1990 many observers were predicting that millions of Sudanese would be at risk from disease and famine. The situation worsened when neither the government nor the SPLM would cooperate with refugee agencies. In mid-December the UN Food and Agriculture Organization (FAO) reported that the current harvest in the Sudan was even poorer than earlier estimates. According to the FAO the nation had a grain shortage of 1.2 million tons and in the Muslim north there was no harvest at all. Unwilling to request Western aid, President Bashir said Sudan would face the crisis in its "own way."

Sudan also faced international financial problems. The government inherited a large international debt from preceding regimes and was unable to improve the economic situation. During 1990, Sudan was declared a noncooperating member of the International Monetary Fund (IMF), and availability of financing for development was reduced further.

International Affairs. Sudan has had close ties with moderate and conservative Arab countries, such as Egypt and Saudi Arabia. However, as the regime became more fundamentalistic, it developed closer ties with more radical Islamic states. By October, Sudan had initiated a process of political integration with Libya and had established closer ties with the Islamic Republic of Iran. In addition, with the buildup of U.S. armed forces in the Persian Gulf region, Bashir adopted a policy that was increasingly sympathetic toward Iraq and Saddam Hussein. In global politics, Sudan moved away from the close ties to the United States that had characterized earlier regimes.

JOHN O. VOLL
University of New Hampshire

SWEDEN

Politics and economic austerity dominated 1990 events in Sweden.

Politics and the Economy. In January the Social Democrats and the Liberals agreed on wide reforms and changes in Sweden's economic system. Effective in 1991, income taxes were to be lowered greatly, taxes on income from

---

SWEDEN • Information Highlights

Official Name: Kingdom of Sweden.
Location: Northern Europe.
Area: 173,730 sq mi (449 960 km²).
Population (mid-1990 est.): 8,500,000.
Chief Cities (Dec. 31, 1989 est.): Stockholm, the capital, 672,187; Göteborg, 431,840; Malmö, 232,908; Uppsala, 164,754.
Government: *Head of state,* Carl XVI Gustaf, king (acceded Sept. 1973). *Head of government,* Ingvar Carlsson, prime minister (elected March 12, 1986). *Legislature* (unicameral)—Riksdag.
Monetary Unit: Krona (5.569 kronor equal U.S.$1, Dec. 13, 1990).
Gross Domestic Product (1989 est. U.S.$): $132,700,-000,000.
Economic Indexes (1989): *Consumer Prices* (1980 = 100), all items, 188.1; food, 213.2. *Industrial Production* (1980 = 100), 120.
Foreign Trade (1989 U.S.$): *Imports,* $48,890,-000,000; *exports,* $51,542,000,000.

---

capital would be higher, a one-year freeze on wages and prices was to be imposed, and the value-added taxes would be increased. In addition, energy would be more expensive and a possible ban on strikes and lockouts would be adopted. Prime Minister Ingvar Carlsson called the program "the biggest and most important reforms" of the post-World War II era.

Strenuously opposed by the Labor Organization but supported by the business community, the austerity package was rejected on February 15. Carlsson's Social Democratic cabinet then resigned but stayed on as a caretaker government. After consultations among the speaker of parliament and political leaders, it became clear that no party except the Social Democrats was prepared or willing to form a government. Thus, on February 27, Carlsson and a straight Social Democratic government, based on a slight parliamentary majority, took office.

Kjell-Olof Feldt, who had been finance minister since 1982 and previously had been minister of commerce, was not included in the new cabinet. Allan Larson, former head of the Labor Movement Board, took over the finance ministry. Other new members of the cabinet were Rune Molin, vice-chairman of the Labor Organization, who became minister of industry, and Mona Sahlin, a 32-year-old leader in parliament, who took office as minister of labor.

A new austerity package, omitting a wage freeze and a ban on strikes and lockouts, was approved in late February. In April the Social Democrats and the Liberals also jointly supported a series of measures to strengthen the economy, dampen inflation, and safeguard employment.

Prime Minister Carlsson was reelected unanimously as chairman of the Social Democratic Party in September. He has held the post since the assassination of Olof Palme in February 1986.

The Swedish cabinet system of government marked its 150th anniversary in May. It was in May 1840 that King Carl XIV Johan set up a number of government ministries with direct responsibility for handling affairs within their spheres. Although the office of prime minister was added in 1876 and the number of government ministries has expanded, the basic organization of the cabinet has remained the same since 1840.

Other Developments. Some 190 participants from 40 countries attended the Fourth International Conference Against Apartheid in Sports in Stockholm in September. The three-day meeting urged a continued boycott of South Africa in all international sports meets, including the Olympics, unless radical changes are made.

Plans for an automobile-railway bridge, linking Denmark and Sweden across Øresund (The Sound), went forward. The Nordic Literary Prize for 1990 was presented to the Swedish poet Tomas Tranströmer, the author of ten collections of poems. Some of his works have been translated into as many as 30 languages.

ERIK J. FRIIS
"The Scandinavian-American Bulletin"

SWITZERLAND

Matters relating to the trial of former Justice Minister Elizabeth Kopp dominated Swiss affairs during 1990.

Kopp Exonerated. On February 23 a five-judge panel of the Federal Supreme Court acquitted Kopp of charges that she knowingly had divulged official state secrets when she warned her husband in October 1988 that his firm was about to be investigated regarding money laundering in connection with the "Lebanese Connection" drug case. The judges ruled that the prosecution had failed to show that Kopp was aware that the information she gave her husband had emanated from within her own ministry, rather than from "banking circle rumors" as she maintained. This was the first time a former Swiss government minister had been tried on criminal charges.

Secret Files. In November 1989 a parliamentary commission investigating the Kopp affair reported the discovery of 900,000 secret federal police files on 200,000 Swiss citizens and foreign residents. In February 1990 it was revealed that both the justice and defense departments had compiled similar files, with no accountability to elected officials regarding their nature or purpose. Although the federal police maintained that their files related only to political extremists and potential terrorists, it was discovered that 70 members of parliament, plus citizens who had traveled for any reason in the Soviet Union, participated in antinuclear demonstrations, or taken a leadership position on feminist issues also were included.

On March 3, 1990, 30,000 persons demonstrated in Berne, demanding an end to the government's surveillance policies. In response the government on March 7 opened the files for personal scrutiny by any person listed. It also pledged to bring forward a new law to place the security police clearly under parliamentary control. The "Stop State Snooping Committee," which had organized the demonstration, also vowed to begin the process necessary for placing the issue before the voters in a binding national referendum.

New Legislation. In another response to the Kopp scandal, parliament on March 19 imposed penalties of up to 1 million Swiss francs (about $375,000) and five years in prison for bankers, accountants, lawyers, and portfolio managers convicted of knowingly engaging in money-laundering activities. Lesser fines and jail terms were authorized for financial professionals who failed to take "due care" in obtaining reliable identification of customers. The law went into effect on August 1.

On June 20 a law was enacted designed to make immigration, already very difficult, even harder. It included a new regulation prohibiting political-asylum applicants from holding a job during the first three months of their stay in Switzerland.

Other Developments. On April 29 male voters of the half-canton of Appenzell Inner-Rhoden voted overwhelmingly for the third time to deny women voting rights in cantonal affairs. This placed the canton in direct violation of the Swiss national equal-rights law and made confrontation in the court system very likely.

Despite French, British, and U.S. action freezing Kuwaiti assets in their countries following the Iraqi invasion of Kuwait, the Swiss government resisted pressure to do the same. However, it announced on August 2 that it would monitor carefully Kuwaiti holdings in Switzerland in order to keep Iraq from seizing them.

PAUL C. HELMREICH, *Wheaton College, MA*

SWITZERLAND • Information Highlights

Official Name: Swiss Confederation.
Location: Central Europe.
Area: 15,942 sq mi (41 290 km²).
Population (mid-1990 est.): 6,700,000.
Chief Cities (Dec. 31, 1988 est.): Bern, the capital, 135,147; Zurich, 345,159; Basel, 170,080.
Government: *Head of state,* Arnold Koller, president (took office Jan. 1990). *Legislature*—Council of States and National Council.
Monetary Unit: Franc (1.2662 francs equal U.S.$1, Dec. 13, 1990).
Gross Domestic Product (1989 est. U.S.$): $119,500,-000,000.
Economic Indexes: *Consumer Prices* (1989, 1980 = 100), all items, 132.5; food, 137.6. *Industrial Production* (1988, 1980 = 100), 115.
Foreign Trade (1989 U.S.$): *Imports,* $58,221,-000,000; *exports,* $51,549,000,000.

SYRIA

Not a great deal changed in the internal situation of Syria in 1990. In foreign relations, however, a substantial series of changes occurred which moved Syria from the isolated position it had occupied for years to a more central and prestigious, though possibly also more risky, role in the Middle East.

Domestic Affairs. The Syrian economy continued to limp badly, but with some signs of modest improvement over previous years. The state has played an excessive role in economic decisions, burdening what was once a flourishing private sector with the weight of an incompetent bureaucracy, but President Hafiz al-Assad in 1990 moved somewhat to open up the state-run economy to private enterprise. Also, there were some gains in oil production and foreign trade. In the fall there were unofficial reports that Saudi Arabia, as a reward for Syria's emphatic opposition to the Iraqi conquest of Kuwait, was to give to Syria substantial subsidies, to the tune of $2 billion.

The authority and control of President Assad and his Baath Party regime appeared unimpaired or even enhanced. A member of the minority Alawi sect, Assad tends to appoint other Alawi members as his most trusted aides and as high officers in the armed services. Assad's continuing sway, of course, has been facilitated, but cannot be explained wholly, by his reputation for total ruthlessness when his rule is threatened. Assad shares this trait with his longtime arch foe, Saddam Hussein of Iraq. Yet Assad generally is considered to be a cooler and more precise political calculator, and also one who employs violence only on occasion and for well-defined political ends.

General Elections. On May 22–23 a general election was held for the fifth People's Assembly or *Majlis al-Sha'ab*, a body which to some extent reflects public opinion in Syria, though it is hardly the seat of power. More than 9,700 candidates competed for the 250-seat assembly, enlarged from 195 since the previous election in 1986. The ruling Baath Party won 134 seats, and the five other parties which together with the Baath constitute the National Progressive Front gained 32. The increased number of successful independent candidates was 84, but the Baath and its allies still had a comfortable majority of 66%.

In Paris on February 21 the formation of an inclusive anti-Assad movement, the ''Patriotic Front for National Salvation,'' was announced. Its objectives were reportedly the overthrow of Assad and the establishment of a multiparty parliamentary system in Syria. The chief novelty here was the full cooperation of the Muslim Brotherhood with a number of other groups, some of them secular. However, the new front is to be based in Baghdad and financed by Iraq, which clearly will taint its

---

SYRIA • Information Highlights

Official Name: Syrian Arab Republic.
Location: Southwest Asia.
Area: 71,498 sq mi (185 180 km²).
Population (mid-1990 est.): 12,600,000.
Chief Cities (1986 est.): Damascus, the capital, 1,219,448; Aleppo, 1,191,151; Homs, 427,500.
Government: *Head of state*, Gen. Hafiz al-Assad, president (took office officially March 1971). *Head of government*, Mahmoud Zubi, prime minister (took office Nov. 1987). *Legislature* (unicameral)—People's Council.
Monetary Unit: Pound (11.225 pounds equal U.S.$1, August 1990).
Gross Domestic Product (1989 est. U.S.$): $18,500,000,000.
Economic Index (Damascus, 1989): *Consumer Prices* (1980 = 100), all items, 599.2; food, 513.7.
Foreign Trade (1989 U.S.$): *Imports*, $2,097,000,000; *exports*, $3,006,000,000.

chances of success; there have been many Iraq-based conspiracies against Assad in the past.

Foreign Relations. The most important motive for the new course in Syrian foreign policy was the waning support from the ailing Soviet Union since 1988. Relations with the United States improved. Syria and Iran have cooperated in obtaining the release of some U.S. hostages in Lebanon. Normal diplomatic relations with Egypt, broken off by Syria in 1977 at the start of Egyptian peace moves toward Israel, had been reestablished in December 1989. On May 2–3, 1990, Egypt's President Hosni Mubarak visited Damascus, the first visit by an Egyptian leader in 13 years. Later in the year, after the Iraqi takeover of Kuwait, relations with Egypt grew even more cordial. As a result of the meeting with Mubarak, Assad agreed to renew contact with PLO leader Yasir Arafat.

In August, Assad moved boldly. He was quick to denounce the Iraqi invasion of Kuwait, played a major role in convening an emergency Arab summit meeting on August 10, and at that meeting lined up with Egypt, Saudi Arabia, and other pro-Western states. On August 20 the first contingent of 1,200 Syrian troops were sent to Saudi Arabia to support the kingdom. These developments reportedly caused some adverse public reactions in Syria but there were no overt outbreaks of dissent. On September 21–24, Assad had prolonged discussions in Tehran with Iran's President Ali Akbar Hashemi Rafsanjani. Syria had been Iran's sole supporter among Arab states throughout the Iraq-Iran war.

Lebanon. On October 13, Assad had his reward for his rapprochement with the United States and Egypt when an all-out Syrian assault in East Beirut finally routed Assad's Lebanese opponent, Christian militia leader Gen. Michael Aoun, who gave up and took refuge in the French embassy. Assad thus obtained his objective of taking control of Lebanon.

ARTHUR CAMPBELL TURNER
University of California, Riverside

Students occupied Chiang Kai-shek Square in Taipei for six days during prodemocracy demonstrations in March 1990. The protesters were demanding the dissolution of Taiwan's National Assembly and a timetable for political reforms.

AP/Wide World

TAIWAN

In 1990, Taiwan reelected its president, held a National Affairs Conference to explore political reforms, and continued to experience difficulty defining its role vis-à-vis mainland China.

Politics and Government. The incumbent president, Lee Teng-hui of the ruling Kuomintang (KMT) or Nationalist Party, was the favored candidate in the election held in March, but KMT conservatives in the National Assembly (which elects the president) did put forward an opposition slate of candidates. Opposition from the other end of the political spectrum took the form of demonstrations involving 10,000–20,000 people, who took to the streets of the capital to protest the process itself and to call for direct presidential elections. In the event, Lee was reelected by an overwhelming majority of the delegates after the opposition slate withdrew prior to the voting.

Following his election, Lee took steps to placate both opposition camps. To those who had demonstrated in favor of increased democratization, he promised to call a broadly representative National Affairs Conference to discuss reconstitution of the political system and redefinition of its relationship with the mainland. To satisfy his conservative opponents, he appointed one of their number, Defense Minister Hau Pei-tsun, to become his prime minister. Although initially regarded by many on Taiwan as a menace to the fledgling process of democratization because of his military background, the new prime minister soon rose in the public esteem as he mounted a campaign against the rising crime rate and attempted to rein in the disruptive behavior of opposition politicians in the legislature.

The National Affairs Conference, held in the early summer, drew together 140 politicians from across the political spectrum. An important result of the conference was the creation of a coalition between the opposition Democratic Progressive Party (DPP) and reform-minded members of the KMT. As expected, the conference recommended a shift to the direct election of the president, of all delegates to the national legislature, and of provincial and county officials. Its mandate for change in the political system was given impetus by a court ruling in June calling on all legislators who have occupied seats since they were elected on the mainland in 1947 to resign by the end of 1991.

Relations With the Mainland. The conference also endorsed President Lee's statement in his inaugural address regarding relations with the People's Republic of China (PRC). He listed four conditions for opening up direct talks. The first was that the talks be conducted on a state-to-state basis, not, as Beijing had proposed, between the Chinese Communist Party and the KMT. Lee's second and third conditions were that the mainland authorities reinstitute reforms leading to the establishment of a democratic political system and a free-market economy. The fourth condition was that the PRC renounce the use of force as a means of reunification.

Although Beijing's reaction was a negative one, Lee's approach succeeded in grasping the initiative in the relationship. Meanwhile, informal interaction between Taiwan and the mainland provinces grew at a rapid pace. Travel to the mainland by Taiwan citizens increased

---

TAIWAN • Information Highlights

Official Name: Taiwan.
Location: Island off the southeastern coast of mainland China.
Area: 13,892 sq mi (35 980 km²).
Population (mid-1990 est.): 20,200,000.
Chief Cities (Dec. 31, 1986): Taipei, the capital, 2,575,180; Kaohsiung, 1,320,552; Taichung, 695,562; Tainan, 646,298.
Government: *Head of state,* Lee Teng-hui, president (installed Jan. 1988). *Head of government,* Hau Pei-tsun, prime minister (appointed March 1990). *Legislature* (unicameral)—Legislative Yuan.
Monetary Unit: New Taiwan dollar (27.10 NT dollars equal U.S.$1, Dec. 31, 1990).
Gross National Product (1989 U.S.$): $121,400,000,000.

significantly once again in 1990 after a lull following the suppression of the democracy movement in June 1989. Although trade and investment did not grow at the same pace as in 1989, the slowdown had more to do with economic conditions on Taiwan than it did with a lack of confidence in the mainland as a source of cheap labor and imports. It seemed possible that, over the next several years, Taiwan might surpass Hong Kong, Japan, and the United States as the principal source of investment capital for mainland China and as its principal trading partner.

Foreign Relations. Taiwan suffered a diplomatic setback during the summer, when Saudi Arabia, Indonesia, and Singapore established new diplomatic ties with the PRC. This left only 27 nations maintaining diplomatic relations with Taipei. While Taiwan has pursued a policy of "flexible diplomacy" designed to find formulas whereby dual recognition can be maintained, the authorities in Beijing have rejected these formulas as promoting the concept of "two Chinas" that they find unacceptable.

Many observers argued, however, that the diplomatic isolation in which Taiwan finds itself today is justified even less than the diplomatic isolation of the PRC during the 1950s and 1960s. With a total two-way trade amounting to $118 billion in 1989, per-capita income approaching $8,000 per year, and foreign-exchange reserves in excess of $63 billion, unrecognized Taiwan has an economic significance in East Asia far outstripping that of the much more widely recognized mainland.

Taking account of this anomaly, a number of member states supported Taiwan's application to join the General Agreement on Tariffs and Trade (GATT) in 1990. The Republic of China was a founding member of GATT in 1947 but abandoned its seat in 1950 after its defeat on the mainland and subsequent move to Taiwan. The government in Beijing applied in 1986 to occupy that seat once again, but because its economy is subject to central planning, its membership has been postponed. Taiwan, meanwhile, has applied for membership as a customs territory—not as the representative of the whole of China. Choosing to ignore this important distinction, Beijing's observer at GATT responded to Taiwan's application as a "wholly illegal" manifestation of a two-China policy.

JOHN BRYAN STARR
Yale-China Association

TANZANIA

Under an Economic Recovery Program (ERP) inspired by the World Bank, Tanzania's economy grew at a rate of 4.4% in 1990. At the same time pressure continued to mount in the nation for political change.

TANZANIA · Information Highlights

Official Name: United Republic of Tanzania.
Location: East coast of Africa.
Area: 364,900 sq mi (945 090 km^2).
Population (mid-1990 est.): 26,000,000.
Chief City (1985 est.): Dar es Salaam, the capital, 1,096,000.
Government: *Head of state,* Ali Hassan Mwinyi, president (took office Nov. 1985). *Head of government,* Joseph S. Warioba, prime minister (took office Nov. 1985). *Legislature* (unicameral)—National Assembly, 233 members.
Monetary Unit: Tanzanian shilling (194.2 shillings equal U.S.$1, June 1990).
Gross Domestic Product (1989 est. U.S.$): $5,920,000,000.
Foreign Trade (1988 U.S.$): *Imports,* $823,000,000; *exports,* $276,000,000.

Economy. The principal elements of the nation's ERP focused on currency devaluations, high interest rates, and a reliance on market forces to structure production. Growing levels of agricultural and industrial output, however, necessitated a new focus on Tanzania's long-neglected social and economic infrastructure.

Prior to the late 1980s-1990, Tanzania's crumbling transportation and communications infrastructure received scant investment and its inability to cope with growing levels of output threatened economic recovery. Rehabilitation activities have centered on expanding capacity and adding a container facility to the port of Dar es Salaam; improving the locomotive capacity and upgrading the Tazara railroad and Tanzama pipeline between Tanzania and Zambia; and improving the regional network of roads. The rehabilitation of Tanzania's transport system also would benefit its landlocked neighbors. In order to stimulate regional trade, Tanzania signed free-trade agreements with Burundi and Zaire in 1990.

To alleviate some of the austerity measures associated with the ERP, President Ali Hassan Mwinyi introduced an economic and social-action program to rehabilitate the educational system, health facilities, and the water-delivery systems in the rural areas.

Politics. Former President Julius Nyerere retired in August as chairman of the ruling Chama Cha Mapinduzi (CCM) Party. President Mwinyi assumed the post. The move brought immediate calls for rapid reform, especially from Oscar Ramadar Mapuri, the Zanzibari minister. Prior to elections scheduled for October more than 250 CCM critics in Zanzibar were detained without trial under the 1964 preventive detention act.

President Mwinyi sacked seven cabinet ministers in October but retained Joseph S. Warioba as premier.

Other. Nelson Mandela, a leader of South Africa's African National Congress (ANC), was in Tanzania in March and Pope John Paul II visited the country in September.

WILLIAM CYRUS REED, *Wabash College*

TAXATION

Although significant tax-reform legislation was not enacted in 1990, the increasing U.S. budget deficit together with new and unexpected expenditure demands forced President George Bush to break his "no new taxes" campaign pledge and to negotiate with the Congress for deficit-reduction tax increases beginning in fiscal year (FY) 1991 (Oct. 1, 1990-Sept. 30, 1991). As a consequence the 1990 fiscal debate between the Bush administration and the U.S. Congress centered on the types and levels of new taxes, rather than on whether or not taxes would be increased. The final compromise budget raised income and excise taxes by more than $140 billion over the next five years. It was designed to reduce the federal-budget deficit by $40 billion in FY 1991 and by about $500 billion total over the next five fiscal years. Many states also changed their tax-revenue collections within existing tax structures in the face of growing expenditure responsibilities.

On the international scene, a proposed 7% goods and services tax in Canada caused considerable controversy and Britain radically changed its local-government tax structure. The imposition of the new poll tax in Britain contributed to the political downfall of Prime Minister Margaret Thatcher.

United States

Federal. Federal-tax collections during FY 1990 were estimated to be about $1,049,000,000,000. The bulk of these estimated collections was composed of individual income, social-insurance taxes and contributions (Social Security and unemployment insurance), and corporation-income taxes. An estimated $489.4 billion in individual income taxes made up 46.7% of total tax revenue, $385.4 billion in social-insurance taxes (payroll taxes) represented 37% of collections, and $112.0 billion in corporation-income taxes made up 11% of total federal-tax collections. The remaining estimated revenues were excise taxes, estate and gift taxes, and customs duties and fees. These taxes comprised only about 5.3% of federal-tax collections.

The last major federal-tax-reform legislation, the Tax Reform Act of 1986 (1986-TRA), transformed the U.S. tax system. First, by eliminating one of the major tax benefits to corporations that invest—the corporation investment tax credit—and by removing the ability of corporations to lower their tax burden through the use of accelerated depreciation accounting techniques, the 1986-TRA reversed the 30-year erosion of the corporation-tax burden. Second, the 1986-TRA eliminated the favored tax treatment of gains that occur as a result of the sale of stocks, bonds, real estate, and other assets. For tax purposes these "capital gains" would be treated identically to regular income. Finally, the 1986-TRA reduced the number of tax-bracket rates applied to personal income (the rate applied to the portion of personal income falling into each bracket) from 15 brackets to two (15% and 28%) and lowered the highest bracket from 50%. Under the legislation enacted during 1986 a married couple filing a joint return in 1990 faced a 15% tax rate on their first $32,400 of taxable income and a 28% rate on any dollar of taxable income greater than $32,400.

However, although the 1986-TRA reduced the number of brackets to two, the advantages of the lower 15% tax bracket on the first $32,400 of income and personal exemptions from taxable income were removed for higher income taxpayers. The result was that taxable income between $78,400 and $185,760 was taxed at a 33% rate. Finally, any income over $78,400 was taxed at 28%. This increase in marginal tax rates for this group in the 33% tax bracket and then the decrease to 28% created the so-called "bubble" in the income-tax brackets. The 1986-TRA also gradually eliminated or limited major personal deductions ("tax loopholes"), including the deduction for interest on personal debt.

The federal-income tax historically has been considered a fair or progressive tax in opinion polls. (In a progressive-tax system, individuals with higher income pay a greater tax as a proportion of their total income. In a regressive tax system, they pay a smaller proportion of their income in taxes.) Since higher marginal tax brackets still are applied to larger incomes and with the increases in the personal exemption and standard deduction and a general decrease in number of "tax loopholes" after the 1986-TRA, the individual-income tax still is considered to be the most progressive federal tax. Social-insurance taxes and contributions (payroll taxes) are considered regressive, since a flat tax rate is applied to only labor income (e.g., interest and capital gains are not covered by this tax) up to a cutoff income level of $51,300 (as of January 1990). No tax is paid on income beyond $51,300. The regressivity of this tax is reduced, however, when the payments from these taxes (Social Security, Medicare, and unemployment insurance) are taken into consideration.

Tax Fairness. One of the major issues in the 1990 budget negotiations between the Bush administration and Congress was the proper distribution of any new deficit-reduction taxes across high-, middle-, and low-income taxpayers. Many members of Congress believed that the bulk of tax benefits in the 1980s (mostly in the form of the lower tax rates in the 1986-TRA and the tax bubble) were skewed toward individuals in the upper income brackets. As a result these members concluded that "tax fairness" required that the bulk of any new deficit-reduction taxes should be borne disproportionately by upper-income individuals. Consequently, many of the congressional budget proposals differed from those of the Bush administration and contained tax measures specifically aimed at individuals in the upper-income brackets.

In his original budget for FY 1991, President Bush proposed the reinstatement of the preferential tax treatment of capital gains (to 15%). The proposal remained a major objective of the administration during the budget negotiations. One argument for preferential treatment is that gains in the value of assets reflect general price-level increases and not real wealth increases. A second argument is that the preferential tax treatment of capital gains will encourage savings and investment. However, Congress refused to reinstate the significant differential treatment of capital gains that was eliminated in the 1986-TRA. The feeling was that since capital gains are realized disproportionately by upper-income individuals, the preferential tax treatment of these gains was unfair. In the completed and accepted five-year budget plan, the difference between income and capital gains was reinstated slightly by setting the top marginal tax rate on capital gains at 28%.

Congress also called for increased marginal tax rates on individuals in the upper-income brackets (or at least the elimination of the tax bubble) as well as increased excise taxes and surcharges on luxury goods. The removal of the tax bubble in the individual-income tax was a major part of the budget negotiations between the administration and Congress. In the enacted five-year budget plan beginning in FY 1991, the top marginal rate was increased to 31% and the tax bubble was eliminated. As a result, taxpayers would pay at the 31% rate on income over $78,400, 28% on income between $32,450 and $78,400, and 15% on income below $32,400. Additional changes in the budget package were increases in excise taxes on gasoline, cigarettes, alcohol, luxury items, airline-passenger tickets, and telephones.

One part of the payroll tax on labor income is designated as a medical-insurance program (Medicare) for the elderly. In another move designed to decrease the regressivity of the payroll tax and to increase tax fairness, the budget agreement increased the cap on employee wages subject to the 1.45% Medicare tax to $125,000 from $51,300.

State and Local. States and municipalities also levy taxes. States get about 75% of their revenue from income taxes on individuals and corporations, sales taxes, and federal grants. State revenues from their own sources (nonfederal grant revenues) amounted to about $250 billion in FY 1990. Local governments receive the bulk of their revenue from property taxes, state grants, and, in a few localities, income taxes.

There are many differences in tax structures and burdens across the states and localities. For example, seven states impose no individual income tax. The numbers of tax brackets and the levels of the tax rates in these brackets vary widely among the states that do have a personal-income tax. In addition a few states do not impose a general sales tax. Of the states that do have a sales tax, many exempt food and/or prescription drugs. Finally, local taxes on property vary across jurisdictions with regards to tax rates, tax base, and definition of property. As a result it is difficult to summarize the tax burden of these state and local levies. It generally is believed, however, that the combined state and local taxes are neither significantly progressive nor regressive.

In FY 1990 several states enacted proposals to increase their own sources of revenue. However, in only nine of the 18 states that changed their personal-income-tax structures were there increases in taxes. The other half either decreased or left unchanged their income-tax-revenue collections. In addition nearly half of all of the states would have to reconsider the discriminatory tax treatment of federal pensions by the state-income-tax laws in the wake of a new U.S. Supreme Court ruling. Sales-tax rates were increased in Connecticut, Georgia, Kansas, Missouri, and North Dakota for FY 1990. Sales-tax revenues increased in 14 other states through the increase in the number of goods subject to the tax. Four other states had sales-tax-revenue reductions. Finally, many states increased their excise taxes on cigarettes, motor fuels, and, to a lesser extent, alcohol. The general reluctance of many states and localities to increase the individual or corporate tax burdens was due to the problem of migration of individuals and corporations out of the state in response to relatively high tax burdens.

International

England. In an important change in the method by which Great Britain pays for local government services, the government adopted a "community tax" to replace a complex local tax-rate system. This tax was first implemented in Scotland in 1989 and then in England and Wales in early 1990. Unlike taxes that are related to economic activity (e.g., sales, excise, and wage taxes) or economic measures (e.g., income, wealth, or property) and are most common in the United States, this community tax is uniform across all adult-age individuals. Because of this characteristic, this community tax commonly is referred to as a "poll tax."

The administration of this poll tax is straightforward. The central government (equivalent to the U.S. federal government) determines how much a local government can be expected to spend on a particular level of local services. The local governments have fiscal autonomy, since they are free to spend above or below the central government's estimations. However, the central government sets a community tax for each local government on the basis of its estimation of local expenditures. The local government multiplies the community tax by the number of adults in the community and this determines the level of poll tax due to the central government. The proceeds of the poll tax are pooled and distributed to local governments based on the central government's estimation of the local government's expenditures. This revenue is combined with the proceeds from a business tax and central-government grants. This means that any increase in the local spending above the revenues provided by the central government must by paid for by local residents out of additional local tax increases.

The early public evaluations of this poll tax have been unfavorable. Because it is not based on some economic measure (e.g., an income tax), it is considered by many individuals to be unfair, and English citizens took to the streets in violent protests over its imposition in early 1990. In addition the administration of these poll taxes has been expensive and incomplete —after five months, more than 8 million poll taxpayers in England were in arrears.

Canada. The Canadian government of Brian Mulroney continued to battle for passage of a 7% goods and services tax (GST) to replace a 13.5% manufacturers' sales tax. Although the House of Commons enacted the change, the GST was considered very unpopular among the Canadian populace. By late 1990 opposition Liberal Party members in the Senate were filibustering to delay a vote on the tax. (*See also* CANADA.)

THOMAS A. HUSTED
The American University

TELEVISION AND RADIO

Showing a resourcefulness born of financial panic, the "Big Three" television networks and the young Fox Network showed spurts of impressive creativity midway through the 1989–90 season. At a time when television ratings fell throughout the industry, surveys showed the American audience rejecting blandness—historically television's most dependable moneymaker—and embracing weirdness.

In other words, the nation was suddenly abuzz with *Twin Peaks* and *The Simpsons*, two new shows of early 1990. The depth to which these hip, quirky shows penetrated the general culture could be measured in the frequency of the question, "Who killed Laura Palmer?"— referring to the central murder case in *Peaks*, the stylishly moody serial on the American

Broadcasting Companies (ABC) network; or by the proliferation of dolls, T-shirts, and other promotional spin-offs from Fox's *Simpsons*, with images of the hapless cartoon family whose eyes seemed permanently goggled with contemporary angst. (*See* page 88.)

At the start of the fall 1990 season, *The Simpsons* moved to a new time slot opposite the National Broadcasting Company's (NBC's) slipping ratings king, *The Cosby Show*, signaling a battle royal for ratings. Interestingly, the creators of the innovative shows had come from areas that once were alien to the sanitized world of television: alternative newspapers (Matt Groening, who first drew *The Simpsons* as a comic strip), and cult movies (David Lynch, whose writing and direction of *Twin Peaks* and feature films won him a *Time* magazine cover and the headline, "Czar of the Bizarre"). The shows' success, however, had little effect on the 1989–90 ratings race, particularly in the case of *Twin Peaks*, which began in April 1990 and relied on a smaller though committed audience rather than mass popularity for its success.

NBC topped the 1989–90 ratings for the fifth straight season with a 14.6 rating and a 24% share of all television sets in use (the network's *Cheers* ranked second, *Cosby* fourth). ABC continued to close the gap, however, with a 12.9 and 21% share, placing *Roseanne*, *America's Funniest Home Videos*, and *Coach* as the first-, third-, and fifth-ranked shows.

Twin Peaks and *The Simpsons* became the point shows for a broad groundswell of programming that moved away from that vanishing breed, the "typical television family," to reflect the diversity and feverish change of American life in the 1990s. Fox Network's *In Living Color*, a revue of outrageous satirical sketches with a black viewpoint, was one such series, and director-star Keenan Ivory Wayans was cited by television critic John J. O'Connor as a prime example of blacks "steadily gaining more control of the finished television product." (The Supreme Court bolstered the trend by rejecting the George Bush administration's charge that federal affirmative-action programs were unconstitutional, affirming preferential licensing for minority-owned broadcast stations.) *Fresh Prince of Bel Air* (NBC), about a hip black street youth comically upending his wealthy relatives' household, and Fox's *True Colors*, about an interracial marriage, were fall 1990 entries that attempted to ride the new ethnic-diversity wave early in the 1990–91 season.

The New Season. As the fall stretched on, critics began to note that television audiences' hunger for change did not run as deep as it first may have appeared. There were many innovative entries among the massive slate of 34 new shows that debuted in the fall of 1990, but most were ratings disappointments in their early weeks of life, including ABC's quickly-canceled *Cop Rock*, a police show with rock 'n' roll numbers; NBC's *Hull High*, another experimental mixing of comedy-drama and choreographed musical segments; the Columbia Broadcasting System's (CBS') *Evening Shade*, a Southern ensemble comedy with sex-and-marriage themes and an all-star cast that included Burt Reynolds, Marilu Henner, Charles Durning, Ossie Davis, and Hal Holbrook; NBC's *Law and Order*, a courtroom/crime drama starring Michael Moriarty; ABC's *Gabriel's Fire*, starring James Earl Jones as a former cop and ex-con turned reluctant investigator; CBS' *The Flash*, a high-tech, comic-strip-based series; and NBC's *Life Stories*, an anthology of realistic medical dramas with no regular stars. The ever-incorrigible *Washington Post* critic Tom Shales labeled the fall crop of shows "the schlock of the new," explaining they were not really as innovative as their trendy tag lines implied.

Industry executives, though jittery, did not immediately toss innovation to the wolves of the marketplace. NBC announced plans for an *NBC Theater* series, commissioning teleplays and a telemusical from respected dramatists Arthur Kopit and George C. Wolfe and theatrical composer Alan Menken; and cable's Turner Network Television (TNT) began work on a *Writer's Cinema*, with a similar premise and a commission for distinguished playwright-screenwriter Horton Foote. Cable superstation TBS contributed a cartoon with a socially redeeming bent—*Captain Planet and the Planeteers*, with the voices of Whoopi Goldberg, Martin Sheen, Meg Ryan, and Phyllis Diller as superheroes out to save the environment.

By contrast, the more conventional, established shows did better than ever in the ratings, including *America's Funniest Home Videos*, *60 Minutes*, *Murphy Brown*, and *Cheers*. There was also a stubborn refusal to abandon the classy dramatic special with women at the center, such as ABC's *The Last Best Year* with Bernadette Peters and Mary Tyler Moore, NBC's *The Love She Sought* with Angela Lansbury, and Public Broadcasting Service (PBS) vehicles for Diana Rigg (*Mother Love*) and British actress Maggie Smith (*see* Biography) (*Bed Among the Lentils*).

The much beleaguered PBS, in fact, amazed observers by offering the one unqualified new smash of the fall. *The Civil War*, five years in the making by 37-year-old filmmaker Ken Burns, was described by some as the finest television documentary ever made. With elegant simplicity, the 11-hour miniseries brought immediacy and power to the war between the states through reenactments of speeches (using celebrity voice-overs), rare and revealing letters, and massive research. It was a huge popular success, reaching the largest audience in PBS history.

The *Civil War* coup seemed to make perfect sense in what one ABC executive called "a pretty crazy season so far." Even CBS scored a weekly ratings victory—its first in six years

AP/Wide World   © CBS Inc.

Among television's major entertainment offerings of 1990 were the established CBS hit Murphy Brown (above), with Emmy winner Candice Bergen (standing) in the title role, and the quirky new ABC production Twin Peaks (left), with (left to right) Joan Chen, Michael Ontkean, Kyle MacLachlan, and Piper Laurie.

TELEVISION | 1990

Some Sample Programs

Barnum—A London stage production of the musical, taped for television. With Michael Crawford. PBS, March 14.

Blind Faith—A two-part, fact-based, 1990 TV movie inspired by the Joe McGinniss bestseller about a prominent New Jersey insurance man accused of killing his wife. With Robert Urich. NBC, Feb. 11.

Bob Hope—Variety special lampoons television and the movies. With Bob Hope. NBC, Feb. 17.

Caroline—A TV movie about a daughter who returns home after 14 years, after being presumed dead. With Stephanie Zimbalist, Dorothy McGuire, George Grizzard, Pamela Reed, Patricia Neal. CBS, April 29.

Challenger—A TV movie dramatizing the events leading up to the explosion of the space shuttle in 1986. With Karen Allen, Barry Bostwick. ABC, Feb. 25.

Changes—An *NBC News Special* featuring people who have gone through significant changes in their lives. With Jane Pauley. NBC, March 13.

The Civil War—Eleven-hour documentary by filmmaker Ken Burns chronicling events and personal histories from the U.S. Civil War. PBS, Sept. 23.

Dancing for Mr. B.: Six Balanchine Ballerinas—A *Great Performances* telecast featuring ballerinas who worked with the late choreographer George Balanchine. PBS, March 30.

Decade of Destruction—Four-part *Frontline* series chronicling the destruction of the Brazilian rain forest. PBS, Sept. 18.

Drug Wars: The Camarena Story—Three-part miniseries, based on a true story about the U.S. war on drugs. With Craig T. Nelson, Elizabeth Pena. NBC, Jan. 7.

Edward R. Murrow: This Reporter—A two-part *American Masters* profile of the legendary Columbia Broadcasting System (CBS) newsman. PBS, July 30.

An Enemy of the People—An *American Playhouse* dramatization of the Henrik Ibsen classic. With John Glover, George Grizzard. PBS, June 13.

Eyes on the Prize II—An eight-part documentary sequel to the 1986 series on the U.S. civil-rights struggle, examining the ideological changes promoted by a new breed of black leaders in the early 1960s, including Malcolm X. PBS, Jan. 15.

Family of Spies—Two-part, fact-based TV movie about a U.S. Navy spy case. With Powers Boothe, Lesley Ann Warren. CBS, Feb. 4.

Goodnight, Sweet Wife: A Murder in Boston—A fact-based TV movie on the Boston murders of Carol Stuart and her prematurely delivered baby. With Ken Olin, Annabella Price. CBS, Sept. 25.

Gunsmoke: The Last Apache—A TV movie featuring the famous television character Matt Dillon. With James Arness, Richard Kiley. CBS, March 18.

Hamlet—A *Great Performances* telecast of Shakespeare's play. With Kevin Kline. PBS, Nov. 2.

The Heat of the Day—A *Masterpiece Theatre* dramatization of the novel by Elizabeth Bowen. With Michael York, Patricia Hodge, Peggy Ashcroft. PBS, Sept. 30.

Hiroshima: Out of the Ashes—A TV movie that dramatizes the event in 1945 that ended World War II. With Max von Sydow. NBC, Aug. 6.

The Image—A made-for-cable movie that presents a look at television journalism. With Albert Finney, Marsha Mason, Swoosie Kurtz. HBO, Jan. 27.

Jeeves and Wooster—A five-part *Masterpiece Theatre* series, based on the stories by P.G. Wodehouse. With Hugh Laurie, Stephen Fry. PBS, Nov. 11.

Jekyll & Hyde—A TV movie based on Robert Louis Stevenson's novella. With Michael Caine, Cheryl Ladd. ABC, Jan. 21.

Kennedys of Massachusetts—Three-part miniseries chronicling 55 years in the Kennedy family history. ABC, Feb. 18.

Largo Desolato—A *Great Performances* telecast of Czech playwright Václav Havel's 1984 absurdist comedy. With F. Murray Abraham. PBS, April 20.

The Last Best Year—A TV movie about a woman with potentially terminal cancer who develops a friendship with her therapist. With Bernadette Peters, Mary Tyler Moore. ABC, Nov. 4.

The Love She Sought—A TV movie about an older woman's quest for romance while on a vacation in Ireland. With

Angela Lansbury, Denholm Elliott, Robert Prosky. NBC, Oct. 21.

Lucky/Chances—A three-part miniseries adapted from two Jackie Collins novels. With Nicollette Sheridan, Vincent Irizarry. NBC, Oct. 7.

Metropolitan Opera Presents—"Der Ring des Nibelungen"—Telecast of Wagner's four-opera cycle: *Das Rheingold*, *Die Walküre*, *Siegfried*, and *Götterdämmerung*. With James Morris, Christa Ludwig, Hildegard Behrens, Jessye Norman, Siegfried Jerusalem. PBS, June 18.

Miracle Planet—Six-part science series exploring the events and forces that formed and continue to shape the Earth. With host Bill Kurtis. PBS, Jan. 15.

Mother Love—A three-part *Mystery* telecast of a psychological thriller. With Diana Rigg, David McCallum, James Grout, James Wilby. PBS, Oct. 25.

Mozart in Salzburg—A *Great Performances* telecast from the 1989 Salzburg Festival, featuring the Vienna Philharmonic under the direction of James Levine. With Jessye Norman. PBS, March 9.

Murder in Mississippi—A TV movie on a tragic event of the 1960s U.S. civil-rights struggle. With Blair Underwood, Tom Hulce, Josh Charles. NBC, Feb. 5.

The Old Man and the Sea—A TV movie based on the Ernest Hemingway novella. With Anthony Quinn. NBC, March 25.

Orpheus Descending—A made-for-cable movie adaptation of the 1957 Tennessee Williams play. With Vanessa Redgrave, Kevin Anderson. TNT, Sept. 24.

Pair of Aces—A TV movie in which a Texas ranger and a safecracker solve a serial-murder case. With Willie Nelson, Kris Kristofferson. CBS, Jan. 14.

Paul McCartney's Long and Winding Road—An expanded edition of *48 Hours* that follows the former Beatle on the Chicago leg of his world tour. CBS, Jan. 25.

Pavarotti Plus!—A *Live from Lincoln Center* telecast, with highlights from various Italian operas. With Luciano Pavarotti, Leona Mitchell, Carol Vaness, Harolyn Blackwell, and Leo Nucci. PBS, Feb. 28.

People Like Us—Two-part drama based on the Dominick Dunne novel, *The Two Mrs. Grenvilles*. With Ben Gazzara, Connie Sellecca, Eva Marie Saint. NBC, May 13.

The Perfect Baby—An *ABC News Special* report on genetics. With Barbara Walters. ABC, July 18.

Perry Mason: The Case of the Poisoned Pen—A TV movie that has Mason solving the murder of a mystery writer. With Raymond Burr. NBC, Jan. 21.

The Phantom of the Opera—Two-part TV movie based on the 1911 novel by Gaston Leroux. With Burt Lancaster, Charles Dance, Teri Polo. NBC, March 18.

Presidency, the Press, and the People—Ten former White House press secretaries from the Kennedy through the Reagan administrations discuss the role of the press secretary. With John Chancellor. PBS, April 9.

Rock Hudson—A TV movie based on actor Rock Hudson's struggle to deal with his homosexuality. With Thomas Ian Griffith. ABC, Jan. 8.

Sammy Davis, Jr.'s 60th Anniversary—An all-star, variety-show celebration of Sammy Davis, Jr.'s 60 years in show business. With Sammy Davis, Jr. ABC, Feb. 4.

Silhouette—A made-for-cable movie in which an architect witnesses a brutal murder. With Faye Dunaway. USA, Nov. 28.

Sinatra 75: The Best Is Yet to Come—A two-hour salute to Frank Sinatra on his 75th birthday. CBS, Dec. 16.

Treasure Island—A made-for-cable adaptation of the Robert Louis Stevenson 1883 classic. With Charlton Heston. TNT, Jan. 22.

Twin Peaks—Premiere two-hour pilot episode of the series, set in a small town in the Pacific Northwest. With Kyle MacLachlan, Piper Laurie, Michael Ontkean, James Hurley, Dana Ashbrook, Sherilyn Fenn, Lara Flynn Boyle, Sheryl Lee. ABC, April 8.

Voices Within: The Lives of Truddi Chase—A two-part, fact-based TV movie about a woman with multiple personalities. With Shelley Long. ABC, May 20.

Voyage of Terror—The Achille Lauro Affair—A two-part dramatization of the 1985 hijacking. With Burt Lancaster, Eva Marie Saint. Independent, May 1.

The Winslow Boy—A *Great Performances* telecast of the prizewinning 1946 Terence Rattigan play. With Christopher Haley, Ian Richardson. PBS, Feb. 9.

You Don't Look 40, Charlie Brown—A *Peanuts* telecast celebrates the characters' 40th anniversary in the comic strips and their 25th TV anniversary. CBS, Feb. 2.

The Legacy of Jim Henson

With fabric cut from his mother's discarded spring coat and a Ping-Pong ball split in half, a tall, quiet, young man created what became the most popular puppet since Pinocchio. That modern day Geppetto was Jim Henson and that very first Muppet was Kermit, a wise and gentle green frog.

One of the most celebrated figures in the history of children's entertainment, James Maury Henson died of pneumonia on May 16, 1990, at the age of 53. Growing up with such TV shows as *Kukla, Fran and Ollie*, he became fascinated with the challenge of using the television screen as a stage for his felt and foam creations. As a freshman at the University of Maryland, he produced a five-minute, late-night TV show, *Sam and Friends*, working with Jane Nebel, first his business partner and later his wife.

But the marriage that made the Muppets a household word was the union in 1969 of Henson and his company of puppeteers with Joan Ganz Cooney's Children's Television Workshop and its vision of the power of television to educate as it entertains. The Henson characters who people *Sesame Street* project his message that "life is basically good." They reach across boundaries of age, language, and nationality to enchant children and their families in more than 80 countries. Through the antics of Oscar the Grouch and Cookie Monster, the vaudeville routines of Bert and Ernie, the songs of Kermit, and the childlike questions of Big Bird, preschoolers learn about the alphabet and animals, counting and caring, and even about birth and death.

Another phenomenally successful program, *The Muppet Show*, introduced on prime-time television in 1976, proved that Henson's magic, augmented by the playful posturing of Miss Piggy, could attract adults. The Emmy-winning show, which reached some 235 million viewers in 100 countries, spawned several feature-length films and an animated children's series, *The Muppet Babies*.

As millions mourned the loss of this beloved entertainer, they hoped that the special worlds Jim Henson helped to create would not disappear, and that the extraordinary band of puppet makers he trained would continue to tickle imaginations. However, negotiations to transfer the assets of Henson Associates, except for the various residents of *Sesame Street,* to the Walt Disney Company were discontinued by joint agreement, it was announced in mid-December 1990.

PEGGY CHARREN, *President*
Action for Children's Television

Documentary filmmaker Ken Burns offered a major hit of television's fall season with his stunning 11-hour, public-television miniseries on the American Civil War.

—as the networks fought an unpredictable back-and-forth ratings battle. And cable's two comedy channels, once considered highly promising with their blend of classic old shows and hip new material, announced their merger in December after struggling financially through the year.

It was a new television decade and suddenly all the old assumptions were in question. The death in October of William S. Paley (*see* OBITUARIES), founder and architect of the CBS broadcasting empire, loomed as a benchmark for industry uncertainties of the 1990s.

News and Public Issues. Questions flew throughout 1990 about the future of television news and the extent to which it would have to compromise to satisfy two growing pangs: the network parent companies' hunger for increased profit and the mass audiences' taste for ever slicker, flashier news.

The appointment of Steve Friedman, former chief producer of *Today*, as executive producer of the struggling *NBC Nightly News with Tom Brokaw* seemed to some the harbinger of a change for the worse. Some applauded Friedman's breezier, more populist style (he ran a Tom Petty rock song behind footage of U.S. soldiers in Saudi Arabia), but his decision to do about six single-topic shows for the year (which began with the November 9 newscast, "The State of America") created controversy.

Similar format changes were expected at the news departments of ABC and CBS, already gasping from budget cuts and competitive pressure from Cable News Network (CNN), and pressured to perform in the ratings like entertainment programs.

Yet the dire expectations were belied somewhat by expansion in news programming. CBS began a new 30-minute, late-night newscast, *America Tonight*, with seasoned anchors Lesley Stahl and Charles Kuralt. It was the network's second attempt in ten years to challenge

the late-night leadership of ABC News and its much-admired *Nightline*, with Ted Koppel. NBC also reportedly was preparing a 24-hour news network to counter the round-the-clock service of CNN, which incidentally was experimenting with an old idea—the newsreel—which had not been produced since television news knocked it off movie screens in the late 1960s. CNN made headlines of its own in early November when it aired brief excerpts from a taped telephone conversation between Panama's Gen. Manuel Noriega and his lawyers made by federal prison authorities. The issue wound up before the U.S. Supreme Court, which upheld a temporary tape ban (lifted in late November).

People. Admitting that pressuring Jane Pauley off the *Today* show in favor of Deborah Norville had been a mistake, NBC attempted to shore up the severe ratings damage by bringing back veteran news- and sportscaster Joe Garagiola. Pauley, meanwhile, appeared to thrive on her *Real Life* newsmagazine and as Brokaw's occasional co-anchor.

Another high-profile newswoman, Connie Chung of CBS, announced that she would seek a lighter work load while attempting to have a baby, which some observers took as a symbol that the hyper-careerism of the 1980s was coming to an end—or at least going out of style.

Andy Rooney, curmudgeonly humorist/commentator of *60 Minutes*, was suspended by CBS News for racist and homophobic remarks attributed to him by a gay-advocacy newspaper. Claiming he was misquoted, Rooney was back on the air after only one month of the three-month suspension, during which time the *60 Minutes* ratings sagged. A comedian often accused of similar insensitivity to women, gays, and minorities, Andrew Dice Clay, who was booked on NBC's *Saturday Night Live*, made news when Irish rock singer Sinéad O'Connor canceled her appearance and program regular Nora Dunne refused to appear on that telecast.

Radio. The new star of talk radio was syndicated commentator Rush Limbaugh, a prickly conservative whose confrontational style led some critics to lump him with the "shock jocks" who continue to set low standards of taste in radio. Other listeners, however, detected an informed seriousness beneath his showmanship.

Armed Forces Radio, taking a cue from the manic disc jockey in the film *Good Morning, Vietnam*, was beginning its broadcasts to troops in the Mideast with "Gooooooooood morning, Saudia Arabia!"

An increasingly popular commercial gimmick was the "talking billboard," fitted with a transmitter that can break into the regular radio broadcasts that passing motorists are hearing.

DAN HULBERT
"The Atlanta Journal and Constitution"

TENNESSEE

The election and a public outcry over a legislative pension hike made headlines in Tennessee during 1990. Encountering only token opposition, Democratic Gov. Ned McWherter was reelected to a second four-year term.

Politics and Government. Boasting that the state government had fewer employees in 1990 than it did when he took office in 1987 in spite of the opening of three new prisons and the expansion of other state services and facilities, Governor McWherter pledged continuing economy in government and attention to the improvement of the public-school system. The governor was noncommittal about taxes throughout the campaign. In other races, the only newcomers elected were three Democratic Supreme Court members, including Criminal Appeals Judge Martha Daugherty, who became the first woman to sit in the high chamber. All of the state's U.S. House incumbents were reelected, including Harold E. Ford, whose bank-fraud trial resulted in a mistrial.

Legislators approved an $8.5 billion budget, gave teachers a 4% raise, and increased the fuel tax. In an otherwise humdrum annual session, lawmakers created a public stir when they enacted legislation giving themselves a 43% pension hike—a measure dubbed by the press as "unpopular," "avaricious," and "arrogant." Opponents showed that the state, ranking 37th in per-capita income, would have one of the highest U.S. pension rates. After permitting the law to remain on the books for a few weeks, legislators finally repealed it.

Crime and Punishment. Federal investigation into gambling and other charges of wrongdoing among public officials resulted during the summer in the conviction of Democratic leader and legislator Tommy Burnett on nine counts of conspiracy, mail fraud, and illegal gambling. Burnett had been convicted as early as 1984 for failure to make timely income-tax reports, but was reelected to the state Senate after serving time in prison. His 1990 conviction carried a five-year sentence. Davidson County Sheriff Fate Thomas was convicted in July of tax evasion, mail fraud, theft, and conspiracy, and joined the list of more than one dozen county sheriffs convicted in recent years.

Statistics released at the end of 1990 indicated that Tennessee ranked first in the nation for alcohol-linked arrests and second when drug charges were added.

Industrial Growth. Industrial expansion, led by Japanese companies, continued across the state. Nissan Motors of Smyrna, a manufacturer of light trucks and Sentra passenger cars, celebrated the completion of a successful decade by announcing a third vehicle to be added to the line in 1991. Nissan also began a plant expansion that when completed would result in a Nissan investment in Tennessee exceeding $1.2 billion. During the summer, General Motors displayed the first of its Saturn cars produced at the new plant near Columbia.

Agriculture. Adequate rains resulted in expanded crop production after a year of severe drought. Farmers, after two consecutive years of poor soybean yields, scaled that crop back in favor of corn. The burley tobacco crop increased substantially—as did the production of beef cattle. Cotton production was at the highest point in more than a decade.

Public Education. Tennessee's community colleges and technical schools experienced sharp gains in enrollment, especially in industrially expanding east Tennessee. The institution at Blountsville, for example, experienced a 70% increase in two years, and Chattanooga State's growth was described as "dramatic."

Otis Floyd, erstwhile president of predominantly black Tennessee State, became chancellor of the State Board of Regents when Tom Garland resigned. Dr. Harry Wagner of Chattanooga was named to a newly created position of executive vice-chancellor.

ROBERT E. CORLEW
Middle Tennessee State University

TENNESSEE • Information Highlights

Area: 42,144 sq mi (109 152 km²).
Population (1990 census prelim.): 4,822,000.
Chief Cities (July 1, 1988 est.): Nashville-Davidson, the capital, 481,400; Memphis, 645,190; Knoxville, 172,080; Chattanooga, 162,670; Clarksville (1980 census), 54,777.
Government (1990): *Chief Officer*—governor, Ned McWherter (D); *General Assembly*—Senate, 33 members; House of Representatives, 99 members.
State Finances (fiscal year 1989): *Revenue,* $8,325,000,000; *expenditure,* $7,742,000,000.
Personal Income (1989): $72,586,000,000; per capita, $14,694.
Labor Force (June 1990): *Civilian labor force,* 2,415,900; *unemployed,* 130,200 (5.4% of total force).
Education: *Enrollment* (fall 1988)—public elementary schools, 585,972; public secondary, 235,608; colleges and universities, 206,406. *Public school expenditures* (1989–90 est.), $2,716,828,000.

TERRORISM

The end of the Cold War and the spread of democratic revolutions to many parts of the world was not accompanied by a decline in dramatic terrorist incidents in 1990. Instead, the year 1990 will be remembered for the largest hostage-taking incident since the Barbary pirates of the late 18th and early 19th centuries.

Iraq. Saddam Hussein's seizing of thousands of foreigners as hostages after Iraq's invasion of Kuwait in August, and his distribution of some of them to strategic sites in Kuwait and Iraq in order to deter an attack by U.S. forces, showed the power of hostage-tak-

© Harriet Logan/Sipa

Officials inspect the damage following an explosion at London's Carlton Club, a gathering place for members of Britain's Conservative Party. The Irish Republican Army claimed responsibility for the blast, which injured eight persons.

ing to influence events. These "human shields" were used to heighten tension and give Hussein a bargaining chip in dealing with the United States. But President Bush indicated that he would not allow the presence of hostages to prevent the United States from taking appropriate military action. In a dramatic turn of events the hostages were released in December.

Middle East. Terrorism in the Middle East also included the February 4 ambush of a Cairo tour bus that killed nine Israelis and wounded 17 others. The Muslim extremist group Islamic Jihad claimed responsibility for the attack, as did several Palestinian extremist groups. On May 30, Israel foiled an attempted raid on Tel Aviv by Palestinian guerrillas. Four Palestinians were killed and 12 captured when they approached the Israeli coast in two speedboats armed with rockets and heavy machine guns. Israel claimed that Libya supplied the Palestinians with weapons, training, and the crew, which piloted the ship from which the speedboats were launched. On July 28 a pipe bomb exploded on a crowded Tel Aviv beach, injuring 15 people. The bomb was hidden under the sand near a lifeguard post.

On November 25 an Egyptian soldier crossed into southern Israel and fired at several vehicles, killing three Israeli soldiers and a bus driver. Twenty-three civilians also were injured in the assault. The gunman fired a Soviet-made AK-47 rifle at the Israelis, and then fled a few hundred yards back across the border to Egypt where he was arrested by Egyptian authorities. That same day, a Lebanese teenage girl died in a suicide attack against Israeli soldiers. The girl carried a bag of explosives toward the group of soldiers in the security zone that Israel has established along its northern border inside Lebanon. Two soldiers and a Lebanese bystander were injured.

IRA. The Irish Republican Army (IRA) staged a diverse array of attacks against British targets. These included the June 25 bombing of a London club frequented by members of the Conservative Party that injured eight people; the explosion of a bomb in July that wrecked part of the London Stock Exchange; and the assassination of Ian Gow, a Conservative member of Parliament, on July 30. The IRA had placed a bomb beneath the driver's seat of Gow's car. Gow, a leading critic of the IRA, had been named in an IRA death list found in a London bomb factory in December 1988.

Meanwhile a "human bomb" attack failed in November when armed men believed to be IRA members kidnapped a man near Newtown Butler, Northern Ireland, tied up his parents, locked them in the house, and forced him to drive a pickup truck containing a 3,500-lb (1 588-kg) bomb to an army checkpoint 10 mi (16 km) away. He was ordered to drive through the checkpoint and detonate the bomb. However, he jumped out and shouted a warning before the bomb could explode. A small explosion occurred, but nobody was injured. A similar IRA-initiated attack in October killed seven people.

Asia. In Asia two U.S. airmen were killed outside Clark Air Base in the Philippines on May 13 when they were shot from behind at point-blank range with .45-caliber handguns as they left a hotel in Angeles, 50 mi (80 km) north of Manila. The Communist New People's Army is believed responsible for the assassination, which occurred only one day before negotiations started on the future of all U.S. military bases in the Philippines. The NPA had threatened to kill U.S. servicemen as part of its campaign to overthrow the Philippine government and force removal of all U.S. military facilities. The NPA also killed a U.S. Marine outside Subic Bay Naval Station early in May, and assassinated the Filipino vice-president of Nestle Philippines in March.

Meanwhile, terrorism associated with separatist movements in Sri Lanka and India continued. In July, 21 Sinhalese villagers were massacred by Tamil separatist guerrillas. The guerrillas also reportedly massacred 62 Muslim villagers on June 22 for allegedly providing information to government troops. In the Punjab, Sikh separatists initiated a new campaign of violence in the fall, forcing authorities to impose a curfew on the town of Jullundur. More than 3,500 people were believed to have been killed in the Punjab in 1990 alone. There also was large-scale violence in Kashmir where Muslim secessionists and Indian security forces clashed. Almost 2,000 people were believed to have been killed in gun battles in that region in 1990. And Hindu mobs attacked a Muslim mosque in the holy city of Ayodhya in November, killing many.

Latin America. Drug-related terrorism continued in Latin America with a car bombing on a highway bridge near Medellín, Colombia, on April 11, which killed at least 21 people and wounded more than 100. Among the dead were officers of the Elite Brigade which operates against drug traffickers and leftist guerrillas. The former leader of the Colombian guerrilla group M-19, Carlos Pizarro, a presidential candidate, was assassinated on April 26. In Peru, *Sendero Luminoso* terrorists were believed responsible for the assassination of former Defense Minister Enrique Lopez Albujar on January 9. Meanwhile, a terrorist shouting ''Viva Noriega'' tossed a grenade into a U.S.-owned disco in Panama City in March, killing a U.S. serviceman and injuring 27 others. A group calling itself the Martyrs of December 20 claimed responsibility. The group takes its name from the date that the United States invaded Panama in 1989, showing how new terrorist groups can be formed to protest specific government actions. In Chile one person was injured when a bomb went off on March 9 in front of the U.S. consulate in Santiago. The Manuel Rodríguez Patriotic Front claimed responsibility. The incident occurred only a few

hours before Patricio Aylwin was to be sworn in as the new Chilean president.

And in Honduras the Morazanista Patriotic Liberation Front claimed responsibility for the wounding of seven U.S. airmen when a bus carrying U.S. servicemen was fired on northwest of Tegucigalpa.

USSR-East Europe. Terrorism also struck the Soviet Union as several planes were hijacked and a man with a sawed-off shotgun fired two shots in the vicinity of Mikhail Gorbachev as the Soviet leader was presiding over a parade in Red Square. Nobody was injured in the November 7 shooting.

On March 27 in suburbs throughout Athens, Greece, explosive devices destroyed 12 cars belonging to diplomats from the Soviet Union, Czechoslovakia, Bulgaria, Hungary, Syria, and a Palestine Liberation Organization representative. The leftist Social Resistance group claimed responsibility. A Polish diplomat and his wife were wounded in Lebanon when extremists belonging to the Revolutionary Action Organization of the Arab Resistance Front opened fire on them. The shooting was in retaliation for the Polish government's offer to help transport Soviet Jews to Israel.

The United States. In the United States, Rabbi Meir Kahane, the founder of the militant Jewish Defense League and former member of the Israeli parliament, was assassinated on November 5 after giving a speech in New York City. He moved to Israel from New York in 1971 and had been the leader of a movement to expel Arabs from Israeli territories. Police believe that Kahane's alleged killer, El Sayyid A. Nosair, an Egyptian-born devout Muslim, acted alone.

In a separate event, Walter Moody was arrested in November for a series of 1989 mail bombings that killed a U.S. federal judge in Atlanta and a civil-rights lawyer in Savannah.

JEFFREY D. SIMON, *The RAND Corporation*

On May 30, 1990, Israeli security forces foiled an attempt by heavily armed Palestinians to land on beaches in central Israel. Four Palestinians were killed and 12 were captured as they approached Israel's coast in two speedboats.

TEXAS

By late 1990, Texas was experiencing a healthy economic upswing. A crisis in the Middle East caused by Iraq's invasion of Kuwait resulted in a $40-per-barrel oil price, and while Texas oilmen rejected that figure as unstable, a price at that level justified renewed drilling activities. A number of successful federal savings-and-loan prosecutions also inspired confidence in the economy. Office and hotel space was at a premium in Houston, Dallas, and San Antonio, and speculative commercial construction was on the rise. Nonetheless, economists tempered these encouraging trends with the cautionary note that unemployment remained stable at 7%, and new housing starts were down. While Texas was not experiencing the doldrums of some states in the Northeast, there was still room for improvement in its economy.

Politics. In a stunning upset in the November election, Democratic state Treasurer Ann Richards (*see* BIOGRAPHY) defeated Republican Clayton Williams in the Texas gubernatorial race. The nearly 4% margin of victory surprised even Richards' most ardent backers. Reflecting voter interest in the contest, some 3.9 million Texans cast a ballot, totaling just more than 50% of those entitled to vote. With Williams spending $20 million on his campaign and Richards $10 million, it became the most expensive race for governor in U.S. history. Williams was endorsed enthusiastically by U.S. President George Bush, who returned to Texas to campaign for him.

The Texas governor's race attracted a great deal of national interest because of the prevalence of "negative" campaigning by both candidates. Williams made reference to his opponent's struggle with alcoholism, while Richards stressed that Williams, an acknowledged millionaire, paid no federal income taxes for

1986. Personalities aside, both candidates agreed that education reform and crime control were the major statewide issues. On abortion, Richards adopted a pro-choice stance, while Williams took a harder line. Because of the 1990 census count, the Democratic state legislature and governor now must draw new election districts for three additional seats in the U.S. House of Representatives.

Democrat Dan Morales, a graduate of Harvard Law School and the first Hispanic elected to statewide office in Texas history, defeated state Sen. Buster Brown in the contest for attorney general, becoming a new political force. Republican Sen. Phil Gramm was returned by a handsome margin over Hugh Parmer, a former mayor of Fort Worth, and all incumbent U.S. representatives except Democrat Marvin Leath, who retired, were returned to Washington. State Sen. Chet Edwards (D) was elected to the House in Leath's 11th District.

Education. Public education remained a controversial matter in Texas. On Oct. 2, 1989, the state Supreme Court had ruled unanimously that the school finance system must be corrected to provide the 1,055 Texas school districts with essentially equal revenues for equal tax effort. After four special sessions of the legislature during 1990, a plan was crafted that appropriated $582 million for school equalization. Despite an election-year pledge against any new taxes, Gov. Bill Clements approved a quarter-cent increase in the state sales tax, plus additional taxes on liquor and cigarettes.

However, on September 26, state District Judge Scott McCown held the new plan unconstitutional since it would leave wealthy school districts with tax revenues far in excess of state assistance to property-poor districts. In conclusion, McCown held that unless the legislature came up with an acceptable plan by Sept. 1, 1991, he would suspend all state and local funding for the schools. The Texas Supreme Court announced that it would hear final arguments on the case before Jan. 1, 1991.

Other News. A Houston jury in May convicted Paul Stedman Cullen of poisoning an historic 500-year-old "Treaty Oak" tree in Austin. Cullen was sentenced to serve nine years in prison and to pay a $1,000 fine.

In June an oil spill occurred off the Texas coast in the Gulf of Mexico, following an explosion and fire on the Norwegian tanker *Mega Borg*. Two crew members died in the accident.

In September a federal appeals court in New Orleans, LA, upheld the Texas system of electing judges, rejecting a suit brought by civil-rights groups charging that the system violated the 1965 Voting Rights Act by electing judges at large rather than in special districts and thus diluting minority voting strength. The court contended that the 1965 act did not apply to judicial elections.

STANLEY E. SIEGEL, *University of Houston*

TEXAS · Information Highlights

Area: 266,807 sq mi (691 030 km²).

Population (1990 census prelim.): 16,825,000.

Chief Cities (July 1, 1988 est.): Austin, the capital, 464,690; Houston, 1,698,090; Dallas, 987,360; San Antonio, 941,150; El Paso, 510,970; Fort Worth, 426,610; Corpus Christi, 260,930.

Government (1990): *Chief Officers*—governor, William Clements (R); lt. gov., William P. Hobby (D). *Legislature*—Senate, 31 members; House of Representatives, 150 members.

State Finances (fiscal year 1989): *Revenue,* $29,389,000,000; *expenditure,* $24,226,000,000.

Personal Income (1989): $266,794,000,000; per capita, $15,702.

Labor Force (June 1990): *Civilian labor force,* 8,548,800; *unemployed,* 539,100 (6.3% of total force).

Education: *Enrollment* (fall 1988)—public elementary schools, 2,392,079; public secondary, 891,628; colleges and universities, 847,192. *Public school expenditures* (1989–90 est.), $12,299,-000,000.

THAILAND

For Thailand, 1990 was marked by high economic growth, labor unrest, political intrigue, and improved prospects for peace in neighboring Cambodia.

Politics. Prime Minister Chatichai Choonhavan faced a series of challenges from former army commander Chaovalit Yongchaiyut, from opposition parties in parliament, from the workers in state enterprises, and from the army itself. It seemed that each time the veteran politician defeated one of his foes, two more would pop up to threaten his government.

Former Gen. Chaovalit Yongchaiyut is 12 years younger than Chatichai, and he made no secret of his impatience to succeed him. While he was army commander, Chaovalit constantly sought to upstage the prime minister by grandiose political initiatives. Even after retiring from the army, he kept alive speculation that he might lead a military coup. In March, Prime Minister Chatichai pulled a coup of his own by inducing Chaovalit to join his government as deputy prime minister and defense minister. Taking advantage of Chaovalit's ambition, Chatichai gave him one difficult task after another—rooting out corruption in Bangkok, developing the barren Northeast, and mediating the civil war in Cambodia. After just ten weeks, Chaovalit resigned, apparently fearing he would bear the blame for any failures while Chatichai would take credit for whatever success he might gain.

Some army officers were unhappy that friends of the prime minister had embarrassed Chaovalit and made it difficult for him to remain in the government. But Prime Minister Chatichai was supported by King Bhumibol Adulyadej and by the new army commander, Gen. Suchinda Kraprayoon. Thus, on the same day that Chaovalit resigned his government posts, Chatichai felt secure enough to fly off to the United States on an important diplomatic mission.

In July, Chatichai faced a vote of no confidence by the opposition parties in parliament. Although his majority was large enough to ensure his survival, the debate on opposition charges of corruption hit home and forced him to shake up his cabinet in August. In November a renewed challenge from the military led to a second cabinet shuffle, and in December, Chatichai was forced to resign but he was reappointed by the king.

Economy. For the third consecutive year, the Thai economy grew at one of the fastest rates in the world. However, there was growing public concern about corruption among the leaders of government, business, and the military, and about the unequal distribution of the country's wealth. Now that the kingdom no longer is threatened seriously from abroad, other concerns, including inflation, AIDS, and pollution, have come to occupy the attention of the Thai public.

In May thousands of workers in state enterprises launched a strike that threatened to cut off supplies of electricity and running water to many of the 5.5 million residents of Bangkok. Although the military tended to side with the workers, because many senior officers are on the boards of state-run utilities, Prime Minister Chatichai managed to line up army support in case the strike got out of hand. In the end, Chatichai won by first demonstrating that the workers lacked public support—and then offering them a generous raise.

In July, Chatichai pushed through parliament the country's first social-security law, which gradually will phase in coverage of many of the country's 10 million workers for accidents, disability, death, maternity leave, retirement, and unemployment. The bill excludes state enterprise workers because they have their own pension and insurance plans. Although it was opposed strongly by military leaders on the boards of utilities, its passage was hailed as a milestone in asserting civilian control over the government.

Foreign Affairs. Siddhi Savetsila, who had served as foreign minister since 1980, was replaced in August by former Commerce Minister Subin Pinkayan. Siddhi was an architect of the policy of resisting Vietnamese influence in Cambodia. This put him increasingly at odds with Prime Minister Chatichai, who personally had opened contact with the Vietnamese-backed government in Phnom Penh. Siddhi's successor was expected to follow Chatichai's lead. The year was also notable for improved relations with the United States, the Soviet Union, and neighboring Laos.

More than 8,000 Thai workers were stranded in Kuwait and Iraq when the Persian Gulf crisis erupted in August, but most managed to get out of the area by year's end.

PETER A. POOLE
Author, "The Vietnamese in Thailand"

THAILAND • Information Highlights

Official Name: Kingdom of Thailand (conventional); Prathet Thai (Thai).
Location: Southeast Asia.
Area: 198,456 sq mi (514 000 km²).
Population (mid-1990 est.): 55,700,000.
Chief City (June 30, 1989 est.): Bangkok, the capital, 5,845,152.
Government: *Head of state,* Bhumibol Adulyadej, king (acceded June 1946). *Head of government,* Chatichai Choonhavan, prime minister (took office August 1988).
Monetary Unit: Baht (25.62 baht equal U.S.$1, July 1990).
Gross National Product (1989 est. U.S.$): $64,500,-000,000.
Economic Index (Bangkok, 1989): *Consumer Prices* (1980 = 100), all items, 147.8; food, 137.3.
Foreign Trade (1989 U.S.$): *Imports,* $25,769,-000,000; *exports,* $20,059,000,000.

Playwright August Wilson's 1990 Pulitzer Prize-winning "The Piano Lesson" starred Charles S. Dutton and S. Epatha Merkerson in their Tony Award-winning roles as a farmer and would-be landowner struggling with his sister over whether to sell the family heirloom, a piano, in order to raise money to buy farmland on which previous generations of the family had been slaves and sharecroppers.

© Gerry Goodstein

THEATER

In a year of shuttered theaters, widespread deficits, falling subscriptions, and runaway playwrights seeking the deeper feed troughs of Hollywood, there was a shining beacon of good news—a 1990 production of *The Grapes of Wrath* that proved the continuing excellence, relevance, and power of the American theater. Staged by the Steppenwolf Theatre of Chicago, it pulled together the best of two worlds—the nonprofit resident theaters, of which Steppenwolf is a leading light, and Broadway, where the production transferred with its Chicago ensemble intact and won national exposure and the 1990 Tony Award for best play. Featuring some of Steppenwolf's most familiar stalwarts (Gary Sinise, Terry Kinney, Jeff Perry, and Lois Smith, as Ma Joad), Frank Galati's elegiac adaptation and staging of John Steinbeck's novel so clearly evoked the tragedy of America's homeless that many left the Cort Theater in tears.

Broadway. But for the Great White Way, the 1989–90 theater season in general was another of those "it could be worse" seasons of small comfort, better than the bleak mid-1980s at roughly 8 million attendance and 35 openings, but puny compared to Broadway's heyday of 20 and 30 years before. By September 1990 the spring triumph, *Wrath*, had closed—and thereby hangs the tale of Broadway's sudden, jolting cycles of boom and bust.

In fact, at year's end the new fall season looked as though it might never come to life at all, with nothing like the surprising spring spurt of plays that *The New York Times* called "Broadway's Bounty" (among them, Craig Lucas' romantic fantasy *Prelude to a Kiss*; the stylishly witty, best-musical Tony winner *City of Angels*; August Wilson's Pulitzer Prize-winning supernatural drama about black history, *The Piano Lesson*; Tommy Tune's Tony Award-winning, perpetual-motion staging and

choreography of *Grand Hotel*; and a fine revival of Tennessee Williams' *Cat on a Hot Tin Roof* that featured a sizzling Kathleen Turner as Maggie and Charles Durning as Big Daddy.)

Superb performances redeemed lesser plays: Britain's Dame Maggie Smith (*see* BIOGRAPHY), beating out Turner for the best-actress Tony as she played a wacky, less-than-accurate tour guide in the Peter Shaffer boulevard comedy, *Lettice and Lovage*; and comeback kid Robert Morse, who as an astoundingly convincing Truman Capote in *Tru*, beat out Dustin Hoffman's inspired Shylock in *The Merchant of Venice* for the best-actor award.

Precious few fall productions generated the kind of excitement of the spring awakening, however. The most notable early entries of the 1990–91 season were *Six Degrees of Separation*, which premiered at Lincoln Center's small Newhouse Theater during the summer and transferred onto the larger Beaumont stage in October; *Once on This Island*, the utterly charming Calypso-flavored musical fable that likewise transferred from an off-Broadway debut at Playwrights Horizons; and *Shadowlands*, by William Nicholson, with Nigel Hawthorne and Jane Alexander as, respectively, the Christian essayist/children's author C.S. Lewis and the American poet Joy Davidman, whose fleeting autumnal romance and marriage is cut short cruelly by her bone cancer.

With his funny and suspenseful comedy-drama, *Six Degrees*, about a wealthy New York couple (Stockard Channing and John Cunningham) who are conned dazzlingly by a mysterious young black man (Courtney B. Vance) claiming to be a friend of their Harvard student son, playwright John Guare seized and defined the moment of urban paranoia in U.S. life.

Other late 1990 Broadway entries, in brief:

• *Shogun*, the musicalization of James Clavell's best-selling novel, was a stupefied sumo wrestler of a show, notable only for its decorative splendor of 16th-century Japan.

• *Oh, Kay!* was a rare revival of a 1920s Gershwin brothers' musical from venerable producer David Merrick, but its creaky book gained no new dimension by simply substituting black actors in the originally white roles.

• *Buddy: The Buddy Holly Story*, as straightforward as its title, was a London hit that transferred to Broadway, and its main asset was bespectacled Paul Hipp capturing the all-American innocence and energy of rock 'n' roll legend Buddy Holly.

Altogether, it was a pretty paltry crop of musicals (true to form also for most of the 1980s) as 1990 ended, made even paltrier by the September closing of *Jerome Robbins' Broadway*, after a disappointing run of less than a year and a half, and the closing of *A Chorus Line*, after its magnificent record-setting run of 15 years. The gaping hole left by *Chorus Line* was a kind of symbolic reproach to a Broadway creative community that had succeeded so rarely in emulating that musical's innovative spirit. (*See* feature article, page 78.)

There was a ferocious curiosity awaiting *Miss Saigon*, due in the spring of 1991. The smash London musical by the creators of *Les Misérables* became the center of an ethnic battleground during 1990 as Asian-American artists (led by *M. Butterfly* author David Henry Hwang) protested the casting of white British actor Jonathan Pryce in the lead Eurasian role, and Actor's Equity threatened to deny him working papers on Broadway. Producer Cameron Mackintosh then canceled the show, which had an advance sale of $25 million and roles for 40 more Asian actors. Finally, Equity gave in, and the booking was reinstated. Both sides of the controversy claimed to represent the same ideal: casting on the basis of talent, without regards to race and ethnicity.

Off-Broadway. Despite the unimpressive Roundabout Theatre production surrounding him, Hal Halbrook gave a worthy performance in the title role of *King Lear*.

Playwright Beth Henley, still struggling to regain the level of 1980's *Crimes of the Heart*, got mixed but respectful notices as she switched gears to a historical epic mode in *Abundance*. The comedy-drama at Manhattan Theatre Club featured Amanda Plummer and Tess Harper as mail-order brides in the Wild West.

Spalding Gray and Eric Bogosian, whose quirky charms helped make the performance-art monologue into a popular theater event in the late 1980s, had hip new entries. Bogosian's *Sex, Drugs, Rock 'n' Roll* looked at an addicted, compulsive society with dark corrosive wit, and Gray's *Monster in a Box* at Lincoln Center captured the mixed delights of traveling the world while lugging an unfinished novel that it seems neither can be finished nor gotten rid of.

Rescued from oblivion, and showing powerful new relevance, was *Machinal*, Sophie Treadwell's pioneering feminist drama of the 1920s suggested by the murder case of Ruth Snyder, the first woman to die in the electric chair. Michael Greif's staging at the New York Shakespeare Festival marvelously captured the urban industrial angst with an Expressionistic starkness of the period.

Resident Theaters. While the United States debated throughout 1990 whether a recession indeed had arrived, the nonprofit resident theaters struggled to deal with that painful reality.

A newspaper survey reported theater closings (the League of Resident Theatres had dropped from 80 members to 68 since the mid-1980s), shortened rehearsal time, curtailed programming, and staff cuts on a widespread basis. Artistic directors complained of stagnating federal-funding levels and of the switching of resources by major philanthropies from the arts to such social issues as the homeless. Young patrons' resistance to committing their time months ahead (a symptom of a more hurried, transient society) was seen as a factor in the continuing decline in subscription sales. Added to those dire factors was the phenomenon of the disappearing playwright, often lured away by the money of screenwriting. The writers whose playwriting drought continued into

The acclaimed "Six Degrees of Separation" involved spouses John Cunningham (right) and Stockard Channing in a life-altering encounter with imposter Courtney Vance.

© Martha Swope

BROADWAY OPENINGS | 1990

MUSICALS

Aspects of Love, music and book adaptation by Andrew Lloyd Webber, from a novel by David Garnett; lyrics by Don Black and Charles Hart; directed by Trevor Nunn; with Michael Ball, Ann Crumb, Kevin Colson, Kathleen Rowe McAllen; April 8–.

Buddy . . . "The Buddy Holly Story," featuring music by Buddy Holly; book by Alan Janes; directed by Rob Bettinson; with Paul Hipp, Fred Sanders, David Mucci, Philip Anthony; Nov. 4–.

A Change in the Heir, music by Dan Sticco; lyrics by George H. Gorham; book by Mr. Gorham and Mr. Sticco; directed by David H. Bell; with Brooks Almy, Judy Blazer, Jeffrey Herbst; April 29–May 13.

Fiddler on the Roof, music by Jerry Bock; book by Joseph Stein; lyrics by Sheldon Harnick; direction reproduced by Ruth Mitchell; with Topol; Nov. 18–.

Oh, Kay!, music by George Gershwin; lyrics by Ira Gershwin; book by Guy Bolton and P.G. Wodehouse; adapted by James Racheff; directed by Dan Siretta; with Brian Mitchell, Angela Teek; Nov. 1–.

Once on This Island, music by Stephen Flaherty; book and lyrics by Lynn Ahrens; directed by Graciela Daniele; with La Chanze, Jerry Dixon; Oct. 18–.

Peter Pan, adapted from book by Sir James M. Barrie; music by Moose Charlap, with additional music by Jule Styne; lyrics by Carolyn Leigh, with additional lyrics by Betty Comden and Adolph Green; directed by Fran Soeder; with Cathy Rigby, Stephen Hanan; Dec. 13–.

Shogun, The Musical, music by Paul Chihara; book and lyrics by John Driver, based on a novel by James Clavell; directed by Michael Smuin; with June Angela, Philip Casnoff, Francis Ruivivar; Nov. 15–.

Those Were the Days, conceived by Zalmen Mlotk and Moishe Rosenfeld; music and lyrics by Abe Ellstein, Ben Bonus, Molly Picon, Gene Raskin, and others; directed by Eleanor Reissa; Nov. 7–.

Truly Blessed: A Musical Celebration of Mahalia Jackson, original music and lyrics by Queen Esther Marrow; additional music and lyrics by Reginald Royal; book by Ms. Marrow; directed by Robert Kalfin; with Ms. Marrow, Carl Hall, Lynette G. DuPré, Doug Eskew, Gwen Stewart; April 22–May 20.

PLAYS

Accomplice, by Rupert Holmes; directed by Art Wolff; with Jason Alexander, Pamela Brull, Michael McKean, Natalia Nogulich; April 26–June 10.

Cat on a Hot Tin Roof, by Tennessee Williams; directed by Howard Davies; with Kathleen Turner, Charles Durning, Polly Holliday, Daniel Hugh Kelly; March 21–Aug. 1.

The Cemetery Club, by Ivan Menchell; directed by Pamela Berlin; with Eileen Heckart, Elizabeth Franz, Doris Belack; May 15–July 1.

The Grapes of Wrath, by John Steinbeck; directed by Frank Galati; with Gary Sinise, Lois Smith, Terry Kinney; March 22–Sept. 2.

Lettice & Lovage, by Peter Shaffer; directed by Michael Blakemore; with Maggie Smith, Margaret Tyzack; March 25–Dec. 23.

Miss Margarida's Way, written and directed by Roberto Athayde; with Estelle Parsons; Feb. 15–25.

The Miser, by Molière; directed by Stephen Porter; with Philip Bosco, Carole Shelley, Mia Dillon; Oct. 11–Dec. 30.

The Piano Lesson, by August Wilson; directed by Lloyd Richards; with Charles S. Dutton, S. Epatha Merkerson; April 16–.

Prelude to a Kiss, by Craig Lucas; directed by Norman René; with Barnard Hughes, John Dossett, Ashley Crow; May 1–.

Shadowlands, by William Nicholson; directed by Elijah Moshinsky; with Nigel Hawthorne, Jane Alexander; Nov. 11–.

Six Degrees of Separation, by John Guare; directed by Jerry Zaks; with Stockard Channing, John Cunningham, Courtney B. Vance; Nov. 8–.

Some Americans Abroad, by Richard Nelson; directed by Roger Michell; with Kate Burton, Frances Conroy, Henderson Forsythe, Nathan Lane, Elizabeth Shue; May 2–June 17.

Stand-up Tragedy, by Bill Cain; directed by Ron Link; with Marcus Chong, Charles Cioffi, Jack Coleman; Oct. 4–16.

Zoya's Apartment, by Mikhail Bulgakov; directed by Boris Morozov; with Bronson Pinchot, Linda Thorson, Robert LuPone; May 10–June 17.

OTHER ENTERTAINMENT

Michael Feinstein, concert in piano and voice; with Michael Feinstein; Oct. 2–27.

Jackie Mason: Brand New, comedy; Oct. 17–.

1990 included Pulitzer Prize winners Sam Shepard, David Mamet, Marsha Norman, and Lanford Wilson.

Nonetheless, artistic energy remained fierce on many fronts in the resident theaters. Multiculturalism, a term that gained wide currency during the *Miss Saigon* controversy, was seen as "the most important single issue of the 1990s," in the words of founding producer-director Zelda Fichandler of Washington's Arena Stage. The trend had many faces and forms, from the well-received Falstaff performed by a woman (Pat Carroll) in *The Merry Wives of Windsor* at the Folger Shakespeare Theatre of Washington, to the casting of black actor Morgan Freeman as a cowboy Petruchio (opposite Tracy Ullman's Kate) in *The Taming of the Shrew* at the New York Shakespeare Festival in Central Park, to the plays offered on alternate days in English and Spanish at the San Diego Repertory Theatre.

Arena was a leader in this multicultural movement, not only with nontraditional casting (a controversial all-black *Glass Menagerie*) but

with new minority representation in all areas of production and administration. (There was even a sociologist attached to the staff to help smooth the changes.) Blacks who were promoted to a welter of new associate directorships with broad policy-making powers included Benny Ambush at American Conservatory Theatre of San Francisco, playwright-director George S. Wolfe (*The Colored Museum*) at the New York Shakespeare Festival, and Tazewell Thompson at the Arena.

Perhaps the most dramatic change was at the 20-year-old Alliance Theatre of Atlanta, a historically conservative white theater that hired 34-year-old black Atlantan Kenny Leon as artistic director. Leon's inaugural production was *Miss Evers' Boys* (based on horrifying true accounts of black sharecroppers used as medical guinea pigs in a nearby Alabama county).

According to the season schedules printed in September by *American Theatre* magazine, two of the most popular plays slated for U.S. productions in 1990–91 were Alfred Uhry's

© Carol Rosegg/Martha Swope Associates

Among 1990 Broadway musicals was "Oh, Kay!," impresario David Merrick's revival of a 1926 Gershwin brothers' musical, using an all-black cast, that opened to mixed reviews in November for a short run prior to beginning a national tour.

Driving Miss Daisy, the 1988 Pulitzer Prize-winning play about an elderly Southern Jewish widow and her black chauffeur; and *The Boys Next Door*, Tom Griffin's funny and moving portrait of a residence for men who are retarded mildly.

Bold, literate new dramas from Britain got wide exposure. David Hare's exposé of the mercenary spirit of Thatcherian Britain, *Rapture*, was staged at the Dallas Theater Center, South Coast Repertory in Costa Mesa, CA, and at Steppenwolf of Chicago. *Our Country's Good* (Timberlake Wertenbaker's play-within-a-play about 18th-century Australian convicts who stage *The Recruiting Officer*) was mounted at the Berkeley (CA) Repertory Theatre, Remains Ensemble of Chicago, Repertory Theatre of St. Louis, and the Hartford Stage.

In Los Angeles the Mark Taper Forum premiered *Hope of the Heart*, a continuation of director Adrian Hall's noted dramatizations of works by his fellow Southerner, Robert Penn Warren. *Hope* was adapted from the 19th-century flashback section of Warren's novel *All the King's Men*.

In Louisville, Actors Theatre under the artistic direction of Jon Jory continued its annual "Classics in Context" series with a "Commedia dell 'Arte" festival, spotlighting the delightful clowning and mime of Geoff Hoyle and Bill Irwin (*Largely New York*).

Chicago played host to its second biennial International Theatre Festival in April, dominated by Britain's Renaissance Theatre Company and its brace of Shakespearean productions (*King Lear*, *A Midsummer Night's Dream*) marked by a muscular straightforwardness, the signature style of artistic director

Kenneth Branagh, whose 1989 film sensation *Henry V* insured a rush on tickets. The star turn of the Chicago fall belonged to Brian Dennehy, playing the Hickey role made famous by Jason Robards in O'Neill's *The Iceman Cometh* at the Goodman Theatre.

Atlanta also hosted a biennial fest: the National Black Arts Festival, where a theatrical highlight was Avery Brooks' stunning performance in *Paul Robeson*. In Cleveland the Great Lakes Theater Festival honored the oeuvre of Texan Horton Foote (*The Trip to Bountiful*) with dozens of stage productions and film and television screenings from his 50-year career.

In Minneapolis the Guthrie Theatre under artistic director Garland Wright marshalled its considerable resources and aptitude for classics with a cycle of Shakespeare history plays (*Richard II*, *Henry IV* parts 1 and 2, *Henry V*) whose scope rivaled the Royal Shakespeare Company's "War of the Roses" cycle of a few seasons earlier.

In Houston at the Alley Theatre, the international craze for musicalizing 19th- and early 20th-century novels (Broadway's *Les Misérables*, *Phantom of the Opera*) continued with a world premiere of the suspense classic *Jekyll and Hyde*, marking librettist Leslie Bricusse's (*Stop the World—I Want to Get Off*) long-awaited return to the musical theater.

Seattle Repertory Theatre, spawning ground in recent seasons for such fine plays as *The Heidi Chronicles* and *Eastern Standard*, won a special 1990 Tony Award for regional theater.

DAN HULBERT
"The Atlanta Journal & Constitution"

Continental Airlines, burdened by massive debt, sought bankruptcy protection through the courts in December 1990 in an effort to reorganize its financial structure while maintaining full operations and employment. A month later Pan American airlines took similar action.

© Howell/Gamma-Liaison

TRANSPORTATION

Traffic and earnings of North American freight and passenger carriers came under increasing pressure during 1990 from the business recession and increases in fuel costs stemming from a crisis in the Persian Gulf following Iraq's invasion of Kuwait.

Airlines. Passengers carried by the 12 major U.S.-based airlines during January-August rose 4.38% over the same period in 1989. Increases, however, were accompanied by a 70% decrease in aggregate net income of the major carriers due to intense fare competition and heavy interest payments on debt. Conditions worsened significantly in the last five months of 1990. Some analysts forecast that the airline industry would suffer an aggregate loss of more than $1 billion by the close of 1990, as sharp increases in fuel prices took full hold, growth in passenger traffic fell below 2%, and unsold seats increased as carriers placed new larger-capacity aircraft into service.

In the face of these conditions, USAir postponed expansion plans and furloughed employees. Eastern Airlines teetered on the brink of extinction, continuing to fly only because the federal court overseeing its bankruptcy proceedings released $135 million on November 27 to meet operating expenses. The funds had been held in escrow to meet creditors' claims, and were released despite creditors' protests.

Continental Airlines, burdened by a more than $6.2 billion debt, filed for bankruptcy court protection from its creditors on December 3. In explaining the filing, Continental emphasized that it planned to maintain full operation of its systems, serving 144 domestic and foreign airports, and avoid cuts in employ-

ment and pay rates while seeking reorganization of its financial structure.

Midway Airlines, one of the very few surviving carriers among those formed after deregulation in 1978, announced on October 19 that it was selling most of its Philadelphia hub assets to USAir for $67.5 million, after having purchased them from Eastern Airlines for $100 million in 1989. Earlier in October, Midway had sold slots at Washington National Airport and New York's LaGuardia Airport to American Airlines. The sales marked Midway's retreat from an attempt to expand beyond its Midway Airport (Chicago) hub with flights radiating from Philadelphia to Toronto, Montreal, Miami, and other points. In doing so Midway encountered below-cost fare cuts and increased flight frequencies by competing airlines. The resulting operating losses, magnified after July by sharp fuel-price increases, threatened Midway's survival.

Pan American World Airways Inc., in its attempts to stay afloat, announced plans in September to eliminate 8.5% of its work force (2,500 employees) by October, cut service, and replace 412-seat Boeing 747–400s with 192-seat Airbus Industrie A310–300s. In November the airline agreed to sell to United Airlines its London hub assets and routes between London and New York, San Francisco, Seattle, Los Angeles, and Washington. Routes from London to various European points also were included in the sale. Despite these efforts, in January 1991 the carrier (which would continue to fly) filed for bankruptcy protection, the third major U.S. airline recently to take that step.

Trans World Airlines (TWA), emulating Pan Am, agreed in December to sell its London assets and routes between London and New

York, Boston, Philadelphia, Baltimore, St. Louis, and Los Angeles to American Airlines' parent AMR Corporation. That same month TWA negotiated to acquire Pan Am. TWA owner Carl Icahn's motives were unclear; if completed the acquisition would combine two weak carriers burdened by debt, deficits, and aging equipment.

Retrenchment and restructuring were not limited to U.S.-based airlines. Airline analysts suggested that the major Canadian air carriers should merge in order to compete effectively. The European Commission permitted Air France to acquire Air Inter and UTA, France's second- and third-largest airlines. In return the commission required that Air France divest its 35% ownership share in TAT, the country's largest regional air carrier. The commission also directed the French government to open France's most important domestic and international air routes to airlines outside the Air France group, and to give priority to carriers outside the Air France group on new international routes not presently operated by a French airline.

The growing financial difficulties of certain U.S. airlines brought pleas for changes in the law that requires that U.S.-based airlines be 75% owned and controlled by U.S. citizens. In response Transportation Secretary Samuel Skinner announced in December that he was considering recommending that Congress make such changes. Proponents of increased foreign ownership view it mainly as a means for maintaining and increasing competition in air transport on a global basis.

In the air-cargo sector, Emery Worldwide, which was formed through the merger of Emery Air Freight and CF AirFreight on April 7, 1989, struggled to reduce its losses and achieve profitability. The struggle included a change in the chief executive officer of Emery's trucking-company parent, Consolidated Freightways. United Parcel Service (UPS), now an air as well as a surface carrier, took firm steps with changes in pricing and service to penetrate the domestic air-express markets dominated by Federal Express Corporation.

Air-freight carriers saw benefits from enactment of the United States' first federal aircraft noise-control law in the fall. While the legislation sets a July 1999 deadline for the replacement of 85% of the airlines' noisier planes with quieter equipment, it also places constraints on locally set aircraft-noise rules. Such rules often restrict airport use during times of heavy cargo-flight operation.

Bus. Greyhound Lines, Inc. (GLI), operator of the only U.S. nationwide intercity bus system, suffered heavy turmoil during 1990. On March 2 the Amalgamated Transit Union, which represented 9,400 GLI employees, struck the company. GLI sought to maintain operations with nonunion drivers and union

members who crossed picket lines. GLI property, personnel, and passengers became targets of extensive vandalism, assaults, and shootings. Service disruptions were severe, and traffic and earnings plummeted, forcing the debt-laden company to seek protection from its creditors under Chapter 11 of the federal bankruptcy code on June 4. Deep cuts in managerial and staff personnel occurred along with demoralization of GLI's commission ticket-sales agents.

Later in the year, traffic rebounded as GLI restored numerous strike-disrupted schedules, and violence and vandalism subsided. The company reported that its revenues for October reached 90% of their October 1989 level and that it lost $105 million on revenues of $475 million in the first nine months of 1990. On November 19, GLI filed a financial reorganization plan with its bankruptcy court, which projected that GLI could be restored to profitable operation, although with heavy losses to the investors who acquired it in a 1987 leveraged (heavily indebted) buyout.

Rail. Intercity passengers carried by Amtrak during its 1990 fiscal year (Oct. 1, 1989-Sept. 30, 1990) increased by 3.73% over the previous year, while passenger miles increased 3.37%. Revenues increased 3.1%. Amtrak's revenue-to-expense ratio (percentage of costs covered by company-generated revenues as distinguished from government subsidies) remained

The issue of air safety remained in the forefront during 1990. In July, Eastern Airlines was indicted for failure to maintain and repair its carriers at three airports.

© Susan Greenwood/Gamma-Liaison

at the 1989 level of 72%. As with other types of carriers, rising fuel prices after July put pressure on Amtrak's cost containment and operational self-sufficiency goals. However, Amtrak was positioned better to withstand this pressure, since fuel costs represented only 3.7% of its total operating costs as compared with approximately 15–20% for airlines.

Equipment remained a major constraint on Amtrak's ability to serve greater numbers of passengers and localities, generate more passenger revenue, and reduce its need for operating subsidies. During the year Amtrak completed design specifications for new bilevel superliner cars and began negotiations with manufacturers for their purchase. These cars must include design features mandated by the Americans with Disabilities Act, passed by Congress in July, which requires that all new rail-passenger cars be accessible to persons with disabilities. The act also affects equipment purchases by other modes of transport, including urban mass transit.

The French National Railways (SNCF) set another world railway speed record on April 18, when an SNCF TGV (*Train à Grande Vitesse*, or train of very high speed) reached a top speed of 320.2 mph (515.3 km/hr) during a series of trial runs between Courtalain and Tours.

Cutbacks in service on Via Rail Canada went into effect in mid-January.

In the freight sector, carloadings on U.S. Class I railroads increased 0.4% in the 50 weeks ended December 15, as compared with the same period in 1989. Ton-mileage grew 1.9% and exceeded 1 trillion for the second successive year. Revenues increased an estimated 1%, from $28.0 to $28.3 billion. Strength in intermodal traffic, which exceeded 6 million trailers and containers (carried on railway flatcars) for the first time, and coal movements helped offset recession-caused weakness in other categories of traffic.

CP Rail, Canada's second-largest freight railway, completed agreements to acquire the bankrupt Delaware & Hudson Railway, giving it access to points in the eastern United States, including the New York-New Jersey port area, Philadelphia, and Washington, DC. Nippon Yusen K.K., a major Japanese ocean carrier, acquired a 5% interest in Rio Grande Industries, parent company of the Denver & Rio Grande Western and the Southern Pacific. Mileage operated by regional and short-line railways increased, as such carriers acquired light- and medium-density line segments from Class I roads such as Conrail, Norfolk Southern, Union Pacific, and Santa Fe.

Shipping. Changing international trade flows and increases in unused vessel and container capacity depressed earnings of liner container-ship operators. In an effort to reduce capacity and costs, Sea-Land Service, P&O Lines, and Nedlloyd announced a program to share containers and container chassis. They already shared trans-Atlantic route vessel capacity. The longtime competitors Sea-Land and American President Lines began talks about vessel sharing and other possible cost-reducing arrangements.

Trucking. Intercity truck ton-miles grew an estimated $778 billion, 3.5% over 1989 volume. Intercity and local trucking revenues reached an estimated $276 billion, 6.5% above 1989. This seeming prosperity masked difficult conditions, which pressed the industry's average profit margin below an estimated 2%. ANR Freight System reduced its scope of operation from a national LTL (less-than-truckload) carrier (focusing on shipments below 10,000 lbs or 4 536 kg) to a specialized regional carrier. P-I-E Nationwide and Transcon Lines, which had been among the top U.S. LTL carriers, suffered financial failure and ceased all operations, along with six smaller LTL carriers. Several mergers and acquisitions occurred in the TL sector (shipments of 10,000 lbs, or 4 536 kg, and above), including absorption of Bulldog Trucking by J.B. Hunt Transport, and Ryder Bulk Transportation by Trimac Transportation Systems.

Urban Transit. Service began on the new 22-mi (35-km) Los Angeles-Long Beach light rail line on July 16. Seattle Metro opened its new 1.3-mi (2.1-km) downtown transit tunnel in September, using buses which operate on electric power in the tunnel and diesel power elsewhere. Transit operators intensified the search for ways in which to comply with the Clean Air Act of 1990, which imposes strict pollution-emission standards on new buses. Compressed natural gas and methanol were among the alternatives to diesel fuel being considered. The Southern California Rapid Transit District began studying the feasibility of converting diesel bus lines to electric trolley-bus operations. In addition to environmental advantages, the relative stability of electricity rates could be attractive to transit systems, which saw diesel-fuel prices increase 72% between August 1 and October 15. This increase, together with state and local budget difficulties and recession-induced ridership declines, resulted in deficits and the specter of service cuts in a number of localities, including New York and Philadelphia.

The federal budget enacted in October authorized a 7% increase in federal mass-transit-program funding. Whether the full authorized amount would be matched by appropriations was unclear at year's end. Transit funding received a major boost in California on June 5, when voters approved bond issues totaling approximately $3 billion to expand both mass transit and intercity rail passenger services within the state.

JOHN C. SPYCHALSKI
The Pennsylvania State University

© Mike Clemmer/Picture Group

With Americans opting for shorter, less expensive vacations, the fast-food restaurant remained as popular as ever. Accordingly, McDonald's opened the Golden Arch Cafe in Huntsville, TN, above, as a test of a new diner-type restaurant.

TRAVEL

The 1990 travel year got off to a promising start, and a rapidly changing Eastern Europe drew U.S. vacationers in record numbers. But as the year progressed, many Americans reacted to economic and political uncertainties by cutting back on leisure travel.

Fear of recession, a weakened U.S. dollar, and escalating fuel prices after Iraq's August invasion of Kuwait all put a damper on vacation plans. By summer—even before the Persian Gulf crisis—numerous U.S. resorts, theme parks, and other major attractions were reporting a downturn in business during what is usually their busiest season. Vacationers seemed to be opting for shorter, less expensive trips close to home. Business travelers began combining trips to cut costs.

On the other hand, favorable exchange rates created bargains for foreign visitors to the United States. Some 40.6 million inbound travelers provided the bright spot in the domestic-travel picture, representing an 11% increase over 1989. While Europe was still the biggest source of overseas visitors (6.7 million), some 4.9 million travelers from Asia and the Middle East also visited the United States, an 11% increase. Canada was once again the largest single market, contributing 17.3 million visitors—a 12% growth. Another 8 million arrivals came from Mexico, an 11% jump.

Outward Bound. Dramatic political changes in Eastern Europe created new travel opportunities and proved a powerful attraction for Americans who wanted to witness history in the making. Other tourists were motivated by their ethnic ties to the region. Tour operators capitalized on the new political climate by organizing "*perestroika* tours" of Eastern Europe and the USSR.

The weak U.S. dollar made overseas travel expensive for Americans, but Europe nonetheless drew some 7.3 million U.S. citizens in 1990, up 5% over the previous year. New air-line routes to secondary destination cities on both sides of the Atlantic—made possible by fuel-efficient smaller aircraft—added impetus to European travel.

Altogether, 44 million Americans traveled outside the country, 6% more than during the year before. Toward year's end, though, rising fuel costs, uneasiness over U.S. involvement in the Middle East, and a slowing of the U.S. economy contributed to a general feeling that the travel industry was in for a slump.

Cruising. Seemingly little affected by recession fears, the cruise industry was claiming 4 million North American passengers by the end of 1990. A dozen new cruise ships were introduced during the year, ranging from intimate vessels designed for adventure cruising to giant superliners.

Among the new "mega-ships" were Princess Cruises' 1,590-passenger *Crown Princess*, Carnival Cruise Lines' 2,600-passenger *Fantasy*, and Royal Caribbean Cruise Line's 2,000-passenger *Nordic Empress*. Crystal Cruises' 960-passenger *Crystal Harmony* expanded cruising's super-deluxe category, offering such amenities as an atrium lobby complete with waterfall, staterooms with private verandas, penthouse suites with Jacuzzis, and three shipboard restaurants.

High-Tech Trends. Electronic technology continued to shape the travel industry. Computer data banks informed travel agents and consumers about everything from snow conditions at ski resorts to cabin availability on cruise ships. More hotels installed machines that let travel agents deliver airline tickets electronically to en-route clients. Some destination promoters even mailed out visitor guides in diskette form for use on home or office computers.

The first electronic travel agency—the Vacation Network's half-hour shopping program offering discounted travel products—debuted on cable television during the year.

PHYLLIS ELVING, *Free-lance Writer*

TUNISIA

In 1990, President Zine El Abidine Ben Ali celebrated the third anniversary of his rise to power (November 7) with his domestic position strengthened by the Persian Gulf crisis. The president, condemning the presence of "foreign forces on Arab soil" and calling for reinforcement of Tunisia's "Arab-Islamic" heritage, won support from a populace that mainly condemned Western military intervention in what was viewed as an inter-Arab conflict.

Governmental Affairs. Response to events in the Gulf also relieved some of the pressure Ben Ali has experienced from Tunisia's powerful Islamic fundamentalists, who remained prohibited from forming a political party. Still, Ben Ali's failure to move ahead with promised democratic reforms contributed to mounting discontent among Tunisia's intellectuals and middle class.

As in legislative elections in 1989, local elections on June 10 resulted in a virtual clean sweep by the ruling Constitutional Democratic Rally (RCD). The results, however, testified more to the lack of an attractive and credible opposition and the fundamentalists' failure to gain official recognition than to the popularity of the party in power.

With neighboring Algeria opening the political door to fundamentalists and pushing ahead with fully democratic national elections, Tunisians expressed increasing impatience with the nation's virtual one-party rule. The September shooting death by police in Tunis of a young fundamentalist passing out leaflets in front of his mosque—and the scattered demonstrations that followed—exemplified the nation's sensitivity.

Rumors circulated in late summer in Tunis that Ben Ali would name a coalition government after he held discussions with two opposition-party leaders. While the president did include several opposition leaders among the emissaries he sent out to foreign capitals to explain Tunisia's position on the Gulf crisis, he brought none of them into the government. In August, Ben Ali replaced his foreign minister, whose views on the Gulf were more sympathetic to Western intervention than his own.

Tunisia was the sole Arab League member to refuse to attend a league meeting in Cairo on August 10 that resulted in a condemnation of Iraq's invasion of Kuwait. The meeting ended in a damaging split between Arab camps and led to a subsequent League vote to hasten the transfer of the organization's headquarters from Tunis to Cairo. In September the League's Tunisian secretary-general resigned.

Economic Affairs. Relations continued to improve with neighboring Maghreb countries a year after creation of the Arab Maghreb Union. Economically, however, relations with Western Europe remained more important, which explained the warm reception of an Italo-Spanish proposal for a regular forum to improve cooperation on economic and security issues between southern Europe and North Africa.

Perhaps Tunisia's single most significant economic event was membership in the General Agreement on Tariffs and Trade (GATT) in August. Officials hoped that GATT membership would help the nation develop its exports of agricultural products and textiles and its fledgling production of electronics components. With the official unemployment rate hovering around 14%, however, the government slowed reforms aimed at opening the economy to stiffer foreign competition. Farm-sector results improved but still suffered from the effects of drought, locust invasions, and poorly performing public farms.

Officials watched nervously as the Gulf crisis threatened to undo Tunisia's nascent economic reprise. More than 500,000 Tunisians work outside the country, and the hundreds who returned from Kuwait to seek work at home provided a foretaste of what might be to come.

HOWARD LAFRANCHI
"The Christian Science Monitor"

TUNISIA • Information Highlights

Official Name: Republic of Tunisia.
Location: North Africa.
Area: 63,170 sq mi (163 610 km²).
Population (mid-1990 est.): 8,100,000.
Chief City (1987 est.): Tunis, the capital, 1,600,000, district population.
Government: *Head of state,* Zine El Abidine Ben Ali, president (took office Nov. 7, 1987). *Head of government,* Hamed Karoui, prime minister (took office Sept. 27, 1989). *Legislature* (unicameral)—National Assembly.
Monetary Unit: Dinar (0.861 dinar equals U.S.$1, August 1990).
Gross Domestic Product (1989 est. U.S.$): $8,700,-000,000.
Economic Index (1989): *Consumer Prices* (1980 = 100), all items, 204.5; food, 210.9.
Foreign Trade (1989 U.S.$): *Imports,* $4,378,000,000; *exports,* $3,027,000,000.

TURKEY

In a year marked by the growth of democracy in Eastern Europe and the Iraqi invasion of Kuwait, foreign affairs occupied the center of the Turkish stage.

External Relations. Turkey's neighbor Bulgaria was one of the Eastern European countries that experienced radical changes in 1990. Tension had arisen between the two nations in the 1980s because of measures taken by Bulgaria's Communist government against ethnic Turks living under its jurisdiction. An understanding was reached with the new non-Communist government in January providing for the repeal of laws forcing ethnic Turks to adopt Bulgarian names, and guaranteeing freedom for the Muslim faith. Nevertheless, continued anti-Turkish agitation by Bulgarian nationalists aroused fears that problems might recur. In the same month there were demonstrations in Istanbul against mistreatment of Muslims by Armenians in Soviet Azerbaijan. Another repercussion of the upheaval in Eastern Europe was a flood of Albanian refugees seeking asylum in Turkish and other embassies.

On a more general level, considerable concern was expressed that the closer connections between the East and Central European countries and Western Europe would lead to increased competition for Turkish workers in Europe, as well as for Turkish exports to the European Community (EC). Many also feared that the easing of Cold War tensions between the United States and the Soviet Union would mean a decline in Turkey's strategic importance and a consequent reduction in U.S. military aid.

On the other hand, the end of the Cold War raised the possibility that Turkish military spending, which rose to 13.6% of the national budget in 1990 from 11.2% in 1989, could be decreased so as to free resources for development projects.

Prospects for Turkish entry into the EC also took a turn for the worse when the EC decided that, while membership was not ruled out in principle, negotiations would be postponed.

Turkey was affected strongly by the Iraqi crisis that began in August. In compliance with United Nations resolutions, the Iraqi oil pipelines to the Turkish port of Yumurtalik were shut. The estimated more than $5 billion in costs to Turkey from lost oil transit fees, overland transport earnings and trade, and from an influx of refugees across the Turkish-Iraqi border were made up only partially by pledges from Kuwait, Germany, and Japan. Turkey also showed its support for the UN resolutions by allowing its air bases to be used by anti-Iraqi forces and by strengthening its own military units along the Iraqi border. The National Assembly also authorized the government to declare a state of war in case Turkey was attacked while the assembly was in recess.

Relations with the United States were strained temporarily when the U.S. Congress again gave serious consideration to a resolution condemning Turkey for its treatment of the Armenians during World War I. When the resolution was defeated narrowly after vigorous Turkish lobbying, Turkey rescinded curbs it had imposed on the use of military bases leased to the United States. In September, on his second visit to Washington in 1990, Turkish President Turgut Ozal was partly successful in obtaining desired reductions in U.S. import barriers against Turkish textiles. Turkey also was gratified that proposals to divert part of its

U.S. military and economic aid to countries in Latin America and Eastern Europe were for the most part not approved by Congress and the Bush administration. Turkey remained the third-largest recipient of U.S. military and economic aid, exceeded only by Israel and Egypt.

On other foreign matters, no progress was made in the Greek-Turkish dispute over Cyprus, and tensions with Greece continued as a result of alleged Greek threats to Turkish residents of western Thrace. The nation was saddened in July, when more than 350 Turkish pilgrims were among those who died in a fire in Mecca.

Domestic Affairs. The economy showed increases in many production and export sectors, and tourism reported record earnings. Inflation, however, continued at an estimated 45%-50%, with the prospect of a further increase when the full impact of the Iraq situation became felt. Signs of widening consumer unrest included a meat boycott in June.

In key cabinet changes, Foreign Minister Mesut Yilmaz was replaced by Ali Bozer and later by Ahmet Kurtcebe Alptemocin and Adnan Kahveci assumed the post of finance minister. The ruling Motherland Party won two local elections, but fared badly in the opinion polls.

At least 16 political killings, including that of Muammer Aksoy, president of the Turkish Law Institute, and Cetin Emec, a leading journalist, revived fears of the kind of extremist violence that had plagued Turkey in the late 1970s. The killings generally were believed to have been carried out by pro-Islamic groups, although there also were reports that leftist extremists claimed credit for some of them.

Unrest continued in the southeast, and clashes between security forces and Kurdish separatists again caused casualties among both. The situation was aggravated further when many Kurdish refugees crossed the Turkish border from Iraq.

TURKEY • Information Highlights

Official Name: Republic of Turkey.
Location: Southeastern Europe and southwestern Asia.
Area: 301,382 sq mi (780 580 km²).
Population (mid-1990 est.): 56,700,000.
Chief Cities (1985 census): Ankara, the capital, 2,235,035; Istanbul, 5,475,982; Izmir, 1,489,772.
Government: Head of state, Turgut Ozal, president (took office November 1989). Head of government, Yildirim Akbulut, prime minister (took office November 1989). Legislature—Grand National Assembly.
Monetary Unit: Lira (2,799 liras equal U.S. $1, Dec. 13, 1990).
Gross Domestic Product (1989 est. U.S.$): $75,000,-000,000.
Economic Index (1989): Consumer Prices (1982 = 100), all items, 1,571.4; food, 1,482.5.
Foreign Trade (1988 U.S.$): Imports, $14,380,-000,000; exports, $11,608,000,000.

A significant achievement was the completion of the Ataturk Dam, part of the Southeast Anatolia Project. (*See also* ENGINEERING.) On environmental issues, there was more progress in cleaning waterways, such as the Golden Horn area of Istanbul and part of the Mediterranean (the latter in cooperation with a consortium of European and North African nations), but serious air pollution continued in Ankara despite major efforts to replace the use of lignite for heat with natural gas. On one occasion it was necessary to close schools and to order a 50% reduction in production by polluting industrial plants.

WALTER F. WEIKER, *Rutgers University*

UGANDA

In 1990, President Yoweri Museveni continued to consolidate his control over Uganda and to receive generous backing from the international community for his program of structural adjustment.

Politics. With elections slated for 1995, Museveni was attempting to build the military (National Resistance Movement, or NRM) into an independent political body. By late 1990 his strategy had centered around expanding the size of the NRM and his cabinet—which had grown to 70 in number—and co-opting political rivals in the now-suspended Democratic Party and the United People's Party.

In July, Museveni signed an agreement with the Uganda Patriotic Democratic Movement (UPDM), incorporating the UPDM's 5,000 troops into the 75,000-man Uganda national army. The agreement also provided an amnesty for UPDM political leaders.

Antigovernment Activity. A great deal of unrest persisted in various parts of the country. In January the government announced that several members of the military had been charged with treason in connection with a plot to overthrow Museveni. Minister of Culture, Youth, and Sport, Brig. Gen. Moses Ali, also was arrested on charges of sedition.

In March a government newspaper reported that, in an attempt to control rebel activity in eastern and western Uganda, the army forcibly relocated some 200,000 civilians, confining them in camps, or "protected centers." Some reports indicated a death rate of 30 to 60 people per day among the detainees due to a lack of food, water, and medical care in the camps. Responding to questions from the press about these allegations, Museveni defended the army's policy, arguing that it was necessary to restore order.

Economy. Uganda's economic policy continued to be guided by the principles of free trade set forth by the International Monetary Fund (IMF). To this end, Uganda permitted three coffee cooperatives to export their products directly, rather than through the government-owned Coffee Marketing Board. Coffee continued to provide 97% of Uganda's export earnings.

With assistance from the World Bank, Uganda established its Third Special Import Program, which allocated $50 million, primarily for agricultural imports. The move also was designed to cut inflation from its current rate of 30% and to close the gap between the official exchange rate and the parallel rate. The parallel rate was more than double the official rate. Uganda also adopted a generous new foreign-investment code.

International Affairs. Uganda continued to receive the generous support of the international donor community. U.S. aid amounted to $29.1 million, including $10.4 million in debt relief. Uganda also signed a $17.2 million barter-trade agreement with Cuba.

Regionally, Uganda signed a nonaggression pact with the Sudanese government. Since the outbreak of the Sudanese civil war in 1989, some 60,000 refugees fled into Uganda and incidents on the Uganda-Sudan border have been a constant source of recrimination. Refugees continued to be a problem with Rwanda; tens of thousands fled that country in October.

Following a strike over a demand for a tenfold increase in wages, agreements with the national airlines of Tanzania, Burundi, and Libya enabled Uganda Airways to maintain air links with neighboring territories while it suspended flights and reorganized operations. Uganda also agreed to increase cooperation with Zaire, particularly in the areas of oil prospecting and bilateral trade.

Perhaps the highlight of the year was a July visit by Nelson Mandela, the leader of the African National Congress (ANC) of South Africa. Museveni, a longtime ally of the ANC, had permitted it to maintain guerrilla-training facilities in Uganda during its struggle against South Africa's white-supremacist government. In April, ANC dissidents in Kenya had charged that prisoners were being tortured in camps that the group still was maintaining in Uganda.

WILLIAM CYRUS REED
Wabash College

UGANDA · Information Highlights

Official Name: Republic of Uganda.
Location: Interior of East Africa.
Area: 91,135 sq mi (236 040 km²).
Population: (mid-1990 est.): 18,000,000.
Chief Cities (1980 census): Kampala, the capital, 458,423; Jinja, 45,060.
Government: *Head of state,* Yoweri Museveni, president (Jan. 29, 1986). *Head of government,* Samson Kisekka, prime minister (Jan. 30, 1986). *Legislature* (unicameral)—National Assembly.
Monetary Unit: Uganda shilling (440 shillings equal U.S. $1, July 1990).
Foreign Trade (1988 U.S.$): *Imports,* $626,000,000; *exports,* $272,000,000.

The year 1990 was a difficult but also a historic one for Mikhail Sergeyevich Gorbachev, left. At home he assumed the office of president of the USSR and faced severe economic problems, cries for more autonomy from the republics, as well as the sudden resignation of his foreign minister. At the same time, he remained extremely popular on the international scene. In October the Norwegian Nobel Committee awarded him the 1990 Nobel Peace Prize.

© Novosti/Sipa

USSR

The year 1990 witnessed the USSR's slide into a deep internal crisis engulfing its political, social, economic, and legal systems. Mikhail Gorbachev's *perestroika* reform program fell into disarray and, by year's end, was ignored increasingly as the country's leadership reached for emergency measures to cope with the domestic crisis. While his conservative party opponent, Yegor Ligachev, went into semiretirement, Gorbachev was besieged by new and formidable critics and challengers to his authority from the direction of the radical leadership of the Russian Republic, Lithuania, and the cities of Moscow and Leningrad (*see* feature article, THE SOVIET REPUBLICS, page 44). By the end of 1990 the battered USSR encompassed a fledgling participatory political system locked in decision-making paralysis, a state structure in the process of rapid disintegration as separatist fever raced through the land, an economy, neither command nor market, in ruinous condition; a legal system which had become part of the problem rather than the solution, and a social system weakened by economic adversity and troubled by ethnic and religious conflict.

In spite of a steady flow of bad news at home and his declining popularity in the public-opinion polls, Gorbachev managed to stay afloat as leader, even accruing to himself more and more power as the year wore on. As in the past, a factor in his political survival was his continuing success as a statesman. Although his foreign successes were no longer convertible into domestic political capital, they did buoy him up at critical moments as he met with President George Bush in Washington and Hel-

sinki, Finland, conferred with the leaders of the West in Paris, played a key role in the Persian Gulf crisis precipitated by Iraq, and capped the year off by winning the Nobel Peace Prize.

Domestic Affairs

The year was marked by political instability, near economic collapse, both social conflict and malaise, and a faltering legal order. Each of these problems contributed to the general crisis of the Soviet system. Though Gorbachev was deluged with criticism and became increasingly irritable and defensive in response, the fact that he successfully navigated through a year of exceptional turmoil was further evidence of his remarkable public skills and his uncanny sense of political balance.

Political Developments. The major political trends of 1990 were the decline of the Communist Party and the rise of the presidential system in the Soviet Union. As the year began, Gorbachev governed principally through his powerful position as general secretary of the Communist Party. When it ended, his primary power stemmed from his new post as president of the USSR, an office in which he gradually accumulated legal authority nearly comparable in scope to the vast, arbitrary power of Stalin. Although he also retained the party leadership, President Gorbachev steadily had shifted the locus of power in the USSR from the Communist Party to the Soviet state.

The party's decline as the dominant force in national politics and decision-making occurred in three steps. During the first quarter of 1990, prodded by General Secretary Gorbachev, the party leadership decided to give up its constitutional monopoly on political power. Action then followed in the Congress of People's Deputies revising Article 6 of the USSR Constitution of 1977, thus laying the groundwork for the possible transition from a one-party to a multiparty political system. Next, at the 28th Congress of the Communist Party of the Soviet Union in July, Gorbachev engineered the separation of the party leadership from government office. Although he retained his dual offices in the party and the state, other senior party officials no longer could hold governmental office simultaneously, effectively divorcing the party from direct control over national policy-making. Finally, the crowning blow to the prestige of the party took place at the end of the Congress when Boris Yeltsin (*see* BIOGRAPHY), a Central Committee member and by then head of the Russian Republic as well, publicly resigned his party membership after nearly 30 years, indicating that as a committed reformer, he no longer could work within the framework of the still conservative Communist Party. Although thousands of rank-and-file members previously had resigned from the party, Yeltsin's dramatic departure accelerated the exodus from the erstwhile ruling party.

However, it should be noted that party organizations at the regional and local level in many parts of the country continued to remain in control in 1990, their authority diminished but their power still intact. The major exceptions were the cities of Moscow and Leningrad where radical reformers won in the spring elections and took control of municipal government from the respective city party committees. To demonstrate their independence, the two re-

An Orthodox religious ceremony is held in the Kremlin in Moscow. In October 1990 the Soviet legislature passed a landmark law guaranteeing religious freedom to all Soviets.

© Laski/Sipa

USSR · Information Highlights

Official Name: Union of Soviet Socialist Republics.
Location: Eastern Europe and northern Asia.
Area: 8,649,498 sq mi (22 402 200 km²).
Population (mid-1990 est.): 291,000,000.
Chief Cities (Jan. 12, 1989 est.): Moscow, the capital, 8,967,000; Leningrad, 5,020,000; Kiev, 2,587,000.
Government: *Head of state and government,* Mikhail S. Gorbachev, president (elected May 1989). *Legislature* (bicameral)—Supreme Soviet and Congress of People's Deputies.
Monetary Unit: Ruble (0.600 ruble equals U.S. $1, February 1990—official rate).
Gross National Product (1989 est. U.S. $): $2,659,500,000,000.
Economic Indexes (1986): *Consumer Prices* (1980 = 100), all items, 106.5; food, 114.2. *Industrial Production* (1989, 1980 = 100), 136.
Foreign Trade (1989 U.S.$): *Imports,* $114,550,000,000; *exports,* $109,212,000,000.

form mayors, Gavriil Popov and Anatoly Sobchak, respectively, followed Yeltsin's example and resigned from the party at the 28th Congress as well.

As the Communist Party's ruling power waned, Gorbachev was forging new governmental institutions through which to govern the USSR. He had entered the year as chairman of the presidium of the parent legislature and its offspring, the new Supreme Soviet of the USSR. To offset the diminution of his party power, Gorbachev in March persuaded the Third Congress of People's Deputies to create constitutionally a new office, the presidency, and to elect him as its first incumbent. As the first Soviet president, Gorbachev acquired immense authority, including the power to issue decrees, and to preempt subnational governments by imposing presidential rule. In addition, two consultative bodies were created subordinate to his new office—the Federation Council, made up of the leaders of the union republics, and the Presidential Council, the members of which served as his advisers.

The instability of the new political arrangements became apparent later in the year. In September as the multiple crises deepened and rumors of a military coup were rife, Gorbachev asked for and received from the Supreme Soviet enormous additional emergency presidential powers designed to run until 1992. Finally in November, in response to legislative complaints at his lack of effective leadership of the country, he proposed another dramatic reorganization of the national political system which by the end of the year still was under consideration. These changes included further strengthening the presidency, abolishing the Congress of People's Deputies and the Presidential Council, creating a National Security Council, and elevating the Federation Council to an active policy-making role. The plan also entailed the establishment of a new office of vice-president to which Gennadi I. Yanayev was elected in late December.

Economic conditions in the USSR deteriorated during 1990. By late in the year there was a general shortage of almost all food items and long lines were prevalent for the limited supplies that were available. Meanwhile a group of Soviets set up a tent city, below, in the center of Moscow to dramatize their plight.

© Gamma-Liaison

The Economic Situation. To a great extent, Gorbachev's continual quest for more legal authority throughout 1990 was in response to the progressively worsening economic situation, the most immediate and constant of the several crises with which he was coping. By the end of summer, once the basically conservative national Communist Party was neutralized, Gorbachev felt freer to lead the growing consensus of economists which advocated moving the Soviet Union toward a market economy. A debate ensued, however, over how to reach the goal, whether by a radical 500-day plan or through a more moderate plan which would mitigate the social pain. Fearing the potential social dislocation of an overly abrupt transition, Gorbachev opted for a synthesis of the two plans, prompting Yeltsin, who favored the radical approach, to comment derisively that the result would be like trying to mate a hedgehog with a snake. Impending winter and widespread public anxiety over shortages forced a suspension of theoretical discussion as Gorbachev found himself buffeted from one consumer crisis to another—a shortage of cigarettes in the summer, a bread shortage in the fall, and shortages of nearly everything after that. With only 20 of 1,100 standard consumer items readily available, widespread strikes, a transportation system no longer able to move goods in timely fashion, customs barriers popping up between republics, and factories reduced to doing business by barter—the public perception was of an economy near collapse, raising the specter of hunger and malnutrition.

Paradoxically, the situation was not as bad as it looked. As Gorbachev pointed out in trying to allay panic, production was at or a little ahead of the previous year's level. The problem was in the distribution system, which had broken down due to producers (under Gorbachev's more liberal economic rules) withholding foodstuffs from the state stores for

© Robert D. Tonsing/Picture Group

higher prices elsewhere, and to extensive corruption by which scarce goods were "diverted" en route to the consumer and rerouted to the black market. Powerless to prevent producers from withholding supplies, Gorbachev attacked the problem of diversion by using the KGB and workers' vigilante groups to protect food shipments in transit. The outcome was inconclusive by year's end.

Meanwhile, desperate consumers spent most of their waking hours foraging for food, which was abundant but too expensive in the private farmer's markets, and cheap (thanks to state subsidies) but absent in the state stores. Rationing was established in many places—including Leningrad, for the first time since the German siege of World War II. As the distribution failure intensified, even rationing was to no avail; in some communities the requisite coupon could not bring forth even the small designated allotment, which often was just not available. When food did appear on store shelves, it was snapped up quickly as hoarding became the norm among the worried and frightened citizenry.

Social Conflict and Malaise. Social conflict, including communal violence, which had become a salient factor in Soviet society in 1989, continued unabated as the days and weeks grew into months of rage. In the history of the multinational Russian and Soviet state, 1990 may be remembered as the time when the contagion of separatism spread throughout the USSR, including not just most of the union republics, but numerous autonomous republics, districts, regions, and even some cities and towns. From the summer on, declarations of sovereignty by one or another jurisdiction became routine. Leaders of the major ethnic groups, and many relatively small and obscure national minorities as well, were rushing to position their constituencies for the anticipated negotiations on the promised new Union treaty redefining center-periphery relationships within the crumbling USSR. A draft version of the treaty was published in late November to an immediate chorus of ethnic criticism. Gorbachev responded by proposing a nationwide referendum on the treaty in 1991. Meanwhile the Congress of People's Deputies nominally passed the treaty in December.

In addition to conflicting separatist movements in a few instances, other sources of direct violence were territorial disputes and economic scarcity. In January the simmering Azeri-Armenian territorial dispute, which already entailed an on-going guerrilla war in the contested area, exploded again. In Baku, capital of Azerbaijan, Azeri mobs went on a rampage, massacring Armenian residents and causing Gorbachev to intervene with troops. This was the first deployment of 1990. By December substantial numbers of peacekeeping riot troops were on duty in 12 areas throughout the USSR. In February riots broke out in a heretofore quiet part of Soviet Central Asia, and in March the Lithuanian union republic formally declared its independence from the Soviet Union. Threatening military action, Gorbachev instead used his new presidential powers to impose a coercive economic embargo on Lithuania until a temporary compromise was agreed to in the summer.

Lithuania's move, though stalemated for now, set off the country-wide dash for sovereignty. By summer independence-minded Moldavia was facing secessionist challenges from two different ethnic minorities within the republic, precipitating an outbreak of violence in the fall. By far the greatest challenge to Gorbachev's leadership during the year was his rival Boris Yeltsin's election as head of the Russian Republic legislature in late May. Yeltsin immediately set Russia on a political, economic, and legal collision course with the central government, a battle of words which dominated Soviet politics and shaped the public discourse for the rest of the year.

All of the foregoing—political paralysis, economic chaos, and a daily diet of conflict of one kind or another, cast a shadow over society, with large parts of the population falling prey to despair and a pervasive malaise. Adults, beset with the endless frustrations of shopping, lived in fear of the crime wave sweeping the cities, while the youth, having lost confidence in the arguing, temporizing leaders of the country, concentrated on short-term gratifications in the absence of hope for a foreseeable, stable and better future. Even the military was not immune to the malaise as its personnel experienced the hardships of everyday life in the USSR. While freedom of religion was proclaimed in law late in the year, the organized religions just were beginning to recover from decades of suppression and were unable as yet to fill the spiritual void.

Soviet Jews, in particular, had a difficult year as anti-Semitism spread and intensified, causing tens of thousands to fear for their safety and leave for Israel and the West.

The Legal Order. When Gorbachev launched *perestroika* in the mid-1980s, it was his intention that all of the proposed reforms would be expressed in law (as against administrative fiat), and set within a new, restructured Soviet legal order. To this end, the restructured legislative system of 1988-89 began to enact a veritable forest of new legislation on the myriad aspects of Gorbachev's program—for instance, the 1990 law on freedom of the press. Problems, however, soon appeared, as the body of new law coexisted uneasily with the much larger domain of old law reinforced by the inveterate administrative habits of the huge bureaucracy charged with implementation. These difficulties were compounded greatly in 1990 as all of the 15 union republics proclaimed their sovereignty and the primacy of republic law over federal legislation. This led to what was referred commonly to in the USSR as the "war of laws," as all-union and republic laws clashed on a variety of issues, resulting in legal gridlock. The new federal Committee on Constitutional Supervision, which began its work during the year, tried to resolve some of the differences, but the volume of legal conflicts became too great for anything but a far-reaching political resolution.

Under these circumstances, law and the legal system in the USSR became in 1990 another part of the general crisis rather than Gorbachev's medium of choice for the rapid and profound social change under way in the system and society. Surveying the Soviet legal order during 1990, then, we find:

• a procuracy (prosecutorial system) overloaded with new tasks.

In November, Mikhail Gorbachev became the first foreign leader to pay a state visit to Germany since its reunification one month earlier. The Soviet president and German Chancellor Helmut Kohl (right) *signed a series of treaties, including friendship and nonaggression pacts.*

© Kessler/Sipa

- a judiciary underqualified for its new caseload.
- a municipal police force confused, demoralized, and undermanned for its new street duties of policing demonstrations, and its increased crime-fighting responsibilities.
- a governmental bureaucracy, slated for deep cuts but determined to survive, with the result that the implementation process was in a state of near collapse.
- rebellious republics, regions, cities, trade unions, and armed bands for whom federal writ no longer merited respect or compliance.
- and, finally, a growing legal vacuum in society in which presidential decrees and federal law fell on deaf ears.

Foreign Affairs

Perhaps no two events better epitomized the chasm between Gorbachev's domestic failures and foreign successes in 1990 than the attempt on his life in Red Square during the November celebration of the anniversary of the Bolshevik Revolution, and the Norwegian parliament's conferral upon him of the Nobel Prize for Peace. During the year, Gorbachev continued his string of accomplishments as a statesman, but the Soviet public, exhausted by the downside of *perestroika*, no longer was paying attention. Even the announcement of the Nobel Prize barely evoked a ripple of interest among the long lines of weary consumers dotting Moscow's urban landscape.

The year included yet another summit with a U.S. president, this time in Washington in June. A host of minor agreements, but no major accords, were ready for the leaders' signatures. Among other commitments, President Bush promised to lower tariffs on Soviet imports once the forthcoming Soviet law on emigration was passed. The lumbering Soviet economy, however, is not likely to produce many exports of interest to the U.S. market in the near future. Further impetus was given to arms reduction negotiations as well, but the main importance of the meeting was a strengthening of the personal relationship between the two leaders.

This proved to be important a few months later in August, when Iraq invaded Kuwait and President Bush responded with an international coalition and economic sanctions. Key to this effort was Soviet cooperation, signaling the first Soviet-U.S. alliance against an aggressor since World War II. The two presidents met again for seven hours in Helsinki, Finland, September 9 to discuss the crisis. Another showcase for Gorbachev's international talents occurred in the fall when the leaders of the 34 member-states of the Commission on Security and Cooperation in Europe, meeting in Paris, celebrated the *perestroika* of international relations that made possible liberation of Eastern Europe and opened up the prospect of incorporating the USSR into the European "common home."

As the year drew to a close, the Soviet Union normalized its economic relations with its erstwhile East European client states, acquiesced in the reunification of Germany, and made tentative moves toward settling its longstanding dispute with Japan over the Kurile Islands. On the downside, however, Soviet Foreign Minister Eduard A. Shevardnadze, in a surprise move, announced his resignation at the end of the year. Looking toward 1991, President Gorbachev was preoccupied with a major domestic issue which rapidly was becoming an international issue—the question of whether the USSR would survive the internal "sovereignty war" as a unified, multinational nation-state.

ROBERT SHARLET, *Union College*

UNITED NATIONS

Iraqi President Saddam Hussein's "Guns of August" invasion of Kuwait shattered the cautious euphoria that characterized United Nations activity during the first seven months of 1990. By year's end, the UN was poised for Security Council-authorized military action against Iraq at any time after Jan. 15, 1991.

Early 1990 Accomplishments. The early months recorded progress on a variety of stubborn issues, much of it attributable to the U.S.-Soviet entente. On January 15 the Security Council's permanent members—the United States, China, France, the Soviet Union, and Britain—agreed on a UN role for solving the 12-year-old Cambodia conflict. The blueprint called for elections under the aegis of a UN Transitional Authority in Cambodia (UNTAC). Cambodian political authority was to be vested in a Supreme National Council (SNC) comprising the four rival Cambodian factions.

By August the accord had been refined to five "indispensable requirements" for peace: transitional arrangements for administering the country in the preelection period, military arrangements during the transitional period, elections under UN auspices, protection of human rights, and international guarantees.

The first seven months also saw breakthroughs on other fronts involving the UN. On February 15, Argentina and Britain announced resumption of diplomatic relations broken during the 1982 Falklands war. Also on February 15, Secretary-General Javier Pérez de Cuéllar announced that after "intensive contacts" with the parties in the Afghanistan conflict he could see a growing commitment to a political solution.

In Nicaragua more than 1.5 million voters went to the polls on February 25 under the first UN-monitored election of an independent country. With UN personnel observing, Violeta Barrios de Chamorro was elected to replace the Marxist government of Daniel Ortega Saavedra. The demobilization by the 1,000-member UN Observer Group in Central America (ONUCA) of some 22,000 Nicaraguan contra rebels ended June 29, under a deadline set by the Security Council. In disarming the rebels, ONUCA collected and destroyed thousands of weapons and ordnance, including SAM-7 surface-to-air missiles, mortars, grenade launchers, machine guns, and more than 15,000 small arms.

El Salvador's decade-long civil war was more resistant to solution than Nicaragua's. Yet in a move described by Alvaro de Soto, the secretary-general's Central America representative, as "positive" and "without precedent," representatives of the government and the rebel Farabundo Martí Liberation Front met in Geneva on April 4 and signed an agreement aimed at a political settlement under UN aus-

pices and with Security Council verification. At subsequent meetings, the two sides agreed on a cease-fire, but the mid-September target date passed without a truce. The secretary-general, nevertheless, said the UN was prepared to take "a broad monitoring and verification role once a cease-fire was in place."

During a good-offices mission in March, Pérez de Cuéllar conferred in Rabat with Morocco's King Hassan II and in Tindouf, Algeria, with leaders of the Polisario rebels—the two adversaries in the Western Sahara conflict. Afterward, the secretary-general said he found "a more propitious atmosphere" for solving the 14-year war over the contested desert territory.

In what the secretary-general called "a psychological breakthrough," Foreign Ministers Tariq Aziz of Iraq and Ali-Akbar Velayati of Iran met face-to-face in Geneva on July 3 for the first time since the UN-crafted cease-fire of Aug. 20, 1988. The encounter paved the way for subsequent steps toward implementing other actions aimed at closing the books on the Iran-Iraq war: the exchange of prisoners and Iraq's withdrawal from captured Iranian territory. By year's end the prisoner exchange was proceeding and the Iraqi withdrawal from Iran virtually was complete.

Under the guidance of the 8,000-member UN Transitional Assistance Group (UNTAG), the onetime German colony of South-West Africa became independent as the sovereign nation of Namibia following the withdrawal of South Africa, which had administered the territory under a UN-invalidated League of Nations trusteeship mandate. Since 1967 the UN Council for Namibia had been the territory's legal administrator. However, it was not until December 1988 that the Pretoria government, under increasingly intense international pressure, signed an agreement to yield the territory.

On March 21, Pérez de Cuéllar swore in Sam Nujoma, leader of the South-West Africa People's Organization resistance front, as Namibia's first president. Hundreds of dignitaries from some 70 countries attended the inauguration at the sports stadium in Windhoek, the capital city. Against a background of pealing church bells, fireworks, and singing and dancing by 30,000 spectators, Nujoma hailed South Africa's President F.W. de Klerk for his "statesmanship and realism" in negotiating the handing over of Namibia.

Only a few weeks before, de Klerk had released Nelson Mandela, the international symbol of resistance to apartheid, from 27 years of imprisonment. On June 22, Mandela appeared before the General Assembly to thank the UN for "what you did over the decades to secure my release and the release of other South African prisoners from Pretoria's dungeons."

At a February 20–23 special session, the General Assembly adopted an action plan for a global attack on illicit narcotics production, trafficking, and consumption.

General Assembly. The 45th General Assembly's regular session opened September 18, under the cloud of the Gulf conflict, which the secretary-general said posed a "tremendous threat (of) global war." Deputy Prime Minister Guido de Marco of Malta was elected by acclamation to succeed Joseph Garba of Nigeria as Assembly president. While the Gulf was the overarching theme, delegates faced an agenda of more than 150 items spanning the range of human activity: debt and development, the environment, drugs, poverty, refugees, apartheid, and human rights.

The UN hosted the most elevated summit ever assembled when more than 70 heads of state or government gathered in the General Assembly hall for the September 29–30 World Summit for Children (*see* page 89). The session produced a pledge by delegates—ranging from Belgium's King Baudouin and Britain's Prime Minister Margaret Thatcher to Grand Duke Jean of Luxembourg and U.S. President George Bush—to put the needs of children in the forefront of development.

UN membership fluctuated throughout the year. After peaking at 160 with Namibia's admission on April 23, it shrank to 159 on May 22 when the two Yemens merged, returned briefly to 160 when Liechtenstein joined on September 18, and dropped back to 159 with German reunification October 3.

Assembly voting changed the Security Council's future composition with the expiration of the two-year terms of five of the nonpermanent members: Canada, Colombia, Ethiopia, Finland, and Malaysia. They were replaced for the 1991–92 period by Austria, Belgium, Ecuador, India, and Zimbabwe. The nonpermanent members with one year more to serve were Cuba, Ivory Coast, Romania, Yemen, and Zaire.

The 45th Assembly ended its 1990 sitting December 21, three days beyond the scheduled recess, after adopting a biennial budget of $1.146 billion. It also elected Mrs. Sadako Ogata of Japan, a university dean in Tokyo, as UN high commissioner for refugees to succeed Thorvald Stoltenberg, who resigned to become Norway's foreign minister.

Security Council. Peacekeeping continued to be a UN preoccupation. During the year the Security Council renewed the mandates of long-established operations in the Middle East and in Cyprus, as well as newer missions in Central America. At the government's request, a UN contingent monitored the December elections in Haiti. Proposals also were voiced for UN peace missions to verify any Iraqi withdrawal from Kuwait and to monitor Israel's treatment of Palestinians in the occupied territories; neither of the proposals had been acted on by year's end.

However, it was the Persian Gulf crisis that dominated the Security Council's proceedings during the second half of 1990. Within hours after Hussein's juggernaut had rolled into Kuwait on August 2, the Council adopted a resolution condemning the invasion and demanding immediate withdrawal. The measure was followed by 11 others, culminating in a November 29 resolution authorizing the use of force unless Iraq complied with all earlier mandates by Jan. 15, 1991. Interim resolutions included invoking a trade embargo, nullifying Iraq's annexation claim over Kuwait, demanding the safe departure from Iraq and occupied Kuwait of foreign nationals, condemning "aggressive acts" against foreign diplomats, and imposing an air embargo.

In the face of arguments equating Iraq's invasion with Israel's occupation of Arab territories, the council renewed pressure on Israel to abide by the Geneva conventions on the treatment of civilians under occupation. The precipitating event was the slaying by Israeli security forces of at least 18 Arabs during a violent clash at Jerusalem's Al Aksa Mosque on October 8. After more than two months of negotiations aimed in part at accommodating U.S. refusal to link the Iraqi invasion and the Israeli occupation, the Security Council unanimously adopted a resolution aimed at providing greater protection for Palestinian civilians in the occupied territories.

To focus attention on the plight of Palestinians, Assembly President de Marco announced that in early 1991 he would confer with national leaders and visit UN refugee camps in Israel, Jordan, and the Israeli-occupied Gaza Strip and West Bank. The camps are operated by the UN Relief and Works Agency for Palestine Refugees (UNRWA). Shortly after de Marco's announcement, Israeli troops shot and killed four Palestinians and wounded scores of others in a series of clashes in Gaza Strip refugee districts. In his last pronouncement of the year, the secretary-general on December 31 expressed deep concern over the incident, which occurred two days earlier, and ordered a report from UNRWA. The incident again thrust the Middle East into the forefront as the most intractable issue on the UN's crisis agenda.

Agencies. The International Labor Organization (ILO) drafted a 1992–93 agenda tailored to the global social and economic changes, notably in Eastern Europe. The UN Children's Fund (UNICEF) set its sights for the 1990s on upgrading the status of the girl child, particularly in health and education. The World Health Organization (WHO) reaffirmed its target of achieving health for all by the year 2000. The year marked the 125th anniversary of the International Telecommunications Union (ITU), the UN's oldest affiliated organization.

TED MORELLO, *United Nations Correspondent*
"The Christian Science Monitor"

ORGANIZATION OF THE UNITED NATIONS

THE SECRETARIAT

Secretary-General: Javier Pérez de Cuéllar (until Dec. 31, 1991)

THE GENERAL ASSEMBLY (1990)

President: Guido de Marco, Malta
The 159 member nations were as follows:

Afghanistan	Cape Verde	Gambia	Lesotho	Panama	Sudan
Albania	Central African	Germany	Liberia	Papua New	Suriname
Algeria	Republic	Ghana	Libya	Guinea	Swaziland
Angola	Chad	Greece	Liechtenstein	Paraguay	Sweden
Antigua and	Chile	Grenada	Luxembourg	Peru	Syria
Barbuda	China, People's	Guatemala	Madagascar	Philippines	Tanzania
Argentina	Republic of	Guinea	Malawi	Poland	Thailand
Australia	Colombia	Guinea-Bissau	Malaysia	Portugal	Togo
Austria	Comoros	Guyana	Maldives	Qatar	Trinidad and Tobago
Bahamas	Congo	Haiti	Mali	Romania	Tunisia
Bahrain	Costa Rica	Honduras	Malta	Rwanda	Turkey
Bangladesh	Cuba	Hungary	Mauritania	Saint Christopher	Uganda
Barbados	Cyprus	Iceland	Mauritius	and Nevis	Ukrainian SSR
Belgium	Czechoslovakia	India	Mexico	Saint Lucia	USSR
Belize	Denmark	Indonesia	Mongolia	Saint Vincent and	United Arab Emirates
Byelorussian SSR	Djibouti	Iran	Morocco	The Grenadines	United Kingdom
Benin	Dominica	Iraq	Mozambique	São Tomé and	United States
Bhutan	Dominican	Ireland	Myanmar	Principe	Uruguay
Bolivia	Republic	Israel	Namibia	Saudi Arabia	Vanuatu
Botswana	Ecuador	Italy	Nepal	Senegal	Venezuela
Brazil	Egypt	Ivory Coast	Netherlands	Seychelles	Vietnam
Brunei Darussalam	El Salvador	Jamaica	New Zealand	Sierra Leone	Western Samoa
Bulgaria	Equatorial Guinea	Japan	Nicaragua	Singapore	Yemen
Burkina Faso	Ethiopia	Jordan	Niger	Solomon Islands	Yugoslavia
Burundi	Fiji	Kenya	Nigeria	Somalia	Zaire
Cambodia	Finland	Kuwait	Norway	South Africa	Zambia
Cameroon	France	Laos	Oman	Spain	Zimbabwe
Canada	Gabon	Lebanon	Pakistan	Sri Lanka	

COMMITTEES

General. Composed of 29 members as follows: The General Assembly president; the 21 General Assembly vice-presidents (heads of delegations or their deputies of Brazil, Canada, China, Cyprus, Egypt, Fiji, France, Ghana, Honduras, Indonesia, Lebanon, Mauritius, Mozambique, Rwanda, Saint Lucia, Senegal, Union of Soviet Socialist Republics, United Arab Emirates, United Kingdom of Great Britain and Northern Ireland, United States, Yugoslavia); and the chairmen of the main committees at right, which are composed of all 159 member countries.

First (Political and Security): Jai Pratap Rana (Nepal)
Special Political: Perezi Karukubiro-Kamunanwire (Uganda)
Second (Economic and Financial): George Papadatos (Greece)
Third (Social, Humanitarian and Cultural): Juan Somavia (Chile)
Fourth (Decolonization): Martin Adouki (Congo)
Fifth (Administrative and Budgetary): E. Besley-Maycock (Barbados)
Sixth (Legal): Václav Mikulka (Czechoslovakia)

THE TRUSTEESHIP COUNCIL

President: Thomas Richardson (United Kingdom)

China[2] France[2] USSR[2] United Kingdom[2] United States[1]

[1] Administers Trust Territory. [2] Permanent member of Security Council not administering Trust Territory.

THE SECURITY COUNCIL

Membership ends on December 31 of the year noted; asterisks indicate permanent membership.

Austria (1992)	France*	United Kingdom*
Belgium (1992)	India (1992)	United States*
China*	Ivory Coast (1991)	Yemen (1991)
Cuba (1991)	Romania (1991)	Zaire (1991)
Ecuador (1992)	USSR*	Zimbabwe (1992)

THE INTERNATIONAL COURT OF JUSTICE

Membership ends on February 5 of the year noted.

President: José María Ruda (Argentina, 1991)
Vice-President: Kéba Mbaye (Senegal, 1991)

Roberto Ago (Italy, 1997)
Andres Aguilar Mawdsley (Venezuela, 2000)
Mohammed Bedjaoui (Algeria, 1997)
Taslim O. Elias (Nigeria, 1994)
Jens Evensen (Norway, 1994)
Gilbert Guillaume (France, 2000)
Robert Y. Jennings (United Kingdom, 2000)
Manfred Lachs (Poland, 1994)

Ni Zhengyu (China, 1994)
Shigeru Oda (Japan, 1994)
Raymond Ranjeva (Madagascar, 2000)
Stephen Schwebel (United States, 1997)
Mohamed Shahabuddeen (Guyana, 1997)
Nikolai Konstantinovich Tarassov (USSR, 1997)
Christopher G. Weeramantry (Sri Lanka, 2000)

THE ECONOMIC AND SOCIAL COUNCIL

President: Kjeld Mortensen (Denmark)
Membership ends on December 31 of the year noted.

Algeria (1992)	Indonesia (1991)	Spain (1993)
Argentina (1993)	Iran (1992)	Sweden (1992)
Austria (1993)	Iraq (1991)	Syria (1993)
Bahamas (1991)	Italy (1991)	Thailand (1991)
Bahrain (1992)	Jamaica (1992)	Togo (1993)
Botswana (1993)	Japan (1993)	Trinidad and Tobago (1993)
Brazil (1991)	Jordan (1991)	
Bulgaria (1992)	Kenya (1991)	Tunisia (1991)
Burkina Faso (1992)	Malaysia (1993)	Turkey (1993)
Cameroon (1991)	Mexico (1992)	Ukrainian Soviet Socialist Republic (1991)
Canada (1992)	Morocco (1993)	
Chile (1993)	Netherlands (1991)	
China (1992)	New Zealand (1991)	USSR (1992)
Czechoslovakia (1991)	Nicaragua (1991)	United Kingdom (1992)
Ecuador (1992)	Niger (1991)	
Finland (1992)	Pakistan (1992)	United States (1991)
France (1993)	Peru (1993)	Yugoslavia (1993)
Germany (1993)	Romania (1992)	Zaire (1992)
Guinea (1993)	Somalia (1993)	Zambia (1991)

INTERGOVERNMENTAL AGENCIES

Food and Agricultural Organization (FAO); General Agreement on Tariffs and Trade (GATT); International Atomic Energy Agency (IAEA); International Bank for Reconstruction and Development (World Bank); International Civil Aviation Organization (ICAO); International Fund for Agricultural Development (IFAD); International Labor Organization (ILO); International Maritime Organization (IMO); International Monetary Fund (IMF); International Telecommunication Union (ITU); United Nations Educational, Scientific and Cultural Organization (UNESCO); United Nations Industrial Development Organization (UNIDO); Universal Postal Union (UPU); World Health Organization (WHO); World Intellectual Property Organization (WIPO); World Meteorological Organization (WMO).

© J.L. Atlan/Sygma

Extensive traveling was a hallmark of George Bush's second year in the White House. The president and congressional leaders spent Thanksgiving in Saudi Arabia visiting with U.S. troops involved in Operation Desert Shield.

UNITED STATES

"The events of the year just ended, the revolution of '89, have been a chain reaction, changes so striking that it marks the beginning of a new era in the world's affairs." So said President George Bush in his State of the Union address on Jan. 31, 1990. The president was referring to the political upheaval in Eastern Europe, symbolized by the dismantling of the Berlin Wall, which marked an end to the Cold War. In the new era taking shape the president foresaw a bright future for the nation. On the international scene, Bush said, "America stands at the center of a widening circle of freedom." Meanwhile at home he vowed to lead the way to "a better America, where there's a job for everyone who wants one . . . and where every one of us enjoys the same opportunity to live, to work, and to contribute to society."

But by year's end this rosy picture had been clouded by the harsh realities 1990 had produced. Abroad, the Iraqi invasion of Kuwait in August had spurred the United States to stage its most massive military buildup since Vietnam, bringing the country to the brink of war (*see* feature articles, page 24). And just as peace was imperiled abroad, so was prosperity endangered at home. The downward plunge of economic indicators sharply eroded public confidence and forced politicians in both political parties and at both ends of Pennsylvania Avenue to confront tough decisions.

Domestic Affairs

The Presidency. Bush had enjoyed favorable poll ratings throughout his first year in the White House and as he began his second year his standing in the public's esteem soared to record heights. According to a *Washington Post/ABC News* survey released January 18, 79% of the public approved of his job performance, a higher score than that achieved by any of the other post-World War II presidents. But critics contended that this achievement was due in part to a run of good fortune, an assessment that seemed to be borne out during the year as Bush's luck appeared to run out, compelling him to make some politically costly choices.

By far the most painful domestic dilemma he faced was the federal budget deficit, a problem Bush had pledged during the 1988 campaign that he would solve without raising taxes. At first the president stuck to his "read my lips" opposition to a tax increase. The $1.23 trillion budget he submitted to Congress on January 29 not only proposed no tax increases, but in fact embodied one major tax reduction, a cut in the capital-gains rate long favored by

© Chick Harrity/"U.S. News & World Report"

Members of the administration and Congress spent months in 1990 trying to agree on a plan for reducing the budget deficit. Many Americans were disillusioned by the affair.

the president. To meet the federal deficit limits established by the Gramm-Rudman-Hollings law, Bush's budget relied on spending cut proposals which Congress had rejected in the past and on assumptions about the economy which many economists disputed.

Indeed, even the White House seemed to share some of the skepticism about its own budget goals, as was evidenced by its surprisingly positive response to the deficit-reduction proposal announced March 11 by House Ways and Means Committee Chairman Daniel Rostenkowski. Although tax increases were part of the Illinois Democrat's proposal, Bush's press secretary, Marlin Fitzwater, called Rostenkowski's approach "serious and thoughtful." Meanwhile, circumstances created mounting pressure on the president to modify his long-standing opposition to a tax increase. On April 6 the General Accounting Office told Congress that the cost of the bailout of the debt-ridden savings and loan industry could run as high as $500 billion over the next decade, about triple the administration's 1989 forecast (*see* BANK-ING AND FINANCE). On April 27 the Commerce Department provided more bleak news—the gross national product (GNP) had grown only 2.1% in the first quarter of the year, while inflation soared to 6.5%, the highest quarterly rate since 1981. And on May 1 the House of Representatives adopted a budget plan, put forward by the Democratic majority, which called for $13.9 billion in tax increases and rejected many of Bush's proposals for cuts in domestic spend-

ing. Republican House leaders did not even put Bush's own budget plan to a vote.

The initial public indication that the president was prepared to be flexible on tax increases came May 9 when congressional leaders announced that the White House had agreed to meet with them to discuss the deficit, "without preconditions," which presumably meant that the possibility of a tax increase would not be ruled out in advance. At first the talks moved slowly, and Democrats complained that Bush so far had failed to explain to the public the seriousness of the deficit crisis and the need for tax increases.

But with economic prospects steadily worsening, thus swelling the anticipated size of the deficit, while the burgeoning savings and loan crisis added tens of billions of dollars to federal expenses, Bush came to realize that he had no choice but to change his antitax stand. On June 26 he released a statement in which he acknowledged that "it is clear to me" that "tax-revenue increases" along with other measures now were necessary to solve the deficit problems.

Some politicians suggested that the president made the change in order to stave off a prolonged recession and boost his reelection prospects in 1992. But in the short run, the move hurt him politically. Democrats immediately charged that his real reason for raising taxes was to ensure that the Treasury had enough funds to pay off his wealthy friends in the savings and loan industry. But the most vociferous protest against the president's shift came from many of his fellow Republicans, who charged that by giving ground on taxes the president had thrown away the issue which best served to define the differences between the Democratic and Republican parties to the GOP's advantage. Indeed, despite Bush's altered stance, a majority of the Republican members of the House went on record as opposing any tax increase.

Bush suffered further political damage when he tried to gain public support for a compromise agreement on the budget which finally had been reached in September by the White House and congressional leaders after weeks of bitter haggling. On October 2 in a nationally televised address from the Oval Office, only the fourth such speech of his presidency, Bush called upon the public to urge Congress to support the plan, warning that "if we fail to enact this agreement our economy will falter, markets may tumble, and recession will follow." Despite this appeal, Republican members were outraged at the $134 billion in tax increases over five years in the measure, while Democrats complained that the tax increases on gasoline and liquor and Medicare were regressive. The plan was rejected by the House on October 5 by a 254-to-179 vote, with 105 out of 176 House Republicans defying the president to vote no.

While negotiations for a new agreement dragged on, Bush caused himself additional political harm on October 9 by first saying he would be willing to accept an increase in income-tax rates on the wealthy, but then only a few hours later rejecting that idea. Eventually a budget agreement, which included an increase in income-tax rates that Bush originally had opposed but did not include the capital-gains tax cut he long had sought was enacted by Congress on October 27 and signed into law.

Bush managed to recover some of the lost ground after the budget debate ended and Congress adjourned, by focusing attention on the Middle East crisis as he campaigned for Republican candidates in the midterm elections (*see* special report, page 548). Nevertheless, a *New York Times/CBS News* poll released November 3 showed that his approval rating had dropped 21 points in little more than a month, to 52%, the lowest score of his presidency. Moreover, the troubles of the economy, like the crisis in the Mideast, still faced him at year's end, casting a shadow over the second half of his presidential term. On November 14 in a Cable News Network interview the president conceded for the first time that the country might sink into a recession, though he added: "Most [of his economic advisers] seem to feel that if we have a recession, it will not be deep and that we'll come out of it relatively soon, six months at most."

The president confronted another controversy October 22 when he vetoed civil-rights legislation passed by Congress to combat discrimination in employment. Bush claimed the act would lead to the imposition of "the destructive force of quotas" in hiring and promotion. The Senate vote to override the veto was 66 to 34, one short of the necessary two-thirds majority, but the veto seemed likely to undermine Bush's efforts to expand his support among black voters for the 1992 campaign.

In the face of his other difficulties, the president was aided by stability in the ranks of his top advisers for much of the year. When Eliz-

abeth Dole resigned October 24 as labor secretary to head the American Red Cross, she became the first member of the cabinet to leave. In mid-December, Lauro F. Cavazos gave up his position as secretary of education. The president named Rep. Lynn Martin, who had lost her bid to unseat Illinois Sen. Paul Simon, to replace Dole and former Tennessee Gov. Lamar Alexander as the new education secretary. Another top administration figure, William Bennett, also resigned as federal drug-policy director. Outgoing Florida Gov. Bob Martinez was selected for the post.

Congress. The bitter struggle over the budget deficit which dominated the final session of the 101st Congress resulted in an agreement with far-reaching implications. The main objective of the plan was to reduce the deficit by nearly $500 billion over five years. But in order to achieve its fiscal goals the agreement reached broadly across U.S. life, establishing a wide range of social and economic guidelines.

The increase in gross revenue over five years would be $164.6 billion, plus a claimed $9.4 billion resulting from tightened tax enforcement measures. Another $18.6 billion from increased user fees on government loans and services would bring the gross increase of revenues to $192.6 billion, a figure that would be offset in part by new tax breaks of $27.4 billion. Along with this net revenue increase of $165.2 billion, lawmakers expected to raise about $100 billion over five years from cuts in federal programs. The rest of the total deficit reduction goal of $500 billion—nearly half— would result from cuts in defense spending to be enacted separately and from savings on the interest payments on the reduced deficit.

The lion's share of the burden fell on the wealthy as a result of an increase in the top personal tax rate to 31% from 28%, a raise in the alternative minimum tax rate to 24% from 21%, a new luxury tax on high-priced cars, airplanes, yachts, and furs, and imposition of a user's fee on owners of recreational boats. In relative terms, lower- and middle-bracket taxpayers would bear a heavy portion of the new revenue load in proportion to their income as a result of increased excise taxes on gasoline, cigarettes, beer, wine, and liquor. But the law cushioned the impact on the poor by providing new tax credits for low-income families with children and expanding Medicaid coverage for such families.

Among the major savings provided for in the agreement: $42.5 billion from Medicare as a result of increased premiums and reduced payments to doctors and hospitals; $14.9 billion from agricultural programs, chiefly price supports; $3.7 billion from veterans' benefits; and $9 billion from increasing the premiums banks and thrifts pay for deposit insurance. The agreement also modified the Gramm-Rud-

(Continued on page 550.)

The 1990 Elections

AP/Wide World

Although there was a strong public cry for new political faces throughout the United States during the 1990 campaign season, incumbents again did well on election day.

By the time voters went to the polls on November 6, the 1990 midterm campaign had gone through a series of drastic twists and turns which made the political debate particularly spasmodic. The ballot choices offered voters on election day had begun to take shape more than a year earlier—in the summer of 1989. At that time the peace and relative prosperity that had helped George Bush win the White House still prevailed and the president's poll ratings were high. Despite the historical tradition that the party controlling the White House loses ground in off-year elections, Republicans hoped at least to hold their own in the House and to gain seats in the Senate, and six Republicans gave up safe House seats to seek election to the Senate, while three others bid for governorships.

But by the late spring of 1990, the economy weakened, raising fears of a recession and underlining the urgency of dealing with the federal deficit. When these pressures forced President Bush to revoke his campaign pledge to resist any tax increase, many in his own party rebelled. Before the Democrats could take full advantage of this split in the GOP, the Mideast crisis erupted in August, diverting attention from domestic issues as the country rallied behind the president. But by fall the focus of public concern shifted again, this time to the prolonged debate on Capitol Hill over the budget. Republicans were hurt because the controversy highlighted the divisions within their own party over tax increases and made the president seem indecisive. The Democrats added to the damage by accusing the GOP of favoring the rich.

The public mood soured, leading to warnings that voters would take wholesale revenge against incumbents in both parties. On election day, though, no such massive revolt developed. Instead, the main result of the election was that Democrats strengthened their already powerful grip on both houses of Congress and on the state level scored successes in key governors' races which bolstered their ability to influence the reapportionment process that would follow the 1990 census.

House and Senate Races. In the House of Representatives the Democrats gained eight seats, extending their majority to 267 against 167 Republicans with one socialist, Bernard Sanders, who was elected in Vermont, expected to caucus with the Democrats. Democrats defeated eight Republican incumbents and won six open seats, five of which had been vacated by Republicans seeking higher office. Though Republicans defeated six Democratic incumbents more than 96% of the 406 House incumbents seeking reelection were returned to office.

In the Senate the Democrats made a net gain of one seat, in Minnesota, where liberal college professor Paul Wellstone defeated two-term Republican incumbent Rudy Boschwitz. Incumbent Democratic senators in Illinois, Rhode Island, Michigan, Iowa, and Hawaii turned back stiff challenges from Republicans who had quit the House of Representatives in hopes of advancing to the Senate. Despite retirements of their incumbents, Republicans held on to Senate seats in Colorado, where Rep. Hank Brown replaced William Armstrong; Idaho, where Rep. Larry Craig replaced James McClure; and New Hampshire, where Rep. Robert Smith took the seat held by Gordon J. Humphrey. In a contest that attracted intense national attention, three-term Republican in-

AP/Wide World

Connecticut's Lowell Weicker, a former Republican U.S. senator who lost a close reelection bid in 1988, ran as an independent and won the governorship. Eunice Groark (left) was the first woman to be elected lieutenant governor in the state.

cumbent and conservative bulwark Jesse Helms staved off a strong bid by Democrat Harvey Gantt, the black former mayor of Charlotte.

Gubernatorial Campaigns. In the governors' races, Democrats, who had 29 governorships before the elections to 21 for the Republicans, emerged with 28 while Republicans, who had 21, wound up with 19. Two former Republicans running as independents won two seats previously held by Democrats, former U.S. Sen. Lowell Weicker in Connecticut and former Gov. Walter J. Hickel in Alaska. A close race in Arizona ended indecisively and a runoff was scheduled for early 1991.

Because of reapportionment the most important Democratic gubernatorial victories were in Florida, which was expected to gain four House seats, and where former U.S. Sen. Lawton Chiles defeated incumbent Republican Gov. Bob Martinez, and Texas, which was expected to pick up three seats, where Democrats elected state Treasurer Ann Richards. But the Republicans held on to the richest single gubernatorial prize of the election, California, which was expected to gain seven House seats, by electing U.S. Sen. Peter Wilson.

In addition to Florida, Democrats ousted Republican incumbents in Nebraska, where Ben Nelson defeated Gov. Kay Orr; Kansas, where state Treasurer Joan Finney beat Gov. Mike Hayden; and Rhode Island, where Bruce Sundlun defeated Gov. Ed DiPrete. In addition to Texas, Democrats elected governors in two states where Republican governors retired,

David Walters in Oklahoma and Bruce King in New Mexico. In two states, Democrats—Zell Miller in Georgia and Barbara Roberts in Oregon—replaced retiring governors from their own party.

Republicans unseated Democratic incumbents in Minnesota, where Arne Carlson defeated Rudy Perpich, and Michigan, where John Engler beat James Blanchard. And Republicans elected governors in three states where incumbent Democrats retired. The winners were former Cleveland Mayor George Voinovich in Ohio, former Gov. Richard Snelling in Vermont, and William Weld in Massachusetts. In Illinois, Republican Secretary of State Jim Edgar replaced a retiring Republican governor.

Initiatives. Though the defeats of several incumbent governors, as well as the surprisingly narrow victory of New Jersey Democratic Sen. Bill Bradley, were attributed to backlash against tax hikes, it was far from clear that a full-scale taxpayers' revolt was under way. In six states, Massachusetts, California, Montana, Nebraska, Colorado, and Utah, voters rejected ballot propositions that would have limited taxes or spending increases. The returns were muddled equally on the question of abortion (*see also* ABORTION). California and Colorado supported measures setting limits on the length of service for elected officials and environmental initiatives went down to defeat in such states as California, New York, Oregon, and Washington.

ROBERT SHOGAN

man-Hollings deficit-reduction law by putting more emphasis on controlling federal spending rather than on specific reductions in the deficit.

Though the budget-deficit controversy generated the most heat and produced the most headlines, Congress enacted major legislation in a number of other policy areas, including clean air, housing, immigration, the disabled, and child care. (*See* page 590.) In other action, the Senate confirmed President Bush's nomination of David H. Souter (*see* BIOGRAPHY) to the Supreme Court, and both Houses approved reauthorization of the National Endowment for the Arts for a period of three years, without including a controversial proposal to bar the endowment for supporting "obscene" art. But the Congress failed to act on proposals for funding the savings and loan bailout, for campaign-finance reform, and for strengthening sanctions against banks which launder money for drug dealers.

Congress also had to devote time to deal with allegations of ethical misconduct against some of its members. On July 25 the Senate "denounced" Republican Sen. David Durenberger of Minnesota for financial improprieties. Durenberger was ordered to pay more than $120,000 in restitution for speaking fees and other funds he had accepted in violation of Senate rules. The House of Representatives reprimanded Massachusetts Democratic Rep. Barney Frank, an acknowledged homosexual, for using his influence to fix parking tickets for a male prostitute he had befriended. Democratic Rep. Gus Savage of Illinois was reproved for making sexual advances to a female Peace Corps volunteer while on an overseas trip, and Republican Rep. Newt Gingrich of Georgia was cleared of major charges of misbehavior stemming from a book-promotion deal but criticized for less serious violations.

The most significant and highly publicized test of congressional ethics rules came after Congress adjourned and was linked to the savings and loan scandal. It stemmed from charges that five senators improperly had used their influence on behalf of Charles H. Keating, Jr., the indicted chairman of the failed California thrift, Lincoln Savings and Loan Association, who had been a major campaign contributor for them. After a nine-month investigation, Robert Bennett, special counsel to the Senate Ethics Committee, recommended clearing two of the senators under investigation, Democrat John Glenn of Ohio and Republican John McCain of Arizona. Bennett said there was "probable cause" to believe that the other three—Democrats Dennis DeConcini of Arizona, Alan Cranston of California, and Donald Riegle of Michigan—had intervened with federal regulators to aid Keating. But the committee disregarded Bennett's advice and in mid-November began holding hearings into the conduct of all five senators.

Meanwhile, the 76-year-old Cranston disclosed that he was suffering from prostate cancer and therefore would not seek reelection when his term expires in 1992 or continue in his post as Democratic Senate whip. His Democratic colleagues elected Wendell Ford of Kentucky to replace him.

Environment. In the wake of 1989's *Exxon Valdez* disaster the threat of oil spills remained a constant concern. On March 22, Joseph J. Hazelwood—captain of the oil tanker which had caused the worst oil spill in U.S. history—was convicted of negligence, a misdemeanor, by an Alaska jury. But Hazelwood was acquitted of the more serious charges of criminal mischief and of operating a vessel while intoxicated.

After a 16-month investigation into the episode the National Transportation Safety Board issued a report July 31 which found plenty of blame to go around. In addition to criticizing Hazelwood and his third mate for faulty seamanship, the report cited Exxon Shipping Company for failing to provide a "fit master and a rested and sufficient crew," the U.S. Coast Guard for inadequate tracking of ships in the area, and Alaska authorities for not assigning a pilot to steer the ship safely past Bligh Reef, with which it collided, causing the spillage of 258,000 barrels of oil.

Meanwhile, spills continued to blight the nation's coast. On January 2 a gash in an Exxon Corp. pipeline caused a major spill in New York harbor between Staten Island and New Jersey. On February 7 the spillage of nearly 400,000 gallons (1.5 million l) of crude oil off Huntington Beach, CA, from a tanker that apparently ran over its own anchor threatened beaches and wildlife sanctuaries. On June 8 an explosion and fire aboard the Norwegian supertanker *Mega Borg* off the Texas Gulf Coast sent 3.9 million gallons (14.8 million l) pouring into Galveston Bay. And on July 28 two barges collided with a Greek tanker in the same waters, causing a 500,000-gallon (1.9 million-l) spill.

Responding to such mishaps, Congress passed tough new legislation aimed at increasing the liability limits of shippers for spills and providing compensation for economic loss. Another new law requires owners of pipelines in the Gulf of Mexico to inspect and rebury exposed lines to prevent tankers from colliding with them. Meanwhile, despite pressure to increase oil supplies because of the Mideast crisis, Congress decided in an agreement linked to the Interior Department appropriations bill to maintain prohibition of oil drilling in 135 million acres (55 million ha) of coastal waters.

On another environmental front, Congress strengthened the federal Clean Air Act (*see* feature article, page 61).

ROBERT SHOGAN
Washington Bureau, "Los Angeles Times"

Congressional Reform

Once again, as the 1990s began, the legislative branch of the U.S. Congress was under attack and cries for its reform were heard throughout the nation. The issue of congressional reform has been a long-standing one in U.S. political history, and periodically Congress has changed its organization and rules of procedure.

History. A major wave of reform occurred in 1910, when the House of Representatives voted to weaken the office of House speaker and give more power to the chairmen of House committees. Prior to this reform, the speaker had been the dominant center of power in the Congress. The House speaker often would put together a legislative program for the House of Representatives and then use his powers to rally support and get it enacted.

The 1910 reforms gave rise to what became known as "committee government." Under this system, committees reviewed proposed legislation in specific areas. Thus the House Ways and Means Committee reviewed legislation in the general area of taxation and recommended new tax laws for adoption. The Senate Armed Services Committee reviewed policies concerning national defense and made legislative recommendations to the full Senate.

Following the 1910 reforms, it was the congressional committees, particularly their chairmen, who had the most to say about what bills would or would not be enacted. Senators and representatives became committee chairmen by seniority—being the member of the majority party with the longest number of years of service on the particular committee. Because they could not be fired from their chairmanships by Senate and House leaders, committee chairmen tended to become individual centers of power.

By the early 1970s, advocates of congressional reform had become as critical of the enlarged powers of committee chairmen as earlier reformers had been of the great powers of the speaker of the House. Because committee chairmen got their jobs through seniority, they tended to be older and more conservative than the average member of Congress. They often were referred to as "autonomous barons" who were unresponsive to other members of Congress and public opinion.

In 1973 another wave of reform swept the Congress. In the House of Representatives, the powers of committee chairmen were reduced greatly. Chairmen no longer would have the power to appoint subcommittees and deter-

mine the jurisdiction of those subcommittees. Instead, each committee member was allowed to select his or her own subcommittee assignment, and every member of the majority party was guaranteed the chairmanship of at least one subcommittee. This reform, hailed as the "Subcommittee Bill of Rights," often is characterized as having replaced "committee government" with "subcommittee government."

As soon as this reform was in place, however, it developed its own critics and still further calls for reform. Giving each member of the majority party a subcommittee chairmanship in the House, critics said, dispersed the power of Congress so broadly that it became almost impossible to get action on controversial issues. The newly empowered subcommittees became multiple decision points that made it much easier to stop than to enact legislation. Most importantly, the subcommittees appeared to be particularly vulnerable to being influenced by the powerful interest groups—primarily business corporations or labor unions—that were affected most by their work.

By 1990 the major criticism of Congress was that its powers were distributed too widely to subcommittees to produce effective legislative action. Such words as "disaggregation" and "particularism" were used to describe a legislative body that appeared to have great difficulty agreeing on policies and programs and enacting them into law. The end result was that the Congress, mired in inaction because its power was dispersed too widely, had lost most of its ability to propose and innovate. Congress spent most of its time reacting to presidential proposals.

Current Proposals. The major reform proposals presented for Congress as the early 1990s began called for restoring congressional ability to act by creating stronger centers of power. One suggestion was to reduce the number of subcommittees, perhaps by as much as 50%. This would enable senators and representatives to spend less time at subcommittee meetings and more time building coalitions with their fellow legislators that could result in coherent congressional action. It also would increase the importance of committees and committee chairmen, and thereby enable them to broker the various competing interests and negotiate the compromises that would produce higher quality legislation from Congress.

Another major reform, widely discussed by political scientists and congressional experts, called for strengthening the power of the majority-party leadership in the Senate and House of Representatives. Under this plan, members of the majority party in each house would caucus and develop a coherent legislative program for a particular session of Congress. It then would be the job of the leadership—the speaker of the House and the majority leader in the Senate—to push this majority-party program through to enactment. The divisive effects of subcommittee government thus would be cured by centralizing power in the party leadership in each house.

Congress also has been criticized for the extent to which it is dominated by major economic interests. In the wave of reform that swept the Congress in the early 1970s, political action committees (PACs) were legalized. These organizations raise money from various economic-interest groups, both business and labor, and contribute it to the reelection campaigns of those members of Congress who support the particular economic-interest group. Most congressmen have denied that PAC contributions could "buy" their vote on a particular bill, but most would acknowledge that they have listened to the problems and desires of heavy PAC contributors and have made an extra effort to represent them.

By the time of the 1988 congressional elections, PACs were contributing more than $100 million to the reelection campaigns of incumbents. Less than $20 million was contributed by PACs to challengers—candidates trying to oust a sitting member of Congress. The final result was that PAC contributions helped to create a phenomenon known as incumbency advantage, the fact that members of Congress are reelected almost automatically unless they retire voluntarily.

Some critics have blamed PACs as another cause of the inability of Congress to act. Senators and representatives in search of PAC contributions do not want to antagonize competing interests, and thus they maneuver to sidestep problems rather than solve them. Also, congressmen have become so dependent on PAC contributions that they spend too much of their time raising money from PACs rather than serving their constituents and studying legislation.

One reform suggested for curbing the influence of PAC donations would be to set a $100,000 limit on the amount of money an individual member of Congress could receive from PACs in any one election campaign. This figure could be adjusted upward for senators from large states. Another idea would be to provide for public financing of congressional election campaigns, such as is done in presidential elections. Some critics have suggested putting

a spending cap on both incumbents and challengers. A sum of $250,000 per candidate per election has been mentioned frequently.

A number of reforms also have been suggested for reducing incumbency advantage. Members of Congress would be made to give up the subsidized postal rates that they use to do mass mailings to their constituents in election years. One unique suggestion would permit taxpayers to earmark $1 of their income taxes to go into a special campaign fund that would be allocated to congressional challengers only.

Congress is criticized every year for its continuing failure to take control of the federal budget and begin reducing the budget deficit. A favorite technique to avoid budgetary responsibility is to give the government temporary spending authority, thereby allowing the government to continue spending money even though the Congress has not yet made the tough decisions concerning the annual budget. Suggested reforms in this key area of concern include going from a one-year to a two-year budget cycle. This would give congressmen more time to find solutions to budget problems and would reduce the large amount of time Congress now spends debating the budget. Congress also could be forced to operate on a strict pay-as-you-go system— any new spending program would have to be accompanied by a tax increase to pay for it or by an offsetting spending cut somewhere else in the budget.

As a basic answer to the question of congressional reform, a national lobby group has begun promoting a constitutional amendment to limit congressional tenure to 12 years. Proponents believe that the era of the "career" congressional politician must end. According to Sen. Gordon Humphrey (R-NH), who retired from the Senate in 1990 after two terms, "no single reform would do more good than to limit terms." Opponents counter that the amendment would limit the effectiveness of many extremely capable legislators and would not come to the heart of the overall issue.

A major problem with congressional reform is that only Congress can change the laws and its own rules to make itself more effective. It would be tough for incumbent members of Congress to vote to limit their PAC contributions, to provide more campaign funds to the candidates who want to defeat them for reelection, and to make themselves behave more responsibly at budget time. Congress would have to consider these reforms, however, if it wanted to quiet the heavy criticism that was coming its way in 1990.

ROBERT D. LOEVY

The Dwight D. Eisenhower Centennial

Dwight David Eisenhower, supreme commander of the Allied Expeditionary Force during World War II and the 34th president of the United States, was the focus of numerous events during 1990 as a variety of groups commemorated the centennial of his birth on Oct. 14, 1890, in Denison, TX.

Ceremonies. A joint session of Congress was held on March 27, 1990, to pay tribute to Dwight D. Eisenhower. Centennial events were held later at Columbia University, Washington's Kennedy Center, and in several European coun-

Copyrighted by The White House Historical Association;
Photograph by the National Geographic Society

tries. Denison, TX, where the Eisenhower Birthplace Foundation operates a museum in the house where "Ike" was born, celebrated the centennial on September 29 and 30.

In 1951, Eisenhower and his wife Mamie Doud Eisenhower, whom he married in 1916, purchased a farm near Gettysburg, PA, where they retired in 1961. The state legislature created an Eisenhower Centennial Commission of Pennsylvania, which sponsored a variety of activities. The Dwight D. Eisenhower Society of Gettysburg organized programs, including a lecture series, an exhibition of Eisenhower papers and paintings, an academic symposium on his presidency (October 11–13), and a banquet and memorial ceremony later that same weekend. Former President Gerald Ford and David Eisenhower, the late president's grandson, joined academicians and Eisenhower colleagues at the symposium. A ceremony also was held at Washington's Kennedy Center.

Ike, who always considered Kansas home, once said that "the proudest thing I can claim is that I am from Abilene." The Kansas legislature also created an Eisenhower Centennial Commission, and it sponsored educational programs for schools, touring exhibits, television and radio spots, several lecture series and symposia, and an exhibit of Eisenhower's paintings. Throughout the year, family members and politicians participated in a variety of activities in Abilene, the site of the Eisenhower Presidential Library complex that includes the graves of the Eisenhowers. Former Presidents Ronald Reagan and Ford visited the site in July and August, respectively. Gen. Colin Powell, the current chairman of the Joint Chiefs of Staff, joined Kansas' two senators, Robert Dole and Nancy Kassebaum, Eisenhower's son John, and a crowd of 25,000–30,000 in Abilene for an October 14 ceremony.

Evaluation of Ike's Presidency. Over the last few decades, the Eisenhower presidency has been reassessed by historians and political scientists. Immediately following his two terms as president, Eisenhower generally was viewed as a fairly mediocre chief executive who was not comfortable with party politics, and as a somewhat ineffective manager. Recent views and rankings of presidents, however, place Eisenhower in the "near great" category. He is viewed as a politician who mastered the art of compromise. Now Eisenhower also is considered a skilled leader who effectively used his subordinates, both as the commander in charge of one of history's largest and most complex military assignments and as president. An example of the latter was his involvement of the scientific community in policy-making related to the U.S. entrance into the "space race."

Eisenhower biographer Stephen E. Ambrose credits Ike with being an excellent fiscal manager and with skillfully handling—without overreacting—a number of "crises" during his administration, such as the armistice in Korea, Hungary's unsuccessful revolt against its Communist leaders in 1956, Egypt's nationalization of the Suez Canal in 1956, the racial unrest in Little Rock, AR, in 1957, and the downing of the U-2 by the USSR in 1960.

Eisenhower always was popular with the general public, particularly among the generations that remember his leadership during World War II. That affection for him endures to the present, as demonstrated by the scope of and the large number of participants in the many centennial events.

PATRICIA A. MICHAELIS

One or Two New States?

The issue of possible statehood for the Commonwealth of Puerto Rico and the District of Columbia was renewed in 1990. Although a vote on statehood for Puerto Rico inched closer to becoming a reality, such a motion stayed out of reach for the District of Columbia. Residents of the District, however, selected their first "shadow senators" on November 6. Their primary function would be to lobby for statehood.

Puerto Rico. The U.S. House of Representatives in October passed a long-fought bill calling for a 1991 referendum on Puerto Rico's relationship with the United States. The bill would allow residents of Puerto Rico to choose among statehood, independence, or an improved commonwealth status for the island. However, a companion bill remained stalled in the Senate, and differences between the two measures prevented final congressional action in 1990. The social and tax benefits available to islanders under the statehood, commonwealth, and independence options varied in the two bills.

A self-governing commonwealth since July 25, 1952, the island elects its own executive, legislative, and judicial officials. Puerto Rico's 3.6 million residents cannot vote in federal elections and pay no federal income taxes. They can serve in the armed forces and migrate freely to the mainland. An estimated 2.5 million Puerto Ricans live in the states. The island's official ties to the United States date to 1898, when it became a U.S. territory after the Spanish-American War. The island's Spanish heritage remains strong in its dominant Spanish-speaking culture.

While President George Bush is a longtime supporter of statehood for Puerto Rico, many Republican members of Congress are not. Puerto Rico's former Gov. Carlos Romero Barceló, president of the Progressive Party, is a leading proponent of statehood. Opponents include Gov. Rafael Hernández Colón of the Popular Democratic Party. Most of the island's elected legislators are members of the party that favors keeping the island a commonwealth. Jaime B. Fuster, the island's resident commissioner and a nonvoting delegate to the U.S. House, also favors commonwealth status. Polls show that the island's residents are divided sharply on the issue. In a 1967 plebiscite, initiated by the island government, residents favored remaining a commonwealth.

Statehood would grant new rights of citizenship in addition to a political say in federal elections. A study for the Congressional Budget Office found that a change in the island's political status could change its economic status. Statehood would mean the island's residents would receive increased federal social-service benefits, including food stamps and Medicaid. But opponents believe that statehood would mean the loss of a tax benefit that is key to its economic development.

Under Section 936 of the U.S. tax code, U.S. companies do not have to pay federal income tax on profits made on their operations in Puerto Rico. The commonwealth further sweetens the tax break by exempting 90% of the companies' profits from local taxes. The congressional study estimated that loss of the tax incentive could cause U.S. companies to pull out. An estimated 100,000 or more jobs would be lost. For an island where the jobless rate stands at 14% and the minimum wage is $3.25, the study provided ammunition for commonwealth supporters. The third option of independence would allow the island to be self-governing. Residents would keep their U.S. citizenship under the proposal.

District of Columbia. The 626,000 residents of the District of Columbia seemed unlikely to gain statehood anytime soon. With no bill calling for DC statehood progressing in Congress, the District's residents on November 6 elected their first two new "shadow senators." The post was created to lobby for statehood for the District. Whether the shadow senators will be admitted to the Senate floor was uncertain late in 1990. The District already had a nonvoting delegate in the House.

Proponents of statehood for the District, including former Democratic presidential candidate Jesse Jackson, argue that the District should have voting representation in Congress, budgetary autonomy, control over its courts, and the rights of self-determination. The District's residents already pay federal taxes amounting to some $1.38 billion annually. Most of the District's budget is funded locally, but the federal government makes special payments in lieu of taxes on federal lands for which city services are provided.

Opponents of DC statehood see the District as the seat of the federal government, requiring special status. [The District became the U.S. capital on Dec. 1, 1800, and was granted a unique status at that time.] Opponents also resist statehood on the basis that the District is essentially a city.

As 1990 ended, it appeared too soon to plan for an additional star or two for the U.S. flag.

ELAINE S. KNAPP

The Economy

The story of the U.S. economy in 1990 was one of steady and persistent erosion and then a sharp descent into recession during the final quarter. At first, many economists and government officials, including some in the White House and the Federal Reserve Board, declined to use the word "recession," but by November the erosion in economic statistics overwhelmed any euphemisms. For the first time since the fall of 1982, the economy was shrinking and it was bringing to an end what often was called the longest peacetime expansion since the end of World War II.

Downturn. Even before the sharp fourth-quarter falloff, the engine had been faltering. A year earlier, in the fourth quarter of 1989, real growth as measured by gross national product (GNP) was a mere 0.3%, rising to 1.7% in the first quarter of 1990, falling back to just 0.4% in the April-June period, and then struggling back to 1.4% in the third quarter. When it tripped and fell in the final quarter it was of a different magnitude, and even the diehards finally conceded a recession was under way.

After having spent many months just above 5%, unemployment in November rose to 5.9%. The index of leading economic indicators fell for the fifth straight month. The manufacturing index fell to its lowest level since 1982, and the output of plants and factories dropped to around 81% of capacity, its lowest in years. Ford Motor posted its first quarterly loss in eight years, as sales by all companies of vehicles built in North America sank to the lowest since 1982. The barrage of bad news undermined consumer morale, and probably added to the woes.

Debt. The usual pre-Christmas spurt in retail sales did not develop as expected, and the newspapers explained that holiday shopping was tempered by fears about the Middle East crisis and federal-tax increases just imposed, on gasoline, and soon to be, on expensive cars and other goods. But there was more to it than that; people were worried about their jobs and big debts. Enormous amounts of credit had financed the long expansion of the 1980s. Now the bills were coming due, and they could not be paid. The delinquency rates for home mortgages, credit-card and bank-card debt, and personal loans rose. In 1990 individuals owed more than $3 trillion, between two and three times what they had owed in 1980. Reflecting this, personal bankruptcies rose 15% in 1990, atop a 10% rise in 1989.

Equally dramatic and ominous was the devastation in business loans, especially among real-estate developers and the institutions that lent to them. Dun & Bradstreet (D&B) found that in the first nine months of the year failures among real-estate companies (the borrowers), financial institutions (who arranged the loans), and insurers (who often bought the high-yield bonds that supposedly backed the debt), rose 31.1% from the year before. Some insurance companies, those institutions that are relied upon to pay off in disaster, were themselves in trouble, and speculation abounded about them being "the next S&Ls [savings and loan associations]" crisis. Some of the biggest banks were forced to write off, sell off, or discount billions of dollars in loans that once they called assets, and the Federal Deposit Insurance Corporation raised its estimate of bank deposit insurance fund losses to $4 billion or more for the year. This came atop an earlier savings and loan debacle that could cost U.S. taxpayers as much as $500 billion, or roughly $2,000 for every person in the country. In all, 43,836 concerns had failed by the end of September.

AP/Wide World

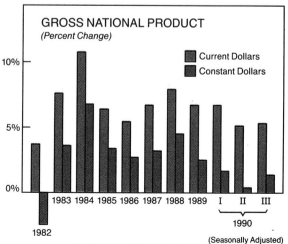

For much of 1990, Federal Reserve Chairman Alan Greenspan (left) avoided the word recession in discussing the economy. In mid-December the Fed lowered the discount rate to 6.5%—an apparent acknowledgment of bad times.

GROSS NATIONAL PRODUCT
(Percent Change)

- Current Dollars
- Constant Dollars

10%

5%

0%

1982 1983 1984 1985 1986 1987 1988 1989 I II III

1990

(Seasonally Adjusted)
U.S. Department of Commerce, Bureau of Economic Analysis

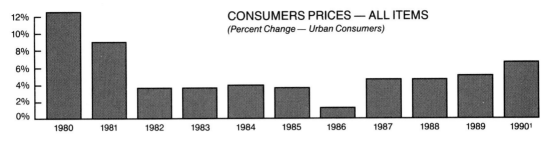

CONSUMERS PRICES — ALL ITEMS
(Percent Change — Urban Consumers)

(Seasonally Adjusted)
[1] November estimate   U.S. Department of Labor, Bureau of Labor Statistics

Moreover, said D&B, the size of the liabilities also was up sharply.

Uncle Sam, too, remained in debt, unable to balance his budget or U.S. foreign payments for two decades. For fiscal 1990, which ended in September, the deficit was $220 billion, and the Congressional Budget Office said the shortfall would rise to $253 billion in fiscal 1991, and to $262 billion in 1992. This was after a torturous round of so-called budget cutting.

The Prime Rate and Home Mortgages. Even the good news was marred. Reacting to the deepening decline, the Federal Reserve Board at first attempted to talk confidence into its member banks, urging them to be freer in making loans. That failed, and on December 18 it lowered by one half of one percentage point to 6.5% the rate at which members can borrow from the central bank. The first such cut since Feb. 24, 1989, it was seen as an effort to encourage banks to lower their highly visible prime interest rate, or lending rate to the nation's best corporate customers. That rate sometimes is used as a measure for other rates, including those to consumers. Analysts noted, however, that banks already were burdened with more loans than they could deal with, were attempting to clear their books of bad business, and were in the process of downsizing rather than expanding operations. Lowering rates, as the Fed wished them to do, meant they would earn smaller returns. In addition, not only was inflation coming under control—except for oil-related products and health-care costs—but deflation actually was beginning to occur. That meant even more stress on borrowers; instead of paying back in cheaper dollars, which is the case when inflation occurs, they would be forced to repay in dollars of equal or greater value.

It was a dilemma, and for a while many banks declined the offer. They needed the money as badly as anyone else. Still, interest rates on government securities did fall, and many homeowners with variable-rate mortgages tied to those securities received immediate relief. In some instances, those with large mortgages benefited to the extent of more than $100 per month in savings, as rates fell well below 10%, a "raise" when few employers were giving them. New fixed-rate, long-term mortgages also fell below 10%; as a result hous-

ing officials expected their severely battered industry might show signs of life by springtime 1991 or before.

Reasons for the Decline. These were among some of the basic problems that weakened the U.S. economy, but none of them was entirely new, and for at least two years the economy had been wavering. What finally triggered the collapse that somehow had been avoided during that time? History will provide the proper perspective, but at least three factors were involved: 1. too much debt, which resulted in overconsumption and overbuilding; 2. a prolonged stalemate between Congress and the White House over budget cuts, finally resolved by an untimely if, some said, necessary agreement to raise taxes; 3. the threat of war in the Middle East, with an attendant sharp rise in energy prices.

Energy prices have a history of causing economic upheaval in the United States, and they did it again. The threat of war over Iraq's conquest of Kuwait drove gasoline pump prices to more than $1.75 per gallon at one point in some areas, and home-heating-oil prices in the Northeast leaped from a summer level below $1 per gallon to as much as $1.60 per gallon. The threat of war presented an additional element of uncertainty, forcing people and industries to delay spending. In addition the tax increase added five cents per gallon to gasoline prices, right at the time everyone was dealing with debts and layoffs.

The Outlook. As the year ended, the barrage of bad news kept consumer morale low and insecurity high. Generally, the news items were even bleaker than anticipated. Just before New Year's Day, for example, the government reported that orders to factories for durable goods, a vast category of products from appliances to cars to industrial machinery, plunged 10.5% in November, equaling a 32-year record drop. To the National Association of Manufacturers it meant "a deepening recession," and economists who just a couple of months before had said the downturn would be short and shallow were reassessing their forecasts. To the esteemed National Bureau of Economic Research, a private organization recognized as the arbiter of business cycles, the recession already might have been months old. In the final week of December it offered the opinion that a recession probably had begun between June and September.

What Americans had feared for at least two years was coming true, and there was very little to remove the gloom. True, interest rates were falling, and that meant homeowners with variable-rate mortgages would have smaller monthly bills; and it meant that business costs might recede a bit. In addition, inflation seemed to have been tamed. But such things were small compensation for big and worsening problems; they were hardly a match for what had become a pervasive mood of caution that compelled individuals to slow abruptly their use of credit cards and businesses to cut commitments to capital spending. Nobody, you might say, was making spending plans; instead, they were developing a survival mode. The old bills had come due, and now the task was to pay them.

JOHN CUNNIFF, *The Associated Press*

Foreign Affairs

In the midst of what some saw as inconsistent presidential leadership on domestic budgetary and tax issues, George Bush seemed to prefer the more personalized world of international diplomacy in 1990. However, it became ever more unmistakable that foreign policies have important domestic connections and consequences; one example was the agreement by the administration and Congress on a sweeping immigration-reform law liberalizing quotas based on skills.

In mid-December 1990, Secretary of State Baker and Eduard Shevardnadze (left) discussed arms control and other issues in Houston. The Soviet foreign minister later resigned.

© Greg Smith/Sipa

Diplomatic Contacts. Having met more than 130 times with heads of state in 1989, President Bush extended diplomatic contacts in 1990 even as far afield as the leaders of Pacific island "microstates," who were reassured about environmental and arms-control concerns in their area. Late in the year, in conjunction with his attendance at the historic 35-nation Conference on Security and Cooperation in Europe (CSCE) in Paris, Bush became the first U.S. president to visit Czechoslovakia. A number of foreign-policy successes were scored, including a European conventional arms agreement, but the administration suffered a major unexpected crisis in the Persian Gulf as Iraq invaded Kuwait on August 2. (*See* feature articles, page 24.)

Fortunately for the administration, European leaders were able to sort out a historic realignment, entailing the reunification of Germany, the collapse of the Warsaw Pact, and Soviet preoccupations with economic reform and domestic ethnic separatism. A harmonious North Atlantic Treaty Organization (NATO) summit in July reduced nuclear-weapons reliance to a "last resort," and cleared the way for the 35-nation CSCE to take on a more institutionalized security role. The arms-control treaty signed at the CSCE in Paris was the culmination of a process begun with the signing of the Helsinki accords in 1973.

However, many observers also saw conflicts within the Western community displacing East-West disputes, as a unifying Euro-market confronted a potential Western Hemisphere market (linking the United States, Canada, Mexico, and possibly South American states), and a Pacific rim of states economically attached to Japan. For a combination of economic and ideological reasons, President Bush was unable to carry through with much-promised economic assistance to the nations of Eastern Europe (except for minor aid to Hungary and Poland and most-favored-nation status for Czechoslovakia), and delayed implementing a new U.S.-Soviet trade agreement and participation in European assistance programs to the hard-pressed Soviet Union until it codifies its emigration policies. At year's end, with gloomy forecasts regarding food shortages in the Soviet Union, however, the president approved up to $1 billion in federally guaranteed loans to Moscow so that the USSR could purchase food and other items.

International Coalition. Soviet support was valued in the international coalition the president helped organize against Iraqi President Saddam Hussein. Washington eased the way for Egypt, Turkey, and several other states to join in a United Nations-sanctioned economic embargo of Iraq, by forgiving major debts and providing additional aid. Oil-rich Arab states provided funds to help finance the effort to counter Iraq. In addition, the administration solicited Germany and Japan for further funds, although neither was able to send troops to the Persian Gulf.

Total U.S. armed forces dispatched to Saudi Arabia were to exceed 400,000—the largest military deployment since Vietnam. U.S. troops were joined by British, French, Egyptian, and Syrian units, along with small contingents from other nations. With the massive buildup, questions were raised in the United States and abroad about the wisdom and legality of authorizing war against Iraq and about the U.S. policy goals involved. The subject of the presidential versus congressional war-making powers again was debated, with the Senate Foreign Relations Committee holding hearings on the issue.

While President Bush brushed aside Arab criticism that the United States did not show equal concern about Israel's occupation of the West Bank, Washington's relations with Israel were strained due to the administration's efforts to maintain Arab support, the failure of Arab-Israeli peace initiatives sponsored by President Bush, declining U.S.-Soviet hostilities, Israel's settlement policies, and the forceful crackdown on Palestinian demonstrators. For the first time in many years, the United States failed to veto an anti-Israeli resolution in the UN Security Council. Many observers feared that the mixture of anti-Israeli and anti-Iraqi sentiment in the Middle East long had posed an explosive threat to U.S. efforts in promoting stable governments in the region. One encouraging note, however, was the Syrian-brokered agreement to end the Lebanese civil war.

Arms Control. President Bush and his Soviet counterpart, Mikhail Gorbachev, nailed down major provisions of both nuclear and conventional arms-control agreements at a late May-early June meeting. U.S.-Soviet long-range nuclear weapons were to be cut by roughly 30%. By October agreements were reached and treaties outlined on the number of alliance forces and weapons to remain stationed in various European countries. The U.S. Senate also ratified two previous treaties limiting the explosive force of underground nuclear tests. Progress was made on a joint chemical-weapons-reduction agreement, but the destruction of weapons and a worldwide agreement were slowed by Iraq's possession of chemical weapons. Despite the progress in arms control, there was worry about political disintegration of the Soviet state, as various republics refused to implement Moscow's directives. The Soviet Union continued to possess one of the world's largest stockpiles of nuclear weapons.

Despite U.S.-Soviet "peace dividends" and the expectation that large numbers of foreign-based U.S. troops eventually would be brought home, the Iraqi crisis spurred Congress to retain every major weapons system in the De-fense Department's budget, although cutting the administration's original budgetary request by approximately 6%. Deeper cuts were expected in later years of a five-year deficit-reduction package.

Drugs and Debt. The Iraqi crisis also pushed antidrug efforts off the front pages, despite an early summit in February with Latin leaders. Southern neighbors were able to convince Washington that direct military confrontation with the drug cartel would be less effective than reducing demand for drugs in the United States, limiting the export of arms and drug-processing chemicals, and providing economic-development aid.

Despite some innovative debt "swap" or buyout programs, most experts rated the overall U.S. debt-relief plans of Secretary of State James Baker and Secretary of the Treasury Nicholas Brady as insufficient to spur enough bank lending to rescue Third World economies. Debt relief and additional lending were left largely to international governmental organizations. Much U.S. assistance went to building Latin military and police forces.

Trade. The heads of the seven major industrialized democracies met in Houston, TX, for their annual economic summit in July, in connection with the Uruguay Round of GATT trade talks. Conflicting demands about reducing agricultural subsidies in order to bring down international-trade barriers were muted in a compromise statement calling for further negotiations. However, the Uruguay Round itself adjourned in early December without agreement because of the dispute over agricultural subsidies. In Houston the seven industrialized democracies generally had supported deficit-reduction efforts and increased environmental cooperation. However, due to economic concerns and despite U.S. claims of leading the environmental movement, Washington along with Moscow refused to join the European nations and Japan in more stringent "greenhouse gas" restrictions to combat "global warming."

As a result of a series of U.S.-Japanese trade talks, Japan found ways to avoid redesignation as an "unfair trading partner" and the sanctions that go with it. (Brazil also was removed from the designation; India was not.) Estimates rated Japanese trade restrictions as accounting for only about 15% of the $49 billion U.S. deficit with Japan, which remained the nation's second-largest trade market. The year also saw a marked decline in the dollar's overseas value because of economic doubts and interest-rate uncertainties. This worked to relieve trade deficits only somewhat in the face of higher oil import prices.

Asia and Africa. Hesitant progress was made in Asian and African regional disputes in 1990. The United States withdrew its recognition of the Cambodian Khmer Rouge rebels

© Dirck Halstead/Gamma-Liaison

During the first stop of a six-day, December 1990 tour of Latin America, President Bush met with Brazil's president and addressed the National Congress. Bush said he would permit Brazil to purchase a high-performance supercomputer.

and consulted with Vietnam. The administration originally had supported several groups of rebels against the Vietnamese-installed regime in Cambodia and the change confused some Asian governments. The UN was called upon to provide a temporary administration for Cambodia pending elections. In the meantime, Thailand and Hong Kong resisted U.S. and Vietnamese requests to delay expulsion of Vietnamese refugees to allow time for "voluntary" repatriation plans.

U.S.-Pakistani relations were strained by the lingering Afghanistan war, Pakistan's border and ethnic tensions with India, and the U.S. restriction of aid because of the Pakistani nuclear-weapons program. The administration also had to deal with the fall of Prime Minister Benazir Bhutto's government. Pakistan joined the United States in supporting Arab Persian Gulf states and opposing Iraq, however.

In 1990 the Philippines began to turn to Japan for economic assistance as talks on new leases for U.S. bases in the Philippines stalled. Officials from both nations indicated that an end to the U.S. military presence in the Philippines is inevitable. The United States, however, reportedly was seeking a gradual ten-year phaseout. Vietnam and Singapore reportedly suggested U.S. access to bases, given the Philippine phaseout.

In Africa an AIDS epidemic and war-related famine still raged. Liberia's government fell in bloody yearlong fighting, with a contingent of U.S. marines sent into the capital city of Monrovia at one point to evacuate U.S. citizens. South Africa released Nelson Mandela, a leader of the African National Congress, from prison after more than 27 years and lifted the ban on antiapartheid political parties. Mandela received a hero's welcome in the United States and South African President F.W. de Klerk was welcomed in Washington. There was hope for progress on dismantling apartheid even as South Africa continued to erupt in ethnic violence.

Latin America. The Bush administration welcomed the various moves toward democracy in Latin America. The election of Violeta Barrios de Chamorro as president of Nicaragua especially was gratifying. In June the president proposed a new plan to encourage economic growth in the area; in November he was in Mexico for conferences with President Carlos Salinas de Gortari; and in December he went on a six-day tour of five nations—Argentina, Brazil, Chile, Uruguay, and Venezuela. Meanwhile, Manuel Noriega was under arrest in the United States following the successful U.S. military action to oust him in late 1989-early 1990. Questions about his detainment and forthcoming trial were being raised in international legal circles.

The United Nations. While the United Nations was called upon to organize collective security against Iraq, investigate Israeli policies in occupied territories, administer Cambodia, and help negotiate African and Central American regional agreements, the United States remained hundreds of millions of dollars behind in assessments (withheld by the Reagan administration). The first UN World Summit for Children was held in September (*see* page 89). Washington, while signing the conference declaration, failed to ratify the International Convention on the Rights of the Child.

Although 1990 saw hopes for a "new world order" in the wake of the end of the Cold War, the world continued to be plagued by regional disputes, the spread of lethal weapons of mass destruction, human-rights violations, and frustrations over the gap between the rich and poor in world politics.

FREDERIC S. PEARSON
Wayne State University

559

URUGUAY

With a new government in place, Uruguay began during 1990 to restructure its economic system toward less state control, a transformation opposed by labor forces. A large part of the foreign debt was to be repurchased on the secondary market.

Politics and Government. Luis Alberto Lacalle was installed as president on March 1 (after winning the election in late 1989) and faced a legislature in which his rightist National Party did not have a majority. Furthermore, the leftist Broad Front coalition had placed its candidate, Tabaré Vásquez, in the mayor's office of the capital, Montevideo, where about half of Uruguay's population lives. Lacalle won the votes necessary to get some of his legislative programs passed by filling four cabinet posts with members of the centrist Colorado Party.

Lacalle's early efforts centered on a program to restart the stagnated economy that in 1989 had a growth rate of only 0.5%. His goal was to halve a 100% inflation rate, and he also expected to bring the budget deficit from 8% of gross domestic product (GDP) to 2.5% through government spending cuts, reduction of the bureaucracy, higher taxation, and sale of managing control of several state-run concerns. By midyear, despite heavy opposition, Lacalle's bill encouraging early retirement of some of the 300,000 public-sector workers with an offer of two years' extra pay was adopted. Among opponents to the new measures were organized labor, which rejected Lacalle's restructuring plan outright, and farmers, who refused to pay doubled land taxes, as they just were recovering from one of the worst droughts on record.

The administration quarreled with the Montevideo government in June over the city budget, which contained pay increases that sometimes doubled salaries, and were to be funded by new levies on vacant lots, expensive city real estate, and cars. Urban-transport fares were hiked by one third. The price of fuels was increased by 30% in April, and a 15% cost-of-living adjustment on wages and salaries was authorized for the third quarter of the year despite the consumer price index's 30% rise in the first four months of 1990.

Economy. A letter of intent with the International Monetary Fund (IMF) in which Uruguay pledged itself to lower the inflation rate and deficit in 1990 was finalized in May. Uruguay also expected to pay $310 million on its public-sector foreign debt of $4.3 billion in 1990. With assistance of $500 million from the IMF, World Bank, Inter-American Development Bank, and Japan, Central Bank President Ramón Díaz announced on May 12 that Uruguay would buy back about $1 billion of its $1.6 billion commercial bank debt, selling at 45% of face value on the secondary market.

Lacalle immediately endorsed an offer forthcoming from U.S. President George Bush on June 27 of eventual free trade. Free-trade zones flourished in the southwest border towns of Colonia and Nueve Palmira, where storage, warehousing, manufacturing, and related financial, data-processing, and professional activities had been granted tax-exempt status. However, in March, Uruguayan custom agents seized purchases made by Uruguayans crossing into Brazil to shop, a consequence of favorable exchange rates on the weaker Brazilian currency.

Labor. Lacalle's efforts to reduce the role of the state in the economy met stiff resistance from unions, dominated by Communist leaders. In his first half-year in office, Lacalle failed to gain a 100-day truce and was confronted by four general strikes and many other stoppages in economic sectors. Labor forces wanted higher wages and opposed reductions in public spending and privatizations and were annoyed particularly by the government's system for adjusting wages to compensate for inflation.

Foreign Relations. As president-elect, Lacalle met with Bush in Washington on February 5, but was unable to obtain a $50 million safety net for lessening the impact of free-market and free-trade policies that he introduced upon assuming office.

LARRY L. PIPPIN
University of the Pacific

URUGUAY · Information Highlights

Official Name: Oriental Republic of Uruguay.
Location: Southeastern coast of South America.
Area: 68,039 sq mi (176 220 km²).
Population (mid-1990 est.): 3,000,000.
Capital (1985 census): Montevideo, 1,246,500.
Government: *Head of state,* Luis Alberto Lacalle, president (took office March 1, 1990). *Legislature* —National Congress: Senate and House of Deputies.
Monetary Unit: Peso (1583.0 pesos equal U.S.$1, financial rate, Dec. 31, 1990).
Gross Domestic Product (1989 est. U.S.$): $8,800,-000,000.
Foreign Trade (1989 U.S.$): *Imports,* $1,203,000,-000; *exports,* $1,599,000,000.

UTAH

Elections and the continuing cold-fusion saga marked the scene in Utah in 1990.

Elections. A resurgence of Utah Democrats characterized the political scene of 1990. In an upset victory in the U.S. congressional 3d District, political newcomer and conservative Democrat William Orton defeated Karl Snow (R). This victory was noteworthy because the district has been considered one of the most Republican in the nation, with the seat being held by a Republican since the district was created in 1982. Orton campaigned vigorously and

UTAH • Information Highlights

Area 84,899 sq mi (219 889 km²).
Population (1990 census prelim.): 1,711,000.
Chief Cities (1980 census): Salt Lake City, the capital (July 1, 1988 est.), 152,740; Provo, 74,108; Ogden, 64,407.
Government (1990): *Chief Officers—*governor, Norman H. Bangerter (R); lt. gov., W. Val Oveson (R). *Legislature—*Senate, 29 members; House of Representatives, 75 members.
State Finances (fiscal year 1989): *Revenue,* $3,693,000,000; *expenditure,* $3,513,000,000.
Personal Income (1989): $22,326,000,000; per capita, $13,079.
Labor Force (June 1990): *Civilian labor force,* 796,600; *unemployed,* 38,600 (4.8% of total force).
Education: *Enrollment* (fall 1988)—public elementary schools, 319,423; public secondary, 111,696; colleges and universities, 107,538. *Public school expenditures* (1989–90 est.), $1,096,242,000.

benefited from a lingering backlash of negative campaigning against Snow during the GOP primary.

In other congressional elections, incumbent Wayne Owens (D-2d District) handily defeated challenger Genevieve Atwood (R) with about 58% of the vote. Incumbent James Hansen (R) retained his seat in the 1st District, withstanding a strong challenge from Democrat Kensley Brunsdale.

Locally, Salt Lake County voters ousted both incumbent Republican commissioners with James Bradley (D) crushing ten-year veteran Bart Barker (R) by about 20 percentage points and Randy Horiuchi (D) narrowly defeating the seven-year incumbent Tom Shimizu (R) by a little more than one half of one percent.

The Republican majority declined in both houses of the state legislature. There now would be 19 Republicans and ten Democrats in the Senate and 44 Republicans and 31 Democrats in the House of Representatives.

A controversial initiative easily defeated by Utah voters was a move, spearheaded by Merrill Cook, leader of the Utah Independent Party, to eliminate the 6.25% sales tax on food. Supporters claimed that with a budget surplus of more than $200 million, the state easily could absorb the revenue loss. In an unusual coalition, Democrats joined the Independents and denounced the tax as immoral and unfair because it placed the heaviest burden on the poor. Opposition, however, came from Gov. Norman H. Bangerter (R), the GOP leadership, the State Board of Regents (representing higher education), the business community, and local governments. They argued that state revenues would be reduced by $90 million and local government revenues by another $23 million.

Cold Fusion. After more than a year of hot debate and laboratory experimentation, the mystery of "cold fusion" persisted. In March 1990 the "First Annual Conference on Cold Fusion" was held at the University of Utah with some 200 scientists and observers gathering to review the data. Although hundreds of scientists have failed to duplicate the claimed achievement of a University of Utah electrochemist and a colleague of nuclear fusion at room temperature, experimentation by others continued to produce perplexing results that, in their view, justified continued research.

Meanwhile, the National Cold Fusion Institute, a nonprofit corporation founded by the University of Utah, at year's end was undergoing a technical evaluation by four outside scientists which might determine the fate of the institute. Additionally, University of Utah faculty members had criticized strongly the university's president, Chase N. Peterson, for his continued support of questionable science and called for his resignation. Under this pressure, Peterson said he would retire at the end of the 1990–91 academic year.

LORENZO K. KIMBALL
University of Utah

VENEZUELA

An unexpected oil-price rise and the first fruits of fundamental economic and political reforms helped Venezuela in 1990 to begin to emerge from nearly a decade of decline. However, lingering hardship and discontent continued to foment some demonstrations and violence.

Unrest. In February the Venezuelan Workers Confederation (CTV) organized more than 10,000 people to protest rising prices in Caracas and other cities, claiming that the January wage increase of 30% did little to compensate for inflation, which surpassed 80% in 1989. CTV also charged that 60,000 workers lost jobs in December 1989, when the government lifted a freeze on dismissals that had been in place since the austerity program began in February 1989.

Soon thereafter, a series of food riots broke out in the eastern coastal state of Anzoátegui and spread throughout the country, where they were joined by students protesting government corruption. The students were incensed by the Supreme Court's decision to revoke the arrest warrants for 12 ministers of the former Lusinchi administration (1984-89), who had been accused of illegally distributing $5 billion in subsidized hard currency to friends and family. The rioting culminated in clashes with government security forces, resulting in the death of one student.

The major opposition party, COPEI, reacted to the continuing economic hardship more moderately by calling for greater consultation by the government, without challenging the basic economic reforms.

Economic Recovery. President Carlos Andrés Pérez was able to claim substantial

Carlos Andrés Pérez (left) *met with George Bush at the White House in April 1990. In December the Venezuelan president served as host to the U.S. chief executive in Caracas.*

AP/Wide World

progress in his second year in office. In March, Venezuela signed an agreement with its foreign creditors that reduced the principal owed to commercial banks by 20% and reduced the debt-service burden in the short term by 50%. The agreement was expected to save Venezuela $12 to $15 billion over the next ten years. The government also liberalized its investment and trade regulations to promote foreign investment. As part of its effort to decrease government control over the economy, Pérez proposed to privatize 70 of the 430 state-owned autonomous institutions, despite the private sector's fears of increasing foreign ownership and organized labor's fears of huge layoffs and undesirable working conditions.

Nevertheless, inflation dropped dramatically, to an estimated 30%, and after declining by a record 8.5% in 1989, the gross domestic product (GDP) was expected to grow 2%-2.5% in 1990. Economic recovery also was stimulated by the dramatic increase in oil prices from $15.60 to around $40 per barrel as a result of the worldwide embargo against Iraqi and Kuwaiti oil beginning in August. The price increase, combined with increased production to help cover the reduction in exports from the Persian Gulf, was expected to bring Venezuela a $4.4 billion windfall in the last five months of 1990 alone, enough to increase reserves of hard currency substantially and possibly eliminate the country's entire fiscal deficit, which amounted to 2.5% of GDP.

Political Reform. The first directly elected governors and mayors in the country took office in 1990. The Presidential Commission for the Reform of the State drafted legislation to decentralize and restructure other areas of political life, such as the political parties, the electoral system, and the civil service. Further progress on approval of these laws was expected during 1991.

Yanomami Indians. President Pérez also took a major step to ensure the future welfare of the 14,000 Yanomami Indians living in Venezuela. The Yanomami had suffered greatly from an outbreak of malaria brought on by the water-blasting techniques used by Brazilians who are mining illegally for gold near the Orinoco River. When ten previously unknown Yanomami villages were discovered in September, Pérez promised that he soon would establish a reserve to protect the primitive population from further threats to their existence from the outside world.

MICHAEL COPPEDGE
Johns Hopkins University

VENEZUELA • Information Highlights

Official Name: Republic of Venezuela.
Location: Northern coast of South America.
Area: 352,143 sq mi (912 050 km²).
Population (mid-1990 est.): 19,600,000.
Chief Cities (June 30, 1989 est., incl. suburbs): Caracas, the capital, 3,373,059; Maracaibo, 1,365,308; Valencia, 1,227,472.
Government: *Head of state and government,* Carlos Andrés Pérez, president (took office February 1989). *Legislature*—National Congress: Senate and Chamber of Deputies.
Monetary Unit: Bolívar (50.6 bolívares equal U.S.$1, floating rate, Dec. 31, 1990).
Gross Domestic Product (1989 est. U.S.$): $52,000,-000,000.
Economic Index (1989): *Consumer Prices* (1984 = 100), all items, 380.2; food, 652.1.
Foreign Trade (1989 U.S.$): *Imports,* $7,837,-000,000; *exports,* $12,890,000,000.

Bernard Sanders, a 49-year-old self-described socialist and registered Independent, and his wife Jane celebrate his election to Vermont's only U.S. House seat. The former Burlington mayor, free-lance writer, and college professor had campaigned on a message condemning Washington's overall political process.

© Peter Blakely/Saba

VERMONT

Vermont made history on Nov. 6, 1990, when former Burlington Mayor Bernard Sanders, a self-styled socialist running as an Independent, defeated the state's first-term Republican Congressman Peter Smith. Sanders' victory, by 56% to 40%, reflected Republican dissatisfaction with the federal budget. The official Democratic candidate, education professor Dolores Sandoval, was abandoned by most Democrats as they endorsed Smith or Sanders. The latter candidate won the votes of conservatives opposed to gun control.

Former four-term Republican Gov. Richard A. Snelling defeated Democrat Peter Welch for the governorship, vacated by retiring Democrat Madeline M. Kunin. Welch, former president pro tem of the state Senate, was defeated despite a last-minute upsurge in his support. The election left the state Senate split evenly between Republicans and Democrats and the

House with 75 Republicans, 73 Democrats, and two Independents.

Economy and the Legislature. Hanging over the state and local governments throughout the year were the clouds of recession, tax revolt, and revenue shortfalls. At town meetings in March, more than 10% of the state's school districts voted down school budgets, while voters in more than one third of all towns endorsed a 5% annual cut in national defense spending. Bitter though inconclusive controversy dogged Act 200, the state's two-year-old effort to tighten regional planning powers over the towns.

The state legislature ended an extended session in mid-May after the House speaker broke a tie vote in favor of a $624.5 million budget. Governor Kunin's farewell address to the legislature noted her disappointment that a clean-air measure, a moratorium on the use of bovine-growth hormones, and a ban on polystyrene all had failed. However, she praised the legislature for establishing a family-court system and mandating that noncustodial parents make child-support payments on a timely basis. Combating the economic downturn with spending freezes and cutbacks, increased taxes, and use of a contingency fund established in the first Kunin administration, the state managed to end fiscal year 1990 in June with the books in balance.

Colleges. Several Vermont colleges underwent leadership changes in 1990. Newly inaugurated Johnson State College President Lynn Veach Sadler resigned in early June upon the request of the chancellor of the state college system. After faculty and students protested her departure, Sadler sued for reinstatement, contending she had been a victim of sexism and that her resignation had not been accepted for-

---

VERMONT • Information Highlights

Area: 9,614 sq mi (24 900 km²).

Population (1990 census prelim.): 560,000.

Chief Cities (1980 census): Montpelier, the capital, 8,241; Burlington, 37,712; Rutland, 18,436.

Government (1990): *Chief Officers*—governor, Madeleine M. Kunin (D); lt. gov., Howard Dean (D). *General Assembly*—Senate, 30 members; House of Representatives, 150 members.

State Finances (fiscal year 1989): *Revenue,* $1,530,000,000; *expenditure,* $1,434,000,000.

Personal Income (1989): $9,283,000,000; per capita, $16,371.

Labor Force (June 1990): *Civilian labor force,* 313,500; *unemployed,* 13,800 (4.4% of total force).

Education: *Enrollment* (fall 1988)—public elementary schools, 66,745; public secondary, 26,719; colleges and universities, 34,467. *Public school expenditures* (1989–90 est.), $522,000,000.

mally. A court ruled the resignation invalid and the Vermont State College Board of Trustees and its chancellor subsequently voted her reinstatement. In October the University of Vermont inaugurated Dr. George Davis as its 22d president, and Dr. Timothy Light was chosen as president of Middlebury College.

Fishing. It was a banner year for sports fishermen. During the summer, work on a long-debated fish hatchery was begun in Grand Isle County, and, after a decade of controversy, lampricides were introduced to reduce the lamprey population in Lake Champlain.

SAMUEL B. HAND and ROBERT V. DANIELS
University of Vermont

VIETNAM

Vietnam improved relations with the United States and China during 1990, but despite some ambitious economic and political reforms, it remained one of the poorest countries in Asia.

Politics. In August the Central Committee of the Communist Party met for two weeks to decide on a new political platform and economic program, marking only the second time since 1930 that the platform has been revised. Official reports led to speculation that the committee was deadlocked over proposals for radical reform as in Eastern Europe. Inflation was listed as one of Vietnam's key problems, but instead of blaming foreigners, as it often has, the committee placed the blame for the stalled economy on "incompetent, corrupt, and indisciplined" officials. No governmental changes were announced by the committee.

Vietnam has struggled in recent years to create and implement a legal code in order to control graft and corruption and lay the groundwork for a market economy. Amnesty International reported that Vietnam had 7,000 political prisoners, including several hundred who were detained, usually without trial, in 1990.

Economics. Vietnam, which began moving toward a market economy in 1986, still lacked many of the institutions and skilled managers to make the recent reforms effective. Few Vietnamese bankers were experienced with large-scale development projects, and the collapse of many credit cooperatives earlier in 1990 nearly destroyed the fragile banking system. Shortages of fertilizer cut rice production in the rich Mekong delta, while in the marketplace more than half of all goods sold reportedly were smuggled from abroad. The return of Vietnamese workers from East Germany, Iraq, and Kuwait also stressed the economy.

Since a foreign-investment code was adopted in 1987, the government has approved 151 projects and $1.07 billion worth of capital has been invested, although fewer than half of

---

VIETNAM • Information Highlights

Official Name: Socialist Republic of Vietnam.
Location: Southeast Asia.
Area: 127,243 sq mi (329 560 km²).
Population (mid-1989 est.): 66,800,000.
Chief Cities (April 1, 1989 prelim. census): Hanoi, the capital, 1,088,862; Ho Chi Minh City, 3,169,135.
Government: Communist Party secretary, Nguyen Van Linh.
Monetary Unit: Dong (5,000 dongs equal U.S.$1, July 1990).
Gross National Product (1989 est. U.S.$): $14,200,-000,000.

---

the projects were operating by 1990. One that was in operation was Ho Chi Minh City's luxurious 200-room Saigon Floating Hotel, built by an Australian firm on an enormous barge on the banks of the Saigon River. In Hanoi, which has only 800 hotel rooms, a multimillion-dollar project to restore the old Metropole Hotel languished because of bureaucratic red tape and financing problems.

Foreign Affairs. With Soviet aid and interest in Indochina declining, Vietnam moved to normalize relations with its former enemy, China. Hanoi also made it clear that it wanted to reestablish relations with the United States and end the Western economic blockade, which began after the 1978 Vietnamese invasion of Cambodia. After Vietnam withdrew its forces from Cambodia in 1989, most U.S. allies began to normalize relations with Vietnam.

In July the United States announced it would engage in direct talks with Vietnam about the future of Cambodia. Meetings at the working level were followed by a meeting of Secretary of State James Baker and Foreign Minister Nguyen Co Thach in September and a visit by Thach to Washington in October. Nonetheless, the George Bush administration decided to keep the trade embargo until a comprehensive peace settlement was achieved in Cambodia.

Le Duc Tho. One of the last members of the first generation of Communist leaders, Le Duc Tho, died in October. He negotiated the end of the war with the United States in 1973.

PETER A. POOLE
Author, "The Vietnamese in Thailand"

VIRGINIA

From his historic inauguration in January 1990, through his position as a national network commentator on the elections in November, Gov. L. Douglas Wilder (*see* BIOGRAPHY), the first black man elected to a state governorship, dominated the news in Virginia in 1990.

Although the governor's campaign for pledge-bond financing for transportation went to defeat at the state polls, Wilder's stature as a possible candidate for national office in 1992 was bolstered by ballot results from other states and a yearlong battle to make up the state's budget deficit without raising taxes.

Governor Wilder. Despite his repeated denials, Wilder spent much of the year seemingly positioning himself for a run for national office. The two most visible aspects, announcing state budget cuts and travel across the United States to stump for other Democratic politicians, occasionally brought him criticism at home. He also was criticized in Virginia for using state aircraft to make some of those political trips. He received national notoriety, and occasional Virginia tongue-clucking, because Pat Kluge, estranged wife of John Kluge, one of the nation's richest men, reportedly accompanied him on a state plane trip.

Budget. Governor Wilder announced in August that Virginia's budget situation was "the worst since World War II"—the state was more than $1 billion short of projected revenues. He told agencies to slash spending, canceled salary increases for state and college employees, and announced layoffs. He said Virginia could be a model for the nation and other states by proving the budget could be balanced without a tax increase.

During a fairly quiet General Assembly session earlier in the year, Wilder had pulled off a last-minute power play to win repeal of the state's 4.5% sales tax on over-the-counter drugs.

Elections. In a year when "throw the rascals out" became a rallying cry that was more sound than fury, Virginia was one of the few states in which an incumbent congressman lost his seat. Republican Stanford E. Parris, elected six times in northern Virginia's 8th District, fell to Alexandria's Democratic Mayor James P. Moran by 52% to 43%. Republican 1st District Rep. Herbert H. Bateman almost fell to the anti-incumbent mood, beating a little-known Democrat, Andrew H. Fox, by only 2% of the vote despite outspending him five to one. The

three other Republicans turned back Democratic challengers more easily, while the five Democratic House members each beat independent candidates without challenge from Republicans. For the first time since the 90th Congress (1967–69), Virginia's ten-man congressional delegation had a Democratic majority of six to four. As recently as 1980, Republicans held nine of the seats.

Republican Sen. John W. Warner won a third term. He had no Democratic opposition and amassed 82% of the vote against an independent candidate.

Labor Settlement. The year started off with the news of the settlement of the longest coal strike in state history. The United Mine Workers strike against Pittston Coal Group, Inc., had idled more than 1,000 Virginians.

ED NEWLAND, *"Richmond Times Dispatch"*

WASHINGTON

Washington's economy started strong in 1990, but stalled as the year progressed. Compared with 1989, employment was up about 4%, largely due to a January increase. Job growth continued shifting from traditional industries such as timber and aerospace to computer software, health services, retail, and foreign trade.

Elections and Government. State voters turned down a strict growth-management measure, and voters in five of six counties rejected a proposed real-estate tax to protect open space. All eight congressional incumbents were reelected.

State Employment Security Commissioner Isiah Turner resigned after a state audit revealed he misused or failed to document $22,000 in travel and expense funds.

Courts. U.S. District Judge Barbara Rothstein in Seattle ruled the flag-protection law passed by the U.S. Congress in 1989 was unconstitutional; her ruling was upheld by the U.S. Supreme Court.

Earl Shriner, 40, was sentenced to 131 years in prison for the sexual mutilation and attempted murder of a 7-year-old Tacoma boy. The case triggered public outrage and prompted passage of a controversial new law that allows authorities to hold sex offenders under civil commitment after their prison terms expire.

Business. A record $11 billion aircraft order from United Airlines enabled the Boeing Company to begin development of its 363-passenger 777 jetliner. But the company's state employment dipped slightly for the year, from 106,700 to 104,000. Thousands of jobs were forecast to be lost in the Northwest's forest-products industry after the U.S. Fish and Wildlife Service declared the northern spotted owl a threatened species.

VIRGINIA • Information Highlights

Area: 40,767 sq mi (105 586 km²).

Population (1990 census prelim.): 6,128,000.

Chief Cities (July 1, 1988 est.): Richmond, the capital, 213,300; Virginia Beach, 365,300; Norfolk, 286,500; Newport News, 160,100; Chesapeake, 147,800.

Government (1990): *Chief Officers*—governor, Douglas L. Wider (D); lt. gov., Donald S. Beyer, Jr. (D). *General Assembly*—Senate, 40 members; House of Delegates, 100 members.

State Finances (fiscal year 1989): *Revenue,* $13,096,000,000; *expenditure,* $11,724,000,000.

Personal Income (1989): $115,408,000,000; per capita, $18,927.

Labor Force (June 1990): *Civilian labor force,* 3,194,800; *unemployed,* 133,800 (4.2% of total force).

Education: *Enrollment* (fall 1988)—public elementary schools, 699,064; public secondary, 283,329; colleges and universities, 321,216. *Public school expenditures* (1989–90 est.), $4,408,386,000.

Four men try to rescue a car being washed away by surging waters in Centralia, WA, in mid-January. Some 3,000 people in southwestern Washington and northern Oregon were forced to vacate their homes as a result of the severe flooding that struck the region.

AP/Wide World

Environment. At the 47-year-old Hanford Nuclear Reservation, 1990 was marked by new revelations about old problems. The federal Department of Energy said thousands of people living near the site in the mid-1940s had been exposed to potentially cancer-causing doses of radiation. And previously unreleased documents showed the site's 177 nuclear-waste storage tanks have leaked hundreds of thousands of gallons of cooling water and radioactive waste over the years. Late in 1990, Energy Secretary James Watkins said the facility no longer would produce plutonium.

Sports. Seven Washington cities hosted the 1990 Goodwill Games. (*See* SPORTS—*The Goodwill Games.*) The University of Washington football team won the Pac Ten championship, earning its first trip to the Rose Bowl since 1982. And the Seattle Mariners became the first major-league baseball team with a father and son in the lineup, playing Ken Griffey, Sr., and Ken Griffey, Jr. (*See* page 481.)

Medicine. A Seattle physician, Dr. E. Donnall Thomas, shared the Nobel Prize in medicine or physiology for research facilitating organ transplants. A 3-year-old Olympia boy, Bryan Peek, received the Northwest's first liver transplant at Children's Hospital and Medical Center in Seattle. And a government report showed Acquired Immune Deficiency Syndrome (AIDS) had become the leading killer of young men in the Seattle area.

Tragedies. Four rodeo cowboys and their pilot died when their small plane crashed on Mount Rainier. Five British Columbia residents were killed when their plane crashed in southwest Washington. Nine crew members of a Seattle-based fishing boat were lost when the boat sank in the Bering Sea.

Record flooding in January and November claimed four lives and forced the evacuation of thousands. Heavy rains also were believed to have contributed to the sinking of a 50-year-old floating bridge between Seattle and suburban Mercer Island.

JACK BROOM
"The Seattle Times"

WASHINGTON • Information Highlights

Area: 68,139 sq mi (176 479 km²).
Population (1990 census prelim.): 4,827,000.
Chief Cities (July 1, 1988 est.): Olympia, the capital (1980 census), 27,447; Seattle, 502,200; Spokane, 170,900; Tacoma, 163,960.
Government (1990): *Chief Officers*—governor, Booth Gardner (D); lt. gov., Joel Pritchard (R). *Legislature*—Senate, 49 members; House of Representatives, 98 members.
State Finances (fiscal year 1989): *Revenue,* $13,507,000,000; *expenditure,* $11,650,000,000.
Personal Income (1989): $84,011,000,000; per capita, $17,647.
Labor Force (June 1990): *Civilian labor force,* 2,564,100; *unemployed,* 122,500 (4.8% of total force).
Education: *Enrollment* (fall 1988)—public elementary schools, 563,100; public secondary, 227,818; colleges and universities, 253,088. *Public school expenditures* (1989–90 est.), $3,641,000,000.

WASHINGTON, DC

The January 1990 cocaine-possession arrest of Mayor Marion Barry after a Federal Bureau of Investigation (FBI) sting radically changed the District of Columbia's political landscape. For the entire year, the city's attention was fixed on Barry's drug-and-alcohol-addiction recovery, his federal trial, and the campaign to succeed him as mayor.

Mayor Marion Barry. Mayor Barry, once considered to be among the nation's most influential black elected officials, for years had denied media reports of alleged drug use, only to have them repudiated in an eight-week trial featuring an FBI videotape of the mayor smoking crack cocaine. The trial burst open a long-festering distrust of whites by some blacks, who claimed that Barry's arrest, prosecution, and

conviction on one misdemeanor drug possession charge would not have occurred had he
been a white mayor.

Days after his trial ended in August with the
one conviction, an acquittal on another misdemeanor charge, and a mistrial declared on 12
counts, three of them felonies, Barry announced his intention not to seek another term
as mayor. Instead, he switched his Democratic
Party affiliation to seek an Independent bid for
the city council; however, he failed to win a
seat in the November election. In October,
Barry was sentenced to six months in prison
and one year on probation; an appeal was
under way at year's end.

The Election. The race to replace Barry included five Democratic candidates who were
unsure for much of the campaign whether
Barry would seek a fourth term. The candidates included city council Chairman David A.
Clarke and council members John Ray and
Charlene Drew Jarvis; District of Columbia
congressional delegate Walter Fauntroy, who
risked losing his nearly 20-year hold on the seat
to enter the mayoral race; and Sharon Pratt
Dixon, a former treasurer of the Democratic
National Committee. Dixon had begun her bid
for the mayoral post in 1988 and was considered to be a long shot with no money and a
young and inexperienced organization. Dixon
was the only political leader to demand that
Barry resign from his office.

By midsummer, Dixon's "clean house"
theme had struck a chord with voters disillusioned by Barry's continuing troubles, a
bloated city government, and a dwindling service delivery system. Dixon upset her four
challengers in a surprising September party primary that ended with front-runner Ray in second place. Ray had been considered the odds-
on favorite because of his $1 million war chest
and bevy of endorsements. Dixon's campaign
had managed on $250,000 and a growing debt.

Former Washington, DC, police chief Maurice T. Turner, Jr., was defeated resoundingly
by Dixon in the general election for mayor despite a heavy infusion of money by the Republican National Committee and personal
campaign appearances by President George
Bush, Mrs. Bush, and Vice-President Dan
Quayle. A lifelong Democrat, Turner had become frustrated with the Barry administration
and had switched to the Republican Party in a
highly publicized White House visit with President Bush.

District of Columbia voters also elected the
Rev. Jesse Jackson to his first political office.
Jackson, who moved to the city in 1989, won
one of two "shadow" U.S. Senate seats. The
new positions are intended to serve as lobbying
posts to persuade Congress to grant statehood
to the district.

In the race to succeed Fauntroy as the congressional delegate, civil-rights veteran and

© J. L. Atlan/Sygma

*Sharon Pratt Dixon, 46, a lawyer and vice-president of an
electric company, is joined by her campaign manager as she
acknowledges her election as mayor of Washington, DC.*

university law professor Eleanor Holmes Norton won in the primary and general election
despite disclosures that her family had failed to
file city tax returns for seven years.

Crime. The city's total homicide figure by
late November 1990, at 436, already had surpassed the record 1989 total of 434. With an
average of one murder per weekday and three
per weekend, city officials were not surprised
that the District had set a homicide record for
the third consecutive year.

Education News. The District of Columbia
board of education decided not to renew the
contract of Superintendent Andrew Jenkins
after media disclosures of erroneous enrollment figures and concerns about his management ability. Meanwhile, students at the
University of the District of Columbia for
nearly two weeks shut down the school's operation in protest of a decision by the board of
trustees that brought the school's accreditation
into jeopardy. Forty-two demands by the students included the resignation of the 15-mem-
ber board and the recision of a piece of art—
The Dinner Party—by Judy Chicago. The artwork would have cost the cash-strapped university $1.6 million to house and display and
contained subject matter considered in poor
taste. Students ended their protest when the
artwork was rescinded and board members resigned.

See also page 554.

VINCENT D. McCRAW
"The Washington Times"

WEST VIRGINIA

The events of 1990 in West Virginia had a familiar ring to them: The economy remained shaky; inefficient management in government persisted; and the fall elections were basically a Democratic sweep.

Politics. Arch Moore, Jr., three-time governor of West Virginia and leader of the state's badly outnumbered Republicans, pleaded guilty in the spring to five charges of mail fraud, public corruption, falsifying his income-tax returns, and obstruction of justice. In July he was sentenced to five years and ten months in federal prison. Moore's plea reportedly spared him from facing more than 20 additional charges.

When the prison doors closed behind former Governor Moore, they spelled doom for the Republican ticket in the fall elections. Sen. Jay Rockefeller (D) and all four Democratic Congressmen—Alan Mollohan, Harley Staggers, Jr., Robert Wise, and Nick Rahall—were reelected. Republicans did increase their membership in the state House from 20 to 23, but won only one seat in the state Senate (a loss of three seats).

Teachers' Strike. A ten-month strike by 16,000 United Mine Workers employees of the Pittston Coal Company finally ended in February, but a wildcat teachers' strike began the same month and picketing on the Capitol lawn kept all eyes on the growing frustration of workers.

Teachers in West Virginia were among the most poorly paid in the United States in 1990. When they followed the wildcat strike with the first general teachers' strike in the state's history one month later, Gov. Gaston Caperton angrily withdrew a proposed 5% pay-raise package and courts imposed a cooling-off period. The teachers went back to work after promises of relief from Charleston. A governor's task force in May proposed a five-part plan aimed at providing $20,000 in raises over a six-year period.

State Management. The 1990 legislative sessions were frustrated by inadequate revenues and proliferating demands by employees. By the end of the summer, modest raises were given to all state workers—including the teachers. The ailing Workmen's Compensation system apparently was rescued from a near-fatal condition. However, the troubled Public Employees Insurance system continued to lag many months behind in its payments, and in the fall proposed increased premiums for individuals and employees and reduced payments for hospitals and physicians.

A national magazine in April labeled West Virginia the nation's worst in overall management, specifically citing its continuing levels of poverty and unemployment, as well as inefficiency and corruption.

Former Governor Moore's conviction was but one result of a continuing federal investigation into misdeeds in high places. Over a two-year period, various charges of corruption and racketeering also were brought against three leaders of the state Senate and an attorney general.

Governor Caperton continued to shuffle department heads and workers to achieve more efficiency and to strengthen the economy. The state also opened an office in Tokyo to promote trade with Japan.

DONOVAN H. BOND
West Virginia University

WISCONSIN

Election upsets and new educational programs highlighted 1990 in Wisconsin.

Elections. Republican Gov. Tommy G. Thompson easily defeated the Democratic State Assembly Speaker Tom Loftus with 58% of the vote to win a second four-year term, but voters again were fiercely independent in casting the rest of their ballots. In the biggest upset, Democratic Congressman Robert Kastenmeier, who represented the 2d District for 32 years, was defeated by former television anchorman Scott Klug. All other incumbent U.S. House members were reelected, bringing five Republicans and four Democrats to the congressional delegation. Republican Attorney General Donald Hanaway lost to Democrat Jim Doyle. State Treasurer Charles Smith, a 20-year veteran, was defeated by Kathy Zeuske (R). The state legislature remained virtually unchanged, with Democrats controlling the senate 19 to 14 and the Assembly 58 to 41.

Legislative Action. In a two-month winter session, the legislature talked a lot about property-tax relief but did little with some controversial issues. With a budget surplus of $306 million, legislators set aside $100 million for future property-tax relief and $13 million to expand the homestead-credit program. By year's

WISCONSIN • Information Highlights

Area: 56,153 sq mi (145 436 km²).
Population (1990 census prelim.): 4,870,000.
Chief Cities (July 1, 1988 est.): Madison, the capital, 178,180; Milwaukee, 599,380; Green Bay (1980 census), 87,899.
Government (1990): *Chief Officers*—governor, Tommy G. Thompson (R); lt. gov., Scott Mc-Callum (R). *Legislature*—Senate, 33 members; Assembly, 99 members.
State Finances (fiscal year 1989): *Revenue,* $13.132,000,000; *expenditure,* $10,514,000,000.
Personal Income (1989): $80,052,000,000; per capita, $16,449.
Labor Force (June 1990): *Civilian labor force,* 2,604,900; *unemployed,* 106,700 (4.1% of total force).
Education: *Enrollment* (fall 1988)—public elementary schools, 535,215; public secondary, 239,642; colleges and universities, 285,227. *Public school expenditures* (1989–90 est.), $3,783,605,000.

end, however, lower-than-expected tax revenue caused an economic downturn resulting in predictions of an $800 million deficit by the end of the 1991–93 budget period. The legislature approved a plan to require local community recycling programs and to ban the bovine-growth hormone, effective June 1, 1991.

Legislators failed to enact much-debated bills to require parental consent for abortion and to facilitate prosecution of drug users and dealers. Sensitive about the controversy over Indian spearfishing, the legislature provided about $10 million in assistance for northern Wisconsin. The subsequent spearfishing season was less confrontational than in 1989. A federal judge ruled that "harvestable natural resources" in northern Wisconsin should be divided equally between Indians and non-Indians. The judge also ruled that the Chippewa could not sue the state for being denied treaty hunting and fishing rights for more than a century.

Education. Faced with high dropout rates and low achievement levels, Wisconsin initiated some innovative and controversial school programs. On a statewide level, Governor Thompson's Learnfare program withstood a court challenge. Under the program, students aged 13 to 19 whose families receive public assistance must attend school or the aid would be reduced. Milwaukee schools initiated a "choice" program in which up to 1,000 pupils from poor families could attend private nonsectarian schools at state expense. Only about one third of that number actually took part in the program at the start. The Milwaukee School Board voted to create two schools, on the elementary and middle-school levels, geared to black males.

The Economy. Total nonfarm employment reached 2.3 million in June 1990, an all-time high. From September 1989 to September 1990, the state created 34,300 new jobs. Major sectors experiencing record employment levels included trade, construction, services, finance, and utilities. Wisconsin's farm income for 1990 was projected to be up modestly from the 1989 level of $4.5 billion, which was a 9% increase over drought-affected 1988.

PAUL SALSINI
"The Milwaukee Journal"

WOMEN

It was predicted that 1990 would be viewed in U.S. politics as the "Year of the Woman," as record numbers of female candidates sought elective office, and several prominent candidates began their campaigns with an edge over their male opponents. As the elections approached, however, the so-called "caring" issues, such as education, child care, and the environment, were replaced on the political agenda by the threat of war in the Middle East and a recession at home.

Politics. The election of women to the governorships of Kansas, Oregon, and Texas represented important victories for female candidates. Democrat Ann Richards (*see* BIOGRAPHY), in winning the Texas gubernatorial race following a close and heated contest with her opponent, Clayton Williams, became the first woman in Texas since the 1930s to hold that post. Oregon's Secretary of State Barbara Roberts, a Democrat, defeated David Frohnmayer for the state's governorship. In Kansas, Democrat Joan Finney defeated the incumbent Gov. Mike Hayden and U.S. Sen. Nancy Kassebaum (R) overwhelmingly won reelection. In addition, a total of 29 women captured U.S. House seats, and voters in Washington, DC, elected Sharon Pratt Dixon as mayor. Less successful were Republican Gov. Kay Orr, who was defeated for reelection; former San Francisco Mayor Dianne Feinstein (D), who lost her bid for the governorship of California; and Representatives Lynn Martin, Patricia Saiki, and Claudine Schneider, all Republicans, who failed to unseat incumbent male senators in Illinois, Hawaii, and Rhode Island, respectively. President Bush later named Representative Martin to succeed Elizabeth Dole, who resigned as secretary of labor.

Internationally, 1990 saw the election of women presidents in Nicaragua and Ireland. Violeta Chamorro (*see* BIOGRAPHY) toppled Nicaragua's Sandinista regime in February elections to become that country's first female leader. Mary Robinson, a feminist lawyer, became Ireland's first woman president on a platform of support for the poor, the homeless, the unemployed, and the women of Ireland. In Norway former Prime Minister Gro Harlem Brundtland headed a new coalition government. The year also saw the departure from the scene of one of the strongest women leaders of the 20th century as Margaret Thatcher resigned

© Chris Rodwell/Gamma-Liaison

Mary Robinson, a 46-year-old attorney and professor of law and a member of the Irish Senate for 20 years, celebrates her November 1990 election as president of Ireland. Inaugurated on December 3, she became the first woman to hold the office.

as Britain's prime minister and Conservative Party leader. Thatcher, who had been prime minister since May 1979 and leader of the Tories since February 1975, had carved her own stamp on recent British history and was one of the most recognized persons throughout the world. Pakistan Prime Minister Benazir Bhutto was removed from power in August and charged, along with her husband, with corruption. Although Bhutto and her husband denied the charges, her Pakistan People's Party was crushed in parliamentary elections in October.

Liberation's Legacy. A 1990 Gallup Organization survey found that the majority of women polled expressed frustration because of unfulfilled expectations about the women's movement. The survey reported that 64% of the women believed that the women's movement made it more difficult for women to combine jobs and families. Some historians believe that such periods of disillusionment may foreshadow a cycle of reform leading to the next stage of social change and possibly a revitalized women's movement. The focus of women's issues in the future was thought likely to be care for dependent children and parents, combating violence against women, and basic changes in the structure of work to allow for more flexible schedules for men and women.

U.S. Labor Department statistics indicated that women were not entering the work force as rapidly as they did in the 1970s and 1980s. The data suggested that the number of women working or job-hunting was restrained by such factors as an incipient national recession and a rising number of births. Economists predicted, however, that the trend could change by the end of the 1990s with the availability of more child-care facilities and the resolution of other issues.

Health Research Gap. Attention was drawn in 1990 to an alarming information gap in research on women's health. In June a General Accounting Office (GAO) report charged that the $7 billion funding system of the National Institutes of Health (NIH) overwhelmingly supported research projects focusing more on men than on women. The Congressional Caucus for Women's Issues, which commissioned the GAO study, introduced a $237 million legislative package in July designed to achieve equity in medical research, and in response to past research biases, an Office of Research on Women's Health was established at NIH in 1990. Also, Dr. Bernadine P. Healy, a renowned cardiologist and past president of the American Heart Association, was nominated to the directorship of the NIH early in 1991.

Women Behind Bars. The number of women in U.S. prisons nearly tripled during the 1980s, resulting in a prison system that was overcrowded and overwhelmed by the unique problems presented by a growing female inmate population. Prison officials estimated that the underlying cause of the imprisonment of 95% of female inmates was drugs—either directly, or indirectly through theft, prostitution, and armed robbery. Unprepared prison officials were learning to deal with the unique psychological and medical needs of women inmates, particularly the needs of their children. Inequities in the correctional system seemed to mirror society, as women inmates often did not receive the same rehabilitation or educational programs as male prisoners.

ELIZABETH MCNALLY, *Free-lance Writer*

WYOMING

The state's centennial, the economy, water-resource issues, and the November elections highlighted 1990 news in Wyoming.

Centennial. Communities throughout the state celebrated Wyoming's 100th birthday on July 10 with a variety of activities, including a Centennial Wagon Train trek from Casper to Cody and a reenactment of statehood day at the Capitol in Cheyenne. A visit from President Bush highlighted the festivities.

The Economy. A mixed economic picture continued in Wyoming in 1990. The crisis in the Middle East and the effects of the Clean Air Act of 1990 boosted coal and oil production in the state. Coal production surpassed 1989's record of 171 million tons and oil prices were up sharply from prices prior to Iraq's invasion of Kuwait. Planned secondary and tertiary recovery processes were expected to invigorate the state's sluggish oil industry. A proposed natural-gas pipeline from southwestern Wyoming to California also was anticipated to spur the economy. The agricultural economy for 1990 continued to be mixed, with beef cattle prices up and the sheep market down.

Wyoming continued to feel the effects of the population out-migration of the 1980s following the mineral boom of the 1970s and early 1980s. Preliminary 1990 census data estimated a population decline to approximately 450,000–482,000 people in the state—a sharp drop from the peak population of 516,000 in 1983. Unemployment figures showed a decline from 6.3% in 1989 to 5.23% in the summer of 1990.

Politics. Incumbent domination proved the rule in the November elections as U.S. Sen. Alan Simpson defeated Democratic challenger Kathy Helling and Rep. Craig Thomas (R) defeated Democrat Pete Maxfield. At the state level, Gov. Mike Sullivan (D) defeated Mary Mead (R) with 65% of the vote. In the race for secretary of state, Democrat Kathy Karpan won easily. In the legislature, Republicans

---

WYOMING • Information Highlights

Area: 97,809 sq mi (253 326 km^2).
Population (1990 census prelim.): 450,000.
Chief Cities (1980 census): Cheyenne, the capital, 47,283; Casper, 51,016; Laramie, 24,410.
Government (1990): *Chief Officers*—governor, Mike Sullivan (D); secretary of state, Kathy Karpan (D). *Legislature*—Senate, 30 members; House of Representatives, 64 members.
State Finances (fiscal year 1989): *Revenue,* $1,843,000,000; *expenditure,* $1,566,000,000.
Personal Income (1989): $6,884,000,000; per capita, $14,508.
Labor Force (June 1990): *Civilian labor force,* 249,000; *unemployed,* 9,600 (3.9% of total force).

Education: *Enrollment* (fall 1988)—public elementary schools, 70,415; public secondary, 27,378; colleges and universities, 26,540. *Public school expenditures* (1989–90 est.), $521,892,000.

---

strengthened their majority, one vote shy of a two-thirds majority in both houses.

The 1990 legislature passed a $785 million budget for the 1990–91 biennium. The Republican-controlled legislature reorganized the state government into 12 departments, passed a mineral tax-reform bill, and joined other states in making the birthday of Martin Luther King, Jr., a holiday.

Water Resources. A 1989 U.S. Supreme Court decision gave Arapaho and Shoshone tribes senior water rights on the Big Wind River. Controversy over water rights and use continued to keep tribal, state, and federal parties at odds in 1990.

The congressional designation of 20.5 mi (33 km) of the Clarks Fork River as a "wild and scenic" river was another topic in the news in arid Wyoming. At issue was whether the federal or state government would determine water levels.

Governor Herschler. Former Gov. Ed Herschler died of cancer on February 5. The popular, three-term Democrat served longer than any other governor. His environmental commitment and resistance to federal intrusion into state affairs made him a legendary figure in state history.

ROBERT A. CAMPBELL
University of Wyoming

YEMEN. *See* MIDDLE EAST.

YUGOSLAVIA

In 1990 ancient ethnic hatreds, disagreements over political and economic liberalization, conflict between republics over federation or confederation, and violent demonstrations that required constant military intervention seemed to have brought Yugoslavia to the brink of civil war and dissolution.

Political Developments. The federal party and governmental structures progressively fragmented during the year. With a bloody revolution going on in neighboring Romania, the Yugoslav League of Communists hastily convened an extraordinary congress, January 20–23. The delegates agreed that the League should relinquish its monopoly of power and accept a pluralist political system, but on little else. There was bitter infighting between two camps. The two more economically developed and liberal republics, Slovenia and Croatia, pressed for Western-style democratization, a loose confederation of republics, rapid movement toward privatization and a free market, and early membership in the European Community. They were opposed by the largest republic, Serbia, which insisted on a more strongly centralized government and Communist Party (with a greater role for Serbia in

A Yugoslav proudly flying an ethnic Albanian flag (right) was an example of the strife that was bringing Yugoslavia to the brink of civil war in 1990.

© Steve McCurry/Magnum

both) and slow changes in the existing economic system. When the Slovene delegation walked out of the congress, it simply was adjourned. Soon afterward, on February 4, the Slovene Communists declared themselves independent of the Yugoslav party and renamed themselves the Democratic Renewal Party. The Croatian League of Communists quickly followed suit.

In April the two northern republics held their first free post-World War II parliamentary and presidential elections. In each case, a center-right coalition of nationalist and anti-communist groups—DEMOS in Slovenia, the Croatian Democratic Union in Croatia—won a strong parliamentary majority. They demanded the transformation of Yugoslavia into a loose confederation of sovereign republics and threatened to hold popular referendums on outright secession if their demands were not met. In May, Borisav Jović, head of the collective federal presidency and a Serb, warned that such "fascist methods," together with ethnic tensions, were threatening Yugoslavia with civil war. On July 2–3, Slovenia became the first republic to declare its full sovereignty, with its constitution and laws taking precedence over federal ones and with control of its own military forces. The federal presidency promptly ordered that the action be rescinded, warning that the government would use any means necessary to save the federation.

In July the Serbian League of Communists finally yielded to popular pressures, renaming itself the Serbian Socialist Party (SSP) and agreeing to permit multiparty elections in December. (Elections also took place in Macedonia and Bosnia-Herzegovina in November and in Montenegro in December.) Running against some 40 other parties, the SSP won a controlling bloc of seats in the new Serbian legislature. Its powerful conservative chief, Slobodan Milošević, campaigning for the protection of Serbian national interests, a strongly centralized Yugoslavia, and economic stability, received 60% of the popular vote for president. On December 23 the government of Slovenia organized a referendum on independence for the republic and received the approval of 95% of the voters. It promptly began to take over all formerly federally controlled functions in Slovenia. At the same time, a new Croatian constitution was promulgated that included provisions for secession from Yugoslavia. The federal presidency labeled Slovenia's referendum illegal, and the Yugoslav army announced that it would reassert its authority over paramilitary units now controlled by the two republics.

Ethnic Strife. These political developments were conditioned heavily by widespread fears of rising Serbian nationalism and Serbia's apparent determination to dominate Yugoslavia. Serbia's harsh treatment of the ethnic Albanian majority in its autonomous province of Kosovo polarized Yugoslavs into pro- and anti-Serbian groups. Beginning on January 24, thousands of armed ethnic Albanians began an almost daily

---

YUGOSLAVIA • Information Highlights

Official Name: Socialist Federal Republic of Yugoslavia.
Location: Southeastern Europe.
Area: 98,764 sq mi (255 800 km^2).
Population (mid-1990 est.): 23,800,000.
Chief Cities (1981 census): Belgrade, the capital, 1,470,073; Osijek, 867,646; Zagreb, 768,700.
Government: *Head of state,* collective state presidency, Slobodan Milošević, president (took office 1989). *Legislature*—Federal Assembly: Federal Chamber and Chamber of Republics and Provinces.
Monetary Unit: Dinar (10.64 dinars equal U.S.$1, Dec. 31, 1990).
Gross National Product (1989 est. U.S.$): $129,500,-000,000.
Economic Indexes (1989): *Consumer Prices* (1980 = 100), all items, 115,148. *Industrial Production* (1980 = 100), 137.
Foreign Trade (1989 U.S.$): *Imports,* $14,802,-000,000; *exports,* $13,363,000,000.

series of demonstrations, general strikes, and violent clashes with security forces in the capital, Priština, and throughout Kosovo. They demanded full autonomy for the province, democratic multiparty elections, and the release of all political prisoners. Acting under a state of emergency existing since March 1989, the federal government sent in army units with tanks and aircraft to maintain order. Milošević threatened to send armed civilian volunteers to protect the Serbian minority and hundreds of thousands of Serbian settlers to "colonize" the province. Huge demonstrations in Serbia and Montenegro backed him, denouncing Albanian "terrorism" and the support the Albanian cause was getting from Croatia and Slovenia. In July, Serbia completed its takeover of Kosovo by assuming all administrative and legislative power there, incorporating its territory into the republic, and taking control of all communications media. In response, the Albanian deputies to the dissolved Kosovo parliament met secretly to declare Kosovo an independent, sovereign republic. Serbia condemned the move.

Serbian minorities in other republics also felt themselves threatened and called for help from Belgrade. In August police had to intervene in Bosnia-Herzegovina, where several hundred thousand Muslims massed to honor their kin killed by the Serbian Chetniks (royal military units) in World War II. In Croatia the large Serbian minority (about 12% of the total population) took up arms, raised barricades, and declared all Serb-populated areas autonomous.

Economy. Defiance of the federal system by the republics and ethnic strife imperiled Prime Minister Ante Marković's plan for Yugoslavia's economic rehabilitation. The first stage, begun in December 1989, reduced the staggering inflation rate of more than 2,600% to 4% through a restructuring of monetary policy. The second stage, unveiled in June 1990, envisioned an 18% cut in state spending, legislation to attract foreign investment, and widespread privatization of state-owned enterprises. The political crisis also undercut Yugoslavia's position in various regional and all-European associations working toward political-economic cooperation and integration, such as the Adriatic-Danube Group, the "Pentagon" Nations, and the Conference on Security and Cooperation in Europe.

JOSEPH FREDERICK ZACEK
State University of New York at Albany

YUKON

During 1990 attention in Yukon was focused on the territory's economic difficulties and the ongoing negotiations about the Yukon Indian land-claims dispute.

YUKON • Information Highlights

Area: 186,660 sq mi (483 450 km²).
Population (September 1990): 26,000.
Chief cities (Sept. 1990): Whitehorse, the capital, 20,721.
Government (1990): *Chief Officers*—commissioner, J. Kenneth McKinnon; premier, Tony Penikett (New Democratic Party); leader of official opposition, Willard Phelps (Progressive Conservative Party). *Legislature*—16-member Legislative Assembly.
Public Finance (1990–91 fiscal year budget est.): *Revenues,* $355,498,000; *expenditures,* $346,-602,000.
Personal Income (average weekly earnings, July 1990): $603.34.
Education (1990–91): *Enrollment*—elementary and secondary schools, 5,240 pupils.
(All monetary figures are in Canadian dollars.)

Economy. Because of cuts in federal government funding and an anticipated nationwide recession, the Yukon government, which depends to a great extent on federal financial support, began preparing to reduce its own spending and curtail some of its programs. In the light of dramatic drops in construction and mineral exploration and a slight dip in tourism, coupled with the introduction of a national 7% goods and services tax as of Jan. 1, 1991, the territory was bracing itself for a period of belt-tightening.

Spending on mineral exploration throughout the territory for 1990 was expected to go no higher than C$10 million, down substantially from C$55 million in 1988. Fluctuating mineral prices on world markets and mounting environmental opposition to new mining developments combined to slow growth and cast several potential hardrock mines in doubt. Meanwhile food costs in the capital city of Whitehorse continued to be the highest in Canada and construction in 1990 was down 26% compared with 1989. However, total value of retail trade in the first quarter of 1990 was C$45 million, up 9.8% compared with the same period in 1989.

Indian Land Claims. Negotiators for the federal and territorial governments and the Council for Yukon Indians moved a step closer to a final constitutionally based land-claims agreement on April 1, 1990, with the initialing of an "umbrella agreement." It followed on the heels of a 1988 agreement-in-principle and provides a more precise legal and technical expression of Indian demands.

The next step in the process—which has been going on since 1973—was to begin band-by-band negotiations over such issues as the division of 16,000 sq mi (41 440 km²) of land, participation in wildlife management, Indian self-government, and about 20 other specific areas of concern. Part of the projected agreement would mean a federal government payment of more than C$230 million to the estimated 5,000 Yukon Indians.

DON SAWATSKY, *Whitehorse*

ZAIRE

With only a 1% annual growth in the gross national product (GNP), high inflation continuing, and the zaire dropping 30% below black-market rates, Zaire's economy was stagnant in 1990. The economic situation and increasing criticism from abroad for human-rights violations led President Mobutu Sese Seko to promise major reforms in the government.

Domestic Policy. In January, Mobutu, responding to pressure, embarked on "a dialog with the people" inviting criticism of the government. He received more than 15,000 messages, most extremely critical. On April 24 the president broadcast his response. He announced an end to the 20-year ban on all parties other than the ruling Popular Movement of the Revolution (MPR). In the undefined future there would be three parties allowed and free elections.

Mobutu said he was stepping down as leader of the MPR but would continue as head of state. There would be an interim government formed to run the state pending adoption of the new constitution. Premier Kengo wa Dondo was dismissed, and Lundu Bululu, a former professor, was called upon in May to head a transitional cabinet of 40 members, none of whom belonged to the opposition. Etienne Tshisekedi wa Mulumba, the leader of the Underground Union for Democracy and Social Progress (UDPS), was released from prison.

Euphoric Zairians took to the streets to celebrate the good news but Mobutu claimed he was misunderstood; political parties were not authorized yet to hold public meetings. Two of the promised parties would be the MPR and an associated party. A rally at Mulumba's home was attacked; two persons were killed and many injured. Beginning in May troops attacked student demonstrators, killing an estimated 50. Mobutu, pressured by his old guard, postponed his promised reforms to a later date.

Foreign and Economic Developments. Responding to criticism from the African National Congress (ANC) and the Organization of African Unity (OAU), Mobutu postponed indefinitely his plan to act as a mediator of South Africa's problems and canceled a summer meeting with President de Klerk of South Africa. Zaire's relations with the United States became more strained as evidence of continued corruption, police brutality, and violations of human rights mounted.

Having received $4 billion in U.S. aid since 1982, Zaire was shocked rudely in June when the U.S. House of Representatives stopped all such support. This followed the World Bank's decision to delay $100 million in loans until more was provided for social services and less for security and government operations. The International Monetary Fund (IMF) also withheld a disbursement of $54 million because Zaire had not met agreed-upon budgetary targets.

HARRY A. GAILEY
San Jose State University

ZIMBABWE

In 1990, Zimbabwe's President Robert Mugabe won endorsement from the electorate and postponed plans to establish a one-party regime. The government also ended the state of emergency and instituted reforms to attract foreign investment.

Elections. On March 28, Zimbabwe's voters went to the polls for a simultaneous presidential and parliamentary election, the second in the country's ten-year history of black-majority rule. At stake were 120 seats in the new 150-seat unicameral parliament; the 30 remaining seats were filled by appointees of President Mugabe. The election campaigns were marred by acts of violence, and the Catholic Commission for Justice and Peace declared prior to the voting that the violence was "already calling into question the freeness and fairness of the election." Former cabinet minister Edgar Tekere's opposition party, the Zimbabwe Unity Movement (ZUM), which had been formed to try to prevent Robert Mugabe from establishing a one-party state, did not live up to expectations in the election. ZUM won only two of the 120 contested parliamentary seats, and Edgar Tekere only one fifth of the presidential vote. Mugabe's party, the Zimbabwe African National Union-Patriotic Front (ZANU-PF) won all but four seats; in the election for president, Mugabe received 2.3 million votes and Tekere 413,840. There were clear signs of apathy with a record low turnout of 54% of the registered voters; more than 90% of the electorate had voted in the elections of 1980 and 1985. However, there was a substantial voter turnout in the eastern border town of Mutare, the stronghold of Edgar Tekere and ZUM.

Cabinet Changes. After the election President Mugabe announced changes in his cabinet. Joshua Nkomo was reappointed as senior minister of state in the president's office until such time as a revision of the constitution

---

ZAIRE • Information Highlights

Official Name: Republic of Zaire.
Location: Central equatorial Africa.
Area: 905,564 sq mi (2 345 410 km²).
Population (mid-1990 est.): 36,600,000.
Chief City (1987 est.): Kinshasa, the capital, 2,500,000.
Government: *Head of state,* Mobutu Sese Seko, president (took office 1965). *Legislature* (unicameral)—National Legislative Council.
Monetary Unit: Zaire (576.308 zaires equal U.S.$1, June 1990).
Foreign Trade (1989 U.S.$): *Imports,* $849,000,000; *exports,* $1,254,000,000.

In March 1990, Zimbabwe President Robert Mugabe (right) joined Nelson Mandela, a leader of the African National Congress, who only weeks before was released from prison, and his wife Winnie at an enthusiastic stadium rally in Harare.

Reuters/Bettmann

would allow him to be named one of two vice-presidents of equal rank. Didymus Mutasa, former speaker of the House of Assembly and ZANU-PF secretary for administration, was appointed to the cabinet for the first time as the senior minister of political affairs. Bernard Chidzero retained his position as minister of finance, economic planning, and development. Edison Zvobgo was appointed minister of state for the public service. Two whites were appointed to the cabinet: Chris Andersen became minister of mines and Dennis Norman, who had been minister of agriculture in the cabinet of 1980, now was named minister of transport and national supplies.

One-Party State. It was anticipated that Robert Mugabe would use the mandate of the election to create a one-party system, but he softened his government's position in September, announcing that ZANU-PF would not legislate a one-party state into being, but would work toward achieving it on a de facto basis. His decision to "leave things as they are" reflected opposition to such a change by the churches and by a large majority of the ZANU-PF Central Committee. Since the merger between the ruling ZANU-PF and Joshua Nkomo's Zimbabwe African Peoples Union (ZAPU) in 1988, the country essentially has been dominated by one party anyway.

State of Emergency Ends. In July the government lifted the state of emergency that had been in effect for 25 years. Initially imposed by Rhodesian white supremacist Premier Ian Smith in 1965, it remained in effect as long as he was in power, and had been continued under black-majority rule.

Economy. High unemployment and a sluggish economy forced the government to ease economic controls in 1990. In an effort to attract foreign investors, Finance Minister Bernard Chidzero announced a major policy change in July: Zimbabwe would move toward an economy in which the state would permit "market forces to operate in directing the pace

ZIMBABWE • Information Highlights

Official Name: Republic of Zimbabwe.
Location: Southern Africa.
Area: 150,803 sq mi (390 580 km²).
Population (mid-1990 est.): 9,700,000.
Chief Cities (1983 est.): Harare (formerly Salisbury), the capital, 681,000; Bulawayo, 429,000; Chitungwiza, 202,000.
Government: *Head of state and government,* Robert Mugabe, executive president (sworn in Dec. 31, 1987). *Legislature*—unicameral Parliament.
Monetary Unit: Zimbabwe dollar (2.482 Z dollars equal U.S.$1, August 1990).
Economic Index (July 1989): *Industrial Production* (1980 = 100), 131.
Foreign Trade (1987 U.S.$): *Imports,* $1,046,000,000; *exports,* $1,419,000,000.

and course of economic activities." He also promised that trade conditions would be liberalized and that unproductive government enterprises would be sold and run privately. In addition, Chidzero recognized the need to cut back the size of the bureaucracy; the country currently employs 190,000 civil servants.

Zimbabwe continued to have a problem with unemployment; for example, in 1990, 300,000 people were competing in a labor market for between 8,000 and 10,000 new jobs. The overall unemployment rate for the country has been estimated at 30% and the inflation rate stood at 20%.

During the year the government indicated that it would force white commercial farmers to sell half of their land for the resettlement of African peasant farmers. There had been considerable pressure on the government to do so because of the slow pace of land reform since the end of white rule. However, by the end of the year the government seemed to be reconsidering this initiative following an outcry by the commercial farmers, who claimed that they employed at least 25% of the country's work force and produced 40% of the foreign exchange, and that serious consequences would ensue if land reform adversely affected them.

PATRICK O'MEARA, *Indiana University*

ZOOS AND ZOOLOGY

The year 1990 seemed to be the age of aquariums. Three major facilities featuring aquatic animals opened to the public during 1990 and one debuted in late 1989.

At the Aquarium Reptile Complex at Riverbanks Zoo in Columbia, SC, which opened in late 1989, 80 exhibits display a variety of creatures in watery habitats. Featured are animals ranging from huge anacondas and strange-looking matamata turtles of the Amazon River Basin, to neon gobies and moray eels in a coral reef, to sea stars and American lobsters from the ocean deep.

On July 6, 1990, the Texas State Aquarium in Corpus Christi unveiled the Jesse H. and Mary Gibbs Jones Gulf of Mexico Exhibit Building—Phase I of a four-part master plan which is to focus on the plants and animals native to the Gulf of Mexico and the Caribbean Sea. Visitors explore the world of marshes and seagrass beds; see the power of wind and waves on barrier islands and delve into the depths of the sea; visit a re-creation of the Flower Gardens Coral Reef, the northernmost coral reef in North America; and view the plant and animal life supported by a full-scale model of an offshore oil platform like those in the Gulf.

Thousands of miles to the west, in Japan, the new $107 million Osaka Aquarium also

© Greg Spaulding/Texas State Aquarium, Corpus Christi

A visitor examines bivalves at the Gulf of Mexico Exhibit at the new Texas State Aquarium, the only U.S. facility to focus on species native to the Gulf and the Caribbean Sea.

opened in July. One of the largest aquatic exhibits in the world, it takes as its theme the Ring of Fire—the dynamic volcanic perimeter of the Pacific Ocean. Starting with giant crabs and other creatures native to Japan and moving downward between walls of water, visitors see 300 kinds of animals that inhabit all levels of the continually changing Pacific ecosystem, in-

The Ring of Fire Aquarium in Osaka, Japan, is devoted to Pacific coastal ecosystems. Designed by Peter Chermayeff of Cambridge Seven Associates, it uses water as an architectural element.

© Fujifotos/The Image Works

cluding sea otters from California's Monterey Bay, squirrel monkeys native to the shores of South America, penguins from Antarctica, moray eels from tropical seas, and the whale shark—the world's largest fish.

Highlighting the Atlantic Ocean in the Western Hemisphere, New Orleans' Aquarium of the Americas opened in August. More than 7,500 animals of about 400 species are exhibited in four major displays: The Caribbean Reef Environment, The Amazon Rainforest Habitat, Mississippi River and Delta Habitat, and The Gulf of Mexico Exhibit. This was the first stage of what eventually will be one of the United States' largest aquariums. Phase II of the aquarium is expected to open in 1994.

Exhibits. Meanwhile, a number of zoos were busy creating new exhibits. On April 21 the Dallas (TX) Zoo unveiled its 25-acre (10.12-ha) Wilds of Africa. A nature trail winds through a forested area inhabited by okapis, which look like a cross between an antelope and a zebra but are extremely rare relatives of the giraffe that live only in the Ituri Forest of Zaire. A two-acre (0.8-ha) reserve has been set aside for lowland gorillas, where visitors can watch these endangered primates from several vantage points and literally peer over the shoulders of scientists studying their behavior in the Jake L. Hamon Gorilla Conservation Research Center. Future plans for the exhibit call for creation of an additional 30 acres (12.15 ha) for lions, rhinos, elephants, lake and swamp exhibits, and more.

The Bronx (NY) Zoo revealed a new display on July 10 for geladas—a type of baboon native to Ethiopia. Mature male geladas can weigh 100 lbs (45.67 kg) and have magnificent long hair flowing over their neck and shoulders. Both sexes have bright red patches of skin on chest and rump. These unusual monkeys graze on grass and live in social groups of as many as 400.

ZooAtlanta (GA) opened two new exhibits for endangered species: Black rhinos were added to its Masai Mara complex, which simulates the savannas of East Africa; and a pair of Sumatran tigers now inhabit the Ketambe Indonesian Rainforest. The Indianapolis (IN) Zoo, which was redesigned completely and reopened in 1988, completed its master plan with the July opening of Living Deserts of the World. The climate-controlled domed conservatory, which measures 80 ft (24.5 m) in diameter, houses cactus wrens, small lizards, radiated tortoises, and 30 other species that live in hot, arid lands.

Endangered Species. Befitting the year in which the world celebrated the 20th anniversary of Earth Day (*see* page 54), there were several breakthroughs in zoology that may help scientists in their efforts to ensure the survival of endangered species. The Henry Doorly Zoo in Omaha, NE, proudly announced the April 27 birth of Mary Alice, a Bengal tiger cub. What makes Mary Alice so special is that she was born to a *Siberian* tiger mother—the first time one of the big cats has been conceived by in-vitro fertilization and embryo transfer. The eventual goal of such reproductive research is to freeze fertilized embryos from zoo animals and transfer them to animals in the wild. This will enable scientists to introduce new genetic material into small populations of rare and endangered species.

Two black-necked cranes hatched on the same day, July 10, but half a world apart. One, called Trung Trung, debuted at the International Crane Foundation (ICF) in Baraboo, WI, and the other made its appearance at Vogelpark, a bird sanctuary in Walsrode, West Germany. The black-necked crane is endangered critically; its wetlands habitat in China is disappearing rapidly and only 1,615 of the birds are known to exist. ICF and Vogelpark are working in cooperation with the Chinese government to breed these cranes in captivity and to protect them in the wild.

Technological Advances. Modern technology is being used successfully by zoologists to identify and study individual animals. At the Bronx Zoo, technicians have implanted microchips, or transponders, into rare species such as snow leopards, parrots, and Chinese alligators. An encoded copper coil in the chip generates a ten-digit readout when a wand is passed over it, in much the same way as bar codes on food products reveal prices. This technique helps scientists keep track of the animals' breeding and health records. In addition, people are having their dogs, cats, horses, and other pets implanted, so in case of loss, they can be identified positively.

At the National Marine Fisheries Service in Galveston, TX, researchers are working on a captive-breeding project to repopulate the Gulf of Mexico with females of the extremely rare Kemp's ridley sea turtle. In the 1940s, as many as 40,000 females came ashore each year to nest, but now, the number is down to only a few hundred. The most reliable method of determining the sex of hatchling turtles requires killing them. Scientists at the University of Tennessee at Memphis, however, recently discovered that a genetic probe that binds to gender-specific DNA fragments can be used to identify the sexes of hatchling ridley and green sea turtles.

Satellite tracking is being tested with a number of animals, from bears in Alaska to caribou in Maine to elephants in Africa. At the Virginia Institute of Marine Science of the College of William and Mary, researchers have followed successfully a loggerhead sea turtle via satellite as it made its 2,000-mi (3,200-km) migration to and from Florida.

DEBORAH A. BEHLER
"Wildlife Conservation" Magazine

Statistical and Tabular Data

Table of Contents

NATIONS OF THE WORLD [1]

A Profile and Synopsis of Major 1990 Developments

Nation, Region	Population in millions	Capital	Area Sq mi (km²)	Head of State/Government
Antigua and Barbuda, Caribbean	0.1	St. John's	170 (440)	Sir Wilfred E. Jacobs, governor-general Vere C. Bird, prime minister

The son of Prime Minister Vere C. Bird, Sr., allegedly was involved in an arms scandal in which a shipment of Israeli arms was sent through the nation on its way to Colombian drug traffickers. Vere C. Bird, Jr., who resigned his cabinet post after the allegations were made public, denied knowing that the arms were destined for use in another country. Gross Domestic Product (GDP) (1989 est.): $353.5 million. Foreign Trade (1988 est.): Imports, $302.1 million; exports, $30.4 million.

Nation, Region	Population in millions	Capital	Area Sq mi (km²)	Head of State/Government
Bahamas, Caribbean	0.2	Nassau	5,382 (13 940)	Sir Henry Taylor, governor-general Lynden O. Pindling, prime minister

A Caribbean Development Bank review, released May 31, 1990, showed that the Bahamas was one of only four member nations which had higher growth rates in 1989 than in 1988, despite suffering hurricane damage. GDP (1988 est.): $2.4 billion. Foreign Trade (1987): Imports, $1.7 billion; exports, $733 million.

Nation, Region	Population in millions	Capital	Area Sq mi (km²)	Head of State/Government
Bahrain, W. Asia	0.5	Manama	239 (620)	Isa bin Salman Al Khalifa, emir Khalifa bin Salman Al Khalifa, prime minister

GDP (1987): $3.5 billion. Foreign Trade (1988 est.): Imports, $2.5 billion; exports, $2.4 billion.

Nation, Region	Population in millions	Capital	Area Sq mi (km²)	Head of State/Government
Barbados, Caribbean	0.3	Bridgetown	166 (430)	Sir Hugh Springer, governor-general L. Erskine Sandiford, prime minister

Barbados was visited in March 1990 by Canadian Prime Minister Brian Mulroney; while there, he met with leaders of the Caribbean Commonwealth nations and announced Canada would forgive $154 million in debt owed by Caribbean nations. GDP (1988 est.): $1.3 billion. Foreign Trade (1988): Imports, $582 million; exports, $173 million.

Nation, Region	Population in millions	Capital	Area Sq mi (km²)	Head of State/Government
Benin, W. Africa	4.7	Porto Novo	43,483 (112 620)	Mathieu Kérékou, president Nicephore Soglo, prime minister

A completely new Benin government was sworn in on March 12, 1990, following President Kérékou's renunciation of Marxism-Leninism in 1989. A 15-member interim cabinet, made up entirely of civilians, was put in place, and a High Council of the Republic, to be in charge of a "democratic resurgence" leading to the "inauguration of democratic institutions" by April 1991 was appointed. Kérékou would remain as head of the armed forces. GDP (1988): $1.7 billion. Foreign Trade (1988): Imports, $413 million; exports, $226 million.

Nation, Region	Population in millions	Capital	Area Sq mi (km²)	Head of State/Government
Bhutan, S. Asia	1.6	Thimphu	18,147 (47 000)	Jigme Singye Wangchuck, king

In July 1990 exiled political leaders demanded a democratic form of government for Bhutan, but the king replied that the nation never would face a prodemocracy movement. The opposition leaders in August called for immediate protests against what they termed a "despotic" regime. Although Bhutan's government continued its efforts to modernize the nation with the aid of foreign expertise, it also continued to isolate the nation further: Monasteries and temples, its main tourist attractions, were closed to foreigners, and visas were limited sharply. GDP (1988 est.): $273 million. Foreign Trade (1989): Imports, $138.3 million; exports, $70.9 million.

[1] Independent nations not covered separately in alphabetical section.

Nation, Region	Population in millions	Capital	Area Sq mi (km²)	Head of State/Government
Botswana, S. Africa	1.2	Gaborone	231,803 (600 370)	Quett Masire, president

Botswana became one of five African nations exempting their countries from the global ban on ivory trading imposed in January 1990. Botswana claimed the controlled sale of legal ivory was an important part of its wildlife-management programs, since it has a flourishing elephant population. Botswana continued as the Western world's most important diamond producer, but despite its wealth, was unable to reduce significantly its economic dependence on South Africa. GDP (1988): $1.87 billion. Foreign Trade (1988): Imports, $1.1 billion; exports, $1.3 billion.

Brunei, S.E. Asia	0.3	Bandar Seri Begawan	2,288 (5 770)	Sir Muda Hassanal Bolkiah, sultan and prime minister

The sultan of Brunei was accused in March of participating in the fraud-based $1 billion takeover of House of Fraser, the owner of the British Harrods department stores; he denied the accusations. A criminal prosecution would not be pursued. Brunei and the other members of the Association of Southeast Nations (ASEAN) issued a statement in July 1990 criticizing the United States for withdrawing its recognition of the rebel coalition in Cambodia and for its policy on Cambodian and Vietnamese refugees, saying the economic and political costs ASEAN nations were suffering for taking in these refugees were unacceptable. GDP (1989 est.): $3.3 billion. Foreign Trade (1987): Imports, $800 million; exports, $2.07 billion.

Burkina Faso, W. Africa	9.1	Ouagadougou	105,869 (274 200)	Blaise Compaoré, president

Pope John Paul II visited Burkina Faso in January 1990. Speaking in Ouagadougou, he begged the more affluent nations to not ignore the needs of poverty-stricken African nations such as Burkina Faso. It was revealed in August that Burkina Faso had been supplying arms and troops to one of the rebel factions in the Liberian civil war. GDP (1988): $1.43 billion. Foreign Trade (1988): Imports, $591 million; exports, $249 million.

Burundi, E. Africa	5.6	Bujumbura	10,745 (27 830)	Pierre Buyoya, president Adrien Sibomana, prime minister

GDP(1988): $1.3 billion. Foreign Trade (1988): Imports, $204 million; exports, $128 million.

Cameroon, Cen. Africa	11.1	Yaoundé	183,568 (475 440)	Paul Biya, president

Conservation efforts continued in the Korup, one of the world's oldest and most pristine tropical rain forests. The British-based World Wide Fund for Nature (WWF) created "buffer zones"—areas of farmland surrounding the forest. Western pharmaceutical companies who are interested in natural "forest medicines" also aided in the efforts. However, conservation efforts were undermined by timber concerns that engaged in indiscriminate logging operations. The Cameroonian government agreed to launch an investigation into multinational timber companies and their activities in the Korup forest. The human-rights group Amnesty International claimed that several persons sentenced to jail were arrested for trying to start a second political party in Cameroon, a legal act under the constitution. GDP (1988): $12.9 billion. Foreign Trade (1988): Imports, $2.3 billion; exports, $2.0 billion.

Cape Verde, W. Africa	0.4	Praia	1,556 (4 030)	Aristides Pereira, president Pedro Pires, prime minister

During a January visit, Pope John Paul II urged wealthier nations to aid and cooperate with poor countries such as Cape Verde. Earnings sent back from Cape Verdeans in the United States provide almost 20% of Cape Verde's gross national product. GDP (1987): $158 million. Foreign Trade (1987): Imports, $124 million; exports, $8.9 million.

Central African Republic, Cen. Africa	2.9	Bangui	240,533 (622 980)	André-Dieudonné Kolingba, president

GDP (1988 est.): $1.27 billion. Foreign Trade (1988 est.): Imports, $285 million; exports, $138 million.

Chad, Cen. Africa	5.0	Ndjamena	495,753 (1 284 000)	Gen. Idris Deby, president

The Patriotic Salvation Movement, a rebel group led by Gen. Idris Deby, in an offensive begun on November 10, toppled the eight-year-old government of Hissein Habré, who fled the country to exile in Sudan on December 1. Although French troops stationed in Chad worked to assure the safety of French nationals, France did not interfere in the dispute. Deby promised to turn the nation into a multiparty democracy and pledged that he would bring freedom and justice to Chad, torn by civil war for more than 20 years. Deby assumed the presidency on December 4 and suspended the constitution, but set no timetable for free elections. Freed political prisoners told tales of torture ordered personally by Habré. Deby denied allegations that his forces had received aid from Libya. GDP (1988): $902 million. Foreign Trade (1988): Imports, $214 million; exports, $432 million.

Comoros, E. Africa	0.5	Moroni	838 (2 170)	Said Mohamed Djohar, president

The first free elections in the Comoros, held Feb. 18, 1990, were fraught with irregularities, including supposedly indelible ink which washed easily off voters' fingers. After unsuccessful opposition demands for the resignation of President Said Mohamed Djohar, second elections were held March 11 in which Djohar defeated his opponent, Mohamed Taki, by a margin of 55.1% to 44.9%. Taki charged that fraud had taken place, but an Organization of African Unity observer endorsed this vote. GDP (1988 est.): $207 million. Foreign Trade (1987): Imports, $52 million; exports, $12 million.

Congo, Cen. Africa	2.2	Brazzaville	132,046 (342 000)	Denis Sassou-Nguesso, president Alphonse Poaty-Souchlaty, prime minister

GDP (1988 est.): $2.2 billion. Foreign Trade (1987): Imports, $494.4 million; exports, $912 million.

Djibouti, E. Africa	0.4	Djibouti	8,494 (22 000)	Hassan Gouled Aptidon, president Barkat Gourad Hamadou, premier

Gross National Product (GNP) (1986): $333 million. Foreign Trade (1986): Imports, $198 million; exports, $128 million.

Dominica, Caribbean	0.1	Roseau	290 (750)	Clarence A. Seignoret, president Eugenia Charles, prime minister

Eugenia Charles was reelected to a third consecutive term as prime minister on May 28. Her Dominica Freedom Party took 11 of 21 elected seats in the House of Assembly, down from 17. The two-year-old United Workers' Party, headed by Edison James, became the official opposition by winning six seats. Four seats were won by the Dominica Labour Party, led by Michael A. Douglas. Charles was disappointed in her reduced majority. GDP (1988 est.): $137 million. Foreign Trade (1987): Imports, $66 million; exports, $46 million.

Dominican Republic, Caribbean	7.2	Santo Domingo	18,815 (48 730)	Joaquín Balaguer Ricardo, president

Presidential elections were held in the Dominican Republic May 16. However, with 95% of the vote counted, such a tiny margin separated candidates Joaquin Balaguer and Juan Bosch Gavino that a recount was agreed to. Despite

Nation, Region	Population in millions	Capital	Area Sq mi (km²)	Head of State/Government

observers' statements that the vote had been honest, there were numerous protests and accusations of fraud by Bosch against Balaguer. After a recount, Balaguer was declared the winner on June 11 by a margin of less than 25,000 votes. However, Balaguer's Social Christian Reformist Party was relegated to minority status in the legislature. He was sworn in to his second consecutive term and sixth overall on August 16. Throughout the year, antigovernment protests and general strikes greeted Balaguer's economic-austerity program, implemented to reduce inflation and bring down the government deficit. A major general strike in November virtually shut down the country. GDP (1988): $5.1 billion. Foreign Trade (1988): Imports, $1.8 billion; exports, $711 million.

Equatorial Guinea, Cen. Africa — 0.4 — Malabo — 10,830 (28 050) — Obiang Nguema Mbasogo, president / Cristino Seriche Bioko, prime minister

Representatives from Equatorial Guinea and the 41 other poorest nations of the world met in Dhaka, Bangladesh, in February 1990 to find new ways to receive increased aid from richer countries and international lending organizations. Representatives then met with donor-nation representatives in Geneva in March, in preparation for a larger international conference scheduled for Paris in September. GNP (1987): $103 million. Foreign Trade (1988 est.): Imports, $50 million; exports, $30 million.

Fiji, Oceania — 0.8 — Suva — 7,054 (18 270) — Sir Penaia Ganilau, president / Sir Kamisese Mara, prime minister

GDP (1989 est.): $1.32 billion. Foreign Trade (1988): Imports, $454 million; exports, $312 million.

Gabon, Cen. Africa — 1.2 — Libreville — 103,348 (267 670) — El Hadj Omar Bongo, president / Casimir Oye Mba, premier

President Bongo stated he was working toward establishing a multiparty democracy, agreeing to demands that parties be allowed to form immediately. The nation currently had only one legal political party. A transition government was installed in May. Gabon had suffered through a wave of violent prodemocracy protests, strikes, and rioting in Libreville and Port Gentil since the beginning of the year. Antigovernment riots erupted in May after the mysterious death of a prominent opposition leader, causing France to send more troops temporarily to its former colony to help restore order. In the nation's first multiparty elections in 22 years, held in September, election officials were attacked and ballot boxes smashed by voters claiming the election was rigged in favor of President Bongo. GDP (1989): $3.2 billion. Foreign Trade (1989): Imports, $0.76 billion; exports, $1.14 billion.

Gambia, W. Africa — 0.9 — Banjul — 4,363 (11 300) — Sir Dawda Kairaba Jawara, president

Gambia contributed troops to a multinational West African military force sent to Liberia in August to help effect a cease-fire in the civil war there. It was the first time in modern history such a cooperative military intervention had been organized within Africa. GDP (1989 est.): $195 million. Foreign Trade (1989): Imports, $105 million; exports, $133 million.

Ghana, W. Africa — 15.0 — Accra — 92,100 (238 540) — Jerry Rawlings, chairman of the Provisional National Defense Council

Five persons, including three military officers, were arrested after trying to destroy evidence linking them to an assassination attempt on Ghanaian leader Jerry Rawlings. Ghana participated during 1990 in the multinational West African military force sent to Liberia to help defend against rebels there. GNP (1988): $5.2 billion. Foreign Trade (1987): Imports, $988 million; exports, $977 million.

Grenada, Caribbean — 0.1 — St. George's — 131 (340) — Sir Paul Scoon, governor-general / Sir Nicholas Brathwaite, prime minister

In national elections on March 13, in which some 60% of eligible Grenada voters participated, Nicholas Brathwaite's National Democratic Congress won seven of 15 parliament seats; Brathwaite was appointed prime minister after then Prime Minister Ben Jones was persuaded by Governor-General Sir Paul Scoon to step down. Brathwaite sought to form a coalition with Jones' National Party, but Jones would not make a commitment. GDP (1988): $129.7 million. Foreign Trade (1988 est.): Imports, $92.6 million; exports, $31.8 million.

Guinea, W. Africa — 7.3 — Conakry — 94,927 (245 860) — Lansana Conté, president

Along with troops from Nigeria, Ghana, Sierra Leone, and Gambia, soldiers from Guinea participated in a multinational West African military force which sought an end to the civil war in Liberia. GDP (1988): $2.5 billion. Foreign Trade (1988 est.): Imports, $509 million; exports, $553 million.

Guinea-Bissau, W. Africa — 1.0 — Bissau — 13,946 (36 120) — João Bernardo Vieira, president

Pope John Paul II, visiting Guinea-Bissau in January, urged an end to "static and conditioned ideologies," thought to refer to the nation's Marxist orientation. The government recently has encouraged more private ownership and freer trade, and is turning its foreign policy somewhat toward the West. The nation remains extremely poor, with a per-capita income of slightly more than $3 per week. In 1990 it was found by the UN to have one of the world's lowest life expectancies—39 years, and an infant mortality rate of 148 per 1,000. GDP (1987): $152 million. Foreign Trade (1987): Imports, $49 million; exports, $15 million.

Guyana, N.E. South America — 0.8 — Georgetown — 83,000 (214 970) — Hugh Desmond Hoyte, president / Hamilton Green, prime minister

GDP (1988 est.): $323 million. Foreign Trade (1988 est.): Imports, $216 million; exports, $215 million.

Ivory Coast, W. Africa — 12.6 — Yamoussoukro — 124,502 (322 460) — Félix Houphouët-Boigny, president

Economic-austerity measures proposed by President Houphouët-Boigny in February led to violent protests, in which demonstrators demanded the removal of Houphouët-Boigny. The government canceled the austerity measures in April and later announced that opposition parties would be allowed to participate in October elections. The first free elections held in Ivory Coast since independence in 1960 were marred, however, by charges of across-the-board cheating by the ruling party. Houphouët-Boigny was said to have won reelection with 81.67% of the votes cast. In parliamentary elections later in 1990, the governing Democratic Party won 163 of 175 seats. Voter turnout was as low as 30% in Abidjan. In September, Pope John Paul II consecrated the controversy-ridden Basilica of Our Lady of Peace in Yamoussoukro, the largest Christian church in the world. GDP (1988): $10.0 billion. Foreign Trade (1988): Imports, $1.3 billion; exports, $2.2 billion.

Kiribati, Oceania — 0.07 — Tarawa — 277 (717) — Ieremia Tabai, president

GDP (1989): $34 million. Foreign Trade (1988): Imports, $21.5 million; exports, $5.1 million.

Nation, Region	Population in millions	Capital	Area Sq mi (km²)	Head of State/Government
Lesotho, S. Africa	1.8	Maseru	11,718 (30 350)	Moshoeshoe II, king Justin Lekhanya, chairman, military council

Military ruler Justin Lekhanya stripped King Moshoeshoe of all his powers in February 1990 after the king refused to approve Lekhanya's choices to replace top military officials who had been dismissed for allegedly plotting against the government. In March the king was sent by Lekhanya into temporary exile in Britain. Lekhanya, who had come to power in a South African-supported coup in 1986, assumed the king's powers, shuffled the cabinet extensively, and announced a political- and economic-reform program. A national council was created to set up a timetable for democratization by 1992. Lekhanya's critics believed, however, that his goal was to consolidate his power and avoid a return to civilian rule. GDP (1989 est.): $412 million. Foreign Trade (1989 est.): Imports, $526 million; exports, $55 million.

Nation, Region	Population in millions	Capital	Area Sq mi (km²)	Head of State/Government
Liechtenstein, Cen. Europe	0.03	Vaduz	62 (160)	Hans Adam, prince Hans Brunhart, prime minister
Luxembourg, W. Europe	0.4	Luxembourg	998 (2 586)	Jean, grand duke Jacques Santer, prime minister

Two units of the Luxembourg-based Bank of Credit & Commerce International Holdings S.A. pleaded guilty in January 1990 in a plea-bargaining agreement to charges of money laundering. The units apparently helped members of Colombia's Medellin drug cartel launder their profits. In May the bank announced a loss of $498 million for 1989 and confirmed that majority control was in the hands of the government of Abu Dhabi, United Arab Emirates. GDP (1989 est.): $6.3 billion. (Luxembourg's foreign trade is recorded with Belgium's.)

Nation, Region	Population in millions	Capital	Area Sq mi (km²)	Head of State/Government
Madagascar, E. Africa	12.0	Antananarivo	226,656 (587 040)	Didier Ratsiraka, president Victor Ramahatra, prime minister

It was announced in March 1990 that the ban on multiparty politics which had been in place since 1975 would be rescinded effective immediately. In May, 11 armed dissidents seized control of a radio station in Antananarivo to broadcast an appeal for a revolt against the 15-year "dictatorship" of Didier Ratsiraka and his family, who they said had impoverished the nation. Security forces soon stormed the station and subdued the rebels. In a first, the Central Bank of Madagascar agreed to allow a private conservation group, Washington, DC-based Conservation International, to pay $5 million of Madagascar's international debt in exchange for a commitment to try to save the island's endangered plants and animals. GDP (1988): $1.7 billion. Foreign Trade (1988): Imports, $319 million; exports, $284 million.

Nation, Region	Population in millions	Capital	Area Sq mi (km²)	Head of State/Government
Malawi, E. Africa	9.2	Lilongwe	45,745 (118 480)	Hastings Kamuzu Banda, president

It was reported by the United Nations Children's Fund that the level of child malnutrition in Malawi was second only to that in Ethiopia. This contradicted President Banda's frequent claims that Malawi was self-sufficient in food production. The nation long had been cited by international organizations as a success story and model for the rest of Africa. Various international groups continued their harsh criticisms of extensive human-rights violations in the country. GDP (1988): $1.4 billion. Foreign Trade (1988): Imports, $402 million; exports, $292 million.

Nation, Region	Population in millions	Capital	Area Sq mi (km²)	Head of State/Government
Maldives, S. Asia	0.2	Malé	116 (300)	Maumoon Abdul Gayoom, president

The leaders of seven South Asian nations held a meeting in Malé in late November 1990 to discuss regional problems and projects. GDP (1988): $136 million. Foreign Trade (1988 est.): Imports, $90.0 million; exports, $47.0 million.

Nation, Region	Population in millions	Capital	Area Sq mi (km²)	Head of State/Government
Mali, W. Africa	8.1	Bamako	478,764 (1 240 000)	Moussa Traoré, president

GDP (1988 est.): $1.94 billion. Foreign Trade (1987): Imports, $493 million; exports, $260 million.

Nation, Region	Population in millions	Capital	Area Sq mi (km²)	Head of State/Government
Malta, S. Europe	0.4	Valletta	124 (320)	Vincent Tabone, president Edward Fenech Adami, prime minister

GDP (1988): $1.9 billion. Foreign Trade (1988): Imports, $1.36 billion; exports, $710 million.

Nation, Region	Population in millions	Capital	Area Sq mi (km²)	Head of State/Government
Mauritania, W. Africa	2.0	Nouakchott	397,954 (1 030 700)	Maaouiya Ould Sid Ahmed Taya, president

The international watchdog group Africa Watch claimed that slavery still was thriving in Mauritania, despite having been abolished legally for the third time in 1980. The group claims that the government has not even attempted to eradicate the practice and quoted former slaves as saying they never had heard of the emancipation law. GDP (1988): $1.0 billion. Foreign Trade (1988): Imports, $365 million; exports, $424 million.

Nation, Region	Population in millions	Capital	Area Sq mi (km²)	Head of State/Government
Mauritius, E. Africa	1.1	Port Louis	718 (1 860)	Sir Veerasamy Ringadoo, governor-general Aneerood Jugnauth, prime minister

Prime Minister Jugnauth called a parliament vote for August on the subject of changing the Mauritian constitution to make the nation a republic and remove the provision making Queen Elizabeth II of England the titular head of state. However, the vote never was taken and Jugnauth's political maneuvering to make his ally Paul Béringer president failed. Mauritius' economy prospered, mainly due to its thriving textile industry and popularity as a vacation spot for well-to-do Europeans. Its economic growth largely is built on its status as an export-processing zone. GDP (1988): $1.9 billion. Foreign Trade (1988): Imports, $1.3 billion; exports, $1.0 billion.

Nation, Region	Population in millions	Capital	Area Sq mi (km²)	Head of State/Government
Monaco, S. Europe	0.03	Monaco-Ville	0.7 (1.9)	Rainier III, prince M. Jean Ausseil, minister of state

Princess Caroline's husband, Italian financier Stefano Casiraghi, 30, was killed October 3 when his speedboat flipped over as he was defending his World Offshore Championship title off the coast of Monaco. The couple, married in 1983, had three children.

Nation, Region	Population in millions	Capital	Area Sq mi (km²)	Head of State/Government
Nauru, Oceania	0.009	Nauru	8 (21)	Bernard Dowiyogo, president

Foreign Trade (1984): Imports, $73 million; exports, $93 million.

Nation, Region	Population in millions	Capital	Area Sq mi (km²)	Head of State/Government
Niger, W. Africa	7.9	Niamey	489,189 (1 267 000)	Ali Saibou, president Aliou Mahamida, prime minister

It was reported in February 1990 that police in Niger had shot ten students to death and injured 50 more during the suppression of a protest against austerity measures and cutbacks planned by the government. Some 4,500 university students went on strike to oppose the measures, and the strike eventually spread to secondary and even primary schools in Niamey. GDP (1988 est.): $2.4 billion. Foreign Trade (1988 est.): Imports, $441 million; exports, $371 million.

Nation, Region	Population in millions	Capital	Area Sq mi (km²)	Head of State/Government
Oman, W. Asia	1.5	Muscat	82,031 (212 460)	Qaboos bin Said, sultan and prime minister

GDP (1987 est.): $7.8 billion. Foreign Trade (1988 est.): Imports, $1.9 billion; exports, $3.6 billion.

Nation, Region	Population in millions	Capital	Area Sq mi (km²)	Head of State/Government
Papua New Guinea, Oceania	4.0	Port Moresby	178,259 (461 690)	Vincent Eri, governor-general Rabbie Namaliu, prime minister

The closure in May 1989 of one of the world's largest copper mines on the island of Bougainville due to militant activity against the mine had forced Papua New Guinea into a financial crisis and spurred its largest-ever military campaign. Militant landowners on the island demanded independence from the nation and $10 billion in compensation for environmental damage. A total of 100 persons died in clashes between the government and the rebels. The government imposed an economic blockade in May 1990. Peace talks led to an interim agreement between the secessionists and the government in August and talks to discuss the future of the mine and the island began in September. GDP (1988 est.): $3.26 billion. Foreign Trade (1988): Imports, $1.2 billion; exports, $1.4 billion.

Qatar, W. Asia	0.5	Doha	4,247 (11 000)	Khalifa bin Hamad Al Thani, emir and prime minister

GDP (1987): $5.4 billion. Foreign Trade (1988 est.): Imports, $1 billion; exports, $2.2 billion.

Rwanda, E. Africa	7.3	Kigali	10,170 (26 340)	Juvénal Habyarimana, president

On September 30 a rebel army of refugee Tutsi tribesmen invaded from Uganda in an attempt to oust the Rwandan government, which was dominated by the rival Hutu tribe. Troops from Belgium, France, and Zaire were sent to aid the Rwandan army. A cease-fire plan proposed by Belgium was accepted October 18, although scattered fighting continued. There were claims, refuted by the government, that Rwandan soldiers indiscriminately had killed residents of Tutsi settlements. In November, President Habyarimana announced he would permit a multiparty political system in 1991. GDP (1988 est.): $2.3 billion. Foreign Trade (1988): Imports, $278 million; exports, $118 million.

Saint Kitts and Nevis, Caribbean	0.04	Basseterre	139 (360)	Clement A. Arrindell, governor-general Kennedy A. Simmonds, prime minister

GDP (1988 est.): $119 million. Foreign Trade (1988): Imports, $94.7 million; exports, $30.3 million.

Saint Lucia, Caribbean	0.2	Castries	239 (620)	Sir Stanislaus A. James, governor-general John Compton, prime minister

GDP (1988 est.): $172 million. Foreign Trade (1987): Imports, $178.1 million; exports, $76.8 million.

Saint Vincent and the Grenadines, Caribbean	0.1	Kingstown	131 (340)	David Jack, governor-general James F. Mitchell, prime minister

GDP (1988): $136 million. Foreign Trade (1986): Imports, $87.3 million; exports, $63.8 million.

San Marino, S. Europe	0.023	San Marino	23 (60)	Co-regents appointed semi-annually

São Tomé and Principe, W. Africa	0.1	São Tomé	371 (960)	Manuel Pinto da Costa, president Celestino Rocha da Costa, prime minister

In the first strikes to take place in São Tomé and Principe since independence, telecommunications workers and plantation workers each staged one-day work stoppages in 1990. Later in the year, the nation's sole political party debated a draft of a revised constitution which would permit multiple political parties; direct, secret elections; a free press; and privatization. GDP (1986): $37.9 million. Foreign Trade (1988 est.): Imports, $17.3 million; exports, $9.1 million.

Senegal, W. Africa	7.4	Dakar	75,749 (196 190)	Abdou Diouf, president

President Abdou Diouf was one of the world leaders who addressed the United Nations World Summit for Children. He stated that alleviation of the plight of children in Third World nations ultimately was linked to a "solution to the debt crisis" and called for "radical solutions," such as debt forgiveness by industrialized nations. GDP (1988 est.): $5 billion. Foreign Trade (1988): Imports, $1.1 billion; exports, $761 million.

Seychelles, E. Africa	0.1	Victoria	176 (455)	France Albert René, president

The government, with the help of the World Bank and the United Nations, drew up a $600 million plan for environmental management, which it hopes will be financed by donor nations. An international conference was planned in Paris for 1991, where donor nations would be asked to make pledges. Although tourism is the source of more than half the foreign-exchange earnings of the Seychelles, the government stated it would limit the number of tourists to 100,000 per year to help preserve the environment. GDP (1988 est.): $255 million. Foreign Trade (1988 est.): Imports, $116 million; exports, $17 million.

Sierra Leone, W. Africa	4.2	Freetown	27,699 (71 740)	Joseph Momoh, president

The government struggled in 1990 with economic reform, devaluing the leone by 300% over a period of one year. The devaluation caused hyperinflation, without apparently boosting the economy. Diamond production continued to decrease, and shortages were rampant. Life expectancy had decreased to 35 years, and the infant mortality rate was 270 per 1,000. The government was depending on proposed European projects to revamp communications and road systems, a dependence a Western diplomat called "the recolonization of Sierra Leone." GDP (1987): $965 million. Foreign Trade (1988): Imports, $167 million; exports, $106 million.

Solomon Islands, Oceania	0.3	Honiara	10,985 (28 450)	Sir George Lepping, governor-general Solomon Mamaloni, prime minister

GDP (1988): $156 million. Foreign Trade (1988): Imports, $101.7 million; exports, $80.1 million.

Somalia, E. Africa	8.4	Mogadishu	246,200 (637 660)	Mohammed Siad Barre, president Mohammed Ali Samantar, premier

In June more than 40 people were arrested for allegedly distributing pamphlets criticizing the government of Mohammed Siad Barre for corruption and human-rights violations. There were reports that at least 65 were killed in July when Somali security forces opened fire on the crowd at a soccer match in Mogadishu after protesters threw rocks at President Barre. The government claimed only three died in the incident. In late December rebels of the United Somali Congress launched an attack against the government in Mogadishu; fighting continued at year's end. GDP (1988): $1.7 billion. Foreign Trade (1988): Imports, $354 million; exports, $58 million.

Nation, Region	Population in millions	Capital	Area Sq mi (km²)	Head of State/Government
Suriname, S. America	0.4	Paramaribo	63,039 (163 270)	Ramsewak Shankar, president

A military coup took place in Suriname on December 24. Longtime military chief Lt. Col. Désiré Bouterse's feud with President Ramsewak Shankar was said to spark the takeover. Military officials promised free elections within 100 days; they claimed popular support and promised President Shankar would be made to resign. Throughout 1990 there had been complaints that Bouterse and his forces were using violence and murder to keep control of the nation. It was estimated that 10% of the population had fled the nation during the past year. GDP (1988 est.): $1.27 billion. Foreign Trade (1988 est.): Imports, $365 million; exports, $425 million.

Nation, Region	Population in millions	Capital	Area Sq mi (km²)	Head of State/Government
Swaziland, S. Africa	0.8	Mbabane	6,703 (17 360)	Mswati III, king Obed Mfanyana, prime minister

GNP (1989 est.): $539 million. Foreign Trade (1988): Imports, $386 million; exports, $394 million.

Togo, W. Africa	3.7	Lomé	21,927 (56 790)	Gnassingbé Eyadéma, president

The government of President Gnassingbé Eyadéma claimed that the people of Togo did not want a multiparty political system. It was said by critics, however, that the results of the interviews conducted across the nation on the question had been shaped by the one-party government. Togo's economy suffered during 1990 as prices for cocoa, its main export crop, continued to fall, but recent economic reforms brought some growth. The government hoped an export-processing plan soon to begin would boost the nation's economy. GDP (1988 est.): $1.35 billion. Foreign Trade (1988): Imports, $369 million; exports, $344 million.

Tonga, Oceania	0.1	Nuku'alofa	289 (748)	Taufa'ahau Tupou IV, king Prince Fatafehi Tu'ipelehake, prime minister

Tonga laid claim in August 1990 to the last 16 unoccupied orbital satellite "parking spaces" over the South Pacific region. The slots could be reserved by almost any nation at no cost. Critics claimed that, since the tiny nation was unlikely to be able to afford to start a satellite system, it had reserved the spots solely to lease them to the highest bidders; it was estimated each slot could be worth up to $2 million per year. The consortium Intelsat, which maintains most of the spaces for its member nations, tried to persuade international authorities to dismiss Tonga's claim. GDP (1989 est.): $86 million. Foreign Trade (1988 est.): Imports, $60.1 million; exports, $9.1 million.

Trinidad and Tobago, Caribbean	1.3	Port-of-Spain	1,981 (5 130)	Noor Hassanali, president Arthur Robinson, prime minister

On July 27, 1990, a Black Muslim group headed by Abu Bakr seized the national television station and parliament building in Port-of-Spain in an attempted coup. Prime Minister Arthur Robinson was taken hostage, along with 40 others; Robinson and some others were wired to explosives. Robinson was freed July 31, and the Muslims surrendered the next day. The rebels were taken into custody and were to be tried on charges of treason and murder. At least 60 were killed during the coup attempt. GDP (1988 est.): $3.75 billion. Foreign Trade (1987): Imports, $1.2 billion; exports, $1.4 billion.

Tuvalu, Oceania	0.009	Funafuti	10 (26)	Sir Tupua Leupena, governor-general Bikenibeu Paeniu, prime minister

GNP (1989 est.): $4.6 million. Foreign Trade (1983 est.): Imports, $2.8 million; exports, $1 million.

United Arab Emirates, W. Asia	1.6	Abu Dhabi	32,278 (83 600)	Zayid bin Sultan Al Nuhayyan, president Rashid bin Said Al Maktum, prime minister

The United Arab Emirates announced after the invasion of Kuwait by Iraq in August 1990 that it would welcome troops from Arab and other nations to help in its national defense. It remained a supporter of the anti-Iraq forces throughout the remainder of the year. GNP (1988): $23.3 billion. Foreign Trade (1988 est.): Imports, $8.5 billion; exports, $10.6 billion.

Vanuatu, Oceania	0.2	Port-Vila	5,699 (14 760)	Frederick Timakata, president Walter Lini, prime minister

GDP (1987 est.): $120 million. Foreign Trade (1988 est.): Imports, $58 million; exports, $16 million.

Vatican City, S. Europe	0.001	Vatican City	0.17 (0.438)	John Paul II, pope

The Vatican and Czechoslovakia restored full diplomatic relations during 1990 after a 40-year lapse, and Pope John Paul II visited that nation April 21–22 in his first visit to a Warsaw Pact country other than his native Poland. Limited ties were resumed with the USSR, and relations were established and improved between the Vatican and several other former Communist nations during the year.

Western Samoa, Oceania	0.2	Apia	1,104 (2 860)	Tanumafili II Malietoa, head of state Tofilau Eti, prime minister

GDP (1989 est.): $112 million. Foreign Trade (1988): Imports, $51.8 million; exports, $9.9 million.

Yemen, S. Asia	13.0	San'a	203,850 (527 970)	Ali Abdullah Saleh, president

Pro-Western North Yemen and Marxist South Yemen merged into the Yemeni Republic in ceremonies on May 22, 1990. Ali Abdullah Saleh, who had been president of North Yemen, was elected president of the new nation by both parliaments. Elections were to be held around the end of 1992. Later in the year, Yemen was seen as taking the side of its ally, Iraq, in the Middle East crisis—although the nation claimed it was neutral. It criticized Saudi Arabia for expelling Yemeni workers and for inviting U.S-led forces into the area. Yemen, with Cuba, voted against the UN Security Council resolution authorizing force against Iraq if it did not withdraw from Kuwait by Jan. 15, 1991. GDP (North—1987): $4.5 billion; (South—1986): $1.01 billion. Foreign Trade (North—1987): Imports, $1.4 billion; exports, $51.1 million; (South —1987 est.): Imports, $497 million; exports, $54 million. See also MIDDLE EAST—The Yemens Merge.

Zambia, E. Africa	8.1	Lusaka	290,583 (752 610)	Kenneth David Kaunda, president Malimba Masheke, prime minister

Nelson Mandela made a triumphant visit to Zambia in late February-early March to meet with officials of the African National Congress. Food riots erupted late in June, leaving at least 23 dead—many of them killed by government forces. An apparent coup attempt on June 30 weakened President Kaunda's leadership. Following the riots, Kaunda announced that a referendum would be held in October to allow the people to choose whether they wanted a multiparty political system. However, after later trying to postpone the referendum, Kaunda announced in September that he would recommend constitutional amendments to legalize multiple parties. The new laws were approved in December, ending 17 years of one-party rule. GDP (1988): $4 billion. Foreign Trade (1988): Imports, $687 million; exports, $1.184 billion.

WORLD MINERAL AND METAL PRODUCTION

ALUMINUM, primary smelter (thousand metric tons)

	1988	1989
United States	3,944	4,030
USSR[e]	2,400	2,400
Canada	1,534	1,555
Australia	1,150	1,244
Brazil	874	935
Norway	864	859
China[e]	800	825
West Germany	744	742
Venezuela	455	546
India	335	423
Spain	323	352
France	328	335
United Kingdom	300	297
Netherlands	278	274
Other countries[a]	3,276	3,210
Total	17,605	18,027

ANTIMONY, mine[b] (metric tons)

	1988	1989
China[e]	30,000	30,000
USSR[e]	9,600	9,600
Bolivia	9,943	8,533
South Africa	6,264	5,201
Canada	3,171	2,882
Mexico	2,185	1,906
Australia	1,320	1,419
Guatemala	921	1,191
Turkey	1,665	1,031
Yugoslavia	725	798
Thailand	445	500[e]
Other countries[a]	1,753	3,014
Total	67,992	66,075

ASBESTOS[c] (thousand metric tons)

	1988	1989
USSR[e]	2,600	2,600
Canada	705	710
Brazil	228	230
Zimbabwe	187	190[e]
China	157	160[e]
South Africa	146	150[e]
Italy	95	95[e]
Other countries[a]	205	190
Total	4,323	4,325

BARITE[c] (thousand metric tons)

	1988	1989
China[e]	1,500	1,750
Mexico	535	566
USSR[e]	540	540
Turkey	388	460[e]
India	393	395[e]
Morocco	322	320[e]
United States	404	290
West Germany[e]	167	160
France	100	100
Other countries[a]	1,132	1,131
Total	5,481	5,712

BAUXITE[d] (thousand metric tons)

	1988	1989
Australia	36,192	38,583
Guinea	15,600	16,523
Jamaica	7,408	9,395
Brazil	7,727	7,894
USSR[e]	5,715	5,684
India	3,415	4,027
China[e]	3,500	4,000
Suriname	3,434	3,530
Yugoslavia	3,034	3,252
Hungary	2,906	2,700[e]
Greece	2,533	2,576
Sierra Leone	1,379	1,548
Guyana	1,774	1,281
Indonesia	513	862
Other countries[a]	3,367	3,291
Total	98,497	105,146

CEMENT[c] (thousand metric tons)

	1988	1989
China	204,144	207,000
USSR	139,499	140,000
Japan	77,554	81,300
United States	70,989	71,268
India	40,716	42,100
Italy	37,257	37,500[e]
South Korea	28,995	30,474
West Germany	26,215	26,500[e]
France	25,272	25,300[e]
Brazil	25,328	25,000[e]
Spain	24,372	24,500[e]
Turkey	22,675	23,800
Mexico	22,513	23,500[e]
Other countries[a]	362,097	367,211
Total	1,107,626	1,125,453

CHROMITE[c] (thousand metric tons)

	1988	1989
South Africa	4,245	4,275
USSR[e]	3,700	3,800
India	759	800[e]
Albania[e]	750	700
Turkey[e]	625	650
Zimbabwe	561	570[e]
Finland	536	499
Brazil[e]	240	225
Philippines	164	188
Other countries[a]	397	416
Total	11,977	12,123

COAL, anthracite and bituminous[c] (million metric tons)

	1988	1989
China	980	1,040
United States	813	838
USSR	600	580
India	189	200[e]
Australia	174	180[e]
Poland	193	178
South Africa	176	176
United Kingdom	104	98
West Germany	73	71
Canada	71	71
North Korea[e]	62	65
Other countries[a]	108	110
Total	3,543	3,607

COAL, lignite[c f] (million metric tons)

	1988	1989
East Germany	310	312
USSR	172	160
West Germany	109	110
Czechoslovakia	102	97
Yugoslavia	73	75
United States	70	72
Poland	74	69[e]
Romania	49	50
Australia	40	42[e]
Other countries[a]	214	215
Total	1,213	1,202

COPPER, mine[b] (thousand metric tons)

	1988	1989
Chile	1,472	1,609
United States	1,420	1,497
Canada	777	732
USSR[e]	640	640
Zambia	475	510
Zaire	530	475
Poland	437	436
Peru	318	384
China[e]	375	375
Australia	244	295
Mexico	280	249
Papua New Guinea	219	204
South Africa	192	197
Philippines	218	193
Other countries[a]	1,035	1,080
Total	8,632	8,876

COPPER, refined, primary and secondary (thousand metric tons)

	1988	1989
United States	1,852	1,954
Chile	1,013	1,071
USSR[e]	1,000	1,000
Japan	955	990
China[e]	510	530
Canada	566	511
West Germany	426	475
Zambia	448	466
Belgium	393	397
Poland	401	390
Australia	218	255
Peru	175	225
Zaire	258	204
South Korea	169	179
Spain	159	166
Other countries	1,644	1,726
Total	10,187	10,539

DIAMOND, natural (thousand carats)

	1988	1989
Australia	35,034	35,080
Zaire	18,227	19,000[e]
Botswana	15,229	15,252
USSR[e]	11,000	11,000
South Africa	8,504	9,116
Angola[e]	1,000	1,000
China[e]	1,000	1,000
Namibia	938	1,000[e]
Other countries[a]	2,414	2,389
Total	93,346	94,837

FLUORSPAR[g] (thousand metric tons)

	1988	1989
China[e]	1,400	1,700
Mexico	828	861[e]
Mongolia[e]	800	800
USSR[e]	410	410
South Africa	328	368
France[e]	183	183
Spain[e]	180	180
Italy	140	140
Other countries[a]	1,023	1,089
Total	5,292	5,731

GAS, natural[h] (billion cubic feet)

	1988	1989
USSR	27,200	28,100
United States	17,808	17,955
Canada	3,144	3,211
Netherlands	2,317	2,350[e]
Algeria	1,585	1,670[e]
Indonesia	1,312	1,400[e]
Mexico	1,219	1,250[e]
Romania	1,165	1,170[e]
United Kingdom	1,299	1,031
Other countries[a]	12,106	12,340
Total	69,155	70,477

GOLD, mine[b] (kilograms)

	1988	1989
South Africa	618,369	605,452
USSR[e]	280,000	285,000
United States	200,914	265,541
Australia	156,950	202,900
Canada	135,889	159,135
Brazil	100,200	100,000[e]
China[e]	78,000	80,000
Papua New Guinea	38,129	31,136
Poland[e]	31,000	31,000
Philippines	32,486	30,627
Colombia	29,020	27,090
Chile	20,614	21,382
Other countries[a]	155,531	159,033
Total	1,877,102	1,998,296

GYPSUM[c] (thousand metric tons)

	1988	1989
United States	14,869	15,988
Canada	9,512	8,700
Iran[e]	8,400	8,400
China[e]	8,100	8,100
Japan[e]	6,300	6,300
Spain[e]	5,500	5,500
Thailand	4,549	5,477
France[e]	5,400	5,400
Mexico	4,126	4,813
USSR[e]	4,800	4,800
United Kingdom[e]	3,700	4,000
West Germany[e]	1,800	1,850
Australia[e]	1,600	1,800
Romania[e]	1,600	1,600
Other countries[a]	15,732	15,855
Total	95,988	98,583

IRON ORE[c] (thousand metric tons)

	1988	1989
USSR	249,737	241,000
Brazil	145,040	153,700
Australia	96,084	105,810
China[e]	99,000	100,000
United States	57,515	58,700
India	49,961	49,487
Canada	38,742	40,900
South Africa	25,248	29,958
Sweden	20,440	21,578
Venezuela	18,218	18,053
Liberia	12,767	11,700[e]
Mauritania	10,004	11,138
France	10,903	10,500
Other countries[a]	72,634	70,776
Total	906,293	923,300

IRON, crude steel (thousand metric tons)

	1988	1989
USSR	163,037	160,000[e]
Japan	105,681	107,909
United States	90,650	88,852
China	59,000	61,200
West Germany	41,023	41,002
Italy	23,760	25,171
Brazil	24,536	25,018
South Korea	19,117	21,800
France	19,003	19,286
United Kingdom	19,013	18,813
Poland	16,873	17,000[e]
Czechoslovakia	15,319	15,465
Canada	14,866	15,458
India	14,309	14,429
Romania	14,000[e]	14,415
Spain	11,685	12,684
Belgium	11,222	10,948
Other countries[a]	115,309	114,773
Total	778,403	784,223

LEAD, mine[b] (thousand metric tons)

	1988	1989
Australia	466	495
USSR[e]	440	440
United States	394	419
China[e]	300	330
Canada	368	275
Peru	149	192
Mexico	171	163
North Korea[e]	110	110
Yugoslavia	103	100
Other countries[a]	908	895
Total	3,409	3,419

LEAD, refined, primary and secondary[i] (thousand metric tons)

	1988	1989
United States	1,128	1,205
USSR	727	735
United Kingdom	374	350
West Germany	345	350
Japan	339	332
China[e]	245	270
France	256	267
Canada	269	245
Australia	183	204
Mexico	203	196
Italy	184	181
Belgium	127	126
Other countries[a]	1,475	1,452
Total	5,855	5,913

MAGNESIUM, primary (thousand metric tons)

	1988	1989
United States	142	152
USSR [e]	91	91
Norway	50	50
France	14	14
Japan	9	11
Canada	8	7
Brazil	6	6
Other countries [a]	14	13
Total	334	344

MANGANESE ORE [c] (thousand metric tons)

	1988	1989
USSR [e]	9,100	8,800
South Africa	3,454	3,623
China [e]	2,750	2,750
Gabon	2,254	2,600 [e]
Australia	1,985	2,124
Brazil	1,945	1,602
India	1,324	1,400 [e]
Other countries [a]	1,094	1,130
Total	23,906	24,029

MERCURY, mine (metric tons)

	1988	1989
USSR [e]	2,300	2,300
Spain	1,380	967
Algeria [e]	700	700
China [e]	700	700
United States [e]	480	430
Mexico	345	345
Other countries [a]	465	460
Total	6,370	5,902

MOLYBDENUM, mine [b] (metric tons)

	1988	1989
United States	43,051	63,105
Chile	15,527	16,550
Canada	13,535	13,654
USSR [e]	11,500	11,500
Mexico	4,456	4,500 [e]
Peru	2,444	3,100
Other countries [a]	3,959	4,055
Total	94,472	116,464

NATURAL GAS LIQUIDS (million barrels)

	1988	1989
United States	595	564
USSR [e]	318	330
Saudi Arabia	150	150 [e]
Mexico	135	135 [e]
Algeria [e]	122	125
Canada	121	125
Other countries [a]	333	340
Total	1,774	1,769

NICKEL, mine [b] (thousand metric tons)

	1988	1989
USSR [e]	215	215
Canada	219	203
New Caledonia	68	102
Australia	62	65
Indonesia	58	60
Cuba	42	43
South Africa	35	34
Dominican Republic	42	31
Other countries [a]	131	135
Total	872	888

NITROGEN, content of ammonia (thousand metric tons)

	1988	1989
USSR [e]	20,100	20,100
China [e]	16,200	17,000
United States	12,544	12,546
India	6,205	6,700 [e]
Canada	3,298	3,332
Netherlands	2,956	3,001
Romania [e]	2,800	2,600
Indonesia	2,367	2,526
Mexico	2,067	2,100
France	1,832	1,476
Other countries [a]	28,145	28,204
Total	98,514	99,585

PETROLEUM, crude (million barrels)

	1988	1989
USSR	4,275	4,146
United States	2,979	2,779
Saudi Arabia	1,935	1,879
Iran	827	1,045
Iraq	968	1,030
China	998	1,007
Mexico	919	915
United Arab Emirates	588	715
Venezuela	696	687
Kuwait	546	657

PETROLEUM, crude (cont'd)

	1988	1989
United Kingdom	817	652
Nigeria	531	616
Canada	589	569
Indonesia	486	502
Libya	386	400
Other countries [a]	3,858	4,104
Total	21,398	21,703

PHOSPHATE ROCK [c] (thousand metric tons)

	1988	1989
United States	45,389	48,866
USSR [e]	34,400	34,400
Morocco	25,015	24,400 [e]
China [e]	15,000	15,500
Tunisia	6,103	6,100 [e]
Jordan	6,611	6,000 [e]
Brazil	4,672	3,655
Togo	3,464	3,355
South Africa	2,850	2,963
Senegal	2,326	2,273
Other countries [a]	14,545	14,831
Total	160,375	162,343

POTASH, K_2O equivalent basis (thousand metric tons)

	1988	1989
USSR	11,301	10,500
Canada	8,311	7,458
East Germany	3,510	3,200
West Germany	2,390	2,240
United States	1,521	1,595
Israel	1,244	1,271
France	1,502	1,200
Other countries [a]	2,329	2,325
Total	32,108	29,789

SALT [c] (thousand metric tons)

	1988	1989
United States	34,506	35,291
China [e]	22,000	28,000
USSR [e]	14,800	14,800
West Germany	13,605	13,100 [e]
Canada	10,687	11,140
India	9,204	9,004 [e]
France	7,925	8,050
Mexico	7,189	7,652
Australia	6,976	7,345
United Kingdom	6,130	5,800
Poland	5,700	5,700 [e]
Romania [e]	5,400	5,000
Brazil	4,356	4,391
Other countries [a]	35,216	35,304
Total	183,694	190,577

SILVER, mine [b] (metric tons)

	1988	1989
Mexico	2,359	2,306
United States	1,661	2,010
Peru	1,552	1,840 [e]
USSR [e]	1,490	1,490
Canada	1,371	1,285
Poland	1,063	1,060
Australia	1,118	1,000 [e]
Chile	507	510
Bolivia	232	267
Spain	221	250
Morocco	226	225
Sweden	193	195
South Africa	200	178
Other countries [a]	1,590	1,486
Total	13,783	14,102

SULFUR, all forms [j] (thousand metric tons)

	1988	1989
United States	10,746	11,592
USSR [e]	10,265	9,350
Canada	6,930	6,625
Poland	5,090	5,090 [e]
China [e]	4,750	4,900
Japan	2,447	2,523
Mexico	2,378	2,367
West Germany	1,795	1,885
Saudi Arabia	1,450	1,400 [e]
Iraq	1,050	1,270 [e]
Spain	1,340	1,235 [e]
France	1,168	1,051
Other countries [a]	8,687	9,060
Total	58,096	58,348

TIN, mine [b] (metric tons)

	1988	1989
Brazil	44,102	50,161
Malaysia	28,866	32,006
Indonesia	29,590	31,263
China [e]	25,000	25,000

TIN, mine (cont'd)

	1988	1989
USSR [e]	16,000	16,000
Bolivia	10,573	15,858
Thailand	14,225	14,683
Australia	7,009	7,776
Other countries [a]	24,785	24,899
Total	200,150	217,646

TITANIUM MINERALS [c] [k] (thousand metric tons)

ILMENITE

	1988	1989
Australia	1,622	1,776
Norway [e]	875	880
Malaysia	486	497 [e]
USSR [e]	460	460
India	140	160
China [e]	150	150
Other countries [a]	270	290
Total	4,003	4,213

RUTILE

	1988	1989
Australia	231	266 [e]
Sierra Leone	126	128
South Africa	55	60
Other countries [a]	22	22
Total	434	476

TITANIFEROUS SLAG

	1988	1989
Canada [e]	1,025	1,040
South Africa [e]	700	725
Total	1,725	1,765

TUNGSTEN, mine [b] (metric tons)

	1988	1989
China [e]	21,000	21,000
USSR [e]	9,200	9,300
Mongolia [e]	2,000	2,200
South Korea	2,029	1,800 [e]
Portugal	1,382	1,300 [e]
Australia	1,281	1,250
Austria	1,235	1,245
Peru	545	1,100
Bolivia	900	1,075 [e]
Thailand	651	700 [e]
Other countries [a]	2,381	2,310
Total	42,604	43,280

URANIUM OXIDE (U_3O_8) [l] (metric tons)

	1988	1989
Canada	14,229	13,637
United States	5,956	6,276
Australia	4,165	4,600 [e]
Niger	3,479	3,506
South Africa	4,583	3,456
France	3,430	3,412
Namibia	3,600	3,400 [e]
Other countries [a]	2,101	2,200
Total	41,543	40,487

ZINC, mine [b] (thousand metric tons)

	1988	1989
Canada	1,352	1,215
USSR [e]	810	810
Australia	766	803
China [e]	527	620
Peru	485	597
United States	256	288
Mexico	262	284
Spain	278	265
Poland	184	170
Ireland	173	169
Sweden	187	168
Other countries [a]	1,735	1,733
Total	7,015	7,122

ZINC, smelter, primary and secondary (thousand metric tons)

	1988	1989
USSR [e]	963	977
Canada	703	670
Japan	678	664
China [e]	425	451
United States	330	359
West Germany	356	354
Australia	307	298
Belgium	298	287
France	274	266
Italy	242	246
Spain	245	246
Netherlands	211	203
Mexico	193	195
Poland	177	164
Other countries [a]	1,748	1,803
Total	7,150	7,183

[a] Estimated in part. [b] Content of concentrates. [c] Gross weight. [d] Includes calculated bauxite equivalent of estimated output of aluminum ores other than bauxite (nepheline concentrate and alunite ores), which are produced for recovery of aluminum only in the USSR. [e] Estimate. [f] Includes coal classified in some countries as brown coal. [g] Gross weight of marketable product. [h] Marketable production (includes gas sold or used by producers as fuel, but excludes gas reinjected to reservoirs for pressure maintenance as well as that flared or vented to the atmosphere and hence not used either as a fuel or an industrial raw material, and thus having no economic value. [i] Data for each country exclude bullion produced for refining elsewhere. [j] Includes: (1) Frasch process sulfur, (2) elemental sulfur mined by conventional means, (3) by-product recovered elemental sulfur, and (4) elemental sulfur equivalent of sulfur recovered in the form of sulfuric acid or other chemicals from pyrite and other materials. [k] Excludes output in the United States, which cannot be disclosed because it is company proprietary information. [l] Excludes output, if any, by Albania, Bulgaria, China, Cuba, Czechoslovakia, East Germany, Hungary, North Korea, Mongolia, Poland, Romania, USSR, and Vietnam.

Compiled by Charles L. Kimbell primarily from data collected by the U.S. Bureau of Mines, but with some additions and modifications based on other sources.

THE UNITED STATES GOVERNMENT

EXECUTIVE BRANCH
(selected listing, as of Dec. 31, 1990)

President: George Bush

Vice-President: Dan Quayle

Executive Office of the President
The White House

Chief of Staff to the President: John H. Sununu

Assistant to the President and Deputy to the Chief of Staff: Andrew H. Card, Jr., and James W. Cicconi

Assistant to the President and Secretary to the Cabinet: Edith E. Holiday

Assistant to the President for Communications: David F. Demarest, Jr.

Assistant to the President and Press Secretary: Max Marlin Fitzwater

Counsel to the President: C. Boyden Gray

Assistant to the President for Legislative Affairs: Frederick D. McClure

Assistant to the President for Management and Administration: J. Bonnie Newman

Assistant to the President for Economic and Domestic Policy: Roger B. Porter

Assistant to the President for National Security Affairs: Gen. Brent Scowcroft, USAF (Ret.)

Assistant to the President and Deputy for National Security Affairs: Robert M. Gates

Assistant to the President for Public Events and Initiatives: Sigmund A. Rogich

Assistant to the President and Director of Presidential Personnel: Charles G. Untermeyer

Office of Management and Budget, Director: Richard G. Darman

Council of Economic Advisers, Chairman: Michael J. Boskin

Office of Policy Development, Deputy Assistant to the President for Domestic Policy and Director: Charles Kolb

Office of United States Trade Representative, United States Trade Representative: Carla A. Hills

Council on Environmental Quality, Chairman: Michael R. Deland

Office of Science and Technology Policy, Assistant to the President for Science and Technology and Director: D. Allan Bromley

Office of National Drug Control Policy, Director: Bob Martinez*

National Critical Materials Council, Chairman: D. Allan Bromley

Office of Administration, Deputy Assistant to the President for Management and Director: Paul W. Bateman

The Cabinet

Department of Agriculture
Secretary: Clayton K. Yeutter
Deputy Secretary: Jack C. Parnell

Department of Commerce
Secretary: Robert A. Mosbacher
Deputy Secretary: Thomas J. Murrin
Bureau of the Census, Director: Barbara E. Bryant

Department of Defense
Secretary: Richard Cheney
Deputy Secretary: Donald J. Atwood
Joint Chiefs of Staff
　Chairman: Gen. Colin L. Powell, USA
　Chief of Staff, Army: Gen. Carl E. Vuono, USA
　Chief of Staff, Air Force: Gen. Merrill A. McPeak, USAF
　Chief of Naval Operations: Adm. C. A. H. Trost, USN
　Commandant, Marine Corps: Gen. A. M. Gray, Jr., USMC
Secretary of the Air Force: Donald B. Rice
Secretary of the Army: Michael P.W. Stone
Secretary of the Navy: H. Lawrence Garrett III

Department of Education
Secretary: Lamar Alexander*

Department of Energy
Secretary: James D. Watkins
Deputy Secretary: W. Henson Moore

Department of Health and Human Services
Secretary: Louis W. Sullivan, M.D.
Undersecretary: Constance Horner
Surgeon General: Antonia Coello Novello
Centers for Disease Control, Director: William L. Roper
National Institutes of Health, Director: Bernadine Healy*
Social Security Administration, Commissioner: Gwendolyn S. King

Department of Housing and Urban Development
Secretary: Jack Kemp
Undersecretary: Alfred DelliBovi

Department of Interior
Secretary: Manuel Lujan, Jr.
Undersecretary: Frank A. Bracken
Assistant Secretary for Indian Affairs: Eddie F. Brown
National Park Service, Director: James M. Ridenour
Bureau of Mines, Director: T. S. Ary

Department of Justice
Attorney General: Richard Thornburgh
Deputy Attorney General: William B. Barr
Solicitor General: Kenneth W. Starr
Federal Bureau of Investigation, Director: W. S. Sessions
Drug Enforcement Administrator: Robert C. Bonner
Immigration and Naturalization Service, Commissioner: Gene McNary
Bureau of Prisons, Director: J. Michael Quinlan

Department of Labor
Secretary: Lynn Martin*
Deputy Secretary: Roderick DeArment
Women's Bureau, Director: Elsie V. Vartanian
Commissioner of Labor Statistics: Janet L. Norwood

Department of State
Secretary: James A. Baker III
Chief of Protocol: Joseph V. Reed, Jr.
Deputy Secretary of State: Lawrence S. Eagleburger
Assistant Secretary for Human Rights and Humanitarian Affairs: Richard Schifter
Assistant Secretary for African Affairs: Herman J. Cohen
Assistant Secretary for East Asian and Pacific Affairs: Richard Solomon
Assistant Secretary for European and Canadian Affairs: Raymond G. H. Seitz
Assistant Secretary for Inter-American Affairs: Bernard W. Aronson
Assistant Secretary for Near Eastern and South Asian Affairs: John H. Kelly
United Nations Representative: Thomas R. Pickering

Department of Transportation
Secretary: Samuel K. Skinner
U.S. Coast Guard, Commandant: Rear Adm. J. W. Kime
Federal Aviation Administrator: James B. Busey IV
Federal Highway Administrator: Thomas D. Larson
Federal Railroad Administrator: Gilbert E. Carmichael

Department of the Treasury
Secretary: Nicholas F. Brady
Deputy Secretary: John E. Robson
Comptroller of the Currency: Robert L. Clarke
Internal Revenue Service, Commissioner: Fred T. Goldberg, Jr.

Department of Veterans Affairs
Secretary: Edward J. Derwinski
Deputy Secretary: Anthony J. Principi

Independent Agencies (selected listing)

ACTION, Director: Jane A. Kenny

Central Intelligence Agency, Director: William H. Webster

Commission on Civil Rights, Chairman: Arthur A. Fletcher

Consumer Product Safety Commission, Chairman: Jacqueline Jones-Smith

Environmental Protection Agency, Administrator: William K. Reilly

Equal Employment Opportunity Commission, Chairman: Evan J. Kemp, Jr.

Export-Import Bank of the United States, President and Chairman: John D. Macomber

Farm Credit Administration, Chairman: Harold B. Steele

Federal Communications Commission, Chairman: Alfred C. Sikes

Federal Deposit Insurance Corporation, Chairman: L. William Seidman

Federal Election Commission, Chairman: Lee Ann Elliott

Federal Emergency Management Agency, Director: Wallace Elmer Stickney

Federal Labor Relations Authority, Chairman: Jean McKee

Federal Maritime Commission, Chairman: Christopher L. Koch

Federal Mediation and Conciliation Service, Director: Bernard E. DeLury

Federal Reserve System, Chairman: Alan Greenspan

Federal Trade Commission, Chairman: Janet D. Steiger

General Services Administrator: Richard G. Austin

Interstate Commerce Commission, Chairman: Edward J. Philbin

National Aeronautics and Space Administration, Administrator: Richard H. Truly

National Foundation on the Arts and Humanities
National Endowment for the Arts, Chairman: John E. Frohnmayer
National Endowment for the Humanities, Chairman: Lynne V. Cheney

National Labor Relations Board, Chairman: James M. Stephens

National Science Foundation, Chairman: Walter Massey*

National Transportation Safety Board, Chairman: James L. Kolstad

Nuclear Regulatory Commission, Chairman: Kenneth Carr

Office of Government Ethics, Director: Stephen D. Potts

Office of Personnel Management, Director: Constance Berry Newman

Peace Corps, Director: Paul D. Coverdell

Postal Rate Commission, Chairman: George W. Haley

Securities and Exchange Commission, Chairman: Richard C. Breeden

Selective Service System, Director: Robert William Gambino

Small Business Administrator: Susan S. Engeleiter

Tennessee Valley Authority, Chairman: Marvin Runyon

U.S. Arms Control and Disarmament Agency, Director: Ronald F. Lehman II

U.S. Information Agency, Director: Bruce S. Gelb

U.S. International Development Cooperation Agency, Director: Ronald W. Roskens, acting

U.S. International Trade Commission, Chairman: Anne E. Brunsdale

U.S. Postal Service, Postmaster General: Anthony M. Frank

THE SUPREME COURT

William H. Rehnquist, chief justice
Byron R. White
Thurgood Marshall

Harry A. Blackmun
John Paul Stevens
Sandra Day O'Connor

Antonin Scalia
Anthony M. Kennedy
David H. Souter

THE 102d CONGRESS

Senate Committee Chairmen

Agriculture, Nutrition, and Forestry: Patrick J. Leahy (VT)
Appropriations: Robert C. Byrd (WV)
Armed Services: Sam Nunn (GA)
Banking, Housing, and Urban Affairs: Donald W. Riegle, Jr. (MI)
Budget: Jim Sasser (TN)
Commerce, Science, and Transportation: Ernest F. Hollings (SC)
Energy and Natural Resources: J. Bennett Johnston (LA)
Environment and Public Works: Quentin N. Burdick (ND)
Finance: Lloyd Bentsen (TX)
Foreign Relations: Claiborne Pell (RI)
Governmental Affairs: John Glenn (OH)
Judiciary: Joseph R. Biden, Jr. (DE)
Labor and Human Resources: Edward Kennedy (MA)
Rules and Administration: Wendell H. Ford (KY)
Small Business: Dale Bumpers (AR)
Special Aging: David Pryor (AR)
Veterans' Affairs: Alan Cranston (CA)

Select Senate Committee Chairmen

Ethics: Howell T. Heflin (AL)
Indian Affairs: Daniel K. Inouye (HI)
Intelligence: David L. Boren (OK)

House Committee Chairmen

Agriculture: E. (Kika) de la Garza (TX)
Appropriations: Jamie L. Whitten (MS)
Armed Services: Les Aspin (WI)
Banking, Finance, and Urban Affairs: Henry B. Gonzalez (TX)
Budget: Leon E. Panetta (CA)
District of Columbia: Ronald V. Dellums (CA)
Education and Labor: William D. Ford (MI)
Energy and Commerce: John D. Dingell (MI)
Foreign Affairs: Dante B. Fascell (FL)
Government Operations: John Conyers, Jr. (MI)
House Administration: Charlie Rose (NC)
Interior and Insular Affairs: Morris K. Udall (AZ)
Judiciary: Jack Brooks (TX)
Merchant Marine and Fisheries: Walter B. Jones (NC)
Post Office and Civil Service: William L. Clay (MO)
Public Works and Transportation: Robert A. Roe (NJ)
Rules: Joe Moakley (MA)
Science, Space, and Technology: George E. Brown, Jr. (CA)
Small Business: John J. LaFalce (NY)
Standards of Official Conduct: Julian C. Dixon (CA)
Veterans' Affairs: G. V. (Sonny) Montgomery (MS)
Ways and Means: Dan Rostenkowski (IL)

Select House Committees

Aging: Edward R. Roybal (CA)
Children, Youth, and Families: George Miller (CA)
Hunger: Tony P. Hall (OH)
Intelligence: Dave McCurdy (OK)
Narcotics Abuse and Control: Charles B. Rangel (NY)

* not confirmed

UNITED STATES: 102d CONGRESS
First Session

SENATE MEMBERSHIP

(As of January 1991: 56 Democrats, 44 Republicans). Letters after senators' names refer to party affiliation—D for Democrat, R for Republican, I for Independent. Single asterisk (*) denotes term expiring in January 1993; double asterisk (**), term expiring in January 1995; triple asterisk (***), term expiring in January 1997. [1]Elected in 1990 to fill unexpired term. [2]Appointed to fill vacancy.

Alabama
*** H. Heflin, D
* R. C. Shelby, D

Alaska
*** T. Stevens, R
* F. H. Murkowski, R

Arizona
** D. DeConcini, D
* J. S. McCain III, R

Arkansas
* D. Bumpers, D
*** D. H. Pryor, D

California
* A. Cranston, D
** J. F. Seymour, R[2]

Colorado
* T. E. Wirth, D
*** H. Brown, R

Connecticut
** C. J. Dodd, D
*** J. I. Lieberman, D

Delaware
** W. V. Roth, Jr., R
*** J. R. Biden, Jr., D

Florida
* B. Graham, D
** C. Mack, R

Georgia
*** S. Nunn, D
* W. Fowler, Jr., D

Hawaii
* D. K. Inouye, D
*** D. K. Akaka, D[1]

Idaho
* S. Symms, R
*** L. E. Craig, R

Illinois
* A. J. Dixon, D
*** P. Simon, D

Indiana
** R. G. Lugar, R
* D. Coats, R

Iowa
* C. E. Grassley, R
*** T. R. Harkin, D

Kansas
* R. J. Dole, R
*** N. L. Kassebaum, R

Kentucky
* W. H. Ford, D
*** M. McConnell, R

Louisiana
*** J. B. Johnston, D
* J. B. Breaux, D

Maine
*** W. Cohen, R
** G. J. Mitchell, D

Maryland
* P. S. Sarbanes, D
* B. A. Mikulski, D

Massachusetts
* E. M. Kennedy, D
*** J. F. Kerry, D

Michigan
* D. W. Riegle, Jr., D
*** C. Levin, D

Minnesota
* D. F. Durenberger, R
*** P. Wellstone, D

Mississippi
*** T. Cochran, R
** T. Lott, R

Missouri
** J. C. Danforth, R
* C. S. Bond, R

Montana
*** M. Baucus, D
** C. Burns, R

Nebraska
*** J. J. Exon, Jr., D
** J. R. Kerrey, D

Nevada
* H. Reid, D
** R. H. Bryan, D

New Hampshire
* W. B. Rudman, R
*** R. C. Smith, R

New Jersey
*** B. Bradley, D
* F. R. Lautenberg, D

New Mexico
*** P. V. Domenici, R
* J. Bingaman, D

New York
** D. P. Moynihan, D
* A. M D'Amato, R

North Carolina
*** J. Helms, R
* T. Sanford, D

North Dakota
** Q. N. Burdick, D
* K. Conrad, D

Ohio
* J. H. Glenn, Jr., D
** H. M. Metzenbaum, D

Oklahoma
*** D. L. Boren, D
* D. L. Nickles, R

Oregon
*** M. O. Hatfield, R
** B. Packwood, R

Pennsylvania
** J. Heinz, R
* A. Specter, R

Rhode Island
*** C. Pell, D
** J. H. Chafee, R

South Carolina
*** S. Thurmond, R
* E. F. Hollings, D

South Dakota
*** L. Pressler, R
* T. A. Daschle, D

Tennessee
** J. R. Sasser, D
*** A. Gore, Jr., D

Texas
** L. Bentsen, D
*** W. Gramm, R

Utah
* J. Garn, R
** O. G. Hatch, R

Vermont
* P. J. Leahy, D
** J. M. Jeffords, R

Virginia
*** J. W. Warner, R
** C. S. Robb, D

Washington
* B. Adams, D
** S. Gorton, R

West Virginia
** R. C. Byrd, D
*** J. D. Rockefeller IV, D

Wisconsin
* R. W. Kasten, Jr., R
** H. Kohl, D

Wyoming
** M. Wallop, R
*** A. K. Simpson, R

HOUSE MEMBERSHIP

(As of January 1991, 267 Democrats, 167 Republicans, 1 independent). "At-L." in place of congressional district number means "representative at large." * Indicates elected Nov. 6, 1990; all others were reelected.

Alabama
1. H. L. Callahan, R
2. W. L. Dickinson, R
3. G. Browder, D
4. T. Bevill, D
5. B. Cramer, D*
6. B. Erdreich, D
7. C. Harris, Jr., D

Alaska
At-L. D. Young, R

Arizona
1. J. J. Rhodes, III, R
2. M. K. Udall, D
3. B. Stump, R
4. J. L. Kyl, R
5. J. Kolbe, R

Arkansas
1. W. V. Alexander, Jr., D
2. R. Thornton, D*
3. J. P. Hammerschmidt, R
4. B. F. Anthony, Jr., D

California
1. F. Riggs, R*
2. W. W. Herger, R
3. R. T. Matsui, D
4. V. Fazio, D
5. N. Pelosi, D
6. B. Boxer, D
7. G. Miller, D
8. R. V. Dellums, D
9. F. H. Stark, Jr., D
10. D. Edwards, D
11. T. P. Lantos, D
12. T. Campbell, R

13. N. Y. Mineta, D
14. J. T. Doolittle, R*
15. G. Condit, D
16. L. E. Panetta, D
17. C. Dooley, D*
18. R. H. Lehman, D
19. R. J. Lagomarsino, R
20. W. M. Thomas, R
21. E. W. Gallegly, R
22. C. J. Moorhead, R
23. A. C. Beilenson, D
24. H. A. Waxman, D
25. E. R. Roybal, D
26. H. L. Berman, D
27. M. Levine, D
28. J. C. Dixon, D
29. M. Waters, D*
30. M. G. Martinez, Jr., D
31. M. W. Dymally, D
32. G. M. Anderson, D
33. D. Dreier, R
34. E. E. Torres, D
35. J. Lewis, R
36. G. E. Brown, Jr., D
37. A. A. McCandless, R
38. R. K. Dornan, R
39. W. E. Dannemeyer, R
40. C. C. Cox, R
41. W. D. Lowery, R
42. D. Rohrabacher, R
43. R. Packard, R
44. R. Cunningham, R*
45. D. L. Hunter, R

Colorado
1. P. Schroeder, D
2. D. Skaggs, D

3. B. N. Campbell, D
4. W. Allard, R*
5. J. M. Hefley, R
6. D. Schaefer, R

Connecticut
1. B. B. Kennelly, D
2. S. Gejdenson, D
3. R. DeLauro, D*
4. C. Shays, R
5. G. Franks, R*
6. N. L. Johnson, R

Delaware
At-L. T. R. Carper, D

Florida
1. E. Hutto, D
2. P. Peterson, D*
3. C. E. Bennett, D
4. C. T. James, R
5. B. McCollum, Jr., R
6. C. B. Stearns, R
7. S. M. Gibbons, D
8. C. W. B. Young, R
9. M. Bilirakis, R
10. A. Ireland, R
11. J. Bacchus, D*
12. T. Lewis, R
13. P. J. Goss, R
14. H. A. Johnston, D
15. E. C. Shaw, Jr., R
16. L. J. Smith, D
17. W. Lehman, D
18. I. Ros-Lehtinen, R
19. D. B. Fascell, D

Georgia
1. R. L. Thomas, D
2. C. F. Hatcher, D
3. R. B. Ray, D
4. B. Jones, D
5. J. R. Lewis, D
6. N. Gingrich, R
7. G. Darden, D
8. J. R. Rowland, D
9. E. L. Jenkins, D
10. D. Barnard, Jr., D

Hawaii
1. N. Abercrombie, D*
2. P. Mink, D

Idaho
1. L. LaRocco, D*
2. R. H. Stallings, D

Illinois
1. C. A. Hayes, D
2. G. Savage, D
3. M. Russo, D
4. G. E. Sangmeister, D
5. W. O. Lipinski, D
6. H. J. Hyde, R
7. C. Collins, D
8. D. Rostenkowski, D
9. S. R. Yates, D
10. J. E. Porter, R
11. F. Annunzio, D
12. P. M. Crane, R
13. H. W. Fawell, R
14. J. D. Hastert, R
15. E. R. Madigan, R
16. J. W. Cox, Jr., D*
17. L. Evans, D

18. R. H. Michel, R
19. T. L. Bruce, D
20. R. Durbin, D
21. J. F. Costello, D
22. G. Poshard, D

Indiana
1. P. J. Visclosky, D
2. P. R. Sharp, D
3. T. Roemer, D *
4. J. Long, D
5. J. P. Jontz, D
6. D. L. Burton, R
7. J. T. Myers, R
8. F. McCloskey, D
9. L. H. Hamilton, D
10. A. Jacobs, Jr., D

Iowa
1. J. Leach, R
2. J. Nussle, R *
3. D. R. Nagle, D
4. N. Smith, D
5. J. R. Lightfoot, R
6. F. L. Grandy, R

Kansas
1. C. P. Roberts, R
2. J. C. Slattery, D
3. J. Meyers, R
4. D. Glickman, D
5. D. Nichols, R *

Kentucky
1. C. Hubbard, Jr., D
2. W. H. Natcher, D
3. R. L. Mazzoli, D
4. J. Bunning, R
5. H. D. Rogers, R
6. L. J. Hopkins, R
7. C. C. Perkins, D

Louisiana
1. R. L. Livingston, Jr., R
2. W. J. Jefferson, D *
3. W. J. Tauzin, D
4. J. McCrery, R
5. T. J. Huckaby, D
6. R. H. Baker, R
7. J. A. Hayes, D
8. C. C. Holloway, R

Maine
1. T. H. Andrews, D *
2. O. J. Snowe, R

Maryland
1. W. T. Gilchrest, R *
2. H. D. Bentley, R
3. B. L. Cardin, D
4. C. T. McMillen, D
5. S. H. Hoyer, D
6. B. B. Byron, D
7. K. Mfume, D
8. C. A. Morella, R

Massachusetts
1. S. O. Conte, R
2. R. E. Neal, D
3. J. D. Early, D
4. B. Frank, D
5. C. G. Atkins, D
6. N. Mavroules, D
7. E. J. Markey, D
8. J. P. Kennedy II, D
9. J. J. Moakley, D
10. G. E. Studds, D
11. B. J. Donnelly, D

Michigan
1. J. Conyers, Jr., D
2. C. D. Pursell, R
3. H. E. Wolpe, D
4. F. S. Upton, R
5. P. B. Henry, R
6. B. Carr, D
7. D. E. Kildee, D
8. B. Traxler, D
9. G. Vander Jagt, R
10. D. Camp, R *
11. R. W. Davis, R
12. D. E. Bonior, D
13. B. R. Collins, D *
14. D. M. Hertel, D
15. W. D. Ford, D
16. J. D. Dingell, D
17. S. M. Levin, D
18. W. S. Broomfield, R

Minnesota
1. T. J. Penny, D
2. V. Weber, R
3. J. Ramstad, R *

4. B. F. Vento, D
5. M. O. Sabo, D
6. G. Sikorski, D
7. C. C. Peterson, D *
8. J. L. Oberstar, D

Mississippi
1. J. L. Whitten, D
2. M. Espy, D
3. G. V. Montgomery, D
4. M. Parker, D
5. G. Taylor, D

Missouri
1. W. L. Clay, D
2. J. K. Horn, D *
3. R. A. Gephardt, D
4. I. Skelton, D
5. A. D. Wheat, D
6. E. T. Coleman, R
7. M. D. Hancock, R
8. W. Emerson, R
9. H. L. Volkmer, D

Montana
1. P. Williams, D
2. R. C. Marlenee, R

Nebraska
1. D. Bereuter, R
2. P. Hoagland, D
3. B. Barrett, R *

Nevada
1. J. H. Bilbray, D
2. B. F. Vucanovich, R

New Hampshire
1. B. Zeliff, R *
2. D. Swett, D *

New Jersey
1. R. E. Andrews, D *
2. W. J. Hughes, D
3. F. Pallone, Jr., D
4. C. H. Smith, R
5. M. S. Roukema, R
6. B. J. Dwyer, D
7. M. J. Rinaldo, R
8. R. A. Roe, D
9. R. G. Torricelli, D
10. D. M. Payne, D
11. D. A. Gallo, R
12. R. A. Zimmer, R *
13. H. J. Saxton, R
14. F. J. Guarini, D

New Mexico
1. S. Schiff, R
2. J. R. Skeen, R
3. W. B. Richardson, D

New York
1. G. J. Hochbrueckner, D
2. T. J. Downey, D
3. R. J. Mrazek, D
4. N. F. Lent, R
5. R. J. McGrath, R
6. F. H. Flake, D
7. G. L. Ackerman, D
8. J. H. Scheuer, D
9. T. J. Manton, D
10. C. E. Schumer, D
11. E. Towns, D
12. M. R. Owens, D
13. S. J. Solarz, D
14. S. Molinari, R
15. B. Green, R
16. C. B. Rangel, D
17. T. Weiss, D
18. J. Serrano, D
19. E. L. Engel, D
20. N. Lowey, D
21. H. Fish, Jr., R
22. B. A. Gilman, R
23. M. R. McNulty, D
24. G. B. Solomon, R
25. S. L. Boehlert, R
26. D. O'B. Martin, R
27. J. T. Walsh, R
28. M. F. McHugh, D
29. F. Horton, R
30. L. M. Slaughter, D
31. B. Paxon, R
32. J. J. LaFalce, D
33. H. J. Nowak, D
34. A. Houghton, R

North Carolina
1. W. B. Jones, D
2. T. Valentine, D

3. H. M. Lancaster, D
4. D. E. Price, D
5. S. L. Neal, D
6. H. Coble, R
7. C. Rose, D
8. W. G. Hefner, D
9. J. A. McMillan, R
10. C. Ballenger, R
11. C. H. Taylor, R *

North Dakota
At-L. B. L. Dorgan, D

Ohio
1. C. Luken, D *
2. W. D. Gradison, Jr., R
3. T. P. Hall, D
4. M. G. Oxley, R
5. P. E. Gillmor, R
6. B. McEwen, R
7. D. L. Hobson, R *
8. J. A. Boehner, R *
9. M. C. Kaptur, D
10. C. E. Miller, R
11. D. E. Eckart, D
12. J. R. Kasich, R
13. D. J. Pease, D
14. T. C. Sawyer, D
15. C. P. Wylie, R
16. R. Regula, R
17. J. A. Traficant, Jr., D
18. D. Applegate, D
19. E. F. Feighan, D
20. M. R. Oakar, D
21. L. Stokes, D

Oklahoma
1. J. M. Inhofe, R
2. M. Synar, D
3. B. Brewster, D *
4. D. McCurdy, D
5. M. Edwards, R
6. G. English, D

Oregon
1. L. AuCoin, D
2. R. F. Smith, R
3. R. Wyden, D
4. P. A. DeFazio, D
5. M. Kopetski, D *

Pennsylvania
1. T. M. Foglietta, D
2. W. H. Gray, III, D
3. R. A. Borski, Jr., D
4. J. P. Kolter, D
5. R. T. Schulze, R
6. G. Yatron, D
7. W. C. Weldon, R
8. P. H. Kostmayer, D
9. B. Shuster, R
10. J. M. McDade, R
11. P. E. Kanjorski, D
12. J. P. Murtha, D
13. L. Coughlin, R
14. W. J. Coyne, D
15. D. L. Ritter, R
16. R. S. Walker, R
17. G. W. Gekas, R
18. R. Santorum, R *
19. W. F. Goodling, R
20. J. M. Gaydos, D
21. T. J. Ridge, R
22. A. J. Murphy, D
23. W. F. Clinger, Jr., R

Rhode Island
1. R. K. Machtley, R
2. J. F. Reed, D *

South Carolina
1. A. Ravenel, Jr., R
2. F. D. Spence, R
3. B. C. Derrick, Jr., D
4. E. J. Patterson, D
5. J. M. Spratt, Jr., D
6. R. M. Tallon, Jr., D

South Dakota
At-L. T. Johnson, D

Tennessee
1. J. H. Quillen, R
2. J. J. Duncan, R
3. M. Lloyd, D
4. J. Cooper, D
5. B. Clement, D
6. B. J. Gordon, D
7. D. K. Sundquist, R
8. J. S. Tanner, D
9. H. E. Ford, D

Texas
1. J. Chapman, D
2. C. Wilson, D
3. S. Bartlett, R
4. R. M. Hall, D
5. J. W. Bryant, D
6. J. L. Barton, R
7. B. Archer, R
8. J. M. Fields, R
9. J. Brooks, D
10. J. J. Pickle, D
11. C. Edwards, D *
12. P. Geren, D
13. B. Sarpalius, D
14. G. Laughlin, D
15. E. de la Garza, D
16. R. D. Coleman, D
17. C. W. Stenholm, D
18. C. Washington, D
19. L. E. Combest, R
20. H. B. Gonzalez, D
21. L. S. Smith, R
22. T. D. DeLay, R
23. A. G. Bustamante, D
24. M. Frost, D
25. M. A. Andrews, D
26. R. K. Armey, R
27. S. P. Ortiz, D

Utah
1. J. V. Hansen, R
2. D. W. Owens, D
3. W. Orton, D *

Vermont
At-L. B. Sanders, I *

Virginia
1. H. H. Bateman, R
2. O. B. Pickett, D
3. T. J. Bliley, Jr., R
4. N. Sisisky, D
5. L. F. Payne, Jr., D
6. J. R. Olin, D
7. D. F. Slaughter, Jr., R
8. J. P. Moran, Jr., D *
9. F. C. Boucher, D
10. F. R. Wolf, R

Washington
1. J. R. Miller, R
2. A. Swift, D
3. J. Unsoeld, D
4. S. W. Morrison, R
5. T. S. Foley, D
6. N. D. Dicks, D
7. J. McDermott, D
8. R. Chandler, R

West Virginia
1. A. B. Mollohan, D
2. H. O. Staggers, Jr., D
3. R. E. Wise, Jr., D
4. N. J. Rahall, II, D

Wisconsin
1. L. Aspin, D
2. S. L. Klug, R *
3. S. C. Gunderson, R
4. G. D. Kleczka, D
5. J. Moody, D
6. T. E. Petri, R
7. D. R. Obey, D
8. T. Roth, R
9. F. J. Sensenbrenner, Jr., R

Wyoming
At-L. C. Thomas, R

AMERICAN SAMOA
Delegate E. F. H. Faleomavaega, D

DISTRICT OF COLUMBIA
Delegate Eleanor Holmes Norton, D *

GUAM
Delegate, Ben Blaz, R

PUERTO RICO
Resident Commissioner
J. B. Fuster, D

VIRGIN ISLANDS
Delegate, Ron de Lugo, D

UNITED STATES: Major Legislation Enacted During the Second Session of the 101st Congress

SUBJECT	PURPOSE
Panamanian Aid	Approves $42 million in emergency aid to Panama and lifts economic sanctions against Panama imposed during Gen. Manuel Antonio Noriega's tenure. Signed February 14. Public Law 101-243.
Eisenhower Centennial	Provides for the commemoration of the 100th anniversary of the birth of Dwight David Eisenhower. Signed March 27. Public Law 101-258.
Crime	Orders a detailed study of crimes motivated by racial, ethnic, religious, or sexual prejudice. Signed April 23. Public Law 101-275.
Environment	Provides for the establishment of the National Commission on Natural Resources Disasters. Signed May 9. Public Law 101-286.
Recreation Area	Establishes the Grand Island National Recreation Area in the state of Michigan. Signed May 17. Public Law 101-292.
Biological Weapons	Imposes new criminal penalties against those who would employ or contribute to the proliferation of biological weapons. Signed May 22. Public Law 101-298.
New Mexico	Establishes the Petroglyph National Monument and the Pecos National Historical Park in New Mexico. Signed June 27. Public Law 101-313.
UN-Zionism	"Calls upon the United Nations" to repeal General Assembly Resolution 3379, which declared Zionism to be a form of racism and racial discrimination. Signed June 29. Public Law 101-317.
The Disabled	Extends to disabled Americans those rights guaranteed to women and racial, ethnic, and religious minorities. Signed July 26. Public Law 101-336. *See page 464.*
Health	Amends the Public Health Service Act to establish a program of grants for the prevention and control of breast and cervical cancer. Signed August 10. Public Law 101-354.
Oil Spills	Provides comprehensive oil-spill liability and compensation, cleanup, and prevention measures and leaves states free to maintain their own cleanup funds and enforce liability laws. Signed August 18. Public Law 101-380.
AIDS	Authorizes emergency assistance to states and cities hardest hit by the AIDS epidemic. Signed August 18. Public Law 101-381.
Hungary	Extends nondiscriminatory treatment to the products of Hungary. Signed August 20. Public Law 101-382.
Vocational Educational	Reauthorizes vocational-educational programs through fiscal year 1995; urges coordination of high-school and postsecondary programs. Signed September 25. Public Law 101-392.
Age Discrimination	Bans age discrimination in employee benefits unless such bias is due to age-based cost differences. Signed October 16. Public Law 101-433.
Advertising	Limits the amount of advertising during children's television programs. Became law without the president's signature on October 17. Public Law 101-437. *See page 94.*
Health	Reauthorizes a 1986 program to provide federal funding for vaccines against childhood diseases. Signed November 3. Public Law 101-502.
Budget	Reduces the federal budget deficit. Signed November 5. Public Law 101-508. *See page 547.*
National Monument	Establishes the Newberry Volcanoes National Monument in Oregon. Signed November 5. Public Law 101-522.
Historic Reserve	Establishes the Vancouver National Historic Reserve in Washington state. Signed November 5. Public Law 101-523.
Nutrition	Requires nutrition labeling on most food packaging and restricts the ability of food manufacturers to make health or nutrition claims about their products. Signed November 8. Public Law 101-535.
Education	Requires institutions of higher education receiving federal aid to provide certain information regarding graduation rates of their student athletes. Signed November 8. Public Law 101-542.
Clean Air	Amends the Clean Air Act. Signed November 15. Public Law 101-549. *See page 61.*
Hydrogen	Establishes a hydrogen research and development program. Signed November 15. Public Law 101-566.
Antarctica	Protects and conserves the continent of Antarctica. Signed November 16. Public Law 101-594.
Aviation	Tightens security measures at major airports. Signed November 16. Public Law 101-604.
Housing	Authorizes a new corporation to support state and local programs for achieving more affordable housing and to increase homeownership. Signed November 28. Public Law 101-625. *See page 267.*
Alaska	Amends the Alaska National Interest Lands Conservation Act and designates certain lands in the Tongass National Forest as wilderness. Signed November 28. Public Law 101-626.
Medical Devices	Improves the regulation of medical devices. Signed November 28. Public Law 101-629.
Homeless	Extends programs providing aid for the homeless. Signed November 29. Public Law 101-645.
Crime	Sets new penalties for bank fraud, certain drug offenses, and child abuse, and authorizes funding increases for law enforcement and prison alternatives. Signed November 29. Public Law 101-647.
Immigration	Reforms the nation's immigration system. Signed November 29. Public Law 101-649. *See page 447.*
Judges	Provides for the appointment of additional federal circuit and district judges. Signed December 1. Public Law 101-650.

Contributors

ADRIAN, CHARLES R., Professor of Political Science, University of California, Riverside; Author, *A History of City Government: The Emergence of the Metropolis 1920–1945;* Coauthor, *A History of American City Government: The Formation of Traditions, 1775–1870, Governing Urban America:* CALIFORNIA; LOS ANGELES

ALDRIDGE, BILL G., Executive Director, National Science Teachers Association: EDUCATION—*The Teaching of Science*

AMBRE, AGO, Economist, Office of Economic Affairs, U.S. Department of Commerce: INDUSTRIAL PRODUCTION

ARNOLD, ANTHONY, Visiting Scholar, Hoover Institution, Stanford, CA; Author, *Afghanistan: The Soviet Invasion in Perspective, Afghanistan's Two-Party Communism: Parcham and Khalq:* AFGHANISTAN

ATTNER, PAUL, National Correspondent, *The Sporting News:* SPORTS—*Basketball, Football, Soccer*

AUSTIN, TERESA, Free-lance Writer: ENGINEERING, CIVIL

BALAKRISHNAN, N., Staff Writer, *Far Eastern Economic Review:* INDONESIA; MALAYSIA; SINGAPORE

BARMASH, ISADORE, Business-Financial Writer, *The New York Times;* Author, *Always Live Better Than Your Clients, More Than They Bargained For, The Chief Executives:* RETAILING; RETAILING—*The Department Store*

BATRA, PREM P., Professor of Biochemistry, Wright State University: BIOCHEMISTRY

BECK, KAY, Department of Communications, Georgia State University: GEORGIA

BEHLER, DEBORAH A., Senior Editor, *Wildlife Conservation* magazine: ZOOS AND ZOOLOGY

BENDER, JOHN R., Assistant Professor, College of Journalism, University of Nebraska—Lincoln: ARTS, THE—*The Question of Obscenity*

BEST, JOHN, Chief, *Canada World News,* Ottawa: NEW BRUNSWICK; PRINCE EDWARD ISLAND; QUEBEC

BLANCHARD, PAUL, Professor of Government, Eastern Kentucky University; Author, *Kentucky State and Local Government, New School Board Members: A Portrait:* KENTUCKY

BOND, DONOVAN H., Professor Emeritus of Journalism, West Virginia University: WEST VIRGINIA

BOULAY, HARVEY, Director of Development, Rogerson House; Author, *The Twilight Cities:* BOSTON; MASSACHUSETTS

BOWER, BRUCE, Behavioral Sciences Editor, *Science News:* ANTHROPOLOGY; ARCHAEOLOGY

BRAMMER, DANA B., Director, Public Policy Research Center, University of Mississippi: MISSISSIPPI

BRANDHORST, L. CARL, and JoANN C., Department of Geography, Western Oregon State College: OREGON

BROOM, JACK, Reporter, *The Seattle Times:* SPORTS—*The Goodwill Games;* WASHINGTON

BURANELLI, VINCENT, Free-lance Writer and Editor; Author, *Thomas Edison, The Trial of Peter Zenger, Louis XIV;* Coauthor, *Spy/Counterspy: An Encyclopedia of Espionage:* ESPIONAGE

BURKS, ARDATH W., Professor Emeritus Asian Studies, Rutgers University; Author, *Japan: A Postindustrial Power:* JAPAN

BUSH, GRAHAM W. A., Associate Professor of Political Studies, University of Auckland; Author, *Local Government & Politics in New Zealand;* Editor, *New Zealand—A Nation Divided?:* NEW ZEALAND

BUTTRY, STEPHEN, Assistant Managing Editor, *The Kansas City Star:* MISSOURI

CAMPBELL, ROBERT, University of Wyoming; Coauthor, *Discovering Wyoming:* WYOMING

CASEY, DAN, *The* (Annapolis) *Capital:* MARYLAND

CASPER, GRETCHEN, Department of Political Science, Texas A&M: PHILIPPINES

CASPER, LEONARD, Professor of English, Boston College; Past Recipient of Fulbright grants to lecture in the Philippines: PHILIPPINES

CASSIDY, SUZANNE, Free-lance Writer; Researcher, London Bureau, *The New York Times:* GREAT BRITAIN; GREAT BRITAIN—*The Arts*

CHARREN, PEGGY, President, Action for Children's Television: TELEVISION—*The Legacy of Jim Henson*

CHRISTENSEN, WILLIAM E., Professor of History, Midland Lutheran College; Author, *In Such Harmony: A History of the Federated Church of Columbus, Nebraska:* NEBRASKA

COLE, JOHN N., Founder, *Maine Times;* Author, *Fishing Came First, In Maine, Striper, Salmon, House Building:* MAINE

COLLINS, BUD, Sports Columnist, *The Boston Globe;* Author, *My Life With The Pros:* SPORTS—*Tennis*

COLTON, KENT W., Executive Vice-President and Chief Executive Officer, National Association of Home Builders, Washington, DC: HOUSING

CONRADT, DAVID P., Professor of Political Science, University of Florida; Author, *The German Polity, Comparative Politics, The Civic Culture Revisited, The West German Party System:* GERMANY

COOPER, MARY H., Staff Writer, *Editorial Research Reports:* ABORTION; FOREIGN AID; INSURANCE, LIABILITY

COPPEDGE, MICHAEL, Assistant Professor, Paul H. Nitze School of Advanced International Studies, Johns Hopkins University: ECUADOR; PERU; VENEZUELA

CORLEW, ROBERT E., Vice-President, Middle Tennessee State University: TENNESSEE

CORNWELL, ELMER E., JR., Professor of Political Science, Brown University: RHODE ISLAND

CUNNIFF, JOHN, Business News Analyst, The Associated Press; Author, *How to Stretch Your Dollar:* BUSINESS AND CORPORATE AFFAIRS; STOCKS AND BONDS—*Junk Bonds;* UNITED STATES—*The Economy*

CURRIER, CHET, Financial Writer, The Associated Press; Author, *The Investor's Encyclopedia, The 15-Minute Investor;* Coauthor, *No-Cost/Low-Cost Investing:* STOCKS AND BONDS

CURTIS, L. PERRY, JR., Professor of History, Brown University: IRELAND

DANIELS, ROBERT V., Professor of History, University of Vermont; former Vermont state senator; Author, *Russia: The Roots of Confrontation:* VERMONT

DARBY, JOSEPH W., III, Reporter, *The Times-Picayune,* New Orleans: LOUISIANA

DASCH, E. JULIUS, NRC/NASA Headquarters; Author of more than 100 papers and abstracts in geology and geochemistry: SPACE EXPLORATION

DASCH, PATRICIA A., NRC/NASA Headquarters: SPACE EXPLORATION

De GREGORIO, GEORGE, Sports Department, *The New York Times;* Author, *Joe DiMaggio, An Informal Biography:* SPORTS—*Boxing, Ice Skating, Skiing, Swimming, Track and Field, Yachting*

DELZELL, CHARLES F., Professor of History Emeritus, Vanderbilt University; Author, *Italy in the Twentieth Century, Mediterranean Fascism, Mussolini's Enemies:* ITALY

591

DENNIS, LARRY, Golf Writer, Creative Communications: BI-OGRAPHY—*Nick Faldo;* SPORTS—*Golf*

DUFF, ERNEST A., Professor of Politics, Randolph-Macon Woman's College; Author, *Agrarian Reform in Colombia, Violence and Repression in Latin America, Leader and Party in Latin America:* COLOMBIA

ELKINS, ANN M., Fashion Director, *Good Housekeeping Magazine:* FASHION; FASHION—*The Fur-Coat Debate, The Halston Legacy*

ELVING, PHYLLIS, Free-lance Travel Writer: TRAVEL

ENSTAD, ROBERT H., Writer, *Chicago Tribune:* CHICAGO; IL-LINOIS

ENTER, JACK E., Program Director, Criminal Justice Coordinating Council: CRIME

EWEGEN, ROBERT D., Editorial Writer, *The Denver Post:* COLORADO

FAGEN, MORTON D., Formerly, AT&T Bell Laboratories; Editor, *A History of Engineering and Science in the Bell System, Vol. 1, The Early Years, 1875–1925, and Vol. II, National Service in War and Peace, 1925–1975:* COMMU-NICATION TECHNOLOGY

FISHER, JIM, Editorial Writer, *Lewiston Morning Tribune:* IDAHO

FRANCIS, DAVID R., Economy Page Editor, *The Christian Science Monitor:* INTERNATIONAL TRADE AND FINANCE; IN-TERNATIONAL TRADE AND FINANCE—*Most-Favored-Nation Status*

FRIIS, ERIK J., Editor and Publisher, *The Scandinavian-American Bulletin:* DENMARK; FINLAND; NORWAY; SWEDEN

GAILEY, HARRY A., Professor of History, San Jose State University; Author, *History of the Gambia, History of Africa, Road to Aba:* LIBERIA; MOZAMBIQUE; NIGERIA; ZAIRE

GEORGE, PAUL S., Department of History, University of Miami; Author, *Florida: Yesterday and Today, A Guide to the History of Florida:* FLORIDA

GIBSON, ROBERT C., Associate Editor, *The Billings Gazette:* MONTANA

GOODMAN, DONALD, Associate Professor of Sociology, John Jay College of Criminal Justice, City University of New York: PRISONS

GORDON, MAYNARD M., Detroit Editor, *Auto Age;* Author, *The Iacocca Management Technique:* AUTOMOBILES

GOUDINOFF, PETER, Member, House of Representatives, Arizona; Professor, Department of Political Science, University of Arizona; Author, *People's Guide to National Defense:* ARIZONA

GRAYSON, GEORGE W., John Marshall Professor of Government and Citizenship, College of William and Mary; Author, *The Politics of Mexican Oil, The United States and Mexico: Patterns of Influence, Oil and Mexican Foreign Policy:* BIOGRAPHY—*Fernando Collor de Mello;* BRAZIL; PORTUGAL; SPAIN

GREEN, MAUREEN, Writer and Publisher, London: LITERA-TURE—*English*

GREGORY, BARBARA J., American Numismatic Association: COINS AND COIN COLLECTING

GROSSMAN, LAWRENCE, Director of Publications, The American Jewish Committee: RELIGION—*Judaism*

GROTH, ALEXANDER J., Professor of Political Science, University of California, Davis; Author, *People's Poland;* Coauthor, *Contemporary Politics: Europe, Comparative Resource Allocation, Public Policy Across Nations:* PO-LAND

HACKER, JEFFREY H., Free-lance Writer and Editor: HIGH-TOPS AND TWO-WHEELERS: RACING INTO THE NINETIES

HAGER, MARY, Correspondent, *Newsweek* magazine: THE ENVIRONMENT: THE GARBAGE CRISIS

HALLER, TIMOTHY G., Assistant Professor, Department of Political Science, University of Nevada, Reno: NEVADA

HALSEY, MARGARET BROWN, Professor of Art History, New York City Technical College: ART; ART—*The Art Market*

HAND, SAMUEL B., Professor of History, University of Vermont: VERMONT

HANDELMAN, GLADYS, Free-lance Writer and Editor: BI-OGRAPHY—*Maggie Smith;* OBITUARIES—*Leonard Bernstein, Sammy Davis, Jr.*

HARLAND, ALAN T., Department of Criminal Justice, Temple University: LAW—*Community Service*

HARMON, CHARLES, American Library Association: LI-BRARIES

HARRIS, DORRAINE, Free-lance Writer, Las Cruces, NM: NEW MEXICO

HARVEY, ROSS M., Executive Director, Television Northern Canada: NORTHWEST TERRITORIES

HELMREICH, ERNST C., Professor Emeritus of History, Bowdoin College; Author, *The German Churches under Hitler: Background, Struggle, and Epilogue:* AUSTRIA

HELMREICH, JONATHAN E., Professor of History, Allegheny College; Author, *Belgium and Europe: A Study in Small Power Diplomacy, Gathering Rare Ores: The Diplomacy of Uranium China in World Acquisition, 1943–54:* BELGIUM

HELMREICH, PAUL C., Professor of History, Wheaton College; Author, *Wheaton College: The Seminary Years, 1834–1912; From Paris to Sèvres: The Partition of the Ottoman Empire at the Peace Conference of 1919–1920:* SWITZERLAND

HILL, EDWARD W., Associate Professor, College of Urban Affairs, Cleveland State University; Coeditor, *Financing Economic Development: An Institutional Response:* BANKING AND FINANCE

HINTON, HAROLD C., Professor of Political Science and International Affairs, The George Washington University; Author, *Korea under New Leadership: The Fifth Republic, Communist China in World Politics, The China Sea: The American Stake in Its Future:* KOREA

HOLLOWAY, HARRY, Professor of Political Science, University of Oklahoma; Coauthor, *Public Opinion: Coalitions, Elites, and Masses, Party and Factional Division in Texas:* OKLAHOMA

HOOVER, HERBERT T., Professor of History, University of South Dakota; Author, *South Dakota Leaders, The Yankton Sioux, To Be an Indian, The Chitimacha People:* SOUTH DAKOTA

HOPKO, THE REV. THOMAS, Assistant Professor, St. Vladimir's Orthodox Theological Seminary: RELIGION—*Orthodox Eastern*

HOWARD, CARLA BREER, Furnishings and Antiques Editor, *Traditional Home:* INTERIOR DESIGN

HOYT, CHARLES K., Senior Editor, *Architectural Record;* Author, *More Places for People, Building for Commerce and Industry:* ARCHITECTURE

HUFFMAN, GEORGE J., Assistant Professor, Department of Meteorology, University of Maryland: METEOROLOGY

HULBERT, DAN, *Atlanta Journal & Constitution:* TELEVISION AND RADIO; THEATER

HUSTED, THOMAS A., Assistant Professor, Department of Economics, The American University: TAXATION

JACKSON, PAUL CONRAD, Editor, *The Calgary Sun;* Columnist, *Saskatoon Star-Phoenix:* ALBERTA; SAS-KATCHEWAN

JONES, H.G., Curator, North Carolina Collection, University of North Carolina at Chapel Hill; Author, *North Carolina Illustrated, 1524–1984:* NORTH CAROLINA

JUDD, DENNIS R., Professor and Chair, Department of Political Science, University of Missouri; Coauthor, *The Development of American Public Policy, Leadership and Urban Regeneration:* CITIES AND URBAN AFFAIRS

JUDD, LEWIS L., Director, National Institute of Mental Health: MEDICINE AND HEALTH—*Mental Health*

KARNES, THOMAS L., Professor of History Emeritus, Arizona State University; Author, *Latin American Policy of the United States, Failure of Union: Central America 1824–1960:* BIOGRAPHY—*Violeta Barrios de Chamorro;* CENTRAL AMERICA

KIMBALL, LORENZO K., Professor Emeritus, Department of Political Science, University of Utah: UTAH

KIMBELL, CHARLES L., Senior Foreign Mineral Specialist, U.S. Bureau of Mines: STATISTICAL AND TABULAR DATA—*Mineral and Metal Production*

KING, PETER J., Professor of History, Carleton University, Ottawa; Author, *Utilitarian Jurisprudence in America:* ONTARIO; OTTAWA

KINNEAR, MICHAEL, Professor of History, University of Manitoba; Author, *The Fall of Lloyd George, The British Voter:* MANITOBA

KISSELGOFF, ANNA, Chief Dance Critic, *The New York Times:* DANCE

KNAPP, ELAINE S., Editor, Council of State Government: UNITED STATES—*One or Two New States?*

KOZINN, ALLAN, Music Critic, *The New York Times;* Author, *Mischa Elman and the Romantic Style, The Guitar: The History, The Music, The Players:* BIOGRAPHY—*Kurt Masur;* MUSIC—*Classical*

KRONISH, SYD, Stamp Editor, The Associated Press: STAMPS AND STAMP COLLECTING

KUNZ, KENEVA, BBC Foreign Correspondent, Reykjavik: ICELAND

LaFRANCHI, HOWARD, Paris Correspondent, *The Christian Science Monitor:* FRANCE; TUNISIA

LAI, DAVID CHUENYAN, Professor of Geography, University of Victoria, British Columbia; Author, *Chinatowns: Towns Within Cities in Canada:* HONG KONG

LANCASTER, CAROL, Director, African Studies Program, Georgetown University; Coeditor, *African Debt and Financing:* AFRICA

LAWRENCE, ROBERT M., Professor of Political Science, Colorado State University; Author, *Strategic Defense Initiative: Bibliography and Research Guide:* ARMS CONTROL AND DISARMAMENT; MILITARY AFFAIRS

LEE, STEWART M., Chairman, Department of Economics and Business Administration, Geneva College; Coauthor, *Personal Finance for Consumers, Consumer Economics: The Consumer in Our Society:* CONSUMER AFFAIRS

LEEPSON, MARC, Free-lance Writer: DRUGS AND ALCOHOL; SOCIAL WELFARE; SOCIAL WELFARE—*The Disabled*

LEVINE, LOUIS, Professor, Department of Biology, City College of New York; Author, *Biology of the Gene, Biology for a Modern Society:* BIOTECHNOLOGY; GENETICS; MICROBIOLOGY

LEWIS, ANNE C., Education Policy Writer: EDUCATION

LEWIS, JEROME R., Director for Public Administration, College of Urban Affairs and Public Policy, University of Delaware: DELAWARE

LOBRON, BARBARA L., Writer, Editor, Photographer: PHOTOGRAPHY

LOESCHER, GIL, Associate Professor of International Relations, University of Notre Dame; Author, *Calculated Kindness: Refugees and America's Half-Open Door, Refugees and International Relations, The Moral Nation: Humanitarianism and U.S. Foreign Policy:* REFUGEES AND IMMIGRATION

LOEVY, ROBERT D., Professor of Political Science, Colorado College; Author, *To End All Segregation: The Politics of the Passage of the Civil Rights Act of 1964:* UNITED STATES—*Congressional Reform*

MABRY, DONALD J., Professor of History, Mississippi State University; Author, *Mexico's Acción Nacional, The Mexican University and the State;* Coauthor, *Neighbors—Mexico and the United States;* Editor, *The Latin American Narcotics Trade and U.S. National Security:* MEXICO

MARCOPOULOS, GEORGE J., Associate Professor of History, Tufts University: CYPRUS; GREECE

MARSDEN, SULLIVAN S., JR., Professor, Petroleum Energy, Stanford University: ENERGY

MATHESON, JIM, Sportswriter, *Edmonton Journal:* SPORTS —*Ice Hockey*

MATHINOS, DEBRA A., Assistant Professor of Education, Bucknell University: EDUCATION—*TV News in the Classroom*

McCORQUODALE, SUSAN, Professor of Political Science, Memorial University of Newfoundland: NEWFOUNDLAND

McCRAW, VINCENT D., *The Washington Times:* WASHINGTON, DC

McGILL, DAVID A., Professor of Marine Science, U.S. Coast Guard Academy: OCEANOGRAPHY

McLAURIN, RONALD D., President, Abbott Associates, Inc.; Author, *The Emergence of a New Lebanon: Fantasy or Reality?, Lebanon and the World in the 1980s:* LEBANON

MEDINGER, DANIEL, Editor, *Catholic Review,* Baltimore: RELIGION—*Roman Catholicism*

MICHAELIS, PATRICIA A., Curator of Manuscripts, Kansas State Historical Society: KANSAS; UNITED STATES—*The Dwight D. Eisenhower Centennial*

MICHIE, ARUNA NAYYAR, Associate Professor of Political Science, Kansas State University: BANGLADESH

MILLER, RANDALL M., Department of History, St. Joseph's University; Author, *Shades of the Sunbelt: Essays on Race, Ethnicity and the Urban South:* ETHNIC GROUPS

MILWARD, JOHN, Free-lance Writer and Critic: "A CHORUS LINE": BROADWAY'S LONGEST RUN; MUSIC—*Popular;* RECORDINGS

MITCHELL, GARY, Professor of Physics, North Carolina State University: PHYSICS

MONASTERSKY, RICHARD, Earth Sciences Editor, *Science News:* GEOLOGY

MORELLO, TED, United Nations Correspondent, *The Christian Science Monitor;* Author, *Official Handbook of the Hall of Fame:* UNITED NATIONS

MORTIMER, ROBERT A., Professor, Department of Political Science, Haverford College; Author, *The Third World Coalition in International Politics:* ALGERIA

MORTON, DESMOND, Professor of History and Principal, Erindale College, University of Toronto; Author, *A Short History of Canada, Bloody Victory: Canadians and the D-Day Campaign, Working People: An Illustrated History of the Canadian Labour Movement, A Military History of Canada, Winning the Second Battle: Canadian Veterans and the Return to Civilian Life, 1915–1930;* Coauthor, *Marching to Armageddon: Canadians in the First World War, 1914–1919:* BIOGRAPHY—*Jean Chrétien, Ramon John Hnatyshyn;* CANADA

MURPHY, ROBERT F., Editorial Writer, *The Hartford Courant:* CONNECTICUT

NAFTALIN, ARTHUR, Professor Emeritus of Public Affairs, University of Minnesota: MINNESOTA

NEUMANN, JIM, Free-lance Writer, Fargo, ND: NORTH DAKOTA

NEWLAND, ED, Assistant City Editor, *Richmond Times-Dispatch:* VIRGINIA

NUZZI, CAROLYN G., Free-lance Writer: BIOGRAPHY—*Brent Scowcroft*

OCHSENWALD, WILLIAM, Professor of History, Virginia Polytechnic Institute; Author, *The Middle East: A History, The Hijaz Railroad, Religion, Society, and the State in Arabia:* BIOGRAPHY—*Saddam Hussein;* SAUDI ARABIA

O'CONNOR, ROBERT E., Associate Professor of Political Science, The Pennsylvania State University; Author, *Politics and Structure: Essentials of American National Government:* PENNSYLVANIA

O'MEARA, PATRICK, Director, African Studies Program, Indiana University; Coeditor, *Africa, International Politics in Southern Africa, Southern Africa, The Continuing Crisis:* ANGOLA; BIOGRAPHY—*F.W. de Klerk, Nelson Mandela;* NAMIBIA; SOUTH AFRICA; ZIMBABWE

PALMER, NORMAN D., Professor Emeritus of Political Science and South Asian Studies, University of Pennsylvania; Author, *Westward Watch: The United States and the Changing Western Pacific, The United States and India: The Dimensions of Influence, Elections and Political Development: The South Asian Experience, The New Regionalism in Asia and the Pacific:* BIOGRAPHY—*V.P. Singh;* INDIA; SRI LANKA

PEARSON, FREDERIC S., Director, Center for Peace and Conflict Studies, and Professor of Political Science, Wayne State University; Author, *International Relations: The Global Condition in the Late Twentieth Century, The Weak State in International Crisis:* UNITED STATES—*Foreign Affairs*

PERETZ, DON, Professor of Political Science, State University of New York at Binghamton; Author, *The West Bank—History, Politics, Society & Economy, Government and Politics of Israel, The Middle East Today:* EGYPT; ISRAEL

PERKINS, KENNETH J., Assistant Professor of History, University of South Carolina: LIBYA; RELIGION—*Islam*

PERRY, DAVID K., Associate Professor, Department of Journalism, The University of Alabama: PUBLISHING

PIPPIN, LARRY L., Professor of Political Science, University of the Pacific; Author, *The Remón Era:* ARGENTINA; PARAGUAY; URUGUAY

PLATT, HERMANN K., Professor of History, Saint Peter's College: NEW JERSEY

POOLE, PETER A., Author, *The Vietnamese in Thailand, Eight Presidents and Indochina;* Coauthor, *American Diplomacy:* CAMBODIA; LAOS; MONGOLIA; THAILAND; VIETNAM

RALOFF, JANET, Environment/Policy Editor, *Science News:* THE ENVIRONMENT: AIR POLLUTION

RAMIREZ, DEBORAH, Reporter, *San Juan Star:* PUERTO RICO

REED, WILLIAM CYRUS, Professor, Department of Political Science, Wabash College: KENYA; TANZANIA; UGANDA

REUNING, WINIFRED, Writer, Polar Program, National Science Foundation: POLAR RESEARCH

RICHTER, LINDA K., Professor, Department of Political Science, Kansas State University; Author, *Land Reform and Tourism Development: Policy-Making in the Philippines, The Politics of Tourism in Asia:* MYANMAR

RICHTER, WILLIAM L., Professor and Head, Department of Political Science, Kansas State University: NEPAL; PAKISTAN

RIGGAN, WILLIAM, Associate Editor, *World Literature Today,* University of Oklahoma; Author, *Picaros, Madmen, Naifs, and Clowns, Comparative Literature and Literary Theory:* LITERATURE—*World*

ROBERTS, SAM, Urban Affairs Columnist, *The New York Times;* Editor, *The New York Times Reader;* Coauthor, *I Never Wanted To Be Vice-President of Anything:* NEW YORK CITY

ROBINSON, LEIF J., Editor, *Sky & Telescope;* Author, *Outdoor Optics:* ASTRONOMY; ASTRONOMY—*The Hubble Space Telescope*

ROSS, RUSSELL M., Professor of Political Science, University of Iowa; Author, *State and Local Government and Administration, Iowa Government and Administration:* IOWA

ROVNER, JULIE, *Congressional Quarterly:* MEDICINE AND HEALTH—*Health Care in the 1990s*

ROWEN, HERBERT H., Professor Emeritus, Rutgers University, New Brunswick; Author, *The Princes of Orange, John de Witt: Statesman of the "True Freedom", The King's State, John de Witt: Grand Pensionary of Holland:* NETHERLANDS

RUBIN, JIM, Supreme Court Correspondent, The Associated Press: BIOGRAPHY—*David Souter;* LAW

RUFF, NORMAN J., Assistant Professor, Department of Political Science, University of Victoria, B.C.; Coauthor, *The Reins of Power: Governing British Columbia:* BRITISH COLUMBIA

SALSINI, PAUL, Staff Development Director, *The Milwaukee Journal:* WISCONSIN

SAVAGE, DAVID, Free-lance Writer: CANADA—*The Arts;* LITERATURE—*Canadian*

SAWATSKY, DON, Free-lance Writer/Broadcaster; Author, *Ghost Town Trails of the Yukon:* YUKON

SCHLOSSBERG, DAN, Baseball Writer; Author, *The Baseball IQ Challenge, The Baseball Catalog, The Baseball Book of Why, Barons of the Bullpen, Baseball Stars 1985, 1986, 1987:* BIOGRAPHY—*José Canseco, Nolan Ryan, George Steinbrenner;* SPORTS—*Baseball*

SCHROEDER, RICHARD, Syndicated Writer, various U.S. newspapers; Consultant to Organization of American States: BOLIVIA; CARIBBEAN; CHILE; HAITI; LATIN AMERICA

SCHWAB, PETER, Professor of Political Science, State University of New York at Purchase; Author, *Ethiopia: Politics, Economics, and Society, Toward a Human Rights Framework:* ETHIOPIA

SEIDERS, DAVID F., Chief Economist and Senior Staff Vice-President, National Association of Home Builders, Washington, DC: HOUSING

SENSER, ROBERT A., Free-lance Labor Writer, Washington, DC: LABOR; LABOR—*Children at Work*

SETH, R.P., Professor of Economics, Mount Saint Vincent University, Halifax: CANADA—*The Economy;* NOVA SCOTIA

SEYBOLD, PAUL G., Professor, Department of Chemistry, Wright State University: CHEMISTRY

SHARLET, ROBERT, Professor of Political Science, Union College; Coeditor, *P.I. Stuchka: Selected Writings on Soviet Law and Marxism, The Soviet Union Since Stalin, Pashukanis: Selected Writings on Marxism and Law:* THE UNION REPUBLICS OF THE USSR; BIOGRAPHY—*Boris Yeltsin;* USSR

SHEPRO, CARL E., Professor, University of Alaska-Anchorage: ALASKA

SHOGAN, ROBERT, National Political Correspondent, Washington Bureau, *Los Angeles Times;* Author, *A Question of Judgment, Promises to Keep:* THE IRAQ CRISIS: THE U.S. VIEWPOINT; UNITED STATES—*Domestic Affairs, The 1990 Elections*

SIEGEL, STANLEY E., Professor of History, University of Houston; Author, *A Political History of the Texas Republic, 1836–1845, Houston: Portrait of the Supercity on Buffalo Bayou:* TEXAS

SIMON, JEFFREY D., The RAND Corporation, Santa Monica, CA: TERRORISM

SIMON, SHELDON W., Professor of Political Science and Faculty Associate, Arizona State University-Tempe; Author, *The Future of Asian-Pacific Security Collaboration, The ASEAN States and Regional Security:* ASIA

SMITH, REX, Albany Bureau Chief, *Newsday:* NEW YORK

SMITH, STEPHEN, Research Assistant, Department of Criminal Justice, Temple University: LAW—*Community Service*

SNODSMITH, RALPH L., Garden Editor, "Good Morning America", ABC-TV; Host, "Garden Hotline"; Author, *Ralph Snodsmith's Tips from the Garden Hotline, Garden Calendar and Record Keeper 1985–1988:* GARDENING AND HORTICULTURE

SPYCHALSKI, JOHN C., Chairman, Department of Business Logistics, College of Business Administration, The Pennsylvania State University; Editor, *Transportation Journal:* TRANSPORTATION

STARR, JOHN BRYAN, Executive Director, Yale-China Association; Author, *Continuing the Revolution: The Political Thought of Mao;* Editor, *The Future of U.S.-China Relations:* CHINA; TAIWAN

STERN, JEROME H., Associate Professor of English, Florida State University; Editor, *Studies in Popular Culture:* BIOGRAPHY—*August Wilson;* LITERATURE—*American*

STEWART, WILLIAM H., Associate Professor of Political Science, The University of Alabama; Coauthor, *Alabama Government and Politics;* Author, *The Alabama Constitution:* ALABAMA

STOUDEMIRE, ROBERT H., Distinguished Professor Emeritus, University of South Carolina: SOUTH CAROLINA

SUTTON, STAN, Sportswriter, *The Courier-Journal,* Louisville, KY: SPORTS—*Auto Racing, Horse Racing*

SYLVESTER, LORNA LUTES, Associate Editor, *Indiana Magazine of History,* Indiana University: INDIANA

TABORSKY, EDWARD, Professor of Government, University of Texas at Austin; Author, *Communism in Czechoslovakia, 1948–1960, Communist Penetration of the Third World:* BIOGRAPHY—*Václav Havel;* CZECHOSLOVAKIA

TAYLOR, WILLIAM L., Professor of History, Plymouth State College: NEW HAMPSHIRE

TESAR, JENNY, Science and Medicine Writer; Author, *Parents as Teachers:* THE BIG BUSINESS OF DIETING; COMPUTERS; MEDICINE AND HEALTH; MEDICINE AND HEALTH—*Generic Drugs*

THEISEN, CHARLES W., Assistant News Editor, *The Detroit News:* MICHIGAN

TURNER, ARTHUR CAMPBELL, Professor of Political Science, University of California, Riverside; Coauthor, *Ideology and Power in the Middle East:* THE IRAQ CRISIS; IRAN; IRAQ; JORDAN; MIDDLE EAST; MIDDLE EAST—*The Yemens Merge;* SYRIA

TURNER, CHARLES H., Free-lance Journalist: HAWAII

TURNER, DARRELL J., Associate Editor, Religious News Service: RELIGION—*Far Eastern, Protestantism*

VAN RIPER, PAUL P., Professor Emeritus and Head, Department of Political Science, Texas A&M University; Editor and Coauthor, *The Wilson Influence on Public Administration:* POSTAL SERVICE

VOLL, JOHN O., Department of History, University of New Hampshire; Author, *Islam: Continuity and Change in the Modern World, Sudan: Unity & Diversity in a Multicultural State:* SUDAN

VOLSKY, GEORGE, Center for Advanced International Studies, University of Miami: CUBA

WALD, MATTHEW L., *The New York Times:* THE ENVIRONMENT: A WORLD OF CHALLENGES

WEAVER, JOHN B., Department of History, Wright State University: OHIO

WEIKER, WALTER F., Professor of Political Science, Rutgers University: TURKEY

WELLER, MARC, Cambridge University Research Centre for International Law; St. Catharine's College, Cambridge: LAW—*International*

WILLIAMS, C. FRED, Professor of History, University of Arkansas at Little Rock; Author, *Arkansas: An Illustrated History of the Land of Opportunity, Arkansas: A Documentary History:* ARKANSAS

WILLIS, F. ROY, Professor of History, University of California, Davis; Author, *France, Germany and the New Europe, 1945–1968, Italy Chooses Europe, The French Paradox:* A VIEW OF EUROPE AS THE COLD WAR ENDS

WILMS, DENISE M., Free-lance Children's Book Reviewer: LITERATURE—*Children's*

WINCHESTER, N. BRIAN, Associate Director, African Studies Program, Indiana University: ANGOLA; NAMIBIA; SOUTH AFRICA

WISNER, ROBERT N., Professor, Iowa State University; Coeditor, *Marketing for Farmers;* Author, *World Food Trade and U.S. Agriculture:* AGRICULTURE; FOOD

WOLF, WILLIAM, New York University; Author, *The Marx Brothers, Landmark Films, The Cinema and Our Century:* MOTION PICTURES

WOLFE, JOHN, New York Bureau Chief, *Advertising Age:* ADVERTISING

YOUNGER, R.M., Journalist and Author; Author, *Australia and the Australians, Australia! Australia! A Bicentennial Record:* AUSTRALIA

ZACEK, JOSEPH FREDERICK, Professor of History, State University of New York, Albany; Author, *Palacky: The Historian as Scholar and Nationalist;* Coauthor, *Frantisek Palacky, 1798–1876: A Centennial Appreciation, The Enlightenment and the National Revivals in Eastern Europe:* ALBANIA; BULGARIA; HUNGARY; ROMANIA; YUGOSLAVIA

Index

Main article headings appear in this index as bold-faced capitals; subjects within articles appear as lower-case entries. Both the general references and the subentries should be consulted for maximum usefulness of this index. Illustrations are indexed herein. Cross references are to the entries in this index.